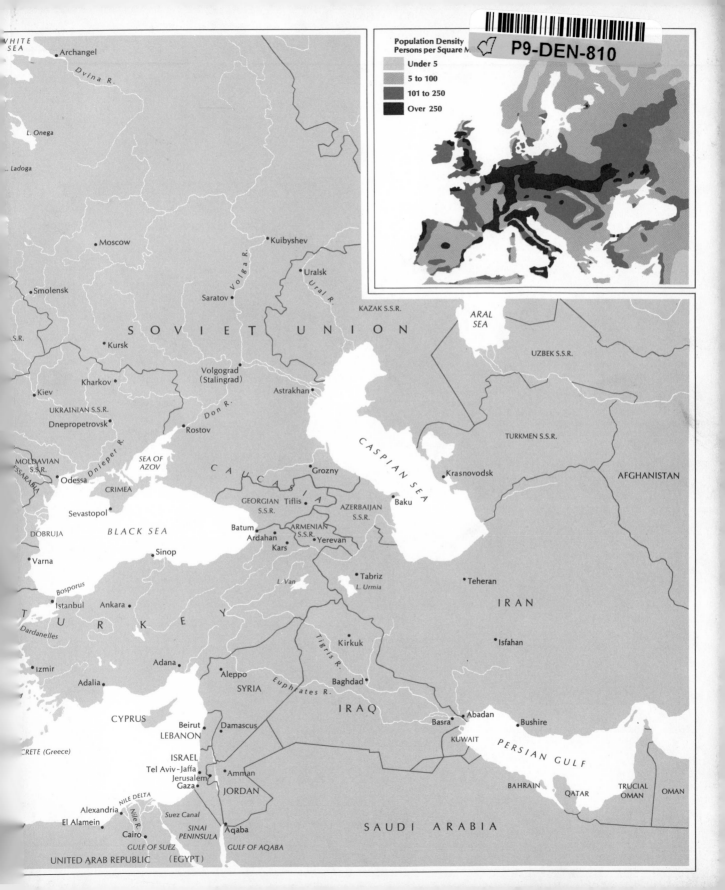

WHITE
SEA

• Archangel

Dvina R.

L. Onega

.. Ladoga

• Moscow

S.R.

• Smolensk

• Kursk

Kharkov •

• Kiev

UKRAINIAN S.S.R.

MOLDAVIAN
S.S.R.
ESSARABIA

• Odessa

DOBRUJA

CRIMEA

• Sevastopol

• Varna

Dnieper R.

SEA OF
AZOV

Volga R.

• Saratov

Volgograd
(Stalingrad)

Don R.

• Rostov

BLACK SEA

Bosporus

• Istanbul   Ankara •

T   U   R   K   E   Y

Dardanelles

• Izmir

• Adalia

• Adana

• Sinop

• Kuibyshev

• Uralsk

Ural R.

KAZAK S.S.R.

• Astrakhan

C   A   U   C   A   S   I   A

• Grozny

GEORGIAN Tiflis
S.S.R.

Batum •   AZERBAIJAN
• Ardahan   ARMENIAN   S.S.R.
   • Kars   S.S.R.
              • Yerevan

CASPIAN SEA

ARAL
SEA

UZBEK S.S.R.

TURKMEN S.S.R.

• Krasnovodsk

• Baku

AFGHANISTAN

L. Van
L. Urmia

• Tabriz

• Teheran

I   R   A   N

Tigris R.

• Kirkuk

• Isfahan

CYPRUS

• Aleppo   • Baghdad
SYRIA   _Euphrates R._

• Beirut   • Damascus
LEBANON

CRETE (Greece)

ISRAEL

Tel Aviv-Jaffa
Jerusalem • Amman
Gaza

JORDAN

I   R   A   Q

Basra •   • Abadan
                   • Bushire
KUWAIT

P   E   R   S   I   A   N   G   U   L   F

BAHRAIN

QATAR

TRUCIAL
OMAN   OMAN

• Alexandria

NILE DELTA

• El Alamein   Nile R.

• Cairo

Suez Canal

SINAI
PENINSULA

GULF OF SUEZ

• Aqaba

GULF OF AQABA

SAUDI   ARABIA

UNITED ARAB REPUBLIC   (EGYPT)

Population Density
Persons per Square M.

Under 5
5 to 100
101 to 250
Over 250

A HISTORY OF THE

A HISTORY OF THE MODERN WORLD

MODERN WORLD

R. R. PALMER
Yale University

JOEL COLTON
Duke University

Fourth Edition
ALFRED A. KNOPF *NEW YORK*

THIS IS A BORZOI BOOK PUBLISHED BY ALFRED A. KNOPF, INC.

Library of Congress Catalog Card Number: 78-123273

Standard Book Number: 394-30356-3

Manufactured in the United States of America

Published July 24, 1950. Reprinted seven times.

Second edition, revised, reset, and printed from new plates, with new maps, 1956. Reprinted fourteen times.

Third edition, revised, with new maps, 1965. Reprinted five times.

Fourth edition, revised, reset, and printed from new plates, with new maps and illustrations, 1971.

Fourth Edition
987654321

Cover photographs, superimposed on a color moiré: the astrolabe by permission of Harcourt Brace Jovanovich, collection of Mr. and Mrs. David H. H. Felix; the Hiroshima clock by Fred Ward for Black Star; the earth from space by NASA.

ACKNOWLEDGMENT IS HEREBY MADE FOR PERMISSION TO QUOTE FROM THE FOLLOWING WORKS:

Lenin: A Biography, by David Shub. Copyright, 1948, by David Shub, and reprinted by permission of Doubleday & Company, Inc.

"The White Man's Burden" from *The Five Nations* by Rudyard Kipling. Copyright, 1903, by Rudyard Kipling, reprinted by permission of Mrs. George Bambridge, Methuen & Company, and Doubleday & Company, Inc.

Three Who Made a Revolution, by Bertram D. Wolfe, by permission of the Dial Press, Inc. Copyright, 1948, by Bertram D. Wolfe.

World Population, by A. N. Carr-Saunders. Clarendon Press, Oxford.

PREFACE

This fourth edition of *A History of the Modern World* appears in a new format, entirely redesigned, more abundantly illustrated, and with maps in color. Without altering the book in any fundamental way, we hope that we have improved it. Originally the work of a single hand, it has become our joint enterprise, and we have worked closely together to respond to criticisms that have been made of it over the years. Mr. Colton, who has general charge of the latter part of the book, has added substantial pages on political and intellectual developments in the twentieth century, and has reworked and brought up to date the concluding chapter on the Contemporary Age. Rewriting and expansion on the Italian Renaissance, the Puritan Revolution, certain demographic topics, the "democratic revolution" of the eighteenth century, and the British parliamentary reform movement have been chiefly the work of Mr. Palmer. Corrections and readjustments have been made throughout, including some which will be detected by friendly critics who have called various points to our attention. More radical critics, of whom there have been some, may remain unsatisfied. It is perhaps enough for any book, when used as a text, if it serves as a base on which teachers and students can construct their own interpretations.

The book is still designed to set forth the modern history of Europe and European civilization as a unit, and in its later chapters attempts to tell the story of an integrated, or at least interconnected, world. Emphasis falls on situations and movements of international scope, or on what Europeans and their descendants have done and faced in common. National histories are therefore somewhat subordinated, and in each national history the points of contact with a larger civilization are treated most fully. Historic regional differences within Europe, as between eastern and western Europe, are brought out, and the history of the Americas is woven into the story at various points, as are developments of the last century in Asia and Africa. A good deal of institutional history is included. Considerable space is given to the history of ideas, not only in special sections devoted to ideas, but throughout the book in close connection with the account of institutions and events. Social and economic development bulks rather large. Since our own age is one in which much depends on political decision, we think of this volume as political history in the broadest sense, in that matters of many kinds, such as religion, economics, social welfare, and international relations, have presented themselves as public questions requiring public action by responsible citizens or public persons. Nor do we hesitate, living in the present age, to dwell at some length on war and revolution. The greater wars and revolutions have perhaps had more profound consequences than are generally acknowledged. In any event, they are good examples of movements that transcend individual nations and affect the course of modern history as a whole.

The increased number of full-page reproductions of paintings, together with the six picture essays introduced in this new edition, should give visual confirmation to some of the ideas set forth in the text. The use of color in the maps should make them more serviceable as well as more inviting. Mr. Colton has personally revised and updated the bibliography, selectively absorbing into it the constant new flow of historical writing. In its topical arrangement, and in its careful indication of availability of books in paperback, he has tried to make it convenient to students at various levels of special interest.

We wish again to express our thanks to all those who, since the first edition, have contributed their ideas to the book as it now stands. Miss Suzanne Thibodeau and Mrs. Shareen Brysac have been especially helpful in the preparation of the present edition. We are again indebted to Shirley Colton for special assistance in many demanding tasks. Only she and Esther Palmer can quite understand how our personal and professional lives have become intertwined in these pages.

R. R. Palmer
Joel Colton

CONTENTS

ILLUSTRATIONS

MAPS

xiv

A HISTORY OF THE MODERN WORLD

I: THE RISE OF EUROPE

The modern world in the closing decades of the twentieth century is a large and complicated affair. The whole earth is included in it, and even more, for the bold earthlings who scrutinize the moon are very much a part of the planet from which they came. The spreading forces of modern life reach into the most impenetrable jungles and the most inaccessible valleys. Persons of all colors and creeds proceed by boat or plane to sit down at the same conferences, or sometimes to fight in the same wars. Over 125 governments from five continents make up the United Nations, whose executive officer may be Swedish at one time and Burmese at another. Intellectuals in Moscow and Peking debate the meaning of a revolutionary philosophy that originated in western Europe; over 2,000 bishops from all parts of the world sit at Rome at a council of the Catholic church; and Protestants have gathered for world-wide assemblies by the shores of Lake Michigan and of the Ganges. For the funeral of an assassinated president of the United States, in 1963, the notables of the whole planet could converge in Washington in a few hours.

It might therefore seem that a history of the modern world should relate the history of all the world's peoples alike. The reader will discover, however, that this book is in the main a history of Europe. Why is this?

Chapter Emblem: The symbolic Chi-Rho, or crossed X and P, standing for the first two letters of the Greek *Khristos.* From a Roman sarcophagus.

Partly it is because America, in which this book is written and will mainly be read, is historically in large measure a projection from Europe. But there are better and less self-centered reasons. There are reasons why Asians and Africans, or Americans whose personal origins lie in Asia or Africa, can understand their own world better if they have a better understanding of Europe. The main reason is that modern civilization, wherever found, has been formed by ideas, institutions, and industries that originated in Europe. Europe itself, to be sure, has always received much from others—from the calendar and Christianity to the use of cotton and potatoes. Europe itself, moreover, became "modernized" by the effects upon it of growing contacts with the earth as a whole, especially after the discovery of America and the ocean trade routes in the days of Columbus. But in the last few centuries Europe has had more influence on the rest of the world than the rest of the world has had upon Europe.

Europe was the first part of the world to become modern. The rest of the world is undergoing a continuing process of modernization, and the modern world is becoming more of an interlocking unity; events on one side of the globe have immediate repercussions on the other. It is a world characterized by modern science, industry, and machines, modern sources of energy, modern transport and communications, modern medicine, sanitation, and methods of raising food. It is filled with states and nations which have fought wars by advanced technical methods and negotiate or maintain peace by certain practices of diplomacy. It is knitted by finance and trade, loans and debts, investments and bank accounts. It is a world that seeks for more democracy, for self-government and representative institutions, for an enlargement of individual liberty and extension of individual well being. It is a world in which common men begin to sense the attractions of a higher standard of living, of better food and housing in return for less laborious and spirit-killing work, to see their ancestral religions and historic rulers in a new light, to shake loose from the past, to form new political parties, to favor revolutionary movements which may be either slow and gradual or abrupt and catastrophic. It is a troubled world, at once materialistic and possessed by new ideals, both dynamic and hard to move, both ruthless and humane.

All these indexes of modernity, if such they may be called, appeared first in the history of Europe, or of the European world in the extended sense in which the United States is included. The present book deals mainly with the growth of European society and civilization, with an increasing attention, in the later chapters, to the earth as a whole.

If "modern" refers especially to a certain complicated way of living, it has also another sense, meaning merely what is recent or current. As a time span the word "modern" is purely relative. It depends on what we are talking about. A modern kitchen may be as much as 5 years old, modern physics is not much over 50 years old, modern science over 300, the modern European languages about 1,000. Modern civilization, the current civilization in which we are living, and which may be passing, is in one sense a product of our own twentieth century, but in other senses it is much older. In general, it is agreed that modern times began in Europe about the year

1500. Modern times were preceded by a period of 1,000 years called the Middle Ages, which set in about A.D. 500, and which were in turn preceded by another 1,000 years of classical Greco-Roman civilization. Before that reached the long histories of Egypt and Mesopotamia, and, further east, of the Indus Valley and of China. All times prior to the European Middle Ages are commonly called "ancient." But the whole framework—ancient, medieval, and modern—is largely a matter of words and convention, without meaning except for Europe. We shall begin our history with a running start, and slow down the pace, surveying the scene more fully in proportion as the times grow more "modern."

Europeans were by no means the pioneers of human civilization. Half of man's recorded history had passed before anyone in Europe could read or write. The priests of Egypt began to keep written records between 4000 and 3000 B.C., but more than two thousand years later the poems of Homer were still being circulated in the Greek city-states by word of mouth. Shortly after 3000 B.C., while the pharaohs were building the first pyramids, Europeans were creating nothing more distinguished than huge garbage heaps. Ironically, like the pyramids, they still endure and are known to archeologists as "kitchen middens." At the time when the Babylonian King Hammurabi, about 2000 B.C., caused the laws of a complex society to be carved on stone, the most advanced Europeans were peoples like the Swiss Lake Dwellers, simple agriculturists who lived in shelters built over the water to protect themselves from beasts and men. In a word, until after 2000 B.C., Europe was in the Neolithic or New Stone Age. This was in truth a great age in man's history, the age in which men learned to make and use sharp tools, weave cloth, build living quarters, domesticate animals, plant seeds, harvest crops, and sense the returning cycles of the months and years. But the Near East—Egypt, the Euphrates and Tigris valley, the island of Crete, and the shores of the Aegean Sea (which belonged more to Asia than to Europe)—had reached and passed the Neolithic two thousand years before Europe. By about 4000 B.C. the Near East had already moved on into the Bronze Age.

After about 2000 B.C., in the dim dark continent that Europe then was, there began to be great changes that are now difficult to trace. The new elements came from Asia, or from Africa by way of Gibraltar. Europeans, too, learned how to smelt and forge metals, with the Bronze Age setting in about 2000 B.C. and the Iron Age about 1000 B.C. The new knowledge passed from tribe to tribe, from east to west. The Iron Age, for example, began in Asia Minor about 1400 B.C., in what is now Austria about 1000 B.C., in England about 400 B.C. At the same time there was a steady infusion of new peoples into Europe. They spoke languages related to languages now spoken in India and Persia, to which similar peoples migrated at about the same time. All these languages (whose interconnection was not known until the nineteenth century) are now referred to as Indo-European, and the people who spoke them, merging with and imposing their speech upon older European stocks, became the ancestors both of the classical Greeks and Romans and of the Europeans of modern times. All European languages today are Indo-European with the exception of Basque, which is thought to be a survival from before the Indo-European invasion, and of Finnish and Hungarian, which were brought into Europe from Asia some centuries later. All that is known of these invading Indo-Europeans is that they diffused over Europe the kind of speech from which the Latin, Greek, Germanic, Slavic, Celtic, and Baltic languages were later derived. What racial or cultural contribution they may have made is most unclear.[1]

The Greek World

The first Indo-Europeans to emerge into the clear light of history, in what is now Europe, were the Greeks. They filtered down through the Balkan peninsula to the shores of the Aegean Sea about 1900 B.C., undermining the older Cretan civilization, and occupying most of what has since been called Greece by 1300 B.C. Beginning about 1150 B.C., other Greek-speaking tribes invaded from the north in successive waves. The newcomers consisted of separate barbaric tribes and their coming ushered in several centuries of chaos and unrest before a gradual stabilization and revival began in the ninth century. The *Iliad* and the *Odyssey*, written down about 800 B.C., but composed and recited much earlier, probably refer to wars between the Greeks and other centers of civilization, of which one was at Troy in Asia Minor. The siege of Troy is thought to have occurred about 1200 B.C.

The Greeks proved to be as gifted a people as mankind has ever produced, achieving supreme heights in thought and letters. They absorbed the knowledge of the, to them, mysterious East, the mathematical lore of the ancient Chaldeans, the arts and crafts that they found in Asia Minor and on voyages to Egypt. They added immediately to everything that they learned. It was the Greeks of the fifth and fourth centuries B.C. who first became fully conscious of the powers of the human mind, who discovered what the Western world has meant by the beautiful, and who first speculated on political freedom.

As they settled down, the Greeks formed tiny city-states, all independent and often at war with one another, each comprising only a few hundred square miles, and typically including a coastal city and its adjoining farmlands. Athens, Corinth, Sparta were such city-states. Many were democratic; all citizens (i.e., all grown men except slaves and "metics" or outsiders) congregated in the market place to elect officials and discuss their public business. Politics was turbulent in the small Greek states. Democracy alternated with aristocracy, oligarchy, despotism, and tyranny. From this rich fund of experience was born systematic political science as set forth in the unwritten speculations of Socrates and in the *Republic* of Plato and the *Politics* of

---

[1] Formerly the term Aryan was sometimes used to denote Indo-European. In Germany, under Adolf Hitler, much nonsense was written about an Aryan race, and the term Aryan was made in practice to mean simply non-Jewish. The grain of truth in all this was simply that Hebrew is not an Indo-European but a Semitic language, closely related to Arabic (which is also Semitic) and less closely to the language of the ancient Egyptians. There is no Indo-European (Aryan) or Semitic "race"; persons speaking these languages no more had to be of one physical descent than are persons who speak English today.

Aristotle in the fourth century before Christ. The Greeks also were the first to write history as a subject distinct from myth and legend. Herodotus, "the Father of History," traveled throughout the Greek world and far beyond, ferreting out all he could learn of the past; and Thucydides, in his account of the wars between Athens and Sparta, presented history as a guide to enlightened citizenship and constructive statecraft.

Perhaps because they were a restless and vehement people, the Greeks came to prize the "classical" virtues, which they were the first to define. For them, the ideal lay in moderation, or a golden mean. They valued order, balance, symmetry, clarity, and control. Their statues revealed their conception of what man ought to be—a noble creature, dignified, poised, unterrified by life or death, master of himself and of his feelings. Their architecture, as in the Parthenon, made use of exactly measured angles and rows of columns. The classical "order," or set of carefully wrought pillars placed in a straight line at specified intervals, represented the firm impress of human reason on the brute materials of nature. The same sense of form was thrown over the torrent of human words. Written language became contrived, carefully planned, organized for effect. The epic poem, the lyric, the drama, the oration, along with history and the philosophic dialogue, each with its own rules and principles of composition, became the "forms" within which, in Western civilization, men long continued to express their thoughts.

Reflecting on the world about them, the Greeks concluded that something more fundamental existed beyond the world of appearances, that true reality was not what met the eye. With other peoples, and with the Greeks themselves in earlier times, this same realization had led to the formation of myths, dealing with invisible but mighty beings known as gods, and with faraway places on the tops

Europe: Physical. *Topographically Europe is a peninsula jutting off from Asia. It is notable for the great number of its sub-peninsulas, inland seas, and offshore islands. The South is generally mountainous, with the ranges running from east to west and enclosing occasional pockets of flat land, as in the Ebro, Po, and middle Danube valleys; but the only point at which one may go from the Mediterranean to the North without climbing mountains is in France, which is the only country that clearly belongs both to the Mediterranean and to the North. A great plain, with branches in England and Sweden, runs from northern France through northern Germany, Poland, and Russia, and on into Asia. The plain is barely interrupted by the Ural Mountains, which, though conventionally the boundary between Europe and Asia, are too low and gradual to form an actual barrier. In any case, the Urals stop 500 miles north of the Caspian Sea, leaving a broad lowland called the Caspian Gate. One might draw a straight line from Amsterdam eastward through the Caspian Gate as far as the borders of western China, and although this line would reach the distance from New York to a point 500 miles west of San Francisco, one would never in traveling along it be higher above sea level than the top of the Empire State Building. Europe, including the Russian plain, is about as large as the United States together with the inhabited regions of Canada. It comprises only one-fifteenth of the earth's land surface. Nevertheless, in the past century, a quarter of the human race has lived in it.*

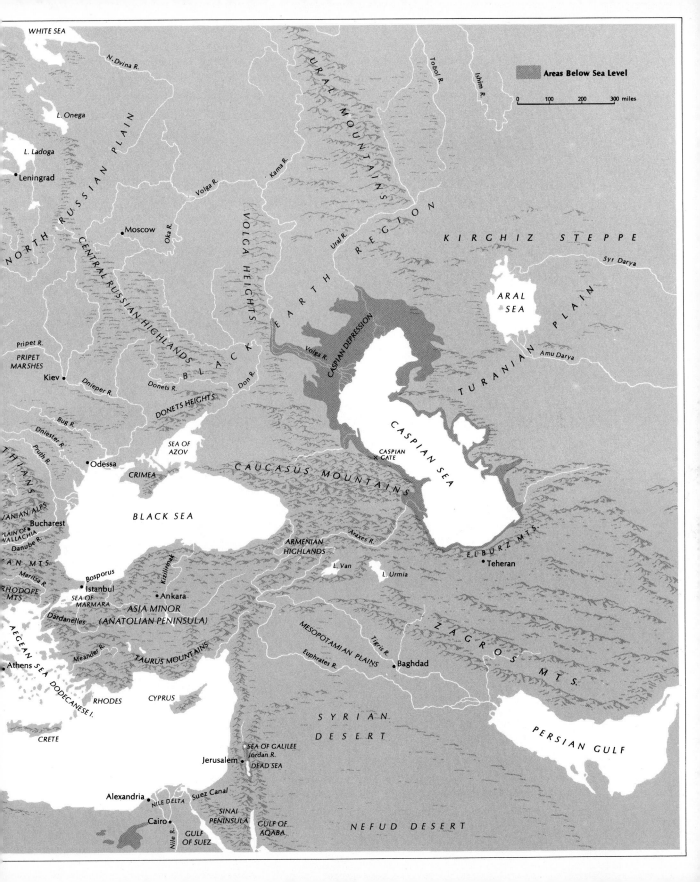

WHITE SEA

N. Dvina R.

L. Onega

L. Ladoga

• Leningrad

NORTH RUSSIAN PLAIN

URAL MOUNTAINS

Tobol R.

Ishim R.

Areas Below Sea Level

0   100   200   300 miles

Volga R.

Kama R.

CENTRAL RUSSIAN HIGHLANDS

• Moscow

Oka R.

VOLGA HEIGHTS

Ural R.

BLACK EARTH REGION

KIRGHIZ STEPPE

Syr Darya

ARAL SEA

Pripet R.

PRIPET MARSHES

Kiev •

Dnieper R.

Donets R.

Don R.

Volga R.

CASPIAN DEPRESSION

TURANIAN PLAIN

Amu Darya

DONETS HEIGHTS

Bug R.

Dniester R.

Pruth R.

Odessa •

SEA OF AZOV

CRIMEA

THIANS

CAUCASUS MOUNTAINS

CASPIAN SEA

NIAN ALPS

AIN OF WALLACHIA

• Bucharest

Danube R.

BLACK SEA

ARMENIAN HIGHLANDS

Araxes R.

CASPIAN × GATE

ELBURZ MTS.

AN MTS

Maritsa R.

RHODOPE MTS.

Kizilirmak

Bosporus

• Istanbul

SEA OF MARMARA

• Ankara

ASIA MINOR (ANATOLIAN PENINSULA)

L. Van

L. Urmia

• Teheran

Dardanelles

AEGEAN SEA

Meander R.

TAURUS MOUNTAINS

MESOPOTAMIAN PLAINS

Tigris R.

ZAGROS MTS.

• Athens

DODECANESE I.

RHODES

CYPRUS

Euphrates R.

• Baghdad

CRETE

SYRIAN DESERT

PERSIAN GULF

SEA OF GALILEE

Jordan R.

• Jerusalem

DEAD SEA

Alexandria •

Suez Canal

NILE DELTA

SINAI PENINSULA

Cairo •

Nile R.

GULF OF SUEZ

GULF OF AQABA

NEFUD DESERT

of mountains, beneath the earth, or in a world that followed death. Greek thinkers set to criticizing the web of myth. They looked for rational or natural explanations of what was at work behind the variety and confusion that they saw. Some, observing human sickness, said that disease was not a demonic possession, but a natural sequence of conditions in the body, which could be identified, understood, foreseen, and even treated in a natural way. Others, turning to physical nature, said that all matter was in reality composed of a very few things—of atoms or elements—which they usually designated as fire, water, earth, and air. Some said that change was a kind of illusion, all basic reality being uniform; some, that only change was real, and that the world was a flux. Some, like Pythagoras, found the enduring reality in "number" or mathematics. The Greeks, in short, laid the foundations for science. Studying also the way in which the mind worked, or ought to work if it was to reach truthful conclusions, they developed the science of logic. The great codifier of Greek thought on almost all subjects in the classical period was Aristotle, who lived in Athens from 384 to 322 B.C.

Greek influence spread widely and rapidly. Hardly were some of the city-states founded when their people, crowded within their narrow bounds, sent off some of their number with equipment and provisions to establish colonies. In this way Greek cities were very early established in south Italy, in Sicily, and even in the western Mediterranean, where Marseilles was founded about 600 B.C. Later the Greek city-states, unable to unite, succumbed to conquest by Philip of Macedon, who came from the relatively crude northern part of the Greek world, and whose son, Alexander the Great (356–323 B.C.), led a phenomenal and conquering march into Asia, across Persia, and on as far as India itself. Alexander's empire did not hold together, but Greek civilization, after having penetrated the raw world of the western Mediterranean, now began to revivify the ancient peoples of Egypt and the Near East. Greek thought, Greek art, and the Greek language spread far and wide. The most famous "Greeks" after the fourth century B.C. and on into the early centuries of the Christian era usually did not come from Greece but from the Hellenized Near East, and especially from Alexandria in Egypt. Among these later Greeks were the great summarizers or writers of encyclopedias in which ancient science was passed on to later generations—Strabo in geography, Galen in medicine, Ptolemy in astronomy. All three lived in the first and second centuries after Christ.

The Roman World

In 146 B.C. the Greeks of Greece were conquered by a new people, the Romans. The Romans, while keeping their own Latin language, rapidly absorbed what they could of the intellectual and artistic culture of the Greeks. Over a period of two or three centuries they assembled an empire in which the whole world of ancient civilization (west of Persia) was included. Egypt, Greece, Asia Minor, Syria all became Roman provinces, but in them the Romans had hardly any deep influence except in a political sense. In the West, in what are now Tunisia, Algeria, Morocco, Spain, Portugal, France, Switzerland, Belgium, and England, the Romans, though ruthless in their methods of conquest, in the long run acted as civilizing agents, transmitting to these hitherto backward countries the age-old achievements of the East and the more recent culture of Greece and of Rome itself. So thorough was the Romanization that in the West Latin even became the currently spoken language. It was later wiped out in Africa by Arabic but survives to this day, transformed by time, in the languages of France, Spain, Italy, and Portugal.

In the Roman Empire, which lasted with many vicissitudes from about 31 B.C. to the latter part of the fifth century A.D., virtually the entire civilized world of the ancient West was politically united and enjoyed generations of internal peace. Rome was the center, around which in all directions lay the "circle of lands," the *orbis terrarum*, the known world. The empire consisted essentially in the coasts of the Mediterranean Sea, which provided the great artery of transport and communication, and from which no part of the empire, except northern Gaul (France), Britain, and the Rhineland, was more than a couple of hundred miles away. Civilization was uniform; there were no distinct nationalities; the only significant cultural difference was that east of Italy the predominant language was Greek, in Italy and west of it, Latin. Cities grew up everywhere, engaged in a busy commercial life and exchange of ideas with one another. They remained most numerous in the East, where most of the manufacturing crafts and the densest population were still concentrated, but they sprang up also in the West—indeed, most of the older cities of France, Spain, England, and western and southern Germany boast of some kind of origin under the Romans.

The distinctive aptitude of the Romans lay in organization, administration, government, and law. Never before had armies been so systematically formed, maintained over such long periods, dispatched at a word of command over such distances, or maneuvered so effectively on the field of battle. Never had so many peoples been governed from a single center. The Romans had at first possessed self-governing and republican institutions, but they lost them in the process of conquest, and the governing talents which they displayed in the days of the empire were of an authoritarian character—talents, not for self-government, but for managing, coordinating and ruling the manifold and scattered parts of one enormous system. Locally, cities and city-states enjoyed a good deal of autonomy. But above them all rose a pyramid of imperial officials and provincial governors, culminating in the emperor at the top. The empire kept peace, the *pax Romana*, and even provided a certain justice as between its many peoples. Lawyers worked on the body of principles known ever afterward as Roman law.

Roman judges had somehow to settle disputes between persons of different regions, with conflicting local customs, for example, two merchants of Spain and Egypt. The Roman law came therefore to hold that no custom is necessarily right, that there is a higher or universal law by which fair decisions may be made, and that this higher, universal, or "natural" law, or "law of nature," will be understandable or acceptable to all men, since it arises from human nature and reason. Here the lawyers drew on Greek philosophy for support. They held also that law derives its force from being enacted by a proper authority (not merely from custom, usage, or former legal cases); this authority to make law they called *majestas* or sovereign power, and they

11

attributed it to the emperor. Thus the Romans emancipated the idea of law from mere custom on the one hand, and mere caprice on the other; they regarded it as something to be formed by enlightened intelligence, consistently with reason and the nature of things; and they associated it with the solemn action of official power. It must be added that Roman law favored the state, or the public interest as seen by the government, rather than the interests or liberties of individual persons. These principles, together with more specific ideas on property, debt, marriage, wills, etc., were in later centuries to have a great effect in Europe.

The Coming of Christianity

The thousand years during which Greco-Roman civilization arose and flourished were notable in another way even more momentous for all the later history of mankind. It was in this period that the great world religions came into being. Within the time bracket 700 B.C.–A.D. 700 the lives of Confucius and Buddha, of the major Jewish prophets, and of Mohammed are all included. At the very midpoint (probably about 4 B.C.), in Palestine in the Roman Empire, was born a man named Jesus believed by his followers to be the Son of God. The first Christians were Jews; but both under the impulse of its own doctrine, which held that all men were alike in spirit, and under the strong leadership of Paul, a man of Jewish birth, Roman citizenship, and Greek culture, Christianity began to make converts without regard to former belief. There were certainly a few Christians in Rome by the middle of the first century. Both Paul and the elder apostle, Peter, according to church tradition, died as martyrs at Rome in the time of the Emperor Nero about A.D. 67.

The Christian teaching spread at first among the poor, the people at the bottom of society, those whom Greek glories and Roman splendors had passed over or enslaved, and who had the least to delight in or to hope for in the existing world. Gradually it reached other classes; a few classically educated and well-to-do people became Christians; in the second century Christian bishops and writers were at work publicly in various parts of the empire. In the third century the Roman government, with the empire falling into turmoil, and blaming the social troubles on the Christians, subjected them to wholesale persecution. In the fourth century (possibly in A.D. 312) the Emperor Constantine was converted to Christianity. By the fifth century the entire Roman world was formally Christian; no other religion was officially tolerated; and the deepest thinkers were also Christians, men who combined Christian beliefs with the now thousand-year-old tradition of Greco-Roman thought and philosophy.

It is impossible to exaggerate the importance of the coming of Christianity. It brought with it, for one thing, an altogether new sense of human life. Where the Greeks had shown man his mind, the Christians showed him his soul; and they taught that in the sight of God all souls were equal, that every human life was sacrosanct and inviolate, and that all worldly distinctions of greatness, beauty, and brilliancy were in the last analysis superficial. Where the Greeks had identified the beautiful and the good, had thought ugliness to be bad, and had shrunk from disease as an imperfection and from everything misshapen as horrible and repulsive, the Christians resolutely saw a spiritual beauty even in the plainest or most unpleasant exterior and sought out the diseased, the crippled, and the mutilated to give them help. Love, for the ancients, was never quite distinguished from Venus; for the Christians, who held that God was love, it took on deep overtones of sacrifice and compassion. Suffering itself was proclaimed by Christians to be in a way divine, since God himself had suffered on the Cross in human form. A new dignity was thus found for suffering that the world could not cure. At the same time the Christians worked to relieve suffering as none had worked before. They protested against the massacre of prisoners of war, against the mistreatment and degradation of slaves, against the sending of gladiators to kill each other in the arena for another's pleasure. In place of the Greek and pagan self-satisfaction with human accomplishments they taught humility in the face of an almighty Providence, and in place of proud distinctions between high and low, slave and free, civilized and barbarian, they held that all men were brothers because all were children of the same God.

On an intellectual level Christianity also marked a revolution. It was Christianity, not rational philosophy, that dispelled the swarm of greater and lesser gods and goddesses, the blood sacrifices and self-immolation, the frantic resort to magic, fortune-telling, and divination, or grim resignation in the temples of Fate and Fortune. The Christians taught that since there was only one God, the pagan gods must be at best lesser demons, and even this idea was gradually given up. The pagan conception of local, tribal, or national gods disappeared. It was now held that for all the world there was only one God, one plan of Salvation, and one Providence, and that all mankind took its origin from one source. The idea of the world as one thing, a "universe," was thus affirmed with a new depth of meaning. The very intolerance of Christianity (which was new to the ancient world) came from this overwhelming sense of human unity, in which it was thought that all men should have, and deserved to have, the one true and saving religion.

It was for their political ideas that the Christians were most often denounced and persecuted. The Roman Empire was a world state; there was no other state but it; no living human being except the emperor was sovereign; no one anywhere on earth was his equal. Between gods and men, in the pagan view, there was moreover no clear distinction. Some gods behaved much like men, and some men were more like gods than others. The emperor was held to be veritably a god, *divus Caesar, semper Augustus*. A cult of Caesar was established, regarded as necessary to maintain the state, which was the world itself. All this the Christians firmly refused to accept. It was because they would not worship Caesar that the Roman officials regarded them as monstrous social incendiaries who must be persecuted and stamped out.

The Christian doctrine on this point went back to the saying gathered from Jesus, that one should render to Caesar the things that were Caesar's, and to God those that were God's. The same dualism was presented more systematically by St. Augustine about A.D. 420 in his *City of God*. Few books have been more influential in shaping the later development of Western civilization.

The "world," the world of Caesar, in the time of St. Augustine, was going to ruin. Rome itself was plundered in 410 by heathen barbarians. Augustine wrote the *City of God* with this event obsessing his imagination. He wrote to show that though the world itself perished there was yet another world that was more enduring and more important.

There were, he said, really two "cities," the earthly and the heavenly, the temporal and the eternal, the city of man and the City of God. The earthly city was the domain of state and empire, of political authority and political obedience. It was a good thing, as part of God's providential scheme for human life, but it had no inherently divine character of its own. The emperor was a man. The state was not absolute; it could be judged, amended, or corrected from sources outside itself. It was, for all its majesty and splendor, really subordinate in some way to a higher and spiritual power. This power lay in the City of God. By the City of God Augustine meant many things, and all sorts of meanings were found by readers in later ages. The heavenly city might mean heaven itself, the abode of God and of blessed spirits enjoying life after death. It might mean certain elect spirits of this world, the good people as opposed to the bad. It might, more theoretically, be a system of ideal values or ideal justice, as opposed to the crude approximations of the actual world. Or it was later thought, by some, to mean the organized church and its clergy.

In any case, with this Christian dualism the Western world escaped from what is called Caesaropapism, the holding by one man of the powers of ruler and of pontiff. The spiritual and the political power were held to be separate and independent. In later times, popes and kings often quarreled with each other; the clergy often struggled for worldly power, and governments at various times (including the twentieth century with its totalitarian systems) have attempted to dictate what men should believe, or love, or hope for. But speaking in general of European history neither side has ever won out, and in the sharp distinction between the spiritual and the temporal has lain the germ of many liberties in the West. At the same time, the idea that no ruler, no government, and no institution is too mighty to rise above moral criticism opened the way to a dynamic and progressive way of living in the West.

As for Augustine himself, he lived to see the world grow worse. He died in A.D. 430. In 429 the Roman province of Africa, where he had been a bishop, was pillaged by a wild Germanic tribe called the Vandals.

2
The Early Middle Ages: The Formation of Europe

There was really no Europe in ancient times. In the Roman Empire we may see a Mediterranean world, or even a West and an East in the Latin- and Greek-speaking portions. But the West included parts of Africa as well as of Europe, and Europe as we know it was divided by the Rhine-Danube frontier, south and west of which lay the civilized provinces of the empire, and north and east the "barbarians" of whom the civilized world knew almost nothing. To the Romans "Africa" meant Tunisia-Algeria, "Asia" meant the Asia Minor peninsula; and the word "Europe," since it meant little, was scarcely used by them at all. It was in the half-millennium from the fifth to the tenth centuries that Europe as such for the first time emerged with its peoples brought together in a life of their own, clearly set off from that of Asia or Africa.

First of all the Roman Empire went to pieces, especially in the West. The Christianizing of the empire did nothing to impede its decline. The Emperor Constantine, who in embracing Christianity undoubtedly hoped to strengthen the imperial system, also took one other significant step. In A.D. 330 he founded a new capital at the old Greek city of Byzantium, which he renamed Constantinople. Thereafter the Roman Empire had two capitals, Rome and Constantinople, and was administered in two halves. Increasingly the center of gravity moved eastward, as if returning to the more ancient centers in the Near East, as if the "modern" experiment of civilizing the West were to be given up as a failure.

Throughout its long life the empire had been surrounded on almost all sides by barbarians, wild Celts in Wales and Scotland, Germans in the heart of Europe, Persians or Parthians in the East ("barbarian" only in the ancient sense of speaking neither Greek nor Latin), and, in the southeast, the Arabs. (In the south the empire simply faded off into the Sahara.) These barbarians, always with the exception of Persia, had never been brought within the pale of ancient civilization. They remained illiterate, unsettled, townless, more or less nomadic, and frequently bellicose. Somewhat like the Chinese, who about 200 B.C. built the Great Wall to solve the same problem, the Romans simply drew a line beyond which they themselves rarely ventured and would not allow the barbarians to pass. Nevertheless the barbarians filtered in. As early as the third century A.D. emperors and generals recruited bands of them to serve in the Roman armies. Their service over, they would receive farmlands, settle down, marry and mingle with the population. By the fourth and fifth centuries a good many individuals of barbarian birth were even reaching high positions of state. At the same time, in the West, for reasons that are not fully understood, the activity of the Roman cities began to falter, commerce began to decay, local governments became paralyzed, taxes became more ruinous, and free farmers were bound to the soil. The army seated and unseated emperors. Rival generals fought with each other. Gradually the West fell into decrepitude and an internal barbarization so that the old line between the Roman provinces and the barbarian world made less and less difference.

The barbarians themselves, after some centuries of relative stability, rather suddenly began to move. Sometimes they first sought peaceable access to the empire, pushed by other peoples from behind, or attracted by the warmer Mediterranean climate, or desiring with a childlike eagerness to share in the advantages of Roman civilization. More often, tribes consisting of a few tens of thousands, men, women, and children, moved swiftly and by force, plundering, fighting, and killing as they went. At first most of the barbarians threatening the empire were Germanic, going under many names. The Angles and Saxons overran Britain about 450, the Franks invaded Gaul at the same time, the Vandals reached as

15

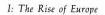

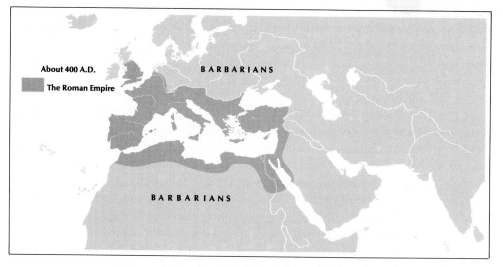

About 400 A.D.

The Roman Empire

BARBARIANS

BARBARIANS

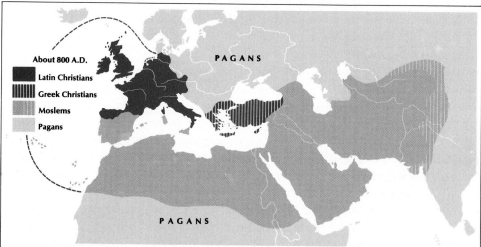

About 800 A.D.

Latin Christians

Greek Christians

Moslems

Pagans

PAGANS

PAGANS

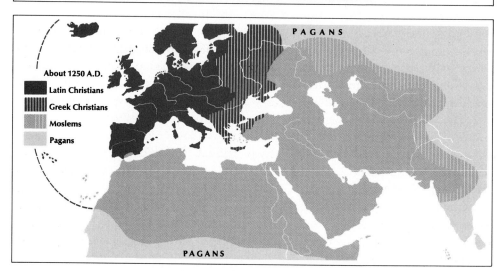

About 1250 A.D.

Latin Christians

Greek Christians

Moslems

Pagans

PAGANS

PAGANS

16

far as Roman Africa in 429, the East Goths appeared in Asia Minor in 382 and in Italy in 493, the West Goths lunged toward Constantinople about 380, tore through Greece in 396, sacked Rome itself in 410, and reached Spain about the year 420. In 476 the last Roman emperor in the West was deposed by a barbarian chieftain. Sometimes in the general upheaval wild Turkman peoples fresh from Asia were intermixed. Of these the most famous were the Huns, who cut through central Europe and France about 450 under their leader Attila, the "scourge of God"—and then disappeared. Nor were these invasions all. Two centuries later new irruptions burst upon the Greco-Roman world on its opposite side, where hitherto outlying peoples poured in from the Arabian deserts. The Arabs, aroused by the new faith of Islam (Mohammed died in 632), fell as conquerors upon Syria, Mesopotamia, Persia, occupied Egypt about 640, the old Roman Africa about 700, and in 711 reached Spain, where they destroyed the Germanic kingdom set up there by the West Goths.

Beneath these blows the old unity of the Greco-Roman or Mediterranean world was broken. The "circle of lands" divided into three segments. Three types of civilization now confronted each other across the inland sea.

One was the Eastern Roman, Later Roman, Greek, or Byzantine Empire (all names for the same thing) with its capital at Constantinople, and now including only the Asia Minor peninsula, the Balkan peninsula, and parts of Italy. It represented the most direct continuation of the immemorial civilization of the Near East. It was Christian in religion and Greek in culture and language. Its people felt themselves to be the truest heirs both of early Christianity and of the Greeks of the golden age. Art and architecture, trades and crafts, commerce and navigation, thought and writing, government and law, while not so creative or flexible as in the classical age, were still carried on actively in the Eastern Empire, on much the same level as in the closing centuries of ancient times. For all Christians, and for heathen barbarians in Europe, the emperor of the East stood out as the world's supreme ruler, and Constantinople as the world's preeminent and almost fabulous city.

The second segment, and the most extensive, was the Arabic and Mohammedan. It reached from the neighborhood of the Pyrenees through Spain and all North Africa into Arabia, Syria, and the East. Arabic was its language; it became, and still remains, the common speech from Morocco to the Persian Gulf. Islam was its religion. It was organized in the caliphate in which all Moslems were included, and

Mediterranean World about 400, 800, and 1250 A.D. *The unified world of Mediterranean civilization, as it existed under the Roman Empire, broke apart into three segments in the early Middle Ages. Each segment developed its own type of life. Each segment also expanded beyond the limits of the ancient Mediterranean civilization. Latin Christendom reached to the Baltic and beyond, Greek Christendom penetrated north of the Black Sea, and the Moslem world spread into inner Asia and into Black Africa. In 1250 and until 1492, the Moslems, or Moors, still held the southern tip of Spain.*

the caliph was regarded as the true religious and military successor to Mohammed himself. The Arabic world, like the Byzantine, built directly upon the heritage of the Greco-Romans. In religion, the early Moslems regarded themselves as successors to the Jewish and Christian traditions. They considered the line of Jewish prophets to be spokesmen of the true God, and they put Jesus in this line. But they added that Mohammed was the last and greatest of the prophets, that the Koran set forth a revelation replacing that of the Jewish Bible, that the New Testament of the Christians was mistaken because Christ was not divine, and that the Christian belief in a Trinity was erroneous because there was in the strictest and most rigid sense only One True God. To the Moslem Arabs, therefore, all Christians were contemptible infidels.

In mundane matters, the Arabs speedily took over the civilization of the lands they conquered. In the caliphate, as in the Byzantine Empire, the civilization of the ancient world went its way without serious interruption. Huge buildings and magnificent palaces were constructed; ships plied the Mediterranean; merchants ventured over the deserts and traversed the Indian Ocean; holy or learned men corresponded over thousands of miles; taxes were collected, laws were enforced, and provinces were kept in order. In the sciences the Arabs not only learned from but went beyond the Greeks. The Greek scientific literature was translated: some of it is known today only through these medieval Arabic versions. Arab geographers had a wider knowledge of the world than anyone had possessed up to their time. Arab mathematicians developed algebra so far beyond the Greeks as almost to be its creator ("algebra" is an Arabic word), and in introducing the "Arabic" numerals (through their contacts with India) they made arithmetic, which in Roman numerals had been a formidably difficult science, into something that every schoolchild can be taught.

The third segment, about A.D. 700, did not look very promising. It was what was left over from the other two—what the Byzantines were unable to hold, and the Arabs unable to conquer. It included only Italy (shared in part with the Byzantines), France, Belgium, the Rhineland, and Britain. Barbarian kings were doing their best to rule small kingdoms, but in truth all government had fallen to pieces. Strange and uncouth peoples milled about. Usually the invading barbarians remained a minority, eventually to be absorbed. Only in England, and in the region immediately west of the Rhine, did the Germanic element replace the older Celtic and Latin. But the presence of the invaders, armed and fierce amid peasants and city-dwellers reduced to passivity by Roman rule, together with the disintegration of Roman institutions that had gone on even before the invasions, left this region in chaos.

The Western barbarians, as noted, were Germanic; and the Germanic influence was to be a distinctive contribution to the making of Europe. Some Germans were Christian by the fourth century, but most were still heathen when they burst into the Roman Empire. Their languages had not been written down, but they possessed an intricate folklore and religion, in which fighting and heroic valor were much esteemed. Though now in a migratory phase, they were an agricultural people who knew how to work iron, and they had a rudimentary knowledge of the crafts of the Romans. They were organized in small tribes, and had a strong sense of tribal kinship, which (as with many primitive peoples) dominated their ideas of leadership and law. They enjoyed more freedom in their affairs than did the citizens of the Roman Empire. Many of the tribes were roughly self-governing in that all free men, those entitled to bear arms, met in open fields to hold council; and often the tribe itself elected its leader or king. They had a strong sense of loyalty to persons, of fealty to the acknowledged king or chief; but they had no sense of loyalty to large or general institutions. They had no sense of the state—of any distant, impersonal, and continuing source of law and rule. Law they regarded as the inflexible custom of each tribe. In the absence of abstract jurisprudence or trained judges, they settled disputes by rough and ready methods. In the ordeal, for example, a person who obstinately floated when thrown into water was adjudged guilty. In trial by battle, the winner of a kind of ritualistic duel was regarded as innocent. The gods, it was thought, would not allow wrong to prevail.

The Germans who overran the old Roman provinces found it difficult to maintain any political organization at more than a local level. Security and civil order all but disappeared. Peasant communities were at the mercy of wandering bands of habitual fighters. Fighters often captured peasant villages, took them under their protection, guarded them from further marauders, and lived off their produce. Sometimes the same great fighting man came to possess many such villages, moving with his retinue of horsemen from one village to another to support himself throughout the year. Thus originated a new distinction between lord and servant, noble and commoner, martial and menial class. Life became local and self-sufficient. People ate, wore, used, and dwelled in only what they themselves and their neighbors could produce. Trade died down, the cities became depopulated, money went out of circulation, almost nothing was bought or sold. The Roman roads fell into neglect; people often used them as quarries for ready-cut building blocks for their own crude purposes. The West not only broke up into localized villages, but also ceased to have habitual contacts across the Mediterranean. It became isolated from the Eastern centers from which its former civilization had always been drawn. The West was reverting. From roughly 500 A.D. on, Europe was in the so-called Dark Ages.

Only one organized institution maintained a tie with the civilized past. Only one institution, reaching over the whole West, could receive news or dispatch its agents over the whole area. This institution was the Christian church. Its framework still stood; its network of bishoprics, as built up in late Roman times, remained intact except in places like England where the barbarian conquest was complete.

In addition, a new type of religious institution was rapidly spreading with the growth of monasteries. The serious and the sensitive, both men and women (though not together, to be sure), rejected the savagery about them and retired into communities of their own. Usually they were left unmolested by rough neighbors who held them in religious awe. In a world of violence they formed islands of quiet and of peace. In a society of burly barbarians they lived the life of contemplation. Their prayers, it was believed, were of use to all the world, and their example might at the least arouse in obstreperous worldlings the pangs of shame. The monastic houses generally adopted the rule of St. Benedict (*c.* 480–543), and were generally governed by an abbot. Dedicated to the same ideals, they formed unifying filaments throughout the chaos of the Latin West.

Bishops, abbots, and monks looked with veneration to Rome as the spot where St. Peter, the first apostle, had been martyred. The bishop of Rome corresponded with other bishops, sent out missionaries (to England, for example), gave advice on doctrine when he could, and attempted to keep in mind the situation throughout the Latin world as a whole. Moreover, with no emperor any longer in Rome, the bishop took over the government and public affairs of the city. Thus the bishop of Rome, while claiming a primacy over all Christians, was not dominated by any secular power. In the East the great church functionaries, the patriarchs, fell under the influence of the emperor who continued to rule at Constantinople, so that a tradition of Caesaropapism grew up in the East; but in the West the independence of the bishop of Rome now confirmed in practice a principle always maintained by the great churchmen of the West—the independence of the spiritual power from the political or temporal.

In this way was built up the authority of the popes. It was fortified by various arguments. St. Peter, it was held, had imparted the spiritual authority given to him by Christ himself to the Roman bishops who were his successors. This doctrine of the "Petrine supremacy" was based on two verses in the Bible, according to which Christ designated Peter as the head of the church, giving him the "power of the keys," to open and close the doors of eternal salvation.[2] As for the pope's temporal rule in Rome, it was affirmed that the Emperor Constantine had endowed the bishop with the government of the city. This "Donation of Constantine" was accepted as historical fact from the eighth century to the fifteenth, when it was proved to be a forgery.

It was the church which incorporated the barbarians into a higher way of life, and when a barbarian embraced a more civilized way of living it was the church that he entered. As early as about A.D. 340, the church sent out Ulfilas to convert the Goths; his translation of the Bible represents the first writing down of any Germanic language. About 496 the king of the Franks, Clovis, was converted to Christianity. A hundred years later, in 597, the king of Kent in southeast England yielded to the persuasions of Augustine of Canterbury, a missionary dispatched from Rome, and the Christianization of the Anglo-Saxons gradually followed. Missionaries from Ireland also, to which Christians of the Roman Empire had fled before the heathen

---

[2]"Thou art Peter, and upon this rock I will build my church; and the gates of hell shall not prevail against it. And I will give unto thee the keys of the kingdom of heaven, and whatsoever thou shalt bind on earth shall be bound in heaven; and whatsoever thou shalt loose on earth shall be loosed in heaven." Matthew xvi, 18–19. In Greek the name Peter meant a "rock"; a play upon words was involved. The pun is still evident in some modern languages, as in French, where *pierre,* a rock, is the same as *Pierre,* Peter.

barbarians, now returned to both Britain and the Continent to spread the gospel. By some such year as A.D. 700, after three centuries of turmoil, the borders of Christianity in the West were again roughly what they had been in late Roman times. Then in 711, as we have seen, the Arabs conquered Spain. They crossed the Pyrenees and raced toward central Europe, but were stopped by a Christian and Frankish army in 732 at Tours on the river Loire. Islam was not destined to reach beyond Spain.

Among the Franks, in what is now northern France and the German Rhineland, there had meanwhile arisen a line of capable rulers of whom the greatest was Charlemagne. The Frankish kings made it their policy to cooperate with the pope. The pope needed a protector against depredations by his barbarian neighbors and against the political claims of the Byzantine Empire upon the city of Rome. The Frankish kings, in return for protection thus offered, won papal support to their side. This made it easier for them to control their own bishops, who were more often seen on horseback than in the episcopal chair, and was of use in pacifying their own domains and in wars of conquest against the heathen. In the year 800, in Rome, the pope crowned Charlemagne as emperor of the West. Frankish king and Roman bishop both believed that if only the Roman Empire could be restored peace and order might once more reign. Church and empire, the spirit and the state, were to be as two mighty swords employed in the same holy cause.

Charlemagne crossed the Pyrenees and won back the northeastern corner of Spain to Christian rule. He overthrew and subordinated the barbarian kings who had set themselves up in Italy. He sent forces down the Danube, penetrated into Bohemia, and proceeded against some of the still heathen Germans (the Saxons) who lived along the river Elbe, and whom he either massacred or converted to Christianity. All these regions he brought within his new empire. Except for England and Ireland, which remained outside, the borders of his empire were coextensive with those of the Latin Christian world.

Once more, to a degree, the West was united. But a momentous change had occurred. Its capital was now not Rome and did not lie in the ancient world of the Mediterranean. Its capital was at Aix-la-Chapelle, or Aachen, near the mouth of the Rhine. Its ruler, Charlemagne, was a German of an ethnic group which ancient civilization had left outside. Its people were Germans, French, and Italians, or the ancestors from whom these nationalities were to be developed. In the Greco-Roman world the north had always been at best provincial. Now the north became a center in its own right. Charlemagne dispatched embassies to the emperor at Constantinople, and to Harun al-Rashid, the great caliph at Baghdad. In intellectual matters, too, the north now became a capital. Centuries of violence and confusion had left ignorance very widespread. Charlemagne himself, though he understood Latin, could barely read and never learned to write. He used his authority to revive the all but forgotten ancient learning and to spread education at least among the clergy. To his palace school came scholars from England, Germany, France, Italy, Spain. They wrote and spoke in Latin, the only Western language in which any complicated ideas could at the time be expressed. Disintegrating ancient manuscripts were copied and then again copied to assure a more abundant supply for study—always by hand, but in a more rapid script than had before been used, the so-called Carolingian minuscule, from which come the small letters of the modern Western. alphabet, only the capitals being Roman. Commerce also, which had virtually disappeared, Charlemagne undertook to foster. He created a new and more reliable coinage, which was based on silver, the gold coins of the Roman Empire having long since vanished. A pound of silver was divided into 20 *solidi* or 240 pennies. This scheme of values, though long used in many parts of Europe, survived longest in the country that remained outside Charlemagne's empire, namely, in England, in its pound sterling of 20 shillings each containing 12 pence.

It is in Charlemagne's empire that we can first see the shape of Europe, as a unit of society and culture distinct from the Mediterranean world of antiquity. The empire did not last. The troubled era was not yet over. New hordes of barbarians assailed Western Christendom in the ninth century. The Magyars (called in Latin "Hungarians") terrified various parts of Europe until they settled down on the middle Danube about the year 900. New Germanic tribes uprooted themselves, coming this time from Scandinavia, and variously known as Norsemen, Vikings, or Danes. Bursting out in all directions, they reached Kiev in Russia in 864, discovered Iceland in 874, and even touched America in 1000. In the Christian world they assaulted the coasts and pushed up the rivers but settled in considerable numbers only in the Danelaw in England and in Normandy in France. Meanwhile the Arabs raided the shores of France and Italy and occupied Sicily. Nowhere was the power of government strong enough to ward off such attacks. Everywhere the harassed local population found its own means of defense or, that failing, was slaughtered, robbed, or carried off into slavery.

Gradually the second wave of barbarians was incorporated as the first had been, by the same process of conversion to Christianity. By the year 1000 the process was nearly complete. In 1001 the pope sent a golden crown to the Magyars to crown St. Stephen as their first king, thus bringing Hungary within the orbit of the Latin West. Poland, Bohemia, and the Scandinavian homelands of the Norsemen were being rapidly Christianized. In older Christian countries, such as France, the last remote and isolated rustics—the "heathen" who lived in the "heath"—were finally ferreted out by missionaries and brought within the Christian fold. In Christian countries Christianity now permeated to every corner, and the historic peoples of western Europe had come together within the spreading system of the Latin church.

Meanwhile West and East continued to drift apart. The refusal of Greek patriarchs at Constantinople to recognize the claims to primacy of the bishop of Rome, whom they regarded as a kind of Western barbarian, and the refusal of the Roman pontiff to acknowledge the political pretensions of the Byzantine Empire, led to the Great Schism of East and West. This schism, after developing for three centuries, became definite in 1054. It divided the Christian world into the Latin or

Roman Catholic and the Greek Orthodox churches. It was from Constantinople that Christianity reached the peoples of Russia. The Russians, like the Balkan peoples, remained out of contact with the West during the centuries when spiritual and intellectual contacts were carried through the clergy. They believed, indeed, that the Latin West was evil, heretical, contumacious, and unholy. The Latin West, at the same time, by the schism, cut one more of its ties with antiquity and emerged the more clearly as an independent center of its own civilization.

By the year 1000, or soon thereafter, the entity that we call Europe had been brought into existence. From the turbulence that followed the collapse of the Greco-Roman civilization had issued the peoples and the countries of modern Europe. A kingdom of France was in being, adjoining the great ill-defined bulk of Germany to the east. There were small Christian kingdoms in northern Spain and a number of city-states in the Italian peninsula. In the north there were now a kingdom of England and a kingdom of Scotland, and Denmark, Norway, and Sweden had taken form. In the east rose the three great kingdoms of Poland, Bohemia, and Hungary, the first two predominantly Slavic, Hungary predominantly Magyar, but all Latin and Catholic in culture and religion, and Western in orientation. The east Slavs, or Russians, and the Slavs and other peoples of the Balkan peninsula, also formed kingdoms of their own. Their way was diverging from the West. Christianized by Byzantine missionaries, they were Greek and Orthodox in culture and religion and oriented toward Constantinople.

The civilization of the West, in the year 1000, was still not much to boast of in the more polished circles of Byzantium or Baghdad. It might still seem that the West would suffer more than the East from their separation. But the West began at this time to experience a remarkable activity, ushering in the European civilization of the High Middle Ages.

S ome historical periods are so dynamic that a person who lives to be fifty years old can remember sweeping changes that have come in his own lifetime. Such a time has been the last century of the modern age. Such a time, also, began in Europe in the eleventh century. A man could see new towns rise and grow before his eyes. He could observe new undertakings in commerce or government. It is hardly too much to say that all the cities that Europe was to know before the modern industrial era sprang up between about 1050 and 1200. The population of western Europe, which had been sparse even in Roman days, and which was even more sparse after 500, suddenly began to grow more dense about the year 1000, expanded steadily for two or three hundred years, and then, from the fourteenth century, did not again abruptly increase until after 1800. The people of the High Middle Ages did not develop the conception of progress, because their minds were set upon timeless values and personal salvation in another world, but the period was nevertheless one of rapid progress in nonreligious or "secular" things. It was a period in which much was created that remained fundamental far into modern times.

3

The High Middle Ages: Secular Civilization

Changes After
A.D. *1000*

The new era was made possible by the process of growth in population which went along with agricultural changes. After the Norse and Magyar inroads had stopped, Europe was spared the assaults of barbarians. There came to be more security of life and limb. A farmer could plant with more confidence that he would reap. A man could build a house and expect to live his life in it and pass it on to his children. Hence there was more planting and building. Sometime before the year 1000 a heavier plow had been invented, which cut a deeper furrow. Better methods of harnessing horses had been found than the ancients had ever known. The Romans had continued simply to throw a yoke over a horse's neck, so that the animal in pulling a weight easily choked. Europeans, before the year 1000, began to use a horse collar that rested on the animal's shoulders. The single horse could pull a greater load, or several horses could now for the first time be hitched in tandem. The amount of available animal power was thus multiplied, at a time when animals were the main source of power other than human muscle. Probably windmills, unknown to the ancients, were developed in the Low Countries about this time. They too offered a new source of power. Thus at the very beginning of a specifically "European" history, one may detect a characteristic of European civilization—a faculty for invention, a quest for sources of power other than man's muscle.

With such labor-saving devices men continued to work very hard, but they obtained more results by their efforts. Probably the use of such inventions, together with the influence of the Christian clergy, accounts for the gradual disappearance of slavery from Europe and its replacement by the less abject and less degrading status of serfdom. It is true that medieval Christians, when they could, continued to enslave whites as they were later to do with blacks. Usually such slaves were captives in war, taken from tribes not yet converted to Christianity, and sometimes exported as a form of merchandise to the Byzantine and Moslem worlds. As the successive European peoples became Christianized, the supply of slaves dried up. Medieval Christians did not enslave each other, nor was slavery essential to any important form of production.

Not only did population increase, and work become more productive, but groups of people became less isolated from one another. Communications improved. The roads remained poor or nonexistent, but bridges were built across the many European rivers, and settlers filled in the wildernesses that had formerly separated the inhabited areas. Trees were felled and land cleared, as long afterward in the United States during the westward movement. But where the forest gave way in America to an agricultural world of detached individual farmsteads, in medieval Europe the rural population clustered in village communities. The "nucleated" village gave more security, more contact between families, and readier access to the blacksmith or the priest. It also made possible a communally organized agriculture.

Better ways of using land were introduced in the "three-field" system, which spread almost everywhere where cereal crops were the staple. In this "system" the peasant village divided its arable fields into three parts. In a given year one part was sown with one crop, such as wheat, a second part with another, such as barley, and the third was left to lie fallow. The three parts were rotated from year to year. Thus soil exhaustion was avoided at a time when fertilizers were unknown. Formerly half or less of the available fields had been cultivated at any one time. With the three-field system two-thirds of the land came into annual use. This fact, reinforced by better plowing and more effective employment of animals, led to a huge increase in the supply of food.

The peace and personal security necessary to agriculture were also advanced, in the absence of effective public authority, by the growth of institutions that we know as "feudalism." Feudalism was intricate and diverse, but in essence it was a means of carrying on some kind of government on a local basis where no organized state existed. After the collapse of Charlemagne's empire the real authority fell into the hands of persons who were most often called "counts." The count was the most important man of a region covering a few hundred square miles. To build up his own position, and strengthen himself for war against other counts, he tried to keep the peace and maintain control over the lesser lords in his county, those whose possessions extended over a few hundred or a few thousand acres. These lesser lords accepted or were forced to accept his protection. They became his vassals, and he became their "lord." The lord-and-vassal relation was one of reciprocal duties. The lord protected the vassal and assured him justice and firm tenure of his land. If two vassals of the same lord disputed the possession of the same village, the lord decided the case, sitting in council (or "court") with all his vassals assembled and judging according to the common memory of customary law of the district. If a vassal died young, leaving only small children, the lord took the family under his "wardship" or guardianship, guaranteeing that the rightful heirs would inherit in due time. Correspondingly the vassal agreed to serve the lord as a fighting man for a certain number of days in the year. From other "unauthorized" fighting and squabbling the vassal was supposed to refrain. The vassal also owed it to the lord to attend and advise him, to sit in his court in the judging of disputes. Usually he owed no money or material payment; but if the lord had to be ransomed from captivity, or when his children married, the vassal paid a fee. The vassal also paid a fee on inheriting an estate, and the income of estates under wardship went to the lord. Thus the lord collected sporadic revenues with which to finance his somewhat primitive government.

This feudal scheme, which probably originated locally, gradually spread. Lords at the level of counts became in turn the vassals of dukes. In the year 987 the great lords of France chose Hugh Capet as their king, and became his vassals. The kings of France enjoyed little real power for another two hundred years, but the descendants of Hugh occupied their throne for eight centuries, until the French Revolution. Similarly the magnates of Germany elected a king in 911; in 962 the German king was crowned emperor, as Charlemagne had been before him; thus originated the Holy Roman Empire of which much will be heard in the following chapters.

To England, in these formative centuries, it was not given to choose a king by election. England was conquered in 1066 by the Duke of Normandy, William. The Normans (the old Norsemen reshaped by a century of Christian and French influence) imposed upon England a centralized and efficient type of feudalism which they had

25

developed in Normandy. In England, from an early date, the king and his central officials therefore had considerable power. In England there was more civil peace and personal security than on the Continent. Within its strong monarchy self-governing institutions could eventually develop with a minimum of disorder.

The notable feature of feudalism was its mutual or reciprocal character. In this it differed from the old Roman imperial principle, by which the emperor had been a majestic and all-powerful sovereign. Under feudalism no one was sovereign. King and people, lord and vassal, were joined in a kind of contract. Each owed something to the other. If one defaulted, the obligation ceased. If a vassal refused his due services, the king had the right to enforce compliance. If the king violated the rights of the vassal, the vassals could join together against him. The king was supposed to act with the advice of the vassals, who formed his council or court. If the vassals believed the king to be exceeding his lawful powers, they could impose terms upon him. It was out of this mutual or contractual character of feudalism that ideas of constitutional government later developed.

Feudalism applied in the strict sense only to the military or noble class. Below the feudal world lay the vast mass of the peasantry. Here, in the village, the lowliest vassal of a higher noble was lord over his own subjects. The village, with its people and surrounding farmlands, constituted a "manor," the estate of a lord. In the eleventh century most people of the manor were serfs. They were "bound to the soil" in that they could not leave the manor without the lord's permission. Few wanted to leave anyway, at a time when the world beyond the village was unknown and dangerous, and filled at best only with other similar manors in which opportunities were no different. The lord, for his part, could not expropriate the villagers or drive them away. He owed them protection and the administration of justice. They in turn worked his fields, and gave him part of the produce of their own. No money changed hands, because there was virtually no money in circulation. The manorial system was the agricultural base on which a ruling class was supported. It supported also the clergy, for the church held much land in the form of manors. It gave the protection from physical violence and the framework of communal living, without which the peasants could not grow crops or tend livestock.

Many consequences flowed from the rise of agricultural productivity. Lords and even a few peasants could produce a surplus, which they might sell if only they could find a market. The country was able to produce enough food for a town population to live on. And since population grew with the increase of the food supply, and since not all the new people were needed in agriculture, a surplus of population also began to exist. Restless spirits among the peasants now wanted to get away from the manor. And many went off to the new towns.

We have seen how the ancient cities had decayed. In the ninth and tenth centuries, with few exceptions, there were none left in western Europe. Here and there one would find a cluster of population around the headquarters of a bishop, a great count, or a king. But there were no commercial centers. There was no merchant class. The simple crafts—weaving, metal working, harness making—were carried on locally on the manors. Rarely, an itinerant trader might appear with such semi-precious goods as he could carry for long distances on donkeys—Eastern silks, or a few spices for the wealthy. Among these early traders Jews were often important, because Judaism, penetrating the Byzantine and Arabic worlds as well as the Western, offered one of the few channels of distant communication that were open.

Long-distance trading was the first to develop. The city of Venice was founded about A.D. 570 when refugees from the barbarians settled in its islands. The Venetians, as time went on, brought Eastern goods up the Adriatic and sold them to traders coming down from central Europe. In Flanders in the north, in what is now Belgium, there developed manufacturers of woolen cloth. Flemish woolens were of a unique quality, owing to peculiarities of the atmosphere and the skill of the weavers. They could not be duplicated elsewhere. Nor could Eastern goods be procured except through the Venetians—or the Genoese or Pisans. Such goods could not possibly be produced locally, yet they were in demand wherever they became known. Merchants traveled in increasing numbers to disseminate them. Money came back into more general circulation; where it came from is not quite clear, since there was little mining of gold or silver in the Middle Ages. Merchants began to establish permanent headquarters, settling within the deserted walls of ghostly Roman towns, or near the seat of a lord or ecclesiastic, whose throngs of retainers might become customers. Craftsmen moved from the overpopulated manors to these same growing centers, where they might produce wares that the lords or merchants would wish to buy. The process once started tended to snowball: the more people settled in such an agglomeration the more they needed food brought to them from the country, and the more craftsmen left the villages the more the country people, lords and serfs, had to obtain clothing and simple tools and utensils from the towns. Hence a busy local trade developed also.

By 1100, or not long thereafter, such centers existed all over Europe, from the Baltic to Italy, from England as far east as Bohemia. Usually there was one about every twenty or thirty miles. The smallest towns had only a few hundred inhabitants, the larger ones two or three thousand, or sometimes more. Each carried on a local exchange with its immediate countryside and purveyed goods of more distant origin to local consumers. But their importance was by no means merely economic. What made them "towns" in the full sense of the word was their acquisition of political rights.

The merchants and craftsmen who lived in the towns did not wish to remain, like the country people, subject to neighboring feudal lords. At worst, the feudal lords regarded merchants as fat possessors of ready money; they might hold them up on the road, plunder their mule trains, collect tolls at river crossings, or extort cash by offering "protection." At best, the most well-meaning feudal lord could not supervise the affairs of merchants, for the feudal and customary law knew nothing of commercial problems. The traders in the course of their business developed a "law merchant" of their own, having to do with money and money changing, debt and bankruptcy, contracts, invoices, and bills of lading. They wished to have their own means of apprehending thieves, runaway debtors or sellers of fraudulent goods. They strove, therefore, to get recognition for their own law, their own courts, their own judges and magistrates. They wished, too, to govern their towns themselves and to avoid payment of fees or taxes to nearby nobles.

Everywhere in Latin Christendom, along about 1100, the new towns struggled to free themselves from the encircling feudalism and to set themselves up as self-governing little republics. Where the towns were largest and closest together—along the highly urbanized arteries of the trade routes, in north Italy, on the upper Danube and Rhine rivers, in Flanders, or on the Baltic coast—they emancipated themselves the most fully. Venice, Genoa, Pisa, Florence, Milan became virtually independent city-states, each governing a substantial tract of its surrounding country. In Flanders also, towns like Bruges and Ghent dominated their localities. Along the upper Danube, the Rhine, the North Sea, the Baltic, many towns became imperial free cities within the Holy Roman Empire, each a kind of small republic owing allegiance to no one except the distant and usually ineffectual emperor. Nuremberg, Frankfurt, Augsburg, Strasbourg, Hamburg, and Lübeck were free cities of this kind. In France and England, where the towns in the twelfth century were somewhat less powerful, they obtained less independence but received charters of liberties from the king. By these charters they were assured the right to have their own town governments and officials, their own courts and law, and to pay their own kind of taxes to the king in lieu of ordinary feudal obligations.

Often towns formed leagues or urban federations, joining forces to repress banditry or piracy or to deal with ambitious monarchs or predatory nobles. The most famous such league was the Hanse; it was formed mainly of German towns, fought wars under its own banner, and dominated the commerce of the North Sea and the Baltic until after 1300. Similar tendencies of the towns to form political leagues, or to act independently in war and diplomacy, were suppressed by the kings in England, France, and Spain.

The fact that Italy, Germany, and the Netherlands were commercially more advanced than the Atlantic countries in the Middle Ages, and so had a more intensive town life, was to be one cause (out of many) preventing political unification. Not until 1860 or 1870 were nationwide states created in this region. In the west, where towns also grew up, but where more of a balance was kept between town and country, the towns were absorbed into nationwide monarchies that were arising under the kings. This difference between central and western Europe was to shape all the subsequent history of modern times.

The liberties won by the towns were corporate liberties. Each town was a collective thing. The townsman did not possess individual rights, but only the rights which followed from being a resident of his particular town. Among these were personal liberty; no townsman could be a serf, and fugitive serfs who lived over a year in a town were generally deemed to be free. But no townsman wanted individual liberty in the modern sense. The world was still too unsettled for the individual to act alone. The citizens wanted to join together in a compact body, and to protect themselves by all sorts of regulations and controls. The most obvious evidence of this communal solidarity was the wall within which most towns were enclosed. The citizens in time of trouble looked to their own defense. As the towns grew they built new walls farther out. Today, in Paris or Cologne, one may still see remains of different walls in use from the tenth to the thirteenth centuries.

Economic solidarity was of more day-to-day importance. The towns required neighboring peasants to sell foodstuffs only in the town market place. They thus protected their food supply against competition from other towns. Or they forbade the carrying on of certain trades in the country; this was to oblige peasants to make purchases in town, and protect the jobs and livelihood of the town craftsmen. They put up tariffs and tolls on the goods of other towns brought within their own walls. Or they levied special fees on merchants from outside who did business in the town. In Italy and Germany they often coined their own money; and the typical town fixed the rates at which various moneys should exchange. The medieval towns, in short, at the time of their greatest liberty, followed in a local way the same policies of protectionism and exclusiveness which national governments were generally to follow in modern times.

Within each town, merchants and craftsmen formed associations or "gilds" for collective supervision of their affairs. Merchants formed a merchant gild. Stonemasons, carpenters, barbers, dyers, goldsmiths, coppersmiths, weavers, hatters, tailors, shoemakers, grocers, apothecaries, etc., formed craft gilds of their own. The gilds served a public purpose, for they provided that work should be done by reliable and experienced persons, and so protected people from the pitfalls of shoddy garments, clumsy barbers, poisonous drugs, or crooked and flimsy houses. They also provided a means of vocational education and marked out a career for young men. Typically a boy became an apprentice to some master, learned the trade, and lived with and was supported by the master's family for a term of years, such as seven. Then he became a journeyman, a qualified and recognized worker, who might work for any master at a stated wage. Last, he might become a master himself, open his own shop, hire journeymen, and take apprentices. So long as the towns were growing, careers remained open, and a boy could reasonably expect to become a master himself; but as early as 1300 many gilds were becoming frozen, and the masters were increasingly chary of admitting new persons to their own status. From the beginning, in any case, it was an important function of the gilds to protect their own members. The masters, assembled together, preserved their reputation by regulating the quality of their product. They divided work among themselves, fixed the terms of apprenticeship, the wages to be paid to journeymen, and the prices at which their goods must be sold. Or they took collective steps to meet or keep out the competition of the same trade in nearby towns.

Whether among individuals within the town itself, or as between town and country, or between town and town, the spirit of the medieval economy was to prevent competition. Risk, adventure, and speculation were not wanted. Almost no one thought it proper to work for monetary profit. The few who did, big merchants trading over large areas, met with suspicion and disapproval wherever they went.

The towns, although in many ways they tried to subject the peasants' interests to their own, nevertheless had an emancipating influence on the country. A rustic by settling in town might escape from serfdom. But the town influence was more widespread, and far out of proportion to the relatively small number of people who could become town dwellers. The growth of towns increased the demand for foods. Lords began to clear new lands. All western Europe set about developing a kind of internal frontier. Formerly villages had been separated by dark tracts of roadless woods, in which wolves roamed freely, shadowed by the gnomes, elves, and fairies of popular folklore. Now pioneers with axes cleared farmlands and built villages in these immemorial forests. The lords who usually supervised such operations (since their serfs were not slaves, and could not be moved at will) offered freer terms to entice peasants to go and settle on the new lands. It was less easy for the lord of an old village to hold his people in serfdom when in an adjacent village, within a few hours' walk, the people were free. The peasants, moreover, were now able to obtain a little money by selling produce in town. The lords now wanted money because the towns were producing more articles which money could buy. It became very common for peasants to obtain personal freedom, holding their own lands, in return for an annual money payment to the lord for an indefinite period into the future. As early as the twelfth century serfdom began to disappear in northern France and southern England, and by the fifteenth century it had disappeared from most of western Europe. The peasant could now, in law, move freely about. But the manorial organization remained; the peasant owed dues and fees to the lord, and was still under his legal jurisdiction.

Meanwhile the kings were busy, each trying to build his kingdom into an organized monarchy that would outlast his life.[3] Monarchy became hereditary; the king inherited his position like any other feudal lord or possessor of an estate. Inheritance of the crown made for peace and order, for elections under conditions of the time were usually turbulent and disputed, and where the older Germanic principle of elective monarchy remained alive, as in the Holy Roman Empire, there was periodic commotion. The kings sent out executive officers to supervise their interests throughout their kingdoms. The kings of England, adopting an old Anglo-Saxon practice, had a sheriff in each of the forty shires; the kings of France created similar officers who were called bailiffs. The kings likewise instituted royal courts, under royal justices, to decide property disputes and repress crime. This assertion of legal jurisdiction, together with the military force to enforce judgments upon obstinate nobles, became a main pillar of the royal power. In England especially, and in lesser degree elsewhere, the kings required local inhabitants to assist royal judges in the discovery of relevant facts in particular cases. They put men on oath to declare what they knew of events in their own neighborhood. It is from

[3] See pp. 25–26.

this enforced association of private persons with royal officers that the jury developed.

The kings needed money to pay for their governmental machinery or to carry on war with other kings. Taxation, as known in the Roman Empire, was quite unknown to the Germanic and feudal tradition. In the feudal scheme each person was responsible only for the customary fees which arose on stated occasions. The king, like other lords, was supposed to live on his own income—on the revenue of manors that he owned himself, the proceeds of estates temporarily under his wardship, or the occasional fees paid to him by his vassals. No king, even for the best of reasons, could simply decree a new tax and collect it. At the same time, as the use of money became more common, the kings had to assure themselves of a money income. In England, in the twelfth century, the customary obligation of the vassal to render military service to the king was being converted into a money payment, called "scutage" or shield money. As the towns grew up, with a new kind of wealth and a new source of money income, they agreed to make certain payments in return for their royal charters.

The royal demands for money, the royal claims to exercise jurisdiction, were regarded as innovations. They were constantly growing and sometimes were a source of abuse. They met with frequent resistance in all countries. A famous case historically (though somewhat commonplace in its own day) was that of Magna Carta in England in 1215, when a group of English lords and high churchmen, joined by representatives of the city of London, required King John to confirm and guarantee their historic liberties.

The king, as has been said, like any lord, was supposed to act in council or "court" with his vassals. The royal council became the egg out of which departments of government were hatched—such as the royal judiciary, exchequer, and military command. From it also was hatched the institution of parliaments. The kings had always, in a rough sort of way, held great parleys or "talks" (the Latin *parliamentum* meant simply a "talking") with their chief retainers. In the twelfth and thirteenth centuries the growth of towns added a new element to European life. To the lords and bishops was now added a burgher class, which, if of far inferior dignity, was too stubborn, free-spirited, and well furnished with money to be overlooked. When representatives of the towns began to be normally summoned to the king's great "talks," along with lords and clergy, parliaments may be said to have come into being.

Parliaments, in this sense, sprouted all over Europe in the thirteenth century. Nothing shows better the similarity of institutions in Latin Christendom, or the inadequacy of tracing the history of any one country by itself. The new assemblies were called *cortes* in Spain, diets in Germany, Estates-General in France, parliaments in the British Isles. Usually they are referred to generically as "estates," the word "parliament" being reserved for Britain, but in origin they were all essentially the same.

The kings called these assemblies as a means of publicizing and strengthening the royal rule. They found it more convenient to explain their policies, or to ask for money, to a large gathering brought together for that purpose than to have a hundred officials make local explanations and strike local bargains in a hundred different places. The kings did not recognize, nor did the assemblies claim, any right of the parliament to dictate to the king and his government. But usually the king invited the parliament to state grievances; his action upon them was the beginning of parliamentary legislation.

The parliaments were considered to represent not the "nation" nor "people" nor yet the individual citizen, but the "estates of the realm," the great collective interests of the country. The first and highest estate was the clergy, the second the landed or noble class; to these older ruling groups were added, as a "third estate," the burghers of the chartered towns. Quite commonly these three types of people sat separately as three distinct chambers. But the pattern varied from country to country. In England, Poland, and Hungary the clergy as a whole ceased to be represented; only the bishops came, sitting with lay magnates in an upper house. Eventually the burghers dropped out in Poland, Bohemia, and Hungary, leaving the landed aristocracy in triumph in eastern Europe. In Castile and Württemberg, on the other hand, the noble estate eventually refused to attend parliament, leaving the townspeople and clergy in the assemblies. In some countries—in Scandinavia, Switzerland, and in the French Estates-General—even peasants were allowed to have delegates.

In England the Parliament developed eventually in a distinctive way. After a long period of uncertainty there came to be two houses, known as the Lords and the Commons. The Lords, as in Hungary or Poland, included both great prelates and lay magnates. The House of Commons developed features not found on the Continent. Lesser landholders, the people who elsewhere counted as small nobles, sat in the same House of Commons with representatives of the towns. The Commons was made up of "knights and burgesses," or gentry and townsmen together, a fact which greatly added to its strength, for the middle class of the towns long remained too weak to act alone. The mingling of classes in England, the willingness of townsmen to follow the leadership of the gentry, and of the gentry to respect the interests of townsmen, helped to root representative institutions in England more deeply than in other countries, in many of which the parliaments tended to die out in later times, in part because of class conflict. Moreover, England was a small country in the Middle Ages, even smaller than it looked on the map because the north was almost wild. There were no provincial or local parliamentary bodies (as in France, the Holy Roman Empire, or Poland), which might jealously cut into the powers of the central body, or with which the king could make local arrangements without violating the principle of representative government. And finally, as a reason for the strength of Parliament in England, the elected members of the House of Commons very early obtained the power to *commit* their constituents. If they voted a tax, those who elected them had to pay it. The king, in order to get matters decided, insisted that the votes be binding. Constituents were not allowed to repudiate the vote of their deputy, nor to punish or harass him when he came home, as often happened in other countries. Parliament thus exercised power as well as rights.

In summary, the three centuries of the High Middle Ages laid foundations both for order and for freedom. Slavery was defunct and serfdom expiring. Politically, the multitude of free chartered towns, the growth of juries in some places, the rise of parliaments everywhere, provided means by which peoples could take some part in their governments. The ancient civilizations had never created a free political unit larger than the city-state. The Greeks had never carried democracy beyond the confines within which people could meet in person, nor had the Romans devised means by which, in a large state, the governed could share any responsibilities with an official bureaucracy. The ancients had never developed the idea of representative government, or of government by duly elected and authorized representatives acting at a distance from home. The idea is by no means as obvious or simple as it looks. It first appeared in the medieval monarchies of the West.

So far in our account of the High Middle Ages we have told the story of Hamlet without speaking of the Prince of Denmark, for we have left aside the church, except, indeed, when some mention of it could not be avoided. In the real life of the time the church was omnipresent. Religion permeated every pore. In feudalism, the mutual duties of lord and vassal were confirmed by religious oaths, and bishops and abbots, as holders of lands, became feudal personages themselves. In the monarchies, the king was crowned by the chief churchman of his kingdom, adjured to rule with justice and piety, and anointed with holy oils. In the towns, gilds served as lay religious brotherhoods; each gild chose a patron saint and marched in the streets on holy days. For amusement the townsmen watched religious dramas, the morality and miracle plays in which religious themes were enacted. The rising town, if it harbored a bishop, took especial care to erect a new cathedral. Years of effort and of religious fervor produced the Gothic cathedrals which still stand as the best known memorials of medieval civilization.

If, however, we turn back to the tenth century, the troubled years before 1000, we find the church in as dubious a condition as everything else. The church reflected the life about it. It was fragmented and localized. Every bishop went his own way. Though the clergy was the only literate class, many of the clergy themselves could not read and write. Christian belief was mixed with the old pagan magic and superstition. The monasteries were in decay. Priests often lived in a concubinage that was generally condoned. It was customary for them to marry, so that they had recognized children, to whom they intrigued to pass on their churchly position. Often rough laymen dominated their ecclesiastical neighbors, with the big lords appointing the bishops, and the little ones the parish priests. When people thought about Rome at all, they sensed a vague respect for something legendary and far away; but the bishop of Rome, or pope, had no influence and was treated in unseemly fashion in his own city. The popes of the tenth century were the creatures of the unruly Roman nobles. Marozia, daughter of a Roman "senator," became the mistress of one pope, by whom she had a son who became pope in turn, until she imprisoned him so that another son, by another father, could claim the papacy also.

The Roman Catholic Church is in fact unrecognizable in the jumble of the tenth century. So far at least as human effort was concerned, it was virtually created in the eleventh century along with the other institutions of the High Middle Ages.

The impulse to reform came from many quarters. Sometimes a secular ruler undertook to correct conditions in his own domains. For this purpose he asserted a strict control over his clergy. In 962 the Holy Roman Empire was proclaimed. This Empire, like the Carolingian and Roman empires which it was supposed to continue, was in theory coterminous with Latin Christendom itself, and endowed with a special mission of preserving and extending the Christian faith. Neither in France nor in England (nor, when they became Christian states, in Spain, Hungary, Poland, or Scandinavia) was this claim of the Holy Roman Empire ever acknowledged. But the Empire did for a time embrace Italy as well as Germany. The first emperors, in the tenth and eleventh centuries, denouncing the outrageous conditions in Rome, strove to make the pope into their appointee.

At the same time a reform movement arose from spiritual sources. Serious Christians took matters into their own hands. They founded a new monastery at Cluny in France, which soon had many daughter houses. It was their purpose to purify monastic life and to set a higher Christian ideal to which all clergy and laity might look up. To rid themselves of immediate local pressures, the greed, narrowness, ignorance, family ambition, and self-satisfied inertia that were the main cause of corruption, the Cluniacs refused to recognize any authority except that of Rome itself. Thus, at the very time when conditions in Rome were at their worst, Christians throughout Europe built up the prestige of Rome, of the idea of Rome, as a means to raise all Latin Christendom from its depths.

As for the popes in Rome, those who preserved any independence of judgment or respect for their own office, it was their general plan to free themselves from the Roman mobs and aristocrats without falling into dependence upon the Holy Roman Emperor. In 1059 Pope Nicholas II issued a decree providing that future popes should be elected by the cardinals. The cardinals, at that time, were the priests of churches in the city of Rome, or bishops of neighboring dioceses. By entrusting the choice of future popes to them, Pope Nicholas hoped to exclude all influence from outside the clergy itself. Popes have been elected by cardinals ever since, though not always without influence from outside.

One of the first popes so elected was Gregory VII, known also as Hildebrand, a dynamic and strong-willed man who was pope from 1073 to 1085. He had been in touch with the Cluniac reformers, and dreamed of a reformed and reinvigorated Europe under the universal guidance of the Roman pontiff.

To understand what followed, the reader must exert his imagination. In his mind's eye he must see a world in which all political barriers have dropped away. In this world people have no nationality. They do not live in the state, as in modern times; they live in the church. Society itself is a great religious community. Its leaders are the clergy, to which all educated persons belong. The public personage with whom people come into most frequent contact is the priest, and the most important public official is the bishop. The chief public buildings are churches, abbeys, and cathedrals. Secular interests, those of kings and dukes, of merchants and artisans, are earthbound and shortsighted. All persons, even kings, in addition to secular interests, have a higher concern. All are living in the religious community and preparing their souls for eternal life. The religious community, or church, reaches in principle as far as the borders of the known world. It is universal, for all men must be saved. At its head stands the bishop of Rome, the Vicar of Christ, the successor to Peter, the keeper of the keys, the *servus servorum Dei*, the servant of the servants of God.

Some such vision filled the mind of Gregory VII, and with it he founded the papal supremacy of the High Middle Ages. He believed that the church should stand apart from worldly society, that it should judge and guide all human actions, and that a pope could judge and punish kings and emperors if he deemed them sinful. His ideal was not a "world state," but its spiritual counterpart, a world church officered by a single-minded and disciplined clergy, centralized under a single authority. He began by insisting that the clergy free itself of worldly involvements. He required married priests to put aside their wives and families. Celibacy of the clergy, never generally established in the Greek Orthodox church, and later rejected by Protestants in the West, became and remained the rule for the Roman Catholic priesthood. Gregory insisted also that no ecclesiastic might receive office through appointment by a layman. In his view only clergy might institute or influence clergy, for the clergy must be independent and self-contained.

Gregory soon faced a battle with that other aspirant to universal supremacy and a sacred mission, the Holy Roman Emperor, who at this time was Henry IV. In Germany the bishops and abbots possessed a great deal of the land, which they held and governed under the emperor as feudal magnates in their own right. To the emperor it was vitally important to have his own men, as reliable vassals, in these great positions. Hence in Germany "lay investiture" had become very common. "Lay investiture" meant the practice by which a layman, the emperor, conferred upon the new bishop the signs of his spiritual authority, the ring and the staff. Gregory prohibited lay investiture. He supported the German bishops and nobles when they rebelled against Henry. Henry proving obstinate, Gregory excommunicated him, i.e., outlawed him from Christian society by forbidding any priest to give him the sacraments. Henry, baffled, sought out the pope at Canossa in Italy to do penance. "To go to Canossa" in later times became a byword for submission to the will of Rome.

In 1122, after both original contenders had died, a compromise on the matter of lay investiture was effected by which bishops recognized the emperor as their feudal head but looked to Rome for spiritual authority. But the struggle between popes and emperors went on unabated. The magnates of Germany, lay lords as well as bishops, often allied with the pope to preserve their own feudal liberties from the emperor. The emperor in Germany was never able to consolidate his domains as did the kings in England and France. In Italy, too, the popes and emperors quarreled, the foes of each commonly siding with the other. The unwillingness of lords and churchmen (and of towns also, as we have seen) to let the emperors build up an effectual government left its mark permanently upon Europe in two ways. It contributed to the centralization of Latin Christendom under Rome, and it blocked national unity in central Europe.

The height of the medieval papacy came with Innocent III, whose pontificate lasted from 1198 to 1216. Innocent virtually realized Gregory's dream of a unified Christian world. He intervened in politics everywhere. He was recognized as a supreme arbiter. At his word, a king of France took a wife, a king of England accepted an unwanted archbishop, a king of León put aside the cousin whom he had married, and a claimant to the crown of Hungary deferred to his rival. Innocent advised the kings of Bohemia, Poland, and Denmark on weighty matters, and the kings of England, Aragon, and Portugal acknowledged him as feudal overlord within their realms. Huge revenues now flowed to Rome from all over Latin Christendom, and an enormous bureaucracy worked there to dispatch the voluminous business of the papal court. As kings struggled to repress civil rebellion, so Innocent and his successors struggled to repress heresy, which, defined as doctrine at variance with that of the church at large, was becoming alarmingly common among the Albigensians of southern France.

In 1215 Innocent called a great church council, the greatest since antiquity, attended by five hundred bishops and even by the patriarchs of Constantinople and Jerusalem. The council labored at the perplexing task of keeping the clergy from worldly temptations. By forbidding priests to officiate at ordeals or trials by battle, it virtually ended these survivals of barbarism. It attempted to regularize belief in the supernatural by controlling the superstitious traffic in relics. It declared the sacraments to be the channel of God's saving grace and defined them authoritatively.[4] In the chief sacrament, the Eucharist or Mass, it promulgated the dogma of transubstantiation, which holds that, in the Mass, the priest converts the substance of bread and wine into the substance of Christ's body and blood. Except for heretics, who were suppressed, the acts of the Fourth Lateran Council were accepted with satisfaction throughout Latin Europe.

Intellectual Life:
The Universities,
Scholasticism

Under the auspices of the church, as rising governments gave more civil security, and as the economy of town and country became able to support men devoted to a life of thought, the intellectual horizon of Europeans began to open. The twelfth and thirteenth centuries saw the founding of the first universities. These originated in the natural and spontaneous coming together of teachers and pupils which had never

---

[4]A sacrament is understood to be the outward sign of an inward grace. In Catholic doctrine the sacraments were and are seven in number: baptism, confirmation, penance, the Eucharist, extreme unction, marriage, and holy orders. Except for baptism, a sacrament may be administered only by a priest. A dogma is the common belief of the church, in which all the faithful share and must share so long as they are members of the church. Dogmas are regarded as implicitly the same in all ages; they cannot be invented or developed, but may from time to time be clarified, defined, promulgated, or proclaimed.

wholly disappeared even in the Dark Ages. By 1200 there was a center of medical studies at Salerno in south Italy, of legal studies at Bologna in north Italy, of theological studies at Paris. Oxford was founded about 1200 by a secession of disgruntled students and professors from Paris, Cambridge shortly thereafter. By 1300 there were a dozen such universities in Latin Europe, by 1500 almost a hundred.

As the early agglomerations of traders developed into organized towns, so the informal concourses of students and teachers developed into organized institutions of learning, receiving the sharp corporate stamp that was characteristic of the High Middle Ages. It was in having this corporate identity that medieval universities resemble our own and differed from the schools of Athens or Alexandria in ancient times. A university, the early University of Paris, for example, was a body of men, young and old, interested in learning and endowed by law with a communal name and being. It possessed definite liberties under some kind of charter, regulated its own affairs through its own officials, and kept its own order among its often boisterous population. It gave, and even advertised, courses and lectures, and it decided collectively which professors were the best qualified to teach. It might consist of distinct schools or "faculties"—the combination of theology, law, and medicine, as at Paris, was the most usual. It held examinations and awarded degrees, whose meaning and value were recognized throughout the Latin West. The degree, which originated as a license to teach, admitted its holder to certain honors or privileges such as those of a craft gild. With it, a professor might readily move from one university to another. Students moved easily also, the language being everywhere Latin and the curriculum much the same. The university, moreover, though typically it began in poverty, was as a corporate body capable of holding property of its own; and the benefactions of pious donors, as the years went on, often built up substantial endowments in lands and manors. So organized, free from outside control, and enjoying property of its own, the university lived on as an institution beyond the lifetime of all living men, through good times and bad, through civil war or disorder, through dreary years when students were few or professors undistinguished, always to some extent fulfilling its role of conserving or diffusing knowledge, and always ready for a periodic wave of reform.

The queen of the sciences was theology, the intellectual study of religion. Many in Europe, by the eleventh century, were beginning to reflect upon their beliefs. They continued to believe but could no longer believe with naive or unthinking acceptance. It was accepted as a fact, for example, that the Son of God had been incarnated as a man in Jesus Christ. But in the eleventh century an Italian named Anselm, who became archbishop of Canterbury, wrote a treatise called *Cur Deus Homo?*—"Why Did God Become Man?"—giving reasoned explanations to show why God had taken this means to save mankind. Soon afterward Abélard, who taught at Paris, wrote his *Sic et non*—"Yes and No" or "Pro and Con"—a collection of inconsistent statements made by St. Augustine and other Fathers of the Church. Abélard's purpose was to apply logic to the inherited mass of patristic writings, show wherein the truth of Christian doctrine really lay, and so make the faith consistent with reason and reflection.

Meanwhile, in the twelfth century a great stream of new knowledge poured into Europe, bringing about a veritable intellectual revolution. It was derived from the Arabs, with whom Christians were in contact in Sicily and Spain. The Arabs, as has been seen, had taken over the ancient Greek science, translated Greek writings into Arabic, and in many ways added further refinements of their own. Bilingual Christians (assisted by numerous learned Jews who passed readily between the Christian and Moslem worlds) translated these works into Latin. Above all, they translated Aristotle, the great codifier of Greek knowledge who had lived and written in the fourth century B.C. The Europeans, barely emerging from barbarism, were overwhelmed by this sudden disclosure of an undreamed of universe of knowledge. Aristotle became The Philosopher, the unparalleled authority on all branches of knowledge other than religious.

The great problem for Europeans was how to digest the gigantic bulk of Aristotle, or, in more general terms, to assimilate or reconcile the body of Greek and Arabic learning to the Christian faith. The universities, with their "scholastic" philosophers or "schoolmen," performed this useful social function. Most eminent of scholastics was Thomas Aquinas (1225–1274), the Angelic Doctor, known also to his own contemporaries as the Dumb Ox from the slow deliberation of his speech. His chief work, appropriately called the *Summa Theologica,* was a survey of all knowledge. The thought of Aquinas, as recently as 1879, was pronounced by Pope Leo XIII to be the foundation of official Catholic philosophy.

The chief accomplishment of Thomas Aquinas was his demonstration that faith and reason could not be in conflict. By reason he meant a severely logical method, with exact definition of words and concepts, deducing step by step what follows and must follow if certain premises are accepted. His philosophy is classified as a form of "realism." It holds, that is, that the general idea is more "real" than the particular—that "man" is more real than this or that man or woman, that "law" as such

The Meeting of St. Anthony and St. Paul *by Sassetta (Italian, 1392–1450)*
Here we can see something of the medieval way of thinking. The picture tells a religious story. St. Anthony appears in three places, walking alone, converting a centaur, and meeting and embracing St. Paul. There is no attempt to present him as a unique individual person; his head and features disappear behind those of St. Paul in the principal scene. The picture gives the "idea" of the story. The two figures are typical saints, with the haloes which conventionally designated sacred persons. The artist has painted the "idea" or "essence" of a forest, i.e., many trees; he has not shown the actual appearance of a particular forest, with underbrush, shadows, trees of different sizes and foliage of different kinds. His hills are hills in general, i.e., mounds of earth; his cave is a cave in general, i.e., a dark hole. When the two saints embrace, their arms and legs are placed where the mind knows that they ought to be, not where the eye would see them concretely in any particular situation. The picture thus illustrates, on a simple level, what is meant by the abstractness or "realism" (the realism of ideas) of medieval thought. A child today, or an artistically untrained adult, draws in the same way, portraying the idea rather than the physical actuality. The idea of a forest is, after all, "many trees"; all else is special or incidental, not of the essence. Courtesy of the National Gallery of Art, Washington, D. C., Samuel H. Kress Collection.

is more real and binding than this or that particular law. He derived his philosophy from what he took to be the nature of God, of man, of law, of reason, of beings in general. He taught a hierarchic view of the universe and of society, of which God was the apex, and in which all things and all men were subordinated to God in a descending order, each bound to fulfill the role set by its own place and nature. It was the emphasis on the superior reality of abstractions that enabled men in the Middle Ages to believe steadfastly in the church while freely attacking individual churchmen, to have faith in the papacy while denouncing the popes as scoundrels—or to accept without difficulty the mystery of transubstantiation, which declared that what admittedly looked and tasted like bread and wine was, in real inner substance, the body of Christ.

The scholastic philosophy, as perfected by Thomas Aquinas, was not very favorable to the growth of natural science, because, in its emphasis on an inner reality, it drew attention away from the actual details and behavior of concrete things. On the other hand, the scholastic philosophy laid foundations on which later European thought was to be reared. It habituated Europeans to great exactness, to careful distinctions, even to the splitting of hairs. It called for disciplined thinking. And it made the world safe for reason. If any historical generalization may be made safely, it may be safely said that any society that believes reason to threaten its foundations will suppress reason. In Thomas' time, there were some who said that Aristotle and the Arabs were infidels, dangerous influences that must be silenced. Any reasoning about the faith, they warned, was a form of weakness. Thomas' doctrine that faith could not be endangered by reason gave a freedom to thinkers to go on thinking. Here Latin Christendom may be contrasted with the Moslem world. It was ruled, in about the time of Thomas Aquinas, that valid interpretation of the Koran had ended with the Four Great Doctors of early Islam. As Moslems said, the Gate was closed. Arabic thought, so brilliant for several centuries, withered away.

Magdalene at the Foot of the Cross *by Sandro Botticelli (Italian, 1444?–1510)*
Botticelli, in his love of the human form, was a typical painter of the Italian Renaissance (see pp. 53–66). But the carrying over of medieval attitudes is also evident in his work. The painting reproduced here is a mysterious one. Its setting is clearly in the natural world, with the city of Florence recognizably in the background, standing in actual space against hills and sky. But the mood is somber. Some have called it a picture of abject grief, in the figure of the woman prostrate at the foot of the cross. Others find the main theme in the avenging angel. Indeed, the painting has been known also under the title of "The Punishment of Heaven for the Murder of Savonarola." Savonarola was a religious leader who in 1494 aroused a strong moral reaction at Florence against the more pagan aspects of the Renaissance. In 1498 he was put to death. Botticelli was his follower. It seems likely that this painting contains an allegory. The angel is represented as scourging a lion cub (the lion was the heraldic device of the city of Florence), while fiendish figures appear darkly through the smoke, and other angels approach from the heavens. There is no exuberance of the Renaissance here, but rather a tragic brooding on wrongs that cannot be undone. Courtesy of the Fogg Art Museum, Harvard University, Gift—Friends of the Fogg Art Museum.

Meanwhile, the West was expanding. Europe in the eleventh century took the offensive against Islam. All Latin Christendom went on the Crusades. War itself was subordinated to the purposes of religion.

The most ambitious, best remembered, and least successful of such expeditions were the Crusades to win back the Holy Land. The First Crusade was preached in 1095 by Pope Urban II, who hoped thereby to advance the Peace of God by draining off belligerent nobles to fight the infidels, and to build up the leadership of Rome, just asserted by Gregory VII, through raising a universal cause of which the pope might be the head. Crusades to the Holy Land, with varying success, and sometimes departing woefully from their religious aims, went on intermittently for two hundred years. It was the growth of Italian shipping in the Mediterranean, the rise of more orderly feudal monarchies, the increasing sense of a Europe-wide common purpose, that made possible the assembly and transport of considerable forces over a great distance. It is sometimes said that the Crusades, by bringing contacts with the East, stimulated the development of civilization in the West, but it seems more likely that, as Europe's counterthrust against Islam, the Crusades were the consequence of Europe's own growing strength. For a century the Latin Christians occupied parts of Palestine and Syria. But in the thirteenth century they had to withdraw, and the Moslems remained in possession.

Other crusades (for such they were) had more lasting results. A party of Normans won Sicily from the Arabs about 1100. Iberian Christians, descending from the mountains of northern Spain, carried on a *reconquista* of two centuries against the Moors. By 1250 they had staked out the Christian kingdoms of Portugal, León, Castile, Aragon, and Valencia, leaving the Moslems only Granada in the extreme south, which was conquered much later, in 1492. An Albigensian crusade in the thirteenth century put down the heretics, those born in the faith but erring from it. Against remaining European heathen, those born in ignorance of the faith, of whom a few were still found along the Baltic coast, crusading expeditions were also launched. The Teutonic Order, a military-religious society of knights founded originally to fight in the Holy Land, transferred its operations to the north. Christianity, and with it the civilization of the Latin West, was brought by the sword to primitive Prussia and the east Baltic regions.

About the year 1250 there developed a new threat of invasion from Asia. As the Huns had burst out of Asia in the fifth century, and the Magyars in the ninth, so now the Tartars appeared in the thirteenth century, to be followed in the fourteenth by the Ottoman Turks. The Tartars (or Mongols) overran and conquered Russia and defeated Polish and Hungarian armies in 1241. But powerful as they were, they penetrated no farther into the Latin West. About 1350, the Moslem Ottoman Turks filtered into the Balkan peninsula and subdued what would today be the whole region from Rumania to Greece. In 1453 Constantinople itself fell to the conquering Turks, ending the thousand-year-old Roman Empire in the East. With the Turks in possession of the Balkan peninsula and Constantinople, and the Tartars (who adopted Islam) controlling the Russian plain, the world of Eastern or Greek Orthodox Christianity now passed completely under the political domination of Moslem overlords.

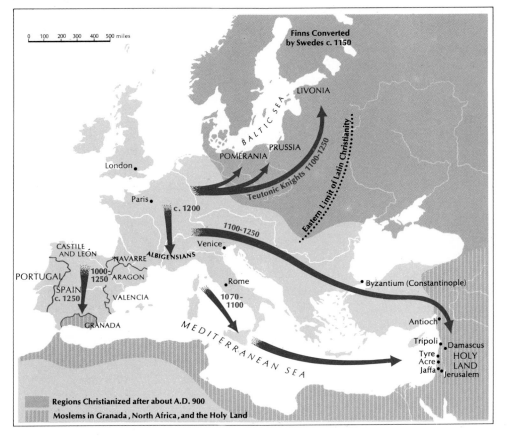

Crusading Activity 1100–1250. *Medieval Christendom expanded geographically until about* A.D. 1250. *Darker regions are those Christianized shortly before and after* A.D. 1000. *Arrows indicate organized military-religious expeditions, which by 1250 had recovered most of Spain from Moslem control, but had failed to do so in the Holy Land. Dates are rounded and very rough.*

The great struggle between Latin Christendom and Islam was not over. We shall see how the Turks long continued to press upon central Europe.[5] But, on the whole, by the thirteenth century, Europe was capable of resistance. Always until then it had lain open, an outlying, backward, thinly populated protuberance from the Eurasian land mass. It had lain open in the remote past to wandering Indo-Europeans, then to Roman imperial conquerors, to Germanic barbarians, to Huns, Magyars, and, in part, the Arabs. All these were assimilated. The blood of all flowed in European veins. In spirit all were assimilated by the Roman church, the Latin language, the common institutions of feudalism, monarchy, a free town life, parliamentary assemblies, scholastic learning, which ran as an almost seamless web from England to Sicily and from Portugal to Poland.

[5] See pp. 76, 81, 225–231, and the Index under Ottoman Empire.

By 1300 the "rise of Europe" was an accomplished fact. The third of the three segments into which the Greco-Roman world had divided, the one which in A.D. 700 had been the most barbarous, now some six hundred years later had a civilization of its own. It had geographically filled out the contours of what we know as Europe, and was able to stand against further penetration from outside. It is not possible to make sweeping comparisons of whole civilizations. In all respects except political unity, however, the Europe of 1300 probably surpassed the Roman Empire. It compared well enough, for the first time, with the older civilizations of the East. It was not in its material culture, in the technical crafts, in the arts of building, in the distances traveled by its merchants, nor in the mere size or magnificence of its cities that Europe in 1300 surpassed the Arabic, Byzantine, Indian, or Chinese civilizations of that time. If it surpassed them at all, if it had any secret that the others did not know, its uniqueness lay in the realm of intangibles. Europe had a political system that blended freedom with more general order; a labor system in which no one was totally enslaved; a spiritual outlook producing a restless activity, because nothing that actually existed was ever believed to be perfect; an intellectual outlook not averse to the new, yet incorporating the old; a diversity of many nations which yet somehow were all the same. The Arabs inherited Greco-Roman civilization, and the Byzantines inherited Christianity as well. In Europe some new element was added in the Middle Ages, something that neither the Greco-Romans nor ancient Christianity had alone supplied, something that cannot be characterized in a few words nor even in many, and yet was decisive in the making of modern Europe.

II: THE REVOLUTION IN THE

CHRISTIAN CHURCH, 1300-1560

In the light of world history, as we see it today, one of the most momentous experiences that can befall any civilization is for it to break loose from its religious base. Today we can observe this process at work everywhere: the Chinese reconsider the age-old teachings of Confucius, the Moslems enter into wider activities than those known to the Koran, the peoples of India attempt to found a society in which neither historic Hindu practices, nor the historic split between Hindu and Moslem, shall form the dominant pattern. It is not, in most cases, that peoples reject their ancestral religion. On the contrary, they often reaffirm it; but they try also to modernize it, to adapt it, to make room for new and nonreligious interests, to bring it about that religion, instead of being the womb or matrix from which all else comes, shall be one interest among many.

Latin Christendom was the first modern society to embark on the momentous, troublesome, and long drawn out process of "secularization." In 1300 Europe was still primarily a religious community. The clergy were the prestige-enjoying class. All else was somehow oriented to or pervaded by religious belief. Three centuries later religion was one interest among many. The church itself was divided. The

Chapter Emblem: A medal struck in honor of Pico della Mirandola, Florentine humanist of the fifteenth century.

Christian faith still stood; indeed it was purified and reaffirmed both by those who became Protestant and by those who remained Catholic. But other interests made equal claims upon men's attention. Government, law, philosophy, science, the arts, material and economic activities were pursued without regard to Christian values. Power, order, beauty, wealth, knowledge, control of nature were all accepted as desirable in themselves.

It is this process of secularization that gives unity to the intricate history set forth in the present chapter.

5

The Decline of the Church

At the close of the thirteenth century the church of the High Middle Ages, centralized in the papacy, stood at its zenith. But the church (as good Catholics always remind us) was staffed by mortal men who were no different from others. The church faced the danger that besets every successful institution—a form of government, an army or navy, a business corporation, a labor union, a university, to choose modern examples—the danger of believing that the institution exists for the benefit of those who conduct its affairs. The papacy, being at the top, was the most liable to this danger. The papacy became "corrupt," set in its ways, absorbed by the possession of wealth and authority, afflicted by a self-perpetuating bureaucracy, out of touch with public opinion, more concerned with maintaining papal grandeur than with spiritual religion, unable to reform itself, and unwilling to let anyone else reform it. At the same time, forces quite outside the papacy or the church, forces which had been growing up for generations before 1300, became too strong after 1300 to be held in the old containers, asserted themselves with ever more insistence, and clashed with the official clergy of the international church. Such forces, especially, were the new national monarchies and the commercial classes in the towns.

The Papacy Divided

The decline of the papacy can be readily dated, from the time when Pope Boniface VIII ran into trouble with the kings of England and of France. These two kings, needing money for war, undertook to tax the clergy in their respective kingdoms, in both of which the clergy were substantial owners of land. Boniface prohibited the taxation of clergy by the civil ruler. In the ensuing altercation, in 1302, he issued the famous bull *Unam Sanctam*,[1] the most extreme of all assertions of papal supremacy, declaring that outside the Roman church there was no salvation, and that "every human creature" was "subject to the Roman pontiff." The French king, Philip the Fair, retorted by sending soldiers to arrest Boniface, who soon died. French influence in the College of Cardinals brought about the election of a pope who was subservient to Philip, and who took up his residence, with his court and officials,

---

[1] Bulls are known by their first one or two Latin words, which in this case mean "one holy (Catholic church)"; a "bull," while the most solemn form of papal edict, does not as such embody a dogma, and it is not Catholic practice today to affirm this policy of Boniface VIII.

at Avignon on the lower Rhone river, on the then borders of France. Thus began the "Babylonian Captivity" of the church. The rest of Europe regarded the popes at Avignon throughout the century as tools of France. The prestige of the papacy as a universal institution was badly dimmed.

Attempts to correct the situation made matters worse. In 1378 the College of Cardinals, torn by French and anti-French factions within it, elected two popes. Both were equally legitimate, being chosen by the cardinals, but one lived at Rome, one at Avignon, and neither would resign. The French and their supporters recognized the Avignon pope, England and most of Germany, the Roman. For forty years both lines were perpetuated. There were now two papacies, estranged by the Great Schism of the West, and it seemed as if the schism might become permanent, as the earlier schism between Rome and Constantinople had proved to be. All agreed that the situation was scandalous and must be ended, but no one in influential position would make the sacrifice necessary to put it to an end.

Never had the papacy been so externally magnificent as in the days of the Captivity and the Schism. The papal court at Avignon surpassed the courts of kings in splendor. The papal officialdom grew in numbers, ignoring the deeper problems while busily transacting each day's business. Papal revenues mounted, and new papal taxes were devised, for example, the "annates," by which every bishop or abbot in Christendom had to transmit to Rome most of the first year's income of his office. In the continuing movement of funds from all over Europe to the papal court, from the thirteenth century on, a new class of international bankers rose and prospered.

But the papacy, never so sumptuous, had never since the tenth century rested on such shaky foundations. People pay willingly for institutions in which they believe, and admire magnificence in leaders whom they respect. But before 1378, with the pope submissive to France, and after 1378, with two popes and two papacies to support, there was growing complaint at the extravagance and worldliness of papal rule. The most pious Christians were the most shocked. To them the behavior of the cardinals was disgraceful. Earnest souls were worried in conscience. To obtain God's grace was to them of all things the most vital, but with two churches under two popes, each claiming to hold the keys of Peter, how could anyone be certain that his church gave him true salvation? In a society that was still primarily a religious community, this sense of religious insecurity was a source of unutterable uneasiness and dread.

Social conditions in the fourteenth century, and on into the fifteenth, were most unsettled. Journeymen in the gilds were turning into life-long wageworkers without a future. The spread of the money economy in the countryside led to peasant restlessness and rebellion, as in Wat Tyler's rebellion in England in 1381. Such rebellions were forcibly suppressed by the upper classes, but the disturbing question ran through men's minds:

> *When Adam delved, and Eve span,*
> *Who was then the gentleman?*

After 1300 for a long time the royal governments developed their organization very slowly. More power fell into the hands of parliaments, diets, and estates, so that the old feudal classes enjoyed a resurgence, and many countries fell into a chronic anarchy of "barons' wars." England and France became locked in the Hundred Years' War (1337–1453), in which bands of destructive English soldiery roamed back and forth across a France divided within itself. Germany and central Europe also were rocked by civil turmoil. To all this were added the horrors of plague. The Black Death, or bubonic plague, swept over Europe from east to west, beginning in 1348. In some places half or more of the population, suddenly and within a few months, died in the squalor and misery of the pesthouse. The plague kept recurring, striking blindly and inexorably, for fifty years.

The old moorings were weakened, the old certainties lost, the wrath of God seemed to be raining upon mankind, and no one had the slightest notion of how the world was going to turn out. Symptoms of mass neurosis appeared. Some people sought refuge in a hectic merriment or brief sensual self-indulgence. Others became preoccupied with grisly subjects. Some frantically performed the Dance of Death in the cemeteries, others furtively celebrated the Black Mass, parodying religion in a mad desire to appease the devil. The Order of Flagellants grew up; its members went through the streets, two by two, beating each other with chains and whips. It was at this time that the great witchcraft delusion, which was to reach its height in the fifteenth and sixteenth centuries, first became important. In a century like the thirteenth, people had believed in witches but had not worried about them because they felt secure in the protection of God's church. Now witches were feared, hunted out, prosecuted, and disposed of by burning alive, a form of punishment which also now became more common than it had been in former times. Nor was the belief entirely unfounded, for there was in fact a social phenomenon of diabolism. Some people actually thought they were in a compact with the devil, and, if they did not thereby become witches, they were nevertheless, in many cases, antisocial beings who meant no good to their neighbors.

It was widely agreed, in this afflicted society, that the true church must be restored in its purity. Led by men like the Italian Marsiglio of Padua, or the Englishmen Ockham and Wycliff, reformers declared that the church consisted in the whole body of the faithful, not merely or even primarily in the clergy. If the clergy, they said, were not performing their spiritual duties to the laity, then either a secular ruler or a general council representing the whole church might enforce reform upon the clergy, and even upon the pope. John Wycliff went even further. He taught, about 1380, that no visible church was needful for salvation, that ordinary persons might obtain divine grace by reading the Bible, without the ministrations of any clergy whatsoever. This doctrine, which, if pursued far enough, would explode any church as an authoritative institution, was promptly branded as heresy. Wycliff nevertheless won many adherents. In England there were "poor men," or Lollards, who might know nothing of Wycliff but sought escape from all forms of established authority. In Bohemia, John Huss took up Wycliff's ideas, and here the doctrine became a national movement. The Hussites were both a religious party and at the same time a Slavic or Czech party protesting against the supremacy of the Germans who lived in Bohemia. The Hussite wars ravaged central Europe for decades in the early part of the fifteenth century.

Settled, influential, educated, and established persons did not turn to heresy, nor yet to witchcraft or flagellation. Their answer to the needs of the day was the conciliar movement. Professors at the universities, advisers to kings, enlightened bishops, thoughtful burghers, about 1400, believed the pope (or rather, popes) to be incapable of reforming existing abuses. They demanded a great Europe-wide council of the entire church at which all the gravest matters that were troubling Christendom might be discussed and decided. They would introduce into the church, that is to say, the type of parliamentary institutions which at this time were functioning in the civil affairs of almost all countries.

In 1409 such a church council met at Pisa. All parts of the Latin West were represented. The council declared both reigning popes deposed, and obtained the due election of another, but since the first two refused to resign there were now three. In 1414 an even greater and more fully attended council met at Constance. Its aims were three: to end the now threefold schism, to extirpate heresy, and to reform the church "in head and members," or from top to bottom. Not much was accomplished in reform. To discourage heresy, John Huss was interrogated, condemned, and burned at the stake. The schism was ended. All three popes were at last persuaded or compelled to withdraw, and another, Martin V, was elected. The unity of the church, under the papacy, was at last restored.

The majority at the Council of Constance wished to make general councils part of the permanent apparatus of the church for all time in the future. They regarded the pope as, so to speak, a constitutional monarch, and the general body of the faithful as self-governing in religious matters. In its decree *Sacrosancta*, the council solemnly declared that a council was superior to a pope, and, in the decree *Frequens*, that councils should be assembled every ten years in the future.

Martin V, however, no sooner elected pope, reaffirmed the prerogatives of the papal office. He dissolved the Council of Constance, and repudiated its decrees. The next thirty years saw a continuing tug of war between successive popes and successive councils. On the one hand, with the pope, stood the papal court and central bureaucracy, supported by the monastic orders, and by scattered individuals for various reasons. On the other, with the councils, stood most Catholic bishops from all countries (outside of Italy), together with representatives of the emperor and the kings. Popes argued that theirs was the true apostolic authority derived from Peter, and that in any case to entrust power to the territorial bishops, exposed as they were to local pressure from kings and princes, would endanger the unity and independence of the church. Councils argued that the bishop of Rome was fundamentally only a bishop like any other; that the authority of Christ was vested in the whole church as a collective body, over which the pope was no more than a symbolic or merely administrative head.

In this acrimonious battle for jurisdiction few reforms could be adopted, and fewer still enforced. Increasingly the life of the church was corrupted by money. No one believed in bribery; but everyone knew that many high churchmen (like many high civil officials of the day) could be bribed. To buy or sell a church office was a crime in the canon law, known as "simony"; but it was a crime which in the fifteenth century could not be suppressed. For churchmen to live with mistresses was considered understandable, if unseemly; the standards of laymen in such matters were not high; but for a bishop or other ecclesiastic to give lucrative church positions to his own children (or other relatives) was the abuse known as nepotism, and it, too, could not be eradicated. To sell divine grace for money, all agreed, was not only wrong but impossible. In 1300 Boniface VIII had given encouragement to the practice of "indulgences." A person, if properly confessed, absolved, and truly repentant, might, by obtaining an indulgence, be spared certain of the temporal punishments of purgatory. One obtained such an indulgence, almost always, in return for a donation of money. Indulgences were never "sold," but many un-enlightened persons thought they were; and a protest arose all over Europe, among both laity and clergy, that the abuse of indulgences was discrediting the sacraments and undermining common morals. But to raise money in this way was fatally easy, and this practice, too, could not be stopped.

The councils insisted that such conditions be reformed, to which popes replied, while agreeing in principle, that the papal authority must be upheld first. Gradually the popes prevailed. The conciliar movement, for Christendom as a whole, was greatly weakened when the powerful French element secured its aims by a local national arrangement. In the Pragmatic Sanction of Bourges, in 1438, the Gallican (or French) church affirmed the supremacy of councils over popes, declared its administrative independence from the Holy See, suppressed the payment of annates to Rome, and forbade papal intervention in the appointment of French prelates. The papacy thus lost influence in France, but the conciliarists themselves were divided. In 1449, with the dissolution of the Council of Basel, the conciliar movement came to an end. In 1450 a great Jubilee was held to celebrate the papal triumph.

The papacy, its prestige and freedom of action thus secured, now passed into the hands of a series of cultivated gentlemen, men of the world, men of "modern" outlook in tune with their times—the famous popes of the Renaissance. Some, like Nicholas V (1447–1455) or Pius II (1458–1464) were accomplished scholars and connoisseurs of books. Some were like Innocent VIII (1484–1492), a pleasant man who was the first pope to dine in public with ladies. Alexander VI (1492–1503) exploited his office in the vain attempt to gratify his avaricious relatives who swarmed from Spain. He schemed also to make his son Caesar Borgia the ruler of all Italy. Julius II (1503–1513) was a capable general, and Leo X (1513–1521) a superb patron of the arts. But we must now describe the Italian Renaissance, in which worthies of this type were elevated to the see of Peter and the vicariate of Christ.

In Italy in the fifteenth century, and especially at Florence, we observe not merely a decay of medieval certainties but the appearance of a new and constructive attitude toward the world. The Renaissance, a French word meaning "rebirth," first received its name from those who thought of the Middle Ages as a dark time from which the human spirit had to be awakened. It was called a *re*birth in the belief that men now, after a long interruption, took up and resumed a civilization like that of the Greco-Romans. Medieval people had thought of the times of Aristotle or Cicero as not sharply distinct from their own. In the Renaissance, with a new historical sense, arose the conception of "modern" and "ancient" times, separated by a long period with a different life style and appropriately called the Middle Ages. Nowadays the Middle Ages are not regarded as dark, at least after the year 1000 or 1100, or even as being especially intermediate on a chronological scale. The word "modern" has taken on conflicting meanings in the twentieth century. It may refer to a very recent tempo of life and society, hardly older than the twentieth century itself, even in the most highly developed countries. Or it may mean a kind of Western civilization that became visible during the Renaissance, but which is undergoing a profound transformation in the twentieth century. In this sense recent times may be referred to as "postmodern." The "modern world" of which this book is a history embraces both meanings of the word.

A few useful distinctions can be made. The basic institutions of Europe, the very languages and nationalities, the great frameworks of collective action in law, government and economic production, all originated in the Middle Ages. But the Renaissance marked a new era in thought and feeling, by which Europe and its institutions were in the long run to be transformed. The origins of modern natural science can be traced more to the medieval universities than to the Renaissance thinkers. But it was in the Italy of the Quattrocento (as Italians call the fifteenth century) that other fields of thought and expression were first cultivated. The Italian influence in other countries, in these respects, remained very strong for at least 200 years. It pertained to high culture, and hence to a limited number of persons, but extended over the whole area represented by literature and the arts—literature meaning all kinds of writing, and the arts including all products of human skill. The effects of the Italian Renaissance, though much modified with the passage of time, were evident in the books and art galleries of Europe and America, and in the architecture of their cities, until the revolution of "modern" art in the early twentieth century. They involved the whole area of culture which is neither theological nor scientific but concerns essentially moral and civic questions, asking what man ought to be or ought to do, and is reflected in matters of taste, style, propriety, decorum, personal character, and education. In particular, it was in Renaissance Italy that an almost purely secular attitude first appeared, in which life was no longer seen by leading thinkers as a brief preparation for the hereafter.

The towns of Italy, so long as trade converged in the Mediterranean, were the biggest and most bustling of all the towns that rose in Europe in the Middle Ages. The crafts of Italy included many refined trades such as those of the goldsmith or stonecarver, which were so zealously pursued that artisanship turned into art, and a delight in the beautiful became common among all classes. Merchants made fortunes in commerce; they lent their money to popes or princes, and so made further fortunes as bankers. They bought the wares of the craftsmen-artists. They rejoiced, not so much in money or the making of money, as in the beautiful things and psychological satisfactions that money could buy; and if they forgot the things that money could not buy, this is only to say again that their outlook was "secular."

The towns were independent city-states. There was no king to build up a government for Italy as a whole, and for several generations the popes were either absent at Avignon or engaged in disputes arising from the Great Schism, so that the influence of Rome was unimportant. The merchant oligarchies, each in its own city, enjoyed an unhampered stage on which to pursue interests other than those of business. In some, as at Milan, they succumbed to or worked with a local prince or despot. In others, as at Florence, Venice, and Genoa, they continued to govern themselves as republics. They had the experience of contending for public office, of suppressing popular revolt or winning popular favor, of producing works of public munificence, of making alliances, hiring armies, outwitting rivals, and conducting affairs of state. In short, Italy offered an environment in which many facets of human personality could be developed.

All this was most especially true in Florence, the chief city of Tuscany. In the fifteenth century it had a population of about 60,000, which made it only moderately large as Italian cities went. Of no other place could the boast of being a modern Athens be so legitimately made. Like Athens, Florence produced an extraordinary sequence of gifted men in a short period. From the days of Dante, Petrarch, and Boccaccio, who all died before 1375, to those of Machiavelli, who lived until 1527, an amazing number of the leading figures of the Italian Renaissance were Florentines. Like Athens also, Florence lost its republican liberty as well as its creative powers. Its history can be summarized in that of the Medici family. The founder of the family fortunes was Giovanni (d. 1429), a merchant and banker of Florence. His son, Cosimo de' Medici (1389–1464), allying himself with the popular element against some of the leading families of the republic, soon became unofficial ruler himself. Cosimo's grandson, Lorenzo the Magnificent (1449–1492), also used his great wealth to govern but is chiefly remembered as a poet, connoisseur, and lavish benefactor of art and learning. In the next century Tuscany became a grand duchy, of which the Medici were hereditary grand dukes until the family died out in 1737. Thus established, they furnished numerous cardinals and two popes to the church, and two Medici women became queens of France.

What arose in Italy, in these surroundings, was no less than a new conception of man himself. The world was so exciting that another world need not be thought of. It seemed very doubtful whether a quiet, cloistered, or celibate life was on a higher plane than an active gregarious life, or family life, or even a life of promiscuity and adventure. It was hard to believe that clergy were any better than laity, or that life led to a stern divine judgment in the end. That man's will and intelligence might mislead him seemed a gloomy doctrine. That man was a frail creature, in need of God's grace and salvation, though perhaps said with the lips, was not felt in the heart. Instead, what captivated the Italians of the Renaissance was a sense of man's tremendous powers.

Formerly, the ideal had been seen in renunciation, in a certain disdain for the concerns of this world. Now a life of involvement was also prized. Formerly, poverty had been greatly respected, at least in Christian doctrine. Now voices were heard in praise of a proper enjoyment of wealth. In the past, men had admired a life of contemplation, or meditative withdrawal. Now the humanist Leonardo Bruni could write, in 1433, "The whole glory of man lies in activity." Often, to be sure, the two attitudes existed in the same person. Sometimes they divided different groups within the same city. As always, the old persisted along with the new. The result might be psychological stress and civil conflict.

The new esteem for human activity took both a social and an individualistic turn. In cities maintaining their republican forms, as at Florence in the early fifteenth century, a new civic consciousness or sense of public duty was expressed. For this purpose the writings of Cicero and other ancients were found to be highly relevant, since they provided an ethics independent of the Christian and medieval tradition. There was also a kind of cult of the great individual, hardly known to the ancients, and one which gave little attention to collective responsibility. Renaissance individualism put its emphasis on outstanding attainments. The great individual shaped his own destiny in a world governed by fortune. He had *virtù*, the quality of being a man (*vir*, "man"), in the sense of successfully demonstrating human powers. A man of *virtù*, in the arts, in war, or in statecraft, was a man who knew what he was doing, who, from resources within himself, made the best use of his opportunities, hewing his way through the world, and excelling in all that he did. For the arts, such a spirit is preserved in the autobiography of Benvenuto Cellini.

The growing preoccupation with things human can be traced in new forms of painting, sculpture, and architecture that arose in Italy at this time. These arts likewise reflected an increasing this-worldliness, a new sense of reality and a new sense of space, of a kind different from that of the Middle Ages, and which was to underlie European thinking almost to our own time. Space was no longer indeterminate, unknowable, or divine; it was a zone occupied by physical human beings, or one in which human beings might at least imagine themselves moving about. Reality meant visible and tangible persons or objects in this space, "objective" in the sense that they looked or felt the same to all normal persons who perceived them. It was a function of the arts to convey this reality, however idealized or suffused by the artist's individual feeling, in such a way that observers could recognize in the image the identity of the thing portrayed.

Architecture reflected the new tendencies. Though the Gothic cathedral at Milan was built as late as 1386, at Florence and elsewhere architects preferred to adapt Greco-Roman principles of design, such as symmetrical arrangements of doors and windows, the classical column, the arch and the dome. More public buildings of a nonreligious character were built, and more substantial town houses were put up by wealthy merchants, in styles meant to represent grandeur, or civic importance, or availability and convenience for human use. Gardens and terraces were added to many such buildings.

Sculpture, confined in the Middle Ages to the niches and portals of cathedrals, now emerged as an independent and free-standing art. Its favored subjects were human beings, now presented so that the viewer could walk around the object and see it from all directions, thus bringing it securely into his own world. The difference from the religious figures carved on medieval churches was very great. Like the architects, the sculptors in parting from the immediate past found much in the Greek and Roman tradition that was modern and useful to their purpose. They produced portrait busts of eminent contemporaries, or figures of great leaders sometimes on horseback, or statues depicting characters from Greco-Roman history and mythology. The use of the nude, in mythological or allegorical subjects, likewise showed a conception of humanity that was more in keeping with the Greek than with the Christian tradition.

Painting was less influenced by the ancients, since the little of ancient painting that had survived was unknown during the Renaissance. The invention of painting in oils opened new pathways for the art. Merchants, ecclesiastics, and princes provided a mounting demand. In subject matter painting remained conservative, dealing most often with religious themes. It was the conception and presentation that were new. The new feeling for space became evident. With the discovery of the mathematics of perspective, space was presented in exact relation to the beholder's eye. The viewer, in a sense, entered into the world of the painting. A three-dimensional effect was achieved, with careful representation of distance through variation of size, and techniques of shading or chiaroscuro added to the illusion of physical volume. Human figures were often placed in a setting of painted architecture, or against a background of landscape or scenery, showing castles or hills,

Portrait of a Condottiere *by Giovanni Bellini (Italian, 1430–1516)*
An emphatic portrayal of Renaissance individualism. Note the artist's ability to present a concrete human being, one who is not merely an abstract type. For the "condottieri" see p. 64. The name of this particular "condottiere" is not known. But the hard expression and set features, the firm lines about the mouth and chin, the bull neck and the unflinching gaze, suggest an aggressive character of considerable "virtù." The face is thoughtful and intelligent but devoid of spirituality. The man is clearly in the habit of depending on himself alone. The artist has heightened the sense of his subject's independence and self-sufficiency by making him stand out from a dark and entirely vacant background. Courtesy of the National Gallery of Art, Washington, D.C., Samuel H. Kress Collection.

which though supposedly far away yet closed in the composition with a knowable boundary. In such a painting everything was localized in place and time; a part of the real world was caught and put in the picture. The idea was not to suggest eternity, as in earlier religious painting, nor yet to express private fantasy or the workings of the unconscious, as sometimes in "postmodern" art, but to present a familiar theme in an understandable setting, often with a narrative content, that is, by the telling of a story. Much of the later course of Western painting was anticipated in Masaccio's *Expulsion of Adam and Eve*, produced at Florence in the 1420s. Here we have two convincingly real human figures, set in a definite garden, visibly moved by grief and shame, represented in depth with three-dimensional accuracy, their nudity justified by the religious story, in the act of departure from Eden, as an avenging angel in the upper middle distance sternly orders them away.

Painters were able also, like the sculptors, by a close study of human anatomy, to show people in distinctive and living attitudes. Faces took on more expression; individual personality was depicted. Differences among men were shown, not merely abstract characteristics that all men or certain kinds of men, such as kings or saints, had in common. Painting became less symbolic, less an intimation of general truths, more a portrayal of concrete realities as they met the eye. In the preceding portrait by Bellini of a *condottiere* the reader can see for himself, though who the man was is not known, how a strong, real, and vivid personality looks out from the canvas. Similarly, the great religious paintings were peopled with human beings. In Leonardo da Vinci's *Last Supper* Christ and his disciples are seen as a group of men each with his own characteristics, Raphael's Madonnas seem to be young Italian women, and in the mighty figures of Michelangelo the attributes of humanity invade heaven itself.

There were always countercurrents that make such generalizations debatable. The main tone of the arts in Renaissance Italy was to take satisfaction in beauty, to present the world as desirable, to be clear-cut, lucid, and finite. But another note, one of danger and horror, is struck in Botticelli's *Magdalene at the Foot of the Cross*. (See page 41.) Many Florentines were troubled by the worldliness and even paganism that had grown up about them. Their anxieties were expressed in a movement for religious reforms led by the priest Savonarola. As it ran its course it became involved in political questions, until Savonarola was tried and burned at the stake in 1498.

Erasmus of Rotterdam *by Hans Holbein, the Younger (German, 1497–1543)*
The classic portrayal of humanism at its best. The portrait was painted in 1523, when Erasmus was fifty-six, and the Lutheran Reformation and Peasant Rebellion were raging in Germany. Holbein has conveyed the mood of tight-lipped calm, or of saddened humanity, felt by a life-long reforming writer who has lived to see violent revolution. The face, finely delineated, and high-lighted against the deeper tones of the cap and cloak, is concentrated upon Erasmus' only weapon, the pen. The picture captures the life of thought; it is a picture of the human mind, as Bellini's "Condottiere" is a picture of the will. Courtesy of the Louvre (Giraudon).

The literary movement in Renaissance Italy is called humanism because of the rising interest in humane letters, *litterae humaniores*. There had indeed been much writing in the later Middle Ages. Much of it had been of a technical character, as in theology, philosophy, or law; some of it had been meant to convey information, as in chronicles, histories, and cosmographical descriptions of the world. Great hymns had been composed, lively student songs had been heard at the universities, plays had been performed in cathedrals, the old legends of King Arthur and Roland had been written down, and occasionally a monk would try his hand at a long narrative poem. Yet it is hardly too much to say that literature, in the modern sense, first appeared in the fourteenth and fifteenth centuries in Italy. There came to be a class of men who looked upon writing as their main life's work, who wrote for each other and for a somewhat larger public, and who used writing to deal with general questions, or to examine their own states of mind, or resolve their own difficulties, or used words to achieve artistic effects, or simply to please and amuse their readers.

The Italian humanists, like their predecessors, wrote a good deal in Latin. They differed from earlier literate persons in that they were not, for the most part, members of the clergy. They complained that Latin had become monkish, barbaric, and "scholastic," a jargon of the schools and universities, and they greatly preferred the classic style of a Cicero or a Livy. In all this there was much that was unfair, much that was merely literary, and something that anticipated the famous twentieth-century problem of the "two cultures," or failure of understanding between persons of humanistic interests and those of more scientific interests. Medieval Latin was a vigorously living language that used words in new senses, many of which have passed into English and the Romance languages as perfectly normal expressions. Yet in the ancient writers the humanists found qualities that medieval writing did not have. They discovered a new range of interests, a new sensibility, discussion of political and civic questions, a world presented without the overarching framework of religious belief. In addition, the Greeks and Romans unquestionably had style—a sense of form, a taste for the elegant and the epigrammatic. They had often also written for practical ends, in dialogs, orations, or treatises that were designed for purposes of persuasion.

If the humanists therefore made a cult of antiquity it was because they saw kindred spirits in it. They sensed a relevancy for their own time. The classical influence, never wholly absent in the Middle Ages, now reentered as a main force in the higher civilization of Europe. The humanists polished their Latin, and increasingly they learned Greek. They made assiduous searches for classical texts hitherto unknown. Many were found; they had of course been copied and preserved by the monks of preceding times.

But while an especial dignity attached to writing in Latin, known throughout Europe, most of the humanists wrote in Italian also. Or rather, they used the mode of speech current in Florence. This had also been the language of Dante in the *Divine Comedy*. To this vast poem the humanists now added many writings in Florentine or Tuscan prose. The result was that Florentine became the standard form of modern

Italian. It was the first time that a European vernacular—that is, the common spoken tongue as opposed to Latin—became thus standardized amid the variety of its dialects and adapted in structure and vocabulary to the more complex requirements of a written language. French and English soon followed, and most of the other European languages somewhat later.

The Florentine exile, Francesco Petrarca, or Petrarch, has been called the first man of letters. The son of a merchant, he spent his life in travel throughout France and Italy. Trained for the law, and ordained to the clergy, he became a somewhat rootless critic of these two esteemed professions, which he denounced for their "scholasticism." He lived in the generation after Dante, dying in 1374, and he anticipated the more fully developed humanism that was to come. His voluminous writings show him to have been the prey of contrary attitudes. He was attracted by life, love, beauty, travel, and connections with men of importance in church and state; he could also spurn all these things as ephemeral and deceptive. He loved Cicero for his common sense and his commitment to political liberty; indeed, he discovered a manuscript of Cicero's letters in 1345. He loved St. Augustine for his otherworldly vision of the City of God. But in Cicero's writings he also found a deep religious concern, and in St. Augustine he esteemed the active man who had been a bishop, a writer heavily engaged in the controversies of his time, and one who taught that for true Christians the world is not evil.

Petrarch wrote sonnets in Italian, an epic in Latin, an introspective study of himself, and a great many letters which he clearly meant to be literary productions. He aspired to literary fame. In all this we see a new kind of writer, who uses language not merely as a practical tool but as a medium of more subtle expression, to commune with himself, to convey moods of discouragement or satisfaction, to clarify doubts, to improve his own understanding of the choices and options that life affords. With Petrarch, in short, literature became a kind of calling, and also a consideration of moral philosophy, still related but no longer subordinate to religion. It was moral philosophy in the widest sense, raising questions of how human beings should adjust to the world, what a good life could be or ought to be, or where the genuine and ultimate rewards of living were to be found.

Petrarch was an indication of things to come. Boccaccio, his contemporary and also a Florentine, wrote the *Decameron* in Italian, a series of tales designed both to entertain and to impart a certain wisdom about human character and behavior. They were followed by the main group of humanists, far more numerous but less well remembered. Men of letters began to take part in public life, to be sought out and asked for advice, to gather pupils and found schools, to serve as secretaries to governing bodies or princes, and even to occupy office themselves. Thus the humanist Coluccio Salutati became chancellor of Florence in 1375. During the following decades Florence was threatened by the expansive ambitions of Milan, where the princely despotism of the Visconti family had established itself. Against such dangers a new and intense civic consciousness asserted itself. Salutati, in addition to the usual duties of chancellor, served the state with his pen, glorifying

Florentine liberty, identifying it with the liberties of ancient republican Rome before they were undermined by the Caesars. He was succeeded as chancellor by two other humanists, Bruni and Poggio. Bruni wrote a history of Florence which marked a new achievement in historical writing, when compared with the annals and chronicles of the Middle Ages. He saw the past as clearly past, different from but relevant to the present; and he introduced a new division of historical periods. On the model of such ancient writers as Livy, he adopted a flowing narrative form. And he used history for a practical political purpose, to show that Florence had a long tradition of liberty and possessed values and attainments worth fighting for against menacing neighbors. History took on a utility that it had had for the Greeks and Romans and was to retain in the future in Europe and eventually America: the function of heightening a sentiment, not yet of nationalism, but of collective civic consciousness or group identity. It was meant to arouse men to a life of commitment and participation. Where Petrarch had chided Cicero for becoming overinvolved in worldly cares, Salutati and Bruni hailed him as a positive source of inspiration, the very model of a philosopher and a literary man who was also a man of action, a good citizen, and a stalwart republican who stood up against despots.

All this literary activity was of a scholarly type, in which authors broadened their understanding as much by reading as by personal experience of the world. And scholarly activity, the habit of attending closely to what a page really said, had consequences that went beyond either pure literature or local patriotism. A new critical attitude developed. Bruni, in his history, showed a new sense of the need for authentic sources. Lorenzo Valla became one of the founders of textual criticism. Gaining a historical sense for the Latin language, he observed that its characteristic words and expressions varied from one time to another. He put this knowledge to the service of the king of Naples in a dispute with the pope. Valla showed, by analysis of the language used in the document, that the Donation of Constantine, on which the papacy then based its temporal claims, could not have been written in Constantine's time in the fourth century, and so was a forgery. Pico della Mirandola and others looked for aspects of truth not revealed in the Christian Scriptures. As men of letters, they put their faith in books, but as men of the Renaissance they were receptive to anything written by men anywhere. A group at the Academy of Florence took a serious interest in the study of Plato. The enthusiastic and very learned young Pico, at the age of twenty-three, in 1486, offered to expatiate publicly on all human knowledge in 900 theses, to be drawn from "the Chaldaic, Arabic, Hebrew, Grecian, Egyptian and Latin sages."

Schooling and Manners

While Italian humanism thus contributed much to literature and scholarship, to classical learning, and to the formation of modern national languages, it also had tangible and lasting effects in education. Here its impact remained in all regions of European civilization until the twentieth century. The medieval universities were essentially places for professional training in theology, medicine, and law. Except in

England this continued to be their primary function. What came to be known as secondary education, the preparation of young men either for the universities or for "life," owes more to the Renaissance. The organized education of women came much later.

Medieval schooling had been chaotic and repetitious. Youngsters of all ages sat together with a teacher, each absorbing from the confusion whatever he could of Latin rules and vocabulary. The Renaissance launched the idea of putting different age groups or levels of accomplishment into separate classes, in separate rooms, each with its own teacher, with periodic promotion of the pupil from one level to the next. Latin remained the principal subject, with Greek now added. But many new purposes were seen in the study of Latin. It was intended to give skill in the use of language, including the pupil's native tongue. Rhetoric was the art of using language to influence others. It heightened communication. Knowledge alone was not enough, said the historian and chancellor Bruni, who also wrote a short work on education: "to make effectual use of what we know we must add the power of expression." Nor was Latin merely the necessary professional tool for the priest, the physician, the lawyer, or the government servant. The student learned Latin (and Greek) in order to read the ancient writings—epics, lyrics, orations, letters, histories, dialogs, and philosophical treatises—and these writings, especially at a time when the modern literatures were undeveloped, opened his horizons in all directions. They had a practical application; and at least as late as the American and French revolutions men found useful lessons in the rise and decline of the Roman republic and the troubles of the Greek city-states. The classics were meant also to have a moral impact, to produce a balanced personality, and to form character. Not everyone could be important or gifted, said the humanist Vittorino, but we all face a life of "social duty," and "all are responsible for the personal influence which goes forth from us." These aims built themselves permanently into the educational system of modern Europe.

Young men were trained also for a more civilized deportment in everyday social living. Personal style in the upper classes became somewhat more studied. Hitherto Europeans had generally acted like big children; they spat, belched, and blew their noses without inhibition, snatched at food with their fingers, bawled at each other when aroused, or sulked when their feelings were offended. It was Italians of the Renaissance who first taught more polite habits. Books of etiquette began to appear, of which the most successful was Castiglione's *Book of the Courtier*. The "courtier" was ancestor to the "gentleman"; "courtesy" was originally the kind of behavior suited to princely courts.

The "courtier," according to Castiglione, should be a man of good birth but is chiefly the product of training. His education in youth, and his efforts in mature years, should be directed toward mixing agreeably in the company of his equals. His clothes should be neat, his movements graceful, his approach to other people perfectly poised. He must converse with facility, be proficient in sports and arms, and know how to dance and appreciate music. He should know Latin and Greek.

With literary and other subjects he should show a certain familiarity but never become too engrossed. For the well-bred man speaks with "a certain carelessness, to hide his art, and show that what he says or does comes from him without effort or deliberation." Pedantry and heaviness must yield to a certain air of effortless superiority, so that even if the "courtier" knows or does something seriously, he must treat it lightly as one of many accomplishments. At its best, the code taught a certain considerateness for the feelings of others, and incorporated some of the moral ideas of the humanists, aiming at a creditable life in active society. Such a code is easy to travesty today in an age that favors both technical specialization and spontaneous self-expression. Castiglione's book was translated into numerous languages, and a hundred editions were printed before 1600. Its ideal was inculcated for centuries by private tutors and in the schools. The conception of the gentleman helped to tame and civilize Europe's upper classes, and in the end all classes so far as they imitated their social betters. Indeed, there was a time, in the eighteenth century, when civilization itself was referred to as "the refinement of manners."

Politics and the Italian Renaissance

The Italian Renaissance, for all its accomplishments, produced no institution or great idea by which masses of men living in society could be held together. Indeed, the greatest of Europe's institutions, the Roman church, in which Europeans had lived for centuries, and without which they did not see how they could live at all, fell into sheer neglect under the Renaissance popes. For decades after breaking the conciliar movement the triumphant papacy made no attempts at reform. Nor did Italy develop any effectual political institutions. Florence during the fifteenth century passed from a high-spirited republicanism to acceptance of one-man rule. Through-out the peninsula the merchants, bankers, connoisseurs, and courtly classes who controlled the city-states could not fight for themselves, nor arouse their citizens to fight for them. They therefore hired professional fighting men, *condottieri,* private leaders of armed bands, who contracted with the various city-states to carry on warfare, and often raised their price or changed sides during hostilities. Italian politics became a tangled web, a labyrinth of subterfuge and conspiracy, a platform on which great individuals might exhibit their *virtù.* "Italian cunning" became a byword throughout Europe. Dictators rose and fell. The Medici became dukes in Florence, the Sforza in Milan, while in Venice and Genoa, where the republics were kept, narrow oligarchies held the rule. These states, along with the states of the church, jockeyed about like pugilists in a ring, held within an intricate, shifting, and purely local balance of power.

Italy was the despair of its patriots, or of such few as remained. One of these was Niccolò Machiavelli, who, in *The Prince* (1513), wrote the most lasting work of the Italian Renaissance. He resembled the other humanists in his dislike of the church and his love of the classics. From Livy's history of ancient Rome he drew many republican lessons, and he kept alive some of the civic concern of Salutati and Bruni. He himself was exiled for opposing the Medici rise to power.

Machiavelli dreamed of the day when the citizens of his native Florence, or indeed of all Italy, should behave like early Romans—show virility in their politics, fight in citizen armies for patriotic causes, and uphold their dignity before Europe. It was outside Italy, in kings Ferdinand of Aragon, Louis XI of France, and Henry VII of England, that Machiavelli was obliged to find his heroes. He admired them because they were successful builders of states. In *The Prince* he produced a handbook of statecraft which he hoped Italy might find useful. He produced also the first purely secular treatise on politics.

Medieval writings on politics, those of Thomas Aquinas or Marsiglio of Padua, for example, had always talked of God's will for the government of men, with such accompanying matters as justice and right, or divine and natural law. All this Machiavelli put aside. He "emancipated" politics from theology and moral philosophy. He undertook to describe simply what rulers actually did, and thus anticipated what was later called the scientific spirit, in which questions of good and bad are ignored, and the observer attempts to discover only what really happens. What really happens, said Machiavelli, is that effective rulers and governments act only in their own political interest. They keep faith or break it, observe treaties or repudiate them, are merciful or ruthless, forthright or sly, peaceable or aggressive, according as they estimate their own political needs. Machiavelli was prepared to admit that such behavior was bad; he only insisted that it was in this way, however regrettably, that successful rulers behaved. He was thought unduly cynical even in an age not characterized by political delicacy. He had nevertheless diagnosed the new era with considerable insight. It was an age when politics was in fact becoming more secular, breaking off from religion, with the building up of states and with state authority emerging as a goal requiring no other justification.

But the most successful states of the time, as Machiavelli saw, were not in Italy. They were what history knows as the New Monarchies, and they owed their strength to something more than princely craft, for they enjoyed a measure of spontaneous loyalty from their own peoples. Italy was politically helpless. Politics in Italy was not about anything vital; it was an affair of *virtù;* and the people of Italy lost interest in politics, as they did in war, becoming "effeminate" in the eyes of outsiders.

So Italy, the sunny land of balmy Mediterranean skies, rich in the busy life of its cities, its moneyed wealth, its gorgeous works of art, lay helplessly open to the depredations of less easy-going peoples, from Spain and the north, who possessed institutions in which men could act together in large numbers. In a new age of rising national monarchies the city-states of Italy were too small to compete. In 1494 a French army crossed the Alps. Italy became a bone of contention between France and Spain. In 1527 a horde of undisciplined Spanish and German mercenaries, joined by foot-loose Italians, fell upon Rome itself. Never, not even from the Goths of the fifth century, had Rome experienced anything so horrible and degrading. The city was sacked, thousands were killed, soldiers milled about for a week in an orgy of rape and loot, the pope was imprisoned, and cardinals were mockingly paraded through the streets facing backward on the backs of mules. By this time religious passions were aroused; we are encroaching on the story of the Reformation.

After the sack of Rome the Renaissance faded away. Politically, for over three hundred years, Italy remained divided, the passive object of the ambitions of outside powers. Meanwhile its culture permeated the rest of Europe.

7
The Renaissance outside Italy

Outside Italy people were much less conscious of any sudden break with the Middle Ages. Developments north of the Alps, and in Spain, were more an outgrowth of what had gone before. There was indeed a Renaissance in the Italian sense. In some of the innovations in painting the Flemish masters preceded those of Italy. A new delight in realistic detail, with the placing of a multitude of figures in a humanized space, could be found in a variety of forms, from the beautiful fifteenth-century miniatures of northern France to the huge altarpiece which Wit Stosz minutely carved in wood for the cathedral at Cracow. In the latter, whole villages with realistic men and women can be seen, with specific plants so exactly presented that they can be botanically identified today. In the north also, as in Italy a little sooner, writers favored a neoclassical Latin, but the modern written languages also began to develop.

But the northern Renaissance was more a blend of the old and the new. In it, above all, the religious element was stronger than in Italy. The most important northern humanists were men like Thomas More in England and the Dutch Erasmus. The French humanism that produced Rabelais also produced John Calvin.

Religious Scholarship and Science

It is customary to distinguish between the "pagan" humanism of Italy and the Christian humanism of the north. In the north, Christian humanists studied the Hebrew and Greek texts of the Bible and read the Church Fathers, both Latin and Greek, in order to deepen their understanding of Christianity and to restore its moral vitality. Among lesser people, too, without pretense to humanistic learning, religion remained a force. Medieval intellectual interests persisted. This is apparent from the continuing foundation of universities. The humanists generally regarded universities as centers of a pedantic, monkish, and "scholastic" learning. Concentrating upon theology, or upon medicine and law, the universities gave little encouragement to experimental science and still less to purely literary studies. In Italy in the fifteenth century no new universities were established. But in Spain, in France, in Scotland, in Scandinavia, and above all in Germany, new universities sprouted up. Between 1386 and 1506 no less than fourteen universities were established in Germany. At one of the newest, Wittenberg, founded in 1502, Martin Luther was to launch the Protestant Reformation.

Germany at this time, on the eve of the great religious upheaval, and before the shift of the commercial artery from central Europe to the Atlantic seaboard, was a main center of European life. Politically, the German-speaking world was an ill-defined and ill-organized region, composed of many diverse parts, from which the

Netherlands and Switzerland were not yet differentiated. Parts of it were infested by robber knights, picturesque in legend, but unpleasant for those who had to live with them in reality. Economically, nevertheless, western and southern Germany enjoyed a lead; the towns traded busily, and German banking families, like the famous Fugger, controlled more capital than any others in Europe. Technical inventiveness was alive; mining was developing; and it was in the Rhineland, at Mainz, that Gutenberg, about 1450, produced the first books printed with movable type. In painting, the western fringe of the Germanic world produced the Flemish masters, and south Germany gave birth to Dürer and the Holbeins.

Intellectually, Germany shared in the Latin culture of Europe, a fact often obscured by the Latinizing of German names. Regiomontanus (the Latin name of Johann Müller) laid the foundations during his short lifetime (1436–1476) for a mathematical conception of the universe. He was probably the most influential scientific worker of the fifteenth century, especially since Leonardo da Vinci's scientific labors remained unknown. Nicholas of Cusa (1401?–1464) was a churchman whose mystical philosophy entered into the later development of mathematics and science. From such a background of mathematical interests came Copernicus (Nikolaus Koppernigk, 1473–1543), who believed that the earth moved about the sun; he was a Pole, but was born and spent most of his life in the mixed German-Polish region of East Prussia. Fortified by the same mathematical interests, Europe's best known cartographers were also Germans, such as Behaim and Schöner, whose world maps the reader may see on page 310. Paracelsus (Latin for Hohenheim) undertook to revolutionize medicine at the University of Basel. His wild prophecies made him a mixture of scientist and charlatan; but, in truth, science was not yet clearly distinguished from the occult, with which it shared the idea of control over natural forces. A similar figure, remembered in literature and the arts, was the celebrated Dr. Faustus. In real life Faust, or Faustus, was perhaps a learned German of the first part of the sixteenth century. He was rumored to have sold his soul to the devil in return for knowledge and power. The Faust story was dramatized in England as early as 1593 by Christopher Marlowe, and, much later, by Goethe in poetry and by Gounod in the opera. In the legend of Faust later generations were to see a symbol of the inordinate striving of modern man. Oswald Spengler published his *Decline of the West* in 1918. Needing a name for the European civilization whose doom he prophesied, he called it "Faustian."

The idea of man's powers to understand and control physical nature, as developed most especially north of the Alps, corresponded in many ways to the more purely Italian and humanistic idea of the infinite richness of human personality. Together, they constituted the new Renaissance spirit, for both emphasized the emancipation of humanity's limitless potentialities. The two ideas constantly interacted; in fact, most of the scientific workers just mentioned—Regiomontanus, Nicholas of Cusa, Copernicus—spent many years in Italy, receiving the stimulus of Italian thought.[2]

[2] On da Vinci, Copernicus, and the rise of modern science in general, see Chapter VII.

In the north a genuine religious impulse, in addition to religious humanistic scholarship, also remained alive. Where in Italy the religious sense, if not extinct, seemed
to pass into the aesthetic, into a joyous and public cult in which God was glorified by works of art, in the north it took on a more mystical and a more soberly
moral tone. Germany in the fourteenth century produced a series of mystics. The
mystic tendencies of Nicholas of Cusa have been mentioned. More typical mystics
were Meister Eckhart (d. 1327) and Thomas à Kempis (d. 1471), author of the *Imitation*
of Christ. The essence of mysticism lay in the belief, or experience, that the individual
soul could in perfect solitude commune directly with God. The mystic had no need
of reason, nor of words, nor of joining with other people in open worship, nor even of
the sacraments administered by the priests—nor even of the church. The mystics did
not rebel against the church; they accepted its pattern of salvation; but at bottom they
offered, to those who could follow, a deeper religion in which the church as a social
institution had no place. All social institutions, in fact, were transcended in
mysticism by the individual soul; and on this doctrine, both profound and socially
disruptive, Martin Luther was later to draw.

For the church, it was significant also that religion was felt deeply outside the
clergy. Persons stirred by religion, who in the Middle Ages would have taken holy
orders, now frequently remained laymen. In the past the church had often needed
reform. But in the past, in the bad times of the tenth century, for example, the church
had found reformers within itself. The church had thus been repeatedly reformed
and renewed without revolution. Now, in the fifteenth and early sixteenth centuries
an ominous line seemed to be increasingly drawn: between the clergy as an
established interest, inert and set in its ways, merely living, and living well, off the
church; and groups of people outside the clergy—religious laymen, religiously
inclined humanists and writers, impatient and headstrong rulers—who were more
influential than ever before, and more critical of ecclesiastical abuses.

Lay religion was especially active in the Netherlands. A lay preacher, Gerard
Groote, attracted followers by his sermons on spiritual regeneration. In 1374 he
founded a religious sisterhood, which was followed by more numerous establishments for religiously minded men. They called themselves Brothers of the
Common Life, and they received papal approval for their mode of living. Their
influence spread among lay groups and in certain monastic communities in the
Rhineland and Germany. The Brothers opened many schools, which were so
successful that they were imitated by others. Such schools taught, besides reading
and writing, a Christian ideal of character and conduct. They paid little attention to
systematic doctrine but emphasized instead such personal qualities as humility,
tolerance, reverence, love of one's neighbor, and conscientiousness in the performance of duty. This Modern Devotion, as it was called, spread very widely in the
Netherlands. By the close of the fifteenth century thousands of laymen throughout
the Rhine valley and Germany had received their schooling from the Brothers. The
Brothers of the Common Life, while critical of worldliness in the clergy, never
opposed the organized church. They simply found that it did not meet their religious
needs.

In this atmosphere grew up the greatest of all the northern humanists, and indeed the most notable figure of the entire humanist movement, Erasmus of Rotterdam (1466–1536). Like all the humanists, Erasmus chose to write in a "purified" and usually intricate Latin style. He regarded the Middle Ages as benighted, ridiculed the scholastic philosophers, and studied deeply the classical writers of antiquity. He had the strength and the limitations of the pure man of letters. To the hard questions of serious philosophy he was largely indifferent; he feared the unenlightened excitability of the common people, and he was almost wholly unpolitical in his outlook. He rarely thought in terms of worldly power or advantage and made too little allowance for those who did. An exact contemporary to the most notorious of the worldly Renaissance popes, Erasmus was keenly aware of the need of a reform of the clergy. He put his faith in education, enlightened discussion, and gradual moral improvement. He led no burning crusade and counseled against all violence or fanaticism. He prepared new Greek and Latin editions of the New Testament. Urging also the reading of the New Testament in the vernacular languages, he hoped that with a better understanding of Christ's teaching people might turn from their evil ways. In his *Praise of Folly* he satirized all worldly pretensions and ambitions, those of the clergy most emphatically. In his *Handbook of a Christian Knight* he showed how a man might take part in the affairs of the world while remaining a devout Christian. Mildness, reasonableness, tolerance, restraint, scholarly understanding, a love of peace, a critical and reforming zeal which, hating nobody, worked through trying to make men think, a subdued and controlled tone from which shouting or bad temper were always excluded—such were the Erasmian virtues.[3]

Erasmus achieved an international eminence such as no man of purely intellectual attainments has ever enjoyed. He corresponded with the great of Europe. He lectured at Cambridge and edited books for a publisher at Basel. The king of Spain named him a councilor, the king of France called him to Paris, Pope Leo X assisted him when he was in trouble. Theologians found fault with Erasmus' ideas (in which, indeed, the supernatural had little importance), but among the chief practical men of the church, the popes and prelates, he had many admirers. Erasmus, it must be noted, attacked only the abuses in the church, the ignorance or sloth of the clergy, the moral or financial corruption of their lives. The essence and principle of the Roman Catholic Church he never called into question. Whether the Erasmian spirit, so widely diffused about 1520, would have sufficed to restore the church without the revolutionary impact of Protestantism is one of the many unanswerable questions of history.

Meanwhile, in Europe outside Italy, kings were actively building up the institutions of the modern state. It was these states, more than any other single factor, that were to determine the course of the religious revolution. Whether a country

---

[3] See the portrait by Hans Holbein on p. 59.

turned Protestant, or remained Catholic, or was divided into separate religious communities, was to depend very largely upon political considerations.

Centralization under the New Monarchies

War, civil war, class war, feudal rebellion, and plain banditry afflicted a good deal of Europe in the middle of the fifteenth century. All this formless violence, which presented itself to contemporaries simply as a series of calamities, goes historically under many names: the Hundred Years' War between England and France (ended in 1453), the Hussite wars in Germany and Bohemia (ended 1436), Jack Cade's rebellion in England in 1450, the Wars of the Roses in England (ended 1485), peasant uprisings or *jacqueries* in France, social restlessness in the cloth towns of Flanders. Central governments were weak or almost nonexistent. The parliamentary bodies, whose establishment at the close of the Middle Ages was noted in the last chapter, enjoyed great influence over the kings. Constitutionally, it was the "golden age" of medieval parliaments. In social reality, since the predominance of these assemblies meant the predominance of feudal nobles and of narrowly localistic towns, it was an age of insecurity and confusion. Even at best, under peaceable conditions, medieval institutions had been either localistic or universal—centered on the one hand in the manor, town, or province, and on the other in the Roman church and Latin culture of Western Christendom as a whole. To the medieval man the intermediate level, that of the nation, was the least real.

With the middle of the fifteenth century appeared a group of kings known as the New Monarchs, who attempted to put down violence, enforce domestic peace, and curb the power of the feudal nobles. The New Monarchs laid the foundations for national, or at least territorial, states. They were not altogether new, for in placing royal authority over feudal authority they resumed the interrupted labors of kings of the High Middle Ages, and they succeeded in laying a basis for national states only where medieval developments had already pointed in this direction, as in England and France and to a lesser degree in Spain.[4]

The New Monarchs offered the institution of monarchy as a guarantee of law and order. They aroused latent sentiments of loyalty to the reigning dynasty, which in most countries was now centuries old. They proclaimed that hereditary monarchy was the legitimate form of public power, which all should accept without turmoil or resistance. They especially enlisted the support of middle-class people in the towns, who were tired of the private wars and marauding habits of the feudal nobles. The middle class was willing to pay taxes in return for peace. They were willing to let parliaments be dominated or even ignored by the king, for parliaments had proved to be too often strongholds of the noble class, or too often had merely accentuated class conflict. The king, receiving money in taxes, was able to organize armies with which to put down the nobles. The use of the pike and the longbow, which enabled the foot soldier to stand against the horseman, was here of great potential value. The king, if only he could get his monarchy sufficiently organized, and his finances into reliable order, could hire great numbers of foot soldiers, who generally came from the

[4]See pp. 25–26, 29–32.

endless ranks of plebeians, unlike the knightly horsemen. But to organize his monarchy, the king had to break down the mass of feudal, inherited, customary, or "common" law in which the rights of the feudal classes were entrenched. For this purpose, at least on the Continent, the New Monarch made use of Roman law, which was now actively studied in the universities.[5] He called himself a "sovereign"—it was at this time that kings began to be addressed as "majesty." The king, said the experts in Roman law, incorporated the will and welfare of the people in his own person—and they would cite the principle *salus populi suprema lex,* "the welfare of the people is the highest law." The king, they added, could *make* law, enact it by his own authority, regardless of previous custom or even of historic liberties—and they would quote, *quod principi placuit legis habet vigorem,* or "what pleases the prince has the force of law."

The New Monarchy came to England with the dynasty of the Tudors (1485–1603), whose first king, Henry VII (1485–1509), after gaining the throne by force, put an end to the civil turbulence of the Wars of the Roses. In these wars the great English baronial families had seriously weakened each other, to the great convenience of the king and the bulk of the citizenry. Henry VII passed laws against "livery and maintenance," the practice by which great lords maintained private armies wearing their own livery or insignia. Since ordinary procedures had recently failed to give security, with witnesses afraid to testify and juries afraid to offend the mighty, Henry VII used his royal council as a new court to deal with property disputes and infractions of the public peace. It met in a room decorated with stars, whence its name, the Star Chamber. It represented the authority of the king and his council, and it dispensed with a jury. Later denounced as an instrument of despotism, it was popular enough at first, because it preserved order and rendered substantial justice. Henry VII, though miserly and unpleasant in person, was accepted as a good ruler. National feeling in England consolidated around the house of Tudor.

In France the New Monarchy was represented by Louis XI (1461–1483), of the Valois line, and his successors. In the five centuries since the first French king had been crowned, the royal domain had steadily expanded from its original small nucleus around Paris through a combination of inheritance, marriage, war, intrigue, and conquest. Louis XI continued to round out the French borders. Internally, he built up a royal army, suppressed brigands, and subdued rebellious nobles. He acquired far greater powers than the English Tudors to raise taxation without parliamentary consent. The Estates-General of France met only once in his reign. On that occasion, remembering the anarchy of the past, they requested the king to govern without them in the future. The king proceeded to legislate on his own, reinforced the prestige of his officials vis-à-vis local magnates in various parts of the country, and broke down the chartered rights and localistic self-regarding attitudes of the numerous towns. Over the first estate of the realm, namely, the clergy, the French monarchy asserted extensive powers. We have seen how, by the Pragmatic Sanction of 1438, the Gallican church had won considerable national independence.[6]

[5] See pp. 11–12.
[6] See p. 52.

Habsburg Dominions
Church Lands
— **Boundary of Holy Roman Empire**

SHETLAND I.
ORKNEY I.
THE HEBRIDES
NORWAY
SWEDEN
FINLAND
Bergen
Oslo
Helsingfors
Stockholm
ESTONIA
LIVONIA
Riga
COURLAND
SCOTLAND
Edinburgh
NORTH SEA
DENMARK
Copenhagen
BALTIC SEA
Danzig
PRUSSIA
Vilna
IRELAND
Dublin
York
ENGLAND
WALES
Hamburg
BRANDENBURG
Berlin
Vistula R.
Warsaw
POLAND
LITHUA
London
Canterbury
Calais
(England)
DUTCH
NETHERLANDS
Antwerp
BELGIAN
NETH.
Brussels
Münster
Cologne
Schmalkalden
Wittenberg
SAXONY
SILESIA
Breslau
POLAND
Cracow
Lemberg
GALICIA
PO
Rhine R.
ATLANTIC OCEAN
St. Malo
Rouen
Paris
LUX.
Trier
PALA-
TINATE
Metz
Worms
Prague
BOHEMIA
MORAVIA
CARPAT
Orléans
F R A N C E
BURGUNDY
Strasbourg
Ratisbon
BAVARIA
Augsburg
Munich
AUSTRIA
Vienna
Danube R.
Bourges
FR.
COMTÉ
Basel
SWISS
CONFEDERATION
TYROL
HUNGARY
Budapest
TRANSYLVANIA
Angoulême
Bordeaux
Geneva
SAVOY
Milan
Trent
Venice
Mohacs
Belgrade
WALLA
Bucha
Bayonne
DAUPHINÉ
Parma
Genoa
VENETIAN REPUBLIC
DALMATIA
BOSNIA
OTTO
Dar
PYRENEES
Avignon
Marseilles
Florence
PAPAL
STATES
Sofia
M
Santiago
NAVARRE
ARAGON
CATALONIA
Barcelona
CORSICA
(Genoa)
Rome
MONTENEGRO
ALBANIA
Adri
Oporto
Burgos
Valladolid
S P A I N
Madrid
Salonica
AEGE
SE
PORTUGAL
Lisbon
C A S T I L E
Escorial
Toledo
Valencia
BALEARIC I.
SARDINIA
(Aragon)
NAPLES
(Aragon)
Naples
GREECE
IONIAN I.
(Venice)
Lepanto
Seville
Granada
GRANADA
Cadiz
MEDITERRANEAN
MOREA
Melilla (Spain)
Algiers
SULTANATE
OF FEZ
SULTANATE OF ALGIERS
Tunis
SULTANATE
OF TUNIS
Palermo
SICILY
(Aragon)
SEA
(Venice)
MALTA (Knights of St. John)
B A R B A R Y   S T A T E S
C
(V

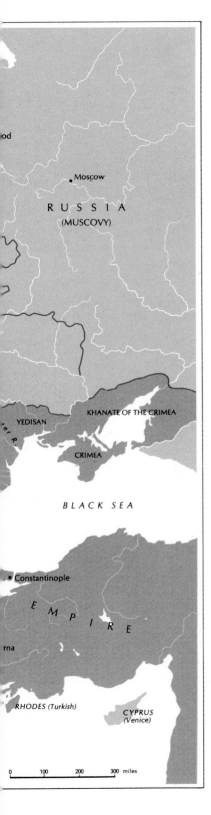

od

• Moscow

R U S S I A
(MUSCOVY)

KHANATE OF THE CRIMEA

YEDISAN

CRIMEA

BLACK SEA

• Constantinople

E M P I R E

rna

RHODES (Turkish)

CYPRUS
(Venice)

0   100   200   300 miles

Europe 1526. *The main feature of the political map of Europe about 1526 is the predominance of the house of Habsburg. Much of Europe was ruled by the Habsburg Emperor Charles V, who was at the same time King Charles I of Spain. As is explained in this and the following chapter, Charles left his possessions in Austria, Hungary, and Bohemia to his brother, those in Spain, the Netherlands, Italy, and America to his son. He thus established the Austrian and Spanish branches of the Habsburg dynasty. France was nearly encircled by Habsburg dominions and habitually formed alliances with various German princes and with Sweden, Poland, and Turkey. The Habsburgs remained the principal power in Europe until after the Thirty Years' War, which ended in 1648.*

In 1516 King Francis I reached an agreement with Pope Leo X, the Concordat of Bologna. By this agreement the Pragmatic Sanction was rescinded; the pope received his "annates," or money income, from French ecclesiastics; the king appointed the bishops and abbots. The fact that, after 1516, the kings of France already controlled their own national clergy was one reason why, in later years, they were never tempted to turn Protestant.

Strictly speaking, there was no kingdom of Spain. Various Spanish kingdoms had combined into two, Aragon and Castile. To Aragon, which lay along the Mediterranean side of the peninsula, belonged the Balearic Islands, Sardinia, Sicily, and the south Italian kingdom of Naples. To Castile, after 1492, belonged the newly discovered Americas. The two were joined in a personal union by the marriage of Ferdinand of Aragon and Isabella of Castile in 1469. The union was personal only; that is, both kingdoms recognized the two monarchs, but they had no common political, judicial, or administrative institutions. There was little or no Spanish national feeling; indeed, the Catalans in northern Aragon spoke a language quite different from Castilian Spanish. The common feeling throughout Spain was the sense of belonging to the Spanish Catholic church. The common memory was the memory of the Christian crusade against the Moors. The one common institution, whose officials had equal authority and equal access to all the kingdoms, was a church court, the Inquisition. The church in Spain was in vigorous condition. Cardinal Ximenes, shortly before 1500, managed to rid it of the abuses and the inertia which debilitated the church in the rest of Europe. The *reconquista* was at last completed. In 1492 Granada, the southern tip of Spain, was conquered from the Moors. Its annexation added to the heterogeneous and undigested character of the Spanish dominions.

In these circumstances the New Monarchy in Spain followed a religious bent. Unification took place around the church. The rulers, though they made efforts at political centralization, worked largely through facilities offered by the church, notably the Inquisition. They insisted on religious conformity. National feeling was church feeling; the sense of "Spanishness" was a sense of Catholicity. Formerly the Spanish had been among the most tolerant of Europeans; Christians, Moslems, and Jews had managed to live together. But in the wave of national (or religious) excitement that accompanied the conquest of Granada both the Jews and the Moors were expelled.[7] All persons in Spain were now supposed to be Christians. In fact, however, Spain was the one country in Europe where a person's Christianity could

[7] The expulsion of the Jews by the decree of 1492 was actually a sign of former toleration in Spain; for the Jews had been expelled from England in 1290 and from France in 1306, nor were they again allowed in England until the mid-seventeenth century, nor in France (with great exceptions) until the French Revolution. It would appear that, in the history of many European peoples, the attainment of a certain degree of national self-consciousness brought a dislike of the Jews as "outsiders." The Jews who left Spain (the Sephardic Jews) went to the Near East, and, in smaller numbers, to the Netherlands and even to southwestern France (one of the exceptions noted above). The Jews who earlier left England and France generally went to Germany, the great center of Ashkenazic Jewry in the Middle Ages. Driven from Germany in the fourteenth century they concentrated in Poland, which remained the great center of European Jewry until the Nazi massacres of the 1940s.

not be taken for granted, because many Spanish families had been Jewish or Moslem for centuries, and had only accepted Christianity to avoid expulsion. Hence arose a fear of false Christians, of an unassimilated element secretly hostile to the foundations of Spanish life. It was feared that Moriscos (Christians of Moorish background) and Marranos (Christians of Jewish background) retained a clandestine sympathy for the religion of their forebears. A distaste for eating pork, or an inclination not to work on Saturday, was enough to arouse suspicion. Thousands of such persons were haled before the Inquisition, where, as in the civil courts under Roman procedure, torture could be employed to extort confessions. Spanish life became rigidly and ostentatiously orthodox. It was safest to be profuse in one's external devotions. It was the way of proving oneself to be a good Spaniard. The national and the Catholic were fused.

The life of Spain remained a great crusade, a crusade within Spain against Moriscos and Marranos, a crusade carried against the Moors into Africa itself, which the Spanish invaded immediately after the conquest of Granada. The crusade crossed the ocean into the Americas, where the Spanish church set about gathering the Indians into the fold. And it was soon to spread to Europe also. Spain was ready, before Protestantism ever appeared, to play its role in the Reformation, to be the avenging angel to extirpate heresy, and the stern apostle demanding Catholic reform.

Ideas of the New Monarchy were at work even in Germany, which is to say, in the Holy Roman Empire. There were three kinds of states in the Empire. There were the princely states—duchies, margraviates, etc.—each a little hereditary dynastic monarchy in itself, such as Saxony, Brandenburg, or Bavaria. There were ecclesiastical states—bishoprics, abbacies, etc.—in which the bishop or abbot, whose rule was of course not hereditary, conducted the government. A large portion of the area of the Empire consisted in these church states, as may be seen from the map on pages 72–73. Third, there were the imperial free cities, some fifty in number; their collective area was not large, but they dominated the commercial and financial life of the country. There was in truth also a fourth category, made up of some thousands of imperial knights, noblemen of minor consequence who possessed a few manors, but who belonged to no state, recognizing the supremacy of none but the emperor.

The states, over the centuries, had prevented the emperor from infringing upon their local liberties. They had taken care to keep the emperorship an elective office, so that with each election local liberties could be reaffirmed. After 1356 the right of electing an emperor was vested in seven electors—namely, four of the princely lords, the Count Palatine, Duke of Saxony, Margrave of Brandenburg, and King of Bohemia (the one king in the Empire), and in three ecclesiastical lords, the archbishops of Mainz, Trier, and Cologne. In 1438 the electors chose the Archduke of Austria to be emperor. His family name was Habsburg. The Habsburgs, by using the resources of their hereditary possessions in Austria (and later elsewhere) and by delicately balancing and bribing the numerous political forces within Germany, managed to get themselves consistently reelected to the Holy Roman Emperorship in every generation, with one exception, from 1438 until 1806.

The principles of New Monarchy were successful mainly in the hereditary princely states of reasonable size. Here the rulers went through the familiar process of quelling their own feudal subordinates, increasing their revenues, enforcing local peace, and letting their own parliamentary bodies fall into abeyance. Thus Brandenburg, Saxony, Bavaria, Württemberg, and a few others, though small, began to take on the semblance of modern states.

The Habsburg emperors also tried to introduce the centralizing principles of the New Monarchy in the Empire as a whole. Under Maximilian I (1493–1519) there seemed to be progress in this direction: the Empire was divided into administrative "circles," and an Imperial Chamber and Council were created, but they were all doomed to failure before the immovable obstacle of states' rights. Maximilian was the author of the Habsburg family fortunes in a quite different way. *Bella gerunt alii; tu, felix Austria, nubes*—"where others have to fight wars, you, fortunate Austria, marry!" Maximilian himself married the heiress of the dukes of Burgundy, who, over the past century, had acquired a number of provinces in the western extremities of the Empire—the Netherlands and the Free County of Burgundy, which bordered upon France. Maximilian by this marriage had a son Philip, whom he married to Joanna, heiress to Ferdinand and Isabella of Spain. Philip and Joanna produced a son Charles. Charles combined the inheritances of his four grandparents: Austria from Maximilian, the Netherlands and Free County from Mary of Burgundy, Castile and Spanish America from Isabella, Aragon and its Mediterranean and Italian possessions from Ferdinand. In addition, in 1519, he was elected Holy Roman Emperor and so became the symbolic head of all Germany.

Charles V of the Empire (he was known as Charles I in Spain) was thus beyond all comparison the most powerful ruler of his day. But still other fortunes awaited the house of Habsburg. The Turks, who had occupied Constantinople in 1453, were at this time pushing through Hungary and menacing central Europe. In 1526 they defeated the Hungarians at the battle of Mohacs. The parliaments of Hungary, and of the adjoining kingdom of Bohemia, hoping to gain allies in the face of the Turkish peril, thereupon elected Charles V's brother Ferdinand as their king. The Habsburg family was now entrenched in central Europe, in the Netherlands, in Spain, in the Mediterranean, in south Italy, in America. No one since Charlemagne had stood so far above all rivals. Contemporaries cried that Europe was threatened with "universal monarchy," with a kind of world-state in which no people could preserve its independence.

The reader who wishes to understand the religious revolution, and consequent emergence of Protestantism, to which we shall now turn, must bear in mind the extraordinarily intricate interplay of the factors that have now been outlined: the decline of the church, the growth of secular and humanistic feeling, the spread of lay religion outside the official clergy, the rise of monarchs who wished to control everything in their kingdoms, including the church, the resistance of feudal elements to these same monarchs, the lassitude of the popes and their fear of church councils, the atomistic division of Germany, the Turkish peril, the zeal of Spain, the preeminence of Charles V, and the fears felt in the rest of Europe, especially in France, of absorption or suffocation by the amazing empire of the Habsburgs.

I t is always misleading to read history backward, and especially the history of the Reformation. Seen in retrospect, since northern Europe became Protestant while the south remained Catholic, it looks as if the north had broken off in a body from a once solid Roman church. The reality was not so simple. Let us for the moment put aside the term "Protestant," and call the adherents of the new religion religious revolutionaries.[8] These revolutionaries were active for a time in almost all parts of Europe. The new ideas leaped over every frontier. It was the entire or "universal" church that the revolutionaries intended to reform. Their aim was not to be let alone to follow their own religion in their own country, but to purify the whole church of Christ itself. Everywhere adherents of the old faith remained active also. No one thought that people should be free to believe individually as they chose. No one regarded religion as a mere opinion. For all parties the issue lay between God's true word and abominable misconceptions, and all saw in the church the supreme institution in which men lived. All maintained (isolated exceptions were few and unimportant) that in so vital a matter as religion people who lived together must believe alike.

For years many thought that old and new ideas of the church might be combined. Many deplored the extremes but gradually in the heat of struggle had to choose one side or the other. The issues became drawn; and each side long aspired to destroy its adversary. For over a century the revolutionaries maintained the hope that "popery" would everywhere fall. For over a century the upholders of the old order worked to annihilate or reconvert their opponents. Only very slowly did Catholics and Protestants come to accept each other's existence as an established fact of European society. Though the religious frontier that was to prove permanent appeared as early as 1560, it was not generally accepted until after the Thirty Years' War, which closed in 1648, and in Hungary the Protestant-Catholic war may be said to have lasted until after 1700.

The Protestant doctrines were revolutionary because they held, not merely that "abuses" in the church must be corrected, but that the Roman church itself, even if perfect by its own ideals, was wrong in principle. The Protestants aimed not to restore the medieval church but to overthrow it. In its place they meant to put a church founded on principles drawn from the Bible.

---

[8] The word "Protestant" arose as an incident in the struggle, at first denoting certain Lutherans who drew up a formal protest against an action of the diet of the Empire in 1529. Only very gradually did the various groups of anti-Roman reformers think of themselves as collectively Protestant, and in recent times some High Church Anglicans, while anti-Roman, have refused to be called Protestant.

The first to formulate the Protestant principles was Martin Luther. He was a monk, a vehement and spiritually uneasy man, with many dark and introspective recesses in his personality, terrified by the thought of the awful omnipotence of God, distressed by his own littleness, apprehensive of the devil, and suffering from the chronic conviction that he was damned. The means offered by the church to allay such spiritual anguish—the sacraments, prayer, attendance at Mass—gave him no satisfaction. From a reading and pondering of St. Paul (Romans i, 17)—"the just shall live by faith"—there dawned upon him a new realization and sense of peace. He developed the doctrine of justification by faith alone. This held that what "justifies" a man is not what the church knew as "works" (prayer, alms, the sacraments, holy living) but "faith alone," an inward bent of spirit given to each soul directly by God. Good works, Luther thought, were the consequence and external evidence of this inner grace, but in no way its cause. A man did not "earn" grace by doing good; he did the good because he possessed the grace of God. With this idea Luther for some years lived content. Even years later some high-placed churchmen believed that in Luther's doctrine of justification by faith there was nothing contrary to the teachings of the Catholic church.

Luther, now a professor at Wittenberg, was brought out of seclusion by an incident of 1517. A friar named Tetzel was traveling through Germany distributing indulgences, authorized by the pope to finance the building of St. Peter's in Rome.[9] In return for them the faithful paid certain stipulated sums of money. Luther thought that people were being deluded, that no one could in this way obtain grace for himself, or ease the pains of relatives in purgatory, as was officially claimed. In the usual academic manner of the day, he posted ninety-five theses on the door of the castle church at Wittenberg. In them he reviewed the Catholic sacrament of penance. Luther held that, after confession, the sinner is freed of his burden not by the priest's absolution, but by inner grace and faith alone. Increasingly, it seemed that the priesthood performed no necessary function in the relation between man and God.

Luther at first appealed to the pope, Leo X, to correct the abuse of indulgences in Germany. When the pope refused action Luther (like many before him) urged the assembly of a general church council as an authority higher even than the pope. He was obliged, however, to admit in public debate that even the decision of a general council might be mistaken. The Council of Constance, he said, had in fact erred in its condemnation of John Huss. But if neither the pope, nor yet a council, had authority to define true Christian belief, where was such authority to be found? Luther's answer was, in effect: There is no such authority. He held that each individual might read the Bible and freely make his own interpretation according to his own conscience. It was the doctrine of the priesthood of all believers. It was as revolutionary, for the church, as would be the assertion today that neither the Supreme Court nor any other body may authoritatively interpret or enforce the Constitution of the United States, since each citizen may interpret the Constitution in his own way.

[9]On indulgences see p. 52.

From his first public appearance Luther won ardent supporters, for there was a good deal of resentment in Germany against Rome. In 1519 and 1520 he rallied public opinion in a series of tracts, setting forth his main beliefs. He declared that the claim of the clergy to be different from the laity was an imposture. He urged people to find Christian truth in the Bible for themselves, and in the Bible only. He denounced the reliance on fasts, pilgrimages, saints, and Masses. He rejected the belief in purgatory. He reduced the seven sacraments to two—baptism and the communion, as he called the Mass. In the latter he repudiated the new and "modern" doctrine of transubstantiation, while affirming that God was still somehow mysteriously present in the bread and wine.[10] He declared that the clergy should marry, upbraided the prelates for their luxury, and demanded that monasticism be eliminated. To drive through such reforms, while depriving the clergy of their pretensions, he called upon the temporal power, the princes of Germany. He thus issued an invitation to the state to assume control over religion, an invitation which, in the days of the New Monarchy, a good many rulers were enthusiastically willing to accept.

Threatened by a papal bull with excommunication unless he recanted, Luther solemnly and publicly burned the bull. Excommunication followed. To the emperor, Charles V, now fell the duty of apprehending the heretic and repressing the heresy. Luther was summoned to appear before a diet of the Empire, held at Worms. He declared that he could be convinced only by Scripture or right reason, otherwise—"I neither can nor will recant anything, since it is neither right nor safe to act against conscience. God help me! Amen." He was placed under the ban of the Empire. But the Elector of Saxony and other north German princes took him under their protection. In safe seclusion, he began to translate the Bible into German.

Luther's excitable obstinacy, intemperate language, and sweeping repudiation of existing authorities antagonized many who had at first looked upon him with favor, and who still hoped for a reform of the church without revolution. Among these was Erasmus, who, as often happens to those who find themselves in the middle, was in his last years looked upon by both sides, Lutheran and Catholic, as a meddlesome friend of the opposition.

Lutheranism, or at least anti-Romanism, swept over Germany, assuming the proportions of a national upheaval. It became mixed with all sorts of political and social revolution. A league of imperial knights, adopting Lutheranism, attacked their neighbors, the church states of the Rhineland, hoping by annexations to enlarge their own meager territories. In 1524 the peasants of a large part of Germany revolted. They were stirred by new religious ideas, worked upon by preachers who went beyond Luther in asserting that any man could see for himself what was right. Their aims, however, were social and economic; they demanded a regulation of rents and security of common village rights and complained of exorbitant exactions and oppressive rule by their manorial overlords. Luther repudiated all connection with the peasants, called them filthy swine, and urged the princes to suppress them by the

[10] See pp. 36, 40.

sword. The peasants were unmercifully put down, but popular unrest continued to stir the country, expressing itself, in a religious age, in various forms of extreme religious frenzy. Various leaders had various followings, known collectively as Anabaptists. Some said that all the world needed was love, some that Christ would soon come again, some that they were saints and could do no wrong, and some that infant baptism was useless, immersion of full-grown adults being required, as described in the Bible. The roads of Germany were alive with obscure zealots, of whom some tens of thousands converged in 1534 on the city of Münster. There they proclaimed the reign of the saints, abolished property, and introduced polygamy as authorized in the Old Testament. A Dutch tailor, John of Leyden, claimed authority from God himself, and, hemmed in by besieging armies, ruled Münster by a revolutionary terror. Luther advised his followers to join even with Catholics to repress such an appalling menace. After a full year Münster was relieved. The "saints" were pitilessly rooted out; John of Leyden died in torture.

Luther, horrified at the way in which religious revolution passed into social revolution, defined his own position more conservatively. He qualified his idea of the priesthood of all believers; restricted, while never denying, the right of private judgment in matters of conscience; and made a larger place for an established clergy, Lutheranized, to be sure, but still established as teachers over the laity. Always well disposed to temporal rulers, having called upon the princes to act as religious reformers, he was thrown by the peasant and Anabaptist uprisings into an even closer alliance with them. Lutheranism took on a character of submissiveness to the state. Christian liberty, Luther insisted, was an internal freedom, purely spiritual, known only to God. In worldly matters, he said, the good Christian owed perfect obedience to established authority. Lutheranism, more than Catholicism and more than the Calvinism which soon arose, came to hold the state in a kind of religious awe as an institution almost sacred in its own right.

In the revolution that was rocking Germany it was not the uprising of imperial knights, nor that of peasants or tailors and journeymen, that was successful, but the rebellion of the higher orders of the Empire against the emperor. Charles V, as Holy Roman Emperor, was bound to uphold Catholicism because only in a Catholic world did the Holy Empire have any meaning. The states of the Empire, always fearing the loss of local liberty, saw in Charles' efforts to repress Luther a threat to their own freedom. Many imperial free cities, and most of the dynastic states of north Germany, now insisted on adding to their other rights and liberties the right, or liberty, to determine their own religion. The *ius reformandi,* they said, the right or power to reform, belonged to member states, not to the Empire itself. They became Lutheran, locally, introducing Lutheran bishops, doctrines, and forms of worship. Where a state turned Lutheran it usually "secularized" (i.e., confiscated) the church properties within its borders, a process which considerably enriched some of the Lutheran princes and gave them a strong material interest in the success of the Lutheran movement. In most of the church states, since the Catholic archbishop or bishop was himself the government, Catholicism prevailed. But a few church states turned Lutheran. A good example of the secularization of a church state was afforded in East Prussia, just outside the Empire.   This territory belonged to the Teutonic _Protestantism_ Order, a Catholic organization of which the grand commander, an elective official, was at this time Albert of Brandenburg.   In 1525 Albert declared for Luther and converted East Prussia into a secular duchy, of which he and his descendants became hereditary dukes.

Against the emperor, a group of Lutheran princes and free cities formed the League of Schmalkald.   The king of France, Francis I, though a Catholic in good standing, allied with and supported the League.   Political interests overrode religious ones.   Against the "universal monarchy" of the swollen Habsburgs the French found alliances where they could, allying with the Turks as with the Lutherans, building up a balance of power against their mighty foe.   It became the studied policy of Catholic France to maintain the religious division of Germany.

Charles V strove to find some basis of agreement by which the permanent religious division of Germany could be avoided.   He was at war with France over certain disputed territories and with the Turks, who in 1529 besieged Vienna itself. Though the Lutheran princes did render a little help at the last moment, it seemed on the whole that the infidels might overrun Germany before the German states would yield their liberties to their own emperor.

Charles appealed to the pope, urging him to assemble a Europe-wide council in which all disputed matters could be considered, the Protestants heard, compromises effected, and church unity and German unity (such as it was) restored.   The king of France schemed at Rome to prevent the pope from calling any such council.   The kings of both France and England urged national councils instead, in which religious questions could be settled on a national basis.   Pope after pope delayed.   The papacy feared that a council of all Latin Christendom might get out of control, since Catholics as much as Protestants demanded reform.   At the very rumor of a council the price of salable offices in Rome abruptly fell.   To the papacy, remembering the Council of Constance, nothing was more upsetting than the thought of a council, not even the Protestants, not even the Turks.   So the popes procrastinated, no council met, years passed, and a new generation grew up in Lutheranism.   Desperately, in 1548, Charles tried to settle matters himself, issuing the _Interim,_ to guide religion in all Germany until a general church council could complete its work.   The _Interim_ upheld the main Catholic doctrines, but, to attract the Protestants, allowed marriage of the clergy and one or two other minor concessions.   Neither side would accept it: Protestants found that it gave too little, and Catholics refused to have their religion tampered with by the temporal power.

Meanwhile the Schmalkaldic League, allied with France, had actually gone to war with the emperor in 1546.   Germany fell into an anarchy of civil struggle between Catholic and Protestant states, the latter aided by France.   The war was ended by the Peace of Augsburg of 1555.

The terms set at Augsburg signified a complete victory for the cause of Lutheranism and states' rights.   Each state of the Empire received the liberty to be either Lutheran or Catholic as it chose—_cuius regio eius religio,_ "whose the region, his the religion."   No individual freedom of religion was permitted; if a ruler decided for

Lutheranism then all his subjects had to be Lutheran. Similarly in Catholic states all had to be Catholic. The churches were state churches, rather more so in the Lutheran than in the Catholic territories, since Lutheranism was set up and maintained in each case by the individual states, while Catholicism retained its connection with Rome and with the Catholic world beyond each state's borders. The Peace of Augsburg provided also, by the so-called Ecclesiastical Reservation, that any Catholic bishop or other churchman who turned Lutheran in the future (or who had turned Lutheran as recently as 1552) should not carry his territory with him, but should turn Lutheran as an individual and move away, leaving his land and its inhabitants Catholic. Since the issues in Germany were still far from stabilized, this proviso was often disregarded in later years.

The Peace of Augsburg was thus, in religion, a great victory for Protestantism, and at the same time, in German politics and constitutional matters, a step in the disintegration of Germany into a mosaic of increasingly separate states. Lutheranism prevailed in the north, and in the south in the duchy of Württemberg and various detached islands formed by Lutheranized free cities. Catholicism prevailed in the south (except in Württemberg and certain cities), in the Rhine valley, and in the direct possessions of the house of Habsburg, which in 1555 reached as far north as the Netherlands. The Germans, because of conditions in the Holy Roman Empire, were the one large European people to emerge from the religious conflict almost evenly divided between Catholic and Protestant.

No rights were granted by the Peace of Augsburg to another group of religious revolutionaries which neither Lutherans nor Catholics were willing to tolerate, namely, the followers of John Calvin.

Lutheranism, it must be pointed out, was adopted by the kings of Denmark and Sweden as early as the 1520s. Since Denmark controlled Norway, and Sweden ruled Finland and the eastern Baltic, all Scandinavia and the Baltic regions became, like north Germany, Lutheran. Beyond this area Lutheranism failed to take root. Like Anglicanism in England (to be described shortly) Lutheranism was too closely associated with established states to spread easily as an international movement. The most successful international form of the Protestant movement was Calvinism.

Calvin and Calvinism

John Calvin was a Frenchman, born Jean Cauvin, who called himself Calvinus in Latin. Born in 1509, he was a full generation younger than Luther. He was trained both as a priest and as a lawyer, and had a humanist's knowledge of Latin and Greek, as well as Hebrew. At the age of twenty-four, experiencing a sudden conversion, or fresh insight into the meaning of Christianity, he joined forces with the religious revolutionaries of whom the best known was then Luther. Three years later, in 1536, he published, in the international language, Latin, his *Institutes of the Christian Religion.* Where Luther had aimed much of his writing either at the existing rulers of Germany, or at the German national feeling against Rome, Calvin addressed his *Institutes* to all the world. He seemed to appeal to human reason itself; he wrote in the severe, logical style of the trained lawyer; he dealt firmly, lucidly, and convincingly with the most basic issues. In the *Institutes* men in all countries, if dissatisfied with the existing Roman church (as many in all countries were), could find cogent expression of universal propositions, which they could apply to their own local circumstances as they required.

With Luther's criticisms of the Roman church, and with most of Luther's fundamental religious ideas, such as justification by faith and not by works, Calvin agreed. In what they retained of the Catholic Mass, the communion or Lord's Supper as they called it, they developed certain doctrinal differences. Both rejected transubstantiation, but where Luther insisted that God was somehow actually present in the bread and wine used in the service ("consubstantiation"), Calvin and his followers tended more to regard it as a pious act of symbolic or commemorative character.

The chief differences between Calvin and Luther were two. Calvin made far more of the idea of predestination. Both, drawing heavily on St. Augustine, held that man by his own actions could earn no merit in the sight of divine justice, that any grace which a man possessed came from the free action of God alone. God, being Almighty, knew and willed in advance all things that happened, including the way in which every life would turn out. He knew and willed, from all eternity, that some were saved and some were damned. Calvin, a severe critic of human nature, felt that those who had grace were relatively few. They were the "elect," the "godly," the little band chosen without merit of their own, from all eternity, for salvation. A person could feel in his own mind that he was among the saved, God's chosen few, if throughout all trials and temptations he persisted in a saintly life. Thus the idea of predestination, of God's omnipotence, instead of turning to fatalism and resignation, became a challenge to unrelenting effort, a sense of burning conviction, a conviction of having a mission, of doing battle for the Lord, of being on the side of that Almighty Power which must in the end be everlastingly triumphant. It was the most resolute spirits that were attracted to Calvinism. Calvinists, in all countries, were militant, uncompromising, perfectionist—or Puritan, as they were called first in England and later in America.

The second way in which Calvinism differed from Lutheranism was in its attitude to society and to the state. Calvinists refused to recognize the subordination of church to state, or the right of any government—king, parliament, or civic magistracy—to lay down laws for religion. On the contrary, they insisted that true Christians, the elect or godly, should Christianize the state. They wished to remake society itself into the image of a religious community, with all people living stern, disciplined, and saintly lives, and kings themselves doing the Lord's work. They rejected the institution of bishops (which both the Lutheran and Anglican churches retained), and provided instead that the church should be governed by presbyteries, elected bodies made up of ministers and devout laymen. By thus bringing an element of lay control into church affairs, they broke the monopoly of priestly power and so promoted secularization. On the other hand, they were the reverse of secular, for they wished to Christianize all society.

Calvin, called in by earlier reformers who had driven out their bishop, was able to set up his model Christian community at Geneva in Switzerland. A body of ministers ruled the church; a consistory of ministers and elders ruled the town. The rule was strict; all loose, light, or frivolous living was suppressed; disaffected persons were driven into exile. The form of worship was severe, and favored the intellectual rather than the emotional or the aesthetic. The service was devoted largely to long sermons elucidating Christian doctrine, and all appeals to the senses—color, music, incense— were rigidly subdued. The black gown of Geneva replaced brighter clerical vestments. Images, representing the saints, Mary, or Christ, were taken down and destroyed. Candles went the way of incense. Chanting was replaced by the singing of hymns. Instrumental music was frowned upon, and many Calvinists thought even bells to be a survival of "popery." In all things Calvin undertook to regulate his church by the Bible. Nor was he more willing than Luther to countenance any doctrine more radical than his own. When a Spanish refugee, Michael Servetus, who denied the Trinity, i.e., the divinity of Christ, sought asylum at Geneva, Calvin pronounced him a heretic and burned him at the stake.

To Geneva flocked reformers of all nationalities, Englishmen, Scots, Frenchmen, Netherlanders, Germans, Poles, and Hungarians, to see and study a true scriptural community so that they might reproduce it in their own countries. Geneva became the Protestant Rome, the one great international center of Reformed doctrine. Everywhere Calvinists made their teachings heard (even in Spain and Italy in isolated cases), and everywhere, or almost everywhere, little groups which had locally and spontaneously broken with the old church found in Calvin's *Institutes* a reasoned statement of doctrine and a suggested method of organization. Thus Calvinism spread, or was adopted, very widely. In Hungary and Bohemia large elements turned Protestant, and usually Calvinist, partly as a way of opposing the Habsburg rule. In Poland there were many Calvinists, along with less organized Anabaptists and Unitarians, or Socinians as those who denied the Trinity were then called. Calvinists spread in Germany, where, opposing both Lutheran and Catholic churches as ungodly impositions of worldly power, they were disliked equally by both. In France the Huguenots were Calvinist, as were the Protestants of what are now Belgium and Holland. John Knox in the 1550s brought Calvinism to Scotland, where Presbyterianism became and remained the established religion. At the same time Calvinism began to penetrate England, from which it was later to reach British America, giving birth to the Presbyterian and Congregationalist churches of the United States.

Calvinism was far from democratic in any modern sense, being rather of an almost aristocratic outlook, in that those who sensed themselves to be God's chosen few felt free to dictate to the common run of mankind. Yet in many ways Calvinism entered into the development of what became democracy. For one thing, Calvinists never venerated the state; they always held that the sphere of the state and of public life was subject to moral judgment. For another, the Calvinist doctrine of the "calling" taught that a man's labor had a religious dignity, and that any form of honest work was pleasing in the sight of God. In the conduct of their own affairs Calvinists developed a type of self-government. They formed "covenants" with one another, and devised machinery for the election of presbyteries. They refused to believe that authority was transmitted downward through bishops or through kings. They were inclined also to a democratic outlook by the circumstance that in most countries they remained an unofficial minority. Only at Geneva, in the Dutch Netherlands, in Scotland, and in New England (and for a few years in England in the seventeenth century) were Calvinists ever able to prescribe the mode of life and religion of a whole country. In England, in France, in Germany, in eastern Europe Calvinists remained in opposition to the established authorities of church and state and hence disposed to favor limitations upon established power.

England was peculiar in that its government broke with the Roman church before adopting any Protestant principles. Henry VIII (1509–1547) in fact prided himself on his orthodoxy. When a few obscure persons, about 1520, began to whisper Luther's ideas in England, Henry himself wrote a *Defense of the Seven Sacraments* in refutation, for which a grateful pope conferred upon him the title of "Defender of the Faith." But the king had no male heir. Recalling the anarchy from which the Tudor dynasty had extricated England, and determined as a New Monarch to build up a durable monarchy, he felt, or said, that before all else he must have a son. In order to remarry, he requested the pope to annul his existing marriage to Catherine of Aragon. Popes in the past had obliged monarchs similarly pressed. The pope now, however, was embarrassed by the fact that Catherine, who objected, was the aunt of the Emperor Charles V, whom the pope was in no position to offend. Henry, not a patient man, drove matters forward. He put in a new archbishop of Canterbury, repudiated the Roman connection, and married the buxom Anne Boleyn. The fact that only three years later he put to death the unfortunate Anne, and thereafter in quick succession married four more wives, for a total of six, threw considerable doubt on the original character of his motives.

Henry acted through Parliament, believing, as he said, that a king was never stronger than when united with representatives of his kingdom. In 1534 Parliament passed the Act of Supremacy, which declared the English king to be the "Protector and Only Supreme Head of the Church and Clergy of England." All subjects were required, if asked, to take the oath of supremacy acknowledging the religious headship of Henry and rejecting that of the pope. For refusing this oath Sir Thomas More, a statesman and humanist best known as the author of *Utopia*, was executed for treason. He received a somewhat delayed reward four centuries later when the Roman church pronounced him to be a saint. Henry, in the next few years, closed all the monasteries in England. The extensive monastic lands, accumulated by never-dying corporations from gifts made over the centuries, were seized by the king, who passed them out to numerous followers, thus strengthening and reconstituting a landed aristocracy which had been seriously weakened in the Wars of the Roses. The new landed gentry remained firm supporters of the house of Tudor and the English national church, whatever its doctrines.

It was Henry's intent not to change the doctrines at all. He simply wished to be the supreme head of an English Catholic church. On the one hand, in 1536, he forcibly suppressed a predominantly Catholic rebellion, and, on the other, in 1539, through the Six Articles, required everybody to believe in transubstantiation, the celibacy of the clergy, the need of confession, and a few other test items of Catholic faith and practice. But it proved impossible to maintain this position, for a great many people in England began to favor one or another of the ideas of Continental Reformers, and a small minority were willing to accept the entire Protestant position.

For three decades the government veered about. Henry died in 1547 and was succeeded by his ten-year-old son, Edward VI, under whom the Protestant party came to the fore. But Edward died in 1553, and was succeeded by his much older sister, Mary, the daughter of Catherine of Aragon and a devout Roman Catholic whose whole life had been embittered by the break with Rome. Mary tried to re-Catholicize England; but she actually made Catholicism more unpopular with the English. In 1554 she married Philip of Spain, who became king of England, though only nominally. The English did not like Philip, nor the Spanish, nor the intense Spanish Catholicism that Philip represented. Under Mary, moreover, some three hundred persons were burned at the stake, as heretics, in public mass executions. It was the first (and last) time that such a thing had happened in England, and it set up a wave of horror. In any event, Mary did not live long. She was succeeded in 1558 by Henry's younger daughter, Elizabeth, the child of Anne Boleyn. Whatever Elizabeth's real views in religion might be (she concealed them successfully and was rumored to have none), she could not be a Roman Catholic. For Catholics she was illegitimate and so unable to be queen.

Under Elizabeth the English became Protestant, gradually and in their own way. The Church of England took on a form of its own. Organizationally, it resembled a Lutheran church. It was a state church, for its existence and doctrines were determined by the temporal power, in this case the monarch acting through Parliament. All English subjects were obliged to belong to it, and laws were passed against "recusants," a term used to cover both the Roman Catholics and the more advanced Calvinists who refused to acknowledge it. With the exception of monasteries and certain other church foundations, the Church of England retained the physical possessions, buildings, and internal organization of the medieval church—the bishops and the archbishops, who continued to sit in the House of Lords, the episcopal courts with their jurisdiction over marriage and wills, the tithes or church taxes paid by all landowners, the parish structure, the universities of Oxford and Cambridge. In religious practice, the Church of England was definitely Protestant: English replaced Latin as the language of the liturgy, there was no cult of the saints, and the clergy married, though Elizabeth confessed to some embarrassment at the thought of an archbishop having a wife. In doctrine, it was Elizabeth's policy to make the dogmas broad and ambiguous, so that persons of all shades of belief could be more readily accommodated. The Thirty-nine Articles (1563) composed by a committee of bishops, defined the creed of the Anglican church. In the light of the burning issues of the day many of the articles were evasive,

though Protestant in tone.   All but one of the Anglican bishops had been newly
appointed by Elizabeth at her accession; many had lived in exile among Continental
Protestants in the reign of Mary Tudor; and except on the matter of church
government through bishops (known as episcopacy) a strong Calvinist impress was
set upon Anglican belief in the time of Elizabeth.   Anglicans, for a century or more,
generally considered themselves closer to Geneva than to Rome, the seat of "popery,"
and regarded Lutherans as "semi-papist."   There remained, however, a High Church
element, emphasizing the Catholic rather than the Protestant character of Anglicanism.

The same ecclesiastical settlement was prescribed for Ireland, where a replica of
the Church of England was established, called the Church of Ireland, which took over
the properties and position of the Roman church in the lesser island.   The native Irish
remained almost solidly Roman Catholic.   As in Hungary or Bohemia people who
resented the Habsburgs were likely to turn Protestant rather than share in the ruler's
religion, so in Ireland the fact that the ruling English were Protestant only confirmed
the Irish in their attachment to the Roman church.   The Catholic priests, deprived of
status, income, and church buildings, and often in hiding, became national leaders of
a discontented people.

Neither in England, nor in Germany, nor in a Europe at large penetrated by in- *The Religious*
ternational Calvinism were the issues regarded as settled in 1560.   Nor had the *Situation by 1560*
Roman church accepted the new situation.   But by 1560 the chief Protestant doctrines
had been affirmed, and geographically Protestantism had made many conquests.
The spiritual unity of Latin Christendom had been broken.   Even without
Protestantism the unity of the late medieval church had been badly disjointed, in
recurring conflicts between conciliarists and upholders of papal power, and in the
tendency of Catholic clergy and Catholic monarchs to assert national autonomy for
their churches, as seen most especially in France.   But whatever spiritual or
administrative unity might still have been derived from the Roman supremacy was
now lost by the Protestant revolt.   Christendom was disintegrating into a purely
intangible ideal.   A world of separate states and nations was taking its place.

Protestants differed with one another, yet there was much that all had in
common.   All rejected the papal authority.   None participated in any effective
international organization; the ascendancy of Geneva was spiritual only and proved to
be temporary.   All Protestants rejected the special, sacerdotal, or supernatural
character of the priesthood; indeed, the movement was perhaps most fundamentally a
revolt against the medieval position of the clergy.   Protestants generally called their
clergy ministers, not priests.   All Protestant clergy could marry.   There were no
Protestant monks, nuns, or friars.   All Protestant churches replaced Latin with the
vernacular in religious services—English, French, German, Czech, as the case might
be.   All Protestants reduced the number of sacraments, usually to two or three; such
sacraments as they retained they regarded more as symbols than as actual carriers of
divine grace; all believed, in one way or another, in justification by faith.   All denied

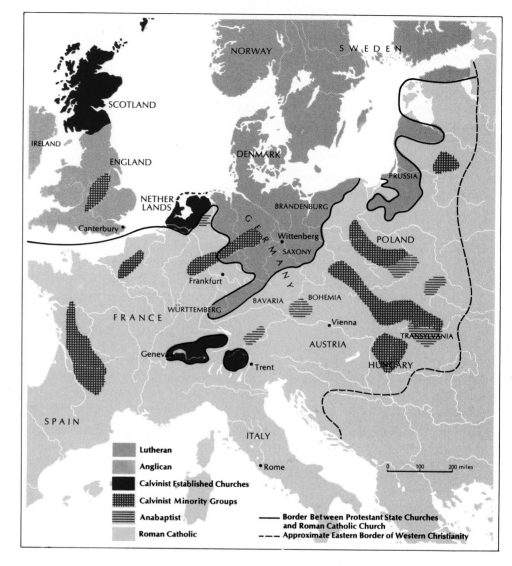

State Religions in Europe about 1560. *It is not possible to draw a religious map of Europe during the Reformation, because persons of different religious belief were intermixed and each group still labored to convert others to its position. Legally, however, by 1560 or 1570, the churches were as indicated above. Many Catholics lived north of the heavy line, especially in Ireland, and many Protestants south of it, especially in France, Bohemia, and Hungary. The Germans, because of political disunity within the Holy Roman Empire, were the one large people of Europe to emerge from the Reformation almost evenly divided. In the other large countries one side or the other, Protestant or Catholic, was ultimately reduced to a small minority.*

transubstantiation, or the miracle of the Mass. All gave up the obligatory confessional, and with it priestly absolution. All gave up the idea of purgatory as a kind of temporal zone between heaven and hell and hence abandoned the practice of saying prayers and Masses for the dead. It need hardly be added that nothing like indulgences remained. All gave up the cult of the saints and of the Virgin Mary, whose intercession in heaven was no longer expected. All declared that the one true source of Christian belief was the Holy Scripture; all, save perhaps the Anglicans, denied any such authority to church tradition, i.e., to the cumulative religious development since ancient times. And while all established Protestant churches, in the sixteenth century, insisted on conformity to their own doctrines, allowing no individual freedom, all Protestants still had some small spark of the spirit first ignited by Luther, so that none flatly, formally, or positively repudiated the right of private judgment in matters of conscience.

In recent times it has often been maintained that one of the motivations in Protestantism was economic—that a new acquisitive, aggressive, dynamic, progressive, capitalistic impulse shook off the restrictions imposed by medieval religion. The fact that Protestant England and Holland soon underwent a rapid capitalistic development gives added likelihood to this idea. The alacrity with which Protestant governments confiscated church lands shows a keen material interest; but in truth, both before and since the Reformation, governments confiscated church properties without breaking with the Roman church. That profound economic changes were occurring at the time will become apparent in the following chapter. Yet it seems that economic conditions were far less decisive than religious convictions and political circumstances. Calvinism appealed not only to the economically advanced, but to the economically backward, as the Scots then were, and as the Poles and Hungarians long remained. Lutheranism spread more successfully in the economically retarded north Germany than in the busy south. The English were for years no more inclined to Protestantism than the French, and in France, while many lords and peasants turned Protestant, Paris and many other towns remained as steadfastly Catholic. It is possible that Protestantism, by casting a glow of religious righteousness over a man's daily business and material prosperity, later contributed to the economic success of Protestant peoples, but it does not seem that economic forces were of any distinctive importance in the first stages of Protestantism.

The Catholic movement corresponding to the rise of Protestantism is known as the Catholic Reformation or the Counter Reformation, the former term being preferred by Catholics, the latter by Protestants. Both are applicable. On the one hand the Catholic church underwent a genuine reform, which would probably have worked itself out in one way or another even if the stimulus of revolutionary Protestantism had been absent. On the other hand the character of the reform, the

10
Catholicism
Reformed
and Reorganized

89

decisions made, and the measures adopted were shaped by the need of responding explicitly to the Protestant challenge; and certainly, also, there was a good deal of purely "counter" activity aimed at the elimination of Protestantism as such.

The demand for reform was as old as the abuses against which it was directed. Characteristically, it had expressed itself in the demand for a general or ecumenical church council. The conciliar movement, defeated by the popes about 1450, showed signs of revival after 1500.[11] But it was almost as hard, even then, to assemble a general council as it is today to create an international body possessing any effective authority.

Several years before Luther had been heard of, Europe's two most important secular rulers, the king of France and the Holy Roman Emperor, jointly convened on their own authority a council at Pisa in 1511. It was their purpose to force reforms upon Pope Julius II, and if necessary depose him. But no delegates from other countries attended; the five cardinals and handful of bishops who came to Pisa were regarded as minions of the two rulers who sent them; the council lacked moral authority, no one listened to it, and it accomplished nothing, never even attaining historically the name of a council. The pope, however, to ward off the danger of a council under secular auspices, himself assembled the Fifth Lateran Council at Rome in 1512. It was supposed to be general, ecumenical, Europe-wide, representing that "spiritual unity" sometimes imagined to have existed in Europe before Luther. In fact, few took it seriously, because it was composed mainly of Italian prelates, who began by denouncing the doctrines of the Council of Constance, and ended by making a few tame resolutions on miscellaneous topics.

Then came the Lutheran upheaval, and the attempts of Charles V, in the interests of German unity, to persuade the pope to assemble a true and adequately empowered council, so that removal of abuses in the church, which no one really defended, would take away the grounds upon which many Germans were turning to Lutheranism. But meanwhile the king of France found reason to favor the pope and to oppose the emperor. The French king, Francis I (1515–1547), could support the pope because he had obtained from the papacy what he wanted, namely, control over the Gallican church, as acquired in the Concordat of Bologna of 1516.[12] And he had reason to oppose Charles V, because Charles V ruled not only in Germany but in the Netherlands, Spain, and much of Italy, thus encircling France and threatening Europe with what contemporaries called "universal monarchy." Francis I therefore actively encouraged the Protestants of Germany as a means of maintaining dissension there, and used his influence at Rome against the calling of a council by which the troubles of the Catholic world might be relieved. The pope was afraid to summon a council against the wishes of Francis I, for fear that Francis, if angered, might take the Gallican church entirely outside the Roman fold as Henry VIII had already taken the Anglican. On so little did the religious destiny of nations seem to depend!

[11] On the conciliar movement see pp. 51–52.
[12] See p. 74.

Gradually, in the curia, there arose a party of reforming cardinals who concluded that the need of reform was so urgent that all dangers of a council must be risked. The pope summoned a council to meet in 1537, but the wars between France and the Empire forced its abandonment. Then a council was called for 1542, but no one came except a few Italians so that it had to be suspended. Finally, in 1545, a council did assemble and begin operations. It met at Trent, on the Alpine borders of Germany and Italy. The Council of Trent, which shaped the destiny of all modern Catholicism, sat at irregular intervals for almost twenty years—in 1545–1547, 1551–1552, 1562–1563.

The council was beset by difficulties of a political nature, which seemed to show that under troubled conditions an international council was no longer a suitable means of regulating Catholic affairs. For one thing, it was poorly attended. Where at the Fourth Lateran Council of 1215, and at Constance in 1415, some five hundred prelates had assembled, the attendance at Trent was never nearly so great; it sometimes fell as low as twenty or thirty, and the important decree on "justification," the prime issue raised by Luther, and one on which some good Catholics had until then believed a compromise to be possible, was passed at a session where only sixty prelates were present. The most regular in attendance were the Italians and Spanish; French and Germans came erratically and in smaller numbers. Even with the small attendance, the old conciliar issue was raised. A party of bishops believed that the bishops of the Catholic church, when assembled in council from all parts of the Catholic world, collectively constituted an authority superior to that of the pope. To stave off this "episcopal" movement was one of the chief duties of the cardinal legates deputed by the pope to preside over the sessions. Moreover, the great Catholic states showed little friendliness. In 1547, the imperial diet of the Holy Roman Empire, in which Catholics still had a majority despite the spread of Lutheranism, requested a "free" council in which bishops should be free from the pope's direction, and urged that the decrees thus far enacted at Trent be reconsidered, since they were making the religious gulf in Germany impossible to bridge. In 1551, the French king announced that France would not be bound by the council at all. In 1562 the Emperor Ferdinand, successor to Charles V, issued a reform program, in which he urged the council, then nearing its end, to reassert the supremacy of council over pope, and impose further controls on the papacy, the cardinals, and the curia.

Thus, to the end of the council, the idea persisted of limiting the papal power. The popes, however, managed successfully to resist, and in the end triumphed, through a final ruling, voted by the council, that no act of the council should be valid unless accepted by the Holy See. It is possible that had the conciliar theory won out, the Catholic church might have become as disunited in modern times as the Protestant. It was clear, at Trent, that the various bishops tended to see matters in a national way, in the light of their own problems at home, and to be frequently under strong influence from their respective secular monarchs. In any case, the papal party prevailed, which is to say that the centralizing element, not the national, triumphed. The Council of Trent in fact marked an important step in the movement which issued, three hundred years later, in the promulgation of the infallibility of the pope in matters of faith and morals. After 1563 no council met at all until the Vatican Council of 1870 at which this papal infallibility was proclaimed.[13] The Council of Trent thus preserved the papacy as a center of unity for the Catholic church and helped prevent the very real threat of its dissolution into state churches. Even so, the council's success was not immediate, for in every important country the secular rulers at first accepted only what they chose of its work, and only gradually did its influence prevail.

Questions of national politics and of church politics apart, the Council of Trent addressed itself to two kinds of labors, to a statement of Catholic doctrine and to a reform of abuses in the church. When the council began to meet, in 1545, the Protestant movement had already gone so far that any reconciliation was probably impossible—Protestants, especially Calvinists, simply did not wish to belong to the church of Rome under any conditions. In any case, the Council of Trent made no concessions.

It declared justification to be by works and faith combined, enumerated the seven sacraments and defined them exactly, affirmed a sacrament to be a vehicle of grace independent of the spiritual state of him who received it, reaffirmed transubstantiation, and declared the priesthood to be a special estate set apart from the laity by the sacrament of holy orders and endowed with a supernatural power transmitted from Christ and the apostles. As sources of Catholic faith, the council put Scripture and Tradition on an equal footing. It thus rejected the Protestant claim to find true faith in the Bible alone and reaffirmed the validity of church development since New Testament times. The Vulgate, a translation into Latin made by St. Jerome in the fourth century, was declared to be the only version of the Bible on which authoritative teaching could be based. The right of individuals to believe that their own interpretation of Scripture was more true than that of church authorities (private judgment) was denied. Latin (as against the national languages) was prescribed as the language of religious worship. Celibacy of all clergy was maintained. Monasticism was upheld. The existence of purgatory was reaffirmed. The theory and correct practice in the grant of indulgences were restated. The veneration of saints, the cult of the Virgin, the use of images, relics, and pilgrimages were approved as spiritually useful and pious actions.

It was easier for a council to define doctrines than to reform abuses, since the latter consisted in the rooted habits of thousands and millions of people's lives. The council decreed, however, a drastic reform of the monastic orders. It acted against the abuse of indulgences while upholding the principle. It ruled that bishops should reside habitually in their dioceses and attend more carefully to their proper duties. It gave bishops more administrative control over clergy in their own dioceses, such as

[13]See p. 656.

mendicant friars, who in the past had been exempt from episcopal jurisdiction, and whose presence had often caused disturbance, or indeed scandal, among the local people. The abuse by which one man had held numerous church offices at the same time (pluralism) was checked, and steps were taken to assure that church officials should be competent. The council ordered, to provide an educated clergy, that a seminary should be set up in each diocese for the training of priests.

As laws in general have little force unless sustained by opinion, so the reform decrees of the Council of Trent would have remained ineffectual had not a renewed sense of religious seriousness been growing up at the same time. Herein lay the inner force of the Catholic Reform. Men of a new type came forward. In Italy, as the Renaissance became more undeniably pagan, and as the sack of Rome, in 1527, showed the depths of hatred felt even by Catholics toward the Roman clergy, the voices of severer moralists began to be heeded. The line of Renaissance popes was succeeded by a line of reforming popes, of whom the first was Paul III (1534–1549). The reforming popes insisted on the primacy of the papal office, but they regarded this office, unlike their predecessors, as a moral and religious force. In many bishoprics, in many countries, bishops began on their own initiative to be more strict. The new Catholic religious sense, unlike the Protestant, and more than in the Middle Ages, centered in a profound reverence for the sacraments, particularly the Mass, as the main avenue of the religious life, and a mystical awe for the church itself as a divine institution which no human sinfulness had ever polluted, and which extended as a seamless web throughout the ages and among all peoples, even those by whom it was flouted. Missionary fervor became more characteristic of Catholics than of Protestants. In Europe it expressed itself as an intense desire to reconvert the Protestant heretics. It showed itself, too, in missions among the poor, as in the work of St. Vincent de Paul among the human wreckage of Paris, for which the established Protestant churches failed to produce anything comparable. In America, as colonies developed in the sixteenth and seventeenth centuries, the Protestant clergy tended to take the layman's view of the Indians, while Catholic clergy labored to convert and preserve them; and the Catholic church generally worked to mitigate the brutality of Negro slavery, to which the pastors in English and Dutch colonies, perhaps because they were more dependent upon the laity, remained largely indifferent, when, indeed, they did not positively declare that black men had no souls at all.

We have seen how in Spain, where the Renaissance had never taken much hold, the very life of the country was a boundless Christian crusade. It was in Spain that much of the new Catholic feeling first developed, and from Spain that much of the missionary spirit first went out. It was Spain that gave birth to St. Ignatius Loyola (1491–1556). A soldier in youth, he too, like Luther and Calvin, had a religious "experience" or "conversion," which occurred in 1521, before he had heard of Luther, and while Calvin was still a boy. It was by reading the life of Christ that he was converted, but his evangelizing zeal proved very different from that of either the

Protestants or of the Catholic mystics who, in the north, had founded the lay Brothers of the Common Life.

Loyola resolved to become a soldier of the church, a militant crusader for the pope and the Holy See. On this principle he established the Society of Jesus, commonly known as the Jesuits. Authorized by Paul III in 1540, the Jesuits constituted a monastic order of a new type, less attached to the cloister, more directed toward active participation in the affairs of the world. Only men of proven strength of character and intellectual force were admitted. Each Jesuit had to undergo an arduous and even horrifying mystical training, set forth by Loyola in his *Spiritual Exercises.* The order was ruled by an iron discipline, which required each member to see in his immediate superior the infallibility of Holy Church. If, said Loyola, the church teaches to be black what the eye sees as white, the mind will believe it to be black. Aside from demanding absolute submission in matters of faith, the Jesuits generally favored rationality and a measure of liberty in the religious life. For two hundred years they were the chief schoolmasters of Catholic Europe, eventually conducting some five hundred schools for boys of the upper and middle classes. In them they taught, besides the faith, the principles of gentlemanly deportment (their teaching of dancing and dramatics became a scandal to more puritanical Catholics), and they carried over the Renaissance and humanist idea of the Latin classics as the main substance of adolescent education. The Jesuits made a specialty of work among the ruling classes. They became confessors to kings and hence involved in political intrigue. In an age when Protestants subordinated the organized church either to the state or to the individual conscience, and when even Catholics frequently thought of the church within a national framework, the Jesuits seemed almost to worship the church itself as a divine institution, the Church Militant and the Church Universal, internationally organized and governed by the Roman pontiff. All full-fledged Jesuits took a special vow of obedience to the pope. Jesuits in the later sessions of the Council of Trent fought obstinately, and successfully, to uphold the position of Rome against that of the national bishops. The high papalism of the Jesuits (later called "ultramontanism") for centuries made them as obnoxious to many Catholics as they were to the Protestants.

By 1560 the Catholic church, renewed by a deepening of its religious life, and by an uncompromising restatement of its dogmas and discipline, had devised also the practical machinery for a counteroffensive against Protestantism. The Jesuits acted as an international missionary force. They recruited members from all countries, including those in which the governments had turned Protestant. English Catholics, for example, trained as Jesuits on the Continent, returned to England to overthrow the heretic usurper, Elizabeth, seeing in the universal church a higher cause than national independence in religion. Jesuits poured also into the most hotly disputed regions where the issue still swayed in the balance—France, Germany, Bohemia, Poland, Hungary. As after every great revolution, many people after an initial burst of Protestantism were inclined to turn back to the old order, especially as the more crying evils within the Catholic church were corrected. The Jesuits reconverted many who thus hesitated.

For the more recalcitrant other machinery was provided. All countries censored books; Protestant authorities labored to keep "papist" works from the eyes of the faithful, and Catholic authorities took the same pains to suppress all knowledge of "heretics." All bishops, Anglican, Lutheran, and Catholic, regulated reading matter within their dioceses. In the Catholic world, with the trend toward centralization under the pope, a special importance attached to the list published by the bishop of Rome, the papal Index of Prohibited Books. Only with special permission, granted to reliable persons for special study, could Catholics read books listed on the Index, on which most of the significant works written in Europe since the Reformation have been included.

All countries, Protestant and Catholic, also set up judicial and police machinery to enforce conformity to the accepted church. In England, for example, Elizabeth established the High Commission to bring "recusants" into the Church of England. All bishops, Protestant and Catholic, likewise possessed machinery of enforcement in their episcopal courts. But no court made itself so dreaded as the Inquisition. In reality two distinct organizations went under this name, the word itself being simply an old term of the Roman law, signifying a court of inquest or inquiry. One was the Spanish Inquisition, established originally, about 1480, to ferret out Jewish and Moslem survivals in Spain. It was then introduced into all countries ruled by the Spanish crown and employed against Protestantism, particularly in the Spanish Netherlands, which was an important center of Calvinism. The other was the Roman or papal Inquisition, established at Rome in 1542 under a permanent committee of cardinals called the Holy Office; it was in a sense a revival of the famous medieval tribunal established in the thirteenth century for the detection and repression of heresy. Both the Spanish and the Roman Inquisition employed torture, for heresy was regarded as the supreme crime, and all persons charged with crime could be tortured, in civil as well as ecclesiastical courts, under the existing laws. In the use of torture, as in the imposition of the harshest sentence, burning alive, the Roman Inquisition was milder than the Spanish. With the growth of papal centralization the Roman Inquisition in principle offered a court to protect purity of faith in all parts of the Catholic world. But the national resistance of Catholic countries proved too strong; few Catholics wished the agents of Rome inquiring locally into their opinions; and the Roman Inquisition never functioned for any length of time outside of Italy. In France no form of the Inquisition was admitted either then or later.

In the "machinery" of enforcing religious belief, however, no engine was to be so powerful as the apparatus of state, of political sovereignty. Where Protestants won control of government, people became Protestant. Where Catholics retained control of governments, Protestants became in time small minorities. And it was in the clash of governments, which is to say in war, for about a century after 1560, that the fate of European religion was worked out. In 1560 the strongest powers of Europe—Spain, France, Austria—were all officially Catholic. The Protestant states were all small or at most middle-sized. The Lutheran states of Germany, like all German states, were individually of little weight. The Scandinavian monarchies were far away. England, the most considerable of Protestant kingdoms, was a country of only four million people, with an independent and hostile Scotland to the north, and with no sign of colonial empire yet in existence. In the precedence of monarchs, as arranged in the earlier part of the century, the king of England ranked just below the king of Portugal, and next above the king of Sicily. Clearly, had a great combined Catholic crusade ever developed, Protestantism could have been wiped out. To launch such a crusade was the dream of the king of Spain. It never succeeded; why, will be seen in the next chapter.

The supreme site of the Italian Renaissance, Florence was both a city lying on either side of the river Arno and an independent republic, with a territory extending, by 1500, for about fifty miles in most directions from Florence itself. The city had grown wealthy in the later Middle Ages from the production of woolens. It developed also an intense civic spirit in its conflicts with other Italian cities. It became a home of merchant princes, of whom the Medici were the most famous. Such families, enriched in earlier generations in the woolen trade, then passing into banking, emerged as an urban patriciate or governing class, the more easily because there was no royalty to overshadow them, and the feudal nobility in the surrounding country was very weak.

Patricians were sometimes opposed by the populace, and sometimes, like the early Medici, they had popular followings of their own. Outbursts of factionalism were therefore very common, compounded by the rivalry with other Italian cities, and by the increasing involvement of the Holy Roman Emperor, the King of France, and the pope. The Medici became dominant in the fifteenth century, were expelled in 1494, restored in 1512, expelled again in 1527, then again restored in 1530, this time permanently, since they remained as hereditary grand dukes of Tuscany until 1737. The following pages suggest something of the wealth, the civic life, and the political crises of Florence until the end of the republic in the 1530s.

More interesting to outsiders than the civil turmoil were Florentine literature and works of art. Writers of a new kind, the humanists, abounded in the city. Reflecting the new interests of the Renaissance, they rejected the church-centered and university-oriented learning of the Middle Ages, and they brought a new spirit to the study of the Latin and Greek classics, in which they found a keen significance for their own times. Of these writers, the best remembered is Machiavelli, who worked to strengthen Florentine republicanism during the period of the Medici exile from 1494 to 1512.

Also born in Florence, either in the city or in the republic, were Michelangelo, Leonardo da Vinci, Masaccio, Donatello, Brunelleschi, Botticelli and Benvenuto Cellini, to name only the most eminent painters and sculptors, in addition to such lesser lights as the historian Guicciardini and the explorer Amerigo Vespucci, Latinized as Americus Vespucius, after whom America was named. Never since ancient Athens had so much talent appeared in so small a place within the short span of three or four generations. Patronage by the ruling elite was reinforced by a high degree of literacy in the general population; a chronicler reports that as early as 1338 there were 8,000 boys and girls in the schools. Such conditions promoted a degree of taste and understanding in which architecture, painting, sculpture, literature and intellectual discussion could flourish.

THE FLORENCE OF THE RENAISSANCE

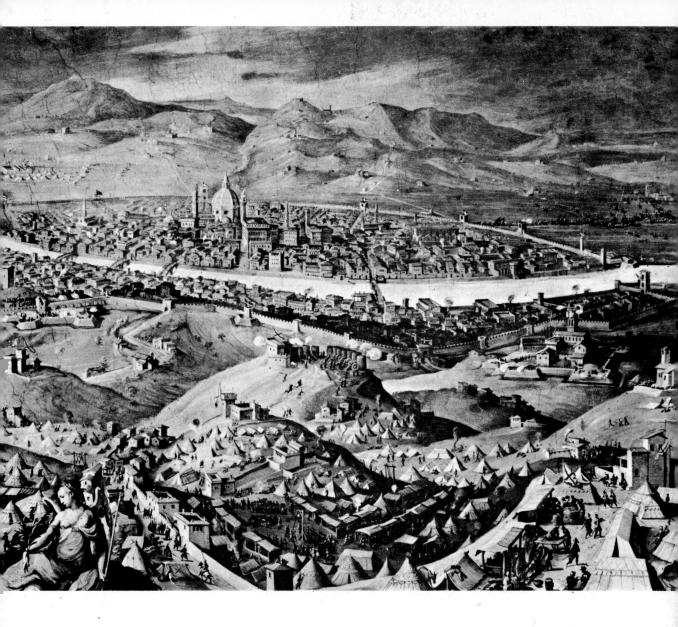

This view of Florence shows the river Arno bisecting it and flowing on into the Tuscan plain. In the right center is the Duomo, or cathedral, dominating the city. The scene, painted by Vasari, shows the situation in 1530, when the city was besieged by the Holy Roman Emperor, Charles V. The defenses were strong, and Michelangelo himself served as one of nine citizens in charge of engineering and fortifications. The Imperial army, shown encamped outside the walls, eventually overcame the resistance and restored the exiled Medici to power.

At the extreme left is the sign of the wool gild of Florence, in which a sheep is appropriately displayed. The near left shows the modest establishment of a fifteenth century banker, engaged in the actual counting or changing of money.

Above, Lorenzo de' Medici, the "Magnificent," examines a model for a villa built for him about 1480 on the outskirts of the city. The Medici town house, or "palace," appears on the last page of the present essay.

At the left is a part of a huge fresco executed for the chapel of the Medici town house by Benozzo Gozzoli in 1469. It is called the Procession of the Three Kings to Bethlehem, but what it really represents is the important personages of Florence at their most resplendent. The presence of an African servant in Italy at this early date is to be noted. He wears his hair in African style and carries a bow. To the right of him is Cosimo de' Medici on a white horse, followed by a throng whose varied complexions and miscellaneous head-gear, including the mitre of a Greek patriarch, suggest the cosmopolitanism of the city.

The three figures at the left are from a painting by Domenico Ghirlandaio, done about 1490 for a chapel in memory of a woman who had died in childbirth. The theme is "Zacharias in the Temple," but the three heads are actually portraits of contemporary Florentine humanists. The painting thus illustrates, like the one by Gozzoli on the preceding pages, the use of religious themes to convey secular subjects, or of everyday observation to convey religious ideas.

Above, the governing council, or "signoria," deliberates on going to war against the neighboring city of Pisa, during the period of republican revival after expulsion of the Medici in 1494. A Nemesis floats over the councillors' heads.

103

Valse el c° della lana a¢s contanti 26 ¥ 13 ß 4 ¥ di p̄

Upper left: Detail of the fall of Troy, enacted in Florentine costume in the streets of Florence. The building at the left is the Medici palace (see the next page). At the right, the African warrior wielding a large bow is Memnon, King of the Ethiopians, who according to an ancient legend fought at Troy on the side of the Trojans.

Lower left: Two wool merchants with their goods, from a book of 1492 on arithmetic. Arabic numerals are visible above, but the bags of wool are marked "CLX" or 160 in Roman numerals.

Above: The Piazza della Signoria showing the burning of Savonarola. The dome of the cathedral is half in view at the left. The arcade at the right is the "loggia dei lanzi," built about 1380 as an open but sheltered place for public assemblies. The "palazzo della signoria," or town hall,. the large square building, very dark in this picture, dates from 1298 and so reflects the medieval fortress-like style, with small windows, crenelated roof lines and high towers that characterized this part of Italy before the classicizing features of Renaissance architecture were adopted.   105

These are town houses, or "palazzi," of Florentine patricians. At the right is the Palazzo Medici, built for Cosimo de' Medici in the 1440s. At the left is the slightly later Palazzo Rucellai. Architects such as Brunelleschi transformed the old fortress-like dwellings of an earlier day into these massive and elegant residences. The new style is evident in the horizontal composition, the long rows of wide, closely spaced, identical windows, the pilasters, and the cornices under the overhanging roof. The interiors were often even more classical, with arches and columns enclosing an open courtyard.

   It was in the Medici Palace that Lorenzo the Magnificent received his following of artists and humanists, and that Pope Leo X (born 1475, pope 1513–1521) and Catherine de' Medici (born 1519, queen of France 1547–1559, queen mother 1559–1589) spent their youth.

III: THE WARS OF RELIGION

1560-1648

It is convenient, when we wish a single phrase, to think of the period of almost a century following 1560 as the age of the Wars of Religion. France, England, the dominions of the king of Spain, and the Holy Roman Empire were all torn by civil struggles in which religion was an issue, and all these powers, with Denmark and Sweden in addition, at one time or another fought international wars in which religion was at stake. Religion was by no means the sole motivating force or cause of conflict. It may even be that the term Wars of Religion is a misnomer. The wars involved political, constitutional, economic, and social issues as well as religious. Often the ideological line became blurred, with Catholics lending aid to Protestants, or vice versa. Nevertheless, the "ideological" element was always important: had the Spanish Armada landed in England, for example, it is entirely conceivable that Catholicism might have been restored there. The wars of the time may be called Wars of Religion somewhat as the wars of our own century might be called, by some future historian, Wars of Social Doctrine—wars in which the "ideology" of democracy, autocracy, capitalism, or communism is an actual issue, and wars in which the social character of many countries has been profoundly affected, yet in which

Chapter Emblem: A mariner's astrolabe, or simplified astrolabe that could be taken to sea and used in determination of latitude.

ideology has been mixed with national interest, political security, political expansionism, or economic need—or greed. So it was with the "ideology" of religion in the Wars of Religion.

But before going further it is necessary to describe basic changes in the economic and social foundation of the European countries.

11

The Opening of the Atlantic

Always until about 1500 the Atlantic Ocean had been a barrier, an end. About 1500 it became a bridge, a starting place. In the Middle Ages, and even in Roman times, small craft had groped from port to port on Europe's Atlantic coast. In 1317 the Venetians established the Flanders galleys, commercial flotillas which regularly made the passage between the Adriatic and the North Sea. In the fifteenth century, with further improvements in shipbuilding, in the rigging and manipulation of sails, and with the adoption of the mariner's compass, it became feasible to sail in the open ocean out of sight of land. It was the Portuguese who first made use of this opportunity. They were perhaps mainly drawn by the simple lure of exploration, but they were certainly tempted, on the material level, by the thought of trading directly with Asia.

For centuries, Asia had been a source for Europe of many highly valued commodities, partly manufactures in which Europe could not compete, such as silk and cotton fabrics, rugs, jewelry, porcelains, and fine steel, and partly raw or semimanufactured drugs and foodstuffs, such as sugar and above all spices. The latter—pepper, cinnamon, cloves, ginger, nutmeg, and many less common ones—were of more importance then than now. They were used in pharmacy, and in the preservation of meat, as in the making of sausages. They added palatability to fresh meats and other foods which easily spoiled in the absence of refrigeration. Europeans had never themselves gone to the sources of supply of Eastern goods. Somewhere, east of Suez, barely known to Europeans, was another world of other merchants, mainly Arabs, who moved the wares of China, India, and the East Indies Spice Islands by caravan over land and by boat through the Red Sea or Persian Gulf to the markets of the eastern Mediterranean. Traders of the two worlds met and did business at such thriving centers as Alexandria or Beirut or Constantinople.

The Portuguese in the East

For some time the Portuguese royal house had sponsored and encouraged exploration of the Atlantic. In 1498 the Portuguese navigator Vasco da Gama, having rounded Africa in the wake of other intrepid explorers, found himself in the midst of the unknown world of Arab commerce. He landed on the Malabar Coast (the southwest coast of India), where he found a busy commercial population of heterogeneous religious background. These people knew at least as much about Europe as Europeans did about India (one Jew was able to act as da Gama's interpreter) and they realized that the coming of the Portuguese would disturb their established channels of commerce. Da Gama, playing upon local rivalries, was able to load his ships with the coveted wares, but on his second voyage, in 1502, he came better prepared, bringing a fighting fleet of no less than twenty-one vessels. A ferocious war broke out between the Portuguese and Arab merchants, the latter supported in one way or another by the Egyptians, the Turks, and even the distant Venetians, all of whom had an interest in maintaining the old routes of trade. For the Portuguese, trained like the Spaniards in long wars against the Moors at home, no atrocities were too horrible to commit against the infidel competitors whom they found at the end of their heroic quest. Cities were devastated, ships burned at their docks, prisoners butchered and their dismembered hands, noses, and ears sent back as derisive trophies. One Brahmin, mutilated in this way, was left alive to bear them to his people. Such, unfortunately, was India's introduction to the West.

In the following years, under the first governor-general, Albuquerque, the Portuguese built permanent fortified stations at Goa on the Malabar Coast, at Aden near the mouth of the Red Sea, at Ormuz near the mouth of the Persian Gulf, and in East Africa. In 1509 they reached Malacca, near the modern Singapore, from which they passed northward into China itself, and eastward to Amboina, the heart of the Spice Islands, just west of New Guinea. Thus an empire was created, the first of Europe's commercial-colonial empires, maintained by superiority of firearms and sea power and with trade alternating with war and plunder. Albuquerque died in 1515, dreaming grandiose and preposterous dreams—to deflect the course of the Nile and so destroy Egypt and Egyptian commerce, and to capture Mecca and exchange it for the Holy Land. It should be added that bold Jesuits soon arrived, led by St. Francis Xavier, who, by 1550, had baptized thousands of souls in India, Indonesia, and even Japan.

By the new route the cost of Eastern goods for Europeans was much reduced, for the old route had involved many transshipments, unloadings, and reloadings, movements by sea and by land, through the hands of many merchants. In 1504 spices could be bought in Lisbon for only a fifth of the price demanded in Venice. The Venetians (who in their desperation even talked of digging a Suez canal) were hopelessly undersold; their trade thereafter was confined to products of the Near East itself. As for the Portuguese, never was a commercial monopoly built so fast. The lower prices added enormously to European demand and consumption. Beginning in 1504, only five years after da Gama's first return, an average of twelve ships a year left Lisbon for the East.

Meanwhile, as every American schoolchild can tell, the same quest for a route to the East had led to the somewhat disappointing discovery of America. Like most such discoveries, this was no chance hit of a queer or isolated genius. Behaim's globe, constructed in 1492,[1] the very year of Columbus' first voyage, could hardly fail to suggest the idea of sailing westward. Nevertheless, it was Christopher Columbus who had the persistence and daring to undertake the unprecedented westward

[1] See p. 310.

voyage. Before the invention of sufficiently accurate clocks (in the eighteenth century) mariners had no way of determining longitude, i.e., their east-west position; and learned geographers, as may be seen from Behaim's map, greatly underestimated the probable distance from Europe westward to Asia. When Columbus struck land, he naturally supposed it to be an outlying part of the Indies. The people were soon called Indians, and the islands where Columbus landed, the West Indies.

Columbus had sailed with the backing of Queen Isabella of Castile, and the new lands became part of the composite dominions of the crown of Spain. The Spaniards, hoping to beat the Portuguese to the East (which da Gama had not yet reached), received Columbus' first reports with enthusiasm. For his second voyage they gave him 17 ships, filled with 1,500 workmen and artisans. Columbus himself, until his death in 1506, kept probing about in the Caribbean, baffled and frustrated, hoping to find something that looked like the fabulous East. Others were more willing to accept the new land for what it was. Churchmen, powerful in Spain, regarded it as a new field for crusading and conversion. The government saw it as a source of gold and silver for the royal exchequer. Foot-loose gentry of warlike habits, left idle by the end of war with the Moors, turned to it to make their fortunes. The *conquistadores* fell upon the new lands. Cortés conquered the Aztecs in Mexico, Pizarro the Incas in Peru. They despoiled the native empires. Mines for precious metals were opened almost immediately. The Indians were put to forced labor, in which many died. The attempts of the church to protect its Indian converts, and restrictions set by the royal authorities on their exploitation, led almost immediately to the importation of African slaves, of whom, it was estimated, 100,000 had been brought to America by 1560.

Explorers began to feel their way along the vast dim bulk that barred them from Asia. A Spanish expedition, led by Magellan, found a southwestern passage in 1520, sailed from the Atlantic into the Pacific, crossed the Pacific, discovered the Philippine Islands, and fought its way through hostile Portuguese across the Indian Ocean back to Spain. The globe was thus circumnavigated for the first time, and an idea of the true size and interconnection of the oceans was brought back to Europe. Geographical experts immediately incorporated the new knowledge, as in the map drawn by Schöner in 1523.[2] Meanwhile others sailing for Spain, the Cabots sailing for England, Jacques Cartier for France, began the long and fruitless search for a

The Geographer *by Jan Vermeer (Dutch, 1632–1675)*
The impact on Europe of the opening of the Atlantic may be seen in this painting and the following one. On the basis of their new ocean-going trade the Dutch built up their remarkable seventeenth-century civilization, in which the brightest luminaries were the painters. Vermeer, in this "Geographer," captures the spirit of the Age of Discovery, in which Dutch navigators, instrument-makers and cartographers played a leading role. For the first time in human history it became possible to conceive, with some accuracy, of the relationships of oceans and continents throughout the globe as a whole. Courtesy of the Städelsches Kunstinstitut, Frankfurt.

   [2]See p. 310.

northwest passage. An English expedition, looking for a northeast passage, discovered the White Sea in 1553. English merchants immediately began to take the ocean route to Russia. Archangel became an ocean port.

For a century it was only the Spanish and Portuguese who followed up the new ocean routes to America and the East. These two peoples, in a treaty of 1494, divided the globe between them. The Philippines, because of Magellan's discovery, went to Spain; Brazil, because it had been discovered by Cabral in 1500, to Portugal. Otherwise Spain received all America, and Portugal all rights of trade in Asia and the East Indies.

The Spanish Empire in America

In the populous and civilized East the Portuguese were never more than a handful of outsiders who could not impose their language, their religion, or their way of life. In America, after the first fiendishness of the *conquista,* the Spanish established their own civilization. In Protestant countries, and also in France, as the years went on, there arose an extremely unfavorable idea of the Spanish regime in America, where, it was noted, the Inquisition was presently established and the native peoples were reduced to servitude by the conquerors. The Spanish themselves came to dismiss this grim picture as a Black Legend concocted by their rivals. The true character of the Spanish empire in America is not easy to portray. The Spanish government (like the home governments of all colonial empires until the American Revolution, and even later) regarded its empire as existing for the benefit of the mother country. The Indians were put into servitude, to work in mines or in agriculture. The government introduced the *encomienda,* a kind of distant analogue to the European manor. The "lord" of the *encomienda* controlled the labor of his Indians, but according to law he could not deprive an Indian of his own parcel of land, and he must make Indians work for him no more than four days a week, leaving them two days to work on their parcels. Such conditions corresponded very closely to those in which the white masses of eastern Europe lived until the nineteenth century. How much the royal regulations were enforced in remote *encomiendas* is another question, on which answers vary. Negro slavery never assumed the importance in Spanish America that it later assumed in the Dutch, French, and English colonies. The white population remained small. Castilian Spaniards looked down on American-born whites, or creoles. Since few women emigrated from Spain, there arose a large class of *mestizos,* of mixed white and Indian descent.

Study of Two Black Heads by *Rembrandt van Rijn (Dutch, 1606–1669)*
One consequence of the new intercontinental travel was the mass transportation to the Americas of black Africans as slaves. Some appeared also in Europe, where they attracted a great deal of personal curiosity and produced much speculation on the diversity of human races. Rembrandt, though he never traveled more than twenty miles from his native Leyden, painted all types of persons who streamed into the Netherlands. The greatest of the Dutch painters, and a profound observer of human beings, he was no doubt fascinated by the dark color tones, rugged features and secret inner feelings of these two men in the strange world into which they had been cast. Courtesy of the Mauritshuis, The Hague (A. Dingjan).

The *mestizos,* along with many pure Indians, adopted to a considerable degree the Spanish language and the faith of the Spanish church. The Indians, while unfree, had usually been unfree under their own tribal chiefs; they were spared from tribal war; and the rigors of the Inquisition were mild compared with the sheer physical cruelty of the Aztecs or Incas. The printing press was brought to Mexico in 1544. By the middle of the sixteenth century Spanish America consisted of two great vice-royalties, those of Mexico and Peru, with twenty-two bishoprics, and with a university in each vice-royalty, the University of Lima established in 1551, that of Mexico in 1553. When Harvard College was founded in New England (in 1636) there were five universities on the European model in Spanish America. In sum, it may be observed not only that the Spanish empire let many Indians survive, but that in all the long record of European expansion the Spanish are the only people, along with the Portuguese in Brazil, who were able in some measure to "Europeanize" a non-European population in its own native environment.

In 1545 a great discovery was made, the prodigiously rich silver deposits at Potosí in Peru. Almost simultaneously, better methods of extracting silver from the ore by the use of mercury were developed. American production of precious metals shot up suddenly and portentously. For years, after the mid-century, half a million pounds of silver flowed annually from America to Spain, and ten thousand pounds of gold. A price revolution followed in Europe. The riches of Potosí financed the European projects of the king of Spain. Peruvian ores, Indian labor, and Spanish management combined to make possible the militant and anti-Protestant phase of the Counter Reformation.

The opening of the Atlantic reoriented Europe. In an age of oceanic communications Europe became a center from which America, Africa, and Asia could all be reached. In Europe itself, the Atlantic coast enjoyed great advantages over the center. No sooner did the Portuguese begin to bring spices from the East Indies than Antwerp began to flourish as the point of redistribution for northern Europe. But for a century after the great discoveries the northern peoples did not take to the oceans. French corsairs did indeed put out from Bayonne or St. Malo, and Dutch prowlers and English "sea dogs" followed at the close of the century, all bent upon plundering the Iberian treasure ships. Still the Spanish and Portuguese kept their monopoly. No organized effort, backed by governments, came from the north until about 1600. For it is by no means geography alone that sets the fate of peoples, and the English, Dutch, and French could not make use of the opportunities with which the opening of the Atlantic provided them until they had cleared up domestic troubles at home and survived the perils and hazards of the Wars of Religion.

12
The Commercial
Revolution

In the period under discussion a great economic readjustment was taking place in Europe in which the opening of ocean trade routes was an important but by no means the only factor. The changes about to be described are usually summarized under the term Commercial Revolution, which in general signifies the rise of a capitalistic economy and the transition from a town-centered to a nation-centered economic system. This "revolution" was an exceptionally slow and protracted one, for it began at least as early as the fourteenth century and lasted into the eighteenth century.

In the Middle Ages the town and its adjoining country formed an economic unit.[3] Craftsmen, organized in gilds, produced common articles for local use. Peasants and lords sold their agricultural products to the local town, from which they bought manufactures. The town protected itself by its own tariffs and regulations. In the workshop the master both owned his "capital"—his house, workbench, tools, and materials—and acted as a workman himself along with half a dozen journeymen and apprentices. The masters owned a modest capital, but they were hardly capitalists. They produced only upon order, or at least for customers whose tastes and number were known in advance. There was little profit, and little risk of loss. There was much social mobility; the journeyman could expect to become a master, and the apprentice might even marry the master's daughter. Journeymen as well as masters could generally vote for town officials.

All this changed with the widening of the trading area, or market. Even in the Middle Ages, as we have seen, there was a certain amount of long-distance trading in articles that could not be produced as well in one place as in another. Gradually more articles came within this category. Where goods were produced to be sold at some time in the future, in faraway places, to persons unknown, the local gildmaster could not manage the operation. He lacked the money (or "capital") to tie up in stocks of unsold wares; he lacked the knowledge of what distant customers wanted, or where, in what quantities, and at what price people would buy. In this type of business a new type of man developed. Economists call him the "enterpriser" or *entrepreneur*. He usually started out as a merchant working in an extensive market, and ended up as a banker. The Italian Medici family has been mentioned.[4] Equally typical were the German Fuggers.

The first of this family, Johann Fugger, a small-town weaver, came to Augsburg in 1368. He established a business in a new kind of cloth, called fustian, in which cotton was mixed, and which had certain advantages over the woolens and linens in which people then clothed themselves. He thus enjoyed a more than local market, and made trips to Venice to obtain the cotton imported from the Near East. Gradually the family began to deal also in spices, silks, and other Eastern goods obtained at Venice. They made large profits, which were invested in other enterprises, notably mining. They lent money to the Renaissance popes. They lent Charles V the money which he spent to obtain election as Holy Roman Emperor in 1519. They became bankers to the Habsburgs in both Germany and Spain. Together with other German and Flemish bankers, the Fuggers financed the Portuguese trade with Asia, either by

[3]See p. 29.
[4]See p. 54.

outright loans, or by providing in advance, on credit, the cargoes which the Portuguese traded for spices. Portugal was not a very productive country, nor did Asian peoples want European manufactures. The Portuguese ships went out loaded mainly with metals, both precious and common, gold, silver, copper, lead, and mercury, produced mainly in Germany and controlled by German capital. The Fuggers, and others like them, through branches established at Lisbon and Antwerp, likewise controlled the distribution in Europe of wares that the Portuguese ships brought back. The wealth of the Fuggers became proverbial, and declined only through repeated Habsburg bankruptcies, and with the general economic decline that beset Germany in the sixteenth century.

Other dealers in cloth, less spectacular than the first Fugger, broke away from the town-and-gild framework in other ways. England until the fifteenth century was an exporter of raw wool and an importer of finished woolens from Flanders. In the fifteenth century certain Englishmen began to develop the spinning, weaving, and dyeing of wool in England. To avoid the restrictive practices of the towns and gilds they "put out" the work to people in the country, providing them with looms and other equipment for the purpose, of which they generally retained the ownership themselves. This "putting out" or "domestic" system spread very widely. In France, the cloth dealers of Rouen, feeling the competition of the new silk trade, developed a lighter, cheaper, and more simply made type of woolen cloth. Various gild regulations in Rouen, to protect the workers there, prohibited the manufacture of this cheaper cloth. The Rouen dealers, in 1496, took the industry into the country, installed looms in peasant cottages, and farmed out the work to the peasants.

This domestic system, or system of rural household industry, remained typical of production in many lines (cloth, hardware, etc.) in western Europe until the introduction of factories in the late eighteenth century. It was clearly capitalistic. On the one hand were the workers, people who worked as the employer needed them, received wages for what they did, and had no interest in or knowledge of more than their own task. Living both by agriculture and by cottage industry, they formed an expansible labor force, available when labor was needed, left to live by farming or local charity when times were bad. On the other hand was the man who managed the whole affair. He had no personal acquaintance with the workers. Estimating how much of his product, let us say woolens, he could sell in a national or even international market, he purchased the needed raw materials, passed out wool to be spun by one group of peasants, took the yarn to another group for weaving, collected the cloth and took it still elsewhere to be dyed, paying wages on all sides for services rendered, while retaining ownership of the materials and the equipment and keeping the coordination and management of the whole enterprise in his own head. Much larger business enterprises could be established in this way than within the municipal framework of gild and town. Indeed, the very master weavers of the gilds often sank to the status of subcontractors, hardly different from wage employees, of the great "clothiers" and "drapers" by whom the business was dominated. The latter, with the widening market, became personages of national or even international repute. And, of course, the bigger the business the more of a capital investment it represented.

Certain other industries, new or virtually new in the fifteenth and sixteenth centuries, could by their nature never fit into a town-centered system and were capitalistic from the start, in that they required a large initial outlay before any income could be received. One such was mining. Another was printing and the book trade; books had a national and even international market, being mainly in Latin; and no ordinary craftsman could afford the outlay required for a printing press, for fonts of type, supplies of paper, and stocks of books on hand. Printers therefore borrowed from capitalists, or shared with them an interest in business. Shipbuilding was so stimulated by the shift to the oceans as almost to be a new industry, and still another was the manufacture of cannons and muskets. For the latter the chief demand came from the state, from the New Monarchies which were organizing national armies. In the rise of capitalism the needs of the military were in fact fundamentally important. Armies, which started out by requiring thousands of weapons, in the seventeenth century required thousands of uniforms, and in the eighteenth century many solidly built barracks and fortifications. These were the first demands for mass production; and where governments themselves did not take the initiative, capitalists stepped in as middlemen between these huge impersonal requirements and the myriads of small handicraft workers by whom, before the industrial age, the actual product was still manufactured.

The new sea route to the East and the discovery of America brought a vast increase in trade not only of luxury items but of bulk commodities like rice, sugar, tea, and other consumer goods. Older commercial activities were transformed by the widening of markets. Spain increasingly drew cereals from Sicily. The Netherlands was fed from Poland, the French wine districts lived on food brought from northern France. With the growth of shipping, the timber, tar, pitch and other "naval stores" of Russia and the Baltic came upon the commercial scene. There was thus an ever growing movement of heavy staple commodities, in which again only men controlling large funds of capital could normally take part.

Not all capital was invested; some was simply lent, either to the church, or to governments, or to impecunious nobles, or, though perhaps this was the least common type of lending in the sixteenth century, to persons engaged in trade and commerce. Bankers and others who lent money expected to receive back, after a time, a larger sum than that of the loan. They expected "interest"; and they sometimes received as much as 30 percent a year. In the Middle Ages the taking of interest had been frowned upon as usury, denounced as avarice, and forbidden in the canon law. It was still frowned upon in the sixteenth century by almost all but the lenders themselves. The Catholic church maintained its prohibitions. The theologians of the University of Paris ruled against it in 1530. Luther, who hated "Fuggerism," continued to preach against usury. Calvin made allowances, but as late as 1640, in capitalist Holland itself, the stricter Calvinist ministers still denounced lending at interest. Nothing could stop the practice. Borrowers compounded with lenders to evade prohibitions, and theologians of all churches began to distinguish between "usury" and a "legitimate return." Gradually, as interest rates fell, as banking became more established, and as loans were made for economically productive uses rather than to sustain ecclesiastics, princes, and nobles in their personal habits, the feeling against a "reasonable" interest died down, and interest became an accepted feature of capitalism. The Bank of Amsterdam, in the seventeenth century, because depositors knew that their money was safe and could be withdrawn at will, was able to attract deposits from all countries by offering a very low rate of interest, which enabled it in turn to make loans, at a low rate, to finance commercial activities.

The net effect of all these developments was a "commercialization of industry." The great man of business was the merchant. Industry, the actual processes of production, still in an essentially handicraft stage, was subordinate to the buyers and sellers. Producers—weavers, hatters, metal workers, gunsmiths, glass workers, etc.—worked to fill the orders of the merchants, and often with capital which the merchants supplied and owned. The man who knew where the article could be sold prevailed over the man who simply knew how to produce it. This commercial capitalism remained the typical form of capitalism until after 1800, when, with the introduction of power machinery, it yielded to industrial capitalism, and merchants became dependent on industrialists, who owned, understood, and organized the machines. In the meantime the merchant, along with the banker, stood near the top of the middle class and indeed of all nonnoble people.

The Price Revolution

With these more purely commercial changes went a transformation in money values by which all classes of society were affected. It has been known as the "price revolution," though in fact it occurred over a long period of time. It was most rapid in the second half of the sixteenth century. It varied from one country to another, but, roughly speaking, prices between 1550 and 1600 approximately doubled, and by 1650 they were more than three times higher than they had been in 1500. In 1500 an Englishman with an annual income of fifty pounds sterling was well-to-do, but in 1650 he was barely middle class. Wheat and hay sold in the Paris market, in 1650, for fifteen times the price of 1500. So it went everywhere. The persistent inflation had the effects that inflation always has: persons whose income was fixed in money value suffered, because the money always bought less; persons whose debts and obligations were fixed in money value benefited, because as years passed the same sum of money was easier to obtain and less of a burden to pay. Or as a Frenchman observed in 1620: "The debtor gains what the creditor has lost."

In this long inflationary trend one of the underlying causes was the flow of precious metals from America, especially after the discoveries at Potosí. Shiploads of silver poured into Spain, from which the Spaniards used it to finance economic wants or political objectives in the rest of Europe. So far as the amount of metal rose faster than the volume of goods or services produced, the result was that the value of metal declined, which is to say that prices rose. The fact that prices rose very unevenly shows that other causes were also at work. Prices for agricultural products went up far more drastically than those for manufactured articles or for such items as salt and building materials. They rose in distant countries, like Sweden, before the impact of

Spanish silver could be felt. The price revolution thus reflected more significant developments than a mere increase in the money supply. With population growing steadily, though not abruptly, less desirable land was brought into use. Costs of production and transportation of foodstuffs therefore rose. Society was becoming not only more numerous but more complicated, with a higher proportion of persons who were not engaged in agriculture, but who still had to be fed. Since agricultural technology did not much improve, the general price increase was most apparent in agriculture.

Governments were caught between fixed income and a mounting need for money. The idea persisted, carried over from the Middle Ages, that kings should normally live "on their own," from the income of the manors and other properties in their crown domain, and from feudal payments or customary taxes, such as import and export duties, whose amount had usually been fixed in money value in the past.[5] At the same time governments were becoming more complex. Kings were maintaining larger armies and fighting frequent wars, of which the costs were always rising. Various kings adopted various expedients. They might simply borrow, as the Habsburgs did from the Fuggers. Often they "devalued" their money or "debased" their coinage, simply declaring that a given weight of silver or gold should be worth a larger number of livres, or reals, or florins. This practice, while temporarily raising a king's income, in the long run added to the inflation. Others, especially in France, sold government offices in return for cash. Or they sold monopolies, or the exclusive privilege of doing a certain kind of business in a certain place or in the country as a whole. Or they encroached on the rights of towns, requiring money payments in return for confirmation of town charters. Or they quarreled with their parliaments, notably in England but also elsewhere, demanding assent to new taxes which parliaments were either unwilling to grant or willing to grant only in return for political concessions. Thus the monetary crisis helped to precipitate a constitutional crisis, with the king increasingly at odds with representative bodies. Out of this constitutional crisis, in the seventeenth century, came the triumph of Parliament in England and of royal absolutism almost everywhere else.

In the towns, inflation accentuated the class differences that were also arising from other causes. Generally it benefited the merchants. The wealth of the merchants was in goods whose value, measured in money, was rising. Merchants and others who owned urban real estate benefited from the increase of rents. Merchants who bought ships or dyeing vats or copper mines found their investment automatically increasing in value as time went by. On the other hand the town wage earners, the journeymen, were consistently worse off because wages rarely rose as fast as prices, especially those for food. Thus the journeyman, whose position had deteriorated in any case for quite different reasons, who could no longer aspire to become an independent master, who competed with peasants under the growing system of domestic industry and who increasingly worked simply as an occasional employee of the merchant, was in addition pinched by purely monetary devel-

[5] See p. 31.

opments. Journeymen formed mysterious organizations of their own, outside the gilds, and to which the masters of the gilds were not admitted; these were the first true labor unions, and they sometimes conducted strikes to obtain better wages. Governments tried to suppress them, but in many places they persisted in secrecy.

Towns everywhere divided into an upper or "bourgeois" and a lower or laboring class. The journeymen lost their voice in civic affairs, and the nearly universal suffrage of townsmen of the Middle Ages gave way to rule by a bourgeois patriciate, oligarchy, or "corporation." The laboring class lived in slums, often in the very buildings built in the thirteenth or fourteenth century. The merchants and bourgeois lived in substantial new houses of brick or stone. In England they began to consider themselves gentlemen; in Holland they ruled the country; in France they called themselves *honnêtes hommes* and on their tombstones left the epitaph that they had "lived nobly."

Social Developments
in Western and
Eastern Europe

But it was chiefly in the country that the price revolution had its most sweeping effects, especially when it is remembered that all parts of Europe remained overwhelmingly agricultural. The effects worked inversely in western and in eastern Europe. In the West, the peasant went up and the lord went down in general position. In the East, the peasant went down and the lord went up.

In western Europe, as early as the fourteenth century, the peasants had very commonly secured manorial lands for themselves by agreeing to pay the lords a set annual sum of money in perpetuity into the future.[6] The sum so set, while not changing in amount, was in real value much less in 1600 than in 1300 or 1400 because of the inflation. Peasants, selling their own farm products, benefited from rising prices and received a higher money income, yet they owed the lord only the same old amount. Peasants, therefore, were proportionately far better off. It was from such peasant dues and fees that, in western Europe, the bulk of the old feudal class, the small nobles, gentry or landed aristocracy, drew most of its income. These lords of manors were usually not farmers themselves; they did not raise and sell agricultural products on their own account; most of the area of their manors was let out to peasants on perpetual and hereditary leaseholds in return for the payments just mentioned. Most nobles and gentry were thus receivers of fixed income, and as such they were faced with ruin.

The period, in the West, was one of a distressed landed aristocracy, of impoverished *hidalgos* in Spain, *hoberaux* in France, squires in England, who met their problem in different ways. Sometimes they borrowed from bankers or merchants, and then lost their lands when unable to pay their debts. Sometimes they sold lands and manors outright to affluent merchants, who thereupon moved into the country, where they "lived nobly," or "like gentlemen." The real noble, the noble of blood and birth, thus losing his patrimony, or unable to live from it if he kept it, drifted off to one kind of activity or another. The large number of uprooted minor nobles, to

[6] See p. 30.

whom war was the one honorable occupation, made a restless element from which all sides were recruited in the civil struggles of the Wars of Religion. Spanish *hidalgos* went off to America. In all countries there were many who took service with the king. In England some went into trade, thus further blurring the class boundaries in England. In England, however, the landed gentry, enriched by farmlands that had formerly belonged to the monasteries, and turning to sheep raising to meet the growing demand for wool, was less hard hit by economic changes than was the corresponding lesser nobility of other countries.

In eastern Europe, it was the lords who benefited from rising prices and the growing market for grain and forest products. Here too the institution of the manor existed; but the peasant land tenures were more precarious than in the West, more dependent on accidents of death or on the wishes of the lord, and the lord worked a larger part of the manor with his own workmen for his own use or profit. The rise of prices and expansion of the Baltic trade gave the lord an incentive to increase his output. In northeast Germany (where such lords were called Junkers), in Poland, in the Baltic region, and as time went on in Russia, and also in Bohemia and Hungary, beginning in the sixteenth century and continuing into the eighteenth, there set in a vast process by which the mass of the peasantry sank into serfdom. It was hastened in many regions by the violence and insecurity of the religious wars. Typically, the peasant lost his parcel of land, or received it back on condition that he render unpaid labor services to the lord. Usually the peasant owed three or four days a week of such forced labor (called *robot* in Bohemia and adjoining territories), remaining free to work during the remainder of the week on his own parcel. Often the number of days of *robot* exacted by the lord was greater, since in eastern Europe, where central monarchy was weak and centralized legal systems almost unknown, the lord himself was the final court of appeal for his people. His people were in fact his "subjects." Serfdom in Germany was not called serfdom, an ill-sounding word, but "hereditary subjection." The serf, or hereditary subject of the manorial lord, by whatever name called throughout eastern Europe, could not leave the manor, marry, or learn a trade without the lord's express permission. The lord, drawing on this large reserve of compulsory labor, using most of it for agriculture but teaching some quick-minded youths the various handcrafts that were needed on the estate, worked the land as his own venture, sold the produce, and retained the profit.

Thus in the East, at the beginning of modern times, the rural masses lost personal freedom and lived in a poverty unknown to the peasants of the West, poor as the latter were. In the West the peasants were already on the way to becoming small farmers. They were free men in the law. They could migrate, marry, and learn trades as opportunity offered. Those who held land could defend it in royal courts, and they raised crops and took part in the market economy on their own account. They owed the lord no forced labor—or virtually none, for the ten days a year of *corvée* still found in parts of France hardly compared with the almost full-time *robot* of the peasant of eastern Europe.

The landlord, in the East, from the sixteenth century onward, was solidly entrenched in his own domain, monarch of all he surveyed, with no troublesome bourgeoisie to annoy him (for towns were few), and with kings and territorial rulers solicitous of his wishes. Travelers from the West were impressed with the lavishness of great Polish and Lithuanian magnates, with their palatial homes, private art galleries, well stocked libraries, collections of jewels, swarms of servants, trains of dependent lesser gentry, gargantuan dinners, and barbaric hospitality. The Junkers of northeast Germany lived with more modesty, but enjoyed the same kind of independence and social superiority. The importance of all this will become evident when, in later chapters, we turn to Prussia, Poland, Russia, and the Austrian lands.

Mercantilism

There was still another aspect of the Commercial Revolution, namely, the various government policies that go historically under the name of mercantilism. Rulers, as we have seen, were hard pressed for money, and needed more of it as it fell in value. The desire of kings and their advisers to force gold and silver to flow into their own kingdoms was one of the first impulses leading to mercantilist regulation. Gradually this "bullionist" idea was replaced by the more general idea of building up a strong and self-sufficient economy. The means adopted, in either case, was to "set the poor on work," as they said in England, to turn the country into a hive of industry, to discourage idleness, begging, vagabondage and unemployment. New crafts and manufactures were introduced, and favors were given to merchants who provided work for "the poor" and who sold the country's products abroad. It was thought desirable to raise the export of finished goods and reduce the export of unprocessed raw materials, to curtail all imports except of needed raw materials, and thus obtain a "favorable" balance of trade so that other countries would have to pay their debts in bullion. Since all this was done by a royal or nationwide system of regulations, mercantilism became in the economic sphere what the state-building of the New Monarchies was in the political, signifying the transition from town to national units of social living.[7]

Mercantilists frowned upon the gilds, with their localistic and conservative outlook. In England the gilds ceased to have any importance. Parliament, in the time of Elizabeth, did on a national scale what gilds had once done locally when it enacted the Statute of Artificers of 1563, regulating the admission to apprenticeship and level of wages in various trades. In France the royal government kept the gilds in being, because they were convenient bodies to tax, but it deprived them of most of their old independence and used them as organizations through which royal control of industry could be enforced. In both countries, the government assisted merchants who wished to set up domestic or cottage industry in the country, against the protests of the town gilds, which in their heyday had forbidden rural people to engage in crafts. Governments generally tried to suppress idleness, especially in Protestant countries where begging was out of favor, and where it was thought unwise to give alms without asking questions. The famous English Poor Law of 1601 (which

[7]On the New Monarchies see pp. 69–76.

remained in effect, with amendments, until 1834) was designed both to force people to work and to relieve absolute destitution.

Governments likewise took steps to introduce new industries. The silk industry was brought from Italy to France under royal protection, to the dismay of French woolen and linen interests. The English government assisted in turning England from a producer of raw wool into a producer of finished woolens, supervising the immigration of skilled Flemish weavers, and even fetching from faraway Turkey, about 1582, two youths who understood the more advanced dyeing arts of the Near East. Generally, under mercantilism, governments fought to steal skilled workers from each other while prohibiting or discouraging the emigration of their own skilled workers, who might take their trade secrets and "mysteries" to foreign parts.

By such means governments helped to create a national market and an industrious nationwide labor supply for their great merchants, and without such government support the great merchants, such as the drapers or clothiers, could never have risen and prospered. The same help was given to merchants operating in foreign markets. Henry VII of England in 1496 negotiated a commercial treaty with Flanders, known as the Intercursus Magnus; and in the next century the kings of France signed a number of treaties with the Ottoman Empire by which French merchants obtained privileges in the Near East. A merchant backed by a national monarchy was in a much stronger position than one backed merely by a city, such as Augsburg or Venice. This backing on a national scale was again given when national governments subsidized exports, paying bounties for goods whose production they wished to encourage, or when they erected tariff barriers against imports to protect their own producers from competition. Thus a national tariff system was superimposed on the old network of provincial and municipal tariffs. These latter were now thought of as "internal tariffs," and mercantilists usually wished to abolish them, in order to create an area of free trade within the state as a whole. But local interests were so strong, and a sense of interprovincial and intertown unity was so slow to develop, that for centuries they were unable to get rid of local tariffs except in England.

In wild or distant parts of the world, or in exotic regions nearer home, such as the Moslem Near East or Russia, it was not possible for individual merchants to act by merely private initiative. Merchants trading with such countries needed a good deal of capital, they often had to obtain special privileges and protection from native rulers, and they had to arm their ships against Barbary or Malay pirates or against hostile Europeans. Merchants and their respective governments came together to found official companies for the transocean trade. In England, soon after the English discovery of the White Sea in 1553, a Russia Company was established. A Turkey Company soon followed. Shortly after 1600 a great many such companies were operating out of England, Holland, and France. The most famous of all were the East India Companies the English founded in 1600, the Dutch in 1602, the French not until 1664. Each of these companies was a state-supported organization, with special rights. Each was a monopoly in that only merchants who belonged to the company could legally engage in trade in the region for which the company had a charter. Each was expected to find markets for the national manufactures, and of most of them it was hoped that they would bring home gold or silver. With these companies the northern peoples began to encroach on the Spanish and Portuguese monopoly in America and the East. With them new commercial-colonial empires were to be launched. But, as has been already observed, before this could happen it was necessary for certain domestic and purely European conflicts and controversies to be settled.

13
The Crusade of Catholic Spain: The Dutch and English

The Ambitions of Philip II

Charles V, having tried in vain for thirty-five years to preserve religious unity in Germany, abdicated his many crowns and retired to a monastery in 1556, the year after the Peace of Augsburg.[8] He left Austria, Bohemia, and Hungary (or the small part of it not occupied by the Turks) to his brother Ferdinand, who was soon elected Holy Roman Emperor.[9] All his other possessions Charles left to his son Philip, who became Philip II of Spain. The Habsburg dynasty remained thereafter divided into two branches, the Austrian and the Spanish. The two cooperated in European affairs. The Spanish for a century was the more important. Philip II (1556–1598) not only possessed the Spanish kingdoms but in 1580 inherited Portugal, so that the whole Iberian peninsula was brought under his rule. He possessed the seventeen provinces of the Netherlands and the Free County of Burgundy, which were member states of the Holy Roman Empire, lying on its western border, adjacent to France. Milan in north Italy and Naples in the south belonged to Philip, and since he also held the chief islands, as well as Tunis, he enjoyed a naval ascendancy in the western Mediterranean which was threatened only by the Turks. For five years, until 1558, he was titular king of England, and in 1589, in the name of his daughter, he laid claim to the throne of France. All America belonged to Philip II, and after 1580 all the Portuguese empire as well, so that except for a few nautical daredevils all ships plying the open ocean were the Spanish king's.

Philip II therefore naturally regarded himself as an international figure, and the more so because he thought in terms not of nationality but of religion. Before all else he was a Catholic, fervid and fanatical, committed to upholding the sway of the universal church, within which all nations were no more than minorities and all heretics no more than rebels. A grave and sober man, of abstemious personal habits, sharing in the moral severity of the Catholic Reform, and in the dark, brooding, and tormented inner world of the Spanish mystics, he took upon himself the headship of a far-flung Catholic counteroffensive, into which he was willing to pour with grim persistence the blood and treasure of all his kingdoms. To economic and material interests he gave no thought, and in such matters Spanish society began to deteriorate in his reign; but for all material problems the wealth of Potosí provided a facile solution, and meanwhile Spain entered upon the Golden Age of its culture.

[8]See pp. 80–82.
[9]See map, pp. 72–73.

In this period, the *siglo de oro*, running in round dates from 1550 to 1650, Cervantes wrote his *Don Quixote* and Lope de Vega his seven hundred dramas, while El Greco, Murillo, and Velasquez painted their pictures, and the Jesuit Suarez composed works on philosophy and law that were read even in Protestant countries. But the essence of Spanish life was its peculiarly intensive Catholicism. The church was vitally present at every social level, from the archbishop of Toledo, who ranked above grandees and could address the king as an equal, down to a host of penniless and mendicant friars, who mixed with the poorest and most disinherited of the people. It is said that about 1600 a third of the population of Spain was in one way or another in the service of the church. Spain, whose whole history had been a crusade, was ideally suited to be Philip's instrument in the re-Catholicizing of Europe.[10]

Philip II built himself a new royal residence ("palace" is hardly the word), the Escorial, which well expressed in solid stone its creator's inner spirit. Madrid itself was a new town, merely a government center, far from the worldly distractions of Toledo or Valladolid. But it was thirty miles from Madrid, on the bleak arid plateau of central Castile, overlooked by the jagged Sierra, that Philip chose to erect the Escorial. He built it in honor of St. Lawrence, on whose day he had won a battle against the French. The great pile of connecting buildings was laid out in the shape of a grill, since according to martyrologists St. Lawrence, in the year 258, had been roasted alive on a grill over burning coals. Somber and vast, angular and unrelieved, made of blocks of granite meant to last forever, and with its highest spire rising three hundred feet from the ground, the Escorial was designed not only as a palace but as a monastery and a mausoleum. The monks moved in before the king, who, when he installed himself, brought with him eight coffins, those of his father, his dead wives, and his children, to remind him of his own. Here, in an atmosphere that could be painted only by El Greco, the king of Spain worked and lived, a slim figure dressed almost like a monk himself, always industrious, avid for detail, dispatching his couriers to Mexico, to Manila, to Vienna, to Milan, his troops and his bars of bullion to Italy and the Netherlands, his diplomats to all courts, and his spies to all countries, wholly and utterly absorbed in his one consuming project.

Let us try to see the events of the time internationally, for though it may be confusing to try to see all nations together, it is distorting to look at only one of them alone. The first years of Philip's reign were also the first years of Elizabeth's reign in England, where the religious issue was still in flux; they were years in which Calvinism agitated the Netherlands, and when France, ruled by teen-aged boys, fell apart into implacable civil war. Religious loyalties that knew no frontiers overlapped all political boundaries. Everywhere there were people who looked for guidance outside their own countries. Calvinists in England, France, and the Netherlands felt closer to one another than to their own monarchs or their own neighbors. Zealous Catholics, in all three countries, welcomed the support of international Catholic forces—the Jesuits, the king of Spain, the pope. National unity threatened to dissolve or was not yet formed. The mere unity of juxtaposition, the sense of mutual trust between people who live side by side, was eaten away; and people who lived not only

[10] See pp. 74–75.

in the same country, but in the same town, the same street, or even the same house, turned against each other in the name of a higher cause.

For about five years, beginning in 1567, it seemed that the Catholic cause might prevail. The great crusade took the offensive on all fronts. In 1567 Philip sent a new and firmer governor-general to the Netherlands, the Duke of Alva, with 20,000 Spanish soldiers; the duke proceeded to suppress religious and political dissidents by establishing a Council of Troubles. In 1569 Philip put down a revolt of the Moriscos in Spain. In the same year the Catholics of northern England, led by the Duke of Norfolk, and sewing the cross of crusaders on their garments, rose in armed rebellion against their heretic queen. In the next year, 1570, the pope excommunicated Elizabeth, and absolved her subjects from allegiance to her, so that English Catholics, if they wished, could henceforth in good conscience conspire to overthrow her. In 1571 the Spanish won a great naval battle against the Turks, at Lepanto off the coast of Greece; on their sails they wove the same cross that had been raised at the other corner of Europe, by the Duke of Norfolk in England; and they themselves believed that they were carrying on the crusades of the Middle Ages. In the next year, 1572, the Catholic leaders of France, with the advice of the pope and of Philip II, decided to make an end of the Huguenots, or French Protestants. Over three thousand were seized and put to death on the eve of St. Bartholomew's Day in Paris alone; and this massacre was followed by lesser liquidations throughout the provinces. At the news of St. Bartholomew Philip II is reported to have laughed aloud, and the pope, Gregory XIII, declaring it "more agreeable than fifty Lepantos," had the scenes in Paris painted by the Italian artist Vasari, and issued a medal, *Ugonotorum strages,* "Destruction of the Huguenots."

But none of these victories proved enduring. The Turkish power was not seriously damaged at Lepanto. In fact, the Turks took Tunis from Philip two years later. The Moriscos were not assimilated. The English Catholic rebellion was stamped out; eight hundred persons were put to death by Elizabeth's government. The revolt in the Netherlands remained very much alive, as did the French Huguenots. Twenty years later England was Protestant, the Dutch were winning independence, a Huguenot had become king of France, and the Spanish fleet had gone to ruin in northern waters. Let us see how these events came to pass.

The Revolt of the
Netherlands

The Netherlands, or Low Countries (they had no other name), roughly comprised the area of the modern kingdoms of the Netherlands and Belgium and the grand duchy of Luxembourg. They consisted of seventeen provinces, which in the fifteenth century, one by one, had been inherited, purchased, or conquered by the dukes of Burgundy, from whom they were inherited by Charles V and his son Philip II. In the mid-sixteenth century neither a Dutch nor a Belgian nationality yet existed. In the northern provinces the people spoke German dialects; in the southern provinces they spoke dialects of French, but neither here, nor elsewhere in Europe, was it felt that language boundaries had anything to do with political borders. The southern provinces had for centuries been busy commercial centers, and we have seen how

Antwerp, having once flourished on trade with Venice, now flourished on trade with Lisbon. The northern provinces, or rather the two of them which were most open to the sea, the counties of Holland and Zeeland, had developed rapidly in the fifteenth century. They had a popular literature of their own, written in their own kind of German, which came to be called Dutch. The lay piety of the Brothers of the Common Life had originated in this region, and here Erasmus of Rotterdam had been born. The wealth of the northern provinces was drawn from deep-sea fishing. Holland, observed one traveler, had no vineyards, yet nowhere was wine more bibulously consumed; it had neither wool nor flax, yet all the world knew its woolen and linen fabrics. Wines, wool, and flax all came originally to Holland in exchange for fish. Amsterdam was said to be built on herring bones, and the Dutch, when they added trading to fishing, still lived by the sea.

The northern provinces felt no tie with each other and no sense of difference from the southern. Each of the seventeen provinces was a small state or country in itself. Each province enjoyed typical medieval liberties, privileges, and immunities, including the right to preserve its own law and consent to its own taxes. This constitution of the Netherlands, for such it was, went under the name of the *Joyeuse Entrée,* from the "joyous entry" made by the reigning duke into Brussels in 1355 after a solemn promise to recognize the liberties of the province of Brabant. The common bond of all seventeen provinces was simply that beginning with the dukes of Burgundy they had the same ruler; but since they had the same ruler they were called upon from time to time to send delegates to an estates-general, and so developed an embryonic sense of federal collaboration. The feeling of Netherlandish identity was heightened with the accession of Philip II, for Philip, unlike his father, was thought of as foreign, a Spaniard who lived in Spain; and after 1560 Spanish governors-general, Spanish officials, and Spanish troops were seen more frequently in the Netherlands. Moreover, since the Netherlands was the crossroads of Europe, with a tradition of earnestness in religion, Protestant ideas took root very early, and after 1560, when the religious wars began in France, a great many French Calvinists fled across the borders. At first, there were probably more Calvinists in the southern provinces than in the northern, more among the people that we now call Belgians than among those that we now call Dutch.

The revolt against Philip II was inextricably political and religious at the same time, and it became increasingly an economic struggle as the years went by. It began in 1566, when some two hundred nobles of the various provinces founded a league to check the "foreign" or Spanish influence in the Netherlands. The league, to which both Catholic and Protestant nobles belonged, petitioned Philip II not to employ the Spanish Inquisition in the Netherlands. They feared the trouble it would stir up; they feared it as a foreign court; they feared that in the enforcement of its rulings the liberties of their provinces would be crushed. Philip's agents in the Netherlands refused the petition. A mass revolt now broke out. Within a week fanatical Calvinists pillaged four hundred churches, pulling down images, breaking stained-glass windows, defacing paintings and tapestries, making off with gold chalices, destroying with a fierce contempt the symbols of "popery" and "idolatry."

The fury spread from town to town, to Antwerp, to Amsterdam, to Armentières (now in France, but then in the Netherlands); it was chiefly journeymen wage earners, numerous in the industrial Netherlands, and aroused by social and economic grievances as well as religious belief, who formed the rank-and-file for these anti-Catholic and anti-Spanish demonstrations. Before such vandalism many of the petitioning nobles recoiled; the Catholics among them, as well as less militant Protestants, unable to control their revolutionary followers, began to look upon the Spanish authorities with less disfavor.

Philip II, appalled at the sacrilege, forthwith sent in the Inquisition, the Duke of Alva, and reinforcements of Spanish troops. Alva's Council of Troubles, nicknamed the Council of Blood, sentenced some thousands to death, levied new taxes, and confiscated the estates of a number of important nobles. These measures united people of all classes in opposition; and what might have been primarily a class conflict took on the character of a national opposition. At its head emerged one of the noblemen whose estates had been confiscated, William of Orange (called William the Silent), Philip II's "stadholder" or lieutenant in the County of Holland. Beginning to claim the authority of a sovereign, he issued letters of marque, or authorizations to ship captains—Dutch, Danes, Scots, English—to make war at sea. Fishing crews, "sea dogs," and downright pirates began to raid the small port towns of the Netherlands and France, descending upon them without warning, desecrating the churches, looting, torturing, and killing, in a wild combination of religious rage, political hatred, and lust for booty. The Spanish reciprocated by renewing their confiscations, their

0 10 20 30 40 50 miles

NORTH SEA

FRIESLAND

IJSSEL MEER

HOLLAND

OVERIJSSEL

Amsterdam

The Hague
Ryswick

Utrecht

Münster

ZEELAND

THE GENERALITY

Rhine R.

Bruges

Antwerp

BRABANT

Calais

Ghent

Meuse R.

FLANDERS

Lille

Brussels

LIÈGE

Cologne

Aix-la-Chapelle

Liège

ARTOIS

Scheldt R.

HAINAULT

FRANCE

LUXEMBOURG

Trier

Spanish (Belgian) Netherlands

United Provinces, Independent, 1572, 1609, 1648

Church Lands

—— Boundary of Holy Roman Empire

The Low Countries 1648. *This group of towns and provinces, along the lower reaches of the Rhine, Meuse and Scheldt rivers, originated in the Middle Ages as part of the Holy Roman Empire. The northern or Dutch provinces were recognized as independent of the Empire in 1648. Early in the seventeenth century a political frontier emerged between the "Dutch" and "Belgian" parts, but the word "Belgium" was not used until much later, the southern or Habsburg provinces being called the Spanish Netherlands in the seventeenth century and the Austrian Netherlands in the eighteenth. The large bishopric of Liège remained a separate church-state until the French Revolution. The language frontier, then as now, ran roughly east and west through Brussels, with French to the south and Flemish (a form of Dutch, and hence Germanic) to the north of the line.*

inquisitorial tortures, and their burnings and hangings. The Netherlands was racked by anarchy, revolution, and civil war. No lines were clear, either political or religious. But in 1576 the anti-Spanish feeling prevailed over religious difference when representatives of all seventeen provinces, putting aside the religious question, formed a union to drive out the Spanish at any cost.

But the Netherlands revolution, though it was a national revolution with political independence as its first aim, was only part of the international politico-religious struggle. All sorts of other interests became involved in it. Queen Elizabeth of England lent aid to the Netherlands, though for many years surreptitiously, not wishing to provoke a war with Spain, in which it was feared that English Catholics might side with the Spaniards. Elizabeth was troubled by having on her hands an unwanted guest, Mary Queen of Scots, a Catholic who had been queen of France until her husband's premature death, and queen of Scotland until driven out by irate Calvinist lords, and who—if the pope, the king of Spain, the Society of Jesus, and many English Catholics were to have their way—would also be queen of England instead of the usurper Elizabeth.[11] Elizabeth under these circumstances kept Mary Stuart imprisoned. Many intrigues were afoot to put Mary on the English throne, some with, and some without, Mary's knowledge.

In 1576 Don Juan, hero of Lepanto, and half-brother of Philip II, became governor-general of the embattled Netherlands. It was his grandiose idea, formed after consultations in Rome, not merely to subdue the Netherlands but to use that country as a base for an invasion of England, and after overthrowing Elizabeth with Spanish troops, to put Mary Stuart on the throne, marry her himself, and so become king of a re-Catholicized England. Thus the security of Elizabethan and Protestant England was coming to depend on the outcome of fighting in the Netherlands. Elizabeth signed an alliance with the Netherlands patriots and countered with another intrigue. The Virgin Queen, throughout her long reign, used the approaches of suitors to political advantage, and it now happened that certain French Huguenots hoped to marry the Duke of Alençon to Elizabeth. Alençon had already led a French force into the Netherlands to assist the anti-Spanish revolutionaries in that country; and his followers believed that, as husband to the queen of England, he would receive enough support from her to set up a Protestant kingdom in the seventeen provinces, with himself as king. Elizabeth gave him grounds for hope, enough to keep him in the field against the Spanish, but in the end rejected his highly political courtship, having no intention of becoming too involved on the Continent.

Don Juan died in 1578 and was succeeded as governor-general of the Netherlands by the prince of Parma. A diplomat as well as a soldier, Parma broke the solid front of the seventeen provinces by a mixture of force and persuasion. He promised that the historic liberties of the *Joyeuse Entrée* would be respected, and he

---

[11] Mary Stuart was the next lawful heir to the English throne after Elizabeth, since Elizabeth had no children, and Mary Stuart was a great-granddaughter of Henry VII.

appealed not only to the more zealous Catholics but to moderates who were wearying of the struggle and repelled by mob violence and religious vandalism. On this basis he rallied the southernmost provinces to his side. The seven northern provinces, led by Holland and Zeeland, responded by forming the Union of Utrecht in 1579. In 1581 they formally declared their independence from the king of Spain, calling themselves the United Provinces of the Netherlands. Thus originated what was more commonly called the Dutch Republic, or simply "Holland" in view of the predominance of that county among the seven. The great Flemish towns, Antwerp, Ghent, and Bruges, at first sided with the Union.

Where formerly all had been turmoil, a geographical line was now drawn. A south rallied to Philip II now faced a still rebellious north. But neither side accepted any such partition. Parma still fought to reconquer the north, and the Dutch, led by William the Silent, still struggled to clear the Spanish out of all seventeen provinces. Meanwhile the two sides fought to capture the intermediate Flemish cities. When Parma moved upon Antwerp, still the leading port of the North Sea, and one from which an invasion of England could best be mounted, Elizabeth at last openly entered the war on the side of the rebels, sending six thousand English troops to the Netherlands under the Earl of Leicester in 1585.

England was now clearly emerging as the chief bulwark of Protestantism and of anti-Spanish feeling in northwestern Europe. In England itself, the popular fears of Spain, the popular resentment against Catholic plots revolving about Mary Stuart, and the popular indignation at "foreign" and "outside" meddling in English matters produced an unprecedented sense of national solidarity. The country rallied to Protestantism and to Elizabeth, and even the Catholic minority for the most part disowned the conspiracies against her. The English were now openly and defiantly allied with the Protestant Dutch. Not only were they fighting together in the Netherlands, but both English and Dutch sea-raiders fell upon Spanish shipping, captured the treasure ships, and even pillaged the Spanish Main, the mainland coast of northern South America. The Dutch were beginning to penetrate East Indian waters. Elizabeth was negotiating with Scotland, with German Calvinists and French Huguenots. At the Escorial it was said that the Netherlands could only be rewon by an invasion of England, that the queen of the heretics must be at last dethroned, that in any case it was cheaper to launch a gigantic attack upon England than to pay the cost of protecting Spanish galleons, year after year, against the depredations of piratical sea dogs.

Philip II therefore prepared to invade England. The English retorted with vigor. Mary Stuart, after almost twenty years' imprisonment, was executed in 1587; an aroused Parliament, more than Elizabeth herself, demanded her life on the eve of foreign attack. Sir Francis Drake, most spectacular of the sea dogs, sailed into the port of Cadiz and burnt the very ships assembling there to join the Armada. This was jocosely described as singeing the beard of the king of Spain.

The great Armada, the *armada católica*, was ready early in 1588. With crosses on the sails, and banners bearing the image of the Holy Virgin, it went forth as to a new Lepanto against the Turks of the north. It consisted of 130 ships, weighing 58,000 tons, carrying 30,000 men and 2,400 pieces of artillery, the most prodigious assemblage of naval power that the world had ever seen. In Spain only the pessimistic observed that its commander was no seaman, that some of its ships were too cumbersome, and some too frail, to weather the gales of the north, that orders had to be issued to its crews in six languages, and the antagonisms of Portuguese, Catalans, Castilians, Irishmen, and émigré English Catholics somehow appeased. The plan was for the fleet to sail to the Netherlands, from which it was to escort the prince of Parma's army across the straits to the English coast. In the Channel the Armada was met by some two hundred English vessels, commanded, under a noble figurehead, by Sir Francis Drake. The English craft, lighter, smaller, and faster, though well furnished with guns, harried the lumbering mass of the Armada, broke up its formations, attacked its great vessels one by one. It found no refuge at Calais, where English fireships drove it out again to sea. Then arose a great storm, the famous "Protestant wind," which blew the broken Armada northward, into seas that to southerners seemed almost polar, around the tip of Scotland, the Orkneys, the Hebrides, and northern Ireland, forbidding coasts which the Spaniards had to skirt without charts or pilots, and which they strewed with their wreckage and their bones.

The war went on for several years. Philip died in 1598, after a long and horrible illness, a frustrated and broken man. In the wars with Spain the English had, above all else, assured their national independence. They had acquired an intense national spirit, a love of "this other Eden, demi-paradise," "this precious stone set in the silver sea," as Shakespeare wrote; and they had become more solidly Protestant, almost unanimously set against "popery." With the ruin of the Armada, they were more free to take to the sea; we have seen how the English East India Company was founded in 1600.

The Results of the Struggle

In the Netherlands, the battle lines swayed back and forth until 1609. In that year a Twelve Years' Truce was agreed to. By this truce the Netherlands were partitioned. The line of partition ran somewhat farther north than it had in Parma's time, for the Spaniards had retaken Antwerp and other cities in the middle zone. The seven provinces north of the line, those that had formed the Union of Utrecht in 1579, were henceforth known as Dutch. The ten provinces south of the line were known as the Spanish Netherlands. Protestants in the south either became Catholics or fled to the north, so that the south (the modern Belgium) became solidly Catholic, while the number of Protestants in the north was increased. Even so, the Dutch were not a completely Protestant people, for probably as many as a third of them remained Catholic. Calvinism was the religion of most Dutch burghers and the religion favored by the state; but in the face of an exceptionally large religious minority the Dutch Netherlands adopted a policy of toleration. The southern Netherlands were ruined by almost forty years of war. The Dutch, moreover, occupied the mouth of the Scheldt and refused to allow ocean-going vessels to proceed upstream to Antwerp or to Ghent. The Scheldt remained "closed" for two centuries, and the Flemish cities never recovered their old position. Amsterdam became the commercial and financial center of northern Europe; it retained its commercial supremacy for a century and its financial supremacy for two centuries. For the Dutch, as for the English, the weakening of Spanish naval power opened the way to the sea. The Dutch East India Company was organized in 1602. Both Dutch and English began to found overseas colonies. Englishmen settled in Virginia in 1607, Dutchmen at New York in 1612.

As for Spain, while it remained the most formidable military power of Europe for another half-century, its internal decline had already begun. At the death of Philip II the monarchy was living from hand to mouth, habitually depending on the next arrival of treasure from the Indies. The productive forces of the country were weakened by inflation, by taxation, by emigration, by depopulation. At Seville, for example, only 400 looms were in operation in 1621, where there had been 16,000 a century earlier. Spain suffered from the very circumstances that made it great. The qualities most useful in leading the Counter Reformation were not those on which a modern society could most easily be built. The generations of crusading against infidels, heathen, and heretics had produced an exceptionally large number of minor aristocrats, chevaliers, dons, and *hidalgos,* who as a class were contemptuous of work, content with small incomes, and generally idle, and who were numerous enough and close enough to the common people to impress their haughty indifference upon the country as a whole. The wealth of America gave the government and some of the upper classes an easy income, leaving them without incentive to encourage commerce or manufacturing and in any case ignorant of real economic questions. With the extreme concentration on religion the ablest men entered the church, and so great was the popular admiration for saints and mystics, missionaries and crusaders, theologians, archbishops, ascetics, and begging friars, that more-secular activities offered little psychological satisfaction or reward.

The very unity accomplished under Ferdinand and Isabella threatened to dissolve. After more than a century of the Inquisition people were still afraid of false Christians and crypto-Moslems. The question of the Moriscos rose again in 1608.[12] The Moriscos included some of the best farmers and most skilled artisans in the country. They lived in almost all parts of Spain; they were in no sense a "foreign" element; they were simply the descendants of those Spaniards who, in the Moslem period, which had begun 900 years before, had adopted the Moslem religion and Arabic language and culture. They were now supposedly Christian, but the true and pure Christians accused them of preserving in secret the rites of Islam and of sympathy for the Barbary pirates. They were thought to be clannish, marrying among themselves; and they were so efficient, sober, and hard-working that they outdistanced other Spaniards in competition. In 1609 some 150,000 Moriscos were driven out of Valencia; in 1610 some 64,000 were driven from Aragon; in 1611 an unknown number were expelled from Castile. All were simply put on boats and sent off with what they could carry. Spain, whose total population was rapidly falling in any case, thus lost one of the most socially valuable, if not religiously orthodox, of all its minorities.

134   [12]See p. 75.

Nor could the Christian kingdoms hold peaceably together. In 1640 Portugal, which had been joined to the Spanish crown since 1580 when its own ruling line had run out, reestablished its independence. That same year Catalonia rose in open rebellion. The Catalan war, in which the French streamed across the Pyrenees to aid the rebels, lasted for almost twenty years. Catalonia was at last reconquered, but it managed to preserve its old privileges and separate identity. Catalan and Castilian viewed each other with increased repugnance. The Spanish kingdoms were hardly more unified, in spirit or in institutions, than in the days of Isabella and Ferdinand. They suffered, too, during the seventeenth century from a line of kings whose mental peculiarities reached the point of positive imbecility. Meanwhile, however, the might of Spain was still to be felt in both Germany and France.

Both France and Germany, in the so-called Wars of Religion, fell into an advanced state of decomposition, France in almost forty years of civil war between 1562 and 1598, Germany in a long period of civil troubles culminating in the Thirty Years' War between 1618 and 1648. From this decomposition France recovered in the seventeenth century, but Germany did not.

14
The Disintegration and Reconstruction of France

Political and Religious Disunity

The Wars of Religion in France, despite the religious ferocity shown by partisans of both sides, were no more religious than they were political and were essentially a new form of the old phenomenon of feudal rebellion against a higher central authority. "Feudal," when the word is used of the sixteenth, seventeenth, or eighteenth century, generally refers not to nobles only, but to all sorts of component groups having rights within the state, and so includes towns and provinces, and even craft gilds and courts of law, in addition to the church and the noble class. It remained to be seen whether all these elements could be welded into one body politic.

In France the New Monarchy, resuming the work of medieval kings, had imposed a certain unity on the country.[13] Normally, or apart from civil war, the country acted as a unit in foreign affairs. The king alone made treaties, and in war his subjects all fought on his side, if they fought at all. Internally, the royal centralization was largely administrative; that is, the king and those who worked for him dealt with subordinate bodies of all kinds, while these subordinate bodies remained in existence with their own functions and personnel. France by the ideas of the time was a very large country. It was three times as large as England and five times as populous. At a time when the traveler could move hardly thirty miles a day it took three weeks of steady plodding to cross the kingdom. Local influence was therefore very strong. Beneath the platform of royalty there was almost as little substantial unity in France as in the Holy Roman Empire. Where the Empire had three hundred "states," France had

[13] See pp. 71–74.

some three hundred areas with their own legal systems. Where the Empire had free cities, France had *bonnes villes,* the king's "good towns," each with its stubbornly defended corporate rights. Where the Empire had middle-sized states like Bavaria, France had provinces as great as some European kingdoms—Brittany, Burgundy, Provence, Languedoc—each ruled by the French king, to be sure, but each with its own identity, autonomy, laws, courts, tariffs, taxes, and parliament or Provincial Estates. To all this diversity, in France as in Germany, was now added diversity of religion. Calvin himself was by birth and upbringing a Frenchman. Calvinism spread in France very rapidly. The difference between Calvinism and Catholicism, let it be repeated, was not a mere difference of opinion, involving only freedom of "thought"; it was a difference on the nature and function of the church, which was still the principal public institution, and it manifested itself in the outward habits of daily life.

France was not much attached to a papal, Rome-centered, or international Catholicism. The French clergy had long struggled for its national or Gallican liberties; the French kings had dealt rudely with popes, ignored the Council of Trent, and allied for political reasons with both the Lutherans and the Turks. Since 1516 the king of France had the right to nominate the French bishops. The fact that both the monarchy and the clergy felt already independent of Rome, and so had less sense of grievance against Rome than was common in Germany in Luther's day, held them back from the revolutionary solutions of Protestantism. The Protestantism which did spread in France was of the most clear-cut and radical kind, namely, Calvinism, which preached at kings, attacked bishops, and smashed religious images and desecrated the churches. Even in countries that became Protestant—England, north Germany, even the Netherlands—this extreme Protestantism was the doctrine of a minority. In France there was no middle-of-the-road Protestantism, no broad and comfortable Anglicanism, no half-way Lutheranism inspired by governments, and in the long run, as will be seen, the middle of the road was occupied by Catholics.

At first, however, the Huguenots, as the French Calvinists were called, though always a minority, were neither a small one nor modest in their demands. In a class analysis, it is clear that it was chiefly the nobility that was attracted to Protestantism, though of course it does not follow that most French Protestants were nobles, since the nobility was a small class. More than a third, and possibly almost a half, of the French nobility was Protestant in the 1560s or 1570s. Frequently the *seigneur,* or lord of one or more manors, believed that he should have the *ius reformandi,* or right to regulate religion on his own estates, as the princes of Germany decided the religion of their own territories. It thus happened that a lord might defy the local bishop, put a Calvinist minister in his village church, throw out the images, simplify the sacraments, and have the service conducted in French. In this way peasants also became Huguenots. Occasionally peasants turned Huguenot without encouragement by the lord. It was chiefly in southwestern France that Protestantism spread as a general movement affecting whole areas. But in all parts of the country, north as well as south, many towns converted to Protestantism. Usually this meant that the bourgeois oligarchy, into whose hands town government had generally fallen, went over to Calvinism and thereupon banned Catholic services, of which the sequel might be either that the journeymen wage earners followed along, or that, estranged by the class differences whose development has been described above, they remained attached to their old priests.[14]   In general, the unskilled laboring mass probably remained the least touched of all classes by Calvinist doctrine.

Both Francis I and Henry II opposed the spread of Calvinism—as did Lutheran and Anglican rulers—for Calvinism, a kind of grassroots movement in religion, rising spontaneously among laity and reforming ministers, seemed to threaten not only the powers of monarchy but the very idea of a nationally established church.   The fact that in France the nobility, a traditionally ungovernable class, figured prominently in the movement only made it look the more like political or feudal rebellion. Persecution of Huguenots, with burnings at the stake, began in the 1550s.

Then in 1559 King Henry II was accidentally killed in a tournament.   He left three sons, of whom the eldest in 1559 was only fifteen.   Their mother, Henry's widow, was Catherine de' Medici, an Italian woman who brought to France some of the polish of Renaissance Italy, along with some of its taste for political intrigue and inclination to vices both natural and unnatural, all of which, for thirty years, she exploited in the attempt to govern a distracted country for her royal sons.   (Their names were Francis II, who died in 1560, Charles IX, who died in 1574, and Henry III, who lasted until 1589.)   The trouble was that, with no firm hand in control of the monarchy, the country fell apart, and that in the ensuing chaos various powerful factions tried to get control of the youthful, effeminate, and entirely ineffectual monarchs for their own purposes.   Among these factions were both Huguenots and Catholics.   The Huguenots, under persecution, were too strong a minority to go into hiding.   Counting among their number a third or more of the professional warrior class, the nobles, they took naturally and aggressively to arms.

Exact history distinguishes no less than nine civil wars in the concluding four decades of the sixteenth century in France, but in this history they will be telescoped together.   They were not civil wars of the kind where one region of a country takes up arms against another, each retaining some apparatus of government, as in the American Civil War or the civil wars of the seventeenth century in England.   They were civil wars of the kind fought in the absence of government.   Roving bands of armed men, without territorial base or regular means of subsistence, wandered about the country, fighting and plundering, joining or separating from other similar bands, in shifting hosts that were quickly formed or quickly dissolved.   The underlying social conditions, the incessant rise of prices, detached many people from their old routines, made it impossible for small gentry or wageworkers to live on their incomes, and threw them into a life of adventure.   The more prominent leaders could thus easily obtain followers, and at the coming of such cohorts the peasants usually took to the woods, while bourgeois would lock the gates of their cities.   Or else peasants would form protective leagues, like vigilantes; and even small towns maintained diminutive armies.

---

[14] See pp. 121–122.

The Huguenots were led by various personages of rank, such as Admiral de Coligny and Henry of Bourbon, king of Navarre, a small independent kingdom at the foot of the Pyrenees between Spain and France. A pronounced Catholic party arose under the Guise family, headed by the Duke of Guise and the Cardinal of Lorraine. Catherine de' Medici was left in the middle, opposed like all monarchs to Calvinism, but unwilling to fall under the domination of the Guises. While the Guises wished to extirpate heresy they wished even more to govern France. Among the Huguenots, some fought for local liberties in religion, while the more ardent spirits hoped to drive "idolatry" and "popery" out of all France, and indeed out of the world itself. Catherine de' Medici for a time tried to play the two parties against each other. But in 1572, fearing the growing influence of Coligny over the king, and taking advantage of a great concourse of leading Huguenots in Paris to celebrate the marriage of Henry of Navarre, she decided to rid herself of the heads of the Huguenot party at a single blow. In the resulting massacre of St. Bartholomew's Day some thousands of Huguenots were dragged from their beds after midnight and unceremoniously murdered. Coligny was killed; Henry of Navarre escaped by temporarily changing his religion.

This outrage only aroused Huguenot fury, and led to a renewal of civil war, with mounting atrocities committed by both sides. The armed bands slaughtered each other and terrorized noncombatants. Both parties hired companies of mercenary soldiers, mainly from Germany. Spanish troops invaded France at the invitation of the Guises. Protestant towns, like Rouen and La Rochelle, appealed to Elizabeth of England, reminding her that kings of England had once reigned over their parts of France, inviting English invasion and a renewal of the horrors of the Hundred Years' War; but Elizabeth was too preoccupied with her own problems to give more than very sporadic and insignificant assistance. Neither side could subdue the other, and hence there were numerous truces, during which fighting still flared up, since no one had the power to impose peace. The truces usually acknowledged the status quo, allowing Protestant worship locally in places where it was actually going on; but the Protestants felt no security in such terms, nor were Catholics satisfied at such recognition of heresy, so that each truce expired in further war.

Gradually, mainly among the more perfunctory Catholics, but also among moderate Protestants, there developed still another group, who thought of themselves as the "politicals" or *politiques*. The *politiques* were men who concluded that too much was being made of religion, that no doctrine was important enough to justify everlasting war, that perhaps after all there might be room for two churches, and that what the country needed above all else was civil order. Theirs was the secular not the religious view. They believed that men lived primarily in the state, not in the church. They were willing to overlook a man's ideas if only he would obey the king and go peaceably about his business. To escape anarchy they put their hopes in the institution of monarchy. Henry of Navarre, now again a Protestant, was at heart a *politique*. Another was the political philosopher Jean Bodin (1530–1596), the first thinker to develop the modern theory of sovereignty. He held that in every society there must be one power strong enough to give law to all others, with their consent if possible, without their consent if necessary. Thus from the disorders of the religious wars in France was germinated the idea of royal absolutism and of the sovereign state.

In 1589 both Henry III, the reigning king, and Henry of Guise, the Catholic party chief who was trying to depose him, were assassinated, each by a partisan of the other. The throne now came by legal inheritance to the third of the three Henrys, Henry of Navarre, the Huguenot chieftain. He reigned as Henry IV. Most popular and most amiably remembered of all French kings, except for medieval St. Louis, he was the first of the Bourbon dynasty, which was to last until the French Revolution.

The civil wars did not end with the accession of Henry IV. The Catholic party refused to recognize him, set up a pretender against him, and called in the Spaniards. Henry, the *politique,* sensed that the majority of the French people were still Catholic, and that the Huguenots were not only a minority but after thirty years of civil strife an increasingly unpopular minority kept going as a political party by obstinate nobles. Paris especially, Catholic throughout the wars, refused to admit the heretic king within its gates. Supposedly remarking that "Paris is well worth a Mass," Henry IV in 1593 abjured the Calvinist faith, and subjected himself to the elaborate processes of papal absolution. Thereupon the *politiques* and less excitable Catholics consented to work with him. The Huguenots, at first elated that their leader should become king, were now not only outraged by Henry's abjuration but alarmed for their own safety. They demanded not only religious liberty, but positive guarantees.

Henry IV in 1598 responded by issuing the Edict of Nantes. The Edict granted to every *seigneur,* or noble who was also a manorial lord, the right to hold Protestant services in his own household. It allowed Protestantism in towns where it was in fact the prevailing form of worship, and in any case in one town of each *baillage* (a unit corresponding somewhat to the English shire) throughout the country; but it barred it from Catholic episcopal towns and from a zone surrounding and including the city of Paris. It promised that Protestants should enjoy the same civil rights as Catholics, the same chance for public office, and access to the Catholic universities. In certain of the superior law courts it created "mixed chambers" of both Protestants and Catholics—somewhat as if a stated minority representation were to be legally required in United States federal courts today. The Edict also gave Protestants their own means of defense, granting them about a hundred fortified towns to be held by Protestant garrisons under Protestant command.

The Huguenot minority, reassured by the Edict of Nantes, became less of a rebellious element within the state. The majority of the French people viewed the Edict with suspicion. The *parlements,* or supreme law courts, of Paris, Bordeaux, Toulouse, Aix, and Rennes all refused to recognize it as the law of the land. It was the king who forced toleration upon the country. He silenced the *parlements,* and subdued Catholic opposition by doing favors for the Jesuits. France's chief minority was thus protected by the central government, not by popular wishes. Where in England the Catholic minority had no rights at all, and in Germany the religious question was settled only by cutting the country into small and hostile fragments, in France a compromise was effected, by which the Protestant minority had both individual and territorial rights. A considerable number of French statesmen, generals, and other important persons in the seventeenth century were Protestants.

Henry IV, having appeased the religious controversy, did everything that he could to let the country gradually recover, to replant, rebuild, transact business, and rediscover the arts of peace. His ideal, as he breezily put it, was a "chicken in the pot" for every Frenchman. He worked also to put the ruined government back together, to collect taxes, pay officials, discipline the army, and supervise the administration of justice. Roads and bridges were repaired, new manufactures were introduced under mercantilist principles, and the export of grain was legalized so that peasant landowners would have a better market. Never throughout his reign of twenty-one years did he summon the Estates-General. A country that had just hacked itself to pieces in civil war was scarcely able to govern itself, and so, under Henry IV, the foundations of the later royal absolutism of the Bourbons were laid down.

Henry IV was assassinated in 1610 by a crazed fanatic who believed him a menace to the Catholic church. Under his widow, Marie de' Medici, the nobility and upper Catholic clergy again grew restless and forced the summoning of the Estates-General, in which so many conflicting and mutually distrustful interests were represented that no program could be adopted, and Marie dismissed them in 1615 to the general relief of all concerned. No Estates-General of the kingdom as a whole thereafter met until the French Revolution. National government was to be conducted by and through the king.

Cardinal Richelieu

In the name of Marie de' Medici and her young son, Louis XIII, the control of affairs gradually came into the hands of an ecclesiastic, Cardinal Richelieu. In the preceding generation Richelieu might have been called a *politique.* It was the state, not the church, whose interests he worked to further. He tried to strengthen the state economically by mercantilistic edicts. He attempted to draw impoverished gentlemen into trade by allowing them to engage in maritime commerce without loss of noble status. For wholesale merchants, as an incentive, he made it possible to become nobles, in return for payments into the royal exchequer. He founded and supported many commercial companies on the Anglo-Dutch model.

For a time it seemed that civil war might break out again. Nobles still feuded with each other and evaded the royal jurisdiction. Richelieu prohibited private warfare and ordered the destruction of all fortified castles not manned and needed by the king himself. He even prohibited dueling, a custom much favored by the d'Artagnans of the day, but regarded by Richelieu as a mere remnant of private war. The Huguenots, too, with their own towns and their own armed forces under the Edict of Nantes, had become something of a state within the state. In 1627 the Duke of Rohan led a Huguenot rebellion, based on the city of La Rochelle, which received military support from the English. Richelieu after a year suppressed the rebellion, and in 1629, by the Peace of Alais, amended the Edict of Nantes. For this highly secularized cardinal of the Catholic church it was agreeable for the Protestants to keep their religion, but not for them to share in the instruments of political power. The Huguenots lost, in 1629, their fortified cities, their Protestant armies, and all their military and territorial rights, but in their religious and civil rights they were not officially molested for another fifty years.

The French monarchy no sooner reestablished itself after the civil wars than it began to recur to the old foreign policy of Francis I, who had opposed on every front the European supremacy of the house of Habsburg.[15] The Spanish power still encircled France at the Pyrenees, in the Mediterranean, in the Free County of Burgundy, and in Belgium. The Austrian branch had pretensions to supremacy in Germany and all central Europe. Richelieu found his opportunity to assail the Habsburgs in the civil struggles which now began to afflict Germany.

T he Holy Roman Empire extended from France on the west to Poland and Hungary on the east. It included the Czechs of Bohemia, and sizable French-speaking populations in what are now Belgium, Lorraine, eastern Burgundy, and western Switzerland; but with these exceptions the Empire was made up of Germans.[16] Language, however, was far less important than religion as the tie which people felt to be basic to a community; and in religion the Empire was almost evenly divided. Where in England, after stabilization set in, Roman Catholics sank to a minority of some 3 percent, and in France the Huguenots fell to not much over 5 percent, in Germany there was no true minority, and hence no majority, and religion gave no ground for national concentration. Possibly there were more Protestants than Catholics in the Empire in 1600, for not only was Protestantism the state religion in many of the 300 states, but individual Protestants were exceedingly numerous in the legally Catholic states of the Austrian Habsburgs. Bohemia had a Protestant majority, rooted in the Czech people, and even in Austria, in meetings of the estates, the Protestants sometimes prevailed. Farther east, outside the Holy Roman Empire, the Hungarian nobles were mainly Protestant, and Transylvania, in the elbow of the Carpathian mountains, was an active center of Calvinism.

In 1500 Germany had led in the life of Europe, but in 1600 it showed evidences of backwardness and provincialism. Literature had declined, and the language itself became barbarized and ungainly. Where both Catholics and Calvinists recognized international affiliations and read with interest books written in other countries, Lutherans were suspicious of the world outside the Lutheran states of Germany and Scandinavia, and hence suffered from a cultural isolation. The German universities, both Lutheran and Catholic, attracted fewer students than formerly, and their intellectual effort was consumed in combative dogmatics, each side demonstrating

15
The Thirty Years' War, 1618–1648: The Disintegration of Germany

---

[15] See map, pp. 72–73; and p. 81.
[16] See maps, pp. 72–73, 148–149.

the truth of its own ideas. Nowhere was superstition so rife as in Germany. More witches were burned there than elsewhere, the popular fairy tales were more gruesome, and the educated were more fascinated by astrology. The commerce of south Germany and the Rhineland was in decay, both because of the shift of trade to the Atlantic and because the Dutch controlled the mouth of the Rhine in their own interests. The Baltic trade was rapidly growing, but it was not the old German Hanseatic towns that benefited. The king of Denmark controlled the Sound, or mouth of the Baltic, and the king of Sweden most of its shores; these two rulers opened the Baltic to the Dutch and English, and the old German trading towns could not compete with merchants who had the backing of national monarchs. German bankers, such as the Fuggers, were of slight importance after 1600. It was now in the West that capital was being formed.

The Peace of Augsburg in 1555, with its principle of *cuius regio eius religio,* had provided that in each state the government could prescribe the religion of its subjects.[17] In some states an abbot or an archbishop or bishop himself constituted the government. In these cases, whenever an incumbent died, there was a race to name his successor, to secure the territory as Lutheran or Catholic. In 1593 a small war was fought for the control of Aix-la-Chapelle, in 1600 another for the control of Cologne. In general, in the decades following the Peace of Augsburg, the Lutherans made considerable gains, putting Lutheran administrators into the church states, or "secularizing" them and converting them into lay principalities. The Catholics did not accept this constant attrition, which violated the Ecclesiastical Reservation of the Peace of Augsburg. In addition, Calvinism spread into Germany. Though Calvinists had no rights under the Peace of Augsburg, a number of states became Calvinist. One of these was the Palatinate, important because it was strategically placed across the middle Rhine, and because its ruler, the Elector Palatine, was one of the seven persons who elected the Holy Roman Emperor. In 1608 the Protestant states, urged on by the Elector Palatine, formed a Protestant union to defend their gains. To obtain support, they negotiated with the Dutch, with the English, and with Henry IV of France. In 1609 a league of Catholic German states was organized by Bavaria. It looked for help from Spain.

The Germans were thus falling apart, or rather coming together, into two parties in anticipation of a religious war, and each party solicited foreign assistance against the other. Other issues were also maturing. The Twelve Years' Truce between Spain and the Dutch, signed in 1609, was due to expire in 1621. The Spanish (whose military power was still unaffected by internal decline) were again preparing to crush the Dutch Republic, or, at the very least, to open the mouth of the Scheldt and to get Dutch traders out of the East Indies. Since the Dutch insisted on independence, and were in any case unwilling to leave the Indies or to remove their stranglehold on the

[17]See pp. 81–82.

port of Antwerp, a renewal of the Dutch-Spanish war appeared to be inevitable. The Spanish also wished to consolidate the Habsburg position in central Europe. From Milan in north Italy they proposed to build up a fork of territory, one of whose prongs would lead through the easternmost of the Swiss cantons direct to Habsburg Austria, the other through the westernmost Swiss cantons to the valley of the Rhine. There, on and near the Rhine, if they could conquer a few states like the Calvinistic Palatinate, they might join the Netherlands and Franche-Comté (the Free County of Burgundy, ruled by Spain) into a large and continuous territorial block.[18] These Spanish designs in the Rhineland and Switzerland naturally aroused the opposition of France. Moreover, the Austrian branch of the Habsburg family was slowly bestirring itself to eradicate Protestantism in its own domains and even to turn the Holy Roman Empire into a more modern and national type of state. The idea of a strong power in Germany was abhorrent to the French. France, through opposition to the Habsburgs, was again put in the position of chief protector of Protestantism. France, as we have observed, was a giant of Europe, five times as populous as England, over ten times as populous as Sweden or the Dutch Republic, incomparably more populous than any single German state. And France after 1600 was at last unified within—at least relatively. As a French writer has observed, speaking of these years, the appearance of the fleur-de-lis upon the Rhine would tumble to the ground the vast projects of the Counter Reformation.

The Thirty Years' War, resulting from all these pressures, was therefore exceedingly complex. It was a German civil war fought over the Catholic-Protestant issue. It was also a German civil war fought over constitutional issues, between the emperor striving to build up the central power of the Empire and the member states struggling to maintain independence. These two civil wars by no means coincided, for Catholic and Protestant states were alike in objecting to imperial control. It was also an international war, between France and the Habsburgs, between Spain and the Dutch, with the kings of Denmark and Sweden and the prince of Transylvania becoming involved, and with all these outsiders finding allies within Germany, on whose soil most of the battles were fought. The wars were further complicated by the fact that many of the generals were soldiers of fortune, who aspired to create principalities of their own, and who fought or refused to fight to suit their own convenience. Allies became fearful of each other's successes and so changed their aims while operations were still in progress. The powers which sought to crush each other were themselves highly vulnerable; France, Spain, and the Austrian realms were all weakened by collusion of their own subjects with the enemy during hostilities. The whole struggle, resembling nothing so much as the croquet game in *Alice in Wonderland* where the players used the necks of flamingoes for mallets and hedgehogs for balls, was too fluctuating, oblique, contradictory, and protracted to be recounted in any detail. Yet it was the greatest of all European wars before the time of the French Revolution.

[18]See map, pp. 148–149.

The fighting began in Bohemia. It is in fact customary to divide the war into four phases, the Bohemian (1618–1625), the Danish (1625–1629), the Swedish (1630–1635), and the Swedish-French (1635–1648).

In 1618 the Bohemians, or Czechs, fearing the loss of their Protestant liberties, dealt with two emissaries from the Habsburg Holy Roman Emperor, Matthias (who was also their king), by a method occasionally used in that country—throwing them out of the window. After this "defenestration of Prague" the king-emperor sent troops to restore his authority, whereupon the Bohemians deposed him and elected a new king. In order to obtain Protestant assistance, they chose the Calvinist Elector Palatine, the head of the Protestant Union. This young man proceeded to Bohemia, where he assumed the title of Frederick V. He brought aid to the Bohemians from the Protestant Union, the Dutch sent money, and the prince of Transylvania harried the Habsburg rear. The Emperor Ferdinand, Matthias' successor, assisted by money from the pope, Spanish troops sent up from Milan, and the forces of Catholic Bavaria, and benefiting from the fears felt by Lutherans in the Protestant Union for the radical Calvinism emerging in Bohemia, managed to overwhelm the Bohemians at the battle of the White Mountain in 1620. Frederick fled, jeered or pitied as the "winter king." His ancestral domains in the Palatinate were overrun by the Spaniards.

Two facts emerged in consequence of the Bohemian war. First, the Spaniards were entrenching themselves in the Rhineland, building up their position against the French and the Dutch. Second, Bohemia was reconquered and revolutionized by the Habsburgs. Ferdinand got himself elected again as king. He confiscated the estates of some half the Bohemian nobles. He granted these lands as endowments for Catholic churches, orders, and monasteries, or gave them out to a swarm of adventurers of all nationalities who had entered his service, and who now became the new landed aristocracy of Bohemia. Jesuits streamed in, and through missions and schools, as well as court proceedings and executions, the re-Catholicization of Bohemia began. In Austria also, which had at first joined Bohemia in rebellion, Protestantism was stamped out.

With Protestant fortunes at a low ebb, and the Protestant Union itself dissolved in 1621, the lead in Protestant affairs was now taken by the king of Denmark, who was also Duke of Holstein, a state of the Holy Roman Empire. His aims were well mixed with politics, for he hoped by acquiring a few bishoprics in Germany to construct a kingdom for his younger son. With a little aid from the Dutch and English, and with promises from Richelieu, he entered the fray. Against him the Emperor Ferdinand raised another army, or, rather, commissioned Albert of Wallenstein to raise one on his own private initiative. Wallenstein assembled a force of professional fighters, of all nationalities, who lived by pillage rather than by pay. His army was his personal instrument, not the emperor's, and he therefore followed a policy of his own, which was so tortuous and well concealed that the name of Wallenstein has always remained an enigma. Possibly he dreamed of a united empire and a revived Germany from which foreigners should be expelled; certainly he dreamed of creating a sizable principality for himself. Wallenstein and other imperial generals soon defeated the king of Denmark, reached the Baltic coast and even invaded the Danish peninsula.

The full tide of the Counter Reformation now flowed over Germany. Not only was Catholicism again seeping into the Palatinate, and again flooding Bohemia, but it rolled northward into the inner recesses of the Lutheran states. By the Edict of Restitution, in 1629, the emperor declared all church territories secularized since 1552 automatically restored to the Catholic church. Two archbishoprics, twelve bishoprics, and over a hundred small territories formerly belonging to monasteries and religious orders were involved. Some, like the bishopric of Lübeck, were as far north as the Baltic. Some had been Protestant since the oldest person could remember. Terror swept over Protestant Germany. It seemed that the whole Protestant Reformation, now a century old, might be undone. In addition, the emperor showed signs of wishing to create a Habsburg monarchy over the whole Empire. He talked of holding the seacoast and of putting Germany on the seas, discussed prospects for a Flemish-Spanish-German commercial company to compete with the Danes, Dutch, and English, and endowed Wallenstein, who was besieging the coastal city of Stralsund, with the magniloquent title of Admiral of the Oceanic and Baltic Seas.

Among those to be alarmed were the French and the Swedes. Richelieu, however, was still putting down fractious nobles and Huguenots. He had not yet consolidated France to his satisfaction and believed that France, without fighting itself, could counter the Habsburg ambitions through the use of allies. He sent diplomats to help extricate the king of Sweden from a war with Poland, and he promised him financial assistance, which soon rose to a million livres a year in return for the maintenance in Germany of 40,000 Swedish troops. The Dutch subsidized the Swedes with some 50,000 florins a month.

The king of Sweden was Gustavus Adolphus, a ruler of superlative ability, who had conciliated all parties in Sweden, worked harmoniously with his Estates-General, and thus created a base from which he could safely conduct overseas operations. He had extended Swedish holdings on the east shore of the Baltic. Using Dutch and other military experts, he had created the most modern army of the times, noted for its firm discipline, high courage, and mobile cannon. Himself a religious man, he had his troops march to battle singing Lutheran hymns. He was ideally suited to be the Protestant champion, a role he now willingly took up, landing in Germany in 1630. Richelieu, besides giving financial help, negotiated with the Catholic states of Germany, playing on their fears of imperial centralization and so sowing discord among German Catholics and isolating the emperor, against whom the Swedish war machine was now hurled.

The Swedes, with military aid from Saxony, won a number of spectacular victories, at Breitenfeld in 1631 and Lützen in 1632, where, however, Gustavus Adolphus was killed. His chancellor, Oxenstierna, carried on. The Swedish army penetrated into Bohemia, and as far south as the Danube. What those in the higher counsels of Sweden were aiming at is not clear. Perhaps they dreamed of a great federal Protestant empire, to include Scandinavia and north Germany, a Lutheran empire confronting a Catholic and Habsburg empire in the south. But the brilliant

145

Swedish victories came to little. Both sides were weakened by disagreement. Wallenstein, who disliked the Spanish influence in Germany, virtually ceased to fight the Swedes and Saxons, with whom he even entered into private talks, hoping to create an independent position for himself. He was finally disgraced by the emperor and assassinated by one of his own staff. On the Swedish-Saxon side, the Saxons decided to make a separate peace. Saxony therefore signed with the emperor the Peace of Prague of 1635. The other German Protestant states concurred in it and withdrew their support from the Swedes. The emperor, by largely annulling the Edict of Restitution, allayed Protestant apprehensions. The Swedes were left isolated in Germany. It seemed that the German states were coming together, that the religious wars might be nearing an end. But, in fact, in 1635, the Thirty Years' War was only well begun. Neither France nor Spain wished peace or reconciliation in Germany.

Richelieu renewed his assurances to the Swedes, paid subsidies even to the wealthy Dutch, hired a German princeling, Bernard of Saxe-Weimar, to maintain an army of Germans in the French service, and, cardinal of the Roman church though he was, at last came out openly and plainly in favor of the German Protestants.

So the fleur-de-lis at last moved toward the Rhine, though not at first with the success for which Frenchmen or Protestants might hope. The Spanish, from their bases in Belgium and Franche-Comté, drove instead deep into France. Champagne and Burgundy were ravaged, and Paris itself was seized with panic. The Spanish also raided the south. The French had a taste of the plunder, murder, burnings, and stealing of cattle by which Germany had been afflicted. But the French soon turned the tables. When Portugal and Catalonia rebelled against Philip IV, France immediately recognized the independence of Portugal under the new royal house of Braganza—as did England, Holland, and Sweden with equal alacrity. French troops streamed over the Pyrenees into Catalonia, spreading the usual devastation. Richelieu even recognized a Catalan republic.

In Germany the last or Swedish-French phase of the war was not so much a civil war among Germans as an international struggle on German soil. Few German states now sided with the French and Swedes. A feeling of national resentment against foreign invasion even seemed to develop, and the emperor had as allies not only Catholic Bavaria but Lutheran Saxony. But these states regarded themselves emphatically as the emperor's allies, not his subordinates. They were willing to negotiate separately with the enemy and even make a separate peace. No centralized German authority or unity of action could be built up. Spanish, French, and Swedish armies cut wide swaths across the country. The Empire had as much to fear from its friends, the Spanish, as from its declared enemies. The Spanish still fought to subdue the Dutch, and to consolidate, within the Empire, a belt of Spanish territory from Milan to the Netherlands. The French, Swedes, and Dutch—not to mention the Hungarians, Portuguese, Catalans, and a good many Germans intriguing behind the scenes—while pursuing different and often contradictory aims had one aim in common, to smash the Habsburgs both Spanish and Austrian.

Peace talks began in 1644 in Westphalia, at the two towns of Münster and Osnabrück. The German states were crying for peace, for a final religious settlement, and for "reform" of the Holy Roman Empire. France and Sweden insisted that the German states should individually take part in the negotiations, a disintegrating principle that the German princes eagerly welcomed and which the emperor vainly resisted. To Westphalia, therefore, hundreds of diplomats and negotiators now repaired, representing the Empire, its member states, Spain, France, Sweden, the Dutch, the Swiss, the Portuguese, the Venetians, many other Italians, and the pope. There had been no such European congress since the Council of Constance, and the fact that a European assemblage had in 1415 dealt with affairs of the church, and now in the 1640s dealt with affairs of state, war, and power, was a measure of the secularization that had come over Europe. The papal nuncio, it may be remarked, was barely listened to at Westphalia, and the pope never signed the treaties.

The negotiations dragged on, because the armies were still fighting, and after each battle one side or the other raised its terms. France and Spain refused to make peace with each other at all and in fact remained at war until 1659. But for the Holy Roman Empire a settlement was agreed to, incorporated in 1648 in the two treaties of Münster and Osnabrück, and commonly known as the Peace of Westphalia.

The Peace of Westphalia represented a general checkmate to the Counter Reformation in Germany. It not only renewed the terms of the Peace of Augsburg, granting each German state the right to determine its own religion, but it added Calvinism to Lutheranism and Catholicism as an acceptable faith. On the controversial issue of church territories secularized after 1552 the Protestants won a complete victory. These lands were to remain in the possession of those who held them in 1624, before the Edict of Restitution. The right of the Austrian Habsburg ruler to reconquer and re-Catholicize his own direct possessions, namely, Austria and Bohemia, was not questioned; here as elsewhere the principle of *cuius regio eius religio* prevailed; and in the Austrian Habsburg lands the Counter Reformation went forward successfully.

The dissolution of the Holy Roman Empire, which had been advanced by the drawing of internal religious frontiers in the days of Luther, was now confirmed in politics and international law. Borderlands of the Empire fell away. The Dutch and Swiss ceased to belong to it, both the United Provinces and Swiss cantons (or Helvetic Body) being recognized as sovereign and independent. The Dutch, in addition, were confirmed in their conquest of both banks of the lower Scheldt, the closure of that river to ocean-going vessels, and hence the commercial destruction of Antwerp. They likewise received, from Portugal, the right to have outposts in Brazil and Indonesia.

From the disintegrating western frontier of the Holy Empire the French cut off small pieces, receiving the sovereignty over three Lorraine bishoprics, which they had occupied for a century, and certain rights in Alsace which were so confused that they later led to trouble. The king of Sweden received the bishoprics of Bremen and Verden and the western half of Pomerania, including the city of Stettin. Sweden

Austrian Habsburgs

Spanish Monarchy

Swedish Dominions

Brandenburg-Prussia

Church Lands

——— Boundary of the Holy Roman Empire

0   100   200   300 miles

SHETLAND I.

ORKNEY I.

NORWAY

Bergen

SWEDEN

FINLAND

Helsingfors

Stockholm

ESTONIA

LIVONIA

Riga

COURLAND

LI

KINGDOM OF
DENMARK AND NORWAY

SCOTLAND

Edinburgh

NORTH SEA

DENMARK

(TO SWEDEN, 1658)
Copenhagen

BALTIC SEA

BRANDENBURG-PRUSSIA

Danzig

DUCHY
OF
PRUSSIA

Belfast

IRELAND

Dublin

Liverpool

ENGLAND
(COMMONWEALTH
1649-1660
UNITED KINGDOM
1707)

SCHLESWIG

HOLSTEIN
Hamburg

Lübeck

SWEDISH
POMERANIA

Stralsund

POMERELIA

Stettin

Vistula R.

ATLANTIC OCEAN

Bristol

London

UNITED
PROVINCES

Amsterdam

Ryswick

Utrecht

Elbe

Bremen

HANOVER

BRANDENBURG

Berlin

GREAT
POLAND

Warsaw

PO

ENGLISH
CHANNEL

SPANISH
NETH.

Brussels

Münster

Rhine

Cologne

Leipzig

SAXONY

Oder R.

Dresden

Breslau

SILESIA

LITTLE
POLAND

Rouen

MINOR
GERMAN STATES

Mainz

Prague

BOHEMIA

Lemberg

GALICIA

Cracow

Rennes

Paris

Trier

Metz

PALATINATE

LORRAINE

ALSACE

Strasbourg

MORAVIA

AUSTRIA

CARPATHIANS

P

Nantes

Orléans

FRANCE

FRANCHE
COMTÉ

BAVARIA

Augsburg

Vienna

SWISS CANTONS

La Coruña

Bordeaux

Lyons

SAVOY

REP. OF VENICE

KINGDOM OF HUNGARY

Budapest

HUNGARY

TRANSYL

León

Montauban

PIEDMONT

Milan

Parma

Venice

SLAVONIA

WA

Oporto

PORTUGAL
(TO SPAIN
1580-1640)

Valladolid

NAVARRE

PYRENEES

Avignon

Marseilles

Genoa

Florence

TUSCANY

PAPAL
STATES

ADRIATIC SEA

BOSNIA

Belgrade

SERBIA

OTTOMAN

B

MONTENEGRO

RU

Lisbon

Escorial

Mérida

Madrid

Saragossa

ARAGON

CATALONIA

Barcelona

CORSICA
(Genoa)

Rome

Aquila

Zara

ALBANIA

Salonica

AE

CASTILE

Toledo

Valencia

SPAIN

BALEARIC I.

MINORCA

SARDINIA

Bari

Naples

NAPLES

IONIAN I.
(Venice)

GREECE

Athens

Seville

Murcia

Cadiz

Malaga

GIBRALTAR

MAJORCA

KINGDOM OF THE
TWO SICILIES

Tangier
(Portugal)

Ceuta (Spain)

Algiers

MEDITERRANEAN

Palermo

SICILY

SEA

Oran (Spain)

Tunis

FEZ AND MOROCCO

ALGERIA

TUNISIA

MALTA (Spain)

B A R B A R Y   S T A T E S

Europe 1648. *The map shows the European states at the time of the Peace of Westphalia. The main feature of the Peace of Westphalia was that the threat of domination of Europe by the Catholic Habsburgs was averted. A plurality of independent sovereign states was henceforth considered normal. The plurality of religions was also henceforth taken for granted for Europe as a whole, though each state continued to require, or at least to favor, religious uniformity within its own borders. By weakening the Habsburgs, and furthering the disintegration of Germany, the Peace of Westphalia opened the way for the political ascendancy of France.*

thus added to its trans-Baltic possessions. The mouths of the imperial rivers were now controlled by non-Germans, the Oder, Elbe, and Weser by Sweden, the Rhine and the Scheldt by the Dutch. In the interior of the Empire Brandenburg received eastern Pomerania, the large archbishopric of Magdeburg, and two smaller bishoprics, while Bavaria also increased its stature, obtaining part of the Palatinate and a seat in the electoral college, so that the Empire now had eight electors.

It was in the new constitution of the Empire itself, not in territorial changes, that the greatest victory of the French and their Swedish and Dutch allies was to be found. The German states, over three hundred in number, became virtually sovereign. Each received the right to conduct diplomacy and make treaties with foreign powers. The Peace of Westphalia further stipulated that no laws could be made by the Empire, no taxes raised, no soldiers recruited, no war declared or peace terms ratified except with the consent of the imperial estates, the 300-odd princes, ecclesiastics, and free cities in the Reichstag assembled. Since it was well known that agreement on any such matters was impossible, the principle of self-government, or of medieval constitutional liberties, was used to destroy the Empire itself as an effective political entity. While most other European countries were consolidating under royal absolutism, Germany sank back into "feudal chaos." A constitution for Germany was written into an international treaty. As people then said, the "German liberties," or German states' rights, became part of the public law of Europe. France and Sweden were made guarantors of the Peace of Westphalia. Though Sweden presently became too weak to exercise this right effectively, France for a century and a half enjoyed a legal basis for intervention in central Europe.

Not only did the Peace of Westphalia block the Counter Reformation, and not only did it frustrate the Austrian Habsburgs and forestall for almost two centuries any movement toward German national unification, but it also marked the advent in international law of the modern European *Staatensystem* or system of sovereign states. The diplomats who assembled at Westphalia represented independent powers which recognized no superior or common tie. No one any longer pretended that Europe had any significant unity, religious, political, or other. Statesmen delighted in the absence of any such unity, in which they sensed the menace of "universal monarchy." Europe was understood to consist in a large number of unconnected sovereignties, free and detached atoms, or states, which moved about according to their own laws, following their own political interests, forming and dissolving alliances, exchanging embassies and legations, alternating between war and peace, shifting position with a shifting balance of power.

Physically Germany was wrecked by the Thirty Years' War. Cities were sacked by mercenary soldiers with a rapacity that their commanders could not control; or the commanders themselves, drawing no supplies from their home governments, systematically looted whole areas to maintain their armies. Magdeburg was besieged ten times, Leipzig five. In one woolen town of Bohemia, with a population of 6,000 before the wars, the citizens fled and disappeared, the houses collapsed, and eight years after the peace only 850 persons were found there. On the site of another small town Swedish cavalry found nothing but wolves. The peasants, murdered, put to flight, or tortured by soldiers to reveal their few valuables, ceased to give attention to farming; agriculture was ruined, so that starvation followed, and with it came pestilence. Even revised modern estimates allow that in many extensive parts of Germany as much as a third of the population may have perished. The effects of fire, disease, undernourishment, homelessness, and exposure in the seventeenth century were the more terrible because of the lack of means to combat them. People lived in piles of debris and ransacked dumps to find food, as they did after the Second World War. But even the Second World War, in sheer depopulation, was not as devastating for Germany as was the Thirty Years' War. It is quite possible for human beings to die like flies without benefit of scientific destruction. The horrors of modern war are not wholly different from horrors that men and women have experienced in the past.

Germany as such, physically wrecked, and politically cut into small pieces, ceased for a long time to play any part in European affairs. A kind of political and cultural vacuum existed in central Europe. On the one hand, the western or Atlantic peoples—French, English, Dutch—began in the seventeenth century to take the lead in European affairs. On the other hand, in eastern Germany, around Berlin and Vienna, new and only half-German power complexes began to form. These themes will be traced in the two following chapters.

◎ With the close of the Thirty Years' War the Wars of Religion came to an end. While in some later conflicts, as in Hungary or in Ireland and Scotland, religion remained an issue, it was never again an important issue in the political affairs of Europe as a whole. In general, by the close of the seventeenth century, the division between Protestant and Catholic had become stabilized. Neither side any longer expected to make territorial gains at the expense of the other. Both the Protestant and the Catholic reformations were accomplished facts. Seen in the long view, each had succeeded, but each also had failed, for Protestants had not freed the whole Christian world of "idolatry," nor had the Catholics been able to exterminate "heresy." A compromise was in the end accepted. Latin Christendom was partitioned. The breaking up of the medieval church, with the accompanying break-up of the medieval view of life and of the world—a process that may be said to have lasted from 1300 to 1650, and was as slow and deeply disrupting as a geological upheaval—perhaps came as near as anything in European history to breaking up Europe itself; but after about 1650 such troubles became past history, and Europe entered upon a new age.

With the Age of Discovery, Europe entered into habitual communication with the "Indies," as Asia, Africa and America were at first vaguely and collectively called.

Europeans found some peoples in these countries less civilized than themselves, and others whom they considered equally civilized or more so, as in India and China. From Asia, while the Europeans at first sought for spices, they soon imported manufactures of a more refined kind than Europe could then produce, such as Indian cottons and Chinese porcelains. In Asia, as in Africa, the Europeans were transients—traders, sailors, missionaries, and officials sent to govern small outposts. There was no settlement of European families except at the Cape of Good Hope. The interior of Africa remained unknown. The Mogul empire in India until after 1700, and the Ming empire in China, succeeded by the Ch'ing or Manchu empire about 1650, long commanded the awe and respect of Europeans. China exerted a special fascination. During the European Enlightenment, in the eighteenth century, China was admired as a huge empire that had no clergy, and was governed by an enlightened literary class, the mandarins, recruited by competitive examination rather than by noble birth.

The aboriginal Americans and the black Africans were regarded by the Europeans as savages, who in any case could not defend themselves against European organization and weapons. The American Indians were either killed off, subjugated or pushed aside. America was valuable to Europeans for its natural resources, whose exploitation required masses of labor which was supplied from Africa. In the ensuing slave trade, the number of Africans who were taken to America, including the two continents and the West Indies, was far greater than the number of Europeans who settled there before 1800. A few Spanish emigrated permanently to New Spain, and a few Portuguese to Brazil, but by the time of the American Revolution the most purely "European" region was the Atlantic coast of North America, where about two million whites lived with half a million blacks and a very few Indians.

Europe itself was transformed by these overseas ventures. A wealthy commercial class grew up in northwestern Europe. Naval power became decisive. The inflow of American gold and silver affected currency values and hence the relationship between social classes. Population grew with the adoption of the American potato. Men took increasing pride in their understanding of the world. There was much speculation on the diversity of human races and cultures, which sometimes led to a new kind of race consciousness on the part of Europeans, and sometimes to a cultural relativism in which European ways were seen as only one variant of human behavior as a whole.

THE WORLD OVERSEAS

Right: "Our Lady of the Navigators," painted about 1535 by Alejo Fernandez for the Casa de Contratacion, or Trade House, at Seville.   The figures to whom the Virgin extends her protection, with their sharply individualized features, are thought to represent various actual explorers; the one to the left may be Columbus.   The picture evokes the combination of religious spirit with adventure and gold-seeking that motivated the early expeditions.

The Spaniards stamped out much of the Indian religion as idolatrous, yet it is to Spanish priests that we owe the preservation of much of our knowledge of the pre-Conquest culture.   The page at the above right is from a book in which a Spaniard wrote down the Aztec language in the Latin alphabet.   A human sacrifice is also depicted.

At the above left is a page from a book published in England, translated from the Dutch.   The author, Johannes Nieuhoff, spent three years in Java and nine in Brazil, where the Dutch had a settlement in the 1640s.   He was thus well qualified to write on the "West and East Indies," whose wonders are suggested by palms, parasols, elephants, and a huge flying bat.

154

"An Episode in the Conquest of America," by Jan Mostaert of Haarlem in Holland. An early visualization of the New World by a painter who died in 1555. The multitude of busy small figures suggests the style of the Flemish Breughel, and the placid livestock is Dutch. The American Indians are seen as naked, helpless and confused—and very different from Europeans.

Opposite, above: Europeans negotiate with an African chief and his council on the Guinea coast. The Europeans have guns, the Africans only spears, but the Africans, in contrast to the American Indians on the preceding page, are fully clothed and seated with dignity in an organized situation. They may be discussing the sale of slaves.

Above, center: Black slaves are stooped over in a diamond-processing operation in Brazil, while overseers watch with whips. The slaves seem to be sifting material in water made to flow through the little compartments.

Above, left: An early advertisement to attract European immigration to what eventually became the United States. This one was published in London two years after the founding of Jamestown, the first permanent English settlement in America. "Planting" meant settling in the seventeenth century.

Right: The headquarters of the Dutch East India Company in 1665 in Bengal, long before the British predominance there. It is wholly walled off from the Indian life around it, with offices, living quarters and spacious gardens for the employees of the Company. A large Dutch flag flies at the corner of the enclosure, and others on the ships in the Hooghly River (in the Ganges delta); these ships kept the Dutch traders in continual touch with Holland, though the voyage took almost a year.

158

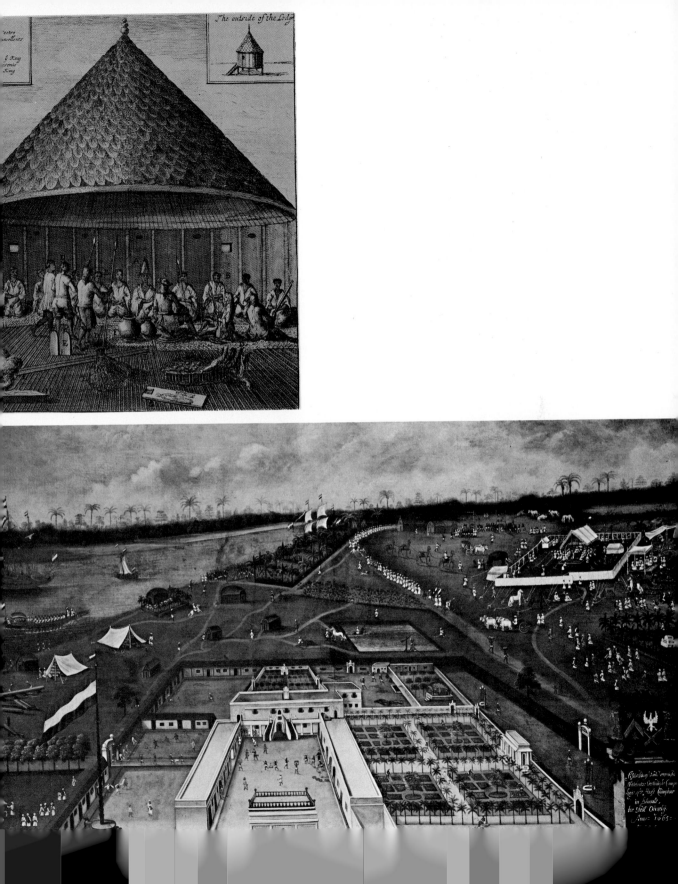

These two prints suggest some results of three centuries of European experience with the world overseas. In China, no Europeans had as yet any territorial foothold. China was seen by Europe as a kind of counterpart civilization to itself. Confucius is shown here in a library of suspiciously European appearance, but holding a book in which Chinese characters are represented. He symbolized for Europeans the great teacher of virtue and wisdom, of social harmony and civic duty, far removed from the theological bickering of European religions.

Meanwhile the settlement at Jamestown had grown into a string of populous colonies. Above, we see Boston Common in 1768. The town seems rural, but has substantial houses with fences and rows of planted trees. British troops have just moved in, because of rising political troubles. They have pitched their tents on the common, where they march and drill in full sight of the citizens. The first fighting of the American Revolution was soon to begin here.

IV: THE ESTABLISHMENT OF

WEST-EUROPEAN LEADERSHIP

If the reader were to take a map of Europe, set one leg of a pair of dividers on the city of Paris, and with the other leg describe a circle having a radius of five hundred miles, he would mark out a zone from which, since about the year 1650, a great deal of modern or "western" civilization has radiated. The circle would not constitute western Europe in a strict geographical sense, since the extreme western parts of Europe—Ireland, Portugal, and Spain—would be left mainly outside it. But it might with considerable accuracy be equated with modern western Europe in a cultural sense. For the zone so traced out, including all of France, England, the Low Countries, and Switzerland, and reaching into Lowland Scotland, western and central Germany and northern Italy, for over two hundred years beginning in the seventeenth century, was the earth's principal center of what anthropologists might call cultural diffusion. Leadership in Europe, in those aspects of civilization deemed worthy of imitation by other Europeans, became concentrated along the Atlantic seaboard north of the Pyrenees, and as Europeans increasingly penetrated the overseas world it was the west-Europeans who did so. Eastern Europe, the Iberian peninsula, colonial America, all in various ways "borrowed" from the zone of greater advancement. A

Chapter Emblem: A commemorative medal, in which Louis XIV receives the homage of Tournai and Courtrai, Flemish towns temporarily annexed in 1667.

secular society, modern natural science, a highly developed capitalism, the centralized state, parliamentary government in its modern form, democratic ideas, machine industry—and much else—if they did not exactly originate, received their first full development or expression in the zone described by the reader's imaginary dividers.

This leadership of western Europe became established in the half-century following the Peace of Westphalia. The fading out of the Italian Renaissance, the subsiding of religious wars, the ruin of the Holy Roman Empire and the decay of Spain all cleared the stage on which the Dutch, English, and French were to be the principal actors. But the Dutch were few in number, and the English during most of the seventeenth century were weakened by domestic discord. It was France that for a time played the most imposing role. The whole half-century following the Peace of Westphalia is in fact often called the Age of Louis XIV.

This king of France inherited his throne in 1643 at the age of five, assumed the personal direction of affairs in 1661 at the age of twenty-three, and reigned for seventy-two years until his death in 1715. No one else in modern history has held so powerful a position for so long a time. Louis XIV was more than a figurehead. For over half a century, during his whole adult life, he was the actual and working head of the French government. Inheriting the achievement of Richelieu,[1] he made France the strongest country in Europe. Using French money, by bribes or other inducements, he built up a pro-French interest in virtually every country from England to Turkey. His policies and the counter-policies that others adopted against him set the pace of public events, and his methods of government and administration, war and diplomacy, became a model for other rulers to copy. During this time the French language, French thought and literature, French architecture and landscape gardens, French styles in clothes, cooking, and etiquette became the accepted standard for Europe. France seemed to be the land of light, and Louis XIV was called by his fascinated admirers Louis the Great, the *Grand Monarque,* and the Sun King. To the internal achievements of France we shall shortly return.

Internationally, the consuming political question of the last decades of the seventeenth century (at least in western Europe—eastern Europe we shall reserve for the next chapter) was the fate of the still vast possessions of the Spanish crown. Spain was what Turkey was later called, "the sick man of Europe." To its social and economic decline[2] was added hereditary physical deterioration of its rulers. In 1665 the Spanish throne was inherited by Charles II, an unfortunate afflicted by many ills of mind and body, impotent, even imbecile, the pitiable product of generations of inbreeding in the Habsburg house. His rule was irresolute and feeble. It was known from the moment of his accession that he could have no children, and that the Spanish branch of the Habsburg family would die out with his own death. The whole future

[1]See pp. 140–141.
[2]See pp. 134–135.

not only of Spain but of the Spanish Netherlands, the Spanish holdings in Italy, and all Spanish America was therefore in question. Charles II dragged out his miserable days until 1700, the object of jealousy and outright assault during his lifetime, and precipitating a new European war by his death.

Louis XIV, who in his youth married a sister of Charles II, intended to benefit from the debility of his royal brother-in-law. His expansionist policies followed two main lines. One was to push the French borders eastward to the Rhine, annexing the Spanish Netherlands (or Belgium) and the Franche-Comté or Free County of Burgundy, a French-speaking region lying between ducal Burgundy and Switzerland.[3] Such a policy involved the further dismemberment of the Holy Roman Empire. The other line of Louis XIV's ambitions, increasingly clear as time went on, was his hope of obtaining the entire Spanish inheritance for himself. By combining the resources of France and Spain he would make France supreme in Europe, in America, and on the sea. To promote these ends Louis XIV intrigued with the smaller and middle-sized powers of Europe. He took various princes of Germany, and for a time a king of England, into his pay. He supported, with complete disregard of ideology, the republicans in Holland against their prince, and the royalists in England against the parliamentary opposition, knowing that in Holland it was the republicans, and in England the partisans of high monarchy, who were most dependent on foreign assistance and most likely to follow his wishes.

Were Louis XIV to succeed in his aims, he would create the "universal monarchy" dreaded by diplomats, that is to say, a political situation in which one state might subordinate all others to its will. The technique used against universal monarchy was the balance of power. Universal monarchy had formerly been almost achieved by the Austro-Spanish Habsburgs. The Habsburg supremacy had been blocked mainly by a balance of power headed by France, and of which the Thirty Years' War and the Peace of Westphalia were the outstanding triumphs. Now the danger of universal monarchy came from France, and it was against France that the balance of power was directed.

The Idea of the Balance of Power

It will be useful to explain what a balance of power was and was not meant to be. The phrase itself, which came into general use at this time, has been employed ever since in different though related senses. In one sense it refers to a condition of equilibrium, or of even balance, in which power is distributed among many separate states. The second sense arises when this equilibrium is disturbed. If one state preponderates, and if others then form a coalition against it, then the coalition itself may be called the "balance," though it is actually the counterweight by which balance or equilibrium is to be restored. In a third sense one speaks of "holding" or "controlling" the balance of power; here the balance refers to that decisive increment of weight or power which one state may bring to bear. Thus if a state is a vitally necessary member of a coalition, more needed by its allies than it is in need of them, it

---

[3] See map, pp. 148–149.

may be said to "hold" the balance. Or if it belongs to no coalition at all, but tries to keep all other states in a condition of equilibrium, so that its own intervention on one side or the other would be decisive, it may also be said to "hold" the balance, although strictly speaking not participating in the balance at all.

The aim of statesmen pursuing policies of balance of power in the seventeenth and eighteenth centuries was generally to preserve their own independence of action to the utmost. Hence the basic rule was to ally against any state threatening domination. If one state seemed to dictate too much, others would shun alliance with it unless they were willing (from ideological sympathy or other reasons) to become its puppets. They would seek alliance with the other weaker states instead. They would thus create a balance or counterweight, or "restore the balance," against the state whose ascendancy they feared. Another more subtle reason for preferring alliance with the weak rather than with the strong was that in such an alliance each member could feel his own contribution to be necessary and valued, hence could preserve his own dignity and prestige, and by threatening to withdraw his support could win consideration of his own policies. Indeed, the balance of power may be defined as a system in which each state tends to throw its weight where it is most needed, so that its own importance may be enhanced.

The purpose of balance-of-power politics was not to preserve peace, but to preserve the sovereignty and independence of the states of Europe, or the "liberties of Europe," as they were called, against potential aggressors. The system was effective as a means to this end in the seventeenth and eighteenth centuries. Combinations were intricate, and alliances were readily made and unmade to deal with emerging situations. One reason for the effectiveness of the system lay in the great number of states capable of pursuing an independent foreign policy. These included not only the greater and middle-sized states of Austria, Spain, France, England, Holland, Sweden, and Bavaria, but a great number of small independent states, such as Denmark, the German principalities, Portugal after 1640, and Savoy, Venice, Genoa, and Tuscany. States moved easily from one alliance to another, or from one side of the balance to another. They were held back by no ideologies or sympathies, especially after the religious wars subsided, but could freely choose or reject allies, aiming only to protect their own independence or enlarge their own interests. Moreover, owing to the military technology of the day, small states might count as important military partners in an alliance. By controlling a strategic location, like the king of Denmark, or by making a contribution of ships or money, like the Dutch Republic, they might add just enough strength to an alliance to balance and overbalance the opposing great power and its allies.

As the ambitions of Louis XIV became bolder, and as the capacity of Spain to resist them withered away, the prevention of universal monarchy under France depended increasingly on combining the states of Europe into a balance of power against him. The balance against Louis XIV was engineered mainly by the Dutch. The most tireless of his enemies, and the man who did more than any other to checkmate him, was the Dutchman William III, the prince of Orange, who in his later years was king of England and Scotland as well.

Let us, after first surveying the Dutch in the seventeenth century, turn to the British Isles, where a momentous conflict occurred between Parliament and king. We shall then examine the French absolute monarchy under Louis XIV and conclude the present chapter with the wars of Louis XIV, particularly the War of the Spanish Succession, in which the great international issues of the time conflicted and were resolved.

The ambassadors of kings, strolling beside a canal at The Hague, might on occasion observe a number of burghers in plain black garments step out of a boat and proceed to make a meal of cheese and herring on the lawn, and they would recognize in these portly figures Their High Mightinesses the Estates-General of the United Provinces, as the Dutch government was known in the diplomatic language of the day. Though noblemen lived in the country, the Dutch were the most bourgeois of all peoples. They were not the only republicans in Europe, since the Swiss cantons, Venice, Genoa, and even England for a few years were republics, but of all republics the United Provinces was by far the most wealthy, the most flourishing, and the most preeminently civilized.

The Dutch acquired a nationality of their own in the long struggle against Spain, and with it a pride in their own freedom and independence. In the later phases of the war with Spain, notably during the Thirty Years' War, they were able to rely more on their wealth, ready money, shipping, and diplomacy than on actual fighting, so that during the whole seventeenth century they enjoyed a degree of comfort, and of intellectual, artistic, and commercial achievement unexcelled in Europe. The classic Dutch poets and dramatists wrote at this time, making a literary language of what had formerly been a dialect of Low German. Hugo Grotius produced, in his *Law of War and Peace*, a pioneering treatise on international law. Baruch Spinoza, of a family of refugee Portuguese Jews, quietly turned out works of philosophy, examining the fundamentals of reality, of human conduct, and of church and state. Spinoza made his living by grinding lenses; there were many other lens grinders in Holland; some of them developed the microscope, and some of these, in turn—Leeuwenhoek, Swammerdam, and others—peering through their microscopes and beholding for the first time the world of microscopic life, became founders of modern biological science. The greatest Dutch scientist was Christian Huyghens (1629–1695), who worked mainly in physics and mathematics; he improved the telescope (a Dutch invention), made clocks move with pendulums, discovered the rings of Saturn, and launched the wave theory of light. A less famous writer, Balthasar Bekker, in his *World Bewitched* (1691) delivered a decisive blow against the expiring superstition of witchcraft.

But the most eternally fresh of the Dutch creations, suffering from no barrier of time or language, were the superb canvases of the painters. Frans Hals produced bluff portraits of the common people. Jan Vermeer threw a spell of magic and quiet dignity over men, and especially women, of the burgher class. Rembrandt conveyed the mystery of human consciousness itself. In Rembrandt's *Masters of the Cloth Hall* (see illustration) we face a group of men who seem about to speak from the canvas, inclined slightly forward, as intent on their business as judges on the proceedings in a courtroom; men of the kind who conducted the affairs of Holland, in both commerce and government; intelligent men, calculating but not cunning, honest but determined to drive a hard bargain, stern rather than mild; and the sober black cloaks, with the clean white collars, set against the carved woodwork and rich table covering of the Cloth Hall, seem to suggest that personal vanity must yield to collective undertakings, and personal simplicity be maintained in the midst of material opulence. And in Vermeer's *Geographer*, painted in 1669 (also reproduced in this book—see page 113), there appears not only an immaculately scrubbed and dusted Dutch interior, but something of a symbol of the modern world in its youth—the pale northern sunlight streaming through the window, the globe and the map, the dividers in the scholar's right hand, instrument of science and mathematics, the tapestry flung over the table (or is it an Oriental rug brought from the East?), the head lifted in thought and eyes resting on an invisible world of fresh discoveries and opening horizons.

In religion, after initial disputes, the Dutch Republic adopted toleration. Early in the seventeenth century the Dutch Calvinists divided. One group favored a modification of Calvinism, with a toning down of the doctrine of absolute and unconditional predestination; it drew its main support from the comfortable burghers and its doctrines from a theologian of Leyden named Arminius. To deal with this Arminian heresy a great international Calvinist synod met in 1618 at Dordrecht in Holland. Of the hundred delegates almost a third came from Scotland, England, Germany, Switzerland, and France. The orthodox party won out at the synod; one old man was put to death; the philosopher Grotius fled to France for safety. But beginning in 1632 the Arminians were tolerated. Rights were granted to the large Catholic minority. Jews had long been welcomed in the republic; and Christian sects despised everywhere else, such as the Mennonites, found a refuge in it. Although none of these people had as many political or economic rights as the Calvinists, the resulting mixture stimulated both the intellectual life and the commercial enterprise of the country.

The Dutch as early as 1600 had 10,000 ships, and throughout the seventeenth century they owned most of the shipping of northern Europe. They were the carriers between Spain, France, England, and the Baltic. Much coastwise shipping between

The Masters of the Cloth Hall *by Rembrandt van Rijn (Dutch, 1606–1669)*
For the subject of this picture see above. These men are "clothiers" or "drapers" such as are described on pp. 117–118 in connection with the Commercial Revolution. Rembrandt over 40 years produced some 600 paintings in addition to etchings and drawings, in which he conveyed all types of experience, from the commercial practicality of the present group to the deeply mystical and the religious. This painting was done on commission for the Cloth Hall, or drapers' gild, at Amsterdam. Courtesy of the Rijksmuseum, Amsterdam.

ports of France was in Dutch hands. They settled in Bordeaux to buy wines, lent money to vintners, and soon owned many vineyards in France itself. They sailed on every sea. They explored the waters around Spitzbergen and almost monopolized Arctic whaling. They entered the Pacific by way of South America, where they rounded Cape Horn and named it after Hoorn in Holland. Organized in the East India Company of 1602, their merchants increasingly replaced the Portuguese in India and the Far East. In Java, in 1619, they founded the city of Batavia—the Latin name for Holland. (It is now called Djakarta.) Finding some Englishmen in 1623 at Amboina, in the midst of the Spice Islands, they tortured and killed them. The English did not return until the days of Napoleon. Not long after 1600 the Dutch reached Japan. But the Japanese, fearing the political consequences of Christian penetration, in 1641 expelled all other Europeans and confined the Dutch to limited operations on an island near Nagasaki. The Dutch remained for over two centuries the sole link of the West with Japan. In 1612 the Dutch founded their first settlement on Manhattan Island, and in 1621 they established a Dutch West India Company to exploit the loosely held riches of Spanish and Portuguese America. They founded colonies at Pernambuco and Bahia in Brazil (lost soon thereafter) and at Caracas, Curaçao, and in Guiana in the Caribbean. In 1652 the Dutch captured the Cape of Good Hope in South Africa from the Portuguese. Dutch settlers soon appeared—men, women, and children. It is here alone, among the modern Afrikaner people, that a kind of overseas Holland, Dutch in language and culture, persists to this day.

In 1609 the Dutch founded the Bank of Amsterdam. European money was a chaos; coins were minted not only by great monarchs but by small states and cities in Germany and Italy, and even by private persons. In addition, under inflationary pressures, kings and others habitually debased their coins by adding more alloy, while leaving the old coins in circulation along with the new. Anyone handling money thus accumulated a miscellany of uncertain value. The Bank of Amsterdam accepted deposits of such mixed money from all persons and from all countries, assessed the gold and silver content, and, at rates of exchange fixed by itself, allowed depositors to withdraw equivalent values in gold florins minted by the Bank of Amsterdam. These were of known and unchanging weight and purity. They thus became an

A Scholar Holding a Thesis on Botany *by Willem Moreelse (Dutch, before 1630–1666) The Netherlands became a great intellectual center in the seventeenth century, with five universities founded during the years of struggle against Spain. The most famous was at Leyden, but the present scholar may be a new doctor of the University of Utrecht, where the little-known painter Willem Moreelse worked. Crowned with laurel, the successful candidate proudly displays his thesis, on which the Latin words announce that "any plant shows the presence of God." The bringing of hitherto unknown plants from the rest of the world to Europe contributed strongly not only to science but to medicine, food supply, and the pleasures of chocolate, tea and coffee. Courtesy*

of The Toledo Museum of Art, Gift of Edward Drummond Libbey, 1962.

internationally sought money, an international measure of value, acceptable everywhere. Depositors were also allowed to draw checks against their accounts. These conveniences, plus a safety of deposits guaranteed by the Dutch government, attracted capital from all quarters and made possible loans for a wide range of purposes. Amsterdam remained the financial center of Europe until the French Revolution.

Under their republican government the Dutch enjoyed great freedom, but it can hardly be said that their form of government met all the requirements of a state. Their High Mightinesses (the *Hooge Moogende*), who made up the Estates-General, were only delegates from their respective seven provinces and could act only as the estates of the provinces gave instructions. The seven provinces, like the states of the Holy Roman Empire in which they had originated, were jealous of their own independence. Each province had, as its executive, an elected stadholder, but there was no stadholder for the United Provinces as a whole. This difficulty was overcome by the fact that most of the various provinces usually elected the same man as stadholder. The stadholder in most provinces was usually the head of the house of Orange, which since the days of William the Silent and the wars for independence had enjoyed exceptional prestige in the republic. The prince of Orange, apart from being stadholder, was simply one of the feudal noblemen of the country, for the United Provinces had a landed feudal aristocracy which was represented in the seven provincial estates. But the aristocratic class had been outdistanced by the commercial, and affairs were generally managed by the burghers. The burghers, intent on making money and enjoying comfort, rarely worried over military questions and hated taxes.

Politics in the Dutch Republic was a seesaw between the burghers, pacifistic and absorbed with business, and the princes of Orange, to whom the country owed most of its military security. When foreigners threatened invasion, the power of the stadholder increased. When all was calm, the stadholder could do little. The Peace of Westphalia produced a mood of confidence in the burghers, followed by a constitutional crisis, in the course of which the stadholder William II died, in 1650. No new stadholder was elected for twenty-two years. The burgher, civilian, and decentralizing tendencies prevailed.

In 1650, eight days after his father's death, was born the third William of the house of Orange, seemingly fated never to be stadholder and to pass his life as a private nobleman on his own estates. William III grew up to be a grave and reserved young man, small and rather stocky, with thin compressed lips and a determined spirit. He learned to speak Dutch, German, English, and French with equal facility, and to understand Italian, Spanish, and Latin. He observed the requirements of his religion, which was Dutch Calvinism, with sober regularity. He had a strong dislike, Dutch and Calvinistic, for everything magnificent or pompous; he lived plainly, hated flattery, and took no pleasure in social conversation. In these respects he was the opposite of his life-long enemy the Sun King, whom he resembled only in his diligent preoccupation with affairs. In 1677 he married the king of England's niece, Mary.

Meanwhile matters were not going favorably for the Dutch Republic. In 1651 the revolutionary government then ruling England passed a Navigation Act. This act may be considered the first of a long series of political measures by which the British colonial empire was built up. It was aimed against the Dutch carrying trade. It provided that goods imported into England and its dependencies must be brought in English ships, or in ships belonging to the country exporting the goods. Since the Dutch were too small a people to be great producers and exporters themselves, and lived largely by carrying the goods of others, they saw in the new English policy a threat to their economic existence. The English likewise, claiming sovereignty of the "narrow seas," demanded that Dutch ships salute the English flag in the Channel. Three wars between the Dutch and English followed, running with interruptions from 1652 to 1674 and generally indecisive, though the English annexed New York.

While thus assaulted at sea by the English, the Dutch were menaced on land by the French. Louis XIV made his first aggressive move in 1667, claiming the Spanish Netherlands and Franche-Comté by alleging certain rights of his Spanish wife, and overrunning the Spanish Netherlands with his army. The Dutch, to whom the Spanish Netherlands were a buffer against France, set into motion the mechanism of the balance of power. Dropping temporarily their disputes with the English, they allied with them instead; and since they were able also to secure the adherence of Sweden, the resulting Triple Alliance was sufficient to give pause to Louis XIV, who withdrew from the Spanish Netherlands, made peace, and renounced his claims, though keeping a few towns in Flanders. It was soon evident that Louis XIV had been only temporarily halted, and that the next time he would pass straight through the Spanish Netherlands into the Dutch provinces themselves. He broke up the Triple Alliance, detaching Sweden from Holland and secretly sending funds to the king of England, who at this time preferred to depend on the king of France rather than on his own Parliament for his income. The Dutch, still under their burgher government, were slow to take alarm and did nothing to strengthen their army. In 1672 Louis XIV rapidly crossed the Spanish Netherlands, attacked with forces five times as large as the Dutch, and occupied three of the seven Dutch provinces.

A popular clamor now arose among the Dutch for William of Orange, demanding that the young prince, who was now twenty-two years of age, be installed in the old office of stadholder, in which his ancestors had defended them against Spain. He was duly elected stadholder in six provinces. In 1673 these six provinces voted to make the stadholderate hereditary in the house of Orange. William, during his whole tenure or "reign" in the Netherlands, attempted to centralize and consolidate his government, put down the feudal liberties of the provinces, and free himself from constitutional checks, moving generally in the direction of absolute monarchy, which by the tests of power and under French example was the successful form of government at the time. He was unable, however, to go far in this course, and the United Provinces remained a decentralized patrician republic until 1795. Meanwhile, to stave off the immediate menace of Louis XIV, William resorted to a new manipulation of the balance of power. He formed an alliance this time with the minor powers of Denmark and Brandenburg (the German margraviate around Berlin) and with the Austrian and Spanish Habsburgs. Nothing could indicate more clearly the new balance of power precipitated by the rise of France than this coming over of the Dutch to the Habsburg side. The alliance was successful to the extent at least of wearying Louis XIV of the war. Peace was signed in 1678 (treaty of Nimwegen), but only at the expense of Spain and the Holy Roman Empire, from which Louis XIV took the long coveted Franche-Comté, together with another batch of towns in Flanders. The Dutch preserved their territory intact.

In the next ten years came the great windfall of William's life. In 1689 he became king of England. He was now able to bring the British Isles into his perpetual combinations against France. Since the real impact of France was yet to be felt, and the real bid of Louis XIV for universal monarchy was yet to be made, and since the English at this time were rapidly gaining in strength, the entrance of England was a decisive addition to the balance formed against French expansion. In this way the constitutional troubles of England, by bringing a determined Dutchman to the English throne, entered into the general stream of European affairs and helped to assure that western Europe and its overseas offshoots should not be dominated totally by France.

After the defeat of the Spanish Armada and recession of the Spanish threat the English were for a time less closely involved with the affairs of the Continent. They played no significant part in the Thirty Years' War, and were almost the only European people, west of Poland, who were not represented at the Congress of Westphalia. At the time of the Westphalia negotiations in the 1640s they were in fact engaged in a civil war of their own. This English civil war was a milder variant of the Wars of Religion which desolated France, Germany, and the Netherlands. It was fought not between Protestants and Catholics as on the Continent, but between the more extreme or Calvinistic Protestants called Puritans and the more moderate Protestants, or Anglicans, adhering to the established Church of England. As in the wars on the Continent, religious differences were mixed indistinguishably with political and constitutional issues. As the Huguenots represented to some extent feudal rebelliousness against the French monarchy, as German Protestants fought for states' rights against imperial centralization, and the Calvinists of the Netherlands for provincial liberties against the king of Spain, so the Puritans asserted the rights of Parliament against the mounting claims of royalty in England.

The civil war in England was relatively so mild that England itself can be said to have escaped the horrors of the Wars of Religion. The same was not true of the British Isles as a whole. After 1603 the kingdoms of England and Scotland, while otherwise separate, were ruled by the same king; the kingdom of Ireland remained, as before, a dependency of the English crown. Between England and Presbyterian Scotland there was constant friction, but the worst trouble was between

England and Catholic Ireland, which was the scene of religious warfare as savage as that of the Continent.

For the English the seventeenth century was an age of great achievement, during which they made their debut as one of the chief peoples of modern Europe. In 1600 only four or five million persons, in England and Lowland Scotland, spoke the English language. The number did not rise rapidly for another century and a half. But the population began to spread. Religious discontents, reinforced by economic pressures, led to considerable emigration. Twenty thousand Puritans settled in New England between 1630 and 1640, and about the same number went to Barbados and other West India islands during the same years. A third stream, again roughly of the same size, but made up mainly of Scottish Presbyterians, settled in northern Ireland under government auspices, driving away or expropriating the native Celts. English Catholics were allowed by the home government to settle in Maryland. A great many Anglicans went to Virginia in the mid-century, adding to the small settlement made at Jamestown in 1607. Except for the movement to northern Ireland, called the "plantation of Ulster," these migrations took place without much attention on the part of the government, through private initiative organized in commercial companies. After the middle of the century the government began deliberately to build an empire. New York was conquered from the Dutch, Jamaica from the Spanish, and Pennsylvania and the Carolinas were established. All the Thirteen Colonies except Georgia were founded before 1700, and there were at that time perhaps half a million people in British North America. Relative to the home population, it was as if the United States should in three generations build up a distant colonial appendage with fifteen million inhabitants.

The English also, like the Dutch, French, and Spanish at the time, were creating their national culture. Throughout western Europe the national languages, encroaching upon international Latin on the one hand and local dialects on the other, were becoming adequate vehicles for the expression of thought and feeling. Shakespeare and Milton projected their mighty conceptions with overwhelming power of words, not since equaled in English or in any other tongue. The English classical literature, rugged in form but deep in content, vigorous yet subtle in insight, majestic, abundant, and sonorous in expression, was almost the reverse of French classical writing, with its virtues of order, economy, propriety, and graceful precision. The English could never thereafter quite yield to French standards, nor be dazzled or dumbfounded, as some peoples were, by the cultural glories of the Age of Louis XIV. There were no painters at all comparable to those on the Continent, but in music it was the age of Campion and Purcell, and in architecture the century closed with the great buildings of Christopher Wren.

Economically the English were enterprising and affluent, though in 1600 far outdistanced by the Dutch. They had a larger and more productive country than the Dutch, and were therefore not as limited to purely mercantile and seafaring occupations. Coal was mined around Newcastle, and was increasingly used, but was not yet a leading source of English wealth. The great industry was the growing of sheep and manufacture of woolens, which were the main export. Weaving was done to a large extent in the country, under the putting-out system, and organized by merchants according to the methods of commercial capitalism.[4] Since 1553 the English had traded with Russia by way of the White Sea; they were increasingly active in the Baltic and eastern Mediterranean; and with the founding of the East India Company, in 1600, they competed with the Dutch in assaulting the old Portuguese monopoly in India and the Far East. But profitable as such overseas operations were, the main wealth of England was still in the land. The richest men were not merchants but landlords, and the landed aristocracy formed the richest class.

Background to the
Civil War: Parliament
and the Stuart Kings

In England, as elsewhere in the seventeenth century, the kings clashed with their old medieval representative bodies. In England the old body, Parliament, won out against the king. But this was not the unique feature in the English development. In Germany the estates of the Holy Roman Empire triumphed against the emperor, and much the same thing, as will be seen, occurred in Poland. But on the Continent the triumph of the old representative bodies generally meant political dissolution or even anarchy. Successful governments were generally those in which kingly powers increased; this was the strong tendency of the time, evident even in the Dutch Republic after 1672 under William of Orange. The unique thing about England was that Parliament, in defeating the king, arrived at a workable form of government. Government remained strong but came under parliamentary control. This determined the character of modern England and launched into the history of Europe and of the world the great movement of liberalism and representative institutions.

What happened was somewhat as follows. In 1603, on the death of Queen Elizabeth, the English crown was inherited by the son of Mary Stuart, James VI of Scotland, who became king of England also, taking there the title of James I. James was a philosopher of royal absolutism. He had even written a book on the subject, *The True Law of Free Monarchy.* By a "free" monarchy James meant a monarchy free from control by Parliament, churchmen, or laws and customs of the past. It was a monarchy in which the king, as father to his people, looked after their welfare as he saw fit, standing above all parties, private interests, and pressure groups. He even declared that kings drew their authority from God, and were responsible to God alone. The doctrine which he represented is known as the divine right of kings.[5]

Probably any ruler succeeding Elizabeth would have had trouble with Parliament, which had shown signs of restlessness in the last years of her reign, but had deferred to her as an aging woman and a national symbol. She had maintained peace within the country and fought off the Spaniards, but these very accomplishments persuaded many people that they could safely bring their grievances into

[4]See p. 118.
[5]See pp. 190–191, 318–319.

the open. James I was a foreigner, a Scot, who lacked the touch for dealing with the English, and who was moreover a royal pedant, the "wisest fool in Christendom," as he was uncharitably called. Not content with the actualities of control, as Elizabeth had been, he read the Parliament tiresome lectures on the royal rights. He also was in constant need of money. The wars against Spain had left a considerable debt. James was far from economical, and, in any case, in an age of rising prices, he could not live within the fixed and customary revenues of the English crown. These were of a medieval character, increasingly quaint under the new conditions—rights of wardship and marriage, escheats, franc-fiefs and fees for the distraint of knighthood, together with "tunnage and poundage," or rights given to the king by Parliament at his accession (and normally unchanged during his reign) to collect specified duties on exports and imports, according to quantity, not value, and hence not rising in proportion to prices.

Neither to James I nor to his son Charles I, who succeeded him in 1625, would Parliament grant adequate revenue, because it distrusted them both. Many members of Parliament were Puritans, dissatisfied with the organization and doctrine of the Church of England.[6] Elizabeth had tried to hush up religious troubles, but James threatened to "harry the Puritans out of the land," and Charles supported the Anglican hierarchy which, under Archbishop Laud, sought to enforce religious conformity. Many members of Parliament were also lawyers, who feared that the common law of England, the historic or customary law, was in danger. They disliked the prerogative courts, the Star Chamber set up by Henry VII, the High Commission set up by Elizabeth.[7] They heard with trepidation the modern doctrine that the sovereign king could make laws and decide cases at his own discretion.[8] Last but not least, practically all members of Parliament were property-owners. Landowners, supported by the merchants, feared that if the king succeeded in raising taxes on his own authority their wealth would be insecure. Hence there were strong grounds for resistance.

In England the Parliament was so organized as to make resistance effective.[9] There was only one Parliament for the whole country. There were no provincial or local estates, as in the Dutch Republic, Spain, France, Germany, and Poland. Hence all parliamentary opposition was concentrated in one place. In this one place, the one and only Parliament, there were only two houses, the House of Lords and the House of Commons. The landed interest dominated in both houses, the noblemen in the Lords and the gentry in the Commons. In the Commons the gentry, who formed the bulk of the aristocracy, mixed with representatives of the merchants and the towns. Indeed the towns frequently chose country gentlemen to represent them. Hence the houses of Parliament did not accentuate, as did the estates on the Continent, the class division within the country. Nor was the church present in Parliament as a separate force. Before Henry VIII's break with Rome the bishops and abbots together had

[6] See pp. 83–87.
[7] See pp. 71, 95.
[8] See p. 71.
[9] See p. 32.

formed a large majority in the House of Lords. Now there were no abbots left, for there were no monasteries. The House of Lords was now predominantly secular; in the first Parliament of James I there were eighty-two lay peers and twenty-six bishops. The great landowners had captured the House of Lords. The smaller landowners of the Commons had been enriched by receiving former monastic lands and had prospered by raising wool. The merchants had likewise grown up under mercantilistic protection. Parliament was strong not only in organization but in the social interests and wealth that it represented. No king could long govern against its will.

In 1629 king and Parliament came to a deadlock. Charles I attempted to rule without Parliament, which could legally meet only at the royal summons. He intended to give England a good and efficient government. Had he succeeded, the course of English constitutional development would have paralleled that of France. But by certain reforms in Ireland he antagonized the English landlords who had interests in that country. By supporting the High Anglicans he made enemies of the Puritans. By attempting to modernize the navy with funds raised without parliamentary consent (called "ship money") he alarmed all property-owners, whose opposition was typified in the famous lawsuit of a country gentleman, John Hampden, in 1637.

The ship-money case illustrates the best arguments of both sides. It was the old custom in England for coastal towns to provide ships for the king's service in time of war. More recently, these coastal towns had provided money instead. Charles I wished to maintain a navy in time of peace and to have ship money paid by the country as a whole, including the inland counties. In the old or medieval view it was the function of the towns which were directly affected to maintain a fleet. In the new view, sponsored by the king, the whole nation was the unit on which a navy should be based. The country gentlemen whom Parliament mainly represented, and most of whom lived in inland counties, wished neither to pay new taxes, nor to depart from old customs which worked in their favor, nor even to maintain a navy in which they saw little advantage to themselves. It was the king who, in the ship-money case, represented the more modern ideas of government and the needs of state. The parliamentary class represented the idea, derived from the Middle Ages, that new taxes must be authorized by Parliament. John Hampden lost his case in court, but he won the sympathy of the politically significant classes of the country. Until the king could govern with the confidence of Parliament, or until Parliament itself was willing, not merely to keep down taxes, but to assume the responsibilities of government under modern conditions, neither a navy nor any effectual government could be maintained.

The Scots were the first to rebel. In 1637 they rioted in Edinburgh against attempts to impose the Anglican religion in Scotland. Charles, to raise funds to put down the Scottish rebellion, convoked the English Parliament in 1640, for the first time in eleven years. When it proved hostile to him he dissolved it and called for new elections. The same men were returned. The resulting body, since it sat theoretically for twenty years without new elections, from 1640 to 1660, is known historically as the Long Parliament. Its principal leaders—men like John Hampden, John Pym, and Oliver Cromwell—were small or moderately well-to-do landowning gentry. The merchant class, while furnishing no leaders, lent its support.

The Long Parliament, far from assisting the king against the Scots, used the Scottish rebellion as a means of pressing its own demands. These were revolutionary from the outset. Parliament insisted that the chief royal advisers be not merely removed but impeached and put to death. It abolished the Star Chamber and the High Commission. The most extreme Calvinist element, the "root and branch" men or "radicals," drove through a bill for the abolition of bishops, revolutionizing the Anglican church. In 1642 Parliament and king came to open war, the king drawing followers mainly from the north and west, the Parliament from the commercially and agriculturally more advanced counties of the south and east. During the war, as the price of support from the Scottish army, Parliament adopted the Solemn League and Covenant. This prescribed that religion in England, Scotland and Ireland should be made uniform "according to the word of God and the example of the best reformed churches." Thus Presbyterianism became the established legal religion of the three kingdoms.

The parliamentary forces, called Roundheads from the close haircuts favored by Puritans, gradually defeated the royalists. The wars brought a hitherto unknown gentleman named Oliver Cromwell to the foreground. A devout Puritan, he organized a new and more effective military force, the Ironsides, in which extreme Protestant exaltation provided the basis for morale, discipline, and the will to fight. Parliament had no sooner defeated the king than it fell out with its own army. The army, in which a more popular class was represented than in the Parliament, became the center of advanced democratic ideas. Many of the soldiers objected to Presbyterianism as much as to Anglicanism. They favored a free toleration for all "godly" forms of religion, with no superior church organization above local groups of like-minded spirits.

Cromwell concluded that the defeated king, Charles I, could not be trusted, that "ungodly" persons of all kinds put their hopes in him (what later ages would call counterrevolution), and that he must be put to death. Since Parliament hesitated, Cromwell with the support of the army broke Parliament up. The Long Parliament, having started in 1640 with some 500 members, had sunk by 1649 to about 150 (for this revolution, like others, was pushed through by a minority); of these Cromwell now drove out almost 100, leaving a Rump of 50 or 60. This operation was called Pride's Purge, after the Colonel Pride who commanded the soldiers by whom Parliament was intimidated; and in subsequent revolutions such excisions have been commonly known as purges, and the residues, sometimes, as rumps. The Rump put King Charles to death on the scaffold in 1649.

England, or rather the whole British Isles, was now declared a republic. It was named the Commonwealth. Cromwell tried to govern as best he could. Religious toleration was decreed except for Unitarians and atheists on the one hand, and except for Roman Catholics and the most obstinate Anglicans on the other—a considerable exception. Cromwell had to subdue both Scotland and Ireland by force. In Scotland the execution of the king, violating the ancient national Scottish monarchy of the Stuarts, had swung the country back into the royalist camp. Cromwell crushed the Scots in 1650. Meanwhile the Protestant and Calvinist fury swept over Ireland. A massacre of newly settled Protestants in Ulster in 1641 had left bitter memories which were now avenged. The Irish garrisons of Drogheda and Wexford were defeated and massacred. Thousands of Catholics were killed; priests were put to the sword, and women and small children dispatched in cold blood. Where formerly, in the "plantation" of Ulster, a whole Protestant population had been settled in northern Ireland, bodily replacing the native Irish, now Protestant landlords were scattered over the country as a whole, replacing the Catholic landlords and retaining the Catholic peasantry as their tenants. What now happened in Ireland was a close parallel to what had happened thirty years before in Bohemia, except that Protestant and Catholic roles were reversed.[10] For the Irish, as for the Czechs, the native religion and clergy were driven underground, a foreign and detested church was established, and a new and foreign landed aristocracy, originally recruited in large measure from military adventurers, was settled upon the country, in which, as soon as it assured the payment of its rents, it soon ceased to reside.

In England itself Cromwell ruled with great difficulty. In external affairs his regime was successful enough, for he not only completed the subjugation of Ireland, but in the Navigation Act of 1651[11] he opened the English attack on the Dutch maritime supremacy, and in a war with Spain, in which the English acquired Jamaica, he opened the English bidding for the inheritance of the Spanish Habsburgs. But he failed to make himself loved by a majority of the English. The Puritan Revolution, like others, produced its extremists. It failed to satisfy the most ardent and could not win over the truly conservative, so that Cromwell found himself reluctantly more autocratic, and more alone.

A party arose called the Levellers, who were in fact what later times would call advanced political democrats. They were numerous in the Puritan army, though their chief spokesman, John Lilburne, was a civilian. Appealing to natural rights and to the rights of Englishmen, they asked for a nearly universal manhood suffrage, equality of representation, a written constitution, and subordination of Parliament to a reformed body of voters. They thus anticipated many ideas of the American and French revolutions over a century later. There were others in whom religious and social radicalism were indistinguishably mixed. George Fox, going beyond Calvinism or Presbyterianism, founded the Society of Friends, or "Quakers," who caused consternation by rejecting various social amenities in the name of the Spirit. A more ephemeral group, the "Diggers," proceeded to occupy and cultivate common lands, or lands privately owned, in a general repudiation of property. The Fifth Monarchy Men were a millennial group who felt that the end of the world was at hand. They were so called from their belief, as they read the Bible, that history had

[10]See pp. 144, 232.
[11]See p. 173.

seen four empires, those of Assyria, Persia, Alexander, and Caesar; and that the existing world was still "Caesar's" but would soon give way to the fifth monarchy, of Christ, in which justice would at last rule.

Cromwell opposed such movements, by which all established persons in society felt threatened. As a regicide and a Puritan, however, he could not turn to the royalist and Anglican interests. Unable to agree even with the Rump, he abolished it also in 1653, and thereafter vainly attempted to govern, as Lord Protector, through representative bodies devised by himself and his followers, under a written consti- tution, the Instrument of Government. Actually, he was driven to place England under military rule, the regime of the "major-generals." These officials, each in his district, repressed malcontents, vagabonds, and "bandits," closed ale houses, and prohibited cock-fighting, in a mixture of moral puritanism and political dictatorship. Cromwell died in 1658; and his son was unable to maintain the Protectorate. Two years later, with all but universal assent, royalty was restored. Charles II, son of the dead Charles I, became king of England and of Scotland.

Cromwell, by beheading a king and keeping his successor off the throne for eleven years, had left a lesson which was not forgotten. Though he favored constitutional and parliamentary government and had granted a measure of religious toleration, he had in fact ruled as a dictator in behalf of a stern Puritan minority. The English people now began to blot from their memories the fact that they had ever had a real revolution. The fervid dream of a "godly" England was dissipated forever. What was remembered was a nightmare of standing armies and major-generals, of grim Puritans and overwrought religious enthusiasts. The English lower classes, for whom politics could still take only a religious form, ceased to have any political consciousness for over a century. Democratic ideas were generally rejected as "levelling." They were generally abandoned in England after 1660 or were cherished by obscure individuals who could not make themselves heard. Such ideas, indeed, had a more continuous history in the English colonies in America, where some leaders of the discredited revolution took refuge.

What was restored in 1660 was not only the monarchy, in the person of Charles II, but also the Church of England and the Parliament. Everything, legally, was supposed to be as it had been in 1640. The difference was that Charles II, knowing the fate of his father, was careful not to provoke Parliament to extremes, and that the classes represented in Parliament, frightened by the disturbances of the past twenty years, were for some time more warmly loyal to the king than they had been before 1640 and more willing to uphold the established church.

Parliament during the Restoration enacted some far-reaching legislation. It changed the legal basis of land tenure, abolishing certain old feudal payments owed by landholders to the king. The possession of land thus came to resemble private property of modern type, and the landowning class became more definitely a propertied aristocracy. In place of the feudal dues to the king, which had been

19
Britain: The Triumph of Parliament

The Restoration, 1660–1688: The Later Stuarts

automatically payable, Parliament arranged for the king to receive income in the form of taxation, which Parliament could raise or reduce in amount. This gave a new power to Parliament and a new flexibility to government. The aristocracy, in short, cleared their property of customary restrictions and obligations and at the same time undertook to support the state by imposing taxes on themselves. The English aristocracy proved more willing than the corresponding classes on the Continent to pay a large share of the expenses of government. Its reward was that, for a century and a half, it virtually ran the government to the exclusion of everyone else. Landowners in this period directed not only national affairs through Parliament, but also local affairs as justices of the peace. The justices, drawn from the gentry of each county, decided small lawsuits, punished misdemeanors, and supervised the parish officials charged with poor relief and care of the roads. The regime of the landlord-justices came to be called the "squirearchy."

Other classes drew less immediate advantage from the Restoration. The Navigation Act of 1651 was renewed and even added to, so that commercial, shipping, and manufacturing interests were well protected. But in other ways the landed classes now in power showed themselves unsympathetic to the business classes of the towns. Many people in the towns were Dissenters, of the element formerly called Puritan, and now refusing to accept the restored Church of England. Parliament excluded Dissenters from the town corporations, forbade any dissenting clergymen to teach school or come within five miles of an incorporated town, and prohibited all religious meetings, called "conventicles," not held according to the forms and by the authority of the Church of England. The effect was that many middle-class townspeople found it difficult or impossible to follow their preferred religion, to obtain an education for their children, either elementary or advanced (for Oxford and Cambridge were a part of the established church), to take part in local affairs through the town corporations, or to sit in the House of Commons, since the corporations in many cases chose the burgesses who represented the towns. The lowest classes, the very poor, were discouraged by the same laws from following sectarian and visionary preachers. Another enactment fell upon them alone, the Act of Settlement of 1662, which decentralized the administration of the Poor Law, making each parish responsible only for its own paupers. Poor people, who were very numerous, were condemned to remain in the parishes where they lived. A large section of the English population was immobilized.

But it was not long after the Restoration that Parliament and king were again at odds. The issue was again religion. There was at this time a tendency throughout Europe for Protestants to return voluntarily to Roman Catholicism, a tendency naturally dreaded by the Protestant churches. It was most conspicuously illustrated when the daughter of Gustavus Adolphus himself, Queen Christina of Sweden, to the consternation of the Protestant world, abdicated her throne and was received into the Roman church. In England the national feeling was excitedly anti-Catholic. No measures were more popular than those against "popery"; and the squires in Parliament, stiffly loyal to the Church of England, dreaded papists even more than Dissenters. The king, Charles II, was personally inclined to Catholicism. He admired the magnificent monarchy of Louis XIV, which he would have liked to duplicate, so far as possible, in England. At odds with his Parliament, Charles II made overtures to Louis XIV. The secret treaty of Dover of 1670 was the outcome. Charles thereby agreed to join Louis XIV in his expected war against the Dutch; and Louis agreed to pay the king of England three million livres a year during the war. He hoped also that Charles II would soon find it opportune to rejoin the Roman church.

While these arrangements were unknown in detail in England, it was known that Charles II was well disposed to the French and to Roman Catholicism. England went to war again with the Dutch. The king's brother and heir, James, Duke of York, publicly announced his conversion to Rome. Charles II, in a "declaration of indulgence," announced the nonenforcement of laws against Dissenters. The king declared that he favored general toleration, but it was rightly feared that his real aim was to promote Roman Catholicism in England, and that his policy might be the opening wedge for the Counter Reformation, which had already swept Protestantism out of Bohemia and Poland and was at this very moment menacing it in France. Parliament retorted in 1673 by passing the Test Act, which required all officeholders to take communion in the Church of England. The Test Act renewed the legislation against Dissenters and also made it impossible for Catholics to serve in the government or in the army and navy. The Test Act remained on the statute books until 1828.

While Charles' pro-French and pro-Catholic policies were extremely unpopular, both among the country gentry who disliked Frenchmen from prejudice, and the merchants who found in them increasingly pressing competitors, still the situation might not have come to a head except for the avowed Catholicism and French orientation of Charles' brother James, due to be the next king since Charles had no legitimate children. A strong movement developed in Parliament to exclude James by law from the throne. The exclusionists—and those generally who were most suspicious of king, Catholics, and Frenchmen—received the nickname of Whigs. The king's supporters were popularly called Tories. The Whigs, while backed by the middle class and merchants of London, drew their main strength from the upper aristocracy, especially certain great noblemen who might expect, if the king's power were weakened, to play a prominent part in ruling the country themselves. The Tories were the party of the lesser aristocracy and gentry, those who were suspicious of the "moneyed interest" of London, and felt a strong loyalty to church and king. These two parties became permanently established in English public life. But all the Whigs and Tories together, at this time, did not number more than a few thousand persons.

James II, despite Whig vexation, became king in 1685. He soon antagonized even the Tories. The Tories were strong Anglicans or Church of England men. As landowners they appointed most of the parish clergy, who imparted Tory sentiments to the rural population, and from their ranks were drawn the bishops, archdeacons, university functionaries, and other higher personnel of the church. The laws keeping

The Revolution of 1688

183

Dissenters and Catholics from office had given Anglicans a monopoly in local and national government and in the army and navy. James II acted as if there were no Test Act, claiming the right to suspend its operation in individual cases, and appointed a good many Catholics to influential and lucrative positions. He offered a program, as his brother had done, of general religious toleration, to allow Protestant Dissenters as well as Roman Catholics to participate in public life. Such a program, whether frankly meant as a secularizing of politics or indirectly intended as favoritism to Catholics, was equally repugnant to the Church of England. Seven bishops refused to endorse it. They were prosecuted for disobedience to the king but were acquitted by the jury. James, by these actions, violated the liberties of the established church, threatened the Anglican monopoly of church and state, and aroused the popular terrors of "popery." He was also forced to take the position philosophically set forth by his grandfather James I, that a king of England could make and unmake the law by his own will. The Tories joined the Whigs in opposition. In 1688, a son was born to James II and baptized into the Catholic faith. The prospect now opened up of an indefinite line of Catholic rulers in England. Leading men of both parties thereupon abandoned James II. They offered the throne to his grown daughter Mary, born and brought up a Protestant before her father's conversion to Rome.

Mary was the wife of William of Orange. William, it will be recalled, had spent his adult life in blocking the ambitions of the king of France, who, it should be recalled likewise, threatened Europe with a "universal monarchy" by absorbing or inheriting the world of Spain. To William III it would be a mere distraction to be husband to a queen of England, or even to be king in his own name, unless England could be brought to serve his own purposes. He was immutably Dutch; his purpose was to save Holland and hence to ruin Louis XIV. His chief interest in England was to bring the English into his balance of power against France. Since the English were generally anti-French, and had chafed under the pro-French tendencies of their kings, William without difficulty reached an understanding with the discontented Whigs and Tories. Protected by a written invitation from prominent Englishmen he invaded England with a considerable army. James II fled, and William was proclaimed co-ruler with Mary over England and Scotland. In the next year, 1690, at the Boyne River in Ireland, a motley army of Dutchmen, Germans, Scots, and French Huguenots under William III defeated a French and Irish force led by James II. Thus the liberties of England were saved. James II fled to France.

Louis XIV of course refused to recognize his inveterate enemy as ruler of England. He maintained James at the French court with all the honors due the English king. It was thereafter one of his principal war aims to restore the Catholic and Stuart dynasty across the Channel. The English, contrariwise, had added reason to fight the French. French victory would mean counterrevolution and royal absolutism in England. The whole revolution of 1688 was at stake in the French wars.

In 1689, Parliament enacted a Bill of Rights, stipulating that no law could be suspended by the king (as the Test Act had been), no taxes raised or army maintained except by parliamentary consent, and no subject (however poor) arrested and detained without legal process. William III accepted these articles as conditions to receiving the crown. Thereafter the relation between king and people was a kind of contract. It was further provided, by the Act of Settlement of 1701, that no Catholic could be king of England; this excluded the descendants of James II, known in the following century as the Pretenders. Parliament also passed the Toleration Act of 1689, which allowed Protestant Dissenters to practice their religion but still excluded them from political life and public service. Since ways of evading these restrictions were soon found, and since even Catholics were not molested unless they supported the Pretenders, there was thereafter no serious trouble over religion in England and Lowland Scotland.

The English Parliament could make no laws for Scotland, and it was to be feared that James II might some day be restored in his northern kingdom. The securing of the parliamentary revolution in England, and of the island's defenses against France, required that the two kingdoms be organically joined. There was little sentiment in Scotland, however, for a merger with the English. The English tempted the Scots with economic advantages. The Scots still had no rights in the English East India Company, nor in the English colonies, nor within the English system of mercantilism and Navigation Acts. They obtained such rights by consenting to a union. In 1707 the United Kingdom of Great Britain was created. The Scots retained their own legal system and established Presbyterian church, but their government and parliament were merged with those of England. The term "British" came into use to refer to both English and Scots.

As for Ireland, it was now feared as a center of Stuart and French intrigue. The Revolution of 1688 marked the climax of a long record of trouble. Ireland had never been simply "conquered" by England, though certain English or rather Anglo-Norman families had carved out estates there since the twelfth century. By the end of the Middle Ages Ireland was organized as a separate kingdom with its own parliament, subordinate to the English crown. During the Reformation the Irish remained Catholic while England turned Protestant, but the monasteries were dissolved in Ireland as in England; and the organized church as such, the established Church of Ireland, with its apparatus of bishoprics, parishes, and tithes, became an Anglican communion in which the mass of native Irish had no interest. Next came the plantation of Ulster, already mentioned, in which a mass of newcomers, mainly Scottish and Presbyterian, settled in the northern part of the island. Then in Cromwell's time, as just seen, English landlords spread through the rest of the country; or rather, a new Anglo-Irish upper class developed, in which English landowning families, residing most often in England, added the income from Irish estates to their miscellaneous revenues. Ireland therefore by the close of the seventeenth century was a very mixed country. Probably two-thirds of its population was Catholic, of generally Celtic ethnic background; perhaps a fifth was Presbyterian, with recent Scottish connections; the small remainder was made up of Anglicans, largely Anglo-Irish of recent or distant origin in England, who controlled most of the land, manned the official church, and were influential in the Irish parliament. It was essentially a landlord and peasant society, in which the Presbyterian as well as the Catholic mass was overwhelmingly agricultural; towns were small, and the middle class scarcely developed.

After the Revolution of 1688, in which the final overthrow of James II took place at the Boyne River, the English feared Ireland as a source of danger to the postrevolutionary arrangements in England. Resistance of the subjugated Catholics had also to be prevented. Hence to the burden of an alien church and absentee landlordism was now added the "penal code." Catholic clergy were banished, and Catholics were forbidden to vote or to sit in the Irish parliament. Catholic teachers were forbidden to teach, and Catholic parents were forbidden to send children overseas to be educated in Catholic schools. No Catholic could take a degree from Dublin University. Catholic Irishmen were forbidden to purchase land, to lease it for more than thirty-one years, to inherit it from a Protestant, or to own a horse worth more than £5. A Catholic whose son turned Protestant found his own property rights limited in his son's favor. Catholics were forbidden to be attorneys, to serve as constables, or, in most trades, to have more than two apprentices. Some disabilities fell on the Protestant Irish also. Thus Irish shipping was excluded from the British colonies, nor could the Irish import colonial goods except through England. Export of Irish woolens and glass manufactures was prohibited. No import tariff on English manufactures could be levied by the Irish parliament. About all that was left to the Irish, in international trade, was the export of agricultural produce; and the foreign exchange acquired in this way went very largely to pay the rents of absentee landlords.

The purpose of the penal code was in part strategic, to weaken Ireland as a potentially hostile country during a long period of wars with France. In part it was commercial, to favor English manufactures by removing Irish competition. And in part it was social, to confirm the position of the Anglican interest, or "ascendancy" as it came to be called. Parts of the code were removed piecemeal in the following decades, and a Catholic merchant class grew up in the eighteenth century; but much remained in effect for a long time, so that, for example, a Catholic could not vote for members of the Irish parliament until 1793, and even then could not be elected to it. In general, the Irish emerged from the seventeenth century as the most repressed people of western Europe.

England, immediately after the expulsion of James II, joined William III's coalition against France. To the alliance England brought a highly competent naval force, together with very considerable wealth. William's government, to finance the war, borrowed £1,200,000 from a syndicate of private lenders, who in return for holding government bonds were given the privilege of operating a bank. Thus originated, in 1694, both the Bank of England and the British national debt. Owners of liquid assets, merchants of London and Whig aristocrats with fat rent rolls, having lent their money to the new regime, had a compelling reason to defend it against the French and James II. And having at last a government whose policies they could control, they were willing to entrust it with money in large amounts. The national debt rapidly rose, while the credit of the government held consistently good; and for many years the Continent was astonished at the wealth that the British government could tap at will, and the quantities of money that it could pour into the wars of Europe.

The events of 1688 came to be known to the English as the Glorious Revolution. The Revolution was considered to have vindicated the principles of parliamentary government, the rule of law, and even the right of rebellion against tyranny. It has often been depicted as the climax in the growth of English constitutional self-government. Political writers like John Locke, shortly after the events, helped to give wide currency to these ideas.[12] There was in truth some justification for these views even though in more recent times some writers have "deglorified" the Revolution of 1688. They point out that it was a class movement, promoted and maintained by the landed aristocracy. The Parliament which boldly asserted itself against the king was at the same time closing itself to large segments of the people. Where in the Middle Ages members of the House of Commons had usually received pay for their services, this custom disappeared in the seventeenth century, so that thereafter only men with independent incomes could sit. After the parliamentary triumph of 1688 this tendency became a matter of law. An act of 1710 required members of the House of Commons to possess private incomes at such a level that only a few thousand persons could legally qualify. This income had to come from the ownership of land. England from 1688 to 1832 was the best example in modern times of a true aristocracy, i.e., of a country in which the aristocratic landowning class not only enjoyed privileges but also conducted the government. But the landowning interest was then the only class sufficiently wealthy, numerous, educated and self-conscious to stand on its own feet. The rule of the "gentlemen of England" was within its limits a regime of political liberty.

20
The France of Louis XIV, 1643–1715: The Triumph of Absolutism

French Civilization in the Seventeenth Century

Having traveled in the outer orbits of the European political system, we come now to its radiant and mighty center, the domain of the Sun King himself, the France against which the rest of Europe felt obliged to combine, and on whose push and pull depended the course of the lesser bodies—the future of the Spanish possessions, the independence of Holland, the maintenance in England of the parliamentary revolution. The France of Louis XIV owed much of its ascendancy to the quantity and the quality of its population. With 19,000,000 inhabitants in 1700 it was four times as populous as England and twice as populous as Spain; and its people were among the most industrious, thrifty, and generally proficient in Europe. Its fertile soil, in an agricultural age, made it exceptionally wealthy; and it also had a great many cities with a busy commercial and capitalistic class, so much so that the French term for the upper elements of townspeople, the *bourgeoisie*, came later to designate this class in all countries. The French in the seventeenth century began trading in India and Madagascar, founded Canada, penetrated the Great Lakes and the Mississippi

---

[12]On John Locke and the philosophy of the Glorious Revolution see pp. 319–321.

Valley, set up plantations in the West Indies, expanded their ancient commerce with the Levant, enlarged their mercantile marine, and for a time had the leading navy of Europe.

The dominance of France meant the dominance not merely of power, but of a people generally admitted to be in the forefront of civilization. They carried over the versatility of the Italy of the Renaissance. In Poussin and Claude Lorrain they produced a notable school of painters, their architecture was emulated throughout Europe, and they excelled in military fortification and general engineering. Much of their literature, though often written by bourgeois writers, was designed for an aristocratic and courtly audience, which had put aside the uncouth manners of an earlier day and prided itself on the refinement of its tastes and perceptions. Corneille and Racine wrote austere tragedies on the fundamental situations of human life. Molière, in his comedies, ridiculed bumbling doctors, new-rich bourgeois, and foppish aristocrats, making the word "marquis" almost a joke in the French language. La Fontaine gave the world his animal fables, and La Rochefoucauld, in his witty and sardonic maxims, a great nobleman's candid judgment on human nature. In Descartes the French produced a great mathematician and scientific thinker, in Pascal a scientist who was also a profound spokesman for Christianity, in Bayle the father of modern skeptics. It was French thought and the French language, not merely the armies of Louis XIV, which in the seventeenth century were sweeping the European world.

The Development of
Absolutism in France

This ascendancy of French culture went along with a regime in which political liberties were at a discount. It was an embellishment to the absolute monarchy of Louis XIV. France had a tradition of political freedom in the feudal sense. It had the same kind of background of feudal liberties as did the other countries of Europe. It had an Estates-General, which had not met since 1615 but was not legally abolished. In some regions Provincial Estates, still meeting frequently, retained a measure of self-government and of power over taxation. There were about a dozen bodies known as parliaments,[13] which, unlike the English Parliament, had developed as courts of law, each being the supreme court for a certain area of the country. The parliaments upheld certain "fundamental laws" which they said the king could not overstep, and they often refused to enforce royal edicts which they declared to be unconstitutional. We have already observed how France, beneath the surface, was almost as composite as Germany.[14] French towns had won charters of acknowledged rights, and many of the great provinces enjoyed liberties written into old agreements with the crown. These local liberties were the main reason for a good deal of institutional complication. There were some 300 "customs" or regional systems of law; it was observed that a traveler sometimes changed laws more often than he changed horses. Internal tariffs ran along the old provincial borders. Tolls were

[13] Often spelled *parlements,* as in French, to distinguish from the English Parliament.
[14] See pp. 135–136 and map, p. 193.

levied by manorial lords. The king's taxes fell less heavily on some regions than on others. Neither coinage nor weights and measures were uniform throughout the country. France was a bundle of territories held together by allegiance to the king.

This older kind of freedom discredited itself in France at the very time when by triumphing in Germany it pulled the Holy Roman Empire to pieces, and when in England it successfully made the transition to a more modern form of political liberty, embodied in the parliamentary though aristocratic state. In France the old medieval, feudal, or local type of liberty became associated with disorder. It has already been related how after the disorders of the sixteenth-century religious wars people had turned with relief to the monarchy and how Henry IV and then Richelieu had begun to make the monarchy strong.[15] The troubles of the Fronde provided additional incentive for absolutism in France.

The Fronde broke out immediately after the Peace of Westphalia, while Louis XIV was still a child, and was directed against Cardinal Mazarin, who was governing in his name. It was an abortive revolution, led by the same elements, the parliaments and the nobility, which were to precipitate the great French Revolution in 1789. The parliaments, especially the Parliament of Paris, insisted in 1648 on their right to pronounce certain edicts unconstitutional. Barricades were thrown up and street fighting broke out in Paris. The nobility rebelled, as it had often in the past. Leadership was assumed by certain prominent noblemen who, roughly like the great Whigs of England, had enough wealth and influence to believe that, if the king's power were kept down, they might govern the country themselves. The nobility demanded a calling of the Estates-General, expecting to dominate over the bourgeoisie and the clergy in that body. Armed bands of soldiers, unemployed since the Peace of Westphalia and led by nobles, roamed about the country terrorizing the peasants. If the nobles had their way, it was probable that the manorial system would fall on the peasants more heavily, as in eastern Europe, where triumphant lords were at this very time exacting increased labor services from the peasants. Finally the rebellious nobles called in Spanish troops, though France was at war with Spain. By this time the bourgeoisie, represented in the parliaments, had withdrawn support from the rebellious nobles. The agitation subsided in total failure, because bourgeoisie and aristocracy could not work together, because the nobles outraged the loyalty of many Frenchmen by joining with a power with which France was at war, and because the *frondeurs*, especially after the parliaments deserted them, had no systematic or constructive program, aiming only at the overthrow of the unpopular Cardinal Mazarin and at obtaining offices and favors for themselves.

After the Fronde, as after the religious wars, the bourgeoisie and peasantry of France, to protect themselves against the claims of the aristocracy, were in a mood to welcome the exercise of strong power by the kings. And in the young Louis XIV they had a man more than willing to grasp all the power he could get. Louis, on Mazarin's death in 1661, announced that he would govern the country himself. He was the

---

[15]See pp. 139–141.

third king of the Bourbon line. It was the Bourbon tradition, established by Henry IV and by Richelieu, to draw the teeth from the feudal aristocrats, and this tradition Louis XIV followed. He was not a man of any transcendent abilities, though he had the capacity, often found among successful executives, of learning a good deal from conversation with experts. His education was not very good, having been made purposely easy; but he had the ability to see and stick to definite lines of policy, and he was extremely methodical and industrious in his daily habits, scrupulously loading himself with administrative business throughout his reign. He was extremely fond of himself and his position of kingship, with an insatiable appetite for admiration and flattery; he loved magnificent display and elaborate etiquette, though to some extent he simply adopted them as instruments of policy rather than as a personal whim.

With the reign of Louis XIV the "state" in its modern form took a long step forward. The state in the abstract has always seemed theoretical to the English-speaking world. Let us say, for simplicity, that the state represents a fusion of justice and power. A sovereign state possesses, within its territory, a monopoly over the administration of justice and the use of force. Private persons neither pass legal judgments on others nor control private armies of their own. For private and unauthorized persons to do so, in an orderly state, constitutes rebellion. This was in contrast to the older feudal practice, by which feudal lords maintained manorial courts and led their own followers into battle. Against these feudal practices Louis XIV energetically worked, though not with complete success, claiming to possess in his own person, as sovereign ruler, a monopoly over the law-making processes and the armed forces of the kingdom. This is the deeper meaning of his reputed boast, *L'état, c'est moi*—"the state is myself." In the France of the seventeenth century, divided by classes and by regions, there was in fact no means of consolidating the powers of state except in a single man.

The state, however, while representing law and order within its borders, has generally stood in a lawless and disorderly relation to other states, since no higher monopoly of law and force has existed. Louis XIV, personifying the French state, had no particular regard for the claims of other states or rulers. He was constantly either at war or preparing for war with his neighbors. The modern state, indeed, was created by the needs of peace at home and war abroad. Machinery of government, as devised by Louis XIV and others, was a means of giving order and security within the territory of the state, and of raising, supporting and controlling armies for use against other states.

The idea that law and force within a country should be monopolized by the lawful king was the essence of the seventeenth-century doctrine of absolutism. Its principal theorist in the time of Louis XIV was Bishop Bossuet. Bossuet advanced the old Christian teaching that all power comes from God, and that all who hold power are responsible to God for the way they use it. He held that kings were God's representatives in the political affairs of earth. Royal power, according to Bossuet, was absolute but not arbitrary: not arbitrary because it must be reasonable and just, like the will of God which it reflected; absolute in that it was free from dictation by parliaments, estates or other subordinate elements within the country. Law, therefore, was the will of the sovereign king, so long as it conformed to the higher law which was the will of God. This doctrine, affirming the divine right of kings, was popularly held in France at the time and was taught in the churches. It was fortified by the principles of Roman law, which also held that laws could be made and unmade, modified, and amended by act of the sovereign power. In addition, the authority of Louis XIV rested on purely practical considerations. Experience showed absolutism to be the corrective to anarchy, and the king was widely believed to represent the interests of the country better than anyone else.

Possibly the most fundamental step taken by Louis XIV was to assure himself of control of the army. Armed forces had formerly been almost a private enterprise. Specialists in fighting, leading their own troops, worked for governments more or less as they chose, either in return for money or to pursue political aims of their own. This was especially common in central Europe, but even in France great noblemen had strong private influence over the troops, and in times of disorder nobles led armed retainers about the country. Colonels were virtually on their own. Provided with a general commission and with funds by some government, they recruited, trained, and equipped their own regiments, and likewise fed and supplied them, often by preying upon bourgeois and peasants in the vicinity. In these circumstances it was often difficult to say on whose side soldiers were fighting. It was hard for governments to set armies into motion and equally hard to make them stop fighting, for commanders fought for their own interests and on their own momentum. War was not a "continuation of policy"; it was not an act of the state; it easily degenerated, as in the Thirty Years' War, into a kind of aimless and perpetual violence.

Louis XIV made war an activity of state. He saw to it that all armed persons in France fought only for him. This produced peace and order in France, while strengthening the fighting power of France against other states. Under the older conditions there was also little integration among different units and arms of the army. Infantry regiments and troops of horse went largely their own way, and the artillery was supplied by civilian technicians under contract. Louis XIV created a stronger unity of control, put the artillery organically into the army, systematized the military ranks and grades, and clarified the chain of command, placing himself at the top. The government supervised recruiting, required colonels to prove that they were maintaining the proper number of soldiers, and assumed most of the responsibility for equipping, provisioning, clothing, and housing the troops. Higher officers, thus becoming dependent on the government, could be subjected to discipline. The soldiers were put into uniforms, taught to march in step, and housed in barracks; thus they too became more susceptible to discipline and control. Armed forces became less of a terror to their own people and a more effective weapon in the hands of government. They were employed usually against other governments but sometimes to suppress rebellion at home. Louis XIV also increased the French army in size, raising it from about 100,000 to about 400,000. These changes, both in size and in degree of government control, were made possible by the growth of a large civilian administration. The heads of this administration under Louis XIV were civilians. They were in effect the first ministers of war, and their assistants, officials, inspectors, and clerks constituted the first organized war ministry.

Louis XIV was not only a vain man but made it a political principle to overawe the country with his own grandeur. He built himself a whole new city at the old village of Versailles about ten miles from Paris. Where the Escorial had the atmosphere of a monastery, Versailles was a monument to worldly splendor. Tremendous in size alone, fitted out with polished mirrors, gleaming chandeliers, and magnificent tapestries, opening on to a formal park with fountains and shaded walks, the palace of Versailles was the marvel of Europe and the envy of lesser kings. It was virtually a public building, much of it used for government offices, and with nobles, churchmen, notable bourgeois, and servants milling about on the king's affairs. The more exclusive honors of the château were reserved for the higher aristocrats. The king surrounded his daily routine of rising, eating, and going to bed (known as the *lever, dîner,* and *coucher*) with an infinite series of ceremonial acts, so minute and so formalized that there were, for example, six different entries of persons at the *lever,* and a certain gentleman at a specified moment held the right sleeve of the king's nightshirt as he took it off. The most exalted persons thought themselves the greater for thus waiting on so august a being. In this way, and by more material favors, many great lords were induced to live habitually at court. Here, under the royal eye, they might engage in palace intrigue but were kept away from real political mischief. Versailles completed the political and moral ruin of the French aristocracy as a class. The king himself was one of the few who could proceed through such rounds of elaborate living and still be able to attend regularly to public affairs. Neither the nobles whom he kept about him nor his own successors Louis XV and Louis XVI were able to carry the burden.

For positions in the government, as distinguished from his personal entourage, Louis XIV preferred to use men who had recently risen from the bourgeois class, who were dependent on him for salaries and careers, and who unlike noblemen could aspire to no independent political influence of their own. He never called the Estates-General, which in any case no one except some of the nobility wanted. Some of the Provincial Estates, because of local and aristocratic pressures, he allowed to remain functioning. He temporarily destroyed the independence of the parliaments, commanding them to accept his orders, as Henry IV had commanded them to accept the Edict of Nantes.[16] He stifled the old liberties of the towns, turning their civic offices into empty and purchasable honors and likewise regulating the operation of the gilds. He developed a strong system of administrative coordination, centering in a number of councils of state, which he attended in person, and in "intendants" who represented these councils throughout the country. Councilors of state and intendants were generally of bourgeois origin. Each intendant, within his district, embodied all aspects of the royal government, supervising the flow of taxes and recruiting of soldiers, keeping an eye on the local nobility, dealing with towns and

[16] See p. 138.

gilds, controlling the more or less hereditary officeholders, stamping out bandits, smugglers, and wolves, policing the market places, relieving famine, watching the local law courts, and often deciding cases himself. In this way a firm and uniform administration was superimposed upon the heterogeneous mass of the old France. In contrast to England, all local questions were handled by agents of the central government, usually honest and often efficient, but essentially bureaucrats constantly instructed by, and referring back to, their superiors at Versailles.

The France of Louis XIV, 1643–1715: The Triumph of Absolutism

To support the reorganized and enlarged army, the panoply of Versailles, and the growing civil administration, the king needed a good deal of money. Finance was always the weak spot in the French monarchy. Methods of collecting taxes were costly and inefficient. Direct taxes passed through the hands of many intermediate officials; indirect taxes were collected by private concessionaires called tax farmers, who made a substantial profit. The state always received far less than what the taxpayers actually paid. But the main weakness arose from an old bargain between the French crown and nobility; the king might raise taxes without consent if only he refrained from taxing the nobles. Only the "unprivileged" classes paid direct taxes, and these came almost to mean the peasants only, since many bourgeois in one way or another obtained exemptions. The system was outrageously unjust in throwing the tax burden on the poor and helpless. It was ruinous to the government, since the

Economic and Financial Policies: Colbert

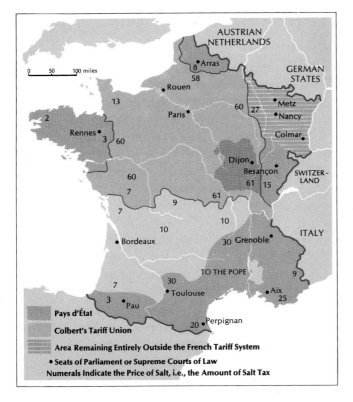

France from the Last Years of Louis XIV to the Revolution of 1789. *The map gives an idea of the diversity of law and administration before the Revolution. Dark areas are "pays d'état," provinces in which representative bodies ("estates") continued to meet. Cities named are the seats of what the French called parliaments (see p. 188). The key indicates Colbert's tariff union, the Five Great Farms (see p. 194). The area marked with hatching remained outside the French tariff system entirely; it continued to trade with the states of the Holy Roman Empire (from which it had been annexed) without interference by the French government. Numerals indicate the price of salt, i.e., the amount of the salt tax, in various regions. In general, it will be seen that regions farthest from Paris enjoyed the most "privileges" or "liberties," preserving their legal and judicial identity, provincial estates, local tariffs, and a favored position in national taxation.*

government could never raise enough money, however hard it taxed the poor, being unable to tap the real source of ready wealth, namely, the wealthier people. It was ruinous also to the French nobility, who in paying no direct taxes lost their hold over the government, lacked incentive to interest themselves in public affairs, and were unable to assume leadership of the bulk of the population. Louis XIV was willing enough to tax the nobles but was unwilling to fall under their control, and only toward the close of his reign, under extreme stress of war, was he able, for the first time in French history, to impose direct taxes on the aristocratic elements of the population. This was a great step toward equality before the law and toward sound public finance, but so many concessions and exemptions were won by nobles and bourgeois that the reform lost much of its value.

Like his predecessors, Louis resorted to all manner of expedients to increase his revenues. He raised the tax rates, always with disappointing results. He devaluated the currency. He sold patents of nobility to ambitious bourgeois. He sold government offices, judgeships, and commissions in the army and navy. For both financial and political reasons the king used his sovereign authority to annul the town charters then sell back reduced rights at a price; this produced a little income but demoralized local government and civic spirit. The need for money, arising from the fundamental inability to tax the wealthy, which in turn reflected the weakness of absolutism, of a government which would not or could not share its rule with the propertied classes, corrupted much of the public life and political aptitude of the French people.

Louis XIV wished, if only for his own purposes, to make France economically powerful. His great minister Colbert worked for twenty years to do so. Colbert went beyond Richelieu in the application of mercantilism, aiming to make France a self-sufficing economic unit and to increase the wealth from which taxes were drawn.[17] He managed to abolish local tariffs in a large part of central France, where he set up a tariff-union oddly entitled the Five Great Farms (since the remaining tolls were collected by tax farmers); and although vested interests and provincial liberties remained too strong for him to do away with all internal tariffs, the area of the Five Great Farms was in itself one of the largest free-trade areas in Europe, being about the size of England. For the convenience of businessmen Colbert promulgated a Commercial Code, replacing much of the local customary law, and long a model of business practice and business regulation. He improved communications by building roads and canals, of which the most famous was one joining the Bay of Biscay with the Mediterranean. Working through the gilds, he required the handicraft manufacturers to produce goods of specified kind and quality, believing that foreigners, if assured of quality by the government, would purchase French products more freely. He gave subsidies, tax exemptions, and other privileges to expand the manufacture of silks, tapestries, glassware, and woolens. He helped to found colonies, built up the navy, and established the French East India Company. Export of some goods, notably foodstuffs, was forbidden, for the government wished to keep

[17]On mercantilism in general, see pp. 124–126.

the populace quiet by holding down the price of bread. Export of other goods, mainly manufactures, was encouraged, partly as a means of bringing money into the country, where it could be funneled into the royal treasury. The growth of the army, and the fact that under Louis XIV the government clothed and equipped the soldiers, and hence placed unprecedentedly large orders for uniforms, overcoats, weapons, and ammunition, greatly stimulated the employment of weavers, tailors, and gunsmiths and advanced the commercial capitalism by which such labors were organized. In general, trade and manufacture developed in France under more direct government guidance than in England. They long gave the English an extremely brisk competition. Not until the age of iron and coal did France begin economically to lag.

The consolidation of France under Louis XIV reached its high point in his policies toward religion. Toward Rome Louis backed the old claims of the Gallican church to enjoy a certain national independence of policy. He repressed the movement known as Jansenism, a kind of Calvinism within the Catholic church, which persisted for almost two centuries. But it was the Protestants who suffered most.

France, in the early years of Louis XIV's reign, still allowed more religious toleration than any other large state in Europe. The Huguenots had lost their separate political status under Richelieu, but they continued to live in relative security and contentment, protected by the Edict of Nantes of 1598.[18] From the beginning, however, toleration had been a royal rather than a popular policy, and under Louis XIV the royal policy changed. The fate of Catholics at the hands of a triumphant Parliament in England suggests that the Protestants in France would have been no better off under more popular institutions.

Bending all else to his will, Louis XIV resented the presence of heretics among his subjects. He considered religious unity necessary to the strength and dignity of his rule. He perhaps envied the right claimed by most governments at the time, Protestant as well as Catholic, to determine the religion of their respective peoples. He fell under the influence of certain Catholic advisers, who, not content with the attrition by which some Protestants were turning back to Catholicism in any case, wished to hasten the process to the greater glory of themselves. Systematic conversion of Huguenots was begun. Life for Protestant families was gradually made unbearable. Finally they were literally "dragooned," mounted infantrymen being quartered in Huguenot homes to reinforce the persuasions of missionaries. In 1685 Louis revoked the Edict of Nantes. During the persecutions a good many Protestants left France, migrating to Holland, Germany, and America. Their loss was a blow to French economic life, for although Protestants were found in all levels of French society, those of the commercial and industrial classes were the most mobile. With the revocation of the Edict of Nantes France embarked on a century of official intolerance (slowly mitigated in practice), under which Protestants in France were in

[18] See pp. 139–141.

much the same position as Catholics in the British Isles. The fact that a hundred years later, when Protestants were again tolerated, many of them were found to be both commercially prosperous and politically loyal indicates that they fared far better than the Catholic Irish.

All things considered, the reign of Louis XIV brought considerable advantages to the French middle and lower classes. His most bitter critics, with the natural exception of Protestants, were disgruntled nobles such as the Duke of Saint-Simon. His use of bourgeois in influential positions and willingness to issue patents of nobility in return for money, while disgusting to the old aristocracy, were gratifying to the middle class. For the common people he did less, but he did save them from falling under the control of the lords. The intendants were assiduous enemies of the manorial courts; they did everything possible to keep the peasants under royal, not feudal, jurisdiction. Hence the French peasantry was kept free from the burden of serfdom that was rising in eastern Europe, and from the submission to rural squires that prevailed in England after the Restoration. Louis XIV, at a heavy and indeed prohibitive cost of privileges to the nobles, yet accomplished something for the cause of equality in France. He was generally popular, and even loved. What finally turned a good many Frenchmen against him in his last years was the strain brought by incessant wars.

From the outset of his reign Louis pursued a vigorous foreign policy. The quarrel between the house of France and the house of Habsburg had gone on for more than a century. The Austrian branch of the Habsburgs had been checkmated at the Peace of Westphalia. With the Spanish branch the French remained at war for another decade, until the Peace of the Pyrenees in 1659. When, two years later, Louis XIV assumed his personal rule, Spanish territories still faced France on three sides, northeast, east, and south; but so weakened was Spain that this fact was no longer a menace to France so much as a temptation to French expansion. Louis XIV could count on popular national feeling to support him, for the dream of a frontier on the Rhine and the Alps was captivating to Frenchmen. He struck in 1667. (The war was called the "War of Devolution," from a legal term used in the preliminary demands.) He was blocked, as noted above, by a Triple Alliance engineered by the Dutch.[19] With strength renewed by reforms at home, and in alliance with Charles II of England, he struck again in 1672 (the "Dutch War"), invading the Dutch provinces on the lower Rhine, and this time raising up his great adversary and inveterate enemy, the prince of Orange.[20] William III, bringing the Austrian and Spanish Habsburgs, Brandenburg, and Denmark into alliance with the Dutch Republic, forced Louis to sign the treaty of Nimwegen in 1678. The French gave up their ambitions against Holland but took from Spain the rich province of Franche-Comté, which outflanked Alsace on the south, and brought French power to the borders of Switzerland.

[19] See p. 173.
[20] See pp. 173–174, 184.

In the very next year, 1679, Louis further infiltrated the dissolving frontier of the Holy Roman Empire, this time in Lorraine and Alsace. By the Peace of Westphalia the French king had rights in this region, but the terms of that treaty were so ambiguous, and the local feudal law so confusing, that claims could be made in contrary directions. Louis XIV now set up *chambres de réunion*, as he called them, law courts in which French judges examined the claims to various parcels of territory and pronounced in favor of the king of France. French troops thereupon moved in. In 1681 French troops occupied the city of Strasbourg, which, as a free city of the Holy Roman Empire, regarded itself as an independent little republic. A protest went up over Germany against this undeclared invasion. But Germany was not a political unity. Since 1648 each German state conducted its own foreign policy, and at this very moment, in 1681, Louis XIV had an ally in the Elector of Brandenburg (forerunner of the kings of Prussia); and the electors of the Rhineland church-states—the archbishops of Cologne, Trier, and Mainz—were on the French payroll, receiving "subsidies" from the French king. The diet of the Holy Roman Empire was divided between an anti-French and a pro-French party. The emperor, Leopold I, was distracted by developments in the East. The Hungarians, incited and financed by Louis XIV, were again rebelling against the Habsburgs. They appealed to the Turks, and the Turks in 1683 moved up the Danube and actually besieged Vienna—as in 1529. Louis XIV, if he did not on this occasion positively assist the Turks, ostentatiously declined to join the proposed crusade against them.

The emperor, with Polish assistance, succeeded in getting the Turkish host out of Austria.[21] Returning to western problems, observing the western border of the Empire constantly crumbling, Franche-Comté already lost, the Spanish Netherlands constantly threatened, Lorraine and Alsace absorbed bit by bit, and the Rhineland archbishops reduced to the status of French puppets, and not forgetting that Louis XIV had designs on the whole of Habsburg Spain, the Emperor Leopold gathered the Catholic powers into a combination against the French. The Protestant states at the same time, aroused by Louis' revocation of the Edict of Nantes in 1685 and by Huguenot émigrés who called down the wrath of God on the perfidious Sun King, began to ally the more readily with William of Orange. Catholic and Protestant enemies of Louis XIV came together in 1686 in the League of Augsburg, which comprised the Holy Roman Emperor, the kings of Spain and of Sweden, the electors of Bavaria, Saxony, and the Palatinate, and the Dutch Republic. In 1686 the king of England was still a protégé of France, but three years later, when William became king in England, that country too joined the League.

The War of the League of Augsburg broke out in 1688. The French armies won battles but could not drive so many enemies from the field. The French navy could not overpower the combined fleets of the Dutch and English. Louis XIV found himself badly strained (it was at this time that he first imposed direct taxes on the French nobles) and finally made peace at Ryswick in the Netherlands in 1697. The Peace of Ryswick, terminating the long "War of the League of Augsburg," left matters about where they had been when the war began.

[21] See pp. 230–231.

In all the warring and negotiating, in the plans of the Augsburg allies and in the maneuvers of Louis XIV, the question had not been merely the fate of this or that piece of territory, nor even the French thrust to the east, but the eventual disposition of the whole empire of Spain. The Spanish king, Charles II, prematurely senile, momentarily expected to die, yet lived on year after year. He was still alive at the time of the Peace of Ryswick. The greatest diplomatic issue of the day was still unsettled.

*The War of the
Spanish Succession*

The War of the Spanish Succession lasted eleven years, from 1702 to 1713. It was less destructive than the Thirty Years' War, for armies were now supplied in more orderly fashion, subject to more orderly discipline and command, and could be stopped from fighting at the will of their governments. Except for the effects of civil war in Spain and of starvation in France, the civilian populations were generally spared, and in this respect the war foreshadowed the typical warfare of the eighteenth century, fought by professional armies rather than by whole peoples. Among wars of the largest scale, the War of the Spanish Succession was the first in which religion counted for little, the first in which commerce and sea power were the principal stakes, the first in which English money was liberally used in Continental politics, and the first that can be called a "world war" in involving the overseas world together with the leading powers of Europe.

The struggle had long been foreseen. The two main aspirants to the Spanish inheritance were the king of France and the Holy Roman Emperor, each of whom had married a sister of the perpetually moribund Charles II, and each of whom could hope to place a younger member of his family on the throne of Spain. During the last decades of the seventeenth century the powers had made various treaties agreeing to "partition" the Spanish possessions. The idea was, by dividing the Spanish heritage between the two claimants, to preserve the balance of power in Europe.[22] But when Charles II finally died, in 1700, it was found that he had made a will, in which he stipulated that the world of Spain should be kept intact, that all Spanish territories without exception should go to the grandson of Louis XIV, and that if Louis XIV refused to accept in the name of his seventeen-year-old grandson, the entire inheritance should pass to the son of the Habsburg emperor in Vienna. Louis XIV decided to accept. With Bourbons reigning in Versailles and Madrid, even if the two thrones were never united, French influence would run from Belgium to the Straits of Gibraltar, and from Milan to Mexico and Manila. At Versailles the word went out: "The Pyrenees exist no longer."

Never, at least in almost two centuries, had the political balance within Europe been so threatened. Never had the other states faced such a prospect of relegation to the sidelines. William III acted at once; he gathered the stunned or hesitant diplomats into the last of his coalitions, the Grand Alliance of 1701. He died the next year, before hostilities began, and with Louis XIV at the seeming apex of his grandeur, but he had in fact launched the engine that was to crush the Sun King. The Grand

[22]On the idea of the balance of power see pp. 165–166.

Alliance included England, Holland, and the emperor, supported by Brandenburg and eventually by Portugal and the Italian duchy of Savoy. Louis XIV could count on Spain, which was generally loyal to the late king's will. Otherwise his only ally was Bavaria, whose rivalry with Austria made it a habitual satellite of France. The Bavarian alliance gave the French armies an advanced position toward Vienna and maintained that internal division, balance of power, or cancellation of forces within Germany which was fundamental to the politics of the time, and of a long time to come.

The war was long, mainly because each side no sooner gained a temporary advantage than it raised its demands on the other. The English, though they sent relatively few troops to the Continent, produced in John Churchill, Duke of Marlborough, a preeminent military commander for the Allied forces. The Austrians were led by Prince Eugene of Savoy. The Allies won notable battles at Blenheim in Bavaria (1704), and at Ramillies (1706), Oudenarde (1708), and Malplaquet (1709) in the Spanish Netherlands. The French were routed; Louis XIV asked for peace but would not make it because the Allied terms were so enormous. Louis fought to hold the two crowns, to conquer Belgium, to get French merchants into Spanish America, and at the worst in self-defense. After minor successes in 1710 he again insisted on controlling the crown of Spain. The Spanish fought to uphold the will of the deceased king, the unity of the Spanish possessions, and even the integrity of Spain itself—for the English moved in at Gibraltar and made a menacing treaty with Portugal, while the Austrians landed at Barcelona and invaded Catalonia, which (as in 1640) again rose in rebellion, recognizing the Austrian claimant, so that all Spain fell into civil war.

The Austrians fought to keep Spain in the Habsburg family, to crush Bavaria, and to carry Austrian influence across the Alps into Italy. The Dutch fought as always for their security, to keep the French out of Belgium, and to close the river Scheldt. The English fought for these same reasons and also to keep the French-supported Catholic Stuarts out of England and preserve the Revolution of 1688. It was to be expected that the Stuarts, if they returned, would ruin the Bank of England and repudiate the National Debt. Both maritime powers, England and Holland, fought to keep French merchants out of Spanish America and to advance their own commercial position in America and the Mediterranean. These being the war aims, the Whigs were the implacable war party in England, the vaguely pro-Stuart and anti-commercial Tories being quite willing to make peace at an early date. As for the minor allies, Brandenburg and Savoy, their rulers had simply entered the alliance to gain such advantages as might turn up.

The Peace of Utrecht

Peace was finally made at the treaties of Utrecht and Rastadt of 1713 and 1714. So fierce was the Whig war spirit in England that ratification of the treaty of Utrecht incidentally marked a step in English constitutional history. The Whigs thought the treaty insufficiently favorable to England. The Tories, pledged to peace, had won the House of Commons in 1710, but the Whigs continued to control the House of Lords.

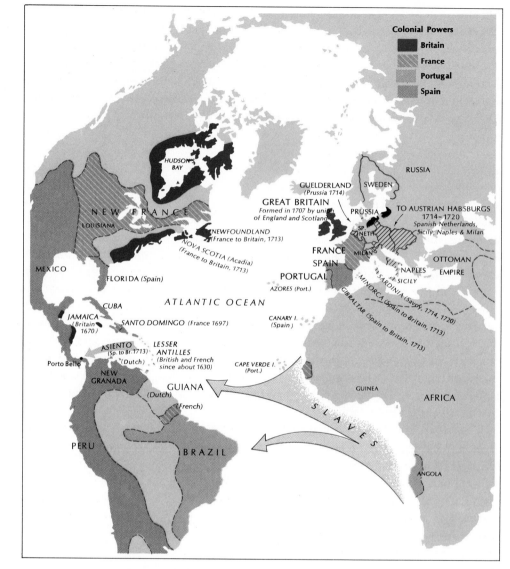

The Atlantic World after the Peace of Utrecht 1713. *The map shows the partitioning of the Spanish empire and the rise of the British. Spain and its American possessions went to the Bourbon Philip V; the European possessions of Spain—the Netherlands, Milan, Naples, and Sicily—went to the Habsburgs. Britain meanwhile was strengthened by the union of England and Scotland, the acquisition of Minorca, Gibraltar and the commercial privilege of the "asiento" from Spain, and of Newfoundland and Nova Scotia from France. (See also map, p. 339.)*

Queen Anne, at the request of Tory leaders and in the interests of peace, raised twelve Tory commoners to the peerage, the number required to give a Tory majority in the Lords and hence to obtain ratification of the treaty. This established itself as a precedent; it became an unwritten article of the British constitution that when the Lords blocked the Commons on an issue of fundamental importance, enough new Lords of appropriate views would be created to make a majority in that House.[23]

The treaty of Utrecht, with its allied instruments, in fact partitioned the world of Spain. But it did not divide it between the two legal claimants only. The British remained at Gibraltar, to the great irritation of the Spaniards, and likewise annexed the island of Minorca. The Duke of Savoy was granted the former Spanish island of Sardinia in return for his contribution to the Allied cause.[24] The rest of the Spanish Mediterranean holdings—Milan, Naples, and Sicily—passed to the Austrian Habsburgs, as did the Spanish Netherlands (or Belgium), subsequently referred to as the Austrian Netherlands—except that the tiny region of Spanish Guelderland was handed over to the Elector of Brandenburg for his pains. In Spain itself, shorn of its European possessions but retaining America, the grandson of Louis XIV was confirmed as king (Philip V of Spain), on the understanding that the French and Spanish thrones should never be inherited by the same person. The Bourbons reigned in Spain, with interruptions, from Philip V to the republican revolution of 1931. French influence was strong in the eighteenth century, for a good many French courtiers, advisers, administrators, and businessmen crossed the Pyrenees with Philip V. They helped somewhat to revive the Spanish monarchy by applying the methods of Louis XIV, and they passed a swelling volume of French manufactures through Seville into Spanish America.

The old objective of William III, to prevent domination by France, was realized at last. The war itself was the main cause of French loss of strength. It produced poverty, misery, and depopulation, exposed Louis XIV to severe criticism at home, and led to a revival of aristocratic and parliamentary opposition. By the peace treaties the French abandoned, for the time being, their efforts to conquer Belgium. They ceased to recognize the Stuart pretender as king of Great Britain. They surrendered to the British two of their colonies, Newfoundland and Nova Scotia (called Acadia), and recognized British sovereignty in the disputed American northwest, known as the Hudson Bay territory. But the French were only checked, not downed. They retained the conquests of Louis XIV in Alsace and the Franche-Comté. Their influence was strong in Spain. Their deeper strength and capacity for recovery were soon evident in renewed economic expansion. Their language and civilization continued to spread throughout Europe.

The Dutch received guarantees of their security. They were granted the right to garrison the "Dutch Barrier," a string of forts in Belgium on the side toward France.

[23] The precedent was invoked in 1832 and 1911, but never since 1713 have the Lords allowed themselves to be swamped by newcomers. They have yielded at the threat.

[24] By the terms of 1713 Sardinia was awarded to Austria and Sicily to Savoy, but Sardinia and Sicily were exchanged in 1720. The kingdom of the Two Sicilies (Naples and Sicily) was thereby reconstituted. Savoy came to be called "Sardinia."

The Wars of Louis XIV: The Peace of Utrecht, 1713

With Belgium transferred to Austria, which was not expected to stimulate Belgian commerce, and with the closure of the river Scheldt reconfirmed at Utrecht, the Dutch could comfortably expect a minimum of competition from their southern neighbors. But the Dutch, strained by the war and outdistanced by England, never again played a primary role in European political affairs. Two other small states ascended over the diplomatic horizon, Savoy and Brandenburg. The rulers of both, for having sided with the victors, were recognized as "kings" by the treaty of Utrecht. Savoy came to be known as "Sardinia," and Brandenburg as "Prussia." More is said of Prussia in the next chapter.

The greatest winners were the British. Great Britain made its appearance as a great power. Union of England and Scotland had taken place during the war. Based at Gibraltar and Minorca, Britain was now a power in the Mediterranean. Belgium, the "pistol pointed at the heart of England," was in the innocuous hands of the Austrians. The Austrians had not especially wanted Belgium; it was too distant from Vienna and too likely to embroil them with France; they had taken it largely at the instigation of the maritime states, Britain and Holland, which saw in transfer to Austria a good solution to the problem. The British added to their American holdings at the expense of France. Far more valuable than Newfoundland or Nova Scotia, won from France, was the *asiento* extorted from Spain. The *asiento* granted the lucrative privilege (which the French had sought) of providing Spanish America with African slaves. Much of the wealth of Bristol and Liverpool in the following decades was to be built upon the slave trade. The *asiento*, by permitting one shipload of British goods to be brought each year to Porto Bello in Panama, also provided opportunities for illicit trade in nonhuman cargoes. The Spanish empire was pried open, and British merchants entered on an era of wholesale smuggling into Spanish America, competing strenuously with the French, who because of their favored position in Spain were usually able to go through more legal channels. Moreover the British, by defeating France, assured themselves of a line of Protestant kings and of the maintenance of constitutional and parliamentary government. The landed aristocracy and their merchant allies could now govern as they saw fit. The result was a rapid increase of wealth in England, precipitating within a few generations a veritable Industrial Revolution.

Except for the addition of England, the same powers were parties to the treaty of Utrecht in 1713 as to the Peace of Westphalia in 1648, and they now confirmed the system of international relations established by Westphalia. The powers accepted each other as members of the European system, recognized each other as sovereign states connected only by free negotiation, war, and treaty, and adjusted their differences through rather facile exchanges of territory, made in the interests of a balance of power, and without regard to the nationality or presumed wishes of the peoples affected. With Germany still in its "feudal chaos," Italy negligible, and Spain subordinated to France, the treaty of Utrecht left France and Great Britain as the two most vigorous powers of Europe and as the two principal carriers and exporters of the type of civilization most characteristic of the modern world. In the next chapter we turn to central and eastern Europe, to see how these regions developed along lines of their own, though under strong influence from the West.

The seventeenth century was an age of high monarchy, or royal absolutism, of which the great exemplar was France. A style of life that developed first in Italy during the Renaissance, and which set high value on patronage of the arts, courtly manners, elaborate clothing and elegant speech, was taken over in France (with some influence from the two Medici queens), and from France was diffused throughout much of Europe. It was especially suited to monarchies, since the kings, with their increasingly organized governments, could afford the necessary expense and even required a palatial atmosphere in which to impress their often unruly subjects. The same applies in a way to the papal monarchy of the church, and the new ideas came as much from papal Rome as from republican Florence. The result is best illustrated by architecture, to which the following pages are devoted.

It was an architecture derived from classical elements of design, but it soon went beyond the Greeks and Romans. The baroque, as it is called, delighted in arches and colonnades, domes and entablatures, and ornamented windows and cornices. Indoors and outdoors flowed together in complexes of façades, staircases, terraces, balustrades, gardens, fountains and formal vistas. Statuary was distributed inside and out. Mirrors, paintings and tapestries adorned the interiors. Great halls were built for state receptions, and paved courtyards for troops of soldiers, throngs of retainers, the arrival of coaches, or simply to provide open views.

Architecture passed over into city planning. Versailles was a new city; the plan of modern Paris also dates from Louis XIV; and Washington, D.C., planned by a Frenchman, with its diagonal streets and circles, punctuated by statues, still reflects these traditions of neoclassical monumentality. On the other hand it was the kings who initiated the movement to the suburbs. Versailles was built ten miles from Paris, away from the clamor and restlessness of the city, and where the king already owned enough land for a new spacious development. When other monarchs imitated Louis XIV they often did likewise. The Habsburgs built Schönbrunn outside Vienna, and the Hohenzollern Frederick II built Sans Souci at Potsdam about twenty miles from Berlin.

The Russian tsars, in their new city of St. Petersburg, and the kings of Sweden in their new royal palace at Stockholm, joined the host of German princes in emulating the royal grandeur of France. It was different where royalty counted for less. The Dutch had no king, and cared little for public magnificence. Sans Souci was hardly more than a wealthy gentleman's home. The English, with their antimonarchical revolutions, built no grandiose royal palaces at this time. But they built Blenheim Palace and presented it to John Churchill, the first Duke of Marlborough, as a reward for his services in the last great war against the *Grand Monarque*.

THE AGE OF GRANDEUR

Above: The Emperor Constantine (d. 337) discusses with Pope Julius II (d. 1513) the building of a new church of St. Peter's in Rome. An older church, of which parts went back to Constantine's time, was torn down to make room for the new one.

The new St. Peter's, seen here in a seventeenth-century print, required a century and a half for completion. The great dome of the church is the work of Michelangelo. The pair of immense semicircular arcades, each four columns thick, was built about a hundred years later by Bernini, one of the great masters of the baroque.

AMBASSADEURS DE SIAM

The château of Versailles was mainly built by Louis XIV in the 1670s, on a site used by his predecessor as a hunting lodge. Thirty thousand workmen were employed at one time in the building operations, which are shown in a contemporary painting at the left above. The painting below shows the château and its adjacent buildings about a hundred years later, shortly before the Revolution. The twin structures in the foreground, left and right of the vast court, were assigned to government offices. The château proper is in the middle distance, with the gardens invisible behind it, except that the long rectangular basin of the Grand Canal can be seen reaching to the horizon.

At Versailles, for thirty years, the Sun King received visitors from all countries in overwhelming splendor. The memorable arrival in 1684 of ambassadors from far-off Siam (now Thailand) is recorded in the print above.

Louis XIV gave sponsorship and subsidies to cultural activities of many kinds, usually organized as academies. At the left, above, he appears on a visit to the Academy of Sciences, founded in 1666. A scientific gentleman is explaining the "philosophical apparatus" to the king. 207

The opera developed as an art form in the seventeenth century and was characteristic of the baroque in its simultaneous use of different arts, its ostentation, and general staginess. At the left, below, Lully's "Alceste" is performed for Louis XIV in the courtyard of a lesser palace before the building of Versailles.

Left, above: Frederick the Great's Sans Souci. The young Frederick had been disciplined by his drill-sergeant father for writing poetry and corresponding with Frenchmen, but after becoming king, in 1740, at the age of twenty-eight, he gave full rein to his French tastes, and after the first Silesian War built this residence, whose name means "carefree." Here he met with Voltaire and other intellectual companions.

Above: There were many buildings in St. Petersburg, now Leningrad, on the model of European palaces of the day, but here we have signs of the Western influences penetrating to Moscow. If the structures seem dreamy and evanescent, it is because they are only temporary pavilions set up in 1775 to celebrate the end of a victorious war with Turkey.

At the left: Schönbrunn Palace, near Vienna. The Habsburg monarchs, as the Turkish menace receded, planned this great edifice to compete with their Bourbon rivals. The plan was never completed, partly because the sensible Maria Theresa (1740–1780) thought that what is seen here was enough. It was here that the six-year-old Mozart astonished the court with his precocious virtuosity.

At the right: Blenheim Palace in Oxfordshire, presented to the Duke of Marlborough for his victories over Louis XIV. Built in the 1720s with funds voted by Parliament, a monument in a way to England's rising greatness, it has always been thought by the English to be a little exaggerated. The architect, Vanbrugh, left everyone dissatisfied. He sacrificed interiors to external splendor, putting the kitchen 400 yards from the dining room. Voltaire said that if only the rooms were as wide as the walls were thick, it would be a convenient little château.

These two buildings were built at the same time for the same purpose, as homes for old and retired soldiers. It was a sign of the growth of royal government to have professional standing armies, in which men might spend their whole lives apart from the civilian population.

At the left is Chelsea Royal Hospital, founded by Charles II; at the right, the Invalides, founded by Louis XIV. The much greater size and imposing dome of the French establishment contrast with the simplicity of the English, and reflect the far greater power of France at that time. The broad avenues radiating beyond the Invalides, then in open country, are now boulevards of central Paris.

V: THE TRANSFORMATION

OF EASTERN EUROPE, 1648-1740

During the century after the Peace of Westphalia of 1648 a development of permanent importance for the modern world took place in central and eastern Europe, the appearance of three new powers—Prussia, Austria, and Russia. The three new states grew at the expense of three older political organizations that were in decay—the Holy Roman Empire, the Republic of Poland, and the empire of the Ottoman Turks.[1] By overrunning the intermediate ground of Poland in the eighteenth century the new states came to adjoin one another and to cover all eastern Europe except the Balkans. It was in this same period that Russia expanded territorially, adopted some of the civilization of the West, and became a power in the affairs of Europe.

East and West are of course relative terms. For the Russians Germany and even Poland were "western." But for Europe as a whole a real though indefinite line ran along the Elbe and the Bohemian mountains to the head of the Adriatic Sea. East of

[1] See maps, pp. 217 and 221.

Chapter Emblem: A Russian medal commemorating the capture of Narva from the Swedes in 1704, and hence the establishment of Russian power on the Baltic.

215

this line towns were fewer than in the West, human labor less productive, the middle classes less strong.   Above all, the peasants were governed by their landlords.[2]   From the sixteenth to the eighteenth century, in eastern Europe in contrast to what happened in the West, the peasant mass increasingly lost its freedom.   The commercial revolution and widening of the market, which in the West raised up a strong merchant or bourgeois class and tended to turn working people into a legally free and mobile labor force, in eastern Europe strengthened the great landlords who produced for export, and who secured their labor force by the institutions of serfdom and "hereditary subjection."   The main social unit was the agricultural estate, which the lord exploited with uncompensated compulsory labor (or *robot*) furnished by his people, who could neither migrate, marry, nor learn a trade except as he permitted, and who, until the eighteenth century, had no legal protector or court of appeal other than himself.   In the East, therefore, the landlords were exceedingly powerful. They were the only significant political class.   And the three new states that grew up—Prussia, Austria, Russia—were alike in being landlord states.

22
Three Aging Empires

In 1648 the whole mainland of Europe from the French border almost to Moscow was occupied by the three large and loosely built structures that have been mentioned—the Holy Roman Empire, the Republic of Poland, and the empire of the Ottoman Turks.[3]   The Turkish power reached to about fifty miles from Vienna, extended over what is now Rumania, and prevailed over the Tartars on the north shore of the Black Sea.   Even so, its European holdings were but a projection from the main mass in Asia and Africa.   Poland extended roughly from a hundred miles east of Berlin to a hundred miles west of Moscow, and virtually from "sea to sea" in the old phrase of its patriots, from the Baltic around Riga almost to the Black Sea coast, which, however, was held by Tartar Khans under the overlordship of the Turkish sultan at Constantinople.   The Holy Roman Empire extended from Poland and Hungary to the North Sea.

[2]See pp. 123–124.
[3]See maps, pp. 217 and 221.

Central and Eastern Europe 1660–1795.   *This complex area is shown in simplified form on p. 221.   The upper panel of the present map indicates boundaries as of 1660, the lower panel those of 1795.   Both panels show the border between the eastern and western agrarian zones, running from the mouth of the Elbe River into central Germany and down to Trieste.   East of this line, from the sixteenth to the eighteenth centuries, the mass of people sank into a kind of serfdom in which they rendered forced labor to their lords on large farms.   West of the line the peasants owed little or no forced labor and tilled small farms which they owned or rented.   This line is one of the most important sociological boundaries in the history of modern Europe.*

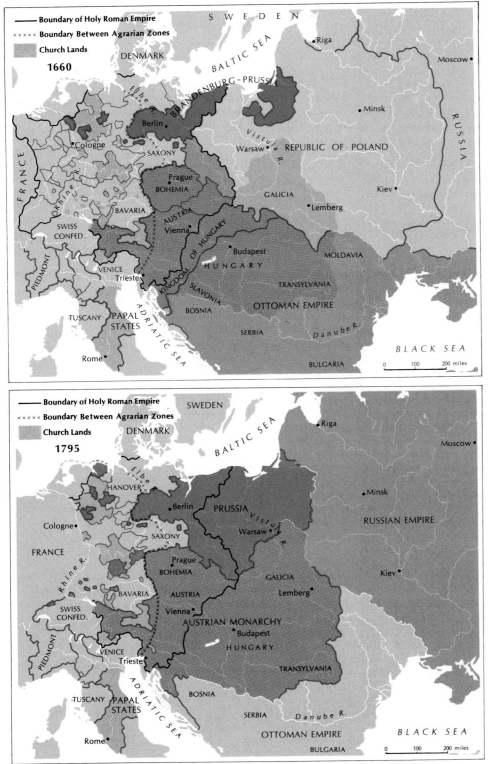

Boundary of Holy Roman Empire

××××× **Boundary Between Agrarian Zones**

Church Lands

1660

SWEDEN

DENMARK

BALTIC SEA

•Riga

Moscow•

•Minsk

BRANDENBURG-PRUSSIA

Berlin•

Elbe R.

FRANCE

Cologne•

SAXONY

Vistula R.

Warsaw•

REPUBLIC OF POLAND

RUSSIA

Rhine R.

Prague•

BOHEMIA

GALICIA

Kiev•

SWISS CONFED.

BAVARIA

AUSTRIA

Vienna•

•Lemberg

KINGDOM OF HUNGARY

Budapest•

MOLDAVIA

PIEDMONT

VENICE

Trieste•

HUNGARY

SLAVONIA

TRANSYLVANIA

TUSCANY

PAPAL STATES

ADRIATIC SEA

BOSNIA

OTTOMAN EMPIRE

SERBIA

Danube R.

BLACK SEA

Rome•

BULGARIA

0   100   200 miles

Boundary of Holy Roman Empire

××××× **Boundary Between Agrarian Zones**

Church Lands

1795

SWEDEN

DENMARK

BALTIC SEA

•Riga

Moscow•

Elbe R.

HANOVER

Berlin•

PRUSSIA

Vistula R.

•Minsk

RUSSIAN EMPIRE

FRANCE

Cologne•

SAXONY

Warsaw•

Rhine R.

Prague•

BOHEMIA

Kiev•

GALICIA

SWISS CONFED.

BAVARIA

AUSTRIA

Vienna•

•Lemberg

AUSTRIAN MONARCHY

Budapest•

PIEDMONT

VENICE

Trieste•

HUNGARY

TRANSYLVANIA

TUSCANY

PAPAL STATES

ADRIATIC SEA

BOSNIA

SERBIA

Danube R.

OTTOMAN EMPIRE

BLACK SEA

Rome•

BULGARIA

0   100   200 miles

217

These three empires were by no means alike. The Holy Empire bore some of the oldest traditions of Christendom. Poland too had old connections with the West. Turkey was a Moslem power, strange to Europe and contemptuous of it. Yet in some ways the three resembled each other. In all of them central authority had become weak, consisting largely of understandings between a nominal head and outlying dignitaries or potentates. All lacked efficient systems of administration and government. All were being put out of date by newer types of state of which France was the leading example. All, but especially Poland and Turkey, were made up of diverse populations, the actual distribution of ethnic or language groups being about as they are today. None of these peoples, nor any combination of them—neither the dominant Germans, Poles, and Turks, nor the submerged Lithuanians, White Russians, Ukrainians, Czechs, Slovaks, Rumanians, Croats, Magyars, Serbs, Bulgars, or Greeks—had been formed into a compact organization. The whole immense area was politically soft. It was malleable in the hands of whoever might become a little stronger than his neighbor. We must try to see in what this softness consisted, and then how newer and harder "state-forms" (as the Germans would say) were created.

The Holy Roman Empire after 1648

With the Holy Roman Empire the reader is already familiar.[4] It was an empire, especially after the Peace of Westphalia, with next to no army, revenues, or working organs of government. Voltaire called it neither holy, Roman, nor an empire. As the seventeenth-century German jurist Pufendorf put it, it was somewhat of an abortion and a monstrosity. Created in the Middle Ages, it was Roman in that it was then believed to continue the imperial sway of the Rome of antiquity, and it was holy in being the secular counterpart to the spiritual empire of the pope. It had been ruined by the Reformation, which left the Germans divided almost evenly between Protestant and Catholic, with each side thereafter demanding special safeguards against the other. The Empire continued, however, to be universal in principle, having no relation to nationality, and theoretically being a form of government suitable to all peoples, although it had never made good this theoretical claim and had shown no expansionist tendency since the Middle Ages. In actuality, the Empire was very roughly coterminous with the German states and the region of the German language, except that it excluded after 1648 the Dutch and Swiss, who no longer considered themselves German; and it likewise excluded those Germans who since the fourteenth century had settled along the eastern shores of the Baltic.

Large parts of the Empire had suffered repeatedly from the Thirty Years' War. Yet the war, and the peace terms which followed it, only accentuated a situation which had long been unfavorable. Postwar revival was difficult; the break-up of commercial connections and the wartime losses of savings and capital were hard to overcome. Germany fell increasingly out of step with western Europe. The burgher class, its ambitions blocked, lost much of its old vitality. No overseas colonies could be founded, for want of strong enough government backing, as was shown when a

[4]See pp. 21, 25, 34, 75–76, 147–150.

colonial venture of Brandenburg came to nothing. There was no stock exchange in Germany until one was established at Vienna in 1771, half a century after those of London, Paris, and Amsterdam. Laws, tariffs, tolls, and coinage were more variegated than in France. Even the calendar varied. It varied, indeed, throughout Europe as a whole, since Protestant states long declined to accept the corrected calendar issued by Pope Gregory XIII in 1582, but in parts of divided Germany the holidays, the date of the month, and the day of the week changed every few miles. The arts and letters, flourishing in western Europe as never before, were at a low ebb in Germany in the seventeenth century. In science the Germans during and after the Thirty Years' War did less than the English, Dutch, French, or Italians, despite the great mathematician and philosopher Leibnitz, one of the great minds of the age. Only in music, as in the work of the Bach family, did the Germans at this time excel. But music was not then much heard beyond the place of its origin. Germany for the rest of the world was a mute country, a byway in the higher civilization of Europe.

After the Thirty Years' War each German state had sovereign rights. These "states" numbered some 300 or 2,000, depending on how they were counted. The higher figure included the "knights of the Empire," found in south Germany and the Rhineland. They were persons who acknowledged no overlordship except that of the emperor himself. The knights had tiny estates of their own, averaging not over a hundred acres apiece, consisting of a castle and a manor or two, enclosed by the territory of a larger state but not forming a part of it. These free knights had arisen in various ways; in Württemberg, for example, the lords simply ceased to attend the diet, won exemption from the duke's jurisdiction, and retired to their own domains, leaving the surface of Württemberg pock-marked with small units politically independent of it. It was as if, in England, the peers had lost interest in the House of Lords and had set up independently, each on his own estates. Since the emperor, whom the knights regarded as their only superior, had in fact no authority, the knights were in effect private persons enjoying sovereign status—the last anomaly of bizarre neo-feudalism and distorted freedom.

But even without the knights there were about three hundred states capable of some independence of action—free cities, abbots without subjects, archbishops and bishops ruling with temporal power, landgraves, margraves and dukes, and one king, the king of Bohemia. The highest ranking were called electors, who had the privilege of electing the emperor. By the Golden Bull of 1356 there were seven electors—three ecclesiastics, the archbishops of Cologne, Mainz, and Trier—and four laymen, the Count Palatine of the Rhine, the Duke of Saxony, the Margrave of Brandenburg, and the King of Bohemia. Bavaria was made an electorate at the Peace of Westphalia, and Hanover at the end of the century, so that finally there were nine electors. The fact that nearly half the electors were Protestants after the Reformation, whereas the Holy Empire had meaning only in a Catholic world, added to the internal confusion and general oddity of the system.

All these states were intent on preserving what were called the "Germanic liberties." They were gladly assisted by outside powers, notably but not exclusively France. The Germanic liberties meant freedom of the member states from control by emperor or Empire. The electors, at each election of an emperor, required the candidate to accept certain "capitulations," in which he promised to safeguard all the privileges and immunities of the states. The Habsburgs, though consistently elected after 1438, had none of the advantages of hereditary rulers, each having to bargain away in turn any gains made by his predecessor. The elective principle meant that imperial power could not be accumulated and transmitted from one generation to the next. It opened the doors to foreign intrigue, the electors being willing to consider whichever candidate would promise them most. The French repeatedly supported a rival candidate to the Habsburgs. After 1648 they had a party in the electoral college, Bavaria and Cologne being the most consistently pro-French. Cardinal Mazarin in 1658 even entertained the thought of making the young Louis XIV Holy Roman Emperor. He had to accept election of a Habsburg, despite liberal use of French money, but the new emperor, Leopold I, undertook not to engage the Empire in any war supporting the Spanish Habsburgs against France. In 1742 the French obtained the elevation of their Bavarian ally to the imperial throne. The office of emperor became the political football of Germans and non-Germans working together.

Nor would the German states, after the Thirty Years' War, allow any authority to the imperial diet. The diet possessed the power to raise troops and taxes for the whole Empire, but the power remained unused. On matters affecting religion, after 1648, either Protestants or Catholics could demand the *ius eundi in partes,* or "right of sitting apart." Each religious group then constituted itself as a chamber, Protestant or Catholic, and since agreement of the two was required, each possessed a veto. The deliberations of the diet became notorious for their wordiness and futility. Many sessions were spent, for example, in attempts to fix for all Germany a common date of Easter, on which the whole calendar depended. In 1663 a diet met to consider measures against a new Turkish advance on the Danube. It was the last diet ever to be convoked, for it lasted "forever," i.e., until the end of the Holy Empire in 1806. It became the "perpetual diet" of Regensburg, never dismissed or renewed, unresponsive to events or issues, the states simply replacing their representatives individually, generation after generation, as at an endless congress of diplomats.

The states which insisted with such obstinacy on their liberties from the Empire gave few liberties to their subjects. The free cities were closed oligarchies, as indeed were most cities in other countries, but in Germany the burgher oligarchs of the free cities were virtually sovereign also. Most of the other states, large or small, developed in the direction of absolutism. Absolutism was checked for Germany as a whole, only to reappear in miniature in hundreds of different places. Each ruler thought himself a little Louis XIV, each court a small Versailles. The rulers raised diminutive standing armies, developed their corps of officials, superintended their churches, planned and regulated economic life within their restricted frontiers. The local princes in many cases gave seed to the peasants and rebuilt villages and towns after the Thirty Years' War. Operating over a small area and a small population, absolutism became more personal and paternalistic than in France, more concerned with and more easily informed of the minutest details in the lives of the people. Subjects became attached by ties of sentiment to their rulers, who almost always lived in the neighborhood and could be readily seen by passers-by. People liked the little courts, the toy armies, the gossipy politics, and the familiar officials of their tiny states. Such localism perhaps gave the Germans a taste for personal and immediate government.

The Empire, for all its faults, had the merit of holding this conglomeration of states in a lawful relation to one another. It was a kind of miniature league of nations. For a century and a half after the Peace of Westphalia infinitesimally small states existed alongside larger ones, or often totally enclosed within them, without serious fear for their security and without losing their independence. Only in power politics and in European or world affairs was the Empire a shadow. For the Germans it was a reality, a world in itself, a thing of sublime tradition and rich and colorful associations, which no one for a long time dreamed of violating or even reforming, for its existence assured a way of life which most Germans were glad to keep.

Yet there were many ambitious rulers in Germany after the Peace of Westphalia. The princes were "on the make." They had won recognition of their sovereignty in 1648. They were busily building absolutist monarchies over their

Aging Empires and New Powers. *The left panel shows the "three aging empires" which occupied much of central and eastern Europe in the seventeenth century. (See pp. 216–228.) Though maintaining themselves with growing difficulty under modern conditions, the Polish Republic lasted until 1795, the Holy Roman Empire until 1806, the Ottoman Empire until 1923. Meanwhile, beginning in the seventeenth century, the political leadership in this area was assumed by three states of more modern type, organized around the institutions of monarchy, the standing army, and the professional bureaucracy or civil service—the reorganized Austrian Empire of the Habsburgs, the Hohenzollern kingdom of Prussia, and the Russian empire of the Romanovs. These are shown in the right panel. All three figured prominently in the affairs of Europe for over two hundred years; all perished in the First World War, 1914–1918.*

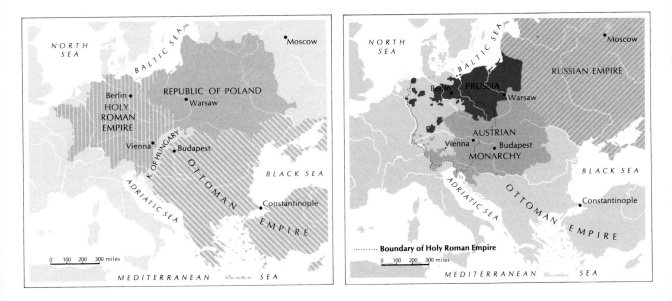

subjects. They aspired also to extend their dominions and cut a greater figure in the world. There were other ways of doing this than by devouring their smaller neighbors outright. One was by marriage and inheritance. The Empire in this respect was a paradise of fortune hunters; the variety of possible marriages was enormous because of the great number of ruling families; and legal claims to inheritance could be pushed in every direction, because territories had shifted back and forth for twenty generations. Another outlet for ambition lay in the high politics of the Empire. The Wittelsbach family, which ruled in Bavaria, managed to win an electorate in the Thirty Years' War; they consistently placed members of the family as archbishop of Cologne and in the other great Rhineland sees, and with the interest thus built up were able to sell their influence to France, which in turn backed them against the Habsburgs. The Guelph family, ruling in Hanover, schemed for years to obtain an electorate, which they finally extorted from the emperor in 1692; in 1714 they inherited the throne of Great Britain, preferred by the British as Protestants to their Catholic Stuart cousins. Two electors of Saxony in these years got themselves crowned king of Poland. The Hohenzollerns, electors of Brandenburg, were extremely fortunate in the seventeenth century in inheriting territories as far apart as the Rhine and the Vistula. The Habsburgs, hereditary rulers in Austria, a mere archduchy, not even an electorate, were confirmed by the Peace of Westphalia as hereditary kings of Bohemia, where they had formerly depended on election.

The half-century after the Peace of Westphalia was a highly critical period in central Europe. The situation in Germany was fluid. No one could tell which, if any, of the half-dozen chief German states would emerge in the lead. Nothing was crystallized; anything might happen. Germany and central Europe, politically chaotic, were a tempting field for dynastic ambition, political calculation, and military adventure. The politics of the Empire was a web zealously woven by half a dozen sizable states and 300 small ones, many of them with foreign connections, and with foreigners constantly interfering in their own interest; a complex mass of family arrangements, private understandings, petty intrigue, and abstruse legal argument harking back to the Middle Ages; a strange contest in which the stakes were sometimes substantial, involving the whole European balance of power, sometimes only archaic titles and obsolete dignities; an abyss which the most expert political observers could study for a lifetime and still not altogether fathom. Two states definitely came forward after 1700, built by the skill and persistence of their rulers—Austria and Prussia. It is a curious and revealing fact that neither really had a name of its own. They were for a long time known most commonly as "houses"—the house of Austria or Habsburg and the house of Brandenburg or Hohenzollern. Each house put together a certain combination of territories. Each would have been as willing to possess any other combination had the course of events been different. By extension of meaning, one came to be called "Austria," which for centuries had been simply an archduchy on the upper Danube, and the other "Prussia," which for centuries had meant only a certain stretch of the Baltic coast. To the development of these two states we shall shortly turn.

Running almost a thousand miles eastward from the Holy Roman Empire in the middle of the seventeenth century lay the vast tract of the Republic of Poland, called a republic because its king was elected, and because the political classes took pride in their constitutional liberties. Its vast size was one cause of its internal peculiarities. No administrative system could have kept up with the expansion of its frontiers, so that a large degree of freedom had always been left to outlying lords. In addition, the population was heterogeneous.

The Polish state was a far more recent and less substantial creation than the Holy Roman Empire. It was made up of two main parts, Poland proper in the west and the Grand Duchy of Lithuania in the east, the two having been joined by a union of their crowns.[5] Only in the extreme west, in the valley of the Vistula River, was there a mass of Polish population. The Duchy of Prussia, a fief of the Polish crown, was peopled by Germans. Further east a White Russian and Ukrainian peasantry was presided over by a scattering of Polish and Lithuanian landlords. Even in Poland itself the urban population was not generally Polish, the townspeople being largely Germans and Jews. The latter spoke Yiddish, a dialect basically German, and were very numerous because a king of Poland, in the later Middle Ages, had welcomed Jewish settlers fleeing from Germany.[6] The Jews did not adopt the Polish language. Tending at first to live in separate communities because of their religion, they were later confined to compulsory ghettoes, islands of Orthodox Jewish life in the Gentile ocean. The Germans too held aloof, resisting assimilation to their less advanced surroundings. An unsurpassable barrier thus existed between town and country. There was no national middle class. The towns were in any case not as flourishing as in the Middle Ages, the old commerce between the Black and Baltic seas having declined. The landlords, the dominant element, lived in most parts of the country as conquerors settled on an alien land, which they felt they had redeemed from occupation by the Turks and Tartars. The official and political language was Latin. Roman Catholicism was the leading religion. There was little literature in the Polish language, and the native arts remained at the level of folk productions.

Poland is interesting as the region in which the landed aristocracy won over all other groups in the country, neither allowing the consolidation of the state on absolutist lines, as happened in France, the German principalities and even Sweden and Denmark in the seventeenth century, nor yet creating an effective constitutional or parliamentary government, as was done in England. The Polish aristocracy, or *szlachta,* made up some 8 percent of the population, a far higher proportion than the aristocracy of any country of western Europe. On this ground the old Polish kingdom has sometimes been considered, especially by later Polish nationalists, as the possessor of an early form of democracy. The aristocracy were sticklers for their liberties, called the "Polish liberties," and resembling the German liberties in consisting largely of a fierce suspicion of central authority and in being a perpetual

[5] See maps, pp. 217 and 221.
[6] See p. 74, note.

invitation to foreign interference.   As in the Holy Roman Empire, the monarchy was elective, and the king upon election had to accept certain contractual agreements, which, like the German "capitulations," made impossible the accumulation of authority by the crown.   As in the Empire, the royal elections were a cockpit of foreign influence, bribery, and intrigue.   The Poles were too factious to accept one of their own number as king.   They were divided into pro-French, pro-Swedish, pro-Russian, and other parties.   From 1572 to the extinction of Poland over two centuries later there were only two native Polish kings who reigned for any length of time, and one of these was the discarded lover of a Russian empress.   The other was the national hero John Sobieski, whose decisive action against the Turks is noted below.

As in Germany, also, the central diet was ineffective and the nuclei of political action were local.   There were no organized states or governments, as in the Empire, but the aristocracy met in fifty or sixty regional diets, turbulent assemblages of warlike gentry, in which the great lords used the little ones for their own purposes. The central diet, from which the towns were excluded, was a periodic meeting of emissaries, under binding instructions, from the regional diets.   It came to be recognized, as one of the liberties of the country, that the central diet could take no action to which any member objected.   Any member, by stating his unalterable opposition, could oblige a diet to disband.   This was the famous *liberum veto*, the free veto, and to use it to break up a diet was called "exploding" the diet.   The first diet was exploded in 1652.   Of fifty-five diets held from that year to 1764, forty-eight were exploded.   Since parliamentary methods were thus unworkable, a right of "confederation" was recognized, by which individuals might band together and take up arms to force acceptance of their program.   This procedure, often justified as the right of resistance to oppression, or on the ground of bringing a stubborn minority to reason, was itself often resorted to by minority factions, sometimes supported by foreign powers.

Government became a fiasco.   The monopoly of law and force, characteristic of the modern state, failed to develop in Poland.   The king of Poland had practically no army, no law courts, no officials, and no income.   The nobility paid no taxes.   By 1750 the revenues of the king of Poland were about one-thirteenth those of the tsar of Russia and one seventy-fifth those of the king of France.   Armed force was in the hands of a dozen or so aristocratic leaders, who also conducted their own individual foreign policies, pursuing their own adventures against the Turks, or bringing in Russians, French, or Swedes to help them against other Poles.   The landlords became local monarchs on their manorial estates, and the mass of the rural population fell deeper into a serfdom scarcely different from slavery, bound to compulsory labor on estates resembling plantations, with police and disciplinary powers in the hands of the lords, and with no outside legal or administrative system to set the limits of exploitation.   Some Polish aristocrats, hiring architects or buying libraries from Germany and western Europe, traveling with trains of servants to Italy or France, masters of many languages and habitually associating with the great, became among the most accomplished and cosmopolitan people in Europe.   A great Polish nobleman could boast of more territory and subjects, and of more international consideration, than many a sovereign princeling of Germany. But the mass of the aristocracy became an impoverished, ill-educated, and unruly body of decayed gentry, dependent on their connections with the powerful families, and indifferent to western Europe.

The huge expanse comprised under the name of Poland was, in short, in modern parlance, a power vacuum, an area of low political pressure; and as centers of higher pressure developed, notably around Berlin and Moscow, the push against the Polish frontiers became steadily stronger. It was facilitated by the centrifugal habits of the Poles themselves. The Polish nobles lacked the means, and their neighbors the will, to preserve the integrity of their sprawling empire. As early as 1660 the East Prussian fief became independent of the Polish crown. As early as 1667 the Muscovites reconquered Smolensk and Kiev. Already there was confidential talk of partitioning Poland, which, however, was deferred for a century. The history of the world would have been different had the Poland of the seventeenth century held together. There would have been no kingdom of Prussia and no Prussian influence in Germany; nor would Russia have become the chief Slavic power or reached so far into central Europe. Such speculations are rather futile, since it is hard to see, in the circumstances, how the great Poland of the seventeenth century could have been maintained; but they do suggest the gravity of the issues at stake, and the full significance of what actually happened.

The Ottoman state, the third of the three empires which together spread over so much of Europe, was larger than either of the others, and in the seventeenth century was more solidly organized. In 1529 the Turks had attacked Vienna and seemed about to burst into Germany.[7] To the Christian world the Turks were a mystery as well as a terror, not only ferocious and merciless fighters but fanatics of a wicked religion, sunk in polygamy and fornication (it being popularly believed that all Turks had several wives), and led by a sultan or Grand Turk whose government was known as the Sublime Porte (French for "lofty gate"), and who ruled through horsetailed pashas, the number of horsetails carried before a dignitary being a badge of his rank.

The Ottoman Turks were in truth among the rougher of the Moslem peoples. They had erupted from central Asia only a few centuries before and owed most of their higher civilization to the Arabs and the Persians. They were within Islam what the Romans had been in the ancient world, a military and conquering people, who subjected but also learned from their more civilized neighbors. In addition, after conquering Constantinople, they fell heir to some traditions of the Christian Byzantine Empire. Their dominions extended, about 1650, from the Hungarian plain and the south Russian steppes as far as Algeria, the upper Nile, and the Persian Gulf. The empire was based to a large degree on military proficiency. Long before Europe the Turks had a standing army, of which the main striking force was the janissaries. The janissaries were originally recruited from Christian children taken from their

[7]See pp. 43, 76, and 81.

families in early childhood, brought up as Moslems, reared in military surroundings, and forbidden to marry; without background or ties, interests, or ambition outside the military organization to which they belonged, they were an ideal fighting material in the hands of political leaders. The Turkish forces were long as well equipped as the Christian, being especially strong in heavy artillery. But by the mid-seventeenth century they were falling behind. They had changed little, or for the worse, since the days of Suleiman the Magnificent a century before, whereas in the better organized Christian states discipline and military administration had been improved, and firearms, land mines, and siegecraft had become more effective.

The comparison of the Turkish empire to the Roman, more or less valid in the matter of army organization and conquest, is in some other ways entirely fallacious. The Turks, unlike the Romans, had no special aptitude for law and no conception of a universal or natural law applying to all peoples and persons. And they cared little about assimilating subject peoples to their language or institutions. Law was religious law derived from the Koran. Law courts and judges were hard to distinguish from religious authorities, for there was no separation between religious and secular spheres. The sultan was also the caliph, the commander of the faithful, and while on the one hand there was no clergy in the European sense, on the other hand religious influences affected all aspects of life. The Turks, for the most part, applied the Moslem law only to Moslems. Non-Moslems, mostly Christians, remained outside this law, having no rights against true believers, disdainfully regarded as "cattle," bearing the burden of the taxes and subject to various forms of extortion.

The Ottoman government left its non-Moslem subjects to settle their own affairs in their own way, not according to nationality, which was generally indistinguishable, but according to religious groupings. The Greek Orthodox church, to which most Christians in the empire belonged, thus became an almost autonomous intermediary between the sultan and a large fraction of his subjects. Armenian Christians and Jews formed other separate bodies. Except in the western Balkans (Albania and Bosnia) there was no general conversion of Christians to Islam during the Turkish rule, although there were many individual cases of Christians turning Moslem to obtain the privileges of the ruling faith. North of the Danube the Christian princes of Transylvania, Wallachia, and Moldavia (later combined in the modern Rumania) continued to rule over Christian subjects. They were kept in office for that purpose by the sultan, to whom they paid tribute. In general, since their subjects were more profitable to them as Christians, the Turks were not eager to proselytize for Islam.

The Ottoman Empire was therefore a relatively tolerant empire, far more so than the states of Europe. Christians in the Turkish empire fared better than Moslems would have fared in Christendom or than the Moors had in fact fared in Spain. Christians were less disturbed in Turkey than were Protestants in France, after 1685, or Catholics in Ireland. The empire was tolerant because it was composite, an aggregation of peoples, religions, and laws, having no drive, as did the Western states, toward internal unity and complete legal sovereignty. The same was evident in the attitude toward foreign merchants.

The king of France had had treaty arrangements with Turkey since 1535, and many traders from Marseilles had spread over the port towns of the Near East. They were exempted by treaty from the laws of the Ottoman Empire and were liable to trial only by their own judges, who though residing in Turkey were appointed by the king of France. They were free to exercise their Roman Catholic religion, and if disputes with Moslems arose, they appeared in special courts where the word of an infidel received equal weight with that of a follower of the prophet. Similar rights in Turkey were obtained by other European states. Thus began "extraterritorial" privileges of the kind obtained by Europeans in later centuries in China and elsewhere, wherever the local laws were regarded as backward. To the Turks of the seventeenth century there was nothing exceptional about such arrangements, and nothing insulting to the dignity of the Sublime Porte. Only much later, under Western influence, did the Turks learn to resent these "capitulations" as impairments of their own sovereignty.

Yet the Turkish rule was oppressive, and the "terrible Turk" was with reason the nightmare of eastern Europe. Ottoman rule was oppressive to Christians if only because it relegated them to a despised position, and because everything they held holy was viewed by the Turks with violent contempt. But it was oppressive also in that it was arbitrary and brutal even by the none too sensitive standards of Europeans. It was worse in these respects in the seventeenth century than formerly, for the central authority of the sultans had become corrupt, and the outlying governors, or pashas, had a virtually free hand with their subjects. The sultans, once virile leaders of armies, now lived in seclusion and self-indulgence in their harems, surrounded by jealous women and eunuchs, fearful of being deceived by their grand viziers, whom therefore they made and unmade, appointed and executed with disconcerting vacillation. They were fearful even for the stability of their own thrones—one sultan about the year 1600 put to death his nineteen brothers to secure himself against rivals. The pashas, never knowing how long they might remain in their governorships, made haste to get rich by the quickest means. From the grand viziers, dependent for life itself on the whims of a morally undisciplined sultan, down through all levels and grades of office the functionaries were exposed to the caprice of those above them, and protected themselves by erratic demands on those below. The military and governing element became a self-sustaining machine, removed both from the old Turkish aristocracy and from the peasant masses, much of it recruited from adventurers, slaves, or persons taken in infancy from Christian families and then brought up in the ruling system. A few reforming voices were heard, mostly harking back to more purely old Turkish traditions, but nothing was accomplished because the real causes of Ottoman decay were not understood.

Those parts of the Ottoman Empire which adjoined the Christian states were among the least firmly attached to Constantinople. The Tartar Khans of south Russia, like the Christian princes of the Danubian principalities, were simply protégés who paid tribute. Hungary was occupied but was more a battlefield than a province. These regions were disputed by Germans, Poles, and Russians. It seemed in the middle of the seventeenth century as if the grip of the Turks might be relaxing. But a dynasty of unusually capable grand viziers, the Kiuprilis, came to power and retained it contrary to Turkish customs for fifty years. Under them the empire again put forth a mighty effort. By 1663 the janissaries were again mobilizing in Hungary. Tartar horsemen were on the move. Central Europe again felt the old terror. The pope feared that the dreaded enemy might break into Italy. Throughout Germany by the emperor's order special "Turk bells" sounded the alarm. The states of the Empire assembled in 1663 as a diet at Regensburg. They voted to raise a small imperial army. The Holy Empire, even in its senility, bestirred itself temporarily against the historic enemy of the Christians. But it was not the Empire, but the house of Austria, under whose auspices the Turks were to be repelled.

23
The Formation of an Austrian Monarchy

Having now surveyed the three very different empires whose occupancy of most of Europe from France to Muscovy kept the whole area politically malleable and soft, we turn to the three new states which consolidated themselves in this region, namely Austria, Prussia, and Russia.

The Recovery and Growth of Habsburg Power, 1648–1740

The Austria which appeared by 1700 was in truth a new creation, though not as obviously so as the two others. The Austrian Habsburgs had long enjoyed an eminent role. Formerly their position had rested on their headship of the Holy Roman Empire and on their family connection with the more wealthy Habsburgs of Spain. In the seventeenth century these two supports collapsed. The hope for an effective Habsburg empire in Germany disappeared in the Thirty Years' War. The connection with Spain lost its value as Spain declined, and vanished when in 1700 Spain passed to the house of France. The Austrian family in the latter half of the seventeenth century stood at the great turning point of its fortunes. It successfully made a difficult transition, emerging from the husk of the Holy Empire and building an empire of its own. At the same time the Habsburgs continued to be Holy Roman Emperors and remained active in German affairs, using resources drawn from outside Germany to maintain their influence over the German princes. The relation of Austria to the rest of Germany became a political conundrum, forcibly solved by Bismarck in 1866 by the exclusion of Austria, only to be raised again by Adolf Hitler in the twentieth century.

The dominions considered by the house of Austria to be its own direct possessions were in three parts. The oldest were the "hereditary provinces"—Upper and Lower Austria, with the adjoining Tyrol, Styria, Carinthia, and Carniola. Second, there was the kingdom of Bohemia—Bohemia, Moravia, and Silesia joined under the crown of St. Wenceslas. Third, there was the kingdom of Hungary—Hungary, Transylvania, and Croatia joined under the crown of St. Stephen. Nothing held all these regions together except the fact that the Austrian Habsburg dynasty, in the seventeenth century, reaffirmed its grip upon them all. The Thirty

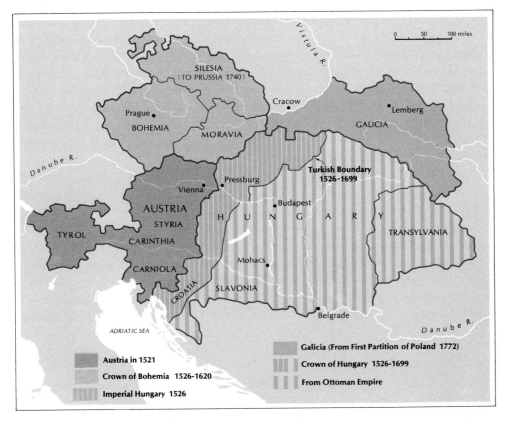

The Growth of the Austrian Monarchy 1521–1772. *The map shows the main body of the Austrian monarchy as it came to be in the eighteenth century and continued until the collapse of the empire in 1918. There were three main parts: (1) a nucleus, composed of Austria and adjoining duchies, often called the "hereditary provinces"; (2) the lands of the Bohemian crown, which became Habsburg in 1526 and where the Habsburgs reasserted their power during the Bohemian phase of the Thirty Years' War; and (3) the lands of the Hungarian crown, where at first the Habsburgs held only the segment called Imperial Hungary, the rest remaining Turkish until reconquered by the Habsburgs in 1699. In the first partition of Poland the Habsburgs annexed Galicia. Silesia was lost to Prussia in 1740. Outlying parts of the empire in the eighteenth century, not shown on the map, were most of what is now Belgium (then the Austrian Netherlands) and the duchy of Milan in Italy. The Italian duchy of Tuscany, where the Medici family died out in 1737, was ruled as a separate state by a Habsburg archduke.*

Years' War, a calamity to the Austrian Habsburgs from their older point of view, in that they failed to re-Catholicize Germany or to maintain the authority of the Holy Empire, was from the newer point of view, that of a new Habsburg monarchy in process of formation, a notable success. During the war the dynasty rooted Protestantism and feudal rebelliousness out of Austria and the hereditary provinces. It reconquered and re-Catholicized Bohemia, with whose rebellion the Thirty Years' War had begun. And in the following decades it conquered Hungary also.

229

Since 1526 most of Hungary had been occupied by the Turks. For generations the Hungarian plain was a theater of intermittent warfare between the armies of Vienna and Constantinople. The struggle flared up again in 1663, when the Kiuprili vizier started Turkish armies moving up the Danube. A mixed force, assembled from the Empire and from all Christendom, obliged the Turks in 1664 to accept a twenty-year truce. But Louis XIV, who in these years was busily dismembering the western frontier of the Empire, stood to profit greatly from a diversion on the Danube. He incited the Turks (old allies of France through common hostility to the Habsburgs) to resume their assaults, which they did as the twenty-year truce came to a close.

In 1683 a vast Turkish host reached the city of Vienna and besieged it. The Turks again, as in 1529, peered into the very inner chambers of Europe. The garrison and people of Vienna, greatly outnumbered, held off the besiegers for two months, enough time for a defending force to arrive. Both sides showed the composite or "international" character of the conflict. The Turkish army included some Christians—Rumanian and Hungarian—the latter being in rebellion against Habsburg rule in Hungary. The Christian force was composed mainly of Poles, Austrian dynastic troops, and Germans from various states of the Empire. It was financed largely by Pope Innocent XI; it was commanded in the field by the Habsburg general, Duke Charles of Lorraine, who hoped to protect his inheritance from annexation by France; and its higher command was entrusted to John Sobieski, king of Poland. It was against the pressure of French agents in Warsaw that Sobieski led his Poles to the Danube. Sobieski contributed greatly to the relief of Vienna, and his bold action represented the last great military effort of the moribund Republic of Poland, but it would be too much to say that it dramatically saved Europe from domination by the Turks. The retrograde Turkish state, even if it had gained a foothold at Vienna, could hardly have long maintained it at such a distance from Constantinople. In any case, the Turks abandoned the siege. A by-product of their defeat was to strengthen Germany against the ambitions of Louis XIV. A general anti-Turkish counteroffensive developed. Forces of the pope, Poland, Russia, and the Republic of Venice joined with the Habsburgs. It was in this war, in fighting between Turks and Venetians, that the Parthenon at Athens, which had survived for two thousand years but was now used as an ammunition dump by the Turks, was blown to ruins.

The Habsburgs, whose luck was proverbial, fighting now on two fronts against Turks and French, had the good fortune to obtain the services of a man of remarkable talent, Prince Eugene of Savoy. Eugene, like many other servants of the Austrian house, was not Austrian at all; he was in fact French by origin and education but like many of the aristocratic class of the time was an international personage. More than anyone else he was the founder of the modern Austrian state. Distinguished both as a military administrator and as a commander in the field, he reformed the supply, equipment, training, and command of the Habsburg forces, along lines laid out by Louis XIV, and in 1697 he won the battle of Zenta, driving the Turks out of Hungary. The English and Dutch offered mediation, since their commerce in the Mediterranean was disturbed by the war, and since they desired Austria to concentrate against

France. At the Peace of Karlowitz (1699) the Turks yielded most of Hungary, together with Transylvania and Croatia, to the Habsburg house.

The Habsburgs were now free to pursue their designs in the west. They entered the War of the Spanish Succession to win the Spanish crown, but although an Austrian archduke campaigned in Spain for years, assisted by the English, they had to content themselves at the treaty of Rastadt in 1714 with the old Spanish Netherlands and with Milan and Naples. Prince Eugene, freed now in the west, again turned eastward. Never before or afterward were the Austrians so brilliantly successful. Eugene captured Belgrade and pushed through the Iron Gate into Wallachia. For a generation the Austrians held what are now western Rumania and central Yugoslavia. Eugene's dream of reaching the Black Sea and Aegean seemed on the point of realization. But Austria was preoccupied elsewhere, nor were the Turks yet helpless; and by the Peace of Belgrade (1739) a frontier was drawn which on the Austrian side remained unchanged until the twentieth century. The Turks continued to hold Rumania and the whole Balkan peninsula except Catholic Croatia, which, incorporated in the Habsburg empire, was again faced toward Europe. The Habsburg government, to open a window on the Mediterranean, developed a seaport at Trieste.

Thus the house of Austria, in two or three generations after its humiliation at the Peace of Westphalia, acquired a new empire of very considerable proportions. Though installed in Belgium and Italy, it was essentially an empire of the middle Danube, with its headquarters at Vienna in Austria proper, but possessing the sizable kingdoms of Hungary and Bohemia, and so filling the basin enclosed by the Alpine, Bohemian, and Carpathian mountain systems. Though German influence was strong, the empire was international or nonnational. At the Habsburg court, and in the Habsburg government and army, the names of Czech, Hungarian, Croatian, and Italian noblemen were very common. It is hard today to see this empire as it was, because it is hard to see it except through the eyes of its enemies. It made enemies of all Protestants. Democrats came to hate it. When the nationalistic movement swept over Europe in the nineteenth century, the empire was denounced as tyrannical by Hungarians, Croats, Serbs, Rumanians, Czechs, Poles, Italians, and even some Germans, whose national ambitions were blocked by its existence. Later, disillusioned by nationalism in central and eastern Europe, some tended to romanticize unduly the old Danubian monarchy, noting that it had at least the merit of holding many discordant peoples together.

The empire was from the first international, based on a cosmopolitan aristocracy of landowners who felt closer to each other, despite difference of language, than to the laboring masses who worked on their estates. Not for many years, until after 1848, did the Habsburg government really touch these rural masses; it dealt with the landed class and with the relatively few cities, and left the landlords to control the peasants. The old diets remained in being in Bohemia, Hungary, and the Austrian provinces. No diet was created for the empire as a whole. The diets were essentially assemblages of landlords; and though they no longer enjoyed their medieval freedom, they retained certain powers over taxation and administration and a sense of constitutional liberty against the crown, like the Provincial Estates in France. So long as they produced taxes and soldiers as needed, and accepted the wars and foreign policy of the ruling house, no questions were asked at Vienna. The peasants remained in, or reverted to, serfdom. The law allowed the lord to exact three days a week of *robot* from his peasants.[8] In France, by way of contrast, where the monarchy checked the feudal interest, the royal courts generally limited such peasant service for the lord to twelve days a year.

The Habsburgs were determined to make their new empire unmistakably hereditary and Catholic. It is understandable that the Austrian house, together with its officials, should have acquired a strong distaste for both Protestantism and elective monarchy. These were the two biggest rocks on which Habsburg ambitions in the Holy Roman Empire had been sunk. In addition the Habsburgs of Austria, like those of Spain, were usually somewhat stodgily pious, and often under the influence of Jesuits, who saw in every realm only a province of the Universal Faith.

The first to feel the blow had been Bohemia. The Czech rebellion had been crushed, as we have seen, at the battle of the White Mountain in 1620.[9] This ended, until 1918, the national independence of a people who had greatly prospered in the Middle Ages. The reigning Habsburg, Ferdinand II, abrogated the elective Bohemian monarchy and declared the kingdom hereditary. He poured Catholic missionaries into the country. He confiscated the estates of the rebel nobles and granted them to a host of adventurers of many nationalities, mostly colonels and generals of the Thirty Years' War. A few of these were Czechs, but most were ignorant of the languages and customs of the people, and they owed their position entirely to the Habsburgs. Yet even under these circumstances he could not rule unconditionally. In 1627 he issued a new charter or constitution to Bohemia, or rather to the pro-Habsburg aristocracy whom he installed there. By this charter the new landlords received considerable liberties, the right to meet in a diet, raise taxes, supervise administration, and conduct the affairs of Bohemia in their own way. Bohemia remained an entirely separate kingdom. Its new aristocracy, while remaining apart from the native peasantry and the towns, soon developed, as the ruling element of the country, a sense of Bohemian autonomy and a desire to be let alone by the central government at Vienna.

Somewhat the same happened in Hungary after its reconquest from the Turks in 1699. Protestantism was widespread in Hungary, where it formed part of the famous Hungarian liberties. Every Hungarian magnate, like princes of the Holy Roman Empire, possessed the *ius reformandi,* or right to reform religion on his own estates. There was thus religious disorder, and religion and politics were mixed. The Turks, during their occupation, favored the Protestants, knowing that Protestants would have no longing for a Catholic Habsburg king. In Hungary, therefore, as in Bohemia,

[8] See pp. 123–124.
[9] See p. 144.

the first step following the reconquest was to repress Protestantism, which was not only detested as heretical but feared as pro-Turkish. The elective monarchy was done away with; the crown of St. Stephen[10] became the hereditary possession of the Habsburgs. The Hungarian nobles lost their constitutional right of armed rebellion. German veterans were settled in the country, the Croats given privileges, and even Serbs imported from across the Danube, all to weaken the grip of the Magyar aristocracy; the effect was to scramble the nationalities in an already heterogeneous region. Hardly had Eugene's armies entered Turkish Hungary when a rebellion against the Habsburgs broke out in 1703, led by Prince Francis Rakoczy, whose name is known to the world through the traditional march bearing his name, and which originated at this time as a patriotic song of the rebels. Rakoczy received help from Louis XIV but was finally crushed by 1711 and spent the rest of his life in France and Turkey. The Hungarians, proud and stubborn, became nationalistic before the era of nationalism. And for all that the Habsburgs could do, Hungary remained a distinct kingdom, and the magnates of Hungary remained the freest-handed aristocracy in Europe, except for the Poles.

Thus, despite the efforts of the Habsburgs, the Austrian monarchy remained a collection of territories held together by a personal union. Inhabitants of Austria proper considered their ruler as archduke, Bohemians saw in him the king of Bohemia, Magyars the apostolic king of Hungary. Each country retained its own law, diet, and political life. No feeling in the people held these regions together, and even the several aristocracies were joined only by common service to the house. For the empire to exist, all crowns had to be inherited by the same person.

After the reconquest of Hungary the king-archduke, Charles VI (1711–1740), devised a form of insurance to guarantee such an undivided succession. This took the form of a document called the Pragmatic Sanction, first issued in 1713. By it every diet in the empire and the various archdukes of the Habsburg family were to agree to regard the Habsburg territories as indivisible and to recognize only one specified line of heirs. The matter became urgent when it developed that Charles would have no children except a daughter, Maria Theresa, and that the direct male line of the Austrian Habsburgs, as of the Spanish a few years before, was about to become extinct. Charles VI gradually won acceptance of the Pragmatic Sanction by all parts of his empire and all members of his family. He then set about having foreign powers guarantee it, knowing that Bavaria, Prussia, or others might well put in claims for this or that part of the inheritance. This process took years, and was accomplished at the cost of many damaging concessions. Charles VI had attempted, for example, to revive Belgium commercially by founding an overseas trading company at Ostend. The British government, before agreeing to guarantee the Pragmatic Sanction, demanded and obtained the abandonment of this commercial project. Finally all powers signed. Charles VI died in 1740, having done all that could be done, by domestic law and international treaty, to assure the continuation of the Austrian empire.

[10] See p. 22.

He was scarcely dead when armed "heirs" presented themselves. A great war broke out to partition the Austrian empire, as the Spanish empire had been partitioned shortly before. Bohemia threw off its allegiance. Hungary almost did the same. But these events belong later in the story.[11] At the moment it is enough to know that by 1740 a populous empire, of great military strength, had been founded on the Danube.

Nothing is more characteristic of the seventeenth century than the way in which very small states were able to play an influential part in European affairs, seemingly out of all proportion to their size. That small population was no barrier to the attainment of a high level of wealth, comfort, and intellectual and artistic activity is perhaps not surprising. Of such high civilization among a small people the Dutch were the conspicuous example. It is more surprising that small population, and even relative economic backwardness, presented no insuperable barrier to military and political strength.

The main reason why small states could act as great powers was that armies were small and weapons simple. Difficulties of supply and communications, the poor state of the roads, the lack of maps, the absence of general staffs, together with many other administrative and technical difficulties, held down the number of soldiers who could be successfully managed in a campaign. The battles of the Thirty Years' War, on the average, were fought by armies of less than 20,000 men. And while Louis XIV, by the last years of his reign, built up a military establishment aggregating some 400,000, the actual field armies in the wars of Louis XIV did not exceed, on the average, 40,000. Armies of this size were well within the reach of smaller powers. If especially well trained, disciplined, and equipped, and if ably commanded and economically employed, the armies of small powers could defeat those of much larger neighbors. On this fact, fundamentally, the German state of Prussia was to be built. But Prussia was not the first to exploit the opportunity with spectacular consequences. The first, it may be said, was Sweden.

*Sweden's Short-Lived
Empire*

Sweden almost, but not quite, formed an empire out of the malleable matter of central and eastern Europe in the seventeenth century. The population of Sweden at the time was not over a million; it was smaller than that of the Dutch Republic. But the Swedes produced a line of extraordinary rulers, ranging from genius in Gustavus Adolphus (1611–1632) to the verge of madness in Charles XII (1697–1718). The elective Swedish kingship was made definitely hereditary, the royal power freed from control by the estates, craftsmen and experts brought from the west, notably Holland, war industries subsidized by the government, and an army created with many novel features in weapons, organization, and tactics.

234   [11]See pp. 281–292.

With this army Gustavus Adolphus crossed the Baltic in the Thirty Years' War, made alliances with Protestant German princes, cut through the yielding mass of the Holy Roman Empire, and helped to ward off unification of Germany by the Habsburgs.[12]   The Swedish crown, by the Peace of Westphalia, received certain coastal regions of Germany—western Pomerania including the city of Stettin, and the former bishoprics of Bremen and Verden on the North Sea.   Subsequently, in a confused series of wars, in which a Polish king claimed to be king of Sweden, and a Swedish king claimed to be king of Poland, the Swedes won control of virtually all the shores and cities of the Baltic.   Only Denmark at the mouth of that sea and the territories of the house of Brandenburg, which had almost no ports, remained independent.   For a time the Baltic was a Swedish lake.   The Russians were shut off from it, and the Poles and even the Germans, who lived on its shores, could reach it only on Swedish terms.

The final Swedish effort was made by the meteoric Charles XII, a young man crazed by military ambition, who led an army for years back and forth across the plains of Poland and Russia, only to be ruined in the end by the Russians, and spend more long years as a guest and protégé of the Turks.[13]   With the death of Charles XII in 1718 the Swedish sphere contracted to Sweden itself, except that Finland and reduced holdings in northern Germany remained Swedish for a century more.   The Swedes in time proved themselves exceptional among European peoples in not harping on their former greatness.   They successfully and peaceably made the transition from the role of a great power to that of a small one.

In the long run it was to be Prussia that dominated this part of Europe and through its later influence on Germany was to play a momentous part in the modern world. The south coast of the Baltic, where Prussia was to arise, was an unpromising site for the creation of a strong political power.   It was an uninviting country, thinly populated, with poor soil and without mineral resources, more backward than Saxony or Bohemia, not to mention the busy centers of south Germany and western Europe. It was a flat open plain, merging imperceptibly into Poland, without prominent physical features or natural frontiers.[14]   The coastal region directly south from Sweden was known as Pomerania.   Inland from it, shut off from the sea, was the electoral margraviate of Brandenburg, centering about Berlin.   In 1417 the Hohenzollern family had come to rule Brandenburg, which was to be the nucleus of modern Prussia.   Brandenburg had been founded in the Middle Ages as a "mark" or "march" of the Holy Roman Empire, to fight the battles of the Holy Empire against the then heathen Slavs.   All Germany east of the Elbe represented a medieval conquest by the German-speaking peoples—the German *Drang nach Osten*, or drive to the East.   From the Elbe to Poland, German conquerors and settlers had replaced the primitive Slavs, eliminating them or absorbing them by intermarriage.

[12] See pp. 145–150.
[13] See p. 251.
[14] See maps, pp. 8–9, 148–149, 217, and 221.

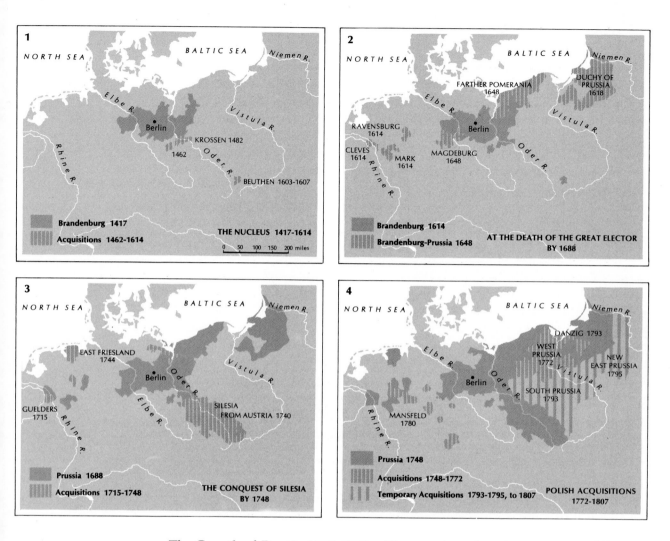

The Growth of Prussia 1417–1918. *The maps shown here give a conspectus of Prussian history from the time when Brandenburg began to expand in the seventeenth century. One may see, by looking at all the panels together, how Prussia was really an east-European state until 1815; its center of gravity shifted westward, in significant degree, only in the nineteenth century. Panel 2 shows the early formation of three unconnected masses; Panel 3, the huge bulk of Silesia relative to the small kingdom that annexed it (pp. 285–286); Panel 4, the fruits of the partitions of Poland (p. 260). Napoleon pared Prussia down (p. 427). The main crisis at the Congress of Vienna, and its resolution, are shown in Panels 6 and 7 (pp. 458–459). Bismarck's enlargement of Prussia appears in Panel 8 (pp. 572–574). The boundaries established by Bismarck remained unchanged until the fall of the Prussian monarchy in 1918.*

Extending eastward from Brandenburg and Pomerania, and outside the Holy Roman Empire, stretched a region inhabited by Slavic peoples and known historically as Pomerelia. Next to the east came "Prussia," which eventually was to give its name

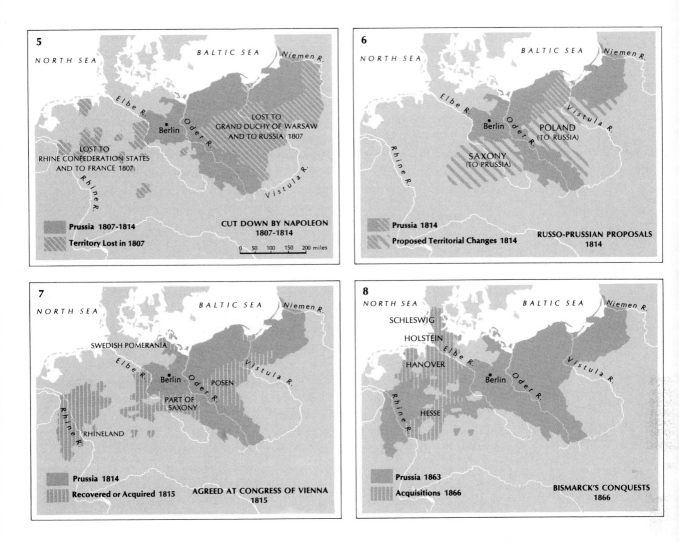

5 CUT DOWN BY NAPOLEON 1807–1814

NORTH SEA · BALTIC SEA · Niemen R. · Elbe R. · Oder R. · Rhine R. · Vistula R.

LOST TO GRAND DUCHY OF WARSAW AND TO RUSSIA 1807

LOST TO RHINE CONFEDERATION STATES AND TO FRANCE 1807

Berlin

◼ Prussia 1807–1814
▨ Territory Lost in 1807

0 50 100 150 200 miles

6 RUSSO-PRUSSIAN PROPOSALS 1814

NORTH SEA · BALTIC SEA · Niemen R. · Elbe R. · Oder R. · Rhine R. · Vistula R.

POLAND (TO RUSSIA)

SAXONY (TO PRUSSIA)

Berlin

▨ Prussia 1814
▨ Proposed Territorial Changes 1814

7 AGREED AT CONGRESS OF VIENNA 1815

NORTH SEA · BALTIC SEA · Niemen R. · Elbe R. · Oder R. · Rhine R. · Vistula R.

SWEDISH POMERANIA

Berlin · POSEN

PART OF SAXONY

RHINELAND

◼ Prussia 1814
▥ Recovered or Acquired 1815

8 BISMARCK'S CONQUESTS 1866

NORTH SEA · BALTIC SEA · Niemen R. · Elbe R. · Oder R. · Rhine R. · Vistula R.

SCHLESWIG
HOLSTEIN
HANOVER
HESSE

Berlin

◼ Prussia 1863
▥ Acquisitions 1866

to all territories of the Hohenzollern monarchy. This original Prussia formed part of the lands of the Teutonic Knights, a military crusading order which had conquered and Christianized the native peoples in the thirteenth century.[15] The name reflected much earlier history, for the earliest Prussians, or Borussians, had been related to the Lithuanians but had disappeared under the impact of Germans and Poles. "Prussia" was already predominantly German in language and culture at the beginning of modern times. The grand master of the Teutonic Knights at the time of the Protestant Reformation happened to be a member of the Hohenzollern family. Turning Protestant, he "secularized" the lands of the Order, which henceforth became the hereditary duchy of Prussia under Polish overlordship.[16] Except for its seacoast along the Baltic, the duchy of Prussia was totally enclosed by the Polish

[15] See p. 42.
[16] See pp. 80–81.

237

kingdom. To the north, along the Baltic, as far as the Gulf of Finland, German minorities lived among undeveloped Lithuanians, Letts, and Estonians. The towns were German, founded as German commercial colonies in the Middle Ages, and many of the landlords were German also, descendants of the Teutonic Knights, and later known as the "Baltic barons." These Germans at that time, since nationalist sentiment scarcely existed, felt no affiliation with the main block of Germans farther west, but they retained their German language and traditions.

Modern Prussia began to appear in the seventeenth century when a number of territories came together in the hands of the Hohenzollerns of Brandenburg, who, we have noted, had ruled in Brandenburg since 1417. In 1618 the Elector of Brandenburg inherited the duchy of Prussia where the ducal family died out after a few generations. This was the first significant step in the growth of Brandenburg-Prussia. Another important development occurred when the old ruling line in Pomerania expired during the Thirty Years' War. Although the Swedes succeeded in taking the better part of Pomerania, including the city of Stettin, the Elector of Brandenburg received at the Peace of Westphalia eastern or Farther Pomerania. Barren, rural and harborless though it was, it at least had the advantage of connecting Brandenburg with the Baltic. The Hohenzollerns no sooner obtained it than they began to dream of joining it to the duchy of Prussia, a task which required the absorption of the intermediate and predominantly Slavic Pomerelia, which was part of Poland. (This task was accomplished in 1772. The Hohenzollern administrators then called the old duchy "East Prussia" and the old Pomerelia "West Prussia"; but by that time, in a general confusion of nomenclature, "Prussia" also referred to all the Hohenzollern provinces taken together.)

Had the duchy of Prussia and Farther Pomerania been the only acquisitions of the Hohenzollerns, their state would have been oriented almost exclusively toward eastern Europe. But at the Peace of Westphalia they received, in addition to Farther Pomerania, the large bishopric of Halberstadt and the still larger archbishopric of Magdeburg, which lay on the west bank of the Elbe. Moreover, through the play of inheritance so common in the Holy Roman Empire, the Hohenzollerns had earlier fallen heir, in 1614, to the small state of Cleves on the Rhine at the Dutch border and a few other small territories also in western Germany. These were separated from the main mass around Brandenburg by many intermediate German principalities. But they gave the Hohenzollerns a direct contact with the more advanced regions of western Europe, and a base from which larger holdings in the Rhineland were eventually to be built up.

In the seventeenth century, meanwhile, the dominions of the house of Brandenburg were in three disconnected masses. The main mass was Brandenburg, with the adjoining Pomerania and Elbe bishoprics. There was a detached eastern mass in ducal Prussia and a small detached western mass on and near the Rhine. The middle and western masses were within the Holy Roman Empire. The eastern mass was outside the Empire, and until 1660, a fief of Poland. To connect and unify the three masses became the underlying long-range policy of the Brandenburg house.

In the midst of the Thirty Years' War, in 1640, a young man of twenty, named Frederick William, succeeded to these diverse possessions. Known later as the Great Elector, he was the first of the men who made modern Prussia. He had grown up under trying conditions. Brandenburg was one of the parts of Germany to suffer most heavily from the war. Its location made it the stamping ground of Swedish and Habsburg armies. In 1640, in the twenty-two years since the beginning of the war, the population of Berlin had fallen from about 14,000 to about 6,000, that of Frankfurt-on-the-Oder perhaps from 12,000 to 2,000. Hundreds of villages had been wiped out. Wolves roamed over the countryside.

Frederick William concluded that in his position, ruling a small and open territory, without natural frontiers or possibility of defense in depth, surrounded by hard-pressing and much more powerful neighbors, he must put his main reliance in a competent army. With an effective army, even if small, he could oblige the stronger states to take him into their calculations, and so could enter with some hope of advantage into the politics of the balance of power. This long remained the program of the Brandenburgers—to have an army but not to use it, to conserve it with loving and even miserly care, to keep an "army in being," and to gain their ends by diplomatic maneuver. Frederick William liquidated the mercenary adventurers employed by his predecessor. By the end of the Thirty Years' War he had a small army of 8,000 men under his own control. He was able thus to get a hearing at the Peace of Westphalia, and to prevent the Swedes from annexing all Pomerania. But even with all its accessions of territory, since north Germany was thinly populated and had been ravaged by war, the Brandenburgers at the death of the Great Elector (in 1688) had fewer than 1,500,000 subjects—less than the Dutch, and not a twelfth as many as the king of France. Brandenburg-Prussia was still a small power, one of half a dozen rising creations in Germany.

The foreign policy of the Great Elector and his successors was like that of the rival German princes after the Peace of Westphalia, that is to say, tortuous in the extreme and forever in search of lucky windfalls. In the south the Brandenburgers played off France against the Habsburgs, to the disadvantage of the Holy Roman Empire, for a pro-French phase in Brandenburg policy made it easier for Louis XIV to absorb Alsace in the 1680s.[17] In the north they played off Sweden against Poland. The Great Elector aspired to make himself sovereign in the duchy of Prussia by ridding himself of feudal dependence on Poland. First he combined with Sweden, signing a secret treaty for a partition of Poland; then, when the Poles defeated these projects, he allied with the Poles against Sweden, demanding as the price of his aid, and obtaining it, the recognition of his sovereignty over ducal Prussia in 1660.

The next step was to become not only sovereign duke of Prussia, but king. This step was successfully taken by the Great Elector's successor, Frederick I. Various German princes were trying to make themselves kings. Since except for Bohemia, which was a special case, there could be no kingdoms in the Holy Roman Empire,

[17] See p. 197.

239

aspirants to royal honors had to cast their hopes outside it. By 1700 the Elector of Saxony was king of Poland, the Elector of Hanover was in line to be king of England, the Elector of Bavaria was intriguing avidly to obtain any crown he could get, and the archduke of Austria had confirmed his position as king of both Hungary and Bohemia. The Brandenburgers were fearful of being outdistanced. In 1701 the Habsburg emperor was preparing to enter the War of the Spanish Succession. He wanted the support of 8,000 Brandenburg troops. The elector named his price: recognition of himself, by the emperor, as king "in Prussia." The emperor yielded; the title, at first explicitly limited to the less honorable king *in* Prussia, soon became king *of* Prussia. Another rent was made in the old fabric of the Holy Empire. There was now a German king above all the other German princes, for where the union between Hanover and England, or between Saxony and Poland, remained a purely personal tie, Brandenburg and Prussia became institutionally joined as a German state. Prussia proper, the old duchy of that name, remained outside the Holy Roman Empire but was fused with the Hohenzollern dominions within the Empire. All the scattered Hohenzollern possessions, from the Rhine to the Lithuanian border, came to be known as the kingdom of Prussia.

The Kingdom of Prussia: The Role of the Army

The new kingdom of Prussia was still the most insignificant kingdom in Europe, with the exception of Savoy in Italy, a state much like Prussia in its ambitions and methods, and whose duke was recognized as king at about the same time. Weak and small, Prussia was created by policy. It let others do its fighting; its efficient new army was seldom risked. In 1720, for example, the king of Prussia won Stettin and part of western Pomerania from the Swedes. But it was Peter the Great of Russia and a Russian force that carried on most of the military operations. The Prussian king gained this service from the tsar by diplomatic jockeying, in which he used Prussian troops very sparingly. Until late in its history Prussia was militaristic but not warlike. It was ambitious but not belligerent. It was far more reluctant to be involved in actual fighting than were its wealthier and stronger neighbors. It was less bellicose than Austria, France, or Great Britain. Yet it was more militaristic than any of these states, for its very essence was its army.

The preoccupation of Prussia with its army was unquestionably defensive in origin, arising from the horrors of the Thirty Years' War. But it outlasted its cause, and became the settled habit and character of the country. Prussia was not unique, in a world of Bourbons and Habsburgs, Swedes, Russians, Turks, and the growing British navy, in the attention it paid to its armed forces. The unique thing about Prussia was the disproportion between the size of the army and the size of the resources on which the army was based. The government, to maintain the army, had to direct and plan the life of the country for this purpose. Nor was Prussia the originator of the "standing" army, kept active in time of peace, and always preparing for war. Most governments imitated Louis XIV in establishing standing armies, not merely to promote foreign ambitions but to keep armed forces out of the hands of nobles and military adventurers, and under control by the state.

But Prussia was unique in that, more than in any other country, the army developed a life of its own, almost independent of the life of the state. It was older than the Prussian state. In 1657 the Great Elector fought a great battle at Warsaw with soldiers from all parts of his dominions. It was the first time that men from Cleves, Brandenburg, and ducal Prussia had ever done anything together. The army was the first "all-Prussian" institution. Institutions of civilian government, common to all Prussia, developed later and largely to meet the needs of the army. And in later generations the army proved more durable than the state. When Prussia collapsed before Napoleon in 1806, the spirit and morale of the Prussian army carried on; and when the Hohenzollern empire finally crashed in 1918, the army still maintained its life and traditions on into the Republic, which again it survived.[18]

In all countries, to some extent, the machinery of the modern state developed as a means of supporting armed forces, but in Prussia the process was exceptionally clear and simple. In Prussia the rulers drew roughly half their income from the crown domain and only about half from taxes. The crown domain, consisting of manors and other productive enterprises owned directly by the ruler as lord, was in effect a kind of government property, for the Prussian rulers used their income almost entirely for state purposes, being personally men of simple and even Spartan habits. The rulers of Prussia, until a century after the accession of the Great Elector, were able to pay the whole cost of their civil government from their own income, the proceeds of the crown domain. To maintain an army, they had to supplement the remaining income from the domain with new income derived from taxes. To develop the domain, increase its productivity, account for and transfer the funds, they created a large body of civilian officials. The domain bulked so large that much of the economy of the country was not in private hands but consisted of enterprises owned and administered by the state. For additional income the Great Elector introduced taxes of the kind used in France, such as excise taxes on consumers' goods and a government monopoly on the sale of salt. These taxes, together with the old land tax, began to be collected during the disorders of the Thirty Years' War by war commissioners, later organized into a general commissariat. In effect, the army itself collected the taxes and determined the purposes for which the funds should be spent. All taxes, for a century after the accession of the Great Elector, were levied for the use of the army.

Economic life grew up under government sponsorship, rather than by the enterprise of a venturesome business class. This was because, for a rural country to maintain an organized army, productive and technical skills had to be imported, mainly from the West. The Great Elector in his youth spent a number of years in Holland, where he was impressed by the wealth and prosperity that he saw. After becoming elector he settled Swiss and Frisians in Brandenburg (the Frisians were almost Dutch); he welcomed Jews from Poland; and when Louis XIV began to persecute the French Protestants, he provided funds and special officials to assist the immigration of 20,000 Huguenots to Brandenburg. Frenchmen for a time formed a

[18] See pp. 447–449, 748–749, 821–824.

sixth of the population of Berlin and were the most advanced element of that comparatively primitive city. The government, as in France under Colbert, initiated and helped to finance various industries; but the importance of such government participation was greater than in France, because the amount of privately owned capital available for investment was incomparably less. Military needs, more than elsewhere, dominated the market for goods, because civilian demand, in so poor a country, was relatively low; so that the army, in its requirements for food, uniforms, and weapons, was a strong force in shaping the economic growth of the country. For all its scraping thrift and careful planning, the government depended on outside financial assistance from western Europe. The Great Elector, for example, in the last fifteen years of his reign, received (as subsidies requiring no repayment) 973,000 thalers from the Empire, 912,000 from the Dutch, 503,000 from France, 467,000 from Spain, and 57,000 from Denmark. With money from France the Great Elector attempted to enter the overseas world, founding a Brandenburg colony in West Africa; but this venture was financially dependent from the beginning and was liquidated as a useless expense by his successor.

The army had a profound effect also on the social development and class structure of Prussia. It became the policy of the rulers to absorb practically the whole landed aristocracy, the Junkers, into military service. They used the army, with conscious purpose, as a means of implanting an "all-Prussian" psychology in the landed families of Cleves, Brandenburg, Pomerania, and the former dominions of the Teutonic Knights. The sense of service to the king or state was exalted as the supreme human virtue. The fact that Prussia was a very recent and artificial combination of territories, so that loyalty to it was not at first a natural sentiment, made it all the more necessary to instill it by obvious and martial means. Emphasis on duty, obedience, service, and sacrifice, morally the best side of the army code, was probably encouraged in Prussia by the Lutheran religion, which, as has been seen, was strongly inclined to teach that Christian freedom was a matter of the inner spirit, and that in earthly affairs men owed a willing obedience to their princes.[19] That military virtues became characteristic of the whole Prussian aristocracy was also due, like so much else, to the small size of the population. In France, for example, with perhaps 50,000 male adult nobles, only a small minority served habitually as army officers. In Prussia there were few Junker families that did not have some of their members in uniform.

Moreover, the Great Elector and his successors, like all absolutist rulers, repressed the estates or parliamentary assemblages in which the landed aristocracy was the main element. To mollify the squires, the rulers promised commissions in the army to men of their class. They promised them also a free hand over their peasants. The Prussian monarchy was largely based on an understanding between the ruler and the landlord gentry—the latter agreed to accept the ruler's government and to serve in his army, in return for holding their own peasants in hereditary

[19]See p. 80.

subjection. Serfdom spread in Prussia as elsewhere in eastern Europe.[20] In East Prussia the condition of the peasants became as deplorable as in Poland.

The Prussian rulers believed that the Junkers made better army officers because they were brought up in the habit of commanding their own peasants. Bourgeois officers, a minority in all armies, were of the utmost rarity in Prussia. To preserve the officer class, legislation forbade the sale of "noble" lands, i.e., manors, to persons not noble. In France, again by way of contrast, where manorial rights had become simply a form of property, bourgeois and even peasants could legally acquire manors and enjoy a lordly or "seigneurial" income. In Prussia this was not possible; classes were frozen by owning nonexchangeable forms of property. It was thus harder for middle-class persons to enter the aristocracy by setting up as landed gentry. The bourgeois class in any case had little spirit of independence. Few of the old towns of Germany were in Prussia. The Prussian middle class was not wealthy. It was not strong by the possession of private property. The typical middle-class man was an official, who worked for the government as an employee or lease-holder of the large crown domain, or in an enterprise subsidized by the state. The civil service in Prussia, from the days of the Great Elector, became notable for its honesty and efficiency. But the middle class, more than elsewhere, deferred to the nobles, served the state, and stood in awe of the army.

These peculiar features of Prussia developed especially under Frederick William I, who was king from 1713 to 1740. He was an earthy, uncouth man, who, were the matter less serious, might almost be regarded as a comical character. He disdained whatever savored of "culture," to which his father and grandfather (the Great Elector) and also his son (Frederick the Great) were all strongly attracted. He begrudged every penny not spent on the army. He cut the expense of the royal household by three-fourths. On his coronation journey to Königsberg he spent 2,547 thalers, where his father had spent five million. He ruled the country in a fatherly German way, supervising it like a private estate, prowling the streets of Berlin in an old seedy uniform, and disciplining negligent citizens with blows of his walking stick. He worked all the time, and expected everyone else to do likewise. He loved the army, which all his policies were designed to serve. He was the first Prussian king to appear always in uniform. He rearranged the order of courtly precedence, pushing army officers up and civilians down. His love of tall soldiers is famous; he collected a special unit, men between six and seven feet high, from all over Europe, and indeed Peter the Great sent him some from Asia. He devised new forms of discipline and maneuver, founded a cadet corps to train the sons of the Junkers, and devised a new system of recruiting and replacement (the canton system, long the most effective in Europe), by which each regiment had a particular district or canton assigned to it as a source of soldiers. He raised the size of the army from 40,000 at his accession to 83,000 at his death. During his reign Berlin grew to be a city of 100,000, of whom 20,000 were soldiers, a proportion probably matched in no other city of Europe. He

[20] See pp. 123–124, 216, 224, 232, 248.

likewise left to his successor (for he fought practically no wars himself) a war chest of 7,000,000 thalers.

With this army and war chest Frederick II, later called the Great, who became king in 1740, startled Europe. Charles VI of Austria had just died. His daughter Maria Theresa entered upon her manifold inheritance. All Europe was hedging on its guarantee of the Pragmatic Sanction. While others waited, Frederick struck. Serving no notice, he moved his forces into Silesia, to which the Hohenzollerns had an old though doubtful claim. Silesia was a part of the kingdom of Bohemia on the side toward Poland, lying in the upper valley of the Oder River, and adjoining Brandenburg on the north. The addition of Silesia to the kingdom of Prussia almost doubled the population and added valuable industries, so that Prussia now, with 6,000,000 people and an army which Frederick raised to 200,000, at last established itself as a great power. But Frederick, as will be seen, had to fight repeatedly to retain Silesia. Having made his great conquest by sudden aggression, and spent his father's war chest, he soon came up against the fundamental problem of Prussia, its relative poverty, and relapsed into the cautious program of his forebears.[21] Only at the beginning was the career of Frederick the Great an exception to the picture of Prussia here set forth—that it was a militaristic but unwarlike and even timid state, preferring to secure its ends by threats, machinations, balance of power policies, and intrigue. It must be added that, judged simply as a human accomplishment, Prussia was a remarkable creation, a state made on a shoestring, a triumph of work and duty.

The affairs of central and eastern Europe, from Sweden to Turkey and from Germany to the Caspian Sea, were profoundly interconnected. The underlying theme of the present chapter, it may be recalled, is that this whole great area was fluid, occupied by the flabby bodies of the Holy Roman Empire, Poland, and Turkey, and that in this fluid area three harder masses developed—the modern Austrian monarchy, the kingdom of Prussia, and the Russian empire. All, too, in varying degree, were modernized by borrowings from the West.

In the century after 1650 the old tsardom of Muscovy turned into modern Russia. Moving out from the region around Moscow, the Russians not only established themselves across northern Asia, reaching the Bering Sea about 1700, but also entered into closer relations with Europe, undergoing especially in the time of Tsar Peter the Great (1682–1725) a rapid process of Europeanization. To what extent Russia became truly European has always been an open question, disputed both by western Europeans and by Russians themselves. In some ways the Russians have been European from as far back as Europe itself can be said to have existed, i.e., from the early Middle Ages. Ancient Russia had been colonized by Vikings, and the Russians had become Christians long before the Swedes, the Lithuanians, or the Finns. But Russia had not been part of the general development of Europe for a

[21]See pp. 282–286, 344–345.

number of reasons. For one thing, Russia had been converted to the Greek Orthodox branch of Christianity; therefore, the religious and cultural influence of Constantinople, not of Rome, had predominated. Second, the Mongol invasions and conquest about 1240 had kept Russia under Asiatic domination for about two hundred and fifty years, until 1480 when a grand duke of Muscovy, Ivan III (1462–1505), was able to throw off the Mongol overlordship and cease payment of tribute.[22] Last, Russian geography, especially the lack of warm-water or ice-free seaports, had made commerce and communication with the West difficult. For these reasons Russia had not shared in the general European development after about 1100, and the changes that took place in the seventeenth and eighteenth centuries may accurately be called Europeanization, or at least a wholesale borrowing of the apparatus of civilization from the West. The Europeanizing or westernizing of Russia was by no means a unique thing. It was a step in the expansion of the European type of civilization and hence in the formation of the modern world as we have known it in the last three hundred years.

In some ways the new Russian empire resembled the new kingdom of Prussia. Both took form in the great plain which runs uninterruptedly from the North Sea into inner Asia. Both lacked natural frontiers and grew by addition of territories to an original nucleus. In both countries the state arose primarily as a means of supporting a modern army. In both the government developed autocratically, in conjunction with a landlord class which was impressed into state service and which in turn held the peasantry in serfdom. Neither Russia nor Prussia had a native commercial class of any political importance. In neither country could the modern state and army have been created without the importation of skills from western Europe. Yet Prussia, with its German connections, its Protestant religion, its universities, and its nearness to the busy commercial artery of the Baltic, was far more "European" than Russia, and the Europeanization of Russia may perhaps better be compared with the later westernization of Japan.[23] In the Russia of 1700, as in the Japan of 1870, the main purpose of the westernizers was to obtain scientific, technical, and military knowledge from the West, in part with a view to strengthening their own states against penetration or conquest by Europeans. Yet here too the parallel must not be pushed too far. Russia became more fully Europeanized than did the peoples of Asia. In time, its upper classes intermarried with Europeans, and Russian music and literature became part of the culture of Europe. Russia developed a unique blend of European and non-European traits.

The Russians in the seventeenth century, as today, were a medley of peoples distinguished by their language, which was of the Slavic family, of the great Indo-European language group.[24] The Great Russians or Muscovites lived around

[22] See pp. 22–23, 42.
[23] See pp. 594–600.
[24] See pp. 5–6, see also map, Languages of Europe, p. 478.

Moscow. Moving out from that area, they had penetrated the northern forests and had also settled in the southern steppes and along the Volga, where they had assimilated various Asiatic peoples known as Tartars. After two centuries of expansion, from roughly 1450 to 1650, the Russians had almost but not quite reached the Baltic and the Black seas. The Baltic shore was held by Sweden. The Black Sea coast was still held by Tartar Khans under the protection of Turkey. In the rough borderlands between Tartar and Russian lived the semi-independent cowboy-like Cossacks, largely recruited from migratory Russians. West of Muscovy were the White Russians (or Bielorussians) and southwest of Muscovy the Little Russians (or Ruthenians or Ukrainians), both in the seventeenth century under the rule of Poland, which was then the leading Slavic power.

The energies of the Great Russians were directed principally eastward. They conquered the Volga Tartars in the sixteenth century, thus reaching the Ural Mountains, which they immediately crossed. Muscovite pioneers, settlers, and townbuilders streamed along the river systems of Siberia, felling timber and trading in furs as they went. In the 1630s, while the English founded Boston and the Dutch New York, the Russians were establishing towns in the vast Asiatic stretches of Siberia, reaching to the Pacific itself. A whole string of settlements, remote, small, and isolated—Tomsk and Tobolsk, Irkutsk and Yakutsk—extended for 5,000 miles across northern Asia.

It was toward the vast heartland of central Asia that Muscovy really faced, looking out upon Persia and China across the deserts. The bazaars of Moscow and Astrakhan were frequented by Persians, Afghans, Kirghiz, Indians, and Chinese. The Caspian Sea, into which flowed the Volga, the greatest of Russian rivers, was better known than was the Baltic. Europe as sensed from Moscow was in the rear. During most of the seventeenth century even Smolensk and Kiev belonged to Poland. And, as has been noted, while the Swedes blocked the Russians from access to the Baltic, the Tartars and Turks barred them from the Black Sea and the Mediterranean. Poles and Swedes, on various occasions, actually discouraged the passage of Europeans into Great Russia, fearing the consequences should their monstrous Eastern neighbor acquire Western arts. Yet the Russians were not totally shut off from Europe. In 1552, when Ivan the Terrible conquered Kazan from the Tartars, he had a German engineer in his army. In the next year, 1553, Richard Chancellor arrived in Moscow from England by the roundabout way of Archangel on the White Sea.[25] Thereafter trade between England and Muscovy was continuous. The tsars valued Archangel as their only inlet from the West, through which military materials could be imported. The English valued it as a means of reaching the wares of Persia.

Russia in the seventeenth century reflected its long estrangement from Europe and its long association with some of the more barbarous peoples of Asia. Women of the upper classes were secluded and often wore veils. Men wore beards and skirted garments that seemed exotic to Europeans. Customs were crude, wild drunkenness

246   [25] See p. 114.

and revelry alternating with spasms of repentance and religious prostration. Dwarfs and fools, no longer the fashion in the West, still amused the tsar and his retainers. Superstition infected the highest classes of church and state. Life counted for little; murder, kidnapping, torture, and elaborate physical cruelty were common. The Russian church supported no such educational or charitable institutions as did the Catholic and Protestant churches of Europe and had developed no such respect for learning or sentiments of humanity. Churchmen feared the incipient Western influences. "Abhorred of God," declared a Russian bishop, "is any who loves geometry; it is a spiritual sin." Even arithmetic was hardly understood in Russia. Arabic numerals were not used, and merchants computed with the abacus. The calendar was dated from the creation of the world. Ability to predict an eclipse seemed a form of magic. Clocks, brought in by Europeans, seemed as wonderful in Russia as they did in China, where they were brought in by Jesuits at about the same time. The principal Russian art was the painting of icons. There was no literature in the Russian language, which was scarcely a written language at all. A few annals, tales, and translations from Greek ecclesiastical literature were written in Slavonic, an artificial, learned language used in the churches. The most notable writer to live in Moscow in the seventeenth century was not a Russian but a Croatian, Yury Krizhanich (who wrote in Latin), founder of the idea that all Slav peoples should act together, and who went all the way to Moscow to win support for his Pan-Slav dream. But the Muscovites were not yet ready for his doctrine. They exiled him to Tobolsk, in Siberia.

Yet this great barbarous Russia, which fronted on inner Asia, was European in some of its fundamental social institutions. It possessed a variant of the manorial and feudal systems. It felt the same wave of constitutional crises that was sweeping over Europe at the same time. Russia had a duma or council of retainers and advisers to the tsar, and the rudiments of a national assembly corresponding to meetings of the estates in western Europe. In Russia as in Europe the question was whether power should remain in the hands of these bodies or become concentrated in the hands of the ruler. Ivan the Terrible, who ruled from 1533 to 1584 and was the first grand duke of Muscovy to assume the title of tsar,[26] was a shrewd observer of contemporary events in Poland. He saw the dissolution that was overtaking the Polish state and was determined to avoid it in Muscovy. His ferocity toward those who opposed him made him literally terrible, but though his methods were not used in Europe, his aims were the aims of his European contemporaries. Not long after his death Russia passed into a period known as the Time of Troubles (1604–1613), during which the Russian nobles elected a series of tsars and demanded certain assurances of their own liberties. But the country was racked by contending factions and civil war, in which, as in the religious wars in France or the Thirty Years' War in central Europe at

---

[26] The Slavic word *tsar,* like the German *Kaiser,* derives from *Caesar,* a title used as a synonym for *emperor* in the Roman, the Holy Roman, and the Byzantine (or Eastern Roman) empires. The spelling *czar,* also common in English, reveals the etymology and, with the initial letter silent, the current English-language pronunciation, *zar.*

approximately the same time, the issue lay between feudal independence and a more modern centralization.

In 1613 a national assembly, hoping to settle the troubles, elected a seventeen-year-old boy as tsar, or emperor, believing him young enough to have no connection with any of the warring factions. The new boy tsar was Michael Romanov, of a gentry family, related by marriage to the old line of Ivan the Terrible. Thus was established, by vote of the political classes of the day, the Romanov dynasty which ruled in Russia until 1917. The early Romanovs, aware of the fate of elective monarchy in Poland and elsewhere, soon began to repress the representative institutions of Russia and set up as absolute monarchs. Here again, though they were more lawless and violent than any European king, they followed the general pattern of contemporary Europe.

Nor can it be said that the main social development of the seventeenth century in Russia, the sinking of the peasantry into an abyss of helpless serfdom, was exclusively a Russian phenomenon. The same generally took place in eastern Europe.[27] Serfdom had long been overtaking the older free peasantry of Russia. In Russia, as in the American colonies, land was abundant and labor scarce. The natural tendency of labor was to migrate over the great plain, to run off to the Cossacks, or to go to Siberia. In the Time of Troubles, especially, there was a good deal of moving about. The landlords wished to assure themselves of their labor force. To this end they obtained the support of the Romanov tsars. The manor, or what corresponded to it in Russia, came to resemble the slave plantation of the New World.[28] Laws against fugitive serfs were strengthened; lords won the right to recover fugitives up to fifteen years after their flight, and finally the time limit was abolished altogether. Peasants came to be so little regarded that a law of 1625 authorized anyone killing another man's peasant simply to give him another peasant in return. Lords exercised police and judicial powers. By a law of 1646 landowners were required to enter the names of all their peasants in government registers; peasants once so entered, together with their descendants, were regarded as attached to the estate on which they were registered. Thus the peasant lost the freedom to move at his own will. For a time he was supposed to have secure tenure of his land; but a law of 1675 allowed the lords to sell peasants without the land, and thus to move peasants like chattels at the will of the owner. This sale of serfs without land, which made their condition almost indistinguishable from slavery as practiced in America, became indeed a distinctive feature of serfdom in Russia, since in Poland, Prussia, Bohemia, and other regions of serfdom, the serf was generally regarded as "bound to the soil," inseparable from the land.

Against the loss of their freedom the rural population of Russia protested as best it could, murdering landlords, fleeing to the Cossacks, taking refuge in a vagrant existence, countered by wholesale government-organized manhunts and by renewed and more stringent legislation. A tremendous uprising was led in 1667 by Stephen Razin, who gathered a host of fugitive serfs, Cossacks, and adventurers, outfitted a

[27] See pp. 123–124, 216, 242–243.
[28] See pp. 268–269.

fleet on the Caspian Sea, plundered Russian vessels, defeated a Persian squadron, and invaded Persia itself. He then turned back, ascended the Volga, killing and burning as he went and proclaiming a war against landlords, nobles, and priests. Cities opened their gates to him; an army sent against him went over to his side. He was caught and put to death in 1671. The consequence of the rebellion, for over a century, was that serfdom was clamped on the country more firmly than ever. But the memory of Razin lived in the folklore of Russian peasants. A hill near the lower Volga was named for him. The legend grew that whoever climbed Razin's hill at night would learn his secret—and that this secret was class war.

Even from the church the increasingly wretched rural people drew little comfort. The Russian Orthodox church at this same time went through a great internal crisis, and ended up as hardly more than a department of the tsardom, useful to the government in instilling a superstitious reverence for Holy Russia. The Russian church had historically looked to the Patriarch of Constantinople as its head. But the conquest of Constantinople by the Turks made the head of the Greek Orthodox church a merely tolerated inferior to the Moslem sultan-caliph, so that the Russians in 1589 set up an independent Russian patriarch of their own. In the following generations the Russian patriarchate first became dependent on, then was destroyed by, the tsarist government.

In the 1650s the Russian patriarch undertook certain church reforms, mainly to correct mistranslations in Russian versions of the Bible and other sacred writings. The changes aroused the horror and indignation of the general body of believers. Superstitiously attached to the mere form of the written word, believing the faith itself to depend on the customary spelling of the name of Jesus, the malcontents saw in the reformers a band of cunning Greek scholars perpetrating the work of Antichrist and the devil. The patriarch and higher church officials forced through the reforms but only with the help of the government and the army. Those who rejected the reforms came to be called Old Believers. More ignorant and fanatical than the established church, agitated by visionary preachers, dividing into innumerable sects, the Old Believers became very numerous, especially among the peasants. Old Believers were active in Stephen Razin's rebellion and in all the sporadic peasant uprisings that followed. The peasants, already put by serfdom outside the protection of law, were also largely estranged from the established religion. A distrust of all organized authority settled over the Russian masses, to whom both church and government seemed mere engines of repression. The Russian Orthodox church meanwhile maintained its position only by support of the tsar.

But while willing enough to modernize to the extent of correcting mistranslations from the Greek, the church officials resisted the kind of modernization that was coming in from western Europe. They therefore opposed Peter the Great at the end of the century. After 1700 no new patriarch was appointed. Peter put the church under a committee of bishops called the Holy Synod, and to the Synod he attached a civil official called the Procurator of the Holy Synod, who was not a churchman but head of a government bureau, and whose task was to see that the church did nothing displeasing to the tsar. Peter thus secularized the church, making himself in effect its head. But while the consequences were more extreme in Russia than elsewhere, it must again be noted that this action of Peter's followed the general pattern of Europe. Secular supervision of religion had become the rule almost everywhere, especially in Protestant countries. Indeed an Englishman of the time thought that Peter the Great, in doing away with the patriarchate and putting the church under his own control, was wisely imitating England, which he visited in his youth.

The Russia in which Peter the Great became tsar, in 1682, was in short fundamentally European in some ways and had in any case been in contact with Westerners for over a century. Without Peter, Russia would have developed its European connections more gradually. Peter, by his tempo and methods, made the process a social revolution.

Peter obtained his first knowledge of the West in Moscow itself, where a part of the city known as the German quarter was inhabited by Europeans of various nationalities, whom Peter often visited as a boy. Peter also in his early years mixed with Westerners at Archangel, still Russia's only port, for he was fascinated by the sea and took lessons in navigation on the White Sea from Dutch and English ship captains. Like the Great Elector of Brandenburg, Peter as a young man spent over a year in western Europe, especially Holland and England, where he was profoundly impressed with the backwardness of his own country. He had considerable talents as a mechanic and organizer. He labored with his own hands as a ship's carpenter in Amsterdam and talked with political and business leaders on means of introducing Western organization and technology into Russia. He visited workshops, mines, commercial offices, art galleries, hospitals, and forts. Europeans saw in him a barbarian of genius, a giant of a man standing a head above most others, bursting with physical vitality and plying all he met with interminable questions on their manner of working and living. He had neither the refinement nor the pretension of Western monarchs; he mixed easily with workmen and technical people, dressed cheaply and carelessly, loved horseplay and crude practical jokes, and dismayed his hosts by the squalid disorder in which he and his companions left the rooms put at their disposal. A man of acute practical mind, he was as little troubled by appearances as by moral scruples.

Peter on his visit to Europe in 1697–1698 recruited almost 1,000 experts for service in Russia, and many more followed later. He cared nothing for the civilization of Europe except as a means to an end, and this end was to create an army and a state which could stand against those of the West. His aim from the beginning was in part defensive, to ward off the Poles, Swedes, and Turks who had long pushed against Russia; and in part expansionist, to obtain seaports or "windows on the West," warm-water ports on the Baltic and Black seas, free from the shortcomings of Archangel, which was frozen a good part of the year and in any case offered only a roundabout route to Europe. For all but two years of his long reign Peter was at war.

The Poles were a receding danger. A Polish prince had indeed been elected tsar of Muscovy during the Time of Troubles, and for a while the Poles aspired to conquer and Catholicize the Great Russians, but in 1667 the Russians had regained Smolensk and Kiev, and the growing anarchy in Poland made that country no longer a menace, except as the Swedes or others might install themselves in it. The Turks and their feudatories the Tartars, though no longer expanding, were still obstinate foes. Peter before going to Europe managed in 1696 to capture Azov at the mouth of the Don, but he was unable to hold any of the Black Sea coast and learned in these campaigns to know the inferiority of the Russian army. The Swedes were the main enemy of Russia. Their army, for its size, was still probably the best in Europe. By occupying Finland, Karelia, and Livonia they controlled the whole eastern shore of the Baltic including the Gulf of Finland. In 1697, the Swedish king having died, Peter entered into an alliance with Poland and Denmark to partition the overseas possessions of the Swedish house.

The new king of Sweden, the youthful Charles XII, though descended from civilized enough forebears, was in some ways as crude as Peter (as an adolescent he had sheep driven into his rooms in the palace in order to enjoy the warlike pleasure of killing them), but he proved also to have remarkable aptitude as a general. In 1700, at the battle of Narva, with an army of 8,000 men, he routed Peter's 40,000 Russians. The tsar thus learned another lesson on the need of westernizing his state and army. Fortunately for the Russians Charles XII, instead of immediately pressing his advantage in Russia, spent the following years in furthering Swedish interests in Poland, where he forced the Poles to elect the Swedish candidate as their king. Peter meanwhile, with his imported officers and technicians, reformed the training, discipline, and weapons of the Russian army. Finally Charles XII invaded Russia with a large and well prepared force. Peter used against him the strategy later used by the Russians against Napoleon and Adolf Hitler; he drew the Swedes into the endless plains, exposing them to the Russian winter, which happened to be an exceptionally severe one, and in 1709, at Poltava in south Russia, he met and overwhelmed the demoralized remainder. The entire Swedish army was destroyed at Poltava, only the king and a few hundred fugitives managing to escape across the Turkish frontier. Peter in the next years conquered Livonia and part of eastern Finland. He landed troops near Stockholm itself. He campaigned in Pomerania almost as far west as the Elbe. Never before had Russian influence reached so deeply into Europe. Prussia, as we have seen, rose with the rise of Russia, receiving Stettin and most of western or Swedish Pomerania through an understanding with Peter and without serious commitment of its own forces. The imperial day of Sweden was now over, terminated by Russia. Peter had won for Russia the Baltic shore and with it warm-water outlets. These significant developments ending the great Northern War (1709–1721) were confirmed in the treaty of Nystadt in 1721.

War is surely not the father of all things, as has been sometimes claimed, but these wars did a good deal to father imperial Russia. The army was transformed from an Asiatic horde into a professional force of the kind maintained by Sweden, France, or Prussia. The elite of the old army had been the *streltsi*, a kind of Moscow guard, composed of nobles and constantly active in politics. A rebellion of the *streltsi* in 1698 had cut short Peter's tour of Europe; he had returned and quelled the mutiny by

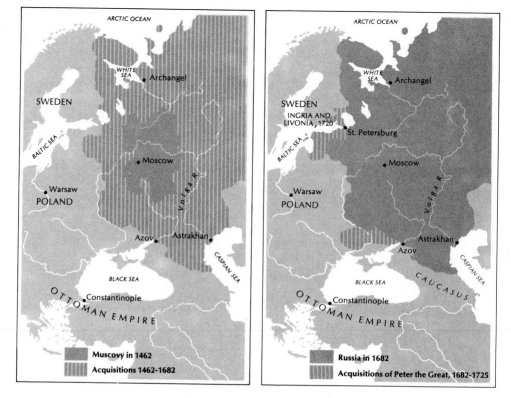

The Growth of Russia in the West. *At the accession of Peter the Great in 1682 the Russian empire, expanding from the old grand duchy of Muscovy, had almost but not quite reached the Black and Baltic seas. Most of Peter's conquests were in the Baltic region where he pushed back the Swedes and built St. Petersburg. Under Catherine the Great (1762–1796) Russia took part in the three partitions of Poland and also reached the Black Sea. The tsar Alexander (1801–1825), thanks largely to the Napoleonic wars, was able to acquire still more of Poland and annex Finland and Bessarabia; he also made conquests in the Caucasus. In the nineteenth century the western boundary of Russia remained stabilized but additional gains were made in the Caucasus. Russia also spread over northern Asia in the seventeenth century, first reaching the Pacific as early as 1630. (See also map, pp. 790–791.)*

ferocious use of torture and execution, killing five of the rebels with his own hands. The *streltsi* were liquidated only two years before the great Russian defeat at Narva. Peter then rebuilt the army from the ground up. He employed European officers of many nationalities, paying them half again as much as native Russians of the same grades. He filled his ranks with soldiers supplied by districts on a territorial basis, somewhat as in Prussia. He put the troops into uniforms resembling those of the West and organized them in regiments of standardized composition. He armed them with muskets and artillery of the kind used in Europe and tried to create a service of

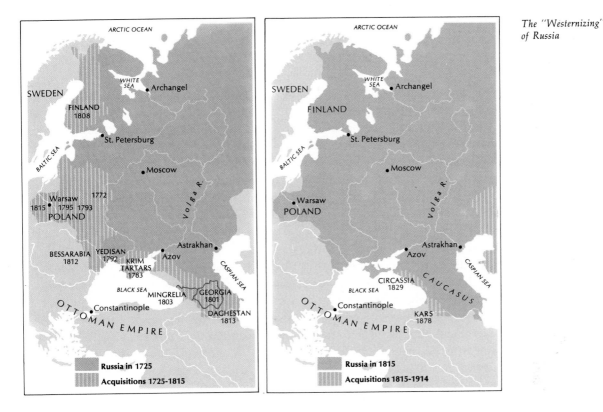

Map legend (left): Russia in 1725 / Acquisitions 1725-1815

Map legend (right): Russia in 1815 / Acquisitions 1815-1914

supply. With this army he had not only driven the Swedes back into Sweden, but also dominated Russia itself. At the very time of the Swedish invasion large parts of the country were in rebellion, as in the days of Stephen Razin, for the whole middle and lower Volga, together with the Cossacks of the Don and Dnieper, rose against the tsar and rallied behind slogans of class war and hatred of the tsar's foreign experts. Peter crushed these disturbances with the usual ruthlessness. The Russian empire, loose and heterogeneous, was held together by military might.

While the war was still in progress, even before the decisive battle of Poltava, Peter laid the foundations of a wholly new city in territory conquered from the Swedes and inhabited not by Russians but by various Baltic peoples. This city is now called Leningrad. Peter named it St. Petersburg after himself and his patron saint. From the beginning it was more truly a city than Louis' spectacular creation at Versailles established at almost the same time. Standing at the head of the Gulf of Finland, it was Peter's chief window on the West. Here he established the offices of government, required noblemen to build town houses, and gave favorable terms to foreign merchants and craftsmen to settle. Peter meant to make St. Petersburg a symbol of the new Russia, a new city facing toward Europe and drawing the minds of the Russians westward, replacing the old capital, Moscow, which faced toward Asia and was the stronghold of opposition to his westernizing program. St. Petersburg soon became one of the leading cities of northern Europe. It remained the capital of Russia until the revolution of 1917 when Moscow resumed its old place.

The new army, the new city, the new and expanding government offices all required money, which in Russia was very scarce. Taxes were imposed on an inconceivable variety of objects—on heads, as poll taxes; on land; on inns, mills, hats, leather, cellars, and coffins; on the right to marry, sell meat, wear a beard, or be an Old Believer. The tax burden fell mainly on the peasants; and to assure the payment of taxes the mobility of peasants was further restricted, and borderline individuals were classified as peasants in the government records, so that serfdom became both more onerous and more nearly universal. To raise government revenues and to stimulate production Peter adopted the mercantilist policies exemplified by Colbert in France. He encouraged exports, built a fleet on the Baltic, and developed mining, metallurgy, and textiles, which were indispensable to the army. He organized mixed groups of Russians and foreigners into commercial companies, provided them with capital from government funds (little private capital being available), and gave them a labor supply by assigning them the use of serfs in a given locality. Serfdom, in origin mainly an agricultural institution, began to spread in Russia as an industrial institution also. The fact that serf owners obtained the right to sell serfs without land, or to move them from landed estates into mines or towns, made it easier for industry in Russia to develop on the basis of unfree labor. Nor were the employers of serfs, in these government enterprises, free to modify or abandon their projects at will. They too were simply in the tsar's service. The economic system rested largely on impressment of both management and labor, not on private profit and wages as in the increasingly capitalistic West. In this way Peter's efforts to force Russia to a European level of material productivity widened the gap between Russia and western Europe.

To oversee and operate this system of tax-collecting, recruiting, economic controls, serf-hunting, and repression of internal rebellion Peter created a new administrative system. The old organs of local self-government wasted away. The duma and the national assembly, decadent anyway in that they could not function without disorder, disappeared. In their place Peter put a "senate" dependent on himself, and ten territorial areas called "governments" or *gubernii*—the very words were not Slavic but Latin and showed imitation of the West. The church he ruled through his Procurator of the Holy Synod.[29] At the top of the whole structure was himself, an absolute ruler, tsar and autocrat of all the Russias. Before his death, dissatisfied with his son, he abolished the rule of hereditary succession to the tsardom, claiming the right for each tsar to name his own successor. Transmission of supreme power was thus put outside the domain of law, and in the following century the accession of tsars and tsarinas was marked by strife, conspiracy, and assassination. The whole system of centralized absolutism, while in form resembling that of the West, notably France, was in fact significantly different, for it lacked legal regularity, was handicapped by the insuperable ignorance of many officials, and was imposed on a turbulent and largely unwilling population. The empire of the Romanovs has been called a state without a people.

[29] See pp. 249–250.

Peter, to assure the success of his westernizing program, developed what was called "state service," which had been begun by his predecessors. Virtually all landowning and serf-owning aristocrats were required to serve in the army or civil administration. Offices were multiplied to provide places for all. In the state service birth counted for nothing. Peter used men of all classes; Prince Dolgoruky was of the most ancient nobility, Prince Menshikov had been a cook, the tax administrator Kurbatov was an ex-serf, and many others were foreigners of unknown background. Status in Peter's Russia depended not on inherited rank which Peter could not control, but on rank in his state service, civilian grades being equated with military, and all persons in the first eight grades being considered gentry. "History," wrote a Scot serving in Peter's army, "scarcely affords an example where so many people of low birth have been raised to such dignities as in tsar Peter's reign, or where so many of the highest birth and fortune have been leveled to the lowest ranks of life." In this respect especially, Peter's program resembled a true social revolution. It created a new governing element in place of the old, almost what in modern parlance would be called a party, a body of men working zealously for the new system with a personal interest in its preservation. These men, during Peter's lifetime and after his death, were the bulwarks against an anti-Western reaction, the main agents in making Peter's revolution stick. In time the new families became hereditary themselves. The priority of state service over personal position was abandoned a generation after Peter's death. Offices in the army and government were filled by men of property and birth. After Peter's revolution, as after some others, the new upper class became merged with the old.

The "Westernizing" of Russia

Revolutionary also, suggesting the great French Revolution or the Russian revolution of 1917, were Peter's unconcealed contempt for everything reminiscent of the old Russia and his zeal to reeducate his people in the new ways. He required all gentry to put their sons in school. He sent many abroad to study. He simplified the Russian alphabet. He edited the first newspaper to appear in Russia. He ordered the preparation of the first Russian book of etiquette, teaching his subjects not to spit on the floor, scratch themselves, or gnaw bones at dinner, to mix socially with women, take off their hats, converse pleasantly, and look at people while talking. The beard he took as a symbol of Muscovite backwardness; he forbade it in Russia, and himself shaved a number of men at his court. He forced people to attend evening parties to teach them manners. He had no respect for hereditary aristocracy, torturing or executing the highborn as readily as the peasants. As for religion, we are told that he was a pious man and enjoyed singing in church, but he was contemptuous of ecclesiastical dignity, and in one wild revel paraded publicly with drunken companions clothed in religious vestments and mocking the priests. Like most great revolutionists since his time he was aggressively secular.

Peter's tactics provoked a strong reaction. Some adhered strictly to the old ways, others simply thought that Peter was moving too fast and too indiscriminately toward the new. Many Russians resented the inescapable presence of foreigners, who often

The Results of Peter's Revolution

looked down on Russians as savages, and who enjoyed special privileges such as the right of free exit from Russia and higher pay for similar employments. One center around which malcontents rallied was the church. Another was Peter's son Alexis, who declared that when he became tsar he would put a stop to the innovations and restore respect for the customs of old Russia. Peter, after some hesitation, finally put his own son to death. He ruled that each tsar should choose his own successor. He would stop at nothing to remake Russia in his own fashion.

Peter died in 1725, proclaimed "the Great" in his own lifetime by his admiring Senate. Few men in all history have exerted so strong an individual influence, which has indirectly become more far-reaching as the stature of Russia itself has grown. Though the years after Peter's death were years of turmoil and vacillation, his revolutionary changes held firm against those who would undo them. It is not simply that he Europeanized Russia and conquered a place on the Baltic; these developments would probably have come about in any case. It is by the methods he used, his impatient forcing of a new culture on Russia, that he set the future character of his empire. His methods fastened autocracy, serfdom, and bureaucracy more firmly upon the country. They perhaps associated the idea of civilization with the idea of force, and they provoked a reaction in which western Europe was viewed with accentuated dislike and distrust. He was able, for all his efforts, to reach only the upper classes. Many of these became more Europeanized than he could dream, habitually speaking French and living spiritually in France or in Italy. But as time went on many upper-class Russians, because of their very knowledge of Europe, became impatient of the stolid immovability of the peasants around them, sensed themselves as strangers in their own country, or were troubled by a guilty feeling that their position rested on the degradation and enslavement of human beings. Russian psychology, always mysterious to the West, could be explained in part by the violent paradoxes set up by rapid Europeanization. As for the peasant masses, they remained outside the system, egregiously exploited, estranged except by force of habit from their rulers and their social superiors, regarded by them as brutes or children, never sharing in any comparable way in their Europeanized civilization. These facts worked themselves out in later times. As for Peter's own time, Russia by his efforts came clearly out of its isolation, its vast bulk was now organized to play a part in international affairs, and its history thenceforward was a part of the history of Europe and increasingly of the world. Russia, like Prussia and the Austrian monarchy, was to be counted among the powers of Europe.

26
The Partitions
of Poland

The fate of Poland in the eighteenth century reaches beyond the time limits of the present chapter, but it illustrates and brings together many of the strands traced in the preceding pages, so that a few words on it at this point may be useful. Poland in the eighteenth century, if Russia is considered non-European, was still by far the largest European state. It still reached from the Baltic almost to the Black Sea and extended eastward for 800 miles across the north-European plain. But it was the classic example, along with the Holy Roman Empire, of an older political structure which failed to develop modern organs of government.[30] It fell into ever deeper anarchy and confusion. Without army, revenues, or administration, internally divided among parties forever at cross purposes, with many Poles more willing to bargain with foreigners than to work with each other, the country was a perpetual theater for diplomatic maneuvering and was finally absorbed by its growing neighbors.

It will be recalled that King John Sobieski, in 1683, drove the Turks from Vienna.[31] The Polish relief of Vienna, the last great effort of the decaying Republic, initiated the general crusade against Turkey of the following years, in which the Habsburgs conquered Hungary and pushed their frontiers temporarily into the Balkans. For Poland itself this turn of affairs was not altogether beneficial. The Turks were the historic enemy of the Poles, and the weaker the historic enemy became the less there was to hold the Polish nobles together. Sobieski, though a national hero, spent his last years in disillusionment at the progressive disorders in his country. He died in 1696.

The Polish royal elections in the eighteenth century were as usual an international auction and the royal election of 1733 actually precipitated a general European war known as the War of the Polish Succession, which lasted in some areas of the fighting until 1739. The war resulted in the confirmation of the Russian candidate Augustus III as king and also in several territorial adjustments in Europe. France, for example, which had backed Louis XV's father-in-law Stanislas for the Polish throne was compensated for the French loss of standing in Poland by the acquisition of Lorraine.

Not long thereafter, by the middle of the eighteenth century, a reforming movement began to gather strength in Poland. Polish patriots hoped to do away with the *liberum veto* and other elements in the constitution which made government impossible. Their efforts were repeatedly frustrated by foreign influence, notably that of Catherine II, tsarina of Russia (1762–1796), who preferred a Poland in which she could intervene at will. On the death of Augustus III in 1763 Catherine strengthened her hold over the country by obtaining the election of another Russian puppet, a Polish nobleman named Stanislas Poniatowski, her former lover, as king. She declared herself protector of the Polish liberties. It was to the Russian advantage to maintain the existing state of affairs in Poland, which enabled Russian influence to pervade the whole country, rather than to divide the country with neighbors who might exclude Russian influence from their own spheres. The Prussians, however, long awaiting the day when they might join the old duchy of Prussia with Brandenburg-Pomerania in one continuous territory, were more willing to entertain the prospect of a partition of Poland. It was the fundamental policy of Prussia to absorb territory without the risk of war. In the War of the Polish Succession, which had involved most of the powers of Europe, the eccentric and army-loving Frederick William had remained quiet, making no overt move to snatch the coveted West Prussia. His successor, Frederick the Great, though he had gone to war for Silesia,

[30] See pp. 223–225 and maps, pp. 217 and 221.
[31] See p. 230.

likewise hoped to obtain West Prussia by diplomatic means. The opportunity finally presented itself in connection with another war between Russia and Turkey, which threw the whole situation in eastern Europe into question. The Turkish empire was now at last showing signs of unmistakable weakness. It too, like Poland, offered the prospect of partition or of control from outside. The Republic of Poland and the Ottoman Empire were in the cauldron together, ready to be melted down and fused with their stronger neighbors. The Russians were successful in the Turkish war which began in 1768. Their troops overran the north coast of the Black Sea and poured into the Danubian principalities, occupying Bucharest. They were in a position, for all the Turks might do, to cross the Danube and stream into the Balkans to Constantinople itself.

What saved Turkey and condemned Poland was the play of the balance of power. The Russians hesitated to cross the Danube, fearing that the Austrians would fall upon their flank, for they knew that the Austrians, too, had designs upon Turkey and would not permit them a monopoly of the spoils. Prussia meanwhile viewed with concern the prospects of a war that might result in a Russian and Austrian partition of the Turkish territories. Such an eventuality would result in an aggrandizement of the other two east-European states to the disadvantage of Prussia and would upset the balance of power in eastern Europe. The Prussians, therefore, came forward with a proposal. It was a proposal designed to prevent an Austro-Russian war and to preserve the east-European balance of power unchanged by leaving Turkey more or less intact but by having all three powers take territory from Poland instead. The proposition was accepted by the three parties.

The Russians called off their war with Turkey. They evacuated the Danubian principalities and most of the Black Sea coast. They did not, indeed, allow the Turkish empire to escape intact. The sultan was obliged to renounce his suzerainty over the Black Sea Tartars, to admit Russian shipping to the Black Sea and the Straits, and to recognize the Russian government as "protector" of Christian interests at Constantinople. These terms were written into the treaty of Kuchuk Kainarji of 1774, a great turning point in the expansion of Russia southward. The Russians soon used the advantage thus gained to absorb the north coast of the Black Sea, to continue their interference in Turkey, and to send naval vessels into the Mediterranean.

Poland since the Eighteenth Century. *The top panel shows, in simplified form, the ethnic composition of the area included in the great Poland of 1772. In addition to languages shown, Yiddish was spoken by the large scattered Jewish population. Note how the line set in 1795 as the western boundary of Russia persists through later transformations. It reappears as the eastern border of Napoleon's Grand Duchy (p. 432), and of Congress Poland (p. 458). After the First World War the victorious Allies contemplated much this same line as Poland's eastern frontier (the dotted line in the fourth panel, known as the Curzon Line); but the Poles in 1920–1921 conquered territory farther east (p. 786). After the Second World War the Russians pushed the Poles back to the same basic line, but compensated Poland with territory taken from Germany, as far west as the river Oder. If the reader will compare the position of Warsaw in each panel he will see how Poland has been shoved westward.*

Languages
Polish
Lithuanian
Lettish
White Russian
Ukrainian
German

BALTIC SEA
Smolensk
Stettin
Warsaw

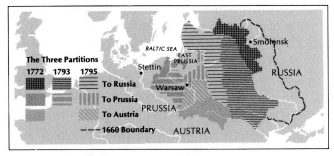

The Three Partitions
1772 1793 1795
To Russia
To Prussia
To Austria
1660 Boundary

BALTIC SEA
EAST PRUSSIA
Stettin
Smolensk
RUSSIA
Warsaw
PRUSSIA
AUSTRIA

During and After
the Napoleonic Era
1808-1831
Grand Duchy of Warsaw,
1808-1814
Congress Poland, 1815-1831
1772 Boundary

BALTIC SEA
PRUSSIA
Stettin
Smolensk
Warsaw
RUSSIA
AUSTRIA

Poland After World War I
Poland, 1922-1939
Curzon Line, 1919
1772 Boundary

BALTIC SEA
Stettin
GERMANY
Warsaw
Smolensk
SOVIET UNION
CZECHOSLOVAKIA

Poland After World War II
Poland After
World War II
1772 Boundary

BALTIC SEA
Stettin
EAST
GERMANY
Warsaw
Smolensk
SOVIET UNION
CZECHOSLOVAKIA

0 100 200 300 miles

Poland was meanwhile sacrificed. By the first partition, in 1772, its outer territories were cut away. Russia took an eastern slice, around the city of Vitebsk. Austria took a southern slice, the region known as Galicia. Prussia took the Pomerelian borderland. The Prussians thus at last realized their old ambition. Prussia now reached continuously as a solid block from the Elbe to the borders of Lithuania.[32] The partition sobered the Poles, who renewed their efforts at a national revival, hoping to create an effective sovereignty which could secure the country against outsiders. But the Polish movement lacked deeper strength, for it was confined mainly to the nobles, who had themselves brought the country to ruin. The mass of the serf population, and the Jews in the towns, did not care whether they were governed by Poles, Russians, or Germans. In addition, the Polish national revival was persistently blocked by the three neighboring powers. In 1792, when Europe was again at war in consequence of the great French Revolution, the three Eastern powers seized the opportunity to finish with Poland. By the second and third partitions, in 1793 and 1795, they absorbed all the remaining Polish territory. Thereafter there was no really independent Polish state until 1918.

The three partitioning powers extenuated their conduct on various grounds. They even took pride in it as a diplomatic achievement, accomplished without war between the partitioners, and preserving the balance of power in eastern Europe. What seemed to be robbery was justified by the argument that the gains were equal; this was the diplomatic doctrine of "compensation." It was argued also that the partitions of Poland put an end to an old cause of international rivalry and war, replacing anarchy with solid government in a large area of eastern Europe. It is a fact that Poland was scarcely more independent before the partitions than after. It is to be noted also, though nationalist arguments were not much used at the time, that on national grounds the Poles themselves had no claim to large parts of the old Poland. The regions taken by Russia, in all three partitions, were inhabited overwhelmingly by White Russians and Ukrainians, among whom the Poles were mainly a landlord class. Russia, even in the third partition, reached only to the true ethnic border of Poland. But later, after the fall of Napoleon, by general international agreement, the Russian sphere was extended deep into the territory inhabited by Poles.

The partitions of Poland, however extenuated, were nevertheless a great shock to the old system of Europe. Many advanced thinkers of the day praised the partitions as a triumph of enlightened rulers, putting an end to an old nuisance. But Edmund Burke, in England, prophetically saw in the first partition the crumbling of the old international order. His diagnosis was a shrewd one. The principle of the balance of power had been historically invoked to preserve the independence of European states, to secure weak or small ones against universal monarchy. It was now used to destroy the independence of a weak but ancient kingdom. Not that Poland was the first to be "partitioned"; the Spanish and Swedish empires had been partitioned, and during the eighteenth century, as will be seen, there were attempts to partition Prussia and the Austrian empire also. But Poland was the first to be partitioned without war

[32] See map, pp. 236–237, panel 4.

and the first to disappear totally.   That Poland was partitioned without war, a source of great satisfaction to the partitioning powers, was still a very unsettling fact.   It was alarming for a huge state to vanish simply by cold diplomatic calculation.   It seemed that no established rights were safe even in peacetime.   The partitions of Poland showed that in a world where great powers had arisen, controlling modern apparatus of state, it was dangerous not to be strong.   They suggested that any area failing to develop a sovereign state capable of keeping out foreign infiltration, and so situated as to be reached by the great powers of Europe, was unlikely to retain its independence.   In this way they anticipated, for example, the partitions of Africa a century later, when Africa too, lacking strong governments, was almost totally divided, without war, among half a dozen states of Europe.

Moreover the partitions of Poland, while maintaining the balance in eastern Europe, profoundly changed the balance of Europe as a whole.   The disappearance of Poland was a blow to France, which had long used Poland, as it had used Hungary and Turkey, as an outpost of French influence in the East.   The three new Eastern powers, especially Prussia and Russia, expanded their territory materially, while France enjoyed henceforth no permanent growth.   Eastern Europe bulked larger than ever before in the affairs of Europe in general.   Likewise in Germany, a kind of Europe in miniature, the eastern Germans, the Prussians and Austrians, bulked larger than ever in purely German affairs.   Prussia, Russia, and the Austrian empire became contiguous by the partitions of Poland.   They had an interest in common, the repression of Polish resistance to their rule.   Polish resistance, dating from before the partitions and continuing after them, was the earliest example of modern revolutionary nationalism in Europe.   The independence of Poland, and of other submerged nationalities, became in time a cause much favored in western Europe, while the three great monarchies of eastern Europe were drawn together in common opposition to nationalist programs; and this fact, plus the fact that the Eastern monarchies were primarily landlord states, accentuated the characteristic division of Europe, in the nineteenth century, between a West that inclined to be liberal and an East that inclined to be reactionary.   But these ideas anticipate a much later part of the story.

VI: THE STRUGGLE FOR

WEALTH AND EMPIRE

In the preceding chapters we have followed the political history of western Europe through the War of the Spanish Succession, terminated in 1713–1714 by the treaties of Utrecht and Rastadt. Affairs of Germany have been traced to 1740. In that year the new kingdom of Prussia and the new or renovated Austrian monarchy each passed into the hands of a new ruler and stood on the eve of a struggle with one another for ascendancy in central Europe, a struggle that merged with the world-wide contest of the mid-eighteenth century between the French and the British for world empire and for commercial supremacy. As for eastern Europe, we have observed the Europeanizing and the expansion of the Russian empire, and seen how the vast area called Poland ceased to form an independent state. Before turning to the great international issues of the mid-eighteenth century, we must first describe the important economic and social developments taking place in Europe and the expanding European world.

Chapter Emblem: A Spanish doubloon or gold coin minted in 1790, showing Charles IV as King of Spain and the Indies.

The opening of the Atlantic in the sixteenth century, it will be recalled, had reoriented Europe. In an age of oceanic communications Europe became a center from which America, Asia, and Africa could all be reached. A global economy had been created. The first to profit had been the Portuguese and the Spanish, and they had retained their monopoly through most of the sixteenth century, but the decline of the Portuguese and Spanish had paved the way for the triumph of the British, the French, and the Dutch. In the eighteenth century the outstanding economic development was the expansion of the global economy and the fact that Europe, or at least the Atlantic region north of Spain, became incomparably wealthier than any other part of the world. The new wealth, in the widest sense, meaning conveniences in every form, was produced by increasing scientific and technical knowledge, which in turn it helped to produce; and the two together, more wealth and more knowledge, helped to form one of the most far-reaching ideas of modern times, the idea of progress. To the increase in scientific knowledge, the idea of progress, and other intellectual developments of this age, we shall return in the chapters that follow.

*Commerce and Industry
in the Eighteenth
Century*

The new wealth of Europe was not like the age-old wealth of the gorgeous East, said by Milton to "shower on her kings barbaric pearl and gold." It consisted of gold, to be sure, but even more of bank deposits and facilities for credit, of more and better devices for mining coal, casting iron, and spinning thread, more productive agriculture, better and more comfortable houses, a wider variety of diet on the table, more and improved sailing ships, warehouses, and docks; more books, more newspapers, more medical instruments, more scientific equipment; greater government revenues, larger armies, and more numerous government employees. In the wealthy European countries, and because of the growing wealth, more people were freed from the necessity of toiling for food, clothing, and shelter, and were enabled to devote themselves to all sorts of specialized callings in government, management, finance, war, teaching, writing, inventing, exploring, and researching, and in producing the amenities rather than the barest necessities of life.

The increase of wealth was brought about by the methods of commercial capitalism and handicraft industry. Only at the close of the eighteenth century, and not really until the nineteenth century, did the use of steam engines and power-driven machinery, and the growth of large factories and great manufacturing cities, begin to bring about the conditions of modern industrialism. The economic system of the eighteenth century, while it contained within itself the seeds of later industrialism, represented the flowering of the older merchant capitalism, domestic industry, and mercantilist government policies which had grown up since the sixteenth century and which have been already described.[1]

Most people in the eighteenth century lived in the country. Agriculture was the greatest single industry and source of wealth. Cities remained small. London and Paris, the largest of Europe, each had a population of 600,000 or 700,000, but the next largest cities did not much exceed 200,000, and in all Europe at the time of the French Revolution (in 1789) there were only fifty cities with as many as 50,000 people. Urbanization, however, was no sign of industrial advancement. Spain, Italy, and even the Balkan peninsula, according to an estimate made in the 1780s, each had more large cities (over 50,000) than did Great Britain. Urbanization did not equate with industry because most industry was carried on in the country, by peasants and part-time agricultural workers who worked for the merchant capitalists of the towns. Thus, while it is true to say that most people still lived in the country, it would be false to say that their lives and labors were devoted to agriculture exclusively. One English estimate, made in 1739, held that there were 4,250,000 persons "engaged in manufactures" in the British Isles, a figure that included women and children, and comprised almost half the entire population. These people worked characteristically in their own cottages, employed as wage earners by merchant capitalists under the "domestic" system.[2] Almost half of them, about 1,500,000, were engaged in the weaving and processing of woolens. Others were in the copper, iron, lead, and tin manufactures; others in leather goods; much smaller were the paper, glass, porcelain, silk, and linen trades; and smallest of all, in 1739, was the manufacture of cotton cloth, which accounted for only about 100,000 workers. The list suggests the importance of nonagricultural occupations in the preindustrial age.

England, even with half its population engaged at least part of the time in manufactures, was not yet the unrivaled manufacturing country that it was to become after 1800. England in the eighteenth century produced no more iron than Russia and no more manufactures than France. The population of England was still small; it began to grow rapidly about 1760, but as late as 1800 France was still twice as populous as England and Scotland together. France, though less intensively developed than England, with probably far less than half its people "engaged in manufactures," nevertheless, because of its greater size, remained the chief industrial center of Europe.

Although foreign and colonial trade grew rapidly in the eighteenth century, it is probable that, in both Great Britain and France, the domestic or internal trade was greater in volume and occupied more people. Great Britain, with no internal tariffs, with an insignificant gild system, and with no monopolies allowed within the country except to inventors, was the largest area of internal free trade in Europe. France, or at least Colbert's Five Great Farms,[3] offered a free-trading internal market hardly less

---

[1] See pp. 116–126.
[2] See p. 118.
[3] See p. 194.

great. A great deal of economic activity was therefore domestic, consisting of exchange between town and town or between region and region. The proportions between domestic and international trade cannot be known. But foreign trade was important in that the largest enterprises were active in it, the greatest commercial fortunes were made in it, and the most capital was accumulated from it. And it was the foreign trade that led to international rivalry and war.

On the international economic scene a great part was still played by the Dutch. After the Peace of Utrecht the Dutch ceased to be a great political power, nor did they become a great economic power in the sense of being an industrial center, for their country was too small to sustain manufactures in any great amount. But their role in commerce, shipping, and finance remained undiminished, or diminished only relatively by the continuing commercial growth of France and Great Britain. They were still the middlemen and common carriers for other peoples. Their freight rates remained the lowest of Europe. They continued to grow rich on imports from the East Indies. To a large extent also, in the eighteenth century, the Dutch simply lived on their investments. The capital they had accumulated over two hundred years they now lent out to French or British or other entrepreneurs. Dutch capital was to be found in every large commercial venture of Europe and was lent to governments far and wide. A third of the capital of the Bank of England in the mid-eighteenth century belonged to Dutch shareholders. The Bank of Amsterdam remained the chief clearing house and financial center of Europe. Its supremacy ended only with the invasion of Holland by a French Revolutionary army in 1795.

The Atlantic trade routes, leading to America, to Africa, and to Asia, tempted the merchants of many nationalities in Europe. A great many East India companies were established—usually to do business in America as well as the East, for the "Indies" at the beginning of the eighteenth century was still a general term for the vast regions overseas. Both the English and the French East India companies were reorganized, with an increased investment of capital, shortly after 1700. A number of others were established—by the Scots, the Swedes, the Danes, the imperial free city of Hamburg, the republic of Venice, Prussia, and the Austrian monarchy. But, with the exception of the Danish company which lasted some sixty years, they all failed after only a few years, either for insufficiency of capital or because they lacked strong diplomatic, military, and naval support. Their failure showed that, in the transocean trade, unassisted business enterprise was not enough. Merchants to succeed in this sphere needed strong national backing. Neither free city, nor small kingdom, nor tiny republic, nor the amorphous Austrian empire provided a firm enough base.

It was the British and French who won out in the commercial rivalry of the eighteenth century. Britain and France were alike in having, besides a high level of industrial production at home, governments organized on a national scale and able to protect and advance, under mercantilist principles, the interests of their merchants in distant countries. For both peoples the eighteenth century—or the three-quarters of a century between the end of the War of the Spanish Succession in 1713 and the beginning of the French Revolution in 1789—was an age of spectacular enrichment and commercial expansion.

Although the trade figures are difficult to arrive at, French foreign and colonial trade may well have grown even more rapidly than the British in the years between the 1720s and the 1780s. In any event, by the 1780s, the two countries were about equal in their total foreign and colonial trade. Of the areas with which they carried on their trade, the British in the 1780s enjoyed proportionately more than the French of the trade with overseas America and Asia; the French enjoyed considerably more of the trade with the rest of Europe and the Near East. The contest for markets played an important part in the colonial and commercial wars between Britain and France all through the eighteenth century and on into the final and climactic struggle, and British triumph, in the time of Napoleon.

In the expanding global economy of the eighteenth century each continent played its special part. The trade with Asia was subject to an ancient limitation. Asia was almost useless as a market for European manufactures. There was much that Europeans wanted from Asia, but almost nothing that Asians wanted from Europe. The peoples of Chinese, Indian, and Malay culture had elaborate civilizations with which they were content; they lacked the dynamic restlessness of Europeans, and the masses were so impoverished (more so even than in Europe) that they could buy nothing anyway. Europeans found that they could send little to Asia except gold. The drain of gold from Europe to Asia had gone on since ancient times and, accumulating over the centuries, was one source of the fabulous treasures of Oriental princes. To finance the swelling demand for Asian products it was necessary for Europeans constantly to replenish their stocks of gold. The British found an important new supply in Africa along the Gulf of Guinea, where one region (the present Ghana) was long called the Gold Coast. The word "guinea" became the name of a gold coin minted in England from 1663 to 1813 and is still used as a fashionable way of saying twenty-one shillings.

What Europeans sought from Asia was still in part spices—pepper and ginger, cinnamon and cloves—now brought in mainly by the Dutch from their East India islands. But they wanted manufactured goods also. Asia was still in some lines superior to Europe in technical skill. It is enough to mention rugs, chinaware, and cotton cloth. The very names by which cotton fabrics are known in English and other European languages reveal the places from which they were thought to come. "Madras" and "calico" refer to the Indian cities of Madras and Calicut, "muslin" to the Arabic city of Mosul. "Gingham" comes from a Malay word meaning "striped"; "chintz," from a Hindustani word meaning "spotted." Most of the Eastern manufactures were increasingly imitated in the eighteenth century in Europe. Axminster and Aubusson carpets competed with Oriental rugs. In 1709 a German named Boettcher discovered a formula for making a vitreous and translucent substance comparable to the porcelain of China; this European "china," made at Sèvres, Dresden, and in England, soon competed successfully with the imported original. Cotton fabrics were never produced in Europe at a price to compete with India until after the introduction of power machinery, which began in England about 1780. Before that date the demand for Indian cotton goods was so heavy that the woolen, linen, and silk interests became alarmed. They could produce nothing like the sheer muslins and bright calico prints which caught the public fancy, and many governments, to protect the jobs and capital involved in the old European textile industries, simply forbade the import of Indian cottons altogether. But it was a time of many laws and little enforcement, the forbidden fabrics continued to come in, and Daniel Defoe observed in 1708 that, despite the laws, cottons were not only sought as clothing by all classes, but "crept into our houses, our closets and bedchambers; curtains, cushions, chairs and at last beds themselves were nothing but calicoes or Indian stuffs." Gradually, in the face of tariff protection for "infant industries" in Europe, and the rapid growth of European cotton manufactures, import of cottons and other manufactures from Asia declined. After about 1770 most of the imports of the British East India Company consisted in tea, which was brought from China.

America in the eighteenth century bulked larger than Asia in the trade of western Europe. The American trade was based mainly on one commodity—sugar. Sugar had long been known in the East, and in the European Middle Ages little bits of it had trickled through to delight the palates of lords and prelates. About 1650 sugar cane was brought in quantities from the East and planted in the West Indies by Europeans. A whole new economic system arose in a few decades. It was based on the "plantation." A plantation was an economic unit consisting of a considerable tract of land, a sizable investment of capital, often owned by absentees in France or England, and a force of impressed labor, supplied by blacks brought from Africa as slaves. Sugar, produced in quantity with cheap labor at low cost, proved to have an inexhaustible market. The eighteenth century was the golden age, economically speaking, of the West Indies. From its own islands alone, during the eighty years from 1713 to 1792, Great Britain imported a total of £ 162,000,000 worth of goods, almost all sugar; imports from India and China, in the same eighty years, amounted to only £ 104,000,000. The little islands of Jamaica, Barbados, St. Kitts, and others, as suppliers of Europe, not only dwarfed the whole mainland of British America but the whole mainland of Asia as well. For France, less well established than Britain on the American mainland and in Asia, the same holds with greater force. The richest of all the sugar colonies, San Domingo, now called Haiti, belonged to France.

The plantation economy, first established in sugar, and later in cotton (after 1800), brought Africa into the foreground. Slaves had been obtained from Black Africa from time immemorial, both by the Roman Empire and by the Moslem world, both of which, however, enslaved blacks and whites indiscriminately. After the European discovery of America, blacks were taken across the Atlantic by the Spanish and Portuguese. Dutch traders landed them in Virginia in 1619, a year before the arrival of the Pilgrim Fathers in Massachusetts. But slavery in the Americas before 1650 may be described as occasional. With the rise of the plantation economy after 1650, and especially after 1700, it became a fundamental economic institution. Slavery now formed the labor supply of a very substantial and heavily capitalized branch of world production.   About 610,000 blacks were landed from Africa in the island of Jamaica alone between 1700 and 1786.   Total figures are hard to give, but it is certain that, until well after 1800, far more Africans than Europeans made the voyage to the Americas.   The transatlantic slave trade in the eighteenth century was conducted mainly by English-speaking interests, principally in England but also in New England, followed as closely as they could manage it by the French.   Yearly export of merchandise from Great Britain to Africa, used chiefly in exchange for slaves, increased tenfold between 1713 and 1792.   As for merchandise coming into Britain from the British West Indies, virtually all produced by slaves, in 1790 it constituted almost a fourth of all British imports.   If we add British imports from the American mainland, including what in 1776 became the United States, the importance of black labor to the British economic system will appear still greater, since a great part of exports from the mainland consisted in agricultural products, such as tobacco and indigo, produced partly by slaves.   It can scarcely be denied that the phenomenal rise of British capitalism in the eighteenth century was based to a considerable extent on the enslavement of Africans.   The town of Liverpool, an insignificant place on the Irish Sea in 1700, built itself up by the slave trade and the trade in slave-produced wares to a busy transatlantic commercial center, which in turn, as will be seen later, stimulated the "industrial revolution" in Manchester and other neighboring towns.[4]

The west-European merchants, British, French, and Dutch, sold the products of America and Asia to their own peoples and those of central and eastern Europe. Trade with Germany and Italy was fairly stable.   With Russia it enormously increased.   To cite the British record only, Britain imported fifteen times as much goods from Russia in 1790 as in 1700, and sold the Russians six times as much.   The Russian landlords, as they became Europeanized, desired Western manufactures and the colonial products such as sugar, tobacco, and tea which could be purchased only from western Europeans.   They had grain, timber, and naval stores to offer in return.   Similarly, landlords of Poland and north Germany, in the seventeenth and eighteenth centuries, found themselves increasingly able to move their agricultural products out through the Baltic and hence increasingly able to buy the products of western Europe, America, and Asia in return.   Landlords of eastern Europe thus had an incentive to make their estates more productive.   "Big" agriculture spread, developing in eastern Europe a system not unlike the plantation economy of the New World.   It had many effects.   It contributed, along with political causes, to reducing the bulk of the east-European population to serfdom.   It helped to civilize and refine, in a word to "Europeanize," the upper classes.   And it helped to enrich the merchants of western Europe.

[4]See pp. 468–469.

The wealth which accumulated along the Atlantic seaboard of Europe was, in short, by no means produced by the efforts of western Europeans only. All the world contributed to its formation. The natural resources of the Americas, the resources and skills of Asia, the gold and manpower of Africa, all alike went into producing the vastly increased volume of goods moving in world commerce. Europeans directed the movement. They supplied capital; they contributed technical and organizing abilities; and it was the demand of Europeans, at home in Europe and as traders abroad, that set increasing numbers of Indians to spinning cotton, Chinese to raising tea, Malays to gathering spices, and Africans to the tending of sugar cane. A few non-Europeans might benefit in the process—Indian or Chinese merchants who dealt locally with Europeans, Indian potentates "subsidized" by the East India companies, African chiefs who captured slaves from neighboring tribes and sold them to Europeans. But the profits of the world economy really went to Europe. The new wealth, over and above what was necessary to keep the far-flung and polyglot labor force in being, and to pay other expenses, piled up in Britain, Holland, and France.

Here it was owned by private persons. It accumulated within the system of private property, and as part of the institutions of private enterprise or private capitalism. Governments were dependent on these private owners of property, for governments, in western Europe, had almost no source of revenue except loans and taxes derived from their peoples. When the wealth-owners gave their support, the government was strong and successful, as in England. When they withdrew support, the government collapsed, as it was to collapse in France in the Revolution of 1789.

In a technical sense there were many "capitalists" in western Europe, persons who had a little savings which they used to buy a parcel of land or a loom or entrusted to some other person to invest at interest. And in a general sense the new wealth was widely distributed; the standard of living rose in western Europe in the eighteenth century. Tea, for example, which cost as much as £ 10 a pound when introduced into England about 1650, was an article of common consumption a hundred years later. But wealth used to produce more wealth, i.e., capital, was owned or controlled in significant amounts by relatively few persons. In the eighteenth century some people became unprecedentedly rich (including some who started quite poor, for it was a time of open opportunity); the great intermediate layers of society became noticeably more comfortable; and the people at the bottom, such as the serfs of eastern Europe, the Irish peasantry, the dispossessed farm workers in England, the poorest peasants and workmen of France, were worse off than they had been before. The poor continued to live in hovels. The prosperous created for themselves that pleasant world of the eighteenth century that is still admired, a world of well-ordered Georgian homes, closely cropped lawns and shrubs, furniture by Chippendale or à la Louis XV, coaches-and-four, family portraits, high chandeliers, books bound in morocco, and a staff of servants "below stairs."

Families enriched by commerce, and especially the daughters, mixed and intermarried with the old families which owned land. The merchant in England or France no sooner became prosperous than he bought himself a landed estate. In France he might also purchase a government office or patent of nobility. Contrariwise, the landowning gentleman, especially in England, no sooner increased his landed income than he invested the proceeds in commercial enterprise or government bonds. The two forms of property, bourgeois and aristocratic, tended to merge. Until toward the end of the century the various propertied interests worked harmoniously together, and the unpropertied classes, the vast majority, were of no political consequence. Hence the period, though one of commercial expansion, was an age of considerable social stability in western Europe.

The foregoing might be illustrated from the lives of thousands of men and women. Two examples are enough, one English and one French. They show the working of the world economic system, the rise of the commercial class in western Europe, and the role of that class in the political life of the Western countries.

Thomas Pitt, called "Diamond" Pitt, was born in 1653, the son of a parish clergyman in the Church of England. He went to India in 1674. Here he operated as an "interloper," trading in defiance of the legal monopoly of the East India Company. Returning to England, he was prosecuted by the company and fined £ 400 but was rich enough to buy the manor of Stratford and with it the borough of Old Sarum, a rotten borough which gave him a seat in the House of Commons without the trouble of an election. He soon returned to India, again as an interloper, where he competed so successfully with the company that it finally took him into its own employment. He traded on his own account, as well as for the company, sent back some new chintzes to England, and defended Madras against the nawab of the Carnatic, buying off the nawab with money. In 1702, though his salary was only £ 300 a year, he purchased a 410-carat uncut diamond for £ 20,400. He bought it from an Indian merchant who had himself bought it from an English skipper, who in turn had stolen it from the slave who had found it in the mines and who had concealed it in a wound in his leg. Back in Europe, Pitt had his diamond cut at Amsterdam and sold it in 1717 to the regent of France for £ 135,000. The regent put it in the French crown; it was appraised at the time of the French Revolution at £ 480,000. A daughter of "Diamond" Pitt became the Countess of Stanhope, one of his sons the Earl of Londonderry. Another son became father to the William Pitt who guided Britain through the Seven Years' War with France, and who was raised to the peerage as the Earl of Chatham. After this Pitt the city of Pittsburgh was named, so that a fortune gained in the East gave its name to a frontier settlement in the interior of America. Chatham's younger son, the second William Pitt, became prime minister at twenty-four. The younger Pitt guided Britain through another and greater war with France, until his death in 1806 during the high tide of the Napoleonic empire.

Jean-Joseph Laborde was born in 1724, of a bourgeois family of southern France. He went to work for an uncle who had a business at Bayonne trading with Spain and the East. From the profits he built up vast plantations and slave-holdings in San Domingo. His ships brought sugar to Europe, and returned with prefabricated building materials, each piece carefully numbered, for his plantations and refineries in the West Indies. He became one of the leading bankers in Paris. His daughter became the Countess de Noailles. He himself received the title of marquis, which he did not use. He bought a number of manors and châteaux near Paris. As a real estate operator he developed that part of Paris, then suburban, now called the Chaussée d'Antin.   During the Seven Years' War he was sent by the French government to borrow money in Spain, where he was told that Spain would lend nothing to Louis XV, but would gladly lend him personally 20,000,000 reals.   In the War of American Independence he raised 12,000,000 livres in gold for the government, to help pay the French army and navy, thus contributing to the success of the American Revolution.   He acted as investment agent for Voltaire, gave 24,000 livres a year to charity, and subscribed 400,000 livres in 1788 toward building new hospitals in Paris. In July 1789 he helped to finance the insurrection which led to the fall of the Bastille and the Revolution.   His son, in June 1789, took the Oath of the Tennis Court, swearing to write a constitution for France.   He himself was guillotined in 1794.   His children turned to scholarship and the arts.

28
Western Europe after Utrecht, 1713–1740

The Peace of Utrecht registered the defeat of French ambitions in the wars of Louis XIV.   The French move toward "universal monarchy" had been blocked.   The European state system had been preserved.   Europe was to consist of a number of independent and sovereign states, all legally free and equal, continuously entering or leaving alliances along the principles of the balance of power.   More specifically, the peace settlement of 1713–1714 placed the Bourbon Philip V on the Spanish throne but partitioned the Spanish empire.[5]   Spain itself, with Spanish America and the Philippines, went to Philip V.   Of the remaining Spanish possessions, Belgium, Milan, and Naples-Sicily went to the Austrian Habsburgs, Sardinia ultimately to the Duke of Savoy, Minorca and Gibraltar to Great Britain.   Britain likewise took from France Newfoundland, Nova Scotia, and the Hudson Bay region.   Great Britain, consolidated during the wars as a combined kingdom of England and Scotland, installed as a naval power in the Mediterranean, winning territory from France and Spain, and receiving trading rights within the hitherto closed domain of Spanish America, emerged as the most dynamic of the Atlantic powers.

Spain and the
Lesser Western
Powers after 1713

For a time Europe was troubled by the unwillingness of many in Spain to accept the treaty.   The Spanish queen, an Italian woman named Elizabeth Farnese, went to great lengths to acquire a kingdom in Italy for her younger son, an operation characteristic enough of the international politics of the day, and one in which she found much support in Spain among patriots who resented the loss of Spanish holdings in Italy and the Mediterranean.   A minor war over this matter broke out in 1719. In the 1730s France and Spain fought Austria in the War of the Polish Succession.[6] As a result of the war Austria ceded the kingdom of the Two Sicilies to the Spanish

[5] See pp. 199–202 and map, p. 200.
[6] See p. 257.

on condition that it never be joined to Spain. A separate Bourbon monarchy was thus established in south Italy, and there were now three Bourbon kingdoms, France, Spain, and the Two Sicilies. In general the period from 1713 to 1740 was one of relative peace in western Europe. Not until after 1740 were the full efforts of the Western peoples again engaged in a military struggle.

Men in authority turned to repairing the damages of war. Spain was somewhat rejuvenated by the French influence under its new Bourbon house. The drift and decadence that had set in under the last Habsburgs were at least halted. The Spanish monarchy was administratively strengthened. Its officials followed the absolutist government of Louis XIV as a model. The estates of the east-Spanish kingdoms, Aragon and Valencia, ceased to meet, going like the Estates-General of France into the limbo of obsolete institutions. They had chosen the losing side in the Spanish civil war that accompanied the War of the Spanish Succession, and their disappearance in the reign of Philip V removed a source of the localism and cross purposes which afflicted Spain. On the whole the French influence in eighteenth-century Spain was intangible. Nothing was changed in substance, but the old machinery functioned with more precision. Administrators were better trained and took a more constructive attitude toward government work; they became more aware of the world north of the Pyrenees, and recovered confidence in their country's future. They tried also to tighten up the administration of their American empire. More revenue officers and coast guards were introduced in the Caribbean, whose zeal led to repeated clashes with smugglers, mainly British. Friction on the Spanish Main, reinforced by Spanish dislike for British occupation of Gibraltar, kept Spain and Britain in a continual ferment of potential hostility.

The Dutch after Utrecht receded from the political stage, though their alliance was always sought because of the huge shipping and financial resources they controlled. The Swiss also became important in banking and financial circles. The Belgians founded an overseas trading company in 1723 on the authority of their new Austrian ruler; this "Ostend Company" sent out six voyages to China, which were highly profitable, but the commercial jealousy of the Dutch and British obliged the Austrian emperor to withdraw his support, so that the enterprise soon came to an end. The Scots began at about this time to play their remarkable role of energizing business affairs in many countries. Union with England gave them access to the British empire and to the numerous commercial advantages won by the English. John Law, the financial wizard of France, was a Scot, as was William Paterson, one of the chief founders of the Bank of England.

Our main attention falls on Britain and France. Though one was the victor and the other the vanquished in the wars ended in 1713, and though one stood for absolutism and the other for constitutionalism in government, their development in the years after Utrecht was in some ways surprisingly parallel. In both countries for some years the king was personally ineffective, and in both the various propertied interests therefore gained many advantages. Both enjoyed the commercial expansion described above. Both went through a short period of financial experimentation and frantic speculation in stocks, the bubble bursting in each case in 1720. Each was thereafter governed by a statesman, Cardinal Fleury in France and Robert Walpole in England, whose policy was to keep peace abroad and conciliate all interests at home. Fleury and Walpole held office for about two decades, toward the end of which the two countries again went to war. But the differences are at least as instructive as the parallels.

In France the new king was a child, Louis XV, the great-grandson of Louis XIV, and only five years old when he began to reign in 1715. The government was entrusted to a regent, the Duke of Orleans, an elder cousin of the young king. Orleans, lacking the authority of a monarch, had to admit the aristocracy to a share in power. Most of the nobles had never liked the absolutism of Louis XIV, and there was much dissatisfaction with absolutism among all classes, because of the ruin and suffering brought by Louis XIV's wars.

The nobles, ousted by Louis XIV, now reappeared in the government. For a time Orleans worked through committees of noblemen, roughly corresponding to ministries, a system lauded by its backers as a revival of political freedom; but the committees proved so incompetent that they were soon abandoned. The old parliaments of France,[7] and especially the Parliament of Paris, which Louis XIV had reduced to silence, vigorously reasserted themselves after his death. The parliaments were primarily law courts, originally composed of bourgeois judges; but Louis XIV and his predecessors, to raise money, had made the judgeships into salable offices, to which they attached titles of nobility to increase the price. Hence in the time of the Regency the judges of the parliaments had bought or inherited their seats, and were almost all nobles. Because they had property rights in their offices, they could not be removed by the king. The Regent conceded much influence to the Parliament of Paris, utilizing it to modify the will of Louis XIV. The parliaments broadened their position, claiming the right to assent to legislation and taxes, through refusing to enforce what they considered contrary to the unwritten constitution or fundamental laws of France. They managed to exercise this right, off and on, from the days of the Regency until the great Revolution of 1789. The eighteenth century, for France, was a period of absolutism checked and balanced by organized privileged groups. It was an age of aristocratic resurgence, in which the nobles won back many powers of which Louis XIV had tried to deprive them.

In Great Britain the Parliament was very different from the French parliaments, and the British aristocracy was more politically competent than the *noblesse* of France. Parliament proved an effective machine for the conduct of public business. The House of Lords was hereditary, with the large exception of the bishops, who were appointed by the government and made up about a quarter of the active members of the upper house. The House of Commons was not at all representative of the country according to modern ideas. Only the wealthy, or those patronized by the wealthy,

[7]See pp. 188–189, 192.

could sit in it,[8] and they were chosen by diverse and eccentric methods, in counties and towns, almost without regard to the size or wishes of the population. Some boroughs were owned outright, like the Old Sarum of the Pitt family. But through the machinations of bosses, or purchase of seats, all kinds of interests managed to get representatives into the Commons. Some members spoke for the "landed interest," others for the "funded interest" (mainly government creditors), others for the "London interest," the "West India interest," the "East India interest" and others. All politically significant groups could expect to have their desires heeded in Parliament, and all therefore were willing to go through parliamentary channels. Parliament was corrupt, slow, and expensive, but it was effective. For Parliament was not only a roughly representative body; it could also act, having acquired, in practice, a sovereign power of legislation.

Queen Anne, the last reigning Stuart, died in 1714. She was succeeded by George I, Elector of Hanover, as provided for by Parliament in the Act of Settlement of 1701.[9] George I was the nearest relative of the Stuarts who was also a Protestant. A heavy middle-aged German who spoke no English, he continued to spend much of his time in Germany, and he brought with him to England a retinue of German ministers and favorites and two ungainly mistresses, dubbed in England the "Elephant and the Maypole." He was never popular in England, where he was regarded as at best a political convenience. He was in no position to play a strong hand in English public life, and during his reign Parliament gained much independence from the crown.

The main problem was still whether the principles of the Revolution of 1688 should be maintained.[10] The agreement of parties which had made that revolution relatively bloodless proved to be temporary. The Whigs, who considered the revolution as their work, long remained a minority made up of a few great landowning noblemen, wealthy London merchants, lesser business people, and Nonconformists in religion. The Whigs generally controlled the House of Lords, but the House of Commons was more uncertain; at the time of the Peace of Utrecht its majority was Tory. We have already noted the significance for English constitutional development of the conflict at that time between the prowar Whig majority in the House of Lords and the Tory majority in Commons, and how the conflict was resolved to help establish the primacy of the House of Commons.[11] After 1714 the two parties tended to dissolve, and the terms "Whig" and "Tory" ceased to have much definite meaning. In general the government, and the Anglican bishops who were close to the government, remained "Whig." Men who were remote from the central government, or suspicious of its activities, formed a kind of country party quite different from the earlier Tories. Gentry and yeomen of the shires and byways were easily aroused against the great noblemen and men of money who led the Whigs. In the established church the lesser clergy were sometimes critical of the Whig bishops. Outside the official church were a group of Anglican clergy who refused the oath of

[8] See p. 187.
[9] See p. 185.
[10] See pp. 183–187.
[11] See pp. 199–201.

loyalty after 1688 and were called Non-Jurors; they kept alive a shadow-church until 1805. In Scotland also, the ancestral home of the Stuarts, many were dis-affected with the new regime.

Tories, Non-Jurors, and Scots made up a milieu after 1688 in which what would now be called counterrevolution might develop. Never enthusiastic for the "Whig wars" against France,[12] critical of the mounting national debt which the wars created, distrustful of the business and moneyed interests, they began to look wistfully to the exiled Stuarts. After 1701, when James II died in France, the Stuart claims devolved upon his son, who lived until 1766, scheming time and again to make himself king of England. His partisans were known as Jacobites, from *Jacobus,* the Latin for James; they regarded him as "James III," where others called him the Pretender. The Jacobites felt that if he would give up his Catholic religion, he should be accepted as Britain's rightful king. To strengthen his claims they kept agitating the theory of divine right.

The Whigs could not tolerate a return of the Stuarts. The restoration of "James III" and his divine-right partisans would undo the principles of the Glorious Revolution—limited monarchy, constitutionalism, parliamentary supremacy, the rule of law, the toleration of dissenting Protestants, in short all that was summarized and defended in the writings of John Locke.[13] Moreover, those who held stock in the Bank of England or who had lent their money to the government would be ruined, since "James III" would surely repudiate a debt contracted by his foes. The Whigs were bound to support the Hanoverian George I. And George I was bound to look for support in a strange country among the Whigs.

George lacked personal appeal even for his English friends. To his enemies he was ridiculous and repulsive. The successful establishment of his dynasty would ruin the hopes of Tories and Jacobites. In 1715 the Pretender landed in Scotland, gathered followers from the Highlands, and proclaimed a rebellion against George I. Civil war seemed to threaten. But the Jacobite leaders bungled, and many of their followers proved to be undecided. They were willing enough to toast the "king over the water" in protest against the Whigs but not willing in a showdown to see the Stuarts, with all that went with them, again in possession of the crown of England. The Fifteen, as the revolt came to be called, petered out. But thirty years later came the Forty-five. In 1745, during war with France, the Pretender's son, "Bonnie Prince Charlie" or the "Young Pretender," again landed in Scotland and again proclaimed rebellion. This time, though almost no one in England rallied, the uprising was more successful. A Scottish force penetrated to within eighty miles of London and was driven back and crushed with the help of Hanoverian regiments rushed over from Germany. The government set out to destroy Jacobitism in the Highlands. The social system of the Highlands was wiped out; the clans were broken up; McDuffs and McDougals were forcibly reorganized according to modern notions of property and of landlord and tenant.[14]

[12] See pp. 199–201.
[13] See pp. 319–321.
[14] See pp. 285, 361–362.

The Jacobite uprisings confirmed the old reputation of England in the eyes of Europe, namely, as Voltaire said, that its government was as stormy as the seas which surrounded it. To partisans of monarchy on the Continent they illustrated the weaknesses of parliamentary government. But their ignominious collapse actually strengthened the parliamentary regime in England. They left little permanent mark and soon passed into an atmosphere of romantic legend. Many Tories, however, continued to believe in the value of a strong and independent ruler. For example, Henry St. John, Viscount Bolingbroke, a Jacobite until after 1715, published in 1749 his *Idea of a Patriot King,* in which he argued that the king should be a popular leader, balancing the interest of the whole country against the special interests of factions or parties. These views influenced George III, who acceded in 1760, and who, as is well known to Americans, by his efforts to "be a king" provoked the rebellion of the American colonists.[15]

Meanwhile, immediately after the Peace of Utrecht, the problem of dealing with a postwar economic situation had to be faced in both England and France. In both countries it meant finding a way to carry the greatly swollen government debt. Organized permanent public debt was new at the time. The possibilities and limitations of large-scale banking, paper money, and credit were not clearly seen. In France there was much amazement at the way in which England and Holland, though smaller and less wealthy than France, had been able to maximize their resources through banking and credit and even to finance the alliance which had eclipsed the Sun King. In addition there was much private demand for both lending and borrowing money. Private persons all over western Europe were looking for enterprises in which to invest their savings. And promoters and organizers, anticipating a profit in this or that line of business, were looking for capital with which to work. Out of this whole situation grew the "South Sea bubble" in England and the "Mississippi bubble" in France. Both bubbles broke in 1720, and both had important long-range effects.

A close tie between government finance and private enterprise was usual at the time, under mercantilist ideas of government guidance of trade. In England, for example, a good deal of the government debt was held by companies organized for that purpose. The government would charter a company, strengthen it with a monopoly in a given line of business, and then receive from the company, after the stockholders had bought up the shares, a large sum of cash as a loan. Much of the British debt, contracted in the wars from 1689 to 1713, was held in this way by the Bank of England, founded in 1694;[16] by the East India Company, reorganized in 1708 in such a way as to provide funds for the government; and by the South Sea Company, founded in 1711. The Bank enjoyed a legal monopoly over certain banking operations in London, the East India Company over trade with the East, the South Sea

[15] See pp. 360–367.
[16] See p. 186.

Company for exploiting the *asiento* [17] and other commercial privileges extorted from Spain. The companies were owned by private investors. Savings drawn from trade and agriculture, put into shares in these companies, became available both for economic reinvestment and for use of the government in defraying the costs of war.

In 1716 the Prince Regent of France was attracted to a Scottish financier, John Law, reputedly by Law's remarkable mathematical system in gambling at cards. Law founded a much needed French central bank. In the next year, 1717, he organized a *Compagnie d'Occident,* popularly called the Mississippi Company, which obtained a monopoly of trade with Louisiana, where it founded New Orleans in 1718. This company, under Law's management, soon absorbed the French East India, China, Senegal, and African companies. It now enjoyed a legal monopoly of all French colonial trade. Law then proposed, and was authorized by the Regent, to assume the entire government debt. The company received from individuals their certificates of royal indebtedness or "bonds," and gave them shares of company stock in return. It proposed to pay dividends on these shares and to extinguish the debt from profits in the colonial trade and from a monopoly over the collection of all indirect taxes in France. The project carried with it a plan for drastic reform of the whole taxation system, to make taxes both more fair to the taxpayer and more lucrative to the government. Shares in the Mississippi Company were gobbled up by the public. There was a frenzy of speculation, a wild fear of not buying soon enough. Quotations rose to 18,000 livres a share. But the company rested only on unrealized projects. Shareholders began to fear for their money. They began to unload. The market broke sharply. Many found their life savings gone. Others lost ancestral estates on which they had borrowed in the hope of getting rich. Those, however, who had owned shares in the company before the rise, and who had resisted the speculative fever, lost nothing by the bursting of inflated prices, and later enjoyed a gilt-edged commercial investment.

Much the same thing happened in England, where it was thought by many that Law was about to provide a panacea for France. The South Sea Company, outbidding the Bank of England, took over a large fraction of the public debt by receiving government "bonds" from their owners in return for shares of its stock. The size and speed of profits to be made in Spanish America were greatly exaggerated, and the market value of South Sea shares rose rapidly for a time, reaching £ 1,050 for a share of £ 100 par value. Other schemes abounded in the passion for easy money. Promoters organized mining and textile companies, as well as others of more fanciful or bolder design: a company to bring live fish to market in tanks, an insurance company to insure female chastity, a company "for an undertaking which shall in due time be revealed." Shares in such enterprises were snatched at mounting prices. But in September 1720 the South Sea stockholders began to sell, doubting whether operations would pay dividends commensurate to £ 1,000 a share. They dragged down the whole unstable structure. As in France, many people found that their savings or their inheritances had disappeared.

[17] See p. 202.

Indignation in both countries was extreme. Both governments were implicated in the scandal. John Law fled to Brussels. The Regent was discredited; he resigned in 1723, and French affairs were afterward conducted by Cardinal Fleury. In England there was a change of ministers. Robert Walpole, a country gentleman of Whig persuasion, who had long sat in the Commons, and who had warned against the South Sea scheme from the beginning, became the principal minister to George I.

Britain recovered from the crisis more successfully than France. Law's bank, a useful institution, was dissolved in the reaction against him. France lacked an adequate banking system during the rest of the century. French investors developed a morbid fear of paper securities and a marked preference for putting their savings into land. Commercial capitalism and the growth of credit institutions in France were retarded. In England the same fears were felt. Parliament passed the "Bubble Act," forbidding all companies except those specifically chartered by the government to raise capital by the sale of stock. In both countries the development of joint-stock financing along the lines of the modern corporation was slowed down for over a century. Business enterprises continued to be typically owned by individuals and partnerships, which expanded by reinvestment of their own profits, and so had another reason to keep profits up and wages down. But in England Walpole managed to save the South Sea Company, the East India Company, and the Bank, all of which were temporarily discredited in the eyes of the public. England continued to perfect its financial machinery.

The credit of the two governments was also shaken by the "bubbles." Much of the French war debt was repudiated in one way or another. Repudiation was in many cases morally justifiable, for many government creditors were unscrupulous war profiteers, but financially it was disastrous, for it discouraged honest people from lending their money to the state. Nor was much accomplished toward reform of the taxes. The nobles continued to evade the taxes imposed on them by Louis XIV, John Law's plans for taxation evaporated with the rest of his project, and when in 1726 a finance minister tried to levy a 2 percent tax on all property, the vested interests, led by the Parliament of Paris, annihilated this proposal also. Lacking an adequate revenue, and repudiating its debts, the French monarchy had little credit. The conception of public or national debt hardly developed in France in the eighteenth century. The debt was considered to be the king's debt, for which no one except a few ministers felt any responsibility. The Bourbon government in fact often borrowed through the church, the Provincial Estates, or the city of Paris, which lenders considered to be better financial risks than the king himself. The government was severely handicapped in its foreign policy and its wars. It could not fully tap the wealth of its own subjects.

In England none of the debt was repudiated. Walpole managed to launch and keep going the system of the sinking fund, by which the government regularly set aside the wherewithal to pay interest and principal on its obligations. The credit of the British government became absolutely firm. The debt was considered a national debt, for which the British people itself assumed the responsibility. Parliamentary government made this development possible. In France no one could tell what the king or his ministers might do, and hence everyone was reluctant to trust them with his money. In England the people who had the money could also, through Parliament, determine the policies of state, decide what the money should be spent for, and levy enough taxes to maintain confidence in the debt. Similarities to France there were; the landowners who controlled the British Parliament, like those who controlled the Parliament of Paris, resisted direct taxation, so that the British government drew two-thirds or more of its revenues from indirect taxes paid by the mass of the population. Yet landowners, even dukes, did pay important amounts of taxes. There were no exemptions by class or rank, as in France. All propertied interests had a stake in the government. The wealth of the country stood behind the national debt. The national credit seemed inexhaustible. This was the supreme trump card of the British in their wars with France from the founding of the Bank of England in 1694 to the fall of Napoleon 120 years later. And it was the political freedom of England that gave it its economic strength.

Fleury in France;
Walpole in England

Fleury was seventy-three years old when he took office, and ninety when he left it. He was not one to initiate programs for the distant future. Louis XV, as he came of age, proved to be indolent and selfish. Public affairs drifted, while France grew privately more wealthy, especially the commercial and bourgeois classes. Walpole likewise kept out of controversies. His motto was *quieta non movere,* "let sleeping dogs lie." It was to win over the Tory squires to the Hanoverian and Whig regime that Walpole kept down the land taxes; this policy was successful, and Jacobitism quieted down. Walpole supported the Bank, the trading companies, and the financial interests, and they in turn supported him. It was a time of political calm, in which the lower classes were quiet and the upper classes not quarreling, favorable therefore to the development of parliamentary institutions.

Walpole has been called the first prime minister and the architect of cabinet government, a system in which the ministers, or executives, are also members of the legislative body. He saw to it, by careful rigging, that a majority in the Commons always supported him. He avoided issues on which his majority might be lost. He thus began to acknowledge the principle of cabinet responsibility to a majority in Parliament, which was to become an important characteristic of cabinet government. And by selecting colleagues who agreed with him, and getting rid of those who did not, he advanced the idea of the cabinet as a body of ministers bound to each other and to the prime minister, obligated to follow the same policies and to stand or fall as a group. Thus Parliament was not only a representative or deliberative body like the diets and estates on the Continent, but one that developed an effective executive organ, without which neither representative government nor any government could survive.

To assure peace and quiet in domestic politics the best means was to avoid raising taxes. And the best way to avoid taxes was to avoid war. Fleury and Walpole both tried to keep at peace. They were not in the long run successful. Fleury was drawn into the War of the Polish Succession in 1733. Walpole kept

England out of war until 1739. He always had a war party to contend with, and the most bellicose were those interested in the American trade—the slave trade, the sugar plantations, and the illicit sale of goods in the Spanish empire. The British official figures show that while trade with Europe, in the eighteenth century, was always less in war than in peace, trade with America always increased during war, except, indeed, during the War of American Independence.

In the 1730s there were constant complaints of indignities suffered by sturdy Britons on the Spanish Main. The war party produced a Captain Jenkins, who carried with him a small box containing a withered ear, which he said had been cut from his head by the outrageous Spaniards. Testifying in the House of Commons, where he "commended his soul to God and his cause to his country," he stirred up a commotion which led to war. So in 1739, after twenty-five years of peace, England plunged with wild enthusiasm into the War of Jenkins' Ear. "They are ringing the bells now," said Walpole; "they will soon be wringing their hands." The war soon became merged in a conflict involving Europeans and others in all parts of the world.

The fighting lasted until 1763, with an uneasy interlude between 1748 and 1756. It went by many names. The opening hostilities between England and Spain were called, by the English, the War of Jenkins' Ear. The Prussians spoke of three "Silesian" wars. The struggle on the Continent in the 1740s was often known as the War of the Pragmatic Sanction. British colonials in America called the fighting of the 1740s King George's War, or used the term "French and Indian Wars," for the whole sporadic conflict. Disorganized and nameless struggles at the same time shook the peoples of India. The names finally adopted by history were the War of the Austrian Succession for operations between 1740 and 1748 and the Seven Years' War for those between 1756 and 1763. The two wars were really one. They involved the same two principal issues, the duel of Britain and France for colonies, trade, and sea power, and the duel of Prussia and Austria for territory and military power in central Europe.

29
The Great War of the Mid-Eighteenth Century: The Peace of Paris, 1763

Eighteenth-Century Warfare

Warfare at the time was in a kind of classical phase, which strongly affected the development of events. It was somewhat slow, formal, elaborate, and indecisive. The enlisted ranks of armies and navies were filled with men considered economically useless, picked up by recruiting officers among unwary loungers in taverns or on the wharves. All governments protected their productive population, peasants, mechanics, and bourgeois, preferring to keep them at home, at work, and paying taxes. Soldiers were a class apart, enlisted for long terms, paid wages, professional in their outlook, and highly trained. They lived in barracks or great forts, and were dressed in bright uniforms (like the British "redcoats"), which, since camouflage was unnecessary, they wore even in battle. Weapons were not destructive; infantry was predominant and was armed with the smooth-bore musket, to which the bayonet could be attached. In war the troops depended on great supply

depots built up beforehand, which were practically immovable with the transportation available, so that armies, at least in central and western Europe, rarely
operated more than a few days' march from their bases. Soldiers fought
methodically for pay. Generals hesitated to risk their troops, which took years to
train and equip, and were very expensive. Strategy took the form not of seeking out
the enemy's main force to destroy it in battle, but of maneuvering for advantages of
position, applying a cumulative and subtle pressure somewhat as in a game of chess.

There was little national feeling, or feeling of any kind. The Prussian army
recruited half or more of its enlisted personnel outside Prussia; the British army was
largely made up of Hanoverian or other German regiments; even the French army had
German units incorporated in it. Deserters from one side were enlisted by the
other. War was between governments, or between the oligarchies and aristocracies
which governments represented, not between whole peoples. It was fought for
power, prestige, or calculated practical interests, not for ideologies, moral principles,
world conquest, national survival, or ways of life. Popular nationalism had
developed farthest in England, where "Rule Britannia" and "God Save the King,"
both breathing a low opinion of foreigners, became popular songs during these
mid-eighteenth-century wars.

Civilians were little affected, except in India or the American wilderness where
European conditions did not prevail. In Europe, a government aspiring to conquer a
neighboring province did not wish to ruin or antagonize it beforehand. The fact that
the west-European struggle was largely naval kept it well outside civilian experience.
Never had war been so harmless, certainly not in the religious wars of earlier times, or
in the national wars initiated later. This was one reason why governments went to
war so lightly. On the other hand governments also withdrew from war much more
readily than in later times. Their treasuries might be exhausted, their trained soldiers
used up; only practical or rational questions were at stake; there was no war hysteria
or pressure of mass opinion; the enemy of today might be the ally of tomorrow.
Peace was almost as easy to make as war. Peace treaties were negotiated, not
imposed. So the eighteenth century saw a series of wars and treaties, more wars,
treaties, and rearrangements of alliances, all arising over much the same issues, and
with exactly the same powers present at the end as at the beginning.

The War of the Austrian Succession was started by the king of Prussia. Frederick
II, or the "Great," was a young man of twenty-eight when he became king in 1740.
His youth had not been happy; he was temperamentally incompatible with his
father. His tastes as a prince had run to playing the flute, corresponding with French
men of letters, and writing prose and verse in the French language. His father, the
sober Frederick William I,[18] thought him frivolous and effeminate, and dealt with him
so clumsily that at the age of eighteen he tried to escape from the kingdom. Caught
and brought back, he was forced to witness the execution, by his father's order, of the

[18]See pp. 243–244.

friend and companion who had shared in his attempted flight. Frederick changed as the years passed from a jaunty youth to an aged cynic, equally undeceived by himself, his friends, or his enemies, and seeing no reason to expect much from human nature. Though his greatest reputation was made as a soldier, he retained his literary interests all his life, became a historian of merit, and is perhaps of all modern monarchs the only one who would have a respectable standing if considered only as a writer. An unabashed freethinker, like many others of his day, he considered all religions ridiculous and laughed at the divine right of kings; but he would have no nonsense about the rights of the house of Brandenburg, and he took a solemn view of the majesty of the state.

Frederick, in 1740, lost no time in showing a boldness which his father would have surely dreaded. He decided to conquer Silesia,[19] and on December 16, 1740, he invaded that province, a region adjoining Prussia, lying in the upper valley of the Oder, and belonging to the kingdom of Bohemia and hence to the Danubian empire of the Habsburgs. The Pragmatic Sanction, a general agreement signed by the European powers, including Prussia, had stipulated that all domains of the Austrian Habsburgs should be inherited integrally by the new heiress, Maria Theresa.[20] The issue was between law and force. Frederick in attacking Silesia could invoke nothing better than "reason of state," the welfare and expansion of the state of which he was ruler. But he was not mistaken in the belief that if he did not attack the Austrians someone else soon would.

The Pragmatic Sanction was universally disregarded. All turned against Maria Theresa. Bavaria and Saxony put in claims. Spain, still hoping to revise the Peace of Utrecht, saw another chance to win back former Spanish holdings in Italy. The decisive intervention was that of France. It was the fate of France to be torn between ambitions on the European continent and ambitions on the sea and beyond the seas. Economic and commercial advantage might dictate concentration on the impending struggle with Britain. But the French nobles were less interested than the British aristocrats in commercial considerations. They were influential because they furnished practically all the army officers and diplomats. They saw in Austria the traditional enemy, in Europe the traditional field of valor, and in Belgium, which now belonged to the Austrians, the traditional object for annexation to France. Cardinal Fleury, much against his will and judgment, found himself forced into war against the Habsburgs.

Maria Theresa was at this time a young woman of twenty-three. She proved to be one of the most capable rulers ever produced by the house of Habsburg. She made full use of her feminine qualities. Graceful and attractive as a young woman, buxom and motherly as she grew older, she commanded an affectionate loyalty from her assistants such as few male rulers ever obtained. She was fond of her husband, bore ten children, and set a model of conscientious family living at a time of much indifference to such matters among the upper classes. She was as devout and as

---

[19] See map, pp. 236–237, panel 3.
[20] See p. 233.

earnest as Frederick of Prussia was irreligious and seemingly flip. She dominated her husband and her grown sons as she did her kingdoms and her duchies. With a good deal of practical sense, she reconstructed her empire without having any doctrinaire program, and she accomplished more in her methodical way than more brilliant contemporaries with more spectacular projects of reform. She knew how to use so-called feminine wiles, charms, moods, and even outbursts or tears to gain her ends. She once remarked to her husband, Francis of Lorraine, that the singer they had just heard at the opera was the greatest actress that ever lived. "Except yourself, Madam," he replied, with a freedom permitted to the husbands even of queens.

She was pregnant when Frederick invaded Silesia, giving birth to her first son, the future emperor Joseph II, in March 1741. She then turned her attention to politics. Her dominions were assailed by half a dozen outside powers, and were also quaking within, for her two kingdoms of Hungary and Bohemia (both of which had accepted the Pragmatic Sanction) were slow to see which way their advantage lay. She betook herself to Hungary to be crowned with the crown of St. Stephen—and to rally support. The Hungarians were still in a grumbling frame of mind, as in the days of the Rakoczy rebellion forty years before.[21] She made a carefully arranged and dramatic appearance before them, implored them to defend an outraged woman, swore to uphold the liberties of the Hungarian nobles and the separate constitution of the kingdom of Hungary. All Europe told how the beautiful young queen, by raising aloft the infant Joseph at a session of the Hungarian parliament, had thrown the dour Magyars into paroxysms of chivalrous resolve. The story was not quite true, but it is true that she made an eloquent address to the Magyars, that she took her baby with her and proudly exhibited him, and that she probably gained more by being a woman than a male Habsburg could possibly have received. The Hungarian magnates pledged their "blood and life," and delivered a hundred thousand soldiers.

The war, as it worked out in Europe, was reminiscent of the struggles of the time of Louis XIV, or even of the Thirty Years' War now a century in the past. It was, again, a kind of civil struggle within the Holy Roman Empire, in which a league of German princes banded together against the monarchy of Vienna. This time they included the new kingdom of Prussia. It was, again, a collision of Bourbons and Habsburgs, in which the French pursued their old policy of maintaining division in Germany, by supporting the German princes against the Habsburgs. The basic aim of French policy, according to instructions given by the French foreign office to its ambassador in Vienna in 1725, was to keep the Empire divided by the principles of the Peace of Westphalia,[22] preventing the union of German powers into "one and the same body, which would in fact become formidable to all the other powers of Europe." This time the Bourbons had Spain on their side. Maria Theresa was supported only by Britain and Holland, which subsidized her financially, but which had inadequate land forces. The Franco-German-Spanish combination was highly successful. In 1742 Maria Theresa, hard pressed, accepted the proposals of Frederick

[21] See p. 233.
[22] See pp. 147–150.

for a separate peace. She temporarily granted him Silesia, and he temporarily slipped out of the war which he had been the first to enter. The French and Bavarians moved into Bohemia and almost organized a puppet kingdom with the aid of Bohemian nobles. The French obtained the election of their Bavarian satellite as Holy Roman Emperor, Charles VII. In 1745 the French won the battle of Fontenoy in Belgium, the greatest battle of the war; they dominated Belgium, which neither the Dutch nor British were able to defend. In the same year they fomented the Jacobite rebellion in Scotland.

But the situation overseas offset the situation in Europe. It was America that tilted the balance. The French fortress of Louisburg on Cape Breton Island was captured by an expedition of New Englanders in conjunction with the British navy. British warships drove French and Spanish shipping from the seas. The French West Indies were blockaded. The French government, in danger of losing the wealth and taxes drawn from the sugar and slave trades, announced its willingness to negotiate.

Peace was made at Aix-la-Chapelle in 1748. It was based on an Anglo-French agreement in which Maria Theresa was obliged to concur. Britain and France arranged their differences by a return to the *status quo ante bellum.* The British restored Louisburg despite the protests of the Americans and relaxed their stranglehold on the Caribbean. The French restored Madras, which they had captured, and gave up their hold on Belgium. The Atlantic powers recognized Frederick's annexation of Silesia and required Maria Theresa to cede some Italian duchies—Parma and Piacenza—to a Spanish Bourbon. Belgium was returned to Maria Theresa at the especial insistence of Britain and the Dutch. She and her ministers were very dissatisfied. They would infinitely have preferred to lose Belgium and keep Silesia. They were required, in the interest of a European or even intercontinental balance of power, to give up Silesia and to hold Belgium for the Dutch against the French.

The war had been more decisive than the few readjustments of the map seemed to show. It proved the weakness of the French position, straddled as it was between Europe and the overseas world. Maintaining a huge army for use in Europe, the French could not, like Britain, concentrate upon the sea. On the other hand, because vulnerable on the sea, they could not hold their gains in Europe or conquer Belgium. The Austrians, though bitter, had reason for satisfaction. The war had been a war to partition the Habsburg empire. The Habsburg empire still stood. Hungary had thrown in its lot with Vienna, a fact of much subsequent importance. Bohemia was won back. In 1745, when Charles VII died, Maria Theresa got her husband elected Holy Roman Emperor, a position for which she could not qualify because she was a woman. But the loss of Silesia was momentous. Silesia was as populous as the Dutch Republic, almost purely German, and industrially the most advanced region east of the Elbe. Prussia by acquiring it doubled its population and more than doubled its resources. Prussia with Silesia was unquestionably a great power. Since Austria was still a great power there were henceforth two great powers in the vague world known as "Germany," a situation which came to be known as the German dualism. But the transfer of Silesia, which doubled the number of Germans ruled by the king of Prussia, made the Habsburg empire less German, more Slavic and

285

Hungarian, more Danubian and international. Silesia was the keystone of Germany. Frederick was determined to hold it, and Maria Theresa to win it back. A new war was therefore foreseeable in central Europe. As for Britain and France, the peace of Aix-la-Chapelle was clearly only a truce.

The next years passed in a busy diplomacy, leading to what is known as the "reversal of alliances" and Diplomatic Revolution of 1756. The Austrians set themselves to nipping off the growth of Prussia. Maria Theresa's foreign minister, Count Kaunitz, perhaps the most artful diplomat of the century, concluded that the time had come to abandon ideas that were centuries old. The rise of Prussia had revolutionized the balance of power. Kaunitz, reversing traditional policy, proposed an alliance between Austria and France—between the Habsburgs and the Bourbons. He encouraged French aspirations for Belgium in return for French support in the destruction of Prussia. The overtures between Austria and France obliged Britain, Austria's former ally, to reconsider its position in Europe; the British had Hanover to protect, and were favorably impressed by the Prussian army. An alliance of Great Britain and Prussia was concluded in January, 1756. Meanwhile Kaunitz consummated his alliance with France. One consequence was to marry the future Louis XVI to one of Maria Theresa's daughters, Marie Antoinette, the "Austrian woman" of Revolutionary fame. The Austrian alliance was never popular in France. Some Frenchmen thought that the ruin of Prussia would only enhance the Austrian control of Germany and so undo the fundamental "Westphalia system." The French progressive thinkers, known as philosophes, believed Austria to be priest-ridden and backward, and were for ideological reasons admirers of the freethinking Frederick II. Dissatisfaction with its foreign policy was one reason for the growth of a revolutionary attitude toward the Bourbon government.

In any case, when the Seven Years' War broke out in 1756, though it was a continuation of the preceding war in that Prussia fought Austria, and Britain France, the belligerents had all changed partners. Great Britain and Prussia were now allies, as were, more remarkably, the Habsburgs and the Bourbons. In addition, Austria had concluded a treaty with the Russian empire for the annihilation of Prussia.

*The Seven Years' War,
1756–1763: In Europe
and America*

The Seven Years' War began in America. Let us turn, however, to Europe first. Here the war was another war of "partition." As a league of powers had but recently attempted to partition the empire of Maria Theresa, and a generation before had in fact partitioned the empires of Sweden and Spain, so now Austria, Russia, and France set out to partition the newly created kingdom of Prussia. Their aim was to relegate the Hohenzollerns to the margraviate of Brandenburg. Prussia, even with Silesia, had less than 6,000,000 people; each of its three principal enemies had 20,000,000 or more. But war was less an affair of peoples than of states and standing armies, and the Prussian state and Prussian army were the most efficient in Europe. Frederick fought brilliant campaigns, won victories as at Rossbach in 1757, moved rapidly along interior lines, eluded, surprised and reattacked the badly coordinated armies opposed to him. He proved himself the great military genius of his day. But genius was scarcely enough. Against three such powers, reinforced by Sweden and the German states, and with no ally except Great Britain (and Hanover) whose aid was almost entirely financial, the kingdom of Prussia by any reasonable estimate had no chance of survival. There were times when Frederick believed all to be lost, yet he went on fighting, and his strength of character in these years of adversity, as much as his ultimate triumph, later made him a hero and symbol for the Germans. His subjects, Junkers and even serfs, advanced in patriotic spirit under pressure. The coalition tended to fall apart. The French lacked enthusiasm; they were fighting Britain, the Austrian alliance was unpopular, Kaunitz would not plainly promise them Belgium. The Russians found that the more they moved westward the more they alarmed their Austrian allies. In 1762 the tsarina Elizabeth died; her successor, Peter III, a somewhat infantile admirer of the soldierly Frederick, immediately called off hostilities—an event often called the "miracle of the house of Brandenburg." Frederick was left to deal only with the implacable Austrians, for whom he was more than a match. By the peace of Hubertusburg in 1763 not only did he lose nothing; he retained Silesia.

For the rest, the Seven Years' War was a phase in the long dispute between France and Great Britain. Its stakes were supremacy in the growing world economy, control of colonies, and command of the sea. The two empires had been left unchanged in 1748 by the peace of Aix-la-Chapelle. Both held possessions in India, in the West Indies, and on the American mainland.[23] In India both British and French possessed only disconnected commercial establishments on the coast, infinitesimal specks on the giant body of India. Both also traded with China at Canton. Both occupied way stations on the route to Asia, the British in St. Helena and Ascension Island in the south Atlantic, the French in the much better islands of Mauritius and Reunion in the Indian Ocean. Frenchmen were active also on the coasts of Madagascar. The greatest way station, the Cape of Good Hope, belonged to the Dutch. In the West Indies the British plantations were mainly in Jamaica, Barbados, and some of the Leeward Islands; the French in San Domingo, Guadeloupe, and Martinique. All were supported by the booming slave trade in Africa.

On the American mainland the French had more territory, the British more people. In the British colonies from Georgia to Nova Scotia lived perhaps two million whites, predominantly English but with strong infusions of Scots-Irish, Dutch, Germans, French, and Swedes. Philadelphia, with some 40,000 people, was as large as any city in England except London. The colonies, in population, bulked about a quarter as large as the mother country. But they were provincial, locally minded, incapable of concerted action. In 1754 the British government called a congress at Albany in New York, hoping that the colonies would assume some collective responsibility for the coming war. The congress adopted an "Albany plan of union" drawn up by Benjamin Franklin, but the colonial legislatures declined to accept it, through fear of losing their independence. The colonials were willing, in a politically immature way, to rely on Britain for military action against France.

---

[23] See maps, pp. 200, 293.

The French were still in possession of Louisburg on Cape Breton Island, a stronghold begun by Louis XIV, located in the Gulf of St. Lawrence. It was designed for naval domination of the American side of the north Atlantic, and to control access to the St. Lawrence River, the Great Lakes, and the vast region now called the Middle West. Through all this tract of country Frenchmen constantly came and went, but there were sizable French settlements only around New Orleans in the south and Quebec in the north. One source of French strength was that the French were more successful than the British in gaining the support of the Indians. This was probably because the French, being few in numbers, did not threaten to expropriate the Indians from their lands, and also because Catholics at this time were incomparably more active than Protestants in Christian missions among non-European peoples.

Both empires, French and British, were held together by mercantilist regulations framed mainly in the interest of the home countries. In some ways the British empire was more liberal than the French; it allowed local self-government and permitted immigration from all parts of Europe. In other ways the British system was more strict. British subjects, for example, were required by the Navigation Acts to use empire ships and seamen—English, Scottish, or colonial—whereas the French were more free to use the carrying services of other nations. British sugar planters had to ship raw sugar to the home country, there to be refined and sold to Europe, whereas French planters were free to refine their sugar in the islands. The mainland British colonials were forbidden to manufacture ironware and numerous other articles for sale; they were expected to buy such objects from England. Since the British sold little to the West Indies, where the slave population had no income with which to buy, the mainland colonies, though less valued as a source of wealth, were a far more important market for British goods. The colonials, though they had prospered under the restrictive system, were beginning to find much of it irksome at the time of the Seven Years' War, and indeed evaded it when they could.

Fighting was endemic even in the years of peace in Europe. Nova Scotia was a trouble spot. French in population, it had been annexed by Britain at the Peace of Utrecht. Its proximity to Louisburg made it a scene of perpetual agitation. The British government in 1755, foreseeing war with France, bodily removed about 7,000 of its people, who called themselves Acadians, scattering them in small numbers through the other mainland colonies. But the great disputed area was the Alleghenies. British colonials were beginning to feel their way westward through the mountains. French traders, soldiers, and empire builders were moving eastward toward the same mountains from points on the Mississippi and the Great Lakes. In 1749, at the request of Virginia and London capitalists, the British government chartered a land-exploitation company, the Ohio Company, to operate in territory claimed also by the French. The French threw up a fort at the point where the Ohio River is formed by the junction of two smaller rivers—Fort Duquesne, later called Pittsburgh. A force of colonials and British regular troops, under General Braddock, started through the wilderness to dislodge the French. It was defeated in July 1755, perhaps through its commander's unwillingness to take advice from the colonial officers, of whom one was George Washington.

A year later France and Britain declared war. The British were brilliantly led by William Pitt, subsequently the Earl of Chatham, a man of wide vision and superb confidence. "I know that I can save the country," he said, "and I know that no one else can." He concentrated British effort on the navy and colonies, while subsidizing Frederick of Prussia to fight in Europe, so that England, as he put it, might win an empire on the plains of Germany. Only the enormous credit of the British government made such a policy feasible. In 1758 British forces successfully took Fort Duquesne. Louisburg fell again in the same year. Gaining entry to the St. Lawrence, the British moved upstream to Quebec, and in 1759 a force under General Wolfe, stealthily scaling the heights, appeared by surprise on the Plains of Abraham outside the fortress, forcing the garrison to accept a battle, which the British won. With the fall of Quebec no further French resistance was possible on the American mainland. The British also, with superior naval power, occupied Guadeloupe and Martinique and the French slave stations in Africa.

Both British and French interests were meanwhile profiting from disturbed conditions in India. As large as Europe without Russia, India was a congested country of impoverished masses, speaking hundreds of languages and following many religions and subreligions, the two greatest being the Hindu and the Moslem. Waves of invasion through the northwest frontier since the Christian year A.D. 1001 had produced a Moslem empire, whose capital was at Delhi and which for a short time held jurisdiction over most of the country. These Moslem emperors were known as Great Moguls. The greatest was Akbar, who ruled from 1556 to 1605, built roads, reformed the taxes, patronized the arts, and attempted to minimize religious differences among his peoples. The Moslem artistic culture flourished for a time after Akbar. One of his successors, Shah Jehan (1628–1658), built the beautiful Taj Mahal near Agra, and at Delhi the delicately carved alabaster palace of the Moguls, in which he placed the Peacock Throne, made of solid gold and studded with gems.

But meanwhile there was restlessness among the Hindus. The Sikhs, who had originated in the fifteenth century as a reform movement in Hinduism, went to war with the Mogul emperor in the seventeenth century. They became one of the most ferociously warlike of Indian peoples. Hindu princes in central India formed a "Mahratta confederacy" against the Moslem emperor at Delhi. Matters were made worse when Aurungzeb, the last significant Mogul emperor (1658–1707), adopted repressive measures against the Hindus. After Aurungzeb, India fell into political dissolution. Many of the modern princely states originated or became autonomous at this time. Hindu princes rebelled against the Mogul. Moslems, beginning as governors or commanders under the Mogul, set up as rulers in their own right. Thus originated Hyderabad, which included the fabulous diamond mines of Golconda, and whose ruler long was called the wealthiest man in the world. Princes and would-be princes fought with each other and with the emperor. New Moslem invaders also poured across the northwest frontier. In 1739 a Persian force occupied Delhi, slaughtered thirty thousand people and departed with the Peacock Throne. Between

1747 and 1761 came a series of forays from Afghanistan, which again resulted in the looting of Delhi and the massacre of uncounted thousands.

The situation in India resembled, on a larger and more frightful scale, what had happened in Europe in the Holy Roman Empire, where also irreconcilable religious differences (of Catholics and Protestants) had torn the country asunder, ambitious princes and city-states had won a chaotic independence, and foreign armies appeared repeatedly as invaders. India, like central Europe, suffered chronically from war, intrigue, and rival pretensions to territory; and in India, as in the Holy Roman Empire, outsiders and ambitious insiders benefited together.

The half-unknown horrors in the interior had repercussions on the coasts. Here handfuls of Europeans were established in the coastal cities. By the troubles in the interior the Indian authorities along the coasts were reduced, so to speak, to a size with which the Europeans could deal. The Europeans—British and French—were agents of their respective East India companies. The companies built forts, maintained soldiers, coined money, and entered into treaties with surrounding Indian powers, under charter of their home governments, and with no one in India to deny them the exercise of such sovereign rights. Agents of the companies, like Indians themselves, ignored or respected the Mogul emperor as suited their own purpose. They were, at first, only one of the many elements in the flux and reflux of Indian affairs.

Neither the British nor the French government, during the Seven Years' War, had any intention of territorial conquest in India, their policy in this respect differing radically from policy toward America. Nor were the two companies imperialistic. The company directors, in London and Paris, disapproved of fantastic schemes of intervention in Indian politics, insisted that their agents should attend to business only, and resented every penny and every sou not spent to bring in commercial profit. But it took a year or more to exchange messages between Europe and India, and company representatives in India, caught up in the Indian vortex, and overcome by the chance to make personal fortunes or by dreams of empire, acted very much on their own, committing their home offices without compunction. Involvement in Indian affairs was not exactly new. We have seen how "Diamond" Pitt, in 1702, purchased the good will of the nawab of the Carnatic, when the nawab threatened, by military force, to reduce the English traders at Madras to submission.[24] But the first European to exploit the possibilities of the situation was the Frenchman Dupleix. Dupleix felt that the funds sent out by the company in Paris, to finance trade in India, were insufficient. His idea seems to have been not empire-building, but to make the company into a local territorial power, in order that, from taxes and other political revenues, it might have more capital for its commercial operations. In any case, during the years of peace in Europe after 1748, Dupleix found himself with about 2,000 French troops in the Carnatic, the east coast around Madras. He lent them out to neighboring native rulers in return for territorial concessions. The first to drill native Indians by European methods, he was the originator of the "sepoys."

[24]See p. 271.

Following a program of backing claimants to various Indian thrones, he built up a clientele of native rulers under obligation to himself. He was very successful, for a few European troops or sepoys could overcome hordes of purely Indian forces in pitched battle. But he was recalled to France in 1754, the company becoming apprehensive of war with Britain and other trouble; and he died in disgrace.

When war came, in 1756, British interests in India were advanced chiefly by Robert Clive. He had come out many years before as a clerk for the company but had shown military talents and an ability to comprehend Indian politics. He had maneuvered, with little success, against Dupleix in the Carnatic in the 1740s. In 1756, on hearing the news of war in Europe, he shifted his attention to Bengal, hoping to drive the French from their trading stations there. The French were favored in Bengal by the local Moslem ruler, Suraja Dowla, who proceeded to anticipate Clive's arrival by expelling the British from Calcutta. Capturing the city, he shut up 146 Englishmen in a small room without windows (soon known as the "Black Hole of Calcutta") and kept them there all night, during which most of them died of suffocation. Clive, soon appearing with a small force of British and sepoys, routed Suraja Dowla at the battle of Plassey in 1757. He put his own puppet on the Bengal throne and extorted huge reparations both for the company and for himself. Back in England he was received with mixed feelings, and again, in India, strove to purify the almost incredible corruption of company employees there, men normal enough but demoralized by irresistible chances for easy riches. Finally he committed suicide in 1774.

It was British sea power, more fundamentally than Clive's tactics, that assured the triumph of British over French ambitions in the East. The British government still had no intention of conquest in India, but it could not see its East India Company forced out by agents of the French company in collaboration with Indian princes. Naval forces were therefore dispatched to the Indian Ocean, and they not only allowed Clive to shift from Madras to Calcutta at will, but gradually cut off the French posts in India from Europe and from each other. By the end of the war all the French establishments in India, as in Africa and America, were at the mercy of the British. The French overseas lay prostrate, and France itself was again detached from the overseas world on which much of its economy rested. In 1761 France made an alliance with Spain, which was alarmed for the safety of its own American empire after the British victories at Quebec and in the Caribbean. But the British also defeated Spain.

The British armed forces had been spectacularly successful. Yet the peace treaty, signed at Paris in February 1763, five days before the Austro-Prussian peace of Hubertusburg, was by no means unfavorable to the defeated. The French Duke of Choiseul was a skillful and single-minded negotiator. The British, Pitt having fallen from office in 1761, were represented by a confused group of parliamentary favorites of the new king, George III. France ceded to Britain all French territory on the North American mainland east of the Mississippi. Canada thereby became British, and the colonials of the Thirteen Colonies were relieved of the French presence beyond the Alleghenies. To Spain, in return for aid in the last days of the war, France ceded all holdings west of the Mississippi and at its mouth. France thereby abandoned the North American continent. But these almost empty regions were of minor commercial importance, and the French, in return for surrendering them, retained many economically more valuable establishments elsewhere. In the West Indies the British planters, and in England the powerful "West India interest," feared competition from the French sugar islands, which produced more cheaply, and wanted them left outside the protected economic system of the British empire. France therefore received back Guadeloupe and Martinique, as well as most of its slave stations in Africa. In India, the French remained in possession of their commercial installations—offices, warehouses, and docks—at Pondicherry and other towns. They were forbidden to erect fortifications or pursue political ambitions among Indian princes—a practice which neither the French nor the British government had hitherto much favored in any case.

The treaties of Paris and Hubertusburg, closing the prolonged war of the mid-century, made the year 1763 a memorable turning point. Prussia was to continue in being. The dualism of Germany was to be lasting; Austria and Prussia eyed each other as rivals. Frederick's aggression of 1740 was legalized and even moralized by the heroic defense that had proved necessary to retain the plunder. Frederick himself, from 1763 until his death in 1786, was a man of peace, philosophical and even benign. But the German crucible had boiled, and out of it had come a Prussia harder and more metallic than ever, more disposed, by its escape from annihilation, to glorify its army as the steel framework of its life.

The Anglo-French settlement was far-reaching and rather curious. Although the war was won overwhelmingly by the British, it resulted in no commercial calamity to the French. French trade with America and the East grew as rapidly after the Seven Years' War as before it, and in 1785 was double what it had been in 1755. For England the war opened up new commercial channels. British trade with America and the East probably tripled between 1755 and 1785.[25] But the outstanding British gains were imperial and strategic. The European balance of power was preserved, the French had been kept out of Belgium, British subjects in North America seemed

[25] See pp. 267–268.

The World in 1763. *At the Peace of Paris of 1763 the British overseas empire triumphed over the French. The French ceded their holdings on the North American mainland east of the Mississippi to Britain, those west of the Mississippi to Spain. Britain also took Florida from Spain in 1763, but lost it, returning it to Spain in 1783, at the close of the War of American Independence. The French retained their sugar islands in the West Indies and their trading stations in India; they were stopped from empire-building but did not greatly suffer commercially from the Seven Years' War. The British proceeded to build their empire in India. (See also map, p. 339.)*

secure, and Britain had again vindicated its command of the sea. British sea power implied, in turn, that British seaborne commerce was safe in peace or war, while the seaborne commerce of the French, or of any others, depended ultimately on the political requirements of the British. But the French still had a few cards to play, and were to play them in the American and French Revolutions.

For America and India the peace of 1763 was decisive. America north of Mexico was to become part of an English-speaking world. In India the British government was drawn increasingly into a policy of territorial occupation; a British "paramount power" eventually emerged in place of the empire of the Moguls. British political rule in India stimulated British business there, until in the greatest days of British prosperity India was one of the main pillars of the British economic system, and the road to India became in a real sense the lifeline of the British empire. But in 1763 this state of affairs was still in the future and was to be reached by many intermediate steps.

The Great War of the Mid-Eighteenth Century: The Peace of Paris, 1763

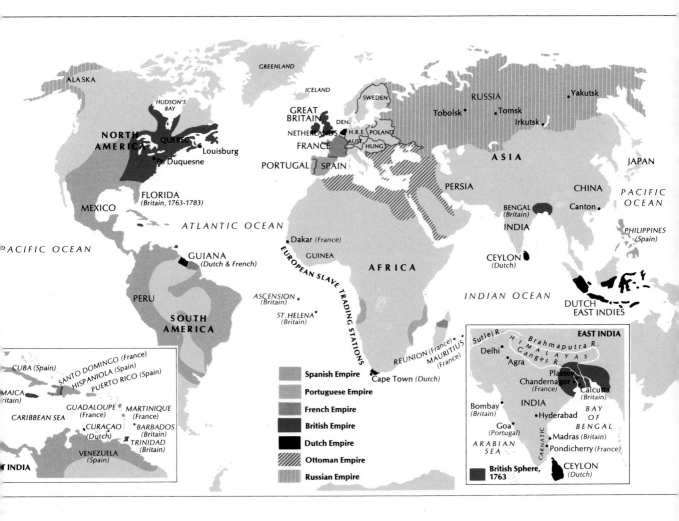

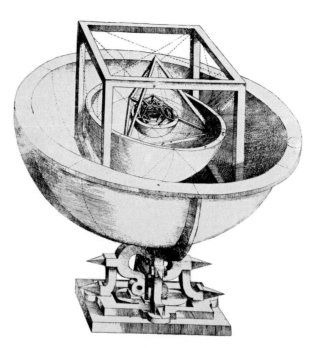

VII: THE SCIENTIFIC VIEW

OF THE WORLD

The seventeenth century has been called the century of genius. One reason is that it was the age when science became "modern." It was the great age of Galileo and Sir Isaac Newton, whose combined lifetimes spanned the century, with Galileo dying and Newton born in the year 1642. When Galileo was young those who probed into the secrets of nature still labored largely in the dark, isolated from one another and from the general public, working oftentimes by methods of trial and error, not altogether clear on what they were trying to do, with their thinking still complicated by ideas not nowadays considered scientific. They had nevertheless accomplished a good deal. Discoveries had been made, and ideas developed, without which the intellectual revolution of the seventeenth century would not have occurred. But in a way all scientific investigators before Galileo seem to be precursors, patient workers destined never to enter into the world toward which they labored. In 1727, when Newton died, all was changed. Scientific men were in continual touch with one another, and science was recognized as one of the principal enterprises of European society. Scientific methods of inquiry had been defined. The store of factual knowledge had become very large. The first modern scientific synthesis, or coherent theory of the physical universe, had been presented by Newton. Scientific knowledge was applied

Chapter Emblem: A Copernican globe designed by Kepler in 1596 to illustrate movement of the planets about the sun.

increasingly to navigation, mining, agriculture, and many branches of manufacture. Science and invention were joining hands. Science was accepted as the main force in the advancement of civilization and progress. And science was becoming popularized; many people who were not themselves scientists "believed" in science and attempted to apply scientific habits of thought to diverse problems of man and society.

The history of science is too great a story to be told in this book, but there are a few ideas about it which even a book of this kind must attempt to make clear. First, science, purely as a form of thought, is one of the supreme achievements of the human mind, and to have a humanistic understanding of man's powers one must sense the importance of science, as of philosophy, literature, or the arts. Second, science has increasingly affected practical affairs, entering into the health, wealth, and happiness of mankind. It has changed the size of populations and the use of raw materials, revolutionized methods of production, transport, business, and war, and so helped to relieve some human problems while producing others. This is especially true of modern civilization since the seventeenth century. Third, in the modern world ideas have had a way of passing over from science into other domains of thought. Many people today, for example, in their notions of themselves, their neighbors, or the meaning of life, are influenced by ideas which they believe to be those of Freud or Einstein—they talk of repressions or relativity without necessarily knowing much about them. Ideas derived from biology and from Darwin—such as evolution and the struggle for existence—have likewise spread far and wide. Similarly the scientific revolution of the seventeenth century had repercussions far beyond the realm of pure science. It changed ideas of religion and of God and man. And it helped to spread certain very deep-seated beliefs, such as that the physical universe in which man finds himself is essentially orderly and harmonious, that the human reason is capable of understanding and dealing with it, and that man can conduct his own affairs by methods of peaceable exchange of ideas and rational agreement. Thus was laid a foundation for belief in free and democratic institutions.

The purpose of this chapter is to sketch the rise of modern science in the seventeenth century and the emergence of the scientific view of the world and of human affairs. The chapter that follows will describe the popularization and application of these ideas in the eighteenth century, in the era generally known as the Age of Enlightenment.

30
Prophets of a Scientific Civilization: Bacon and Descartes

Science Before the Seventeenth Century

The scientific view became characteristic of European society about the middle of the seventeenth century. There had, indeed, been a few in earlier times who caught glimpses of a whole civilization reared upon science. To us today the most famous of these is Leonardo da Vinci (1452–1519), the universal genius of the Italian Renaissance, who had been artist, engineer, and scientific thinker all in one. Leonardo, by actual dissection of dead bodies, had obtained an accurate knowledge of human anatomy; he had conceived of the circulation of the blood and the movement of the earth about the sun; and he had drawn designs for submarines and airplanes and speculated on the use of parachutes and poison gases. But Leonardo had not published his scientific ideas. He was known almost exclusively as an artist. His work in science remained outside the stream of scientific thought, without influence on its course. It was not even known until the discovery of his private notebooks in recent years. Leonardo thus figures in the history of science as an isolated genius, a man of brilliant insights and audacious theories, which died with their author's death, whereas science depends on a transmission of ideas in which men build upon one another's discoveries, test one another's experiments, and fill in the gaps in one another's knowledge.

A century after the death of Leonardo da Vinci educated Europeans were by no means scientifically minded. Among thoughtful persons many currents were stirring. On the one hand there was a great deal of skepticism, a constantly doubting frame of mind, which held that no certain knowledge is possible for human beings at all, that all beliefs are essentially only customs, that some people believe one thing and some another, and that there is no sound way of choosing between them. This attitude was best expressed by the French essayist Montaigne (1533–1592), whose thought distilled itself into an eternal question, *Que sais-je?* "What do I know?" with the always implied answer, "Nothing." Montaigne's philosophy led to a tolerant, humane, and broad-minded outlook; but as a system of thought it was not otherwise very constructive. On the other hand, there was also a tendency to over-belief, arising from the same inability to distinguish between true and false. There was no accepted line between chemistry and alchemy, or between astronomy and astrology; all alike were regarded as ways of penetrating the "secrets" of nature. The sixteenth century had been a great age of charlatans, such as Nostradamus and Paracelsus, some of whom, notably Paracelsus, mixed magic and valid science in a way hardly understandable to us today.[1] As late as the seventeenth century, especially in central Europe where the Thirty Years' War produced chaos and terror, kings and generals kept private astrologers to divine the future. The two centuries from about 1450 to about 1650 were also the period when fear of witches was at its height. The witchcraft panic lasted longest in Germany and central Europe, probably kept alive by the insecurities engendered by the Thirty Years' War. But about twenty persons were hanged as witches in Massachusetts as late as 1692, for the English colonies, as a remote and outlying part of the European world, were among the last to feel some of the waves originating in Europe. It was in Scotland, another outlying region of Europe, that the last known execution for witchcraft took place, in 1722.

It was by no means clear, in the early part of the seventeenth century, which way Europe was going to develop. It might conceivably have fallen into a kind of chaos, as India did at about this time. We have seen that much of Europe was racked by chronic and marauding violence, to which an end was put by the consolidation of the modern state and the conversion of armed bands into organized and disciplined armies. Similarly, in things of the mind, there was no settled order. Doubt went with superstition, indifference with persecution. Science in time provided Europe

[1] See p. 67.

with a new faith in itself. The rise of science in the seventeenth century possibly saved European civilization from petering out in a long postmedieval afterglow, or from wandering off into the diverse paths of a genial skepticism, ineffectual philosophizing, desultory magic, or mad fear of the unknown.

Bacon and Descartes   Two men stand out as prophets of a world reconstructed by science. One was the Englishman Francis Bacon (1561–1626), the other the Frenchman René Descartes (1596–1650). Both published their most influential books between 1620 and 1640. Both addressed themselves to the problem of knowledge. Both asked themselves how it is possible for human beings to know anything with certainty or to have a reliable, truthful, and usable knowledge of the world of nature. Both shared in the doubts of their day. They branded virtually all beliefs of preceding generations (outside religion) as worthless. Both ridiculed the tendency to put faith in ancient books, to cite the writings of Aristotle or others, on questions having to do with the workings of nature. Both attacked earlier methods of seeking knowledge; they rejected the methods of the "schoolmen" or "scholastics," the thinkers in the academic tradition of the universities founded in the Middle Ages. On the whole, medieval philosophy had been rationalistic and deductive.[2] That is, its characteristic procedure was to start with definitions and general propositions and then discover what further knowledge could be logically deduced from the definitions thus accepted. Or it proceeded by affirming the nature of an object to be such-and-such (e.g., that "man is a political animal") and then describing how objects of such a nature do or should behave. These methods, which owed much to Aristotle and other ancient codifiers of human thought, had generally ceased to be fruitful in discovery of knowledge of nature. Bacon and Descartes held that the medieval (or Aristotelian) methods were backward. They held that truth is not something that we postulate at the beginning, and then explore in all its ramifications, but that it is something which we find at the end, after a long process of investigation, experiment, or intermediate thought.

Bacon and Descartes thus went beyond mere doubt. They offered a constructive program, and though their programs were different, they both became heralds or philosophers of a scientific view. They maintained that there was a true and reliable method of knowledge. And they maintained in addition that once this true method was known and practiced, once the real workings of nature were understood, men would be able to use this knowledge for their own purposes, control nature in their own interests, make undreamed of useful inventions, improve their mechanical arts, and add generally to their wealth and comfort. Bacon and Descartes thus announced the advent of a scientific civilization.

Francis Bacon planned a great work in many volumes, to be known as the *Instauratio Magna* or "Great Renewal," calling for a complete new start in science and civilization. He completed only two parts. One, published in 1620, was the

[2]See pp. 37–39.

Novum Organum or new method of acquiring knowledge. Here he insisted on *inductive* method. In the inductive method we proceed from the particular to the general, from the concrete to the abstract. For example, in the study of leaves, if we examine millions of actual leaves, of all sizes and shapes, and if we assemble, observe, and compare them with minute scrutiny, we are using an *inductive* method in the sense meant by Bacon; if successful, we may arrive at a knowledge, based on observed facts, of the general nature of a leaf as such. If, on the other hand, we begin with a general idea of what we think all leaves are like, i.e., all leaves have stems, and then proceed to describe an individual leaf on that basis, we are following the *deductive* method; we draw logical implications from what we already know, but we learn no more of the nature of a leaf than what we knew or thought we knew at the beginning. Bacon advised men to put aside all traditional ideas, to rid themselves of prejudices and preconceptions, to look at the world with fresh eyes, to observe and study the innumerable things that are actually perceived by the senses. Men before Bacon used the inductive method, but he formalized it as a method and became a leading philosopher of empiricism. This philosophy, the founding of knowledge on observation and experience, has always proved a useful safeguard against fitting facts into preconceived patterns. It demands that we let the patterns of our thought be shaped by actual facts as we observe them.

The other completed part of Bacon's great work, published in 1623, was called in its English translation *The Advancement of Learning*. Here Bacon developed the same ideas and especially insisted that true knowledge was useful knowledge. In *The New Atlantis* (1627), he portrayed a scientific utopia in which men enjoyed a perfect society through their knowledge and command of nature. The usefulness of knowledge became the other main element in the Baconian tradition. In this view there was no sharp difference between pure science and applied science or between the work of the purely scientific investigator and that of the mechanic or inventor who in his own way probed into nature and devised instruments or machines for putting natural forces to work. The fact that knowledge could be used for practical purposes became a sign or proof that it was true knowledge. For example, the fact that men could aim their cannon and hit their targets more accurately in the seventeenth century became a proof of the theory of ballistics which had been scientifically worked out. Enthusiastic Baconians believed that knowledge was power. True knowledge could be put to work, if not immediately at least in the long run, after more knowledge was discovered. It was useful to mankind, unlike the "delicate learning" of the misguided scholastics. In this coming together of knowledge and power arose the far-reaching modern idea of progress. And in it arose many of the problems of modern men, since the power given by scientific knowledge can be either bad or good.

But Bacon, though a force in redirecting the European mind, never had much influence on the development of actual science. Kept busy as Lord Chancellor of England and in other government duties, he was not even fully abreast of the most advanced scientific thought of his day. Like the public generally of his lifetime, he was undisturbed by the new theories of astronomers holding the earth to move about the sun. Bacon's greatest weakness was his failure to understand the role of mathematics. Mathematics, dealing with pure abstractions and proceeding deductively from axioms to theorems, was not an empirical or inductive method of thought such as Bacon demanded. Yet science in the seventeenth century went forward most successfully in subjects where mathematics could be applied. Even today the degree to which a subject is truly scientific depends on the degree to which it can be made mathematical. We have pure science where we have formulas and equations, and the scientific method itself is both inductive and deductive.

Descartes was a great mathematician in his own right. He is considered the inventor of coordinate geometry. He showed that by use of coordinates (or graph paper, in simple language) any algebraic formula could be plotted as a curve in space, and contrariwise that any curve in space, however complex, could be converted into algebraic terms and thus dealt with by methods of calculation. And one effect of his general philosophy was to create belief in a vast world of nature that could be reduced to mathematical form.

Descartes set forth his ideas in his *Discourse on Method,* in 1637, and in many more technical writings. He advanced the principle of systematic doubt. He began by trying to doubt everything that could reasonably be doubted, thus sweeping away past ideas and clearing the ground for his own "great renewal," to use Bacon's phrase. He held that he could not doubt his own existence as a thinking and doubting being (*cogito ergo sum,* "I think, therefore I exist"); he then deduced, by systematic reasoning, the existence of God and much else. He arrived at a philosophy of dualism, the famous "Cartesian dualism," which held that God has created two kinds of fundamental reality in the universe. One was "thinking substance"—mind, spirit, consciousness, subjective experience. The other was "extended substance"—everything outside the mind and hence objective. Of everything except the mind itself the most fundamental and universal quality was that it occupied a portion of space, minute or vast. Space itself was conceived as infinite, and everywhere geometric.

This philosophy had profound and long-lasting effects. For one thing, the seemingly most real elements in human experience, color and sound, joy and grief, seemed somehow to be shadowy and unreal, or at least illusive, with no existence outside the mind itself. But all else was quantitative, measurable, reducible to formulas or equations. Over all else, over the whole universe or half-universe of "extended substance," the most powerful instrument available to the human understanding, namely, mathematics, reigned supreme. "Give me motion and extension," said Descartes, "and I will build you the world."

Descartes also, with French genius, expressed the Baconian idea. Instead of the "speculative philosophy of the schools," he wrote in the *Discourse on Method,* men might discover a "practical philosophy by which, understanding the forces and action of fire, water, air, the stars and heavens and all other bodies that surround us, as distinctly as we understand the mechanical arts of our craftsmen, we can use these forces in the same way for all purposes for which they are appropriate, and so make ourselves the masters and possessors of nature. And this is desirable not only for the invention of innumerable devices by which we may enjoy without trouble the fruits of the earth and the conveniences it affords, but mainly also for the preservation of health, which is undoubtedly the principal good and foundation of all other good things in this life."

Meanwhile actual scientific discovery was advancing on many fronts. It did not advance on all with equal speed. Some of the sciences were, and long remained, dependent mainly on the collection of specimens. Botany was one of these; Europe's knowledge of plants expanded enormously with the explorations overseas, and botanical gardens and herb collections in Europe became far more extensive than ever before, bringing important enlargements in the stock of medicinal drugs. Other sciences drew their impetus from intensive and open-minded observation. The Flemish Vesalius, by a book published in 1543, *The Structure of the Human Body*, renewed and modernized the study of anatomy. Formerly anatomists had generally held that the writings of Galen, dating from the second century A.D., contained an authoritative description of all human muscles and tissues.[3] They had indeed dissected cadavers but had dismissed those not conforming to Galen's description as somehow abnormal or not typical. Vesalius put Galen behind him and based his general description of the human frame on actual bodies as he found them. In physiology also, dealing with the functioning rather than the structure of living bodies, there was considerable progress. Here the method of laboratory experiment could be profitably used. William Harvey, after years of laboratory work, including the vivisection of animals, published in 1628 a book *On the Movement of the Heart and Blood*. Here he set forth the doctrine, confirmed by evidence, of the continual circulation of the blood through arteries and veins. The Italian Malpighi, using the newly invented microscope, confirmed Harvey's findings by the discovery of capillaries in 1661. The Dutch Leeuwenhoek, also by use of the microscope, was the first to see blood corpuscles, spermatozoa, and bacteria, of which he left published drawings.

These sciences, and also chemistry, although work in them went continually on, did not come fully into their own until after 1800. They were long overshadowed by astronomy and physics. Here mathematics could be most fully applied, and mathematics underwent a rapid development in the seventeenth century. Decimals came into use to express fractions, the symbols used in algebra were improved and standardized, and in 1614 logarithms were invented by the Scot John Napier. Co-ordinate geometry was mapped out by Descartes, the theory of probabilities developed by Pascal, and calculus invented simultaneously in England by Newton and in Germany by Leibnitz. These advances made it more generally possible to think about nature in purely quantitative terms, to measure with greater precision, and to perform complex and laborious computations. Physics and astronomy were remark-

[3] See p. 10.

ably stimulated, and it was in this field that the most astonishing scientific revolution of the seventeenth century took place.

From time immemorial, since the Greek Ptolemy had codified ancient astronomy in the second century A.D.,[4] educated Europeans had held a conception of the cosmos which we call Ptolemaic. The cosmos in this view was a group of concentric spheres, a series of balls within balls each having the same center. The innermost ball was the earth, made up of hard, solid, earthy substance such as men were familiar with underfoot. The other spheres, encompassing the earth in series, were all transparent. They were the "crystalline spheres" made known to us by the poets; their harmony was the "music of the spheres." These spheres all revolved about the earth, each sphere containing, set in it as a jewel, a luminous heavenly body or orb which moved about the earth with the movement of its transparent sphere. Nearest to the earth was the sphere of the moon; then, in turn, the spheres of Mercury and Venus, then the sphere of the sun, then those of the outer planets. Last came the outermost sphere containing all the fixed stars studded in it, all moving majestically about the earth in daily motion, but motionless with respect to each other because held firmly in the same sphere. Beyond the sphere of the fixed stars, in general belief, lay the "empyrean," the home of angels and immortal spirits; but this was not a matter of natural science.

A man standing on the earth, and looking up into the sky, thus felt himself to be enclosed by a dome of which his own position was the center. In the blue sky of day he could literally see the crystalline spheres; in the stars at night he could behold the orbs which these spheres carried with them. All revolved about him, presumably at no very alarming distance. The celestial bodies were commonly supposed to be of different material and quality from the earth. The earth was of heavy dross; the stars and planets and the sun and moon seemed made of pure and gleaming light, or at least of a bright ethereal substance almost as tenuous as the crystal spheres in which they moved. The cosmos was a hierarchy of ascending perfection. The heavens were purer than the earth.

This system corresponded to actual appearances, and except for scientific knowledge would be highly believable today. It was formulated also in rigorous mathematical terms. Ever since the Greeks, and becoming increasingly intricate in the Middle Ages, a complex geometry had grown up to explain the observed motion of the heavenly bodies. The Ptolemaic system was a mathematical system. And it was for purely mathematical reasons that it first came to be reconsidered. There was a marked revival of mathematical interest at the close of the Middle Ages, in the fourteenth and fifteenth centuries, a renewed concentration on the philosophical traditions of Pythagoras and Plato. In these philosophies could be found the doctrine that numbers might be the final key to the mysteries of nature. With them went a metaphysical belief that simplicity was more likely to be a sign of truth than com-

[4]See p. 10.

plication, and that a simpler mathematical formulation was better than a more complex one.

These ideas motivated Nicholas Copernicus, born in Poland of German and Polish background, who, after study in Italy, wrote his epochal work *On the Revolutions of the Heavenly Orbs.* In this book, published in 1543 after his death, he held the sun to be the center of the solar system and fixed stars, and the earth to be one of the planets revolving in space around it. This view had been entertained by a few isolated thinkers before. Copernicus gave a mathematical demonstration. To him it was a purely mathematical problem. With increasingly detailed knowledge of the actual movement of the heavenly bodies it had become necessary to make the Ptolemaic system more intricate by the addition of new "cycles" and "epicycles," until, as John Milton expressed it later, the cosmos was

> *With Centric and Concentric scribbled o'er,*
> *Cycle and Epicycle, Orb in Orb.*

Copernicus needed fewer such hypothetical constructions to explain the known movements of the heavenly bodies. The heliocentric or sun-centered theory was mathematically a little simpler than the geocentric or earth-centered theory hitherto held.

The Copernican doctrine long remained a hypothesis known only to experts. Most astronomers for a time hesitated to accept it, seeing no need, from the evidence yet produced, of so overwhelming a readjustment of current ideas. Tycho Brahe (1546–1601), the greatest authority on the actual positions and movements of the heavenly bodies in the generations immediately after Copernicus, never accepted the Copernican system in full. But his assistant and follower, John Kepler (1571–1630), not only accepted the Copernican theory but carried it further.

Kepler, a German, was a kind of mathematical mystic, part-time astrologer, and scientific genius. He felt ecstasy at the mysterious harmonies of mathematical forms. He built upon the exact observations of Tycho Brahe. Copernicus had believed the orbits of the planets about the sun to be perfect circles. Tycho showed that this belief did not fit the observable facts. Kepler discovered that orbits of the planets were ellipses. The ellipse, like the circle, is an abstract mathematical figure with knowable properties. Kepler demonstrated that, as a planet moves in its elliptical path about the sun, the straight line connecting it with the sun sweeps through an area of space proportional to the time taken by the planet's motion; that is, that a planet sweeps equal areas in equal times; or, more simply, that the closer a planet is to the sun in its elliptical orbit, the faster it moves. Kepler further showed that the length of time in which the several planets revolve about the sun varies proportionately with their distance from the sun: the square of the time is proportional to the cube of the distance.

It is not possible for most people to understand the mathematics involved, but it is possible to realize the astounding implications of Kepler's laws of planetary motion. Kepler showed that the actual world of stubborn facts, as observed by Tycho, and the purely rational world of mathematical harmony, as surmised by Copernicus, were not really in any discrepancy with each other; that they really corresponded exactly. Why they should he did not know; it was the mystery of numbers. He digested an overwhelming amount of hitherto unexplained information into a few brief statements. He showed a cosmic mathematical relationship between space and time. And he described the movement of the planets in explicit formulas, which any competent person could verify at will.

The next step was taken by Galileo (1564-1642). So far the question of what the heavenly bodies were made of had hardly been affected. Indeed, they were not thought of as bodies at all, but rather as orbs. Only the sun and moon had any dimension; stars and planets were only points of light; and the theories of Copernicus and Kepler, like those of Ptolemy, might apply to insubstantial luminous objects in motion. In 1609 Galileo built a telescope. Turning it to the sky, he perceived that the moon had a rough and apparently mountainous surface, as if made of the same kind of material as the earth. Seeing clearly the dark side of the moon in its various phases, and noting that in every position it only reflected the light of the sun, he concluded that the moon was not itself a luminous object, another indication that it might be made of earth-like substance. He saw spots on the sun, as if the sun were not pure and perfect. He found that the planets had visible breadth when seen in the telescope, but that the fixed stars remained only points of light, as if incalculably further away. He discovered also that Jupiter had satellites, moons moving around it like the moon around the earth. These discoveries reassured him of the validity of the Copernican theory, which he had in any case already accepted. They suggested also that the heavenly bodies might be of the same substance as the earth, masses of matter moving in space. Contrariwise, it became easier to think of the earth as itself a kind of heavenly body revolving about the sun. The difference between the earth and the heavens was disappearing. This struck a terrifying blow at all earlier philosophy and theology. Some professors were afraid to look through the telescope, and Galileo was condemned and forced to an ostensible recantation by his church.

Moreover, where Kepler had found mathematical laws describing the movement of planets, Galileo found mathematical laws describing the movement of bodies on the earth. Formerly it had been thought that some bodies were by nature heavier than others, and that heavier bodies fell to the ground faster than light ones. Galileo in 1591, according to the story, dropped a ten-pound and a one-pound weight simultaneously from the top of the Leaning Tower of Pisa. The truth of this story has been questioned, but in any case Galileo showed that despite all previous speculation on the subject two bodies of different weights, when allowance was made for differences in air resistance due to differences of size or shape, struck the ground at the same time. His further work in dynamics, or the science of the motion of bodies, took many years to accomplish. He had to devise more refined means for measuring small intervals of time, find means of estimating the air resistance, friction, and other impediments which always occur in nature, and conceive of pure or absolute motion, and of force and velocity, in abstract mathematical terms. He arrived at the conception of inertia, holding that motion and rest are equally natural states of matter. Only *change* in motion, he thought, required physical explanation, for bodies in motion would move forever in a straight line at the same speed except as acted on by an external force. This dispensed with the need of an Unmoved Mover felt in the older philosophy. Of bodies moving on the earth, Galileo discovered that when falling freely they fall with a velocity that increased according to mathematical formula.

It was the supreme achievement of Newton to bring Kepler and Galileo together, that is, to show that Kepler's laws of planetary motion and Galileo's laws of terrestrial motion were two aspects of the same laws. Galileo's findings, holding that moving bodies move uniformly in a straight line unless deflected by a definite force, made it necessary to explain why the planets, instead of flying off in straight lines, tend to fall toward the sun, the result being their elliptical orbits—and why the moon, similarly, tends to fall toward the earth. Newton seems early to have suspected that the answer would be related to Galileo's laws of falling bodies—that is, that gravity, or the pull of the earth upon objects on earth, might be a form of a universal gravitation, or similar pull, characterizing all bodies in the solar system. Great technical difficulties stood in the way, but finally, after inventing calculus, and using a new measurement of the size of the earth made by a Frenchman and experiments with circular motion made by the Dutch Huyghens on the pendulum, Newton was able to bring his calculations to fruition, and to publish, in 1687, his *Mathematical Principles of Natural Philosophy.*

This stupendous book showed that all motion that could then be timed and measured, whether on the earth or in the solar system, could be described by the same mathematical formulas. All matter moved as if every particle attracted every other particle with a force proportional to the product of the two masses, and inversely proportional to the square of the distance between them. This "force" was universal gravitation. What it was Newton did not pretend to explain. For two hundred years the law stood unshaken, always verified by every new relevant discovery. Only in the last century have its limitations been found; it does not hold good in the infinitesimal world of subatomic structure or in the macrocosm of the whole physical universe as now conceived.

With Newton's work (which affected other fields than are here mentioned) the promise of science seemed fulfilled. Even in purely practical affairs conveniences followed, as anticipated by the Baconians. The tides could now be understood and predicted by the gravitational interplay of earth, moon, and sun. Exact mathematical knowledge of the solar system was of great help to navigation. In the eighteenth century chronometers were developed, making possible the finding of precise longitude at sea. Merchant ships and naval squadrons could thus operate with more assurance. Better determination of longitude, at sea and on land, was of great value to cartography, the science of map-making. Eighteenth-century Europeans were the first human beings to have a fairly accurate idea of the shapes and sizes of continents and oceans. Or again, mathematical advance, including the development of calculus, which allowed an exact treatment of curves and trajectories, reinforced by technical discoveries in the working of metals, led to an increased use of artillery. Armies in 1750 used twice as many cannon per soldier as in 1650. Naval ordnance also improved. These were items making armed forces more expensive to maintain, requiring governments to increase their taxes, and hence producing constitutional crises. Improved firearms likewise heightened the advantage of armies over insurrectionists or private fighting bands, thus strengthening the sovereignty of the state. They gave Europeans the military advantage over other peoples, in America, India, or elsewhere, on which the world ascendancy of Europe in the European age was built. This example, chosen somewhat at random, suggests the almost inconceivable ramifications of the practical consequences of science.

The instance of the steam engine may also be cited. Steam power was eventually almost literally to move the world. In 1700 it was a cloud no bigger than a man's hand. Yet it was in sight on the horizon. A Frenchman, Denis Papin, in 1681 invented a device in which steam moved a piston, but it produced so little power that it was used only in cooking. British scientists turned their minds to it. Robert Boyle, discoverer of "Boyle's law" on the pressure of gases, studied the problem; scientists, mechanics, and instrument makers collaborated. In 1702 Thomas Newcomen, a man without scientific training but associated with scientists, produced the steam engine known thereafter as Newcomen's engine, from which, as will be seen, James Watt developed the steam engine as we know it. Newcomen's engine was primitive according to later ideas. It burnt so much fuel that it could be used only in coal mines. But it was used. Not long after 1700 it was widely employed to pump water from the coal pits. It saved labor, cheapened production, and opened hitherto unusable deposits to exploitation. It was the first application of steam to an economic purpose.

The faith in natural knowledge was becoming institutionalized. Organized bodies of men, possessing equipment and funds, were engaged in scientific study. Most notable of these were the Royal Society of London, founded in 1662, and the Academy of Sciences in France, founded in 1666. Both originated when earlier and informal groups, usually gentlemen of the landed classes, received charters from their governments to pursue scientific interests. Scientific periodicals began to be published. Scientific societies provided the medium for prompt interchange of ideas indispensable to the growth of scientific knowledge. They published articles not only on the natural sciences and mathematics, but also on paleography, numismatics, chronology, legal history, and natural law. The work of the learned had not yet yielded to specialization. All felt a common interest in the advance of all fronts of knowledge. It is to be noted also how the scientific movement was an international one, shared in by all central and western Europe except Portugal and Spain. Men of many nationalities constantly made use of each other's hypotheses or discoveries. Many or even most of the books written in this age were first published in Latin, still the international language of science and learning, and many articles in the new scientific journals were written in Latin also.

It was perhaps in the world of thought that the revolution accomplished from Copernicus to Newton was most profound. It has been called the greatest spiritual readjustment that men have been required to make. The old heavens were exploded. Man was no longer the center of creation. The luminaries of the sky no longer shone to light his way or to give him beauty. The sky itself was an illusion, its color a thing in the mind only, for when a man now looked upward he was really looking only into the darkness of endless space. The old cosmos, comfortably enclosed and ranked in an ascending order of purity, gave way to a new cosmos which seemed to consist in an infinite emptiness through which particles of matter were distributed. Man was the puny denizen of a material object swinging in space along with other very distant material objects of the same kind. About the physical universe there was nothing especially Christian, nothing that the God portrayed in the Bible would be likely to have made. The gap between Christianity and natural science, always present yet always bridged in the Middle Ages, now opened wider than ever. It was felt with anguish by some in the seventeenth century, notably by the Frenchman Blaise Pascal, a considerable scientist, preeminent mathematician, and deep and troubled Christian believer. He left a record of his state of mind in his *Pensées* or *Thoughts*, jottings from which he hoped some day to write a great book on the Christian faith. "I am terrified," he said in one of these jottings, "by the eternal silence of these infinite spaces."

But on the whole the reaction was more optimistic. Man might be merely a reed, as Pascal said, but Pascal added, "a thinking reed." Man might be no longer the physical center of the world. But it was man's mind that had penetrated the world's laws. The Newtonian system, as it became popularized, a process which took about fifty years, led to a great intellectual complacency. Never had confidence in human powers been so high. As Alexander Pope put it,

> *Nature and nature's laws lay hid in night;*
> *God said, "Let Newton be," and all was light.*

Or, according to another epigram on the subject, there was only one universe to discover, and this universe had been discovered by Newton. Everything seemed possible to the human reason. The old feeling of dependency upon God lost much of its force, or became something to be discussed by clergymen in church on Sunday. Man was not really a little creature, a wayfarer in a world that was alien to him, yearning for the reunion with God that would bring him peace. Man was a dignified creature, one of great capacity in his own right, living in a world that was understandable and manageable by him, and in which he might install himself with quite adequate comfort. These ideas contributed greatly to the secularizing of European society, pushing religion and churches to the sidelines.

The scientific discoveries also reinforced the old philosophy of natural law. This philosophy, developed by the Greeks and renewed in the Middle Ages, held that the universe is fundamentally orderly, and that there is a natural rightness or justice, universally the same for all people, and knowable by reason. It was very important in political theory, where it stood out against arbitrariness and the mere claims of power. The laws of nature as discovered by science were somewhat different, but they taught the same lesson, namely, the orderliness and minute regularity of the world. It was reassuring to feel that everywhere throughout an infinite space, whether or not yet discovered and probed by man, every particle of matter was quietly attracting every other particle by a force proportionate to the product of the masses and inversely proportional to the square of the distance. The physical universe laid bare by science—orderly, rational, balanced, smoothly running, without strife or rivalry or contention—became a model on which many thinkers, as time went on, hoped to refashion human society. They hoped to make society also fulfill the rule of law.

In some ways it would be possible to exaggerate the impact of pure science. Scientists themselves did not usually apply their scientific ideas to religion and society. Few suffered the spiritual torment of Pascal. Both Descartes and Newton wrote placid tractates arguing for the truth of certain ecclesiastical doctrines. Bacon and Harvey were conservative politically, upholders of king against Parliament. The Englishman Joseph Glanvill, in the 1660s, used the Cartesian dualism to demonstrate the probable existence of witches. Descartes, despite his systematic doubt, held that the customs of one's country were to be accepted without question. Natural science, in the pure sense, was not inherently revolutionary or even upsetting. If Europeans in the seventeenth century began to waver in many old beliefs it was not only because of the stimulus of pure science, but also because of an increasing knowledge and study of man himself.

H ere one of the most potent forces at work was the discovery and exploration of the world overseas. Europe was already becoming part of the world as a whole, and could henceforth understand itself only by comparison with non-European regions. Great reciprocal influences were at work. The influences of European expansion on other parts of the world are easily seen: the Indian societies of America were modified or extinguished, the indigenous societies of Africa were dislocated and many of their members enslaved and transported; in the long run even the ancient societies of Asia were to be undermined. From the beginning the counter-influence of the rest of the world upon Europe was equally great. It took the form not only of new medicines, new diseases, new foods, new and exotic manufactures brought to Europe, and the growth of material wealth in west-European countries. It affected European thinking also. It undermined the old Europe and its ideas, just as Europe was undermining the old cultures beyond the oceans. Vast new horizons opened before Europeans in the sixteenth and seventeenth centuries. Europeans of this

32
New Knowledge
of Man and Society

period were the first men to whom it was given to know the globe as a whole, or to realize the variety of the human race and its multifarious manners and customs.

This realization was very unsettling. The realization of human differences had the effect, in Europe, of breaking what anthropologists call the "cake of custom." A new sense of the relative nature of social institutions developed. It became harder to believe in any absolute rightness of one's own ways. Montaigne, already mentioned, expressed the relativist outlook clearly, and nowhere more clearly than in his famous essay on cannibals. The cannibals, he said humorously, did in fact eat human flesh; that was their custom, and they have their customs as we have ours; they would think some of our ways odd or inhuman; peoples differ, and who are we to judge? Travelers' books spread the same message increasingly through the seventeenth century. As one of them observed (whether or not rightly), in Turkey it was the custom to shave the hair and wear the beard, in Europe to shave the beard and wear the hair; what difference does it really make? That the ways of non-Europeans might be good ways was emphasized by Jesuit missionaries. Writing from the depths of the Mississippi Valley or from China, the Jesuit fathers often dwelt on the natural goodness and mental alertness of the native peoples they encountered, perhaps hoping in this way to gain support in Europe for their missionary labors. Sometimes strange people appeared in Europe itself. In 1684 a delegation of aristocratic Siamese arrived in Paris, followed by another in 1686. The Parisians went through a fad for Siam; they recounted how the king of Siam, when asked by a missionary to turn Christian, replied that divine Providence, had it wished a single religion to prevail in the world, could easily have so arranged it. The Siamese seemed civilized, wise, philosophic; they allowed Christians to preach in their own country, whereas it was well known what would happen to a Siamese missionary who undertook to preach in Paris. China also was seen through an ideal glow. By 1700 there were even professors of Arabic, at Paris, Oxford, and Utrecht, who said that Islam was a religion to be respected, as good for Moslems as Christianity was for Christians.

Thus was created a strong current of skepticism, holding that all beliefs are relative, varying with time and place. Its greatest spokesman at the end of the century was Pierre Bayle (1647–1706). Bayle was influenced by the scientific discoveries also; not exactly that he understood them, for he was an almost purely literary scholar, but he realized that many popular beliefs were without foundation. Between 1680 and 1682 a number of comets were seen. The one of 1682 was studied by a friend of Newton's, Edmund Halley, the first man to predict the return of a comet. He identified the one of 1682 with the one observed in 1302, 1456, 1531, and 1607, and predicted its reappearance in 1757 (it appeared in 1759); it was last seen in 1910 and is still called Halley's Comet. In the 1680s people were talking of comets excitedly. Some said that comets emitted poisonous exhalations, others that they were supernatural omens of future events. Bayle, in his *Thoughts on the*

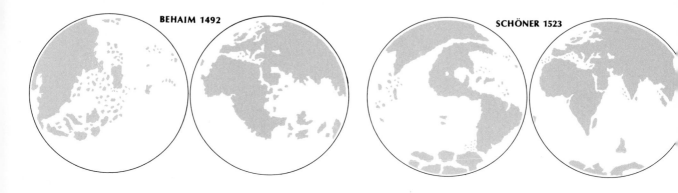

BEHAIM 1492　　　　　　　　　　　　　**SCHÖNER 1523**

The Growth of Geographical Knowledge. *The four maps show the best scientific knowledge at their respective dates. Behaim has no inkling of the existence of America and has filled in the hemisphere opposite to Europe with a mass of islands, representing what he has heard of the East Indies and Japan. He knows pretty well the limits of Africa. Schöner in 1523 fills in America and even distinguishes two American continents. He knows of the Gulf of Mexico but fails to realize the narrowness of the Isthmus of Panama. He knows of the Straits of Magellan (but not Cape Horn) and hopefully fills in a corresponding Northwest Passage in the north. His*

Comet, argued at great length that there was no basis for any such beliefs except human credulity. In 1697 he published his *Historical and Critical Dictionary,* a tremendous repository of miscellaneous lore, conveying the message that what is called truth is often mere opinion, that most people are amazingly gullible, that many things firmly believed are really ridiculous, and that it is very foolish to hold too strongly to one's own views. Bayle's *Dictionary* remained a reservoir on which skeptical writers continued to draw for generations. Bayle himself, having no firm basis in his own mind for settled judgment, mixed skepticism with an impulse to faith. Born a Protestant, he was converted to Rome, then returned to his Calvinist background. In any case his views made for toleration in religion. For Bayle, as for Montaigne, no opinion was worth burning your neighbor for.

The New Sense of Evidence

But in the study of man, as in the study of physical nature, Europeans of the seventeenth century were not generally content with skepticism. They were not possessed by a mere negative and doubting mood, important and salutary as such an attitude was. In the subjects collectively called the humanities, as in pure science, they were looking not for disbelief but for understanding. They wanted new means of telling the true from the false, a new method for arriving at some degree of certainty of conviction. And here, too, a kind of scientific view of the world arose, if that term be understood in a general sense. It took the form of a new sense of evidence. Evidence is that which allows one to believe a thing to be true, or at least

310

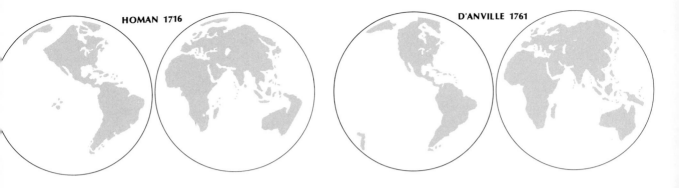

conception of the Indian Ocean is quite accurate. To Homan, two centuries later, the size and shapes of oceans and continents are well known, but he believes New Guinea joined to Australia and is frankly ignorant of the northwest coast of North America, representing it by a straight line. D'Anville in 1761 has no island of Tasmania, does not understand that Alaska is a peninsula, and believes the American polar regions to be impassable by sea. Otherwise his map is indistinguishable from one on the same scale today.

truer than something else for which the evidence is weaker. And if to believe without evidence is the sign of primitive or irrational thinking, to require evidence before believing is in a way to be scientific, or at least to trust and use the power of human intelligence.

The new sense of evidence, and of the need of evidence, revealed itself in many ways. One of the clearest was in the law. The English law of evidence, for example, began to take on its modern form at the close of the seventeenth century. Previously the belief had been that the more atrocious the crime the less evidence should be necessary in arriving at a verdict of guilty; this was thought necessary to protect society from the more hideous offenses. From the end of the seventeenth century, in English law, the judge lost his power of discretion in deciding what should constitute evidence, and the same rules of evidence were applied in all forms of accusation, the essential question being recognized as always the same—did such-and-such a fact (however outrageous) occur or did it not? After 1650 mere hearsay evidence, long vaguely distrusted, was ruled definitely out of court. After 1696 even persons charged with felony were allowed legal counsel.

The new sense of evidence was probably the main force in putting an end to the delusions of witchcraft. What made witchcraft so credible and so fearsome was that many persons confessed themselves to be witches, admitting to supernatural powers and to evil designs upon their neighbors.[5] Many or most such confessions

[5]See p. 50.

311

were extracted under torture. Reformers urged that confessions obtained under torture were not evidence, that people would say anything to escape unbearable pain, so that no quantity of such confessions offered the slightest ground for believing in witches. As for the voluntary confessions, and even the boastings of some people of their diabolical powers, it was noted that such statements often came from half-demented old women, or from persons who would today be called hysterical or psychotic. Witches came to be regarded as self-deluded. Their ideas of themselves were no longer accepted as evidence. But it must be added that, except in England, the use of legal torture lasted on through most of the eighteenth century, in criminal cases in which the judge believed the accused to be guilty.

*History and
Historical Scholarship*

What are called the historical sciences also developed rapidly at this time. History, like the law, depends on the finding and using of evidence. The historian and the judge must answer the same kind of question—did such-and-such a fact really occur? All knowledge of history, so far as it disengages itself from legend and wishful thinking, rests ultimately on pieces of evidence, written records, and other works of man created in the past and surviving in some form or other in the present. On this mass of material the vast picture of the past is built, and without it men would be ignorant of their own antecedents or would have only folk tales and tribal traditions.

There was much skepticism about history in the seventeenth century. Some said that history was not a form of true knowledge because it was not mathematical. Others said that it was useless because Adam, the perfect man, had neither had nor needed any history. Many felt that what passed for history was only a mass of fables. History was distrusted also because historians were often pretentious, claiming to be high-flying men of letters, writing for rhetorical or inspirational appeal or for argumentative reasons, disdaining the hard labor of actual study. History was losing the confidence of thinking people. How was it possible, they asked, to feel even a modicum of certainty about alleged events that had happened long before any living person had been born?

This doubting attitude itself arose from a stricter sense of evidence, or from a realization that there was really no proof for much of what was said about the past. But scholars set to work to assemble what evidence there was. They hoped to create a new history, one that should contain only reliable statements. Europe was littered with old papers and parchments. Abbeys, manor houses, royal archives were full of written documents, many of them of unknown age or unknown origin, often written in a handwriting which people could no longer read. Learned and laborious enthusiasts set to work to explore this accumulation. They added so much to the efforts of their predecessors as virtually to create modern critical scholarship and erudition. The French Benedictine monk Jean Mabillon, in 1681, in his book *On Diplomatics* (referring to ancient charters and "diplomas") established the science of paleography, which deals with the deciphering, reading, dating, and authentication

312

of manuscripts. The Frenchman DuCange in 1688 published a dictionary of medieval Latin which is still used. Others, like the Italian Muratori, spent whole lifetimes exploring archives, collecting, editing, or publishing masses of documents, comparing manuscript copies of the same text and trying to discover what the author had really said, rejecting some as fabrications or forgeries, pronouncing others to be genuine pieces of historical evidence. Others made themselves experts in ancient coins, many of which were far more ancient than the oldest manuscripts; they founded the science of numismatics. Still others, or indeed the same ones, turned to a critical examination of the inscriptions on old buildings and ruins.

Another important but little-known historical "science," namely, chronology, was greatly stimulated also. Chronology deals with the age of the world and with finding a common denominator between the dating systems of various peoples. Probably it is not natural for the human mind to think in terms of dates at all. For simple people it is enough to know that some things happened "long ago." In the seventeenth century the new interest in numbers, evident in physical science, turned also to the human past. Archbishop James Usher, an Anglican prelate of Ireland, after much study of the Bible, announced the date of 4004 B.C. as that of the creation of the world. His chronological system was later printed in the margins of the Authorized Version of the English Bible, and is still adhered to by some fundamentalists as if part of the Bible itself. But Usher's system was not accepted by scholars even in his own time. Geographical knowledge was revealing China and its dynasties to Europe; historical knowledge was beginning to discover ancient Egypt. The Chinese and Egyptian records claimed a greater antiquity for their countries than the Old Testament seemed to allow for the human race. There was much erudite conjecture; one scholar about 1700 counted seventy estimates of the age of the world, ranging as high as 170,000 years, a figure which then seemed fantastic and appalling.

The difficulty was not only in the language of the Old Testament. It was in finding the correspondence between the chronological systems of different peoples. A Chinese system of dating by dynasties might be coherent within itself, but how could it be equated with the European system of dating from the birth of Christ, a date as unknown to the Chinese as the date of Wu Wang was to Europeans? Even European records presented the same difficulty; the Romans counted by consulships, or from the supposed year of the founding of Rome; many medieval documents told only the year of some obscure ruler's reign. Only infinite patience, interminable research, and endless calculation could reduce such a jumble to the simple system of modern textbooks. This is of more importance than may be at first thought. A common system of dating is a great aid to thinking of human history as an interconnected whole. An overall conception of the human race is made easier by the dating of all events according to the Christian era. This itself, it may be pointed out, is an arbitrary and conventional scale, since Christ is now thought to have been born not in A.D. 1, but in 4 B.C.

Common dating was of importance in practical affairs as well as in historical knowledge. Europe was disunited even on the Christian calendar. Protestant and some Orthodox countries followed the old or Julian calendar, Catholic countries the corrected or Gregorian calendar, issued in the sixteenth century under authority of Pope Gregory XIII. The two calendars varied in the seventeenth century by ten days. Only gradually was the Gregorian calendar accepted, by England in 1752, by Russia in 1918. Most other peoples today, in China, India, the Arabic world, and elsewhere, use or recognize the Gregorian calendar. Without a uniform way of specifying days and years it would be less easy to transact international affairs, hold international conferences, make plans, or pay and receive money. This common dating, easily taken for granted, was a consequence of the predominance of Europe in modern times. It is a sign of growing unity in world civilization.

The Questioning of
Traditional Beliefs

The historical sciences provided a foundation on which a knowledge of man's activities in the past could be built, and the growing geographical knowledge spread a panorama of man's diverse activities and peculiarities in the present. This new knowledge of man shared with natural science, and probably derived from it, or from philosophers of science like Descartes and Bacon, the view that many traditional ideas were erroneous, but that much could be known by a disciplined use of the human mind. The humanities and the sciences were alike in demanding evidence for belief and in trusting to the power of reason. In their impact on the old certainties of European life, the studies of man exerted possibly a greater direct force than those of nature. Pascal, in his attempt to defend the Christian faith, feared the spirit of Montaigne, the mood of skepticism and denial, which he felt himself, more than he feared the findings of mathematical and physical science. And the movement of historical thought, with its insistence on textual criticism, threw doubt on much of the Christian religion, or at least on the sacred history related in the Bible, which was considered to be part and parcel of religion itself.

In 1678 a French priest, Richard Simon, published a pioneering work in Biblical criticism, his *Critical History of the Old Testament*. Though his book was condemned both by the church and by the government of Louis XIV, Richard Simon always felt himself to be orthodox; Catholic faith, he insisted, depended more on church tradition than on the literal statements of the Bible. He simply applied to the Old Testament the methods of textual criticism which others were applying to secular documents. He concluded that the Old Testament, as known, rested on medieval manuscripts many of which were of unknown or doubtful origin, that monkish copyists had brought in errors and corruptions, and that the books thought to have been written by Moses could not have been written by him, since they contained obvious contradictions and matter clearly inserted after his death. Others went further, questioning not merely the evidence of the Biblical text, but the very possibility of some events that it related. From the scientific idea of the absolute regularity of nature on the one hand, and from a strong sense of human credulity on the other, they denied that miracles had ever occurred and looked upon oracles and prophecies among either the Greeks or the Hebrews with a dubious eye.

The most profoundly disturbing of all thinkers of the time was Baruch Spinoza (1632–1677), the lens grinder of Amsterdam, a Jew who was excommunicated by his own synagogue and who refused a professorship at the University of Heidelberg, craving only the quiet to think in peace. Spinoza drew on both the scientific and humanistic thought of his day. He arrived at a philosophy holding that God had no existence apart from the world, that everything was itself an aspect of God, a philosophy technically called pantheism but considered by many to be really atheistic. He denied the inspiration of the Bible, disbelieved in miracles and the supernatural, rejected all revelation and revealed religion, Jewish or Christian, and held that few if any governments of the day were really just. He taught a pure, stern, and intellectual ethical code, and one which had few consolations for the average man. His name became a byword for impiety and horrendous unbelief. People were literally afraid to read his works, even when they could find them, which was not often because of the censorship. His influence spread slowly, through the mediation of other writers.

More widely read, less abstruse, more reassuring, dwelling on the merits of common sense, were the writings of the Englishman John Locke (1632–1704), who summarized many of the intellectual trends of his lifetime and exerted a strong influence for the following hundred years. He combined practical experience and theoretical interests. Educated in medicine, he kept in touch with the sciences and was acquainted with Newton. He was associated with the great Whig noblemen who were the main authors of the English revolution in 1688. For political reasons he spent several years in the 1680s in the Netherlands, where he became familiar with thought on the Continent. He wrote on many subjects—finance, economics, education, religious policy, political theory, general philosophy—always with an engaging directness and sober air of the sensible man of the world. In his *Letter on Toleration* (1689) he advocated an established church, but with toleration of all except Roman Catholics and atheists; these he held to be dangerous to society, the former because of a foreign allegiance, the latter because they lacked a basis of moral responsibility. In his *Reasonableness of Christianity* he argued that Christianity, rightly considered, is after all a reasonable form of religion; this softened the friction between religion and natural knowledge but tended to shut out the supernatural and merge religious feeling into an unruffled common sense.

Locke's deepest book was his *Essay Concerning the Human Understanding* (1690). Here he faced the great problem of the day, the problem of knowledge; he asked what it was possible for men to know with certainty, and how certain knowledge was arrived at. His answer was that true or certain knowledge is derived from experience—from perceptions of the sense organs and reflection of the mind on these perceptions. Locke at the end of the century thus echoed Bacon at the beginning; they became the two great pillars of empirical philosophy, insisting on experience and observation as the source of truth. Locke denied Descartes' doctrine of innate ideas, or inevitable disposition of the human mind to think in certain ways. He held that the mind at birth is a blank tablet or *tabula rasa,* and that what a man comes to think or believe depends on the environment in which he lives. Locke's environmentalist philosophy became fundamental to liberal and reforming thought in later years. It seemed that false ideas or superstitions were the result of bad environment and bad education. It seemed that the evil in human actions was due to bad social institutions, and that an improvement in human society would improve human behavior. This philosophy, whether or not wholly true in the final analysis, was largely true with respect to many practical conditions. It gave confidence in the possibility of social progress and turned attention to a sphere in which planned and constructive action was possible, namely, the sphere of government, public policy, and legislation. Here we touch on political theory, to which Locke contributed *Two Treatises of Government.* These are discussed below.

33
Political Theory:
The School of
Natural Law

Political theory can never be strictly scientific. Science deals with what does exist or has existed. It does not tell what ought to exist. To tell what society and government ought to be like, in view of man's nature and his capacity to be miserable or contented, is a main purpose of political theory. Political theory is in a sense more practical than science. It is the scientists and scholars who are most content to observe facts as they are. Practical men, and scientists and scholars so far as they have practical interests, must always ask themselves what ought to be done, what policies ought to be adopted, what measures taken, what state of affairs maintained or brought about. Conservatives and radicals, traditionalists and innovators, are alike in this respect. It is impossible in human affairs to escape the word "ought."

But political theory was affected by the scientific view. The Renaissance Italian, Niccolò Machiavelli (1469–1527), had opened the way in this direction.[6] Machiavelli too had his "ought"; he preferred a republican form of government in which citizens felt a patriotic attachment to their state. But in his book, *The Prince,* he disregarded the question of the best form of government, a favorite question of Christian and scholastic philosophers of the Middle Ages. He separated the study of politics from theology and moral philosophy. He undertook to describe how governments and rulers actually behaved. He observed that successful rulers behaved as if holding or increasing power were their only object, that they regarded all else as means to this end. Princes, said Machiavelli, kept their promises or broke them, they told the truth or distorted or colored it, they sought popularity or ignored it, they advanced public welfare or disrupted it, they conciliated their neighbors or destroyed them, depending merely on which course of action seemed the best means of advancing their political interests. All this was bad, said Machiavelli; but that was not the question, for the question was to find out what rulers really did. Machiavelli, in *The Prince,* chose to be nonmoral in order to be scientific. To most readers he seemed to be simply immoral. Nor was it possible to draw the line between *The Prince* as a scientific description of fact and *The Prince* as a book of maxims of conduct. In telling how

[6]See pp. 64–65.

successful rulers obtained their successes, Machiavelli also suggested how rulers *ought* to proceed. And though governments did in fact continue to behave for the most part as Machiavelli said, most people refused to admit that they ought to.

Political theory in the seventeenth century did not embrace the cynicism attributed to Machiavelli. Nor did it fall into the skepticism of those who said that the customs of one's country should be passively accepted, or that one form of government was about as good as another. It directly faced the question, What is right? The seventeenth century was the classic age of the philosophy of natural right or of natural law.

The idea of natural law has underlain a good deal of modern democratic development, and its decline in the last century has been closely connected with many of the troubles of recent times. It is not easy to say in what the philosophy of natural law essentially consisted. It held that there is, somehow, in the structure of the world, a law that distinguishes right from wrong. It held that right is "natural," not a mere invention of men. This right is not determined, for any country, by its heritage, tradition, or customs, nor yet by its actual laws (called "positive" laws) of the kind that are enforced in the law courts. All these may be unfair or unjust. We detect unfairness or injustice in them by comparing them with natural law as we understand it; thus we have a basis for saying that cannibalism is bad, or that a law requiring forced labor from orphan children is unjust. Nor is natural law, or the real rightness of a thing, determined by the authority of any person or people. No king can make right that which is wrong. No people, by its will as a people, can make just that which is unjust. Right and law, in the ultimate sense, exist outside and above all peoples. They are universal, the same for all. No one can make them up to suit himself. A good king, or a just people, is a king or people whose actions correspond to the objective standard. But how, if we cannot trust our own positive laws or customs, or our leaders or even our collective selves, can we know what is naturally right? How do we discover natural law? The answer, in the natural law philosophy, is that we discover it by reason. Man is considered to be a rational animal. And all men are assumed to have, at least potentially and when better enlightened, the same powers of reason and understanding—Germans or English, Siamese or Europeans. This view favored a cosmopolitan outlook and made international agreement and general world progress seem realizable goals. As time went on, the premises of this philosophy came to be questioned. By the twentieth century it was widely thought that man was not an especially rational being but was motivated by drives or urges or instincts, and that human differences were so fundamental that men of different nationalities or classes could never expect to see things in the same way. When this happened the older philosophy of natural law lost its hold on many minds.

In the seventeenth and eighteenth centuries it was generally accepted. Some, carrying over the philosophy of the Middle Ages, thought of natural law as an aspect of the law of God. Others, more secular in spirit, held that the natural law stood of itself. These included even some churchmen; a group of theologians, mainly Jesuits, were condemned by the pope in 1690 for holding that universal right and wrong might exist by reason only, whether God existed or not. The idea of natural law and the faith in human reason went side by side, and both were fundamental in the thought of the time. They were to be found everywhere in Europe, in their religious or their secular form.

On the basis of natural law some thinkers tried to create an international law or "law of nations," to bring order into the maze of sovereign territorial states, great and small, that was developing in Europe. Hugo Grotius, in 1625, published the first great book devoted exclusively to this subject, his *Law of War and Peace.* Samuel Pufendorf followed with his *Law of Nature and of Nations* in 1672. Both held that sovereign states, though bound by no positive law or authority, should work together for the common good, that there was a community of nations as of individuals, and that in the absence of a higher international sovereignty they were all still subordinate to natural reason and justice. Certain concrete doctrines, such as the freedom of the seas or the immunity of ambassadors, were put forward. The principles of international law remained those of natural law. The content came to include specific agreements between governments, certain kinds of admiralty and maritime law, and the terms of treaties such as the treaties of Westphalia, Utrecht, and others. The means of enforcement, to be sure, remained weak or nonexistent in crises.

Hobbes and Locke   In domestic affairs the philosophy of natural law, though it rather favored constitutionalism, was used to justify both constitutional and absolutist governments. Right itself was held to be in the nature of things, beyond human power to change. But forms of government were held to be means to an end. No philosopher at the time thought the state to have an absolute value in itself. The state had to be "justified," made acceptable to the moral consciousness or the reason. There were, indeed, important competing philosophies. On the side of absolutism was the doctrine of the divine right of kings. On the side of constitutionalism were arguments based on heritage or custom, emphasizing the charters, bulls, or compacts of former times and the historic powers of parliaments and estates. But neither the supernatural argument of the divine right of kings, nor the historical argument pointing back to liberties of the Middle Ages, was entirely satisfactory in the scientific atmosphere of the seventeenth century. Neither carried complete conviction to the reason or moral sense of the most acute thinkers. Both were reinforced by arguments of natural law. Two Englishmen stand out above all others in this connection. Absolutism was philosophically justified by Thomas Hobbes, constitutionalism by John Locke.

Hobbes (1588–1679) followed the scientific and mathematical discoveries of his time with more than an amateur interest. In philosophy he held to a materialistic and even atheistic system. In English politics he sided with king against Parliament; he disliked the disorder and violence of the civil war of the 1640s and the unstable conditions of the English republic of the 1650s.[7] He concluded that men have no capacity for self-government. His opinion of human nature was low; he held that men in the "state of nature," or as imagined to exist without government, were quarrelsome and turbulent, forever locked in a war of all against all. In his famous phrase, life in the state of nature was "solitary, poor, nasty, brutish and short." From fear of each other, to obtain order, and enjoy the advantages of law and right, men came to a kind of agreement or "contract" by which they surrendered their freedom of action into the hands of a ruler. It was necessary for this ruler to have unrestricted or absolute power. Only thus could he maintain order. It was intolerably dangerous, according to Hobbes, for anyone to question the actions of government, for such questioning might reopen the way to chaos. Government must in fact be a kind of Leviathan (the monster mentioned in the Bible, Job 41); and it was by the word *Leviathan* that Hobbes entitled his principal book, published in 1651, two years after the execution of King Charles I.

By this book Hobbes became the leading secular exponent of absolutism and one of the principal theorists of the unlimited sovereignty of the state. His influence on later thinkers was very great. He accustomed political theorists to the use of purely natural arguments. He quoted freely from the Bible, but the Bible had no influence on his thought. After Hobbes, all advanced political theorists regarded government as a thing created by human purpose. It was no longer considered, except popularly and except by professional theologians, as part of a divine dispensation of God to man. Hobbes also affected later theorists by his arguments for a sovereign authority, and, more negatively, by obliging them to refute his idea of an unlimited personal sovereign. But he was never a popular writer. In England the cause which he favored was lost. In those Continental countries where royal absolutism prevailed his arguments were received with secret gratification, but his irreligion was too dangerous to make public, and the absolutist argument, on the popular level, remained that of the divine right of kings. In any case Hobbes's arguments were in some ways insufficient for real monarchs. Hobbes abhorred struggle and violence. His case for absolutism required absolutism to produce civil peace, individual security, and a rule of law. He also held that absolute power depended on, or had at least originated in, a free and rational agreement by which people accepted it. An absolute monarchy that flagrantly violated these conditions could with difficulty be justified even by the doctrines of Hobbes. It is in these respects that Hobbes differs from totalitarian theorists of recent times. For Hobbes, in the final analysis, absolute power was an expedient to promote individual welfare. It was a means necessary to the realization of natural law.

John Locke (1632–1704), as has been seen, also stood in the main current of scientific thought and discovery. But in his political philosophy he carried over many ideas of the Middle Ages, as formulated in the thirteenth century by St. Thomas Aquinas [8] and kept alive in England by successive thinkers of the Anglican church. Medieval philosophy had never favored an absolute power. With Hobbes,

[7] See pp. 179–181.
[8] See pp. 38–40.

Locke shared the idea that good government is an expedient of human purpose, neither provided by divine Providence nor inherited by a national tradition. He held, too, like Hobbes and the whole school of natural law, that government was based on a kind of contract, or rational and conscious agreement upon which authority was based. In contrast to Hobbes, he sided with Parliament against king in the practical struggles of politics. About 1680, in the course of these disputes, he wrote *Two Treatises of Government*, which however were not published until shortly after the parliamentary revolution of 1688–1689.[9]

Locke took a more genial view of human nature than Hobbes. As he showed in his other books, he believed that a moderate religion was a good thing, and above all that men could learn from experience and hence could be educated to an enlightened way of life. These ideas favored a belief in self-government. Locke declared (in contradiction to Hobbes) that men in the "state of nature" were reasonable and well disposed, willing to get along with one another though handicapped by the absence of public authority. Men likewise had a moral sense, quite independently of government; and they also possessed by nature certain rights, quite apart from the state. These rights were the rights to life, liberty, and property. Locke threw very heavy emphasis on the right of property, by which he usually meant the possession of land. His philosophy can in fact be regarded as an expression of the landed classes of England in their claims against the king; it should be noted that land ownership in England was more widespread in 1690 than it later became. Men, as individuals in the state of nature, are not altogether able, according to Locke, to win general respect for their individual natural rights. They cannot by their own efforts protect what is "proper" to them, i.e., their property. They agree to set up government to enforce observance of the rights of all. Government is thus created by a contract, but the contract is not unconditional, as claimed by Hobbes. It imposes mutual obligations. The people must be reasonable; only rational beings can be politically free. Liberty is not an anarchy of undisciplined will; it is the freedom to act without compulsion by another. Only rational and responsible creatures can exercise true freedom; but adult human beings, according to Locke, are or can be educated to be rational and responsible. They therefore can and should be free. On government, also, certain conditions and obligations are imposed. If a government breaks the contract, if it threatens the natural rights which it is the sole purpose of government to protect, if, for example, it takes away a man's property without his consent, then the governed have a right to reconsider what they have done in creating the government and may even in the last extremity rebel against it. The right to resist government, Locke admits, is very dangerous, but it is less dangerous than its opposite, which would lead to enslavement; and in any case we are talking about reasonable and responsible people.

If Locke's ideas seem familiar, especially to Americans, it is because of the wide popularizing of his philosophy in the century after his death. Nowhere was

[9]See pp. 183–187.

his influence greater than in the British colonies. The authors of the American Declaration of Independence and of the Constitution of the United States knew the writings of Locke very thoroughly. Some phrases of the Declaration of Independence echo his very language. In Great Britain also, and in France and elsewhere, in the course of time, Locke's influence was immense.

What Locke did was to convert an episode in English history into an event of universal meaning. In England, in 1688, certain great lords, winning the support of the established church, gentry, and merchants, put out one king and brought in another. On the new king they imposed certain obligations, specified in the Bill of Rights of 1689, and all dealing with legal or technical interpretations of the English constitution. The revolution of 1688 was a very English affair. England in 1688 was still little known to the rest of Europe. The proceedings in England, so far as known, might seem no different from a rebellion of the magnates of Hungary. Locke, in arguing that Parliament had done right to eject James II, put the whole affair on a level of reason, natural right, and human nature. It thus came to have meaning for everyone. At the same time, Locke made the English Revolution a sign of progress rather than reaction. The new and modern form of government in 1690 was royal absolutism, with its professional bureaucracy and corps of paid officials. Almost everywhere there was resistance to the kings, led by landed interests and harking back to earlier freedoms. Such resistance seemed to many Europeans to be feudal and medieval. Locke made the form taken by such resistance in England, namely, the revolution of 1688 against James II, into a modern and forward-looking move. He checked the prestige of absolutism. He gave new prestige to constitutional principles. He carried over, in modified form, many ideas from the scholastic philosophers of the Middle Ages, who had generally maintained that kings had only a relative and restricted power and were responsible to their peoples. To these ideas he added the force of the newer scientific view of the world. He did not rest his case on supernatural or providential arguments. He did not say that constitutional government was the will of God. He said that it rested on experience and observation of human nature, on recognition of certain individual rights and especially the right of property, and on the existence of a purely natural law of reason and justice. He was an almost entirely secular thinker.

One must not claim too much for Locke, or for any writer. England was in fact, in 1688, more modern in many ways than other countries in Europe. The Glorious Revolution was in fact not exactly like uprisings of the landed and propertied classes elsewhere. England in the following century did in fact create a form of parliamentary government that was unique. But facts go together with the theories that give them an understandable meaning. Events in England, as explained by Locke, and as seen in other countries and even in England and its colonies through Locke's eyes, launched into the main stream of modern history the superb tradition of constitutional government, which has been one of the main themes in the history of the modern world ever since.

By 1700, at the close of the "century of genius," some beliefs that were to be characteristic of modern times had clearly taken form, notably a faith in science, in human reason, in natural human rights, and in progress. The following period, generally known as the Age of Enlightenment, was to be a time of clarifying and popularizing ideas which the more creative seventeenth century had produced. These ideas were eventually to revolutionize Europe, America, and the world. They were also in subsequent years to be modified, amended, challenged, and even denied. But they are still very much alive today.

VIII: THE AGE OF ENLIGHTEN

MENT

The eighteenth century, or at least the years of that century preceding the French Revolution of 1789, is commonly known as the Age of Enlightenment, and though that name has more than the usual difficulties by which such sobriquets are always attended, still there is no other that describes so many features of the time so well. People strongly felt that theirs was an enlightened age, and it is from their own evaluation of themselves that our term Age of Enlightenment is derived. Everywhere there was a feeling that Europeans had at last emerged from a long twilight. The past was regarded as a time of barbarism and darkness. The sense of progress was all but universal among the educated classes. It was the belief both of the forward-looking thinkers and writers known as the philosophes and of the forward-looking kings and empresses, the "enlightened despots," together with their ministers and officials.

Chapter Emblem: A French snuff-box showing miniature portraits on tortoiseshell of three famous philosophers, Voltaire, Rousseau, and Benjamin Franklin.   325

The spirit of the eighteenth-century Enlightenment was drawn from the scientific and intellectual revolution of the seventeenth century. The Enlightenment carried over and popularized the ideas of Bacon and Descartes, of Bayle and Spinoza, and, above all, of Locke and Newton. It carried over the philosophy of natural law and of natural right. Never was there an age so skeptical toward tradition, so confident in the powers of human reason and of science, so firmly convinced of the regularity and harmony of nature, and so deeply imbued with the sense of civilization's advance and progress.

The idea of progress is often said to be the dominant or characteristic idea of European civilization from the seventeenth century to the twentieth. It is a belief, a kind of nonreligious faith, that the conditions of human life become better as time goes on, that in general each generation is better off than its predecessors and will contribute by its labors to an even better life for generations to come, and that in the long run all mankind will share in the same advance. All the elements of this belief had been present by 1700. It was after 1700, however, that the idea of progress became explicit. In the seventeenth century it had shown itself in a more rudimentary way, in a sporadic dispute, among men of letters in England and France, known as the quarrel of Ancients and Moderns. The Ancients held that the works of the Greeks and Romans had never been surpassed. The Moderns, pointing to science, art, literature, and invention, declared that their own time was the best, that it was natural for men of their time to do better than the ancients because they came later and built upon their predecessors' achievements. The quarrel was never exactly settled, but a great many people in 1700 were Moderns. Europeans had always felt themselves better off than the ancients in being Christians where the ancients were pagans. Now, for the first time in the history of Europe, a great many Europeans felt that in purely worldly ways they had outdone the noble Greeks and Romans. And many felt that this progress need never cease.

Far-reaching also was the faith of the age in the natural faculties of the human mind. Pure skepticism, the negation of reason, was overcome. Nor were the educated, after 1700, likely to be superstitious, terrified by the unknown, or addicted to magic. The witchcraft mania abruptly died. Indeed all sense of the supernatural became dim. "Modern" people not only ceased to fear the devil; they ceased also to fear God. They thought of God less as a Father than as a First Cause of the physical universe. There was less sense of a personal God, or of the inscrutable imminence of divine Providence, or of man's need for saving grace. God was less the God of Love; He was the inconceivably intelligent being who had made the amazing universe now discovered by man's reason. The great symbol of the Christian God was the Cross, on which a divine being had suffered in human form. The symbol which occurred to people of scientific view was the Watchmaker. The intricacies of the physical universe were compared to the intricacies of a watch, and it was argued that just as a watch could not exist without a watchmaker, so the universe as discovered by Newton could not exist without a God who created it and set it moving by its mathematical law. It was almighty intelligence that was thought divine.

All this promoted the spirit of secularism in Europe. Intellectual developments reinforced social and economic causes in turning people away from the old religion. Churches and churchmen lost out in leadership and prestige. Economics and politics, business and the state, were no longer subordinated to religious ends. They threw off the restraints imposed by moral or religious judgments. At the same time religious toleration spread. Persecution of religious minorities became less common. In any case, in their attempts to enforce acceptance of religious doctrine, churches no longer used the barbaric methods of former times, such as the fagot and the stake. Barbaric methods as used by the state, against persons suspected or convicted of crimes or political offenses, also came increasingly into disrepute.

It was through the philosophes that the ideas of the Enlightenment were spread. The philosophes were not essentially philosophers in the usual sense of the word. They were rather popularizers or publicists. They read the great books which most people did not read and reworded the ideas in such a way as to hold the interest of the average reader. They were primarily "men of letters." Formerly authors had generally been gentlemen of leisure, or talented protégés of aristocratic or royal patrons, or professors or clerics supported by the income from religious foundations. In the Age of Enlightenment a great many were free-lancers, grub-streeters, or journalists. They wrote for "the publick."

The reading public had greatly expanded. The educated middle class, commercial and professional, was much larger than ever before. Country gentlemen were putting off their rustic habits, and even noblemen wished to keep informed. Newspapers and magazines multiplied, and people who could not read them at home could read them in coffee houses or in reading rooms organized for that purpose. There was a great demand also for dictionaries, encyclopedias, and surveys of all fields of knowledge. The new readers wanted matters made interesting and clear. They appreciated wit and lightness of touch. From such a public, literature itself greatly benefited. The style of the eighteenth century became admirably fluent, clear, and exact, neither ponderous on the one hand nor frothy on the other. And from writings of this kind the readers benefited also, from the interior of Europe to the America of Benjamin Franklin. The bourgeois middle class was becoming not only educated but thoughtful. But the movement was not a class movement only.

There was another way in which writings of the day were affected by social conditions. They were all written under censorship. The theory of censorship was to protect people from harmful ideas as they were protected from shoddy merchandise or dishonest weights and measures. In England the censorship was so mild as to have little effect. Other countries, such as Spain, had a powerful censorship but few original writers. France, the center of the Enlightenment, had both a complicated censorship and a large reading and writing public. The church, the Parliament of Paris, the royal officials, and the printers' gilds all had a hand in the censoring of books. French censorship, however, was very loosely administered, and after 1750 writers were disturbed by it very little. It cannot be compared to censorship in some countries in the twentieth century. Yet in one way it had an unfavorable effect on French thought and letters. It discouraged writers from addressing themselves, in a common-sense way, to a serious consideration of concrete public questions. Legally forbidden to criticize church or state, they threw their criticisms on an abstract level. Debarred from attacking things in particular, they tended to attack things in general. Or they talked of the customs of the Persians and the Iroquois but not the French. Their works became full of double meanings, sly digs, innuendoes, and jokes, by which an author, if questioned, could declare that he did not mean what all the world knew he did mean. As for readers, they developed a taste for forbidden books, which were always easy enough to obtain through illicit channels. No one wanted to read merely authorized literature, and Parisians who heard that a book was frowned upon by the archbishop or the Parliament could hardly wait to read it and talk about it. Ideas were prized because they were daring, or even merely naughty. French thought was made radical by the halfway measures used to control it.

Paris was the heart of the movement. There ladies in their *salons* held evening parties at which wits, men of letters, and people of society talked brilliantly on many topics. In Paris, too, was published the most serious of all philosophe enterprises, the *Encyclopédie,* edited by Denis Diderot in seventeen large volumes and completed over the years 1751 to 1772. It was a great compendium of scientific, technical, and historical knowledge, carrying a strong undertone of criticism of existing society and institutions and epitomizing the skeptical, rational, and scientific spirit of the age. It was not the first encyclopedia, but it was the first to have a distinguished list of contributors or to be conceived as a positive force for social progress. Virtually all the French philosophes contributed—Voltaire, Montesquieu, Rousseau, d'Alembert (who assisted in the editing), Buffon, Turgot, Quesnay, and many others, all sometimes collectively called the Encyclopedists.

Another group of thinkers was the Physiocrats, whom their critics called "economists," a word originally thought to be mildly insulting. They included Quesnay, physician to Louis XV, Turgot, minister to Louis XVI, and Dupont de Nemours, founder of the industrial family of the Du Ponts in the United States. The Physiocrats concerned themselves with fiscal and tax reform, and with measures to increase the national wealth of France. The first to use the term *laissez faire* ("let things alone"), they believed that wealth would increase if there were greater freedom for investment and for the trade and circulation of goods, though they insisted on the planning authority of an "enlightened" government.

Men and women who considered themselves philosophes, or close to the philosophes in spirit, were found all over Europe. Frederick the Great was an eminent philosophe; not only was he the friend of Voltaire and host to a circle of literary and scientific men at Potsdam, but he himself wrote epigrams, satires, dissertations, and histories, as well as works on military science, and he had a gift of wit, a sharp tongue, and a certain impishness toward the traditional and the pompous. Catherine the Great, empress of Russia, was also a philosophe for much the same reasons. Maria Theresa, of Austria, was not a philosophe; she was too religious and too little concerned with general ideas. Her son Joseph, on the other hand, as we shall see, proved to be a philosophe enthroned. In England Bishop Warburton was considered by some of his friends as a philosophe; he held that the Church of England of his day, as a social institution, was exactly what pure reason would have invented. The Scottish skeptical philosopher David Hume counted as a philosophe, as did Edward Gibbon, who shocked the pious by his attacks on Christianity in his famous *Decline and Fall of the Roman Empire*. Dr. Samuel Johnson was not a philosophe; he worried over the supernatural, adhered to the established church, deflated pretentious authors, and even declared that Voltaire and Rousseau were bad men who should be sent "to the plantations." There were also Italian and German philosophes, like the Marquis di Beccaria who sought to humanize the criminal law, or Baron Grimm who sent a literary newsletter from Paris to his many subscribers.

Most famous of all philosophes were the French trio, Montesquieu (1689–1755), Voltaire (1694–1778), and Rousseau (1712–1778). They differed vehemently with each other. All were hailed as literary geniuses in their own day. All turned from pure literature to works of political commentary and social protest. All thought that the existing state of society could be improved.

Montesquieu, twice a baron, was a landed aristocrat, *seigneur* or manorial lord of southern France. He inherited from his uncle a seat in the Parliament of Bordeaux and sat actively in that parliament in the days of the Regency.[1] He was part of the noble resurgence which followed the death of Louis XIV and continued on through the eighteenth century. Although he shared many of the ideas in the stream of aristocratic and antiabsolutist thought, he went beyond a mere self-centered class philosophy. In his great work, *The Spirit of Laws*, published in 1748, he developed two principal ideas. One was that forms of government varied according to climate and circumstances, for example, that despotism was suited only to large empires in hot climates, and that democracy would work only in small city-states. His other great doctrine, aimed against royal absolutism in France (which he called "despotism"), was the separation and balance of powers. In France he believed that power should be divided between the king and a great many "intermediate bodies"—parliaments, provincial estates, organized nobility, chartered towns, and even the church. It was natural for him, a judge in parliament, a provincial and a nobleman, to favor the first three and reasonable for him to recognize the position of the bourgeoisie of the towns; as for the church, he observed that, while he took no stock in its teachings, he thought it useful as an offset to undue centralization of government. He greatly admired the English constitution as he understood it, believing that England carried over, more successfully than any other country, the feudal liberties of the early Middle Ages. He

[1] See p. 274.

thought that in England the necessary separation and balance of powers was obtained by an ingenious mixture of monarchy, aristocracy, and democracy (king, lords, and commons) and by a separation of the functions of the executive, legislature, and judiciary. This doctrine had a wide influence and was well known to the Americans who in 1787 wrote the Constitution of the United States. Montesquieu's own philosophe friends thought him too conservative and even tried to dissuade him from publishing his ideas. He was, indeed, technically a reactionary, favoring a scheme of things that antedated Louis XIV, and he was unusual among contemporaries in his admiration of the "barbarous" Middle Ages.

Voltaire was born in 1694 into a comfortable bourgeois family and christened François-Marie Arouet; "'Voltaire," an invented word, is simply the most famous of all pen names. Until he was over forty he was known only as a smart writer of epigrams, tragedies in verse, and an epic. Thereafter he turned increasingly to philosophical and public questions. His strength throughout lay in the facility of his pen. He is the easiest of all great writers to read. He was always trenchant, logical, and incisive, sometimes scurrilous; mocking and sarcastic when he wished, equally a master of deft irony and of withering ridicule. However serious in his purpose, he achieved it by creating a laugh.

In his youth Voltaire spent eleven months in the Bastille for what was considered to be impertinence to the Regent, who, however, in the next year rewarded him with a pension for one of his dramas. He was again arrested after a fracas with a nobleman, the Chevalier de Rohan. He remained an incorrigible bourgeois, while never deeply objecting to the aristocracy on principle. Through his admirer Mme. de Pompadour (another bourgeois, though the king's favorite) he became a gentleman of the bedchamber and royal historian to Louis XV. These functions he fulfilled *in absentia*, when at all, for Paris and Versailles were too hot for him. He was the personal friend of Frederick the Great, with whom he lived for about two years at Potsdam. The two finally quarreled, for no stage was big enough to hold two such prima donnas for very long. Voltaire made a fortune from his writings, pensions, speculations, and practical business sense. In his later years he purchased a manor at Ferney near the Swiss frontier. Here he became, as he said, the "hotel keeper of Europe," receiving the streams of distinguished admirers, favor hunters, and distressed persons who came to seek him out. He died at Paris in 1778, at the age of eighty-four, by far the most famous man of letters in Europe. His collected writings fill over seventy volumes.

Voltaire was mainly interested in the freedom of thought. Like Montesquieu, he was an admirer of England. He spent three years in that country, where, in 1727, he witnessed the state funeral accorded to Sir Isaac Newton and his burial in Westminster Abbey. Voltaire's *Philosophical Letters on the English* (1733) and *Elements of the Philosophy of Newton* (1738) not only brought England increasingly before the consciousness of the rest of Europe, but also popularized the new scientific ideas—the inductive philosophy of Bacon, the physics of Newton, and the sensationalist psychology of Locke,[2] whose doctrine that all true ideas arose from sense experience

[2] See pp. 315–316.

undercut the authority of religious belief. What Voltaire mainly admired in England was its religious liberty, its relative freedom of the press, and the high regard paid to men of letters like himself. Political liberty concerned him much less than it did Montesquieu. Louis XIV, a villain for Montesquieu and the neo-aristocratic school, was a hero for Voltaire, who wrote a laudatory *Age of Louis XIV* (1751) praising the Sun King for the splendor of art and literature in his reign. Voltaire likewise continued to esteem Frederick the Great, though he quarreled with him personally. Frederick was in fact almost his ideal of the enlightened ruler, a man who sponsored the arts and sciences, recognized no religious authority, and granted toleration to all creeds, welcoming Protestants and Catholics on equal terms if only they would be socially useful.

After about 1740 Voltaire became more definitely the crusader, preaching the cause of religious toleration. He fought to clear the memory of Jean Calas, a Protestant put to death on the charge of murdering a son to prevent his conversion to Rome. He wrote also to exonerate a youth named La Barre, who had been executed for defiling a wayside cross. *Écrasez l'infâme!* became the famous Voltairean war cry—"crush the infamous thing!" The *infâme* for him was bigotry, intolerance, and superstition, and behind these the power of an organized clergy. He assaulted not only the Catholic church but the whole traditional Christian view of the world. He argued for "natural religion" and "natural morality," holding that belief in God and the difference between good and evil arose from reason itself. This doctrine had in fact long been taught by the Catholic church. But Voltaire insisted that no supernatural revelation in addition to reason was desirable or necessary, or rather, that belief in a special supernatural revelation made men intolerant, stupid, and cruel. He was the first to present a purely secular conception of world history. In his *Essai sur les moeurs,* or "Universal History," he began with ancient China and surveyed the great civilizations in turn. Earlier writers of world history had put human events within a Christian framework. Following the Bible, they began with the Creation, proceeded to the Fall, recounted the rise of Israel and so on. Voltaire put Judeo-Christian history within a sociological framework. He represented Christianity and all other organized religions as social phenomena or mere human opinions. Spinoza had said as much; Voltaire spread these ideas through Europe.

In matters of politics and self-government Voltaire was neither a liberal nor a democrat. His opinion of the human race was about as low as his friend Frederick's. If only a government was enlightened he did not care how powerful it was. By an enlightened government he meant one that fought against sloth and stupidity, kept the clergy in a subordinate place, allowed freedom of thought and religion, and advanced the cause of material and technical progress. He had no developed political theory, but his ideal for large civilized countries approached that of enlightened or rational despotism. Believing that only a few could be enlightened, he thought that these few, a king and his advisers, should have the power to carry their program against all opposition. To overcome ignorance, habit, credulity, and priestcraft it was necessary for the state to be strong. It may be said that what Voltaire most desired was liberty for the enlightened.

Jean-Jacques Rousseau was very different. Born in Geneva in 1712, he was a Swiss, a Protestant, and almost of lower-class origin. He never felt at ease in France or in Paris society. Neglected as a child, a runaway at sixteen, he lived for years by odd jobs, such as copying music, and not until the age of forty did he have any success as a writer. He was always the little man, the outsider. In addition, his sex life was unsatisfactory; he finally settled down with an uneducated girl named Thérèse Levasseur, and with her mother, who kept interfering with his affairs. By Thérèse he had five children, whom he deposited at an orphanage. He had no social status, no money, and no sense of money, and after he became famous he lived largely by the generosity of his friends. He was pathetically and painfully maladjusted. He came to feel that he could trust no one, that those who tried to befriend him were deriding or betraying him behind his back. He suffered from what would now be termed complexes; possibly he was paranoiac. He talked endlessly of his own virtue and innocence and complained bitterly that he was misunderstood.

But unbalanced though he was, he was possibly the most profound writer of the age and was certainly the most permanently influential. Rousseau felt, from his own experience, that in society as it existed a good man could not be happy. He therefore attacked society, declaring that it was artificial and corrupt. He even attacked reason, calling it a false guide when followed alone. He felt doubts on all the progress which gave satisfaction to his contemporaries. In two "discourses," one on the *Arts and Sciences* (1750), the other on the *Origin of Inequality Among Men* (1753), he argued that civilization was the source of much evil, and that life in a "state of nature," were it only possible, would be much better. As Voltaire said, when Rousseau sent him a copy of his second discourse (Voltaire who relished civilization in every form), it made him "feel like going on all fours." To Rousseau the best traits of human character, such as kindness, unselfishness, honesty, and true understanding, were products of nature. Deep below reason, he sensed the presence of feeling. He delighted in the warmth of sympathy, the quick flash of intuition, the clear message of conscience. He was religious by temperament, for though he believed in no church, no clergy, and no revelation he had a respect for the Bible, a reverent awe toward the cosmos, a love of solitary meditation, and a belief in a God who was not merely a "first cause" but also a God of love and beauty. Rousseau thus made it easier for serious-minded people to slip away from orthodoxy and all forms of churchly discipline. He was feared by the churches as the most dangerous of all "infidels" and was condemned both in Catholic France and at Protestant Geneva.

In general, in most of his books, Rousseau, unlike so many of his contemporaries, gave the impression that impulse is more reliable than considered judgment, spontaneous feeling more to be trusted than critical thought. Mystical insights were for him more truthful than rational or clear ideas. He became the "man of feeling," the "child of nature," the forerunner of the coming age of romanticism, and an important source of all modern emphasis on the nonrational and the subconscious.

In the *Social Contract* (1762) Rousseau seemed to contradict all this. In it he held, somewhat like Hobbes,[3] that the "state of nature" was a brutish condition without law

[3] See pp. 318–319.

or morality. In other works he had held that the badness of men was due to the evils of society. He now held that good men could be produced only by an improved society. Earlier thinkers, such as John Locke, for example, had thought of the "contract" as an agreement between a ruler and a people. Rousseau thought of it as an agreement among the people themselves. It was a social, not merely a political, contract. Organized civil society, i.e., the community, rested upon it. It was an understanding by which all individuals surrendered their natural liberty to each other, fused their individual wills into a combined General Will, and agreed to accept the rulings of this General Will as final. This General Will was the sovereign; and true sovereign power, rightly understood, was "absolute," "sacred," and "inviolable." Government was secondary; kings, officials, or elected representatives were only delegates of a sovereign people. Rousseau devoted many difficult and abstruse pages to explaining how the *real* General Will could be known. It was not necessarily determined by vote of a majority. "What generalizes the will," he said, "is not the number of voices but the common interest that unites them." He said little of the mechanism of government and had no admiration for parliamentary institutions. He was concerned with something deeper. Maladjusted outsider that he was, he craved a commonwealth in which every person could feel that he belonged. He wished a state in which all persons had a sense of membership and participation.

By these ideas Rousseau made himself the prophet of both democracy and nationalism. Indeed, in his *Considerations on Poland,* written at the request of Poles who were fighting against the partitions, Rousseau applied the ideas of the *Social Contract* in more concrete form and became the first systematic theorist of a conscious and calculated nationalism.[4] In writing the *Social Contract* he had in mind a small city-state like his native Geneva. But what he did, in effect, was to generalize and make applicable to large territories the psychology of small city republics—the sense of membership, of community and fellowship, of responsible citizenship and intimate participation in public affairs—in short, of common will. All modern states, democratic or undemocratic, strive to impart this sense of moral solidarity to their peoples. Whereas in democratic states the General Will can in some way be identified with the sovereignty of the people, in dictatorships it becomes possible for individuals (or parties) to arrogate to themselves the right to serve as spokesmen and interpreters of the General Will. Both totalitarians and democrats have regarded Rousseau as one of their prophets.

The *Social Contract* was little read and almost unknown in its own time. Rousseau's influence on his contemporaries was spread by his other writings and especially his novels, *Émile* (1762) and the *Nouvelle Héloïse* (1760). The novels were widely read in all literate classes of society, especially by the women, who made a kind of cult of Jean-Jacques, while he was living and after his death, which occurred in 1778. He was a literary master, able to evoke shades of thought and feeling that no writer had touched before, and by his literary writings he spread in the highest circles a new respect for the common man, a love of common things, an impulse of human pity and compassion, a sense of artifice and superficiality in aristocratic life. Women took to nursing their own babies. Even men spoke of the delicacy of their sentiments. Tears became the fashion. The queen, Marie Antoinette, built herself a village in the gardens at Versailles where she pretended to be a simple milkmaid. In all this there was much that was ridiculous or shallow. Yet it was the wellspring of modern humanitarianism, the force leading to a new sense of human equality. Rousseau estranged the French upper classes from their own mode of life. He made many of them lose faith in their own superiority. That was his main direct contribution to the French Revolution.

Main Currents of
Enlightenment Thought

It is clear that the currents of thought in France and Europe were divergent and inconsistent. Most people believed in progress, reason, science, and civilization. Rousseau had his doubts and praised the beauties of character. Montesquieu thought the church useful but did not believe in religion; Rousseau believed in religion but saw no need of any church. Montesquieu was concerned over practical political liberty; Voltaire would surrender political liberty in return for guarantees of intellectual freedom; Rousseau wanted emancipation from the trivialities of society and sought the freedom that consists in merging willingly with nature and with one's fellows. Most philosophes were closest to Voltaire.

The most active center of ideas in the Age of Enlightenment, it has become clear, was France. French philosophes traveled all over Europe. Frederick II and Catherine II invited French thinkers to their courts. French was the language of the academies of St. Petersburg and Berlin. Frederick wrote his own works in the French language. There was a uniform, cosmopolitan culture among the upper classes of most of Europe, and this culture was predominantly French. But England was important also. Hitherto somewhat on the outer fringes of the European consciousness, England now moved closer to the center. Montesquieu and Voltaire may be said to have "discovered" England to Europe. Through them the ideas of Bacon, Newton, and Locke, and the whole theory of English law and parliamentary government became matters for general discussion and comment. The rise of Britain in wealth and empire gave irresistible prestige to these ideas. And as English families grew more affluent their sons increasingly made the "grand tour" on the Continent, until the *milords anglais* became familiar figures to Europeans, never quite understood but often secretly envied. All such influences, French and English, added to the leadership of western Europe in modern civilization.

The thought of the Enlightenment was completely secular. The church was considered, at most, a socially useful institution. To the more militant it was a survival of barbarism. Churchmen themselves, in the established churches, often looked with distrust on the religious zeal that did appear. For everywhere, it is true, there were religious stirrings, forms of revivalist religion, urging a new and fresh realization of gospel teachings: Jansenism continued in France, Pietism developed in Germany, the Methodist movement began in England, the "great awakening" took place in the Anglo-American colonies. But these revivalist movements had their greatest success among the least comfortable classes. The official churches, Anglican, Lutheran, Catholic, did not wish to be disturbed. Bishops were cultivated and enlightened gentlemen of the age and reasoned like enlightened gentlemen.

By intellectual leaders all churches were pushed aside. Toleration in religion, or even indifference, became the mark of progress. The older Christian view seemed no longer to be necessary. Thinkers provided theories of society, world history, human destiny, and of the nature of good and evil in which Christian explanations had no part. Old Christian virtues, such as humility, chastity, or the patient bearing of pain and sorrow, ceased to be regarded as significant (except in some ways by Rousseau). Christian love was transformed and secularized into humanitarian good will. The most important virtue was to be socially useful. The progress of society, from generation to generation, toward a more comfortable and decent life on earth, became the dominant idea that gave meaning to the history and destiny of mankind. It was a faith summarized by one of the later philosophes, the Marquis de Condorcet, when he wrote, shortly before committing suicide in the French Revolution, his *Outline of the Progress of the Human Mind.*

The main instrument of progress was thought to be the state. Whether in the form of limited monarchy on the English model favored by Montesquieu, or of the enlightened despotism preferred by Voltaire, or of the ideal republican commonwealth portrayed by Rousseau, the rightly ordered society was considered the best guarantee of social welfare. It was to the enlightened state that people now looked for salvation, and all hope of progress rested upon political reform, education, and the creation of an enlightened environment.

Though they thought in terms of reform by the state, the thinkers of the time were not nationalists but "universalists." They believed in the unity of mankind and held that all men subsisted under the same natural law of right and reason. In this they carried over the classical and Christian outlook in a new way. They supposed that all men would participate alike in the same progress, that in the long run all men would agree, and that the outcome of history would be one uniform civilization in which all peoples and races would share equally. No nation was thought to have a peculiar message. French ideas enjoyed a wide currency, but no one thought of them as peculiarly French, arising from a French "national character." It was simply thought that the French at the time, as the most civilized people, had most fully developed the capacities of the human mind. Never since the Age of Enlightenment has there been such unquestioning belief in the potential similarity of all human beings.

All the thinking of the time was designed to make men free. All thought of the Enlightenment, in one way or another, was concerned with the problem of liberty. Montesquieu wanted guarantees against despotism. Rousseau wanted freedom from the artificialities and restraints of society as he knew it. For Voltaire and most of the philosophes, liberty meant freedom from the church and from intolerance, freedom of the mind, freedom from misconception and ignorance, the most insidious of all forms of enslavement. To clear the ground, to shake people out of the habits of ages, to repress the forces which he believed to endanger this liberation of the spirit, Voltaire and others were willing to trust to a powerful and well-disposed government, i.e., to an "enlightened despot." Enlightened despotism, somewhat in the manner favored by Voltaire and most of the philosophes, became the characteristic tone of government in Europe after about 1740.

35

Enlightened Despotism: France, Austria, Prussia

The Meaning of Enlightened Despotism

Enlightened despotism is hard to define, because it grew out of the earlier absolutism represented by Louis XIV or Peter the Great. Characteristically, the enlightened despots drained marshes, built roads and bridges, codified the laws, repressed provincial autonomy and localism, curtailed the independence of church and nobles, and built up a trained and salaried officialdom. All these things had been done by kings before. The typical enlightened despot differed from his "un-enlightened" predecessor mainly in attitude and tempo. He said little of a divine right to his throne. He might even not emphasize his hereditary or dynastic family right. He justified his authority on grounds of usefulness to society, calling himself, as Frederick the Great did, the "first servant of the state."

Enlightened despotism was secular; it claimed no mandate from heaven and recognized no especial responsibility to God or church. The typical enlightened despot consequently favored toleration in religion, and this was an important new emphasis after about 1740; but here again there was precedent in the older absolutism, for the rulers of Prussia had been inclined toward toleration long before Frederick, and even the French Bourbons had recognized a degree of religious liberty for almost a century following the Edict of Nantes.[5] The secular outlook of the enlightened governments is again seen in the common front they adopted against the Jesuits. High papalists and ultramontanes,[6] affirming the authority of a universal church, and at the same time intellectually and in other ways the strongest religious order in the Catholic world, the Jesuits were distasteful to the enlightened monarchs and their civil officials and in the 1760s were expelled from almost all Catholic countries. In 1773 the pope was persuaded to dissolve the Society of Jesus entirely. The various governments concerned, in France, Austria, Spain, Portugal, and Naples, confiscated the Jesuit property and took over the Jesuit schools. Not until 1814 was the order reconstituted.

Enlightened despotism was also rational and reformist. The typical despot set out to reconstruct his state by the use of reason. Sharing the current view of the past as benighted, he was impatient of custom and of all that was imbedded in custom or claimed as a heritage from the past, such as systems of customary law and the rights and privileges of church, nobles, towns, gilds, provinces, assemblies of estates, or, in France, the judicial bodies called parliaments. The complex of such institutions was disparagingly referred to as "feudalism." Monarchs had long struggled against feudalism in this sense, but in the past they had usually compromised. The

[5] See pp. 139–140, 141, 195–196.
[6] See p. 94.

enlightened despot was less willing to compromise, and herein lay the difference in tempo. The new despot acted abruptly, desiring quicker results.

Enlightened despotism, in short, was an acceleration of the old institution of monarchy, which now put aside the quasi-sacred mantle in which it had clothed itself and undertook to justify itself in the cold light of reason and secular usefulness. In theory even the dynastic claim was awkward, for it rested on inheritance from the past. Under enlightened despotism the idea of the state itself was changing, from the older notion of an estate belonging by a kind of sanctified property right to its ruler, to a newer notion of an abstract and impersonal authority exercised by public officers, of whom the king was simply the highest.

The trend to enlightened despotism after 1740 owed a great deal to writers and philosophes, but it arose also out of a very practical situation, namely, the great war of the mid-eighteenth century.[7] War, in modern history, has usually led to concentration and rationalizing of government power, and the wars of 1740–1748 and 1756–1763 were no exception. Under their impact even governments where the rulers were not considered by philosophes to be enlightened, notably those of Louis XV and Maria Theresa, and even the government of Great Britain, which was certainly not despotic, embarked on programs which all bear features in common. They attempted to augment their revenues, devise new taxes, tax persons or regions hitherto more or less tax-exempt, limit the autonomy of outlying political bodies, and centralize and renovate their respective political systems. The workings of enlightened despotism might be seen in many states, in Habsburg Tuscany under Leopold, in Bourbon Naples and Spain under Charles III, in Portugal under the minister Pombal, in Denmark under Struensee. But it seems best to consider only the more important countries at some length—France and Austria, Prussia and Russia—and then the rather different, yet not wholly different, course of events in the British empire.

It was in France that enlightened despotism had the least success. Louis XV, who had inherited the throne in 1715 and lived until 1774, though by no means stupid, was indifferent to most serious questions, absorbed in the daily rounds at Versailles, disinclined to make trouble for people that he saw personally, and interested in government only by fits and starts. His remark, *après moi le déluge,* whether or not he really said it, sufficiently characterizes his personal attitude to conditions in France. Yet the French government was not unenlightened, and many capable officials carried on its affairs all through the century. These men generally knew what the basic trouble was. All the practical difficulties of the French monarchy could be traced to its system of taxation. The most important impost, the taille, a kind of land tax, was generally paid only by the peasants. Nobles were exempt from it on principle, and office-holders and bourgeois, for one reason or another, were generally exempt also. In addition, the church, which owned between 5 and 10

[7] See pp. 281–293.

percent of the land of the country, insisted that its property was not taxable by the state; it granted to the king a periodic "free gift" which, though sizable, was less than the government might expect from direct taxation.   The consequence of the tax exemptions was that, although France itself was wealthy and prosperous, the government was chronically poor, because the social classes which enjoyed most of the wealth and prosperity did not pay taxes corresponding to their incomes.   Louis XIV, under pressure of war, had tried to tax everybody alike by creating new levies, the capitation or poll tax and the *dixième* or tenth, both of which were assessed in proportion to income; but these taxes had been widely evaded.   A similar effort was made in 1726, but it too had failed.   The propertied classes resisted taxation because they thought it degrading.   France had succumbed to the appalling principle that to pay direct taxes was the sure mark of inferior status.   Nobles, churchmen, and bourgeois also resisted taxation because they were kept out of policymaking functions of government and so had no sense of political responsibility or control. There were good historical reasons for this, but the result was financially ruinous.[8]

In 1748, under pressure of the heavy war costs, and at the prompting of Mme. de Pompadour, Louis XV bestirred himself to appoint a controller-general of finance who devised a tax to be paid by all persons receiving income from property—land, manorial rights, business investments, and offices such as parliamentary judge-ships—irrespective of class status, provincial liberties, or previous exemptions of any kind.   A clamor arose from the Parliament of Paris, the eleven provincial parliaments, the estates of Brittany, and the church.   All these were dominated by noblemen and because of the aristocratic resurgence that had begun with the Regency, were politically stronger than in the days of Louis XIV.   They could also now cite Montesquieu to justify their opposition to the crown.   The Parliament of Paris ruled the new tax unconstitutional, or incompatible with the laws of France and liberties of Frenchmen.   The estates of Brittany, and of other *pays d'états*, i.e., provinces having assemblies of estates, declared that their customary and historic liberties were being outraged.   The church protested with vehemence.   After several years of wrangling, Louis XV decided to push the matter no further; he withdrew his support from his finance minister, and the whole project collapsed.

The 1750s and 1760s saw continued friction between the ministry and the various semiautonomous bodies within the country.   Meanwhile came the enormous costs and humiliating reverses of the Seven Years' War.   The government renewed its determination to win effective centralized control.   It was decided to eliminate the parliaments as a political force, and for this purpose, in 1768, Louis XV called to the chancellorship a man named Maupeou, who simply abrogated the old parliaments and set up new ones in their place.   Maupeou had the sympathy of Voltaire and most

[8]See pp. 73–74, 188–190, 193–194.

Europe 1740. *Boundaries are as of 1740.   Thereafter, until the wars of the French Revolution began in 1792, there were no major changes except the transfer of Silesia from Austria to Prussia, and the first partition of Poland.   France obtained Corsica in 1768.*

Bourbon Dominions

Habsburg Dominions

— Boundary of Holy Roman Empire

SWEDEN

NORWAY

St. Petersburg

SCOTLAND

KINGDOM OF
DENMARK AND NORWAY

• Edinburgh

NORTH SEA

• Riga

IRELAND

GREAT BRITAIN

DENMARK

• Copenhagen

BALTIC SEA

• Memel

PRUSSIA

LITHUANIA

Dublin • Liverpool •

ENGLAND

SCHLESWIG

• Stockholm

Danzig • EAST PRUSSIA

• Minsk

WALES

UNITED
PROVINCES

Bremen • Hamburg •

Elbe R.

HANOVER
(Britain)

BRANDENBURG

• Thorn

• London

Amsterdam •

• Utrecht

Magdeburg •

Berlin •

POLAND

• Warsaw

ANTIC OCEAN

AUSTRIAN
NETHERLANDS

Oudenarde •

Antwerp •

Cologne •

MINOR
GERMAN STATES

Leipzig • SAXONY

SILESIA

Breslau •

Oder R.

• Lublin

CHANNEL I.
(Britain)

CAPE
DE LA HOGUE

Malplaquet •

Ramillies •

Rhine R.

Frankfurt •

Dresden •

Prague •

• Lemberg

• Cracow

Rouen •

Reims •

Metz •

PALATI-
NATE

BOHEMIA

MORAVIA

PODOLIA

Paris •

Seine R.

• Orléans

LORRAINE
(France 1766)

Strasbourg •

Blenheim •

AUSTRIA

• Munkacz

Quiberon •

Loire R.

• Tours

Besançon •

Bavaria

Munich •

Vienna •

• Pressburg

• Budapest

FRANCE

SWITZERLAND

TYROL

AUSTRIAN MONARCHY

TRANSYLVANIA

• Limoges

Geneva •

Bordeaux •

Lyons •

Garonne R.

Rhone R.

SAVOY

PO R.

MILAN

PAR-
MA

VENETIA

Venice •

CROATIA

Save R.

KINGDOM
OF HUNGARY

BANAT

• Belgrade

WALLACHIA

Toulouse •

Turin •

Genoa •

Bologna •

BOSNIA

SERBIA

Danube R.

OTTOMAN EMPIRE

Avignon •

Marseilles •

Toulon •

KINGDOM OF SARDINIA

TUSCANY

PAPAL
STATES

DALMATIA
(Venice)

ADRIATIC SEA

MONTENEGRO

• Sofia

antiago

• León

Pamplona •

CATALONIA

ARAGON

Barcelona •

CORSICA
(Genoa)

Rome •

ALBANIA

• Salonica

Burgos •

Ebro R.

Benevento ⊙

SPAIN

Tagus R.

Madrid •

Toledo •

BALEARIC I.

MINORCA
(Britain)

Naples •

NAPLES

IONIAN I.
(Venice)

• Athens

bon

TUGAL

Guadalquivir R.

Almanza •

MAJORCA
(Spain)

SARDINIA

MOREA

Cadiz •

Seville •

• Granada

Cagliari •

MEDITERRANEAN

KINGDOM
OF THE TWO SICILIES

Palermo •

Tangier •

Gibraltar (Britain)

SEA

SICILY

MOROCCO
(Independent)

Algiers •

ALGERIA
(Turkish)

Tunis •

TUNISIA
(Turkish)

MALTA (Knights of St. John)

0   100   200   300 miles

VIII: The Age of
Enlightenment

of the philosophes. In the "Maupeou parliaments" the judges had no property rights in their seats but became salaried officials appointed by the crown with assurances of secure tenure, and they were forbidden to reject government edicts or to pass on their constitutionality, being confined to purely judicial functions. Maupeou likewise proposed to make the laws and judicial procedure more uniform throughout the whole country. Meanwhile, with the old parliaments out of the way, another attempt was made to tax the privileged and exempted groups.

But Louis XV died in 1774. His grandson and successor, Louis XVI, though far superior in personal habits to his grandfather, and possessed by a genuine desire to govern well, resembled Louis XV in that he lacked sustained will power and could not bear to offend the people who could get to see him personally. In any case he was only twenty in 1774. The kingdom resounded with outcries against Maupeou and his colleagues as minions of despotism and with demands for the immediate restoration of the old Parliament of Paris and the others. Louis XVI, fearful of beginning his reign as a "despot," therefore recalled the old parliaments and abolished those of Maupeou. The abortive Maupeou parliaments represented the farthest step taken by enlightened despotism in France. It was arbitrary, high-handed, and despotic for Louis XV to destroy the old parliaments, but it was certainly enlightened in the sense then connoted by the word, for the old parliaments were strongholds of aristocracy and privilege and had for decades blocked programs of reform.

Louis XVI, in recalling the old parliaments in 1774, began his reign by pacifying the privileged classes. At the same time he appointed a reforming ministry. At its head was Turgot, a philosophe and Physiocrat and a widely experienced government administrator. Turgot undertook to suppress the gilds, which were privileged municipal monopolies in their several trades. He allowed greater freedom to the internal commerce in grain. He planned to abolish the royal *corvée* (a requirement that certain peasants labor on the roads a few days each year), replacing it by a money tax which would fall on all classes. He began to review the whole system of taxation and was known even to favor the legal toleration of Protestants. The Parliament of Paris, supported by the Provincial Estates and the church, vociferously opposed him, and in 1776 he resigned. Louis XVI, by recalling the parliaments, had made reform impossible. In 1778 France again went to war with Britain. The same cycle was repeated: war costs, debt, deficit, new projects of taxation, resistance from the parliaments and other semiautonomous bodies. In the 1780s the clash led to revolution.[9]

*Austria: The Reforms
of Maria Theresa
(1740–1780) and of
Joseph (1780–1790)*

For Maria Theresa the war of the 1740s proved the extraordinary flimsiness of her empire.[10] Had the Continental allies won a more smashing victory, not only would Silesia have been lost to Prussia, but Belgium would have gone to France, Bohemia

[9] See pp. 380–383.
[10] See pp. 282–286.

and Austria to the elector of Bavaria supported by France, and the emperorship of the Holy Roman Empire, long a source of prestige to the Habsburgs, would have passed permanently in all probability to a Bavarian or other pro-French German prince. Maria Theresa would have become queen of Hungary only. Nor did her subjects show much inclination to remain together under her rule. In Breslau, the capital of Silesia, after the Prussian attack of 1740, the citizens stood so stubbornly by their town liberties that they would not admit her army within their walls. In Bohemia almost half the nobles welcomed the invading Franco-Bavarians. In Hungary Maria Theresa won support but only by confirming the historic Hungarian liberties. The empire was only a loose bundle of territories, without common purpose or common will. The Pragmatic Sanction devised by Charles VI, it should be recalled, had been meant not only to guarantee the Habsburg inheritance against foreign attack, but also to secure the assent of the several parts of the empire to remain united under the dynasty.[11]

The war of the 1740s led to internal consolidation. The reign of Maria Theresa set the course of all later development of the Austrian empire and hence of the many peoples who lived within its borders. She was aided by a notable team of ministers, whose origin illustrated the nonnational character of the Habsburg system. Her most trusted adviser in foreign relations, the astute Kaunitz,[12] was a Moravian; her main assistants in domestic affairs were a Silesian and a Bohemian-Czech. They worked smoothly with the German archduchess-queen and with German officials in Vienna. Their aim was primarily to prevent dissolution of the monarchy by enlarging and guaranteeing the flow of taxes and soldiers. This involved breaking the local control of territorial nobles in their several diets, which corresponded somewhat to the French Provincial Estates. Hungary, profoundly separatist, was let alone. But the Bohemian and Austrian provinces were welded together. The kingdom of Bohemia, in 1749, lost the constitutional charter which it had received in 1627.[13] The several Bohemian and Austrian diets lost their right to consent to taxes. The separate offices, or "chancelleries," by which their affairs had been separately handled at Vienna, were abolished. Formerly local affairs, recruiting, and tax collecting had been dominated by committees of the diets, made up of landed noblemen of the neighborhood, gentlemen amateurs who were often negligent or indifferent, and who, since they served without pay, were impervious to official discipline, reprimand, or coordination. They were replaced by salaried administrators. Bureaucracy took the place of local self-government. Officials (following a form of mercantilist doctrine called "cameralism" in central Europe) planned to augment the economic strength of the empire by increasing production. They checked the local gild monopolies, suppressed brigandage on the roads, and in 1775 produced a tariff union of Bohemia, Moravia, and the Austrian duchies. This region became the largest area of free trade on the European continent, since even France was still divided by internal

[11] See pp. 233, 283–284.
[12] See p. 286.
[13] See p. 232.

tariffs. Bohemia, industrially the most advanced part of the empire, benefited substantially; one of its cotton manufacturing plants, at the end of Maria Theresa's reign, employed 4,000 persons.

The great social fact, both in the Habsburg lands and in all eastern Europe, was the serfdom into which the rural masses had progressively fallen during the past 200 years.[14] Serfdom meant that the peasant belonged more to his landlord than to the state. The serf owed labor to his lord, often unspecified in amount or kind. The tendency, so long as the landlords ruled locally through their diets, was for the serf to do six days a week of forced labor on the lord's land. Maria Theresa, from humane motives, and also from a desire to lay hands on the manpower from which her armies were recruited, launched a systematic attack on the institutions of serfdom, which meant also an attack on the landed aristocracy of the empire. With the diets reduced in power, the protests of the nobles were less effective; still, the whole agricultural labor system of her territories was involved, and Maria Theresa proceeded with caution. Laws were passed against abuse of peasants by lords or their overseers. Other laws regularized the labor obligations, requiring that they be publicly registered and usually limiting them to three days a week. The laws were often evaded. But the peasant was to some extent freed from arbitrary exactions of the lord. Maria Theresa accomplished more to alleviate serfdom than any other ruler of the eighteenth century in eastern Europe, with the single exception of her own son, Joseph II.

The great archduchess-queen died in 1780, having reigned for forty years. Her son, who had been co-regent with his mother since 1765, had little patience with her methods. Maria Theresa, though steady enough in aim, had always been content with partial measures. Instead of advertising her purposes by philosophical generalization she disguised or understated them, never carrying matters to the point of arousing an unmanageable reaction or of uniting against her the vested interests that she undermined. She backed and filled, watched and waited. Joseph II would not wait. Though he thought the French philosophes frivolous, and Frederick of Prussia a mere clever cynic, he was himself a pure representative of the Age of Enlightenment, and it is in his brief reign of ten years that the character and the limitations of enlightened despotism can best be seen. He was a solemn, earnest, good man, who sensed the misery and hopelessness of the lowest classes. He believed existing conditions to be bad, and he would not regulate or improve them; he would end them. Right and reason, in his mind, lay with the views which he himself adopted; upholders of the old order were self-seeking or mistaken and to yield to them would be to compromise with evil.

"The state," said Joseph, anticipating the Philosophical Radicals in England, meant "the greatest good for the greatest number." He acted accordingly. His ten years of rule passed in a quick succession of decrees. Maria Theresa had regulated serfdom. Joseph abolished it. His mother had collected taxes from nobles as well as peasants, though not equally. Joseph decreed absolute equality of taxation. He

[14]See pp. 123–124, 216, 232, 242–243.

insisted on equal punishment for equal crimes whatever the class status of the offender; an aristocratic army officer, who had stolen 97,000 gulden, was exhibited in the pillory, and Count Podstacky, a forger, was made to sweep the streets of Vienna chained to common convicts. At the same time many legal punishments were made less physically cruel. Joseph granted complete liberty of the press. He ordered toleration of all religions, except for a few popular sects which he thought too ignorant to allow. He granted equal civic rights to the Jews, and equal duties, making Jews liable, for the first time in Europe, to service in the army. He even made Jewish nobles, an amazing phenomenon to those of aristocratic "blood." He clashed openly and rudely with the pope, supporting a movement called Febronianism which urged more national independence from Rome for German Catholic prelates, on the model of the French Gallican liberties. He demanded increased powers in the appointment and supervision of bishops, and he suppressed a good many monasteries, using their property to finance secular hospitals in Vienna, and thus laying the foundations of Viennese excellence as a medical center. He attempted also to develop the empire economically and built up the port of Trieste, where he even established an East India Company, which soon failed for obvious reasons—neither capital nor naval support being forthcoming from central Europe. His attempts to reach the sea commercially through Belgium, like those of his grandfather at the time of the Ostend Company, were blocked by the Dutch and British interests.

To force through his program Joseph had to centralize his state, like earlier rulers, except that he went farther. Regional diets and aristocratic self-government fared even worse than under his mother. Where she had always sagaciously let Hungary go its own way, he applied most of his measures to Hungary also—what was right must be right everywhere. His ideal was a perfectly uniform and rational empire, with all irregularities smoothed out as if under a steam roller. He thought it reasonable to have a single language for administration and naturally chose German; this led to a program of Germanizing the Czechs, Poles, Magyars, and others, which in turn aroused their nationalistic resistance. Using the German language, pushing the emperor's program against regional and class opposition, was a hard-pressed, constantly growing, and increasingly disciplined body of officials. Bureaucracy became recognizably modern, with training courses, promotion schedules, retirement pensions, efficiency reports, and visits by inspectors. The clergy likewise were employed as mouthpieces of the state to explain new laws to their parishioners and teach due respect for the government. To watch over the whole structure Joseph created a secret police, whose agents, soliciting the confidential aid of spies and informers, reported on the performance of government employees, or the ideas and actions of nobles, clergy, or others from whom trouble might be expected. The police state, so infamous to the liberal world, was first systematically built up under Joseph as an instrument of enlightenment and reform.

Joseph II, the "revolutionary emperor," anticipated much that was done in France by the Revolution and under Napoleon. He could not abide "feudalism" or "medievalism"; he personally detested the nobility and the church. But few of his reforms proved lasting. He died prematurely in 1790, at the age of forty-nine, disillusioned

343

and broken-hearted. Hungary and the Belgian provinces were in revolution against him. They held that their old constitutional liberties had been outraged—that they were being governed without their consent. In Hungary all the good will won by Maria Theresa seemed to be lost; in Belgium the provinces stood stubbornly by the same medieval privileges, the old *Joyeuse Entrée*, which they had vindicated 200 years before against the king of Spain.[15] Noble landlords throughout the Habsburg empire, having lost their control over labor by the abolition of serfdom, and their caste status by legal and fiscal reforms, naturally were indignant. The church believed itself to be prostituted and despoiled. The peasants were grateful for their new personal liberty but balked at the official attitude of condescending uplift, and often, in real life, sympathized with their priests and their gentlefolk. The officials were unequal to the task demanded of them. There were too few bourgeois in most parts of the empire to staff the civil service, so that many functionaries were members of the landowning nobility which Joseph humiliated; and in any case they frequently found the directives that flowed from Vienna impossible to enforce or even to understand. Joseph was a revolutionist without a party. He failed because he could not be everywhere and do everything himself. His reign demonstrated the limitations of a merely despotic enlightenment. It showed that a legally absolute ruler could not really do as he pleased. It suggested that drastic and abrupt reform could only come with a true revolution, on a wave of public opinion, and under the leadership of men who shared in a coherent body of ideas.

Joseph was succeeded by his brother Leopold, one of the ablest rulers of the century, who for many years as grand duke of Tuscany had given that country the best government known in Italy for generations, and who now, in 1790, was plagued by outcries from his sister, Marie Antoinette, caught in the toils of a real revolution in France.[16] He refused to interfere in French affairs; in any case, he was busy dealing with the uproar left by Joseph. He abrogated most of Joseph's edicts, but he did not yield entirely. The nobles did not win back full powers in their diets. The peasants were not wholly consigned to the old serfdom; Joseph's efforts to provide them with land and to rid them of forced labor had to be given up, but they remained personally free, in law, to migrate, marry, or choose an occupation at will. Leopold died in 1792 and was followed by his son Francis II. Under Francis the aristocratic and clerical reaction gathered strength, terrified by the memory of Joseph II and by the spectacle of revolutionary France, with which Austria went to war soon after Leopold's death.

Prussia under Frederick the Great (1740–1786)

In Prussia, Frederick the Great continued to reign for twenty-three years after the close of the Seven Years' War. "Old Fritz," as he was called, spent the time peaceably, writing memoirs and histories, rehabilitating his shattered country, promoting agriculture and industry, replenishing his treasury, drilling his army, and assimilating his huge conquest of Silesia, and, after 1772, that part of Poland which

[15]See pp. 129, 131.
[16]See p. 393.

fell to him in the first partition. Frederick's fame as one of the most eminent of enlightened despots rests, however, not so much on his actual innovations as on his own intellectual gifts, which were considerable, and on the admiring publicity which he received from such literary friends as Voltaire. "My chief occupation," he wrote to Voltaire, "is to fight ignorance and prejudices in this country. . . . I must enlighten my people, cultivate their manners and morals, and make them as happy as human beings can be, or as happy as the means at my disposal permit." He did not conceive that sweeping changes were necessary to happiness in Prussia. The country was docile, for its Lutheran church had long been subordinate to the state, its relatively few burghers were largely dependents of the crown, and the independence of the Junker landlords, as expressed in provincial diets, had been curtailed by Frederick's predecessors.[17] Frederick simplified and codified the many laws of the kingdom and made the law courts cheaper, more expeditious, and more honest. He kept up a wholesome and energetic tone in his civil service. He gave religious freedom, and he decreed, though he did not realize, a modicum of elementary education for all children of all classes. Prussia under Frederick was attractive enough for some 300,000 immigrants to seek it out.

But society remained stratified in a way hardly known in western Europe. Nobles, peasants, and burghers lived side by side in a kind of segregation. Each group paid different taxes and owed different duties to the state, and no person could buy property of the type pertaining to one of the other two groups. Property was legally classified, as well as persons; there was little passing from one group to another. The basic aim of these policies was military, to preserve, by keeping intact their respective forms of property, a distinct peasant class from which to draw soldiers and a distinct aristocratic class from which to draw officers. The peasants, except in the western extremities of the kingdom, were serfs holding patches of land on precarious terms in return for obligations to labor on the estates of the lords. They were likewise considered the lord's "hereditary subjects" and were not free to leave the lord's estate, to marry, or to learn a trade except with his permission. Frederick in his early years considered steps to relieve the burden of serfdom. He did relieve it on his own manors, those belonging to the Prussian crown domain, which comprised a quarter of the area of the kingdom. But he did nothing for serfs belonging to the private landlords or Junkers. No king of Prussia could fundamentally antagonize the Junker class which commanded the army. On the other hand, even in Prussia, the existence of a monarchical state was of some advantage to the common man; the serf in Prussia was not so badly off as in adjoining areas—Poland, Livonia, Mecklenburg, or Swedish Pomerania—where the will of the landlords was the law of the land, and which therefore have not inaptly been called Junker republics. In these countries cases came to light in which owners sold their serfs as movable property, or gambled or gave them away, breaking up families in the process, as Russian landlords might do with their serfs or American plantation-owners with their slaves. Such abuses were unknown in Prussia.

[17] See pp. 242–243.

Frederick's system was centralized not merely at Potsdam but in his own head. He himself attended to all business and made all important decisions. None of his ministers or generals ever achieved an independent reputation. As he said of his army, "no one reasons, everyone executes"—that is, no one reasoned except the king himself. Or again, as Frederick put it, if Newton had had to consult with Descartes he would never have discovered the law of universal gravitation. To have to take account of other people's ideas, or to entrust responsibilities to men less capable than himself, seemed to Frederick wasteful and anarchic. He died in 1786, after ruling forty-six years and having trained no successors. Twenty years later Prussia was all but destroyed by Napoleon.[18] It was not surprising that Napoleon should defeat Prussia, but Europe was amazed, in 1806, to see Prussia collapse totally and abruptly. It was then concluded, in Prussia and elsewhere, that government by a mastermind working in lofty and isolated superiority did not offer a viable form of state under modern conditions.

**36
Enlightened
Despotism: Russia**

The Russian empire has long been out of sight in the preceding pages. There are reasons for its absence, for it played no part in the intellectual revolution of the seventeenth century, and its role in the struggle for wealth and empire which reached a climax in the Seven Years' War was somewhat incidental. In the Age of Enlightenment the role of Russia was passive. No Russian thinker was known to Europe. But European thinkers were well known in Russia. The French-dominated cosmopolitan culture of the European upper classes spread to the upper classes of Russia. The Russian court and aristocracy took over French as their common conversational language. With French (German was also known, and sometimes English, for the Russian aristocrats were remarkable linguists) all the ideas boiling up in western Europe streamed into Russia. The Enlightenment, if it did not affect Russia profoundly, yet affected it significantly. It continued the westernization so forcibly pushed forward by Peter and carried further the estrangement of the Russian upper classes from their own people and their own native scene.

*Russia after
Peter the Great*

Peter the Great died in 1725.[19] To secure his revolution he had decreed that each tsar should name his successor, but he himself had named none and had put to death his own son Alexis to prevent social reaction. Peter was succeeded by his wife, a woman of peasant origin, who reigned for two years as Catherine I. Then came the boy Peter II, son of Alexis and grandson of Peter I. Peter II reigned only from 1727 to 1730. He was followed by Anna, 1730–1740; in her reign the old native Russian party, in an attempt to undo the Petrine revolution, tried to surround the tsardom with various constitutional checks. They failed; Anna was followed by Ivan VI, who was

[18]See pp. 426–427, 447.
[19]See pp. 255–256.

tsar for a few months only, during which his mother, a German woman, ran affairs according to the views of the German party in Russia, which was indispensable to the westernization program and was resented by the Russian nativists. A palace revolution in 1741 brought to the throne Peter the Great's daughter, Elizabeth, who managed to hold power until her death twenty-one years later. She was so ignorant that she thought England could be reached by land, but in her reign the military power of Russia expanded, and she entered into European diplomacy and joined in the Seven Years' War against Prussia, fearing that the continued growth of Prussia would endanger the new Russian position on the Baltic. It was Elizabeth's death in 1762 that so decisively relieved the pressure on Frederick.[20] Her nephew, Peter III, was so odd that at twenty-six he still played with paper soldiers and is said to have solemnly tried and hanged a rat which gnawed some of them during the night. Peter III, soon after making peace with Prussia, was dethroned and probably assassinated by a group acting in the name of his wife Catherine, who was proclaimed the Empress Catherine II and is called "the Great." She enjoyed a long reign from 1762 to 1796, during which she acquired a somewhat exaggerated reputation as an enlightened despot.

Enlightened Despotism: Russia

The names of the tsars and tsarinas between Peter I and Catherine II are of slight importance. But their violent and rapid sequence tells a story. With no principle of succession, dynastic or other, the empire fell into a lawless struggle of parties, in which plots against rulers while living alternated with palace revolutions upon their death. The underlying issue was always the westernizing revolution of Peter— whether it should be repudiated or maintained, and, if maintained, by what party, German or native Russian or a faction or subgrouping of these. To western Europe Russia still seemed Byzantine and barbaric.

Catherine the Great was a German woman, of a small princely house of the Holy Roman Empire. She had gone to Russia at the age of fifteen to be married. She had immediately cultivated the good will of the Russians, learned the language, and embraced the Orthodox church. Early in her married life, disgusted with her moronic husband, she foresaw the chance of becoming empress herself. She was nothing like her feminine contemporary Maria Theresa, except possibly in having much the same practical sense. Mannish, hearty, and boisterous, she wore out a long succession of many lovers, mixing them freely with politics and using them in positions of state. When she died at the age of sixty-seven, of a stroke of apoplexy, she was still living with the last of these venturesome paramours. Her intellectual powers were as remarkable as her physical vigor; even after becoming empress she often got up at five in the morning, lighted her own fire, and turned to her books, making a digest, for example, of Blackstone's *Commentaries on the Laws of England*, published in 1765. She corresponded with Voltaire and invited Diderot, editor of the *Encyclopédie*, to visit her at St. Petersburg, where, she reported, he thumped

Catherine the Great (1762–1796): Domestic Program

[20] See p. 287.

347

her so hard on the knee in the energy of his conversation that she had to put a table between them. She bought Diderot's library, allowing him to keep it during his lifetime, and in other ways won renown by her benefactions to the philosophes, whom she probably regarded as useful press agents for Russia. Her gifts to them were substantial, though dwarfed by the £12,000,000 she is estimated to have bestowed on her lovers.

When she first came to power she publicized an intention to make certain enlightened reforms. She summoned a kind of constitutional convention, called a Legislative Commission, which met in the summer of 1767. Nothing much came of its deliberations, though it sat for a year and a half, except that Catherine obtained a good deal of information on conditions in the country and concluded, from the profuse loyalty exhibited by the deputies, that though a usurper and a foreigner she possessed a strong hold upon Russia. The reforms which she subsequently enacted consisted in a measure of legal codification, restrictions on the use of torture, and a certain support of religious toleration, though she would not allow Old Believers to build their own chapels. Such innovations were enough to raise an admiring chorus from the philosophes, who saw in her, as they saw retrospectively in Peter the Great, the standard-bearer of civilization among a backward people. Like other enlightened despots, Catherine turned assiduously to administrative questions also. Consolidating the machinery of state, she replaced Peter's ten *gubernii* with fifty, each subdivided into districts, and all equipped with appropriate sets of governors and officials.

Whatever ideas Catherine may conceivably have had at first, as a thoughtful and progressive young woman, on the fundamental subject of reforming serfdom in Russia, did not last long after she became empress, and dissolved with the great peasant insurrection of 1773, known as Pugachev's rebellion. The condition of the Russian serfs was deteriorating. Serf-owners were increasingly selling them apart from land, breaking up families, using them in mines or manufactures, disciplining and punishing them at will, or exiling them to Siberia. The serf population was restless, worked upon by Old Believers and cherishing distorted popular memories of the mighty hero, Stephen Razin, who a century before had led an uprising against the landlords.[21] Class antagonism, though latent, was profound, nor was it made less when the rough *moujik*, in some places, heard the lord and his family talking French so as not to be understood by the servants or saw them wearing European clothes, reading European books, and adopting the manners of a foreign and superior way of life. Hope stirred among the peasants at the convocation of the Legislative Commission, in which even serfs were represented and at which the problem of serfdom was thoroughly discussed. Yet nothing happened.

In 1773 a Don Cossack, Emelian Pugachev, a former soldier, appeared at the head of an insurrection in the Urals. Following an old Russian custom, he announced himself as the true tsar, Peter III (Catherine's deceased husband), now returned after long travels in Egypt and the Holy Land. He surrounded himself with duplicates of

[21] See pp. 248–249.

the imperial family, courtiers, and even a secretary of state. He issued an imperial manifesto proclaiming the end of serfdom and of taxes and military conscription. Tens and hundreds of thousands, in the Urals and Volga regions, Tartars, Kirghiz, Cossacks, agricultural serfs, servile workers in the Ural mines, fishermen in the rivers and in the Caspian Sea, flocked to Pugachev's banner. The great host surged up the Volga, capturing town after town, burning and pillaging, killing priests and landlords. The upper classes in Moscow were terrified; 100,000 serfs lived in the city as domestic servants or industrial workers, and their sympathies went out to Pugachev and his horde. Armies were at first unsuccessful. But famine along the Volga in 1774 dispersed the rebels. Pugachev, betrayed by some of his own followers, was brought to Moscow in an iron cage. Catherine forbade the use of torture at his trial, but he was executed by the drawing and quartering of his body, a punishment, it should perhaps be noted, used at the time in western Europe in cases of flagrant treason.

Pugachev's rebellion was the most violent peasant uprising in the history of Russia, and the most formidable mass upheaval in Europe in the century before 1789. Catherine replied to it by repression. She conceded more powers to the landlords. The nobles shook off the last vestiges of the compulsory state service to which Peter had bound them. The peasants were henceforth the only bound or unfree class. As in Prussia, the state came more than ever to rest on an understanding between ruler and gentry, by which the gentry accepted the monarchy, with its laws, officials, army, and foreign policy, and received from it, in return, the assurance of full authority over the rural masses. Government reached down through the aristocracy and the scattered towns, but it stopped short at the manor; there the lord took over and was himself a kind of government in his own person. Under these conditions the number of serfs increased, and the load on each became more heavy. Catherine's reign saw the culmination of Russian serfdom, which now ceased to differ in any important respect from the chattel slavery to which Negroes were subject in the Americas. One might read in the Moscow *Gazette* such advertisements as the following: "For sale, two plump coachmen; two girls eighteen and fifteen years, quick at manual work. Two barbers: one, twenty-one, knows how to read and write and play a musical instrument; the other can do ladies' and gentlemen's hair."

Territorially Catherine was one of the main builders of Russia. When she became tsarina in 1762 the empire reached to the Pacific and into central Asia, and it touched upon the Gulf of Riga and the Gulf of Finland on the Baltic, but westward from Moscow one could go only 200 miles before reaching Poland, and no one standing on Russian soil could see the waters of the Black Sea.[22] Russia was separated from central Europe by a wide band of loosely organized domains, extending from the Baltic to the Black Sea and the Mediterranean and nominally belonging to the Polish and Turkish states. Poland was an old enemy, which had once threatened Muscovy,

[22] See map, pp. 252–253.

and both in Poland and in the Ottoman Empire there were many Greek Orthodox
Christians, with whom Russians felt an ideological tie, and whose stories of
mistreatment in Poland at the hands of Roman Catholics, and in Turkey by Moslems,
always aroused a crusading spirit in Russia. In western Europe the disposal of the
whole Polish-Turkish tract, which stretched over into Asia and Africa, came to be
called the Eastern Question. Though the name went out of use after 1900, the question itself has never ceased to exist.

Catherine's supreme plan was to penetrate the entire area, Turkish and Polish
alike. If successful, she would reach into Europe as far as Silesia and the Adriatic.
We have already seen what happened to this plan.[23] In 1763 Catherine put a
discarded lover, Stanislas Poniatowski, on the Polish throne. This led to armed
disputes among the Poles, some of whom favored Russia, some Prussia, some Austria,
some France, and some even Turkey. In 1768 the Turkish sultan went to war with
Russia. Catherine retorted with her "Greek project," a scheme looking to no less
than the overthrow of the Ottoman government and revival of the medieval Greek or
Byzantine Empire, in which the "Greeks," i.e., members of the Greek Orthodox
church, would replace the Moslems as the ruling element in the Near East. Since
these "Greeks" would be guided and counseled from Holy Russia, Russian
supremacy would be established at Constantinople and run through the Balkans, the
eastern Mediterranean, and the Levant. In the war which began in 1768 the Russians
overcame all Turkish opposition. Catherine seemed about to dominate Turkey as
she did Poland.

But the European balance of power now lumbered into play. Catherine could
hardly expect such a gigantic aggrandizement without war with Austria or even with
Europe. Frederick II, seeing a chance to win Pomerelia without risk and playing
on Catherine's disinclination for a general war, proposed that in return for letting
Turkey off lightly she annex a portion of Poland, and that, to keep the proper balance
in eastern Europe, Prussia and the Austrian monarchy absorb parts of Poland also.
The partition was effected in 1772. Frederick took Pomerelia, which he renamed
West Prussia; Catherine took parts of White Russia, Maria Theresa, Galicia.[24]
Frederick digested his portion with relish, realizing an old dream of the Brandenburg
house; Catherine swallowed hers with somewhat less appetite, since she had
satisfactorily controlled the whole of Poland before; to Maria Theresa the dish was
distasteful, and even shocking, but she could not see Russia and Prussia go ahead
without her, and she shared in the feast by suppressing her moral scruples. "She
wept," said Frederick cynically, "but she kept on taking." Catherine, in 1774, signed
a peace treaty with the defeated Turks at Kuchuk Kainarji on the Danube. The sultan
ceded his rights over the Tartar principalities on the north coast of the Black Sea to the
tsarina, admitted Russian ships to the Straits, and recognized Russia as the special
protector of Christians in the Ottoman Empire.

Catherine had only delayed, not altered, her plans with respect to Turkey. She
decided to neutralize the opposition of Austria. She invited Joseph II to visit her in

[23] See pp. 257–260.
[24] See map, p. 259.

Russia, and the two sovereigns proceeded together on a tour of her newly won Black Sea provinces. Her favorite of the moment, Potemkin, constructed artificial one-street villages along their way and produced throngs of cheering and happy-looking villagers to greet them, all of which enriched mankind with nothing except the phrase "Potemkin villages" to mean bogus evidence of a nonexistent prosperity. At Kherson the two monarchs passed through a gate marked "The Road to Byzantium." "What I want is Silesia," said Joseph II, but the tsarina induced him to join in a war of conquest against Turkey. This war was interrupted by the French Revolution. Both governments reduced their commitments in the Balkans to await developments in western Europe. It became Catherine's policy to incite Austria and Prussia into a war with France, in the name of monarchy and civilization, in order that she might have a free hand in the Polish-Turkish sphere.[25] Meanwhile she contributed to killing off the nationalist and reforming movement among the Poles. In 1793 she arranged with Prussia for the second partition and in 1795 with both Prussia and Austria for the third. She was the only ruler who lived to take part in all three partitions of Poland. The Polish kingdom was now extinct, and the Russian-Polish frontier set at about the line it was to follow after 1945. But Catherine's ideas were not yet exhausted, though her judgment seems to have failed her in the last months of her life. In 1796 she allowed her then favorite, Platon Zubov, to dispatch an army of 20,000 men on a mad expedition to conquer India by way of Persia. This force was immediately recalled after her death.

Catherine's foreign policy was purely expansionist and unscrupulous, and the net effect of her domestic policy, aside from a few reforms of detail, was to favor the half-Europeanized aristocracy and to extend serfdom among the people. Her own protestations of enlightenment tempt one to an ironical judgment of her career, but in her defense it may be observed that unscrupulous expansion was the accepted practice of the time, and that, domestically, probably no ruler could have corrected the social evils from which Russia suffered. If there was to be a Russian empire it had to be with the consent of the serf-owning gentry, which was the only politically significant class. As Catherine observed to Diderot on the subject of reforms: "You only write on paper, but I have to write on human skin, which is incomparably more irritable and ticklish." She had reason to know how easily tsars and tsarinas could be unseated and even murdered, and that the danger of overthrow came not from the peasants but from cliques of army officers and landlords.

She therefore yielded, but at least she never yielded her mind. She never said that slavery was a positive good. She never said that there were two or more worlds, subject to different moral codes or different laws of civilization. She never thought that the peculiar institutions of her own country should be cherished and elaborated as a contribution to human welfare. Ideas of this kind, in the following century, gained ground in both Europe and America, to justify conditions which the philosophy of the Enlightenment impatiently condemned. Catherine continued at least to recognize the standards of the Enlightenment as standards. Her mind became somewhat compartmentalized, if not hypocritical, with one part for the play

[25] See pp. 393–394.

of ideas and another part for the administration of Russia. But she seems not to have abandoned the hope that some day Russia might share in the one swelling stream of human progress. At least, in her later years, she gave careful attention to her favorite grandson, Alexander, closely supervising his education, which she planned on the Western model. She gave him as a tutor the Swiss philosophe La Harpe, who filled his mind with humane and liberal sentiments on the duties of princes. Trained by Catherine as a kind of ideal ruler, Alexander I was destined to cut a wide circle in the affairs of Europe, to defeat Napoleon Bonaparte, preach peace and freedom, and suffer from the same internal divisions and frustrations by which educated Russians seemed characteristically to be afflicted.

The Limitations of Enlightened Despotism

Enlightened despotism, seen in retrospect, foreshadowed an age of revolution and even signified a preliminary effort to revolutionize society by authoritative action from above. People were told by their own governments that reforms were needed, that many privileges, special liberties, or tax exemptions were bad, that the past was a source of confusion, injustice, or inefficiency in the present. The state rose up as more completely sovereign, whether acting frankly in its own interest or claiming to act in the interest of its people. All old and established rights were brought into question—rights of kingdoms and provinces, orders and classes, legal bodies and corporate groups. Enlightened despotism overrode or exterminated the Society of Jesus, the Parliament of Paris, the autonomy of Bohemia, and the independence of Poland. Customary and common law was pushed aside by authoritative legal codes. Governments, by opposing the special powers of the church and the feudal interests, tended to make all persons into uniform and equal subjects. To this extent enlightened despotism favored equality before the law. But it could go only a certain distance in this direction. The king was after all a hereditary aristocrat himself, and no government can be revolutionary to the point of breaking up its own foundations.

Even before the French Revolution enlightened despotism had run its course. Everywhere the "despots," for reasons of politics if not of principle, had reached a point beyond which they could not go. In France Louis XVI had appeased the privileged classes, in the Austrian empire Joseph's failure to appease them threw them into open revolt, in Prussia and in Russia the brilliant reigns of Frederick and Catherine wound up in an aggravation of landlordism for the mass of the people. Almost everywhere there was an aristocratic and even feudal revival. Religion also was renewing itself in many ways. Many were again saying that kingship was in a sense divine, and a new alliance was forming between "the throne and the altar." The French Revolution, by terrifying the old vested interests, was to accelerate and embitter a reaction which had already begun. Monarchy in Europe, ever since the Middle Ages, had generally been a progressive institution, acting along the line that Europe seemed destined to take, and in any case setting itself against the feudal and ecclesiastical powers. Enlightened despotism was the culmination of the historic institution of monarchy. After the enlightened despots, and after the French Revolution, monarchy became on the whole nostalgic and backward-looking,

supported most ardently by the churches and aristocracies that it had once tried to
subdue and least of all by those who felt in themselves the surge of the future.

I t was not only by monarchs and their ministers, however, that the older privileged,
feudal, and ecclesiastical interests were threatened. Beginning about 1760 they were
challenged also in more-popular quarters. Growing out of the Enlightenment, and
out of the failure of governments to cope with grave social and fiscal problems, a new
era of revolutionary disturbance was about to open. It was marked above all by the
great French Revolution of 1789, but the American Revolution of 1776 was also of
international importance. In Great Britain, too, the long-drawn-out movement for
parliamentary reform which began in the 1760s was in effect revolutionary in
character, though nonviolent, since it questioned the foundations of traditional
English government and society. In addition, in the last third of the eighteenth
century, there was revolutionary agitation in Switzerland, Belgium and Holland, in
Ireland, Poland, Hungary, Italy, and in lesser degree elsewhere. After 1800 revolutionary ferment was increasingly evident in Germany, Spain, and Latin America.
This general wave of revolution may be said not to have ended until after the revolutions of 1848.

For the whole period the term "Atlantic Revolution" has sometimes been used,
since countries on both sides of the Atlantic were affected. It has been called also an
age of "Democratic Revolution," since in all the diversity of these upheavals, from the
American Revolution to those of 1848, certain principles of the modern democratic
society were in one way or another affirmed. In this view, the particular revolutions,
attempted revolutions, or basic reform movements are seen as aspects of one great
revolutionary wave by which virtually the whole area of Western civilization was
transformed. The contrary is also maintained, namely, that each country presented a
special case, which is misunderstood if viewed only as part of a vague general
international turmoil. Thus the American Revolution, it is argued, was essentially a
movement for independence, even essentially conservative in its objectives, and thus
entirely different from the French Revolution, in which a thorough renovation of all
society and ideas was contemplated; and both were utterly different from what
happened in England, where there was no revolution at all. There is truth in both
contentions, and it need only be affirmed here that the American revolutionaries, the
French Jacobins, the United Irish, the Dutch Patriots, and similar groups elsewhere,
though differing from each other, yet shared much in common that can only be
characterized as revolutionary and as contributing to a revolutionary age.

*Onset of an Age of
"Democratic Revolution"*

It is important to see in what ways the movement that began about 1760 was and
was not "democratic." It did not generally demand universal suffrage, though a
handful of persons in England did so as early as the 1770s and some of the American
states practiced an almost universal male suffrage after 1776, as did the more militant

French revolutionaries in 1792. It did not aim at a welfare state, nor question the
right of property, though there were signs pointing in these directions in the extreme
wing of the French Revolution. It was not especially directed against monarchy as
such. The quarrel of the Americans was primarily with the British Parliament, not
the king; the French proclaimed a republic by default in 1792, three years after their
revolution began; the revolutionary Poles after 1788 tried to strengthen their king's
position, not weaken it; and revolutionary groups could come into action where no
monarchy existed at all, as in the Dutch provinces before the French Revolution, and
the Swiss cantons, the Venetian Republic, or again in Holland, under French influence
after 1795. Indeed the first revolutionary outbreak of the period occurred in 1768 at
Geneva, a very nonmonarchical small city-republic, ruled by a close-knit circle of
hereditary patricians. Royal power, where it existed, became the victim of
revolutionaries only where it was used to support various privileged social groups.

The revolutionary movement announced itself everywhere as a demand for
"liberty and equality." It favored declarations of rights and explicit written
constitutions. It proclaimed the sovereignty of the people, or "nation," and it
formulated the idea of national citizenship. In this context the "people" were
essentially classless; it was a legal term, the obverse of government, signifying the
community over which public authority was exercised and from which government
itself was in principle derived. To say that citizens were equal meant originally that
there was no difference between noble and common. To say that the people were
sovereign meant that neither the king, nor the British Parliament, nor any group
of nobles, patricians, regents or other elite possessed power of government in their
own right; that all public officers were removable and exercised a delegated authority within limits defined by the constitution. There must be no "magistrate" above
the people, no self-perpetuation or cooptation in office, no rank derived from birth
and acknowledged in the law. Social distinctions, as the French said in their
Declaration of Rights of 1789, were to be based only "on common utility." Elites
of talent or function there might be, but none of birth, privilege, or estate. "Aristocracy" in every form must be shunned. In representative bodies, there could be
no special representation for special groups; representatives should be elected by

The Hon. Mrs. Graham *by Thomas Gainsborough (English, 1727–1788)*
*The meaning of aristocracy is abundantly evident in this picture of a young gentlewoman, whose
title, "The Honorable," is still used in Great Britain for the daughters of viscounts and barons.
Wealth is apparent in the brooch, the plumes, the silks, bows and ruffles, and in the pearls which
are both worn in strings and sewn on the hat and garments. The meticulous coiffure and
complexities of dress suggest the constant attentions of lady's maids. The tall stature, delicate
hands, refined mouth and haughty expression all reveal high breeding, and the classical colonnade
on which the lady so casually rests her arm lends an air of familiarity with magnificent
surroundings. Perhaps the aristocrats of the eighteenth century did not often look like this, but this
is the way they liked to imagine themselves and to be portrayed for posterity. In Gainsborough, Sir
Joshua Reynolds, and Sir Thomas Lawrence, England had an unparalleled group of artists who
specialized in painting the upper class. Courtesy of the National Gallery of Scotland.*

frequent elections, not indeed usually by universal suffrage, but by a body of voters, however defined, in which each voter should count for one in a system of equal representation. Representation by numbers, with majority rule, replaced the older idea of representation of social classes, privileged towns, or other corporate groups.

In short, everything associated with absolutism, feudalism, or inherited right (except the right of property) was repudiated. Likewise rejected was any connection between religion and citizenship, or civil rights. The Democratic Revolution undermined the special position of the Catholic church in France, the Anglican in England and Ireland, the Dutch Reformed in the United Provinces; this was also the great period of what has been called Jewish "emancipation." The whole idea that government, or any human authority, was somehow willed by God and protected by religion faded away. A general liberty of opinion on all subjects was countenanced, in the belief that it was necessary to progress. Here again the secularism of the Enlightenment carried on.

On the whole, the Democratic Revolution was a middle-class movement, and indeed the term "bourgeois revolution" was later invented to describe it. Many of its leaders in Europe were in fact nobles who were willing to forego the historic privileges of nobility; and many of its supporters were of the poorer classes, especially in the great French Revolution. But the middle classes were the great beneficiaries, and it was a kind of middle-class or bourgeois society that emerged. Persons of noble ancestry continued to exist after the storm was over, but the world of noble values was gone; and they either took part in various activities on much the same terms as others or retreated into exclusive drawing rooms to enjoy their aristocratic distinctions in private. The main drive of the working classes was still to come.

The English-Speaking Countries: Parliament and Reform

If the American Revolution was the first act of a larger drama, it must be understood also in connection with the broader British world of which the American colonies formed a part. The British Empire in the middle of the century was decentralized and composite. Thirty-one governments were directly subordinate to Westminster, ranging from the separate kingdom of Ireland through all the crown and charter colonies to the various political establishments maintained in the East by the East

Mrs. Isaac Smith *by John Singleton Copley (American, then English, 1737–1815)*
Mrs. Smith may be contrasted with the Hon. Mrs. Graham. The wife of a Boston merchant, she and her husband both had their portraits painted by Copley in 1769. The picture may be taken to typify, in its portrayal of a middle-aged woman, the bourgeois family background from which came much of the leadership of the American and French revolutions. In general, it was a background of substance, comfort and hard work. Mrs. Smith's costume and surroundings, though less elegant than Mrs. Graham's, suggest her high station in New England society. Her expression is between the prim and the pleasant. She clearly represents, and expects from others, a settled standard of behavior and decorum. Copley, troubled by the rising revolutionary agitation, left America in 1774 and spent the rest of his long life in England. Courtesy of the Yale University Art Gallery, Gift of Maitland Fuller Griggs.

India Company. The whole empire, with about 15,000,000 people of all colors in 1750, was less populous than France or the Austrian monarchy. The whole tract of the American mainland from Georgia to Nova Scotia compared in the number of its white population with Ireland or Scotland—or with Brittany or Bohemia—a figure of about 2,000,000 being roughly applicable in each case.

England had its own way of passing through the Age of Enlightenment. There was general contentment with the arrangements that followed the English Revolution of 1688—it has often been remarked that nothing is so conservative as a successful revolution. British thought lacked the asperity of thought on the Continent. The writers who most resembled French philosophes, such as Hume and Gibbon, were innocuously moderate in their political ideas. The prevailing mood was one of complacency, a self-satisfaction in the glories of the British constitution, by which Englishmen enjoyed liberties unknown on the Continent.

In Britain, Parliament was supreme, as in most Continental countries, the monarch. It had the power, as one facetious journalist put it, to do all things except change a man into a woman. The British Parliament was as sovereign as any European ruler, and indeed more so, since less that could be called feudalism remained in England than on the Continent. Nor was there any "despotism" in England, enlightened or otherwise. The young George III, who inherited the throne in 1760, did feel himself to be a "patriot king." He did wish to heighten the influence of the crown and to overcome the factionalism of parties.[26] But it was through Parliament that he had to work. He had to descend into the political arena himself, buy up or otherwise control votes in the Commons, grant pensions and favors, and make promises and deals with other parliamentary politicians. What he did in effect was to create a new faction, the "king's friends." This faction was in power during the ministry of Lord North from 1770 to 1782. It is worth noting that all factions were factions of Whigs, that the Tory party was practically defunct, that Britain did not yet have a two-party system, and that the word "Tory," as it came to be used by American revolutionaries, was little more than a term of abuse.

While Parliament was supreme, and constitutional questions apparently settled, there were nevertheless numerous undercurrents of discontent. These were expressed, since the press was freer in England than elsewhere, in many books and pamphlets which were read in the American colonies and helped to form the psychology of the American Revolution. There was, for example, a school of Anglo-Irish Protestant writers, who argued that since Ireland was in any case a separate kingdom, with its own parliament, it ought to be less dependent on the central government at Westminster. The possibility of a similar separate kingdom, remaining within the British Empire, was one of the alternatives considered by Americans before they settled on independence. In England there was the considerable body of Dissenters, or Protestants not accepting the Church of England, who had enjoyed religious toleration since 1689 but continued to labor (until 1828) under various forms of political exclusion. They overlapped with two other

[26]See pp. 275–277.

amorphous groups, a small number of "commonwealthmen" and a larger and growing number of parliamentary reformers. The commonwealthmen, increasingly eccentric and largely ignored, looked back nostalgically to the Puritan Revolution and the republican era of Oliver Cromwell.[27] They kept alive memories of the Levellers and ideals of equality, well mixed with a pseudo-history of a simple Anglo-Saxon England that had been crushed by the despotism of the Norman Conquest. The commonwealthmen had less influence in England than in the American colonies and especially New England, which had originated in close connection with the Puritan Revolution. The parliamentary reformers were a more diverse and influential group. They were condemned in the eighteenth century to repeated frustration; not until the First Reform Bill of 1832 was anything accomplished.

The very power of Parliament meant that political leaders, the king, his ministers, or others, had to take strong measures to assure its votes. Those measures were generally denounced by their critics as "corruption," on the grounds that Parliament, whether or not truly representative, should at least be free. Control of Parliament, and especially of the House of Commons, was assured by various devices, such as patronage or the giving of government jobs (called "places"), or awarding contracts, or having infrequent general elections (every seven years after 1716), or the fact that in many constituencies there were no real elections at all. Many boroughs were "corrupt"; a few were populous and democratic but easily run by political managers; a great many, authorized in the Middle Ages or by the Tudors to send members to Parliament, now had few inhabitants or none, so that the members were designated by "borough-mongers," with whom political leaders could make arrangements. Despite shifts of population, no new borough was created between the Revolution of 1688 and the Reform Bill of 1832.

The reform movement began in England before the American Revolution, with which it was closely associated. Since complaints were diverse, it attracted people of different kinds. The first agitation centered about John Wilkes. Having attacked the policies of George III, been vindicated when the courts pronounced the arrest of his publisher illegal, and been expelled by a House of Commons dominated by the king's supporters, Wilkes became a hero and was three times reelected to the House, which, however, refused to seat him. In a whirl of protests and public meetings, reams of petitions supported him against the House. His followers in 1769 founded the Supporters of the Bill of Rights, the first of many societies dedicated to parliamentary reform. His case raised the question whether the House of Commons should be dependent on the electorate and the propriety of mass agitation "out of doors" on political questions. It was in this connection, also, that debates in Parliament for the first time came to be reported in the London press. Parliament stood on the eve of a long transition, by which it was to be converted from a select body meeting in private to a modern representative institution answerable to the public and its constituents. Wilkes himself, in 1776, introduced the first of many reform bills of which none passed for over half a century. Meanwhile Major John

Cartwright, called the "father of reform," had begun a long series of pamphlets on the subject; he lived to be eighty-four but not quite long enough to see the Reform Act of 1832. Dissenting intellectuals, such as Richard Price and Joseph Priestley, joined in the movement. Price, a founder of actuarial statistics, announced in 1776 that only 5,723 persons chose half the membership of the House of Commons. Many London merchants favored reform. So did a great many landowners and country gentry, especially in the north of England, led by Christopher Wyvil. These men objected to the fact that four-fifths of the members of the House of Commons sat for the boroughs and only one-fifth for the shires or counties. They rightly thought that the boroughs were more easily manipulated by the government; they thought that county elections were more honest; and they initiated in 1780 a movement of county associations to promote change in the electoral system.

The important Whig leaders, who had previously managed Parliament by much the same methods, began to sense "corruption" after control passed to George III and his "friends." Their most eloquent spokesman was Edmund Burke. Other reformers called for more frequent elections, "annual parliaments," a wider and more equal or even universal male suffrage, with dissolution of some boroughs in which no one was really represented. Burke favored none of these things; in fact he came strenuously to oppose them. A founder of philosophical conservatism, he was yet in his way a reformer. He was more concerned that the House of Commons should be independent and responsible than that it should be mathematically representative. He thought that the landowning interest should govern. But he pleaded for a strong sense of party in opposition to royal encroachments, and he argued that members of Parliament should follow their own best judgment of the country's interests, bound neither by the king on the one hand nor by their own constituents on the other. Like other reformers, he objected to "placemen," or jobholders dependent on their ministerial patrons, and he objected to the use made, for political purposes, of a bewildering array of pensions, sinecures, honorific appointments, and ornamental offices, ranks, and titles. In his Economical Reform of 1782 he got many of these abolished.

The reform movement, though ineffectual, remained strong. Even William Pitt, as prime minister in the 1780s, gave it his sponsorship. It took on new strength at the time of the French Revolution, spreading then to more popular levels, as men of the skilled artisan class were aroused by events in France and demanded a more adequate "representation of the people" of England. They then had upper-class support from Charles James Fox and a minority of the Whigs. But conservatism, satisfaction with the British constitution, patriotism engendered by a new round of French wars, and reaction against the French Revolution all raised an impassable barrier. Reform was delayed for another generation.

After the American Revolution, which in a way was a civil struggle within the English-speaking world, the English reformers generally blamed the trouble with America on King George III. This was less than fair, since Parliament on the American question was never dragooned by the king. The most ardent reformers later argued that if Parliament had been truly representative of the British people, the Americans would not have been driven to independence. This seems unlikely. In any case, reformers of various kinds, from Wilkes to Burke, were sympathetic to the complaints of the American colonials after 1763. There was much busy correspondence across the Atlantic. Wilkes was a hero in Boston as well as London. Burke pleaded for conciliation with the colonies in a famous speech of 1775. His very insistence on the powers and dignity of Parliament, however, made it hard for him to find a workable solution; and after the colonies became independent he showed no interest in the political ideas of the new American states. It was the more radical reformers in England, as in Scotland and Ireland, who most consistently favored the Americans, both before and after independence. They of course had no power. On the American side, for a decade before independence, the increasingly discontented colonials, reading English books and pamphlets and reports of speeches, heard George III denounced for despotism and Parliament accused of incorrigible corruption. All this seemed to confirm what Americans had long been reading anyway in the works of English Dissenters or old commonwealthmen, now on the fringes of English society but sure of a receptive audience in the American colonies. The result was to make Americans suspicious of all actions by the British government, to sense tyranny everywhere, to magnify such things as the Stamp Act into a kind of plot against American liberties.

The real drift in England in the eighteenth century, however, despite the chronic criticism of Parliament, was for Parliament to extend its powers in a general centralization of the empire. The British government faced somewhat the same problems as governments on the Continent. All had to deal with the issues raised by the great war of the mid-century, in its two phases of the Austrian Succession and Seven Years' War. Everywhere the solution adopted by governments was to increase their own central power. We have seen how the French government, in attempting to tap new sources of revenue, tried to encroach on the liberties of Brittany and other provinces and to subordinate the bodies which in France were called parliaments. We have likewise seen how the Habsburg government, also in an effort to raise more taxes, repressed local self-government in the empire and even abrogated the constitution of Bohemia.[28] The same tendency showed itself in the British system. The revocation of the charter of Bohemia in 1749 had its parallel in the revocation of the charter of Massachusetts in 1774. The disputes of the French king with the estates of Brittany or Languedoc had their parallel in the disputes of the British Parliament with the provincial assemblies of Virginia or New York.

There were also problems nearer home. Scotland proved a source of weakness in the War of the Austrian Succession. The Lowlanders were loyal enough, but the Highlanders revolted with French assistance in the Jacobite rising of 1745, and by

[28] See pp. 338–340, 341.

invading England threatened to take the British government in the rear as it was locked in the struggle with France.[29] The Highlands had never really been under any government, even under the old Scottish monarchy before the union of 1707 with England. Social organization, in the Highland fastnesses, followed the primitive principle of physical kinship. Men looked to their chiefs, the heads of the clans, to tell them whom and when to fight. The chiefs had hereditary jurisdiction, often including powers of life and death, over their clansmen. A few leaders could throw the whole region to the Stuarts or the French. The British government, after 1745, proceeded to make its sovereignty effective in the Highlands. Troops were quartered there for years. Roads were pushed across the moors and through the glens. Law courts enforced the law of the Scottish Lowlands. Revenue officers collected funds for the treasury of Great Britain. The chiefs lost their old quasi-feudal jurisdiction. The old system of land tenure was broken up. The holding of land from clannish chiefs was ended. The clansman swayed by his chief was turned into the subject of the crown of Great Britain. He was turned also, in many cases, into an almost landless "crofter," while some of the chiefs, or their sons, emerged as landed gentlemen of the English type. Fighting Highlanders were incorporated into newly formed Highland regiments of the British army, under the usual discipline imposed by the modern state on its fighting forces. For thirty years the Scots were forbidden to wear the kilt or play the bagpipes.

In Ireland the process of centralization worked itself out more slowly. How Ireland was subjected after the battle of the Boyne has already been described.[30] It was a French army that had landed in Ireland, supported James II, and been defeated in 1690. The new English constitutional arrangements, the Hanoverian succession, the Protestant ascendancy, the church and the land settlement in Ireland, together with the prosperity of British commerce were all secured by the subordination of the smaller island. The native or Catholic Irish remained generally pro-French. The Presbyterian Irish disliked both Frenchmen and popery, but they were alienated from England also; many in fact emigrated to America in the generation before the American Revolution. The island remained quiet in the mid-century wars. When the trouble began between the British Parliament and the American colonies the Presbyterian Irish generally took the American side. They were greatly stirred by the example of American independence. Thousands formed themselves into Volunteer Companies; they wore uniforms, armed, and drilled; they demanded both internal reform of the Irish parliament (which was even less representative than the British) and greater autonomy for the Irish parliament as against the central government at Westminster. Faced with these demands, and fearing a French invasion of Ireland during the War of American Independence, the British government made concessions. It allowed an increase of power to the Irish parliament at Dublin. But from this parliament Catholics were still excluded. In the next war between France and Great Britain, which began in 1793, many Irish felt a warm sympathy for the French Revo-

---

[29] See p. 276.
[30] See pp. 185–186.

lution. Catholics and Presbyterians, at last combining, formed a network of United Irish societies throughout the whole island. They sought French aid, and the French barely failed to land a sizable army. Even without French military support, the United Irish rose in 1798 to drive out the English and establish an independent republic. The British, suppressing the rebellion, now turned to centralization. The separate kingdom of Ireland, and Irish parliament, ceased to exist. The Irish were thereafter represented in the imperial Parliament at Westminster. These provisions were incorporated in the Act of Union of 1801, creating the United Kingdom of Great Britain and Ireland, which lasted until 1922.

British establishments in India also felt the hand of Parliament increasingly upon them. At the close of the Seven Years' War the various British posts in and around Bombay, Madras, and Calcutta were unconnected with each other and subordinate only to the board of directors of the East India Company in London. Company employees interfered at will in the wars and politics of the Indian states and enriched themselves by such means as they could, not excluding graft, trickery, intimidation, rapine, and extortion.[31] In 1773 the ministry of Lord North passed a Regulating Act, of which the main purpose was to regulate, not Indians, but the British subjects in India, whom no Indian government could control. The company was left with its trading activities, but its political activities were brought under parliamentary supervision. The act gathered all the British establishments under a single governor-general, set up a new supreme court at Calcutta, and required the company to submit its correspondence on political matters for review by the ministers of His Majesty's Government. Warren Hastings became the first British governor-general in India. He was so high-handed with some of the Indian princes, and made so many enemies among jealous Englishmen in Bengal, that he was denounced at home, impeached, and subjected to a trial which dragged on for seven years in the House of Lords. He was finally acquitted. After Clive, he was the main author of British supremacy in India. Meanwhile, in 1784, by a new India Act of that year, the post of Secretary of State for India, together with an India office, was created in the British ministry at home. The governor-general henceforth ruled the growing British sphere in India almost as an absolute monarch but only as the agent of the ministry and Parliament of Great Britain.

Thus the trend in the British world was to centralization. Despite the flutter of royalism under George III, it was to a centralization of all British territories under authority of the Parliament. What was happening in empire affairs, as in domestic politics in England, was a continuing application of the principles of 1689. The parliamentary sovereignty established in 1689 was now, after the middle of the eighteenth century, being applied to regions where it had heretofore had little effect. And it was against the British Parliament that the Americans primarily rebelled. Some at the time, including Jefferson and Franklin in America and Burke in England, conceived plans by which the Americans, while remaining under the British crown, should possess a kind of parliament of their own. They sketched out the "dominion

[31] See pp. 290–291.

status" later enjoyed by Canada and Australia. What effect the adoption of such a federal or decentralizing scheme might have had has long been a subject of speculation. It was scarcely a practical possibility at the time. Not only was the trend, for good reason, toward greater centralization of the powers of government. It also seemed, before the revolution itself taught them otherwise, that the American colonials were incapable of responsible self-rule.

38
The American
Revolution

*Background to
the Revolution*

The behavior of the Americans in the Seven Years' War left much to be desired.[32] The several colonial legislatures rejected the Albany Plan of Union drafted by Franklin and commended to them by the British officials. During the war it was the British regular army and navy, financed by taxes and loans in Great Britain, that drove the French out of America. The war effort of the Anglo-Americans was desultory at best. After the defeat of the French the colonials had still to reckon with the Indians of the interior, who preferred French rule to that of their new British and British-colonial masters. Many tribes joined in an uprising led by Pontiac, a western chief, and they ravaged as far eastward as the Pennsylvania and Virginia frontiers. Again, the colonials proved unable to deal with a problem vital to their own future, and peace was brought about by officials and army units taking their orders from Great Britain.

The British government tried to make the colonials pay a larger share toward the expenses of the empire. The colonials had hitherto paid only local taxes. They were liable to customs duties, of which the proceeds went in principle to Great Britain; but these duties were levied to enforce the Acts of Trade and Navigation, to direct the flow of commerce, not to raise revenue; and they were seldom paid, because the Acts of Trade and Navigation were persistently ignored. American merchants, for example, commonly imported sugar from the French West Indies, contrary to law, and even shipped in return the iron wares which it was against the law for Americans to manufacture for export. Disregard of law was commonplace in the eighteenth century, when governments freely enacted general legislation without succeeding in or even caring about enforcement in particular cases—one is reminded of the French censorship or the British ban on Indian cloth. Yet the British Americans were possibly the least law-abiding of all the more civilized European peoples. Their illicit trade went on outside the revenue system. Receipts from customs duties fell short even of paying the salaries and other emoluments of the customs officials. The colonial in practice paid only such taxes as were approved by his own local legislature for local purposes. The Americans in effect enjoyed a degree of tax exemption within the empire, and it was against this form of provincial privilege that Parliament began to move.

By the Revenue Act of 1764 (the "Sugar" Act), the British ministry, while reducing and liberalizing the customs duties payable in America, entered upon a program of actual and systematic collection. In the following year the ministry at-

[32]See pp. 287–288.

tempted to extend to British subjects in America a tax peaceably accepted by those in Great Britain and commonplace in most of Europe. This imposed on all uses of paper, as in newspapers and commercial and legal documents, the payment of a fee which was certified by the affixing of a stamp. The Stamp Act aroused violent and concerted resistance in the colonies, especially among the businessmen, lawyers, and editors who were the most articulate class. It therefore was repealed in 1766. In 1767 Parliament, clumsily casting about to find a tax acceptable to the Americans, hit upon the "Townshend duties," which taxed colonial imports of paper, paint, lead, and tea. Another outcry went up, and the Townshend duties were repealed, except the one on tea, which was kept as a token of the sovereign power of Parliament to tax all persons in the empire.

The colonials had proved stubborn, the government pliable but lacking in constructive ideas. The Americans argued that Parliament had no authority to tax them because they were not represented in it. The British replied that Parliament represented America as much as it represented Great Britain. If Philadelphia sent no actually elected deputies to the Commons, so this argument ran, neither did Manchester in England, yet both places enjoyed a "virtual representation," since members of the Commons did not in any case merely speak for local constituencies but made themselves responsible for imperial interests as a whole. To this many Americans retorted that if Manchester was not "really" represented it ought to be, which was of course also the belief of the English reformers. Meanwhile the strictly Anglo-American question subsided after the repeal of the Stamp Act and the Townshend program. There had been no clarification of principle on either side. But in practice the Americans had resisted significant taxation, and Parliament had refrained from making any drastic use of its sovereign power.

The calm was shattered in 1773 by an event which proved, to the more dissatisfied Americans, the disadvantages of belonging to a global economic system in which the main policies were made on the other side of the ocean. The East India Company was in difficulties. It had a great surplus of Chinese tea,[33] and in any case it wanted new commercial privileges in return for the political privileges which it was losing by the Regulating Act of 1773. In the past the company had been required to sell its wares at public auction in London; other merchants had handled distribution from that point on. Now, in 1773, Parliament granted the company the exclusive right to sell tea through its own agents in America to American local dealers. Tea was a large item of business in the commercial capitalism of the time. The colonial consumer might pay less for it, but the intermediary American merchant would be shut out. The company's tea was boycotted in all American ports. In Boston, to prevent its forcible landing, a party of disguised men invaded the tea ships and dumped the chests into the harbor. To this act of vandalism the British government replied by measures far out of proportion to the offense. It "closed" the port of Boston, thus threatening the city with economic ruin. It virtually rescinded the charter of Massachusetts, forbidding certain local elections and the holding of town meetings.

[33] See p. 268.

And at the same time, in 1774, apparently by coincidence, Parliament enacted the Quebec Act. The wisest piece of British legislation in these troubled years, the Quebec Act provided a government for the newly conquered Canadian French, granting them security in their French civil law and Catholic religion, and laying foundations for the British Empire that was to come. But the act defined the boundaries of Quebec somewhat as the French themselves would have defined them, including in them all territory north of the Ohio River—the present states of Wisconsin, Michigan, Illinois, Indiana, and Ohio. These boundaries were perfectly reasonable, since the few white men in the area were French, and since, in the age before canals or railways, the obvious means of reaching the whole region was by way of the St. Lawrence valley and the Lakes. But to the Americans the Quebec Act was a pro-French and pro-Catholic outrage, and at a time when the powers of juries and assemblies in the old colonies were threatened, it was disquieting that the Quebec Act made no mention of such representative institutions for the new northern province. It was lumped with the closing of an American port and the destruction of an American government as one of the "Intolerable Acts" to be resisted.

And indeed the implications of parliamentary sovereignty were now apparent. The meaning of centralized planning and authority was now clear. It was no longer merely an affair of taxation. A government that had to take account of the East India Company, the French Canadians, and the British taxpayers, even if more prudent and enlightened than Lord North's ministry of 1774, could not possibly at the same time have satisfied the Americans of the thirteen seaboard colonies. These Americans, since 1763 no longer afraid of the French empire, were less inclined to forego their own interests in order to remain in the British. British policies had aroused antagonism in the coastal towns and in the backwoods, among wealthy land speculators and poor squatter frontiersmen, among merchants and the workingmen who depended on the business of merchants. The freedom of Americans to determine their own political life was in question. Yet there were few in 1774, or even later, prepared to face the thought of independence.

The War of
American Independence

After the "Intolerable Acts" self-authorized groups met in the several colonies and sent delegates to a "continental congress" in Philadelphia. This body adopted a boycott of British goods, to be enforced on unwilling Americans by local organizers of resistance. Fighting began in the next year, 1775, when the British commander at Boston sent a detachment to seize unauthorized stores of weapons at Concord. On the way, at Lexington, in a brush between soldiers and partisans or "minutemen," someone fired the "shot heard round the world." The Second Continental Congress, meeting a few weeks later, proceeded to raise an American army, dispatched an expedition to force Quebec into the revolutionary union, and entered into overtures with Bourbon France.

The Congress was still reluctant to repudiate the tie with Britain. But passions grew fierce in consequence of the fighting. Radicals convinced moderates that the choice now lay between independence and enslavement. It appeared that the French, naturally uninterested in a reconciliation of British subjects, would give help if the avowed aim of American rebels was to dismember the British Empire. In January 1776 Thomas Paine, in his pamphlet *Common Sense,* made his debut as a kind of international revolutionary; he was to figure in the French Revolution and to work for revolution in England. He had come from England less than two years before, and he detested English society for its injustices to men like himself. Eloquent and vitriolic, *Common Sense* identified the independence of the American colonies with the cause of liberty for all mankind. It pitted freedom against tyranny in the person of "the royal brute of Great Britain." It was "repugnant to reason," said Paine, "to suppose that this Continent can long remain subject to any external power. . . . There is something absurd in supposing a Continent to be perpetually governed by an island." *Common Sense* was read everywhere in the colonies, and its slashing arguments unquestionably spread a sense of proud isolation from the Old World. On July 4, 1776, the Congress adopted the Declaration of Independence, by which the United States assumed its separate and equal station among the powers of the earth.

The War of American Independence thereupon turned into another European struggle for empire. For two more years the French government remained ostensibly noninterventionist but meanwhile poured munitions into the colonies through an especially rigged up commercial concern. Nine-tenths of the arms used by the Americans at the battle of Saratoga came from France. After the American victory in this battle the French government concluded, in 1778, that the insurgents were a good political risk, recognized them, signed an alliance with them, and declared war on Great Britain. Spain soon followed, hoping to drive the British from Gibraltar and deciding that its overseas empire was more threatened by a restoration of British supremacy in North America than by the disturbing example of an independent American republic. The Dutch were drawn into hostilities after recognizing American independence. Other powers, Russia, Sweden, Denmark, Prussia, Portugal, and Turkey, irked at British employment of blockade and sea power in time of war, formed an "Armed Neutrality" to protect their commerce from dictation by the British fleet. The French, in a brief revival of their own sea power, landed an expeditionary force of 6,000 men in Rhode Island. Since the Americans suffered from the internal differences inseparable from all revolutions and were in any case still unable to govern themselves to any effect, meeting with the old difficulties in raising both troops and money, it was the participation of regiments of the French army, in conjunction with squadrons of the French fleet, which made possible the defeat of the armed forces of the British Empire and so persuaded the British government to recognize the independence of the United States. By the peace treaty of 1783, though the British were still in possession of New York and Savannah, and though the governments befriending the Americans would just as soon have confined them east of the mountains, the new republic obtained territory as far west as the Mississippi. Canada remained British. It received an English-speaking population by the settlement of over 60,000 refugee Americans who remained loyal to Great Britain.

The upheaval in America was a revolution as well as a war of independence. The cry for liberty against Great Britain raised echoes within the colonies themselves. The Declaration of Independence was more than an announcement of secession from the empire; it was a justification of rebellion against established authority. Curiously, although the American quarrel had been with the Parliament, the Declaration arraigned no one but the king. One reason was that the Congress, not recognizing the authority of Parliament, could separate from Great Britain only by a denunciation of the British crown; another reason was that the cry of "tyrant" made a more popular and flaming issue. Boldly voicing the natural right philosophy of the age, the Declaration held as "self-evident," i.e., as evident to all reasonable men, that "all men are created equal, that they are endowed by their Creator with certain unalienable rights, that among these are life, liberty, and the pursuit of happiness." These electrifying words leaped inward into America, and outward to the world.

In the new states democratic equality made many advances. It was subject, however, to a great limitation, in that it long really applied only to white persons of European origin. The Indians were few in number, but the black population at the time of the Revolution comprised about a fifth of the whole. It was much larger proportionately than it became later, after mass immigration from Europe raised the proportion of whites. Many American whites of the revolutionary generation were indeed troubled by the institution of slavery. It was abolished outright in Massachusetts, and all states north of Maryland took steps toward its gradual extinction. But to apply the principles of liberty and equality without regard to race was beyond the powers of Americans at the time. In the South, all censuses from 1790 to 1850 showed a third of the population to be slaves. In the North, free blacks found that in fact, and often in law, they were debarred from voting, from adequate schooling, and from the widening opportunities in which white Americans saw the essence of their national life and their superiority to Europe.

For the white majority the Revolution had a democratizing effect in many ways. Lawyers, landowners and businessmen who led the movement against England needed the support of numbers and to obtain it were willing to make promises and concessions to the lower classes. Or the popular elements, workmen and mechanics, farmers and frontiersmen, often dissidents in religion, extorted concessions by force or threats. There was a good deal of violence, as in all revolutions; the new states confiscated property from the counterrevolutionaries, called Tories, some of whom were in addition tarred and feathered by infuriated mobs. The dissolution of the old colonial governments threw open all political questions. In some states more men became qualified to vote. In some, governors and senators were now popularly elected, in addition to the lower houses of the legislatures as in colonial times. The principle was adopted, still unknown to the parliamentary bodies of Europe, that each member of a legislative assembly should represent about the same number of citizens. Primogeniture and entail, which landed families aspiring to an aristocratic mode of life sometimes favored, went down before the demands of democrats and small property owners. Tithes were done away with, and the established churches,

Anglican in the South, Congregationalist in New England, lost their privileged position in varying degree. But the Revolution was not socially as profound as the revolution soon to come in France, or as the revolution in Russia in 1917. Property changed hands, but the law of property was modified only in detail. There had been no such thing in British America as a native nobleman or even a bishop; clergy and aristocracy had been incomparably less ingrained in American than in European society, and the rebellion against them was less devastating in its effect.

The main import of the American Revolution remained political and even constitutional in a strict sense. The American leaders were themselves part of the Age of Enlightenment, sharing fully in its humane and secular spirit. But probably the only non-British thinker by whom they were influenced was Montesquieu, and Montesquieu owed his popularity to his philosophizing upon English institutions. The Americans drew heavily on the writings of John Locke, but their cast of mind went back before Locke to the English Puritan movement of the first half of the seventeenth century. Their thought was formed not only by Locke's ideas of human nature and government, but, as already noted, by the dissenting literature and the neo-republican writings that had never quite died out in England. The realities of life for five generations in America had sharpened the old insistence upon personal liberty and equality. When the dispute with Britain came to a head, the Americans found themselves arguing both for the historic and chartered rights of Englishmen and for the timeless and universal rights of man, both of which were held up as barriers against the inroads of parliamentary sovereignty. The Americans came to believe, more than any other people, that government should possess limited powers and operate only within the terms of a fixed and written constitutional document.

All thirteen of the new states lost no time in providing themselves with written constitutions (in Connecticut and Rhode Island merely the old charters reaffirmed), all of which enshrined virtually the same principles. All followed the thought stated in the great Declaration, that it was to protect "unalienable" rights that governments were instituted among men, and that whenever government became destructive to this end the people had a right to "institute new government" for their safety and happiness. All the constitutions undertook to limit government by a separation of governmental powers. All appended a bill of rights, stating the natural rights of the citizens and the things which no government might justly do. None of the constitutions were as yet fully democratic; even the most liberal gave some advantage in public affairs to the owners of property.

Federalism, or the allocation of power between central and outlying governments, went along with the idea of written constitutions as a principal offering of the Americans to the world. Like constitutionalism, federalism developed in the atmosphere of protest against a centralized sovereign power. It was a hard idea for Americans to work out, since the new states carried over the old separatism which had so distracted the British. Until 1789 the states remained banded together in the Articles of Confederation. The United States was a union of thirteen independent republics. Disadvantages in this scheme becoming apparent, a constitutional convention met at Philadelphia in 1787 and drew up the constitution which is today the world's oldest written instrument of government still in operation. In it the United States was conceived not merely as a league of states, but as a union in which individuals were citizens of the United States of America for some purposes and of their particular states for others. Persons, not states, composed the federal republic, and the laws of the United States fell not merely on the states but on the people.

The consequences of the American Revolution can hardly be overstated. By overburdening the French treasury the American war became a direct cause of the French Revolution. Beyond that, it ushered in the age of predominantly liberal or democratic revolution which lasted through the European revolutions of 1848. The American doctrine, like most thought in the Age of Enlightenment, was expressed in universal terms of "man" and "nature." All peoples regardless of their own history could apply it to themselves, because, as Alexander Hamilton once put it in his youth, "the sacred rights of man are not to be rummaged for among old parchments or musty records. They are written, as with a sunbeam, in the whole volume of human nature, by the hand of Divinity itself, and can never be erased or obscured by mortal power." The Americans, in freeing themselves, had done what all men ought to do.

The revolt in America offered a dramatic judgment on the old colonial system, convincing some, in England and elsewhere, that the empires for which they had long been struggling were hardly worth acquiring, since colonies in time, in the words of Turgot, fell away from the mother country "like ripe fruit." The idea spread, since trade between Britain and America continued to prosper, that one could do business with a country without exerting political influence or control, and this idea became fundamental to the coming movement of economic liberalism and free trade. By coincidence, the book that became the gospel of the free trade movement, Adam Smith's *Wealth of Nations,* was published in England in the year 1776. The American example was pointed to by other peoples wishing to throw off colonial status—first by the Latin Americans, then by the peoples of the older British dominions, and, finally, in the twentieth century, by those of Asia and Africa also. In Europe, the American example encouraged the type of nationalism in which subjugated nations aspire to be free. And at home the Revolution did much to determine the spirit and method by which the bulk of the North American continent was to be peopled and the attitudes for which the United States, when it became a leading power a century and a half later, was to stand before the world.

More immediately, the American example was not lost on the many Europeans who sojourned in the new states during and after the war. Of these the Marquis de Lafayette was the most famous, but there were many others: Thomas Paine, who returned to Europe in 1787; the future French revolutionist Brissot; the future Polish national leader Kosciusko; the future marshals of Napoleon, Jourdan and Berthier; the future reformer of the Prussian army Gneisenau. Contrariwise various Americans went to Europe, notably the aging Benjamin Franklin, who in the 1780s was incredibly lionized in the fashionable and literary world of Paris.

The establishment of the United States was taken in Europe to prove that many ideas of the Enlightenment were practicable. Rationalists declared that here was a people, free of past errors and superstitions, who showed how enlightened beings could plan their affairs. Rousseauists saw in America the very paradise of natural equality, unspoiled innocence, and patriotic virtue. But nothing so much impressed Europeans, and especially the French, as the spectacle of the Americans meeting in solemn conclave to draft their state constitutions. These, along with the Declaration of Independence, were translated and published in 1778 by a French nobleman, the Duke de la Rochefoucauld. They were endlessly and excitedly discussed. Constitutionalism, federalism, and limited government were not new ideas in Europe. They came out of the Middle Ages and were currently set forth in many quarters, for example, in Hungary, the Holy Roman Empire, and the Parliament of Paris. But in their prevailing form, and even in the philosophy of Montesquieu, they were associated with feudalism and aristocracy. The American Revolution made such ideas progressive. The American influence, added to the force of developments in Europe, made the thought of the later Enlightenment more democratic. The United States replaced England as the model country of advanced thinkers. On the Continent there was less passive trust in the enlightened despotism of the official state. Confidence in self-government was aroused.

The American constitutions seemed a demonstration of the social contract. They offered a picture of men in a "state of nature," having cast off their old government, deliberately sitting down to contrive a new one, weighing and judging each branch of government on its merits, assigning due powers to legislature, executive, and judiciary, declaring that all government was created by the people and in possession of a merely delegated authority, and listing specifically the inalienable rights of men—inalienable in that they could not conceivably be taken away, since men possessed them even if denied them by force. And these rights were the very same rights that many Europeans wanted secured for themselves—freedom of religion, freedom of press, freedom of assembly, freedom from arbitrary arrest at the discretion of officials. And they were the same for all, on the rigorous principle of equality before the law. The American example crystallized and made tangible the ideas that were strongly blowing in Europe, and the American example was one reason why the French, in 1789, began their revolution with a declaration of human rights and with the drafting of a written constitution.

And more deeply still, America became a kind of mirage or ideal vision for Europe, a land of open opportunity and of new beginnings, free from the load of history and of the past, wistfully addressed by Goethe:

> *America, thou hast it better*
> *Than has our Continent, the old one.*

It is evident that this was only part of the picture. The United States, as its later history was to show, bore a heavy load of inherited burdens and unsolved problems, 371 especially racial.   But in a general way, until new revolutionary movements set in a century later, America stood as a kind of utopia of the common man, not only for the millions who emigrated to it but for other millions who stayed at home, who often wished that their own countries might become more like it, and many of whom might even agree with Abraham Lincoln in calling it the last best hope of earth.

IX: THE FRENCH REVOLUTION

In 1789 France fell into revolution, and the world has never since been the same. The French Revolution was by far the most momentous upheaval of the whole revolutionary age. It replaced the "old regime" with "modern society," and at its extreme phase it became very radical, so much so that all later revolutionary movements have looked back to it as a predecessor to themselves. At the time, in the age of the Democratic or Atlantic Revolution from the 1760s to 1848, the role of France was decisive. Even the Americans, without French military intervention, would hardly have won such a clear settlement from England or been so free to set up the new states and new constitutions that have just been described. And while revolutionary disturbances in Ireland and Poland, or among the Dutch, Italians, and others, were by no means caused by the French example, it was the presence or absence of French aid that usually determined whatever successes they enjoyed.

The French Revolution, unlike the Russian or Chinese revolutions of the twentieth century, occurred in what was in many ways the most advanced country of the day. France was the center of the intellectual movement of the Enlightenment. French science then led the world. French books were read everywhere, and the

Chapter Emblem: A cockade worn during the French Revolution, with the famous motto, and the fleur-de-lis of the monarchy embellished by the cap of liberty.

newspapers and political journals which became very numerous after 1789 carried a message which hardly needed translation. French was a kind of international spoken language in the educated and aristocratic circles of many countries. France was also, potentially before 1789 and actually after 1793, the most powerful country in Europe. It may have been the wealthiest, though not per capita. With a population of some 24,000,000 the French were the most numerous of all European peoples under a single government. Even Russia was hardly more populous until after the partitions of Poland. The Germans were divided, the subjects of the Habsburgs were of diverse nationalities, and the English and Scots together numbered only 10,000,000. Paris, though smaller than London, was over twice as large as Vienna or Amsterdam. French exports to Europe were larger than those of Great Britain. It is said that half the goldpieces circulating in Europe were French. Europeans in the eighteenth century were in the habit of taking ideas from France; they were therefore, depending on their position, the more excited, encouraged, alarmed or horrified when revolution broke out in that country.

39
Backgrounds

*The Old Regime:
The Three Estates*

Some remarks have already been made about the Old Regime, as the prerevolutionary society came to be called after it disappeared, and about the failure of enlightened despotism in France to make any fundamental alteration in it.[1] The essential fact about the Old Regime was that it was still legally aristocratic and in many ways feudal. Everyone belonged legally to an "estate" or "order" of society. The First Estate was the clergy, the Second Estate the nobility, and the Third Estate included everyone else—from the wealthiest business and professional classes to the poorest peasantry and city workers. These categories were important in that the individual's legal rights and personal prestige depended on the category to which he belonged. Politically, they were obsolescent; not since 1614 had the estates assembled in an Estates-General of the whole kingdom, though in some provinces they had continued to meet as provincial bodies. Socially, they were obsolescent also, for the threefold division no longer corresponded to the real distribution of interest, influence, property, or productive activity among the French people.

Conditions in the church and the position of the clergy have been much exaggerated as a cause of the French Revolution. The church in France levied a tithe on all agricultural products, but so did the church in England; the French bishops often played a part in government affairs, but so did bishops in England through the House of Lords. The French bishoprics of 1789 were in reality no wealthier than those of the Church of England were found to be when investigated forty years later. In actual numbers, in the secular atmosphere of the Age of Enlightenment, the clergy, especially the monastic orders, had greatly declined, so that by 1789 there were probably not more than 100,000 Catholic clergy of all types in the entire population.

376   [1] See pp. 337–340.

But if the importance of the clergy has often been overemphasized, still it must be said that the church was deeply involved in the prevailing social system. For one thing, church bodies—bishoprics, abbeys, convents, schools, and other religious foundations—owned between 5 and 10 percent of the land of the country, which meant that collectively the church was the greatest of all landowners. Moreover, the income from church properties, like all income, was divided very unequally, and much of it found its way into the hands of the aristocratic occupants of the higher ecclesiastical offices. For while the mass of the parish clergy was of lower-class origin (more so than in the Church of England), the better positions were reserved for the nobles. Every bishop of Louis XVI's time was a nobleman—a state of affairs unknown before the eighteenth century. It need only be added that in the Age of Enlightenment the church no longer expressed the ideas of many thinking—and unthinking—people.

The noble order, which in 1789 comprised about 400,000 persons, including women and children, had enjoyed a great resurgence since the death of Louis XIV in 1715.[2] The intendants, usually commoners a century before, were now usually nobles. Government service, higher church offices, army, parliaments, and most other public and semipublic honors were almost monopolized by the titled aristocracy in the time of Louis XVI, who, it will be recalled, had mounted the throne in 1774. Repeatedly, through parliaments, Provincial Estates, or the assembly of the clergy dominated by the noble bishops, the aristocracy had blocked royal plans for taxation and shown a desire to control the policies of state. At the same time the bourgeoisie, or upper crust of the Third Estate, had never been so influential. The fivefold increase of French foreign trade between 1713 and 1789 suggests the growth of the merchant class and of the legal and governmental classes associated with it. As members of the bourgeoisie became stronger, more widely read, and more self-confident, they resented the distinctions enjoyed by the nobles. Some of these were financial: nobles were exempt from the most important direct tax, the taille, on principle, whereas bourgeois obtained exemption with more effort; but so many bourgeois enjoyed tax privileges that purely monetary self-interest was not primary in their psychology. The bourgeois resented the nobleman for his superiority and his arrogance. What had formerly been customary respect was now felt as humiliation. And they felt that they were being shut out from office and honors, and that the nobles were seeking more power in government as a class. The Revolution was the collision of two moving objects, a rising aristocracy and a rising bourgeoisie.

The common people, below the commercial and professional families in the Third Estate, were probably as well off as in most countries. But they were not well off compared with the upper classes. Wage earners had by no means shared in the wave of business prosperity. Between the 1730s and the 1780s the prices of consumers' goods rose about 65 percent, whereas wages rose only 22 percent. Persons dependent on wages were therefore badly pinched, but they were less numerous than today, for in the country there were many small farmers and in the

---

[2] See p. 274.

towns many small craftsmen, both of which groups made a living not by wages but by selling the products of their own labor at market prices. Yet in both town and country there was a significant wage-earning or proletarian element, which was to play a decisive part in the Revolution.

The Agrarian System of the Old Regime

Over four-fifths of the people were rural. The agrarian system had developed so that there was no serfdom in France, to be sure, as it was known in eastern Europe.[3] The relation of lord and peasant in France was not the relation of master and man. The peasant owed no labor to the lord—except a few token services in some cases. The peasant worked for himself, either on his own land or on rented land; or he worked as a sharecropper (*métayer*); or he hired himself out to the lord or to another peasant.

The manor, however, still retained certain surviving features of the feudal age. The noble owner of a manor enjoyed "hunting rights," or the privilege of keeping game preserves, and of hunting on his own and the peasants' land. He usually had a monopoly over the village mill, bakeshop, or wine press, for the use of which he collected fees, called *banalités*. He possessed certain vestigial powers of jurisdiction in the manorial court and certain local police powers, from which fees and fines were collected. These seigneurial privileges were of course the survivals of a day when the local manor had been a unit of government, and the noble had performed the functions of government, an age that had long passed with the development of the centralized modern state.

There was another special feature to the property system of the Old Regime. Every owner of a manor (there were some bourgeois and even wealthy peasants who had purchased manors) possessed what was called a right of "eminent property" with respect to all land located in the manorial village. This meant that lesser landowners within the manor "owned" their land in that they could freely buy, sell, lease, and bequeath or inherit it; but they owed to the owner of the manor, in recognition of his "eminent property" rights, certain rents, payable annually, as well as transfer fees that were payable whenever the land changed owners by sale or death. Subject to these "eminent property" rights, landownership was fairly widespread. Peasants directly owned about two-fifths of the soil of the country; bourgeois a little under a fifth. The nobility owned perhaps a little over a fifth, and the church somewhat under a tenth, the remainder being crown lands, wastelands, or commons. Finally, it must be noted that all property rights were subject also to certain "collective" rights, by which villagers might cut firewood or run their pigs in the commons, or pasture cattle on land belonging to other owners after the crops were in, there being usually no fences or enclosures.

All this may seem rather complex, but it is important to realize that property is a changing institution. Even today, in industrialized countries, a high proportion of all

[3]See pp. 30, 123–124, 216.

property is in land, including natural resources in and below the soil. In the eighteenth century property meant land even more than it does today. Even the bourgeois class, whose wealth was so largely in ships, merchandise, or commercial paper, invested heavily in land, and in France in 1789 enjoyed ownership of almost as much land as the nobility, and of more than the church. The Revolution was to revolutionize the law of property by freeing the private ownership of land from all the indirect encumbrances described—manorial fees, eminent property rights, communal village agricultural practices, and church tithes. It also was to abolish other older forms of property, such as property in public office or in masterships in the gilds, which had become useful mainly to closed and privileged groups. In final effect the Revolution established the institutions of private property in the modern sense and benefited, therefore, most especially the landowning peasants and the bourgeoisie.

The peasants not only owned two-fifths of the soil, but occupied almost all of it, working it on their own initiative and risk. That is to say, land owned by the nobility, the church, the bourgeoisie, and the crown was divided up and leased to peasants in small parcels. France was already a country of small farmers. There was no "big agriculture" as in England, eastern Europe, or the plantations of America. The manorial lord performed no economic function. He lived not by managing an estate and selling his own crops and cattle, but by receiving innumerable dues, quitrents, and fees. During the eighteenth century, in connection with the general aristocratic resurgence, there took place a phenomenon often called the "feudal reaction." Manorial lords, faced with rising living costs and acquiring higher living standards because of the general material progress, collected their dues more rigorously or revived old ones that had fallen into disuse. Leases and sharecropping arrangements also became less favorable to the peasants. The farmers, like the wage earners, were under a steadily increasing pressure. At the same time the peasants resented the "feudal dues" more than ever, because they regarded themselves as in many cases the real owners of the land and the lord as a gentleman of the neighborhood who for no reason enjoyed a special income and a status different from their own. The trouble was that much of the property system no longer bore any relation to real economic usefulness or activity.

The political unity of France, achieved over the centuries by the monarchy, was likewise a fundamental prerequisite, and even a cause, of the Revolution. Whatever social conditions might have existed, they could give rise to nationwide public opinion, nationwide agitation, nationwide policies, and nationwide legislation only in a country already politically unified as a nation. These conditions were lacking in central Europe. In France a French state existed. Reformers did not have to create it but only capture and remodel it. Frenchmen in the eighteenth century already had the sense of membership in a political entity called France. The Revolution saw a tremendous stirring of this sense of membership and of fraternity, turning it into a passion for citizenship, civic rights, voting powers, use and application of the state and its sovereignty for the public advantage. At the very outbreak of the Revolution people saluted each other as *citoyen* and shouted *vive la nation!*

The Revolution was precipitated by a financial collapse of the government. What overloaded the government was by no means the costly magnificence of the court of Versailles. Only 5 percent of public expenditures in 1788 was devoted to the upkeep of the entire royal establishment. What overloaded all governments was war costs, both current upkeep of armies and navies and the burden of public debt, which in all countries was due almost totally to the war costs of the past. In 1788 the French government devoted about a quarter of its annual expenditure to current maintenance of the armed forces and about a half to the payment of its debts. British expenditures showed almost the same distribution. The French debt stood at almost four billion livres. It had been greatly swollen by the War of American Independence. Yet it was only half as great as the national debt of Great Britain, and less than a fifth as heavy per capita. It was less than the debt of the Dutch Republic. It was apparently no greater than the debt left by Louis XIV three-quarters of a century before. At that time the debt had been lightened by repudiation. No responsible French official in the 1780s even considered repudiation, a sure sign of the progress in the interim of the well-to-do classes, who were the main government creditors.

Yet the debt could not be carried, for the simple reason that the French budget did not balance. Taxes and other revenues fell short of necessary expenditures. This in turn was not due to national poverty, but to the tax exemptions and tax evasions of privileged elements, especially the nobles. We have already described how the most important tax, the taille, was generally paid only by the peasants—the nobles being exempt by virtue of their class privilege, and office holders and bourgeois obtaining exemption in various ways.[4] The church too insisted that its property was not taxable by the state; and its periodic "free gift" to the king, though substantial, was less than might have been obtained from direct taxation of the church's land. Thus, although the country itself was prosperous, the government treasury was empty. The social classes which enjoyed most of the wealth of the country did not pay taxes corresponding to their income, and, even worse, they resisted taxation as degrading.

A long series of responsible persons—Louis XIV himself, John Law, Maupeou, Turgot—had seen the need for taxing the privileged classes. Jacques Necker, a Swiss banker made director of the finances in 1777 by Louis XVI, made moves in the same direction, and, like his predecessors, was dismissed. His successor, Calonne, as the crisis mounted, came to even more revolutionary conclusions. In 1786 he produced a program in which enlightened despotism was tempered by a modest resort to representative institutions. He proposed, in place of the taille, a general tax to fall on all landowners without exemption, a lightening of indirect taxes and abolition of internal tariffs to stimulate economic production, a confiscation of some properties of the church, and the establishment, as a means of interesting the propertied elements

[4]See pp. 193–194, 337–340.

in the government, of provincial assemblies in which all landowners, noble, clerical, bourgeois, and peasant, should be represented without regard to estate or order.

This program, if carried out, might have solved the fiscal problem and averted the Revolution. But it struck not only at privileges in taxation—noble, provincial, and others—but at the threefold hierarchic organization of society. Knowing from experience that the Parliament of Paris would never accept it, Calonne in 1787 convened an "assembly of notables," hoping to win its endorsement of his ideas. The notables insisted on concessions in return, for they wished to share in control of the government. A deadlock followed; the king dismissed Calonne and appointed as his successor Loménie de Brienne, the exceedingly worldly-wise archbishop of Toulouse. Brienne tried to push the same program through the Parliament. The Parliament rejected it, declaring that only the three estates of the realm, assembled in an Estates-General, had authority to consent to new taxes. Brienne and Louis XVI at first refused, believing that the Estates-General, if convened, would be dominated by the nobility. Like Maupeou and Louis XV, Brienne and Louis XVI tried to break the parliaments, replacing them with a modernized judicial system in which the law courts should have no influence over policy. This led to a veritable revolt of the nobles. All the parliaments and Provincial Estates resisted, army officers refused to serve, the intendants hesitated to act, noblemen began to organize political clubs and committees of correspondence. With his government brought to a standstill, and unable to borrow money or collect taxes, Louis XVI on July 5, 1788, promised to call the Estates-General for the following May. The various classes were invited to elect representatives and also to draw up lists of their grievances.

Since no Estates-General had met in over a century and a half, the king asked all persons to study the subject and make proposals on how such an assembly should be organized under modern conditions. This led to an outburst of public discussion. Hundreds of political pamphlets appeared, many of them demanding that the old system by which the three estates sat in separate chambers, each chamber voting as a unit, be done away with, since under it the chamber of the Third Estate was always outnumbered. But in September 1788 the Parliament of Paris, restored to its functions, ruled that the Estates-General should meet and vote as in 1614, in three separate orders.

The nobility, through the Parliament, thus revealed its aim. It had forced the summoning of the Estates-General, and in this way the French nobility initiated the Revolution. The Revolution began as another victory in the aristocratic resurgence against the absolutism of the king. The nobles actually had a liberal program: they demanded constitutional government, guarantees of personal liberty for all, freedom of speech and press, freedom from arbitrary arrest and confinement. Many now were even prepared to give up special privileges in taxation; this might have worked itself out in time. But in return they hoped to become the preponderant political element in the state. It was their idea not merely to have the Estates-General meet in 1789, but for France to be governed in all the future through the

Estates-General, a supreme body in three chambers, one for nobles, one for a clergy in which the higher officers were also nobles, and one for the Third Estate.

This was precisely what the Third Estate wished to avoid. Lawyers, bankers, businessmen, government creditors, shopkeepers, artisans, workingmen, and peasants had no desire to be governed by lords temporal and spiritual. Their hopes of a new era, formed by the philosophy of the Enlightenment, stirred by the revolution in America, rose to the utmost excitement when "good king Louis" called the Estates-General. The ruling of the Parliament of Paris in September 1788 came to them as a slap in the face—an unprovoked class insult. The whole Third Estate turned on the nobility with detestation and distrust. The abbé Sieyès in January 1789 launched his famous pamphlet, *What Is the Third Estate?*, declaring that the nobility was a useless caste which could be abolished without loss, that the Third Estate was the one necessary element of society, that it was identical with the nation, and that the nation was absolutely and unqualifiedly sovereign. Through Sieyès the ideas of Rousseau's *Social Contract* entered the thought of the Revolution. At the same time, even before the Estates-General actually met, and not from the books of philosophes so much as from the actual events and conditions, nobles and commoners viewed each other with fear and suspicion. The Third Estate, which had at first supported the nobles against the "despotism" of the king's ministers, now ascribed to them the worst possible motives. Class antagonism poisoned the Revolution at the outset, made peaceful reform impossible, and threw many bourgeois without delay into a radical and destructive mood. And the mutual suspicion between classes, produced by the Old Regime and inflamed by the Revolution, has troubled France ever since.

The Estates-General met as planned in May 1789 at Versailles. The Third Estate, most of whose representatives were lawyers, boycotted the organization in three separate chambers. It insisted that deputies of all three orders should sit as a single house and vote as individuals; this procedure would be of advantage to the Third Estate, since the king had granted it as many deputies as the other two orders combined. For six weeks a deadlock was maintained. On June 13 a few priests, leaving the chamber of the First Estate, came over and sat with the Third. They were greeted with jubilation. On June 17 the Third Estate declared itself the "National Assembly." Louis XVI, under pressure from the nobles, closed the hall in which it met. The members found a neighboring indoor tennis court, and there, milling about in a babel of confusion and apprehension, swore and signed the Oath of the Tennis Court on June 20, 1789, affirming that wherever they foregathered the National Assembly was in existence, and that they would not disband until they had drafted a constitution. This was a revolutionary step, for it assumed virtually sovereign power for a body of men who had no legal authority. The king ordered members of the three estates to sit in their separate houses. He now somewhat tardily presented a reforming program of his own, too late to win the confidence of the disaffected, and in any case continuing the organization of French society in legal classes. The self-entitled National Assembly refused to back down. The king faltered, failed to enforce his commands promptly, and allowed the Assembly to remain in being. In the following days, at the end of June, he summoned about 18,000 soldiers to Versailles.

What had happened was that the king of France, in the dispute raging between nobles and commoners, chose the nobles. It was traditional in France for the king to oppose feudalism. For centuries the French monarchy had drawn strength from the bourgeoisie. All through the eighteenth century the royal ministers had carried on the struggle against the privileged interests. Only a year before, Louis XVI had been almost at war with his rebellious aristocracy. In 1789 he failed to assert himself. He lost control over the Estates-General, exerted no leadership, offered no program until too late, and provided no symbol behind which parties could rally. He failed to make use of the profound loyalty to himself felt by the bourgeoisie and common people, who yearned for nothing so much as a king who would stand up for them, as in days of yore, against an aristocracy of birth and status. He tried instead, at first, to compromise and postpone a crisis; then he found himself in the position of having issued orders which the Third Estate boldly defied; and in this embarrassing predicament he yielded to his wife, Marie Antoinette, to his brothers, and to the court nobles with whom he lived, and who told him that his dignity and authority were outraged and undermined. At the end of June Louis XVI undoubtedly intended to dissolve the Estates-General by military force. But what the Third Estate feared was not a return to the old theoretically absolute monarchy. It was a future in which the aristocracy should control the government of the country. There was now no going back; the revolt of the Third Estate had allied Louis XVI with the nobles, and the Third Estate now feared the nobles more than ever, believing with good reason that they now had the king in their hands.

The country meanwhile was falling into dissolution. The lower classes, below the bourgeoisie, were out of hand. For them too the convocation of the Estates-General had seemed to herald a new era. The grievances of ages, and those which existed equally in other countries than France, rose to the surface. Short-run conditions were bad. The harvest of 1788 had been poor; the price of bread, by July 1789, was higher than at any time since the death of Louis XIV. The year 1789 was also one of depression; the rapid growth of trade since the American war had suddenly halted, so that wages fell and unemployment spread while scarcity drove food prices up. The government, paralyzed at the center, could not take such measures of relief as were customary under the Old Regime. The masses were everywhere restless. Labor trouble broke out; in April a great riot of workingmen devastated a wallpaper factory in Paris. In the rural districts there was much disorder. Peasants declared that they would pay no more manorial dues and were likewise refusing taxes. In the best of times the countryside was troubled by vagrants, beggars, rough characters, and smugglers who flourished along the many tariff frontiers. Now the business depression reduced the income of honest peasants who engaged in weaving or other domestic industries in their homes; unemployment and indigence spread in the country; people were uprooted; and the result was to raise the number of vagrants to terrifying proportions. It was believed, since nothing was too bad to believe of the aristocrats (though it was not true), that they were secretly recruiting these "brigands" for their own purposes to intimidate the Third Estate. The economic and social crisis thus became acutely political.

The towns were afraid of being swamped by beggars and desperadoes. This was true even of Paris, the largest city in Europe except London. The Parisians were also alarmed by the concentration of troops about Versailles. They began to arm in self-defense. All classes of the Third Estate took part. The banker Laborde, whose career was noted in an earlier chapter,[5] and whose son sat in the Assembly at Versailles, was one of many to provide funds. Crowds began to look for weapons in arsenals and public buildings. On July 14 they came to the Bastille, a stronghold built in the Middle Ages to overawe the city, like the tower of London in England. It was used as a place of detention for persons with enough influence to escape the common jails but was otherwise in normal times considered harmless; in fact there had been talk, some years before, of tearing it down to make room for a public park. Now, in the general turbulence, the governor had placed cannon in the embrasures. The crowd requested him to remove his cannon and to furnish them with arms. He refused. Through a series of misunderstandings, reinforced by the vehemence of a few firebrands, the crowd turned into a mob, which assaulted the fortress, and which, when helped by a handful of trained soldiers and five artillery pieces, persuaded the governor to surrender. The mob, enraged by the death of ninety-eight of its members, streamed in and murdered six soldiers of the garrison in cold blood. The governor was murdered while under escort to the Town Hall. The mayor of Paris met the same fate. Their heads were cut off with knives, stuck on the ends of pikes, and paraded about the city. While all this happened the regular army units on the outskirts of Paris did not stir, their reliability being open to question, and the authorities being in any case unaccustomed to firing on the people.

The capture of the Bastille, though not so intended, had the effect of saving the Assembly at Versailles. The king, not knowing what to do, accepted the new situation in Paris. He recognized a citizens' committee, which had formed there, as the new municipal government. He sent away the troops that he had summoned and commanded the recalcitrants among nobles and clergy to join in the National Assembly. In Paris and other cities a bourgeois or national guard was established to keep order. The Marquis de Lafayette, "the hero of two worlds," received command over the guard in Paris. For insignia he combined the colors of the city of Paris, red and blue, with the white of the house of Bourbon. The French tricolor, emblem of the Revolution, thus originated in a fusion of old and new.

In the rural districts matters went from bad to worse. Vague insecurity rose to the proportions of panic in the Great Fear of 1789, which spread over the country late in July in the wake of travelers, postal couriers, and others. The cry was relayed from

[5] See pp. 271–272.

point to point that "the brigands were coming," and peasants, armed to protect their homes and crops and gathered together and working upon each other's feelings, often turned their attention to the manor houses, burning them in some cases, and in others simply destroying the manorial archives in which fees and dues were recorded. The Great Fear became part of a general agrarian insurrection, in which peasants, far from being motivated by wild alarms, knew perfectly well what they were doing. They intended to destroy the manorial regime by force.

The Assembly at Versailles could restore order only by meeting the demands of the peasants. To wipe out all manorial payments would deprive the landed aristocracy of most of its income. Many bourgeois also owned manors. There was therefore much perplexity. A small group of deputies prepared a surprise move in the Assembly, choosing an evening session from which many would be absent. Hence came the "night of August 4." A few liberal noblemen, by prearrangement, arose and surrendered their hunting rights, their *banalités*, their rights in manorial courts, and feudal and seigneurial privileges generally. What was left of serfdom and all personal servitudes were declared ended. Tithes were abolished. Other deputies repudiated the special privileges of their provinces. All personal tax privileges were given up. On the main matter, the dues arising from "eminent property" in the manors, a compromise was adopted. These dues were all abolished, but compensation was to be paid by the peasants to the former owners. The compensation was in most cases never paid. Eventually, in 1793, in the radical phase of the Revolution, the provision for compensation was repealed. In the end French peasant landowners rid themselves of their manorial obligations without cost to themselves. From the cocoon of the manor the French peasant democracy emerged intact, in contrast to what later happened in most other countries, where the peasants, when in turn liberated from manorial obligations, either lost part of their land or were crushed under installment payments lasting many years.

The decree summarizing the resolutions of August 4 announced flatly that "feudalism was abolished." In its place the Assembly proceeded to map out the new order. The first step was to issue, on August 26, 1789, the Declaration of the Rights of Man and Citizen. This document affirmed the principles of the new state, which were essentially the rule of law, equal individual citizenship, and collective sovereignty of the people. "Men are born and remain," declared article I, "free and equal in rights." Man's natural rights were held to be "liberty, property, security, and resistance to oppression." Freedom of thought and religion were guaranteed; no one might be arrested or punished except by process of law; all persons were declared eligible for any public office for which they met the requirements. Liberty was defined as the freedom to do anything not injurious to others, which in turn was to be determined only by law. Law must fall equally upon all persons. Law was the expression of the general will, to be made by all citizens or their representatives. The only sovereign was the nation itself, and all public officials and armed forces acted only in its name. Taxes might be raised only by common consent, all public servants were accountable for their conduct in office, and the powers of government should be separated among different branches. Finally, the state might for public purposes, and under law, confiscate the property of private persons, but only with fair compensation. The Declaration, printed in thousands of leaflets, pamphlets, and books, read aloud in public places, or framed and hung on walls, became the catechism of the Revolution in France, and translated into other languages it soon carried the same message to all of Europe.

Division began to appear, among those who had thus far led the Revolution, when, in September 1789, the Assembly began the actual planning of the new government. Some wanted a strong veto power for the king and a legislative body in two houses, as in England. Others, the "patriots," wanted only a suspensive veto for the king and a legislative body of one chamber. Here again, it was suspicion of the aristocracy that proved decisive. The "patriots" were afraid that an upper chamber would bring back the nobility as a collective force, and they were afraid to make the king constitutionally strong, by giving him a full veto, because they believed him to be in sympathy with the nobles. He was, at the moment, hesitating to accept both the August 4th decrees and the Declaration of Rights. His brother, the Count of Artois, followed by many aristocrats, had already emigrated to foreign parts and, along with these other émigrés, was preparing to agitate against the Revolution with all the governments of Europe. The patriot party would concede nothing, the more conservative party could gain nothing. The debate was interrupted again, as in July, by insurrection and violence. On October 4, a crowd of market women and revolutionary agitators, followed by the Paris national guard, took the road from Paris to Versailles. Besieging and invading the château, they obliged Louis XVI to take up his residence in Paris, where he could be watched. The National Assembly also shifted itself to Paris, where it too soon fell under the influence of radical elements in the city. The champions of a one-chamber legislative body and of a suspensive veto for the king won out.

The more conservative revolutionaries, if such they may be called, disillusioned in seeing constitutional questions settled by mobs, began to drop out of the Assembly. Men who on June 20 had bravely sworn the Oath of the Tennis Court now felt that the Revolution was falling into unworthy hands. Some even emigrated, forming a second wave of émigrés that would have nothing to do with the first. So the counterrevolution gathered strength. But those who wanted still to go forward, and they were many, began to organize in clubs. Most important of all was the Society of Friends of the Constitution, called the Jacobin club for short, since it met in an old Jacobin monastery in Paris. The dues were at first so high that only substantial bourgeois belonged; they were later lowered but never enough to include persons of the poorest classes, who therefore formed lesser clubs of their own. The most advanced members of the Assembly were Jacobins and used the club as a caucus in which to discuss their policies and lay their plans. More will soon be said of the Jacobins.

In the two years from October 1789 to September 1791 the National Assembly (or the Constituent Assembly, as it had come to be called because it was preparing a constitution) continued its work of simultaneously governing the country, devising a written constitution, and destroying in detail the institutions of the Old Regime. The old ministries, the old organization of government bureaus, the old taxes, the old property in office, the old titles of nobility, the old parliaments, the hundreds of regional systems of law, the old internal tariffs, the old provinces, and the old urban municipalities all went into the discard. Contemporaries, like Edmund Burke, were appalled at the thoroughness with which Frenchmen seemed determined to eradicate their national institutions. Why, asked Burke, should the French fanatics cut to pieces the living body of Normandy or Provence? The truth is that the provinces, like everything else, were impacted in the whole system of special privilege and unequal rights. All had to disappear if the hope of equal citizenship under national sovereignty was to be attained. In place of the provinces the Constituent divided France into eighty-three equal "departments." In place of the old towns, with their quaint old magistrates, it introduced a uniform municipal organization, all towns henceforth having the same form of government, varying only according to size. All local officials, even prosecuting attorneys and tax collectors, were elected locally. Administratively the country was decentralized to the last degree in reaction against the bureaucracy of the Old Regime. No one outside Paris now really acted for the central government, and local communities enforced the national legislation, or declined to enforce it, as they chose. This proved ruinous when the war came, and although the "departments" created by the Constituent Assembly still exist, it has been traditional in France since the Revolution, as it was before, to keep local officials under strong control by ministers in Paris.

Under the constitution that was prepared, sometimes called the Constitution of 1791 because it went into effect at that date, the sovereign power of the nation was to be exercised by a unicameral elected assembly, called the Legislative Assembly. The king was given only a suspensive veto power by which legislation desired by the Assembly could be postponed. In general, the executive branch, i.e., king and ministers, was kept weak, partly in reaction against "ministerial despotism," partly from a well-founded distrust of Louis XVI. In July 1791 Louis attempted, in the "flight to Varennes," to escape from the kingdom, join with émigré noblemen, and seek help from foreign powers. He left behind him a written message in which he explicitly repudiated the Revolution. Arrested at Varennes in Lorraine, he was brought back to Paris and forced to accept his status as a constitutional monarch. The attitude of Louis XVI greatly disoriented the Revolution, for it made impossible the creation of a strong executive power and left the country to be ruled by a debating society which under revolutionary conditions contained more than the usual number of hotheads.

Not all this machinery of state was democratic. In the granting of political rights the abstract principles of the great Declaration were seriously modified for practical reasons. Since most people were illiterate it was thought that they could have no reasonable political views. Since the small man was often a domestic servant or shop assistant it was thought that in politics he would be a mere dependent of his employer. The Constituent therefore distinguished in the new constitution between "active" and "passive" citizens. Both had the same civil rights, but only active citizens had the right to vote. These active citizens chose "electors," on the basis of one elector for every hundred active citizens. The electors convened in the chief town of their new "department," and there chose deputies to the national legislature as well as certain local officials. Males over twenty-five years of age, and well enough off to pay a small direct tax, qualified as "active" citizens; well over half the adult male population could so qualify. Of these, men paying a somewhat higher tax qualified as "electors"; even so, almost half the adult males qualified for this role. In practice, what limited the number of available electors was that, to function as such, a man had to have enough education, interest and leisure to attend an electoral assembly, at a distance from home, and remain in attendance for several days. In any case, only about 50,000 persons served as electors in 1790–1791 because a proportion of one for every hundred active citizens yielded that figure. In a sense, these 50,000 men were the governing class of the first phase of the Revolution. They might include former nobles and substantial peasants, but they were mainly of the middle class or bourgeoisie. In some ways the new regime represented the rule of the bourgeoisie. Wealth, in the new legally equal society, remained a legal distinction between man and man.

Economic Policies

Economic policies that were adopted had little to attract the lowest classes. The public debt had precipitated the Revolution, but the revolutionary leaders, even the most extreme Jacobins, never disowned the debt of the Old Regime. The reason is that the bourgeois class, on the whole, were the people to whom the money was owed. To secure the debt, and to pay current expenses of government, since tax collections had become very sporadic, the Constituent Assembly as early as November 1789 resorted to a device by no means new in Europe, though never before used on so extensive a scale. It confiscated all the property of the church. Against this property, it issued negotiable instruments called assignats, first regarded as bonds and issued only in large denominations, later regarded as currency and issued in small bills. Holders of assignats could use them, or any money, to buy parcels of the former church lands. None of the confiscated land was given away; all was in fact sold at fairly high prices, since the interest of the government was fiscal rather than social. The peasants, even when they had the money, could not easily buy land because the lands were sold at distant auctions or in large undivided blocks. The peasants were disgruntled, though they did acquire a good deal of the former church lands through middlemen. Peasant landowners were likewise expected, until 1793, to pay compensation for their old quitrents and many other manorial fees. And the landless peasants were aroused when the government, with its bourgeois ideas, encouraged the dividing up of the village commons and extinction of various collective village rights, in the interest of individual private property.

The revolutionary bourgeoisie favored free economic individualism. It had had enough, under the Old Regime, of government regulation over the sale or quality of goods and of privileged companies and other economic monopolies. Reforming economic thought at the time, not only in France but in England, where Adam Smith had published his epoch-making *Wealth of Nations* in 1776, held that organized special interests were bad for society, and that all prices and wages should be determined by free arrangement between the individuals concerned. The more prominent leaders of the French Revolution believed firmly in this freedom from control. The Constituent Assembly abolished the gilds, which were mainly monopolistic organizations of small businessmen or master craftsmen, interested in keeping up prices and averse to new machinery or new methods. There was also, in France, a rather highly organized labor movement. Since the masterships in the gilds had become practically hereditary (as a form of property and privilege), the journeymen had become lifelong wageworkers. They had formed their own associations, or trade unions, called *compagnonnages*, outside the gilds.[6] Many trades were so organized—the carpenters, plasterers, paper workers, hatters, saddlers, cutlers, nail-makers, carters, tanners, locksmiths, and glassworkers. Some were organized nationally, some only locally. All these journeymen's unions had been illegal under the Old Regime, but they had flourished nevertheless. They collected dues and maintained officers. They often dealt collectively with the gild masters or other employers, requiring the payment of a stipulated wage or amendment of working conditions. Sometimes they even imposed closed shops. Organized strikes were quite common. The labor troubles of 1789 continued on into the Revolution. Business fell off in the atmosphere of disorder. In 1791 there was another wave of strikes. The Assembly, in the Le Chapelier law of that year, renewed the old prohibitions of the *compagnonnages*. The same law restated the abolition of the gilds and forbade the organization of special economic interests of any kind. All trades, it declared, were free for all to enter. All men, without belonging to any organization, had the right to work at any occupation or business they might choose. All wages were to be settled privately by the workman and his employer. This was not at all what the workingman, at that time or any other, really wanted. Nevertheless the provisions of the Le Chapelier law remained a part of French law for three-quarters of a century. The embryonic trade unions continued to exist secretly, though with more difficulty than under the hit-and-miss law enforcement of the Old Regime.

Most fatefully of all, the Constituent Assembly quarreled with the Catholic church. The confiscation of church properties naturally came as a shock to the clergy. The village priests, whose support had made possible the revolt of the Third Estate, now found that the very buildings in which they worshiped with their parishioners on

[6] See pp. 121–122.

Sunday belonged to the "nation." The loss of income-producing properties undercut the religious orders and ruined the schools, including the 40,000 scholarships by which boys were assisted in getting an education before the Revolution. Yet it was not on the question of material wealth that the church and the Revolution came to blows. Members of the Constituent Assembly took the view of the church that the great monarchies had taken before them. The idea of separation of church and state was far from their minds. They regarded the church as a form of public authority and as such subordinate to the sovereign power. They frankly argued that the poor needed religion if they were to respect the property of the more wealthy. In any case, having deprived the church of its own income, they had to provide for its maintenance. For the schools many generous and democratic projects of state-sponsored education were drawn up, though under the troubled conditions of the time little was accomplished. For the clergy the new program was mapped out in the Civil Constitution of the Clergy of 1790.

This document went far toward setting up a French national church. Under its provisions the parish priests and bishops were elected, the latter by the same 50,000 electors who chose other important officials. Protestants, Jews, and agnostics could legally take part in the elections, purely on the ground of citizenship and property qualifications. Archbishoprics were abolished, and all the borders of existing bishoprics were redrawn. The number of dioceses was reduced from over 130 to 83, so that one would be coterminous with each department. Bishops were allowed merely to notify the pope of their elevation; they were forbidden to acknowledge any papal authority in their assumption of office, and no papal letter or decree was to be published or enforced in France except with government permission. All clergy received salaries from the state, the average income of bishops being somewhat reduced, that of parish clergymen being raised. Sinecures, plural holdings, and other abuses by which noble families had been supported by the church were done away with. The Constituent Assembly (independently of the Civil Constitution) also prohibited the taking of religious vows and dissolved all monastic houses.

Some of all this was not in principle alarmingly new, since before the Revolution the civil authority of the king had designated the French bishops and passed on the admission of papal documents into France. French bishops, in the old spirit of the "Gallican liberties," were traditionally jealous of papal power in France.[7] Many were now willing to accept something like the Civil Constitution if allowed to produce it on their own authority. The Assembly refused to concede so much jurisdiction to the Gallican church and applied instead to the pope, hoping to force its plans upon the French clergy by invoking the authority of the Vatican. But the Vatican pronounced the Civil Constitution a wanton usurpation of power over the Catholic church. Unfortunately, the pope also went further, condemning the whole Revolution and all its works. The Constituent Assembly retorted by requiring all French clergy to swear an oath of loyalty to the constitution, including the Civil Constitution of the Clergy. Half took the oath and half refused it, the latter half including all but seven of the

[7]See pp. 52, 71–74, 90, 136, 194.

bishops. One of the seven willing to accept the new arrangements was Talleyrand, soon to be famous as foreign minister of numerous French governments.

There were now two churches in France, one clandestine, the other official, one maintained by voluntary offerings or by funds smuggled in from abroad, the other financed and sponsored by the government. The former, comprising the nonjuring, unsworn or "refractory" clergy, turned violently counterrevolutionary. To protect themselves from the Revolution they insisted, with an emphasis quite new in France, on the universal religious supremacy of the Roman pontiff. They denounced the "constitutional" clergy as schismatics who spurned the pope and as mere careerists willing to hold jobs on the government's terms. The constitutional clergy, those taking the oath and upholding the Civil Constitution, considered themselves to be patriots and defenders of the rights of man; and they insisted that the Gallican church had always enjoyed a degree of liberty from Rome. The Catholic laity were terrified and puzzled. Many were sufficiently attached to the Revolution to prefer the constitutional clergy; but to do so meant to defy the pope, and Catholics who persisted in defying the pope were on the whole those least zealous in their religion. The constitutional clergy therefore stood on shaky foundations. Many of their followers, under stress of the times, eventually turned against Christianity itself.

Good Catholics tended to favor the "refractory" clergy. The outstanding example was the king himself. He personally used the services of refractory priests, and thus gave a new reason for the revolutionaries to distrust him. Whatever chance there was that Louis XVI might go along with the Revolution was exploded, for he concluded that he could do so only by endangering his immortal soul. Former aristocrats also naturally preferred the refractory clergy. They now put aside the Voltairean levities of the Age of Enlightenment, and the "best people" began to exhibit a new piety in religious matters. The peasants, who found little in the Revolution to interest them after their own insurrection of 1789 and the consequent abolition of the manorial regime, also favored the old-fashioned or refractory clergy. Much the same was true of the urban working-class families, especially the women. The Constituent Assembly, and its successors, were at their wits' end what to do. Sometimes they shut their eyes at the intrigues of refractory clergy; the constitutional clergy then became fearful. Sometimes they hunted out and persecuted the refractories; in that case they only stirred up religious fanaticism.

The Civil Constitution of the Clergy has been called the greatest tactical blunder of the Revolution. Certainly its consequences were unfortunate in the extreme, and they spread to much of Europe. In the nineteenth century the church was to be officially antidemocratic and antiliberal;[8] and democrats and liberals in most cases were to be violently and outspokenly anticlerical. The main beneficiary was the papacy. The French church, which had clung for ages to its Gallican liberties, was thrown by the Revolution into the arms of the pope. Even Napoleon, when he healed the schism a decade later, acknowledged powers in the papacy that had never been acknowledged by the French kings. These were steps in the process, leading through

[8]See pp. 526, 655–656.

the proclamation of papal infallibility in 1870,[9] by which the affairs of the modern Catholic church became increasingly centralized at the Vatican.

With the proclamation of the constitution in September 1791, the Constituent Assembly disbanded. Before dissolving, it ruled that none of its members might sit in the forthcoming Legislative Assembly. This body was therefore made up of men who still wished to make their mark in the Revolution. The new regime went into effect in October 1791. It was a constitutional monarchy in which a unicameral Legislative Assembly confronted a king unconverted to the new order. Designed as the permanent solution to France's problems, it was to collapse in ten months, in August 1792, as a result of popular insurrection four months after France became involved in war. A group of Jacobins, known as Girondins, for a time became the left or advanced party of the Revolution and in the Legislative Assembly led France into war.

42

The Revolution and Europe: The War and the "Second" Revolution, 1792

The International Impact of the Revolution

The European governments were long reluctant to become involved with France. They were under considerable pressure. On the one hand, pro-French and pro-revolutionary groups appeared immediately in many quarters. The doctrines of the French Revolution, as of the American, were highly exportable: they took the form of a universal philosophy, proclaiming the rights of man regardless of time or place, race or nation. Moreover, depending on what one was looking for, one might see in the first disturbances in France a revolt of either the nobility, the bourgeoisie, the common people, or the entire nation. In Poland those who were trying to reorganize the country against further partition hailed the French example. The Hungarian landlords pointed to it in their reaction against Joseph II. In England, for a time, those who controlled Parliament complacently believed that the French were attempting to imitate them.

But it was the excluded classes of European society who were most inspired. The hard-pressed Silesian weavers were said to hope that "the French would come." Strikes broke out at Hamburg, and peasants rebelled elsewhere. One English diplomat found that even the Prussian army had "a strong taint of democracy among officers and men." In Belgium, where the privileged elements were already in revolt against the Austrian emperor, a second revolt broke out, inspired by events in France and aimed at the privileged elements. In England the newly developing "radicals," men like Thomas Paine and Dr. Richard Price, who wished a thorough overhauling of Parliament and the established church, entered into correspondence with the Assembly in Paris. Businessmen of importance, including Watt and Boulton, the pioneers of the steam engine, were likewise pro-French since they had no representation in the House of Commons. The Irish too were excited and presently revolted. Everywhere the young men were aroused, the young Hegel in Germany, or in England

[9]See p. 656.

the young Wordsworth, who later recalled the sense of a new era that had captivated so many spirits in 1789:

> *Bliss was it in that dawn to be alive,*
> *But to be young was very heaven!*

On the other hand the anti-Revolutionary movement gathered strength. Edmund Burke, frightened by the French proclivities of English radicals, published as early as 1790 his *Reflections on the Revolution in France.* For France, he predicted anarchy and dictatorship. For England, he sternly advised the English to accept a slow adaptation of their own English liberties. For all the world, he denounced a political philosophy that rested on abstract principles of right and wrong, declaring that every people must be shaped by its own national circumstances, national history, and national character. He drew an eloquent reply and a defense of France from Thomas Paine in the *Rights of Man.* Burke soon began to preach the necessity of war, urging a kind of ideological struggle against French barbarism and violence. His *Reflections* were translated and widely read. In the long run his book proved an influential work in the history of thought. In the short run it fell on willing ears. The king of Sweden, Gustavus III, offered to lead a monarchist crusade. In Russia old Catherine was appalled; she forbade further translations of her erstwhile friend Voltaire, she called the French "vile riffraff" and "brutish cannibals," and she packed off to Siberia a Russian named Radishchev, who in his *Voyage from St. Petersburg to Moscow* pointed out the evils of serfdom. It is said that Russians were even forbidden to speak of the "revolutions of the heavenly spheres." The terrors were heightened by plaintive messages from Louis XVI and Marie Antoinette, and by the émigrés who kept bursting out of France, led as early as July 1789 by the king's own brother, the Count of Artois. The émigrés, who at first were nobles, settled in various parts of Europe and began using their international aristocratic connections. They preached a kind of holy war. They bemoaned the sad plight of the king, but what they most wanted was to get back their manorial incomes and other rights. They hinted that Louis XVI himself was a dangerous revolutionary and much preferred his brother, the unyielding Count of Artois.

In short, Europe was soon split by a division that overran all frontiers. The same was true of America also: in the United States the rising party of Jefferson was branded as Jacobin and pro-French, that of Hamilton as reactionary and pro-British; while in colonial Spanish America ideas of independence were strengthened, and the Venezuelan Miranda became a general in the French army. In all countries of the European world, though least of all in eastern and southern Europe, there were revolutionary or pro-French elements that were feared by their own governments. In all countries, including France, there were implacable enemies of the French Revolution. In all countries were people whose loyalties lay abroad. There had been no such situation since the Protestant Reformation, nor was there anything like it again until after the Russian Revolution of the twentieth century.

393

Yet the European governments were slow to move. Catherine had no intention of becoming involved in western Europe. She only wished to involve her neighbors. William Pitt, the British prime minister, resisted the war cries of Burke. Son of the Earl of Chatham, prime minister since 1784, chief founder of the new Tory party, Pitt had a reforming program of his own; he had tried and failed to carry a reform of Parliament and was now concentrating on a policy of orderly finance and systematic economy. His program would be ruined by war. He insisted that the domestic affairs of France were of no concern to the British government. The key position was occupied by the Habsburg emperor, Leopold II, brother to the French queen. Leopold at first answered Marie Antoinette's pleas for help by telling her to adjust herself to conditions in France. He resisted the furious demands of the émigrés, whom he understood perfectly, having inherited from Joseph II a fractious aristocracy himself.

Still, the new French government was a disturbing phenomenon. It openly encouraged malcontents all over Europe. It showed a tendency to settle international affairs by unilateral action. For example, it annexed Avignon at the request of local revolutionaries but without the consent of its historic sovereign, the pope. Or again, in Alsace there had been much overlapping jurisdiction between France and Germany ever since the Peace of Westphalia.[10] The Constituent Assembly abolished feudalism and manorial dues in Alsace as elsewhere in France. To German princes who had feudal rights in Alsace the Assembly offered compensation, but it did not ask their consent; and the German princes concerned, deprived by a revolutionary decree of rights guaranteed them by past treaties, appealed to the Holy Roman Emperor to protest the infringement of international understandings. Moreover, after the arrest of Louis XVI at Varennes, after his attempted flight in June 1791, it became impossible to deny that the French king and queen were prisoners of the revolutionaries.

In August Leopold met with the king of Prussia at Pillnitz in Saxony. The resulting Declaration of Pillnitz rested on a famous *if:* Leopold would take military steps to restore order in France if all the other powers would join him. Knowing the attitude of Pitt, he believed that the *if* could never materialize. His aim was mainly to rid himself of the French émigrés. These perversely received the Declaration with delight. They used it as an open threat to their enemies in France, announcing that they would soon return alongside the forces of civilized Europe to punish the guilty and right the wrongs that had been done to them.

In France the upholders of the Revolution were alarmed. They were ignorant of what Leopold really meant and took the dire menaces of the émigrés at their face value. The Declaration of Pillnitz, far from cowing the French, enraged them against all the crowned heads of Europe. It gave a political advantage to the then dominant faction of Jacobins, known to history as the Girondins. These included the philosophe Condorcet, the humanitarian lawyer Brissot, and the civil servant Roland and his more famous wife, Mme. Roland, whose house became a kind of headquarters of the group. They attracted many foreigners also, such as Thomas Paine and the

[10]See maps, pp. 148–149, 193, 339.

German Anacharsis Cloots, the "representative of the human race." In December 1791 a deputation of English radicals, led by James Watt, son of the inventor of the steam engine, received a wild ovation at the Paris Jacobin club.

The Girondins became the party of international revolution. They declared that the Revolution could never be secure in France until it spread to the world. In their view, once war had come, the peoples of states at war with France would not support their own governments. There was reason for this belief, since revolutionary elements, antedating the French Revolution, already existed in both the Dutch and the Austrian Netherlands, and to a lesser degree in parts of Switzerland, Poland, and elsewhere. Some Girondins therefore contemplated a war in which French armies should enter neighboring countries, unite with local revolutionaries, overthrow the established governments, and set up a federation of republics. War was also favored by a very different group, led by Lafayette, which wished to curb the Revolution by holding it at the line of constitutional monarchy. This group mistakenly believed that war might restore the much damaged popularity of Louis XVI, unite the country under the new government, and make it possible to put down the continuing Jacobin agitation. As the war spirit boiled up in France, the Emperor Leopold II died. He was succeeded by Francis II, a man much more inclined than Leopold to yield to the clamors of the old aristocracy. Francis resumed negotiations with Prussia. In France all who dreaded a return of the Old Regime listened more readily to the Girondins. Among the Jacobins as a whole, only a few, generally a handful of radical democrats, opposed the war. On April 20, 1792, without serious opposition, the Assembly declared war on "the king of Hungary and Bohemia."

The war intensified the existing unrest and dissatisfaction of the unpropertied classes. Both peasants and urban workers felt that the Constituent and the Legislative Assembly had served the propertied interests and had done little for them. Peasants were dissatisfied at the inadequate measures taken to facilitate land distribution; workers felt especially the pinch of soaring prices, which by 1792 had greatly risen. Gold had been taken out of the country by the émigrés; paper money, the assignats, was almost the sole currency, and the future of the government was so uncertain that it steadily lost value. Peasants concealed their food products rather than sell them for depreciating paper. Actual scarcity combined with the falling value of money to drive up the cost of living. The lowest income groups suffered the most. But dissatisfied though they were, when the war began they were threatened with a return of the émigrés and a vindictive restoration of the Old Regime, which at least for the peasants would be the worst of all possible eventualities. The working classes—peasants, artisans, mechanics, shopkeepers, wageworkers—rallied to the Revolution but not to the revolutionary government in power. The Legislative Assembly and the constitutional monarchy lacked the confidence of large elements of the population.

In addition, the war at first went very unfavorably for the French. Prussia joined immediately with Austria, and by the summer of 1792 the two powers were on the point of invading France. They issued a proclamation to the French people, the Brunswick Manifesto of July 25, declaring that if any harm befell the French king and queen the Austro-Prussian forces, upon their arrival in Paris, would exact the most severe retribution from the inhabitants of that city. Such menaces, compounding the military emergency, only played into the hands of the most violent activists. Masses of the French people, roused and guided by bourgeois Jacobin leaders, notably Robespierre, Danton, and the vitriolic journalist Marat, burst out in a passion of patriotic excitement. They turned against the king because he was identified with powers at war with France, and also because, in France itself, those who still supported him were using the monarchy as a defense against the lower classes. Republicanism in France was partly a rather sudden historical accident, in that France was at war under a king who could not be trusted, and partly a kind of lower-class or quasi-proletarian movement, in which, however, many bourgeois revolutionaries shared.

Feeling ran high during the summer of 1792. Recruits streamed into Paris from all quarters on their way to the frontiers. One detachment, from Marseilles, brought with them a new marching song, known ever since as the *Marseillaise,* a fierce call to war upon tyranny. The transient provincials stirred up the agitation in Paris. On August 10, 1792, the working-class quarters of the city rose in revolt, supported by the recruits from Marseilles and elsewhere, stormed the Tuileries against resistance by the Swiss Guard, many of whom were massacred, and seized and imprisoned the king and the royal family. A revolutionary municipal government, or "Commune," was set up in Paris. Usurping the powers of the Legislative Assembly, it forced the abrogation of the constitution, and the election, by universal male suffrage, of a Constitutional Convention that was to govern France and prepare a new and more democratic constitution. The very word Convention was used in recollection of the American Constitutional Convention of 1787. Meanwhile hysteria, anarchy, and terror reigned in Paris; a handful of insurrectionary volunteers, declaring that they would not fight enemies on the frontiers until they had disposed of enemies in Paris, dragged about 1,100 persons—refractory priests and other counterrevolutionaries—from the prisons of the city and killed them after drumhead trials. These are known as the "September massacres."

A Woman of the Revolution by *Jacques-Louis David* (*French, 1748–1825*)
Here is something of what historians mean by the "working class," and it may be compared with the representations of aristocracy and of the middle class already shown. The coarse garments and untended hair, the colorless lips, the lined forehead and the evidences of suffering in the eyes, all reveal a life of much labor and few amenities. The woman seems to be observing something with an interest mixed with suspicion, and her air of determination and even of defiance suggests the political-mindedness aroused even in the poorest classes in time of revolution. David painted this portrait in 1795, a year after the Terror in France. He was himself an active revolutionary, a member of the Convention and of the Committee of General Security. It is rare to find portraits of people of this class of society done with so much realism, sympathy, and force. Courtesy of the Musée des Beaux-Arts, Lyon (J. Camponogara).

For over two and a half years, since October 1789, there had been an abatement of popular violence. Now the coming of the war and the dissatisfaction of the lower classes with the course of events so far had led to new explosions. The insurrection of August 10, 1792, the "second" French Revolution, initiated the most advanced phase of the Revolution.

43

The Emergency Republic, 1792–1795: The Terror

The National Convention

The National Convention met on September 20, 1792; it was to sit for three years. It immediately proclaimed the Year One of the French Republic. The disorganized French armies, also on September 20, won a great moral victory in the "cannonade of Valmy," a battle that was hardly more than an artillery duel, but which induced the Prussian commander to give up his march on Paris. The French soon occupied Belgium (the Austrian Netherlands), Savoy (which belonged to the king of Sardinia who had joined with the Austrians) and Mainz and other cities on the German Left Bank of the Rhine. Revolutionary sympathizers in these places appealed for French aid. The National Convention decreed assistance to "all peoples wishing to recover their liberty." It also ordered that French generals, in the occupied areas, should dissolve the old governments, confiscate government and church property, abolish tithes, hunting rights and seigneurial dues, and set up provisional administrations. Thus revolution spread in the wake of the successful French armies.

The British and Dutch prepared to resist. Pitt, still insisting that the French might have any domestic regime that they chose, declared that Great Britain could not tolerate the French occupation of Belgium. The British and Dutch began conversations with Prussia and Austria, and the French declared war on them on February 1, 1793. Within a few weeks the Republic had annexed Savoy and Nice, as well as

The Gleaners *by Jean-François Millet (French, 1814–1875)*

As an illustration of a social class this picture may be compared with the three preceding ones. When first exhibited in Paris in 1857 it raised an outcry. One irate critic found that "behind these three gleaning-women, against the leaden horizon, the pikes, riots and scaffolds of '93 are silhouetted." Millet denied any such political implication. The three women here are of the poorest of the French peasantry. Bowed with labor, reaching out with strong muscular hands, clutching their few stalks of grain, they are exercising a legal right, "glanage," by which poor people were allowed to glean the fields after the owners had taken in their harvest. "Glanage" was one of the collective village rights, originally common to France, England, and most of Europe (pp. 378, 388–389, 465), which tended to disappear with the spread of modern private-property institutions into the country. Note how the fields in the picture are "open"; there has yet been no "enclosure" by walls or fences, though the land is privately owned, mainly by the more well-to-do peasants. Courtesy of the Louvre (Giraudon).

Belgium, and had much of the German Rhineland under its military government.[11] Meanwhile, in eastern Europe, while denouncing the rapacity of the French savages, the rulers of Russia and Prussia came to an arrangement of their own, each appropriating a portion of Poland in the second partition in January 1793.[12] The Austrians, excluded from the second partition, became anxious over their interests in the East. The infant French Republic, now at war with all Europe, was saved by the weakness of the Coalition, for Britain and Holland had no land forces of consequence, and Prussia and Austria were too jealous of each other, and too preoccupied with Poland, to commit the bulk of their armies against France.

In the Convention all the leaders were Jacobins, but the Jacobins were again splitting. The Girondins were no longer the most advanced revolutionary group as they had been in the Legislative Assembly. Beside the Girondins appeared a new group, whose members preferred to sit in the highest seats in the hall, and therefore were dubbed the "Mountain" in the political parlance of the day. The leading Girondins came from the great provincial cities; the leading Montagnards, though mostly of provincial birth, were representatives of the city of Paris and owed most of their political strength to the radical and popular elements in that city.

These popular revolutionists, outside the Convention, proudly called themselves *sans-culottes* since they wore the workingman's long trousers, not the knee-breeches or *culottes* of the middle and upper classes. They were the working class of a pre-industrial age, shopkeepers and shop assistants, skilled artisans in various trades, including some who were owners of small manufacturing or handicraft enterprises. For two years their militancy and their activism pressed the revolution forward. They demanded an equality that should be meaningful for people like themselves, they called for a mighty effort against foreign powers that presumed to intervene in the French Revolution, and they denounced the now deposed king and queen (correctly enough) for collusion with the Austrian enemy. The *sans-culottes* feared that the Convention might be too moderate. They favored direct democracy in their neighborhood clubs and assemblies, together with a mass rising if necessary against the Convention itself. The Girondins in the Convention began to dismiss these popular militants as anarchists. The group known as the Mountain was more willing to work with them, so long at least as the emergency lasted.

The Convention put Louis XVI on trial for treason in December 1792. On January 15 it unanimously pronounced him guilty, but on the next day, out of 721 deputies present, only 361 voted for immediate execution, a majority of one. Louis XVI died on the guillotine forthwith. The 361 deputies were henceforth branded for life as regicides; never could they allow, in safety to themselves, a restoration of the Bourbon monarchy in France. The other 360 deputies were not similarly compromised; their rivals called them Girondins, "moderatists," counterrevolutionaries. All who still wanted more from the Revolution, or who feared that the slightest wavering would bring the Allies and the émigrés into France, now looked to the Mountain wing of the Jacobins.

[11] See map, p. 411.
[12] See pp. 258–260, 351.

In April 1793 the most spectacular French general, Dumouriez, who had won the victories in Belgium five months before, defected to Austria. The Allied armies now drove the French from Belgium and again threatened to invade France. Counter-revolutionaries in France exulted. From the revolutionaries went up the cry, "We are betrayed!" Prices continued to rise, the currency fell, food was harder to obtain, and the working classes were increasingly restless. The *sans-culottes* demanded price controls, currency controls, rationing, legislation against the hoarding of food, and requisitioning to enforce the circulation of goods. They denounced the bourgeoisie as profiteers and exploiters of the people. While the Girondins resisted, the Mountain went along with the *sans-culottes*, partly from sympathy with their ideas, partly to win mass support for the war, and partly as a maneuver to get rid of the Girondins. On May 31, 1793, the Commune of Paris, under *sans-culotte* pressure, assembled a host of demonstrators and insurrectionists who invaded the Convention and forced the arrest of the Girondin leaders. Other Girondins fled to the provinces, including Condorcet, who, while in hiding, and before his suicide, found occasion to write his famous book on the *Progress of the Human Mind.*[13]

The Mountain now ruled in the Convention, but the Convention itself ruled very little. Not only were the foreign armies and the émigrés at the gates bent on destroying the Convention as a band of regicides and social incendiaries, but the authority of the Convention was widely repudiated in France itself. In the west, in the Vendée, the peasants had revolted against military conscription; they were worked upon by refractory priests, British agents, and royalist emissaries of the Count of Artois. The great provincial cities, Lyons, Bordeaux, Marseilles and others, had also rebelled, especially after the fugitive Girondins reached them. These "federalist" rebels demanded a more "federal" or decentralized republic. Like the Vendéans, with whom they had no connection, they objected to the ascendancy of Paris, having been accustomed to more regional independence under the Old Regime. These rebellions became counterrevolutionary, since all sorts of foreigners, royalists, émigrés, and clericals streamed in to assist them.

The Convention had to defend itself against extremists of the Left as well. To the genuine mass action of the *sans-culottes* were now added the voices of even more excited militants called *enragés.* Various organizers, enthusiasts, agitators and neighborhood politicians declared that parliamentary methods were useless. Generally they were men outside the Convention—and also women, for women were particularly sensitive to the crisis of food shortage and soaring prices, and an organization of Revolutionary Republican Women caused a brief stir in 1793. All such activists worked through units of local government in Paris and elsewhere, and in thousands of "popular societies" and provincial clubs throughout the whole country. They also formed "revolutionary armies," semimilitary bands of men who scoured the rural areas for food, searched the barns of peasants, denounced suspects and preached revolution.

[13]See p. 335.

As for the Convention, while it cannot be said ever to have had any commanding leaders, the program it followed for about a year was on the whole that of Maximilien Robespierre, himself a Jacobin but not one to go along forever with popular revolution or anarchy. Robespierre is one of the most argued about and least understood men of modern times. Persons accustomed to stable conditions dismiss him with a shudder as a bloodthirsty fanatic, dictator, and demagogue. Others have considered him an idealist, a visionary, and an ardent patriot whose goals and ideals were at least avowedly democratic. All agree on his personal honesty and integrity and on his revolutionary zeal. He was by origin a lawyer of northern France, educated with the aid of scholarships in Paris. He had been elected in 1789 to sit for the Third Estate in the Estates-General, and in the ensuing Constituent Assembly played a minor role, though calling attention to himself by his views against capital punishment and in favor of universal suffrage. During the time of the Legislative Assembly, in 1791–1792, he continued to agitate for democracy and vainly pleaded against the declaration of war. In the Convention, elected in September 1792, he sat for a Paris constituency. He became a prominent member of the Mountain and welcomed the purge of the Girondins. He had always kept free of the bribery and graft in which some others became involved and for this reason was known as the Incorruptible. He was a great believer in the importance of "virtue." This term had been used in a specialized way among the philosophes: both Montesquieu and Rousseau had held that republics depended upon "virtue," or unselfish public spirit and civic zeal, to which was added, under Rousseauist influence, a somewhat sentimentalized idea of personal uprightness and purity of life. Robespierre was determined, in 1793 and 1794, to bring about a democratic republic made up of good citizens and honest men.

The Program of the Convention, 1793–1794: The Terror

The program of the Convention, which Robespierre helped to form, was to repress anarchy, civil strife, and counterrevolution at home and to win the war by a great national mobilization of the country's people and resources. It would prepare a democratic constitution and initiate legislation for the lower classes, but it would not yield to the Paris Commune and other agencies of direct revolutionary action. To conduct the government, the Convention granted wide powers to a Committee of Public Safety, a group of twelve members of the Convention who were reelected every month. Robespierre was an influential member; others were the youthful St. Just, the partially paralyzed Couthon, and the army officer Carnot, "organizer of victory."

To repress the "counterrevolution," the Convention and the Committee of Public Safety set up what is popularly known as the "Reign of Terror." Revolutionary courts were instituted as an alternative to the lynch law of the September massacres. A Committee of General Security was created as a kind of supreme political police. Designed to protect the Revolutionary Republic from its internal enemies, the Terror struck at those who were in league against the Republic, and at those who were merely suspected of hostile activities. Its victims ranged from Marie Antoinette and other royalists to the former revolutionary colleagues of the Mountain, the Girondin leaders; and before the year 1793–1794 was over, some of the old Jacobins of the

Mountain who had helped inaugurate the program also went to the guillotine. The number of persons who lost their lives in the Terror, from the late summer of 1793 to July 1794, has often been exaggerated. By the standards of the twentieth century, in which governments have undertaken to extirpate whole classes or races, the Terror was fairly mild. Yet about 40,000 persons died in it; and additional hundreds of thousands were at one time or another arrested and held in custody. Most executions took place in the Vendée, at Lyons, and in other places in open rebellion, and were directed against persons in insurrection in time of war. The Terror showed no respect for, or interest in, the class origins of its victims. About 8 percent were nobles, but the nobles as a class were not molested unless suspected of political agitation; 14 percent of the victims were classifiable as bourgeois, mainly of the rebellious southern cities; 6 percent were clergy, while no less than 70 percent were of the peasant and laboring classes. A democratic republic, founded on the Declaration of the Rights of Man, was in principle to follow the Terror once the war and the emergency were over, but meanwhile, the Terror was inhuman at best and in some places atrocious, as at Nantes where 2,000 persons were loaded on barges and deliberately drowned. The Terror left long memories in France of antipathy to the Revolution and to republicanism.

To conduct the government in the midst of the war emergency the Committee of Public Safety operated as a joint dictatorship or war cabinet. It prepared and guided legislation through the Convention. It gained control over the "representatives on mission," who were members of the Convention on duty with the armies and in the insurgent areas of France. It established the *Bulletin des loix,* so that all persons might know what laws they were supposed to enforce or to obey. It centralized the administration, converting the swarm of locally elected officials, left over from the Constituent Assembly, and who were royalists in some places, wild extremists in others, into centrally appointed "national agents" named by the Committee of Public Safety.

To win the war the Committee proclaimed the *levée en masse,* calling on all able-bodied men to rally to the colors. It recruited scientific men to work on armaments and munitions. The most prominent French scientists of the day, including Lagrange and Lamarck, worked for or were protected by the government of the Terror, though one, Lavoisier, "father of modern chemistry," was guillotined in 1794 because he had been involved in tax farming before 1789. For military reasons also the Committee instituted economic controls, which at the same time met the demands of the *enragés* and other working-class spokesmen. The assignats ceased to fall during the year of the Terror. Thus the government protected both its own purchasing power and that of the masses. It did so by controlling the export of gold, by confiscating specie and foreign currency from French citizens, to whom it paid assignats in return, and by legislation against hoarding or the withholding of goods from the market. Food and supplies for the armies, and for civilians in the towns, were raised and allocated by a system of requisitions, centralized in a Subsistence Commission under the Committee of Public Safety. A "general maximum" set ceilings for prices and wages. It helped to check inflation during the crisis, but it did not work very well; the Committee believed, on principle, in a free market economy and lacked the technical and administrative machinery to enforce thorough controls. By 1794 it was giving freer rein to private enterprise and to the peasants, in order to encourage production. It tried also to hold down wages and in that respect failed to win the adherence of many working-class leaders.

In June 1793 the Committee produced, and had adopted by the Convention, a republican constitution which provided for universal male suffrage. But the new constitution was suspended indefinitely, and the government was declared "revolutionary until the peace," "revolutionary" meaning extraconstitutional or of an emergency character. In other ways the Committee showed intentions of legislating in behalf of the lower economic classes. The price controls and other economic regulations answered the demands of the *sans-culottes*. The last of the manorial regime was done away with; the peasants were relieved of having to pay compensation for the obligations that had been abolished at the opening of the Revolution. Purchase of land by the peasants was made somewhat easier. There were even moves, in the Ventôse laws of March 1794, to confiscate the property of suspects (not merely of the church or convicted émigrés), and to give such property gratis to "indigent patriots"; but these laws were drafted in unworkable form, never received much support from the ruling Committee, and came to very little. The Committee busied itself also with social services and measures of public improvement: it issued pamphlets to teach farmers to improve their crops, selected promising youths to receive instruction in useful trades, opened a military school for boys of all classes, even the humblest, and certainly intended to introduce universal elementary education. It was at this time, also, that slavery was abolished in the French colonies, free blacks having already received civic rights.

The Committee of Public Safety wished to concentrate the Revolution in itself. It had no patience with unauthorized revolutionary violence. With a democratic program of its own, it disapproved of the turbulent democracy of popular clubs and local assemblies. In the fall of 1793 it arrested the leading *enragés*. Extreme revolutionism thereafter took the name of Hébertism, after Hébert, an officer of the Paris Commune. The Hébertists were a large and indefinable group and included many members of the Convention. They indiscriminately denounced merchants and bourgeoisie. They were the party of extreme Terror; an Hébertist brought about the drownings at Nantes. Believing all religion to be counterrevolutionary, they launched the movement of Dechristianization. Even a Republican calendar was adopted by the Convention. Its main purpose was to blot out from men's minds the Christian cycle of Sundays, saints' days, and such holidays as Christmas and Easter. It counted years from the founding of the French Republic, divided each year into new months of thirty days each, and even abolished the week, which it replaced with the *décade*.[14]

---

[14]Though not adopted until October 1793, the revolutionary calendar dated the Year I of the French Republic from September 22, 1792. The names of the months, in order, were Vendémiaire, Brumaire, Frimaire (autumn); Nivôse, Pluviôse, Ventôse (winter); Germinal, Floréal, Prairial (spring); Messidor, Thermidor, Fructidor (summer).

Another form taken by Dechristianization was the cult of reason which sprang up all over France at the end of 1793. In Paris the bishop resigned his office, declaring that he had been deluded; and the Commune put on ceremonies in the cathedral of Notre Dame, in which Reason was impersonated by an actress who was the wife of one of the city officials. But Dechristianization was severely frowned upon by Robespierre. He believed that it would alienate the masses from the Republic and ruin such sympathy as was still felt for the Revolution abroad. The Committee of Public Safety, therefore, ordered the toleration of peaceable Catholics, and in June 1794 Robespierre introduced the "Worship of the Supreme Being," a kind of national and naturalistic cult, in which the Republic was declared to recognize the existence of God and the immortality of the soul. Robespierre hoped that both Catholics and agnostic anticlericals could become reconciled on this ground. But Catholics were now beyond reconciliation, and the freethinkers, appealing to the tradition of Voltaire, regarded Robespierre as a reactionary and a mystery-monger and were instrumental in bringing about his fall.

Meanwhile the Committee proceeded relentlessly against the Hébertists, whose main champions it sent to the guillotine in March 1794. The paramilitary "revolutionary armies" were repressed. The extreme Terrorists were recalled from the provinces. The revolutionary Paris Commune was destroyed. Robespierre filled the municipal offices of Paris with his own appointees. This Robespierrist commune disapproved of strikes and tried to hold down wages, on the plea of military necessity; it failed to win over the ex-Hébertists and working-class spokesmen, who became disillusioned in the Revolution and dismissed it as a bourgeois movement. Probably to prevent just such a conclusion, and to avoid the appearance of deviation to the right, Robespierre and the Committee, after liquidating the Hébertists, also liquidated certain right-wing members of the Mountain who were known as Dantonists. Danton and his followers were accused of financial dishonesty and of dealing with counterrevolutionaries; the charges contained some truth but were not the main reason for the executions.

By the spring of 1794 the French Republic possessed an army of 800,000 men, the largest ever raised up to that time by a European power. It was a national army, representing a people in arms, commanded by officers who had been promoted rapidly on grounds of merit, and composed of troops who felt themselves to be citizens fighting for their own cause. Its intense political-mindedness made it the more formidable and contrasted strongly with the indifference of the opposing troops, some of whom were in fact serfs and none of whom had any sense of membership in their own political systems. The Allied governments, each pursuing its own ends, and still distracted by their ambitions in Poland, where the third partition was impending, could not combine their forces against France. In June 1794 the French won the battle of Fleurus in Belgium. The Republican hosts again streamed into the Low Countries; in six months their cavalry rode into Amsterdam on the ice.

Military success made the French less willing to put up with the dictatorial rule and economic regimentation of the Terror. Robespierre and the Committee of Public

Safety had antagonized all significant parties. The working-class radicals of Paris would no longer support him, and after the death of Danton the National Convention was afraid of its own ruling committee. A group in the Convention obtained the "outlawing" of Robespierre on 9 Thermidor (July 27, 1794); he was guillotined with some of his associates on the following day. Many who turned against Robespierre believed they were pushing the Revolution farther forward, as in destroying the Girondins the year before. Others thought, or said, that they were stopping a dictator and a tyrant. All agreed, to absolve themselves, in heaping all blame upon Robespierre. The idea that Robespierre was an ogre originated more with his former colleagues than with conservatives of the time.

The Thermidorian Reaction

The fall of Robespierre stunned the country, but its effects manifested themselves during the following months as the "Thermidorian reaction." The Terror subsided. The Convention reduced the powers of the Committee of Public Safety, and it closed the Jacobin club. Businessmen, landowning peasants, army suppliers, speculators in land and currency made their voices heard. Price control and other regulations were removed. Inflation resumed its course, prices again rose, and the disoriented and leaderless working classes suffered more than ever. Sporadic risings broke out, of which the greatest was the insurrection of Prairial in the Year III (May 1795), when a mob all but dispersed the Convention by force. Troops were called to Paris for the first time since 1789. Insurrectionists in the working-class quarters threw up barricades in the streets. The army prevailed without much bloodshed, but the Convention arrested, imprisoned, or deported ten thousand of the insurgents. A few organizers were guillotined, including one militant black. The affair of Prairial gave a foretaste of modern social revolution.

The triumphant element was the bourgeois class which had guided the Revolution since the Constituent Assembly and had not been really unseated even during the Terror. To the old solid bourgeois of the Old Regime new elements were now added, *parvenus* and *nouveaux riches*, speculators and profiteers, often noisy, ostentatious, and vulgar, and whose women, nicknamed the *merveilleuses*, were commonly overdressed or underdressed in the extreme. Young bourgeois often joined with former aristocrats in a "white terror" against the Jacobins. But the bourgeoisie, disreputable though a few of them were, had not lost faith in the Revolution. Democracy they associated with red terror and mob rule, but they still believed in individual legal rights and in a written constitution. Conditions were rather adverse, for the country was still unsettled, and although the Convention made a separate peace with Spain and Prussia, France still remained at war with Great Britain and the Habsburg empire. But the bourgeois of the Convention were determined to make another attempt at constitutional government. They set aside the democratic constitution written in 1793 (and never used) and produced the Constitution of the Year III, which went into effect at the end of 1795.

The first formally constituted French Republic, known as the Directory, lasted only four years. Its weakness was that it rested on an extremely narrow social base, and that it presupposed certain military conquests. The new constitution applied not only to France but also to Belgium, which was regarded as incorporated constitutionally into France, though the Habsburgs had not yet ceded these "Austrian Netherlands," nor had the British yielded in their refusal to accept French occupation. The constitution of 1795 thus committed the republic to a program of successful expansion. At the same time it restricted the politically active class. It gave almost all literate citizens the vote, but voters voted only for "electors," for whom about the same qualifications were set as in the constitution of 1789–1791. Persons chosen as electors were usually men of some means, able to give their time and willing to take part in public life; this in effect meant men of the upper middle class, since the old aristocracy was disaffected. The electors chose all important department officials and also the members of the national Legislative Assembly, which this time was divided into two chambers. The lower chamber was called the Council of Five Hundred, the upper, composed of 250 members, the Council of Ancients—"ancients" being men over forty. The chambers chose the executive, which was called the Directory (whence the whole regime got its name) and was made up of five Directors.

The government was thus constitutionally in the hands of substantial property-owners, rural and urban, but its real base was narrower still. In the reaction after Thermidor many people began to consider restoring the monarchy. The Convention, to protect its own members, ruled that two-thirds of the men initially elected to the Council of Five Hundred and Council of Ancients must be ex-members of the Convention. This interference with the freedom of the elections provoked serious disturbances in Paris, instigated by persons called royalists; but the Convention, having now accustomed itself to using the army, instructed a young general who happened to be in Paris, named Bonaparte, to put down the royalist mob. He did so with a "whiff of grapeshot." The constitutional republic thus made itself dependent on military protection at the outset. As it turned out, 506 *Conventionnels,* or almost all surviving members of the Convention, reappeared among the 741 elected to the new legislative chambers, in which therefore they had a comfortable majority. They were derisively called "perpetuals" by their opponents. The new republic, to its critics, seemed to be a storm cellar for regicides. All the old faces reappeared in new positions.

The regime had enemies to both right and left. On the right, undisguised royalists agitated in Paris and even in the two councils. Their center was the Clichy club, and they were in continuous touch with the late king's brother, the Count of Provence, whom they regarded as Louis XVIII (Louis XVI's son, who died in prison, being counted as Louis XVII). Louis XVIII had installed himself at Verona in Italy, where he headed a propaganda agency financed largely by British money. The worst obstacle to the resurgence of royalism in France was Louis XVIII himself. In 1795, on assuming the title, he had issued a Declaration of Verona, in which he announced his intention to restore the Old Regime and punish all involved in the Revolution back to 1789. It has been said, correctly enough in this connection, that the Bourbons "learned nothing and forgot nothing." Had Louis XVIII offered in 1795 what he offered in 1814, it is quite conceivable that his partisans in France might have brought about his restoration and terminated the war. As it was, the bulk of the French adhered not exactly to the republic as set up in 1795, but more negatively to any system that would shut out the Bourbons and former nobility, prevent a reimposition of the manorial system, and secure the new landowners, peasant and bourgeois, in the possession of the church properties which they had purchased.

The Left was made up of persons from various levels of society who still favored the more democratic ideas expressed earlier in the Revolution. Some of them thought that the fall of Robespierre had been a great misfortune. A tiny group of extremists formed the Conspiracy of Equals, organized in 1796 by "Gracchus" Babeuf. His intention was to overthrow the Directory and replace it with a dictatorial government which he called "democratic," in which private property would be abolished and equality decreed. For these ideas, and for his activist program, he has been regarded as an interesting precursor to modern communism. The Directory repressed the Conspiracy of Equals without difficulty and guillotined Babeuf and one other. Meanwhile it did nothing to relieve the distress of the lower classes, who showed little inclination to follow Babeuf but did suffer from the ravages of scarcity and inflation.

The Political Crisis of 1797

In March 1797 occurred the first really free election ever held in France under republican auspices. A third of the membership of the two councils was to be renewed. Some 216 "perpetuals" retired, of whom about 150 stood for reelection. Only thirteen were reelected. The successful candidates were for the most part constitutional monarchists or at least vaguely royalist. A change of the balance within the Five Hundred and the Ancients, in favor of royalism, seemed to be impending. This was precisely what most of the republicans of 1793, including the regicides, could not endure, even though they had to violate the constitution to prevent it. Nor was it endurable, for other reasons, to General Napoleon Bonaparte.

Bonaparte had been born in 1769 into the minor nobility of Corsica, shortly after the annexation of Corsica to France. He had studied in French military schools and been commissioned in the Bourbon army but would never have reached high rank under the conditions of the Old Regime. In 1793 he was a fervent young Jacobin officer, who had been useful in driving the British from Toulon, and who was consequently made a brigadier general by the government of the Terror. In 1795, as noted, he rendered service to the Convention by breaking up a demonstration of royalists. In 1796 he received command of an army, with which, in two brilliant campaigns, he crossed the Alps and drove the Austrians from north Italy. Like other generals he got out of control of the government in Paris, which was financially too harassed to pay his troops or to supply him. He lived by local requisitions in Italy, became self-supporting and independent, and in fact made the civilian government in Paris dependent on him.

He developed a foreign policy of his own. Many Italians had become dissatisfied with their old governments, so that the arrival of the French republican armies threw north Italy into a turmoil, in which the Venetian cities revolted against Venice, Bologna against the pope, Milan against Austria, and the Sardinian monarchy was threatened by uprisings of its own subjects. Combining with some of these revolutionaries, while rejecting others, Bonaparte established a "Cisalpine" Republic in the Po valley, modeled on the French system, with Milan as its capital, and composed mainly of former Habsburg and papal territories. Where the Directory, on the whole, had originally meant to return Milan to the Austrians in compensation for Austrian recognition of the French conquest of Belgium, Bonaparte insisted that France hold its position in both Belgium and Italy. He therefore needed expansionist republicans in the government in Paris and was perturbed by the elections of 1797.

The Austrians negotiated with Bonaparte because they had been beaten by him in battle. The British also, in conferences with the French at Lille, discussed peace in 1796 and 1797. The war had gone badly for England; a party of Whigs led by Charles James Fox had always openly disapproved it, and the pro-French and republican radicals were so active that the government suspended habeas corpus in 1794, and thereafter imprisoned political agitators at its discretion. In 1795 an assassin fired on George III, breaking the glass in his carriage. Crops were bad, and bread was scarce and costly; it was in the 1790s that Britain became permanently dependent on the importation of food. England too suffered from inflation, for Pitt at first financed the war by extensive loans, and a good deal of gold was shipped to the Continent to finance the Allied armies. In February 1797 the Bank of England suspended gold payments to private citizens. Famine threatened, the populace was restless, and there were even mutinies in the fleet. Ireland was in rebellion; the French came close to landing a republican army in it, and it could be supposed that the next attempt might be more successful. The Austrians, Britain's only remaining ally, were routed by Bonaparte, and at the moment the British could subsidize them no further. The British had every reason to make peace. Many were inclined to settle for colonial conquests, regarding the war as a renewal of the eighteenth-century struggle for empire. The conferees at Lille reached the point of considering an arrangement by which Britain should recognize the French annexation of Belgium, in return for the cession of Ceylon, the Cape of Good Hope, and Trinidad to Great Britain. These were, in truth, not French to cede; Ceylon and the Cape were Dutch, and Trinidad Spanish; but the Spanish monarchy had become allied with the French Republic through the old fear of Great Britain, and a revolution in Holland in 1795, creating the Batavian Republic, had produced in that country also a government allied to France.

Prospects for peace seemed good in the summer of 1797, but, as always, it would be peace upon certain conditions. It was the royalists in France that were the peace party, since a restored king could easily return the conquests of the republic and would in any case abandon the new republics in Holland and the Po valley. The republicans in the French government could make peace with difficulty, if at all. They were constitutionally bound to retain Belgium. They were losing control of their own generals. Nor could the supreme question be evaded: Was peace dear enough to purchase by a return of the Old Regime, such as Louis XVIII had himself promised?

The coup d'état of Fructidor (September 4, 1797) resolved all these many issues. It was the turning point of the constitutional republic and was decisive for all Europe. The Directory asked for help from Bonaparte, who sent one of his generals, Augereau, to Paris. While Augereau stood by with a force of soldiers, the councils annulled most of the elections of the preceding spring. Two Directors were purged; one of them, Lazare Carnot, "organizer of victory" in the Committee of Public Safety, and now in 1797 a strict constitutionalist, was driven into exile. On the whole, it was the old republicans of the Convention who secured themselves in power. Their justification was that they were defending the Revolution, keeping out Louis XVIII and the Old Regime. But to do so they had violated their own constitution and quashed the first free election ever held in a constitutional French republic. And they had become more than ever dependent on the army.

After the coup d'état the "Fructidorian" government broke off negotiations with England. With Austria it signed the treaty of Campo Formio on October 17, 1797, incorporating Bonaparte's ideas. Peace now prevailed on the Continent, since only France and Great Britain remained at war, but a peace full of trouble for the future. By the new treaty Austria recognized the French annexation of Belgium (the former Austrian Netherlands), the French right to incorporate the Left Bank of the Rhine, and the French-dominated Cisalpine Republic in Italy. In return, Bonaparte allowed the Austrians to annex Venice and most of mainland Venetia. The Venetian possessions in the Ionian Islands, off the coast of Greece, went to France.

In the following months, under French auspices, revolutionary republicanism spread through much of Italy. The old patrician republic of Genoa turned into a Ligurian Republic on the French model. At Rome the pope was deposed from his temporal power and a Roman Republic was established. In southern Italy a Neapolitan Republic, also called Parthenopean, was set up. In Switzerland at the same time, Swiss reformers cooperated with the French to create a new Helvetic Republic.

The Left Bank of the Rhine, in the atomistic Holy Roman Empire, was occupied by a great many German princes who now had to vacate. The treaty of Campo Formio provided that they be compensated by church territories in Germany east of the Rhine, and that France have a hand in the redistribution. The German princes turned greedy eyes on the German bishops and abbots, and the almost 1,000-year-old Holy Empire, hardly more than a solemn form since the Peace of Westphalia, sank to the level of a land rush or real estate speculation, while France became involved in the territorial reconstruction of Germany.

NORTH SEA

BALTIC SEA

RÜGEN

ENGLAND

Hamburg

BATAVIAN
REPUBLIC

Berlin

PRUSSIA

BELGIUM
(ANNEXED 1792)

Lille

Fleurus

Rhine R.

OTHER GERMAN STATES

Pillnitz

SILESIA

RHINELAND

Paris
Versailles

Seine R.

Varennes

Lunéville

Loire R.

BADEN

FRANCE

Basel

Lyons

HELVETIC REPUBLIC

SAVOY

PIEDMONT

Milan

Marengo

Vienna

Danube R.

Budapest

AUSTRIA

Campo
Formio

Verona

CISALPINE REPUBLIC

Venice

Po R.

Avignon

Genoa
LIGURIAN
REPUBLIC

Marseilles

Nice

TUSCANY

ROMAN
REPUBLIC

ADRIATIC SEA

OTTOMAN EMPIRE

SPAIN

CORSICA

Rome

SARDINIA

PARTHENOPEAN
REPUBLIC
(1799)

IONIAN I.

MEDITERRANEAN

SEA

French Republic 1798

Dependent Republics 1798

German Church States to be Absorbed by Other German States

The French Republic and its Satellites 1798–1799. *By 1798 the revolutionary French
Republic had annexed Belgium and the German Left Bank of the Rhine and had created, with the
aid of native sympathizers, a group of lesser revolutionary republics in the Netherlands, Switzerland, and most of Italy. The map also shows the church-states of Germany which, by the treaty
of Campo Formio, were to be absorbed by various German rulers under French auspices.*

411

After Fructidor the idea of maintaining the republic as a free or constitutional government was given up. There were more uprisings, more quashed elections, more purgings both to Left and Right. The Directory became a kind of ineffective dictatorship. It repudiated most of the assignats and the debt but failed to restore financial confidence or stability. Guerrilla activity flared up again in the Vendée and other parts of western France. The religious schism became more acute; the Directory took severe measures toward the refractory clergy.

Meanwhile Bonaparte waited for the situation to ripen. Returning from Italy a conquering hero, he was assigned to command the army in training to invade England. He concluded that invasion was premature and decided to strike indirectly at England, by threatening India in a spectacular invasion of Egypt. In 1798, outwitting the British fleet, he landed a French army at the mouth of the Nile. Egypt was part of the Ottoman Empire, and the French occupation of it alarmed the Russians, who had their own designs on the Near East. The Austrians objected to the French rearrangement of Germany. A year and a half after the treaty of Campo Formio, Austria, Russia, and Great Britain formed an alliance known as the Second Coalition. The Republic was again involved in a general war. And the war went unfavorably, for in August 1798 the British fleet had cut off the French army in Egypt by winning the battle of the Nile (or Aboukir), and in 1799 Russian forces, under Marshal Suvorov, were operating as far west as Switzerland and north Italy, where the Cisalpine Republic went down in ruin.

General Bonaparte's opportunity had come. He left his army in Egypt and, again slipping through the British fleet, reappeared unexpectedly in France. He found that certain civilian leaders in the Directory were planning a change. They included Sieyès, of whom little had been heard since he wrote *What Is the Third Estate?* ten years before, but who had sat in the Convention, voted for the death of Louis XVI, and was in fact one of the "perpetuals." Sieyès' formula was now "confidence from below, authority from above"—what he now wanted of the people was acquiescence, and of the government, power to act. This group was looking about for a general, and their choice fell on the sensational young Bonaparte, who was still only thirty. Dictatorship by an army officer was repugnant to most republicans of the Five Hundred and the Ancients. Bonaparte, Sieyès, and their followers resorted to force, executing the coup d'état of Brumaire (November 9, 1799), in which armed soldiers drove the legislators from the chambers. They proclaimed a new form of the republic, which Bonaparte entitled the Consulate. It was headed by three consuls, with Bonaparte as the First Consul.

T he next chapter takes up the affairs of Europe as whole in the time of Napoleon Bonaparte, the purpose at present being only to tell how he closed, in a way, the Revolution in France.

It happened that the French Republic, in falling into the hands of a general, fell also to a man of such remarkable talents as are often denominated genius. Bonaparte was a short dark man, of Mediterranean type, who would never have looked impressive in civilian clothing. He was temperamentally high-strung, yet could sleep at will; talkative or taciturn as his mood changed, and on occasion eloquent, as in the haranguing of troops. His manners were rather coarse; he lost his temper, cheated at cards, and pinched people by the ear in a kind of formidable play—he was no "gentleman." A child of the Enlightenment and the Revolution, he was entirely emancipated not only from customary ideas but from moral scruples as well. He regarded the world as a flux to be formed by his own mind. He had an exalted belief in his own destinies, which became more mystical and exaggerated as the years went on. He claimed to follow his "star." His ideas of the good and the beautiful were rather blunt, but he was a man of extraordinary intellectual capacity, which impressed all with whom he came in contact. "Never speak unless you know you are the ablest man in the room," he once advised his stepson, on making him viceroy of Italy, a maxim which, if he followed it himself, still allowed him to do most of the talking. His interests ran to solid subjects, history, law, military science, public administration. His mind was tenacious and perfectly orderly; he once declared that it was like a chest of drawers, which he could open or close at will, forgetting any subject when its drawer was closed and finding it ready with all necessary detail when its drawer was opened. He had all the masterful qualities associated with leadership; he could dazzle and captivate those who had any inclination to follow him at all. Some of the most humane men of the day, including Goethe and Beethoven in Germany, and Lazare Carnot among the former revolutionary leaders, at first looked on him with high approval. He inspired confidence by his crisp speech, rapid decisions, and quick grasp of complex problems when they were newly presented to him. He was, or seemed, just what many Frenchmen were looking for after ten years of upheaval.

Under the Consulate France reverted to a form of enlightened despotism, and Bonaparte may be thought of as the last and most eminent of the enlightened despots. Despotic the new regime undoubtedly was from the start. Self-government through elected bodies was ruthlessly pushed aside. Bonaparte delighted in affirming the sovereignty of the people; but to his mind the people was a sovereign, like Voltaire's God, who somehow created the world but never thereafter interfered in it. He clearly saw, as Frederick the Great and Joseph II had seen more dimly, that a government's authority was greater when it was held to represent the entire nation. In the weeks after Brumaire he assured himself of a popular mandate by devising a written constitution and submitting it to a general referendum or "plebiscite." The voters could take it—or nothing. They took it by a majority officially reported as 3,011,007 to 1,562.

The new constitution set up a make-believe of parliamentary institutions. It gave universal male suffrage, but the citizens merely chose "notables"; men on the lists of notables were then appointed by the government itself to public position. The notables had no powers of their own. They were merely available for appointment to office. They might sit in a Legislative Body, where they could neither initiate nor discuss legislation, but only mutely reject or enact it. There was also a Tribunate which discussed and deliberated but had no enacting powers. There was a

Conservative Senate, which had rights of appointment of notables to office ("patronage" in American terms), and in which numerous storm-tossed regicides found a haven. The main agency in the new government was the Council of State, imitated from the Old Regime; it prepared the significant legislation, often under the presidency of the First Consul himself, who always gave the impression that he understood everything. The First Consul made all the decisions and ran the state. The regime did not openly represent anybody, and that was its strength, for it provoked the less opposition. In any case, the political machinery just described fell rapidly into disuse.

Bonaparte entrenched himself also by promising and obtaining peace. The military problem, at the close of 1799, was much simplified by the attitude of the Russians, who, for reasons given in the following chapter, in effect withdrew from the war with France.[15] In the Italian theater Bonaparte had to deal only with the Austrians, whom he again defeated, by again crossing the Alps, at the battle of Marengo in June 1800. In February 1801 the Austrians signed the treaty of Lunéville, in which the terms of Campo Formio were confirmed. A year later, in March 1802, peace was made even with Britain.

Peace was made also at home. Bonaparte kept internal order, partly by a secret political police, but more especially through a powerful and centralized administrative machine, in which a "prefect," under direct orders of the minister of the interior, ruled firmly over each of the departments created by the Constituent Assembly. The new government put down the guerrillas in the west. Its laws and taxes were imposed on Brittany and the Vendée. Peasants there were no longer terrorized by marauding partisans. A new peace settled down on the factions left by the Revolution. Bonaparte offered a general amnesty and invited back to France, with a few exceptions, exiles of all stripes from the first aristocratic émigrés to the refugees and deportees of the republican coups d'état. Requiring only that they work for him and stop quarreling with each other, he picked reasonable men from all camps. His Second Consul was Cambacérès, a regicide of the Terror, his Third Consul Lebrun, who had been Maupeou's colleague in the days of Louis XV.[16] Fouché emerged as minister of police; he had been an Hébertist and extreme terrorist in 1793 and had done as much as any man to bring about the fall of Robespierre. Before 1789 he had been an obscure bourgeois professor of physics. Talleyrand appeared as minister of foreign affairs; he had spent the Terror in safe seclusion in the United States, and his principles, if he had any, were those of constitutional monarchy. Before 1789 he had been a bishop and was of an aristocratic lineage almost unbearably distinguished—no one who had not known the Old Regime, he once said, could realize how pleasant it had been. Men of this sort were now willing, for a few years beginning in 1800, to forget the past and work in common toward the future.

Disturbers of the new order the First Consul ruthlessly put down. Indeed, he concocted alarms to make himself more welcome as a pillar of order. On Christmas

[15] See p. 423.
[16] See p. 338.

Eve, 1800, on his way to the opera, he was nearly killed by a bomb, or "infernal machine," as people then said. It had been laid by royalists, but Bonaparte represented it as the work of a Jacobin conspiracy, being most afraid at the moment of some of the old republicans; and over a hundred former Jacobins were again deported. Contrariwise, in 1804, he greatly exaggerated certain royalist plots against him, invaded the independent state of Baden, and there arrested the Duke of Enghien, who was related to the Bourbons. Though he knew Enghien to be innocent, he had him shot. His purpose now was to please the old Jacobins by staining his own hands with Bourbon blood; Fouché and the regicides concluded that they were secure so long as Bonaparte was in power.

For all but the most convinced royalists and republicans, reconciliation was made easier by the establishment of peace with the church. Bonaparte himself was a pure eighteenth-century rationalist. He regarded religion as a convenience. He advertised himself as a Moslem in Egypt, as a Catholic in France, and as a freethinker among the professors at the Institute in Paris. But a Catholic revival was in full swing, and he saw its importance. The refractory clergy were the spiritual force animating all forms of counterrevolution. "Fifty émigré bishops, paid by England," he once said, "lead the French clergy today. Their influence must be destroyed. For this we need the authority of the pope." Ignoring the horrified outcries of the old Jacobins, in 1801 he signed a concordat with the Vatican.

Both parties gained from the settlement. The autonomy of the prerevolutionary Gallican church came to an end. The pope received the right to depose French bishops, since before the schism could be healed both constitutional and refractory bishops had to be obliged to resign. The constitutional or prerevolutionary clergy came under the discipline of the Holy See. Publicity of Catholic worship, in such forms as processions in the streets, was again allowed. Church seminaries were again permitted. But Bonaparte and the heirs of the Revolution gained even more. The pope, by signing the concordat, virtually recognized the Republic. The Vatican agreed to raise no question over the former tithes and the former church lands. The new owners of former church properties thus obtained clear titles. Nor was there any further question of Avignon, an enclave within France, formerly papal, annexed to France in 1791. Nor were the papal negotiators able to undermine religious toleration; all that Bonaparte would concede was a clause that was purely factual, and hence harmless, stating that Catholicism was the religion of the majority of Frenchmen. The clergy, in compensation for loss of their tithes and property, were assured of receiving salaries from the state. But Bonaparte, to dispel the notion of an established church, put Protestant ministers of all denominations on the state payroll also. He thus checkmated the Vatican on important points. At the same time, simply by signing an agreement with Rome, he disarmed the counterrevolution. It could no longer be said that the Republic was godless. Good relations did not, indeed, last very long, for Bonaparte and the papacy were soon at odds. But the terms of the concordat proved lasting.

With peace and order established, the constructive work of the Consulate turned to the fields of law and administration. The First Consul and his advisers combined what they conceived to be the best of the Revolution and of the Old Regime. The modern state took on clearer form. It was the reverse of everything feudal. All public authority was concentrated in paid agents of government, no person was held to be under any legal authority except that of the state, and the authority of government fell on all persons alike. There were no more estates, legal classes, privileges, local liberties, hereditary offices, gilds, or manors. Judges, officials, and army officers received specified salaries. Neither military commissions nor civil offices could be bought and sold. Citizens were to rise in government service purely according to their abilities. This was the doctrine of "careers open to talent"; it was what the bourgeoisie had wanted before the Revolution, and a few persons of quite humble birth profited also.

Another deep demand of the French people, deeper than the demand for the vote, was for more reason, order, and economy in public finance and taxation. The Consulate gave these also. Taxes were henceforth collected, not by local persons who allocated quotas upon individual taxpayers at their own discretion, but by professional collectors who were employed by the central government and dealt directly with each individual taxpayer. There were no tax exemptions because of birth, status, or special arrangement. Everyone was supposed to pay, so that no disgrace attached to payment, and there was less evasion. In principle these changes had been introduced in 1789; after 1799 they began to work. For the first time in ten years the government really collected the taxes which it levied and so could rationally plan its financial affairs. Order was introduced also into expenditure, and accounting methods were improved. There was no longer a haphazard assortment of different "funds," on which various officials drew independently and confidentially as they needed money, but a concentration of financial management in the treasury, and even in a kind of budget. An element of irresponsibility remained because the Consulate never published any clear or candid financial statements. But Bonaparte probably understood his own finances better than any official of the Old Regime had ever done, even though they remained a mystery to the public of his own time, and to historians since. The revolutionary gyrations in the value of money were also ended. Because the Directory had shouldered the odium of repudiating the currency and government bonds, the Consulate was able to establish a relatively sound currency and secure national debt. To assist in government financing, one of the banks of the Old Regime was revived and established as the Bank of France.

Like all enlightened despots, Bonaparte codified the laws, and of all law codes since the Romans the Napoleonic codes are the most famous. To the 300 legal systems of the Old Regime, and the mass of parliamentary and royal ordinances, were now added the thousands of laws enacted but seldom implemented by the revolutionary assemblies. This jumble was now collated, digested, condensed, and made consistent. Five codes emerged, the Civil Code (often called simply the Code Napoleon), the codes of civil and of criminal procedure, and the commercial and penal codes. The codes made France legally and judicially uniform. They assured legal equality; all French citizens had the same civil rights. They embodied the principle of reason, for they held that custom, local practice, or decision in earlier cases was insufficient to make a rule actually lawful, and that positive law must somehow correspond to a natural law of abstract and considered justice. They formulated the new law of property, made landed property a more exclusively private right than under the Old Regime, and set forth the law of contracts, debts, leases, stock companies, and similar matters in such a way as to create the legal framework for an economy of private enterprise. They repeated the ban of all previous regimes on organized labor unions and were severe with the individual workingman, his word not being acceptable in court against that of his employer—a significant departure from equality before the law. The criminal code was somewhat freer in giving the government the means to detect crime than in granting the individual the means of defending himself against legal charges. As for the family, the codes recognized civil marriage and divorce but left the wife with very restricted powers over property, and the father with extensive authority over minor children. The codes reflected much of French life under the Old Regime. They also set the character of France as it has been ever since, socially bourgeois, legally equalitarian, and administratively bureaucratic.

In France, with the Consulate, the Revolution was over. If its highest hopes had not been accomplished, the worst evils of the Old Regime had at least been cured. The beneficiaries of the Revolution felt secure. The country was a combination of peasant democracy and bourgeois paradise. Even former aristocrats were rallying. The proletarian movement, always weak because the number of true wage earners was small, and repeatedly frustrated under all the revolutionary regimes, now vanished from the political scene, to reappear as socialism thirty years later. What the Third Estate had most wanted in 1789 was now both codified and enforced, with the exception of parliamentary government, which after ten years of turmoil many people were temporarily willing to forego. Moreover, in 1802, the French Republic was at peace with the papacy, Great Britain, and all Continental powers. It reached to the Rhine and had dependent republics in Holland and Italy. So popular was the First Consul that in 1802, by another plebiscite, he had himself elected consul for life. A new constitution, in 1804, again ratified by plebiscite, declared that "the government of the republic is confided to an emperor." The Consulate became the Empire, and Bonaparte emerged as Napoleon I, Emperor of the French.

But France, no longer revolutionary at home, was revolutionary outside its borders. Napoleon became a terror to the patricians of Europe. They called him the "Jacobin." And the France which he ruled, and used as his arsenal, was an incomparably formidable state. Even before the Revolution it had been the most populous in Europe, perhaps the most wealthy, in the front rank of scientific enterprise and intellectual leadership. Now all the old barriers of privilege, tax exemption, localism, caste exclusiveness, and routine-mindedness had disappeared. The new France could tap the wealth of its citizens and put able men into position without inquiring into their origins. Every private, boasted Napoleon, carried a marshal's baton in his knapsack. The French looked with disdain on their caste-ridden adversaries. The principle of civic equality proved not only to have the magnificent appeal of justice, but also to be politically useful, and the resources of France were hurled against Europe with a force which for many years nothing could check.

X: NAPOLEONIC EUROPE

Bonaparte is the name of a French army officer and dictator. Napoleon is a name in the history of the European world. The French emperor came nearer than any man has ever come to imposing a political unity on the European continent, nearer even than the German conqueror Adolf Hitler, with whom it is both illuminating and misleading to compare him. Of his ascendancy of fifteen years, from 1799 to 1814, two stories are to be told. One is a story of international relations—of coalitions, wars and treaties, sea power and land power, shifts of alliances and rearrangements of frontiers, all reflecting the diverse interests of the states of Europe. The other is a story of internal development of the European peoples, for all were profoundly affected by the Napoleonic domination. In some countries, notably western Germany and Italy, native reformers worked with Napoleon to introduce the changes that he demanded. In others, notably Prussia east of the Elbe, it was the resistance to Napoleon and to the French that gave the incentive for internal reorganization.

It is convenient to think of the fighting from 1792 to 1814 as a "world war," as indeed it was, affecting not only all of Europe but places as remote as Spanish

Chapter Emblem: An Italian cameo of 1810, showing the idealized head of Napoleon crowned with laurels as law-giver and culture-hero.

America, where the wars of independence began, or the interior of North America, where the United States purchased Louisiana in 1803 and attempted a conquest of Canada in 1812. But it is important to realize that this world war was actually a series of wars, most of them quite short, sharp, and distinct. Only Great Britain remained continually at war with France, except for about a year of peace in 1802–1803. Never were the four great powers, Britain, Austria, Russia, and Prussia, simultaneously in the field against France until 1813.

The history of the Napoleonic period would be much simpler if the European governments had fought merely to protect themselves against the aggressive French. Each, however, in its way, was as dynamic and expansive as Napoleon himself. For some generations Great Britain had been building a commercial empire, Russia pushing upon Poland and Turkey, Prussia consolidating its territories and striving for leadership in north Germany. Austria was less aggressive, being somewhat passively preoccupied by the rise of Prussia and Russia, but the Austrians were not without dreams of ascendancy in Germany, the Balkans, and the Adriatic. None of these ambitions ceased during the Napoleonic years. Governments, in pursuit of their own aims, were quite as willing to ally with Napoleon as to fight him. Only gradually, and under repeated provocation, did they conclude that their main interest was to dispose of the French emperor entirely.

46

The Formation of the French Imperial System

The Dissolution of the First and Second Coalitions, 1792–1802

The conflicting purposes of the powers had been apparent from the beginning. Leopold of Austria, in issuing the Declaration of Pillnitz, in 1791, had believed a general European coalition against France to be impossible. When the First Coalition was formed in 1792, the Austrians and Prussians kept their main forces in eastern Europe, more afraid of each other and of Russia, in the matter of Poland, than of the French revolutionary republic. Indeed, the main accomplishment of the First Coalition was the extermination of the Polish state.[1]

In 1795 the French broke up the coalition. The British withdrew their army from the Continent. The Prussians made a separate peace; the French bought them off by recognizing them as "protectors" of Germany north of the river Main. Spain also made a separate peace in 1795. The world saw the spectacle, outrageous to all ideology or principle, of an alliance between Bourbon Spain and the republic which had guillotined Louis XVI and kept Louis XVIII from his monarchic rights. Spain simply reverted to the eighteenth-century pattern, in allying with France because of hostility to Great Britain, whose possession of Gibraltar, naval influence in the Mediterranean, and attitude toward the Spanish empire were disquieting to the Spanish government. When Austria signed the peace of Campo Formio in 1797 the First Coalition was totally dissipated, only British naval forces remaining engaged with the French.[2]

[1] See pp. 394, 400.
[2] See p. 410.

The Second Coalition of 1799 fared no better. Russia joined it because Bonaparte's expedition to Egypt introduced a Western military force into the Near East.[3] The Russians had their own ambitions in the Mediterranean. A Russian fleet in 1799 passed through the Turkish straits and occupied the Ionian Islands off the coast of Greece, lately taken by Bonaparte from Venice.[4] The Russians set up a puppet republic of their own in the islands. They looked with interest also farther west to Malta, for the Knights of Malta had elected the tsar Paul, Catherine's son, their grand commander, hoping for his protection against France and Britain. But the British installed themselves in Malta (taking over from the French) and also defeated the French fleet in the battle of the Nile, cutting off the French army in Egypt.

The Russians now feared the British more than the French as rivals within the weakening Ottoman Empire. Veering around, they became anti-British and hence mildly pro-French. They recalled Suvorov's army from western Europe, being unable to agree with the Austrians, and in 1801 they joined in the Armed Neutrality to protect their shipping from search and seizure by British sea power. The acceptance by Austria of the peace of Lunéville in 1801 dissolved the Second Coalition. In 1802 Great Britain signed the peace of Amiens. For the only time between 1792 and 1814 no European power was at war with another—though the British, to be sure, were at war with some Indian princes, the Russians with some Caucasian tribesmen, and the French with Toussaint l'Ouverture, the black ex-slave who was attempting to found an independent republic in Haiti.

The Formation of the French Imperial System

Never had a peace been so advantageous to France as the peace of 1802. Austria had again agreed to the conditions of Campo Formio. The British, in the treaty of Amiens, accepted terms less favorable than those they had rejected five years before.[5] France retained Belgium and the Left Bank of the Rhine as integral parts of the Republic and won recognition for its satellites, the Batavian Republic in Holland, the Helvetic Republic in Switzerland, the Ligurian Republic at Genoa, and the Cisalpine Republic in the Po valley. Britain agreed to withdraw from Malta, Minorca, Elba, Trinidad, and the French Caribbean islands and to retain only Dutch Ceylon.[6] The peace of Amiens was so repugnant to British war aims that probably it would not have lasted in any case. But Bonaparte gave it no chance. He used peace as he did war to advance his interests. He dispatched a sizable army to Haiti, ostensibly to win back a rebellious French colony, but with the further thought (since Louisiana had been ceded back by Spain to France in 1800) of reviving the French colonial empire in America. He reorganized the Cisalpine Republic into an "Italian" Republic with himself as president. He reorganized the Helvetic Republic, making himself "mediator" of the Confederation of Switzerland. He reorganized Germany; that is to

Peace Interim, 1802–1803

[3] See p. 412.
[4] See p. 410.
[5] See p. 409.
[6] See maps, pp. 293 and 411.

say, he and his agents closely watched the rearrangement of territory which the Germans themselves had been carrying out since 1797.

By the treaty of Campo Formio,[7] it will be recalled, German princes of the Left Bank of the Rhine, expropriated by the annexation of their dominions to the French Republic, were to receive new territories on the Right Bank. The result was a scramble called by patriotic German historians the "shame of the princes." The German rulers, far from opposing Bonaparte or upholding any national interests, competed desperately for the absorption of German territory, each bribing and fawning upon the French (Talleyrand made over 10,000,000 francs in the process) to win French support against other Germans. The Holy Roman Empire was fatally mauled by the Germans themselves. Most of its ecclesiastical principalities and forty-five out of its fifty-one free cities disappeared, annexed by their larger neighbors. The number of states in the Holy Empire was greatly reduced, especially of the Catholic states, so that it could be foreseen that no Catholic Habsburg would again be elected emperor. Prussia, Bavaria, Württemberg, and Baden consolidated and enlarged themselves. These arrangements were ratified in February 1803 by the diet of the Empire. The enlarged German states now depended on Bonaparte for the maintenance of their new position.

Formation of the
Third Coalition in 1805

In these circumstances Britain refused to evacuate Malta; Bonaparte protested; and Britain declared war in May 1803. Bonaparte, his communications with America menaced by the British navy, and his army in Haiti decimated by disease and by rebellious blacks, suspended his ideas for re-creating an American empire and sold Louisiana to the United States. Great Britain began to seek allies for a Third Coalition. In May 1804 Napoleon pronounced himself Emperor of the French to assure the hereditary permanency of his system, though he had no son. Francis II of Austria, seeing the ruin of the Holy Roman Empire, promulgated the Austrian Empire in August 1804. He thus advanced the long process of integrating the Danubian monarchy. In 1805 Austria signed an alliance with Great Britain. The Third Coalition was completed by the accession of the Russian Tsar Alexander I, who, after Napoleon himself, was to become the most considerable figure on the European stage.

Alexander was the grandson of Catherine the Great, educated by her to be a kind of enlightened despot on the eighteenth-century model.[8] The Swiss tutor of his boyhood, La Harpe, later turned up as a pro-French revolutionary in the Helvetic Republic of 1798. Alexander became tsar in 1801, at the age of twenty-four, through a palace revolution which implicated him in the murder of his father Paul. He still corresponded with La Harpe, and he surrounded himself with a circle of liberal and zealous young men of various nationalities, of whom the most prominent was a Polish youth, Czartoryski. Alexander regarded the still recent partitions of Poland as a crime.[9] He wished to restore the unity of Poland with himself as its constitutional

[7] See p. 367.
[8] See p. 352.
[9] See pp. 256–261, 400.

king.   In Germany many who had first warmed to the French Revolution, but had been disillusioned, began to hail the new liberal tsar as the protector of Germany and hope of the future.   Alexander conceived of himself as a rival to Napoleon in the destinies of Europe in an age of change.   With a genuine concern for reform, constitutional government, international peace, and the extension of modern enlightenment, he was an autocratic humanitarian, who wished mankind to owe its blessings to himself.   Regarding the extension of his personal influence as identical with the progress of human freedom, he in effect carried over, in more seductive form, the expansionist program of Catherine and Peter.   Moralistic, self-righteous, impressionable, and unstable, given to flights of religious mysticism and perhaps to brooding over his father's death, he puzzled and disturbed the statesmen of Europe, who generally saw, behind his humane and republican utterances, either the familiar specter of Russian aggrandizement or an enthroned leader of all the "Jacobins" of Europe.

Yet Alexander, more than his contemporaries, formed a conception of international collective security and the indivisibility of peace.   He was shocked when Napoleon in 1804, in order to seize the Duke of Enghien, rudely violated the sovereignty of Baden.[10]   He declared that the issue in Europe was clearly between law and force—between an international society in which the rights of each member were secured by international agreement and by international organization, and a society in which no state was secure but all trembled before the rule of cynicism and conquest embodied in the French usurper.

Alexander was therefore ready to enter a Third Coalition with Great Britain. The war aims of the Third Coalition, though not accomplished, suggest what was at stake in the ten years that followed and anticipated much of the final peace settlement of 1814.   Alexander and William Pitt did not in truth commit themselves specifically to much.   But Pitt did not reject Alexander's idea that, after the war, some kind of organized international body should enforce the peace.   Alexander's interest in the "freedom of the seas," which in plain terms meant international controls on the use of British sea power in wartime, aroused no corresponding interest in London.   It was somewhat vaguely agreed that French ascendancy in Germany and Italy should cease; that the French should be driven from Belgium, and Belgium combined with Holland in a strong buffer state against France; and that Prussia should be strengthened on the Rhine.   It was understood that England should receive territory overseas, and Alexander revealed some of his plans for reuniting Poland.   The tsar pictured himself as the future arbiter of central Europe. On the Ottoman Empire and the Mediterranean he kept his ideas secret, but he hoped, after the destruction of Napoleon, to partition the Ottoman Empire, take over Constantinople, put Russian garrisons in Malta and Corfu (the chief of the Ionian Islands), and establish a league of Balkan states under Russian protection.   The Anglo-Russian treaty, signed in April 1805, said little or nothing of these matters; but Britain undertook to pay Russia £1,250,000 for each 100,000 soldiers that the Russians raised.

[10]See p. 415.

Napoleon meanwhile, since the resumption of hostilities in 1803, had been making preparations to invade England. He concentrated large forces on the Channel coast, together with thousands of boats and barges, in which he gave the troops amphibious training in embarkation and debarkation. He reasoned that if his own fleet could divert or cripple the British fleet for a few days he could place enough soldiers in the defenseless island to force its capitulation. The British, sensing mortal danger, lined their coasts with lookouts and signal beacons and set to drilling a home guard. Their main defense was twofold: the Austro-Russian armies and the British fleet under Lord Nelson. The Russian and Austrian armies moved westward in the summer of 1805. In August Napoleon relieved the pressure upon England, shifting seven army corps from the Channel to the upper Danube. On October 15 he surrounded an Austrian force of 50,000 men at Ulm in Bavaria, forcing it to surrender without resistance. On October 21 Lord Nelson, off Cape Trafalgar on the Spanish coast, caught and annihilated the main body of the combined fleets of France and Spain.

The battle of Trafalgar established the supremacy of the British navy for over a century—but only on the proviso that Napoleon be prevented from controlling the bulk of Europe, which would furnish an ample base for eventual construction of a greater navy than the British. And to control Europe was precisely what Napoleon proceeded to do. Moving east from Ulm he came upon the Russian and Austrian armies in Moravia, where on December 2 he won the great victory of Austerlitz. The broken Russian army withdrew into Poland, and Austria made peace. By the treaty of Pressburg Napoleon took Venetia from the Austrians, to whom he had given it in 1797, and annexed it to his kingdom of Italy (the former Cisalpine and Italian Republic), which now included a good deal of Italy north of Rome. Venice and Trieste soon resounded with the hammers of shipwrights rebuilding the Napoleonic fleet. In Germany, early in 1806, the French emperor raised Bavaria and Württemberg to the stature of kingdoms and Baden to a grand duchy. The Holy Roman Empire was finally, formally, and irrevocably dissolved. In its place Napoleon began to gather his German client states into a new kind of Germanic federation, the Confederation of the Rhine, of which he made himself the "protector."

Prussia, at peace with France for ten years, had declined to join the Third Coalition. Napoleon held off the Prussians diplomatically, making them all sorts of promises, such as the cession of Hanover, which belonged to the king of England. But as Napoleon's program for controlling Germany became clear after Austerlitz the war party in Prussia became irresistible, and the Prussian government, outwitted and distraught, went to war with the French unaided and alone. The French smashed the famous Prussian army at the battles of Jena and Auerstädt in October 1806. The French cavalry galloped all over north Germany unopposed. The Prussian king and his government took refuge in the east, at Königsberg, where the tsar and the re-forming Russian army might protect them. But the terrible Corsican pursued the Russians also. Marching through western Poland and into East Prussia, he met the Russian army first at the sanguinary but indecisive battle of Eylau and then defeated it on June 14, 1807, at Friedland. Alexander I was unwilling to retreat into Russia. He was unsure of his own resources; if the country were invaded there might be a revolt of the nobles or even of the serfs—for people still remembered Pugachev's rebellion.[11] He feared also merely playing the game of the British. He put aside his war aims of 1804 and signified his willingness to negotiate with Napoleon. The Third Coalition had gone the way of the two before it.

The Formation of the French Imperial System

The Emperor of the French and the Autocrat of All the Russias met privately on a raft in the Niemen River, not far from the border between Prussia and Russia, the very easternmost frontier of civilized Europe, as the triumphant Napoleon gleefully imagined it. The hapless Prussian king, Frederick William III, paced nervously on the bank. Bonaparte turned all his charm upon Alexander, denouncing England as the author of all the troubles of Europe and captivating him by flights of Latin imagination, in which he set before Alexander a boundless destiny as Emperor of the East, intimating that his future lay toward Turkey, Persia, Afghanistan, and India. The result of their conversations was the treaty of Tilsit of July 1807, in many ways the high point of Napoleon's success. The French and Russian empires became allies, mainly against Great Britain. Ostensibly this alliance lasted for five years. Alexander accepted Napoleon as a kind of Emperor of the West. As for Prussia, Napoleon seems to have considered eradicating it entirely but concluded by leaving it in existence, as a buffer between himself and Alexander, and at Alexander's earnest pleadings for his friend the king; but he continued to occupy Berlin with his troops, and he took away all Prussian territories west of the Elbe, combining them with others taken from Hanover to make a new kingdom of Westphalia, which became part of his Confederation of the Rhine.

The Continental System and the War in Spain

Hardly had the "peace of the continent" been reestablished, on the foundation of a Franco-Russian alliance, when Napoleon began to have serious trouble. He was bent on subduing the British who, secure in their island, seemed beyond his reach. Since the French naval disaster at Trafalgar, there was no possibility of invading England in the foreseeable future. Napoleon therefore turned to economic warfare. He would fight sea power with land power, using his political control of the Continent to shut out British goods and shipping from all European ports. He would destroy the British trade in exports to Europe, both exports of British products and the profitable British reexport of goods from America and Asia. Thereby, he hoped, he would ruin British commercial firms and cause a violent business depression, marked by overloaded warehouses, unemployment, runs on the banks, a fall of the currency, rising prices, and revolutionary agitation, in which the British government, which would simultaneously be losing revenues from its customs duties, would find itself unable to carry the enormous national debt, or to borrow additional funds from its subjects, or to continue its financial subsidies to the military powers of Europe. This same strategy had been adopted by the republicans of 1793; they, too, had prohibited the importation into France of goods originating in the British Empire. The same prohibition had been sporadically extended to regions conquered by the French.

[11] See pp. 348–349.

Napoleon simply made it more systematic and more universal. At Berlin, in 1806, after the battle of Jena, he issued the Berlin Decree, forbidding the importation of British goods into any part of Europe allied with or dependent on himself. He thus formally established the Continental System.

To make the Continental System effective Napoleon believed that it must extend to all continental Europe without exception. By the treaty of Tilsit, in 1807, he required both Russia and Prussia to adhere to it. They agreed to exclude all British goods; in fact, in the following months Russia, Prussia, and Austria all declared war on Great Britain. Napoleon then ordered two neutral states, Denmark and Portugal, to adhere. Denmark was an important entrepôt to all central Europe, and the British, fearing Danish compliance, dispatched a fleet to Copenhagen, bombarded the city for four days, and took captive the Danish fleet. The outraged Danes allied with Napoleon and joined the Continental System. Portugal, long a satellite of Britain, refused compliance; Napoleon invaded it. To control the whole European coastline from St. Petersburg around to Trieste he now had only to control the ports of Spain. By a series of deceptions he got both the Bourbon Charles IV and his son Ferdinand to abdicate the Spanish throne. He made his brother Joseph king of Spain in 1808 and reinforced him with a large French army.

He thus involved himself in an entanglement from which he never escaped. The Spanish regarded the Napoleonic soldiers as godless villains who desecrated churches. Fierce guerrillas took the field. Cruelties of one side were answered by atrocities of the other. The British sent an expeditionary force of their small regular army, eventually under the Duke of Wellington, to sustain the Spanish guerrillas; the resulting Peninsular War dragged on for five years. But from the beginning the affair went badly for Napoleon. In July 1808 a French general, for the first time since the Revolution, surrendered an army corps, without fighting, by the capitulation at Baylen. In August another French force surrendered to the British army in Portugal. And these events raised hopes in the rest of Europe. An anti-French movement swept over Germany. It was felt strongly in Austria, where the Habsburg government, undaunted by three defeats, and hoping to lead a general German national resistance, prepared for a fourth time since 1792 to go to war with France.

The Austrian War
of Liberation, 1809

Napoleon summoned a general congress which met at Erfurt in Saxony in September 1808. His main purpose was to talk with his ally of a year, Alexander; but he assembled numerous dependent monarchs as well, by whose presence he hoped to overawe the tsar. He even had Talma, the leading actor of the day, play in the theater of Erfurt before "a parterre of kings." Alexander was unimpressed. He was hurt in a sensitive spot because Napoleon, a few months before, had made moves to re-create a Polish state, setting up what was called the Grand Duchy of Warsaw. He had found Napoleon unwilling, despite the grandiose language of Tilsit, really to support his expansion into the Balkans. In addition, Alexander was taken aside by Talleyrand, Napoleon's foreign minister. Talleyrand had concluded that Napoleon was overreaching himself and said so confidentially to the tsar, advising him to wait.

Talleyrand thus acted as a traitor, betraying the man whom he ostensibly served, and preparing a safe place for himself in the event of Napoleon's fall; but he acted also as an aristocrat of the prenationalistic Old Regime, seeing his own country as only one part of the whole of Europe, believing a balance among the several parts to be necessary, and holding that peace would be possible only when the exaggerated position of French power should be reduced. For France and Russia, the two strongest states, to combine against all other states was contrary to all principles of the older diplomacy.[12] What Napoleon, at Erfurt, most wanted from Alexander was his support in the impending war against Austria, which would catch him under the disadvantage of reverses in Spain. Almost in desperation, he promised the tsar to evacuate Poland and to recognize Russian annexation of the Danubian principalities. Alexander was unmoved; he hoped for more from the French emperor's fall. The Franco-Russian alliance, now tested, failed to hold.

Austria proclaimed a war of liberation in April 1809. Napoleon advanced rapidly along the familiar route to Vienna. The German princes, indebted to the French, declined to join in a general German war against him. Alexander stood watchfully on the sidelines. Napoleon won the battle of Wagram in July. In October Austria made peace. The short war of 1809 was over. The Danubian monarchy, by no means as fragile as it seemed, survived a fourth defeat at the hands of the French without internal revolution or disloyalty to the Habsburg house. From it, in punishment, Napoleon took considerable portions of its territory. Part of Austrian Poland was used to enlarge Napoleon's Grand Duchy of Warsaw, and parts of Dalmatia, Slovenia, and Croatia, on the south, were erected into a new creation which Napoleon called the Illyrian Provinces.[13] Both these moves, the one enlarging Napoleonic Poland, the other bringing Bonaparte within the edges of the Balkans, naturally worsened his relations with the tsar.

Napoleon in 1809 successfully weathered a severe crisis, for the Austrians, had they resisted longer, might have been joined by the Russians and by others. The next two years saw the Napoleonic empire at its peak. In Austria after the defeat of 1809 the conduct of foreign affairs fell to a man who was to retain it for forty years. His name was Clemens von Metternich. He was a German from west of the Rhine, whose ancestral territories had been annexed to the French Republic, but he had entered the Austrian service and even married the granddaughter of Kaunitz,[14] the old model of diplomatic savoir-faire, of which Metternich now became a model himself. Austria had been repeatedly humiliated and even partitioned by Napoleon, most of all in the treaty of 1809. But Metternich was not a man to conduct diplomacy by grudges. Believing that Russia was the really permanent problem for a state situated in the Danube valley, Metternich thought it wise to renew good relations with

[12] See pp. 165–166.
[13] See map, p. 431.
[14] See p. 286.

France. He was quite willing to go along with Napoleon, whom he knew personally, having been Austrian ambassador to Paris before the short war of 1809.

The French emperor, who in 1809 was exactly forty, was increasingly concerned by the fact that he was childless. He had made an empire which he pronounced hereditary. Yet he had no son. Between him and his wife Josephine whom he had married in youth, and who was six years his senior, there had long since ceased to be affection or even fidelity on either side. He divorced her in 1809, though since she had two children by a first husband she naturally protested that Napoleon's childlessness was not her fault. He intended to marry a younger woman who might bear him offspring. He intended also to make a spectacular marriage, to extort for himself, a self-made Corsican army officer, the highest and most exclusive recognition that aristocratic Europe could bestow. He debated between Habsburgs and Romanovs, between an archduchess and a grand duchess. Tactful inquiries at St. Petersburg concerning the availability of Alexander's sister were tactfully rebuffed; the tsar intimated that his mother would never allow it. The Russian alliance again showed its limitations. Napoleon was thrown into the arms of Metternich—and of Marie Louise, the buxom eighteen-year-old daughter of the Austrian emperor and niece of another "Austrian woman," Marie Antoinette. They were married in 1810. In a year she bore him a son, whom he entitled the King of Rome.

Napoleon assumed ever more pompous airs of imperial majesty. He was now, by marriage, the nephew of Louis XVI. He showed more consideration to French noblemen of the Old Regime—only they, he said, knew really how to serve. He surrounded himself with a newly made hereditary Napoleonic nobility, hoping that the new families, as time went on, would bind their own fortunes to the house of Bonaparte. The marshals became dukes and princes, Talleyrand the Prince of Benevento, and the bourgeois Fouché, an Hébertist of '93, and more latterly a police official, was now solemnly addressed as the Duke of Otranto. In foreign affairs also the cycle had been run. With one significant exception all the powers of the successive coalitions were allied with the French, and the Son of the Revolution now gravely referred to the emperor of Austria as "my father."

47

The Grand Empire: Spread of the Revolution

The Organization of the Napoleonic Empire

Territorially Napoleon's influence enjoyed its farthest reach in 1810 and 1811, when it comprehended the entire European mainland except the Balkan peninsula. The Napoleonic domain was in two parts. Its core was the French empire; then came thick layers of dependent states, which together with France comprised the Grand Empire. In addition, to the north and east were the "allied states," not under Napoleon's direct rule but under their traditional governments—the three great powers, Prussia, Austria, and Russia, and also Denmark and Sweden. The allied

Europe 1810. *In 1810 Napoleon dominated the whole of the continent of Europe except the Balkan peninsula. A British expeditionary force was fighting the French in Portugal, and the British controlled all the islands.*

ALTIC SEA

Napoleon's Russian Campaign
June to December, 1812

0   100   200 miles

Moscow
Borodino
Riga
COURLAND Vitebsk
Vilna   Smolensk
Tilsit
Königsberg Kovno   Borisov
RUSSIAN EMPIRE
Warsaw
Brest-Litovsk

FINLAND

NORWAY

SWEDEN

St. Petersburg

Stockholm

ESTONIA

LIVONIA

SCOTLAND

KINGDOM OF DENMARK
AND NORWAY

COURLAND

Memel
Tilsit   Niemen R.
Königsberg Friedland Vilna
Danzig   Eylau

IRELAND

GREAT
BRITAIN

ENGLAND

NORTH SEA

DENMARK   Copenhagen

HELIGOLAND
(Britain)

Lübeck

SWEDISH
POMERANIA

Edinburgh

PRUSSIA

RUSSIA

ATLANTIC OCEAN

London

Plymouth   Dover

ENGLISH CHANNEL
CHANNEL I.
(Britain)

Boulogne
Cherbourg

Amsterdam

KINGDOM OF
HOLLAND

Hamburg
Bremen

MECKLEN-
BURG

Berlin

Posen

Warsaw

Brest-Litovsk

Rhine R.

Antwerp
Brussels

Cologne

BERG

K. OF
WESTPHALIA

K. OF
SAXONY

Dresden

Breslau

GRAND DUCHY
OF WARSAW

Elbe R.

Vistula R.

Oder R.

Amiens

Mainz

Auerstadt
Erfurt Jena

Leipzig

Cracow

GALICIA

Tarnopol

Paris
Versailles
Fontainebleau

Valmy

Metz

CONFEDERATION
OF THE
RHINE

Prague

BOHEMIA

Seine R.

Nantes

Loire R.

Orléans

Strasbourg

BADEN

WÜRTTEM-
BERG

Ulm

Austerlitz

Danube R.

Wagram

FRENCH EMPIRE

Munich

Hohenlinden

K. OF BAVARIA

Vienna

AUSTRIA

Rochefort

Basel

SWITZERLAND

AUSTRIA

Budapest

HUNGARY

Bordeaux

Lyons

SAVOY

Garonne R.

Rhone R.

Drave R.

Toulouse

Avignon

PIEDMONT

Po R.

LOMBARDY
Milan

VENETIA

KINGDOM
OF
ITALY

Trieste

ILLYRIAN

SLOVENIA

CROATIA

Save R.

WALLACHIA

Marseilles

Nice
Toulon

Genoa

LUCCA
Leghorn

Florence

PROVINCES
DALMATIA

BOSNIA

Belgrade

SERBIA

Danube R.

CORSICA

ELBA

ADRIATIC SEA

OTTOMAN EMPIRE

Rome

MONTENEGRO

Valencia

BALEARIC I.
(Spain)

MINORCA

MAJORCA

IVIZA

Barcelona

KINGDOM OF
SARDINIA

Bari

Taranto

ALBANIA

Salonica

SPAIN

Madrid
Ocana

Talavera

La Coruña
GALICIA

Burgos

Ebro R.

Ciudad Rodrigo
Saragossa

Douro R.

orto

UGAL
Almeida

sbon

Tagus R.

Elvas

Albuera Guadiana R.

Cadiz

ANDALUSIA
Seville

Baylen

ALGAR ×
Gibraltar (Britain)

Tangier

MOROCCO

Algiers

ALGERIA
(Turkish)

Cagliari

Naples

Palermo

KINGDOM OF
SICILY

STRAIT OF MESSINA

KINGDOM
OF NAPLES

CORFU

CORFU
(Britain)

IONIAN I.

MOREA

CERIGO

French Empire

Grand Empire

Allied with Napoleon

0   100   200   300 miles

Tunis

TUNISIA
(Turkish)

MALTA (Britain)

MEDITERRANEAN SEA

states were at war with Great Britain, though not engaged in positive hostilities; their populations were supposed to do without British goods under the Continental System, but otherwise Napoleon had no direct lawful influence upon their internal affairs.

The French empire, as successor to the French Republic, included Belgium and the Left Bank of the Rhine.[15] In addition, by 1810, it had developed two appendages which on a map looked like tentacles outstretched from it. When he proclaimed France an empire, and turned its dependent republics into kingdoms, Napoleon had set up his brother Louis as king of Holland; but Louis had shown such a tendency to ingratiate himself with the Dutch, and such a willingness to let Dutch businessmen trade secretly with the British, that Napoleon dethroned him and incorporated Holland into the French empire. In his endless war upon British goods he found it useful to exert more direct control over the ports of Bremen, Hamburg, Lübeck, Genoa, and Leghorn; he therefore annexed directly to the French empire the German coast as far as the western Baltic, and the Italian coast far enough to include Rome. Rome he desired for its imperial rather than its commercial value. Harking back to traditions as old as Charlemagne, he considered Rome the second city of his empire and entitled his son the "King of Rome"; and when Pope Pius VII protested, Napoleon took him prisoner and interned him in France. The whole French empire, from Lübeck to Rome, was governed directly by departmental prefects who reported to Paris, and the eighty-three departments of France, created by the Constituent Assembly, had risen in 1810 to a hundred and thirty.

The dependent states, forming with France the Grand Empire, were of different kinds. The Swiss federation remained republican in form. The Illyrian Provinces, which included Trieste and the Dalmatian coast, were administered in their brief two years almost like departments of France. In Poland, since the Russians objected to a revived kingdom of Poland, Napoleon called his creation the Grand Duchy of Warsaw. The duchy was composed of Polish fragments taken from Prussia in 1807 and from Austria in 1809, and it included most of the area within which the majority of the population was undeniably Polish. Napoleon gave the duchy to his protégé the king of Saxony as grand duke. Among the most important of the dependent states in the Grand Empire were the German states organized into the Confederation of the Rhine. Too modestly named, the Confederation included all Germany between what the French annexed on the west and what Prussia and Austria retained on the east. It was a league of all the German princes in this region that were regarded as sovereign, and who now numbered only about twenty, the most important being the four newly made kings—of Saxony, Bavaria, Württemberg, and Westphalia. Westphalia was an entirely new and synthetic state, made up of Hanoverian and Prussian territories and of various atoms of the old Germany. Its king was Napoleon's youngest brother Jerome. Westphalia was only one of the group of dependent states in which Napoleon placed a relative of his on the throne.

For Napoleon used his family as a means of rule. The Corsican clan became the Bonaparte dynasty. His brother Joseph from 1804 to 1808 functioned as king of

[15] See pp. 407, 410.

Naples and after 1808 as king of Spain. Louis Bonaparte was for six years king of Holland. Jerome was king of Westphalia. Sister Caroline became queen of Naples after brother Joseph's transfer to Spain; for Napoleon, running out of brothers (having quarreled with his remaining brother Lucien), gave the throne of Naples to his brother-in-law, Joachim Murat, a madcap cavalry officer who was Caroline's husband. In the "Kingdom of Italy," which in 1810 included Lombardy, Venetia, and most of the former papal states, Napoleon himself retained the title of king, but set up his stepson, Eugene Beauharnais (Josephine's son) as viceroy. "Uncle Joseph," Napoleon's mother's brother, became Cardinal Fesch. The mother of the Bonapartes, Letitia, who had brought up all these children under very different circumstances in Corsica, was suitably installed at the imperial court as Madame Mère. According to legend she kept repeating to herself, "If only it lasts!"; she outlived Napoleon by fifteen years.

In all the states under French domination the same course of events tended to repeat itself. First came the stage of military conquest and occupation by French troops. Then came the establishment of a native satellite government with the support of local persons who were willing to collaborate with the French and who helped in the drafting of a constitution specifying the powers of the new government and regularizing its relationships with France. In some areas these two stages had been accomplished under the revolutionary governments before Napoleon came into power. In certain regions, in some of which French control began as late as 1808, no more than these two stages was ever really completed, notably in Spain, which was never pacified, and the Grand Duchy of Warsaw, which remained hardly more than an armed outpost against Russia. But Italy and Germany witnessed a third stage, that of sweeping internal reform and reorganization, modeled on Bonaparte's reforms in France and hence derivatively on the French Revolution.[16] Belgium and the German territories west of the Rhine, annexed directly to France in the years before Napoleon's rise to power, may be said to have reached even a fourth stage and to have felt most strongly the impact of the French and of the Revolution.

*Napoleon
and the Spread
of the Revolution*

Napoleon considered himself a great reformer and man of the Enlightenment. He called his system "liberal," and though the word to him meant almost the reverse of what it meant later to liberals, he was possibly the first to use it in a political sense. He believed also in "constitutions"; not that he favored representative assemblies or limited government, but he wanted government to be rationally "constituted," i.e., deliberately mapped out and planned, not merely inherited from the jumble of the past. Man on horseback though he was, he believed firmly in the rule of law. He insisted with the zeal of conviction on transplanting his Civil Code [17] to the dependent states. This code he considered to be based on the very nature of justice and human relationships and to be applicable, therefore, to all countries with no more than minor adaptation. The idea that a country's laws must mirror its peculiar national character

---

[16] See pp. 385–389, 416–417.
[17] See pp. 416–417.

and history was foreign to his mind, for he carried over the rationalist and universalist outlook of the Age of Enlightenment. He thought that people everywhere wanted, and deserved, much the same thing. He undoubtedly believed in a unity of European civilization, to be furthered by a regime of uniform law in all countries under the authoritarian but impartial sanction of himself. He wrote to Jerome in 1807, on making him king of Westphalia:

> You will find enclosed the constitution of your kingdom. . . . You must faithfully observe it. . . . What the peoples of Germany impatiently demand is that men who are not nobles, but who do have ability, should have an equal right to your favor and your employment, and that every kind of serfdom, or of feudal powers between the sovereign and the lowest class of his subjects, should be entirely done away with. The benefits of the Code Napoleon, public trial and the introduction of juries, will be so many distinctive features of your monarchy. . . . What people will want to return under the arbitrary Prussian rule, once it has tasted the benefits of a wise and liberal administration? The peoples of Germany, as of France, Italy and Spain, want equality and liberal ideas. For some years now I have managed the affairs of Europe, and I am convinced that the cackling of the privileged classes was everywhere disliked. Be a constitutional king. Even if reason and the enlightenment of the age were not sufficient cause, it would be good policy for one in your position.

Nowhere does Napoleon better reveal himself—peremptory and dictatorial but not merely cynical, believing in certain reforms as an instrument of policy to rally support for himself but also because they were obviously reasonable, just, and enlightened.

The same plan of reform was initiated, with some variation, in all the dependent states from Spain to Poland and from the mouth of the Elbe to the Straits of Messina. The reforms were directed, in a word, against everything feudal. They established the legal equality of individual persons, and gave governments more complete authority over their individual subjects. Legal classes were wiped out, as in France in 1789; the theory of a society made up of "estates of the realm" gave way to the theory of a society made up of legally equal individuals. The nobility lost its privileges in taxation, office-holding, and military command. Careers were "opened to talent."

The manorial system, bulwark of the old aristocracy, was virtually liquidated. Lords lost all legal jurisdiction over their peasants; peasants became subjects of the state, personally free to move, migrate, or marry, and able to bring suit in the courts of law. The manorial fees, along with tithes, were generally abolished, as in France in 1789. But whereas in France the peasants escaped from these burdens without having to pay compensation, because they had themselves risen in rebellion in 1789 and because France passed through a radical popular revolution in 1793, in other parts of the Grand Empire the peasants were committed to payment of indemnities, and the former feudal class continued to receive income from its abolished rights. Only in Belgium and the Rhineland, incorporated into France under the republic, did the manorial regime disappear without compensation as it did in France, leaving a numerous entrenched class of small landowning farmers. East of the Rhine Napoleon had to compromise with the aristocracy which he assailed. In Poland, the only country in the Grand Empire where a thoroughgoing serfdom had prevailed, the

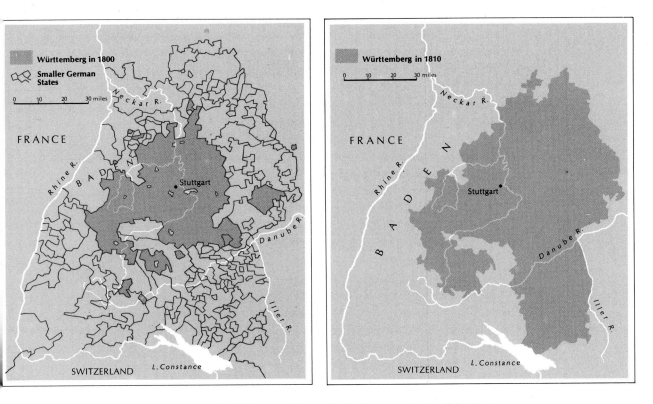

Napoleonic Germany. *In the panel at the left are shown, by shading, territories of the Duchy of Württemberg in 1800. Note how Württemberg had "islands" of territory unconnected with its main mass, and "holes" or enclaves formed by smaller states enclosed within the mass of Württemberg. Note, too, how Württemberg, itself only fifty miles wide, was surrounded by a mosaic of tiny jurisdictions—free cities, counties, duchies, principalities, abbacies, commanderies, bishoprics, archbishoprics, etc.—all "independent" within the Holy Roman Empire. The right-hand panel shows the Kingdom of Württemberg as consolidated and enlarged in the time of Napoleon. Similar consolidations all over Germany greatly reduced the number of states and added to the efficiency of law and government.*

peasants received legal freedom during the French occupation; but the Polish landlords remained economically unharmed, since they owned all the land. Napoleon had to conciliate them, for there was no other effective class in Poland to which he could look for support. In general, outside of France, the assault upon feudalism was not socially as revolutionary as it had been in France. The lord was gone, but the landlord remained.

Everywhere in the Grand Empire the church lost its position as a public authority alongside the state. Church courts were abolished or restricted; the Inquisition was outlawed in Spain. Tithes were done away with, church property confiscated, monastic orders dissolved or severely regulated. Toleration became the law; Catholics, Protestants, Jews and unbelievers received the same civil rights. The state

435

was to be based not on the idea of religious community but on the idea of territorial residence. With the nobility, or on economic matters, Napoleon would compromise; but he would not compromise with the Catholic clergy on the principle of a secular state. Even in Spain he insisted on these fundamentals of his system, a sure indication that he was not actuated by expediency only, since it was largely his religious program that provoked the Spanish populace to rebellion.

Gilds were generally abolished or reduced to empty forms, and the individual's right to work was generally proclaimed. Peasants, gaining legal freedom, might learn and enter any trade as they chose. The old town oligarchies and bourgeois patriciates were broken up. Towns and provinces lost their antique liberties and came under general legislation. Internal tariffs were removed, and free trade within state frontiers was encouraged. Some countries shifted to a decimal system of money; and the heterogeneous weights and measures which had originated in the Middle Ages, and of which the Anglo-American bushels, yards, ounces, and pints are living survivals, yielded to the Cartesian regularities of the metric system. Ancient and diverse legal systems gave way to the Napoleonic codes. Law courts were separated from the administration. Hereditary office and the sale of office were done away with. Officials received salaries large enough to shield them from the temptations of corruption. Kings were put on civil lists, with their personal expenses separated from those of the government. Taxes and finances were modernized. The common tax became a land tax, paid by every landowner; and governments knew how much land each owner really owned, for they developed systematic registration of property and systematic methods of appraisal and assessment. Tax farming was replaced by direct collection. New methods of accounting and of collecting statistics were introduced.

In general, in all countries of the Grand Empire, some of the main principles of the French Revolution were introduced under Napoleon, with the notable exception that there was no self-government through elected legislative bodies. In all countries Napoleon found numerous natives willing to support him, mainly among the commercial and professional men, who were read in the writers of the Enlightenment, often anticlerical, desirous of more equality with the nobility, and eager to break down the old localisms that interfered with trade and with the exchange of ideas. He found supporters also among many progressive nobles and, in the Confederation of the Rhine, among the native rulers. His program appealed to a certain class of men everywhere, and in all parts of the Grand Empire was executed mainly by local persons. Repression went with it, though hardly on a scale to which the twentieth century has become accustomed. There were no vast internment camps, and Fouché's police were engaged more in spying and submitting reports than in the brutalizing of the disaffected. The execution of a single Bavarian bookseller, named Palm, became a famous outrage.

There was, in short, at first, a good deal of pro-Napoleonic feeling in the Grand Empire. The French influence (outside Belgium and the Rhineland) struck deepest in north Italy, where there were no native monarchist traditions, and where the old Italian city-states had produced a strong and often anticlerical burgher class. In south Germany also the French influence was profound. The French system had the least appeal in Spain, where Catholic royalist sentiment produced a kind of counterrevolutionary movement of independence. Nor did it appeal to agrarian eastern Europe, the land of lord and serf. Yet even in Prussia, as will be seen, the state was remodeled along French lines. In Russia, during the Tilsit alliance, Alexander gave his backing to a pro-French reforming minister, Speranski. The Napoleonic influence was pervasive because it carried over the older movement of enlightened despotism and seemed to confer the advantages of the French Revolution without the violence and the disorder. Napoleon, it seemed to Goethe, "was the expression of all that was reasonable, legitimate and European in the revolutionary movement."

But the Napoleonic reforms were also weapons of war. As in France itself, so in Bavaria, Baden, or Italy, the state obtained more freedom in the use of its human and material resources. With the feudal barriers down, and equality enforced, the state raised taxes more abundantly and more quickly and could recruit, train, officer, and equip its armies with regard only to military efficiency. All the dependent states were required by Napoleon to supply him with money and soldiers. Germans, Dutch, Belgians, Italians, Poles, and even Spaniards fought in his armies. In addition, the dependent states defrayed much of the cost of the French army, most of which was stationed outside France. This meant that taxes in France could remain low, to the general satisfaction of the propertied interests that had issued from the Revolution.

Beyond the tributary states of the Grand Empire lay the countries nominally independent, joined under Napoleon in the Continental System. Napoleon thought of his allies as at best subordinate partners in a common project. The great project was to crush Great Britain, and it was for this purpose that the Continental System had been established. But the crushing of Britain became in Napoleon's mind a means to a further end, the unification and mastery of all of Europe. This in turn, had he achieved it, would doubtless have merely opened the way to further conquests.

At the point where he stood in 1807 or 1810 the unification of continental Europe seemed a not impossible objective. He cast about for an ideology to inspire both his Grand Empire and his allies. His problem was to breathe a spirit into a half-articulated body. It was to find some other basis than force, some common ground of consent and teamwork on which Europeans could combine. He held out the cosmopolitan doctrines of the eighteenth century, spoke endlessly of the enlightenment of the age, urged all peoples to work with him against the medievalism, feudalism, ignorance, and obscurantism by which they were still surrounded. And while appealing to the sense of modernity he dwelt also on the grandeur of Roman times. The Roman inspiration reflected itself in the arts of the day. The massive "empire" furniture, the heroic canvases of David, the church of the Madeleine in Paris, resembling a classical temple and converted to a Temple of Glory, the Arch of Triumph in the same city, begun in 1806, all evoked the atmosphere of far-spreading majesty in which Napoleon would have liked the peoples of Europe to live. His inclination to the Roman showed itself in the very

48

The Continental System: Britain and Europe

terminology that he employed—his consuls, prefects, tribunate, and senate, his Legion of Honor, Cisalpine Republic, and Illyrian Provinces, and indeed the term "empire" itself. But Europe was not to be converted by archaism. To arouse a European feeling, Napoleon worked upon the latent hostility to Great Britain.

The British, in winning out in the eighteenth-century struggle for wealth and empire, had made themselves disliked in many quarters. There was the natural jealousy felt toward the successful and resentment against the high-handedness by which success had been won and was maintained. Such feelings were present among almost all Europeans. For over a century the British Navigation Acts had been aimed against Continental shipping.[18] Beginning with the Seven Years' War, as their naval supremacy became established, the British also developed a theory of the use of sea power, or so at least it seemed to Europeans, though it was not the English habit to theorize on such matters, and the doctrine was only explicitly formulated much later by the American Admiral Mahan. The British held, in effect, that naval forces were characterized by extreme mobility and striking power, so that warships would be wastefully employed if one or two of them were stationed at every enemy port to blockade it; and that, instead, British war vessels should have the right to stop neutral vessels anywhere on the high seas, inspect their cargoes, and remove or destroy such as were contraband of war, contraband being defined by the British. Opponents contemptuously rejected these doctrines as mere theories of "paper blockade." They held that a country was truly and lawfully blockaded only insofar as warships patrolled its ports. Against the incipient doctrine of command of the sea, naturally entertained by the British since the British had the principal navy, the neutrals and lesser naval powers put forward the idea of "freedom of the seas," claiming extensive rights for neutrals to trade with all belligerents in time of war. The strength of anti-British sentiment was shown in the two leagues of Armed Neutrality of 1780 and 1801.[19]

British Blockade and Napoleon's Continental System

It was believed that the British were really using their sea power to win a larger permanent share of the world's seaborne commerce for themselves. Nor, in truth, was this belief mistaken. The British, in the Revolutionary and Napoleonic wars, when they declared France and its allies in a state of blockade, did not expect either to starve them or to deprive them of necessary materials of war. Western Europe was still self-sufficient in food, and armaments were to a large extent produced locally, from simple materials like iron, copper, and saltpeter. Europe required almost nothing indispensable from overseas. The chief aim of the British blockade was not, therefore, to keep imports out of enemy countries; it was to keep the trade in such imports out of enemy hands. It was to kill off enemy commerce and shipping, in order, in the short run, to weaken the war-making powers of the enemy government by undermining its revenues and its navy, and in the long run to weaken the enemy's position in the markets of the world. Economic warfare was trade warfare. The

[18]See pp. 173, 180, 182.
[19]See pp. 367, 422–423.

British were willing enough to have British goods pass through to the enemy either by smuggling or by the mediation of neutrals. This in turn was because British exports had limited military value. Great Britain, through the Napoleonic wars, concentrated heavily on the production of civilian-type manufactures, notably on cotton yarn and cloth, then being revolutionized by the application of power machinery.[20] Export of cottons, woolens, pottery, and cutlery was of limited military significance, and the large reexport of colonial products—sugar, tobacco, tea, coffee, chocolate, dyestuffs, drugs, spices—had almost no military significance whatsoever. Hence, the more the British could sell to Europe the better.

As early as 1793 the French republicans had denounced England as the "modern Carthage," a ruthless mercantile and profit-seeking power which aspired to enslave Europe to its financial and commercial system. With the wars, the British in fact obtained a monopoly over the shipment of overseas commodities into Europe. At the same time, being relatively advanced in the industrial revolution, they could produce cotton cloth and certain other articles, by power machinery, more cheaply than other peoples of Europe, and so threatened to monopolize the European market for such manufactured goods. There was much feeling in Europe against the modern Carthage, especially among the bourgeois and commercial classes who were in competition with it. The upper classes were perhaps less hostile, not caring where the goods that they consumed had originated, but aristocracies and governments were susceptible to the argument that Britain was a money power, a "nation of shopkeepers" as Napoleon put it, which fought its wars with pounds sterling instead of blood and was always in search of dupes in Europe.

It was on all these feelings that Napoleon played, reiterating time and again that England was the real enemy of all Europe, and that Europe would never be prosperous or independent until relieved of the incubus of British "monopoly." To prevent the flow of goods into Britain was no more the purpose of the Continental System than to prevent the flow of goods into France was the purpose of the British blockade. England could indeed have been more readily starved than Europe; it had begun to depend habitually on imports of food. But Napoleon, to drain off British gold reserves, actually shipped food to his enemy. The purpose of the Continental System, as of the British blockade, was to destroy the enemy's commerce, credit, and public revenues by the destruction of his exports—and also to build up markets for oneself.

To destroy British exports Napoleon prohibited, by the Berlin Decree of 1806, the importation of British goods into the continent of Europe. Counted as British, if of British or British colonial origin, were goods brought to Europe in neutral ships as the property of neutrals. The British, in response, ruled by an "order in council" of November 1807 that neutrals might enter Napoleonic ports only if they first stopped in Great Britain, where the regulations were such as to encourage their loading with British goods. The British thus tried to move their exports into enemy territory through neutral channels, which was precisely what Napoleon intended to prevent.

[20] See pp. 466–468.

He announced, by the Milan Decree of December 1807, that any neutral vessel that had stopped at a British port, or submitted to search by a British warship at sea, would be confiscated upon its appearance in a Continental harbor.

With all Europe at war, virtually the only trading neutral was the United States, which could now trade with neither England nor Europe except by violating the regulations of one belligerent or the other. It would thus become liable to reprisals, and hence to involvement in war. President Jefferson, to avoid war, attempted a self-imposed policy of commercial isolation, which proved so ruinous to American foreign trade that the United States government took steps to renew trade relations with whichever belligerent first removed its controls over neutral commerce. Napoleon offered to do so, on condition that the United States would defend itself against the enforcement of British controls. At the same time an expansionist party among the western Americans, ambitious to annex Canada, considered that with the British army engaged in Spain the time was ripe to complete the War of Independence by driving Britain from the North American mainland. The result was the Anglo-American war of 1812, which had few results, except to demonstrate the distressing inefficiency of military institutions in the new republic.

But the Continental System was more than a device for destroying the export trade of Great Britain. It was also a scheme—today it would be called a "plan"—for developing the economy of continental Europe, around France as its main center. Before the wars, as has been seen, Europe had imported more from France than from Great Britain.[21] Now, by doing entirely without British goods, Europeans were to become economically more powerful and self-sufficient. The System carried over the older policies of mercantilist states of the past two hundred years. But where mercantilist governments had worked to create national economies in place of the old local economies,[22] the Continental System, if successful, would replace the national economies with an integrated economy for the Continent as a whole. It would create the framework for a European civilization. And it would ruin the British sea power and commercial monopoly; for a unified Europe, Napoleon thought, would itself soon take to the sea.

The Failure of the Continental System

But the Continental System failed; it was worse than a failure, for it caused widespread antagonism to the Napoleonic regime. The dream of a united Europe, under French rule, was not sufficiently attractive to inspire the necessary sacrifice—even a sacrifice more of comforts than of necessities. As Napoleon impatiently said, one would suppose that the destinies of Europe turned upon a barrel of sugar. It was true, as he and his propagandists insisted, that Britain monopolized the sale of sugar, tobacco, and other overseas goods, but people preferred to deal clandestinely with the British rather than go without them. The charms of America destroyed the Continental System.

[21] See p. 267.
[22] See pp. 124–126.

British manufactures were somewhat easier than colonial goods to replace. Raw cotton was brought by land from the Levant through the Balkans, and the cotton manufactures of France, Saxony, Switzerland, and north Italy were stimulated by the relief from British competition. There was a great expansion of Danish woolens and German hardware. The cultivation of sugar beets, to replace cane sugar, spread in France, central Europe, Holland, and even Russia. Thus infant industries and investments were built up which, after Napoleon's fall, clamored for tariff protection. In general, the European industrial interests were well disposed toward the Continental System.

Yet they could never adequately replace the British in supplying the market. One obstacle was transportation. Much trading between parts of the Continent had always been done by sea; this coastal traffic was now blocked by the British. Land routes were increasingly used, even in the faraway Balkans and Illyrian Provinces, through which raw cotton was brought; and improved roads were built through the Simplon and Mont Cenis passes in the Alps. No less than 17,000 wheeled vehicles crossed the Mont Cenis pass in 1810. But land transport, at best, was no substitute for the sea. Without railroads, introduced some thirty years later, a purely Continental economy was impossible to maintain.

Another obstacle was tariffs. The idea of a Continental tariff union was put forward by some of his subordinates, but Napoleon never adopted it. The dependent states remained insistent on their ostensible sovereignty. Each had widened its trading area by demolishing former internal tariffs, but each kept a tariff against the others. The kingdoms of Italy and Naples enjoyed no free trade with each other nor did the German states of the Confederation of the Rhine. France remained protectionist; and when Napoleon annexed Holland and parts of Italy to France he kept them outside the French customs. At the same time Napoleon forbade the satellite states to raise high tariffs against France. France was his base, and he meant to favor French industry, which was much crippled by its loss of its Near Eastern and American markets. His program was for "France First" within Europe, and the Continental System, in one of its aspects, was a struggle of French manufacturers to capture Continental markets from the British.

Shippers, shipbuilders, and dealers in overseas goods, a powerful element of the older bourgeoisie, were ruined by the System. The French ports were idle and their populations distressed and disgruntled. The same befell all ports of Europe where the blockade was strictly enforced; at Trieste, total annual tonnage fell from 208,000 in 1807 to 60,000 in 1812. Eastern Europe was especially hard hit. In the West there was the stimulus to new manufactures. The East, long dependent on western Europe for manufactured goods, could no longer obtain them from England legally, nor from France, Germany, or Bohemia because of the difficulties of land transport and the British control of the Baltic. Nor could the landowners of Prussia, Poland, and Russia market their produce. The aristocracy of eastern Europe, which was the principal spending and importing class, had additional reason to dislike the French and to sympathize with the British.

As a war measure against Britain the Continental System also failed. The British occupied practically all the islands, even those in sight of the French armies. The flow of goods into Europe was augmented when Napoleon, for his own convenience, issued licenses for the import of British products. It even came about that the French army wore overcoats made in England. Nevertheless, British trade with Europe was significantly reduced. But the loss was made up elsewhere because of British control of the sea. Exports to Latin America rose from £300,000 in 1805 to £6,300,000 in 1809. Here again the existence of the overseas world frustrated the Continental System. Despite the System, export of British cotton goods, rising on a continuous tide of the industrial revolution, more than doubled in four years from 1805 to 1809. And while part of the increase was due to mere inflation and rising prices, it is estimated that the annual income of the British people more than doubled in the Revolutionary and Napoleonic wars, leaping from £140,000,000 in 1792 to £335,000,000 in 1814.

49

The National Movements: Germany

The Resistance to Napoleon: Nationalism

From the beginning, as far back as 1792, the French met with resistance as well as collaboration in the countries they occupied. There was resentment when the invading armies plundered and requisitioned upon the country, when the newly organized states were required to pay tribute of men and money, when their policies were dictated by French residents or ambassadors, and when the Continental System was used for the especial benefit of French manufacturers. Europeans began to feel that Napoleon was employing them merely as tools against England. And in all countries, including France itself, people grew tired of the peace that was no peace, the wars and rumors of war, the conscription and the taxes, the aloof bureaucratic government from on high, the obviously growing and insatiable appetite of Napoleon for power and self-exaltation. Movements of protest and independence showed themselves even within the Napoleonic structure. We have seen how the dependent states protected themselves by tariffs. Even the emperor's proconsuls tried to root themselves in local opinion, as when Louis Bonaparte, king of Holland, tried to defend Dutch interests against Napoleon's demands, or when Murat, king of Naples, appealed to Italian sentiment to secure his own throne.

Nationalism, as it was to be known in all the later history of Europe, developed as a movement of resistance against the forcible internationalism of the Napoleonic empire. It arose in protest against the Napoleonic idea, to which Napoleon himself was by no means faithful, of a European continent united by uniform law and administration, with a Continental economic system of its own, a single foreign policy, and all its armies combined in a Grand Army under one command. Since the international system was essentially French, the nationalistic movements were anti-French; and since Napoleon was an autocrat, they were antiautocratic. The nationalism of the period was a mixture of the conservative and the liberal. Some nationalists, predominantly conservative, insisted on the value of their own peculiar institutions, customs, folkways, and historical development, which they feared might be obliterated under the French and Napoleonic system. Others, or indeed the same ones, insisted on more self-determination, more participation in government, more representative institutions, more freedom for the individual against the bureaucratic interference of the state. Both conservatism and liberalism rose up against Napoleon, destroyed him, outlasted him, and shaped the history of the following generations.

Nationalism was thus very complex and appeared in different countries in different ways. In England the profound solidarity of the country exhibited itself; all classes rallied and stood shoulder to shoulder against "Boney"; and ideas of reforming Parliament or tampering with historic English liberties were resolutely put aside. It is possible that the Napoleonic wars helped England through a very difficult social crisis, for the industrial revolution was causing dislocation, misery, unemployment, and even revolutionary agitation among a small minority, all of which were eclipsed by the patriotic need of resistance to Bonaparte. In Spain, nationalism took the form of implacable resistance to the French armies that desolated the land. Some Spanish nationalists were liberal; a bourgeois group at Cadiz, rebelling against the French regime, proclaimed the Spanish constitution of 1812, modeled on the French constitution of 1791. But Spanish nationalism drew its greatest strength from sentiments that were counterrevolutionary, aiming to restore the clergy and the Bourbons. When the French government only a decade later, in 1822, sent a French army into Spain to protect the church and the Bourbons, it met with no serious resistance. Spain under Napoleon was a kind of Vendée within the Grand Empire—the Vendée, it will be recalled, being the region within France where Catholic and royalist peasants had risen up against the armies and the officials of the French Republic.[23] In Italy the Napoleonic regime was better liked and national feeling was less anti-French than in Spain. Bourgeois of the Italian cities generally prized the efficiency and enlightenment of French methods, and often shared in the anticlericalism of the French Revolution. The French regime, which lasted in Italy from 1796 to 1814, broke the habit of loyalty to the various duchies, oligarchic republics, papal states, and foreign dynasties by which Italy had long been ruled. Napoleon never unified Italy, but he assembled it into only three parts, and the French influence brought the notion of a politically united Italy within the bounds of reasonable aspiration. With the Poles Napoleon positively encouraged national feeling. He repeatedly told them that they might win a restored and united Poland by faithfully fighting in his cause. A few Polish nationalists, like the aging patriot Kosciuzsko, never trusted Napoleon, and some others, like Czartoryski, looked rather to the Russian tsar for a restoration of the Polish kingdom; but in general the Poles, for their own national reasons, were exceptionally devoted to the emperor of the French and lamented his passing.

By far the most momentous national movement took place in Germany. Napoleonic Germany was a seedbed that was to fertilize, fructify, and also to poison much of the later development of Europe. The Germans rebelled not only against the Napo-

[23] See p. 401.

leonic rule but against the century-old ascendancy of French civilization. They rebelled not only against the French armies but against the philosophy of the Age of Enlightenment. The years of the French Revolution and Napoleon were for Germany the years of its greatest cultural efflorescence, the years of Beethoven, Goethe and Schiller, of Herder, Kant, Fichte, Hegel, Schleiermacher, and many others. German ideas fell in with all the ferment of fundamental thinking known as "romanticism," which was everywhere challenging the "dry abstractions" of the Age of Reason and about which more will be said in this and the following chapter. Germany became the most "romantic" of all countries, and German influence spread throughout Europe. In the nineteenth century the Germans came to be widely regarded as intellectual leaders, somewhat as the French had been in the century before. And most of the distinctive features of German thought were somehow connected with nationalism in a broad sense.

Formerly, especially in the century following the Peace of Westphalia, the Germans had been the least nationally minded of all the larger European peoples.[24] They prided themselves on their world-citizenship or cosmopolitan outlook. Looking out from the tiny states in which they lived, they were conscious of Europe, conscious of other countries, but hardly conscious of Germany. The Holy Roman Empire was a shadow. The German world had no tangible frontiers; the area of German speech simply faded out into Alsace or the Austrian Netherlands, or into Poland, Bohemia, or the upper Balkans. That "Germany" ever did, thought, or hoped anything never crossed the German mind. There was scarcely even a developed language, for the speech habits of Berlin and Vienna were more different than those of London and New York today. The upper classes, becoming contemptuous of much that was German, took over French fashions, dress, etiquette, manners, ideas, and language, regarding them as an international norm of civilized living. Frederick the Great hired French tax collectors and wrote his own books in French.

About 1780 signs of a change set in. Even Frederick, in his later years, predicted a golden age of German literature, proudly declaring that Germans could do what other nations had done. In 1784 appeared a book by J. G. Herder, called *Ideas on the Philosophy of the History of Mankind*. Herder was an earnest soul, a Protestant pastor and theologian who thought the French somewhat frivolous. He concluded that imitation of French ways, or of any foreign ways, made people shallow and artificial. He declared that German ways were indeed different from French but not for that reason the less worthy of respect. All true culture or civilization, he held, must arise from native roots. It must arise also from the life of the common people, the *Volk*, not from the cosmopolitan and denatured life of the upper classes. Each people, he thought, meaning by a people a group sharing the same language, had its own attitudes, spirit, or genius. A sound civilization must express a national character or *Volksgeist*. And the character of each people was special to itself. Herder did not believe the nations to be in conflict; quite the contrary, he simply insisted that they

[24] See pp. 218–222.

were different. He did not believe German culture to be the best; many other peoples, notably the Slavs, later found his ideas applicable to their own needs. His philosophy of history was very different from Voltaire's. Voltaire and the philosophes had expected all peoples to progress along the same path of reason and enlightenment toward the same civilization. Herder thought that all peoples should develop their own genius in their own way, each slowly unfolding with the inevitability of plant-like growth, avoiding sudden change or distortion by outside influence, and all ultimately reflecting, in their endless diversity, the infinite richness of humanity and of God.

The idea of the *Volksgeist*, possibly the most significant single German idea of these agitated years, was reinforced from other and non-German sources and soon passed to other countries in the general movement of romantic thought. Like much else in romanticism, it emphasized genius or intuition rather than reason. It stressed the differences rather than the similarity of mankind. It broke down that sense of human similarity which had been characteristic of the Age of Enlightenment,[25] and which revealed itself in French and American doctrines of the rights of man, or again in the law codes of Napoleon. In the past it had been usually thought that what was good was good for all peoples. Good poetry was poetry written according to certain classical principles or "rules" of composition, which were the same for all writers from the Greeks on down. Now, according to Herder and to romantics in all countries, good poetry was poetry that expressed an inner genius, either an individual genius or the genius of a people—there were no more "rules." Good and just laws, according to the older philosophy of natural law, somehow corresponded to a standard of justice that was the same for all men. But now, according to Herder and the romantic school of jurisprudence, good laws were those that reflected local conditions or national idiosyncrasies. Here again there were no "rules," except possibly the rule that each nation should have its own way.

Herder's philosophy set forth a cultural nationalism, without political message. The Germans had long been a nonpolitical people. In the microscopic states of the Holy Empire they had had no significant political questions to think about; in the more sizable ones they had been excluded from public affairs. The French Revolution made the Germans acutely conscious of the state. It showed what a people could do with a state, once they took it over and used it for their own purposes. For one thing, the French had raised themselves to the dignity of citizenship; they had become free men, responsible for themselves, taking part in the affairs of their country. For another, because they had a unified state which included all Frenchmen, and one in which a whole nation surged with a new sense of freedom, they were able to rise above all the other peoples of Europe. Many in Germany were beginning to feel humiliation at the paternalism of their governments. The futilities of the Holy Roman Empire, which had made Germany for centuries the battlefield of Europe, now filled them with shame and indignation. They saw with disgust how their German princes, forever squabbling with each other for control over German

[25] See p. 335.

subjects, disgraced themselves before the French to promote their own interests. The national awakening in Germany, which set in strongly after 1800, was therefore directed not only against Napoleon and the French, but also against the German rulers and many of the half-Frenchified German upper classes. It was democratic in that it stressed the superior virtue of the common people.

Germans became fascinated by the idea of political unity and national greatness, precisely because they had neither. A great national German state, expressing the deep moral will and distinctive culture of the German people, seemed to them the solution to all their problems. It would give moral dignity to the individual German, solve the vexatious question of the selfish petty princes, protect the deep German *Volksgeist* from violation, secure the Germans from conquest and subjection by outside powers. The nationalist philosophy remained somewhat vague, because in practice there was little that one could do. "Father" Jahn organized a kind of youth movement and became the inventor of what might be termed political gymnastics, having his young men do calisthenics for the Fatherland; he led them on open-air expeditions into the country, where they made fun of aristocrats in French costume; and he taught them to be suspicious of foreigners, Jews, and internationalists, and indeed of everything that might corrupt the purity of the German *Volk*. Most Germans thought him too extreme. Others collected wonderful stories of the rich medieval German past. There was an anonymous anti-French work *Germany in Its Deep Humiliation,* for selling which the publisher Palm was put to death. Others founded the Moral and Scientific Union, generally known as the *Tugendbund* or league of virtue or manliness, whose members, by developing their own moral character, were to contribute to the future of Germany.

The career of J. G. Fichte illustrates the course of German thought in these years. Fichte was a moral and metaphysical philosopher, a professor at the University of Jena. His doctrine, that the inner spirit of the individual creates its own moral universe, was much admired in many countries. In America, for example, it entered into the transcendental philosophy of Ralph Waldo Emerson. Fichte at first was practically without national feeling. He enthusiastically approved of the French Revolution, as did Jahn and Arndt. In 1793, with the Revolution at its height and many foreign observers turning against it, Fichte published a laudatory tract on the French Republic. He saw it as an emancipation of the human spirit, a step upward in the elevation of human dignity and moral stature. He accepted the idea of the Terror, that of "forcing men to be free"; and he shared Rousseau's conception of the state as the embodiment of the sovereign will of a people. He came to see the state as the means of human salvation. In 1800, in his *Closed Commercial State,* he sketched a kind of totalitarian system in which the state planned and operated the whole economy of the country, shutting itself off from the rest of the world in order that, at home, it might freely develop the character of its own citizens. When the French conquered Germany Fichte became intensely and self-consciously German. He took over the idea of the *Volksgeist:* not only did the individual spirit create its own moral universe, but the spirit of a people created a kind of moral universe as well, manifested in its language, arts, folkways, customs, institutions, and ideas.

At Berlin, in 1808, Fichte delivered a series of *Addresses to the German Nation*, declaring that there was an ineradicable German spirit, a primordial and immutable national character, more noble than that of other peoples (thus going beyond Herder), to be kept pure at all costs from all outside influence, either international or French. The German spirit, he held, had always been profoundly different from that of France and western Europe; it had never yet really been heard from but would be some day. The French army commander then occupying the city thought the lectures too academic to be worth suppression. They had, in fact, few hearers; Fichte was considered a firebrand by most Germans; but they later regarded him as a national hero.

The movement of thought in Napoleonic Germany did not solve the political problem of the Germans themselves. It did rally feeling against the French. It laid the way for the fall of Napoleon. It raised up a democratic sentiment against the ruling dynasties of the Fatherland. It made Germans dream of a great united and awakened Germany of the future. And the same movement of ideas profoundly influenced, indirectly, the whole of Europe. The Germans became interested not only in their own national history, but in history itself as a fundamental method of thought, and they thus launched an intellectual revolution, through the philosophy of Hegel and by other means, which is described in a later chapter.[26]

Politically, in the revolt against the French, the main transformations came in Prussia. Prussia after the death of Frederick the Great had fallen into a period of satisfied inertia, such as is likely to follow upon rapid growth or spectacular success. Then in 1806, at Jena-Auerstädt, the kingdom collapsed in a single battle. No great European power ever came so near extinction as Prussia in the following years. Its western and most of its Polish territories were taken away. It was relegated by Napoleon to its old holdings east of the Elbe. Even here the French remained in occupation, for Napoleon stationed his Ninth Corps in Berlin. But in the eyes of German nationalists Prussia had a moral advantage. Of all the German states it was the least compromised by collaboration with the French; for except for the Austrians, who in 1810 allied themselves with Napoleon by marriage, all the other German states were French satellites in the Confederation of the Rhine. Prussia, ruined by Napoleon, was an unwilling ally in his Continental System, and toward Prussia, as toward a haven, German patriots made their way. East-Elbian Prussia, formerly the least German of German lands, became the center of an all-German movement for national freedom. The years after Jena were decisive in the long historic process of the "Prussianizing" of Germany; but it is to be observed that neither Fichte nor Hegel, Gneisenau nor Scharnhorst, Stein nor Hardenberg, all rebuilders of Prussia, was a native Prussian.

The main problem for Prussia was military, since Napoleon could be overthrown only by military force. And as always in Prussia, the requirements of the army

[26] See p. 480.

shaped the form taken by the state.[27] The problem was conceived to be one of morale and personnel. The old Prussia of Frederick, which had fallen ingloriously, had been mechanical, arbitrary, soulless; its people had lacked the sense of membership in the state, and in the army had had no hope of promotion, no patriotism, and no spirit. To produce this spirit was the aim of the army reformers, Scharnhorst and Gneisenau. Gneisenau, a Saxon, had served in one of the British "Hessian" regiments in the War of American Independence, during which he had observed the military value of patriotic feeling in the American soldiers. He was a close observer also of the consequences of the French Revolution. He wrote in 1807, blending ideas of the *Volksgeist* with ideas taken from the French:

> The Revolution has awakened all forces in the French and given to each force its proper sphere of action. Heroes rose to head the army, statesmen to the chief positions in administration. . . .
>
> What infinite power lies sleeping undeveloped and unused within the womb of the nation! Within the breasts of thousands there lives a great genius, but their lowly condition prevents its flowering. . . . Why did not the courts make use of the simplest and surest means, that of providing a career for this genius, wherever it may be, and of encouraging these talents and virtues, no matter from what class or rank they might come? . . .
>
> The Revolution has set in action the national energy of the entire French people, putting the different classes on an equal social and fiscal basis. . . . If the other states wish to establish the former balance of power, they must open up and use these same resources. They must take over the results of the Revolution, and so gain the double advantage of being able to place their entire national energies in opposition to the enemy and of escaping from the dangers of a revolution. . . .

Democracy, in the sense of legal equality and free opportunity, had proved itself not only just but useful. It had survival value. It made the state stronger; it strengthened the army. Democratic, in this sense, the new Prussia should therefore be. Prussia would learn from the enemy. It would adapt from the Revolution what it needed. And for two reasons: to destroy the enemy and to prevent revolution in Prussia.

The reconstruction of the state, prerequisite to the reconstruction of the army, was initiated by Baron Stein and continued by his successor, Hardenberg. Like Metternich, Stein came from western Germany; he had been an imperial knight of the late Holy Empire, who from a bridge near his castle had beheld the domains of no less than eight German princes in one sweep of the eye. Stateless himself, he thought of Germany as a whole; he was long hostile to what he considered the barely civilized Prussia, but finally resorted to it as the hope of the future. Deeply committed to the philosophy of Kant and Fichte, he dwelt on the concepts of duty, service, moral character, and responsibility. He thought that the common people must be awakened to moral life, raised from a brutalized servility to the level of self-determination and membership in the community. This, he believed, required an equality more of duties than of rights.

[27] See pp. 239–244, 344–346.

Under Stein the old caste structure of Prussia came to an end. Property became interchangeable between classes; bourgeois were allowed to buy land and serve as officers in the army. The burghers, to develop a sense of citizenship and participation in the state, were given extensive freedom of self-government in the cities; the municipal system of Prussia, and later of Germany, became a model for much of Europe in the following century. Stein had ideas for parliamentary institutions in Prussia as a whole, thinking they would strengthen the country, but he left office before acting upon them.

His most famous work was the "abolition of serfdom." It was naturally impossible, since the whole reform program aimed at strengthening Prussia for a war of liberation against the French, to antagonize the Junkers who commanded the army. Stein's ordinance of 1807 abolished serfdom only in that it abolished the "hereditary subjection" of peasants to their manorial lords.[28] It gave peasants the right to move and migrate, marry and take up trades without the lord's approval. If, however, the peasant remained on the land, he was still subject to all the old services of forced labor in the fields of the lord. Peasants enjoying small tenures of their own continued to be liable for the old dues and fees. By an edict of 1810, a peasant might convert his tenure into private property, getting rid of the manorial obligations, but only on condition that one-third of the land he had held should become the private property of the lord. In the following decades many such conversions took place, of which the result was that the estates of the Junkers grew considerably larger. The reforms in Prussia somewhat reduced the old patriarchal powers of the lords and gave legal status and freedom of movement to the mass of the population, thus laying the foundation for a modern state and modern economy. But the peasants tended to become mere hired agricultural laborers; and the position of the Junkers was heightened, not reduced. Prussia avoided the Revolution. Stein himself, because Napoleon feared him, was obliged to go into exile in 1808, but his reforms endured.

T he situation at the close of 1811 may be summarized as follows. Napoleon had the mainland of Europe in his grip. Russia and Turkey were at war on the Danube, but otherwise there was no war except in Spain, where four years of fighting remained inconclusive. The Continental System was working badly. Britain was hurt by it only negatively, in that, without it, British exports to Europe would have risen rapidly in these years. Well launched in the industrial revolution, Great Britain was amassing a vast store of national wealth, accumulating the wherewithal to assist European governments financially against Napoleon. The peoples of Europe were increasingly restless, dreaming increasingly of national freedom. In Germany, especially, many awaited the opportunity to rise in a war of independence. But Napoleon could be overthrown only by the destruction of his army, with which neither British wealth nor British sea power, nor the European patriots and

50

The Overthrow of Napoleon: The Congress of Vienna

[28] See p. 123.

nationalists, nor the Prussian nor the Austrian armed forces were able to cope. All eyes turned to Russia. Alexander I had long been dissatisfied with his French alliance. He had obtained from it nothing but the annexation of Finland in 1809. He received no assistance from France in his war with Turkey; he saw Napoleon marry into the Austrian house; he had to tolerate the existence of a French-oriented Poland at his very door. The articulate classes in Russia, namely, the landowners and serf-owners, loudly denounced the French alliance and demanded a resumption of open trade relations with England. An international clientele of émigrés and anti-Bonapartists, including Baron Stein, also gradually congregated at St. Petersburg, where they poured into the tsar's ears the welcome message that Europe looked to him for its salvation.

The Russian Campaign and the War of Liberation

On December 31, 1810, Russia formally withdrew from the Continental System. Anglo-Russian commercial relations were resumed. Napoleon resolved to crush the tsar. He concentrated the Grand Army in eastern Germany and Poland, a vast force of 700,000 men, the largest ever assembled up to that time for a single military operation. It was an all-European host. Hardly more than a third was French; another third was German, from German regions annexed to France, from the states of the Confederation of the Rhine, and with token forces from Prussia and Austria; and the remaining third was drawn from all other nationalities of the Grand Empire, including 90,000 Poles. Napoleon at first hoped to meet the Russians in Poland or Prussia. This time, however, they decided to fight on their own ground, and they needed in any case to delay until their forces on the lower Danube could be recalled. In June 1812 Napoleon led the Grand Army into Russia.

He intended a short, sharp war, such as most of his wars had been in the past, and carried with him only three weeks' supplies. But from the beginning everything went wrong. It was Napoleon's principle to force a decisive battle; but the Russian army simply melted away. It was his principle to live on the country, so as to reduce the need for supply trains; but the Russians destroyed as they retreated, and in any case, in Russia, even in the summer, it was hard to find sustenance for so many men and horses. Finally, not far from Moscow, Napoleon was able to join battle with the main Russian force at Borodino. Here again everything miscarried. It was his principle always to outnumber the enemy at the decisive spot; but the Grand Army had left so many detachments along its line of march that at Borodino the Russians outnumbered it. It was Napoleon's principle to concentrate his artillery, but here he scattered it instead, and to throw in his last reserves at the critical moment, but at Borodino, so far from home, he refused the risk of ordering the Old Guard into action. Napoleon won the battle, at a cost of 30,000 men, as against 50,000 lost by the Russians; but the Russian army was able to withdraw in good order.

On September 14, 1812, the French emperor entered Moscow. Almost immediately the city broke into flames. Napoleon found himself camping in a ruin, with troops strewn along a long line all the way back to Poland, and with a hostile army maneuvering near at hand. Baffled, he tried to negotiate with Alexander, who refused all overtures. After five weeks, not knowing what to do, and fearful of remaining isolated in Moscow over the winter, Napoleon ordered a retreat. Prevented by the Russians from taking a more southerly route, the Grand Army retired by the same way as it had come. The cold weather set in early and was unusually severe. For a century after 1812 the retreat from Moscow remained the last word in military horror. Men froze and starved, horses slipped and died, vehicles could not be moved, and equipment was abandoned. Discipline broke down toward the end; the army dissolved into a horde of individual fugitives, speaking a babel of languages, harassed by bands of Russian irregulars, picking their way on foot over ice and snow, most of the time in the dark, for the nights are long in these latitudes in December. Of 611,000 who entered Russia 400,000 died of battle casualties, starvation, and exposure, and 100,000 were taken prisoner. The Grand Army no longer existed.

Now at last all the anti-Napoleonic forces rushed together. The Russians pushed westward into central Europe. The Prussian and Austrian governments, which in 1812 had half-heartedly supplied troops for the invasion of Russia, switched over in 1813 and joined the tsar, Prussia quickly and eagerly, Austria more slowly and reluctantly, for Metternich was fearful of the rising Russian colossus, suspicious of the perfervid nationalism of Germany, and still willing to see Napoleon on the throne of a trimmed-down France. Throughout Germany the patriots, often half-trained boys, marched off in the War of Liberation. Anti-French riots broke out in Italy. In Spain Wellington at last pushed rapidly forward; in June 1813 he crossed the Pyrenees into France. The British government, in three years from 1813 to 1815, poured £32,000,000 as subsidies into Europe, more than half of all the funds granted during the twenty-two years of the wars. An incongruous alliance of British capitalism and east-European agrarian feudalism, of the British navy and the Russian army, of Spanish clericalism and German nationalism, of divine-right monarchies and newly aroused democrats and liberals, combined at last to bring the Man of Destiny to the ground.

Napoleon, who had left his army in Russia in December 1812, and rushed across Europe to Paris, by sleigh and coach, in the remarkable time of thirteen days, raised a new army in France in the early months of 1813. But it was untrained and unsteady, and he himself had lost some of his genius for command. His new army was smashed in October at the battle of Leipzig, known to the Germans as the Battle of the Nations, the greatest battle in number of men engaged ever fought until the twentieth century. The allies drove Napoleon back upon France. But the closer they came to defeating him the more they began to fear and distrust each other.

The coalition already showed signs of splitting. Should the allies, together or singly, negotiate with Napoleon? How strong should the France of the future be? What should be its new frontiers? What form of government should it have? There was no agreement on these questions. Alexander wanted to dethrone Napoleon and dictate peace in Paris, in dramatic retribution for the destruction of Moscow. He had a scheme for giving the French throne to Bernadotte, a former French marshal, now crown prince of Sweden, who as king of France would depend on Russian support. Metternich preferred to keep Napoleon or his son as French emperor, after clearing the French out of central Europe; for a Bonaparte dynasty in a reduced France would be dependent on Austria. The Prussian counsels were divided. The British declared that the French must get out of Belgium, and that Napoleon must go; they held that the French might then choose their own government but believed a restoration of the Bourbons to be the best solution. The three Continental monarchies had no concern for the Bourbons, and both Alexander and Metternich, if they could make France dependent respectively on themselves, were willing to see it remain strong to the extent of including Belgium. In November 1813 Metternich communicated to Napoleon a proposition known as the "Frankfurt proposals," by which Napoleon would remain French emperor, and France would retain its "natural" frontier on the Rhine. There was a chance of peace on this basis, for the allies could not shake off their old fear of Napoleon, the Prussians could be compensated elsewhere, and among the Russians many of the generals and others were impatient to go home. The British, their diplomatic influence reduced by the fact that they had few troops in Europe, faced the appalling prospect that the Continent would again make peace without them—and a peace in which France should again keep Belgium.

The British foreign minister, Viscount Castlereagh, arrived in person on the Continent in January 1814. He held a number of strong cards. For one thing, Napoleon rejected the Frankfurt proposals. He continued to fight, and the allies therefore continued to ask for British financial aid. Castlereagh skillfully used the promise of British subsidies to win acceptance of the British war aims. In addition, he found a common ground for agreement with Metternich, both Britain and Austria fearing the domination of Europe by Russia. Castlereagh's first great problem was to hold the alliance together, for without Continental allies the British could not defeat France. He succeeded, on March 9, 1814, in getting Russia, Prussia, Austria, and Great Britain to sign the treaty of Chaumont. Each power bound itself for twenty years to a Quadruple Alliance against France, and each agreed to provide 150,000 soldiers to enforce such peace terms as might be arrived at. For the first time since 1792 a solid coalition of the four great powers now existed against France. Three weeks later the allies entered Paris, and on April 4 Napoleon abdicated at Fontainebleau.

He was forced to this step by lack of support in France itself. Twenty years before, in 1793 and 1794, France had fought off the combined powers of Europe—minus Russia. It could not and would not do so in 1814. The country cried for peace. Even the imperial marshals advised the emperor's abdication. But what was to follow him? For over twenty-five years the French had had one regime after another. Now there were some who wished a republic, some who wished the empire under Napoleon's infant son, some who wished a constitutional monarchy, and some even who longed for the Old Regime. Talleyrand stepped into the breach. The "legitimate" king, he said, Louis XVIII, was after all the man who would provoke the least factionalism and opposition. The powers, likewise, had by this time concluded in favor of the Bourbons. A Bourbon king would be peaceable, under no impulse to win back the conquests of the republic and empire. He would also, as the native and rightful king of France, need no foreign support to bolster him up, so that the control of France would not arise as an issue to divide the victorious powers.

So the Bourbon dynasty was restored. Louis XVIII, ignored and disregarded for a whole generation, both by most Frenchmen and by the governments of Europe, returned to the throne of his brother and his fathers. He issued a "constitutional charter," partly at the insistence of the liberal tsar, and partly because, having actually learned from his long exile, he sought the support of influential people in France. The charter of 1814 made no concession to the principle of popular or national sovereignty. It was represented as the gracious gift of a theoretically absolute king. But in practice it granted what most Frenchmen wanted. It promised legal equality, eligibility of all to public office without regard to class, and a parliamentary government in two chambers. It recognized the Napoleonic law codes, the Napoleonic settlement with the church, and the redistribution of property effected during the Revolution. It carried over the abolition of feudalism and privilege, manorialism and tithes. It confined the vote, to be sure, to a very few large landowners; but for the time being, except for a few irreconcilables, France settled down to enjoy the blessings of a chastened revolution—and peace.

It was with the government of the restored Bourbons that the powers, on May 30, 1814, signed a treaty. This document, the "first" treaty of Paris, confined France to its boundaries of 1792, those obtaining before the wars. The allied statesmen disregarded cries for vengeance and punishment, imposed no indemnity or reparations, and even allowed the works of art gathered from Europe during the wars to remain in Paris. It was not the desire of the victors to handicap the new French government on which they placed their hopes. Napoleon meanwhile was exiled to the island of Elba on the Italian coast.

To deal with other questions, the powers had agreed, before signing the Alliance of Chaumont, to hold an international congress at Vienna after defeating Napoleon. The recession of the French flood left the future of much of Europe—Belgium, Holland, Germany, Poland, Italy, Spain—fluid and uncertain. There were many other debatable questions also; the Russian annexation of Finland and ambitions on the Danube, the disintegration of the Spanish American empire, the British occupation of French, Dutch, and Spanish possessions, the troublesome issue of the freedom of the seas.

Both Russia and Great Britain, before consenting to a general conference, specified certain matters that they would decide for themselves as not susceptible to international consideration. The Russians refused to discuss Turkey and the Balkans; they retained Bessarabia as the prize of their recent war with the Turks. They also kept Finland, as an autonomous constitutional grand duchy, as well as certain recent conquests in the Caucasus almost unknown to Europe. The British refused any discussion of the freedom of the seas. They also barred all colonial and overseas questions. The revolts in Spanish America were left to run their course.

The British government simply announced to Europe which of its colonial and insular conquests it would keep and which it would return.

In Europe, the British remained in possession of Malta, the Ionian Islands, and Heligoland. In America, they kept St. Lucia, Trinidad, and Tobago in the West Indies and reasserted their claims to the Pacific Northwest, or Oregon country, to which claims were also made by Russia, Spain, and the United States. Of former French possessions, the British kept the island of Mauritius in the Indian Ocean. Of former Dutch territories, they kept the Cape of Good Hope and Ceylon, but returned the Netherlands Indies. During the Revolutionary and Napoleonic wars in Europe the British had also made extensive conquests in India, bringing much of the Deccan and the upper Ganges valley under their rule. The British emerged, in 1814, as the controlling power in both India and the Indian Ocean.

Indeed, of all the colonial empires founded by Europeans in the sixteenth and seventeenth centuries, and whose rivalry had been a recurring cause of war in the eighteenth, only the British now remained as a growing and dynamic system. The old French, Spanish, and Portuguese empires were reduced to mere scraps of their former selves; the Dutch still held vast establishments in the East Indies, but all the intermediate positions, the Cape, Ceylon, Mauritius, Singapore, were now British. Nor, in 1814, did any people except the British have a significant navy. With Napoleon and the Continental System defeated, with the industrial revolution bringing power machinery to the manufacturers of England, with no rival left in the contest for overseas dominion, and with a virtual monopoly of naval power, whose use they studiously kept free from international regulation, the British embarked on their century of world leadership, which may be said to have lasted from 1814 to 1914.

The Congress of Vienna assembled in September 1814. Never had such a brilliant gathering been seen. All the states of Europe sent representatives; and many defunct states, such as the formerly sovereign princes and ecclesiastics of the late Holy Roman Empire, sent lobbyists to urge their restoration. But procedure was so arranged that all important matters were decided by the four triumphant Great Powers. Indeed it was at the Congress of Vienna that the terms great and small powers entered clearly into the diplomatic vocabulary. Europe was at peace, a treaty having been signed with the late enemy; France also was represented at the Congress, by none other than Talleyrand, now minister to Louis XVIII. Castlereagh, Metternich, and Alexander spoke for their respective countries; Prussia was represented by Hardenberg. The Prussians hoped, as always, to enlarge the kingdom of Prussia. Alexander was a question mark: he wanted Poland, he wanted constitutional governments in Europe, he wanted some kind of international system of collective security. Castlereagh and Metternich, with support from Talleyrand, were most especially concerned to produce a balance of power on the Continent. Aristocrats of the Old Regime, they applied eighteenth-century diplomatic principles to the existing problem. They by no means desired to restore the territorial boundaries obtaining before the wars. They did desire, as they put it, to restore the "liberties of Europe," meaning the freedom of European states from domination by a single power.[29] The threat of "universal monarchy," a term which diplomats still sometimes used to signify such a system as Napoleon's, was to be offset by an ingenious calculation of forces, a transfer of territory and "souls" from one government to another, in such a way as to distribute and balance political power among a number of free and sovereign states. It was hoped that a proper balance would also produce a lasting peace.

The chief menace to peace, and most likely claimant for the domination of Europe, naturally seemed to be the late trouble-maker, France. The Congress of Vienna, without much disagreement, erected a barrier of strong states along the French eastern frontier. The historic Dutch Republic, extinct since 1795, was revived as the kingdom of the Netherlands, with the house of Orange as a hereditary monarchy; to it was added Belgium, the old Austrian Netherlands with which Austria had long been willing to part. It was hoped that the combined Dutch-Belgian kingdom would be strong enough to discourage the perennial French drive into the Low Countries. On the south, the Italian kingdom of Sardinia was restored and strengthened by the incorporation of the defunct republic of Genoa, extinct since 1797. Behind the Netherlands and Sardinia, and further to discourage a renewal of French pressure upon Germany and Italy, two great powers were installed. Almost all the German Left Bank of the Rhine was ceded to Prussia. Prussia was to be, in Castlereagh's words, a kind of "bridge" spanning central Europe, a bulwark against both France in the West and Russia in the East. With the Rhineland Prussia received, by international agreement, an accession of territory as significant as Silesia, which it had conquered in war, or the Polish territories, which it had appropriated in the partitions. In Italy, again as a kind of secondary barrier against France, the Austrians were firmly installed. They not only took back Tuscany and the Milanese, which they had held before 1796, but also annexed the extinct republic of Venice (as by the treaty of Campo Formio with Bonaparte in 1797); the Austrian Empire now included a Lombardo-Venetian kingdom in north Italy, which lasted for almost half a century. In the rest of Italy the Congress recognized the restoration of the pope in the papal states and of former rulers in the smaller duchies; but it did not insist on a restoration of the Bourbons in the kingdom of Naples. There Napoleon's brother-in-law Murat, with support from Metternich, managed for a time to retain his throne. The Bourbons and Braganzas restored themselves, respectively, in Spain and Portugal and were recognized by the Congress.

As for Germany, the Congress made no attempt to put together again the Humpty Dumpty of the Holy Roman Empire. The pleas of the former princelings went unheeded. The French and Napoleonic reorganization of Germany was substantially confirmed. The kings of Bavaria, Württemberg, and Saxony kept the royal crowns that Napoleon had bestowed on them. The king of England, George III, was now recognized as king, not "elector," of Hanover. The German states, thirty-nine in number, including Prussia and Austria, were joined in a loose

---

[29] See pp. 165–166.

Boundary of the German Confederation

0   100   200 miles

FINLAND
(Russia, 1808)

KINGDOM OF NORWAY
AND SWEDEN

Oslo•

•St. Petersburg

•Stockholm

•Reval   Novgorod•

•Novgorod•

•Riga

LITHUANIA

•Smolensk

SCOTLAND

•Edinburgh

NORTH SEA

BALTIC SEA

Copenhagen•
DENMARK

SCHLESWIG
HOLSTEIN

Niemen R.

EAST
PRUSSIA
Danzig•

UNITED KINGDOM
OF GREAT BRITAIN AND IRELAND

IRELAND   •Dublin

ENGLAND

WALES

•London

HELIGOLAND
(Britain)

Hamburg•
HANOVER

Elbe

KINGDOM OF THE
NETHERLANDS

Vistula R.

•Warsaw

Berlin•

Oder

KINGDOM OF
POLAND
(1815-1831)

•Kiev

UKRA

ENGLISH CHANNEL

BELGIUM
(Ind. 1831)

•Cologne
LUX.
HESSE

SAXON
STATES SAXONY

Breslau•

•Cracow

GALICIA

Dniester R.

ATLANTIC OCEAN

Rouen•

•Paris

Seine R.

Metz•
Strasbourg•

LORRAINE

ALSACE

BADEN

WÜRT-
TEMBERG

Prague•

BAVARIA

Munich•

AUSTRIA

Vienna•

•Pressburg

AUSTRIAN EMPIRE

•Budapest

HUNGARY

TRANSYLVANIA

BESSARABIA
(Russia 1812)

MOLDAVIA
(Autonomous 1829)

Loire R.

Tours•

FRANCE

Lyons•

Rhone R.

SWITZERLAND
Berne•

TYROL

CROATIA

WALLACHIA
(Autonomous 1829)

DC

Bordeaux•

SAVOY

LOM-
BARDY

VENETIA

Milan•

Po R.

DALMATIA

Belgrade•

SERBIA
*(Autonomous
1829)*

Danube R.

Toulouse•

PYRENEES

Ebro R.

Marseilles•
Toulon•

Nice•

PIEDMONT

Genoa•
LUCCA

PARMA

MODENA

TUSCANY

BOSNIA

MONTENEGRO

•Sofia

OTTOMA

BULGARIA

•Constantir

Burgos•

PORTUGAL

Lisbon•

Tagus R.

Madrid•

SPAIN

•Valencia

Barcelona•

ELBA

CORSICA
(France)

Rome•

KINGDOM OF SARDINIA

PAPAL
STATES

ADRIATIC SEA

Salonica•

AEGEAN SEA

•Athens

•Seville

Cadiz•

•Gibraltar *(Britain)*

BALEARIC I.
(Spain)

SARDINIA

Naples•

KINGDOM OF THE
TWO SICILIES

IONIAN I.
(Britain)

GREECE
(Independent 1829)

RH

CRETE

Algiers•

Palermo•

SICILY

MALTA
(Britain)

MOROCCO

ALGERIA *(France, 1830)*

TUNIS
(Turkish)

MEDITERRANEAN SEA

TRIPOLI

TRIPOLI

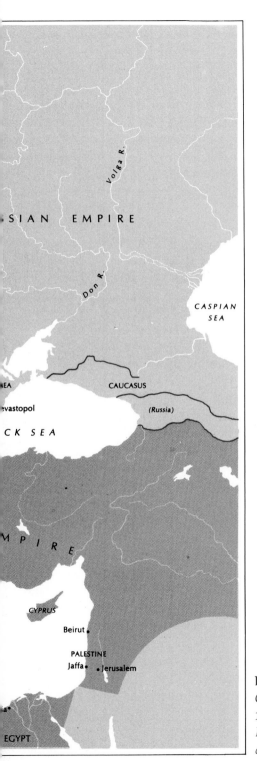

Europe 1815. *Boundaries are those set by the Congress of Vienna in 1815. Outside the Balkans they remained basically unchanged until the Italian war of 1859, except that Belgium became independent and the separate kingdom of Poland disappeared in 1830–1831 (p. 499). For the great crisis of the Congress of Vienna, the Polish-Saxon question, see panels 6 and 7 of the map on pp. 236–237.*

confederation in which the members remained virtually sovereign, and which did nothing to solve the Austro-Prussian dualism or rivalry. The Congress ignored the yearnings of German nationalists for a great unified Fatherland; Metternich especially feared nationalistic agitation; and in any case the nationalists themselves had no practical answer to concrete questions, such as the institutions of government and the frontiers that a united Germany should have. The Congress did declare, somewhat ineffectually, that in each of the German states there should be a representative legislative body.

The question of Poland, reopened by the fall of Napoleon's Grand Duchy of Warsaw, brought the Congress almost to disaster. Alexander still insisted on undoing the crime of the partitions, which to his mind meant reconstituting the Polish kingdom with himself as constitutional king, in a merely personal union with the Russian empire. A similar arrangement was being initiated in the Grand Duchy of Finland, where Alexander reigned as a constitutional grand duke. To reunite Poland required that Austria and Prussia surrender their respective segments of the old Poland, most of which they had in any case lost to Napoleon. The Prussians were willing, with the proviso, which Alexander supported, that Prussia receive instead the whole of the kingdom of Saxony, which was considered available because the king of Saxony had been the last German ruler to abandon Napoleon. The issue presented itself as the Polish-Saxon question, with Russia and Prussia standing together to demand all Poland for Russia, and all Saxony for Prussia.

Such a prospect horrified Metternich. For Prussia to absorb Saxony would raise Prussia prodigiously in the eyes of all Germans, and it would greatly lengthen the common frontier between Prussia and the Austrian Empire. Furthermore, for Alexander to become king of all Poland, and incidentally the protector of an extended Prussia, would incalculably augment the influence of Russia in the affairs of Europe. Metternich found that Castlereagh shared these views. To Castlereagh it seemed that the main problem at Vienna was to restrain Russia. The British had not fought the French emperor only to have Europe fall to the Russian tsar. For months the Polish-Saxon question was debated, Metternich and Castlereagh exploring every device of argument to dissuade the Russo-Prussian combination from its expansionist designs. Finally they accepted the proffered assistance of Talleyrand, who shrewdly used this rift between the victors to bring France back into the diplomatic circle as a power in its own right. On January 3, 1815, Castlereagh, Metternich, and Talleyrand signed a secret treaty, pledging themselves to go to war if necessary against Russia and Prussia. So, in the very midst of the peace conference, war again reared its head; and, in the very deliberations of the victors, one party among them allied itself with the vanquished.

No sooner had news of the secret treaty leaked out than Alexander offered to compromise. In his mixed nature he was, among other things, a man of peace, and he agreed to content himself with a reduced Polish kingdom. The Congress therefore created a new Poland (called "Congress Poland," which lasted for fifteen years); Alexander became its king, and he gave it a constitution; it comprised much the same area as Napoleon's Grand Duchy, representing in effect a transfer of this region from French to Russian control. It reached 250 miles farther west into Europe than had the Russian segment of the third partition of 1795. Some Poles still remained in Prussia and some in the Austrian Empire; Poland was not reunited. With the tsar thus content, Prussia too had to back down. It received about two-fifths of Saxony, the rest remaining to the Saxon king. The addition of both Saxon and Rhenish territories brought the Prussian monarchy into the most advanced parts of Germany. The net effect of the peace settlement, and of the Napoleonic wars, in this connection, was to shift the center of gravity of both Russia and Prussia farther west, Russia almost to the Oder, Prussia to the borders of France.[30]

With the solution of the Polish-Saxon question the main work of the Congress was completed. Other incidental matters were taken up. The Congress initiated international regulation of certain rivers. It issued a declaration against the Atlantic slave trade, which, however, remained ineffective, since the Continental powers were unwilling to grant the British navy free powers of search at sea, and the British were unwilling to put naval forces at the disposal of an international body. Committees of the Congress set to work to draft the Final Act. And at this point the whole settlement was brought into jeopardy.

Napoleon escaped from Elba, landed in France on March 1, 1815, and again proclaimed the empire. In the year since the return of the Bourbons discontent had been spreading in France. Louis XVIII proved to be a sensible man, but a swarm of unreasonable and vindictive émigrés had come back with him. Reaction and a "white terror" were raging through the country. Adherents of the Revolution rallied to the emperor on his dramatic reappearance. Napoleon reached Paris, took over the government and army, and headed for Belgium. He would, if he could, disperse the pompous assemblage at Vienna. To the victors of the year before, and to most of Europe, it seemed that the Revolution was again stirring, that the old horror of toppling thrones and recurring warfare might not after all be ended. The opposing forces met in Belgium at Waterloo, where the Duke of Wellington, commanding an allied force, won a great victory. Napoleon again abdicated, and was again exiled, this time to distant St. Helena in the south Atlantic. A new peace treaty was made with France, the "second" treaty of Paris. It was more severe than the first, since the French seemed to have shown themselves incorrigible and unrepentant. The new treaty imposed minor changes of the frontiers, an indemnity of 700,000,000 francs, and an army of occupation.

The effect of the Hundred Days, as the episode following Napoleon's return from Elba is called, was to renew the dread of revolution, war, and aggression. Britain, Russia, Austria, and Prussia, after being almost at war with each other in January, again joined forces to get rid of the apparition from Elba, and in November 1815 they solemnly reconfirmed the Quadruple Alliance of Chaumont, adding a provision that no Bonaparte should ever govern France. They agreed also to hold future congresses

[30] See maps on pp. 236–237, 252–253, 259.

to review the political situation and enforce the peace. No change was made in the arrangements agreed to at Vienna, except that Murat, who fought for Napoleon during the Hundred Days, was captured and shot, and an extremely unenlightened Bourbon monarchy was restored in Naples. In addition to the Quadruple Alliance of the Great Powers, bound specifically to enforce or amend the terms of the peace treaty by international action, Alexander devised a vaguer scheme which he called the Holy Alliance. Long attracted to the idea of an international order, appalled by the return of Napoleon, and influenced at the moment by the pietistic Baroness von Krüdener, the tsar proposed, for all monarchs to sign, a statement by which they promised to uphold Christian principles of charity and peace. All signed except the pope, the sultan, and the prince regent of Great Britain. The Holy Alliance, probably sincerely meant by Alexander as a condemnation of violence, and at first not taken seriously by the others who signed it, and who thought it absurd to mix Christianity with politics, soon came to signify, in the minds of liberals, a kind of unholy alliance of monarchies against liberty and progress.

The peace of Vienna, including generally the treaty of Vienna itself, the treaties of Paris, and the British and colonial settlement, was the most far-reaching diplomatic agreement between the Peace of Westphalia of 1648 and the Peace of Paris which closed the First World War in 1919. It had its strong points and its weak ones. It produced a minimum of resentment in France; the late enemy accepted the new arrangements. It ended almost two centuries of colonial rivalry; for sixty or seventy years no colonial empire seriously challenged the British. Two other causes of friction in the eighteenth century—the control of Poland and the Austro-Prussian dualism in Germany—were smoothed over for fifty years. With past issues the peace of 1815 dealt rather effectively; with future issues, not unnaturally, it was less successful. The Vienna treaty was not illiberal in its day; it was by no means entirely reactionary, for the Congress showed little desire to restore the state of affairs in existence before the wars. The reaction that gathered strength after 1815 was not written into the treaty itself.

But the treaty gave no satisfaction to nationalists and democrats. It was a disappointment even to many liberals, especially in Germany. The transfer of peoples from government to government, without consultation of their wishes, opened the way under nineteenth-century conditions to a good deal of subsequent trouble. The peacemakers were in fact hostile both to nationalism and to democracy, the potent forces of the coming age; they regarded them, with reason, as leading to revolution and war. The problem to which they addressed themselves was to restore the balance of power, the "liberties of Europe," and to make a lasting peace. In this they were successful. They restored the European state system, or system in which a number of sovereign and independent states existed without fear of conquest or domination. And the peace which they made, though some details broke down in 1830, and others in 1848, on the whole subsisted for half a century; and not for a full century, not until 1914, was there a war in Europe that lasted longer than a few months, or in which all the great powers were involved. No international disturbance comparable in magnitude to that created by the French Revolution and Napoleonic empire has yet been followed by such a protracted period of peace.

XI: REACTION VERSUS

PROGRESS, 1815-1848

Emerging in 1815 from a generation of warfare, the European world proceeded to roll along the broad avenue of the nineteenth century, which, seen in retrospect, stands as one of the most remarkable periods of material progress in the history of the human race. Postwar economic troubles there were, due to the sudden stopping of war production, to the readjustment of markets after the collapse of the Continental System, and to the enormously swollen government debts and inflated prices. These troubles were overcome. Europe was shaken by the wars but not ruined. The injury to Europe produced by the wars of our own century was to be incomparably greater. One reason why Europe came out of the wars of 1792–1815 with relatively so little damage is that warfare was then incomparably less destructive. Another is that Europe was carried on the wave of an expanding economy. The economic expansion which had been going on for centuries was now, in the years around 1815, accentuated and accelerated by the phenomenon generally known as the Industrial Revolution.

The processes of industrialization in the long run were to revolutionize the lives of men everywhere. In the short run, in the generation following the peace of Vienna, the same processes had pronounced political effects. The Industrial Revolution, by

Chapter Emblem: A medal commemorating the Congress of Vienna, showing the victorious rulers of Austria, Russia, and Prussia.

greatly enlarging both the business and the wage-earning classes, doomed all attempts at "reaction," attempts, that is, to undo or check the consequences of the French Revolution. Industrialization made the flood of progress too powerful for conservatism to dam up. It hastened the growth of that world-wide economic system whose rise in the eighteenth century has already been observed. And since industrialization first took place in western Europe, one of its early effects was to widen the difference between eastern and western Europe, and so weaken the efforts made, after the defeat of Napoleon, to organize a kind of international union of Europe.

**51
The Industrial
Revolution**

On the whole, from the beginning of history until about 1800, the work of the world was done with hand tools. Since then it has been increasingly done by machines. Before about 1800 power was supplied by human or animal muscle, reinforced by levers or pulleys, and supplemented by the force of running water or moving air. Since then power has been supplied by the human manipulation of more recondite natural forces found in steam, electricity, the combustion of gases, and most recently within the atom. The process of shifting from hand tools to power machinery is what is meant by the Industrial Revolution. Its beginning cannot be dated exactly. It grew gradually out of the technical practices of earlier times. It is still going on, for in some countries industrialization is barely beginning, and even in the most highly developed it is still making advances. Indeed the technological advances in our own time and the spread of industry to all parts of the globe are among the most spectacular as well as far-reaching developments of the contemporary age. But the first country to be profoundly affected by industrialization was Great Britain, where its effects became manifest in the half-century following 1780.

It seems likely, despite the emphasis placed on revolutionary upheavals by historians, that people are habitually quite conservative. Workingmen do not put off their old way of life, move to strange and overcrowded towns, or enter the deadly rounds of mine and factory except under strong incentive. Well-to-do people, living in comfort on assured incomes, do not risk their wealth in new and untried ventures except for good reason. The shifting to modern machine production requires in any country a certain mobility of people and of wealth. Such mobility may be produced by state planning, as in the industrialization of the Soviet Union in recent times. In England a high degree of social mobility existed in the eighteenth century in consequence of a long historical development.

*The Agricultural
Revolution in Britain*

The English Revolution of 1688, confirming the ascendancy of Parliament over the king, meant in economic terms the ascendancy of the more well-to-do property-owning classes.[1] Among these the landowners were by far the most

[1] See p. 187.

important, though they counted the great London merchants among their allies. For a century and a half, from 1688 to 1832, the British government was substantially in the hands of these landowners—the "squirearchy" or "gentlemen of England." The result was a thorough transformation of farming, an Agricultural Revolution without which the Industrial Revolution could not have occurred.

Many landowners, seeking to increase their money incomes, began experimenting with improved methods of cultivation and stock-raising. They made more use of fertilizers (mainly animal manure); they introduced new implements (such as the "drill seeder" and "horse-hoe"); they brought in new crops, such as turnips, and a more scientific system of crop rotation; they attempted to breed larger sheep and fatter cattle. An improving landlord, to introduce such changes successfully, needed full control over his land. He saw a mere barrier to progress in the old village system of open fields, common lands, and semicollective methods of cultivation. Improvement also required an investment of capital, which was impossible so long as the soil was tilled by numerous poor and custom-bound small farmers.

The old common rights of the villagers were part of the common law. Only an act of Parliament could modify or extinguish them. It was the great landowners who controlled Parliament, which therefore passed hundreds of "enclosure acts," authorizing the enclosure, by fences, walls, or hedges, of the old common lands and unfenced open fields. Land thus came under a strict regime of private ownership and individual management. At the same time small owners sold out or were excluded in various ways, the more easily since the larger owners had so much local authority as justices of the peace. Ownership of land in England, more than anywhere else in central or western Europe, became concentrated in the hands of a relatively small class of wealthy landlords, who let it out in large blocks to a relatively small class of substantial farmers. This development, though in progress throughout the eighteenth century, reached its height during the Napoleonic wars.

One result was greatly to raise the productivity of land and of farm labor. Fatter cattle yielded more meat, more assiduous cultivation yielded more cereals. The food supply of England was increased, while a smaller percentage of the population was needed to produce it. Labor was thus released for other pursuits. Socially, the results were distressing. Oliver Goldsmith reflected upon them in *The Deserted Village:*

> *Ill fares the land, to hastening ills a prey,*
> *Where wealth accumulates, and men decay.*
> *Princes and lords may flourish. . . .*
> *But a bold peasantry, their country's pride,*
> *When once destroyed, can never be supplied.*

The yeomanry, or small landowners—the "bold peasantry"—disappeared as a class. The greater number of the English country people became wage earners, working as hired men for the farmers and landlords, or spinning or weaving in their cottages for merchants in the towns. The English workingman (and woman) was dependent on daily wages long before the coming of the factory and the machine. English working people became mobile; they would go where the jobs were, or where the wages were slightly higher. They also became available, in that fewer of them were needed on the land to produce food. Such conditions hardly obtained except in Great Britain. On the Continent agricultural methods were less productive, and the rural workers were more established on the soil, whether by institutions of serfdom as in eastern Europe, or by the possession of property or firm leaseholds as in France.[2]

Industrialism in Britain: Incentives and Inventions

Meanwhile, as the Agricultural Revolution ran its course in the eighteenth century and into the nineteenth, the British had conquered a colonial empire, staked out markets all over the Americas and Europe, built up a huge mercantile marine, and won command of the sea. The British merchant could sell more, if only more could be produced. He had the customers, he had the ships, and moreover he had the capital with which to finance new ideas. The profit motive prompted the search for more rapid methods of production. The old English staple export, woolen cloth, could be marketed indefinitely if only more of it could be woven. The possibilities in cotton cloth were enormous. The taste of Europeans for cottons had been already formed by imports from Asia. By hand methods Europeans could not produce cotton in competition with the East. But the market was endless if cotton could be spun, woven, and printed with less labor, i.e., by machines. Capital was available, mobile, and fluid, because of the rise of banking, credit, and stock companies. Funds could be shifted from one enterprise to another. Wealthy landowners could divert some of their profits to industry. If an invention proved a total loss, as sometimes happened, or if it required years of development before producing any income, still the investment could be afforded. Only a country already wealthy from commerce and agriculture could have been the first to initiate the machine age. England was such a country.

These conditions induced a series of successful inventions in the textile industry. In 1733 a man named John Kay invented the fly shuttle, by which only one man instead of two was needed to operate a loom. The resulting increase in the output of weaving set up a strong demand for yarn. This was met in the 1760s by the invention of the spinning jenny, a kind of mechanized spinning wheel. The new shuttles and jennies were at first operated by hand and used by domestic workers in their homes. But in 1769 Richard Arkwright patented the water frame, a device for the multiple spinning of many threads. At first it was operated by water power, but in the 1780s Arkwright introduced the steam engine to drive his spinning machinery. Thus requiring a considerable installation of heavy equipment, he gathered his engines, frames, and workers into large and usually dismal buildings, called "mills" by the English, or "factories" in subsequent American usage. Mechanical spinning now for a time overwhelmed the hand weavers with yarn. This led to the development of the power loom, which became economically practicable

466   [2]See p. 216.

shortly after 1800. Weaving as well as spinning was therefore done increasingly in factories. These improvements in the finishing process put a heavy strain on the production of raw cotton. An ingenious Connecticut Yankee, Eli Whitney, while acting as a tutor on a plantation in Georgia, in ten days produced a cotton gin, which by speeding up the removal of seeds greatly increased the output of cotton. The gin soon spread through the American South, where the almost decaying plantation economy was abruptly revived, becoming an adjunct to the Industrial Revolution in England. British imports of raw cotton multiplied fivefold in the thirty years following 1790. In value of manufactures, cotton rose from ninth to first place among British industries in the same years. By 1820 it made up almost half of all British exports.

The steam engine, applied to the cotton mills in the 1780s, had for a century been going through a development of its own.[3] Scientific and technical experiments with steam pressures had been fairly common in the seventeenth century, but what gave the economic impetus to invention was the gradual dwindling away of Europe's primeval stocks of timber. The wood shortage became acute in England about 1700, so that it was more difficult to obtain the charcoal needed in smelting iron, and smelters turned increasingly to coal. Deeper coal shafts could not be sunk until someone devised better methods of pumping out water. About 1702 Thomas Newcomen built the first economically significant steam engine, which was soon widely used to drive pumps in the coal mines. It consumed so much fuel in proportion to power delivered that it could generally be used only in the coal fields themselves. In 1763 James Watt, a technician at the University of Glasgow, began to make improvements on Newcomen's engine. He formed a business partnership with Matthew Boulton. Boulton, originally a manufacturer of toys, buttons, and shoe buckles, provided the funds to finance Watt's rather costly experiments, handmade equipment, and slowly germinating ideas. By the 1780s the firm of Boulton and Watt was eminently successful, manufacturing steam engines both for British use and for the export trade.

At first, until further refinements and greater precision could be obtained in the working of iron, the engines were so cumbersome that they could be used as stationary engines only, as in the new spinning mills of Arkwright and others. Soon after 1800 the steam engine was successfully used to propel river boats, notably on the Hudson in 1807, by Robert Fulton, who employed an imported Boulton and Watt engine. Experiments with steam power for land transportation began at the same time. As it was in the coal fields of England a century before that Newcomen's engine had been put to practical uses, so now it was in the coal fields that Watt's engine first became a "locomotive." Well before 1800 the mines had taken to using "rail ways," on which wagons with flanged wheels, drawn by horses, carried coal to canals or to the sea. In the 1820s steam engines were successfully placed on moving vehicles. The first fully satisfactory locomotive was George Stephenson's *Rocket*, which in 1829, on the newly built Liverpool and Manchester Railway, not only reached an impressive

[3] See p. 306.

speed of sixteen miles per hour but met other more important tests as well. By the 1840s the era of railroad construction was under way in both Europe and the United States.

The Industrial Revolution in Great Britain in its early phase, down to 1830 or 1840, took place principally in the manufacture of textiles, with accompanying developments in the exploitation of iron and coal. The early factories were principally textile factories, and indeed mainly cotton mills; for cotton was an entirely new industry to Europe and hence easily mechanized, whereas the long established woolen trade, in which both employers and workers hesitated to abandon their customary ways, was mechanized more slowly. The suddenness of the change must not be exaggerated. It is often said that the Industrial Revolution was not a revolution at all. As late as the 1830s only a small fraction of the British working people were employed in factories. But the factory and the factory system were even then regarded as the coming mode of production, destined to grow and expand, mighty symbols of the irresistible march of progress.

Some Social Consequences of Industrialism in Britain

The Britain that emerged fundamentally unscathed and in fact strengthened from the wars with Napoleon was no longer the "merrie England" of days of yore. The island was becoming crowded with people, as was the lesser island of Ireland. The combined population of Great Britain and Ireland tripled in the century from 1750 to 1850, rising from about 10,000,000 in 1750 to about 30,000,000 in 1850. The growth was distributed very unevenly. Formerly, in England, most people had lived in the south. But the coal and iron, and hence the steam power, lay in the Midlands and the north. Here whole new cities rose seemingly out of nothing. In 1785 it was estimated that in England and Scotland, outside of London, there were only three cities with more than 50,000 people. Seventy years later, the span of one lifetime, there were thirty-one British cities of this size.

Preeminent among them was Manchester in Lancashire, the first and most famous of industrial cities of modern type. Manchester, before the coming of the cotton mills, was a rather large market town. Though very ancient, it had not been significant enough to be recognized as a borough for representation in Parliament. Locally it was organized as a manor. Not until 1845 did the inhabitants extinguish the manorial rights, buying them out at that time from the last lord, Sir Oswald Mosley, for £200,000 or about 1,000,000 dollars. In population Manchester grew from 25,000 in 1772 to 455,000 in 1851. But until 1835 there was no regular procedure in England for the incorporation of cities. Urban organization was more backward than in Prussia or France. Unless inherited from the Middle Ages, a city had no legal existence. It lacked proper officials and adequate tax-raising and law-making powers. It was therefore difficult for Manchester, and the other new factory towns, to deal with problems of rapid urbanization, such as provision of police protection, water and sewers, or the disposal of garbage.

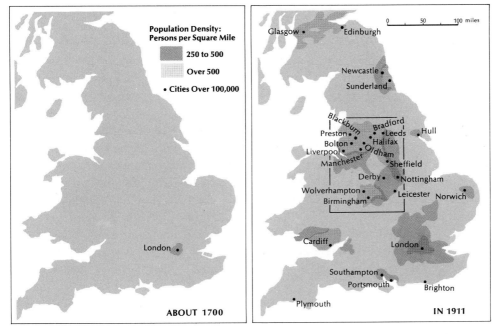
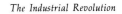

England before and after the Industrial Revolution. *In 1700 England, Scotland, and Wales had only one city with a population of more than 100,000. In 1911 they had nearly thirty. The area within the small rectangle in the right-hand panel, roughly the Midlands, is almost exactly the area of Massachusetts.*

The new urban agglomerations were drab places, blackened with the heavy soot of the early coal age, settling alike on the mills and the workers' quarters, which were dark at best, for the climate of the Midlands is not sunny. Housing for workers was hastily built, closely packed, and always in short supply, as in all rapidly growing communities. Whole families lived in single rooms, and since working-class women commonly worked all day in the factories, family life and common morals went to pieces. A police officer in Glasgow observed that there were whole blocks of tenements in the city each swarming with a thousand ragged children who had first names only, usually nicknames—like animals, as he put it.

The distressing feature of the new factories was that for the most part they required unskilled labor only. Skilled workers found themselves degraded in status. Hand weavers and spinners, thrown out of work by the new machines, either languished in a misery that was the deepest of that of any class in the Industrial Revolution or else went off to a factory to find a job. The factories paid good wages by the standards for unskilled labor at the time. But these standards were very low, too low to allow a man to support his wife and children. This had generally been true for unskilled labor, in England and elsewhere, under earlier economic systems also. In the new factories the work was so mechanical that women and children as young as six years old were often preferred. They worked for less and were often more adept

469

at handling a bobbin. Most male workingmen objected indignantly to this situation; a few lived shamelessly by the spawning of large families.

Hours in the factories were long, fourteen a day or occasionally more; and though such hours were familiar to persons who had worked on farms, or at domestic industry in rural households, they were more tedious and oppressive in the more regimented conditions that were necessary in the mills. Holidays were few, except for the unwelcome leisure of unemployment, which was a common scourge, because the short-run ups and downs of business were very erratic during this period of bewildering expansion. A day without work was a day producing nothing to live on, so that even where the daily wage was relatively attractive the worker's real income was chronically insufficient. Workers in the factories, as in the mines, were almost entirely unorganized. They were a mass of recently assembled humanity without traditions or common ties. Each bargained individually with his employer, who, usually a small businessman himself, facing a ferocious competition with others, often in debt for the equipment in his factory, or determined to save money in order to purchase more, held his "wages bill" to the lowest possible figure that he could manage.

The factory owners, the new "cotton lords," were the first industrial capitalists. They were often self-made men, who owed their position to their own intelligence, persistency, and foresight. They lived in comfort without ostentation or luxury, saving from each year's income to build up their factories and their machines. Hard-working themselves, they thought that landed gentlemen were usually idlers and that the poor tended to be lazy. They were usually honest, in a hard and exacting way; they would make money by any means the law allowed, but not beyond it. They were neither brutal nor knowingly hard-hearted. They gave to charitable and philanthropic causes. They believed that they did "the poor" a favor by furnishing them with work and by seeing to it that they worked diligently and productively. Most of them disapproved of public regulation of their business, though a few, driven by competition to expedients that they did not like, such as the employment of small children, would have accepted some regulation that fell on all competitors equally. It was a cotton magnate, the elder Robert Peel, who in 1802 pushed the first Factory Act through Parliament. This act purported to regulate the conditions in which pauper children were employed in the textile mills, but it was a dead letter from the beginning, since it provided no adequate body of factory inspectors. The English at this time, alone among the leading European peoples, had no class of trained, paid, and professional government administrators; nor did they yet want such a class, preferring self-government and local initiative. To have inspectors for one's affairs smacked of Continental bureaucracy. The fact that the older methods of economic regulation were obsolescent, actually unsuited to the new age, had the effect of discrediting the idea of regulation itself. The new industrialists wanted to be let alone. They considered it unnatural to interfere with business and believed that, if allowed to follow their own judgment, they would assure the future prosperity and progress of the country.

The industrialists were strengthened in these beliefs by the emerging science of "political economy." In 1776 Adam Smith published his epochal *Wealth of Nations*, which criticized the older mercantilism, with its regulatory and monopolistic practices, and urged, though with moderation, that certain "natural laws" of production and exchange be allowed to work themselves out. Smith was followed by Thomas R. Malthus, David Ricardo, and the so-called Manchester School. Their doctrine was dubbed (by its opponents) laissez faire and in its elaborated form is still called the classical economics. It held, basically, that there is a world of economic relationships autonomous and separable from government or politics. The economic world, in this view, is regulated within itself by certain "natural laws," such as the law of supply and demand or the law of diminishing returns. All persons should follow their own enlightened self-interest; each knows his own interest better than anyone else; and the sum total of individual interests will add up to the general welfare and liberty of all. Government should do as little as possible; it should confine itself to preserving security of life and property, providing reasonable laws and reliable courts, and so assuring the discharge of private contracts, debts, and obligations. Not only business, but education, charity, and personal matters generally should be left to private initiative. There should be no tariffs; free trade should reign everywhere, for the economic system is world-wide, unaffected by political barriers or national differences. As for the workingman, according to classical economists before about 1850, he should not expect to make more than a bare minimum living; an "iron law of wages" brings it about that as soon as the worker receives more than a subsistence wage he breeds more children, who eat up the excess, so that he reduces himself, and the working class generally, again to a subsistence level. The workingman, if discontented, should see the folly of changing the system, for this *is* the system, the natural system—there is no other. Political economy as taught in grim Manchester was not without reason called the "dismal science."

For working people in England the Industrial Revolution was a hard experience. It should be remembered, however, that neither low wages, nor the fourteen-hour day, nor the labor of women and children, nor the ravages of unemployment were anything new. All had existed for centuries, in England and western Europe, as agricultural and commercial capitalism replaced the more self-sufficient economies of the Middle Ages. The factory towns were in some ways better places to live than the rural slums from which many of their people came. Factory routine was psychologically deadening, but the textile mills were in some ways not worse than the domestic sweatshops in which manufacturing processes had previously been carried on. The concentration of working people in city and factory opened the way to improvement in their condition. It made their misery apparent; philanthropic sentiment was gradually aroused among the more fortunate. Gathered in cities, workers obtained more knowledge of the world. Mingling and talking together they developed a sense of solidarity, class interest, and common political aims; and in time they became organized, establishing labor unions by which to obtain a larger share of the national income.

Britain after the fall of Napoleon became the workshop of the world. Though factories using steam power sprang up in France, Belgium, New England, and elsewhere, it was really not until after 1870 that Great Britain faced any industrial competition from abroad. The British had a virtual monopoly in textiles and machine tools. The English Midlands and Scottish Lowlands shipped cotton thread and steam engines to all the world. British capital was exported to all countries, there to call new enterprises into being. London became the world's clearinghouse and financial center. Progressive people in other lands looked to Britain as their model, hoping to learn from its advanced industrial methods, and to imitate its parliamentary political system. Thus more foundations of the nineteenth century were laid.

The combined forces of industrialization and of the French Revolution led after 1815 to the proliferation of doctrines and movements of many sorts. These broke out in a general European revolution in 1848. As for the thirty-three years from 1815 to 1848, there is no better way of grasping their long-run meaning than to reflect on the number of still living "isms" that arose at that time.

So far as is known the word "liberalism" first appeared in the English language in 1819, "radicalism" in 1820, "socialism" in 1832, "conservatism" in 1835. The 1830s first saw "individualism," "constitutionalism," "humanitarianism," and "monarchism." "Nationalism" and "communism" date from the 1840s. Not until the 1850s did the English-speaking world use the word "capitalism" (French *capitalisme* is much older); and not until even later had it heard of "Marxism," though the doctrines of Marx grew out of and reflected the troubled times of the 1840s.

The rapid coinage of new "isms" does not in every case mean that the ideas they conveyed were new. Many of them had their origin in the Enlightenment, if not before. Men had loved liberty before talking of liberalism and been conservative without knowing conservatism as such. The appearance of so many "isms" shows rather that people were making their ideas more systematic. To the "philosophy" of the Enlightenment were now added an intense activism and a partisanship generated during the French Revolution. People were being obliged to reconsider and analyze society as a whole. The social sciences were taking form. An "ism" (excluding such words as "hypnotism" or "favoritism") may be defined as the conscious espousal of a doctrine in competition with other doctrines. Without the "isms" created in the thirty-odd years after the peace of Vienna it is impossible to understand or even talk about the history of the world since that event, so that a brief characterization of some of the most important is in order.

One of the "isms" was not political. It was called "romanticism," a word first used in English in the 1840s to describe a movement then half a century old. Romanticism was primarily a theory of literature and the arts. Its great exponents included Wordsworth, Shelley, and Byron in England, Victor Hugo and Chateaubriand in France, Schiller and the Schlegels and many others in Germany. As a theory of art it raised basic questions on the nature of significant truth, on the importance of various human faculties, on the relation of thought and feeling, on the meaning of the past and of time itself. Representing a new way of sensing all human experience, it affected most thinking on social and public questions.

Possibly the most fundamental romantic attitude was a love of the unclassifiable—of moods or impressions, scenes or stories, sights or sounds or things concretely experienced, personal idiosyncrasies or peculiar customs which the intellect could never classify, box up, explain away, or reduce to an abstract generalization. The romantics, characteristically, insisted on the value of feeling as well as of reason. They were aware of the importance of the subconscious. They were likely to suspect a perfectly lucid idea as somehow superficial. They loved the mysterious, the unknown, the half-seen figures on the far horizon. Hence romanticism contributed to a new interest in strange and distant societies and in strange and distant historical epochs. Where the philosophes of the Enlightenment had deplored the Middle Ages as a time of intellectual error, the romantic generation looked back upon them with respect and even nostalgia, finding in them a fascination, a colorfulness, or a spiritual depth which they missed in their own time. The "Gothic," which rationalists thought barbarous, had a strong appeal for romantics. A Gothic Revival set in in the arts, of which one example was the British Parliament buildings, built in the 1830s.

In medieval art and institutions, as in the art and institutions of every age and people, the romantics saw the expression of an inner genius. The idea of original or creative genius was in fact another of the most fundamental romantic beliefs. A genius was a dynamic spirit that no rules could hem in, one that no analysis or classification could ever fully explain. Genius, it was thought, made its own rules and laws. The genius might be that of the individual person, such as the artist, writer, or Napoleon-like mover of the world. It might be the genius or spirit of an age. Or it might be the genius of a people or nation, the *Volksgeist* of Herder, an inherent national character making each people grow in its own distinctive way, which could be known only by a study of its history, and not by ratiocination.[4] Here again romanticism gave a new impetus to study of the past. Politically, romantics could be found in all camps, conservative and radical. Let us turn to the more purely political "isms."

The first Liberals, calling themselves by that name (though Napoleon used that word for his own system, as has been seen[5]), arose in Spain among certain opponents of the Napoleonic occupation. The word then passed to France, where it denoted opposition to royalism after the restoration of the Bourbons in 1814. In England many Whigs became increasingly liberal, as did even a few Tories, until the great

[4] See pp. 444–445.
[5] See p. 433.

Liberal party was founded in the 1850s. Nineteenth-century, or "classical," liberalism varied from country to country, but it showed many basic similarities.

Liberals were generally men of the business and professional classes, together with enterprising landowners wishing to improve their estates. They believed in what was modern, enlightened, efficient, reasonable, and fair. They had confidence in man's powers of self-government and self-control. They set a high value on parliamentary or representative government, working through reasonable discussion and legislation, with responsible ministries and an impartial and law-abiding administration. They demanded full publicity for all actions of government, and to assure such publicity they insisted on freedom of the press and free rights of assembly. All these political advantages they thought most likely to be realized under a good constitutional monarchy. Outside of England they favored explicit written constitutions. They were not democrats; they opposed giving every man the vote, fearing the excesses of mob rule or of irrational political action. Only as the nineteenth century progressed did liberals gradually and reluctantly come to accept the idea of universal manhood suffrage. They subscribed to the doctrines of the rights of man as set forth in the American and French revolutions, but with a clear emphasis on the right of property, and in their economic views they followed the British Manchester School or the French economist J. B. Say.[6] They favored laissez faire, were suspicious of the ability of government to regulate business, wanted to get rid of the gild system where it still existed, and disapproved of attempts on the part of the new industrial laborers to organize unions. Internationally they advocated freedom of trade, to be accomplished by the lowering or abolition of tariffs, so that all countries might exchange their products easily with each other and with industrial England. In this way, they thought, each country would produce what it was most fitted for, and so best increase its wealth and standards of living. From the growth of wealth, production, invention, and scientific progress they believed that the general progress of humanity would ensue. They generally frowned upon the established churches and landed aristocracies as obstacles to advancement. They believed in the spread of tolerance and education. They were also profoundly civilian in attitude, disliking wars, conquerors, army officers, standing armies, and military expenditures. They wanted orderly change by processes of legislation. They shrank before the idea of revolution. Liberals on the Continent were usually admirers of Great Britain.

Radicalism, Republicanism, Socialism

Radicalism, at least as a word, originated in England, where about 1820 the Philosophical Radicals proudly applied the term to themselves. These Radicals in the 1820s included not only the few working-class leaders who were beginning to emerge but also many of the new industrial capitalists, who were still unrepresented in Parliament. They took up where such English "Jacobins" as Thomas Paine had left

[6]See p. 471.

off a generation earlier, before the long crisis of the French wars had discredited all radicalism as pro-French.[7]

The Philosophical Radicals were a good deal like the French philosophes before the Revolution. They were followers of an elderly sage, Jeremy Bentham, who in prolific writings from 1776 to 1832 undertook to reform the English criminal and civil law, church, Parliament, and constitution. The English Radicals professed to deduce the right form of institutions from the very nature and psychology of man himself. They impatiently waved aside all arguments based on history, usage, or custom. They went to the "roots" of things. They wanted a total reconstruction of laws, courts, prisons, poor relief, municipal organization, rotten boroughs, and fox-hunting clergy. Their demand for the reform of Parliament was vehement and insistent. They detested the Church of England, the peerage, and the squirearchy. Many radicals would just as soon abolish royalty also; not until the long reign of Queen Victoria (1837–1901) did the British monarchy become undeniably popular in all quarters. Above all, radicalism was democratic; it demanded a vote for every adult Englishman. After the Reform Bill of 1832 the industrial capitalists generally turned into liberals, but the working-class leaders remained radical democrats, as will be seen.

On the Continent radicalism was represented by militant republicanism. The years of the First French Republic, which to liberals and conservatives signified horrors associated with the Reign of Terror, were for the republicans years of hope and progress, cut short by forces of reaction. Republicans were a minority even in France; elsewhere, as in Italy and Germany, they were fewer still, though they existed. Mostly the republicans were drawn from intelligentsia such as students and writers, from working-class leaders protesting at social injustice, and from elderly veterans, or the sons and nephews of veterans, to whom the Republic of '93, with its wars and its glory, was a living thing. Because of police repression, republicans often joined together in secret societies. They looked with equanimity on the prospect of further revolutionary upheaval, by which they felt that the cause of liberty, equality, and fraternity would be advanced. Strong believers in political equality, they were democrats demanding universal suffrage. They favored parliamentary government but were much less primarily concerned with its successful operation than were the liberals. Most republicans were bitterly anticlerical. Remembering the internecine struggle between the church and the republic during the French Revolution, and still facing the political activity of the Catholic clergy (for republicanism was most common in Catholic countries), they regarded the Catholic church as the implacable enemy of reason and liberty. Opposed to monarchy of any kind, even to constitutional monarchy, intensely hostile to church and aristocracy, conscious heirs of the great French Revolution, organized in national and international secret societies, not averse to overthrowing existing regimes by force, the more militant republicans were considered by most people, including the liberals, to be little better than anarchists.

[7] See pp. 392–393, 409.

Republicanism shaded off into socialism. Socialists generally shared the political attitudes of republicanism but added other views besides. The early socialists, those before the revolution of 1848, were of many kinds, but all had certain ideas in common. All of them regarded the existing economic system as aimless, chaotic, and outrageously unjust. All thought it improper for owners of wealth to have so much economic power—to give or deny work to the worker, to set wages and hours in their own interests, to guide all the labors of society in the interests of private profit. All therefore questioned the value of private enterprise, favoring some degree of communal ownership of productive assets—banks, factories, machines, land, and transportation. All disliked competition as a governing principle and set forth principles of harmony, coordination, organization, or association instead. All flatly and absolutely rejected the laissez faire of the liberals and the political economists. Where the latter thought mainly of increasing production, without much concern over distribution, the early socialists thought mainly of a fairer or more equal distribution of income among all useful members of society. They believed that beyond the civil and legal equality brought in by the French Revolution a further step toward social and economic equality had yet to be taken.

One of the first socialists was also one of the first cotton lords, Robert Owen (1771–1858) of Manchester and the Scottish Lowlands. Appalled at the condition of the millhands, he created a kind of model community for his own employees, paying high wages, reducing hours, sternly correcting vice and drunkenness, building schools and housing and company stores for the cheap sale of workers' necessities. From such paternalistic capitalism in his early years he passed on to a long lifetime spent in crusading for social reforms, in which he was somewhat handicapped, not only by the opposition of industrialists, but by his unpopular radicalism in matters of religion.

Most of the early socialists were Frenchmen, spurred onward by the sense of an uncompleted revolution. One was a nobleman, the Count de Saint-Simon (1760–1825), who had fought in the War of American Independence, accepted the French Revolution, and in his later years wrote many books on social problems. He and his followers, who called themselves not socialists but Saint-Simonians, were among the first clear exponents of a planned society. They advocated the public ownership of industrial equipment and other capital, with control vested in the hands of great captains of industry or social engineers, who should plan vast projects like the digging of a canal at Suez, and in general coordinate the labor and resources of society to productive ends. Of a different type was Charles Fourier (1772–1837), a somewhat doctrinaire thinker who subjected all known institutions to a sweeping condemnation. His positive program took the form of proposing that society be organized in small units which he termed "phalansteries." Each of these he conceived to contain 1,620 persons, each doing the work suited to his natural inclination. Among the practical French no phalanstery was ever successfully organized. A number were established in the United States, still the land of Europe's utopian dream; the best known, since it was operated by literary people, was the Brook Farm "movement" in Massachusetts, which ran through a troubled existence of five years from 1842 to

1847. Robert Owen also, in 1825, had founded an experimental colony in America, at New Harmony, Indiana, on the then remote and unspoiled banks of the Wabash; it, too, lasted only about five years. Such schemes, presupposing the withdrawal of select spirits to live by themselves, really had little to say on the problems of society as a whole in an industrial age.

Politically the most significant form of antediluvian socialism—before the "deluge" of 1848—was the movement stirring among the working classes of Paris, a compound of revolutionary republicanism and socialism. The politically minded Paris workingmen had been republican since 1792. For them the Revolution, in the 1820s, 1830s, 1840s, was not finished but only momentarily interrupted. Reduced to political impotence, discriminated against in their rights in the law courts, obliged to carry identity papers signed by their employers, goaded by the pressures of industrialization as it spread to France, they developed a deep hostility to the owning classes of the bourgeoisie. They found a spokesman in the Paris journalist Louis Blanc, editor of the *Revue de progrès* and author of the *Organization of Work* (1839), one of the most constructive of the early socialist writings. He proposed a system of "social workshops," or state-supported manufacturing centers, in which the workers should labor by and for themselves without the intervention of private capitalists. Of this kind of socialism we shall hear more as the story unfolds.

As for "communism," it was at this time an uncertain synonym for socialism. A small group of German revolutionaries, mainly exiles in France, took the name for themselves in the 1840s. They would have been historically forgotten had they not included Karl Marx and Friedrich Engels among their members. Marx and Engels consciously used the word in 1848 to differentiate their variety of socialism from that of such utopians as Saint-Simon, Fourier, and Owen. But the word "communism" went out of general use after 1848, to be revived after the Russian Revolution of 1917, at which time it received a new meaning.

Nationalism, since it arose so largely in reaction against the international Napoleonic system, has already been discussed in the preceding chapter.[8] It was the most pervasive and the least crystallized of the new "isms." In western Europe—Britain, France, or Spain—where national unity already existed, nationalism was not a doctrine so much as a latent state of mind, easily aroused when national interests were questioned, but normally taken for granted. Elsewhere—in Italy, Germany, Poland, the Austrian and Turkish empires—where peoples of the same nationality were politically divided or subject to foreign rule, nationalism was becoming a deliberate and conscious program. It was undoubtedly the example of the West, of Great Britain and France, successful and flourishing because they were unified nations, that stimulated the ambitions of other peoples to become unified nations too. The period after 1815 was in Germany a time of rising agitation over the national question, in Italy of the Risorgimento or "resurgence," in eastern Europe of the Slavic Revival.

[8] See pp. 442–449.

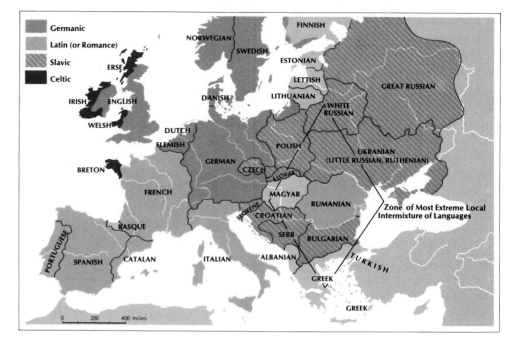

Languages of Europe. *There are three main European language-families—Germanic, Latin, and Slav. It will be seen that they cover most of Europe. Language areas are shown as they were in the first part of the twentieth century, at which time they had not changed much in over five centuries. The map cannot show local complications which have been a leading source of political trouble—such as the overlapping of adjoining languages, bilingual areas, and the existence of small language "pockets," as of Turkish in the Balkans, Greek in Asia Minor, Yiddish in Poland, or German in scattered parts of eastern Europe. For the area within the diamond-shaped zone no map on the present scale can give a realistic idea; the reader must consult an atlas. In any case, during the past decades, many language-pockets have been wiped out through exchange, transportation, or extermination of peoples.*

The movement was led by intellectuals, who often found it necessary to instill in their compatriots the very idea of nationality itself. They seized upon Herder's conception of the *Volksgeist* or national spirit, each applying it to his own people.[9] Usually they began with a cultural nationalism, holding that each people had a language, history, world view, and culture of its own, which must be preserved and perfected. They then usually passed on to a political nationalism, holding that in order to preserve this national culture, and to assure liberty and justice to its individual members, each nation should create for itself a sovereign state. Governing authorities, they held, should be of the same nationality, i.e., language, as those they governed. All persons of the same nationality, i.e., language, should be encompassed within the same state.

[9]See pp. 444–445.

Since such ideas could not be fully realized without the overthrow of every government in Europe east of France, thoroughgoing nationalism was inherently revolutionary. Outspoken nationalists were discountenanced or persecuted by the authorities and consequently formed secret societies in large numbers. The Carbonari, organized in Italy in the time of Napoleon, were the best known. There were many others, the *Veri Italiani,* the Apophasimenes, the Sublime and Perfect Masters, etc. In some regions Masonic lodges might serve the same purpose. In many of the societies nationalism was mixed with liberalism, socialism, or revolutionary republicanism in an as yet undifferentiated way. Members were initiated by a complex ritual intended to impress upon them the dire consequences of betraying the society's secrets. They used special grips and passwords and adopted revolutionary names to conceal their identity and baffle the police. They were usually so organized that the ordinary member knew the identity of only a few others, and never of the higher-ups, so that if arrested he could reveal nothing important. The societies kept busy, circulating forbidden literature and generally maintaining a revolutionary ferment. Conservatives dreaded them, but they were not really dangerous to any government that enjoyed the support of its people.

Best known of the nationalist philosophers in western Europe was the Italian Joseph Mazzini (1805–1872), who spent most of his adult life in exile in France and England. In his youth he joined the Carbonari, but in 1831 he founded a society of his own, called Young Italy, and he edited and smuggled into Italy copies of a journal of the same name. Young Italy was soon imitated by other societies of similar aim, such as Young Germany. In 1834, from a base in Switzerland, Mazzini organized a kind of filibustering expedition against the kingdom of Sardinia, hoping that all Italy would rise and join him. Undeterred by its total failure, he continued to organize, to conspire, and to write. For Mazzini nationality and revolution were a holy cause in which the most generous and humane qualities were to find expression. He was a moral philosopher, as may be judged from the title of his most widely read book, *The Duties of Man,* in which he placed a pure duty to the nation intermediate between duty to family and duty to God. Mazzini sympathized with the national aspirations of all peoples, but his own feelings went out to his own Italian homeland, which he believed had a special mission to lead humanity against oppression. Mazzini was lionized by liberals in England; but being a republican he was distrusted by liberals in Italy, many of whom hoped to unify Italy without revolution, by federation of the existing monarchical and papal states under some kind of constitutional monarchy.

To the Germans, divided and frustrated, nationality became almost an obsession. It affected everything from folklore to metaphysics. *Grimm's Fairy Tales,* for example, was first published in 1812. It was the work of the two Grimm brothers, founders of the modern science of comparative linguistics, who traveled about Germany to study the popular dialects and in doing so collected the folk tales that for generations had been current among the common people. They hoped in this way to find the ancient, native, indigenous "spirit" of Germany, deep and unspoiled in the bosom of the *Volk.* The same preoccupation with nationhood revealed itself in the philosophy of Hegel (1770–1831), possibly the most stupendous of all nineteenth-century thinkers.

To Hegel, with the spectacle of the Napoleonic years before him, it was evident that for a people to enjoy freedom, order, or dignity it must possess a potent and independent state. The state, for him, became the institutional embodiment of reason and liberty—the "march of God through the world," as he put it, meaning not an expansion in space through vulgar conquest, but a march through time and through the processes of history. Hegel conceived of reality itself as a process, an unfolding development, a growth having an inner logic and necessary sequence of its own. He thus broke with the more static and mechanical philosophy of the eighteenth century, with its fixed categories of unchangeable right and wrong. He became an evolutionary philosopher before the scientific theories of biological evolution were successfully framed. The pattern of change he held to be the "dialectic," or irresistible tendency of the mind to proceed by the creation of opposites. A given state of affairs (the "thesis") would in this view inevitably produce the conception of an opposite state of affairs (the "antithesis"), which would equally inevitably be followed by a reconciliation and a fusion of the two (the "synthesis"). Thus it could be thought that the very disunity of Germany, by producing the idea of unity, would inevitably bring about the creation of a German state.

The Hegelian dialectic was soon to be appropriated by Karl Marx to new uses, but meanwhile Hegel's philosophy, with other currents in Germany, made the study of history more philosophically meaningful than it had ever been before. History, the study of time process, seemed to be the very key with which to unlock the true significance of the world. Historical studies were stimulated, and the German universities became centers of historical learning, attracting scholars from many countries. Most eminent of the German historians was Leopold von Ranke (1795–1886), founder of the "scientific" school of historical writing. Ranke, too, though intellectually scrupulous to the last degree, owed much of his incentive to his national feeling. His first youthful work was a study of the *Latin and Teutonic Peoples;* and one of his main ideas, throughout his long life, was that Europe owed its unique greatness to the coexistence and interplay of several distinct nations, which had always resisted the attempts of any one nation to control the whole. By the latter Ranke really meant France—the France of Louis XIV and Napoleon. The Germans, said Ranke in 1830, had a mission from God to develop a culture and a political system entirely different from those of the French. They were destined to "create the pure German state corresponding to the genius of the nation." Whether Western constitutional, parliamentary, and individualist principles were suited to the national character of Germany seemed to Ranke very doubtful. The Germans, to free themselves spiritually from the French, became subtly and deeply counterrevolutionary, in that much of their most profound thought consisted in a critique of the French eighteenth-century Enlightenment and of the French Revolution and all its works.

In economics Friedrich List, in his *National System of Political Economy* (1841), came to much the same conclusion. He held that political economy as taught in England, far from being a valid science, was only a British national opinion. It was suited only to England. It was not an abstract truth but a body of ideas developed in a certain historical stage in a certain country. List thus became a founder of the historical or institutional school of economics. The doctrine of free trade, he said, was designed to make England the world's industrial center by keeping other countries in the status of suppliers of raw material and food. But any country, he held, if it was to be civilized and develop its own national culture, must have cities, factories, industries and capital of its own. It must therefore put up high tariffs (at least temporarily, in theory) to protect itself from the British, since at the moment no one else could compete with the factories that were already humming in England. List, it should be remarked, had developed his ideas during a sojourn in the United States, where Henry Clay's "American system" was in fact a national system of political economy.

In eastern Europe the Poles and the Magyars had long been active political nationalists, the Poles wishing to undo the partitions and reestablish their Polish state, the Magyars insisting on autonomy of their kingdom of Hungary within the Habsburg empire.[10] But for the most part nationalism in eastern Europe long remained more cultural than political. Centuries of development had tended to submerge the Czechs, Slovaks, Ruthenians, Rumanians, Serbs, Croats, Slovenes —and even the Poles and Magyars in lesser degree. Their upper classes spoke German or French and looked to Vienna or to Paris for their ideas. The native languages had remained peasant languages, and the cultures peasant cultures, barely known to civilized Europeans. It seemed that many of these languages would disappear, as native Irish was disappearing before English.

But early in the nineteenth century the process began to reverse itself. Patriots began to demand the preservation of their historic cultures. They collected the folk tales and ballads; they studied the languages, composing grammars and dictionaries, often for the first time; and they took to writing books in their mother tongues. They urged their own educated classes to give up "foreign" ways. They wrote histories showing the famous exploits of their several peoples in the Middle Ages. A new nationalism stirred the Magyars; in 1837 a national Hungarian theater was established at Budapest. In what was to become Rumania a former Transylvanian peasant youth named George Lazar began as early as 1816 to teach at Bucharest. He lectured in Rumanian (to the surprise of the upper classes, who preferred Greek), telling how Rumania had a distinguished history back to the Roman emperor Trajan. As for the Greeks, they entertained visions of restoring the medieval Greek empire (known to Westerners as the Byzantine Empire) in which persons of Greek language or Greek Orthodox religion should become the predominant people of the Balkans.

The most far-reaching of the east-European movements was the Slavic Revival. The Slavs included the Russians, Poles, and Ruthenians; the Czechs and Slovaks; and the South Slavs, consisting of the Slovenes, Croats, Serbs, and Bulgars. They had

[10] On the Poles, see pp. 256–261, 401; on the Magyars, pp. 232–233, 284, 343.

never had any especial consciousness of Slavdom. The Croatian Krizhanich, an early Pan-Slav of the seventeenth century, had found no response for his ideas.[11] The Napoleonic empire excited the sparsely strewn intellectuals of the Slavic world. Many were thrilled by the denouement of 1812–1814, when the mighty emperor's armies had been destroyed in Slavic Russia, and a Russian tsar had ridden in triumph into Paris.

All branches of the Slavs began to come to life. In 1814 the Serb Vuk Karajich published a grammar of his native tongue and a collection of *Popular Songs and Epics of the Serbs;* he worked out a Serbian alphabet, translated the New Testament, and declared that the dialect of Ragusa (now Dubrovnik) should become the literary language of all South Slavs. He was opposed by the Serbian clergy, who preferred to have writing confined to Slavonic, a purely learned language, like Latin; but he found much support outside Serbia, including that of the brothers Grimm. The Czechs had always been a more advanced people than the Serbs, but educated Czechs were usually half Germanized. In 1836 the historian Palacky published the first volume of his *History of Bohemia.* It was designed to give the Czechs a new pride in their national past. A widely instructed man, who knew German, French, and English, Palacky first wrote his book in German, the common reading language of educated Czechs. But he soon recast it into Czech, significantly reentitling it a *History of the Czech People.* Among Poles the poet and revolutionary Adam Mickiewicz may be mentioned. Arrested by the Russians in 1823 for membership in a secret society, he was soon allowed by the tsarist government to pass into western Europe. From 1840 to 1844 he taught Slavic languages at the Collège de France, using his lecture platform as a rostrum to deliver eloquent pleas for the liberation of all peoples and overthrow of autocracy. He wrote epic poems on Polish historical themes and continued to be active among the revolutionary Polish exiles settled in France.

Russia itself, which Poles and Czechs regarded as very backward, was slower to develop a pronounced national sense. Under the Tsar Alexander I a Western or European orientation prevailed, but in Alexander's last years and after his death the doctrines of Slavophilism began to spread. Russian Slavophilism, or the idea that Russia possessed a way of life of its own, different from and not to be corrupted by that of Europe, was simply the application to Russia of the fundamental idea of the *Volksgeist.* Such views in Russia were at least as old as the opposition to the reforms of Peter the Great.[12] In the nationalistic nineteenth century they crystallized more systematically into an "ism," and they tended to merge into Pan-Slavism, which made substantially the same assertions for the Slavic peoples as a whole. But Pan-Slavism, before 1848, was no more than embryonic.

Other "Isms"   Liberalism, radical republicanism, socialism, and nationalism were after 1815 the political forces driving Europe onward toward a future still unknown. Of other

[11] See p. 247.
[12] See pp. 255–256, 347.

"isms" less need be said. Conservatism, too, remained strong. Politically, on the Continent, conservatism upheld the institutions of absolute monarchy, aristocracy, and church and opposed the constitutional and representative government sought by liberals. As a political philosophy, conservatism built upon the ideas of Edmund Burke, who had held that every people must change its institutions by gradual adaptation, and that no people could suddenly realize in the present any freedoms not already well prepared for in the past.[13] This doctrine lacked appeal for those to whom the past had been a series of misfortunes. Conservatism sometimes passed into nationalism, since it stressed the firmness and continuity of national character. But nationalists at this time were more often liberals or republicans. "Monarchism" was conservative and even reactionary. Gone was the enlightened despotism of the last century, when kings had boldly irritated their nobles and defied their churches. After the thunders of the French Revolution aristocracy and monarchy huddled together, and their new watchword was to maintain "the throne and the altar."

Deeper than other "isms," a feeling shared in varying ways by people of all parties was the profound current of humanitarianism. It consisted in a heightened sense of the reality of cruelty inflicted upon others. Here the thought of the Age of Enlightenment suffered no reversal. Torture was gone, and even backward governments showed no inclination to restore it. Conditions in prisons, hospitals, insane asylums, and orphanages improved. People began to be moved by the misery of pauper children, chimney sweeps, women in the mines, and Negro slaves. Russian serf-owners and American slave-owners began to show psychological signs of moral doubt. To degrade a human being, use him as a work animal, torture him, confine him unjustly, hold him as a hostage for others, tear apart his family, and punish his relatives were regarded by Europeans as foreign to true civilization, something distant, "Turkish" or "Asiatic," like the castration of eunuchs, the impressment of janissaries, or the burning of widows. The Christian sense of the inviolability of the human person was now again, in a mundane way, beginning to relieve the sufferings of humanity.

I t is time now to resume the narrative of political events, broken off at the close of the last chapter with the peace settlement of 1814–1815. The governments that defeated Napoleon wanted to assure themselves above all else that the disturbances of the past twenty-five years would not be renewed. In France the restored Bourbon king, Louis XVIII, aspired to keep his throne for himself and his successors. In Great Britain the Tory governing class hoped to preserve the old England that they had so valiantly saved from the clutches of Bonaparte. In Germany, Austria, Italy, and central Europe the chief aim of Metternich, who for another thirty-three years remained the mastermind of these regions, was to maintain a system in which the prestige of the Habsburg dynasty should be supreme. The aims of the tsar, Alexander, were less clear. He was feared by representatives of the other powers as a

53
The Dike and
the Flood: Domestic

[13] See p. 393.

dreamer, a self-chosen world savior, a man who said he wanted to bring Christianity into politics, a crowned Jacobin, and even a liberal. It became one of Metternich's chief hopes to convert Alexander to conservatism.

The arrangements made by the victorious powers were in some ways moderate, at least when the provocations they had undergone in the late wars are considered. Partly by the tsar's insistence written constitutions existed after 1814 in France and in Russian or "Congress" Poland. Some of the rulers of south German states allowed a measure of representative government. Even the king of Prussia promised a representative assembly for his kingdom, though the promise was not kept. But it was difficult to maintain any kind of stability. The forces of the political right, the privileged classes (or in France the former privileged classes) denounced all signs of liberalism as dangerous concessions to revolution. Those of the political left—liberals, nationalists, republicans—regarded the newly installed regimes as hopelessly reactionary and inadequate. Statesmen were jittery on the subject of revolution, so that they met every sign of agitation with attempts at repression, which though they might drive agitation temporarily underground really only made it worse by creating additional grievances. A vicious circle was set endlessly revolving. "Kings will be tyrants from policy when subjects are rebels from principle," as Edmund Burke had sagaciously remarked in 1790; but a less conservative observer might have put the idea in reverse form with equal truth: that subjects would be rebels from principle when governments were repressive by policy. Both statements describe what happened in the years immediately following the peace of Vienna.

Reaction After 1815: France, Poland

In France Louis XVIII in 1814 granted an amnesty to the regicides of 1793. But the regicides, like all republicans, found the France of 1814 an uncomfortable place to live in, exposed as they were to the unofficial vengeance of counterrevolutionaries, and in 1815 most of them rallied to Napoleon when he returned from Elba. This exasperated the royalist counterrevolutionaries beyond all measure. A brutal "white terror" broke out. Upper-class youths murdered Bonapartists and republicans, Catholic mobs seized and killed Protestants at Marseilles and Toulouse. The Chamber of Deputies chosen in 1815 (by the tiny electorate of 100,000 well-to-do landowners) proved to be more royalist than the king—*plus royaliste que le roi*. The king himself could not control the mounting frenzy of reaction, which he was sensible enough to realize would only infuriate the revolutionary element still further, as in fact happened. In 1820 a fanatical workingman assassinated the king's nephew, the Duke de Berry. Those who said that all partisans of the French Revolution were criminal extremists seemed to be justified. The reaction deepened, until in 1824 Louis XVIII died and was succeeded by his brother Charles X. Not only was Charles X the father of the recently murdered Duke de Berry, but for over thirty years he had been the acknowledged leader of implacable counterrevolution. As the Count of Artois, youngest brother of Louis XVI, he had been among the first to emigrate in 1789. He had always remained the leader of the émigrés during the Revolution and was in fact the favorite Bourbon among the most obstinate ex-seigneurs, nobles, and churchmen. He regarded himself as hereditary absolute monarch by the grace of God, had himself crowned as Reims with all the romantic pomp of ages past, and proceeded to stamp out not only revolutionary republicanism but liberalism and constitutionalism as well.

In Poland, it will be recalled, the Vienna settlement created a constitutional kingdom, with Alexander as king, joined in merely personal union with the Russian empire. The new machinery did not work very well. The Polish constitution provided for an elected diet, a very wide suffrage by the standards of the day, the Napoleonic civil code, freedom of press and religion, and exclusive use of the Polish language. But the Poles discovered that Alexander, though favoring liberty, did not like to have anyone disagree with him. They could make little use of their much touted freedom in any actual legislation. The elected diet could not get along with the viceroy, who was a Russian. In Russia the serf-owning aristocracy viewed Alexander's idea of a constitutional kingdom in Poland with a jaundiced eye. They wanted no experimentation with liberty on the very borders of Russia. The Poles themselves played into the hands of their enemies. For the Poles were nationalist at least as much as they were liberal. They were dissatisfied with the boundaries accorded to Congress Poland. They dreamed of the vast kingdom that had existed before the First Partition and so agitated the interminable question of the Eastern Border, laying claim to huge territories in the Ukraine and White Russia.[14] Alexander actually took steps to transfer parts of the Eastern Border to Poland; to him it made no difference, so long as he ruled both Poland and Russia, but it produced a violent reaction among the Russians. At the University of Vilna, in the Border region, the tsar himself encouraged the systematic study of Polish culture and history. He was dismayed when professors and students began to join secret societies. Some members of these societies were revolutionaries aiming at driving out Alexander, reuniting with Prussian and Austrian Poland, and reconstituting an independent Polish state. It was in the discovery and breaking up of one such society, the Philarets of Vilna, that Adam Mickiewicz was arrested in 1823. Reaction and repression now struck the University of Vilna.

In Germany those who had felt national stirrings during the Wars of Liberation were disillusioned by the peace treaty, which maintained the several German principalities about as Napoleon had left them and purposely united them only in a loose federation or Bund. National ideas were most common in the numerous universities, where students and professors were more susceptible than most people to the doctrines of an eternal *Volksgeist* and a far-flung *Deutschtum*. National ideas, being a glorification of the German common people, carried with them a kind of liberal-democratic opposition to aristocrats, princes, and kings. Students in many of the universities in 1815 formed college clubs, called collectively the *Burschenschaft,*

[14] See map, p. 259.

which, as centers of serious political discussion, were to replace the older clubs devoted to drinking and dueling. The *Burschenschaft,* a kind of German youth movement, held a nation-wide congress at Wartburg in 1817. Students listened to rousing speeches by patriotic professors, marched about in "Teutonic" costume, and burned a few reactionary books. This undergraduate performance was no immediate threat to any established state, but the nervous governments took alarm. In 1819 a theology student assassinated the German writer Kotzebue, known as an informer in the service of the tsar. The assassin received hundreds of letters of congratulation, and at Nassau the head of the local government barely escaped the same fate at the hands of a pharmacy student.

Metternich now chose to intervene. He had no authority in Germany except in that Austria was a member of the Germanic federation. He regarded all these manifestations of German national spirit, or of any demand for a more solidly unified Germany, as a threat to the favorable position of the Austrian Empire and to the whole balance of Europe. He called a conference of the principal German states at Carlsbad in Bohemia; the frightened conferees adopted certain resolutions, proposed by Metternich, which were soon enacted by the diet of the Bund. These Carlsbad Decrees (1819) dissolved the *Burschenschaft* and the equally nationalistic gymnastic clubs (some of whose members thereupon joined secret societies); and they provided for government officials to be placed in the universities to watch them and for censors to control the contents of books and of the periodical and newspaper press. The Carlsbad Decrees remained in force for many years, and they imposed a rather effective check on the growth of liberal and nationalist ideas in Germany, especially since they seem not to have been very strongly resisted by any substantial element of the population.

Metternich was unable to persuade the south German rulers to retract the constitutions they had granted. The rulers here, in Bavaria, Württemberg, and elsewhere, found that with representative government they could rally popular support as well as assimilate the numerous new territories that they had obtained from Napoleon. But in general, throughout Germany, after 1820, repression of new or unsettling ideas was the rule. Still more so was this true of the Austrian Empire, which Metternich could more directly control. So manifold were the regulations governing Austrian intercourse with the outside world, so rigid was Metternich's stand against change or innovation of any kind, that Austria came to be known as the China of Europe.

Nor did Great Britain escape the dreary rounds of agitation and repression. As elsewhere, radicalism produced reaction, and vice versa. Britain after Waterloo was still a country of the old regime but one afflicted by the most advanced social evils. In 1815, at the close of the wars, the landed classes feared an inrush of imported agricultural products and consequent collapse of farm prices and rentals. The gentry who controlled Parliament enacted a new Corn Law, raising the protective tariff on imports of grains to the point where importation became impossible unless prices were very high. Landlords and their farmers benefited, but wage earners found the price of breadstuffs soaring out of reach. At the same time there was a postwar depression in industry. Wages fell and many were thrown out of work. These conditions naturally contributed to the spread of political radicalism, which looked first of all to a drastic reform of the House of Commons, in order that thereafter a radical program of social and economic legislation might be enacted.

A riot broke out in London in December 1816. In the following February the Prince Regent was attacked in his carriage. The government suspended habeas corpus and employed *agents provocateurs* to obtain evidence against the agitators. Industrialists of Manchester and the new factory towns, determined to force through the reform of parliamentary representation, took the chance offered by the distress of the working classes to organize mass meetings of protest. At Birmingham a crowd elected a mock member of Parliament. At sprawling Manchester 80,000 people staged an enormous demonstration at St. Peter's Fields in 1819; they demanded universal male suffrage, annual election of the House of Commons, and the repeal of the Corn Laws. Although perfectly orderly they were fired upon by soldiers; 11 persons were killed and about 400 wounded, including 113 women. Radicals called this episode the Peterloo massacre in derisive comparison with the battle of Waterloo. The frightened government thanked the soldiers for their brave upholding of the social order. Parliament rushed through the Six Acts (1819), which outlawed "seditious and blasphemous" literature, put a heavy stamp tax on newspapers, authorized the search of private houses for arms, and rigidly restricted the right of public meeting. A group of revolutionaries thereupon plotted to assassinate the whole cabinet at a dinner; they were caught in Cato Street in London in 1820—whence the name "Cato Street Conspiracy." Five of them were hanged. Meanwhile, for publishing the writings of Thomas Paine, Richard Carlisle spent seven years in prison.

"Our example," wrote the Duke of Wellington to a Continental correspondent in 1819, "will be of value in France and Germany, and it is to be hoped that the world will escape from the general revolution with which we all seem to be threatened."

In summary, reactionary policies entrenched themselves everywhere in the years following the peace. The reaction was due only in part to memories of the French Revolution. It was due even more to the living fear of revolution in the present. This fear, though exaggerated, was no mere hallucination. Sensing the rising flood, the established interests desperately built dikes against it in every country. The same is true of international politics at the time.

A t the Congress of Vienna the powers agreed to hold meetings in the future to enforce the treaty and take up new issues as they arose. A number of congresses of the Great Powers resulted, which are of significance as an experimental step toward international regulation of the affairs of Europe. The congresses resembled, in a tentative and partial way, the League of Nations that arose after the First World War of 1914–1918, or the United Nations that arose during and after the war of 1939–1945. The powers had also, in 1815, in alarm after the return of Napoleon,

54
The Dike and the
Flood: International

subscribed to Alexander I's Holy Alliance, which became the popular term for the collaboration of the European states in the congresses.[15]   The Holy Alliance, on the face of it a statement of Christian purpose and international concord, gradually became an alliance for the suppression of revolutionary and even liberal activity, following in that respect the trend of the governments which made it up.

The Congress of Aix-la-Chapelle, 1818

The first general postwar assemblage of the powers took place at the Congress of Aix-la-Chapelle (or Aachen) in 1818.   The principal item on the agenda was to withdraw the allied army of occupation from France.   The French argued that Louis XVIII would never be popular in France so long as he was supported by a foreign army.   The other powers, since they all desired the French to forget the past and accept the Bourbons, withdrew their military forces without disagreement.   They arranged also to have private bankers take over the French reparations debt (the 700,000,000 francs imposed by the second treaty of Paris); the bankers paid the allied governments, and the French in due time paid the bankers.   On a few other smaller matters international collective action proved successful.   The congress heard a request from the elector of Hesse, who asked that he be granted the title of king, arguing that the title of elector was meaningless since the dissolution of the Holy Roman Empire, and that the former electors of Bavaria, Saxony, and Hanover now were kings.   His request was refused.   The congress also considered a plea from Napoleon's mother, who urged that her sick son be allowed to return to Europe.   It was decided to keep Napoleon at St. Helena.

The Tsar Alexander was still the most advanced internationalist of the day.   He suggested at Aix-la-Chapelle a kind of permanent European union and even proposed the maintenance of international military forces to safeguard recognized states against changes by violence.   Governments if thus reassured against revolution, he argued, would more willingly grant constitutional and liberal reforms. But the others demurred, especially the British foreign minister Lord Castlereagh. The British declared themselves willing to make international commitments against specified contingencies, such as a revival of aggression on the part of France.   But they would assume no obligations to act upon indefinite and unforeseeable future events.   They reserved the right of independent judgment in foreign policy. Concretely, the congress addressed itself to the problems of the Atlantic slave trade and of the recurring nuisance of the Barbary pirates.   It was unanimously agreed that both should be suppressed.   To suppress them required naval forces, which only the British possessed in adequate amount, and it meant also that naval captains must be authorized to stop and search vessels at sea.   The Continental states, always touchy on the subject of British sea power, refused to countenance any such uses of the British fleet. They feared for the freedom of the seas.   As for the British, they would not even discuss placing British warships in an international naval pool or putting

[15]See pp. 459–460.

British squadrons under the authority of an international body. Nothing therefore was done; the slave trade continued, booming illicitly with the endless demand for cotton; and the Barbary pirates were not disposed of until the French occupied and annexed Algeria some years later. The growth of international institutions was blocked by the separate interests of the sovereign states.

Scarcely had the Congress of Aix-la-Chapelle disbanded when revolutionary agitation came to a crisis in southern Europe. It was not that revolutionary or liberal sentiment was stronger here than in the north, in the sense of having more followers, but rather that the governments in question, those of Spain, Naples, and the Ottoman Empire, were inefficient, ignorant, flimsy, and corrupt. In 1820 the governments of Spain and Naples collapsed with remarkable ease before the demonstrations of the revolutionaries. The kings of both countries reluctantly took oaths to the Spanish constitution of 1812, itself modeled on the French revolutionary constitution of 1789–1791.[16]

Metternich considered Italy, since the ejection of Napoleon, to be within the legitimate sphere of influence of the Austrian Empire. He saw the insurrections as the first symptoms of a new revolutionary seizure against which Europe should be quarantined. It was a fact that revolutionary agitation was international, easily leaping across frontiers, because of the operations of secret societies and of political exiles, and because in any case the same ideas had been aroused in all countries by the French Revolution. Metternich therefore called a meeting of the Great Powers at Troppau, hoping to use the authority of an international congress to put down the revolution in Naples. The governments of Great Britain and France, not eager to play Austria's game, sent only observers to the congress. Metternich's main problem was, as usual, Alexander. What would be the attitude of the liberal tsar, the friend and patron of constitutions, toward the idea of a constitutional monarchy in Naples? At an inn in Troppau Metternich and Alexander met alone, and there held a momentous interview over the tea cups. Metternich reviewed the horrors of revolutionism, the unwisdom of granting any concessions lest revolutionaries be encouraged. Alexander was already somewhat disillusioned by the ungrateful feelings of the Poles. He was troubled by rumors of disaffection among officers in his own army. He had always believed that constitutions should be granted by legitimate sovereigns, not extorted from them by revolutionaries, as had happened in Naples. He allowed himself to be persuaded by Metternich. He declared that he had always been wrong, and that Metternich had always been right; and he announced himself ready to follow Metternich's political judgment. The triumph of the Austrian chancellor was complete. The radical tsar now turned reactionary.

Thus fortified, Metternich drew up a document, the protocol of Troppau, for consideration and acceptance by the five Great Powers. It held that all recognized

[16] See pp. 387–388.

European states should be protected by collective international action, and in the interests of general peace and stability, from internal changes brought about by force. The protocol read:

States belonging to the European alliance, which have undergone in their internal structure an alteration brought about by revolt, whose consequences may be dangerous to other states, cease automatically to be members of the alliance. [If such states] cause neighboring states to feel an immediate danger, and if action by the Great Powers can be effective and beneficial, the Great Powers will take steps to bring the disturbed area back into the European system, first of all by friendly representations, and secondly by force if force becomes necessary to this end.

The protocol was a statement of collective security against revolution. Neither France nor Great Britain accepted it. Castlereagh wrote to Metternich that if Austria felt her interests to be threatened in Naples she should intervene in her own name only. It was not the repression of the Neapolitan revolution that the Tories of 1820 objected to, so much as the principle of a binding international collaboration. Metternich could get only Russia and Prussia to endorse his protocol, in addition to Austria. These three, acting as the Congress of Troppau, authorized Metternich to dispatch an Austrian army into Naples. He did so; the Neapolitan revolutionaries were arrested or put to flight; the incompetent and brutal Ferdinand I was restored as "absolute" king; the demon of revolution was seemingly exorcised. Reaction won out. But the Congress of Troppau, ostensibly a Europe-wide international body, had in effect functioned as an antirevolutionary alliance of Austria, Russia, and Prussia. A gap opened between the three Eastern autocracies and the two Western powers—even when the latter consisted of Tories and Bourbons.

Spain, Spanish America, the Near East: Verona, 1822

Thousands of revolutionaries and liberals fled from the terror raging in Italy. Many went to Spain, now dreaded by conservatives as the main seat of revolutionary infection. During the Napoleonic domination of Spain, a few Spanish Americans had seized the opportunity to launch the rebellions that led to wars of independence in both North and South America. In the years before 1815, Simon Bolívar and other leaders long dissatisfied with Spanish colonial rule and influenced by the examples of the American and French revolutions had temporarily established independent states. After major setbacks, these independence movements slowly recovered during the years after 1816. To crush the rebellions in America and regain absolute power in Spain became the twin objectives of the Spanish king.

The Near East also seemed about to ignite in conflagration. Alexander Ypsilanti, a Greek who had spent his adult life in the military service of Russia, in 1821 led a band of armed followers from Russia into Rumania (still a part of Turkey), hoping that all Greeks and pro-Greeks in the Turkish empire would join him. He expected Russian support, since the penetration of Turkey by the use of Greek Christians had long been a pet project of Russian foreign policy. The possibility of a Turkish empire converted into a "Greek" empire and dependent on Russia was naturally unpleasant to Metternich. To deal with all these matters an international congress met at Verona in 1822.

Alexander, in shifting from liberal to reactionary views, had not changed his belief in the need of international government. Had pure power politics determined his decisions he would doubtless have favored Ypsilanti's Grecophile revolution. But he stood by the principle of international solidarity against revolutionary violence. He disowned Ypsilanti, who found less enthusiasm for Greek culture among the Rumanians and Balkan peoples than he had expected and was soon defeated by the Turks. As for intervention to repress the Greek uprising, the question did not arise, since the Turkish government proved quite able for a time to handle the matter itself.

Further to advance the cause of international solidarity Alexander urged that the Congress of Verona mediate between Spain and its revolting colonies. This was a euphemistic way of suggesting military intervention in Spanish America, following the principle of the protocol of Troppau. The British objected. They had penetrated the Spanish empire commercially for over a century. During the Napoleonic wars they had increased their exports to Latin America twentyfold.[17] This advantage they intended to retain, and even the Tory government favored the break-up of the Spanish empire into independent states, with which free-trade treaties might be negotiated. Without at least benevolent neutrality from the British fleet no armed force could sail to America. The Spanish Americans therefore maintained their independence, thanks in part to the use made by the British of their sea power on this occasion.

The new republics received strong moral support from the United States also. In December 1823 President James Monroe, in a message to Congress, announced the "Monroe Doctrine." It stated that attempts by European powers to return parts of America to colonial status would be viewed as an unfriendly act by the United States. The British foreign minister George Canning (who had just succeeded Castlereagh) had at first proposed a joint statement by Great Britain and the United States against the Eastern powers on the Spanish American question. President Monroe, at the advice of his secretary of state John Quincy Adams, decided instead to make a unilateral statement in the form of a message to Congress. They intended to aim their "doctrine" at Great Britain as well as the Continental states, since the British, with their command of the sea, were in fact the only power by which the independence of American states could in practice be threatened. Canning, having no such threats in mind, and concerned more with the Congress of Verona, accepted the line taken by the United States. Indeed, he declared with a flourish that he had "called the New World into existence to redress the balance of the Old." The Monroe Doctrine, at its inception, was a kind of counterblast to the Metternich doctrine of the protocol of Troppau. Where the latter announced the principle of intervention against revolution, the Monroe Doctrine announced that revolutions in America, if they resulted in regimes recognized by the United States, were outside the

[17] See p. 442.

pale of attention by European powers. In any case the efficacy of the Monroe Doctrine long depended on the tacit cooperation of the British fleet.

The question of the revolution in Spain was settled in a different way. The Bourbon regime in France had no taste for a Spain in which revolutionaries, republicans, political exiles, and members of secret societies might be harbored. The French government proposed to the Congress of Verona that it be authorized to dispatch an army across the Pyrenees. The Congress welcomed the offer, and despite many dire predictions of ruin, arising from memories of Napoleon's disaster, a French army of 200,000 men moved into Spain in 1823. The campaign proved to be a military promenade through a cheering country. Not many Spanish liberals, constitutionalists, or revolutionaries could be found. The mass of the people saw the invasion as a deliverance from Masons, Carbonari, and heretics and shouted with satisfaction at the restoration of church and king. Ferdinand VII, unscrupulous and narrow-minded, repudiated his constitutional oath and let the vindictive ecclesiastics, grandees, and hidalgos have their way. The late revolutionaries were savagely persecuted, exiled, or jailed.

The End of the Congress System

After the Congress of Verona no more such meetings were held. The attempt at a formal international regulation of European affairs was given up. In the broadest retrospect, the congresses failed to make progress toward an international order because, especially after Alexander's conversion to conservatism, they came to stand for nothing except preservation of the status quo. They made no attempt at accommodation with the new forces that were shaping Europe. It was not the policy of the congresses to forestall revolution by demanding that governments institute reforms. They simply repressed or punished all revolutionary agitation. They propped up governments that could not stand on their own feet. They supported the reactionary Bourbon monarchies of Spain and Naples, corrupt regimes that were too unsteady to hold up against small handfuls of revolutionaries, and which were becoming an offense to the moral conscience of the European world.

In any case the congresses never succeeded in subordinating the separate interests of the Great Powers. Perhaps Alexander's repudiation of Ypsilanti was a sacrifice of Russian advantage to international principle; but when the Austrian government intervened to crush the revolution in Naples, and when the French government crushed the revolution in Spain, though in both cases they acted with an international mandate, each was really promoting what it conceived to be its own interests. The interest of Great Britain was to pull away from the system entirely. As defined by Castlereagh and by Canning after him, it was to stand aloof from permanent international commitments, to preserve a free exercise of sea power and foreign policy, and to take a benevolent view toward revolution in other countries. Since France eventually pulled away also, the Holy Alliance ceased to be even ostensibly a European system and became no more than a counterrevolutionary league between the three Eastern autocracies. With a majority of the five Great Powers highly illiberal, the cause of liberalism in Europe was advanced by the collapse of the international system. At the same time the collapse of the system opened the way to the uncontrolled nationalism of the sovereign states. "Things are getting back to a wholesome state again," wrote George Canning in 1822; "Every nation for itself and God for us all!"

Alexander I, "the man who defeated Napoleon," the ruler who had led his armies from Moscow to Paris, who had frightened the diplomats by the Russian shadow that he threw over the Continent, and who yet in his way had been the great pillar of constitutional liberalism and international order, died at Taganrog in 1825. His death was the signal for revolution in Russia. Officers of the Russian army, during the campaigns of 1812–1815 in Europe, had become acquainted with many unsettling ideas. Secret societies were formed even in the Russian officer corps; their members held all sorts of conflicting ideas, some wanting a constitutional tsardom in Russia, some demanding a republic, some even dreaming of an emancipation of the serfs. When Alexander died it was for a time uncertain which of his two brothers, Constantine or Nicholas, should succeed him. The restless coteries in the army preferred Constantine, who was thought to be more favorable to innovations in the state. In December 1825 they proclaimed Constantine at St. Petersburg, having their soldiers shout "Constantine and Constitution!" The soldiers, it is said, thought that Constitution was Constantine's wife. But the fact was that Constantine had long before abdicated in favor of Nicholas, who was the rightful heir. The uprising, known as the Decembrist revolt, was soon put down. Five of the mutinous officers were hanged; many others were condemned to forced labor or interned in Siberia. The Decembrist revolt was the first manifestation of the modern revolutionary movement in Russia—of a revolutionary movement inspired by an ideological program, as distinguished from the elemental mass upheavals of Pugachev or Stephen Razin. But the immediate effect of the Decembrist revolt was to clamp repression upon Russia more firmly. Nicholas I (1825–1855) maintained an unconditional and despotic autocracy.

Ten years after the defeat of Napoleon the new forces issuing from the French Revolution seemed to be routed, and reaction, repression, and political immobility seemed everywhere to have prevailed. The dike—a massive dike—seemed to be containing the flood.

The dike broke in 1830, nor in western Europe was the stream thereafter stopped. The seepage, indeed, had already begun. By 1825 Spanish America was independent. The British and the French had pulled away from the congress system. The Greek nationalist movement against the Turks had broken out in the early 1820s.

With the defeat of Ypsilanti in 1821 the Greek nationalists turned somewhat away from the idea of a neo-Greek empire and more toward the idea of independence for Greece proper, the islands and peninsulas where Greek was the predominant language. The Tsar Nicholas was more willing than Alexander to assist this movement. The governments of Great Britain and France were not inclined to let Russia stand as the only champion of Balkan peoples. Moreover, liberals in the West thought of the embattled Greeks as ancient Athenians fighting the modern oriental despotism of the Turkish empire.

The result was a joint Anglo-French-Russian naval intervention, which destroyed the Turkish fleet at Navarino Bay in 1827. Russia again, as often in the past, sent armies into the Balkans. A Russo-Turkish war and a great Near Eastern crisis followed, in the course of which the rival powers agreed in 1829 to recognize Greece as an independent kingdom. The Balkan states of Serbia, Wallachia, and Moldavia were also recognized as autonomous principalities within the badly shaken Ottoman Empire.[18] From the same crisis Egypt emerged as an autonomous region under Mohammed Ali. Egypt in time became a center of Arabic nationalism, which cut down Ottoman power in the south just as Balkan nationalism did in the north.

France, 1824–1830: The July Revolution, 1830

It was in 1830, and first of all in France, that the wall of reaction really collapsed. Charles X became king in 1824.[19] In the next year the legislative chambers voted an indemnity, in the form of perpetual annuities totaling 30,000,000 francs a year, to those who as émigrés thirty-odd years before had had their property confiscated by the revolutionary state. Catholic clergy began to take over classrooms in the schools. A law pronounced the death penalty for sacrilege committed in church buildings. But the France of the restored Bourbons was still a free country, and against these apparent efforts to revive the Old Regime a strong opposition developed in the newspapers and in the chambers. In March 1830 the Chamber of Deputies, in which the bankers Laffitte and Casimir-Périer led the "leftist" opposition, passed a vote of no-confidence in the government. The king, as was his legal right, dissolved

[18]See maps, pp. 456–457, 684.
[19]See pp. 484–485.

Liberty Leading the People *by Eugène Delacroix (French, 1798–1863)*
Delacroix, a founder of the romantic school of painting, painted this picture soon after the July Revolution in Paris in 1830 (see pp. 494–496). It well illustrates the idealistic conception of revolution which prevailed among revolutionaries before 1848, in sharp contrast to the "realistic," "scientific," or "materialistic" conception of revolution that set in after 1848 and was typified by Karl Marx. (See pp. 534–535, 537–542.) Revolution is shown as a noble and moral act. The figures express determination and courage, but show no sign of hatred or even anger. They are not a class (note how the costume varies from the top hat to the semi-nude); they are the People, affirming the rights of man. Liberty, holding the tricolor aloft, is a composed and even rational goddess. Romantic though the painter was, he represents the insurgents as realizing an abstract idea—Liberty or the Republic. It is to this idea that the half-recumbent and presumably wounded figure directs his gaze. Courtesy of the Louvre (Giraudon).

the Chamber and called for new elections. The elections repudiated the king's policies. He replied on July 26, 1830, with four ordinances issued on his own authority. One dissolved the newly elected Chamber before it had ever met; another imposed censorship on the press; the third so amended the suffrage as to reduce the voting power of bankers, merchants, and industrialists and to concentrate it in the hands of the old-fashioned aristocracy; the fourth called for a new election on the new basis.

These July Ordinances produced on the very next day the July Revolution. The upper bourgeois class was of course desperate at being thus brazenly ousted from political life. But it was the republicans—the nucleus of revolutionary workingmen, students, and intelligentsia in Paris—that actually moved. For three days, from July 27 to 29, barricades were thrown up in the city, behind which a swarming populace defied the army and the police. Most of the army refused to fire. Charles X, in no mood to be made captive by a revolution like his long-dead brother Louis XVI, precipitately abdicated and headed for England.

The revolutionary students and workingmen wished to proclaim a democratic republic. The bankers, merchants, and industrialists thought differently. They had been satisfied in general with the constitutional charter of 1814; it was only to the policies and personnel of the government that they had objected, and they wished now to continue with constitutional monarchy, somewhat liberalized, and with a king whom they could trust. A solution to the deadlock was found by the elderly Marquis de Lafayette, the aging hero of the American and the French revolutions, who now came forward as symbol of national unity. Lafayette produced the Duke of Orleans on the balcony of the Paris Hôtel de Ville, embraced him before a great concourse of people, and offered him as the answer to France's need. The duke was a collateral relative of the Bourbons; he had also, as a young man, fought in the republican army of 1792. The militant republicans accepted him, willing to see what would develop; and the Chamber on August 7 offered him the throne, on condition that he observe faithfully the constitutional charter of 1814. He reigned, until 1848, under the title of Louis-Philippe.

The regime of Louis-Philippe, called the Orleanist, bourgeois, or July monarchy, was viewed very differently by different groups in France and in Europe. To the other states of Europe and to the clergy and legitimists within France, it seemed shockingly revolutionary. The new king owed his throne to an insurrection, to a

Big Investments *by Honoré Daumier (French, 1808–1879)*
The Revolution of 1830, romanticized by Delacroix, was in fact followed by a period of money-making and business ferment (as well as genuine economic development) made famous in the novels of Balzac and the graphic art of Daumier. This lithograph of 1837 shows a financier, with bundles of stock certificates piled beside him, offering to sell shares in factories, foundries, breweries, etc., to a skeptical client. Daumier was a satirist and caricaturist of bourgeois society. Where Rembrandt in the seventeenth century could portray businessmen with a high seriousness (as on p. 169 above), artists since the 1830s have been generally alienated from such subjects. Courtesy of

the Bibliothèque Nationale, Paris.

Grand placement d'actions.

aujourd'hui de bien bonnes actions à placer! Mr Desrognures, en voulez vous? — C'est selon. Ça avez-vous en actions?
— 3000 actions de fonderies. — Affaire fondue! — 3000 actions des usines — Use use! — 10.000 actions des
... opérations magnifiques — ... faites les mousser! — J'ai ai du recueil des connaissances. — Connu...
... Enfin combien cela fait-il en bloc — Un milliard ou deux pas plus — Un milliard ... le papier...
... cela doit donner ... livres à 4 sous ... ça vaut 3 francs — Deux milliards poser 2 francs
... vous mon cher? — Mettez au moins 25 francs! — Pas un liard. — Allons enlevez. Vous faites
... che à or. — Sacreué vous ne dites tous les jours la même chose

bargain made with republicans, and to promises made to a parliament. He called himself not king of France but king of the French, and he flew not the Bourbon lily but the tricolor flag of the Revolution. The latter produced an effect on the established classes not unlike that of the hammer and sickle of a later day. He cultivated a popular manner, wore sober dark clothing (the ancestor of the modern "business suit"), and carried an umbrella. Though in private he worked stubbornly to maintain his royal position, in public he adhered scrupulously to the constitution.

The constitution remained substantially what it had been in 1814. The main political change was one of tone; there would be no more absolutism, with its notion that constitutional guarantees could be abrogated by a reigning prince. Legally the main change was that the Chamber of Peers ceased to be hereditary, to the chagrin of the old nobility, and that the Chamber of Deputies was to be elected by a somewhat enlarged body of voters. Where before 1830 there had been 100,000 voters, there were now about 200,000. The right to vote was still based on the ownership of a considerable quantity of real estate. About one-thirtieth of the adult male population (the top thirtieth in the possession of real property) now elected the Chamber of Deputies. The beneficiaries of the new system were the upper bourgeoisie—the bankers, merchants, and industrialists. The big property-owners constituted the *pays légal,* the "legal country," and to them the July monarchy was the consummation and stopping place of political progress. To others, and especially to the radical democrats, it proved as the years passed to be a disillusionment and an annoyance.

Revolutions of 1830:
Belgium, Poland,
and Elsewhere

The immediate effect of the three-day Paris revolution of 1830 was to set off a series of similar explosions throughout Europe. These in turn, coming after the collapse of the Bourbons in France, brought the whole peace settlement of 1815 into jeopardy. It will be recalled that the Congress of Vienna had joined Belgium with the Dutch Netherlands to create a strong buffer state against a resurgent France and had also done what it could to prevent direct pressure of Russian power upon central Europe by way of Poland.[20] Both these arrangements were now undone.

The Dutch-Belgian union proved economically beneficial, for Belgian industry complemented the commercial and shipping activity of the Dutch, but politically it worked very poorly, especially since the Dutch king had absolutist and centralizing ideas. The Belgians, though they had never been independent, had always stood stiffly for their local liberties under former Austrian rulers (and Spanish before them); now they did the same against the Dutch. The Catholic Belgians disliked Dutch Protestantism; those Belgians who spoke French (the Walloons) objected to regulations requiring the use of Dutch. About a month after the July Revolution in Paris disturbances broke out in Brussels. The leaders asked only for local Belgian self-government, but when the king took arms against them they went on to proclaim independence. A national assembly met and drafted a constitution.

Nicholas of Russia wished to send troops to stamp out the Belgian uprising. But he could not get his forces safely through Poland. In Poland, too, in 1830, a

[20]See pp. 455–458.

revolution broke out. The Polish nationalists saw in the fall of the French Bourbons a timely moment for them to strike. They objected also to the appearance of Russian troops bound presumably to suppress freedom in western Europe. One incident led to another, until in January 1831 the Polish diet proclaimed the dethronement of the Polish king (i.e., Nicholas), who thereupon sent in a large army. The Poles, outnumbered and divided among themselves, could put up no successful resistance. They obtained no support from the West. The British government was unsettled by agitation at home. The French government, newly installed under Louis-Philippe, had no wish to appear disturbingly revolutionary, and in any case feared the Polish agents who besought its backing as international firebrands and republicans. The Polish revolution was therefore crushed. Congress Poland disappeared; its constitution was abrogated, and it was merged into the Russian empire. Thousands of Poles settled in western Europe, where they became familiar figures in republican circles. In Poland the engines of repression rolled. The tsar's government exiled some thousands to Siberia, began to Russify the Eastern Border, and closed the universities of Warsaw and Vilna. Since meanwhile it was too late for the tsar any longer to contemplate intervention in Belgium, it may be said that the sacrifice of the Poles contributed to the success of the west-European revolution of 1830, as it had done to that of the great French Revolution of 1789–1795.[21]

It was true enough, as Nicholas maintained, that an independent Belgium presented great international problems. Belgium for twenty years before 1815 had been part of France. A few Belgians now favored reunion with it, and in France the republican left, which regarded the Vienna treaty as an insult to the French nation, saw an opportunity to win back this first and dearest conquest of the First Republic. In 1831, by a small majority, the Belgian national assembly elected as their king the son of Louis-Philippe, who, however, not wishing trouble with the British, forbade his son to accept it. The Belgians thereupon elected Leopold of Saxe-Coburg, a German princeling who had married into the British royal family and become a British subject. He was in fact the uncle of a twelve-year-old girl who was to be Queen Victoria. The British negotiated with Talleyrand, sent over by the French government (it was his last public service); and the result was a treaty of 1831 (confirmed in 1839) setting up Belgium as a perpetually neutral state, incapable of forming alliances and guaranteed against invasion by all five of the Great Powers. The aim intended by the treaty of Vienna, to prevent the annexation of Belgium to France, was thus again realized in a new way. Internally Belgium presently settled down to a stable parliamentary system, somewhat more democratic than the July monarchy in France but fundamentally offering the same type of bourgeois and liberal rule.

Revolutionary disturbances also took place in 1830 in Germany, Italy, Switzerland, Spain, and Portugal. To trace them in any detail is not necessary. In a word, a greater measure of liberalism was established in Switzerland; Spain entered a long period of tortuous parliamentary development confused by civil wars, which arose from a disputed succession to the throne; and in Italy and Germany the 1830

[21] See pp. 400, 405, and map on p. 259.

uprisings were quickly put down, showing only the continuance of a radical dissatisfaction still held in check by the authorities. It was in Great Britain that sweeping changes really came.

Reform in Great Britain

The three-day Paris revolution of 1830 had direct repercussions across the Channel. The quick results following on working-class insurrection gave radical leaders in England the idea that threats of violence might be useful. On the other hand, the ease and speed with which the French bourgeoisie gained the upper hand reassured the British middle classes, who concluded that they might unsparingly embarrass the government without courting a mass upheaval.

The Tory regime in England had in fact already begun to loosen up. A group of younger men came forward in the 1820s in the Tory party, notably George Canning, the foreign minister, and Robert Peel, son of one of the first cotton manufacturers.[22] This group was sensitive to the needs of British business and to the doctrines of liberalism.[23] They began to clear out the untended garden of antiquated laws. They abolished capital punishment for about a hundred different offenses. They introduced a professional police force in London in place of the old "watch"—it is after Robert Peel that London policemen are called "bobbies." They allowed an opening wedge for the organization of labor unions. They reduced tariff duties and liberalized the old Navigation Acts, permitting British colonies to trade with countries other than Britain. By repealing certain old statutes, they made it lawful for skilled workmen to emigrate from England, taking their skills with them to foreign parts, and for manufacturers to export machinery to foreign countries, even though English industrial secrets would thus be given away. By such measures they advanced the liberal conception of a freely exchanging international economic system; they moved toward freedom of trade. The Liberal Tories also undermined the legal position of the Church of England, forwarding the conception of a secular state, though such was hardly their purpose. They repealed the old laws (which dated from the seventeenth century) forbidding dissenting Protestants to hold public office except through a legal fiction by which they pretended to be Anglicans.[24] They even allowed the Test Act of 1673 to be repealed and Catholic Emancipation to be carried. Catholics in both Great Britain and Ireland received the same rights as others; or rather, the old Catholic-Protestant issue at last became immaterial in a constitutional sense. The gulf between Anglican and Dissenter likewise ceased to have legal sanction, though it remained important in English social life.

There were two things that the Liberal Tories could not do. They could not question the Corn Laws, and they could not reform the House of Commons. By the Corn Laws, the tariff on imported grain, raised to new heights in 1815, the gentlemen of England protected their rent rolls; and by the existing structure of the House of

[22] See p. 470.
[23] See pp. 473–474.
[24] See pp. 182–183.

Commons they governed the country, expecting the working classes and the business interests to look to them as natural leaders.

Never in the five hundred years of its history had the Commons been so unrepresentative. No new borough had been created since the Revolution of 1688. The boroughs, or urban centers having the right to elect members of Parliament, were heavily concentrated in southern England. With the industrial revolution, population was shifting noticeably to the north. The new factory towns were unrepresented. Of the boroughs, many had decayed over the centuries; some were quite uninhabited, and one was under the waters of the North Sea. In a few boroughs real elections took place, but in some of them it was the town corporation, and in others the owners of certain pieces of real estate, that had the right to name members of Parliament. Each borough was different, carrying over the local liberties of the Middle Ages. Many boroughs were entirely dominated by influential persons called boroughmongers by their critics. As for the rural districts, the "forty-shilling freeholders" chose two members of Parliament for each county, in a convivial assembly much influenced by the gentlefolk. It was estimated about 1820 that less than 500 men, most of them members of the House of Lords, really selected a majority of the House of Commons.

Some two dozen bills to reform the House of Commons had been introduced in the half-century preceding 1830. They had all failed to pass. In 1830, after the Paris revolution, the issue was again raised by the minority party, the Whigs. The Tory prime minister, the Duke of Wellington, the victor of Waterloo and a most extreme conservative, so immoderately defended the existing system that he lost the confidence even of some of his own followers. The existing methods of election in England, he declared, were more perfect than any that human intelligence could contrive at a single stroke. After this outburst a Whig ministry took over the government. It introduced a reform bill. The House of Commons rejected it. The Whig ministry thereupon resigned. The Tories, fearing popular violence, refused to take the responsibility for forming a cabinet. The Whigs resumed office and again introduced their reform bill. This time it passed the Commons but failed in the House of Lords. An angry roar went up over the country. Crowds milled in the London streets, rioters for several days were in control at Bristol, the jail at Derby was sacked, and Nottingham castle burned. Only the passage of the bill, it seemed, could prevent an actual revolution. Using this argument the Whigs got the king to promise to create enough new peers to change the majority in the House of Lords.[25] The Lords yielded rather than be swamped, and in April 1832 the bill became law.

The Reform Bill of 1832 was a very English measure. It adapted the English or medieval system rather than following new ideas let loose by the French Revolution. On the Continent, where constitutions existed at all (as in France), the idea was that each representative should represent roughly the same number of voters, and that voters should qualify to vote by a flat uniform qualification, usually the payment of a stated amount of property taxes. The British held to the idea that members of the

[25]See note, p. 201.

House of Commons represented boroughs and counties, in general without regard to size of population (with exceptions); in other words, no attempt was made to create equal electoral districts. The qualification for voting was enormously simplified, but it still remained rather complex. The franchise, or right to vote, depended on whether one lived in a borough or in a county. It was defined also very largely in terms of rents, because in England, with the high concentration of landownership in the old landowning class, many important people did not own any land at all.

In a borough, under the new law, a man could vote for a member of Parliament if he occupied premises for which he paid £ 10 annual rental. In a county (a rural area or a small town not considered a borough), a man could vote if he paid £ 10 annual rental for land held on a long-term sixty-year lease; but he had to pay as high as £ 50 rental for land occupied on a shorter-term lease in order to be eligible to vote. If he himself owned the land, he could vote if its annual rental value was £ 2 a year (the old forty-shilling freehold). Thus the vote was nicely distributed according to evidences of economic substance, reliability, and permanence. The total effect on the size of the electorate was to raise the number of voters in the British Isles from about 500,000 to about 813,000. Some persons actually lost their votes, namely, the poorer elements in the handful of old boroughs which had been fairly democratic, like the borough of Westminster in greater London.

The most important thing was not the increased size of the electorate but its redistribution by region and by class. The Reform Bill reallocated the seats in the House of Commons. Fifty-six of the smallest older boroughs were abolished, their inhabitants thereafter voting as residents of their counties. Thirty other small boroughs kept the right to send only one burgess to Parliament instead of the historic two. The 143 seats thus made available were given to the new industrial towns. Here it was the £ 10-householders who voted, i.e., the middle classes—factory-owners and businessmen and their principal employees; doctors, lawyers, brokers, merchants, and newspaper people; relatives and connections of the well-to-do.

The Reform Bill of 1832 was more sweeping than the Whigs would have favored except for their fear of revolution. It was more conservative than the democratic radicals would have accepted, except for their belief that the suffrage might be widened in the future. Great Britain in 1830 was probably nearer to real revolution than any country of Europe—for the revolutions of 1830 on the Continent were in reality only insurrections and readjustments. In Britain a distressed mass of factory workers, and of craft workers thrown out of employment by factory competition, was led by an irate manufacturing interest, grown strong by industrial changes and determined no longer to tolerate its exclusion from political life. Had these elements resorted to general violence a real revolution would have occurred. Yet there was no violent revolution in Britain. The reason probably lies first of all in the existence of the historic institution of Parliament, which, erratic though it was before the Reform Bill, provided the means by which social changes could be legally accomplished and continued, in principle, to enjoy universal respect. Conservatives, driven to the wall, would yield; they could allow a revision of the suffrage because they could expect to remain themselves in public life. Radicals, using enough violence to scare the established interest, did not thereafter face a blank wall; they could expect, once the breach was made, to carry some day a further democratization of Parliament and with it their social and economic program by orderly legislation.

But the Reform Bill of 1832 was in its way a revolution. The new business interests, created by industrialization, took their place alongside the old aristocracy in the governing elite of the country. The aristocratic Whigs who had carried the Reform Bill gradually merged with formerly radical industrialists and with a few Liberal Tories to form the Liberal party. The main body of the Tories, joined by a few old Whigs and even a few former radicals, gradually turned into the Conservative party. The two parties alternated in power at short intervals from 1832 to the First World War, this being the classic period in Great Britain of the Liberal-Conservative two-party system.

In 1833 slavery was abolished in the British Empire. In 1834 a new Poor Law was adopted. In 1835 the Municipal Corporations Act, second only to the Reform Bill in basic importance, modernized the local government of English cities; it broke up the old local oligarchies and brought in uniform electoral and administrative machinery, enabling city-dwellers to grapple more effectively with the problems of urban life. In 1836 the House of Commons allowed the newspapers to report how its members voted; a long step toward publicity of government proceedings was thus taken. Meanwhile an ecclesiastical commission reviewed the affairs of the Church of England; financial and administrative irregularities were corrected, together with the grosser inequalities between the income of upper and lower clergy, all of which had made the church formerly a kind of closed preserve for the landed gentry.

The Tories, thus assaulted in their immemorial strongholds of local government and the established church, carried a counteroffensive into the strongholds of the new liberal manufacturing class, namely, the factories and the mines. Tories became champions of the industrial workers. Landed gentlemen, of whom the most famous was Lord Ashley, later seventh Earl of Shaftesbury, took the lead in publicizing the social evils of a rapid and indeed ruthless industrialization. They received some support from a few humanitarian industrialists; indeed, the early legislation tended to follow practices already established by the best or strongest business firms. A Factory Act of 1833 forbade the labor of children less than nine years old in the textile mills. It was the first effective piece of legislation on the subject, for it provided for paid inspectors and procedures for enforcement. An act of 1842 initiated significant regulation in the coal mines; the employment underground of women and girls, and of boys under ten, was forbidden.

The greatest victory of the working classes came in 1847 with the Ten Hours Act, which limited the labor of women and children in all industrial establishments to ten hours a day. Thereafter men commonly worked only ten hours also, since the work of men, women, and young people was too closely coordinated for the men to work alone. The great Liberal, John Bright, Quaker and cotton magnate, called the Ten Hours Act "a delusion practiced on the working classes." To regulate the hours of labor was contrary to the accepted principles of laissez faire, economic law, the free market, freedom of trade, and individual liberty for employer and workman. Yet the Ten Hours Act stood, and British industry continued to prosper.

Gathering their strength, the Whig-liberal-radical combination established in 1838 an Anti-Corn-Law League. Wage earners objected to the Corn Laws because the tariff on grain imports kept up the price of food. Industrial employers objected to them because, in keeping up food prices, they also kept up wages and cost of production in England, thus working to England's disadvantage in the export trade. Defenders of the Corn Laws argued that protection of agriculture was necessary to maintain the natural aristocracy of the country (most land being owned by peers and gentry, as has been seen), but they also sometimes used more widely framed economic arguments, affirming that Britain should preserve a balanced economy as between industry and farming, and avoid becoming too exclusively dependent on imported food. The issue became a straight contest between the industrialists, acting with working-class support, and the aristocratic and predominantly Tory landowning interest. The Anti-Corn-Law League, whose headquarters were at Manchester, operated like a modern political party. It had plenty of money, supplied by large donations from manufacturers and small ones from laboring people. It sent lecturers on tour, agitated in the newspapers, and issued a stream of polemical pamphlets and educational books. It held political teas, torchlight processions, and open-air mass meetings. The pressure proved irresistible and received a final impetus from a famine in Ireland. It was a Tory government, headed by Sir Robert Peel, which in 1846 yielded before so vociferous a demand.

The repeal of the Corn Laws in 1846 stands as a symbol of the change that had come over England. It reaffirmed the revolutionary consequences of the Reform Bill of 1832. Industry was now a governing element in the country. Free trade was henceforth the rule. Great Britain, in return for the export of manufactures, became deliberately dependent on imports for its very life. It was committed henceforth to an international and even world-wide economic system. The first to undergo the Industrial Revolution, possessing mechanical power and methods of mass production, the British could produce yarn and cloth, machine tools and railroad equipment, more efficiently and more cheaply than any other people. In Britain, the workshop of the world, people would pour increasingly into mine, factory, and city, live by selling manufactures, coal, shipping, and financial services to the other peoples of the earth, and obtain raw cotton, rare ores, meat, cereals, and thousands of lesser but still vital necessities from the rest of the earth in exchange. The welfare of Britain depended on the maintenance of a freely exchanging world-wide economic system.

It depended also, more than ever, on British control of the sea, which was rarely mentioned by the civilian-minded Anti-Corn-Law League, but which, firmly established in the long duel with Napoleon, was now an assumed postulate of economic discussion. No one understood this better than Lord Palmerston, a flamboyant Anglo-Irish Whig aristocrat, who by risky and audacious moves that alarmed his colleagues and threw Queen Victoria into consternation, came forward as the very British bulldog in defense of Britain's name. For example, in 1850 a

Moroccan Jew known as Don Pacifico, who was a British subject, got into trouble in Greece because of certain debts owed to him by the Greek government. Though the claim was not above question, Palmerston unloosed the thunders of the British fleet. He sent a squadron to the Piraeus, the port of Athens, and forbade Greek vessels the use of their own harbor until the matter was settled. Criticized in Parliament, Palmerston made a stirring speech climaxed by the Latin phrase, *civis Romanus sum.* Just as in ancient times the Roman citizen everywhere commanded respect, so now, according to Palmerston, any British subject had behind him the might of the British navy anywhere in the world. On another occasion, in 1856, when Chinese authorities arrested a Chinese ship called the *Arrow,* which, though without due right, was flying the British flag, Palmerston again called on the navy, which proceeded to bombard Canton and precipitated the Second Anglo-Chinese War. In other connections, as a good mid-nineteenth-century liberal, Palmerston favored movements for national independence, including that of the Confederate States of America, expecting them to result in the further extension of free trade.

I n both Great Britain and France (as also in Belgium) the revolutionary agitation of 1830–1832 ushered in a period of ascendancy for the bourgeois or propertied classes. The reigning liberal doctrine was the "stake in society" theory: those should govern who have something to lose. In the France of the July monarchy (1830–1848) about one adult male in thirty could vote, in the Britain of the first Reform Bill (1832–1867) about one in eight. In Britain virtually the whole middle class was now enfranchised, in France only the most well-to-do. In Britain the continuation of the Tory landed interests in politics somewhat blunted the edge of capitalist and managerial rule, resulting in the passage of significant legislation for the protection of industrial labor. In France the aristocratic landed interest, weaker and less public spirited than in England in any case, lost much of its influence by the revolution of 1830. France under Louis-Philippe was a more purely bourgeois country than Great Britain, and less was done to relieve the condition of labor.

In general, the decades following 1830 may be thought of as a kind of golden age of the west-European bourgeoisie. The businessman of Britain, France, and Belgium, while he had established himself against the man of birth, had as yet hardly to reckon politically with the man of toil. By its upholders the system was regarded as perfect and final. Two examples may be given, François Guizot in France and Thomas Babington Macaulay in England, both active in the parliaments of their respective countries, both brilliant writers of history, both proud of the triumphs of modern civilization and of the industrious and intelligent middle classes from which they came—and both convinced that political democracy would lead to ruin.

The bourgeois era left its mark on Europe in many ways. For one thing, western Europe continued to accumulate capital and build up its industrial plant. National income was constantly rising, but a relatively small share went to the laboring class, and a relatively large share went to owners of capital. This meant that less was spent

**56
Triumph of
the West-European
Bourgeoisie**

on consumers' goods—housing, clothing, food, recreation—and that more was saved and available for reinvestment. New stock companies were constantly formed, and the law of corporations was amended, allowing for the extension of corporate enterprise to new fields. The factory system spread from Britain to the Continent and within Britain from the textile industry to other lines of production. The output of iron, a good index to economic advancement in this phase of industrialism, rose about 300 percent in Great Britain between 1830 and 1848 and about 65 percent in France between 1830 and 1845. (All the German states combined, at the latter date, produced about a tenth as much iron as Great Britain, and less than half as much as France.) Railroad building set in in earnest after 1840. In 1840 Samuel Cunard put four steamships in regular transatlantic service. Much capital was exported; as early as 1839 an American estimated that Europeans (mainly British) owned $200,000,000 worth of stocks in American companies. Such investments financed the purchase of British and other goods and helped to rivet together a world economic system, in which western Europe and especially England took the lead, with other regions remaining in a somewhat subordinate status.

The Frustration and Challenge of Labor

The bourgeois age had the effect also of estranging the world of labor. The state in Britain and France was as near as it has ever been to what Karl Marx was soon to call it—a committee of the bourgeois class. Already in France people spoke worriedly of the *prolétaires,* those at the bottom of society, who had nothing to lose. Republicans in France, radical democrats in Britain, felt cheated and imposed upon in the 1830s and 1840s. They had in each country forced through a virtual revolution by their insurrections and demonstrations and then in each country had been left without the vote. Some lost interest in representative institutions. Excluded from government they were tempted to seek political ends through extragovernmental, which is to say revolutionary or utopian, channels. Social and economic reforms seemed to the workingman far more important, as a final aim, than mere governmental innovations. The workingman was told by respected economists that he could not hope to change the system in his own favor. He was tempted therefore to destroy the system, to replace it utterly with some new system conceived mainly in the minds of thinkers. He was told by the Manchester School, and by its equivalent in France, that the income of labor was set by ineluctable natural laws, that it was best and indeed necessary for wages to remain low, and that the way to rise in the world was to get out of the laboring class altogether, by becoming the owner of a profitable business and leaving working people about where they were.[26]

The reigning doctrine emphasized the conception of a labor market. The workman sold labor, the employer bought it. The price of labor, or wage, was to be agreed upon by the two individual parties. The price would naturally fluctuate according to changes in supply and demand. When a great deal of a certain kind of labor was required the wage would go up, until new persons moved into the market of-

[26]See pp. 471, 474.

fering more labor of this type, with the result that something like the old wage would again be established. When no labor was needed none should be bought, and persons who could not sell labor might then subsist for a time by poor relief. The new Poor Law of 1834 was especially repugnant to the British working classes. It corrected crying evils in the old system, which had pauperized and demoralized millions of people. But the new law followed the stern precepts of the dismal science; its main principle was to safeguard the labor market by making relief more unpleasant than any job. It granted relief only to persons willing to enter a workhouse, or poorhouse; and in these establishments the sexes were segregated and life was in other ways made noticeably less attractive than in the outside world. The workers considered the new law an abomination. They called the workhouses "bastilles." They resented the whole conception of a labor market, in which labor was to be bought and sold (or remain unsold) like any other commodity.

There were two means of escape. One was to improve the position of labor in the market. This led to the formation of labor unions for control of the labor supply and collective bargaining with employers. Such unions, illegal in France, were barely legal in Great Britain after 1825, though it was still illegal in both countries to strike. The other means of escape was to repudiate the whole idea of a market economy and of the capitalist system. It was to conceive of a system in which goods were to be produced for use, not for sale; and in which working people should be compensated according to need, not according to the requirements of an employer. This was the basis of most forms of socialism.[27]

Socialism spread rapidly among the working classes after 1830. In France it blended with revolutionary republicanism. There was a revival of interest in the great Revolution and the democratic Republic of 1793. Cheap reprints of the writings of Robespierre began to circulate in the working-class quarters of Paris. Robespierre was now seen as a people's hero. The socialist Louis Blanc, for example, who in 1839 published his *Organization of Work*, recommending the formation of "social workshops," also wrote a long history of the French Revolution, in which he pointed out the democratic ideals that had inspired the National Convention in 1793. In Britain, as befitted the different background of the country, socialistic ideas blended in with the movement for further parliamentary reform. This was advanced by the working-class group known as the Chartists, from the People's Charter which they drafted in 1838. Between the British Chartists and the French socialists there was considerable coming and going. One Chartist, the Irish-born journalist Bronterre O'Brien, translated a French book on the "conspiracy of Babeuf" of 1796, which itself was a source and inspiration of the rising socialism of France.[28]

Chartism was far more of a mass movement than the French socialism of the day. Only a few Chartists were clearly socialists in their own minds. But all were

[27] See pp. 476–477.
[28] See p. 408.

anticapitalistic. All could agree that the first step must be to win working-class representation in Parliament. The Charter of 1838 consisted of six points. It demanded (1) the annual election of the House of Commons by (2) universal suffrage for all adult males, through (3) a secret ballot and (4) equal electoral districts; and it called for (5) the abolition of property qualifications for membership in the House of Commons, which perpetuated the old idea that Parliament should be composed of gentlemen of independent income, and urged instead (6) the payment of salaries to the elected members of Parliament, in order that people of small means might serve. A convention composed of delegates sent by labor unions, mass meetings, and radical societies all over the country met in London in 1839. "Convention" was an ominous word, with French revolutionary and even terrorist overtones; some members of this British convention regarded it as the body really representing the people, and favored armed violence and a general strike, while others stood only for moral pressure upon Parliament.

A petition bearing over a million signatures, urging acceptance of the Charter, was submitted to the House of Commons. The violent and revolutionary wing, or "physical force" Chartists, precipitated a wave of riots which were effectively quelled by the authorities. In 1842 the petition was again submitted. This time, according to the best estimate, it was signed by 3,317,702 persons. Since the entire population of Great Britain was about 19,000,000 it is clear that the Charter, whatever the exact number of signatures, commanded the explicit adherence of half the adult males of the country. The House of Commons nevertheless rejected the petition by 287 votes to 49. It was feared, with reason, that political democracy would threaten property rights and the whole economic system as they then existed. The Chartist movement gradually died down in the face of firm opposition by the government and the business classes, and was weakened by mutual fears and disagreements among its own supporters. It had not been entirely fruitless; for without popular agitation and the publicizing of working-class grievances, the Mines Act of 1842 and the Ten Hours Act of 1847 might not have been enacted. These measures in turn alleviated the distress of industrial workers and kept alive a degree of confidence in the future of the economic system. Chartism revived briefly in 1848, as will be seen in the next chapter; but in general, in the 1840s, British working people turned from political agitation to the forming and strengthening of labor unions, by which they could deal directly with employers without having to appeal to the government. Not until 1867 was the suffrage extended in Great Britain, and it took about eighty years to realize the full program of the Charter of 1838, except for the annual election of Parliament, for which there soon ceased to be any demand.

◎ It is not easy to summarize the history of Europe between 1815 and 1848. Between all the forces set free by the French and Industrial Revolutions—liberalism, conservatism, nationalism, republicanism, democracy, socialism—no stabilization had been achieved. No international system had been created; Europe had rather fallen into two camps, composed of a West in which liberal conceptions moved forward, and an East in which three autocratic monarchies held sway. Western

Europe favored the principles of nationality; governments in central and eastern Europe still opposed them. The West was growing collectively richer, more liberal, more bourgeois. Middle-class people in Germany, central Europe, and Italy (as well as in Spain and Portugal) did not enjoy the dignities and emoluments that they enjoyed in Great Britain or France. But the West had not solved its social problem; its whole material civilization rested upon a restless and sorely tried working class. Everywhere there was repression, in varying degree, and everywhere apprehension, more in some places than in others; but there was also hope, confidence in the progress of an industrial and scientific society, and faith in the unfinished program of the rights of man. The result was the general Revolution of 1848.

XII: 1848: A REVOLUTION THAT

MISFIRED

Fears haunting the established classes of Europe for thirty years came true in 1848. Governments collapsed all over the Continent. Remembered horrors appeared again, as in a recurring dream, in much the same sequence as after 1789 only at a much faster rate of speed. Revolutionaries milled in the streets, kings fled, republics were declared, and within four years there was another Napoleon. Soon thereafter came a series of wars.

Never before or since has Europe seen so truly universal an upheaval as in 1848. While the French Revolution of 1789 and the Russian Revolution of 1917 both had immediate international repercussions, in each of these cases a single country took the lead. In 1848 the revolutionary movement broke out spontaneously from native sources from Copenhagen to Palermo and from Paris to Budapest. Contemporaries sometimes attributed the universality of the phenomenon to the machinations of secret societies, and it is true that the faint beginnings of an international revolutionary movement existed before 1848; but the fact is that revolutionary plotters had little influence upon what actually happened, and the nearly simultaneous fall of governments is quite understandable from other causes. Many people in Europe

Chapter Emblem: A medal showing St. Paul's Church at Frankfurt, then a new building in the neo-classic style, where the German National Assembly met in 1848–1849.

wanted substantially the same things—constitutional government, the independence and unification of national groups, an end to serfdom and manorial restraints where they still existed. With some variation, there was a common body of ideas among politically conscious elements of all countries. Some of the powers that the new forces had to combat were themselves international, notably the Catholic church and the far-spreading influence of the Habsburgs, so that resistance to them arose independently in many places. In any case, only the Russian empire and Great Britain escaped the revolutionary contagion of 1848, and the British received a very bad scare.

But the Revolution of 1848, though it shook the whole Continent, was lacking in basic driving strength. It failed almost as rapidly as it succeeded. Or, more accurately, it misfired. It hit some of its objectives, but missed others, and it set off long chains of consequences that were not aimed at. It was the unintended consequences of the Revolution of 1848 that were among the most far-reaching. Within the nationalist turmoil of central Europe could be discerned fierce national jealousies that would persist, and elements of Pan-Germanism and Pan-Slavism. In the social turmoil appeared class hatreds and the first features of modern Marxism, as well as doctrines of nationalism and Bonapartism claiming to bridge the gulf between classes.

57
Paris: The Specter of Social Revolution in the West

The July Monarchy in France was a platform of boards built over a volcano. Under it burned the repressed fires of the republicanism put down in 1830, which since 1830 had become steadily more socialistic.[1] Republicanism had its strength in Paris and a few other great cities. But the French political system was so centralized, the prefects instituted by Napoleon in the several departments were so accustomed to taking orders from the Ministry of the Interior, the whole French public was so much in the habit of following the ways of the capital, that Paris was in effect a kind of fuse that might explode the whole country.

Politics in the July Monarchy became increasingly more unreal. So few interests were represented in the Chamber of Deputies that the most basic issues were seldom debated. Even most of the bourgeois class had no representation. Graft and corruption were more common than they should have been, as economic expansion favored stockjobbing and fraud by business promoters and politicians in combination. A strong movement set in to give the vote to more people instead of to only one man in thirty. Radicals wanted universal suffrage and a republic, but liberals asked only for a broadening of voting rights within the existing constitutional monarchy. The king, Louis-Philippe, and his prime minister, Guizot, instead of allying with the latter against the former, resolutely and obtusely opposed any change whatsoever.

[1]See pp. 496–498, 506–507.

Reformers, against the king's expressed wishes, planned a great banquet in Paris for February 22, 1848, to be accompanied by demonstrations in the streets. The government on February 21 forbade all such meetings. That night barricades were built in the working-class quarters. These consisted of paving-blocks, building stones, or large pieces of furniture thrown together across the narrow streets and intersections of the old city, and constituting a maze within which insurgents prepared to resist the authorities. The government called out the National Guard, which refused to move. The king now promised electoral reform, but republican firebrands took charge of the semimobilized working-class elements, which held a demonstration outside the house of Guizot. Someone shot at the guards placed around the house; the guards replied, killing twenty persons. The republican organizers put some of the corpses on a torch-lit cart and paraded them through the city, which, armed and barricaded, soon began to swarm in an enormous riot. On February 24 Louis-Philippe, like Charles X before him, abdicated and made for England. The February Revolution of 1848, like the July Revolution of 1830, had unseated a monarch in three days.

The constitutional reformers hoped to carry on with Louis-Philippe's young grandson as king, but the republicans, now aroused and armed, poured into the Chamber of Deputies and forced the proclamation of the Republic. Republican leaders set up a provisional government of ten men, pending election by all France of a Constituent Assembly. Seven of the ten were "straight" republicans, the most notable being the poet Lamartine. Three were "social" republicans, the most notable being Louis Blanc. A huge crowd of workingmen appeared before the Hôtel de Ville, or city hall, demanding that France adopt the new socialist emblem—the red flag. They were dissuaded by the eloquence of Lamartine, and the tricolor remained the republican standard.

Louis Blanc urged the Provisional Government to push through a bold economic and social program without delay. But since the "social" republicans were in a minority in the Provisional Government (though probably not among Paris republicans generally), Louis Blanc's ideas were very much watered down in the application. He wanted a Ministry of Progress to organize a network of "social workshops," the state-supported and collectivist manufacturing establishments that he had projected in his writings. All that was created was a Labor Commission, with limited powers, and a system of shops significantly entitled "national" rather than "social." The National Workshops, as they are always called in English (though "workshop" suggests something more insignificant than Louis Blanc had in mind), were agreed to by the Provisional Government only as a political concession, and no significant work was ever assigned them to do, for fear of competition with private enterprise and dislocation of the economic system. Indeed, the man placed in charge of them admitted that his purpose was to prove the fallacies of socialism. Meanwhile the Labor Commission was unable to win public acceptance for the ten-hour day, which the British Parliament had enacted the year before.

The National Workshops became in practice only an extensive project in unemployment relief. Men of all trades, skilled and unskilled, were set to work digging on the roads and fortifications outside of Paris. They were paid two francs a day. The number of legitimate unemployed increased rapidly, for 1847 had been a year of depression and the revolution prevented the return of business confidence; and a certain number of common idlers naturally presented themselves for remuneration, especially since there were soon too many men for the amount of "work" that was made available. There were 25,000 enrolled in the workshops by the middle of March, 66,000 by the middle of April, and about 120,000 by the middle of June, by which time there were also in Paris 50,000 other unemployed men whom the bulging workshops could no longer accommodate. In June there were probably almost 200,000 essentially idle but able-bodied men in a city of about a million people.

The Constituent Assembly, elected in April by universal suffrage throughout France, met on May 4. It immediately replaced the Provisional Government with a temporary executive board of its own. The main body of France, a land of provincial bourgeois and peasant landowners, was not socialist in the least. The new temporary executive board, chosen by the new Constituent Assembly in May, included no "social" republicans. All five of its members, of whom Lamartine was the head, were known as outspoken enemies of Louis Blanc. Blanc and the socialists could no longer expect even the grudging and insincere concessions that they had so far obtained.

The battle lines were now drawn, after only three months of revolution, somewhat as they had been drawn in 1792 after three years.[2] Paris was pitted against the country at large. Still the largest city on the Continent, Paris stood for a degree of revolutionary action that the rest of the country was not prepared to accept. Revolutionary leaders in Paris, in 1848 as in 1792, were unwilling to accept the processes of majority rule or slow parliamentary deliberation. But the crisis in 1848 was more acute than in 1792. A larger proportion of the Paris population were wage earners. Under a system of predominantly merchant capitalism, in which machine industry and factory concentration were only beginning, they were tormented by the same evils as the more industrialized working classes of England. Hours were if anything longer, and pay less, in France than in Great Britain; insecurity and unemployment were at least as great; and the feeling that a capitalist economy held no future for the laboring man was the same. In addition, where the English workingman shrank from the actual violation of Parliament, the French workingman saw nothing very sacrilegious in the violation of elected assemblies. Too many regimes in France since 1789, including those preferred by the comfortable classes, had been based on insurrectionary violence for the French workingman to feel much compunction over using it for his own ends.

The "June Days"
of 1848

On the one hand stood the nationally elected Constituent Assembly. On the other, the National Workshops had mobilized in Paris the most distressed elements of the working class. Tens of thousands had been brought together where they could talk, read journals, listen to speeches, and concert common action. Agitators and or-

[2]See pp. 395–396.

ganizers naturally made use of the opportunity thus presented to them. Men in the workshops began to feel desperate, to sense that the social republic was slipping from them perhaps forever. On May 15 they attacked the Constituent Assembly, drove its members out of the hall, declared it dissolved, and set up a new provisional government of their own. They announced that a social revolution must follow the purely political revolution of February. But the National Guard, a kind of civilian militia, turned against the insurgents and restored the Constituent Assembly. The Assembly, to root out socialism, prepared to get rid of the National Workshops. It offered those enrolled in them the alternatives of enlistment in the army, transfer to provincial workshops, or being put out of Paris by force. The whole laboring class of the city began to resist. The government proclaimed martial law, the civilian executive board resigned, and all power was given to General Cavaignac and the regular army.

There followed the "Bloody June Days"—June 24–26, 1848—three days during which a terrifying class war raged in Paris. Over twenty thousand men from the workshops took to arms (more would doubtless have done so had not the government continued to pay wages in the workshops during the insurrection), and they were joined by other unnumbered thousands from the working-class districts of the city. Half or more of Paris became a labyrinth of barricades defended by determined men and equally stubborn women. Military methods of the time made it possible for civilians to shoot it out openly with soldiers; small arms were the main weapons, and armies had no armored vehicles or even any very devastating artillery. The soldiers found it a difficult operation, even several generals being killed, but after three days the outcome was in doubt no longer. Ten thousand persons had been killed or wounded. Eleven thousand insurgents were taken prisoner. The Assembly, refusing all clemency, decreed their immediate deportation to the colonies.

The June Days sent a shudder throughout France and Europe. Whether the battle in Paris had been a true class struggle, how large a portion of the laboring class had really participated (it was large in any case), how much they had fought for permanent objectives, and how much over the temporary issue of the workshops—all these are secondary questions. It was widely understood that a class war had in fact broken out. Militant workers were confirmed in a hatred and loathing of the bourgeois class, in a belief that capitalism existed in the last analysis by the callous shooting of laboring men in the streets. People above the laboring class were thrown into a panic. They were sure that they had narrowly escaped a ghastly upheaval. The very ground of civilized living seemed to have quaked. After June 1848, wrote a Frenchwoman of the time, society was "a prey to a feeling of terror incomparable to anything since the invasion of Rome by the barbarians."

Nor were the signs in England much more reassuring. There the Chartist agitation was revived by the February Revolution in Paris.[3] "France is a Republic!" cried the Chartist Ernest Jones; the Chartist petition was again circulated and was soon said to have 6,000,000 signatures. Another Chartist Convention met,

[3] See pp. 507–508.

considered by its leaders to be the forerunner of a Constituent Assembly as in France. The violent minority was the most active; it began to gather arms and to drill. The old Duke of Wellington swore in 70,000 special constables to uphold the social order. Clashes occurred at Liverpool and elsewhere; in London the revolutionary committee laid plans for systematic arson and organized men with pick-axes to break up the pavements for barricades. Meanwhile the petition, weighing 584 pounds, was carried in three cabs to the House of Commons, which estimated that it contained "only" 2,000,000 signatures and again summarily rejected it. The revolutionary menace passed. One of the secret organizers in London proved to be a government spy; he revealed the whole plan at the critical moment, and the revolutionary committee was arrested on the day set for insurrection. Most Chartists had in any case refused to support the militants. All now became discouraged. Tens of thousands emigrated to the United States. The net effect in Great Britain was somewhat as in France. Many of the upper and middle classes felt a sense of unthinkable dangers barely escaped. Soon, however, since there was no actual revolution in Britain in 1848, at a time when the whole Continent was rocking, the prevailing outlook became a complacent satisfaction with the stability of British institutions. The belief that no change or improvement was necessary was entrenched more firmly. But the truculent minority of radical workingmen and journalists had a deeper sense of envenomed class-consciousness. The word "proletarian" was imported from France. "Every proletarian," wrote the Chartist editor of *Red Revolution*, "who does not see and feel that he belongs to an enslaved and degraded class is a *fool*."

The specter of social revolution thus hung over western Europe in the summer of 1848. Doubtless it was unreal; in all probability there could have been no successful socialist revolution at the time. But the specter was there, and it spread a sinking fear among all who had something to lose. This fear shaped the whole subsequent course of the Second Republic in France and of the revolutionary movements that had by this time begun in other countries as well.

The Emergence of Louis-Napoleon Bonaparte

In France, after the June Days, the Constituent Assembly (keeping General Cavaignac as a virtual dictator) set about drafting a republican constitution. It was decided, in view of the disturbances just passed, to create a strong executive power in the hands of a president to be elected by universal suffrage. It was decided also to have this president elected immediately, even before the rest of the constitution was finished. Four candidates presented themselves: Lamartine, Cavaignac, Ledru-Rollin—and Louis-Napoleon Bonaparte. Lamartine stood for a somewhat vaguely moral and idealistic republic, Cavaignac for a republic of disciplined order, Ledru-Rollin for somewhat chastened "social" ideas. What Bonaparte stood for was not so clear. He was, however, elected by an avalanche of votes in December 1848, receiving over 5,400,000, to only 1,500,000 for Cavaignac, 370,000 for Ledru-Rollin and a mere 18,000 for Lamartine.

Thus entered upon the European stage the second Napoleon. Born in 1808, Louis-Napoleon Bonaparte was the nephew of the great Napoleon. His father, Louis Bonaparte, was at the time of his birth the king of Holland. When Napoleon's own son died in 1832 Louis-Napoleon assumed the headship of the Bonaparte family. He resolved to restore the glories of the empire. With a handful of followers he tried to seize power at Strasbourg in 1836 and at Boulogne in 1840, leading what the following century would know as *Putsches.* Both failed ridiculously. Sentenced to life imprisonment in the fortress of Ham, he had escaped from it as recently as 1846 by simply walking off the grounds dressed as a stonemason. He expressed advanced social and political ideas, had probably joined the Carbonari in his youth, and had taken part in the Italian revolutionary uprising of 1830. He wrote two books, one called *Napoleonic Ideas,* claiming that his famous uncle had been misunderstood and checkmated by reactionary forces, and one called the *Extinction of Poverty,* a somewhat anticapitalistic tract like so many others of its time. But he was no friend of "anarchists," and the spring of 1848, at which time he was still a refugee in England, found him enrolled as one of Wellington's special constables to oppose the Chartist revolution. He soon returned to France. He was compromised neither by the June Days nor by their repression; he was supposed to be a friend of the common man and at the same time a believer in order; and his name was Napoleon Bonaparte.

For twenty years a groundswell had been stirring the popular mind. It is known as the Napoleonic Legend. Bored with the drab bourgeois monarchy, Frenchmen began to dream upon the past. Victor Hugo wrote poems, and Adolphe Thiers histories, in which the name of Napoleon gleamed like a waving sword. Peasants put up pictures of the emperor in their cottages, fondly imagining that it had been Napoleon who gave them the free ownership of their land. The completion of the Arch of Triumph in 1836 drove home the memory of imperial glories, and in 1840 the remains of the emperor were brought from St. Helena and majestically interred at the Invalides on the banks of the Seine. All this happened in a country where, government being in the hands of a few, most people had no political experience or political sense except what they had gained in revolution. When millions were suddenly, for the first time in their lives, asked to vote for president in 1848, the name of Bonaparte was the only one they had ever heard of. "How should I not vote for this gentleman," said an old peasant, "I whose nose was frozen at Moscow?"

So Prince Louis-Napoleon became president of the republic, by an overwhelming and indubitable popular mandate, in which an army officer, General Cavaignac, was his only even faintly successful rival. He soon saw the way the wind was blowing. The Constituent Assembly dissolved itself in May 1849 and was replaced by the Legislative Assembly provided for in the new constitution. It was a strange assembly for a republic. It may be recalled that in 1797 the first normal election in the First Republic had produced a royalist majority.[4] Now in the Second Republic, under universal suffrage, the result was the same. Five hundred of the deputies, or two-

[4]See p. 408.

thirds, were really monarchists, but they were divided into irreconcilable factions—the Legitimists, who favored the line of Charles X, and the Orleanists, who favored that of Louis-Philippe. One-third of the deputies called themselves republicans. Of these, in turn, over two-thirds, or about 180, were socialists of one kind or another; and only about 70 were "straight" or old-fashioned republicans to whom the main issue was the form of government rather than the form of society itself. The fear that followed the June Days, together with a taxation policy by which peasants paid more taxes under the republic than under the July Monarchy, had thrown the mass of the voters into the hands of the monarchists.

The president and the Assembly at first combined to conjure away the specter of socialism, with which republicanism itself was now clearly associated. An abortive insurrection of June 1849 provided the chance. The Assembly, backed by the president, ousted thirty-three socialist deputies, suppressed public meetings, and imposed controls on the press. In 1850 it went so far as to rescind universal suffrage, taking the vote away from about a third of the electorate—naturally the poorest and hence most socialistic third. The Falloux law of 1850 put the schools at all levels of the educational system under supervision of the Catholic clergy; for, as M. Falloux said in the Assembly, "lay teachers have made the principles of social revolution popular in the most distant villages," and it was necessary "to rally around religion to strengthen the foundations of society against those who want to divide up property." The French Republic, now actually an antirepublican government, likewise intervened against the revolutionary republic established by Mazzini in the city of Rome. French military forces were sent to Rome to protect the pope; they remained there twenty years.

To the conservatives Bonaparte knew that he was virtually indispensable. They were sharply divided between two sets of monarchists—Legitimist and Orleanist—who so detested each other that each would accept any antisocialist regime rather than yield to the other faction. Bonaparte's problem was to win over the radicals. He did so by urging in 1851 the restoration of universal suffrage, which he had himself helped repeal in 1850. He now posed as the people's friend, the one man in public life who trusted the common man. He let it be thought that greedy plutocrats controlled the Assembly and hoodwinked France. He put his lieutenants in as ministers of War and of the Interior, thus controlling the army, the bureaucracy, and the police. On December 2, 1851, the anniversary of Austerlitz, he sprang his coup d'état. Placards appeared all over Paris. They declared the Assembly dissolved and the vote for every adult Frenchman reinstated. When members of the Assembly tried to meet, they were attacked, dispersed, or arrested by the soldiers. The country did not submit without fighting. One hundred and fifty persons were killed in Paris, and throughout France probably 100,000 were put under arrest. But on December 20 the voters elected Louis-Napoleon president for a term of ten years, by a vote officially stated as 7,439,216 to 646,737. A year later the new Bonaparte proclaimed the empire, with himself as emperor of the French. Remembering Napoleon's son, he called himself Napoleon III.

How the empire functioned will be seen below. Not only the republic was dead. The republic as republicans understood it, an equalitarian, anticlerical regime with socialist or at least antibourgeois tendencies, had been dead since June 1848. Feeble anyway, it was killed by its reputation for radicalism. Liberalism and constitutionalism were dead also. Bourgeois and property-owning monarchists were greater sticklers for constitutional liberalism than were the republicans or the Bonapartists or than town laborers or rural peasants. But the monarchists, hopelessly divided among themselves, were now pushed aside. For the first time since 1815 France ceased to have any parliamentary life. It was ruled by a dictatorship, more demagogic, more calculating, more hollow, and more modern than any that the first Napoleon had ever imagined.

The Austrian Empire of the Habsburgs, with its capital at Vienna, was in 1848 the most populous European state except Russia. Its peoples, living principally in the three major geographical divisions of the empire, Austria, Bohemia, and Hungary, were of about a dozen recognizably different nationalities or language groups— Germans, Czechs, Magyars, Poles, Ruthenians, Slovaks, Serbs, Croats, Slovenes, Dalmatians, Rumanians, and Italians.[5] In some parts of the empire the nationalities lived in solid blocks, but in many regions two or more were interlaced together, the language changing from village to village, or even from house to house, in a way quite unknown in western Europe.

Germans, the leading people, occupied all of Austria proper and considerable parts of Bohemia, and were scattered also in small pockets throughout Hungary. The Czechs occupied Bohemia and the adjoining Moravia. The Magyars were the dominant group in the historic kingdom of Hungary, which contained a mixture of nationalities with a considerable number of Slavic peoples. Two of the most advanced parts of Italy also belonged to the empire—Venetia, with its capital at Venice, and Lombardy, whose chief city was Milan.

The Czechs, Poles, Ruthenians, Slovaks, Serbs, Croats, Slovenes, and Dalmatians in the empire were all Slavs; i.e., their languages were all related to one another and to the several forms of Russian. Neither the Magyars nor the Rumanians were Slavs. The Magyars, as national sentiment grew, prided themselves on the uniqueness of their language in Europe and the Rumanians on their linguistic affiliations with the Latin peoples of the West. Rumanians, Magyars, and Germans formed a thick belt separating the South Slavs (in later years called Yugoslavs) from those of the north. Germans and Italians within the empire were in continual touch with Germans and Italians outside. The peoples of the empire represented every cultural level known to Europe. Vienna, where the Waltz King Johann Strauss was reigning, recognized no peer except Paris itself. Milan was a great center of trade. Bohemia had long had a

[5]See maps, pp. 229, 456–457, 478; and pp. 228–233, 283–286, 340–344, 429–430, 458–459.

textile industry of importance, which was beginning to be mechanized in the 1840s; but 200 miles to the south a Croatian intellectual remarked, about the same time, that the first steam engine he ever saw was in a picture printed on a cotton handkerchief imported from Manchester. In 1848, some denied that any such people as the Ruthenians existed at all. Nor was it clear exactly what groups made up the South Slavs. No such word as Yugoslavia or Czechoslovakia had been invented, and Rumania was a term used only by professors.

Thus the empire ruled from Vienna included, according to political frontiers established seventy years later, in 1918, all of Austria, Hungary, and Czechoslovakia, with adjoining portions of Poland, Rumania, Yugoslavia, and Italy. But the political authority of Vienna reached far beyond the borders of the empire. Austria since 1815 had been the most influential member of the German confederation, for Prussia in these years was content to look with deference upon the Habsburgs. The influence of Vienna was felt throughout Germany in many ways, as in the enactment and enforcement of the Carlsbad Decrees mentioned in the last chapter.[6] It reached also through the length of Italy. Lombardy and Venetia were part of the Austrian Empire. Tuscany, ostensibly independent, was governed by a Habsburg grand duke. The kingdom of Naples or the Two Sicilies, comprising all Italy south of Rome, was virtually a protectorate of Vienna. The papal states looked politically to Vienna for leadership, at least until 1846, when the College of Cardinals elected a liberal-minded pope, Pius IX—the one contingency upon which Metternich confessed he had failed to reckon. In all Italy there was only one state ruled by a native Italian dynasty and attempting any consistent independence of policy—the kingdom of Sardinia (called also Savoy or Piedmont) tucked away in the northwest corner around Turin. Italy, said Metternich blandly, was only a "geographical expression," a mere regional name. He might have said the same of Poland, or even of Germany, though Germany was tenuously joined in the Bund, or loose confederation, of 1815.

These peoples since the turn of the century had all felt the flutters of the *Volksgeist*, persistent stirrings of a cultural nationalism, and among Germans, Italians, Poles, and Hungarians a good deal of political agitation and liberal reformism had been at work. Metternich, in Vienna, had discouraged such manifestations for over thirty years, ominously predicting that if allowed to break out they would produce the *bellum omnium contra omnes*—"the war of all against all." As a prophet he was not wholly mistaken, but if it is the business of statesmanship not merely to prophesy events but to control them it cannot be said that the regime of Metternich was very successful. The whole nationalities question was evaded. The fundamental problem of the century, the bringing of peoples into some kind of mutual and moral relationship with their governments—the problem of which nationalism, liberalism, constitutionalism, and democracy were diverse aspects—remained unconsidered by the responsible authorities of central Europe. All that Metternich offered was the idea that a reigning house, with an official bureaucracy, should rule benevolently over peoples with whom it need have no connection and who need have no connection

[6]See p. 486.

with each other. They were the ideas of the eighteenth century, dating from before the French Revolution and best suited to an agricultural and localistic society.

Trouble in the Austrian realms was an old story. The Polish and Hungarian gentry had been nationalistic for generations. In Italy there had been brief and futile revolutions in 1820 and 1830. In 1846 a revolt broke out in Austrian Poland—Galicia. It was the Polish landowners who were the nationalists, but some of them were not wealthy and in exile in western Europe had picked up hazy "communistic" ideas. To win over the masses they promised emancipation of the serfs. But the serfs fought against the landlords, especially in eastern Galicia, where the lower classes were mainly not Polish but Ruthenian. A class war between lord and serf devastated Galicia. The Vienna government backed up the peasants, offered a bounty of ten florins to any peasant capturing a seditious landlord alive or dead, and hesitatingly made a few reforms to protect the serf against the lord. At least 162 landlords are known to have been killed by peasants, often with indescribable cruelty. Polish nationalism again faded out. In Russian Poland it was held down by police repression. This is the reason why in the almost universal rising of 1848 so little is heard of Poland.

Elsewhere in the Austrian system, in March 1848, everything collapsed with incredible swiftness. At that time the diet of Hungary had been sitting for some months, considering constitutional reforms and, as usual, debating further means of keeping German influence out of Hungary. Then came news of the February Revolution in Paris. The radical party in the Hungarian diet was aroused. Its leader, Louis Kossuth, on March 3 made an impassioned speech on the virtues of liberty. This speech was immediately printed in German and read in Vienna, where restlessness was also heightened by the news from Paris. On March 13 workingmen and students rose in insurrection in Vienna, manned barricades, fought off soldiers, and invaded the imperial palace. So flabbergasted and terrified was the government that Metternich, to the amazement of Europe, resigned and fled in disguise to England.

The fall of Metternich proved that the Vienna government was entirely disoriented. Revolution swept through the empire and through all Italy and Germany. On March 15 rioting began in Berlin; the king of Prussia promised a constitution. The lesser German governments collapsed in sequence. On the last day of March a Pre-Parliament met to arrange the calling of an all-German national assembly. In Hungary, aroused by Kossuth's national party, the diet on March 15 enacted the March Laws, by which Hungary assumed a position of complete constitutional separatism within the empire, while still recognizing the Habsburg house. The harassed Emperor Ferdinand a few days later granted substantially the same status to Bohemia. At Milan between March 18 and 22 the populace drove out the Austrian garrison. Venice proclaimed itself an independent republic. Tuscany drove out its grand duke and also set up as a republic. The king of Sardinia, Charles Albert (who, stimulated by the Paris revolution, had granted a constitution to his small country on March 4) declared war on Austria on March 23 and invaded Lombardy-Venetia, hoping to bring that area under the house of Savoy. Italian troops streamed up from Tuscany, from Naples (where revolution had broken out as early as January), and even from the papal states (the new pope being in some sympathy with national and liberal aims) to join in an all-Italian war against the seemingly helpless Austrian government.

Thus in the brief span of these phenomenal March Days the whole structure based on Vienna went to pieces: the Austrian Empire had fallen into its main components, Prussia had yielded to revolutionaries, all Germany was preparing to unify itself, and war raged in Italy. Everywhere constitutions had been wildly promised by stupefied governments, constitutional assemblies were meeting, and independent or autonomous nations struggled into existence. Patriots everywhere demanded liberal government and national freedom—written constitutions, representative assemblies, responsible ministries, a more or less extended suffrage, restrictions upon police action, jury trial, civil liberty, freedom of press and assembly. And where it still existed—in Prussia, Galicia, Bohemia, Hungary—serfdom was declared abolished and the peasant masses became legally free from control by their local lords.

The Turning of
the Tide after June

The revolution, as in France, surged forward until the month of June, and then began to ebb. For its steady reflux there are many reasons. The old governments had been only stunned in the March Days, not really broken. They merely awaited the opportunity to take back promises extorted by force. The force originally imposed by the revolutionaries could not be sustained. The revolutionary leaders were not really very strong. Middle-class, bourgeois, property-owning, and commercial interests were nowhere nearly as highly developed as in western Europe. The revolutionary leaders were to a large extent writers, editors, professors, and students, men of ideas rather than spokesmen for large positive interests. In Vienna, Milan, and a few other cities the working class was numerous and socialist ideas fairly common; but the workers were not as literate, organized, politically conscious, or irritated as in Paris or Great Britain. They were strong enough, however, to disquiet the middle classes; and especially after the specter of social revolution rose over western Europe, the middle-class and lower-class revolutionaries began to be afraid of each other. The liberated nationalities also began to disagree. The peasants, once emancipated, had no further interest in revolution. Nor were the peasants at this time conscious of nationality; nationalism was primarily a doctrine of the educated middle classes or of the landowning classes in Poland and Hungary. Since the old internationally minded aristocracy furnished the bulk of officers in the armies, and the peasants the bulk of the soldiers, the armies remained almost immune to nationalist aspirations. This attitude of the armies was decisive.

The tide first turned in Prague. The all-German national assembly met at Frankfurt-on-the-Main in May. Representatives from Bohemia had been invited to come to Frankfurt, since many Germans had always lived in Bohemia, and since Bohemia formed part of the confederation of 1815 as it had of the Holy Roman Empire before it. But the idea of belonging to a national German state, a Germany based on the principle that the inhabitants were Germans (which had not been the principle of the Holy Roman Empire or of the confederation of 1815) did not appeal to the Czechs in Bohemia. They refused to go to the all-German congress at Frankfurt. Instead, they called an all-Slav congress of their own. At Prague, in June 1848, this first Pan-Slav assembly met. Most of the delegates were from the Slav communities within the Austrian Empire, but a few came from the Balkans and non-Austrian Poland. Only one Russian was present, the anarchist revolutionary Michael Bakunin. Slavs generally did not at this time look with favor upon Russia, the oppressor of Poles; nor did the tsarist government, under Nicholas I, think well of Pan-Slavism, seeing in it a subversive popular agitation.

The spirit of the Prague congress was that of the Slavic Revival described in the last chapter;[7] the Czech historian Palacky was in fact one of its most active figures. The congress was profoundly anti-German, since the essence of the Slavic Revival was resistance to Germanization. But it was not profoundly anti-Austrian or anti-Habsburg. A few extremists, indeed, maintained that Slavdom should be the basis of political regeneration, and that the world therefore had no place for an Austrian empire. But the great majority at the Prague congress were Austroslavs. Austroslavism held that the many Slavic peoples, pressed on two sides by the population masses of Russians and Germans, needed the Austrian Empire as a political frame within which to develop their own national life. It demanded that the Slavic peoples be admitted as equals with the other nationalities in the Austrian Empire, enjoying local autonomy and constitutional guarantees.

The Germans of Bohemia, the Sudeten Germans, were of course attracted to the Frankfurt Assembly. They were eager to be included in the unified Germany about to be formed. As the Bohemian Czechs would be a minority in a German Germany, so the Bohemian Germans would be a minority in a Czech Bohemia. Minorities questions are often also questions of frontiers. There was therefore friction among the mixed people of Bohemia and in Prague, a bilingual city.

The German-Slav issue in the Austrian Empire did not seem altogether insuperable. The March revolution produced not only projects for constitutions for the major parts of the empire, but also a project for a federal constitution for the empire as a whole. An assembly sitting at Kremsier in Moravia, and including delegates from almost all parts of the empire except Hungary and north Italy, finally after much heated argument produced a federal plan. By this Kremsier constitution the Germans of the empire, i.e., some of the liberal Germans brought forward by the revolution, acknowledged the main principles of Austroslavism. The empire, as they saw it, should become a federation of equal nationalities. All persons should be assured in their right to have schools, law courts, and a public press in their own

[7]See pp. 481–482.

language. The empire should be decentralized, with wide powers given to local and municipal authorities. At the same time it should hold together as a federal system under a constitutional monarchy of the house of Habsburg.

But the Emperor Ferdinand, and the advisors on whom he chose to rely, would have nothing to do with Kremsier constitutions and Austroslavism. These national schemes were also liberal, bristling with restrictions upon the powers of the state. All therefore were to be resisted. The first victory of the old government came at Prague. In that city a Czech insurrection broke out on June 12, at the time when the Slav congress was sitting, and made worse by local animosities between Czechs and Germans. Windischgrätz, the local army commander, bombarded and subdued the city. The Slav congress dispersed. The Habsburg army was in control.

The next victory of the counterrevolution came in north Italy in the following month. Only Lombardy-Venetia, of all parts of the empire, had declared independence from the Habsburgs during the upheavals of March. The diminutive kingdom of Sardinia had supported them and had declared war on Austria. Italians from all over the peninsula had flocked in to fight; and until after the June Days in Paris it seemed not impossible that republican France might intervene, to befriend fellow revolutionaries, as in 1796. But in France no radical or expansionist revolution succeeded. In Italy the republicans and the king of Sardinia distrusted each other, a principal belief of republicans being that there should be no kings, and of kings that republicans were dangerously subversive. The troops sent from Naples were recalled to suppress the revolution there. The pope decided that he ought not to be participating in a war. The north Italians were left to themselves. Radetsky, the Austrian commander in Italy, overwhelmingly defeated the king of Sardinia at Custozza on July 25. The Sardinian king, Charles Albert, retreated into his own country. Lombardy and Venetia were restored with savage vengeance to the Austrian Empire. In Vienna some of the German revolutionaries (for not all entertained the broad views of Kremsier) expressed a nationalistic delight at this new German suppression of Italian rebels. To some of them liberty meant liberty for Germans, and they failed to perceive that the victorious imperial army would soon be turned against themselves.

The third victory of the counterrevolution came in September and October. The Hungarian radical party of Louis Kossuth was liberal and even democratic in many of its principles, but it was a Magyar nationalist party above all else. Triumphant in the March Days, it completely shook off the German connection. It moved the capital from Pressburg near the Austrian border to Budapest in the center of Hungary. It changed the official language of Hungary from Latin to Magyar. Less than half the people of Hungary were Magyars, and Magyar is an extremely difficult language, quite alien to the Indo-European tongues of Europe. It soon became clear that one must be a Magyar to benefit from the new liberal constitution, and that the Magyars intended to denationalize and Magyarize all others with whom they shared the country. Slovaks, Rumanians, Germans, Serbs, and Croats violently resisted, each group determined to keep its own national identity unimpaired. The Croats, who had enjoyed certain Croatian liberties before the Magyar revolution, took the lead under Count Jellachich, the "ban," or provincial governor, of Croatia. In September Jellachich raised a civil war in Hungary, leading a force of Serbo-Croatians, supported by the whole non-Magyar half of the population. Half of Hungary, alarmed by Magyar nationalism, now looked to the Habsburgs and the empire to protect them. Emperor Ferdinand made Jellachich his military commander against the Magyars. Hungary dissolved into the war of all against all.

At Vienna the more clear-sighted revolutionaries, who had led the March rising, now saw that Jellachich's army, if successful against the Magyars, would soon be turned against them. They therefore rose in a second mass insurrection in October 1848. The emperor fled; never had the Viennese revolution gone so far. But it was already too late. The Austrian military leader Windischgrätz brought his intact forces down from Bohemia. He besieged Vienna for five days and forced its surrender on October 31.

With the recapture of Vienna the upholders of the old order took heart. Counterrevolutionary leaders—large estate holders, Catholic clergy, high-ranking army men—decided to clear the way by getting rid of the Emperor Ferdinand, considering that promises made in March by Ferdinand might be more easily repudiated by his successor. Ferdinand abdicated and on December 2, 1848, was succeeded by Francis Joseph, a boy of eighteen, destined to live until 1916 and to end his reign in a crisis even more shattering than that in which he began it.

For a time in the first part of 1849 the revolution in many places seemed to blaze more fiercely than ever. Republican riots broke out in parts of Germany. In Rome someone assassinated the reforming minister of Pius IX; the pope fled from the city, and a radical Roman Republic was proclaimed under three Triumvirs, one of whom was Mazzini, who hastened from England to take part in the republican upheaval. In north Italy Charles Albert of Sardinia again invaded Lombardy. In Hungary, after the revived Habsburg authorities repudiated the new Magyar constitution, the Magyars, led by the flaming Kossuth, went on to declare absolute independence. But all these manifestations proved short-lived. German republicanism flickered out. Mazzini and his republicans were driven from Rome, and Pius IX was restored, by intervention of the French army.[8] The Sardinian king was again defeated by Radetsky at Novara on March 23, 1849. In Hungary the Magyars put up a terrific resistance, which the imperial army and the anti-Magyar native irregulars could not overcome. The Habsburg authorities now renewed the procedures of the Holy Alliance. The new Emperor Francis Joseph invited the Tsar Nicholas to intervene. Over a hundred thousand Russian troops poured over the mountains into Hungary, soon defeated the Magyars, and laid the prostrate country at the feet of the court of Vienna. This was in August 1849.

[8] See p. 518.

The nationalist upheaval of 1848 in central Europe and Italy was now over. The Habsburg authority had been reasserted over Czech nationalists in Prague, Magyars in Hungary, Italian patriots in north Italy, and liberal revolutionists in Vienna itself. Reaction, or antirevolutionism, became the order of the day. Pius IX, the "liberal pope" of 1846, resumed the papal throne disillusioned in his liberal ideas. The breach between liberalism and Roman Catholicism, which had opened wide in the first French Revolution, was made a yawning chasm by the revolutionary violence of Mazzini's Roman Republic and by the measures taken to repress it. Pius IX now reiterated the anathemas of his predecessors. He codified them in 1864 in the *Syllabus of Errors*, which warned all Catholics, on the authority of the Vatican, against everything that went under the names of liberalism, progress, and civilization. As for the nationalists in Italy, many were disillusioned with the firecracker methods of romantic republicans and inclined to conclude that Italy would be liberated from Austrian influence only by an old-fashioned war between established powers.

In the Austrian Empire, under Prince Schwarzenberg, the emperor's chief minister, the main policy was now to oppose all forms of popular self-expression, with a sophistication, in view of the events of 1848, that Metternich had never known, and with a candid reliance on military force. Constitutionalism was to be rooted out, as well as all forms of nationalism—Slavism, Magyarism, Italianism, and also Germanism, which would draw the sentiments of Austrian Germans from the Habsburg empire to the great kindred body of the German people. The regime came to be called the Bach system, after Alexander Bach, the minister of the interior. Under it, the government was rigidly centralized. Hungary lost the separate rights it had had before 1848. The ideal was to create a perfectly solid and unitary political system. Bach insisted on maintaining the emancipation of the peasants, which had converted the mass of the people from subjects of their landlords into subjects of the state. He drove through a reform of the legal system and law courts, created a free trading area of the whole empire with only a common external tariff, and subsidized and encouraged the building of highways and railroads. The aim, as in France at the same time under Louis-Napoleon, was to make people forget liberty in an overwhelming demonstration of administrative efficiency and material progress. But some, at that time, would not forget. A liberal said of the Bach system that it consisted of "a standing army of soldiers, a sitting army of officials, a kneeling army of priests, and a creeping army of informers."

59 Frankfurt and Berlin: The Question of a Liberal Germany

The German States

Meanwhile, from May 1848 to May 1849, the Frankfurt Assembly was sitting at the historic city on the Main. It was attempting to bring a unified German state into being, one which should also be liberal and constitutional, assuring civil rights to its citizens and possessing a government responsive to popular will as manifested in free elections and open parliamentary debate. The failure to produce a democratic Germany has been one of the overshadowing facts of modern times.

The convocation of the Frankfurt Assembly was made possible by the collapse of the existing German governments in the March Days of 1848. These governments, the thirty-nine states recognized after the Congress of Vienna, were the main obstacles in the way of unification. The reigning princes and their ministers enjoyed a heightened political stature from political independence. The German states resisted the surrender of sovereignty to a united Germany just as national states in the next century were to resist the surrender of sovereignty to a United Nations. In another way Germany was a miniature of the political world. It consisted of both great and small powers. Its great powers were Prussia and Austria. Austria was the miscellaneous empire described above; Prussia after 1815 included the Rhineland, the central regions around Berlin, West Prussia and Posen acquired in the partitions of Poland, and historic East Prussia. The former Polish areas were inhabited by a mixture of Germans and Poles.[9] Neither of these great powers could submit to the other or allow the other to dominate its lesser German neighbors. The small German powers, in turn, upheld their own independence in the balance between the two great ones.

Frankfurt and Berlin: The Question of a Liberal Germany

This German "dualism," or polarity between Berlin and Vienna, had been somewhat abated under the common menace of the Napoleonic empire. Then from 1815 to 1848 the Prussian kings, Frederick William III and Frederick William IV, had adopted a deferential respectfulness toward the house of Austria. Sharing the ideology of conservatism, they had made no open issue of Metternich's influence in the lesser states. The whole German question had lain dormant, so far as the governments were concerned, nor did it agitate the old aristocracies. In Prussia the Junkers, the owners of great landed estates east of the Elbe, were singularly indifferent to the all-German dream. Their political feeling was not German but Prussian. They were making a good thing of Prussia for themselves and could expect only to lose by absorption into Germany as a whole, for in Germany west of the Elbe the small peasant holding was the basis of society, and there was no landowning element corresponding to the Junkers. The rest of Germany looked upon Prussia as somewhat uncouth and Eastern; but this feeling, too, had been abated in the time of Napoleon, when patriots from all over Germany enlisted in the Prussian service.[10]

Prussia was illiberal but not backward. Frederick William III repeatedly evaded his promise to grant a modern constitution.[11] His successor, Frederick William IV, who inherited the throne in 1840, and from whom much was at first hoped by liberals, proved to be a somewhat cloudy and neomedieval romantic, equally determined not to share his authority with his subjects. At the same time the government, administratively speaking, was efficient, progressive, and fair. The universities and elementary school system surpassed those of western Europe. In few places was literacy so high. The government followed in mercantilist traditions of evoking,

Berlin: Failure of the Revolution in Prussia

[9] See maps, pp. 236–237, 456–457; and see pp. 235–244, 256–261, 459.
[10] See p. 447.
[11] See p. 484.

planning, and supporting economic life.[12] In 1818 it initiated a tariff union, at first with tiny states (or enclaves) wholly enclosed within Prussia. This tariff union, or *Zollverein*, was extended in the following decades until by 1848 almost all Germany, outside of Austria and Bohemia, was joined in an economic union led by Prussia. Compared with the "China of Europe," the unmoving Austria of Metternich, Prussia seemed progressive and forward-looking.

On March 15, 1848, as noted above, rioting and street fighting broke out in Berlin. For a time it seemed as if the army would master the situation. But the king, Frederick William IV, a man of notions and projects, and erratically conscientious, called off the soldiers and allowed his subjects to elect the first all-Prussian legislative assembly. Thus though the army remained intact, and its Junker officers unconvinced, revolution proceeded superficially on its way. The Prussian Assembly proved surprisingly radical, since it was dominated by anti-Junker lower-class extremists from East Prussia. These men were supporting Polish revolutionaries and exiles who sought the restoration of Polish freedom. Their main belief was that the fortress of reaction was tsarist Russia—that the whole structure of Junkerdom, landlordism, serf-owning, and repression of national freedom depended ultimately on the armed might of the tsarist empire. (The subsequent intervention of Russia in Hungary indicated the truth of this diagnosis.) Prussian radicals, like many elsewhere, hoped to smash the Holy Alliance by raising an all-German or even European revolutionary war against Russia, to precipitate which they supported the claims of the Poles.

Meanwhile the radical-dominated Berlin Assembly granted local self-government to the Poles in the formerly Polish areas of West Prussia and Posen. But in those areas Germans and Slavs had long lived side by side. The Germans in Posen refused to respect the authority of Polish officials. Prussian army units stationed in Posen supported the German element. As early as April 1848, a month after the "revolution," the army crushed the new pro-Polish institutions set up in Posen by the Berlin Assembly. It was clear where the only real power lay. By the end of 1848, in Prussia as in Austria, the revolution was over. The king again changed his mind; and the old authorities, acting through the army, were again in control.

The Frankfurt Assembly

Meanwhile a similar story was enacted on the larger stage of Germany as a whole. The disabling of the old governments left what is known in modern parlance as a power vacuum. A self-appointed committee convoked a Pre-Parliament, which in turn arranged for the election of an all-German assembly. Bypassing the existing sovereignties, voters throughout Germany sent delegates to Frankfurt to create a federated super-state. The strength and weakness of the resulting Frankfurt Assembly originated in this manner of its election. The Assembly represented the moral sentiment of people at large, the liberal and national aspirations of many Germans. It stood for an idea. Politically it represented nothing. The delegates had no power to commit anybody to do anything. There was no one to whom they could

[12]See pp. 124–126, 241–242, 344.

issue orders and expect compliance. Superficially resembling the National Assembly which met in France in 1789, the German National Assembly at Frankfurt was really in a very different position. There was no preexisting national structure for it to work with. There was no all-German army or civil service for the Assembly to take over. The whole history of the Frankfurt Assembly may be summarized in the remark that, having no power of its own, it became dependent on the power of the very sovereign states that it was attempting to supersede.

The Assembly met in May 1848. Its members with a handful of exceptions were not at all revolutionary. They were overwhelmingly professional people—professors, judges, lawyers, government administrators, clergy both Protestant and Catholic, and prominent businessmen. They wanted a liberal, self-governing, federally unified, and "democratic" though not equalitarian Germany. Their outlook was earnest, peaceable, and legalistic; they hoped to succeed by persuasion. Violence was abhorrent to them. They wanted no armed conflict with the existing German states. They wanted no war with Russia. They wanted no general international upheaval of the working classes. The example of the June Days in Paris, and of the Chartist agitation in Great Britain, coinciding with the early weeks of the Frankfurt Assembly, increased the dread of that body for radicalism and republicanism in Germany. The tragedy of Germany (and hence of Europe) lies in the fact that this German revolution came too late, at a time when social revolutionaries had already begun to declare war on the bourgeoisie, and the bourgeoisie was already afraid of the common man. It is the common man, not the professor or respectable merchant, who in unsettled times actually seizes firearms and rushes to shout revolutionary utterances in the streets. Without lower-class insurrection not even middle-class revolutions have been successful. The combination effected in France between 1789 and 1794, an unwilling and divergent combination of bourgeois and lower-class revolutionaries, was not and could not be effected in Germany in 1848. One form of revolutionary power—controlled popular turbulence—the Germans of the Frankfurt Assembly would not or could not use. Quite the contrary: when radical riots broke out in Frankfurt itself in September 1848 the Assembly undertook to repress them. Having no force of its own, it appealed to the Prussian army. The Prussian army put down the riots, and thereafter the Assembly met under its protection.

But the most troublesome question facing the Frankfurt Assembly was not social but national. What, after all, was this "Germany" which so far existed only in the mind? Where was the line really to be drawn in space? Did Germany include Austria and Bohemia, which belonged to the Bund of 1815 and had in former days belonged to the Holy Roman Reich? [13] Did it include all Prussia, although eastern Prussia had lain outside the Reich and did not now belong to the Bund? On the side toward Denmark, did it include the duchies of Schleswig and Holstein, which belonged to the Danish king, who was therefore himself, as ruler of Holstein, a member of the 1815 confederation? And if, as poets said, the Fatherland existed wherever the German tongue was spoken, what of the German communities in Hungary and Moravia, or along the upper Baltic and in the city of Riga, or in some of the Swiss cantons and the

[13] See maps, pp. 456–457, 570.

529

city of Zurich, or for that matter in Holland, which had left the Holy Empire only two hundred years before—not long as time is measured in Europe.

These last and most soaring speculations, though they had already been launched by a few bold spirits, were put out of mind by the men of the Frankfurt Assembly. The other questions remained. The men at Frankfurt, eager to create a real Germany, naturally could not offer one smaller than the shadow Germany that they so much deplored. Most therefore were Great Germans; they thought that the Germany for which they were writing a constitution should include the Austrian lands, except Hungary. This would mean that the federal crown must be offered to the Habsburgs. Others, at first a minority, were Little Germans; they thought that Austria should be excluded, and that the new Germany should comprise the smaller states and the entire kingdom of Prussia. In that case the king of Prussia would become the federal emperor. Under Great German auspices, the Pre-Parliament had invited Bohemian delegates to come to Frankfurt, had met with the refusal from the Czechs described above, and had precipitated the calling of the Prague Assembly in reply. These manifestations of Slavism were annoying to the Germanists at Frankfurt. Nationally minded Germans, both moderate and radical, believed that the Slavs west of Russia were destined for assimilation to German culture, following the Sorbs, Wends, Polabs, Kashubes, and other extinct or nearly extinct Slavonic peoples. They would point to the United States, where the English-speaking element gradually assimilated all others. And in truth the civilizing influence of Germans in eastern Europe was a historical fact, though German nationalists greatly idealized it.

The desire of the Frankfurt Assembly to retain non-German peoples in the new Germany, at a time when these peoples also were feeling national ambitions, was another reason for its fatal dependency upon the Austrian and Prussian armies. The Frankfurt Assembly applauded when Windischgrätz broke the Czech revolution. It expressed its satisfaction when Prussian forces put down the Poles in Posen. On this matter the National Assembly at Frankfurt and the Prussian Assembly at Berlin did not agree. The men of Frankfurt, thinking the Prussian revolutionary assembly too radical and pro-Polish, and wanting no war with Russia, in effect supported the Prussian army and the Junkers against the Berlin Revolution, without which the Frankfurt Assembly itself could never have existed.

A still clearer case arose over Schleswig-Holstein. These duchies belonged to the Danish king. Schleswig, the northern of the two, had a mixed population of Danes and Germans. The Germans in Schleswig rebelled in March 1848; and the Danes, who also had a constitutional upheaval at the time, proceeded to incorporate Schleswig integrally into their modernized Danish state. When the Frankfurt Assembly met, it found that the Pre-Parliament had already declared an all-German war upon Denmark in defense of fellow Germans in Schleswig. Having no army of its own, the Frankfurt Assembly invited Prussia to fight the war; and the revolutionary Prussian government in Berlin was at first able to persuade the Prussian generals to initiate a campaign. Great Britain and Russia prepared to intervene to keep control of the mouth of the Baltic out of German hands. The Prussian army simply withdrew from the war. Its officers had no desire to antagonize Russia or to advance the interests of nationalist revolutionaries in Germany. The Frankfurt Assembly, humiliated and helpless, was obliged to accept the armistice concluded by the Prussian generals. Radical socionationalistic riots broke out against the Junkers, the tsar, and the Frankfurt Assembly; and it was at this time that the Assembly called in Prussian forces for its own protection.

By the end of 1848 the débacle was approaching. The nationalists had check-mated each other. Everywhere in central Europe, from Denmark to Naples and from the Rhineland to the Transylvanian forests, the awakening nationalities had failed to respect each other's aspirations, had delighted in each other's defeats, and by quarreling with each other had hastened the return of the old absolutist and nonnational order. At Berlin and at Vienna the counterrevolution, backed by the army, was in the saddle. At this very time, in December, the Frankfurt Assembly at last issued a Declaration of the Rights of the German People. It was a humane and high-minded document, announcing numerous individual rights, civil liberties, and constitutional guarantees, much along the line of the French and American declarations of the eighteenth century, but with one significant difference—the French and Americans spoke of the rights of man, the Germans of the rights of Germans. In April 1849 the Frankfurt Assembly completed its constitution. It was now clear that Austria must be excluded, for the simple reason that the restored Habsburg government refused to come in. The Danubian empire, as already seen, was as profoundly opposed to Germanism as to any other nationalistic movement. The Little Germans in the Assembly therefore had their way. The hereditary headship of a new German Reich or empire, a constitutional and federal union of German states minus Austria, was now offered to Frederick William IV, the king of Prussia.

Frederick William was tempted. The Prussian army officers and East-Elbian landlords were not. They had no wish to lose Prussia in Germany. The king himself had his scruples. If he took the proffered crown he would still have to impose himself by force on the lesser states, which the Frankfurt Assembly did not represent and could not bind, and which were in fact still the actual powers in the country. He could also expect trouble with Austria. He did not wish war. Nor was it proper for an heir to the Hohenzollerns to accept a throne circumscribed with constitutional limitations and representing the revolutionary conception of the sovereignty of the people. Declaring that he could not "pick up a crown from the gutter," he turned it down. It would have to be offered freely by his equals, the sovereign princes of Germany.

Thus all the work of the Frankfurt Assembly went for nothing. Most members of the Assembly, having never dreamed of using violence in the first place, concluded that they were beaten and went home. A handful of extremists remained at Frankfurt, promulgated the constitution on their own authority, urged revolutionary outbreaks, and called for elections. Riots broke out in various places. The Prussian army put them down—in Saxony, in Bavaria, in Baden. The same army drove the rump Assembly out of Frankfurt, and that was the end of it.

But the king of Prussia, like Caesar, really craved the crown he spurned. He devised a German union of his own, a federation of the German princes without Austria. A united Germany of any kind, even monarchist and conservative, was distasteful to Schwarzenberg's government at Vienna, and at least equally so to a mightier potentate, the Russian tsar. For centuries, indeed, the division of Germany had been basic to the whole political structure of Europe. At a conference at Olmütz in 1850 the three Eastern monarchies reached an agreement: the king of Prussia would drop his German plan, and the loose confederation of 1815 would be restored. This incident, under the influence of Prusso-German writers of later years, passed into the history books as the "humiliation" of Olmütz.

In summary, Germany in 1848 failed to solve the problem of its unification in a liberal and constitutional way. Liberal nationalism failed, and a less gentle kind of nationalism soon replaced it. The German movement of 1848, like so much else in German history, in the long run contributed to a fateful estrangement between Germany and the West. Thousands of disappointed German liberals and revolutionaries migrated to the United States, which came to know them as the "Forty-eighters." They brought to the new country, besides a ripple of revolutionary agitation, a stream of men trained in science, medicine, and music, and of highly skilled craftsmen like silversmiths and engravers.

In Prussia itself the ingenious monarch undertook to placate everybody by issuing a constitution of his own, one that should be peculiarly Prussian. It remained in effect from 1850 to 1918. It granted a single parliament for all the miscellaneous regions of Prussia. The parliament met in two chambers. The lower chamber was elected by manhood suffrage, not along the individualist or equalitarian principles of the West, but by a system that in effect divided the population into three estates—the wealthy, the less wealthy, and the general run of the people. Division was made according to payment of taxes. Those few big taxpayers who together contributed a third of the tax returns chose a third of the members of district electoral colleges, which in turn chose deputies to the Prussian lower house. In this way one large property-owner had as much voting power as hundreds of working people. Large property in Prussia in 1850 still meant mainly the landed estates of the East-Elbian Junkers, but as time went on it came to include industrial property in the Rhineland also. The Junkers likewise were not harmed by the final liquidation of serfdom. They increased the acreage of their holdings, as after the reforms of Stein; [14] and the former servile agricultural workers turned into free wage earners economically dependent on the great landowners.

For 1850 the Prussian constitution was fairly progressive. If the mass of the people could elect only a relatively small number of deputies under the indirect system described, the mass of the British people, until 1867 or even 1884, could elect no deputies to Parliament at all. But the Prussian constitution remained in force until

[14] See p. 449.

1918. By the close of the nineteenth century, with democratic advances making their appearance elsewhere, the electoral system in Prussia, remaining unchanged, came to be reactionary and illiberal, giving the great landowners and industrialists an unusual position of special privilege within the state.

The Revolution of 1848 failed not only in Germany but also in Hungary, in Italy, and in France. The dreams of half a century, visions of a humanitarian nationalism, aspirations for liberalism without violence, ideals of a peaceful and democratic republican commonwealth, were all blasted in 1848. Everywhere the cry had been for constitutional government, but only in a few small states—Denmark, Holland, Belgium, Switzerland, Sardinia—was constitutional liberty more firmly secured by the Revolution of 1848. Everywhere the cry had been for the freedom of nations, to unify national groups or rid them of foreign rule; but nowhere was national liberty more advanced in 1850 than it had been two years before. France obtained manhood suffrage in 1848, and kept it permanently thereafter; but it did not obtain democracy; it obtained a kind of mass dictatorship under Louis-Napoleon Bonaparte. One accomplishment, however, was real enough. The peasantry was emancipated in the German states and the Austrian Empire. Serfdom and manorial restraints were abolished, nor were they reimposed after the failure of the revolution. This was the most fundamental accomplishment of the whole movement. The peasant masses of central Europe were thereafter free to move about, find new jobs, enter a labor market, take part in a money economy, receive and spend wages, migrate to growing cities—or even go to the United States. But the peasants, once freed, showed little concern for constitutional or bourgeois ideas; and peasant emancipation in fact strengthened the forces of political counterrevolution.

Possibly the failure of the 1848 revolution frustrated the democratic development of Europe. Possibly its failure saved Europe from ruin. Had the more zealous revolutionists been more successful, there might indeed have been a spread of democratic institutions, but there might also have been war with Russia, turning into a general European war, inflamed class violence, and nationalistic strife. Possibly the balance of successes and failures gave Europe a half-century of respite for the constructive development of its civilization. The tradition of slow and unforced parliamentary change was confirmed in England. Constitutionalism was established permanently in the small states of the West. The propertied classes of Europe—bourgeois, landlords, small landowning peasants—were secured. The 1850s initiated a period of rising prices and wages, of general economic prosperity as compared with the 1840s; the working classes quieted down, and revolutionary agitation subsided. But the Revolution of 1848 had deposited some deeply laid time bombs—class hatred and national jealousy, Pan-Germanism and Pan-Slavism, a dictatorship in France betraying certain features later called "fascist," and last but not least the philosophy of Karl Marx.

60
Consequences of the 1848 Movements: The New Toughness of Mind

The Results of 1848

The most immediate and far-reaching consequence of the 1848 revolution was a moral reorientation. Idealism was discredited. Ideas themselves were seen in a new way. It had been proved insufficient to have only an idea (or "ideal") of Germany, or an idea of Austroslavism, or an idea of constitutional liberty, or of a socialized community, or of a free and equal republic. It had been shown that an idea could not be realized unless one had the means to achieve it. Emphasis therefore began to fall upon the means. It had been shown everywhere, but most clearly and unmistakably in Germany, that no political aim could be accomplished without power. People therefore became interested in power itself, in what it was, and how to obtain it.

Formerly men had prided themselves on being idealistic—on holding and working for ideas because they believed them to be right. Even conservatives of the old school, like Metternich and Wellington, believed in principle in the old order of things which they defended. Now, as the years passed after 1848, men prided themselves on being realistic, emancipated from illusions, willing to face facts as they were. Whether an idea was "right" became a somewhat irrelevant if not unanswerable question. The question was whether it was workable. A good idea was one that would succeed. The test was to be found in practical results. In any case, it now seemed, ideas had no especial validity in themselves. They were mere products, results of causes, outgrowths of social conditions. The question was not whether representative government was right or reasonable, suited to the nature of free and rational human beings. That was the old eighteenth-century way of thinking. The questions on representative government were, rather, what form of society it was suited for, what social classes demanded it, what they proposed to do with it, how they would advance their interests if they had it.

Everywhere after 1848 could be detected a new toughness of mind. It was an insistence on seeing facts, viewing things as they are rather than as they ought to be. In literature and the arts it was called "realism." Writers and painters broke away from romanticism, which they said colored things out of all relation to the real facts. They attempted to describe and reproduce life exactly as they found it, without intimation of a better or more noble world. More and more people came to trust science, not merely for an understanding of nature, but for insights into the true meaning of man and society. In religion the movement was toward skepticism, renewing the skeptical trend of the eighteenth century, which had been somewhat halted during the intervening period of romanticism. It was variously held, not by all but by many, that religion was unscientific and hence not to be taken seriously; or that it was a mere historical growth among peoples in certain stages of development and hence irrelevant to modern civilization; or that one ought to go to church and lead a decent life, without taking the priest or clergyman too seriously, because religion was necessary to preserve the social order against radicalism and anarchy. To this idea the radical counterpart was of course that religion was a bourgeois invention to delude the people.

In basic philosophy the new mental toughness appeared as materialism, holding that everything mental, spiritual, or ideal, was an outgrowth of physical or physiological forces. It appeared as positivism, holding that to have reliable knowledge one should concentrate on concrete facts and avoid abstract ideas. Its great exponent was the French philosopher Auguste Comte. It appeared also as voluntarism, deriving from a profound work published as long ago as 1819, but ignored for thirty years, *The World as Will and Idea* by the German Arthur Schopenhauer. Schopenhauer, much influenced by the philosophy of India (which became known to Europe as the British Empire advanced there), held that the underlying reality of the universe was will—a blind, instinctual, dynamic, driving will-to-live. Ideas formed in the mind, he thought, were rather shadowy representations, more or less useful, projected by this will for its own purposes. Schopenhauer himself taught that men could only be happy and at peace if the will-force was suppressed. But what the world learned from him was that thought and reason were offshoots of interests, urges, and drives. Since urges and interests were facts, would it not be "unrealistic" and "unscientific" to suppress them? And how would one know which facts to suppress and which to encourage, without going back to merely "idealistic" ideas of reason and right?

In politics the new toughness of mind was called by the Germans *Realpolitik.* This simply meant a "politics of reality." In domestic affairs it meant that people should give up utopian dreams, such as had caused the débacle of 1848, and content themselves with the blessings of an orderly, honest, hardworking government. For radicals it meant that people should stop imagining that the new society would result from goodness or the love of justice, and that social reformers must resort to the methods of politics—power and calculation. In international affairs it meant that governments should not be guided by ideology, or by any system of "natural" enemies or "natural" allies, or by any desire to defend or promote any particular view of the world; but that they should follow their own practical interests, meet facts and situations as they arose, make any alliances that seemed useful, disregard tastes and scruples, use any practical means to achieve their ends. The same men who, before 1848, had been not ashamed to express pacifist and cosmopolitan hopes now dismissed such ideas as a little soft-headed. War, which governments since the overthrow of Napoleon had successfully tried to prevent, was accepted in the 1850s as an obvious means sometimes necessary to achieve a purpose. It was not especially glorious; it was not an end in itself; it was simply one of the tools of the statesman. *Realpolitik* was by no means confined to Germany, despite its German name and although Bismarck became its most famous practitioner. Two other tough-minded thinkers, each in his way, were Louis-Napoleon Bonaparte and Karl Marx.

Marxism, which a century later was to command the assent of hundreds of millions in all parts of the world, first made its appearance in January 1848 with the publication of an obscure tract called *The Communist Manifesto.* It was written by two Germans, Karl Marx and Friedrich Engels, for an organization that called itself the Communist League. Marx (1818–1883), son of a lawyer in the Prussian Rhineland, was a democratic-radical newspaperman, who had studied law and philosophy.

Marx and Engels:
The Communist
Manifesto, 1848

Engels (1820–1895) was the son of a well-to-do German textile manufacturer who owned a factory at Manchester, which the young Engels went to England to manage. Marx and Engels met in Paris in 1844. There they began a collaboration in thinking and writing that lasted for forty years. In 1847 they joined the Communist League.

This League, which had also called itself the League of the Just, was a tiny secret group of revolutionaries, mainly Germans in exile in the more liberal western Europe. The League, according to Engels, was at first "not actually much more than the German branch of the French secret societies." It aspired to become international and worked by tactics of infiltration. In 1840, for example, a group of German workingmen living in London had founded the German Workers' Educational Association. This society, wrote Engels later, was used by the League as a recruiting ground,

and since, as always, the Communists were the most active and intelligent members of the Association, it was a matter of course that its leadership lay entirely in the hands of the League. The League soon had several local sections, or, as they were still called, "lodges," in London. The same obvious tactics were followed in Switzerland and elsewhere. Where workers' associations could be founded, they were utilized in like manner. Where this was forbidden by law, one entered choral societies, gymnastic clubs and the like.

Though the *Manifesto* published in January 1848 passed quite unnoticed, and had no influence on the upheaval that soon occurred, members of the League agitated like those of other societies during the Revolution of 1848. They issued a set of "Demands of the Communist Party in Germany," which urged a unified indivisible German republic, democratic suffrage, universal free education, arming of the people, a progressive income tax, limitations upon inheritance, state ownership of banks, railroads, canals, mines, etc., and a degree of large-scale, scientific, collectivized agriculture. It was such obscurely voiced radicalism that alarmed the Frankfurt Assembly. With the triumph of counterrevolution in Germany the Communist League was crushed. Engels returned to his factory at Manchester, and Marx also settled in England, spending the rest of his life in London, where, after long labors in the British Museum, he finally produced his huge work called *Capital,* of which the first volume was published in German in 1867.

Marxism played no real role in the Revolution of 1848. Not for another twenty years was Marxian socialism at all well known even to socialists. As a historical force Marxism set in in the 1870s. But it grew out of and exactly reflected the conditions of the 1840s. The main positions of Marxism were all mapped out in the *Communist Manifesto* and in contemporary studies which Marx and Engels made of the 1848 revolution. One of these, *Germany: Revolution and Counterrevolution,* first appeared as a series of dispatches to the *New York Tribune* in 1851 and 1852, for which Horace Greeley paid five dollars apiece. Another, *The Eighteenth Brumaire of Louis Bonaparte,* was also first published in 1852 in the United States, in a German-language paper called *Die Revolution.*

Marxism may be said to have had three sources or to have merged three national streams: French revolutionism, the British Industrial Revolution, and German philosophy. Without the massive fact of the Great French Revolution standing at the opening of the nineteenth century it is doubtful whether anyone would have developed so improbable a doctrine as the abrupt and total renovation of human affairs by The Revolution. But revolution had in fact occurred; it therefore might occur again. What the bourgeois class had done, the workers could do too. And Marxism along with all early forms of socialism saw an unredeemed promise in the French Revolution, believing that social and economic equality should follow the civil and legal equality already won.[15] In addition, and in keeping with the general movement of romanticism, the concept of liberty began also to mean a more personal emancipation. Marx, especially in his youthful writings, developed the idea of psychological alienation, a state of mind produced when a human being becomes divorced from the object on which he works, through the historic process of mechanization and commercialization of labor.

The revolutionary outbreaks of 1848, coming within a few weeks of the publication of the *Communist Manifesto,* naturally confirmed Marx and Engels in their beliefs, and the actual class war that shook Paris in the June Days was taken by them as a manifestation of a universal class struggle. But Marx was no mere insurrectionary schemer, like the "revolution-makers," as he contemptuously called them. His mature thought was a system for producing revolution, but it showed how the future revolution must come by the operation of vast impersonal forces.

Engels, a Manchester factory owner, possessed a personal knowledge of the new industrial and factory system in England. He was in touch with a few of the most radical Chartists, though he had no respect for Chartism itself as a revolutionary movement. In 1844 he published a revealing book on *The Condition of the Working Classes in England.* The depressed condition of labor, to which Marxism like all forms of socialism called emphatic attention, was an actual fact.[16] It was a fact that labor received a relatively small portion of the national income, and that much of the product of society was being reinvested in capital goods, which belonged as private property to private persons. Government and parliamentary institutions, also as a matter of fact, were in the hands of the well-to-do in both Great Britain and France. Religion was commonly held to be necessary to keep the lower classes in order. The churches at the time, as a matter of fact, took next to no interest in problems of the workers. At best, evangelical sects taught the poor that they must be patient. The family, as an institution, was in fact disintegrating among laboring people in the cities, through employment of women and children and the overcrowding in inadequate and unsanitary living quarters. All these facts were seized upon and dramatized in the *Communist Manifesto:* The worker is deprived of the wealth he has himself created! The state is a committee of the bourgeoisie for the exploitation of the people! Religion

[15] See pp. 475–477, 506.
[16] See pp. 468–470, 506–507.

is a drug to keep the workingman quietly dreaming upon imaginary heavenly rewards! The worker's family, his wife and children, have been prostituted and brutalized by the bourgeoisie! It seemed to Marx and Engels that the uprooted workingman should be loyal to nothing—except his own class. Even country had become meaningless. The proletarian had no country. Workers everywhere had the same problems and faced everywhere the same enemy. Therefore "let the ruling classes tremble at a communist revolution. The proletarians have nothing to lose but their chains. They have a world to win. Workingmen of all countries, unite!" So closed the *Manifesto*.

It was from English sources that Marx also took over much of his economic theory. From British political economy he adopted the subsistence theory of wages, or Iron Law, which orthodox economists presently abandoned since wages did in fact begin to rise.[17] It held that the average workingman could never obtain more than a minimum level of living—of which the corollary, for those who wished to draw it, was that the existing economic system held out no future for the laboring class as a class. Marx likewise took over from orthodox economists the labor theory of value, holding that the value of any man-made object depended ultimately on the amount of labor put into it—capital being regarded as the stored up labor of former times. Orthodox economists soon discarded the labor theory of value, preferring the theory that value is determined psychologically by satisfaction of human wants or tastes. Marx, from the labor theory, developed his doctrine of surplus value. This was very intricate; but "surplus value" meant in effect that the workingman was being robbed. He received in wages only a fraction of the value of the product which his labor produced. The difference was "expropriated" by the bourgeois capitalists—the private owners of the factories and the machines. And since workers never received in wages the equivalent of what they produced, capitalism was constantly menaced by overproduction, the accumulation of goods that people could not afford to buy. Hence it ran repeatedly into crises and depressions and was obliged also to be constantly expanding in search of new markets. It was the depression of 1847, according to Marx, that had precipitated the Revolution of 1848; and with every such depression during the rest of his lifetime Marx hoped that the day of the great social revolution was drawing nearer.

What brought all these observations together in a unified and compelling doctrine was the philosophy of dialectical materialism. By dialectic, Marx meant what the German philosopher Hegel had meant,[18] that all things are in movement and in evolution, and that all change comes through the clash of antagonistic elements. The word itself, coming from the Greek, meant originally a way of arriving at a higher conclusion through debate. The implications of the dialectic, for both Hegel and Marx, were that all history, and indeed all reality, is a process of development through time, a single and meaningful unfolding of events, necessary, logical, and deterministic; that every event happens in due sequence for good and sufficient reason (not by chance); and that history could not and cannot happen any differently from

[17] See pp. 471, 644.
[18] See p. 480.

the way it has happened and is still happening today. This, it need hardly be said, cannot be demonstrated on any basis of knowable fact.

Marx differed from Hegel in one vital respect. Whereas Hegel emphasized the primacy of "ideas" in social change, Marx gave emphasis to the primacy of material conditions. By materialism, Marx meant that the basic element in society is economic. It is not primarily by having ideas that men create the social world in which they live. On the contrary, their form of society, especially their economic institutions, predisposes them to have certain ideas. At bottom, it is the "relations of production" (technology, invention, natural resources, property systems, etc.) that determine what kind of religions, philosophies, governments, laws, and moral values men accept. To believe that ideas precede and generate actualities was, according to Marx, the error of Hegel. Hegel had thought, for example, that the mind conceives the idea of freedom, which it then realizes in the Greek city-state, in Christianity, in the French Revolution, and in the kingdom of Prussia. Not at all, according to Marx: the idea of freedom, or any other idea, is generated by the actual economic and social conditions. Conditions are the roots, ideas the trees. Hegel had held the ideas to be the roots and the resulting actual conditions to be the trees. Or as Marx and Engels said, they found Hegel standing on his head and set him on his feet again.

Dialectical materialism, or Marxian dialectic, offered an explanation of everything that had ever happened or could happen on earth. It is known also as economic determinism or as the materialist conception of history. As a philosophy of history, it raised the passing events of 1848 and of Marx's lifetime to a higher level of cosmic meaning. It gave Marxism the universal aspects of a religion. It made Marxian socialism into a dogma and a faith.

The picture of historical development offered by Marxism was somewhat as follows. Material conditions, or the relations of production, give rise to economic classes. Agrarian conditions produce a landholding or feudal class, but with changes in trade routes, money, and productive techniques a new commercial or bourgeois class arises. Each class, feudal and bourgeois, develops an ideology suited to its needs. Prevailing religions, governments, laws, and morals reflect the outlook of these classes. The two classes inevitably clash. Bourgeois revolutions against feudal interests break out—in England in 1642, in France in 1789, in Germany in 1848, though the bourgeois revolution in Germany proved abortive. Meanwhile, as the bourgeois class develops, it inevitably calls another class into being, its dialectical antithesis, the proletariat. The bourgeois is defined as the private owner of capital, the proletarian as the wage worker who possesses nothing but his own hands. The more a country becomes bourgeois, the more it becomes proletarian. The more production is concentrated in factories, the more the revolutionary laboring class is built up. Under competitive conditions the bourgeois tend to devour and absorb each other; ownership of the factories, mines, machines, railroads, etc. (capital), becomes concentrated into very few hands. Others sink into the proletariat. In the end the proletarianized mass simply takes over from the remaining bourgeois. It "expropriates the expropriators," abolishes the old private property in the means of production. The social revolution is thus accomplished. It is inevitable. A classless society results, because class arises from economic differences which have been done away with. The state and religion, being outgrowths of bourgeois interests, also disappear. For a time, until all vestiges of bourgeois interests have been rooted out, or until the danger of counterrevolution against socialism has been overcome, there will be a "dictatorship of the proletariat." After that the state will "wither away," since there is no longer an exploiting class to require it.

Meanwhile the call is to war. Bourgeois and proletarian are locked in a universal struggle. It is really war, and as in all war all other considerations must be subordinated to it. Periods of social calm are not peace; they are merely interludes between battles. The workers must not be allowed to grow soft or conciliatory, any more than an army should be allowed to forget its primary function of fighting. Workingmen and labor unions must be kept in a belligerent and revolutionary mood. They must never forget that the employer is their class enemy, and that government, law, morality, and religion are merely so much artillery directed against them. Morals are "bourgeois morals," law is "bourgeois law," government is an instrument of class power, and religion is a form of psychological warfare, a means of providing "opium" for the masses. The worker must not let himself be fooled; he must learn how to detect the class interest underlying the most exalted institutions and beliefs. In this piece of military intelligence, ferreting out the ways of the enemy, he will be helped by an understanding of dialectical materialism and will receive aid from intellectuals especially trained in explaining it to him. Like all fighting forces, the workers need a disciplined solidarity. The individual must lose himself in the whole—in his class. It is a betrayal of his class for a worker to rise above the proletariat, to "improve himself," as the bourgeois says. It is dangerous for labor unions merely to obtain better wages or hours by negotiation with employers, for by such little gains the war itself may be forgotten, the worker may lose interest in his own ultimate emancipation by revolution and in the plight of his fellow workers with whom his gains have not been shared. It is likewise dangerous, and even treasonous, for workers to put faith in the state, to be content with democratic machinery or "social legislation," for the state, an engine of repression, can never be made into an instrument of welfare. Law is the will of the stronger (i.e., the stronger class); "right" and "justice" are thin emanations of class interest. We must hold, wrote Marx in 1875, to "the realistic outlook which has cost so much effort to instill into the party, but which has now taken root in it"; and we must not let this outlook be perverted "by means of ideological nonsense about 'right' and other trash common among the democrats and French Socialists."

The Appeal of Marxism: Its Strength and Weaknesses

Marxism was a hard doctrine, with many advantages and many handicaps in the winning of adherents. One of its advantages was its claim to be scientific. Marx classified early and rival forms of socialism[19] as utopian: they rested on moral indignation, and their formula for reforming society was for men to become more just,

[19]See pp. 476–477.

or for the upper classes to be converted to sympathy for the lower. His own doctrine, Marx insisted, had nothing to do with ethical ideas; it was purely scientific, resting upon the study of actual facts and real processes, and it showed that socialism would be not a miraculous reversal but a historical continuation of what was already taking place. He also considered it utopian and unscientific to describe the future socialist society in any detail. It would be classless, with neither bourgeois nor proletarian; but to lay any specific plans would be idle dreaming. Let the revolution come, and the socialism would take care of itself.

The dialectical philosophy was another great advantage in the spreading of Marx's ideas. It disintegrated the foundations on which the world believed itself to be standing. State, church, law, morals became merely "bourgeois." Everything became a phase or manifestation of something else. Permanent things were made to look transient and absolute things to look relative, as in the great religions. But where in religion it was the idea of God before which all else became transitory and relative, in Marxism it was the idea of the everlasting class war. Class was the one enduring reality in a world of flux—until the Revolution, at which time class, the motivating force of all history, would suddenly cease to exist, a "utopian" element in Marxism that has often been pointed out, but which has never had a discouraging effect upon the winning of followers—rather the contrary. At the same time the dialectical philosophy, while disintegrating the "bourgeoisie," integrated the "proletariat." As Engels wrote:

Communism among the French and Germans, Chartism among the English, now no longer appeared as matters of chance that could just as well not have occurred. These movements now presented themselves as the movement of a modern oppressed class, the proletariat . . . but distinguished from all earlier class struggles by this one thing, that the present-day oppressed class, the proletariat, cannot achieve its emancipation without emancipating society as a whole from division into classes and therefore from class struggles. And communism now no longer meant the concoction by means of the imagination of an ideal society as perfect as possible, but the understanding of the nature and conditions . . . of the struggle waged by the proletariat.

In short, Marxism was a strong compound of the scientific, the historical, the metaphysical, and the apocalyptic.

But some elements of Marxism stood in the way of its natural propagation. The working people of Europe were not really in the frame of mind of an army in battle. They hesitated to subordinate all else to the distant prospect of a class revolution. They were not exclusively class-men, nor did they behave as such. Enough of Christianity was still alive in them, and of older natural-law ideas, to inhibit the belief that morality was a class weapon, or right and justice "trash." They had national loyalties to country; they could with difficulty associate themselves emotionally with a world proletariat in an unrelenting struggle against their own neighbors.

The cure for the revolutionism of 1848 proved in time to be the admission of the laboring classes to a fuller membership in society. Wages generally rose after 1850, labor unions were organized, and by 1870 in the principal European countries the workingman very generally had a vote. Through their unions, workers were often able to get better wages and working conditions by direct pressure upon employers. Having the vote, they gradually formed working-class parties, and as they proceeded to act through the state they had less inclination to destroy it. Marx's word for such maneuvers was "opportunism." Opportunism, the tendency of working people to better themselves by dealing with employers and by obtaining legislation through existing government channels, was the most dangerous of all dangers to the Revolution. For in war people do not negotiate or pass laws; they fight. From Marxism the working classes absorbed much, including a watchful hostility to employers and a sense of working-class solidarity; but on the whole, as Marxism spread at the close of the nineteenth century it ceased to be really revolutionary.[20] Had the old Europe not gone to pieces in the twentieth-century wars, and had Marxism not been revived by Lenin and transplanted to Russia, it is probable that Marx's doctrines would have been domesticated into the general body of European thought, and that much less would be said about them in this book.

We have seen how Louis-Napoleon Bonaparte, elected president of the republic in 1848, in 1852 made himself emperor of the French with the title of Napoleon III.[21] Those willing to fight for the parliamentary and liberal institutions which he crushed in 1851 proved to be a helpless minority. There is no doubt that he became "dictator" on a wave of popular acclaim.

*Political Institutions
of the Second Empire*

Indeed the dubious title of first modern dictator fits Napoleon III far better than it fits Napoleon I. The new Napoleon was not at all like his great uncle. He was no soldier, no administrator, and though intelligent enough he had no especial distinction or force of mind. He was a politician. He had led *Putsches* against the July monarchy, for which he had been imprisoned. The first Napoleon came to power in the course of a war which he had not started. The second Napoleon made himself dictator in time of peace, by playing on social fears in a country divided by an abortive revolution. The first Napoleon, it is hardly too much to say, never in his life condescended to make a public speech. Louis-Napoleon made them all the time; the political rostrum was his natural habitat. Public opinion was more of a force in 1850 than in 1800. Louis-Napoleon recognized it as an opportunity, not merely as a nuisance. He appealed to the masses by promises and by pageantry; he cultivated, solicited, directed, and manufactured popular favor. He understood perfectly that a single leader exerts more magnetism than an elected assembly. And he knew that a Europe still shuddering over the June Days was hoping desperately for order in France.

[20]See pp. 643–645.
[21]See pp. 516–519.

He gloried in modern progress. Toward the changes coming over Europe the monarchs of the old school usually showed an attitude of timidity and doubt if not positive opposition. Napoleon III boldly offered himself as the leader in a brave new world. Like his uncle, he announced that he embodied the sovereignty of the people. He believed, probably sincerely, that he had found a solution to the problem of mass democracy. In all the other great Continental states and in Great Britain, in 1852, universal suffrage was thought to be incompatible with intelligent government and economic prosperity. Napoleon III claimed to put them together. Like Marx and other "realists" after 1848 he held that elected parliamentary bodies, far from representing an abstract "people," only accentuated class divisions within a country. He declared that the regime of the restored Bourbons and the July monarchy had been dominated by special interests, that the Republic of 1848 had first been violent and anarchic, then fallen into the hands of a distrustful assembly that robbed the laboring man of his vote, and that France would find in the empire the permanent, popular, and modern system for which it had been vainly searching since 1789. He affirmed that he stood above classes and would govern equally in the interests of all. In any case, like many others after 1848, he held that forms of government were less important than economic and social realities. Like Marxism or the Bach system in Austria, the Bonapartism of Napoleon III put a low value on political freedom. It was as a leader in a great march toward material progress that the new Napoleon proposed himself to the French people. As he said at Bordeaux, while still "selling" the idea of the empire:

We have immense territories to cultivate, roads to open, harbors to deepen, canals to dig, rivers to make navigable, railroads to complete. . . . That is how I interpret the empire, if the empire is to be restored. Such are the conquests I contemplate; and you, all of you who surround me, and who wish our country's good, you are my soldiers.

But in this great enterprise the government must be untroubled by party politics and the vacillations and reversals of elected assemblies.

The political institutions of the Second Empire were therefore authoritarian, modeled on those of the Consulate of the first Bonaparte. There was a Council of State, composed of experts who drafted legislation and advised on technical matters. There was an appointive senate with few significant functions. There was a Legislative Body elected by universal suffrage. The elections were carefully managed. The government put up an official candidate for each seat whom all office-holders in the district were required to support. Other candidates might offer themselves for election, but there could be no political meetings of any kind, and if the independent candidate put up posters he had to use a different kind of paper from the official candidate. Few ventured in these circumstances to differ with the government.

The Legislative Body had no independent powers of its own. It could not initiate legislation but only consider what was submitted to it by the emperor's will. It had no control over the budget, for the emperor was legally free to borrow money as he saw fit. It had no power over the army or the foreign office or the making of war and peace. To publish speeches made in the legislative chamber was against the law. Any five members, by requesting a secret session, could exclude the public from the galleries. Parliamentary life sank toward absolute zero, and democracy meant that the citizen enjoyed the occasional pleasure of registering his approval of the regime. The newspapers were carefully muzzled, only those authorized by the government being permitted. Professorships of history and philosophy, which seem always to frighten dictatorial governments, were regulated or suppressed.

To captivate public attention and glorify the Napoleonic name the new emperor set up a sumptuous court at the Tuileries. Balked in the ambition to marry into one of the great dynasties, Napoleon III chose as his empress a young Spanish beauty, Eugénie, who was destined to outlive the empire by fifty years, dying in 1920. It was said to be a love match—a sure sign of popularized royalty. The court life of the empire was brilliant, gay, luxurious, and showy beyond anything known at the time in St. Petersburg or Vienna. The note of pageantry was further struck in the embellishment of the city of Paris. Baron Haussmann, one of the most creative of city planners, gave Paris much of the appearance that it has today. He built roomy railway stations with broad approaches, and he constructed a system of boulevards and public squares offering long vistas ending in fine buildings or monuments, as at the Place de l'Opéra. The building program, like the expensive court, had the additional advantage of stimulating business and employment. And the cutting of wide avenues through the crooked streets and congested old houses would permit easier military operations against insurrectionists entrenched behind barricades, should the events of 1848 ever be repeated.

Economic Developments
Under the Empire

It was as a great social engineer that Napoleon III preferred to be known. In his youth he had tried to read the riddle of modern industrialism, and now, as emperor, he found some of his main backers in former Saint-Simonians, who called him their "socialist emperor." Saint-Simon, it may be recalled, had been among the first to conceive of a centrally planned industrial system.[22] But the Saint-Simonians of the 1850s shared in the new sense of being realistic, and their most signal triumph was the invention of investment banking, by which they hoped to guide economic growth through the concentration of financial resources. They founded a novel kind of banking institution, the *Crédit Mobilier*, which raised funds by selling its shares to the public, and with the funds thus obtained bought stock in such new industrial enterprises as it wished to develop. A land bank, or *Crédit Foncier*, was likewise established to lend funds to landowners for the improvement of agriculture.

The times were exceedingly favorable for expansion, for the discovery of gold in California in 1849, and in Australia soon afterward, together with the newly organized credit facilities, brought a substantial increase in the European money supply, which had a mildly inflationary effect. The steady rise of prices and all money values encouraged company promotion and investment of capital. Railway mileage,

[22]See p. 476.

increasing everywhere in the Western world, increased in France from 3,000 to 16,000 kilometers in the 1850s. The demand for rolling stock, iron rails, auxiliary equipment, and building materials for stations and freight houses kept the mines and factories busy. The railway network was rationalized, fifty-five small lines in France being merged into six big regional trunks. Iron steamboats replaced wooden sailing ships. Between 1859 and 1869 a French company built the Suez Canal, which it continued to own for almost a century, though the British government after 1875 was the principal stockholder.

Large corporations made their appearance, in railroads and banking first of all. In 1863 the law granted the right of "limited liability," by which a stockholder could not lose more than the par value of his stock, however insolvent or debt-burdened the corporation might become. This encouraged investment by persons of small means, and by capitalists large and small in enterprises of which they knew very little; thus the wealth and savings of the country were more effectively mobilized and put to work. Stocks and shares became more numerous and diversified. The Stock Exchange boomed. Financiers—those whose business was to handle money, credit, and securities—assumed a new eminence in the capitalistic world. A good many people became very rich, richer perhaps than anyone had ever been in France before. Real industrial growth went along with a sag in morals, a scramble for easy money, a frenzy of speculation, and a rather vulgar taste for ostentatious living—anticipating the age of the tycoons that began in the United States some twenty years later. The Second Empire, in this respect, was even more "bourgeois" than the July monarchy.

The emperor aspired also to do something for the workingman, within the limits of the existing system. The land bank was of some use to the more substantial peasants. Jobs were plentiful and wages good, by the ideas of the day, at least until the temporary depression of 1857. The emperor had a plan, as did some of the Saint-Simonians, for organizing forces of workers in military fashion and setting them to clear and develop uncultivated land. Not much was done in this direction. More was accomplished in the humanitarian relief of suffering. Hospitals and asylums were established, and free medicines were distributed. The outlines of a social-service state began somewhat vaguely to appear. Meanwhile the workers were building up unions. All combinations of workingmen had been prohibited during the French Revolution, and the Le Chapelier law of 1791 was deemed to be still in force.[23] Gradually the ambiguous legal position of labor unions was clarified. In 1864 it even became legal for organized workingmen to go on strike. Large labor units, or unions, and large business units, or corporations, were thus legalized at the same time. Napoleon III hardly did enough for labor to rank as a working-class hero, but he did enough to be suspected as "socialistic" by many middle-class people of the day.

More recent dictatorships, bent like the Second Empire on a program of economic development, have usually been highly protectionist, unwilling to face open competition with the rest of the world. Napoleon III believed in freedom of international trade. He had a project for a tariff union with Belgium, which some

[23] See p. 389.

Belgians also supported. Belgium was already well industrialized, and a Franco-Belgian union, especially since Belgium had the coal which France lacked, would have formed a trading area of very great strength. But the plan was blocked by private interests in both countries, and strongly opposed by both Great Britain and the German *Zollverein*. The emperor then turned to an all-around reduction of import duties. Since the repeal of the Corn Laws in 1846 the free-traders were in power in England.[24] They were eager to abolish trade barriers between Britain and France. Napoleon III, overriding opposition in his Legislative Body, concluded a free trade treaty with Great Britain in 1860. He set aside 40,000,000 francs of government funds to assist French manufacturers to make adjustments in the face of British competition; but this sum was never spent in full, and it has hence been concluded that French industry was able to compete successfully with the more intensively mechanized industry of Britain. The Anglo-French treaty was accompanied by lesser trade agreements with other countries. It looked, in the 1860s, as if Europe might actually be about to enter the promised land of freedom of trade.

Internal Difficulties and War

But by 1860 the empire was running into trouble. It took a few years to overcome the depression of 1857. By his free trade policy the emperor made enemies among industrialists in certain lines. The Catholics did not like his policy in Italy.[25] After 1860 opposition mounted. The emperor granted more leeway to the Legislative Body. The 1860s are called the decade of the Liberal Empire—all such terms being relative. How the empire would have fared had purely internal causes been left free scope we shall never know. Louis-Napoleon actually ruined himself by war. His empire evaporated on the battlefield in 1870. But he was at war long before that.

"The empire means peace," he had assured his audiences in 1852: *l'empire, c'est la paix*. But war is after all the supreme pageantry (or was then); France was the strongest country of Europe, and the emperor's name was Napoleon. Less than a year and a half after the proclamation of the empire France was at war with a European state for the first time since Waterloo. The enemy was Russia, and the war was the Crimean War. Napoleon III did not alone instigate the Crimean War. Many forces in Europe after 1848 made for war; but Napoleon III was one of these forces. In 1859 the new Napoleon was fighting in Italy, from 1862 to 1867 in Mexico, and in 1870 in France itself, in a war with Prussia which he could easily have avoided. These wars form part of the story of the following chapter.[26]

It is enough to say here that in 1870 the Second Empire went the way of the First, into the limbo of governments tried and discarded by the French. It had lasted eighteen years, exactly as long as the July monarchy, and longer than any other regime known in France, up to that time, since the fall of the Bastille. Not until the 1920s and 1930s, when dictators sprouted all over Europe, did the world begin to suspect what Louis-Napoleon had really been, an omen of the future rather than a bizarre reincarnation of the past. It is only right to add that some, like Alexis de Tocqueville, suspected it even then.

[24] See p. 504.
[25] See p. 564.
[26] See pp. 559–561, 564, 572–574; for Mexico, see p. 675.

Industrialization, as it appeared first in England in the nineteenth century, rested on a combination of coal and iron, of which the steam engine was the most portentous offspring. Steam engines provided power to the textile mills, and when put on wheels they revolutionized transportation. In the factories a new kind of wage-earning working class was assembled. The railway train, powered by steam, running on rails at first made of wood, then of iron, then of steel, carried people and goods at a speed and in a volume never known in the past. It made possible the concentration of population in cities, both gigantic cities such as London, and clusters of smaller cities in which manufacturing processes were carried on. In this urban world, while polite architecture ran through a series of classical, Gothic, Renaissance and other revivals, more utilitarian structures of a novel kind were built of iron, and then of structural steel. The new habitat provided luxury for a few, comfort for some, and misery for all too many.

Class conflict therefore raged throughout the nineteenth century, but most acutely in the first half. One difficulty was that, though there had long been talk of the progress of science and invention, the actual difficulties of industrialization had been unforeseen. As the first people to undergo the Industrial Revolution, the English had no experience on which to draw. The English imagination dwelt by preference on rural rather than urban themes, especially in the early part of the century, and under the influence of literary romanticism. Government until 1832 was in the hands of a landed aristocracy and country gentry, made conservative in their politics by the French Revolution. Priding themselves on their English liberties, and fearing anything like Continental bureaucracy, the English only gradually endowed their government with adequate powers of regulation, inspection, enforcement and police.

After 1850 some of the more favorable consequences of modern industry and technology became apparent. While poverty remained chronic, and the working class struggled to better itself, the middle classes grew in numbers and enjoyed new amenities and conveniences. The following pages illustrate the life of social classes in England, and also in France, in this new Age of Iron. The medium here is part of the message, since the nineteenth-century innovations of lithography, photography and low-cost printing for a wide market are to be observed.

EARLY INDUSTRIALISM
AND SOCIAL CLASSES

At the left, this piece of popular art (a song-book cover) points up the exciting contrast between new and old. An express train rushes at night, on a high bridge, with the city behind it, through an English countryside illuminated by the moon.

Above: The newly organized London police, in the 1840s, await the arrival of a Chartist procession. Between 1832 and 1848 the Chartists organized mass demonstrations in the vain attempt to democratize the electoral laws and so obtain legislation designed to favor the working classes. The government introduced a more modern and better disciplined police force as a measure of crowd control, and to avoid the kind of chaotic confrontation shown on the following page. The men are in a kind of civilian uniform complete with stovepipe hats.

Upper left: The "Peterloo Massacre" of 1819, as caricatured by Cruikshank. A peaceable crowd in St. Peter's Fields, Manchester, was fired upon and dispersed by the yeomanry, a militia of nonprofessional part-time soldiers, mostly rural people out of sympathy with modern cities.

Lower left: These primitive trains, about 1840, are running on wooden rails with "guidance wheels" at an apparently crazy angle to help keep them on the track.

Above: London, or rather one of its poorer quarters, as seen by the French artist Gustave Doré about 1880. The omnipresent railroad is in the background, while in the foreground the mass housing, with the little yards, or rather pens, evokes the atmosphere of a prison.   551

Upper left: A workers' meeting in Paris, as seen by the painter Jean Béraud in 1884. The audience is probably hearing some socialist speeches.

Lower left: The future King Edward VII, then Prince of Wales, with his wife, comfortably installed in box seats, observes the new Bessemer steel-making process at Sheffield in 1875.

Above: The Bon Marché department store in Paris about 1880. The new era is evident in the vast expanse, the proliferation of merchandise, and the presence of affluent women, who have come downtown with their children to shop.

Buildings of cast iron and glass, appearing about 1850, represented the most significant technical innovation in architecture in centuries. The department store on the preceding page was of this kind. At the left, above, is the famous Crystal Palace in Hyde Park, London, built to house the Great Exhibition of 1851. The world's fair, or industrial exposition, was another product of the revolution in transportation.

Lower left: The Café de la Rotonde in Paris about 1860. The new French café was designed to be large, airy, open, cosmopolitan, suitable for ladies, and not necessarily alcoholic.

Above: The Eiffel Tower, built for the Paris exposition of 1889, with elevators to carry visitors to the top 984 feet above the ground, long remained the world's highest structure, and still stands as a symbol of nineteenth-century civilization. It was at first criticized as ungainly and vulgarly colossal. A later generation, accustomed to an architecture of concrete slabs and oblong cages, sees its graceful curves and the delicate tracery of its four immense legs.

555

XIII: THE CONSOLIDATION O

ARGE NATION-STATES, 1859-1871

Only a dozen years, from 1859 to 1871, were enough to see the formation of a new German empire, a unified kingdom of Italy, a Dual Monarchy of Austria-Hungary, drastic internal changes in tsarist Russia, the triumph of central authority in the United States, the creation of a united Dominion of Canada, and the revolutionizing and "Europeanization" of the empire of Japan. All these disparate events reflected profound changes brought in by the railroad, steamship, and telegraph, which made the communication of ideas, exchange of goods, and movement of people over wide areas more frequent and easier than ever before. Politically, all represented the advancing principle of the nation-state.

Before 1860 there were two prominent nation-states—Great Britain and France. Spain, united on the map, was internally so miscellaneous as to belong to a different category. Portugal, Switzerland, the Netherlands and the Scandinavian countries were nation-states, but small and peripheral. The characteristic political organ-

Chapter Emblem: Medallion to celebrate the Prussian defeat of Austria in 1866, and featuring the King of Prussia William I, who later became first German Emperor.

izations were small states comprising fragments of a nation, such as were strewn across the middle of Europe—Hanover, Baden, Sardinia, Tuscany, or the Two Sicilies —and large sprawling empires made up of all sorts of peoples, distantly ruled from above by dynasties and bureaucracies, such as the Romanov, Habsburg, and Ottoman domains.[1] Except for recent developments in the Americas the same mixture of small nonnational states and of large nonnational empires was to be found in most of the rest of the world.

Since 1860 or 1870 a nation-state system has prevailed. The consolidation of large nations became a model for other peoples large and small. In time, in the following century, other large peoples undertook to establish nation-states in India, Pakistan, Indonesia and Nigeria. Small and middle-sized peoples increasingly thought of themselves as nations, entitled to their own sovereignty and independence; the result, also accomplished in the following century, was the appearance of such states as Czechoslovakia, the Turkish republic, Eire, or Israel. Some of these sovereignties comprise fewer people than a large modern city. The idea of the nation-state has served both to bring people together into larger units and to break them apart into smaller ones. In the nineteenth century, outside the disintegrating Ottoman Empire, from which Greece, Serbia, Bulgaria, and Rumania became independent, and in which an Arabic national movement also began to stir, the national idea served mainly to create larger units in place of small ones. The map of Europe, from 1871 to 1918, was the simplest it has ever been before or since.[2]

About the idea of the nation-state and the movement of nationalism much has been said already in this book. Earlier chapters have described the ferment of national ideas and movements stirred up by the French Revolution and by the Napoleonic domination of Europe, the nationalist agitation and repression of the years after 1815, and the frustration and failure of patriotic aspirations in Germany, Italy, and central Europe in the Revolution of 1848.[3] For many in the nineteenth century, nationalism, the winning of national unity and independence and the creation of the nation-state, became a kind of secular faith.

A nation-state may be thought of as one in which supreme political authority somehow rests upon and represents the will and feeling of its inhabitants. There must be a people, not merely a swarm of human beings. The people must basically will and feel something in common. They must sense that they belong—that they are members of a community, participating somehow in a common life; that the government is their government, and that outsiders are "foreign." The outsiders or foreigners are usually (though not always) those who speak a different language. The nation is usually (though not always) composed of all persons sharing the same speech. A nation may also possess a belief in common descent or racial origin (however mistaken), or a sense of a common history, a common future, a common religion, a common geographical home, or a common external menace. Nations take

[1] See map, pp. 456–457.
[2] See map, pp. 576–577.
[3] See pp. 379, 392–393, 442–449, 477–500, 519–535.

form in many ways. But all are alike in feeling themselves to be communities, permanent communities in which individual persons, together with their children and their children's children, are committed to a collective destiny on earth.

In the nineteenth century governments found that they could not effectively rule, or develop the full powers of state, except by enlisting this sense of membership and support among their subjects. The consolidation of large nation-states had two distinguishable phases. Territorially, it meant the union of preexisting smaller states. Morally and psychologically it meant the creation of new ties between government and governed, the admission of new segments of the population to political life, through the creation or extension of liberal and representative institutions. This happened even in Japan and in tsarist Russia. National consolidation favored constitutional progress. Although there was considerable variation in the real power of the new political institutions and in the extent of self-government actually realized, parliaments were set up for the new Italy, the new Germany, the new Japan, the new Canada; and the movement in Russia was in the same direction. In Europe, some of the aims which the revolutionists of 1848 had failed to achieve were now realized by the established authorities.

They were realized, however, only in a series of wars. To create an all-German or an all-Italian state, as the revolutions of 1848 had already shown, it was necessary to break the power of Austria, render Russia at least temporarily ineffective, and overthrow or intimidate those German and Italian states which refused to surrender their sovereignty. In the United States, to maintain national unity as understood by President Lincoln, it was necessary to repress the movement for Southern independence by force of arms. For forty years after 1814 there had been no war between established powers of Europe. Then in 1854 came the Crimean War, in 1859 the Italian War, in 1864 the Danish War, in 1866 the Austro-Prussian War, in 1870 the Franco-Prussian War. Concurrently the Civil War raged in the United States. After 1871, for forty-three years there was again no war between European powers.

Before moving on to the first of the national consolidation movements, the Italian, we must examine the Crimean War which, though seemingly remote and unconnected, helped to make possible the success of the European national movements. Its chief significance in the story of the present chapter is that it seriously weakened both Austria and Russia, the two powers most bent on preserving the peace settlement of 1815 and on preventing national changes; it provided also an opportunity for the presentation of Italian grievances to an international forum at the peace congress which ended the war. The war was significant in other ways too. It was the first war covered by newspaper correspondents. It was the first war in which women, led by Florence Nightingale, established their position as army nurses. It was the first war in centuries in which France and Great Britain were on the same side. France and Britain came together because they believed their interests in the eastern Mediterranean to be threatened by Russia.

The pressure of Russia upon Turkey was an old story. Every generation saw its Russo-Turkish war.[4] In the last Russo-Turkish war, to go back no further, that of 1828–1829, the Tsar Nicholas I protected the independence newly won by Greece and annexed the left bank of the mouth of the Danube. Now, in 1853, Nicholas again made demands upon the still large but decaying Ottoman Empire, moving in on the two Danubian principalities, Wallachia and Moldavia (later to be known as Rumania), with military forces.[5] The dispute this time ostensibly involved the protection of Christians in the Ottoman Empire, including the foreign Christians at Jerusalem and in Palestine. Over these Christians the French also claimed a certain protective jurisdiction. The French had for centuries been the principal Western people in the Near East: they had often furnished money and advisers to the sultan, they carried on a huge volume of trade, they staffed and financed Christian missions, and they were continually talking of building a Suez canal. Napoleon III had especial reason to resent the Tsar Nicholas, who regarded him as a revolutionary adventurer. Napoleon III encouraged the Turkish government to resist Russian claims to protect Christians within Turkey. War between Russia and Turkey broke out late in 1853. In 1854 France joined the side of the Turks, as did Great Britain, whose settled policy was to uphold Turkey and the Near East against penetration by Russia. The two Western powers were soon joined by a diminutive and somewhat ridiculous ally, which had no visible interest in the issues—the small mountain kingdom of Sardinia, which entered the war mainly for the purpose of raising the Italian question at the peace conference.

The British fleet successfully blockaded Russia in both its Baltic and Black Sea outlets. French and British armies invaded Russia itself, landing in the Crimean peninsula, to which all the important fighting was confined. The Austrian Empire had its own reasons not to wish Russia to conquer the Balkans and Constantinople, or to see Britain and France master the situation alone; Austria therefore, though not yet recovered from the upheaval of 1848–1849, mobilized its armed forces at a great effort to itself and occupied Wallachia and Moldavia, which the Russians evacuated under this threat of attack by a new enemy. The Tsar Nicholas died in 1855, and his successor Alexander II sued for peace.

A congress of all the great powers made peace at Paris in 1856. By the treaty the powers pledged themselves jointly to maintain the "integrity of the Ottoman Empire." The Russian tide ebbed a little. Russia ceded the left bank of the mouth of the Danube to Moldavia and gave up its claim to the special protection of Christians in the Turkish empire. Moldavia and Wallachia (united as "Rumania" in 1858), together with Serbia, were recognized as self-governing principalities under protection of the European powers. It was agreed that Russia should maintain no warships on the Black Sea, and that the Danube should be an international river open to commercial shipping of all nations. The British, who had found it easy to blockade Russia, and were now mainly concerned with commercial prosperity and free trade,

[4]See pp. 250–251, 349–351, 423, 425, 450, 490–491, 493–494.
[5]See maps, pp. 456–457, 684.

even relaxed their doctrine of sea power, agreeing that "free ships make free goods." What the Continent called the freedom of the seas, the rights of neutrals to trade in wartime, opposed by Britain in its struggle with Napoleon, was now written (temporarily) into international law. At the Congress of Paris all seemed harmonious. There seemed to be such a thing as Europe, undertaking collective obligations, protecting small states, rationally and peaceably conducting its affairs.

But trouble was in the making. Napoleon III needed glory. The Italians wanted some kind of unified Italy. The Prussians, who had done nothing in the Crimean War, and were only tardily invited to the Congress of Paris, feared that their status as a great power might be slipping away. Napoleon III, the Italian nationalists, the Prussians, all stood to gain by change. Change in central Europe and Italy meant a tearing up of the treaty of Vienna of 1815, long guarded by Metternich and unsuccessfully challenged by the revolutionaries of 1848. Now, after the Crimean War, the forces opposing change were very weak. It was the Russian and Austrian empires that had stood firmly for the status quo. It was the victory of counterrevolution in Vienna, with the aid of Russian intervention in Hungary, that had doomed the Revolution of 1848 not only in the Habsburg empire but in Germany and Italy also. It was Russia and Austria, at Olmütz in 1850, that had forbidden the king of Prussia to create a German union according to his own notions. But Austria, though it had not fought, was badly strained by the effort of mobilization in the Crimean War. Russia was in defeat. The two powers which had most seriously attempted to uphold the Vienna settlement could do so no longer. The first proof came in Italy.

In Italy there had long been about a half dozen sizable states, together with a few very small ones. Several of them had dissolved in the Italian movements that accompanied the wars of the French Revolution. All had been reorganized, first by Napoleon and then by the Congress of Vienna. In the northwest lay Sardinia, called also Savoy or Piedmont; its royal house was the only native Italian dynasty in Italy. East of it lay Lombardy, and east of that, Venetia. Since 1814 Lombardy and Venetia belonged to the Austrian Empire. South of Lombardy, in the northwest corner of the "leg" of the peninsula, was the duchy of Tuscany with its capital at Florence. The smaller duchies of Modena, Parma, and Lucca filled the interstices between Tuscany and the northern states. Across the middle of the peninsula were spread the papal states, the hereditary temporal possession of the Roman See. Further south, comprising half of all Italy, lay the large kingdom of Naples or the Two Sicilies, ruled since 1735 by a branch of the Bourbons. The governments of these states were generally content with their separate independence. But the governments were remote from their peoples.

There was a widespread disgust in Italy with the existing authorities and a growing desire for a liberal national state in which all Italy might be embodied and which might resurrect the Italian grandeur of ancient times and of the Renaissance.

64
Cavour and the
Italian War
of 1859: The
Unification of Italy

Italian Nationalism:
The Program of Cavour

This sentiment, the dream of an Italian Risorgimento, or resurgence, had become very heated at the time of the French Revolution and Napoleon, then had been transformed into a moral purpose by the writings of Mazzini.[6] Mazzini, who had invested the cause of Italian unity with almost a holy character, had seen his hopes for a unified republican Italy elevated for a brief moment and then blasted in the general débacle of 1848. In the stormy events of 1848 the papacy had been frightened off by the radical romantic republicanism of Mazzini, Garibaldi, and other firebrands and could no longer be expected to support the cause of Italian nationalism. And in the same events the kingdom of Sardinia had failed in its vow to oust Austria from the Italian peninsula without the aid of any outside great power.[7]

These lessons were not lost on the prime minister of Sardinia, which was ruled since 1848 as a constitutional monarchy and was now under King Victor Emmanuel. This prime minister of Sardinia after 1852 was Camillo di Cavour, one of the shrewdest political tacticians of that or any age. Cavour was a liberal of Western type. He tried to make Sardinia a model of progress, efficiency, and fair government that other Italians would admire. He worked hard to plant constitutional and parliamentary practices in Sardinia. He favored the building of railroads and docks, the improvement of agriculture, and emancipation of trade. He followed a strongly anticlerical policy, cutting down the number of religious holidays, limiting the right of church bodies to own real estate, abolishing the church courts—all without negotiation with the Holy See. A liberal and constitutional monarchist, a loyal servant of the house of Savoy, a wealthy landowner in his own right, he had no sympathy for the revolutionary and republican nationalism of Mazzini. To him it did not seem that Italy would be united by the methods of conspiracy and secret societies, by hortatory literature smuggled in from political exiles, or by the proclamation of idealistic radical republics, as in 1848, which alarmed the most influential people in the country.[8]

Cavour shared in that new toughness of mind described in the last chapter. He embraced a "politics of reality." He did not approve of republicans but was willing to work with them surreptitiously. He did not idealize war but was willing to make war to unify Italy under the Sardinian king. With unruffled calculation, he took Sardinia into the Crimean War, sending troops to Russia, in the hope of winning a place at the peace table and raising the Italian question at the Congress of Paris. It was evident to

[6]See p. 479.
[7]See pp. 521–522, 524, 525–526.
[8]See p. 526.

Nation Building 1859–1867. *In eight years from 1859 to 1867 Italy was unified (except for the city of Rome annexed in 1870), the Habsburg government tried to solve its nationalities problem by creating a Dual Monarchy of Austria-Hungary, the United States affirmed its unity by defeating the Southern secessionist movement, and the Dominion of Canada was formed to include all British North America (with dates shown for accession of provinces) except Newfoundland and Labrador, which were added in 1949.*

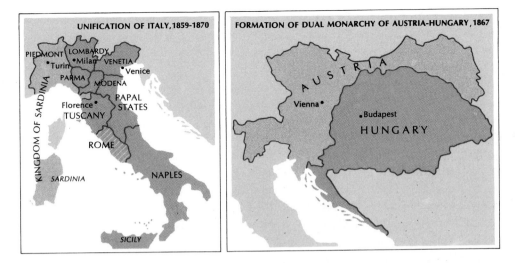

UNIFICATION OF ITALY, 1859-1870

PIEDMONT
LOMBARDY
•Turin •Milan VENETIA
•Venice
PARMA
MODENA
KINGDOM OF SARDINIA
Florence• PAPAL STATES
TUSCANY
ROME
SARDINIA
NAPLES
SICILY

FORMATION OF DUAL MONARCHY OF AUSTRIA-HUNGARY, 1867

AUSTRIA
Vienna•
•Budapest
HUNGARY

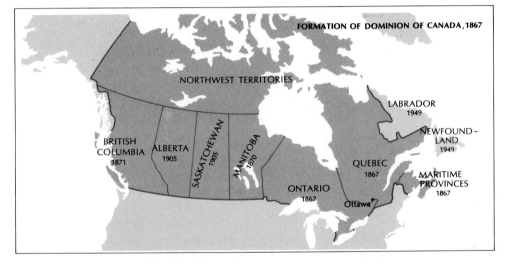

FORMATION OF DOMINION OF CANADA, 1867

NORTHWEST TERRITORIES
LABRADOR
1949
BRITISH COLUMBIA
1871
ALBERTA
1905
SASKATCHEWAN
1905
MANITOBA
1870
NEWFOUND-LAND
1949
QUEBEC
1867
ONTARIO
1867
Ottawa•
MARITIME PROVINCES
1867

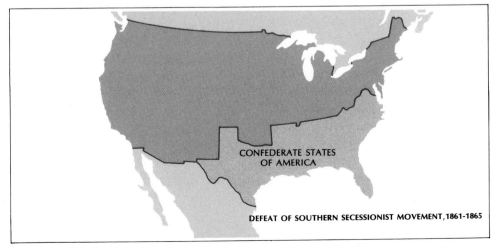

CONFEDERATE STATES
OF AMERICA

DEFEAT OF SOUTHERN SECESSIONIST MOVEMENT, 1861-1865

him that against one great power one must pit another, and that the only way to get Austria out of Italy was to use the French army. It became his master plan deliberately to provoke war with Austria, after having assured himself of French military support.

It was not difficult to persuade Napoleon III to collaborate. The Bonapartes looked upon Italy as their ancestral country, and Napoleon III, in his adventurous youth, had traveled in conspiratorial Italian circles and even participated in an Italian insurrection in 1831. Now, as emperor, in his role of apostle of modernity, he entertained a "doctrine of nationalities" which held the consolidation of nations to be a forward step at the existing stage of history. To fight reactionary Austria for the freedom of Italy would also mollify liberal opinion in France, which in other ways Napoleon was engaged in suppressing. The last note in persuasion was furnished by an Italian republican named Orsini, who in 1858, finding the French emperor too slow to make up his mind, attempted to assassinate him with a bomb. Napoleon III reached a secret agreement with Cavour. In April 1859, Cavour tricked Austria into a declaration of war. The French army poured over the Alps.

There were two battles, Magenta and Solferino, both won by the French and Sardinians. But Napoleon III was now in a quandary. The Prussians began to mobilize on the Rhine, not wishing France to create an Italian sphere of influence for itself. In Italy, with the defeat of the Austrians, revolutionary agitation broke out all over the peninsula, as it had a decade before—and the French emperor was no patron of popular revolution. The revolutionaries overthrew or denounced the existing governments and clamored for annexation to Sardinia. In France, as elsewhere, the Catholics, fearful that the pope's temporal power would be lost, upbraided the emperor for his godless and unnecessary war. The French position was indeed odd, for while the bulk of the French army fought Austria in the north, a detachment of it was still stationed in Rome, sent there in 1849 to protect the pope against Italian republicanism.[9] Napoleon III, in July 1859, at the height of his victories, stupefied Cavour. He made a separate peace with the Austrians.

The Franco-Austrian agreement gave Lombardy to Sardinia but left Venetia within the Austrian Empire. It offered a compromise solution to the Italian question, in the form of a federal union of the existing Italian governments, to be presided over by the pope. This was not what Cavour, or the Sardinians, or the more fiery Italian patriots wanted. Revolution continued to spread. Tuscany, Modena, Parma, and Romagna drove out their old rulers. They were annexed to Sardinia, after plebiscites or general elections in these regions had shown an overwhelming popular favor for this step. Since Romagna belonged to the papal states the pope excommunicated the organizers of the new Italy. Undeterred, representatives of all north Italy except Venetia met at the Sardinian capital of Turin in 1860 in the first parliament of the enlarged kingdom. The British government hailed these events with enthusiasm, and Napoleon III also recognized the expanded Sardinian state, in return for the transfer to France of Nice and Savoy, where plebiscites disclosed enormous majorities for annexation to France.

     [9]See p. 518.

There were now, in 1860, a north Italian kingdom, the papal states in the middle, and the kingdom of the Two Sicilies still standing in the south. The latter was being undermined by revolutionary agitation, as often in the past.[10] A Sardinian republican, Giuseppe Garibaldi, brought matters to a head. Somewhat like Lafayette, Garibaldi was a "hero of two worlds," who had fought for the independence of Uruguay, lived in the United States, and been one of the Triumvirs in the short-lived Roman Republic of 1849. He now organized a group of about 1,150 personal followers—"Garibaldi's Thousand," or the Red Shirts—for an armed expedition to the south. Cavour, unable openly to favor such filibustering against a neighboring state, connived at Garibaldi's preparations and departure. Garibaldi landed in Sicily and soon crossed to the mainland. Revolutionists hastened to join him, and the government of the Two Sicilies, backward and corrupt, commanding little loyalty from its population, collapsed before this picturesque intrusion.

Garibaldi now prepared to push from Naples up to Rome. Here, of course, he would meet not only the pope but the French army, and the international scandal would reverberate throughout the globe. Cavour decided that so extreme a step must be averted, but that Garibaldi's successes must at the same time be used. Anticipating Garibaldi, a Sardinian army entered the papal states, carefully avoiding Rome, and proceeded onward into Naples. The kingdom conquered from its king by Garibaldi was now conquered from Garibaldi by the Sardinian army and the ingenuity of Cavour. The conquest was peaceful; for Garibaldi, though somewhat disposed to bargain, and though he vainly demanded Cavour's resignation, finally yielded. The chief of the Red Shirts, the foe of kings, consented to ride in an open carriage with Victor Emmanuel through the streets of Naples amid cheering thousands. Plebiscites held in the Two Sicilies showed an almost unanimous willingness to join with Sardinia. In the remainder of the papal states, except for Rome and its environs, plebiscites were held also, with the same result. A parliament representing all Italy except Rome and Venetia met in 1861, and the Kingdom of Italy was formally proclaimed, with Victor Emmanuel II as king "by grace of God and the will of the nation." Venetia was added in 1866, as a prize for Italian aid to Prussia in a war against Austria, and Rome was annexed in 1870 after the withdrawal of French troops in the Franco-Prussian War of 1870.[11]

So Italy was "made," as the phrase of the time expressed it. It had been made by the long high-minded apostolate of Mazzini, the audacity of Garibaldi, the cold policy of Cavour, by war and insurrection, by armed violence endorsed by popular vote.

Very little was settled or ended by unification. Even territorially, the more pronounced nationalists refused to believe that Italian unity was completed. They looked beyond, to regions of mixed population where Italians were numerous or preponderant—to the Trentino, to Trieste, to certain Dalmatian islands, or to Nice and Savoy. They saw in these regions an *Italia irredenta*, "an unredeemed Italy," awaiting

[10] See pp. 489–490, 522.
[11] See pp. 571, 572, 574, 656.

in its turn the day of incorporation. "Irredentism" even passed into the English language as a word signifying a vociferous demand, on nationalist grounds, for annexation of regions beyond one's own frontiers.

The occupation of Rome in 1870 by the Italian government opened the rift between church and state still wider. The pope, deprived of territories he had held for a thousand years, renewed his condemnations and chose to remain in lifelong seclusion in the Vatican. His successors followed the same policy until 1929. Hence good Italian patriots were bound to be anticlerical, and good Catholics were bound to look upon the Italian state with unfriendly eyes. The regional differences between northern and southern Italy did not disappear with unification. The north looked upon the agrarian south, the land of priest, landlord, and impoverished peasant, as disgracefully backward. Lawlessness in Sicily and Naples did not disappear with the overthrow of the Bourbons.

The new Italy was parliamentary but not democratic. At first the vote was only given to some 600,000 persons out of more than 20,000,000. Not until 1913 was the suffrage significantly broadened. Meanwhile parliamentary life, confined to a few, was somewhat unrealistic and frequently corrupt. With the mass of the population excluded from the vote, which in any case they were incapable of exercising, the revolutionary agitation continued unabated after the unification. Garibaldi himself, in the 1860s, made two more attempts to seize Rome by violence. In general, the revolutionary movement shifted from the older republican nationalism to the newer forms of Marxian socialism, anarchism or syndicalism.

But the dream of ages was realized. Italy was one. The period that seemed so shameful to patriots, the long centuries that had elapsed since the Renaissance, were now terminated in the glories of a successful Risorgimento.

65
Bismarck: The Founding of a German Empire

To play upon the divisions among the Germans, keeping them in rivalry with each other and dependent upon outside powers, had been the policy of France ever since the Reformation and of Russia since it began to take part in the affairs of Europe. The pulverization of the Germanic world was in fact a kind of negative prerequisite to the development of modern history as we know it, for without it the economic and cultural leadership of Europe would hardly have become concentrated along the Atlantic seaboard, or a great military empire have arisen in Russia and spread along the Baltic and into Poland.

Gradually, as we have seen, the Germans became dissatisfied with their position. They became nationalistic.[12] Many German thinkers held that Germany was different from the West, destined some day to work out a peculiarly German way of life and political system of its own. To the Slavs the Germans felt immeasurably superior. German philosophy, as shown most clearly in Hegel, took on a certain

[12]See pp. 442–447, 479–481.

characteristic tone. It pronounced individualism to be Western; it skipped lightly over individual liberty; it tended to glorify group loyalties, collectivist principles, and the state. It made a great to-do about History, which in the thought of Hegel, and after him Marx, became a vast force almost independent of human beings. History was said to ordain, require, necessitate, condemn, justify, or excuse. What one did not like could be dismissed as a mere historical phase, opening into a quite different and more attractive future. What one wanted, in the present or future, could be described as historically necessary and bound to come.

Bismarck: The Founding of a German Empire

In 1848 a series of revolutions unseated the several governments of Germany. At the Frankfurt Assembly a group composed essentially of private citizens undertook to organize a united Germany by constitutional methods. They failed because they had no power. Hence after 1848 the Germans began to think in terms of power, developing a somewhat extreme admiration for *die Macht*. The men of Frankfurt failed also, perhaps, because they were insufficiently revolutionary. The Germans were a sober, orderly, and respectful people. They were still attached emotionally to their several states. What happened in Italy, a revolutionary extermination of all the old governments except that of Sardinia, could not happen in Germany.[13]

The German States after 1848

After the failure of the 1848 revolution German nationalists and liberals were confused. By 1850 the old states were restored—Austria and Prussia, the kingdoms of Hanover, Saxony, Bavaria, and Württemberg, together with about thirty other states ranging in size down to the free cities of Hamburg and Frankfurt. The loose confederation of 1815, linking all these states together, was restored also.[14] But within this framework great economic and social changes were occurring. Between 1850 and 1870 the output of both coal and iron in Germany multiplied sixfold. In 1850 Germany produced less iron than France, in 1870 more. Germany was overcoming the economic and social lag which had characterized it for three hundred years. A *Zollverein*, or tariff union, initiated by Prussia in 1818, had come to include almost all Germany outside of Austria and Bohemia and provided a large measure of economic unity. The German cities were growing, bound together by railroad and telegraph, requiring larger supporting areas on which to live. Industrial capitalists and industrial workingmen were becoming more numerous. With the advantages of unity more obvious than ever, with the ideals of 1848 badly compromised, with an exaggerated respect for the state and for power, and with a habit of accepting the successful event as the "judgment of history," the Germans were ripe for what happened. They did not unify themselves by their own exertions. They fell into the arms of Prussia.

[13] See pp. 526–532.
[14] See pp. 455–458, 531–532, and map, p. 570.

Prussia had always been the smallest and most precarious of the great powers. Ruined by Napoleon, it had risen again. It owed its international influence and internal character to its army. Actually it had fought rather fewer wars than other great powers, but, with its army in being, it had followed a program of expansion by conquest or diplomacy. The taking of Silesia in 1740, of parts of Poland in the 1770s and 1790s, of the Rhineland in 1815 by an international bargain were the highlights of Prussian growth.[15] After 1850 those who controlled the destinies of Prussia were apprehensive. Their state had been shaken by revolution. At Olmütz in 1850 they had to yield to the Austrian emperor and the tsar. In the Crimean War and at the Congress of Paris they were hardly more than spectators. Italy was unified without any Prussian saying yes or no. It seemed as if the hard-won and still relatively recent position of Prussia might be waning. It likewise seemed easy to enlarge the army. Since 1815 the population of Prussia had grown from eleven to eighteen million, but the size of the army had not changed. A mere enforcement of existing principles of conscription would therefore almost double the army. But this would require increased financial appropriations. After 1850 Prussia had a parliament.[16] It was a parliament, to be sure, dominated by the men of wealth; but some of the wealthy Prussians, notably the capital-owners of the Rhineland, were liberals who wished the parliament to have control over government policies. These men did not like professional armies and considered the Prussian Junkers, from whom the officer corps was recruited, as their main rivals in the state. The parliament refused the necessary appropriations. The king and his war minister, von Roon, were in despair. The army reforms, considered by them as necessary to the future of Prussia, could not be effected. The king at this juncture, in 1862, on von Roon's recommendation, appointed a new chief minister, Otto von Bismarck.

Bismarck was a Junker from old Brandenburg east of the Elbe. He cultivated the gruff manner of an honest country squire, though he was in fact an accomplished man of the world. Intellectually he was far superior to the rather slow-witted landlord class from which he sprang, and for which he often felt an impatient contempt. He shared in many Junker ideas. He advocated, and even felt, a kind of stout Protestant piety. Although he cared for the world's opinion, it never deterred him in his actions; criticism and denunciation left him untouched. He was in fact obstinate. He was not a nationalist. He did not look upon all Germany as his Fatherland. He was a Prussian. His social affinities, as with the Junkers generally, lay to the East with corresponding landowning elements of the Baltic provinces and Russia.[17] The West, including the bulk of Germany, he neither understood nor trusted; it seemed to him revolutionary, turbulent, freethinking, materialistic. Parliamentary bodies he considered ignorant and irresponsible as organs of government. Individual liberty seemed to him disorderly selfishness. Liberalism, democracy, socialism were repugnant to him. He preferred to stress duty, service, order, and the fear of God. The idea of forming a new German union developed only gradually in his mind and

[15] See maps, pp. 236–237.
[16] See pp. 532–533.
[17] See map, p. 217.

then as an adjunct to the strengthening of Prussia. A real and complete German national union, one including the Germans of Austria and Bohemia, who were as German as any, was impossible in Bismarck's eyes. It would bring in another great power to dispute with Prussia. It might create a Catholic majority. It would strengthen south against north. In it the East-Elbian Junkers would be outnumbered and lost.

Bismarck thus had his predilections, and even his principles. But no principle bound him, no ideology seemed to him an end in itself. He became the classic practitioner of *Realpolitik.* The time came when the Junkers thought him a traitor to his class, when even the king was afraid of him, when he outraged and then mollified the august house of Habsburg, when he made friends with liberals, democrats, and even socialists, and in turn made enemies of them. First he made wars, then he insisted upon peace. Enmities and alliances were to him only matters of passing convenience. The enemy of today might be the friend of tomorrow. Far from planning out a long train of events, then following it step by step to a grand consummation, he seems to have been practical and opportunistic, taking advantage of situations as they emerged and prepared to act in any one of several directions as events might suggest.

In 1862, as minister president, it was his job, or duty, to outface the liberals in the Prussian parliament. For four years, from 1862 to 1866, Bismarck waged this "constitutional struggle." The parliament refused to vote the proposed taxes. The government collected them anyway. The taxpayers paid them without protest—it was the orderly thing to do, and the collectors represented public authority. The limitations of Prussian liberalism, the docility of the population, the respect for officialdom, the belief that the king and his ministers were wiser than the elected deputies, all clearly revealed themselves in this triumph of military policy over the theory of government by consent. The army was enlarged, reorganized, retrained, and reequipped. Bismarck fended off the showers of abuse from the liberal majority in the chamber. The liberals declared that the government's policy was flagrantly unconstitutional. The constitution, said Bismarck, could not have been meant to undermine the state. The government, said the liberals, was itself undermining Prussia, for the rest of Germany hoped to find in Prussia, as Italy had found in Sardinia, a model of political freedom. What the Germans admired in Prussia, replied Bismarck coldly, was not her liberalism but her power. He declared that the Prussian boundaries as set in 1815 were unsound, that Prussia must be prepared to seize favorable opportunities for further growth.[18] And he added one of his most memorable utterances: "Not by speeches and majority votes are the great questions of the day decided—that was the great error of 1848 and 1849—but by blood and iron."

A favorable opportunity was not long in presenting itself. The Schleswig-Holstein question arose again. We have seen how it had arisen in 1848, and how even the

[18]See maps, pp. 237, 570.

NORTH SEA

BALTIC SEA

SCHLESWIG

EAST PRUSSIA

HOLSTEIN

Hamburg

MECKLENBURG

Elbe R.

HANOVER

P   R   U   S   S   I   A

POSEN

Vistula R.

Berlin

Oder R.

Rhine R.

HESSE-
CASSEL

THURINGIA

SAXONY

P

NASSAU

HESSE-DARMSTADT

Frankfurt

BOHEMIA

(to Bavaria)

Cracow

ALSACE

BADEN

WÜRTT-
EMBERG

B   A   V   A   R   I   A

MORAVIA

A   U   S   T   R   I   A   N   E   M   P   I   R   E

Vienna

Danube R.

AUSTRIA

Budapest

TYROL

German Confederation,
1815–1866

Prussia, 1815–1866

Annexed to Prussia, 1866

Joined with Prussia in North German Confederation, 1867

South German States Joined in German Empire, 1871

Alsace-Lorraine, Ceded by France to German Empire, 1871

Austrian Dominions Excluded From German Confederation, 1866

Bismarck's
German Empire, 1871

0   100   200 miles

The German Question 1815–1871. *From 1815 to 1866 there were thirty-nine states in Germany (of which only the largest are shown) joined in the Confederation of 1815. At the Frankfurt Assembly in 1848 (see p. 529) two groups developed: the Great Germans who adhered to the idea of an all-German union, including the Austrian lands except Hungary; and the Little Germans who were willing to exclude Austria and her empire. Bismarck was a Little German but a Great Prussian. He (1) enlarged Prussia by conquest in 1866, (2) joined Mecklenburg, Saxony, etc., with his enlarged Prussia in a North German Confederation of 1867, (3) combined this in turn with Bavaria, Württemberg, etc., to form the German empire of 1871, (4) conquered Alsace-Lorraine from France, and (5) ejected Austria. The boundaries of Bismarckian Germany remained unchanged until 1918. See also maps, pp. 236–237, 456–457, 760–761.*

mild men of Frankfurt had insisted, to the point of war, upon the incorporation of the two duchies into their German union.[19]   Now in 1863 the story was repeated. The Danes, engaged in a process of national consolidation of their own, wished to make Schleswig an integral part of Denmark.   The population of Schleswig was part Dane and part German.   The diet of the German confederation, unwilling to see Germans thus annexed outright to Denmark, called for an all-German war upon the Danes, just as the revolutionary Frankfurt Assembly had done.   Bismarck had no desire to support or strengthen the existing German confederation.   He wanted not an all-German war but a Prussian war.   To disguise his aims he acted jointly with Austria.   In 1864 Prussia and Austria together went to war with Denmark, which they soon defeated.   It was Bismarck's intention to annex both Schleswig and Holstein to Prussia, gaining whatever other advantages might present themselves from future trouble with Austria.   He arranged a provisional occupation of Schleswig by Prussia, and of Holstein by Austria.   Disputes soon arose over rights of passage, the keeping of internal order, and other problems with which occupying forces are commonly afflicted.   While pretending to try to regulate these disputes he allowed them to ripen.

He now proceeded to discredit and isolate Austria.   The British government was at the time following a policy of nonintervention in the affairs of the Continent.   The Russian empire was in no position for action; it was divided internally by a reform program then at its height; it was in a mood of hostility to Austria because of events of the Crimean War and well disposed toward Prussia and Bismarck, because Bismarck in 1863 took care to support it against an uprising of Russian Poles.   To win over the new kingdom of Italy Bismarck held out the lure of Venetia.   As for France, Napoleon III was embarrassed by domestic discontents and had his army committed to adventures in Mexico.   In addition, Bismarck charmed him at a confidential interview at Biarritz, where vague oral intimations of French expansion were exchanged, and the two men seemed to agree to a needed modernization of the map of Europe.   To weaken Austria within Germany, Bismarck presented himself as a democrat.   He proposed a reform of the German confederation, recommending that it have a popular chamber elected by universal suffrage.   He calculated that the mass of the German people were wedded neither to the well-to-do capitalistic liberals, nor to the existing government structures of the German states, nor to the house of Habsburg.   He would use "democracy" to undermine all established interests that stood in his way.

Meanwhile the occupying powers continued to quarrel over Schleswig-Holstein.   Austria finally raised the matter formally in the German federal diet, one of whose functions was to prevent war between its members.   Bismarck declared that the diet had no authority, accused the Austrians of aggression, and ordered the Prussian army to enter Holstein.   The Austrians called for federal sanctions in the form of an all-German force to be sent against Prussia.   The result was that Prussia, in 1866, was at war not only with Austria, but with most of the other German states. The Prussian army soon proved its superiority.   Trained to an unprecedented

---

[19]See pp. 530–531.

precision, equipped with the new needle-gun, by which the infantryman could deliver five rounds a minute, brought into the zone of combat by an imaginative strategy that made use of the new railroads, commanded by the skill of von Moltke, the Prussian army overthrew the Austrians at the Battle of Sadowa (or Königgrätz) and defeated the other German states soon thereafter. The Austro-Prussian, or Seven Weeks' War, was amazing in its brevity. Bismarck hastened to make peace before the other European powers, which he had first hoodwinked and now stunned, could realize what had happened.

Prussia annexed outright, together with Schleswig-Holstein, the whole kingdom of Hanover, the duchies of Nassau and Hesse-Cassel and the free city of Frankfurt. Here the old governments simply disappeared before the axe of the "red reactionary." The German federal union disappeared likewise. In its place, in 1867, Bismarck organized a North German Confederation, in which the newly enlarged Prussia joined with twenty-one other states, all of which combined it greatly outweighed. The German states south of the river Main—Austria, Bavaria, Baden, Württemberg, and Hesse-Darmstadt—remained outside the new organization, with no kind of union among themselves. Meanwhile the kingdom of Italy annexed Venetia.

For the North German Confederation Bismarck produced a constitution. The new structure, though a federal one, was much stronger than the now defunct Confederation of 1815. The king of Prussia became its hereditary head. Ministers were responsible to him. There was a parliament with two chambers. The upper chamber, as in the United States, represented the states as such, though not equally. The lower chamber, or Reichstag, was deemed to represent the people and was elected by universal suffrage. Such flirting with democracy seemed madness to both conservative Junker and liberal bourgeois. It was indeed a bold step, for only France at the time illustrated universal suffrage in Europe on a large scale, and in the France of Napoleon III neither old-fashioned conservatives nor genuine liberals could take much satisfaction. As for Great Britain, where voting rights were extended in this same year, 1867, they were still given to less than half the adult male population. Bismarck sensed in the "masses" an ally of strong government against private interests. He negotiated even with the socialists, who had arisen with the industrialization of the past decade, and who, in Germany at this time, were mainly followers of Ferdinand Lassalle. The Lassallean socialists, unlike the Marxian, believed it theoretically possible to improve working-class conditions through the action of existing governments. To the great annoyance of Marx, then in England (his *Capital* first appeared in 1867), the bulk of the German socialists reached an understanding with Bismarck. In return for a democratic suffrage they agreed to accept the North German Confederation. Bismarck, for his part, by making use of democratic and socialist sentiment, won popular approval for his emerging empire.

The Franco-Prussian War, 1870

It was clear that the situation was not yet stable. The small south German states were left floating in empty space; they would sooner or later have to gravitate into some orbit or other, Austrian, Prussian, or French. In France there were angry criticisms of Napoleon III's foreign policy. French intervention in Mexico had proved a fiasco.[20] A united Italy had been allowed to rise on France's borders. And now, contrary to all principles of French national interest observed by French governments for hundreds of years, a strong and independent power was being allowed to spread over virtually the whole of Germany. Everywhere people began to feel that war was coming between France and Prussia. Bismarck played on the fears of France felt in the south German states. South Germany, though in former times it had often been a willing satellite to France, was now sufficiently nationalistic to consider such subservience to a foreign people disgraceful. To Bismarck it seemed that a war between Prussia and France would frighten the small south German states into a union with Prussia, leaving only Austria outside—which was what he wanted. To Napoleon III, or at least to some of his advisers, it seemed that such a war, if successful, would restore public approval of the Bonapartist empire. In this inflammable situation the responsible persons of neither country worked for peace.

Meanwhile a revolution in Spain had driven the reigning queen into exile, and a Spanish provisional government invited Prince Leopold of Hohenzollern, the king of Prussia's cousin, to be constitutional king of Spain. To entrench the Prussian royal house in Spain would naturally be distasteful to France. Three times the Hohenzollern family refused the Spanish offer. Bismarck, who could not control such family decisions, but who foresaw the possibility of a usable incident, deviously persuaded the Spanish to issue the invitation still a fourth time. On July 2, 1870, Paris heard that Prince Leopold had accepted. The French ambassador to Prussia, Benedetti, at the direction of his government, met the king of Prussia at the bathing resort of Ems, where he formally demanded that Prince Leopold's acceptance be withdrawn. It was withdrawn on July 12. The French seemed to have their way. Bismarck was disappointed.

The French government then took a further step, hoping to win a resounding diplomatic triumph. Benedetti received further instructions: he should again approach the king at Ems and demand that at no time in the future would a Hohenzollern become a candidate for the Spanish throne under any conditions. The king politely declined any such commitment and telegraphed a full report of the conversation to Bismarck at Berlin. Bismarck, receiving the telegram, which became famous as the "Ems dispatch," saw a new opportunity, as he put it, to wave a red flag before the Gallic bull. He condensed the Ems telegram for publication, so reducing and abridging it that it seemed to newspaper readers as if a curt exchange had occurred at Ems, in which the Prussians believed that their king had been insulted, and the French that their ambassador had been snubbed. In both countries the war party demanded satisfaction. On July 19, 1870, on these trivial grounds, and with the ostensible issue of the Spanish throne already settled, the irresponsible and decaying government of Napoleon III declared war on Prussia.

Again the war was short. Again Bismarck had taken care to isolate his enemy in advance. The British generally felt France to be in the wrong. They had been

---

[20] See p. 675.

alarmed by French operations in Mexico, which suggested an ambition to re-create a French American empire. The Italians had long been awaiting the chance to seize Rome; they did so in 1870, when the French withdrew their troops from Rome for use against Prussia. The Russians had been awaiting the chance to upset the clause of the Peace of 1856 which forbade them to keep naval vessels in the Black Sea. They did so in 1870. It was Austria, defeated in 1866, that might most probably have combined with France in 1870 to stop the rise of Prussia. But Bismarck had purposely granted lenient terms to Austria in 1866. The Austrians detested Napoleon III for his part in Italian unification. The Austrian Empire was undergoing an internal reorganization, in which the Magyars of Hungary obtained more influence in affairs of state. Since the days of Maria Theresa the military power of the empire had rested very largely on the Magyars, and the Magyars were now inclined to take the part of Bismarck and of Prussia, because the more the Habsburg monarchy was pushed out of Germany, the better the position of the Magyars within it became.

So the War of 1870, like the others of the time, failed to become a general European struggle. Prussia was supported by the south German states. France had no allies. The French army proved to be technically backward compared with the Prussian. War began on July 19; on September 2, after the battle of Sedan, the principal French army surrendered to the Germans. Napoleon III was himself taken prisoner. On September 4 an insurrection in Paris proclaimed the Republic. The Prussian and German forces moved into France and laid siege to the capital. Though the French armies dissolved, Paris refused to capitulate. For four months it was surrounded and besieged.

The German Empire,
1871

With their guns encircling Paris, the German rulers or their representatives assembled at Versailles. The château and gardens of Versailles, since Louis XVI's unceremonious departure in October 1789, had been little more than a vacant monument to a society long since dead. Here, in the most sumptuous room of the palace, the resplendent Hall of Mirrors, where the Sun King had once received the deferential approaches of German princes, Bismarck on January 18, 1871, caused the German Empire to be proclaimed. The king of Prussia received the hereditary title of German emperor. The other German rulers (excepting, to be sure, the ruler of Austria, and those whom Bismarck had himself dethroned) accepted his imperial authority. Ten days later the people of Paris, shivering, hungry, and helpless, opened their gates to the enemy. France had no government with which Bismarck could make peace. It was not at all clear what kind of government the country wanted. Bismarck insisted on the election of a Constituent Assembly by universal suffrage. He demanded that France pay the German Empire a war indemnity of five billion gold francs (then an enormous and unprecedented sum) and cede to it the border region of Alsace and most of Lorraine. Though the Alsatians spoke German, most of them felt as Frenchmen, having shared in the general history of France since the seventeenth century. There was strong local protest at the transfer to Germany, and the French never reconciled themselves to this cold-blooded amputation of their frontier. The peace dictated by Bismarck was embodied in the treaty of Frankfurt of May 10, 1871. Thereafter, as will be seen, the French Constituent Assembly gradually proceeded to construct the Third Republic.[21]

The consolidation of Germany transformed the face of Europe. It reversed the dictum not only of the Peace of Vienna but even of the Peace of Westphalia.[22] The German Empire, no sooner born, was the strongest state on the continent of Europe. Rapidly industrialized after 1870, it became more potent still. Bismarck, by consummate astuteness, by exploiting the opportunities offered by a Europe in flux, and with no more fighting than that involved in a few weeks in three short wars, had brought about what European statesmen of many nationalities had long said should at all costs be prevented. He outwitted everybody in turn, including the Germans. The united all-German state that issued from the nationalist movement was a Germany conquered by Prussia. Prussia, with its annexations of 1866, embraced almost all Germany north of the Main. Within the empire it had about two-thirds of the area. In Prussia the liberals capitulated before Bismarck's unanswerable success. In 1867 the Prussian parliament passed an "indemnity act"; the gist of it was that Bismarck admitted to a certain high-handedness during the constitutional struggle but that the parliament legalized the disputed tax collections *ex post facto,* agreeing to forgive and forget, in view of the victory over Austria and its consequences. Thus liberalism withered away before nationalism. The quick victory over France confirmed the same tendency. All nations respect the methods to which they attribute their successes, and to the Germans it seemed that one should be "realistic" and that an effective army is the mainstay of the state.

The German Empire received substantially the constitution of the North German Confederation. It was a federation of monarchies, each based in theory on divine or hereditary right. At the same time, in the Reichstag elected by manhood suffrage, it rested on a kind of mass appeal and was in a sense democratic. Yet the country's ministers were responsible to the emperor and not to the elected chamber. Moreover, it was the rulers who joined the empire, not the peoples. There were no popular plebiscites as in Italy. Each state kept its own laws, government, and constitution. The people of Prussia, for example, remained for Prussian affairs under the rather illiberal constitution of 1850,[23] while in affairs of the Reich, or empire, they

---

[21] See pp. 627–628.
[22] See p. 150, and map, pp. 148–149.
[23] See pp. 532–533.

Europe 1871. *The new features on this map, as compared to the Europe of 1815 (see pp. 456–457), are the existence of a unified German Empire and a unified Kingdom of Italy. The German domain was enlarged by the incorporation of Schleswig (in the neck of the Danish peninsula) and the annexation from France of Alsace and parts of Lorraine, the regions respectively around Strassburg (French Strasbourg) and Metz on the map. From 1871 to 1914 Europe had fewer separate states, fewer land frontiers and a simpler political geography than at any other time in its history. Except for the voluntary separation of Norway and Sweden in 1905 there were no changes in this period outside the Balkans. (See map, p. 728.)*

ARCTIC OCEAN

ICELAND
(Denmark)

NORWAY
AND
SWEDEN

SHETLAND I.
(Britain)

Kristiania

Stockho

GREAT BRITAIN

SCOTLAND

NORTH SEA

DENMARK

Copenhagen

Belfast

IRELAND

Dublin

Liverpool

HELIGOLAND
(Britain)

Da

Hamburg

ATLANTIC OCEAN

ENGLAND

NETHERLANDS

Amsterdam

Bremen

Rhine R.

Elbe R.

Berlin

London

GERMAN EMPIRE

English Channel

Brussels

BELGIUM

Cologne

Dresden

Prague

Reims

LUX.

Seine R.

Paris

Metz

AUS

Vienna

Loire R.

Strassburg

Munich

Tours

FRANCE

SWITZERLAND

Bordeaux

Lyons

Milan

CROATIA-
SLOVENI

Bilbao

Rhone R.

Turin

Venice

Ebro R.

Marseilles

ADRIATIC

PORTUGAL

Tagus R.

Madrid

CORSICA
(France)

Rome

Lisbon

SPAIN

Barcelona

ITALY

Naples

BALEARIC I.
(Spain)

SARDINIA

Seville

Gibraltar (Britain)

Tangier

Algiers

Tunis

SICILY

Fez

MALTA (

MEDITERRANE

MOROCCO

ALGERIA
(France)

TUNISIA

577

enjoyed an equal vote by universal suffrage. The emperor, who was also the king of Prussia, had legal control over the foreign and military policy of the empire. The German Empire in effect served as a mechanism to magnify the role of Prussia, the Prussian army, and the East-Elbian Prussian aristocracy in world affairs.

66

**The Dual
Monarchy of
Austria-Hungary**

*The Habsburg Empire
After 1848*

Bismarck united Germany, but he also divided it, for he left about a sixth of the Germans outside his German Empire. These Germans of Austria and Bohemia had now to work out a common future with the dozen other nationalities in the Danubian domain.

The clumsiness of the old Habsburg multinational empire is clear enough, but more impressive is its astonishing capacity to live and to survive. Prussia and France, in the 1740s, had tried unsuccessfully to dismember it. Smashed four different times by the French between 1796 and 1809, it outlived this crisis, and after 1815, under Metternich, it guided the counsels of Europe.[24] Broken up in 1848, restored by the intervention of Russia in 1849, dislocated by its effort at mobilization in 1855, attacked by Napoleon III in 1859 and by Bismarck in 1866, it still continued to hold together and disappeared finally only in 1918 in the cataclysm of the First World War.[25] But the events of the 1850s and 1860s greatly altered its character.

The essential question, in a nationalist age, was how the Habsburg government would react to the problems raised by national self-expression. The nationalities did not wish to destroy the empire. Among the Hungarians after 1848–1849, only a handful of extreme radicals dreamed of a Hungary entirely independent. Most of them followed Francis Deak, desiring constitutional autonomy for Hungary but not denying the link with Vienna. Slav opinion, at the Slav Congress of Prague in 1848, went basically no further than Austroslavism.[26] The peoples of the empire, while increasingly insistent on certain national rights—such as a degree of local self-government, and schools, law courts, and administration in their own lan-gauge—felt an underlying need for the larger political structure which the empire gave.

By Habsburg, in this period, one means primarily Francis Joseph, who as emperor from 1848 to 1916 reigned even longer than his famous contemporary, Queen Victoria. Francis Joseph, like many others, could never shake off his own tradition. His thoughts turned on his house and on its rights. Buffeted unmercifully by the waves of change, he cordially disliked everything liberal, progressive, or modern. He allied himself with the Catholic hierarchy and the Vatican, which also, for decades after 1848, and for understandable reason, set itself bluntly against compromise with the new age. Personally, Francis Joseph was incapable of enlarged views, ambitious projects, bold decisions, or persevering action. And he lived in a

[24] See pp. 282–286, 409–410, 423–424, 426, 428–430, 483–493.
[25] See pp. 519–526, 560–561, 564, 569–572, 748.
[26] See pp. 522–524.

pompous dream world, surrounded in the imperial court by great noblemen, high churchmen, and bespangled personages of the army.

Yet the government was not idle; it was, if anything, too fertile in devising new deals and new dispensations. Various expedients were tried after 1849, but none was tried long enough to see if it would work. For several years the ruling idea was centralization, to govern the empire through the German language and with German efficiency, maintaining the abolition of serfdom as accomplished in 1848 (and which required a strong official control over the landlords if it was to work in practice) and favoring the building of railroads and other apparatus of material progress.[27] This Germanic and bureaucratic centralization was distasteful to the non-German nationalities, and especially to the Magyars. It is important to say Magyars, not Hungarians, because the Magyars composed less than half the very mixed population of Hungary within its then-existing borders. Nevertheless the Magyars, as the strongest of the non-German groups, and hence the most able to maintain a political system of their own, felt the Germanic influence as most oppressive. In the war of 1859 the Magyars sympathized with the Italians.

The war, which took away Lombardy, proved the inability of the empire to defend itself under existing conditions. The government concluded that it must solicit the support of its subjects. In 1860 a kind of federative scheme was adopted, but in 1861 this was dropped for a new form of centralization, one in which, alongside the old officialdom, there should be a parliament for the whole empire. In the parliament the nationalities were to be represented proportionately. But the Magyars boycotted the parliament. They declined to merge the separate identity of Hungary in any higher structure, either absolutist or parliamentary. After four years during which the machinery of state ground to a halt, the Vienna government opened negotiations with the Magyars. In 1866 the war with Prussia revealed the impossible handicaps under which the empire labored. In 1867 the Vienna authorities concluded an agreement with the Magyars, and one which lasted as long as the house of Habsburg.

The Compromise of 1867, commonly known as the *Ausgleich*, was essentially a bargain between the Germans of Austria-Bohemia and the Magyars of Hungary. It worked to the common disadvantage of the Slavs. Both Germans and Magyars looked upon the Slavs somewhat as many whites in the United States then looked upon blacks, seeing in them a people useful for labor, naturally slovenly, who had shown no aptitude for civilization except under tutelage. In fact the word "slave" in many languages (German *Sklave*) had originated from the word "Slav." As Count Beust, the Austrian negotiator, put it in 1867, the idea of the Compromise was that each people, Germans and Magyars, should thereafter govern its own barbarians in its own way.

The Compromise created a Dual Monarchy, of a kind unparalleled in Europe. West of the river Leith was the Empire of Austria, east of it the Kingdom of Hungary.

[27] See p. 526.

The two were now judged exactly equal. Each had its own constitution and its own parliament, to which in each country the governing ministry was henceforth to be responsible. The administrative language of Austria would be German, of Hungary, Magyar. Neither state might intervene in the other's affairs. The two were joined by the fact that the same Habsburg ruler should always be emperor in Austria and king in Hungary. Yet the union was not personal only; for, though there was no common parliament, delegates of the two parliaments were to meet together alternately in Vienna and Budapest, and there was to be a common ministry for finance, foreign affairs, and war. To this common ministry of Austria-Hungary both Austrians and Hungarians were to be appointed.

In effect, the Compromise treated Austria as a kind of German nation-state and Hungary as a Magyar nation-state. It furnished each with parliamentary and constitutional organs, by which the leading nationality was made to feel a sense of participation in government. But the Germans formed less than half the people of Austria, as did the Magyars of Hungary. Austria included the Slovenes, Czechs, Poles, and Ruthenians (and a few Italians); Hungary the Slovaks, the Croats and Serbs, and the Transylvanians, who were essentially Rumanians.[28] All these peoples felt aggrieved.

In later years the Germans of Austria proved more liberal toward their minorities than did the Magyars, though never quite liberal enough to allay the discontents. In 1871 Francis Joseph even prepared to recognize the Czechs, agreeing to place Bohemia on the same footing as Hungary. He abandoned the idea in the face of protests from the Germans, especially the Sudeten Germans who lived in Bohemia and who wanted no Czechish state, and also of the Magyars, who feared that the autonomy of Bohemia would be an unsettling example to their own "barbarians." The idea of a Triple Monarchy thereafter never died, but neither did it ever come to life. The Slavs of the Dual Monarchy remained submerged. A man of Slavic birth could hold high office and enjoy the satisfactions of public activity only by adopting the German or Magyar language and culture. Thus frustrated, the Slavs were increasingly tempted to agree with their most radical nationalists.

The Germans of Austria, kept out of Germany by Bismarck, were kept out of Hungary by the Magyars. It was the Magyars who were the great beneficiaries of the Compromise. Somewhat as Bismarck's empire was a mechanism to magnify the rule of East-Elbian Prussia, so the Dual Monarchy became a mechanism to enlarge the influence of the great Hungarian landowners. It was Hungary that adjoined the explosive Balkan peninsula. It was the ruling Magyars, stubbornly refusing concessions to the other peoples, and working through the joint ministry of Austria-Hungary, that transmitted into Europe the shocks originating in the Balkans.

Both Austria and Hungary, under the Dual Monarchy, were in form constitutional parliamentary states, although the principle of ministerial responsibility was not consistently honored. Neither was democratic. In Austria, after much juggling with voting systems, a true universal manhood suffrage was instituted in

[28] See maps, pp. 478, 576–577.

1907. In Hungary, when the First World War came in 1914, still only a quarter of the adult male population had the vote. Socially, the great reform of 1848, the abolition of serfdom, was not allowed to lead on to upsetting conclusions. The owners of great landed estates, especially in Hungary (but also in parts of the Austrian Empire) remained the unquestionably dominant class. They were surrounded by landless peasants, an agrarian proletariat, composed partly of lower classes of their own nationality, and partly of entire peasant peoples, like the Slovaks and Serbs, who had no educated or wealthy class of their own. National and social questions therefore came together. For some nationalities, and for none more than the Magyars, not only a national but a social and economic ascendancy was at stake. Landlordism became the basic social issue. A landowning class, educated and civilized, faced a peasant mass that was generally ignorant, rude, and left out of the advancing civilization of the day.

For Russia also the Crimean War set off a series of changes. The ungainly empire, an "enormous village" as it has been called, stretching from Poland to the Pacific, had proved unable to repel a localized attack by France and Great Britain, into which neither of the Western powers had put anything like its full resources. Alexander II (1855–1881), who became tsar during the war, was no liberal by nature or conviction. But he saw that something drastic must be done. The prestige of western Europe was at its height. There the most successful and even enviable nations were to be found. The reforms in Russia therefore followed, at some distance, the European model.

Imperial Russia was a political organization very difficult to describe. Its own subjects did not know what to make of it. Some, called Westernizers in the mid-nineteenth century, believed Russia destined to become more like Europe. Others, the Slavophiles, believed Russia to be entrusted with a special destiny of its own, which imitation of Europe would only weaken or pervert.

That Russia differed from Europe at least in degree was doubted by nobody. The leading institution was the autocracy of the tsar. This was not exactly the absolutism known in the West. In Russia certain very old European conceptions were missing, such as the idea that spiritual authority is independent of even the mightiest prince or the old feudal idea of reciprocal duties between king and subject.[29] The notion that men have rights, claims for justice at the hands of power, which no one in Europe had ever expressly repudiated, was in Russia a somewhat doctrinaire importation from the West. The tsardom did not rule by law; it ran the country by ukase, police action, and the army. The tsars, since Peter and before, had built up their state very largely by importing European technical methods and technical experts, often against strong objection by native Russians of all classes, upon whom the new methods were, when necessary, simply forced. More than any state in Europe, the Russian empire was a machine superimposed upon its people without organic connection—bureaucracy pure and simple. But as the contacts with

67
Liberalization in
Tsarist Russia:
Alexander II

Tsarist Russia
After 1856

---

[29]See pp. 14, 25–26.

Europe were joined, many Russians acquired European ideas of a kind in which the autocracy was not interested—ideas of liberty and fraternity, of a just and classless society, of individual personality enriched by humane culture and moral freedom. Many people, with such sentiments, found themselves chronically critical of the government and of Russia itself. The government, massive though it seemed, was afraid of such people. Any idea arising outside of official circles seemed pernicious, and the press and the universities were as a rule severely censored.

A second fundamental institution, which had grown up with the tsardom, was legalized bondage or serfdom. The bulk of the population were serfs dependent upon masters. Russian serfdom was more onerous than that found in east-central Europe until 1848.[30] It resembled the slavery of the Americas in that serfs were "owned"; they could be bought and sold and used in other occupations than agriculture. Some serfs worked the soil, rendering unpaid labor service to the gentry. Others could be used by their owners in factories or mines or rented out for such purposes. Others were more independent, working as artisans or mechanics, and even traveling about or residing in the cities, but from their earnings they had to remit certain fees to the lord, or return home when he called them. The owners had a certain paternalistic responsibility for their serfs, and in the villages the gentry constituted a kind of personal local government. The law, as in the American South, did little or nothing to interfere between gentry and servile mass, so that the serf's day-to-day fortunes depended on the personality or economic circumstances of his owner.

By the mid-nineteenth century both conservative and liberal Russians were agreeing that serfdom must some day end. Serfdom was in any case ceasing to be profitable; some two-thirds of all the privately owned serfs (i.e., those not belonging to the tsar or state) were mortgaged as security for loans at the time of Alexander II's accession. Increasingly serfdom was recognized as a bad system of labor relations, making the *moujiks* into illiterate and stolid drudges, without incentive, initiative, self-respect, or pride of workmanship, and also very stupid soldiers for the army.

Educated Russians, full of Western ideas, were estranged from the government, from the Orthodox church, which was an arm of the tsar, and from the common people of their own country. They felt ill at ease in a mass of ignorance and obscurantism and a pang of guilt at the virtual slavery on which their own position rested. Hence arose, at about the time under discussion, what may almost be called another Russian institution, the "intelligentsia." In Russia it was thought so remarkable to be educated, to have ideas, to subscribe to magazines, or engage in critical conversation that the intelligentsia sensed themselves as a class apart. They were made up of students, university graduates, and persons who had a good deal of leisure to read. Such people, while not very free to think, were more free to think than to do almost anything else. The Russian intelligentsia tended to sweeping and all-embracing philosophies. They believed that intellectuals should play a large role in society. They formed an exaggerated idea of the direct influence of thinkers upon

[30]See pp. 248, 348–349.

the course of historical change. Their characteristic attitude was one of opposition. Some, overwhelmed by the mammoth immobility of the tsardom and of serfdom, turned to revolutionary and even terroristic philosophies. This only made the government more repressive. Russia became the land of intimidation, of violent and jarring ideas and lawless acts.

Alexander II, on becoming tsar, attempted to enlist the support of the liberals among the intelligentsia. He gave permission to travel outside of Russia, eased the controls on the universities, and allowed the censorship to go relatively unenforced. Newspapers and journals were founded, and those written by Russian revolutionaries abroad, like the *Polar Star* of Alexander Herzen in London, penetrated more freely into the country. The result was a great outburst of public opinion, which was agreed at least on one point, the necessity of emancipating the peasants. This was in principle hardly a party question. Alexander's father, Nicholas I, had been a noted reactionary, who abhorred Western liberalism and is memorable for having organized, as the "Third Section" of his chancellory, a system of secret political police until then unparalleled in Europe for its ruthlessness. Yet Nicholas I had taken serious measures to alleviate serfdom. Alexander II, basically conservative on Russian affairs, proceeded to set up a special branch of the government to study the question. The government did not wish to throw the whole labor system and economy of the country into chaos, nor to ruin the gentry class without which it could not govern at all. After many discussions, proposals, and memoranda, an imperial ukase of 1861 declared serfdom abolished and the peasants free.

By this great decree the peasants became legally free in the Western sense. They were henceforth subjects of the government, not subjects of their owners. It was hoped that they would be stirred by a new sense of human dignity. As one enthusiastic official put it shortly after emancipation: "The people are erect and transformed; the look, the walk, the speech, everything is changed." The gentry lost their old quasi-manorial jurisdiction over the villages. They could no longer exact forced and unpaid labor or receive fees arising from servitude.

It is important to realize what the Act of Emancipation did and did not do. Roughly (with great differences from region to region) it allocated about half the cultivated land to the gentry and half to the former serfs. The latter had to pay redemption money for the land they received and for the fees and services which the gentry lost. The Russian aristocracy was far from weakened; in place of a kind of human property largely mortgaged anyway, they now had clear possession of some half the land, they received the redemption money, and were rid of obligations to the peasants.

The peasants, on the other hand, now owned some half the arable land in their own right—a considerable amount by the standards of almost any European country. They did not, however, possess it according to the principles of private property or independent farming that had become prevalent in Europe. The peasant land, when redeemed, became the collective property of the ancient peasant village or *mir*. The

583

village, as a unit, was responsible to the government for payment of the redemption and for collection of the necessary sums from its individual members. The village commune, in default of collection, might require forced labor from the defaulter or a member of his family; and it could prevent peasants from moving away from the village, lest those remaining bear the whole burden of payment. It could (as in the past) assign and reassign certain lands to its members for tillage and otherwise supervise cultivation as a joint concern. To keep the village community intact, the government presently forbade the selling or mortgaging of land to persons outside the commune. This tended to preserve the peasant society but also to discourage the investment of outside capital, with which equipment might be purchased, and so to retard agricultural improvement and the growth of wealth. Not all peasants within the village unit were equal. As in France before the Revolution, some had the right to work more land than others. Some were only day laborers. Others had rights of inheritance in the soil (for not all land was subject to reassignment by the commune) or rented additional parcels of land belonging to the gentry. These lands they worked by hiring other peasants for wages. These more substantial peasants, as agricultural entrepreneurs, resembled farmers of the "bourgeois" type found in France or the United States. None of the Russian peasants, however, after the emancipation, possessed full individual freedom of action. In their movements and obligations, as in their thoughts, they were restricted by their village communes as they had once been restricted by their lords.

Alexander II proceeded to overhaul and westernize the legal system of the country. With the disappearance of the lord's jurisdiction over his peasants a new system of local courts was needed in any case, but the opportunity was taken to reform the courts from bottom to top. The arbitrariness of authority and defenselessness of the subject were the inveterate evils. They were greatly mitigated by the edict of 1864. Trials were made public, and private persons received the right to be represented in court by lawyers of their own choosing. All class distinctions in judicial matters were abolished, although in practice peasants continued to be subject to harsh disadvantages. A clear sequence of lower and higher courts was established. Requirements were laid down for the professional training of judges, who henceforth received stated salaries and were protected from administrative pressure. A system of juries on the English model was introduced.

While thus attempting to establish a rule of law, the tsar also moved in the direction of allowing self-government. He hoped to win over the liberals and to shoulder the upper and middle classes with some degree of public responsibility. He created, again by an edict of 1864, a system of provincial and district councils called zemstvos. Elected by various elements, including the peasants, the zemstvos gradually went into operation and took up matters of education, medical relief, public welfare, food supply, and road maintenance in their localities. Their great value was in developing civic sentiment among those who took part in them. Many liberals urged a representative body for all Russia, a Zemsky Sobor or Duma, which, however, Alexander II refused to concede. After 1864 his policy became more cautious. A rebellion in Poland in 1863 inclined him to take advice from those who favored repression. He began to mollify the vested interests that had been disgruntled by the reforms and to whittle down some of the concessions already granted. But the essence of the reforms remained unaffected.

The autocrat who thus undertook to liberalize Russia barely escaped assassination in 1866, had five shots fired at him in 1873, missed death by half an hour in 1880 when his imperial dining room was dynamited, and in 1881 was to be killed by a bomb. The revolutionaries were not pleased with the reforms, which if successful would merely strengthen the existing order. Dissatisfied intelligentsia in the 1860s began to call themselves "nihilists": they believed in "nothing"—except science—and took a cynical view of the reforming tsar and his zemstvos. The peasants, saddled with heavy redemption payments, remained basically unsatisfied, and intellectuals toured the villages fanning this discontent. Revolutionaries developed a mystic conception of the revolutionary role of the Russian masses. They reminded the peasants of the vast rebellions of Stephen Razin and Pugachev, in which they saw a native Russian revolutionary tradition.[31] Socialists, after the failure of socialism in Europe in the Revolution of 1848, came in many cases to believe, as Alexander Herzen wrote, that the true and natural future of socialism lay in Russia, because of the very weakness of capitalism in Russia and the existence of a kind of collectivism already established in the village commune.

More radical than Herzen were the anarchist Bakunin and his disciple Nechaiev. In their *People's Justice* these two called for terrorism not only against tsarist officials but against liberals also. As they wrote in their *Catechism of a Revolutionist*, the true revolutionary "is devoured by one purpose, one thought, one passion—the revolution. . . . He has severed every link with the social order and with the entire civilized world. . . . Everything which promotes the success of the revolution is moral, everything which hinders it is immoral." Terrorism (which is really to say assassination) was rejected by many of the revolutionaries, especially by those who in the 1870s took up the scientific socialism of Karl Marx. To Marx it did not seem that frantic violence would advance an inevitable social process. But other groups, recognizing the inspiration of men like Bakunin and Nechaiev, organized secret terroristic societies. One of these, the People's Will, determined to assassinate the tsar. In an autocratic state, they held, there was no other road to justice and freedom.

Alexander II, alarmed by this underground menace, which of course did not escape the attention of the police, again turned for support to the liberals. The liberals, who were themselves threatened by the revolutionaries, had become estranged from the government by its failure to follow through with the reforms of the early 1860s. Now, in 1880, to rally support, the tsar again relaxed the autocratic system. He abolished the dreaded Third Section or secret police set up by his father, allowed the press to discuss most political subjects freely, and encouraged the zemstvos to do the same. Further to associate representatives of the public with the

[31] See pp. 248–249, 348–349.

government, he proposed, not exactly a parliament, but two nationally elected commissions to sit with the council of state. He signed the edict to this effect on March 13, 1881, and on the same day was assassinated, not by a demented individual acting wildly and alone, but by the joint efforts of the highly trained members of the People's Will.

Alexander III, upon his father's death, abandoned the project for elected commissions and during his whole reign, from 1881 to 1894, reverted to a program of brutal resistance to liberals and revolutionaries alike. The new regime established by peasant emancipation, judicial reform, and the zemstvos was nevertheless allowed to continue. How Russia finally received a parliament in 1905 is explained below in the chapter on the Russian Revolution. At present it is enough to have seen how even tsarist Russia, under Alexander II, shared in a liberal movement that was then at its height. The abolition of serfdom, putting both aristocracy and peasant more fully on a money economy, opened the way for capitalistic development within the empire. And between the two confining walls of autocracy and revolutionism—equally hard and unyielding—European ideas of law, liberty, and humanity inserted themselves in a tentative way.

68
The United States: The American Civil War

The history of Europe, long interconnected with that of the rest of the world, by the early twentieth century became merged with it entirely. Similarly the development of non-European regions, long a collection of separate stories, was to fuse into a single world-wide theme, to which later chapters of this book are largely devoted. It is no great leap at this point to pass to a treatment of areas overseas (as seen from Europe), some of which underwent in the 1860s the same process of national consolidation, or attempted consolidation, already traced in Italy and Germany, Austria, Hungary, and the Russian empire. In particular, foundations were laid for two new "powers" like those of Europe—the United States of America and the Empire of Japan. The huge Dominion of Canada was also established.

Growth of the United States

As in the time of the American Revolution and Napoleon, the history of the United States in the nineteenth century reflected that of the European world of which it formed a part. The most basic fact, besides territorial expansion, was rapid growth. This was so obvious as to lead a French observer in the 1830s, Alexis de Tocqueville, to make a famous prediction: that within a century the United States would have a hundred million people and would, along with Russia, be one of the two leading powers of the world. By 1860, with 31,000,000, the United States was almost as populous as France and more so than Great Britain.

The growth in numbers was due to a prolific birth rate, but also to the arrival of immigrants, who became prolific in their turn. The immigrants—except for an uncounted, because illegal, importation of slaves—came entirely from Europe, and before 1860 almost entirely from Great Britain, Ireland, and Germany. The immigrants did not desire to surrender their native ways. The Catholicism of many of them, especially at a time when Catholicism was at odds with liberalism and republicanism in Europe, was unpopular and even abhorrent to many native Americans. What Europe would call a national question therefore developed. A secret, antiforeign, native-American movement, calling itself the "Know-nothing" or "American" party, even entered briefly into national politics in the 1850s. It quickly collapsed, in the face of more burning issues, and with the refusal of most native Americans to believe themselves actually menaced.

It was of course true that the constant arrival of Europeans was transforming the United States. The transformation was in some ways indisputably for the better, as when educated Germans, in flight from counterrevolution after 1848, brought a knowledge of the sciences, medicine, music, and the most skilled mechanical arts which the new country greatly needed. In other ways it presented a true social problem, obliging peoples to live together without common tradition and landing in the United States many who had been a problem at home. On the whole, it appears that the native Americans accepted the reshaping of their country more calmly than most Europeans would have done in similar circumstances. Few concessions were made. English was the language of the public schools, the police, law courts, local government, and public notices and announcements. Usually the immigrant had to know some English to hold a job. On the other hand no one was exactly forced to become "Americanized"—the new arrivals were free to maintain churches, newspapers, and social gatherings in their own tongues. The fact that the English, Scots, and Irish already spoke English, and that the Germans readily learned it, alleviated the language issue. The immigrants did not constitute minorities in the European sense. They were more than willing to embrace American national attitudes as formed in the eighteenth century—the national traditions of republicanism and self-government, of individual liberty, free enterprise, and unbounded opportunity for self-improvement. The old America impressed itself on the new, being somewhat impressed itself in the process. In this sense a new nationality was being consolidated.

But at the same time the nation was falling to pieces. North and South became completely estranged. The Industrial Revolution had contrary effects on the two regions. It turned the South into an economic associate of Great Britain. The South became the world's chief producer of raw cotton for the Lancashire mills. The Southerners, living by the export of a cash crop, and producing virtually no manufactures, wished to purchase manufactured goods as cheaply as possible. Hence they favored free trade, especially with Great Britain. In the North, the Industrial Revolution led to the building of factories. Northern factory owners, usually backed by their workmen, demanded protection from the inflow of British goods, with which no other country at the time could easily compete. The North therefore favored a high tariff which the South declared to be ruinous.

More fundamental was the difference in the status of labor. As the demand for raw cotton reached astronomical magnitudes the South fell more deeply under the hereditary curse of the Americas—the slave and plantation system.[32] In the nineteenth century slavery increasingly revolted the moral conscience of the white man's world. It was abolished in the British colonies in 1833, in the French colonies in 1848, in the Latin American republics at different dates in the first half of the century. Similarly, serfdom was abolished in the Habsburg possessions in 1848 and in Russia in 1861. The American South could not, and after about 1830 no longer even wished to shake the system off. The South was the Cotton Kingdom whose "peculiar institution" was unfree labor of blacks. Whites were hurt by the system as well as blacks. Few free men could prosper alongside a mass of subservient and virtually uncompensated labor. The incoming Europeans settled overwhelmingly in the North, the South remaining more purely "Anglo-Saxon"—except that in its most densely peopled areas some half of the people were of African descent.

In the movement westward, common to North and South, the pressure in the South came mainly from planters wishing to establish new plantations, in the North from persons hoping to set up small farms and from businessmen bent on building railroads and creating markets. As once France and Great Britain had fought for control beyond the Alleghenies so now North and South fought for control beyond the Mississippi. In 1846 the United States made war upon Mexico by methods at which Bismarck would not have blushed. The North widely denounced the war as an act of Southern aggression, but was willing enough to take the ensuing conquests, which comprised the region from Texas to the Pacific. The first new state created in this region, California, prohibited slavery. Since 1820 the United States had held together precariously by the "Missouri Compromise," under which new states, as set up in the West, were admitted to the Union in pairs, one "slave" and one "free," so that a rough equality was maintained in the Senate and in the presidential electoral vote. With the creation of California this balance of power was upset in favor of the North, so that in return, by the "compromise of 1850," the North agreed to enforce the laws on runaway slaves to the satisfaction of the South. But the new strictness toward fugitive slaves ran against mounting sentiment in the North. Attempts to arrest blacks in the free states and return them to slavery aroused abolitionist sentiment to a higher pitch. The abolitionists, a branch of the humanitarian movement then sweeping the European world, and somewhat resembling the radical democrats who came forward in Europe in 1848, demanded the immediate and total elimination of slavery, without concession, compromise, or compensation for the property interests of the slave-owners. Abolitionists denounced the Union itself as the unholy accomplice in a social abomination.

By 1860 a sense of "sectionalism" had developed in the South not different in principle from the nationalism felt by many peoples in Europe. In their proud insistence on states' rights and constitutional liberties, their aristocratic and warlike codes of ethics, their demand for independence from outside influence and for

[32] See pp. 268–269.

freedom in ruling their own subject people, the Southern whites suggested nothing in Europe so much as the Magyars of the Austrian Empire. They now wondered whether their way of life could be safely maintained within the Union which they had helped to create. They sensed Northerners as outsiders, unsympathetic, foreign, hostile, and the South as potentially as independent and distinct nation. They were aware that within the Union they were increasingly a minority; for where in 1790 North and South had been approximately equal, by 1860 the North had outrun the South in population, in part because of the stream of migration from Europe. The incipient nationalism of the South was of the type of the small nation struggling against the great empire. In the North, nationalism was a sentiment in favor of maintaining the whole existing territory of the United States. Northerners by 1860, with a few exceptions, refused to admit that any state of the Union could withdraw, or secede, for any reason.

In 1860 the new Republican party elected Abraham Lincoln president. It advanced a program of free Western lands for small farmers, a higher tariff, transcontinental railroad building, and economic and capitalistic development on a national scale. The new party's radical wing, to which Lincoln himself did not belong, was vehemently abolitionist and anti-Southern in sentiment. Southern leaders, after the election of Lincoln, brought about the solemn withdrawal of their states from the United States of America and the creation of a Confederate States of America reaching from Virginia to Texas. Lincoln ordered the armed forces to defend the territory of the United States, and the resulting Civil War, or war of Southern independence, lasting for four years and involving battles as great as those of Napoleon, was the most harrowing struggle of the nineteenth century with the possible exception of the Tai-ping rebellion in China.[33]

European governments, while never recognizing the Confederacy, were partial to the South. The United States stood for principles still considered revolutionary in Europe, so that, while the European working classes generally favored the North, the upper classes were willing enough to see the North American republic end in collapse and failure. In addition, Great Britain and France saw in the break-up of the United States the same advantages that they had formerly seen in the break-up of the Spanish empire.[34] In the Confederate States the British, and the French to a lesser degree, expected to find another free trade country, supplying western Europe with raw materials and buying its manufactures; in short, not a competitor like the North, but a complementary partner to the industry of the Old World. It was likewise during the American Civil War that a French army sent by Napoleon III invaded Mexico to create a puppet empire under an Austrian archduke.[35] Thus the only serious attempt to ignore the Monroe Doctrine, violate the independence of Latin America, and revive European colonialism in the Americas occurred at the time when the United States was in dissolution.

[33] See pp. 699–702.
[34] See pp. 202, 490–492.
[35] See p. 675.

But the North won the war and the Union was upheld. The Mexicans rid themselves of their unwanted emperor. The Tsar Alexander II sold Alaska to the United States. The war ended the idea of the Union as a confederation of member states from which members might withdraw at will. In its place triumphed the idea that the United States was a national state, composed not of member states but of a unitary people irrevocably bound together. This doctrine was written explicitly into the Fourteenth Amendment to the Constitution, which pronounced all Americans to be citizens not only of their several states but of the United States and forbade any state to "deprive any person of life, liberty or property without due process of law"—"due process" to be determined by authority of the national government. The new force of central authority was felt first of all in the South. President Lincoln, using his war powers, issued the Emancipation Proclamation in 1863, abolishing slavery in areas engaged in hostilities against the United States. The Thirteenth Amendment in 1865 abolished slavery everywhere in the country. No compensation was paid to the slave-owners, who were therefore ruined. The legal authority of the United States was thus used for an annihilation of individual property rights without parallel (outside of modern communism) in the history of the Western world; for neither the nobility in the French Revolution, nor the Russian serf-owners in 1861, nor the slave-owners of the West Indies in the nineteenth century, nor the owners of businesses nationalized by twentieth-century socialists in western Europe had to face such a total and overwhelming loss of property values as the slave-owners of the American South.

After the Civil War:
Reconstruction;
Industrial Growth

The assassination of Lincoln in 1865 by a fanatical Southern patriot strengthened those radical Republicans who said that the South must be drastically reformed. With the old Southern upper class completely ruined, Northerners of many types poured into the defeated country. Some came to represent the federal government, some to dabble in local politics, some to make money, and a great many out of democratic and humanitarian impulses, to teach the debased ex-slaves the elements of reading and writing or of useful trades. Blacks in the South voted, sat in legislatures, occupied public office. This period, called Reconstruction, may be compared to the most advanced phase of the French Revolution, in that "radical republicans" undertook to press liberty and equality upon a recalcitrant country, under conditions of emergency rule and under the auspices of a highly centralized national government with a mobilized army. The Southern whites strenuously objected, and the Northern radicals discredited themselves and gradually lost their zeal. Reconstruction was abandoned in the 1870s, and, by what Europeans would call a counterrevolution, the Southern whites gradually regained control.

The Northern business interests—financiers, bankers, company promoters, railway builders, manufacturers—expanded greatly with the wartime demand for munitions and military provisioning. They received protection by the Morrill tariff of 1861. In the next year, partly as a war measure, the Union Pacific Railroad was incorporated, and in 1869, at a remote spot in Utah, the last spike was driven in the first railroad to span the American continent. The Homestead Act, providing farms to settlers on easy conditions, and the granting of public lands to certain colleges (ever since called "land-grant colleges"), largely for the promotion of agricultural sciences, encouraged the push of population and civilization into the West. Vast tracts of land were given by the government to subsidize railway building. With the destruction of the Southern slaveholders, who before the war had counterbalanced the rising industrialists, it was now industry and finance that dominated national politics in the increasingly centralized United States. The Fourteenth Amendment, for many years, was mainly interpreted not to protect the civil rights of individual persons, but the property rights of business corporations against restrictive legislation by the states. The shift of political power from the states to the federal government accompanied and protected the shift of economic enterprise from local businesses to far-flung and continent-embracing corporations. As in France under Napoleon III, there was a good deal of corruption, fraud, speculation, and dishonestly or rapaciously acquired wealth; but industry boomed, the cities grew and the American mass market was created. On Fifth Avenue in New York, and in other Northern cities, rose the pretentious and gaudy mansions of the excessively rich.

In short, the American Civil War, which might have reduced English-speaking America to a scramble of jealously competing minor republics, resulted instead in the economic and political consolidation of a large nation-state, liberal and democratic in its political principles, and committed enthusiastically to private enterprise in its economic system.

69
The Dominion of Canada, 1867

North of the United States, at the time of the Civil War, lay a number of British provinces unconnected with one another, and each in varying degree dependent on Great Britain. The population had originated in three great streams. One part was French, settled in the St. Lawrence valley since the seventeenth century. A second part was made up of descendants of United Empire Loyalists, old seaboard colonists who, remaining faithful to Britain, had fled from the United States during the American Revolution.[36] They were numerous in the Maritime Provinces and in Upper Canada, as Ontario was then called.[37] A third part consisted of recent immigrants from Great Britain, men and women of the working classes who had left the home country to improve themselves in America.

The French firmly resisted assimilation to the English-speaking world around them. Their statute of freedom was the Quebec Act of 1774, which had been denounced as "intolerable" by the aroused inhabitants of the Thirteen Colonies, but which put the French civil law, French language, and French Catholic church under the protection of the British Crown.[38] The French looked with apprehension upon the

[36] See p. 367.
[37] See map, p. 563.
[38] See p. 366.

stream of immigrants, English-speaking and Protestant, which began to flow into Canada about 1780 and thereafter never stopped. There was constant irritation between the two nationalities.

The British government tried various expedients. In 1791 it created two provinces in the St. Lawrence and Great Lakes region—a Lower Canada to remain French, and an Upper Canada to be English. They received the same form of government as that enjoyed by the Thirteen Colonies before their break from the empire. Each colony, that is, had a locally elected assembly with certain powers of taxation and law-making, subject to veto by the British authorities, as represented either by the governor or by the London government itself. For many years there was no objection to these arrangements. The War of 1812, in which the United States embarked on the conquest of Canada, aroused a national sentiment among both French and English in that country, together with a willingness to depend politically upon Great Britain for military security. But the internal political differences continued. In Lower Canada the French feared the English-speaking minority. In Upper Canada the old aristocracy of United Empire Loyalists, who had carved the province from the wilderness, hesitated to share control with the new immigrants from Great Britain. Between the provinces there were grievances also, since Lower Canada stood in the way of Upper Canada's outlet to the sea. In 1837 a superficial rebellion broke out in both provinces. It was put down virtually without bloodshed.

Lord Durham's Report

In Great Britain at this time the reforming Whigs were busily renovating many ancient English institutions.[39] Some of them had definite views on the administration of colonies. In general, they held that it was not necessary to control a region politically in order to trade with it. This was an aspect of the free trade doctrine, separating economics from politics, business from power. The Whig reformers were rather indifferent to empire, unconcerned with military, naval, or strategic considerations. A few even thought it natural for colonies, when mature, to drop away entirely from the mother country. Whigs, liberals, and radicals all wished to economize on military expenditure, to relieve British taxpayers by cutting down British garrisons overseas.

After the Canadian insurrection of 1837 the Whig government sent out the Earl of Durham as governor. Durham, one of the framers of the parliamentary Reform Bill of 1832, published his views on Canadian affairs in 1839. Durham's Report has ever since been regarded as one of the classic documents in the rise of the British Commonwealth of Nations. He held that in the long run French separatist feeling in Canada should be extinguished and all Canadians brought to feel a common citizenship and national character. He therefore called for the reuniting of the two Canadas into one province. To consolidate this province he proposed an intensive development of railways and canals. In political matters he urged the granting of virtual self-government for Canada and the introduction of the British system of

---

[39] See pp. 503–504.

"responsible government," in which the elected assembly should control the executive ministers in the province, the governor becoming a kind of legal and ceremonial figure like the king in Great Britain.

Most of Durham's Report was accepted immediately, and a united Canada was given the machinery of self-government in 1840. The British army was withdrawn. The Canadians undertook to maintain their own military establishment, still regarded as necessary, since the era of the famous undefended frontier between Canada and the United States had not yet dawned. The Webster-Ashburton treaty of 1842 put an end to the long dispute over the Maine border. But as late as 1866 the Canadians had to repel armed invaders from the United States, when several hundred Irish Americans, members of the Fenians, an Irish republican secret society, staged a Garibaldi-like attempt to detach Canada from the British Empire. Local Canadian forces proved sufficient to this threat.

The principle of responsible government was established in the late 1840s, the governors of Canada allowing the elected assembly to adopt policies and appoint or remove ministers as it chose. Responsible government, still confined to internal matters, worked satisfactorily from the beginning. But one feature of the new plan, the union of the two Canadas, began to produce friction as the English-speaking immigration continued. The French were afraid of being outnumbered in their own country. Many Canadians therefore turned to the idea of a federation, in which the French and English areas might each conduct its own local affairs, while remaining joined for larger purposes in a superior government.

Federalism in Canada was thus partly a decentralizing idea, aimed at satisfying the French element by a redivision into two provinces, and in part a plan for a new centralization or unification, because it contemplated bringing all the provinces of British North America into union with the St. Lawrence and Great Lakes region, to which alone the term Canada was then applied. While British North Americans discussed federation the Civil War was disrupting the United States. In the face of this unpleasant example, the British North Americans formed a strong union in which all powers were to rest in the central government except those specifically assigned to the provinces. The federal constitution, drafted in Canada by Canadians, was passed through the British Parliament in 1867 as the British North America Act. British advice prevailed in one significant matter; for where the Canadians had decided to call their union the Kingdom of Canada, the British government suggested instead the term "dominion," to spare the well-known sensibilities of the United States on the matter of "kingdoms" in the Americas. The British North America Act of 1867 constitutionally established the Dominion of Canada.

The new dominion received a common parliament, in which the majority party controlled a responsible ministry according to British principles of cabinet government. The original provinces were Quebec and Ontario, formed from the old Canada, and Nova Scotia and New Brunswick, which joined on the understanding that a railroad be built to connect them with Quebec. The old Hudson's Bay

Company, founded in 1670, transferred its rights of government over the vast Northwest to the dominion in 1869. From these territories the province of Manitoba was created in 1870 and British Columbia in 1871. To link them solidly with the rest of the dominion the Canadian Pacific Railway was completed in 1885. It made possible the development of the prairies, where the provinces of Saskatchewan and Alberta were added in 1905.

The Dominion of Canada, though not large in population, possessed from the beginning a significance beyond the mere number of its people. It was the first example of successful devolution, or granting of political liberty, within one of the European colonial empires. It embodied principles which Edmund Burke and Benjamin Franklin had vainly recommended a century before to keep the Thirteen Colonies loyal to Great Britain. The dominion after 1867 moved forward from independence in internal matters to independence in such external affairs as tariffs, diplomacy, and the decisions of war and peace. It thus pioneered in the development of "dominion status," working out precedents later applied in Australia (1901), New Zealand (1907), the Union of South Africa (1910), and in the 1920s, temporarily, in Ireland. By the middle of the twentieth century the same idea, or what may be called the Canadian idea, was even applied to the world-wide problem of colonialism as it affected non-European peoples, notably in India, Pakistan, Ceylon, and the former British colonies in Africa, until all these peoples chose to become republics, though still loosely and voluntarily joined together and to Great Britain in a Commonwealth of Nations.

More immediately, in America, the founding of the dominion, a solid band of self-governing territory stretching from ocean to ocean, stabilized the relations between British North America and the United States. The United States regarded its northern borders as final. The withdrawal of British control from Canadian affairs furthered the United States conception of an American continent entirely free from European political influence. The founding of the dominion and the purchase of Alaska, coming in the same year, rounded out the Monroe Doctrine to the north. The Dominion of Canada filled up politically, in a way more than satisfactory to the United States, the huge territorial vacuum lying between the inhabited regions of North America and the Arctic Sea.

70
Japan and the West

594

T he Japanese, when they allowed the Westerners to discover them, were a highly civilized people living in a complex society. They had many large cities, they enjoyed the contemplation of natural scenery, they went to the theater, and they read novels. With their stylized manners, their fans and their wooden temples, their lacquer work and their painting on screens, their tiny rice fields and their curious and ineffectual firearms, they seemed to Europeans to be the very acme of everything quaint. This feeling is immortalized in *The Mikado* of Gilbert and Sullivan, first performed in 1885. Not long thereafter the idea of Japanese quaintness, like the idea of the

Germans as an impractical people given mainly to music and metaphysics, had to be revised. The Europeans, in "opening" Japan, opened up more than they knew.

In 1853, the American Commodore Perry forced his way with a fleet of naval vessels into Yedo Bay, insisted upon landing, and demanded of the Japanese government, somewhat peremptorily, that it engage in commercial relations with the United States and other Western powers. In the next year the Japanese began to comply, and in 1867 an internal revolution took place, of which the most conspicuous consequence was a rapid westernizing of Japanese life and institutions. But if it looked as if the country had been "opened" by Westerners, actually Japan had exploded from within.

For over two centuries Japan had followed a program of self-imposed isolation. No Japanese was allowed to leave the islands or even to build a ship large enough to navigate the high seas. No foreigner, except for handfuls of Dutch and Chinese, was allowed to enter. Japan remained a sealed book to the West. The contrary is not quite so true, for the Japanese knew rather more about Europe than Europeans did about Japan. The Japanese policy of seclusion was not merely based upon ignorance. Initially, at least, it was based on experience.

The first Europeans—three Portuguese in a Chinese junk—are thought to have arrived in Japan in 1542. For about a century thereafter there was considerable coming and going. The Japanese showed a strong desire to trade with the foreigners, from whom they obtained clocks and maps, learned about printing and shipbuilding, and took over the use of tobacco and potatoes. Thousands also adopted the Christian religion as preached to them by Spanish and Portuguese Jesuits. Japanese traveled to the Dutch Indies and even to Europe. The Japanese in fact proved more receptive to European ideas than other Asiatic peoples. But shortly after 1600 the government began to drive Christianity underground; in 1624 it expelled the Spaniards, in 1639 the Portuguese, and in 1640 all Europeans except for a few Dutch merchants who were allowed to remain at Nagasaki under strict control. From 1640 to 1854 these few Dutch at Nagasaki were the only channel of communication with the West.[40]

The reasons for self-seclusion, as for its abandonment later, arose from the course of political events in Japan. The history of Japan showed an odd parallel to that of Europe. In Japan, as in Europe, a period of feudal warfare was followed by a period of government absolutism, during which civil peace was kept by a bureaucracy, an obsolescent warrior class was maintained as a privileged element in society, and a commercial class of native merchants grew wealthier, stronger and more insistent upon its position.

When the first Europeans arrived the islands were still torn by the wars and rivalries of the numerous clans into which the Japanese were organized. Gradually one clan, the Tokugawa, gained control, taking over the office of "shogun." The

---

[40] See p. 170.

shogun was a kind of military head who governed in the name of the emperor, and the hereditary Tokugawa shogunate, founded in 1603, lasted until 1867. The early Tokugawa shoguns concluded from a good deal of evidence that the Europeans in Japan, both merchants and missionaries, were engaged in feudal or interclan politics and even aspiring to dominate Japan by helping Christian or pro-European Japanese to get into power. The first three Tokugawa shoguns, to establish their own dynasty, to pacify and stabilize the country, and to keep Japan free from European penetration, undertook to exterminate Christianity and adopted the rigid policy of nonintercourse with the rest of the world.

Under the Tokugawa Japan enjoyed peace, a long peace, for the first time in centuries. The Tokugawa shoguns completed the detachment of the emperor from politics, building him up as a divine and legendary being, too august and too remote for the hurly-burly of the world. The emperor remained shut in at Kyoto on a modest allowance furnished by the shoguns. The shoguns established their own court and government at Yedo (later called Tokyo); and as Louis XIV brought nobles to Versailles, or Peter the Great forced his uncouth lords to build town houses in St. Petersburg, so the shoguns required the great feudal chieftains and their men-at-arms to reside at least part of the year in Yedo.

The shoguns administered the country through a kind of military bureaucracy or dictatorship. This formidable instrument of state watched over the great lords (called daimyo), who, however, retained a good deal of feudal authority over their subjects in the regions most distant from Yedo. The great lords and their armed retainers (the samurai), having no further fighting to occupy them, turned into a landed aristocracy which spent a good deal of its time in Yedo and other cities. As a leisure class, they developed new tastes and standards of living and hence needed more income, which they obtained by squeezing the peasants, and which they spent by buying from the merchants.

The merchant class greatly expanded by catering to the government and the gentry. Japan in the seventeenth century passed on to a money economy. Many lords fell seriously into debt to the merchants. Many samurai, like lesser nobles in France or Poland at the time, were almost ridiculously impoverished, hard-pressed to keep up appearances, with nothing except social status to distinguish them from commoners. The law, as in Europe under the Old Regime, drew a sharp line between classes. Nobles, merchants, and peasants were subject to different taxes and were differently punished for different offenses. What was a crime for a commoner would be excusable for a samurai; or what in a samurai would be a punishable breach of honor would be accepted in a common person. The samurai had the right to carry two swords as a mark of class and could in theory cut down an impudent commoner without arousing further inquiry. In practice the shoguns repressed violence of this kind, but there was much less development of law and justice than in the European monarchies of the Old Regime. Economically the merchants and artisans prospered. By 1723 Yedo was a city with 500,000 people; by 1800 with over 1,000,000, it was larger than London or Paris, and twenty times as large as the largest city in the United States. After 1800 some merchants were able to purchase the rank of samurai for money. The old class lines were beginning to blur.

Though deliberately secluded, the economic and social life of Japan was thus by no means static. The same is true of its intellectual life. Buddhism, the historic religion, lost its hold on many people during the Tokugawa period, so that Japan in its way underwent, like the West, a "secularization" of ideas. As a code of personal conduct there was a new emphasis on Bushido, the "way of the warrior," a kind of nonreligious moral teaching which exalted the samurai virtues of honor and loyalty. With the decline of Buddhism went also a revival of the cult of Shinto, the "way of the gods," the ancient indigenous religion of Japan, which held, among much else, that the emperor was veritably the Son of Heaven. There was much activity in the study and writing of history, arousing, as in Europe, an acute interest in the national past. History, like Shinto, led to a feeling that the shoguns were usurpers and that the emperor, obscurely relegated to Kyoto, was the true representative of everything highest and most lasting in the life of Japan.

Meanwhile, through the crack left open at Nagasaki, Western ideas trickled in. The shogun Yoshimune in the mid-eighteenth century permitted the importation of Occidental books, except those relating to Christianity. A few Japanese learned Dutch and began to decipher Dutch books on anatomy, surgery, astronomy, and other subjects. In 1745 a Dutch-Japanese dictionary was completed. For European manufactures also—watches, glassware, velvets, woolens, telescopes, barometers—there came to be an eager demand, satisfied as much as possible by the methodical Dutch. Nor were the Japanese wholly uninformed about politics in the West. While the most assiduous Westerner could learn nothing of the internal affairs of Japan, an educated Japanese could, if he wished, arrive at some idea of the French Revolution, or know who was president of the United States.

When Perry in 1853 made his unwanted visit he therefore had many potential allies within Japan. There were nobles, heavily in debt, unable to draw more income from agriculture, willing to embark upon foreign trade and to exploit their property by introducing new enterprises. There were penurious samurai, with no future in the old system, ready and willing to enter upon new careers as army officers or civil officials. There were merchants hoping to add to their business by dealing in Western goods. There were scholars eager to learn more of Western science and medicine. There were patriots fearful that Japan was becoming defenseless against Western guns. Spiritually the country was already adrift from its moorings, already set toward a course of national self-assertion, restlessly susceptible to hazily understood new ideas. Under such pressures, and from downright fear of a bombardment of Yedo by the Americans, which if it would not subdue Japan would at least ruin the declining prestige of the shogunate, the shogun Iesada in 1854 signed a commercial treaty with the United States. Similar treaties were soon signed with the Europeans.

In the following years were sown the seeds of much later misunderstanding between Japan and the West. The whites in those days—European and American—were somewhat trigger-happy in the discharge of naval ordnance against backward peoples. The Japanese, a proud and elaborately civilized nation, soon found that the whites considered them backward. They found, for example, as soon as they learned more of the West by reading and travel, that the treaties they signed in the 1850s were not treaties between equals as understood in the West. These first treaties provided that Japan should maintain a low tariff on imports and not change it except with the consent of the foreign powers. To give outsiders a voice in determining tariff policy was not the custom among sovereign states of the West. The early treaties also provided for extraterritoriality. This meant that Europeans and Americans residing in Japan were not subject to Japanese law but remained under the jurisdiction of their respective homelands as represented by consular officials. Such extraterritorial provisions had long been established in Turkey and were currently taking root in China.[41] Europeans insisted upon them in countries where European principles of property, debt, or security of life and person did not prevail. At the same time, of course, no civilized state ever permitted a foreign power to exercise jurisdiction within its borders. Extraterritoriality was a mark of inferiority, as the Japanese soon discovered.

A strong antiforeign reaction developed after 1854. It was at first led by certain nobles of the western islands, the lords of Choshu and Satsuma, who had never been fully subordinated to the shogun at Yedo, and who now dreamed of overturning the Tokugawa shogunate and leading a national revival with the emperor as its rallying point. Their first idea was to check Western penetration (as two and a half centuries before) by driving the Westerners out. But in 1862 some Englishmen unintentionally violated a small point of Japanese etiquette. One of them was killed. The British government demanded punishment for the offending Japanese who were followers of the lord of Satsuma. The shogun proved unable to arrange this, and the British navy thereupon itself sailed up and bombarded the capital of Satsuma. In the same year the lord of Choshu, who commanded the straits of Shimonoseki with some ancient artillery, ordered it to fire on passing vessels. The British, French, Dutch, and United States governments immediately protested, and, when the embarrassed shogun proved unable to discipline Choshu, dispatched an allied naval force to Shimonoseki. The forts and shipping of Choshu were destroyed, and in indemnity of $3,000,000 was imposed. These incidents were remembered in Japan long after they were forgotten in Europe and the United States. It was likewise remembered that the Western powers, discovering that the shogun was not the supreme ruler of the country, sent a naval expedition to Kyoto itself and required the emperor to confirm the treaties signed by the shogun and to reduce import duties, under threat of naval bombardment.

[41] See pp. 227, 702–703.

The lords of Choshu and Satsuma now concluded that the only way to deal with the West was to adopt the military and technical equipment of the West itself. They would save Japan for the Japanese by learning the secrets of the Western power. First they forced the resignation of the shogun, whose prestige had long been undermined anyway, and who had now discredited himself first by signing undesirable treaties with the West and then failing to protect the country from outrage. The last shogun abdicated in 1867. The reformers declared the emperor restored to his full authority. It was their intention to use the plenitude of imperial power to consolidate and fortify Japan for its new position in the world. In 1868 a new emperor inherited the throne; his name was Mutsuhito, but according to Japanese custom a name was given to his reign also, which was called Meiji. The Meiji era (1868–1912) was the great era of the westernization of Japan.

Japan turned into a modern national state. Feudalism was abolished, most of the great lords voluntarily surrendering into the emperor's hands their control over samurai and common people. "We abolish the clans and convert them into prefectures," declared one imperial decree. The legal system was reorganized and equality before the law introduced, in the sense that all persons became subject to the same rules regardless of class. In part with the hope of getting rid of extra-territoriality, the reformers recast the criminal law along Western lines, deleting the bizarre and cruel punishments which Europeans considered barbaric. A new army was established, modeled mainly on the Prussian. The samurai in 1871 lost his historic right to carry two swords; he now served as an army officer, not as the retainer of a clannish chief. A navy, modeled on the British, followed somewhat later. Control of money and currency passed to the central government, and a national currency, with decimal units, was adopted. A national postal service began to function and above all a national school system, which soon brought a high rate of literacy to Japan. Buddhism was discouraged, and the property of Buddhist monasteries was confiscated. Shinto was the cult favored by the government. Shinto gave a religious tincture to national sentiment and led to a renewed veneration of the imperial family. In 1889 a constitution was promulgated. It confirmed the civil liberties then common in the West and provided for a parliament in two chambers, but it stressed also the supreme and "eternal" authority of the emperor, to whom the ministers were legally responsible. In practice, in the new Japan, the emperor never actively governed. He remained aloof, as in the past; and political leaders, never fully responsible to the parliament, tended to govern freely in what they conceived to be the interests of the state.

Industrial and financial modernization went along with and even preceded the political revolution. In 1858 the first steamship was purchased from the Dutch. In 1859 Japan placed its first foreign loan, borrowing 5,000,000 yen by a bond issue floated in England. In 1869 the first telegraph connected Yokohama and Tokyo. The first railroad, between the same two cities, was completed in 1872. In 1870 appeared the first spinning machinery. Foreign trade, almost literally zero in 1854, was valued at $200,000,000 a year by the end of the century. The population rose from 33,000,000 in 1872 to 46,000,000 in 1902. The island empire, like Great Britain, became dependent on exports and imports to sustain its dense population at the level of living to which it aspired.

The westernization of Japan still stands as the most remarkable transformation ever undergone by any people in so short a time. It recalls the westernizing of Russia under Peter over a century before, though conducted somewhat less brutally, more rapidly, and with a wider consent among the population. For Japan, as formerly for Russia, the motive was in large measure defense against Western penetration, together with an admiration for Western statecraft and an ambition to become a "power." [42] What the Japanese wanted from the West was primarily science, technology, and organization. They were content enough with the innermost substance of their culture, their moral ideas, their family life, their arts and amusements, their religious conceptions, though even in these they showed an uncommon adaptability. Essentially it was to protect their internal substance, their Japanese culture, that they took over the external apparatus of Western civilization. This apparatus—science, technology, machinery, arms, political and legal organization—was the part of Western civilization for which other peoples generally felt a need, which they hoped to adopt without losing their own spiritual independence, and which therefore, though sometimes rather scornfully dismissed as materialistic, became the common ground for the interdependent world-wide civilization that emerged at the close of the nineteenth century.

◎ In brief, to conclude a long chapter, the world between 1850 and 1870, revolutionized economically by the railroad and steamship, was revolutionized politically by the formation of large and consolidated nation-states. These states at the time all embodied certain liberal and constitutional principles, or at least the machinery of parliamentary and representative government. But the whole earth had also become an arena in which certain mighty beings, called nations or powers, were to act. The Great Powers in 1871 were Great Britain, Germany, France, Austria-Hungary, and Russia. Britain had produced a daughter nation in Canada. Whether Italy was to be called a Great Power was not yet clear. No one knew what Japan would do. All agreed that the United States would one day play a large role in international politics, but the time was not yet.

[42] See pp. 244–256.

XIV: EUROPEAN CIVILIZATION

1871-1914

Half a century elapsed between the period of national consolidation described in the last chapter and the outbreak of the First World War in 1914. In this half-century Europe in many ways reached the climax of the modern phase of its civilization, and also exerted its maximum influence upon peoples outside Europe. The present chapter will attempt a description of European civilization in these years, the next chapter an account of the world-wide ascendancy which Europe enjoyed at this time.

For Europe and the European world the years 1871 to 1914 were marked by hitherto unparalleled material and industrial growth, international peace, domestic stability, the advance of constitutional, representative, and democratic government, and continued faith in science, reason, and progress. But in these very years, in politics, economics, and basic thinking there were forces operating to undermine the liberal premises and tenets of this European civilization. Most of the present chapter will be devoted to the continuing triumphs of liberalism, but the signs of its transformation and wane will be pointed out too.

Chapter Emblem: A painting called "The Last of England," dated 1852, by Ford Madox Brown, showing two emigrants looking back from their departing ship.

*Materialistic and
Nonmaterialistic Ideals*

With the extension of the nation-state system Europe was politically more divided than ever. Its unity lay in the sharing by all Europeans of a similar way of life and outlook, which existed also in such "European" countries as the United States, Australia, and New Zealand. Europe and its offshoots constituted the "civilized world." Other regions—Africa, China, India, the up-country of Peru—were said to be "backward." (They are today referred to as "underdeveloped.") Europeans were extremely conscious and inordinately proud of their civilization in the half-century before 1914. They believed it to be the well-deserved outcome of centuries of progress. Feeling themselves to be the most advanced branch of mankind in the important areas of human endeavor, they assumed that all peoples should respect the same social ideals—that so far as they were unwilling or unable to adopt them they were backward, and that so far as they did adopt them they became civilized in their turn.

These ideals of civilization were in part materialistic. If Europeans considered their civilization to be better in 1900 than in 1800, or better in 1900 than the ways of non-Europeans at the same time, it was because they had a higher standard of living, ate and dressed more adequately, slept in softer beds, and had more satisfactory sanitary facilities. It was because they possessed oceanliners, railroads, and streetcars, and after about 1880 telephones and electric lights. But the ideal of civilization was by no means exclusively materialistic. Knowledge as such, correct or truthful knowledge, was held to be a civilized attainment—scientific knowledge of nature, in place of superstition or demonology; geographical knowledge, by which civilized people were aware of the earth as a whole with its general contours and diverse inhabitants. The ideal was also profoundly moral, derived from Christianity, but now secularized and detached from religion. An Englishman, Isaac Taylor, in his *Ultimate Civilization* published in 1860, defined this moral ideal by listing the contrasting "relics of barbarism" which he thought were due to disappear— "Polygamy, Infanticide, Legalized Prostitution, Capricious Divorce, Sanguinary and Immoral Games, Infliction of Torture, Caste and Slavery." The first four of these had been unknown to the approved customs of Europe at least since the coming of

Train in the Snow *by Claude Monet (French, 1840–1926)*
With the Impressionists, and notably with Claude Monet, some of the conventions of Western painting since the Renaissance began to fade. Emphasis shifted from the representation of objects to the perception of them as experienced through the eye. Solid masses melted into the play of light under a variety of atmospheric conditions. The railway age, which developed rapidly in Monet's youth, furnished many subjects to excite his imagination. In this picture the solid iron of the locomotive merges into the indeterminate grays of a dull day in winter. The chill and the low visibility are conveyed as much as the visual images themselves. Courtesy of the Musée Marmottan, Paris (Giraudon). Permission S.P.A.D.E.M. 1970 by French Reproduction Rights, Inc.

Christianity. Torture went out of use about 1800, even in the illiberal European states; and legalized caste and slavery in the course of the nineteenth century. But there were few non-European peoples, in 1860, among whom two or three of Taylor's "relics" could not be found.

There are certain other indices, more purely quantitative, worked out by sociologists to show the level of advancement of a given society. One of these is the death rate, or number of persons per thousand of population who die each year. In England, France, and Sweden the "true" death rate (or death rate regardless of the proportion of infants and old people, who are most susceptible to death) is known to have fallen from about 25 before 1850, to 19 in 1914 and 18 in the 1930s. Indeed, before the Second World War, it stood seemingly stabilized at about 18 in all countries of northwestern Europe, the United States, and the British dominions. Death rates in countries not "modern" run over 40 even in favorable times. A closely related index is infant mortality, which fell rapidly after 1870 in all countries affected by medical science. Thus a woman under civilized conditions had to go through pregnancy and childbirth less often to produce the same number of surviving children. Another index is life expectancy, or the number of years of age which a person has an even chance of attaining. In England the expectation of life at birth rose from 40 years in the 1840s to 59 in 1933 and 69 in 1970. In India in 1931 it was less than 27 years. It had risen to about 42 in 1970. Still another index is the literacy rate, or proportion of persons above a certain age (such as ten) able to read and write. In northwestern Europe by 1900 the literacy rate approached 100. In some countries it still does not rise very far above zero. A further basic index is the productivity of labor, or amount produced by one worker in a given expenditure of time. This is difficult to compute, especially for earlier periods for which statistical data are lacking. In the 1930s, however, the productivity of a farmer in Denmark was over ten times that of a farmer in Albania. All northwestern Europe was above the European average in this respect with the exception of Ireland, whereas Ireland, Spain, Portugal, Italy, and all eastern Europe were below it.

Sunday Afternoon on the Island of La Grande Jatte *by Georges Seurat (French, 1859–1891) This picture of sunny calm, painted in 1886, suggests something of the well-being brought to a great many people by the European civilization of the late nineteenth century. Whether boating, or idly fishing, or quietly sitting and watching, or strolling alone or in pairs or in families with their children, the figures seem to live in a peaceable world which a later age of war, speed and mechanical amusements has made to seem far away. Technically this is one of the most remarkable pictures ever painted. The artist, an impressionist, created it without the use of lines by filling the canvas with thousands of minute dots of the primary colors, which so blur and mix in the eye as to produce the forms and hues of nature. As a result it seems to be a picture of light itself, with an actual shimmer on the water, an astonishing "grassiness" in the grass, with shadows that seem to be real shadows, and distant figures looking really distant as if seen through the intervening air. Courtesy of The Art Institute of Chicago.*

The essence of civilized living doubtless is in the intangibles, in the way in which men use their minds, and in the attitudes they form toward others or toward the conduct and planning of their own lives. The intangibles, however, are not always agreed upon by persons of different culture or ideology. On the quantitative criteria there is less disagreement; all men, with few exceptions, wish to lower the death rate, raise the literacy rate, and increase the productivity of human exertion. Even if we apply quantitative or sociological indices alone, we can say that after 1870 there was in fact, and not merely in the opinion of Europeans, a civilized world of which Europe was the center.

The "Zones"
of Civilization

Or rather, a certain region of Europe was the center. For there were really two Europes, an inner zone and an outer. A Frenchman writing in the 1920s, describing the two Europes that had risen since 1870, called the inner zone the "Europe of steam," and bounded it by an imaginary line joining Glasgow, Stockholm, Danzig, Trieste, Florence, and Barcelona. It included not only Great Britain but Belgium, Germany, France, northern Italy, and the western portions of the Austrian Empire. Virtually all heavy European industry was located in this zone. Here the railway network was thickest. Here was concentrated the wealth of Europe, in the form both of a high living standard and of accumulations of capital. Here likewise were almost all the laboratories and all the scientific activity of Europe. Here, in the same zone, lay the strength of constitutional and parliamentary government and of liberal, humanitarian, socialist, and reformist movements of many kinds. In this zone the death rate was low, life expectancy high, conditions of health and sanitation at their best, literacy almost universal, productivity of labor very great. To the same zone, for practical purposes, belonged certain regions of European settlement overseas, especially the northeastern part of the United States.

The "outer zone" included most of Ireland, most of the Iberian and Italian peninsulas, and all Europe east of what was then Germany, Bohemia, and Austria proper. The outer zone was agricultural, though the productivity of agriculture, per farm worker or per acre, was far less than in the inner zone. The people were poorer, more illiterate and more likely to die young. The wealthy were landlords, often absentees. The zone lived increasingly after 1870 by selling grain, livestock, wool, or lumber to the more industrialized inner zone but was too poor to purchase many manufactured products in return. To obtain capital it borrowed in London or Paris. Its social and political philosophies were characteristically imported from Germany and the West. It borrowed engineers and technicians from the first zone to build its bridges and install its telegraph systems and sent its youth to universities in the first zone to study medicine or other professions. Many areas of European settlement overseas, for example in Latin America and the southern part of the United States, may also be thought of as belonging to this outer zone.

Beyond the European world lay a third zone, the immense reaches of Asia and Africa, all "backward" by the standards of Europe, with the exception of the recently Europeanized Japan, and all destined, with the exception of Japan, to become heavily dependent upon Europe in the half-century after 1870. Much of the world's history since 1870 could be written as the story of relations among these three zones; but it is necessary in all human things to guard against formulas that are too simple.

72
Basic Demography:
The Increase of
the Europeans

European and
World Population
Growth, 1650–1970

All continents except Africa grew enormously in population in the three centuries following 1650, but it was Europe that grew the most. There is little doubt that the proportion of Europeans in the world's total reached its maximum for all time between 1850 and the Second World War. Estimates are given in the table below, beginning with 1650. (Experts believe that before 1650 the greater population masses had long been either stationary or increasing very slowly.)

The causes of sudden rise in world population after 1650 are not known. Some of them must obviously have operated in Asia as well as Europe. All students agree in attributing the increase to falling death rates rather than to increasing birth rates. Populations grew because more people lived longer, not because more were born. It is probable that a better preservation of civil order reduced death rates in both Asia and Europe. In Europe the organized sovereign states, as established in the seventeenth century, put an end to a long period of civil wars, stopping the chronic violence and marauding, with the accompanying insecurity of agriculture and of family life, which were more deadly than wars fought by armies between governments. Similarly, the Tokugawa kept peace in Japan, and the Manchu dynasty brought a long period of order to China. The British rule in India, and that of the Dutch in Java, by curbing famine and violence, allowed the populations to mount very rapidly. Only in Africa, where the slave trade removed over 10,000,000 persons of the child-bearing ages in three or four centuries, and where slave raiding led to intertribal warfare and the disruption of African cultures, did the growth of population fail to keep pace with the world's average. The fate of the American aborigines was somewhat the same, but they were never very numerous.

In Europe, sooner than in Asia, other causes of growth were at work beyond the maintenance of civil peace. They included the liberation from certain endemic diseases, beginning with the subsiding of bubonic plague in the seventeenth century and the retreat of smallpox in the eighteenth; the improvement of agricultural output, beginning notably in England about 1750; the improvement of transportation, which, by road, canal, and railroad, made localized famine a thing of the past since food could be moved into areas of temporary shortage; and, last, the development of machine industry, which allowed large populations to subsist in Europe by trading with peoples overseas.

Consequently, while it seems that the death rate fell in Asia as well as in Europe after 1650, it fell much more substantially in Europe, and since the European birth rate long remained at a high level, the result was a tremendous swelling of population. Approximate figures are given in the following table. Asia, by these estimates, increased less than threefold in population between 1650 and 1900, but Europe increased fourfold, and the total number of Europeans, including the descendants of

Europeans who migrated to other continents, increased almost fivefold. In 1650 the Europeans comprised only about a fifth of the world's population. In 1900 the proportion of "Europeans" in all continents was approaching a third of the human race. Since 1900 this proportion has been falling. But the ascendancy of European civilization, or roughly of the white races, in the two or three centuries after about 1650, was due in some measure to merely quantitative growth.

Estimated Population of the World by Continental Areas

	1650	1750	1850	1900	1950	1970
	M I L L I O N S					
Europe	100	140	266	401	540	646
United States and Canada	1	1	26	81	166	228
Australasia-Oceania	2	2	2	6	13	19
Predominantly "European"	103	143	294	488	719	893
Latin America	12	11	33	63	163	282
Africa	100	95	95	120	222	352
Asia	330	479	749	937	1,420	2,081
Predominantly "Non-European"	442	585	877	1,120	1,805	2,715
World Total	545	728	1,171	1,608	2,524	3,608
	P E R C E N T A G E S					
Europe	18.3	19.2	22.7	24.9	21.4	18.0
United States and Canada	.2	.1	2.3	5.1	6 6	6.3
Australasia-Oceania	.4	.3	.2	.4	.5	.5
Predominantly "European"	18.9	19.6	25.2	30.4	28.5	24.8
Latin America	2.2	1.5	2.8	3.9	6.5	7.8
Africa	18.3	13.1	8.1	7.4	8.8	9.7
Asia	60.6	65.8	63.9	58.3	56.2	57.7
Predominantly "Non-European"	81.1	80.4	74.8	69.6	71.5	75.2
World Total	100.0	100.0	100.0	100.0	100.0	100.0

SOURCE: Figures for 1650–1900 are from A. N. Carr-Saunders, *World Population,* p. 42, Oxford, 1936. Those for 1950 and 1970 are from the *United Nations Statistical Yearbook.* Neither source attempts a breakdown between "Europeans" and "non-Europeans," which as presented here is significant only in very rough outline for comparative purposes. Figures for the U.S.S.R. are divided in the table between Europe and Asia. Population of the United States and Canada before the eighteenth century, and of Australasia before the nineteenth, was of course almost entirely non-European. Distinctions are further blurred when it is remembered that millions of Europeans (i.e., Russians) have long lived in the Asian parts of the U.S.S.R., that there are about 3,000,000 whites in South Africa, that the population of the United States has always been of both European and African descent, and that Latin America is so mixed that it could as accurately be placed, especially on cultural grounds, in the European category.

This advantage of a higher growth rate began to disappear in the middle of the twentieth century. As early as 1910 it was possible to anticipate that the population of Europe, or, more accurately, of the most advanced "inner zone," would soon grow less rapidly, because the children being born about 1910, who would become the parents of 1940, were not sufficiently numerous to maintain growth at the birth rates which then existed. At the same time death rates began to fall dramatically in Asia. With a large population base to begin with, non-Europeans by the mid-twentieth century were pulling ahead of Europeans.

Stabilization and relative decline of European population followed from a fall in the birth rate. We have seen how the persistence of high birth rates, while death rates fell, accounted for a long period of rapid expansion. But European birth rates began to fall about 1880. As early as 1830 they began noticeably to drop in France, with the result that France, long the most populous European state, was surpassed in population by Russia in the eighteenth century, by Germany about 1870, by the British Isles about 1895, and by Italy about 1930. France, once thought to be decadent for this reason, was in fact only the leading country in a population cycle through which the European countries seemed to pass. The birth rate, which had fallen below 30 per 1,000 in France in the 1830s, fell to that level in Sweden in the 1880s, in England in the 1890s, and in Germany, Bohemia, and the Netherlands between 1900 and 1910. After the First World War, it fell below 30 in Italy, Spain, and eastern Europe, leaving in 1939 only the Soviet Union with a birth rate above 30 per 1,000. What the permanent effect may be of the revived birth rate manifesting itself in many countries after the Second World War is not yet clear.

The reduced birth rate is not a mere dry statistical item, nor does it affect populations merely in the mass. It is one of the indices of modern civilization, first appearing in that inner European zone in which the other indices were also highest, and thence spreading outward in a kind of wave. Concretely, a low birth rate means that families average from two to four children, where in former times, or today under conditions not "modern," families are commonly found to consist of ten children or even more. The low birth rate means the small family system, than which few things are more fundamental to modern life. The principal means used to hold down the birth rate, or to limit the family, is the practice of contraception. But the true causes, or reasons why parents wish to limit their families, are deeply embedded in the codes of modern society.

The French peasants after the Revolution, many of them owners of land, and obliged by the Napoleonic Code to divide inheritances among their children, soon began to limit themselves to two or three children, in order that each child (by inheritance, marriage, and dowries) might remain in as high an economic and social status as its parents. It was thus economic security and the possession of a social standard that led to the reduced birth rate in France. In the great cities of the nineteenth century, in which standards of life for the working classes often collapsed, the effect was at first an unthinking proliferation of offspring. But life in the city, under crowded conditions of housing, also set a premium on the small family. There were many amusements in the city which people with many children could with difficulty enjoy. After about 1880 child labor became much less frequent among the working classes. When children ceased to earn part of the family income parents tended to have fewer of them. About the same time governments in the advanced countries began to require universal compulsory schooling. The number of years spent in education, and hence in economic dependency upon parents, grew longer and longer, until it became common even for young adults to be still engaged in study. Each child represented many years of expense for its parents. The ever rising idea of what it was necessary to do for one's children, and the desire of parents to give them every possible advantage in a competitive world, were probably the most basic causes of voluntary limitation of the family. Hardly less basic was the desire to lighten the burdens upon mothers. The small family system, together with the decline of infant mortality, since they combined to free women from the interminable bearing and tending of infants, probably did more than anything else to improve the position of civilized women.

Most causes for the falling birth rate may be summarized under the idea of welfare. It is in those countries, in those periods, and in those classes of society in which well-being and living standards have been relatively high that the birth rate fell and still falls. The small family is also the sign of a society that looks mainly to the well-being of individuals. It is for the sake of individual parents, especially mothers, and of individual children and their preparation and opportunity in life, that the number of children is held to two or three. Before 1914 liberalism and individualism were in the ascendant, and no government attempted to check the fall in the birth rate by legislation. But the small family system produced a fateful paradox. Even an average of three children for each married pair is barely enough to maintain a population without decline. Those societies in which individual welfare is most highly prized, by the very means they take to promote it, become smaller than the societies which value mass and collective strength.

But the effects of the small family system upon total population became manifest only slowly. More people lived on into the middle and older age groups, and the fall of the birth rate was gradual, so that in all the leading countries total numbers continued to rise, except in France, which hardly grew between 1900 and 1945. The persistent note was one of superabundant increase. In five generations, between 1800 and 1950, some 200,000,000 "Europeans" grew into 700,000,000. Since productivity increased even more rapidly, the standard of living for most of these "Europeans" rose in spite of the increase of numbers, and there was no general problem of overpopulation.

Growth of Cities
and Urban Life

Where did so many people go? Some stayed in the rural areas where most people had always lived. Rural populations in the "inner zone" became more dense, turning to the more intensive agriculture of truck gardening or dairy farming, leaving products like wool and cereal grains to be raised elsewhere and then imported. But it is estimated that of every seven persons added to the western European population only one stayed on the land. Of the other six, one left Europe altogether, and five went to the growing cities.

The modern city is mostly the child of the railroad, for with the railroads it became possible for the first time to concentrate manufacturing in large towns, to which bulky goods such as foods and coal could now be moved in great volume. The growth of cities between 1850 and 1914 was phenomenal. In England two-thirds of the people lived in places of 20,000 or less in 1830; in 1914 two-thirds lived in places of 20,000 or more.[1] Germany, the historic land of archaic towns carried over from the Middle Ages, after 1870 rivaled England in modern industrial urbanization. Whereas in 1840 only London and Paris had a million people, the same could be said by 1914 of Berlin, Vienna, St. Petersburg, and Moscow.[2] Some places, like the English Midlands and the Ruhr valley in Germany, became a mass of contiguous smaller cities, vast urban agglomerations divided only by municipal lines.

The great city set the tone of modern society. City life was impersonal and anonymous; people were uprooted, less tied to home or church than in the country. They lacked the country person's feeling of deference for aristocratic families. They lacked the sense of self-help characteristic of older rural communities. The hungry, the jobless, the miserable could expect little comfort from neighbors. To correct minor nuisances or to rescue people in emergencies one relied on the police—an epileptic, for example, could lie in a busy street without attracting much notice. It was in the city that the daily newspaper press, which spread rapidly in the wake of the telegraph after 1850, found its most habitual readers. The so-called yellow or sensational press appeared about 1900. Articulate public opinion was formed in the cities, and city people were on the whole disrespectful of tradition, receptive to new ideas, having in many cases deliberately altered their own lives by moving from the country or from smaller towns. That socialism spread among the industrial masses of European cities is hardly surprising. It is less often realized that some of the more blatant nationalism that arose after 1870 was stimulated by city life, for people felt increasingly detached from all institutions except the state. At the same time city life, by its greater facilities for schooling, reading, and discussion, made for a more alert and informed public opinion of an enlightened kind.

During the same period in which the cities were rising, approximately 60,000,000 people left Europe altogether, of whom possibly a fifth sooner or later returned. This Atlantic Migration—aptly so called, because all crossed the ocean except those who moved from European to Asiatic Russia—towers above all other historical migrations in magnitude, and possibly also in significance, for it was the means by which earlier colonial offshoots of Europeans were transformed into new Europes alongside the old. All parts of Europe contributed, as is shown in the table on page 615, which comprises the years from 1846 to 1932. Before 1846 the movement had scarcely

---

[1] See map, p. 469.

[2] And, outside Europe, of New York, Chicago, Philadelphia, Rio de Janeiro, Buenos Aires, Calcutta, Tokyo, and Osaka.

begun, though over 1,000,000 immigrants had entered the United States at that time since the close of the Napoleonic wars. After 1932 it was greatly reduced, except into Soviet Asia.

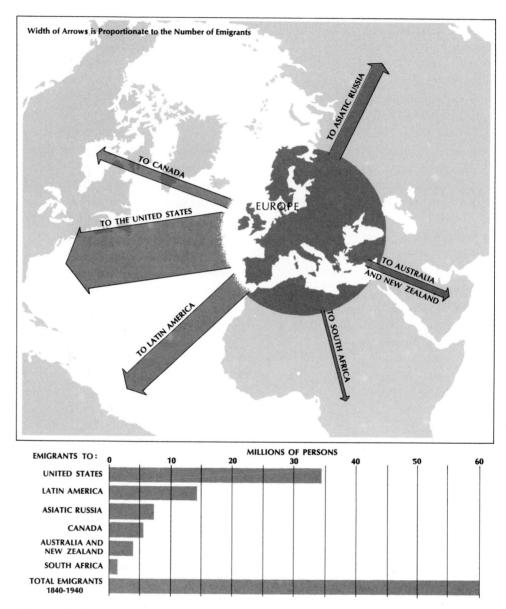

Migration from Europe 1840–1940. *Over 60,000,000 people left Europe in the century preceding the Second World War, distributing themselves as shown in the diagram above. (See figures on p. 615.) About half went to the United States. This huge wave of settlement built up, outside of Europe, populous "European" countries which produced foods and raw materials for Europe and borrowed capital and bought manufactures from Europe, thus helping to support the increasingly dense European population and to build up a world-wide economic system.*

Migration from Europe,* 1846–1932

FROM:		
	Great Britain and Ireland	18,000,000
	Italy	10,100,000
	Russia †	9,200,000
	Austria-Hungary	5,200,000
	Germany	4,900,000
	Spain	4,700,000
	Portugal	1,800,000
	Sweden	1,200,000
	Norway	850,000
	Poland ‡	640,000
	France	520,000
	Denmark	390,000
	Finland	370,000
	Switzerland	330,000
	Holland	220,000
	Belgium	190,000
	Total	58,610,000

* Carr-Saunders, *op. cit.,* pp. 49 and 56.

† Including 7,000,000 from European to Asiatic Russia up to 1914 only. It is thought that 3,000,000 went from European to Asiatic parts of the U.S.S.R. between 1926 and 1939.

‡ 1920–32 only.

The British and Irish (inseparable in the statistical records) went to the British dominions and to the United States. The Italians divided between the United States and Latin America. Spaniards settled overwhelmingly in the Spanish American republics, and Portuguese in Brazil. The Germans moved overwhelmingly to the United States, though some went to the Argentine and Brazil. The new countries received the following influxes of people:

Immigration into Other Countries from Europe*

TO:		
	United States	34,000,000
	Asiatic Russia (to 1914 only)	7,000,000
	Argentina	6,400,000
	Canada	5,200,000
	Brazil	4,400,000
	Australia	2,900,000
	Cuba	860,000
	South Africa	852,000
	Uruguay	713,000
	New Zealand	594,000

* Carr-Saunders, *op. cit.,* p. 49.

The extraordinary preponderance of the United States is apparent. At the same time, it is well to rectify the impressions of most Americans on the subject. Almost half the European migration was directed elsewhere than to the United States. Asiatic Russia was second only to the United States in the receipt of new settlers. Germany was by no means a chief source of emigration, especially in proportion to total national population from which emigrants came. Canada received fewer immigrants than the Argentine, Australia fewer than Brazil, New Zealand fewer than Uruguay. The new worlds were not peculiarly Anglo-Saxon.

The exodus from Europe was due to a remarkable and temporary juxtaposition of causes. Hardship in Europe was by no means the principal one; for several years after the Second World War Europeans had better reason to emigrate than before 1914, yet did not do so. One fundamental cause, or precondition, was that before 1914 the new countries welcomed immigration. Hands were wanted to farm the land, build houses, dig in the mines. This was least true of Australia and New Zealand, which preferred to limit themselves to English-speaking settlers, and which also pioneered as social democracies, becoming models, even before 1900, of legislation to protect the working classes. One result was that no inrush of outsiders to compete for jobs at low wages was desired. A similar combination of national preferences and labor protectionism led to laws restricting immigration in the United States in 1921 and 1924. Thereafter immigrants could enter only under quotas, and the quotas were lowest for eastern and southern Europe from which most emigration was then forthcoming.

In Europe there were many conditions propelling emigrants outward. Physically, the steamship made it easier and cheaper to cross the sea, and the railroad helped people to get to the ports as well as to distribute themselves after landing in the new countries. Economically, people in the mass could for the first time afford a long journey. People migrated to improve their material circumstances; but the great crests in the wave of emigration coincided with crests in the business cycle in Europe, when jobs in Europe were plentiful and wages at their highest. Of the opposite case, of actual flight from economic ruin or starvation, the emigration from Ireland after 1846 is the best example. After the revolutions of 1848 a certain number left Europe for political reasons, and, later on, to avoid compulsory military service. The best example of flight from actual persecution is that of the Jews of Russia and Russian Poland, of whom a million and a half moved to the United States in the fifteen years preceding the First World War.

But perhaps most basic in the whole European exodus was the underlying liberalism of the age. Never before (nor since) had people been legally so free to move. Old laws requiring skilled workmen to stay in their own countries were repealed, as in England in 1824.[3] The old semicommunal agricultural villages, with collective rights and obligations, holding the individual to his native group, fell into disuse except in Russia. The disappearance of serfdom allowed the peasant of

[3] See p. 500.

eastern Europe to change his residence without obtaining a lord's permission.[4] Governments permitted their subjects to emigrate, to take with them their savings of shillings, marks, kronen, or lire, and to change nationality by becoming naturalized in their new homes. The rise of individual liberty in Europe, as well as the hope of enjoying it in America, made possible the great emigration. For so huge a mass movement the most remarkable fact is that it took place by individual initiative and at individual expense. Individuals and family groups (to borrow the metaphor of one authority) detached themselves atom by atom from the mass of Europe, crossed the seas on their own, and reattached themselves atom by atom to the accumulating mass of the New World.

Ｈow did the swelling population of Europeans manage to feed itself? How, in fact, did it not merely feed itself but enjoy an incomparably higher standard of living in 1900 than in 1800? By science, industry, transportation, and communications. And by organization—in business, finance, and labor.

The Industrial Revolution entered upon a new phase. The use of steam power, the growth of the textile and metallurgical industries, and the advent of the railroad had characterized the early part of the century. Now, after 1870, new sources of power were tapped, the already mechanized industries expanded, new industries appeared, and industry spread geographically.

The "New Industrial Revolution"

The steam engine itself was refined and improved. By 1914 it still predominated over other power machinery, but electricity with its incomparable advantages came into use. The invention of the internal combustion (or gasoline) engine and the Diesel engine gave the world automobiles, airplanes, and submarines in the two decades before 1914; the advent of the automotive and aviation industries made oil one of the most coveted of natural resources. In the new chemical industries industrial research laboratories were replacing the individual inventor. Chemists discovered new fertilizers, and from coal tar alone produced a bewildering array of new products ranging from artificial food flavors to high explosives. With the latter the first great tunnels were built, the Mount Cenis in 1873, the Simplon in 1906—both in the Alps; and great new canals, the Suez in 1869, the Kiel in 1895, the Panama in 1914. Chemistry made possible the production of synthetic fabrics like rayon which revolutionized the textile industry. Electricity transformed all indoor and outdoor lighting. There was a communications revolution too. The telephone appeared in the 1870s. Marconi brought the continents closer together, successfully transmitting wireless signals across the Atlantic in 1901. The moving picture and the radio modestly presented themselves before 1914. Medicine ran a tongue-twisting

[4]See pp. 522, 533.

alphabetical gamut from anesthetics to X-rays; yellow fever was overcome. Vastly improved processes for refining iron ore made possible a great expansion in the production of steel, the key product of the new industrial age; aluminum and other metal alloys were also being produced. Railroad mileage multiplied; the European network, including the Russian, increased from 140,000 miles in 1890 to 213,000 in 1914.

In the new phase of the Industrial Revolution machine industry spread geographically from Britain and Belgium, the only truly industrial countries in 1870, to France, Italy, Russia, Japan, and, most markedly, to Germany and the United States. In Europe industrial production was concentrated in the "inner zone." The three powers alone—Britain, Germany, and France—accounted in 1914 for more than seven-tenths of all European manufactures and produced over four-fifths of all European coal, steel, and machinery. Of the major European powers Germany was now forging ahead. To use steel alone as a criterion, in 1871 Germany was producing annually three-fifths as much steel as Britain; by 1900 she was producing more, and by 1914 she was producing twice as much as Britain—but only half as much as the new industrial giant, the United States. By 1914 American steel output was greater than that of Germany, Britain, and France combined. Britain, the pioneer in mechanization, was being outstripped in both the old world and the new. The three European powers increased their industrial production by about 50 percent in the two decades before 1914, but the United States had a far higher annual growth rate from 1870 to 1913, 4.3 percent as compared to the next leading powers, Germany with 2.9 percent, Britain with 2.2 percent, and France with 1.6 percent.[5] By 1914 the United States had moved ahead of Europe in the mechanization of agriculture, in manufactures, and in coal and steel production, in which she was producing over two-fifths of the world's output. The Americans were pioneering also in assembly-line, conveyor-belt techniques for the mass production of automobiles and all kinds of consumer goods.

Free Trade and
the European
"Balance of Payments"

It was Britain in the mid-nineteenth century, then the workshop of the world, that had inaugurated the movement toward free trade. It will be recalled that in 1846, by the repeal of the Corn Laws, the British embarked upon a systematic free trade policy, deliberately choosing to become dependent upon overseas imports for their food.[6] France adopted free trade in 1860.[7] Other countries soon followed. It is true that by 1880 there was a movement back to protective tariffs, except in Britain, Holland, and Belgium. But the tariffs were impediments rather than barriers, and until 1914 the characteristic of the economic system was the extreme mobility of goods across political frontiers. Politically, Europe was more than ever nationalistic; but economic activity, under generally liberal conditions in which business was

[5] *The new Cambridge Modern History,* Volume XII (Cambridge: Cambridge University Press, rev. ed., 1968), p. 40.
[6] See p. 504.
[7] See pp. 545–546.

supposed to be free from the political state, remained predominantly international and globe-encircling.

Broadly speaking, the great economic accomplishment of Europe before 1914 was to create a system by which the huge imports used by industrial Europe could be acquired and paid for. All European countries except Russia, Austria-Hungary, and the Balkan states imported more than they exported. It was the British again that had led in this direction. Britain had been a predominantly importing country since the close of the eighteenth century. That is to say, despite the expanding export of cotton manufactures and other products of the Industrial Revolution, Britain consumed more goods from abroad than it sent out. Industrialization and urbanization in the nineteenth century confirmed the same situation. Between 1800 and 1900 the value of British exports multiplied eightfold, but the value of imports into Great Britain multiplied tenfold, and in the decade before 1914 the British had an import surplus of about three-quarters of a billion dollars a year. Great Britain and the industrial countries of Europe together (roughly Europe's "inner zone"), at the beginning of the twentieth century, were drawing in an import surplus, measured in dollars, of almost $2,000,000,000 every year (the dollar then representing far more goods than it came to represent later). The imports into Europe's inner zone consisted of raw materials for its industries and of food and amenities for its people.

How were the imports paid for? How did Europe enjoy a favorable "balance of payments" despite an unfavorable balance of trade in commodities? Export of European manufactures paid for some imports, and even most, but not all. It was the so-called invisible exports that made up the difference, that is, shipping and insurance services rendered to foreigners, and interest on money lent out or invested, all bringing in foreign exchange. Shipping and insurance were important. An Argentine merchant in Buenos Aires, to ship hides to Germany, might employ a British vessel; he would pay the freight charges in Argentine pesos, which might be credited to the account of the British shipowner in an Argentine bank; the British shipowner would sell the pesos to someone, in England or elsewhere in Europe, who needed them to buy Argentine meat. The far-flung British merchant marine thus earned a considerable amount of the food and raw materials needed by Britain. To insure themselves against risks of every conceivable kind people all over the world turned to Lloyds of London. With the profits drawn from selling insurance the British could buy what they wished. Governments or business enterprises borrowed money in Europe, and mainly in England; the interest payments, putting foreign currencies into European and British hands, constituted another invisible export by which an excess of imports could be financed. But the lending of money to foreigners is only part of a larger phenomenon, the export of capital.

The migration of millions of Europeans had the effect of creating new societies, basically European in character, which both purchased manufactures from Europe and produced the food, wool, cotton, and minerals that Europe needed. It could not have had this effect if Europe had exported people only, especially people of such small means as most emigrants were. Europe also exported the capital necessary to get the new settlers and the new worlds into production.

The export of capital meant that an older and wealthier country, instead of using its whole annual income to raise its own standard of living, or to add to its own capital by expanding or improving its houses, factories, machinery, mines, transportation, etc., diverted some of its income to expanding or improving the houses, factories, machinery, mines and transportation of foreign countries. It meant that British, French, Dutch, Belgian, Swiss, and eventually German investors in the desire to increase their income bought the stocks of foreign business enterprises and the bonds of foreign businesses and government; or they organized companies of their own to operate in foreign climes; or their banks granted loans to banks in New York or Tokyo, which then lent the funds to local users. Capital arose in Europe to some extent from the savings of quite small people, especially in France, where peasants and modest bourgeois families were notably thrifty. But most capital accumulated from savings by the well-to-do. The owners of a business concern, for example, instead of spending the concern's income by paying higher wages, took a portion of it in profits or dividends, and instead of spending all this on their own living, reinvested part of it in domestic or foreign enterprises. The gap between rich and poor was thus one cause of the rapid accumulation of capital, though the accumulation of capital, in the nineteenth century, produced in turn a steady rise of living standards for the working classes. In a sense, however, the common man of western Europe, by foregoing the better housing, diet, education, or pleasures which a more democratic society might have planned for him, made possible the export of capital and hence the financing and building up of other regions of the world.

The British were the chief exporters of capital, followed at some distance by the French, and at the close of the century by the Germans. As early as the 1840s half the annual increase of wealth in Great Britain was going into foreign investments. By 1914 the British had $20,000,000,000 in foreign investments, the French about $8,700,000,000, the Germans about $6,000,000,000. A quarter of all the wealth owned by the inhabitants of Great Britain consisted in 1914 of holdings outside the country. Almost a sixth of the French national wealth lay in investments outside of France. All three countries had given hostages to fortune, and fortune proved unkind, for in the First World War the British lost about a quarter of their foreign investments, the French about a third, the Germans all.

These huge sums, pouring out from Europe's inner zone for a century before 1914, at first went mainly to finance the Americas and the less affluent regions of Europe.[8] No country except Great Britain completely built its railways with its own resources. In the United States the railway system was built very largely with capital borrowed from England. In central and eastern Europe British companies often constructed the first railways, then sold out to native operating companies or to governments which subsequently ran them. In the Argentine Republic the British

---

[8]The penetration of European capital into Asia and Africa, after about 1890, is considered in the following chapter.

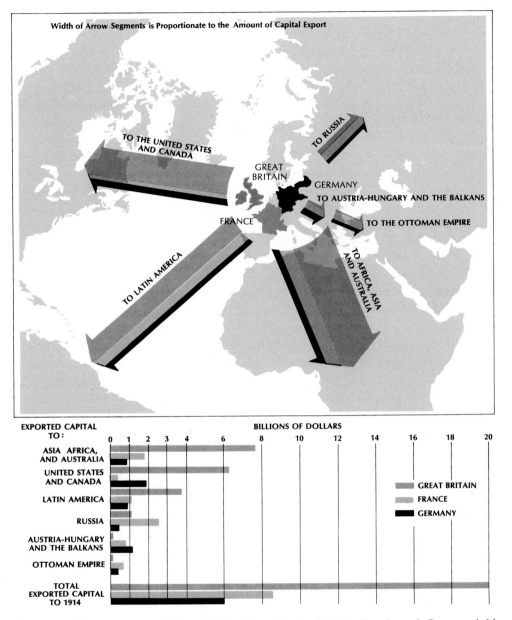

Width of Arrow Segments is Proportionate to the Amount of Capital Export

TO THE UNITED STATES AND CANADA

TO RUSSIA

GREAT BRITAIN

GERMANY

TO AUSTRIA-HUNGARY AND THE BALKANS

FRANCE

TO THE OTTOMAN EMPIRE

TO LATIN AMERICA

TO AFRICA, ASIA AND AUSTRALIA

EXPORTED CAPITAL TO:

BILLIONS OF DOLLARS

0 1 2 3 4 6 8 10 12 14 16 18 20

ASIA AFRICA, AND AUSTRALIA

UNITED STATES AND CANADA

LATIN AMERICA

RUSSIA

AUSTRIA-HUNGARY AND THE BALKANS

OTTOMAN EMPIRE

TOTAL EXPORTED CAPITAL TO 1914

GREAT BRITAIN
FRANCE
GERMANY

Export of European Capital to 1914. *In 1914 the British, French, and Germans held upwards of $30,000,000,000 in foreign and colonial loans and investments, distributed as shown on the map. Dutch investments, especially in the Netherlands Indies, together with Swiss, Belgian, and Scandinavian holdings, would add several billion dollars more. Proceeds from such investments helped Europeans to pay for the excess of their imports over exports. New and undeveloped countries were built up by capital borrowed from Europe. British capital predominated in the overseas world, while the less advanced regions of eastern Europe and the Near East were financed mainly from Germany and France. Most of the investment shown on this map was lost or expended in the First World War. See pp. 751, 757.*

not merely financed and built the railways, but continued thereafter to operate and own them. In addition, up to 1914 the British sold about 75,000,000 tons of coal a year to South America to keep the railways going, not to mention items for replacement and upkeep of equipment. Docks, warehouses, mines, plantations, processing and manufacturing establishments all over the world were similarly built up with capital drawn from Europe. European capital also helped emigrants in the new countries to live in civilized fashion. In the United States, for example, state and local governments very commonly sold their bonds in Europe, to build roads, pave streets, or construct school systems for the westward-moving population. A few of these American bonds proved a partial or total loss to European investors. On the whole, by 1914, the United States had paid back a good deal of its indebtedness. Even so, in 1914, Americans still owed about $4,000,000,000 to Europeans—a sum three times as large as the national debt of the United States at the time.

An International
Money System:
The Gold Standard

The international economy rested upon an international money system, based in turn upon the almost universal acceptance of the gold standard. England had adopted the gold standard in 1816, when the pound sterling was legally defined as the equivalent of 113 grains of fine gold. Western Europe and the United States adopted an exclusively gold standard in the 1870s. A person holding any "civilized" money—pounds, francs, dollars, marks, etc.—could turn it into gold at will, and a person holding gold could turn it into any money. The currencies were like so many different languages all expressing the same thing. All had substantially the same value, and until 1914 the exchange rates between currencies remained highly stable. It was assumed that no civilized country's currency ever "fell"; such things might happen in Turkey or China, or in the French Revolution, but not in the world of practical men, modern progress, and civilized affairs.

The important currencies were all freely exchangeable. A Frenchman, selling silks to a German, and hence receiving German marks, could turn the marks into francs, pounds sterling, or dollars. That is, he was not obliged to buy from Germany or spend his money in Germany but could use the proceeds of his German sale to buy French, British, or American goods or services as he chose. Trade was multilateral. A country needing imports from another country, such as American cotton, did not have to sell to that country to obtain them; it could sell its own goods anywhere and then import according to its needs. Thus Europe, which as time went on sold fewer manufactures to the United States, was still able to buy from the United States by selling manufactures to Brazil or the Dutch East Indies; and Americans correspondingly could buy Brazilian coffee or East Indian rubber by selling to Europe.

It was the acceptance of the gold standard, and the fact that all important countries possessed a sufficient share of gold to support their currencies, that made possible so fluid an interchange. At the same time the gold standard had less wholesome effects. It was hard on countries that lacked gold. And it produced a gradual fall of prices, especially between 1870 and 1900, because (until the gold discoveries in South Africa, Australia, and Alaska in the 1890s) the world's production of gold lagged behind the expanding production of industrial and agricultural goods. Persistently declining prices were a hardship to those who habitually worked with borrowed money—many farmers, many businessmen, and debtor nations as a whole. A famous speech of William Jennings Bryan in the United States in 1896, declaring that mankind should not be crucified "upon this cross of gold," expressed a restlessness that was world-wide. But falling prices were an advantage to the wage-earning class, which generally improved its position in these years, and also to the wealthy, the owners and lenders of capital, the bankers and financiers, who so long as prices were falling were repaid in money of more value than that which they had lent.

The center of the global economic and financial system was London. The London banks came forward in consequence of the defeat of Napoleon, the older financial centers in Amsterdam having been ruined in the Revolutionary and Napoleonic wars. It may be recalled also that the victors in 1815 imposed upon France an indemnity of 700,000,000 francs, which in 1818 was taken over by a syndicate of private bankers; the London banks played a leading part in this affair and so developed their connections with many government treasuries.[9] In the Crimean War of 1854-1856, with England at war with Russia, the London banks floated loans for the Russian government—so independent were business and politics at the time. The early adoption of the gold standard in England meant that many people, British and foreign, kept their funds in the form of sterling on deposit in London, where quantities of available capital therefore accumulated.

The banks, too, grew up in the financing of the British export trade, itself borne on the tide of the Industrial Revolution. A small Lancashire manufacturer, for example, might receive an order for a gross of scissors from an unknown merchant in Trieste. He would draw a bill or "sight draft" against the Trieste merchant, and take this bill to a financial institution known as an acceptance house. The acceptance house, which in the course of its business had acquired a microscopic knowledge of the credit of thousands of individuals and firms in all parts of the world, would then "discount" the bill, giving cash to the Lancashire manufacturer and collecting from the Trieste merchant through international banking channels. In this way the bank took a burden off the British manufacturer, and extended short-term credit to foreigners for the purchase of British goods. Many acceptance houses gradually went into the business of long-term foreign lending also. London became the apex of a pyramid which had the world for its base. It was the main center of exchange of currencies, the clearinghouse of the world's debts, the depository from which all the world borrowed, the banker's bank, the insurance man's resort for reinsurance, as well as the world's shipping center and the headquarters of many international corporations.

Never had the earth been so unified economically, with each region playing its due role in a global specialization. Western Europe, and in 1870 mainly Great Britain,

[9] See p. 488.

was the world's industrial workshop. Other parts of the earth supplied its many needs. Stanley Jevons, an English economist, wrote in awestruck tones as early as 1866:

The several quarters of the globe are our willing tributaries. The plains of North America and Russia are our cornfields; Chicago and Odessa our granaries; Canada and the Baltic our forests; Australia contains our sheep farms, and in South America are our herds of oxen. Peru sends her silver, and the gold of California and Australia flows to London; the Chinese grow tea for us; and coffee, sugar and spice arrive from the East Indian plantations. Spain and France are our vineyards, and the Mediterranean our fruit garden; our cotton grounds, which formerly occupied the southern United States, are now everywhere in the many regions of the earth.

To a degree only less than Great Britain the rest of Europe's "inner zone" could have made the same boast before the First World War.

A true world market had been created. Goods, services, money, capital, people moved back and forth almost without regard to national boundaries. Articles were bought and sold at uniform world prices. Dealers in wheat, for example, followed prices in Minneapolis, Liverpool, Buenos Aires, and Danzig as reported by telegraph and cable from day to day. They bought where it was cheapest, and sold where it was dearest. In this way the world's wheat supply was distributed roughly according to need or ability to pay. The workingman of Milan, if the Italian crop was poor and prices high, was fed from another source. On the other hand, the Italian wheat grower would in this case feel the pinch of world competition. The world market, while it organized the world into a unified economic system, at the same time brought distant regions into competition for the first time. The producer—whether businessman, factory employee, farmer, or coffee planter—had no secure outlet for his product, as had generally been true in the past. He was in competition not only with the man across the street or down the road, but with the world.

The creation of an integrated world market, the financing and building up of countries outside of Europe, and the consequent feeding and support of Europe's increasing population were the great triumphs of the nineteenth-century system of unregulated capitalism. The system was intricate, with thousands and even millions of individuals and business firms supplying each other's wants without central planning. But it was extremely precarious, and the position of most people in it was exceedingly vulnerable. Region competed against region, and person against person. A fall of grain prices in the American Middle West, besides ruining a few speculators, might oblige the Prussian or Argentine wheat grower to sell at a price at which he could not live. A factory owner might be driven out of business if his competitor successfully undersold him or if a new commodity made his own product obsolete. The workingman, hired only when needed by an employer, faced unemployment when business slackened, or the permanent disappearance of his job by the next labor-saving invention. The system went through cycles of boom and depression, the most notable example of the latter being the long depression that set in about

1873 and lasted to about 1893. It rested on expansion and on credit; but sometimes people could not pay their debts, so that credit collapsed, and sometimes expansion failed to keep pace with expectations, and anticipated profits proved to be losses. To combat the essential insecurity of private capitalism, all manner of devices were resorted to. Governments adopted protective tariffs on the one hand and social insurance and welfare legislation on the other; trade unionism and socialist movements grew; business mergers took place. These and other measures, to which we shall return, signalized the gradual decline in the years after 1880 of nineteenth-century unregulated, laissez-faire capitalism.

A great change came over capitalism itself about 1880 or 1890. Formerly characterized by a very large number of very small units, small businesses run by individuals, partnerships, or small companies, it was increasingly characterized by large and impersonal corporations. The attractions of the "limited liability" corporation as a form of business organization and as a means of encouraging investment arose from laws, enacted by most countries in the nineteenth century, which limited the individual investor's personal loss in the event of a bankruptcy to the amount of his shares of stock in the enterprise. The corporation, in its modern form appearing first with the railroads, became the usual form of organization for industry and commerce. As machinery grew more complicated only a large pool of capital could finance it. And as corporations grew in size and number, relying on the sale of stock and the issue of bonds, the influence of banking and financial circles was enhanced. Financiers, using not so much their own money as the savings of others, had a new power to create or to extinguish, to stimulate, discourage, or combine corporate enterprises in various industries. Industrial capitalism brought finance capitalism with it.[10]

Corporate organization made it possible to concentrate economic processes under unified management. In retail commerce, large department stores appeared about 1890 in the United States and France. In industry, steel offers a good example. Steel became in any case a big business when heavy blast furnaces were introduced. It was not safe for the steel business, or for the blast furnaces, to rely for iron and coal on independent producers who might sell to whomsoever they pleased. The steel works therefore began to operate mines of their own or to buy out or otherwise reduce coal and iron mines to subsidiary status. Some, to assure their markets, began to produce not merely steel but steel manufactures as well—steel ships, railway equipment, naval and military ordnance. Thus entire processes from mining to finished product became concentrated in a "vertical" integration. By "horizontal" integration concerns at the same level combined with each other to reduce competition and to protect themselves against fluctuations in prices and in markets. Some fixed prices, some agreed to restrict production, some divided up markets among themselves. They were called trusts in the United States, cartels in

[10]See pp. 544–545, 590–591.

Europe. They were common in many of the new industries at the close of the century, such as chemicals, aluminum, and oil. In steel such combinations produced the great interests of Krupp in Germany, Schneider-Creusot in France, Vickers-Armstrong in Great Britain. It was in the United States that such big business developed furthest, headed by "captains" of industry and "titans" of finance. Andrew Carnegie, by origin a poor Scottish immigrant boy, produced more steel than all England; in 1901 he sold out to an even more colossal organization, the United States Steel Corporation, formed by the financier J. P. Morgan. It was in the United States, too, that concern over monopoly and the power of big business in general was felt most strongly; antitrust legislation, beginning with the Sherman Act of 1890, was enacted but never with any substantial effect.

Many of the new combinations were beneficial in making the ups and downs of business less erratic, and so providing more stable prices and more continuous and secure employment. Generally they reduced the costs of production; but whether the savings went into higher profits, higher wages, or lower prices depended on numerous factors. Some trusts were more greedy than others or confronted with only weakly organized or unorganized labor. In any case, for good or ill, decisions rested with management and finance. A new kind of private power had arisen, which its critics liked to call "feudal." Since no economic system had ever been so centralized up to that time, never in fact had so few people exercised so much economic power over so many. The middle class, with the rise of great corporations, came typically to consist of salaried employees; the salaried man might spend a lifetime with the same company, and feel toward it, in its disputes with labor or government, a loyalty not unlike that of a lord's retainer in feudal times. The laboring class was less amenable; labor attempted to organize unions capable of dealing with increasingly gigantic employers. It also after about 1880 played an increasingly decisive role in the politics of all advanced nations.

74
The Advance of Democracy: Third French Republic, United Kingdom, German Empire

In the years from 1815 to 1870 European political life had been marked by liberal agitation for constitutional government, representative assemblies, responsible ministries, and guarantees of individual liberties. In the years from 1871 to 1914, even where these liberal objectives were not fully achieved but remained as goals, the most notable political development was the democratic extension of the vote to the working class—the adoption of universal manhood suffrage, which in turn meant for the first time the creation of mass political parties and the need for political leaders to appeal to a wide electorate. The extension of the suffrage in these years did not take place because of popular agitation as in the days of the Chartists or of the radical reformers in France; governments for a variety of reasons extended the suffrage on their own. Often democratization took place in a continuing monarchical and aristocratic framework, but almost everywhere by 1914 the machinery at least of democratic self-government was being established. In addition, to counter the growing strength of socialism after 1871, and for humanitarian reasons, governments were also assuming responsibility for the social and economic problems arising from industrialism. The welfare state in its modern form was taking shape.

In France the democratic republic was not easily established, and its troubled early years left deep cleavages within the country. It will be recalled that in September 1870, when the empire of Napoleon III revealed its helplessness in the Franco-Prussian War, insurrectionaries in Paris, as in 1792 and 1848, again proclaimed the Republic.[11] A provisional government of national defense sought desperately to continue the war, but the cause was hopeless. By January 1871, a bitter siege of Paris came to an end and an armistice was signed. Bismarck, insisting that only a properly constituted government could make peace, permitted the election, by universal male suffrage, of a National Assembly which was to consider his peace terms and draft a constitution for the new French state. When the elections were held in February, it was found, as in 1848 (and, indeed, 1797), that republicanism was so distrusted by the French people as a whole, and most especially in the provinces and rural areas, that a free election brought monarchist elements into power.[12] Republicanism was still thought to be violent—bellicose in its foreign policy, turbulent in its political workings, unfriendly to the church, and socialistic or at least equalitarian in its views of property and private wealth. The new Assembly contained only about 200 republicans out of more than 600 deputies.

But the Paris republicans, who had defended France when Napoleon III failed to do so, who for four months had been besieged, starved, and frozen by the Germans, and who still refused to make peace on the harsh terms imposed by Bismarck and about to be accepted by the Assembly, refused to recognize the latter's authority. A civil war broke out between the National Assembly, now sitting at Versailles, and the city of Paris, where a revolutionary municipal council or "Commune" was set up. Paris, so lately attacked by German soldiers, was now attacked by French.

The Paris Commune, which lasted from March to May 1871, seemed to be another explosion of social revolution. Actually, it was in essence a revival of the Jacobinism of 1793. It was fiercely patriotic and republican, anti-German, opposed to wealthy bourgeois, aristocrats, and clergy, in favor of government controls upon prices, wages, and working conditions, but still not socialist in any sweeping or systematic way. Among its leaders, however, filtered in a few of the new international revolutionary socialists, who saw in a Jacobin or democratic republic a step toward their new order. Marx in England, and others elsewhere, hopefully read into the Commune the impending doom of the bourgeoisie. This was precisely what more conservative elements feared. To many of the French middle and peasant class, and to people like them all over Europe, it seemed that the "Communards" were wild and savage destroyers of nineteenth-century civilization. The fighting in Paris was atrocious beyond anything known in any preceding French revolution. The

[11] See p. 574.
[12] See pp. 408, 517–518.

Communards, in final desperation, burned a number of public buildings and put to death the archbishop of Paris, whom they held as a hostage. The forces of the National Assembly, when finally triumphant, were determined to root out the inveterate revolutionism of Paris. Some 330,000 persons were denounced, 38,000 arrested, 20,000 put to death, and 7,500 deported to New Caledonia. The Third Republic was born in an atmosphere of class hate and social terror.

The form of government for the new regime still had to be established. The monarchist majority in the Assembly was itself evenly divided between those who favored a restoration of the Bourbon family and those who favored the Orleanist. In the end, even after they were reconciled, the Bourbon candidate alienated everyone by his stiff insistence on a return to the white flag of the Bourbons. The monarchists checkmated each other. Meanwhile, after extended discussion of various constitutional projects, the Assembly adopted in 1875 not a constitution, but certain constitutive laws. By a margin of one vote, a resolution indirectly amounting to the establishment of a republic was passed. The new laws provided for a president, a parliament in two chambers, and a council of ministers, or cabinet, headed by a premier. The Senate was to be elected by a complicated and indirect system of election, the Chamber of Deputies by universal, direct, manhood suffrage.

Within two years, in 1877, the role of the president, the ministers, and the parliament was further clarified as a result of an unsuccessful attempt by an early president, Marshal MacMahon, to dismiss a premier of whom he did not approve but who had the backing of the Chamber. MacMahon proceeded to dissolve the Chamber and to hold new elections, but the example of Napoleon III's transformation of the Second Republic into a personal dictatorship was still fresh. The elections vindicated the principle of parliamentary primacy and of the responsibility of the premier and his cabinet to the legislature, a responsibility which in France meant generally but not exclusively to the lower house. The true executive in republican France was to be the premier and his cabinet, themselves held strictly to account by a majority of the legislature. Unfortunately, that majority, in a parliament where a dozen or so parties were represented, was always difficult to form and could be created only by unstable, temporary, shifting party alliances, coalitions, or blocs. No president, and indeed no premier, could henceforth dissolve the Chamber in order to hold new elections and consult the country as could be done in Britain. Actually, under the Third Republic the substantial machinery of state—ministries, prefectures, law courts, police, army, all under highly centralized control—was carried over virtually untouched as in all upheavals since the time of Napoleon I. France in the nineteenth century, so volatile in appearance, in effect underwent less revolutionary reorganization than any other leading country in Europe.

Yet the Third Republic was precarious. The government had changed so often since 1789 that all forms of government seemed to be transitory. Questions which in other countries were only party questions became in France questions of "regime"—monarchy versus republic. Many people, especially those influenced by the upper classes, the Catholic clergy, and the professional army officers, continued to feel a positive aversion to the republic. On the other hand, the unmerciful and vindictive repression of the Commune made many middle-class people sympathetic to the republicans. Many turned republican simply because no other form of government established itself, or because it was the form of government that divided the country the least. As republicanism took in wider elements of society, it became less revolutionary and less fearsome. In 1879, for the first time, republicans won control of both houses of the government. They proved mild indeed, in the light of memories of 1871, 1848, or 1793. In the 1880s their radicalism hardly went further than the founding of a democratic and compulsory school system at government expense and the passage of anticlerical legislation intended to curb church influence in education.

For over a quarter of a century, however, republican energies had to be expended in defense of republican institutions in order to ensure the survival of the regime. An initial crisis arose in 1886–1889, when General Boulanger gathered around him an incongruous following which included not only Bonapartists, monarchists, and aristocrats but also extreme radical republicans, who wished a war of revenge against Germany, and workingmen disgruntled over their general lot. Boulanger became a popular figure and seemed for a moment about to seize power as a dictator. But the menace collapsed in a comical failure as the general lost heart at the crucial hour and fled into exile. Meanwhile, in the 1880s and 1890s scandals and revelations of corruption in high quarters provided ammunition for the antirepublicans. A president's son-in-law was discovered trafficking in Legion of Honor decorations. A number of deputies and senators were implicated in the failure of the Panama Canal venture, which had gone bankrupt because of dishonesty and mismanagement. For a time, however, especially after the Boulanger fiasco, it seemed that unsympathetic French Catholics would rally to the republic, as they were urged to do by French prelates and by Pope Leo XIII in 1892. The hope that they would accept the republic was shattered by the Dreyfus Affair, which in the late 1890s rocked the country and indeed the world.

In 1894 Captain Dreyfus, a Jewish army officer, was found guilty of treason by a military court and deported to Devil's Island. Evidence accumulated showing his innocence and pointing to the guilt of another officer, a Major Esterhazy, an adventurer known to be riddled with gambling debts. But the army refused to reopen the case, unwilling to admit it had erred; a staff officer, Major Henry, even forged documents to confirm Dreyfus's guilt. Meanwhile anti-Semites, royalists, traditionalists, militarists, and most of the "best" people fought the reopening of the case, deeming it unpatriotic to shake the nation's confidence in the army and wishing also to disgrace the republican regime. The partisans of Dreyfus stubbornly upheld him, both because they believed in justice and because they wished to discredit their adversaries. The country was deeply split. Finally, in 1899, Dreyfus was pardoned, and in 1906, fully exonerated. In the aftermath of the affair the left republicans and socialists revenged themselves by blocking the promotions of antirepublican officers and by anticlerical legislation. In 1905, in a series of laic laws, they "separated" church and state, ending the close relationship established under Napoleon's concordat a century earlier.

The Strength
and Weakness
of the Republic

The Third Republic, when the war came in 1914, a test which it was successfully to meet, had lasted over twice as long as any French regime since 1789. Born unwanted and accidentally, though it still had its opponents, it now commanded the loyalty of the overwhelming mass of the French people. What it had done, since 1870, was to domesticate democratic republicanism in Europe. Republicanism, one of the most militant of revolutionary movements down to 1870, had been shown in France to be compatible with order, law, parliamentary government, economic prosperity, and a mutual tolerance between classes, to the extent at least that they no longer butchered each other in the streets. Industrial workers were in many ways less well off than in England or Germany, but there were fewer of them; and for most people France in these years was a pleasant country, full of painters, writers, scholars, and scientists, full of bankers, bourgeois and well-established farmers, a country living comfortably and unhurriedly on the savings of generations, and one in which, in a close-knit family group, the average man could plan securely for his own and his children's future.

But the very comforts and values of bourgeois France were not those that would equip it for leadership in the modern age of technology and industrial power. Though substantial economic progress was made, the country lagged behind Germany in industrial development; the French entrepreneur showed little inclination to take the business risks needed for industrial growth. Politically, the fragmentation of political parties, itself a democratic reflection of a divided public opinion, and the distrust for historic reasons of a strong executive power led to the rise and fall of numerous short-lived ministries—no fewer than fifty in the years between 1871 and 1914. Ministerial instability was to be a chronic symptom of the Third Republic both before and after 1914; continuity of government policy was, however, generally maintained because of stability in certain key ministries and because of the permanent civil service.

French labor remained a steady source of discontent. Although French workingmen benefited from some labor legislation in the two decades after 1890, they continued to feel frustrated at the failure to establish a "social republic." Socialist representation in the Chamber grew. However, the most important single party of the republic, the Radicals, or Radical Socialists, were in actuality radical republicans—patriotic, anticlerical, spokesmen for the small shopkeepers and the lesser propertied interests; they drew the line at the advanced social legislation that labor expected from them, and on occasion their leaders even took positive steps to prevent unionization and to suppress strikes. Since some of these Radicals had started out as socialists, the distrust of French workingmen for all politicians and even for political processes was intensified. But the difficulties of the republic went deeper. The political energies of the republican statesmen had gone into liquidating the past, into curbing the political strength of the monarchists, the church, and the army; by the turn of the century, even before these older issues were fully resolved, the republic was compelled to meet the challenge of labor and to face other domestic and international pressures that were to try it sorely. The Third Republic was to weather the crisis of the First World War but not that of the Second.

The British constitutional monarchy in the half-century before 1914 was the great exemplar of reasonable, orderly, and peaceable self-government through parliamentary methods.   For over sixty years, spanning two-thirds of the nineteenth century, Victoria reigned (1837–1901) and gave her name to a distinguished era of material progress, literary accomplishment, and political stability.   The two great parties, Liberal and Conservative, the heirs roughly of the Whigs and Tories, took form in the 1850s, the former producing its great leader in William E. Gladstone, the latter, a series of leaders of whom the most colorful was Benjamin Disraeli.

The advance toward an equalitarian political democracy in Britain was more cautious and slower than in France.   The Reform Bill of 1832 had granted the vote to about an eighth of the adult male population.   The democratic Chartist agitation of the 1830s and 1840s came to nothing.[13]   In 1867, in response to continued demand for a wider suffrage, the Second Reform Bill was passed, Conservatives as well as Liberals outdoing one another in an effort to satisfy the country and to win new political strength for their own party.   The Bill, adopted under Disraeli's Conservative ministry, extended the suffrage from about 1,000,000 eligible voters to about 2,000,000, or over a third of the adult males in the United Kingdom, reaching down far enough to include most workingmen in the cities.   The Conservative critic Lord Derby called it a "leap in the dark."   In 1884, under Liberal auspices, the suffrage was again broadened, this time in the rural areas, adding some 2,000,000 additional voters and enfranchising over three-fourths of all adult males in the country.   The suffrage still excluded agricultural workers who did not have a fixed residence, servants living with employers, and such people as unmarried grown sons who lived in the homes of their parents.   Although the franchise was now broad, it could not yet be equated with universal manhood suffrage.   Not until 1918 did Great Britain adopt universal manhood suffrage, as generally understood; and at that time women over thirty were given the vote too.

Despite the extension of the suffrage, the leadership of the country at the turn of the century was still in the hands of the upper and wealthier classes.   Until 1911 the government paid no salaries to members of the House of Commons, who therefore, in both great parties, were usually gentlemen with private incomes, possessing the same family background and education.   An attitude of sportsmanship and good feeling was characteristic of British politics.   The two parties alternated in power at regular intervals, each indulgent toward the other, carrying over and developing rather than reversing the policies of its predecessor in office.   Both parties sought support where they could find it, the Liberals leaning somewhat more on the industrial and

[13] See pp. 507–508, 515–516.

commercial interests, the Conservatives on the landed aristocracy; both sought and succeeded in winning their share of the new working-class vote. It was in these years that both parties, when parliamentary reversals occurred, increasingly appealed to the country in general elections; the traditional crown and cabinet basis of British parliamentary government was being transformed into crown, cabinet, and country.

The Liberals were usually the more willing to pioneer, the first of the four ministries of Gladstone being especially notable in this respect. Gladstone in this first ministry (1868–1874) developed the principle of state-supported public education for all classes under the Forster Education Act of 1870, introduced the secret ballot, formally legalized labor unions, promoted competitive examinations for civil service posts, reorganized the upper judiciary, eliminated the purchase and sale of commissions in the army (a form of property in office), and by abolishing religious tests enabled persons not members of the Church of England to graduate from Oxford and Cambridge. The Conservative party, less sensitive to pressure from business interests for a laissez-faire policy in economic matters and continuing the tradition of early Tory reformers, took the initiative in further labor legislation. Under Disraeli's second ministry (1874–1880), the existing acts regulating public sanitation and conditions in mines and factories were extended and codified, safety measures were enacted to protect sailors, and the first attempt to regulate housing conditions for the poorer classes was initiated. But the Liberals, it must be added, protected the workers' interests too. In Gladstone's second ministry (1880–1885) workingmen were assured of compensation for injuries not of their own responsibility, and in 1892, before the formation of his fourth ministry (1892–1894), Gladstone campaigned to shorten labor hours and to extend employers' liability in accidents.

British Political Changes after 1900

At the turn of the century important changes were discernible on the British political scene. Labor emerged as an independent political force, the Labour party itself being organized shortly after 1900.[14] The rise of labor had a deep impact upon the Liberal party, and indeed upon liberalism itself. With many persons insisting that protective measures be taken to counteract the poor health, low income, and economic insecurity of the British working people, the Liberals abandoned their traditional position of laissez faire and sponsored a policy of government intervention and social legislation in behalf of the workingman. The Liberals, though they acted in part for humanitarian reasons, were aware that with the emergence of the Labour party workingmen who customarily had voted for them might readily transfer their allegiance.

In control of the government from 1906 to 1916, with Herbert Asquith as prime minister and David Lloyd George as chancellor of the exchequer during most of this time, the Liberals put through a spectacular program of social welfare. Sickness,

[14]See p. 641.

accident, old-age, and a degree of unemployment insurance were adopted, and a moderate minimum wage law was enacted. Labor exchanges, or employment bureaus, were set up over the country. Restrictions on strikes and other trade union activities were removed. To meet the costs of the new program as well as of other government expenditures, Lloyd George's budget of 1909 called for progressive income and inheritance taxes: the wealthier the taxpayer, the higher the rate at which he was taxed. He was in effect advancing the then novel idea of using taxation to modify the extremes of wealth and poverty. It was a "war budget," he said, intended "to wage war against poverty." Its fiscal measures were directed primarily at the landed aristocracy, and it aroused great opposition, especially in the House of Lords, where the contest over the budget led to a further constitutional curtailment of the power of the upper house. The Parliament Act of 1911 deprived the Lords of all veto power in money matters and of all but a two-year delaying veto on action of the Commons in other legislation. At this time, too, the government voted to pay salaries to members of the House of Commons, making it possible for workingmen and others without independent incomes to take seats in Parliament. This last measure was enacted to circumvent a court ruling, the Osborne Judgment of 1909, that trade unions could not pay the salaries of workingmen elected to Parliament.

The Liberal party was embracing a program of positive state intervention in social and economic matters that the older liberalism, nurtured on the doctrines of laissez faire and the Manchester School, would not have accepted. With the Liberals actively seeking the support of labor and altering much in their traditional program, the Conservatives in the twentieth century tended to become the party of industry as well as of landed wealth and to replace the Liberals as the champions of economic liberalism and laissez faire. In the next generation, after the First World War, the Conservatives were to remain one of the two major parties of the country; the Liberals were to be far outstripped by the Labour party.

Meanwhile, despite its gains, labor was not pacified. Real wages showed a tendency to fall after 1900, and great coal and railway strikes broke out in 1911 and 1912. The British capacity to survive crises without violence, while still conspicuous, was being strained. An even more serious threat came from Ireland.

Britain suffered from one of the worst minorities questions in Europe—the Irish question. After 1801 Britain was known as the United Kingdom of Great Britain and Ireland, Ireland having been incorporated into the United Kingdom as a defensive measure against pro-French sympathies in Ireland during the wars of the French Revolution.[15] The Irish representatives who sat in Parliament were generally obstructionist in their tactics. The Irish had many substantial grievances, among which two were conspicuous. The Irish peasant was defenseless against his landlord, far more so, for example, than the French peasant before 1789; and the Irish people, though predominantly Catholic, were obliged to pay tithes to the established Church

The Irish Question

of Ireland (an Anglican sister church to the Church of England), which also owned a good deal of the land.

Gladstone, in his first ministry, disestablished the Church of Ireland. He also initiated measures to protect the Irish farm tenant. By 1900, under Conservative auspices, the Irish tenant was being assisted by the British government to buy out his landlord—often an Englishman or an Anglicized and absentee Irishman. The Irish also wanted home rule, or a parliament of their own. Gladstone, in trying to give it to them in 1886, split his Liberal party, part of which went along with the Conservatives, not wishing political division of the British Isles. Home rule was finally granted to Ireland in 1914. But the Ulstermen, Presbyterians of north Ireland, objected vehemently to inclusion in an autonomous Ireland, in which they would be outnumbered by the Catholics of the south. The latter, however, insisted with equal vehemence on the inclusion of Ulster, not wishing a political division of Ireland.

The Ulstermen, backed by British Conservatives, started arming and drilling to resist the act of Parliament that authorized home rule. Great Britain, in 1914, was about to see a civil war on its own doorstep. It suffered from something of the insoluble nationalistic disputes that afflicted Austria-Hungary. During the First World War home rule was suspended, and after considerable violence on both sides Catholic Ireland (Eire) in 1922 received dominion status, but eventually dissolved all ties with Britain. Ulster remained in the United Kingdom, but agitation by its Catholic minority persisted. Although both the United Kingdom and Ireland had been "partitioned," a satisfactory solution had not yet been found to the "Irish question."

Bismarck and the German Empire, 1871–1890

The German Empire, as put together by Bismarck in 1871 with William I, king of Prussia, as Kaiser, was a federation of monarchies, a union of twenty-five German states, in which the weight of monarchical Prussia, the Prussian army, and the Prussian landed aristocracy was preponderant. It developed neither the strong constitutionalism of England nor the democratic equality that was characteristic of France. To win popular support for his projects, Bismarck exploited existing democratic and socialist sentiment and provided that members of the Reichstag, the lower chamber, be elected by universal manhood suffrage.[16] Remaining chancellor of the united empire for some twenty years, from 1871 to 1890, he usually tried to have a majority in the Reichstag on his side, but he recognized no dependence on a majority in principle, holding to the doctrine that it was the emperor and his chancellor who were to govern the country. Moreover, in practice, the legislative powers of the lower house were severely restricted, and the upper chamber, representing the princes and not the people, and favored by the government, tended to be more important. Despite the nature of the empire, the Prussian conservatives, the East-Elbian Junker landlords, were at first by no means enthusiastic over Bismarck's unified Germany.[17] They opposed his democratic concessions and were left horrified when in 1872 he

[16] See pp. 572, 575.
[17] See pp. 527, 568–569.

undertook to extinguish what was left of their manorial jurisdiction over their peasants.

Bismarck in the 1870s therefore leaned not on the Conservatives but on the National Liberals. With their aid he put through a number of economic and legal measures designed to consolidate the unity of the new empire. Bismarck's first serious conflict developed with the Catholic church. At the very time that he was bent on subordinating all groups within the state to the sovereign power of the new empire, the church had spoken out. In 1864 in the *Syllabus of Errors*, it denounced the encroachment of all governments on educational and church affairs; in 1870 the new dogma of papal infallibility made it incumbent on Catholics to accept unreservedly the pope's pronouncements in matters of faith and morals.[18] To many, the implication was that the new empire could not count on the undivided loyalty of its Catholic citizens. To defend Catholic interests and those of the south German states where Catholicism predominated, Catholic elements had organized the strong Center party, which now upheld the church pronouncements. In 1871 Bismarck launched the so-called *Kulturkampf*, or "battle for modern civilization." The Liberals joined in eagerly. Like nineteenth-century liberals elsewhere (Gladstone's campaign against Anglican privilege and the French laic laws have just been mentioned), they were strongly anticlerical and disapproved of the influence of organized churches in public and private life. Laws were put through imposing restrictions upon Catholic worship and education, the Jesuits were expelled, and many Catholic bishops throughout Germany were arrested or went into exile. But Bismarck gradually concluded that the anti-Catholic legislation was fruitless, that he had overestimated the danger to the state of organized Catholicism, and realized that he needed the support of the Center party for other parts of his program.

In 1879, with the support of the Center and Conservative parties but to the dismay of many of his erstwhile Liberal allies, Bismarck abandoned free trade and adopted a protective tariff that provided needed revenues for the government and gave satisfaction both to agricultural and industrial interests. Meanwhile, with the country's rapid and spectacular industrial expansion, the German working class had been growing and, to the alarm of Bismarck, socialism had been spreading among the German masses.

The German Social Democratic party had been founded in 1875 by a fusion of Marxian socialists and the reformist followers of Ferdinand Lassalle on an essentially moderate program which Marx had denounced. But even a moderate socialism was mistrusted by Bismarck. He shared in the European horror at the recent Paris Commune, he feared socialism as anarchy, and he knew that socialism was in any case republican, and in that alone a potentially revolutionary movement in an empire of monarchies. Two radical attempts on the emperor's life (in neither case by Social Democrats) provided him with all the excuse he needed. In 1878, having already made peace with the Catholics, he set out to exterminate socialism. Antisocialist laws from 1878 to 1890 prohibited socialist meetings and socialist newspapers. For twelve

---

[18] See p. 656.

years socialism was driven underground. But repression was not his only weapon; he turned also to another tactic. Bismarck sought to persuade the workers to place their faith in him and the German Empire rather than in Marx and the prophets of socialism. To that end, in the 1880s, he initiated an extensive program of social legislation. Workmen were insured by the state against sickness, accident, and incapacity in old age. "Our democratic friends," said Bismarck, "will pipe in vain when the people see princes concerned with their well-being." In social insurance imperial Germany was, from whatever motives, years ahead of more democratic England, France, and the United States.

Bismarck failed to kill socialism. The number of socialists elected to the Reichstag was greater in 1890 than in 1878—for Bismarck's antisocialist campaign, in deference to the then current standards of civilized government, never suppressed the voter's freedom to vote as he chose. It seems, however, that Bismarck by the later 1880s was more apprehensive than ever of social revolution that would destroy his empire and contemplated some kind of coup d'état in which the Reichstag would be throttled. He never reached this point because in 1890, at the age of seventy-five, he was obliged by the new emperor, William II, to retire.

The German Empire
after 1890: William II

William I died in 1888 and was succeeded by his son Frederick III who, incurably ill of cancer, died some three months after his accession. Frederick's son, William II, the last king of Prussia and the last German Kaiser, began his reign (1888–1918) as a young man of twenty-nine, full of startling ideas about his personal power and privileges. He was uncomfortable in the presence of an elder statesman who had made the German Empire, who had been his grandfather's aide and adviser, and whom he regarded partly with veneration and partly as an old fogy. William soon quarreled with Bismarck over continuation of the antisocialist laws and over matters of foreign affairs. When Bismarck forbade his ministers to meet with the emperor on policy matters unless he was present, William resolved that he, and not Bismarck, would rule the empire, and in 1890 he ordered Bismarck to resign, "dropping the pilot," in the celebrated phrase. Under the four chancellors who succeeded Bismarck, it was William who dominated policy.

After 1890 Germany embarked upon what was termed a "new course." In foreign affairs this meant a more aggressive and ambitious colonial, naval, and diplomatic policy, as will appear in the next two chapters. In domestic affairs it meant a more conciliatory attitude toward the masses. The antisocialist laws were dropped, and the system of social security legislation was enlarged and codified. But no democratic adjustment seemed possible. William II believed in the divinely ordained prerogatives of the house of Hohenzollern, and the empire still rested on the power of the federated princes, on the Junkers, the army, and the new industrial magnates. But the Social Democrats, the Progressive party, and other democratic forces were growing in strength. They demanded, for Prussia, a reform of the illiberal constitution of 1850,[19] and for the Reich, real control over the federal

[19]See pp. 532–533.

chancellor by the majority party in the Reichstag. In the election of 1912 the Social Democrats reached a new high by polling four and a quarter million votes, about one-third of the total, and by electing 110 members to the Reichstag, in which they now formed the largest single party; yet they were excluded from the highest posts of government. Even had war not come in 1914, it is clear that the imperial Germany created by Bismarck was moving toward a constitutional crisis in which political democracy would be the issue.

Of political developments in other European states before 1914, something has already been said in the preceding chapter. Italy had become a constitutional monarchy in the 1860s and completed its unification by the forceful seizure of Rome in 1870.[20] Despite parliamentary forms, Italian political life in substance was characterized by unstable, opportunistic maneuvers and alliances manipulated by party chieftains, the best known of whom were Francesco Crispi, Agostino Depretis, and Giovanni Giolitti, moderate liberals who maintained themselves in office for long periods of time by shuffling and balancing political coalitions and by controlling elections in a form of parliamentary politics that received the name *trasformismo.* Giolitti, who headed five cabinets in all, governed with few interruptions from 1903 down to 1914. The liberal leaders were anticlerical, and the quarrel with the papacy over the seizure of the papal territories remained unsettled. The popes refused to recognize the Italian kingdom and forbade Catholics to participate in its affairs or even to vote in elections. Catholics voted nonetheless and in 1907 bishops in each diocese were permitted to relax the ban, as they increasingly did.

Industry had begun to make an appearance in the northern cities like Milan. More as a matter of expediency than out of any democratic impulse, the government moved to extend the franchise to the working classes. The narrow suffrage of 1861 was broadened, first in 1882, and then in 1912, when the new reform increased the number of eligible voters from three to eight million, or virtually universal manhood suffrage. Because of illiteracy and political inertia not all of the newly enfranchised hastened to exercise their voting privilege. The social problem remained serious, too, despite some modest social legislation. Poverty and illiteracy, especially in the agrarian south, were grievous problems and radical unrest appeared in the industrial cities. In 1900 Victor Emmanuel's son and successor Humbert was assassinated. The first manifestations of an antiparliamentary ideology, chauvinistic nationalism, and explosive irrationalism appeared in the writings and political activism of literary men like Gabriele d'Annunzio and Filippo Marinetti, the latter publishing in 1909 the manifesto of a violently nihilistic movement he called futurism. The machinery of political democracy was established in Italy but there could be no assurances about the direction Italian parliamentary democracy was taking.

In the Dual Monarchy of Austria-Hungary, created by the Compromise of 1867, Austria and Hungary were each in form constitutional parliamentary states.[21] In

[20] See pp. 565, 574, 656.
[21] See pp. 579–581.

theory, the Emperor-King Francis Joseph ruled through ministries responsible to the legislature in each state. However, in the important sphere of matters affecting the empire as a whole, such as foreign affairs and military questions, there was little parliamentary restraint on the emperor. Here he had virtually final authority; moreover, in all matters he still had broad powers to govern by decree, which he exercised. As in Germany, the tide of socialism was held back both by repressive laws and by social insurance and benevolent legislation. The most serious problem in the empire remained not socialism but agitation by the various subject nationalities, the Czechs and other Slavic peoples. Political democracy took a different course in Austria than in Hungary. In the former, partly as an effort to placate nationalist sentiment, universal male suffrage was introduced in 1907. In the latter it was bitterly and successfully resisted by the Magyars, who saw in it a weapon that could be employed by the Slavs to contest and destroy their preponderance. Austria itself, despite the democratic suffrage, was ruled very much like the German Empire, the legislature able to debate and criticize but not control policy.

Of other countries it can be said that the political forms of democracy showed signs of advancing everywhere. Universal manhood suffrage was adopted in Switzerland in 1874, in Belgium in 1893 (though plural voting was still permitted), in the Netherlands in 1896; and in the next few years in Norway and Sweden (Norway was peacefully separated in 1905 from Sweden). In southern Europe, besides Italy, universal suffrage was introduced in Spain, Greece, Bulgaria, Serbia, and after the revolt of 1908, in Turkey. Although both Spain and Portugal were beset by civil wars, constitutional forms were eventually adopted in both countries, universal male suffrage being introduced in Spain in 1890 and a liberal suffrage in Portugal under a republic in 1911. Even tsarist Russia, after the Revolution of 1905, received a Duma, or national parliament, elected on a wide franchise but on an indirect and undemocratic class basis, and with narrow powers.[22]

Among states west of the Russian empire, only Hungary and Rumania confined the vote to a minority of the population on the eve of the First World War. Women voted in certain western states of the United States, in Australia, New Zealand, and Norway. In 1918 woman suffrage was introduced with certain restrictions in Great Britain; in 1920 it became general in the United States through constitutional amendment. Use of the secret or "Australian" ballot, palladium of the small voter's electoral freedom, also spread very widely in the decades after 1880. In Australia and New Zealand and in the Scandinavian states political democracy was coupled with considerable social legislation; they served as models for the welfare state.

The progress of representative and democratic institutions did not mean an end to the rule of monarchs, landed aristocrats, and other minority interests. For one thing, with the exception of France and Switzerland, Europe remained monarchical. Second, despite the growing importance of parliaments, parliamentary control over political life was far from guaranteed; emperors and kings still ruled through their chancellors and prime ministers. Of the major world powers it was mainly in the

[22]See p. 777.

United States (at least for whites), Britain, and France that democratic and popular control was a reality. But the extension of the suffrage, by the relaxation of property qualifications, had a dynamic of its own and was altering the framework of politics everywhere; mass political parties, including socialist parties and confessional, or religious-oriented parties, were replacing the older narrowly oligarchic political organizations, and support now had to be sought on a wider electoral basis. In almost all Europe, and in many of the outlying areas peopled by European descendants, democracy was advancing, even within the older framework. By 1871, most European nations, with the notable exception of Russia, had already won written constitutions, guarantees of personal freedom, parliamentary and representative institutions, and limitations on absolutism; in the years between 1871 and 1914 the most significant new political factor was the advance of the democratic suffrage.

The artisan and laboring classes had never viewed with much pleasure the rise of capitalism or of "bourgeois" liberalism. They had always been doubtful of free competition, unrestrained private enterprise, the Manchester School, laissez faire, the laws of supply and demand, the free market for goods and labor, the idea of an economy independent of states and governments. These were the ideas of middle-class liberals, not of radical democrats. Popular leaders had opposed them in the French Revolution in 1793. The English Chartists had been outspokenly anticapitalistic, and on the Continent the ideas of socialism had been spreading. In 1848 there was a strong movement among the working classes for a "social" republic, and, though the social revolution failed in 1848, the force of it was enough to terrify the possessing classes and shape the philosophy of Karl Marx.[23] With the advent of the ballot, workers pressed for social legislation and used their political power to gain a greater measure of social democracy.

But in addition, before and after obtaining the ballot, working people resorted to other devices for the improvement of their position. Against the owners of capital, who controlled the giving of jobs, there were two principal lines of action. One was to abolish the capitalists, the other to bargain with them. The former led to socialism, the latter to the formation of labor unions. Socialism, in logic, meant the extinction of the private employer as such.[24] Trade unionism, in logic, meant that the workingman had every reason to keep his employer prosperously in business in order that bargaining with him might produce more results. The working-class movement thus contained an internal contradiction which was never completely resolved.

Middle-class and educated people who took up the workers' cause, the "intellectuals" of the movement—Karl Marx, Friedrich Engels, Louis Blanc, Ferdinand Lassalle, and thousands of less famous names—tended more to socialism than to unionism. They thought of society as a whole, they saw the economic system

[23] See pp. 506–509, 512–516, 535–537.
[24] See pp. 476–477, 507.

as a system, they thought of the future in long-run terms, and their time scale allowed generously for whole historical epochs to come and go. The actual workingman, put to work at an early age, barely educated if at all, with the waking hours of his adult life spent on a manual job, was inclined to keep his attention more on unionism than on socialism. To earn a shilling more every week beginning next week, to be spared the nervous strain and physical danger of constant exposure to unprotected machinery, to have fifteen minutes more every day for lunch, were likely to seem more tangible and important than far-reaching but distant plans for a reconstructed society. The worker looked on the intellectual as an outsider, however welcome; the intellectual looked on the worker as shortsighted and timid, however much in need of help.

After the failures of 1848 the socialist and trade union movements diverged for a generation. The 1850s, compared with the hungry forties, were a time of full employment, rising wages, and increasing prosperity for all classes. Workingmen set to organizing unions, socialist thinkers to perfecting their doctrines.

The Trade Union Movement and Rise of British Labor

Organizations of wage workers, or labor unions in the modern sense (as distinguished from medieval craft gilds), had long maintained a shadowy and sporadic existence, as in the old French journeymen's associations.[25] But they had always been extra-legal, frowned upon or actually prohibited by governments. French revolutionaries in the Le Chapelier Act of 1791, British Tories in the Combination Act of 1799, had been as one in forbidding workers to unite. It was the rise of "bourgeois" liberalism, so insensitive to the worker in most ways, that first gave legal freedom to labor unions. The British unions received a tacit recognition from the Liberal Tories in 1825 and explicit recognition from Gladstone's Liberal ministry in 1871. French unions were recognized by Napoleon III in 1864, then restrained in the reaction caused by the Commune, then fully legalized in 1884. In Germany Bismarck negotiated with labor leaders to find support against the vested interests that stood in his way.

The prosperity of the 1850s favored the formation of unions, for workingmen can always organize most easily when employers are most in need of their services. The craft union—or union of skilled workers in the same trade, such as carpenters—was at first the typical organization. It was most fully developed in England, where a "new model" unionism was introduced by the Amalgamated Society of Engineers (i.e., machinists) in 1851. It was the policy of the "new model" union officials to take the unions out of politics, to forget the semisocialism of the Chartists, to abandon Robert Owen's grandiose idea of "one big union" for all workers, and to concentrate on advancing the interests of each separate trade. The new leaders proposed to be reasonable with employers, avoid strikes, accumulate union funds, and build up their membership. In this they were very successful; the unions took root; and the two governing parties in England, reassured by the unexpected moderation of working-class spokesmen, combined to give the town workman the vote in 1867.

[25] See pp. 121–122, 389, 545.

In the 1880s, and especially with the great London dock strike of 1889, which closed the port of London for the first time since the French Revolution, unions of unskilled workers began to form. Industrial unionism, or the joining in one union of all workers in one industry, such as coal or transportation, regardless of the skill or job of the individual worker, began to take shape at the same time. In some cases the older skilled unions joined with unskilled laborers who worked beside them. Thus gradually arose, for example, the Transport Workers Union, which half a century later was to give a Foreign Secretary to the government in the person of Ernest Bevin. By 1900 there were about 2,000,000 union members in Great Britain, compared with only 850,000 in Germany and 250,000 in France.

It was largely because the British workingman was so far advanced in trade unionism, and so successful in forcing collective bargaining upon his employer, that he was much slower than his Continental counterpart in forming a workers' political party. By the 1880s, when avowed socialists were already sitting in French, Belgian, and German parliaments, the only corresponding persons in Britain were a half-dozen Lib-Labs, as they were called, laboring men elected on the Liberal ticket. The British Labour party was formed at the turn of the century by the joint efforts of trade union officials and middle-class intellectuals.[26] Where on the Continent the labor unions were often led, and even brought into being, by the socialist political parties, in Britain it was the labor unions that brought into being, and subsequently led, the Labour party. Hence for a long time the Labour party was less socialistic than working-class parties on the Continent. Its origin and rapid growth were due in large measure to a desire to defend the unions as established and respectable institutions. The unions were threatened in their very existence by a ruling of the British courts in 1901, the Taff Vale decision, which held a union financially responsible for business losses incurred by an employer during a strike. The shortest and most orderly strike, by exhausting a union's funds, might ruin the union. The year before, steps had been taken to bring together the unions and all other existing labor and socialist organizations into a labor representation committee, in preparation for the elections of 1900; the effort was not very successful and only two of the fifteen labor candidates were returned. But the Taff Vale decision unified all ranks and precipitated the formation of the modern Labour party. In the election of 1906 the new Labour party sent twenty-nine members to Parliament, which thereupon overruled the Taff Vale decision by new legislation. The social legislation put through Parliament by the Liberal party government in the next few years, in good part under pressure from labor, has already been described.[27]

As for socialism, which had so frightened the middle and upper classes in 1848, it seemed in the 1850s to go into abeyance. Karl Marx, after issuing the *Communist Manifesto* with Engels in 1848, and agitating as a journalist in the German revolution

[26] See p. 643.
[27] See pp. 632–633.

of that year, withdrew to the secure haven offered by England and spent the rest of his life in London, where, after years of painstaking research in the British Museum, he published the first volume of his *Capital* in 1867. This work, of which the succeeding volumes were published after his death, gave body, substance, and argument to the principles announced in the *Manifesto*.[28] Marx, during more than thirty years in London, scarcely mixed with the labor leaders then building up the English unions. Hardly known to the English, he associated mainly with political exiles and temporary visitors of numerous nationalities.

In 1864 there took place in London the first meeting of the International Working Men's Association, commonly known as the First International. It was sponsored by a heterogeneous group, including the secretary of the British carpenters' union, Robert Applegarth; the aging Italian revolutionary, Mazzini; and Karl Marx. With the union officials absorbed in union business, leadership in the Association gradually passed to Marx, who used it as a means of publicizing the ideas about to appear in his *Capital*. At subsequent annual congresses, at Geneva, Lausanne, Brussels, and Basel, Marx built up his position. He made the Mazzinians unwelcome, and he denounced the German Lassalleans for their willingness to cooperate with Bismarck, arguing that it was not the business of socialists to cooperate with the state but to seize it. His sharpest struggle was with the Russian Bakunin. With his background in tsarist Russia, Bakunin believed the state to be the cause of the common man's afflictions; he was hence an "anarchist," holding that the state should be attacked and abolished. To Marx anarchism was abhorrent; the correct doctrine was that the state—tsarist or bourgeois—was only a product of economic conditions, a tool in the class struggle, a weapon of the propertied interests, so that the true target for revolutionary action must be not the state but the capitalist economic system. Marx drove Bakunin from the International in 1872.

Meanwhile members of the First International watched with great excitement the Paris Commune of 1871, which they hoped might be the opening act of a European working-class upheaval. Members of the International infiltrated into the Commune, and the connection between the two, though rather incidental, was one reason why the French bourgeois repressed the Commune with such terrified ferocity. But the Commune actually killed the First International. The Commune had been bloody and violent; it had been an armed rebellion against the democratically elected National Assembly of France. Marx praised it as a stage in the international class war. He even saw in it a foretaste of what he was coming to call the "dictatorship of the proletariat." He thus frightened many possible followers away. Certainly British trade unionists, sober and steady men, could have nothing to do with such doings or such doctrines. The First International faded out of existence after 1872.

But in 1875, at the Gotha conference, Marxian and Lassallean socialists effected enough of a union to found the German Social Democratic party, whose growth thereafter, against Bismarck's attempts to stop it, has been already seen. About 1880

[28] See pp. 537–538.

socialist parties sprouted up in many countries. In Belgium, highly industrialized, a Belgian Socialist party appeared in 1879. In the industrial regions of France some workingmen were attracted to Jules Guesde, a self-taught worker, former Communard, and now a rigid Marxist, who held it impossible to emancipate the working class by compromise of any sort; others followed the "possibilist" Dr. Brousse, who thought it possible for workers to arrive at socialism through parliamentary methods; still others supported Jean Jaurès, who eloquently linked social reform to the French revolutionary tradition and the defense of republican institutions. Not until 1905 did the socialist groups in France form a unified Socialist party. In England, in 1881, H. M. Hyndman founded a Social Democratic Federation on the German model and with a Marxist program; it never had more than a handful of members. In 1883 two Russian exiles in Switzerland, Plekhanov and Axelrod, who had just been converted to Marxism, founded the Russian Social Democratic party, from which the communism of the following century was eventually to be derived. The socialist parties all came together to establish an international league in 1889, known as the Second International, which thereafter met every three years and lasted until 1914.

The new socialist parties of the 1880s were all Marxist in inspiration. Marx died in 1883. Marxism or "scientific socialism," by the force of its social analysis, the mass of Marx's writings over forty years, and an attitude of unyielding hostility to competing socialist doctrines, had become the only widely current form of systematic socialism. Strongest in Germany and France, Marxism was relatively unsuccessful in Italy and Spain, where the working class, less industrialized anyway, more illiterate, unable to place its hopes in the ballot, and habituated to an excitable insurrectionism in the manner of Garibaldi, turned more frequently to the anarchism preached by Bakunin.

Nor was Marxism at all successful in England; the worker stood by his trade unions, and middle-class critics of capitalism followed the Fabian Society, established in 1883. The Fabians (so called from the ancient Roman general Fabius Cunctator, the "delayer," or strategist of gradual methods) were very English and very un-Marxist. George Bernard Shaw, H. G. Wells, and Sidney and Beatrice Webb were among early members of the Society. For them socialism was the social and economic counterpart to political democracy, as well as its inevitable outcome. They held that no class conflict was necessary or even existed, that gradual and reasonable and conciliatory measures would in due time bring about a socialist state, and that improvement of local government, or municipal ownership of such things as waterworks and electric lighting, were steps toward this consummation. The Fabians, like the trade union officials, were content with small and immediate satisfactions. They joined with the unions to form the Labour party. At the same time, by patient and detailed researches into economic realities, they provided a mass of practical information on which a legislative program could be based.

The Marxist or Social Democratic parties on the Continent grew very rapidly. Marxism turned into a less revolutionary "parliamentary socialism"—except indeed for the Russian Social Democratic party, since Russia had no parliamentary government. For the growth of socialist parties meant that true workingmen, and not merely intellectuals, were voting for socialist candidates for the Reichstag, Chamber of Deputies, or whatever the lower house of parliament might be called; and this in turn meant that the psychology and influence of labor unions within the parties was increased. The workers, and their union officials, might in theory consider themselves locked in an enormous struggle with capital; but in practice their aim was to get more for themselves out of their employers' business. They might believe in the internationalism of the worker's interests; but in practice, acting through the parliaments of national states, they would work for orderly legislation benefiting the workers of their own country only—social insurance, factory regulation, minimum wages, or maximum hours. Nor was it possible to deny, by the close of the century, that Marx's anticipations (based initially on conditions of the 1840s) had not come true, at least not yet; the bourgeois was getting richer, but the proletarian was not getting poorer. Real wages—or what the wage earner's income would actually buy, even allowing for the losses due to unemployment—are estimated to have risen about 50 percent in the industrialized countries between 1870 and 1900. The increase was due to the greater productivity of labor through mechanization, the growth of the world economy, the accumulation of capital wealth, and the ever stronger pressure of organized labor upon employers.

Repeatedly, but in vain, the Second International had to warn its component socialist parties against collaboration with the bourgeoisie. Marxism began in the 1890s to undergo a movement of revisionism, led in France by Jean Jaurès, socialist leader in the Chamber of Deputies, and in Germany by Eduard Bernstein, social democratic member of the Reichstag and author in 1898 of *Evolutionary Socialism*, an important tract setting forth the new views. The revisionists held that the class conflict might not be absolutely inevitable, that capitalism might be gradually transformed in the workers' interest, and that now that the workers had not only the vote, but a political party of their own, they could obtain their ends through democratic channels, without revolution and without any dictatorship of the proletariat. Most socialists or social democrats followed the revisionists.

This tendency to "opportunism"[29] among Marxists drove the really revolutionary spirits into new directions. Thus there arose revolutionary syndicalism, of which the main intellectual exponent was a Frenchman, Georges Sorel. Syndicalism is simply the French word for trade unionism (*syndicat*, a union), and the idea was that the workers' unions might themselves become the supreme authoritative institutions in society, replacing not only property and the market economy, but government itself. The means to this end was to be a stupendous general strike, in which all workers in all industries should simultaneously stop work, thus paralyzing society and forcing acceptance of their will. Syndicalism made most headway where the unions were weakest, as in Italy, Spain, and France, since here the unions had the least to lose and were most in need of sensational doctrines to attract members. Its strongest base was in the French General Confederation of Labor, founded in 1895.

[29] See p. 542.

Among orthodox Marxists there was also a revival of Marxian fundamentals in protest against revisionism. In Germany Karl Kautsky arraigned the revisionists as compromisers who betrayed Marxism for petty-bourgeois ends. In 1904 he and other rigorists prevailed upon the Second International to condemn the political behavior of the French socialist Alexandre Millerand who in 1899 had accepted a ministerial post in a French cabinet. Socialists might use Parliament as a forum, the International ruled, but socialists who entered the government itself were unpardonably identifying themselves with the enemy bourgeois state. Not until the First World War did socialists henceforth join the cabinet of any European country. In the Russian Social Democratic party the issue of revisionism came to a head in 1903, at a party congress held in London—for the Russian Marxists were mainly exiles. Here a group led by Lenin demanded that revisionism be stamped out. Lenin won a majority, at the moment at least, and hence the uncompromising Marxists were called Bolsheviks (from the Russian word for majority), while the revisionist or conciliatory Russian Marxists, those willing to work with bourgeois liberals and democrats, were subsequently known as Mensheviks or the "minority" group.[30] But in 1903 the Russian Marxists were considered very unimportant.

In general, in Europe's "inner zone," by the turn of the century, most people who called themselves Marxists were no longer actively revolutionary. As revolutionary republicanism had quieted down in the Third French Republic, so revolutionary Marxism seemed to have quieted down into the milder doctrines of social democracy. What would have happened except for the coming of war in 1914 cannot be known; possibly social revolutionism would have revived, since real wages no longer generally rose between 1900 and 1914, and considerable restlessness developed in labor circles, punctuated by great strikes. But in 1914 the working class as a whole was in no revolutionary mood. Workers still sought a greater measure of social justice, but the social agitation so feared or hoped for in 1848 had subsided. There seem to have been three principal reasons: capitalism had worked well enough to raise the worker's living standard above what he could remember of his father's or grandfather's; the worker had the vote and so felt that he participated in the state, could expect to benefit from the government, and had little to gain by its overthrow; and third, he had his interests watched over by organized and increasingly powerful unions, by which a larger share in the national income could be demanded and passed on to the worker.

Faith in the powers of natural science has been characteristic of modern society for over three centuries, but never was there a time when this faith spread to so many people, or was held so firmly, so optimistically, and with so few qualms or mental reservations as in the half-century preceding the First World War. Science lay at the bottom of the whole movement of industrialization; and if science became positively popular after about 1870, in that persons ignorant of science came to look upon it as an oracle, it was because it manifested itself to everybody in the new wonders of

[30] See pp. 772–773.

daily life. Hardly had the world's more civilized regions digested the railroad, the steamship, and the telegraph when a whole series of new inventions already described[31] had begun to unfold itself. In thirty years following 1875 the number of patents tripled in the United States, quadrupled in Germany, and multiplied in all the civilized countries. The scientific and technical advance was as completely international (though confined mainly to the "inner zone") as any movement the world has ever seen. Never had the rush of scientific invention been so fundamentally useful, so helpful to the constructive labors and serious problems of mankind, and in that sense human.

In more basic scientific thinking important changes set in about 1860 or 1870. Up to that time, generally speaking, the underlying ideas had been those set forth by Isaac Newton almost two centuries before.[32] The law of universal gravitation reigned unquestioned, and with it, hardly less so, the geometry of Euclid and a physics that was basically mechanics. The ultimate nature of the universe was thought to be regular, orderly, predictable, and harmonious; it was also timeless, in that the passage of ages brought no change or development. By the end of the epoch considered here, that is, by 1914, the old conceptions had begun to yield on every side.

The Impact
of Evolution

In impact upon general thinking the greatest change came in the new emphasis upon biology and the life sciences. Here the great symbolic date is the publication by Charles Darwin of the *Origin of Species* in 1859. Evolution, after Darwin, became the order of the day. Evolutionary philosophies, holding that the way to understand anything was to understand its development, were not new in 1859. Hegel had introduced the evolutionary conception into metaphysics; and he and Marx, into theories of human society.[33] The idea of progress, taken over from the Age of Enlightenment, was a kind of evolutionary philosophy; and the great activity in historical studies, under romantic and nationalistic auspices, had made people think of human affairs in terms of a time-process.[34] In the world of nature, the rise of geology after 1800 had opened the way to evolutionary ideas, and venturesome biologists had allowed themselves to speculate on an evolutionary development of living forms. What Darwin did was to stamp evolution with the seal of science, marshaling the evidence for it and offering an explanation of how it worked. In 1871, in his *Descent of Man,* he applied the same hypotheses to human beings.

By evolution, Darwin meant that species are mutable; that no species is created to remain unchanged once and for all; and that all species of living organisms, plant and animal, microscopic or elephantine in dimensions, living or extinct, have developed by successive small changes from other species that went before them. An important corollary was that all life was interrelated and subject to the same laws. Another

[31] See pp. 617–618.
[32] See pp. 305–308.
[33] See pp. 480, 538–541.
[34] See pp. 326, 335, 444–445, 479–480.

corollary was that the whole history of living things on earth, generally held by scientists in Darwin's time to be many millions of years, was a unified history unfolding continuously in a single meaningful process of evolution.

Darwin thought that species changed, not by any intelligent or purposeful activity in the organism, but essentially by a kind of chance. Individual organisms, through the play of heredity, inherited slightly different characteristics, some more useful than others in food-getting, fighting, or mating; and the organisms that had the most useful characteristics tended to survive, so that their characteristics were passed on to offspring, until the whole species gradually changed. Certain phrases, not all of them invented by Darwin, summed up the theory. There was a "struggle for existence" resulting in the "survival of the fittest" through "natural selection" of the "most favored races"—races meaning not human races but the strains within a species. The struggle for existence referred to the fact that, in nature, more individuals were born in each species than could live out a normal life span; the "fittest" were those individual specimens of a species having the most useful characteristics, such as fleetness in deer or ferocity in tigers; "natural" selection meant that the fittest survived without purpose in themselves or in a Creator; the "favored races" were the strains within a species having good survival powers.

Darwin's ideas precipitated a great outcry. Scientists rushed to defend and churchmen to attack him. The biologist T. H. Huxley became the chief spokesman for Darwin—"Darwin's bulldog." He debated with, among others, the bishop of Oxford. Darwin was denounced, with less than fairness, for saying that men came from monkeys. It was feared that all grounds of human dignity, morality, and religion would collapse. Darwin himself remained complacent on this score; under civilized conditions, he said, the social and cooperative virtues were useful characteristics assisting in survival, so that "we may expect that virtuous habits will grow stronger, becoming perhaps fixed by inheritance." Much of the outburst against Darwin was somewhat trivial, nor were those who attacked him generally noted for spiritual insight; yet they were not mistaken in sensing a profound danger.

That Darwinism said nothing of God, Providence, or salvation was not surprising; no science ever did. That evolution did not exactly square with the first chapter of Genesis was disturbing but not fatal; much of the Old Testament was already regarded as symbolic, at least outside certain fundamentalist circles. Even the idea that man and the animals were of one piece was not ruinous; the animal side of human nature had not escaped the notice of theologians. The novel and upsetting effect of evolutionary biology was to change the conception of nature. Nature was no longer a harmony, it was a scene of struggle, "nature red in tooth and claw." Struggle and elimination of the weak were natural, and as means toward evolutionary development they might even be considered good. There were no fixed species or perfected forms, but only an unending flux. Change was everlasting; and everything seemed merely relative to time, place, and environment. There were no norms of good and bad; a good organism was one that survived where others perished; adaptation replaced virtue; outside of it there was nothing "right." The test was, in short, success; the "fit" were the successful; and here Darwinism merged with that toughness of mind, or *Realpolitik,* which came over Europe at the same time from other causes.[35]

Such at least were the implications if one generalized from science, carrying over scientific findings into human affairs, and the prestige of science was so great that this is precisely what many people wished to do. With the popularization of biological evolution, a school known as Social Darwinists actively applied the ideas of the struggle for existence and survival of the fittest to human society. Social Darwinists were found all over Europe and the United States. Their doctrines were put to various uses, to show that some peoples were naturally superior to others, such as whites to blacks, or Nordics to Latins, or Germans to Slavs (or vice versa), or non-Jews to Jews; or that the upper and middle classes, comfortable and contented, deserved these blessings because they had proved themselves "fitter" than the shiftless poor; or that big business in the nature of things had to take over smaller concerns; or that some states, such as the British or German Empire, were bound to rise; or that war was morally a fine thing, proving the virility and survival value of those who fought.

Anthropology and
Psychology

The newer life sciences, such as anthropology and psychology, developed very rapidly in the latter part of the nineteenth century. Their effect upon the civilization of the day was not unlike that of Darwinism. Both accepted biological evolution. Both, as the price of being truly scientific, eschewed standards of right and wrong and set themselves to finding out and explaining the mere facts of human behavior.

Anthropology set itself the task of studying the physical and cultural characteristics of all branches of mankind. Physical anthropologists became interested in the several human "races," some of which they considered might be "favored" in the Darwinian sense, that is, superior in inheritance and survival value. It was often concluded, even by scientists at the time, that the whites were the most competent race, and among the whites the Nordics, Teutons, or Germans and Anglo-Saxons. The public, more or less exaggerating such ideas, became more race-conscious than Europeans had ever been before. On the other hand the cultural anthropologists, surveying all manner of primitive or complex societies with scientific disinterest, seemed sometimes to teach a more deflating doctrine. Scientifically, it seemed, no culture or society was "better" than any other, all being adaptations to an environment, or merely a matter of custom—of the *mores,* as people said in careful distinction from "morals." The effect was again a kind of relativism or skepticism—a negation of values, a belief that right and wrong were matters of social convention, psychological conditioning, mere opinion, or point of view. We are describing, let it be repeated, not the history of science itself but the effects of science upon European civilization at the time.

The impact of anthropology was felt keenly in religion too. Sir James Frazer (1854–1941) in his multivolumed *The Golden Bough* could demonstrate that some of the most sacred practices, rites, and ideas of Christianity were not unique but could be

[35]See pp. 534–535.

found among primitive societies, and that, moreover, only the thinnest of lines divided magic from religion. Anthropology, Darwinian evolution, and other developments went far to upset traditional religious beliefs.

Psychology, as a science of human behavior, led to thoroughly upsetting implications about the very nature of man. It was launched in the 1870s as a natural science by the German physiologist Wilhelm Wundt (1832–1920), who based his work on laboratory experiments with animals. The Russian Ivan Pavlov (1849–1936), also working with animals, conducted a famous series of experiments in which he "conditioned" dogs to salivate automatically at the ringing of a bell once they had become accustomed over a period of time to associate the sound with the serving of their food. Pavlov's observations were important; they implied that a great part of animal behavior, and presumably human behavior, could be explained on the basis of conditioned responses. In the case of human beings these would be responses which men have been trained to make automatically by virtue of their environment and upbringing, and which they do not make through choice or conscious reasoning. Most significant of all the developments in psychology was the work of Sigmund Freud (1856–1939) and those inspired by him. Freud, a Viennese physician, came to the conclusion that certain forms of mental disturbance like hysteria could be traced to earlier completely forgotten episodes of a patient's life, perhaps even to his infancy. From this Freud began to explore the drives, frustrations, and repressions, especially sexual, that influence every individual's behavior without his even being aware of it. Freud and the new schools of psychology all laid great stress on the subconscious. Revealing the wide areas of human behavior that lie outside conscious control, they showed the ways in which man was not a rational being; they suggested in essence that man was not primarily a rational being at all.

The New Physics

The revolution in biology of the nineteenth century was soon to be matched and surpassed by the revolution in physics. In the late 1890s physics was on the threshold of a revolutionary transformation. Like Newtonian mechanics in the seventeenth century and Darwinian evolution in the nineteenth, the new physics represented one of the great scientific revolutions of all time. There was no single work comparable to Newton's *Principia* or Darwin's *Origin of Species* unless Albert Einstein's theory of relativity, propounded in a series of scientific papers in 1905 and 1916, might be considered as such. Instead there was a series of discoveries and findings, partly mathematical and then increasingly empirical, that threw new light on the nature of matter and energy. In Newtonian physics the atom, the basic unit of all matter, which the Greeks had hypothesized in ancient times, was like a hard, solid, unstructured billiard ball, permanent and unchanging; and matter and energy were separate and distinct. But a series of discoveries from 1896 on profoundly altered this view. In 1896 the French scientist Antoine Henri Becquerel discovered radioactivity, observing that uranium emitted particles or rays of energy. In the years immediately following, from the observations and discoveries of the French scientists Pierre and Marie Curie and the Englishmen J. J. Thomson and Lord Rutherford, there emerged the notion that atoms were not simple but complex, and, moreover, that various radioactive atoms were by nature unstable, releasing energy as they disintegrated. The German physicist Max Planck demonstrated in 1900 that energy was emitted or absorbed in specific and discrete units or bundles, each called a quantum; moreover, energy was not emitted smoothly and continuously as previously thought, nor was it as distinguishable from matter as once supposed. In 1913, the Danish physicist Niels Bohr postulated an atom consisting of a nucleus of protons surrounded by electrically charged units, called electrons, rotating around the nucleus, each in its orbit, like a minuscule solar system.

With radioactivity scientists were being brought back to the idea long rejected, the favored view of the alchemists, that matter was transmutable; in a way undreamed of even by the alchemists, it was convertible into energy. This the German-born Jewish scientific genius Albert Einstein (1879–1955) propounded in a famous formula $e = mc^2$. From his theory of relativity, developed in 1905 and in 1916, emerged also the profoundly revolutionary notion that time, space, and motion were not absolute in character but were all relative to the observer and the observer's own movement in space. In later years, in 1929 and in 1954, Einstein brought together into one common set of laws, as Newton formerly had done, a unified field theory, an explanation of gravitation, electromagnetism, and subatomic behavior. Difficult as it was to grasp, and a great deal was still the subject of scientific controversy, it modified much that had been taken for granted since Newton. The Newtonian world was being replaced by a four-dimensional world, a kind of space-time continuum; and in mathematics, non-Euclidean geometries were being developed. It turned out, too, that neither cause and effect nor time and space nor Newton's law of universal gravitation meant very much in the subatomic world nor indeed in the cosmos when objects moved with the speed of light. It was impossible, as the German scientist Werner Heisenberg demonstrated a little later, in 1927, by his principle of uncertainty, or indeterminacy, to ascertain simultaneously both the position and the velocity of the individual electron. On these foundations established before the First World War there developed the new science of nuclear physics and the tapping of the atom's energy. The atom was soon discovered to be even more complex than conceived of before 1914, and its potentialities even greater.

The step from pure science to philosophy is a long one, but one that many were prepared to take. Not only was the faith in science widespread but it was widely held that science was the only means of certain knowledge, and that anything unknowable to science must remain unknowable forever—a doctrine called agnosticism, or the acknowledgment of ignorance. Herbert Spencer (1820–1903) in England and Ernst Haeckel (1834–1919) in Germany were widely read popularizers of agnosticism; both also pictured a universe governed by Darwinian evolution. For Spencer especially, all philosophy could be unified, organized, and coordinated through the doctrine of evolution; this doctrine he applied not only to all living things but to sociology, government, and economics as well. The evolution of society, he felt, was toward the increasing freedom of the individual, the role of governments being merely to maintain freedom and justice; they were not to interfere with natural social and economic processes, nor to coddle the weak and unfit. Yet, like Darwin himself, Spencer believed that altruism, charity, and good will as individual ethical virtues were themselves useful and laudable products of evolutionary development.

These latter views were not shared by another of the serious writers of the age, also much influenced by evolutionary ideas, the German philosopher Friedrich Nietzsche (1844–1900). More a philosopher of art than of science, and drawing from many intellectual currents of the century, Nietzsche was an unsystematic and unclear thinker to whom it is easy to do less than justice. It is evident, however, that his opinion of mankind was a low one, and that from a background of evolutionary thinking he developed some kind of doctrine of a Superman, a noble being who, in a final triumph of world history, should issue from, lead, dominate, and dazzle the multitude. Qualities of humility, patience, brotherly helpfulness, hope, and love, in short the specifically Christian virtues, Nietzsche described as a slave morality concocted by the weak to disarm the strong. Qualities of courage, love of danger, intellectual excellence, and beauty of character he considered much better. Such views, for better or worse, were actually a new form of paganism. Nietzsche was neither much read nor much respected by his contemporaries, who considered him unbalanced or even insane; but he nevertheless, as a philosopher should, expressed with unshrinking frankness many ideas implied in the outlook of his day.

As in the sciences, so in works of creative imagination—pure literature and the fine arts—the changes at the dawn of the twentieth century ushered in the contemporary age. Some writers, like Zola in France or Ibsen in Scandinavia, turned to the portrayal of social problems, producing a realistic literature dealing with industrial strife, strikes, prostitution, divorce, or insanity. Freudian and other views of psychology slowly made themselves felt in works of fiction; the new novels were often more lifelike than the old even though they added little to one's faith in human nature. The arts followed the intellectual developments of the age, reflecting, as they do today, attitudes of relativism, irrationalism, social determinism, and interest in the subconscious. On the other hand, never had artist and society been so far apart. The painter, Gauguin, an extreme case, fled to the South Seas, went primitive, and reveled in the stark violence of tropical colors. Others became absorbed in technicalities or mere capricious self-expression. Art at its extreme fringe became incomprehensible, and the average man was deprived of a means (as old as the cave paintings of the Stone Age) of perceiving, seizing, and enjoying the world about him. After the First World War, and on into the present, the same trends of subjectivism in the arts attracted a wider, if still skeptical, audience. People read books without punctuation (or with peculiar punctuation), listened to music called atonal and deliberately composed for effects of discord and dissonance, and studied intently abstract or "nonobjective" paintings and sculpture to which the artists themselves often refused even to give titles.

The problem of communication remained serious. The arts suffered from the specialization of the modern world. The artist was not thought of as a collective spokesman or creator of something for common use but as a specialist plying his own trade and pursuing his own concerns. Society itself was divided into busy, self-centered groups, unable to communicate except on superficial matters, and hence in the long run less able to work in common.

The Churches and
the Modern Age

Religion, too, was displaced. It was now a long time since almost everyone had looked to religion for guidance. But religion was more threatened after 1860 or 1870 than ever in the past, because never before had science, or philosophies drawing upon science, addressed themselves so directly to the existence of life and of man. Never before had so many of the fundamental premises of traditional religion been questioned or denied. Darwinian evolution had challenged the traditional picture of Creation, and anthropologists had questioned the uniqueness of the most sacred Christian tenets. There developed also the "higher" criticism of the Bible, an effort to apply to the Scriptures the techniques of scholarship long applied to secular documents, to incorporate archeological discoveries, and to reconstruct a naturalistic, historical account of ancient religious times. The movement, going back at least to the seventeenth century,[36] now took on significant proportions and was applied both to the Old Testament and the New. In the case of the Old Testament the patient scrutiny of style and language cast doubt on the validity of certain prophecies; and in the New the inconsistencies of the several Gospel sources were made patent. The German theologian David Friedrich Strauss (1808–1874), one such critical scholar, was the author of a widely discussed *Life of Jesus,* in which many miraculous and supernatural episodes were reverently but firmly explained away as "myth." The sensitive French historian and man of letters Ernest Renan (1823–1892) in a somewhat similar vein wrote on the origins of Christianity and on the life of

[36] See p. 314.

Painting #198 (Autumn) *by Vasily Kandinsky (Russian, then in Germany and France, 1866–1944)*
What is loosely called modern art dates from the early twentieth century. Where the Impressionists continued to represent objects while losing interest in objective representation, in the next generation many painters gave up the objects themselves, thus launching various nonobjective or "abstract" styles. This "Painting #198" was done in 1914 by Kandinsky, one of the first practitioners of purely abstract painting. Since it is meant to convey color, without reference to physical objects, it does not lend itself to the kind of reproduction here used. Color at this time had a deep and vital meaning for Kandinsky, though he later turned to the invention of geometric or linear images as well. For the commonly perceived world of external objects he substituted a universe of his own. "To create a body of artistic work," he said, "is to create a world." Or again, speaking of nature, "it is not enough to see it; we must live it." With such sentiments Kandinsky shared in the antirationalist or vitalistic philosophies of the period. Courtesy of The Solomon R. Guggenheim Museum. Permission A.D.A.G.P. 1970 by French Reproduction Rights, Inc.

ancient Israel. The ordinary person's long-established articles of faith were being further undermined. Moreover, the whole tenor of the time, its absorption in material progress, likewise kept people away from church; and the wholesale uprooting, the movement from country to city, often broke religious ties.

The Protestant churches were less successful than the Catholic in protecting their membership from the disintegrating effects of the age. Church attendance among Protestants became increasingly casual, and the doctrines set forth in sermons seemed increasingly remote. Protestant laymen traditionally trusted their own private judgment and regarded their clergy as their own agents, not as authoritative teachers placed above them. Protestants also had always set special emphasis on the Bible as the source of religious belief; and as doubts accumulated on the literal truth of Biblical narratives there seemed no other source on which to rely.

Protestants tended to divide between modernists and fundamentalists. The fundamentalists, as they were called in the United States, in an effort to defend the literal word of Scripture were often obliged to deny the most indubitable findings of science. The modernists were willing enough to be scientific and to interpret much of the Bible as allegory, but only with difficulty could they recapture any spirituality or urgent feeling of Christian truth. Most Protestant churches were slow to face the social problems and wholesale injustices produced by the economic system, though a group of "Christian socialists" developed, notably within the Church of England. And as education and the care of orphans, aged, sick, and insane persons passed to the state, Protestant groups had less to do in the relief of suffering and upbringing of the young. Protestantism, to the regret of many Protestants, became increasingly a customary observance by people whose minds were elsewhere. Not until after the First World War could a strong Protestant revival be discerned, with a reaffirmation of basic doctrines by thinkers like Karl Barth, and a movement on the part of divergent Protestant churches to combine.

The Roman Catholic Church proved more resistant to the trends of the age. We have seen how Pope Pius IX (1846–1878), after being driven from Rome by

Composition with the Ace of Clubs *by Georges Braque (French, 1882–1963)*
This painting, of about the same date as the preceding one by Kandinsky, represents a quite different direction in modern art. It is one of the great works of the Cubist movement. Where the Kandinsky painting presents color without line and seeks to express life and feeling, Braque and the Cubists break up the visual world into lines and planes, in a more analytic and intellectual fashion. Objects recede or disappear, not into an impressionist blur nor a burst of color, but into a carefully contrived and almost mathematical pattern. In the new movement, it made sense to "see" things from more than one direction at a time, as the mind conceives them. Perception is not enough; as Braque once wrote, "the senses deform, but the mind forms." In any case, innovative artists after 1900 turned away from the main concerns of Western painting since the Renaissance: realistic representation of persons, places or objects; natural color; illusionistic three-dimensional volume; a humanly occupied space with perspectives, horizons, location and distance as seen by the eye from a single fixed viewpoint. Courtesy of the Musée d'Art Moderne, Paris (Service Photographique). Permission A.D.A.G.P. 1970 by French Reproduction Rights, Inc.

republicans in 1848, gave up his inclinations to liberalism.[37]   In 1864, in the *Syllabus of Errors*, he denounced as erroneous a long list of widely current ideas, including the faith in rationalism and science, and he vigorously denied that the head of the church "should reconcile and align himself with progress, liberalism, and modern civilization."   The *Syllabus* was in form a warning to Catholics, not a matter of dogma incumbent upon them to believe.   In dogma, the Immaculate Conception of the Virgin Mary was announced as dogmatic truth in 1854; a century later, in 1950, the bodily assumption of Mary into heaven was proclaimed.   Thus the Catholic church reaffirmed in a skeptical age, and against Christian modernists, its faith in the supernatural and miraculous.

Pius IX also convened an ecumenical church council (the first since the Council of Trent) which met at the Vatican in 1870.   The Vatican Council proclaimed the dogma of papal infallibility, which holds that the pope, when speaking *ex cathedra* on matters of faith and morals, speaks with a final and supernatural authority which no Catholic may question or reject.   The Vatican Council, and the acceptance of papal infallibility by Catholics, was only the climax of centuries of development within the church.   In brief, as the world grew more national, Catholicism became more international.   As state sovereignty and secularism grew, Catholic clergy looked increasingly to the spiritual powers of Rome for protection against alien forces.   Much in the past three hundred years had made Catholics distrustful of their own governments or of non-Catholics in their midst—the Protestantism and the state churches of the sixteenth century, the Jansenist movement of the seventeenth, the anticlericalism of enlightened despotism in the eighteenth, the hostility to the church shown by the French Revolution, and by liberalism, republicanism, and socialism in the nineteenth century.   By 1870 the net effect was to throw Catholics into the arms of the Holy See.   Ultramontanism, the unconditional acceptance of papal jurisdiction, prevailed over the old Gallican and other national tendencies within the church.

In 1870, while the 600 prelates of the Vatican Council were sitting, the new Italian state unceremoniously entered and annexed the city of Rome.[38]   The pope's temporal power thus disappeared.   It is now widely agreed that with the loss of local temporal interests the spiritual hold of the papacy on Catholics throughout the world has been enhanced.   The popes long refused, however, to recognize the loss of Rome; and each pope in turn, from 1870 to 1929, adopted a policy of self-imprisonment in the Vatican grounds.   By the Lateran treaty of 1929 the papacy finally recognized the Italian state, and Italy conceded, along with much else, the existence of a Vatican City about a square mile in area, as an independent state not legally within Italy at all.   The papacy thus gained that independence from national or secular authority deemed necessary by Catholics to the performance of its role.

Pius IX's successor, Leo XIII (1878–1903), carried on the counteroffensive against irreligion, and instituted a revival of medieval philosophy as represented by Thomas Aquinas.[39]   But Leo XIII is chiefly remembered for formulating Catholic social

[37] See p. 526.
[38] See p. 574.
[39] See pp. 38–41.

doctrine, especially in the encyclical *Rerum Novarum* ("of modern things") of 1891, to which subsequent pontiffs have adhered, and from which various movements of Catholic socialism are derived. *Rerum Novarum* upheld private property as a natural right, within the limits of justice; but it criticized capitalism for the poverty, insecurity, and even degradation in which many of the laboring classes were left. It declared that much in socialism was Christian in principle; but it criticized socialism insofar as (like Marxism) it was materialistic and antireligious. The pope therefore recommended that Catholics, if they wished, form socialist parties of their own, and that Catholic workingmen form labor unions under Catholic auspices. Since the 1830s there had been individual Catholics and Catholic clergy who were socialists, or at least severe critics of the then emerging social order; these were encouraged by the encyclical of 1891, and Catholic (or Christian, as they were often called) socialist parties and labor unions began to appear at the turn of the century. The Roman church thus undertook to free itself from dependency upon capitalism. At the same time it took steps to insure that a future society, if socialist, might be Catholic also.

The next pope, Pius X (1903–1914), stamped out "modernism," or the belief that the church should modify its basic doctrines, to make them consistent with modern science. Modernism in this sense, defined as heresy in 1907, has disappeared among Catholics; but, since much of modern science is declared to be irrelevant to spiritual truth, Catholics have generally been able to embrace such scientific ideas as they wished. The church, as an organized institution, undertook to emancipate itself from science as it did from capitalism and from non-Catholic socialism, marking out instead a way of its own, and never surrendering its ancient position, much battered by the secularism of modern times, that all worldly concerns should be subordinated to a spiritual authority, transmitted from Christ himself, and exercised by a Catholic hierarchy headed by the bishop of Rome.

As for Judaism, the Jews were a small minority, but their condition had always been a kind of barometer reflecting changes in the atmosphere of Europe as a whole. In the nineteenth century the basic trend was toward "emancipation" and "assimilation." Science and secularism had the same dissolving effect upon Orthodox Judaism as upon traditional Christianity. Reform Judaism grew up as the Jewish counterpart to "modernism" in other faiths. Individual Jews increasingly gave up their old distinctive Jewish way of life. In society at large, the prevalence of liberalism allowed them to act as citizens and to enter business or the professions like everybody else. Jews were thus freed from old legal discriminations that had been imposed on them for centuries.

Toward the end of the century two tendencies, counter to assimilation, became evident. One, a cultural and political nationalism, originated with Jews themselves, some of whom feared an assimilation that would lead to a loss of Jewish identity and perhaps even the disappearance of Judaism itself. The other countertendency, or barrier to assimilation, was the rise of anti-Semitism, noticeable in many quarters by 1900. Racist theories, dislike for Jewish competitors in business and the professions, socialist scorn for Jewish capitalists like the Rothschilds, upper-class fears of Jewish revolutionaries and Marxists, together with a growth of ethnic nationalism, which held that France should be purely French and Latin, Germany purely German and Nordic, or Russia purely Russian and Slav, all combined to raise an anti-Semitic hue and cry. In Russia there were actual pogroms, or massacres of Jews. In France the Dreyfus case, dragged out from 1894 to 1906, revealed unsuspected depths of anti-Semitic fury. Many Jews were forced by such hostility into a new sense of Jewish identity. The Hungarian-born Jewish journalist Theodor Herzl was one. Appalled by the turbulence of the Dreyfus affair in civilized France, which he observed first-hand as a reporter for a Vienna newspaper, he founded modern, or political, Zionism when he organized the first international Zionist congress at Basel in 1897. Zionists hoped to establish a Jewish state in Palestine, in which Jews from all the world might find refuge, although there had been no independent Jewish state there since ancient times.

Many Jews, wishing civic assimilation yet despairing of obtaining it, began to sympathize with the Jewish nationalist movement, looking to Zionism and a Jewish renascence as a way to maintain their own dignity. Others insisted that Judaism was a religious faith, not a nationality by itself; that Jews and non-Jews within the same country shared in exactly the same nationality, citizenship, and political and social outlook. Liberals and democrats were of the same opinion. On the integration of Jews into the larger community the traditions of the Enlightenment, the American and French revolutions, the empire of Napoleon I, and the liberalism of the nineteenth century all agreed.

77
The Waning of Classical Liberalism

The net effect of the political, economic, and intellectual trends described above was twofold. There was a continued advance of much that was basic to liberalism and at the same time a weakening of the grounds on which liberalism had firmly rested ever since the seventeenth and eighteenth centuries. A third effect might be noted too. Even where the essentials of liberalism persisted, in program and doctrine it underwent important changes; liberalism persisted but the classical type of liberalism was in eclipse.

Classical liberalism, the liberalism in its heyday in the nineteenth century, went back at least as far as John Locke in the seventeenth century and the philosophes of the eighteenth and found its highest nineteenth-century expression in the writings of men like John Stuart Mill and in the political outlook of men like William Gladstone. Classical liberalism had as its deepest principle the liberty of the individual person.[40] Man, each man or specimen of mankind, according to liberals, was or could become a free-standing human being. He was not a class-man, nor a race-man, nor a church-man, nor a nation-man, nor a state-man. Morally, he was independent of all such things; he did not owe his nature or being to any of them; he did not have such-and-such ideas because he belonged to such-and-such a group. He was capable of the free use of reason or of thinking things out independently, apart from his own

[40] See pp. 473–474.

interests, prejudices, or subconscious drives. And, since this was so, people of different interests could reasonably and profitably discuss their differences, make compromises, and reach solutions by peaceable agreement. It was because they thought all men potentially reasonable that liberals favored education. They opposed all imposition of force upon the individual, from physical torture to mental indoctrination.

In religion, liberals thought each individual should adopt any faith or no faith as he chose, and that churches and clergy should play little or no part in public affairs. In politics, they thought that governments should be constitutional and limited in power, with individuals governing themselves through their chosen representatives, with issues presented, discussed, and decided by the use of intelligence, both by the voters in election campaigns and by elected deputies in parliamentary debate. The will of a majority, or larger number of individuals, was taken as decisive, with the understanding that the minority might become a majority in its turn through individual changes of opinion. At first distrustful of democracy, fearing the excesses of popular rule, and eager to limit political power and the suffrage to the propertied classes, in the course of the nineteenth century liberals had accepted the democratic principle of universal manhood suffrage. In economics, liberals thought of the whole world as peopled by individuals doing business with one another—buying and selling, borrowing and lending, hiring and firing—without interference from governments and without regard to religion or politics, both of which were thought to impose superficial differences upon the underlying uniformity of mankind. The practical consequences of liberalism were toleration, constitutionalism, laissez faire, free trade, and an international or nonnational economic system. It was thought that all peoples would progress to these same ends.

There never was a time, even in one country, when all liberal ideas were simultaneously triumphant. Pure liberalism has never existed except as a doctrine. Advancing in one way, liberalism would be blocked or reversed in another. On the whole, Europe before 1914 was predominantly liberal. But signs of the wane of liberalism set in clearly about 1880; some, like the changing conceptions of human behavior, have already been mentioned.

The free economy produced many hardships. The workingman tossed by the ups and downs of a labor market, the producer tossed by those of a world commodity market, alike clamored for protection against exposure. A severe depression in 1873 sent prices and wages into collapse, and the economy did not fully recover until 1893. European farmers, both small French farm owners and big Junker landlords of East Germany, demanded tariff protection: they could not compete with the American Middle West or the steppes of South Russia, both opened up by rail and steamship, and both of which after 1870 poured their cereals at low prices into Europe. The revival of tariffs, and decline of free trade, very marked in Europe about 1880, thus began with the protection of agricultural interests. Industry soon demanded the same favors. In Germany the Junkers and the rising Rhineland industrialists joined forces in 1879 to extort a tariff from Bismarck. The French in 1892 adopted a high tariff to shelter both manufacturing and agricultural interests. The United States, rapidly industrializing, also put up protective tariffs beginning in the 1860s, the earliest of all.

The Industrial Revolution was now definitely at work in other countries than Great Britain. There was an increasing resistance to buying manufactures from England, selling only raw materials and foodstuffs in return. Everywhere there was a revival of the arguments of the German economist Friedrich List, who a half-century before, in his *National System of Political Economy* (1840), had branded free trade as a system mainly advantageous to the British and declared that no country could become strong, independent, or even fully civilized if it remained a semi-rustic supplier of unfinished goods.[41] With Germany, the United States, and Japan manufacturing for export, a nationalist competition for world markets set in, contributing also to the drive for colonies and the phenomena of imperialism described in the next chapter. The new imperialism was another sign of the waning of liberalism, which had been largely indifferent to colonies.

In all these respects the division between politics and economics, postulated by liberals, began to fade. A kind of neomercantilism arose, recalling the attempts of governments in the seventeenth and eighteenth centuries to subordinate economic activity to political ends. A better term is economic nationalism, which became noticeable by 1900. Nations struggled to better themselves by tariffs, by trade rivalries, and by internal regulation, without regard to the effect upon other nations. And for the individual worker or businessman also, in purely economic matters, it now made a great difference to what nation he belonged, by what government he was backed, and under what laws he lived.

It was of course to protect themselves against insecurity and abuse as individuals that workers formed labor unions. It was likewise to protect themselves against the uncertainties of uncontrolled markets that business interests began to merge, to concentrate in large corporations, or to form monopolies, trusts, or cartels. The rise of big business and organized labor undermined the theory and practice of individual competition to which classical liberalism had been attached. Organized labor, socialist parties, universal manhood suffrage, and a sensitivity to social distress all obliged political leaders to intervene increasingly in economic matters. Factory codes became more detailed and better enforced. Social insurance, initiated by Bismarck, spread to other countries. Governments regulated the purity of food and drugs. The social service state developed, a state assuming responsibility for the social and economic welfare of the mass of its own subjects. The "new" liberalism, that of the Liberals in England of the David Lloyd George era, of the Republican President Theodore Roosevelt and the Democratic President Woodrow Wilson in the United States, accepted the enlarged role of the government in social and economic matters. Both Theodore Roosevelt and Wilson, and others, sought also to reestablish economic competition by government action against monopolies and trusts. The new liberals

[41]See pp. 480–481.

were generally less well disposed toward business than toward workingmen and the depressed classes; the improvement of the worker's lot would vindicate the old humanitarian concern of liberalism with the dignity and worth of the individual person. The welfare state, remote as it was from the older liberalism, was the direction taken by the new liberals. Others, liberal and otherwise, viewed with concern the growing power of governments and centralized authority and were apprehensive for individual liberties.

Liberalism, both old and new, was undermined also by many developments in the field of thought described earlier in this chapter—Darwinian evolution, the new psychology, trends in philosophy and the arts. Paradoxically, this great age of science found that man was not a rational animal. Darwinian theory implied that man was merely a highly evolved organism whose faculties were merely adaptations to an environment. Psychology seemed to teach that what was called reason was often only rationalization, or a finding of alleged "reasons" to justify material wants or emotional and unconscious needs, and that conscious reflection dominated only a narrow part of human behavior. Ideas themselves were said to be the products of conditioning. There were English ideas or Anglo-Saxon ideas, or bourgeois or progressive or reactionary ideas. Politically, it began to be felt that parties or nations with conflicting interests could never reasonably agree on a program common to both, since neither could ever get beyond the limitations of its own outlook. It became common to dismiss the arguments of an adversary without further thought and without any expectation that thought could overcome difficulties. This insidious "anti-intellectualism" was destructive to liberal principles. If, because of prior conditioning, it was impossible for anyone to change his mind, then there was no hope of settling matters by persuasion.

From the view that man was not essentially a rational being, which in itself was only a scientific attempt at a better understanding of human behavior, it was but a short step deliberately to reject reason and to emphasize and cultivate the irrational, to stress the will, intuition, impulse, and emotion, and to place a new value on violence and conflict. A philosophy of "realism," a kind of unrealistic faith in the constructive value of struggle and a tough-minded rejection of ideas and ideals, spread. It was not new. Marxism, since the 1840s, had taught that class war, latent or open, was the motivating power of history. Schopenhauer earlier in the century had written that the underlying reality of the universe was a blind, instinctual, dynamic will to survive.[42] In this age Nietzsche rejected the ordinary virtues in favor of courage and daring; the Social Darwinists glorified the successful and the dominant in all phases of human activity as the "fit" in the perpetual struggle for existence. Other thinkers embraced a frank irrationalism. Among these may be mentioned Georges Sorel, the philosopher of syndicalism, who, in his *Reflections on Violence* in 1908, declared that violence was good irrespective of the end accomplished (so much

---

[42] See p. 535.

did he hate existing society), and that workingmen should be kept alert in the class war through believing in the "myth" of a future general strike, even though such a strike, with its attendant débacle of bourgeois civilization, was in fact known to be only a "myth." The function of thought, in this philosophy of the social myth, was to keep people agitated and excited and ready for action, not to achieve any correspondence with rational or objective truth. Such ideas passed into the fascism and other activist movements of the twentieth century.

Thus the end of the nineteenth century, the greatest age of peace in Europe's history, abounded in philosophies glorifying struggle. Men who had never heard a shot fired in anger solemnly announced that world history moved forward by violence and antagonism. They said not merely that struggle existed (which would have been a purely factual statement) but that struggle was a positive good through which progress was to be accomplished. The popularity of struggle was due not only to the intellectuals but in part to actual historical events. People remembered that before 1871 certain weighty questions had been settled by force, that the movements of social revolution in 1848 and in the Paris Commune of 1871 had been put down by the military, and that the unity of Italy and Germany, as well as of the United States, had been confirmed by war. In addition, after 1871, all continental European states maintained large standing armies, the largest ever maintained until then in time of peace.

In economic and political matters, even in England, the homeland of liberalism, there were numerous signs between 1900 and 1914 that the older liberalism was on the wane. Joseph Chamberlain led a movement to return to tariff protection (to repeal, so to speak, the repeal of the Corn Laws); it failed at the time, but was strong enough to disorient the Conservative party in 1906. The Liberal party abandoned its traditional laissez-faire policy in sponsoring the labor legislation of the years following 1906. The new Labour party required its members in Parliament to vote as directed by the party, thus initiating a system of party solidarity, eventually copied by others, that hardened the lines of opposition, denied that individuals should freely change sides, and hence reduced the practical significance of parliamentary discussion. The Irish nationalists had long used unparliamentary methods; in 1914, when Parliament at last enacted Irish home rule, the anti-Irish and Conservative interests prepared to resist parliamentary action by force. The suffragettes, as women pioneering for woman suffrage were called, despairing of ever getting the men to listen to reason, resorted to amazingly "un-English" and unreasonable arguments. They chained themselves to public buildings, smashed the store fronts in Bond Street, threw acids into mailboxes, and broke porcelains in the British Museum; when arrested they went on hunger strikes threatening self-starvation, to which the police replied by "forcible feeding" through tubes lowered into the ladies' stomachs. And in 1911 and 1912 great railway and coal strikes disclosed the sheer power of organized labor.

Still, it is the persistence of liberalism rather than its wane that should be emphasized at the close of a chapter on European civilization in the half-century before 1914. Tariffs existed, but goods still circulated freely in world trade.

Nationalism was heightened, but there was nothing like totalitarianism. Racist ideas were in the air, but they had little political importance. Anti-Semitism was sometimes vocal; but all governments except the Russian protected the rights of Jews, and the years from 1848 to 1914 were in fact the great period of Jewish integration into general society. The laissez-faire state was disappearing, but social legislation continued the humanitarian strain that had always been the essence of liberalism. A few advanced revolutionaries preached social catastrophism, but social democrats and laboring men were overwhelmingly revisionist, loyal to parliamentary procedures and to their existing states. Doctrinaires exalted the grim beauty of war, but all governments down to 1914 tried to prevent war among the great powers. And there was still a supreme faith in progress.

ADVENTVS·AVGVSTI·IN·AEGYPTVM
OB·APERIVNDAM·FOSSAM·SVEZIANAM
MDCCCLXIX

XV: EUROPE'S WORLD

SUPREMACY

A century ago the great segments of mankind still lived apart. China was a world in itself, India a world, Black Africa a world, Islam a world, penetrating, to be sure, each of the three others. Europe and its American offshoot formed the Western world. Each of these several worlds had developed its own way of life, most deeply differentiated by the religion it had long ago adopted, in the millennium running from Confucius and Buddha through Jesus to Mohammed. Within each of these worlds there was much coming and going—Moslems, for example, could move from Morocco to the East Indies—but each world remained mysterious and unknown to the others. It was the European white men who first brought them all into an interconnected society.

European civilization, as described in the last chapter, spread to and influenced the whole earth, especially after about 1870. The large nation-states, whose consolidation was traced in the chapter before last, gained empires for themselves in Africa, Asia, and the islands of the sea. In opposition to these empires, non-European and subject peoples began to assert ideas learned from Europe—ideas of liberty, democracy, independence, nationalism, sovereignty, and of an anticapitalism that might pass easily into socialism. They brought into Asia, and more slowly into Africa, the substance of the European revolutions of 1789 and 1848. European history broadened out into the history of the world.

The emergence of an interrelated world civilization was obviously a fact of momentous import. But the process was barely begun, and it created innumerable dislocations and difficulties. Tribal societies and complex old civilizations were alike penetrated by the West. Modern science, modern weapons of warfare, modern machine industry, modern communications, modern capitalism and wage labor, modern forms of taxation, law enforcement, and debt-collecting, modern practices in medicine and sanitation (along with certain "modern" diseases such as syphilis or alcoholism) were suddenly pressed in an overwhelming mass upon bewildered peoples who for generations could neither resist them, adjust to them, nor control them.

All peoples were drawn into a world economy and a world market. But it was the Europeans who reaped the reward in the form of rising material standards of living. In India, China, or Africa the native industries often suffered, and many people found it harder than ever to subsist even at a low level. The building of railways in China, for example, threw boatmen, carters, or innkeepers out of work. In India, the hand spinners and weavers of cotton could not compete in their own villages with the machine-made products of Lancashire. In parts of Africa, native tribes which had lived by owning herds of cattle, moving from place to place to obtain grazing lands, found white farmers or plantation or mine owners occupying their country and were often forced by the white man's law to give up their migratory habits. Peoples of all races began to produce for export—rubber, raw cotton, jute, copra, tin, gold—and hence were exposed to the rise and fall of world prices. A depression tended to become a world depression, dragging all down alike.

Neither the world economy, nor the world market, nor the international investment of capital or movement of people, nor the spread and exchange of scientific or technical or military or medical ideas, absolutely presupposed any one kind of political system or domination by any one part of the world. Presumably, the tendencies toward a world-wide civilization will continue despite all political changes. In the period from 1870 to 1914 they went along with imperialism, which may be briefly defined as the government of one people by another. European imperialism (including that of the United States and Japan) was the first phase in the spread of the industrial and scientific civilization which originated in Europe's "inner zone."[1] That it was not the last phase became clear as the twentieth century unfolded. The subordinated peoples, forcibly introduced to the West by imperialism, came to feel a need for modernizing and industrializing their own countries and for the aid of European or American science, skill and capital; but they wished to get rid of imperialists, govern themselves, and control the conditions under which modernization and borrowing should take place. The present chapter deals only with the imperialist phase.

 [1]See p. 608.

uropean civilization had always shown a tendency to expand. In the Middle Ages Latin Christendom spread by conquest and conversion to include the whole area from Spain to Finland. Then came the age of overseas discoveries and the founding of colonial empires, whose struggles filled the seventeenth and eighteenth centuries, and of which the Europeanization of the Americas was the most far-reaching consequence. At the same time European culture spread among the upper classes of Russia. The defeat of Napoleon left only one of the old colonial empires standing in any strength, namely, the British. For sixty years after 1815 there were no significant colonial rivalries. In many circles there was an indifference to overseas empire. Under principles of free trade, it was thought unnecessary to exercise political influence in areas in which one did business. Actually, in these years, the French moved into Algeria, the British strengthened their Indian empire, the Dutch developed Java and the neighboring islands more intensively, and the Western powers "opened" Japan and began to penetrate China. But there was no overt conflict among Europeans, and no systematic program, doctrine or "ism."

Rather suddenly, about 1870 or 1880, colonial questions came again to the fore. In the short space of two decades, by 1900, the advanced countries partitioned most of the earth among themselves. A world map by 1900 showed their possessions in some eight or ten colors.

The New Imperialism

The new imperialism differed both economically and politically from the colonialism of earlier times. The older empires had been maritime and mercantile. The European trader, in India, Java, or Canton, had simply purchased the wares brought to him by native merchants as produced by native methods. He operated on a kind of cash-and-carry basis. European governments had had no territorial ambitions beyond the protection of way stations and trading centers. To these generalizations America had been an exception; it had neither native states which Europeans respected, nor native industries in which Europeans were interested, and Europeans therefore developed territorial claims, and invested capital and brought in their own methods of production and management, most especially in the then booming sugar islands of the West Indies.[2]

Under the new imperialism Europeans were by no means content simply to purchase what native merchants provided. They wanted goods of a kind or in a quantity that preindustrial handicraft methods could not supply. They moved into the "backward" countries more thoroughly. They invested capital in them, setting up mines, plantations, docks, warehouses, factories, refineries, railroads, river steamships, banks. They built offices, homes, hotels, clubs, and cool mountain resorts suitable for white men in the tropics. Taking over the productive life of the

[2]See p. 268.

country, they transformed large elements of the local population into the wage employees of foreign owners and so introduced the class problems of industrial Europe in a form accentuated by racial difference. Or they lent money to native rulers—the khedive of Egypt, the shah of Persia, the emperor of China—to enable them to hold up their tottering thrones or simply to live with more pleasure and magnificence than they could pay for from their usual revenues. Europeans thus developed a huge financial stake in governments and economic enterprises outside the pale of Western civilization.

To secure these investments, and for other reasons, in contrast to what had happened under the older colonialism, the Europeans now aspired to political and territorial domination. Some areas became outright "colonies," directly governed by white men. Others became "protectorates": here the native chief, sultan, bey, rajah, or prince was maintained and guaranteed against internal upheaval or external conquest. A European "resident" or "commissioner" usually told him what to do. In other regions, as in China or Persia, where no single European state could make good its claims against the others, they arranged to divide the country into "spheres of influence," each European power having advisory privileges and investment and trade opportunities within its own sphere. The sphere of influence was the vaguest of all forms of imperial control; supposedly, it left the country independent.

An enormous differential opened up, about 1875, between the power of European and non-European states. Queen Elizabeth had dealt with the Great Mogul with genuine respect. Even Napoleon had pretended to regard the shah of Persia as an equal. Then came the Industrial Revolution in Europe, iron and steel ships, heavier naval guns, more accurate rifles. Democratic and nationalistic movements produced large and solid European peoples, united in the service of their governments as no "backward" people ever was. Seemingly endless wealth, with modern administration, allowed governments to tax, borrow and spend almost without limit. The civilized states loomed as enormous power complexes without precedent in the world's history. At the same time it so happened that all the principal non-European empires were in decay. They were receiving a minimum of support from their own subjects. As in the eighteenth century the disintegration of the Mogul empire had enabled the British to take over in India,[3] so in the nineteenth century the decrepitude of the sultan of Turkey, the sultan of Zanzibar, the shah of Persia, the emperor of China, and the shogun of Japan made European intervention easy. Only the Japanese were able to revolutionize their government in time to ward off imperialist penetration. Even the Japanese, thanks to early treaties, remained unfree to determine their own tariff policy until after 1900.[4]

So great was the difference in the sheer mechanics of power that usually a mere show of force allowed the white men to impose their will. A garrison of only 75,000 white troops long held India for the British. Numerous sporadic little wars were constantly fought—Afghan wars, Burmese wars, Zulu wars—which passed unnoticed by Europeans in the home country and were no more like true war than the operations

[3] See pp. 289–290, 363.
[4] See p. 598.

of the United States army against the Indians of the western plains. The Spanish-American War of 1898 and the Boer War of 1899 were also wars of colonial type, fought between entirely unequal parties. Often a show of naval strength was enough. It was the classic age of the punitive or minatory bombardment. We have seen how the American Commodore Perry threatened to bombard Tokyo in 1854.[5] In 1856 the British consul at Canton, to punish acts of violence against Europeans, called upon the local British admiral to bombard that Chinese city. In 1863 the British bombarded Satsuma, and in 1864 an allied force including Americans bombarded Choshu—precipitating revolution in Japan.[6] Similarly, Alexandria was bombarded in 1882 and Zanzibar in 1896. The usual consequence was that the local ruler signed a treaty, reorganized his government, or accepted a European (usually British) adviser.

Behind the aggressiveness lay many pressures. Europeans could not maintain, for themselves in Europe, the style of life to which they had become accustomed, except by bringing the rest of the world within their orbit. But many other needs felt in Europe drove men into distant and savage places. Catholic and Protestant groups sent growing numbers of missionaries to regions increasingly remote and wild. The missionaries sometimes got into trouble with the natives; sometimes they were killed; and while the missionaries themselves might regard these as normal risks, and even disapprove of political intervention, public opinion in the home countries, soon learning of such events by ocean cable, might clamor for political action to suppress such vestiges of barbarism. Similarly, science required scientific expeditions for geographical exploration, or for botanical, zoölogical, or mineral discoveries or for astronomical or meteorological observations. Wealthy persons traveled more, now that travel was so easy; they hunted tigers or elephants, or simply went to see sights. It seemed only reasonable, at the close of the nineteenth century, that all civilized persons wherever they might choose to go should enjoy the security of life and limb and the orderly procedures that only European supervision could provide.

Economically, European life required material goods, many of which only tropical regions could supply. Even the working classes now drank tea or coffee every day. After the American Civil War Europe relied for its cotton increasingly on Africa and the East. Rubber and petroleum became staple needs. The lowly jute, which grew only in India, was used to make burlap, twine, carpets, and the millions of jute bags employed in commerce. The lordly coconut tree had innumerable common uses, which led to its intensive cultivation in the Dutch Indies. Various parts of it could be eaten, or manufactured into bags, brushes, cables, ropes, sails, or doormats or converted into copra and coconut oil, which in turn went into the making of candles, soap, margarine, and many other products.

Industrial countries also attempted to sell their own products, and one of the reasons given by imperialists, in support of imperialism, was the urgent necessity of

[5] See pp. 595, 597.
[6] See pp. 505, 598–600.

finding new markets. The industrialization of Germany, the United States, Japan, and other countries, after about 1870, meant that they competed with each other and with Great Britain for foreign trade. The slowly declining price level after 1873 meant that a business firm had to sell more goods to turn over the same amount of money. Competition was more intense. The advanced countries raised tariffs to keep out each other's products. It was therefore argued that each industrial country must develop a colonial empire dependent on itself, an area of "sheltered markets," as the phrase went in England, in which the home country would supply manufactured goods in return for raw materials. The idea was to create a large self-sufficient trading unit, embracing various climates and types of resources, protected if necessary from outside competition by tariffs, guaranteeing a market for all its members, and wealth and prosperity for the home country. This phase of imperialism is often called neomercantilism, since it revived in substance the mercantilism of the eighteenth and earlier centuries.[7]

Purely financial considerations also characterized the new imperialism. Money invested in "backward" countries, by the close of the nineteenth century, brought a higher rate of return than if invested in the more civilized ones. For this there were many reasons, including the cheap labor of non-European regions, the heavy and unsatisfied demand for non-European products, and the greater risk of losses in half-unknown areas where European ideas of law and order did not prevail. By 1900 western Europe and the northeastern United States were equipped with their basic industrial apparatus. Their railway networks and first factories were built. Opportunities for investment in these countries became stabilized. At the same time, these countries themselves accumulated capital seeking an outlet. In the mid-century most exported capital was British-owned. By the close of the century more French, German, American, Dutch, Belgian, and Swiss investors were investing or lending outside their own borders. In 1850, most exported capital went to build up Europe, the United States, Canada, Australia, or the Argentine—the white man's world. By 1900 more of it was going to the backward regions. This capital (unlike much of the capital exported after 1945, which was usually furnished by governments) was the property of small private savers or of large banking combinations. Investors preferred "civilized" political control over the parts of Asia, Africa, or Latin America in which their railroads, mines, plantations, government loans, or other investments were situated. Hence the profit motive, or desire to invest "surplus" capital, promoted imperialism.

This analysis was put forward by critics like the English socialist J. A. Hobson, who wrote an influential book on imperialism in 1903, and later by Lenin, in his *Imperialism, the Highest Stage of World Capitalism*, written in 1916. They ascribed imperialism primarily to the accumulation of surplus capital and condemned it on socialist grounds. Argued Hobson especially, if more of the national income went to workers as wages, and less of it to capitalists as interest and dividends, or if wealthy people were more heavily taxed and the money used for social welfare, there would

[7] See pp. 124–126, 264–269.

be no surplus of capital and no real imperialism. Since the working class, if this were done, would also have more purchasing power, it would be less necessary to look endlessly for new markets outside the country. But the "surplus-capital" explanation of imperialism was not entirely convincing. That investors and exporters were instrumental in the rise of imperialism was of course very true. That imperialism arose essentially from the capitalists' pressure to invest abroad was more doubtful. Perhaps even more basic was Europe's need for imports—only by enormous imports could Europe sustain its dense population, complex industry, and high standard of living. It was the demand for such imports—cotton, cocoa, coffee, copper, or copra drawn from "the colonies"—that made investment in the colonies financially profitable. Moreover, non-Europeans themselves often asked for the capital, glad though the European lenders were to lend it at high rates; in 1890 this might mean merely that a shah or sultan wanted to build himself a new palace, but the need of non-Europeans for Western capital was basic, nor was it to decline as the world became more democratic. Lastly, the imperialism of some countries, notably Russia and Italy, which had little capital and few modern-type capitalists of their own, could not reasonably be attributed to pressure for lucrative foreign investments.

For the British, however, the capitalistic incentive was of great importance. We have seen how the British, in 1914, had $20,000,000,000 invested outside of Great Britain, a quarter of all their wealth.[8] About half, or $10,000,000,000, was invested in the British Empire. Only a tenth of French foreign investments was in French colonies. French investment in the colonial world in general, however, including Egypt, Suez, South Africa, and Asia in addition to the French colonies, amounted to about a fifth of all French foreign investments. Only an infinitesimal fraction of German foreign investment in 1914 was in German colonies, which were of slight value. A fifth of German foreign investments, however, was placed in Africa, Asia, and the Ottoman Empire. These sums are enough to suggest the pressures upon the European governments to assert political influence in Africa, Turkey, or China.

In addition, French investors (including small bourgeois and even affluent peasants) had in 1914 a huge stake in the Russian empire. Russia, an imperial power with respect to adjoining countries in the Balkans and Asia, occupied an almost semicolonial status with respect to western Europe. The tsardom in its last twenty years, not unlike the Ottoman sultanate or the Manchu dynasty, was kept going by foreign loans, predominantly French. The French in 1914 had lent over $2,000,000,000 to Russia, more than to all colonial regions combined. For these huge outlays the motivation was at least as much political as economic. The French government often urged French banks to buy Russian bonds. The aim was not merely to make a profit for bankers and savers, but to build up and hold together a military ally against Germany.

Politics went along with economics in the whole process of imperialist expansion. National security, both political and economic, was as important an aim as the accumulation of private wealth. So, too, was the growing concern in many

[8]See p. 620.

quarters over the economic security and welfare of the working classes. The ideas of the British statesman Joseph Chamberlain (1836–1914) illustrated how these motives entered into imperialist thinking.

Chamberlain, father of Neville Chamberlain who was to be prime minister of Britain in the years just prior to the Second World War, began as a Birmingham manufacturer, the type of man who a generation before would have been a staunch free-trader and upholder of laissez faire. Discarding the old individualism, he came to believe that the community should and could take better care of its members, and, in particular, that the British community (or empire) could advance the welfare of Britons. As mayor of Birmingham, he introduced a kind of municipal socialism, including civic ownership of utilities. As colonial secretary from 1895 to 1903, he preached Britain's need for a great empire in an age of rising international competition—"a great self-sustaining and self-protecting empire" as he said in 1896—a world-wide British trading area whose resources would be developed by British capital and which would give a secure source of raw materials and food, secure markets for exports, and a secure level of profits, wages, and employment.

Chamberlain saw with misgivings the tendencies toward independence in Canada, New Zealand, and the Australian Commonwealth. For these dominions he favored complete self-government, but he hoped that, once assured of virtual independence, they would reknit their ties with each other and with Great Britain. Such a reintegration of the empire he called "imperial federation." Britain and its dominions, in Chamberlain's view, should pool their resources first of all for military defense but also for economic well-being. The dominions had already levied tariffs against British manufactures in order to build up their own. Chamberlain, to favor British exports, urged the dominions to charge a lower duty on British wares than on the same wares coming from foreign countries. To have something in return to offer the dominions Chamberlain even proposed that Great Britain adopt a protective tariff, so that it might then favor Canadian or Australian goods by imposing on them a lower rate. His plan was to bind the empire together by economic bonds, making it a kind of tariff union, or system of "imperial preference." Since Britain imported mainly meat and cereals from the dominions, Chamberlain was obliged to recommend a tariff even upon these—to "tax the people's food," repudiating the very ark of the covenant of Free Trade upon which the British economy had rested for half a century.[9] The proposal was rejected. Chamberlain died in 1914, his goal unaccomplished. But after the First World War the British Empire, or Commonwealth of Nations, followed closely along the lines he had mapped out.[10]

Whether the economic welfare and security of the European working classes was advanced by imperialism is still debated. It is probable that the workingman in western Europe did benefit from imperialism. Socially conservative imperialists were joined in this belief by thinkers of the extreme Left. Marx himself, followed by Lenin, thought that the European worker obtained higher real wages through the inflow of low-priced colonial goods. To Marxists this was unfortunate, for it gave

[9] See pp. 504, 618–619.
[10] See p. 844.

European workers a vested interest in imperialism, made the European proletariat "opportunistic" (i.e., unrevolutionary), and blocked the formation of a true international world proletariat of all races.

Another imperialist argument much heard at the time held that European countries must acquire colonies to which surplus population could migrate without altogether abandoning the native land. It seemed unfortunate, for example, that so many Germans or Italians emigrating to the United States should be lost to the fatherland. This argument was purely specious. No European country after 1870 acquired any colony to which European families in any numbers wished to move. There were not, and never have been, in all tropical Africa, India, and the Far East, more than handfuls of Europeans, almost all transients. The millions who still left Europe, up to 1914, persisted in heading for the Americas, where in the circumstances no European colony could be founded.[11]

The competitive nature of the European state system introduced other almost exclusively political elements. The European states had to guard their security against each other. They had to keep some kind of balance among themselves, in the overseas world as in Europe. Hence, as in the scramble for Africa, one government often hurriedly annexed territory simply for fear that another might do so first. Or again, colonies came to have an intangible but momentous value in symbolism and prestige. To have colonies was a normal criterion of greatness. It was the sign of having arrived as a Great Power. Britain and France had had colonies for centuries. Therefore the new powers formed in the 1860s—Germany, Italy, Japan, and in a sense the United States—had to have colonies also.

Imperialism arose from the commercial, industrial, financial, scientific, political, journalistic, intellectual, religious, and humanitarian impulses of Europe compounded together. It was an outthrust of the whole white man's civilization. It would bring civilization and enlightened living to those who still sat in darkness. Faith in "modern civilization" had become a kind of substitute religion. Imperialism was its crusade.

So the British spoke of the White Man's Burden, the French of their *mission civilisatrice,* the Germans of diffusing *Kultur,* the Americans of the blessings of Anglo-Saxon protection. Social Darwinism and popular anthropology taught that white races were "fitter" or more gifted than colored.[12] Others argued, more reasonably, that the backwardness of non-Europeans was due to historical and hence temporary causes, but that for a long period in the future the civilized whites must keep a guardianship over their darker protégés. In the psychology of imperialism there was much that was not unworthy. Young men of good family left the pleasant lands of Devonshire or Poitou, where, for them, all was temperate, ordered, clean, calm, and congenial, to spend long and lonely years in hot and savage places, sustained by the thought that they were advancing the work of humanity. It was a

[11] See map, p. 614.
[12] See p. 648.

good thing to bring clearer ideas of justice to barbaric peoples, to put down slave-raiding, torture, and famine, to combat degrading superstitions or fight the diseases of neglect and filth. But these accomplishments, however real, went along all too obviously with self-interest and were expressed with unbearable complacency and gross condescension to the larger part of the human race. As Rudyard Kipling wrote in 1899:

> *Take up the White Man's burden—*
> *Send out the best ye breed—*
> *Go bind your sons to exile,*
> *To serve your captives' need;*
> *To wait in heavy harness,*
> *On fluttered folk and wild—*
> *Your new-caught sullen peoples,*
> *Half devil and half child.*

79
The Americas

After the general considerations above, let us turn to each of the earth's great regions in turn.

In America the break-up of the Spanish and Portuguese empires in the first quarter of the nineteenth century, during and after the Napoleonic wars, left the vast tract from Colorado to Cape Horn very unsettled. Most of the people were Indian or a mixture of Indian and white (*mestizo*), with clusters here and there of pure European stock, which the nineteenth-century immigration was greatly to increase.[13] Except in inaccessible spots, the Spanish culture and language predominated. In Brazil the culture was Portuguese, and the country, though independent after 1822, remained a monarchy or "empire" until 1889, when it became a republic. In the former Spanish domains the disappearance of royal control left a large number of flaccid and shifting republics, chronically engaged in border disputes with one another. Fortunately for these republics, at the time of independence in the 1820s, European imperialism was at a low ebb. We have seen how the Congress of Verona considered ways of returning them to Spain but was opposed by Great Britain; and how the United States, in 1823, supplemented the British action by announcing the Monroe Doctrine.[14] For many years no European power took the Monroe Doctrine very seriously. As George Canning, the British foreign minister, noted in 1823, "the doctrine, if such it can be called . . . is absolutely unacceptable to my government and to France." It was British policy, however, largely for commercial reasons, to keep outside influence out of Spanish America. British sea power therefore gave the new republics a chance to grow. Nor was the Monroe Doctrine much liked by the Spanish Americans, who

---

[13] See pp. 114–116.
[14] See pp. 490–492.

674

noted that it proclaimed no bar against the ambitions of the United States. And it was by the United States that one of the new republics was first threatened from the outside.

Mexico, on becoming independent of Spain, reached almost to the Mississippi and the Rocky Mountains. Hardly was it independent when landseekers from the United States swarmed over its northeastern borders. They brought with them their slaves, to grow the cotton so voraciously demanded in industrial England. The Mexican Republic did not allow slavery. The newcomers proclaimed their own republic, which they called Texas. Agitation developed for annexation to the United States. Mexico objected, but in 1845 the United States annexed Texas. A war followed, in which Mexico lost to the United States not only Texas but the whole region from Texas to the California coast. As is usual in such affairs, the loser preserved a longer memory than the winner. It soon seemed only natural in the United States to possess these regions; in Mexico many decades had to pass before the wound was healed. Mexico had lost half its territory within the first generation of its independence. It was argued at the time that the United States had far better facilities than Mexico for civilizing the region.

The next threat to Mexico came from Europe. A certain pretender to government in Mexico, named Miramón, backed by Mexican churchmen and landowners, contracted large loans in Europe on exorbitant terms, the European lenders rightly estimating his credit to be highly unsound. He soon collapsed, though not before seizing certain British properties at the British legation. His successor, the liberal Juarez (a pure-blooded Indian, at least racially "non-European"), repudiated the Miramón loan. European bondholders demanded satisfaction from their governments. The United States was paralyzed by the Civil War. Great Britain, France, and Spain, which had never recognized the Monroe Doctrine, in 1861 sent combined military forces to Vera Cruz. The British proposed seizure of the customs houses in Mexican ports, and appropriation of the customs revenues to pay off the debt (an expedient introduced in China three years before); but the French had more ambitious designs. Unknown both to the British, who wanted only to collect debts, and to the Spanish, who dreamed of setting up a new Bourbon monarchy in Mexico, the Emperor Napoleon III had a secret project for establishing a French satellite state in Mexico, which French capital and exports might subsequently develop. He planned to create a Mexican empire with the Austrian archduke Maximilian as its figurehead emperor. The British and Spanish disapprovingly withdrew their forces. The French army proceeded into the interior. Maximilian reigned for some years, but Napoleon III gradually concluded that conquest of Mexico was impossible, or too expensive. It further appeared, by 1865, that the United States was not going to collapse after all, as expected and even hoped for by the European governing classes. The United States protested strongly to the French government. The French withdrew, Maximilian was captured and shot, and Juarez and the Mexican liberals came back to power.

United States pressure, before 1870, had thus in turn both despoiled and protected the adjoining part of Latin America. This ambivalent situation became characteristic of the New World. As the United States became a great power the Monroe Doctrine became an effective barrier to European territorial ambitions. Latin America never became subject to imperialism as completely as did Asia and Africa. On the other hand, the United States became the imperialist power feared above all others south of the border. It was the *Yanqui* menace, the Colossus of the North.

In the 1870s in the course of its turbulent politics, both natives of Mexico and foreign residents were obliged to pay forced loans to rival leaders. The State Department at Washington demanded that American citizens be reimbursed by the Mexican government. The double standard characteristic of imperialism—one standard for civilized and one for uncivilized states—became clear in the exchange of notes. The Mexican government, now under Porfirio Diaz, attempted to lay down the principle that "foreigners locating in a country accepted the mode of life of the people . . . and participated not only in the benefits of such residence but also in the adversities. Foreigners should enjoy the same guarantees and the same legal protection as natives, but no more." The Mexicans observed that the United States had never recognized the claims of foreigners for losses sustained in its Civil War. The United States, under President Hayes, held on the other hand that citizens of advanced states, operating in more primitive regions, should continue to enjoy the security of property characteristic of their home countries. When on another occasion the United States sent troops to the border, and when the Mexicans objected, the Secretary of State remarked on "the volatile and childish character of these people and their incapacity to treat a general question with calmness and without prejudice." Mexico retorted that the United States had "disregarded all the rules of international law and practice of civilized nations and treated the Mexicans as savages, as Kaffirs of Africa."

It was, in fact, a principle of international law, in the nineteenth century, that civilized states might not intervene in each other's affairs but had the right of intervention in backward countries. In the dispute of 1877 the United States classified Mexico as backward, "volatile and childish." What the Mexicans objected to was being treated like "savages and Kaffirs." They differed on which of the two standards should apply.

*United States
Imperialism in
the 1890s*

The 1890s saw a crescendo of imperialism both in Europe and in the United States. In 1895, in a resounding restatement of the Monroe Doctrine, President Cleveland forbade the British to deal directly with Venezuela in a boundary dispute affecting British Guiana. The British were obliged to accept international arbitration. When, however, the adjacent Colombia faced a revolution in the Isthmus of Panama the United States supported the revolutionaries and, consulting nobody, recognized Panama as an independent republic. Here the United States leased and fortified a Canal Zone, and proceeded to build the Panama Canal. Panama became in effect what Europeans would call a protectorate of the United States.

Meanwhile what was left of the old Spanish American empire, confined to Cuba and Puerto Rico, was agitated by revolutionary disturbances looking to independence. Sympathies in the United States lay with the revolutionaries. Every sign of the new imperialism showed itself unmistakably. Americans had fifty million dollars invested in Cuba. They bought the bonds issued by Cuban revolutionaries in New York. Cuban sugar, whose production was interfered with by political troubles, was necessary to the famed American standard of living. An orderly and amenable Cuba was vital to American strategic interests in the Caribbean, in the soon to be built Canal, and in the Pacific. The barbarity of the Spanish authorities was deplored as an outrage to modern civilization. The newspapers, especially the new "yellow" press, roused the American public to a fury of moral indignation and imperial self-assertion. The climax came when an American warship, the *Maine,* sank under mysterious circumstances in Havana harbor.

The United States easily won the ensuing war with Spain in 1898. Puerto Rico was annexed outright, as were the Philippine Islands on the other side of the world. Cuba was set up as an independent republic, subject to the Platt Amendment, a series of provisions by which the United States obtained the right to oversee Cuba's relations with foreign powers, and to intervene in Cuba in matters of "life, property, individual liberty" and "Cuban independence." Thus the United States obtained another protectorate in the Caribbean. The right of intervention in Cuba was exercised several times in the following two decades, until the growth of Cuban nationalism and subsiding of American imperialism led to abrogation of the Platt Amendment in 1934. Later, after the Second World War, the Philippines formally received independence in 1946 and Puerto Rico became a self-governing commonwealth in 1952.

It was under President Theodore Roosevelt, the peppery "hero of San Juan hill," that the imperial greatness of the United States was most emphatically trumpeted. He announced in 1904 that weakness or misbehavior "which results in a general loosening of the ties of civilized society may . . . require intervention by some civilized nation," and that the Monroe Doctrine might force the United States "to the exercise of an international police power." In the following year Santo Domingo fell into such financial disorder that European creditors were alarmed. To forestall any pretext for European intervention, the United States sent a financial administrator to Santo Domingo, reformed the economy of the country, and impounded half the customs receipts to pay its debts. Roosevelt declared—it came to be known as the "Roosevelt corollary" to the Monroe Doctrine—that, since the United States would not permit European states to intervene in America to collect debts, it must itself assume the duty of intervention to safeguard the investments of the civilized world. The Monroe Doctrine, initially a negative warning to Europe, now stood with the new corollary as a positive notice of supervision of all America by the United States. A quarter of a century of "dollar diplomacy" followed, in which the United States repeatedly intervened, by military or other means, in the Caribbean and Mexico. But the Roosevelt corollary, like the Platt Amendment, created so much bad feeling in Latin America that the Washington government finally repudiated it. Gradually, the United States substituted what came to be known in the 1930s as the "good neighbor" policy, which was designed to respect the sovereignty of the Latin American countries, to treat them as equals of the United States, and to encourage joint, or Pan-American, solutions to common problems.

The story of the Hawaiian Islands was as typical of the new imperialism as any episode in the history of any of the European empires. Known originally to outsiders as the Sandwich Islands, these spots of land long enjoyed isolation in the vastnesses of the mid-Pacific. The growth of navigation in the nineteenth century introduced them to the world. Sailors, whalers, missionaries, and vendors of rum and cloth filled Honolulu by 1840. The native ruler, confused and helpless in the new situation, almost accepted a British protectorate in 1843 and in 1875 did accept a virtual protectorate by the United States, which guaranteed Hawaiian independence against any third party, obtained trading privileges, and acquired Pearl Harbor as a naval base. American capital and management entered the island. They created huge sugar and pineapple industries, entirely dependent on export to, and investment by, the United States. In 1891, when Queen Liliuokalani came to the throne, she tried to check westernization and Americanization. The American interests, endangered by her nativist policies, overthrew the queen and set up an independent republic, which soon sought annexation to the United States. It was the story of Texas reenacted. For several years the issue hung in the balance because of lingering disapproval in the United States for such strong-arm methods. But with Japan revealing imperial designs in 1895, the rush of the other powers into China, the Spanish-American War, acquisition of the Philippines, and plans for the Panama Canal, the United States "accepted its destiny" in the Pacific, and annexed the Hawaiian republic by joint resolution of Congress in 1898.

The United States, as the twentieth century opened, possessing a broad sphere of influence in America, strategic and economic outposts in the Pacific, an active policy in the Far East, and a growing navy, was one of the Great Powers of the world. Canada formed an autonomous dominion within the British Empire. Latin America, while exposed to the indignities of dollar diplomacy, was spared the outright conquest or subjugation to which competitive imperialism reduced most of the rest of the world.

80. The Dissolution of the Ottoman Empire

The Ottoman Empire in the 1850s

Of all parts of the non-European world, the Ottoman, or Turkish, Empire was the nearest to Europe, and with it Europeans had for centuries had close relations. It had for long extended from Hungary and the Balkan peninsula to the south Russian steppes and from Algeria to the Persian Gulf. The empire was not at all like a European state. Immense in extent, it was a congeries of religious communities. Most of its people were Moslem, including both orthodox Moslems and such reform sects as Druses and Wahabis; some were Jews who had always lived in the Near East; many were Christian, principally Greek Orthodox. The Turks were the ruling class and Islam the dominant religion. Only Moslems, for example, could serve in the army; non-Moslems were known as *raya*, the "flock" or "herd"—they paid the taxes. Persons of different religion lived side by side, each under the laws, courts, and customs of his own religious group. Religious officials—patriarchs, bishops, rabbis, imams, ulemas—were responsible to the Turkish government for their own people, over whom therefore they had a great deal of authority.[15]

Western Europeans had their own special rights. Roman Catholic clergy, living mainly in Palestine, looked to the pope in religion and to France for a mundane protector. Western merchants enjoyed the regime of the "capitulations," or special rights granted by the Ottoman government in numerous treaties going back to the sixteenth century. By the capitulations Turkey could not levy a tariff of more than 8 percent on imported goods. Europeans were exempt from most taxes. Cases involving two Europeans, civil or criminal, could be settled only in a court held by a European consul under European law. Disputes between a European and an Ottoman subject were settled in Turkish courts, but in the presence of a European observer.

The Ottoman Empire, in short, completely lacked the European idea of nationalism or national unity. It lacked the European idea of sovereignty and a uniform law for all its peoples. It lacked the European idea of the secular state or of law and citizenship separated from religion. And it had fallen behind Europe in scientific, mechanical, material, humanitarian, and administrative achievements.

Turkey was the "sick man of Europe," and its long decline constituted the Eastern Question. Since the loss of Hungary in 1699 the Ottoman Empire had entered on a long process of territorial disintegration. That the empire lasted another two centuries was due to the European balance of power. The first partition of Poland, in 1772, had been contrived to keep the Russians from overrunning Turkey, and the empire had survived the Napoleonic wars only because the Russians, British, and French deadlocked each other's designs upon it.[16] But by the 1850s the empire was falling away at the edges. Russia had advanced in the Crimea and the Caucasus. Serbia was autonomous, Greece independent, and Rumania recognized as a self-governing principality. The French occupied Algeria. A native Arab dynasty, the Sauds, of the Wahabi reform sect, ruled over much of Arabia. A former Turkish governor of Egypt, Mohammed Ali, had established his family as hereditary "khedives" in the Nile valley.[17] Notwithstanding these changes, the Ottoman Empire in the 1850s was still huge. It encompassed not only the Turkish or Anatolian peninsula (including Armenia and territory south of the Caucasus) but also the central portion of the Balkan peninsula from Constantinople to the Adriatic where many

[15] See pp. 225–226.

[16] See pp. 258, 349–351, 423, 428–429.

[17] See p. 494. The Egyptian ruler, as viceroy under the Ottoman Empire, did not adopt the title of "khedive" until 1867; he was called "sultan" from 1914 to 1922; and thereafter "king" until the overthrow of the monarchy in 1952.

Christians of Slavic nationality lived, Tripoli (Libya) in North Africa, and the islands of Crete and Cyprus. Egypt and Arabia, though autonomous, were still under the nominal suzerainty of the sultan.

The Crimean War of 1854–1856 opened a new phase in Ottoman history as in that of Europe.[18] We have seen how this war was followed by the consolidation of great nation-states in Europe, and how even the United States, Canada, and Japan consolidated or modernized themselves at the same time. The Turks tried to do the same between 1856 and 1876.

In the Crimean War the Turks were on the winning side, but the war affected them as it affected Russia, the loser. Exposing their military and political weakness, it pointed up the need of reorganization. The outcome of the war was taken to prove the superiority of the political system of England and France. It was therefore on Western lines that Turkish reformers wished to remodel. It was not merely that they wished to defend themselves against another of the periodic wars with Russia. They wished also to avoid being periodically saved from Russia by the West, a process which if continued could lead only to French or British control of Turkey.

In 1856 the Ottoman government issued the Hatt-i Humayun, the most far-reaching Turkish reform edict of the century. Its purport was to create an Ottoman national citizenship for all persons in the empire. It abolished the civil authority of religious hierarchs. Equality before the law was guaranteed as was eligibility to public office without regard to religion. The army was opened to Christians and Moslems alike and steps were even taken to include both in nonsegregated military units. The edict announced a reform of taxes, security of property for all, abolition of torture, and reform of prisons. It promised to combat the chronic evils of graft, bribery, and extortion by public officials.

For twenty years there were serious efforts to make the reform decree of 1856 a reality. Western and liberal ideas circulated freely. Newspapers were founded. Writers called for a national Turkish revival, threw off the old Persian style in literature, composed histories of the Ottomans, translated Montesquieu and Rousseau. Foreign loans entered the country. Railroads joined the Black Sea and the Danube. Abdul Aziz (1861–1876), the first sultan to travel in Europe, visited Vienna, London, and the great Paris world's fair of 1867.

Very powerful resistance developed against such radical changes, more radical indeed than anything that the great French Revolution had attempted, since the essential character of the empire was to be reversed. The most obstinate resistance came not from conservative Turks but from the religious leaders whose authority over their own communities was being taken away. The patriarch of Constantinople, for example, controlled the enormous properties of the Greek church (seven-eighths of the land in the Rumanian provinces), and since, under the old Ottoman regime, excommunication meant virtual outlawry, he also possessed an unlimited power over

[18]See pp. 559–561.

all Greek Christians. The religious heads, Christian, Jewish, and Moslem, had every reason to prefer the old regime to the new conception of a secular state, individual freedom, or Ottoman nationality. Many Christians in the empire, however, at odds with their own higher clergy, cooperated with the Turkish reformers to reduce clerical control. But basically, the Christians were beginning to think of themselves as belonging to a nationality rather than to a religion—as Bulgars, Rumanians, Greeks, Serbs, or Armenians. As such, they had no interest in a reformed Ottoman Empire. They even blocked proposals made in 1872 to federalize the empire with local autonomy for the Balkan peoples. On the other hand, the best efforts of the Turkish reformers miscarried. There were too few Turks with skill or experience in the work required. Abdul Aziz took to spending his borrowed money somewhat too freely for purposes of the harem. In 1874 the Ottoman government, having recklessly overborrowed, repudiated half its debt.

A new and more determined reforming minister, Midhat Pasha, goaded by opposition and desperate at the weight of inertia, deposed Abdul Aziz in 1876, deposed the latter's nephew three months later, and set up Abdul Hamid II as sultan. The new sultan at first briskly went along with the reform movement, proclaiming a new constitution in 1876. It declared the Ottoman Empire to be indivisible, and promised personal liberty, freedom of conscience, freedom of education and the press, and parliamentary government. The first Turkish parliament met in 1877. Its members earnestly addressed themselves to reform. But they reckoned without Abdul Hamid, who in 1877 revealed his true intentions. He got rid of Midhat, packed off the parliament and threw away the constitution.

Abdul Hamid reigned for thirty-three years, from 1876 to 1909. For all this time he lived as a terrified animal, fighting back blindly and ferociously against forces that he could not understand. Once when a consignment of dynamos reached the Turkish customs it was held up by fearful officials, because the contents were declared to make several hundred revolutions per minute. Again, chemistry books for use in the new American college were pronounced seditious, because their chemical symbols might be a secret cipher. The sultan sensed that tampering with the old Ottoman way would lead to ruin. He dreaded any moves to check his own whim or power. He was thrown into a panic by Turkish reformers and westernizers, who became increasingly terroristic in the face of his opposition. Driven away by Abdul Hamid, some tens of thousands of Young Turks, the men of the reform era before 1876, or their sons and successors, lived in exile in Paris, London, or Geneva, plotting their return to Turkey and vengeance upon Abdul the Damned. The sultan was frightened also by agitation among his non-Turkish subjects. Nationalist zealots, Armenians, Bulgars, Macedonians, or Cretans, constantly taunted and defied the Ottoman authorities, even precipitating the slaughter of their own people to dramatize their sufferings in the eyes of Europe. The Bulgarian massacres of 1876, the Armenian massacres of 1894, horrible butcheries of thousands of peasants by Ottoman troops, came as a shock to a Europe unused to such violence and were blamed entirely on the allegedly exceptional barbarity of the terrible Turk. Lastly, and with good reason, Abdul Hamid lived in a creeping fear of the designs of the imperialist European powers upon his dissolving empire.

A thoroughly reformed, consolidated, and modernized Ottoman Empire was the last thing that European governments desired. They might wish for humanitarian reforms in Turkey, for more efficiency and honesty in Turkish government and finance, and even for a Turkish parliamentary system. Such demands were eloquently expressed by liberals like Gladstone in England. But no one wanted what Turkish reformers wanted, a reinvigorated Ottoman Empire that could deal with Europe politically as an equal.

The Russo-Turkish War of 1877–1878: The Congress of Berlin

In Russia, since the time of Catherine II, many had dreamed of installing Russia on the shores of the Bosporus.[19] Constantinople they called Tsarigrad, the Imperial City, which Orthodoxy was to liberate from the infidel. Crusading motives, in a nationalist and imperialist age, reappeared anew in the form of Pan-Slavism. The first Pan-Slav congress, in 1848, had been a phenomenon of revolution, liberal in its aims, confined to the Western Slavs including the Poles, and hence anti-tsarist and anti-Russian.[20] Twenty years later Pan-Slavism was preached by leading Russians, including the novelist Dostoievski, the poet Tyutchev, and the publicist Danilevsky. Danilevsky's *Russia and Europe*, published in 1871, predicted a long war between Europe and Russia, to be followed by a grand federation of the East, in which not only all Slavs, but Greeks, Hungarians, and parts of Asiatic Turkey would be included under Russian control. This type of Pan-Slavism was favored and patronized by the Russian government; it diverted attention from internal and revolutionary troubles. As for the Slav peoples of the Ottoman Empire, they were willing to use Russian Pan-Slavism, not especially because they approved of it, but as a means of combating their Turkish rulers. Insurrection against the Turks (and pro-Turkish Slavs) broke out in Bosnia in 1875, in Bulgaria in 1876. In 1877 Russia declared war on Turkey. Russia was again on the move against the Ottoman Empire for the sixth time in a hundred years.

The British, who had fought Russia over Turkey in 1854, were prepared to do so again. A number of recent developments added to their apprehension. The Suez Canal was completed in 1869. It was within the territory of the Ottoman Empire. It restored the Near East to its ancient position as a crossroads of world trade. The British also took alarm when Russia, in 1870, in the confusion of the Franco-Prussian war, repudiated a clause in the treaty of 1856 and began to build a fleet on the Black Sea. In 1874 Benjamin Disraeli, a Conservative and an imperialist, became prime minister of Great Britain. By a sudden coup in the following year he was able to buy up, from the almost bankrupt khedive of Egypt, 44 percent of the shares of the Suez Canal Company. In 1876, in a dramatic affirmation of imperial splendor, he had

[19] See p. 560.
[20] See pp. 522–523.

Queen Victoria take the title of empress of India. British commercial and financial interests in India and the Far East were growing, and the Suez Canal, of which the British government was now the principal stockholder, was becoming the "lifeline" of empire. But the Ottoman state, and hence the whole Near East, was now collapsing before the Russians, whose armies advanced rapidly through the Balkans in 1877, reached Constantinople, and forced the Turks to sign a treaty, the treaty of San Stefano. By this treaty Turkey ceded to Russia Batum and Kars on the south side of the Caucasus mountains, gave full independence to Serbia and Rumania, promised reforms in Bosnia, and granted autonomy to a new Bulgarian state, whose boundaries were to be very generously drawn, and which everyone expected to be dominated by Russia. England seethed with a popular clamor for war against Russia. The outcry gave the word "jingoism" to the language:

> We don't want to fight, but by jingo, if we do,
> We've got the men, we've got the ships, we've
> got the money too.

It now appeared that the weakness of Turkey, its inability to fend off foreigners from its borders, would precipitate at least an Anglo-Russian and possibly a general European war. But war was averted by diplomacy. Bismarck assembled a congress of all the European great powers at Berlin. Once again Europe attempted to assert itself as a unity, to restore life to the much-battered Concert of Europe by dealing collectively with the common problem presented by the Eastern Question. The immediate need was to mediate between the Russians and Turks and to placate the British. To prevent any single power from gaining unequal advantage, and to win the acceptance of all powers for the arrangements agreed to, it was deemed necessary to give something to all, or almost all. The congress in effect initiated a partition of the Ottoman domain. It kept peace in Europe at the expense of Turkey. The European balance now both protected and dismembered Turkey at the same time.

The Russians were persuaded at Berlin to give up the treaty of San Stefano that they had imposed on the Turks, but they still obtained Batum and Kars and won independence for the Serbs and Rumanians. Montenegro, too, was recognized as an independent state. They compromised on Bulgaria, which was divided into three zones with varying degrees of autonomy, all still nominally within the Ottoman Empire. Austria-Hungary was authorized by the congress to "occupy and administer" Bosnia (but not annex it) in the interests of civilization and in compensation for the spread of Russian influence in the Balkans. To the British (Disraeli boasted he brought home "peace with honor") the Turks ceded Cyprus, a large island not far from the Suez Canal. The French were told that they might expand from Algeria into Tunisia. To the Italians (who counted least) it was more vaguely hinted that some day, somehow, they might expand across the Adriatic into Albania. As Bismarck put it, "the Italians have such a large appetite and such poor teeth." Germany took nothing. Bismarck said he was the "honest broker," with no interest except in European peace.

The Dissolution of the Ottoman Empire 1699–1914. *Beginning in 1699, with the loss of Hungary to the House of Austria, the Ottoman Empire entered upon a long process of territorial disintegration which lasted for over two hundred years. Dates shown are those at which territories dropped away. In general, regions lost from 1699 to the fall of Napoleon, 1812–1815, were annexed directly by Austria and Russia. European territories lost in the nineteenth century emerged as independent states, owing to the rise of nationalism and the balance among the great European powers. In the Arabic world, reaching from Algeria to the Persian Gulf, regions lost before the First World War were absorbed into European colonial empires; those lost in the First World War (1918) were at first mostly assigned to France and Britain as mandates, but after the Second World War emerged as independent Arabic states. During the First World War Britain, France, Italy, Russia, and Greece took steps to partition Turkey proper, but a Turkish nationalist movement blocked these designs and established a Turkish republic (pp. 738–739, 830–831).*

The treaty of Berlin of 1878 dispelled the immediate threat of war. But it left many continuing problems for later statesmanship to deal with, problems which, because they were not dealt with successfully, became a principal cause of the First World War thirty-six years later. Neither the Balkan nationalists nor the Russian Pan-Slavs were satisfied. The Turks, both reactionaries like Abdul Hamid and the revolutionary Young Turks in exile, were indignant that peace had been made by

684

further dismemberment of their territory. The demonstrated weakness of Turkey was a constant temptation not only to Russians, Austrians, Serbs, Bulgars, Greeks, and Armenians, but also to the British, French, Italians, and finally the Germans, who found imperialist penetration into its nominal borders irresistibly easy. In the years before 1914 German influence grew. Germans and German capital entered Turkey, projecting, and partially completing, a great Berlin to Bagdad railway to be accompanied by the exploitation of Near Eastern natural resources. The railroad was all but completed before 1914 despite the protests and representations of the Russians, the French, and particularly the British, who saw in it a direct threat to their empire in India.

Abdul Hamid, whose reign began with the Russian war and the Berlin congress, not unreasonably regarded all the nationalistic agitation against him as inspired by foreign imperialists. He repressed all agitation with unblushing despotism and unabashed brutality. He held his empire together by playing the Europeans against one another, for which they accused him of Oriental duplicity. He both lost and gained from the influence of foreign capital. In 1881, overcome with war debts, he had virtually to hand over the whole taxation system of his empire to the agents of foreign bankers, but on the other hand the bondholders, mainly French, could not willingly see the total collapse of a sultan to whom they had lent so much money. He tried also to combat nationalism and revolutionism by a religious revival. He reasserted the dormant powers of the Ottoman sultan as caliph, or commander of the faithful, the universal spiritual head of all Islam. He hoped to rouse a militant neo-Islam against the common menace of the so-called Christian world. But although waves of Pan-Islamism, of neo-Moslem and anti-Christian feeling were in fact stirring all Islam at this time, neo-caliphism appealed to very few. Arabs and Persians, the learned doctors at Mecca, the Moslems of India and the East Indies remained unstirred by a caliph who was also the Turkish sultan. Nevertheless, Abdul Hamid for thirty years hung on to his empire, except in North Africa.

For Egypt, technically autonomous within the Ottoman Empire, the 1850s and 1860s were a time of progress in the Western sense as they had been for the empire as a whole. The Egyptian government modernized its administration, court system, and property law, cooperated with the French in building the Suez Canal, encouraged shipping on the Red Sea, and let British and French interests construct railroads. Between 1861 and 1865, while the American South was unable to export raw cotton, the annual export of Egyptian cotton rose from 60,000,000 to 250,000,000 pounds. Egypt more than Turkey was drawn into the world market, and the khedive more than the sultan became a Western type of man. The khedive Ismail built himself a fine new opera house in Cairo, where, in 1871, two years after the opening of the Suez Canal, Verdi's *Aïda,* written at the khedive's request, was resoundingly performed for the first time.

Such improvements cost a good deal of money, borrowed in England and France. The Egyptian government was soon in financial straits, only temporarily relieved by the sale of Canal shares to Disraeli. By 1879 matters reached the point where Western banking interests forced the abdication of Ismail and his replacement by Tewfik, who, with a childlike fascination for the new Western marvels, soon let himself become thoroughly enmeshed by his creditors. This led to nationalistic protests within Egypt, headed by Colonel Arabi. In a pattern repeated in many parts of the colonial world, especially in Manchu China, the nationalists opposed both the foreigners and their own government, charging it with being a mere front for foreign interests. Arabi's movement, nationalistic and religious, neo-Moslem and anti-foreign, led to riots in Alexandria, where Europeans had to flee aboard British and French shipping in the harbor. A British squadron then unceremoniously bombarded Alexandria. British troops (the French, though invited to take part, refused) disembarked in 1882 at Suez and Alexandria, defeated Arabi, and took Tewfik under their protection. The military intervention of 1882 was said by the British to be temporary, but British troops remained there for a long time, through two world wars and well into the twentieth century, not leaving until 1956.

Egypt became a British protectorate. The British protected the khedive from discontent within his own country, from the claims of the Ottoman Porte, and from the rival attentions of other European powers. The British resident from 1883 to 1907, an exceptionally capable administrator named Evelyn Baring, the first Earl of Cromer, reconstructed the economy of the country, reformed its taxation, eased the burdens on the peasants and raised their productivity, encouraged the growth of raw materials wanted by England, and assured regular payment of interest to British, French, and other holders of Egyptian bonds.

The French strenuously objected when the British stayed on so long in Egypt. It had long been the French who had the greatest investments in the Near East, and Near Easterners who were at all westernized—Egyptian, Syrian, Turkish—overwhelmingly preferred the French language and culture to the English. The French, harboring deep suspicion of British designs in Egypt, compensated themselves by building a North African empire farther west. They developed Algeria, assumed a protectorate over Tunisia, and began to penetrate Morocco. Upon these French advances the British, and soon the Germans, looked with unmitigated disfavor. Rivalry for the spoils of the Ottoman Empire thus created enmity among the Great Powers and constituted a fertile source of the war scares, fears, and diplomatic maneuvers that preceded the First World War. These are related in the following chapter.

The dissolution of the Ottoman Empire became indistinguishable from the whole chronic international crisis before 1914. It is enough to say here, to keep the fate of the Ottoman Empire in focus, that Abdul Hamid's frantic policies came to nothing and that the Young Turks won control of the Ottoman government in 1908. They forced the restoration of the constitution of 1876 and introduced many reforms. In the midst of the revolutionary disturbances of 1908 Bulgaria proclaimed its full independence and Austria annexed Bosnia. In the Turco-Italian War of 1911–1912 Italy took Libya and the Dodecanese Islands from the Turks. In two successive Balkan Wars (1912–1913) Turkey lost nearly all its territory in Europe to Bulgaria, Serbia, Greece, and Albania, the latter becoming an independent state in

1912. Finally, when all Europe became involved in war in 1914, Russia again declared war on Turkey, and the Turks came into the war on the side of Germany, whose political and economic influence in the empire had been steadily growing. During the war, with British aid, the Arabs detached themselves from the empire, becoming eventually independent Arab states. Egypt, too, ended all connections with the empire. In 1923 a Turkish Republic was proclaimed. It was confined to Constantinople and the Anatolian peninsula, where the bulk of the true Turkish people lived. The new republic proceeded to undergo a thorough nationalist and secular revolution.[21]

South of Mediterranean Africa lay the Sahara, and south of that lay Black Africa, the Dark Continent for Europeans. For centuries Europeans knew only its coasts—the Gold Coast, Ivory Coast, Slave Coast—to which from an inexhaustible interior had come shackled processions of captive slaves, as well as the swelling waters of enormous rivers, like the Nile and the Congo, whose sources in the dim hinterland were a subject of romantic speculation. The population was black, except that Arabic-speaking whites were found on the east coast, and in the southern part of the continent (at the time of the founding of the Union of South Africa in 1910) about 1,100,000 Europeans lived along with about 5,000,000 blacks. The native peoples were agricultural or pastoral, and without written language or enduring political states but with bold and remarkable art forms.

81
The Partition
of Africa

Missionaries, explorers, and individual adventurers first opened this world to Europe. The historic pair, Livingstone and Stanley, well illustrate the drift of events. Long before the imperialist age, in 1841, the Scot David Livingstone arrived in southeast Africa as a medical missionary. He gave himself to humanitarian and religious work, with a little occasional trading, and much travel and discovery, but without political or true economic aims. Exploring the Zambesi River, he was the first white man to look upon the Victoria Falls. Fully at home in inner Africa, safe and on friendly terms with its native people, he was quite content to be let alone. But the hectic forces of modern civilization sought him out. Word spread in Europe and America that Dr. Livingstone was lost. The New York *Herald*, to manufacture news, sent the roving journalist H. M. Stanley to "find" him, which he did in 1871. Livingstone soon died, deeply honored by the natives. Stanley was a man of the new era. Seeing vast possibilities in Africa, he went to Europe to solicit backers. In 1878 he found a man with the same ideas, who happened to be a king, Leopold II, king of the Belgians.

Leopold, for all his royalty, was at heart a promoter. China, Formosa, the Philippines, and Morocco had in turn attracted his fancy, but it was the central African basin of the Congo that he decided to develop. Stanley was exactly the man

The Opening of Africa

[21] See pp. 830–831.

Pre-Colonial Africa: Sites and Peoples. *This map is meant to show Africa before pene-*
tration by the Europeans in the nineteenth century. It does not refer to any particular date.
Names in brown designate ancient or medieval centers, like the Ghana and Mali empires, which no
longer existed in modern times. Even the most extensive African kingdoms had indefinite and
shifting boundaries which are hard to indicate on a map. Bantu peoples were moving toward the
southern tip of the continent in the nineteenth century, at the time when Europeans began to move
northeastward into the interior from the Cape.

he was looking for, and the two founded at Brussels, with a few financiers, an
International Congo Association in 1878. It was a purely private enterprise; the
Belgian government and people had nothing to do with it. All Africa inland from the
coasts was considered to be, like America in the time of Columbus, a *terra nullius*,
without government and claimed by nobody, wide open to the first civilized persons
who might arrive. Stanley, returning to the Congo in 1882, in a year or two concluded
treaties with over 500 chiefs, who in return for a few trinkets or a few yards of cloth

put their crude marks on the mysterious papers and accepted the blue-and-gold flag of the Association.

Since the Dark Continent was still innocent of internal frontiers, no one could tell how much ground the Association might soon cover by these methods. The German explorer Karl Peters, working inland from Zanzibar, was signing treaties with the chiefs of east Africa. The Frenchman Brazza, departing from the west coast and distributing the tricolor in every village, was claiming on the Congo River itself a territory larger than France. The Portuguese aspired to join their ancient colonies of Angola and Mozambique into a trans-African empire, for which they required a generous portion of the interior. Britain supported Portugal. In every case the home governments in Europe were still hesitant over involvement in the African wilds, but they were pushed on by small organized minorities of colonizing enthusiasts, and they faced the probability that if they missed the moment it would be too late.

Bismarck, who personally thought African colonies an absurdity, but was sensitive to the new pressures, called another conference at Berlin in 1885, this time to submit the African question to international regulation. Most European states, as well as the United States, attended. The Berlin conference attempted to do two things: to set up the territories of the Congo Association as an international state, under international auspices and restrictions; and to draft an international code governing the way in which European powers wishing to acquire African territory should proceed.

The Congo Free State, which in 1885 took the place of the International Congo Association, was not only an international creation but embodied, in principle, what was to be known in the next century as international trusteeship for backward peoples. The Berlin conference specified that the new state should have no connection with any power, including Belgium. It delegated the government to Leopold. It drew the boundaries, making the Congo Free State almost as large as the United States east of the Mississippi, and it added certain specific provisions: the Congo River was internationalized, persons of all nationalities should be free to do business in the Congo state, there should be no tariff levied on imports, and the slave trade should be suppressed. Leopold in 1889 reassembled the signatory powers in a second conference, held at Brussels. The Brussels conference took further steps to root out the slave trade, which remained a stubborn though declining evil, because the Moslem world was several generations behind the Christian in abolishing slavery. The Brussels conference also undertook to protect native rights, correct certain glaring abuses, and reduce the traffic in liquor and firearms.

This attempt at internationalism failed, because Europe had no international machinery by which the hard daily work of executing general agreements could be carried out. Leopold went his own way in the Congo. His determination to make it commercially profitable led him to unconscionable extremes. Europe and America demanded rubber, and the Congo was at the time one of the world's few sources of supply. The Congo people, among the least advanced in Africa, and afflicted by the disease and enervation of a lowland equatorial climate, could be made to tap enough rubber trees only by inhuman severity and compulsion. The trees themselves were destroyed without thought of replacement. Leopold, by ravaging its resources and virtually enslaving its people, was able to draw from the Congo a princely income to be spent in Brussels, but he could never make the enterprise self-supporting. Consumed with debt, he borrowed another 25,000,000 francs from the kingdom of Belgium, agreeing that Belgium should inherit the Congo on his death if the debt was unpaid. In 1908, the reluctant Belgians thus found themselves heirs to some "tropical gardens" to which they had been consistently indifferent. The Free State became the Belgian Congo, and under Belgian administration the worst excesses of Leopold's regime were removed.

The Berlin conference of 1885 had also laid down, for expansion in Africa, certain rules of the game—a European power with holdings on the coast had prior rights in the back country; occupation must not be on paper only, through drawing lines on a map, but must consist in real occupation by administrators or troops; and each power must give proper notice to the others as to what territories it considered its own. A wild scramble for "real occupation" quickly followed. In fifteen years the entire continent was parceled out. The sole exceptions were Ethiopia and, technically, Liberia, founded in 1822 as a colony for emancipated American slaves and virtually a protectorate of the United States ever since.

Everywhere a variant of the same process was repeated. First, somewhere in the wilderness, would appear a handful of white men, bringing their inevitable treaties—sometimes printed forms. To get what they wanted, the Europeans commonly had to ascribe powers to the chief which by the customs of the tribe he did not possess—powers to convey sovereignty, sell land, or grant mining concessions. Thus the Africans were baffled at the outset by foreign legal conceptions. Then the Europeans would build up the position of the chief, since they themselves had no influence over the people. This led to the widespread system of "indirect rule," by which colonial authorities acted through the existing chiefs and tribal forms. There were many things that only the chief could arrange, such as security for isolated Europeans, porter services, or gangs of workmen to build roads or railroads.

Labor was the overwhelming problem. For pure slavery Europeans now had an abhorrence, and they abolished it wherever they could. But the African, so long as he lived in his traditional way, did not react like the free wage earner postulated in civilized business and economics. He had little sense of individual gain and almost no use for money. Generally he did not work very hard according to European ideas; work, continuous and laborious work, was in many African societies left to the women. The result was that Europeans all over Africa resorted to forced labor. For road building, systems like the French *corvée* before the Revolution reappeared. Or the chief would be required to supply a quota of able-bodied men for a certain length of time, and frequently he did so gladly to raise his own importance in the eyes of the whites. More indirect methods were also used. The colonial government might levy a hut tax or a poll tax, payable only in money, to obtain which the native would have to seek a job. Or the new government, once installed, might allocate so much land to Europeans as private property (another foreign conception) that the local tribe could no longer subsist on the lands that remained to it. Or the whole tribe might be

690

moved to a reservation, like Indians in the United States. In either case, while the women tilled the fields or tended the stock at home, the men would move off to take jobs under the whites for infinitesimal pay. The men then lived in "compounds," away from family and tribal kindred; they became demoralized; and the labor they gave, unintelligent and unwilling, would scarcely have been tolerated in any more civilized community. In these circumstances everything was done to uproot the African, and nothing was done to westernize him. The old tribal or village society collapsed, and nothing replaced it.

Conditions improved with the twentieth century, as traditions of enlightened colonial administration were built up. Colonial officials even came to serve as buffers or protectors of the natives against the white man's interest. Throughout, it was part of the ethos of imperialism to put down slavery, tribal warfare, superstition, disease, and illiteracy. Slowly a westernized class of Africans grew—chiefs and the sons of chiefs, Catholic priests and Protestant ministers, warehouse clerks and government employees. Young men from Nigeria or Uganda appeared as students at Oxford, the University of Paris, or Howard University in the United States, which emerged as the world's leading black institution of learning as black peoples throughout the world became aware of a common identity. Westernized Africans usually resented both exploitation and paternalism. They showed signs of turning nationalistic, like corresponding persons in the Ottoman Empire or Asia. If they wanted westernization, it was at a pace and for a purpose of their own. As the twentieth century progressed, nationalism in Africa grew more vocal and more intense.

Meanwhile, in the fifteen years from 1885 to 1900, the Europeans in Africa came dangerously near to open blows. The Portuguese annexed huge domains in Angola and Mozambique. The Italians took over two barren tracts, Italian Somaliland and Eritrea on the Red Sea. They then moved inland, in quest of more imposing possessions, to conquer Ethiopia and the headwaters of the Nile. Some 80,000 Ethiopians, however, slaughtered and routed 20,000 Italians in pitched battle at Adowa in 1896. It was the first time that native Africans successfully defended themselves against the whites, and it discouraged invasion of Ethiopia by the Italians (or other Europeans) for forty years. Italy and Portugal, like the Congo Free State and Spain (which retained a few vestiges of former days), were able to enjoy sizable holdings in Africa because of mutual fears among the principal contenders. The principal contenders were Great Britain, France, and Germany. Each preferred to have territory held by a minor power rather than by one of its significant rivals.

The Germans were latecomers in the colonial race, which Bismarck entered with reluctance. By the 1880s all the usual imperialist arguments were heard in Germany, though most of them, such as the need of new markets, of outlets for emigration, or for the investment of capital, had little or no application in tropical Africa. The Germans established colonies in German East Africa, and in the Cameroons and Togo on the west coast, not to mention an unpleasant desert called German Southwest

Africa. It did not escape the notice of German imperial planners that some day the Congo and the Portuguese colonies might be joined with German East Africa and the Cameroons in a solid German belt across the African heartland. The French controlled most of west Africa, from Algeria across the Sahara and the Sudan to various points on the Guinea coast. They also occupied Obok on the Red Sea, and after the Italian defeat in 1896 their influence in Ethiopia grew. French planners therefore dreamed of a solid French belt across Africa from Dakar to the Gulf of Aden. The French government in 1898 dispatched Captain J. B. Marchand with a small party eastward from Lake Chad, to hoist the tricolor far away on the upper Nile, in the southern part of the Sudan, which no European power as yet "effectively" occupied.

The two presumptive east-and-west belts, German and French, were cut (presumptively) by a north-and-south belt, projected in the British imperial imagination as an "Africa British from the Cape to Cairo." From the Cape of Good Hope Cecil Rhodes pushed northward into Rhodesia. Kenya and Uganda in the mid-continent were already British. In Egypt, a British protectorate since 1882, the British began to support old Egyptian claims to the upper Nile. The first venture proved a disaster, when in 1885 a British officer, "Chinese Gordon," leading an Egyptian force, was killed by aroused Moslems at Khartoum. In the following decade British opinion turned imperialist in earnest. Another British officer, General Kitchener (with a young man named Winston Churchill under his command) again started southward up the Nile and defeated the local Moslems in 1898 at Omdurman. He then pushed on further upstream. At a place called Fashoda he met Marchand.

The ensuing Fashoda crisis brought Britain and France to the verge of war. Already at odds over Egypt and Morocco,[22] the two governments used the encounter at Fashoda to force a showdown. It was a test of strength, not only for their respective plans for all Africa, but for their relative position in all imperialist and international issues. Both at first refused to yield. The British virtually threatened to fight. The French, fearful of their insecurity against Germany in Europe, at last decided not to take the risk. They backed down and recalled Marchand from Fashoda. A wave of hatred for the British swept over France.

The British no sooner won this Pyrrhic victory than they became involved in more unpleasantness at the other end of the African continent. In 1890 Cecil Rhodes had become prime minister of the Cape Colony. He was a principal sponsor of the Cape-to-Cairo dream. Two small independent neighboring republics, the Transvaal and the Orange Free State, stood in his way. Their people were Afrikaners—Dutch who had originally settled the Cape in the seventeenth century, then after 1815, when England annexed the Cape of Good Hope, had made the "great trek" to escape from British rule. The Boers, as the English called them, from the Dutch word for "farmer," were simple, obstinate, and old-fashioned. They thought slavery not ungodly and disliked promoters, fortune hunters, footloose adventurers, mining-camp people, and other Uitlanders.

[22]See pp. 685–686.

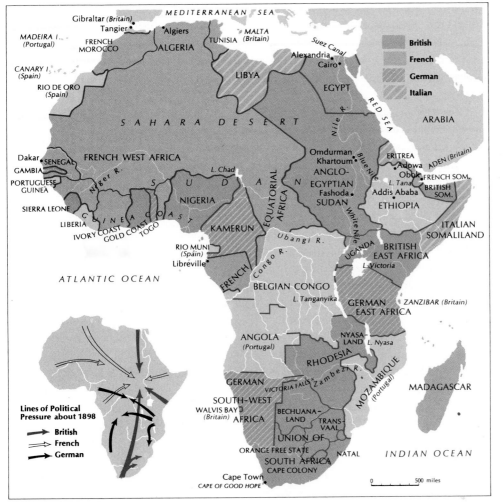

Africa 1914. *The map shows the recognized holdings of the Powers in 1914. The inset suggests the directions of political pressure about 1898. These pressures led to the Fashoda crisis in 1898 and the Boer War in 1899. In 1898 the British and German governments held secret discussions on the possible partitioning of the Portuguese colonies, which, however, never came to pass since the British greatly preferred to have the Portuguese colonies remain in the hands of Portugal.*

The discovery of diamonds and gold in the Transvaal brought the issue to a head. British capital and British people poured in. The Transvaal refused to pass legislation needed by the mining corporations and their employees. In 1895 Rhodes, attempting to precipitate revolution in the Transvaal, sent a party of armed irregulars, under Dr. Jameson, over its borders. This Jameson Raid was a failure, but in Europe a great cry went up against British bullying of a small inoffensive republic. The German emperor, William II, dispatched a famous telegram to Paul Kruger, president of the Transvaal, congratulating him on his driving off the invaders "without having to call for the support of friendly powers"—i.e., Germany. Three years later the

British Empire went to war with the two Boer republics. It took another three years to subdue them. Once conquered and brought within the British Empire they were left with their self-governing institutions, and in 1910 they were joined with the predominantly English colonies of Natal and Cape Colony into the Union of South Africa, which received a semi-independence along the lines of the Dominion of Canada.

The Fashoda crisis and the Boer War, coming in rapid succession, revealed to the British the bottomless depths of their unpopularity in Europe. All European governments and peoples were pro-Boer; only the United States, involved at the time in a similar conquest of the Philippines, showed any sympathy for the British. The British, after the Boer War, began to rethink their international position, as will soon be seen.

As in the case of the Ottoman Empire, rivalry between the Great Powers over the spoils of Africa embittered international relations and helped prepare the way for the First World War. The rivalry over Morocco involving France and Germany entered into the general prewar crisis and will be related in the following chapter. As for Africa as a whole, there was little territorial change after the Boer War, although in 1911 Italy took Libya, in North Africa, from the Turks. In 1914 the Germans were excluded from their short-lived empire. Had the Germans won the First World War, the map of Africa would probably have been greatly revised, but since they lost it the only change was to assign the German colonies, under international mandate, to the French and British. With this change, and except for Italy's conquest of Ethiopia in 1935, a conquest which did not survive the Second World War, the map of Africa remained what the brief years of partition had made it until the spectacular end of the European empires in the 1950s and 1960s.[23]

82
Imperialism in Asia: The Dutch, the British, and the Russians

The Dutch East Indies and British India

B ritish India and the Dutch East Indies, in the half-century before the First World War, were the world's ideal colonies. They illustrated the kind of empire that all imperialists would have wished to have, and a glance at them suggests the goal toward which imperialism was logically moving.

Whereas all countries of western Europe showed a surplus of imports, receiving more goods from the rest of the world than they sent out, India and Indonesia invariably, year after year and decade after decade, showed a surplus of exports, sending out far more goods than they took in. This export surplus was the hallmark of the developed colonial area, geared closely into the world market, with low purchasing power for the natives and kept going by foreign investment and management. Both regions, in addition, were so large as to have a good deal of internal business—commerce, insurance, banking, transportation—which never appeared in the statistics for world trade, but which, being dominated by Europeans, added immeasurably to their profits. Both had rich and varied natural resources,

[23] See pp. 960–966, and map, p. 963.

tropical in character, so that they never competed with the products of Europe—though India even before 1914 showed tendencies to industrialization. In both regions the people were adept and quick to learn. But they were divided by religion and language, so that, once conquered, they were relatively easy for the whites to govern. Neither region before the First World War had any self-government at the highest levels. Both were ruled by a civil service, honest and highminded by its own lights, in which the most illustrious, most influential, and best paying positions were reserved for the whites. Hence upper-class families in England and the Netherlands valued their empires as fields of opportunity for their sons—somewhat as they had formerly valued an established church. In both India and Indonesia the governments were more or less benevolent despotisms, which, by curbing warfare, plague, and famine, at least allowed the population to grow in numbers. Java, with 5,000,000 people in 1815, had 48,000,000 in 1942. India's population in the same years probably grew from less than 200,000,000 to almost 400,000,000. Finally, as the last virtue of a perfect colony, no foreign power directly challenged the British in India or the Dutch in their islands.

The Dutch in 1815 occupied little more than the island of Java itself.[24] In the following decades the British moved into Singapore, the Malay peninsula, and north Borneo, and made claims to Sumatra; the French in the 1860s appeared in Indochina; the Germans in the 1880s annexed eastern New Guinea and the Marshall and Solomon islands. Ultimately it was the mutual jealousy of these three that preserved the Dutch position. The Dutch, however, took the initiative themselves. To forestall occupation by other Europeans, and to put down native pirates and find raw materials that the world demanded, the Dutch spread their rule over the whole 3,000-mile extent of the archipelago. They created an empire, in place of the old chain of trading posts concerned only with buying and selling. Revolts were suppressed in 1830, 1849, 1888; not till the twentieth century were northern Sumatra or the interior of Celebes brought under control. For some decades the Dutch exploited their huge empire by a kind of forced labor, the "culture system," in which the authorities required farmers to deliver, as a kind of tax, stated amounts of stated crops, such as sugar or coffee. After 1870 a freer system was introduced. The Dutch also, as an important matter of policy, favored instruction in the Malay and Javanese languages, not in Dutch. This preserved the native cultures from westernizing disintegration but at the same time meant that Western ideas of nationalism and democracy entered more slowly. The strongest resistance to Dutch imperialism (as later to the equally foreign doctrines of Marxism) came from the Islamic religion of the people. By 1914, thanks to Western steamship lines, 20,000 Indonesians a year were making the pilgrimage to Mecca. Pan-Islamism, the idea that all Islam should stand united against the Christians (an idea that Abdul Hamid used in vain by reasserting the caliphate), made rapid progress in Indonesia.

In India, in 1857, the British faced a dangerous rebellion, commonly called the Indian Mutiny, as if it had been a revolt of undisciplined soldiers only. The Indian

[24]See p. 170.

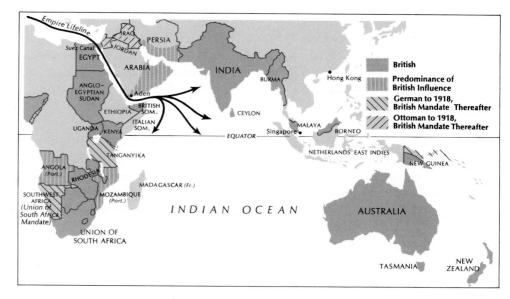

"The British Lake" 1918. *This small map shows almost half the surface of the earth. All the most important parts of the British Empire are visible except Canada and the United Kingdom itself. All shores of the Indian Ocean are shown to be British, except for French Madagascar, the politically weak Portuguese, Italian, and Dutch colonies, and the Arabian and Persian coasts, in which British influence was strong. It is easy to see why the Mediterranean and the Suez Canal, leading from Europe into this half-world, were called the lifeline of the British Empire.*

army, with its sepoys, was the only organization through which Indians could exert any collective pressure. The proportion of sepoys in the army was high in 1857 (about five-sixths) because British units had been withdrawn for the Crimean War and for action in China. Many Indians, outside the army, had been restless for decades. Rulers had been conquered and dethroned. Landowners had lost their property and been replaced by new ones more friendly to the British. Religious sentiments were inflamed. The British too obviously regarded Indian beliefs as repulsive: they had outlawed suttee, or widow-burning, suppressed the Thugs, a small sect of holy assassins, and one British officer even declared that in ten years the government would abolish caste. The Moslems were agitated by Wahabi fundamentalism. Mysterious propaganda circulated over India. It infiltrated the sepoys, announcing to Moslem soldiers that certain newly issued cartridges were greased with the fat of a pig and to Hindus that the same cartridges were greased with the fat of a cow. Since for Hindus the cow was sacred, and for Moslems to touch pork was profane, much agitation was produced. The sepoys mutinied in the Ganges valley; and with them the other injured interests, including the far-faded Great Mogul and his court, rose against the British.

The British put down the rebellion, aided by the fact that western and southern India took no part in it. But the uprising persuaded the British to a radically new course of policy, pursued basically until the end of the Indian empire almost a century later. The British East India Company and the Mogul empire were both finally and forever done away with. British authorities ruled directly. But the British concluded that they must rule India with and through the Indians themselves, not against them. This in practice meant a collaboration between the imperial power and the Indian upper classes. The British began to shelter Indian vested interests. They supported the Indian landlords and became more indulgent toward Indian "superstition." Where before 1857, when they conquered an Indian state, they had simply abolished it and incorporated its territories, after the Mutiny they kept the remaining Indian states as protectorates. States existing in 1857, such as Hyderabad and Kashmir and over 200 others, with their galaxy of rajahs and maharajahs, carried on to the end of British rule in 1947. It was largely to provide a fitting summit for this mountain of Indian royalty that Queen Victoria was proclaimed empress of India in 1877.

India had been a considerable manufacturing country by preindustrial standards. Indian merchants had once been important throughout the Indian Ocean, and before 1800 Indian exports to Europe had included many textiles and other finished goods.[25] The native crafts collapsed before modern industrialism reinforced by political power. "India," observed a British expert in 1837, "can never again be a great manufacturing country, but by cultivating her connection with England she may be one of the greatest agricultural countries in the world." Free trade (made possible by military superiority, usually overlooked by the economists) turned Britain into the world's workshop and India into a supplier of raw materials. Indian exports, in the latter part of the nineteenth century, consisted increasingly in raw cotton, tea, jute, oilseeds, indigo, and wheat. The British shipped their manufactures in return. Business in India boomed; India came to have the densest railway network outside of Europe and North America. It is important to note, however, as a commentary on dealing with poor countries, that Britain in 1914 did far more trading with the 6,000,000 high-standard white people of Australia and New Zealand than with the 315,000,000 impoverished people of India.

The British, in contrast to the Dutch, decided in 1835 to favor instruction in English, not in the native languages. The historian Macaulay, one of the commission to make this recommendation, branded the Indian languages as vehicles of barbarous and unenlightened ideas—a bar to progress. The British also, after the Mutiny, admitted Indians to the civil service and to governors' councils—sparingly indeed, but more than the Dutch in Indonesia. There were also many Indian businessmen. A class of westernized Indians grew up, speaking perfect English, and often educated in England. They demanded more of a role in the affairs of their country. In 1885 the predominantly Hindu Indian National Congress was organized; in 1906, the All India Moslem League. Moslem separatism, while favored by the British and sometimes even blamed upon them, was natural to India and exploited by some Indian leaders. Nationalism spread. It became increasingly anti-British, and radical nationalism turned also against the Indian princes, capitalists, and businessmen, as accomplices in imperialism, and so took on the color of socialism. In the period of the First World

---

[25] See pp. 267–268.

War, under nationalist pressure, the British granted more representation to Indians, especially in provincial affairs, but the movement toward self-rule was never fast enough to overcome the basic anti-British feeling of the Indian peoples.

Conflict of Russian and British Interests

While no outsider yet threatened the British in India, British statecraft discerned in the northern sky a large cloud which was clearly approaching. The Russian empire had occupied northern Asia since the seventeenth century.[26] About 1850 Russian pressure on inner Asia was resumed. It was a type of imperialism in which neither the demand for markets nor for raw materials, nor for the investment of capital, counted for much. In these matters Russia was itself semicolonial with respect to the West. The Russians had, like the Westerners, a sense of spreading their type of civilization; but Russian expansion was distinctively political in that most of the initiative came from the government. Russia was an ice-bound empire, craving "warm-water ports." It was a land-locked empire, so that whichever way it turned it moved toward one ocean or another. The ocean was the domain of the Westerners, and in particular the British. In the large picture, Russia pushed by land against the Ottoman Empire, Persia, India, and China, all of which the British (and others) reached by sea. In 1860, on the shores of the Sea of Japan, the Russians founded Vladivostok, the farthest-flung of all Slavic cities, whose name meant Lord of the East. But their advance in the mid-century was mainly in the arid and thinly settled regions of western Asia. The British had already fought two Afghan wars to keep Afghanistan as a no man's land between Russia and India. In 1864 the Russians took Tashkent, in Turkestan. A decade later they touched India itself but were kept away by an Anglo-Russian agreement, which allotted a long tongue of land to Afghanistan and so separated the Indian and Russian empires by twenty miles—the new frontier, in the high Pamirs, on the Roof of the World, was to be sure, scarcely adapted to military operations.

Russian advances in Turkestan, east of the Caspian, increased the pressure on Persia, which had long felt the same pressure west of the Caspian, where cities like Tiflis and Baku, now Russian, had once been Persian. If Tiflis and Turkestan could fall to the Russian empire, there was no reason why Persia should not do so next—except that Persia had a seacoast and so might also be available for occupancy by the British. In 1864 a British company completed the first Persian telegraph, as part of the line from Europe to India. Other British investments and interests followed. Oil became important about 1900. In 1890, to bolster the Persian government against Russia, the British granted it a loan—taking the customs in Persian Gulf ports as collateral. In 1900 the Russian government granted the same favor, making its own loan to Persia, and appropriating as security all Persian customs except those of the Gulf. Russian ships appeared in the Persian Gulf in 1900, a demonstration soon countered by a state visit to Persia of the Viceroy of India, Lord Curzon. Clearly Persia was losing control of its own affairs, falling into zones, turning ripe for

[26] See p. 246.

partition. A Persian nationalist revolution, directed against all foreigners and against the subservient government of the shah, broke out in 1905 and led to the assembly of the first parliament but hardly settled the question of Persian independence. In 1907 the British recognized a Russian "sphere of influence" in northern Persia, the Russians a British sphere in the south.[27]

Imperial ambitions had deepened the hostility between Great Britain and Russia, with disputes over Persia and the Indian borderlands adding fuel to the quarrel they had long waged over the Ottoman Empire. We have seen how the struggle for Africa had at the same time estranged Britain from France and indeed from all Europe.

But the biggest bone of imperialist contention was offered by China. On this bone every Great Power without exception tried to bite. The Manchu dynasty held a suzerainty over the whole area affected by Chinese civilization, from the mouth of the Amur River (as far north as Labrador) to Burma and Indochina (as far south as Panama), and from the ocean westward into Mongolia and Tibet. In the old Chinese view China was the world itself, the Middle Kingdom between the upper and nether regions. The Europeans were outlandish barbarians. A few had trickled through to China since the European Middle Ages. But the Chinese people persistently wanted nothing to do with them.

China was moving into an upheaval of its own even before Western influence became of any importance. For 2,000 years the country had seen dynasties come and go in a kind of cycle. The Manchu dynasty in the nineteenth century was clearly nearing its end. It was failing to preserve order or to curb extortion. About 1800 a White Lotus Society revolted and was suppressed. In 1813 a Heavenly Reason Society attempted to seize Peking. In the 1850s a Moslem rebellion set up a temporary independent state in the southwest. Greatest of all the upheavals was the Tai-ping Rebellion of 1850, in which as many as 20,000,000 people, approximately the population of Great Britain at the time, are thought to have perished. Except that some fragmentary Christian ideas, obtained from missionaries, were expressed by some of the Tai-pings, the rebellion was due entirely to Chinese causes. The rebels

83
Imperialism in Asia: China and the West

China Before Western Penetration

[27] See p. 724.

Imperialism in Asia 1840–1914. *Boundaries and possessions are as of 1914. During these years the British and Dutch filled out their holdings in India and the East Indies, in each case moving outward from establishments founded long before. The Russians, who had long occupied Siberia, pressed southward in Central Asia, founded Vladivostok in 1860, and penetrated Manchuria at the close of the century. The French built an empire in Indochina, while the United States acquired the Philippines, and the Germans, as latecomers, were confined to miscellaneous parts of the western Pacific. The Japanese won control of Korea and replaced the Russians as the chief outside influence in Manchuria. Meanwhile all obtained special rights and concessions in China. A bid for such concessions by Italy was refused.*

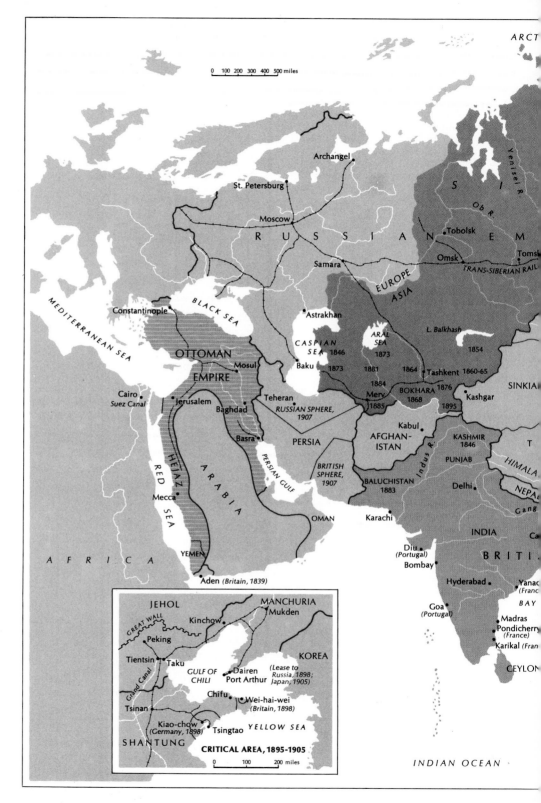

0 100 200 300 400 500 miles

ARCT

Archangel

St. Petersburg

Moscow

R U S S I A N   E M

Tobolsk

Samara

Omsk

Tomsk

TRANS-SIBERIAN RAIL

EUROPE

ASIA

Yenisei R.

Ob R.

S I

MEDITERRANEAN SEA

BLACK SEA

Constantinople

Astrakhan

CASPIAN
SEA

Baku

1846

1873

ARAL
SEA

1873

1881

1884

1864

1860-65

Tashkent

L. Balkhash

1854

SINKIA

OTTOMAN

EMPIRE

Mosul

Teheran

Merv

1885

BOKHARA

1868

1876

1895

Kashgar

RUSSIAN SPHERE,
1907

Cairo

Suez Canal

Jerusalem

Baghdad

Basra

PERSIA

BRITISH
SPHERE,
1907

Kabul

AFGHAN-
ISTAN

Indus R.

KASHMIR
1846

PUNJAB

HIMALA

T

RED
SEA

HEJAZ

A R A B I A

PERSIAN GULF

BALUCHISTAN
1883

Delhi

NEPA

Gang

Mecca

OMAN

Karachi

INDIA

BRITI

A F R I C A

YEMEN

Aden (Britain, 1839)

Diu
(Portugal)

Bombay

Hyderabad

Goa
(Portugal)

Ca

Yanac
(Franc

BAY

Madras
Pondicherr
(France)

Karikal (Fran

CEYLON

JEHOL

MANCHURIA

GREAT WALL

Kinchow

Mukden

Peking

Tientsin   *Taku*

GULF OF
CHILI

Dairen
Port Arthur

KOREA

(Lease to
Russia, 1898;
Japan, 1905)

Chifu

Wei-hai-wei
(Britain, 1898)

Grand Canal

Tsinan

Kiao-chow
(Germany, 1898)

Tsingtao

YELLOW SEA

SHANTUNG

CRITICAL AREA, 1895-1905

0   100   200 miles

INDIAN OCEAN

ALASKA
(Purchased by U.S.A.
from Russia, 1867)

BERING SEA

ALEUTIAN I. (U.S.A., 1867)

KAMCHATKA

Yakutsk

R I A

*SEA OF
OKHOTSK*

Lena R.

SAKHALIN

*KURILE I.
(Japan, 1875)*

AMUR PROVINCE
1858

*KARAFUTO
(Japan, 1905)*

Khabarovsk

Amur R.

MANCHURIA

MARITIME
PROVINCE
(Russia, 1868)

L. Baikal Chita

Irkutsk

Harbin

Vladivostok
1860

JAPANESE EMPIRE

*SEA OF
JAPAN*

Urga

Mukden

OUTER MONGOLIA
omous, 1912 Russian Sphere)

INNER MONGOLIA

JEHOL

KOREA
(Japan, 1905, 1910)

Tokyo

Peking

Tientsin

Port Arthur
(Japan, 1905)

Kiao-chow
(Germany, 1898)

PACIFIC OCEAN

Huang Ho

Nanking

Shanghai
(Britain, 1842)

C H I N A   Hankow

Ningpo
1842

*EAST
CHINA
SEA*

Chungking

Yangtse R.

Foochow

RYUKYU I.

Amoy

Canton
Britain, 1842

FORMOSA *(Japan, 1895)*

PESCADORES *(Japan, 1895)*

*MARIANA I.
(Germany, 1899)*

YÜNNAN

KWANGSI
(French Sphere)

Hong Kong *(Britain, 1842)*

Maçao *(Portugal, 1557)*

*GUAM
(U.S.A., 1898)*

BURMA
ritain, 1852, 1885)

Hanoi

ANNAM

Kwang-chow
(Lease to France, 1898)

HAINAN

*DIA
1852*

Mekong R.

FRENCH
INDOCHINA
1884, 1907

Manila

PHILIPPINE I.
(U.S.A., 1898, 1899)

*CAROLINE I.
(Germany, 1899)*

angoon

SIAM

1826

Bangkok

Saigon

*SOUTH
CHINA
SEA*

YAP

PALAU I.

*AMAN I.
itain)*

GAL

BRITISH
NORTH BORNEO
1888

NEW GUINEA

KAISER WILHEMSLAND
(Germany, 1884)

SARAWAK
1888

MALAY STATES
(Britain, 1800, 1824)

BORNEO

CELEBES

Singapore
(Britain, 1819)

SUMATRA

D U T C H   E A S T   I N D I E S

(Portugal, 1859)

TIMOR Darwin

Batavia

JAVA

AUSTRALIA

701

attacked the Manchus, who had come from Manchuria two centuries before, as corrupt foreigners ruling over China. Their grievances were poverty, extortion, rack-renting, and absentee landlords. The Tai-pings at first set up a state in south China, and their armies were at first disciplined, but the fighting lasted so long that both the Tai-ping leaders and the Manchu commanders sent against them got out of control, and much of the country sank into chronic banditry and disorder. It was in this period that China's war lords, men controlling armed forces but obeying no government, took their rise. The Manchus managed to put down organized Tai-ping resistance after fourteen years, with some European assistance, led by the British General Gordon, the "Chinese Gordon" who later died at Khartoum. But it is clear that Chinese social confusion, agrarianism, and nationalism (the latter at first only anti-Manchu) antedated the impact of European imperialism. They were to remain after the Europeans had come and gone.

Into this distracted China the Europeans began to penetrate about 1840. It became their policy to extort concessions from the Manchu empire but at the same time to defend the Manchu empire against internal opposition, as was shown by the exploits of Gordon. This was because they needed some kind of government in China with which they could make treaties, legalizing their claims and binding upon the whole country.

The Opening of China to the West

The modern phase of Chinese relations with the West was inauspiciously opened by the Opium War of 1841. We have already observed how, though Europeans wanted Chinese products, the Chinese had no interest in buying European products in return. Trade therefore was difficult, and the British East India Company had for decades solved the problem of getting Chinese tea for Europe by shipping Indian-grown opium in return, since opium was one available commodity for which a Chinese demand existed.[28] When the Chinese government attempted to control the inflow of opium the British government went to war. Fifteen years later, in 1857, Britain and France combined in a second war upon China to force the Chinese to receive their diplomats and deal with their traders. The Chinese proving contumacious, 17,000 French and British soldiers entered Peking and deliberately burned the emperor's very extensive Summer Palace, an appalling act of vandalism from which soldiers brought back so much loot—vases, tapestries, porcelain, enamels, jades, wood carvings—as to set a fashion in Europe and America for Chinese art.

From the first of these wars arose the treaty of Nanking (1842), from the second the treaties of Tientsin (1857), whose terms were soon duplicated in still other treaties signed by China with other European powers and with the United States. The resulting complex of interlocking agreements imposed certain restrictions on China, or conferred certain rights upon foreigners, which came to be known as the "treaty system." To the British in 1842 the Chinese ceded Hong Kong outright. They opened over a dozen cities, including Shanghai and Canton, to Europeans as "treaty

[28] See pp. 267–268, 365.

ports." In these cities Europeans were allowed to make settlements of their own, immune to all Chinese law. Europeans traveling in the Chinese empire remained subject only to their own governments, and European and American gunboats began to police the Yangtse River. The Chinese likewise paid large war indemnities, though it was they themselves who suffered most of the damages. They agreed to levy no import duty over 5 percent and so became a free trade market for European products. To administer and collect the customs a staff of European experts was introduced. Money from the customs, collected with a new efficiency, on a swelling volume of imports, went in part to the British and French in payment of the indemnities, but part remained with the Manchu government, which, as noted, the Europeans had no desire to overthrow.

While China was thus permeated at the center like an aging cheese, by extraterritorial and other insidious privileges for Europeans, whole slabs of it were cut away at the outer rim. The Russians moved down the Amur River, established their Maritime Province, and founded Vladivostok in 1860. The Japanese, now sufficiently westernized to behave like Europeans in such matters, in 1876 recognized the independence of Korea. The British annexed Burma in 1886. The French in 1883 assumed a protectorate over Annam despite Chinese protests; they soon combined five areas—Annam, Cochin China, Tonkin, Laos, and Cambodia—into French Indochina. (The first three were known also as Vietnam, a word not familiar in the West until after the Second World War.) These outlying territories had never, it is true, been integral parts of China proper; but it was with China that they had had their most important political and cultural relations and to the Chinese emperor that they had paid tribute.

Japan, whose modernization has been described already, lost little time in developing an imperialistic urge.[29] An expansionist party already looked to the Chinese mainland and to the south. Japanese imperialism first revealed itself to the rest of the world in 1894, when Japan went to war with China over disputes in Korea. The Japanese soon won, equipped as they were with modern weapons, training, and organization. They obliged the Chinese to sign the treaty of Shimonoseki in 1895, by which China ceded Formosa and the Liaotung peninsula to Japan and recognized Korea as an independent state. The Liaotung was a tongue of land reaching down from Manchuria to the sea; at its tip was Port Arthur. Manchuria was the northeastern part of China itself.

This sudden Japanese triumph precipitated a crisis in the Far East. No one had realized how strong Japan had become. All were astounded that a people who were not "European," i.e., white, should show such aptitude for modern war and diplomacy. It was to be supposed that Japan had designs on Manchuria.

Now it so happened that Russia, not long before, in 1891, had begun to build the Trans-Siberian Railway, whose eastern terminus was to be Vladivostok, the Lord of

[29] See pp. 594–600.

the East. Manchuria extended northward in a great hump between central Siberia and Vladivostok. The Russians, whether or not they ever dominated Manchuria themselves, could not allow its domination by another Great Power. It happened also that Germany was at this time looking for a chance to enter the Far Eastern arena, and that France had formed an alliance with Russia, whose good will it was eager to retain.[30]

Russia, Germany, and France therefore registered an immediate joint demurrer with the Tokyo Foreign Office. They demanded that Japan give up the Liaotung peninsula. The Japanese hesitated; they were indignant, but they yielded. The Liaotung went back to China.

In China many alert people were humiliated at the defeat by the Japanese whom they had despised. The Chinese government, at last facing the inevitable, began madly to plan westernization. Huge loans were obtained from Europe—the customs being pawned as security, following the pattern well established in Turkey, Persia, and Santo Domingo. But the European powers did not wish China to become consolidated too soon. Nor had they forgotten the sudden apparition of Japan. The result was a frantic scramble for further concessions in 1898.

It seemed in 1898 as if the Chinese empire in its turn would be partitioned. The Germans extorted a ninety-nine-year lease on Kiaochow Bay, plus exclusive rights in the Shantung peninsula. The Russians took a lease on the Liaotung peninsula from which they had just excluded Japan; they thus obtained Port Arthur and rights to build railroads in Manchuria to interlock with their Trans-Siberian system. The French took Kwangchow and the British Wei-hai-wei, in addition to confirming their sphere of influence in the Yangtze Valley. The Italians demanded a share but were refused. The United States, fearing that all China might soon be parceled out into exclusive spheres, announced its policy of the Open Door. The idea of the Open Door was that China should remain territorially intact and independent, and that powers having special concessions or spheres of influence should maintain the 5 percent Chinese tariff and allow businessmen of all nations to trade without discrimination. The British supported the Open Door, as a means of discouraging actual annexations by Japan or Russia, which, as the only Great Powers adjacent to China, were the only ones that could dispatch real armies into its territory. The Open Door was a program not so much of leaving China to the Chinese, as of assuring that all outsiders should find it literally "open."

If the reader will imagine what the United States would be like if foreign warships patrolled the Mississippi as far as St. Louis, if foreigners came and went throughout the country without being under its laws, if New York, New Orleans, and other cities contained foreign settlements outside its jurisdiction, but in which all banking and management were concentrated, if foreigners determined the tariff policy, collected the proceeds, and remitted much of the money to their own governments, if the western part of the city of Washington had been burned (the Summer Palace), Long Island and California annexed to distant empires (Hong Kong

[30]See p. 723.

and Indochina), and all New England were coveted by two immediate neighbors (Manchuria), if the national authorities were half in collusion with these foreigners and half victimized by them, and if large areas of the country were the prey to bandits, guerrillas, and revolutionary secret societies conspiring against the helpless government and occasionally murdering some of the foreigners—then he can understand how observant Chinese felt at the end of the last century, and why the term "imperialism" came to be held by so many of the world's peoples in abomination.

One Chinese secret society, its name somewhat literally translated as the Order of Literary Patriotic Harmonious Fists, and so dubbed the Boxers by the amused Westerners, broke out in insurrection in 1899. The Boxers pulled up railway tracks, fell upon Chinese Christians, besieged the foreign legations, and killed about 300 foreigners. The European powers, joined by Japan and the United States, sent a combined international force against the insurgents, who were put down. The victors imposed still more severe controls on the Chinese government and inflicted an indemnity of $330,000,000. Of this the United States received $24,000,000, of which, however, in 1924, it canceled the balance that was still due. On the other hand, as a consequence of the Boxer Rebellion, the Manchu officials strove desperately to strengthen themselves by westernization, while at the same time the revolutionary movement in China, aiming at expulsion of Manchus and foreigners alike, spread rapidly throughout the country, especially in the south, under the leadership of Sun Yat-sen.

M

eanwhile Russia and Japan opposed each other's intrigues in Manchuria and Korea. The Japanese felt a need for supplying their new factories with raw materials and markets on the Asiatic mainland, for employment for their newly westernized army and navy, for recognized status as a Great Power in the Western sense. The Russian government needed an atmosphere of crisis and expansion to stifle criticism of tsarism at home; it could not abide the presence of a strong power directly on its East Asian frontier; it could use Manchuria and Korea to strengthen the exposed outpost of Vladivostok, which was somewhat squeezed against the sea, and land-locked by Japanese waters. The Russians had obtained a concession from China to build the Chinese Eastern Railway to Vladivostok across the heart of Manchuria. A railway, in Manchuria, implied special zones, railway guards, mining and timber rights, and other auxiliary activities. The Japanese saw the fruits of their successful war of 1895 against China greedily enjoyed by their rival. In 1902 Japan signed a military alliance with Great Britain. We have seen how the British were alarmed by their diplomatic isolation after Fashoda and the Boer War, and how for many years, in the Far East, the Middle East, and the Near East, they had been expecting to have trouble with Russia. The Anglo-Japanese military alliance lasted twenty years.

**84
The Russo-Japanese
War and Its
Consequences**

Northeast China and Adjoining Regions, 1895–1914. *This area has long been one of the world's trouble zones. Note how Vladivostok is shut off from the ocean by the Japanese islands and Korea, and almost shut off from the mass of Russia by the intervening bulk of Manchuria. Manchuria, which began to be industrialized about 1900, became an object of dispute between China, to which it belonged historically, the Russian empire, to which it had strategic value and offered an access to the open ocean, and the Japanese empire, which found in it an outlet for commercial and military expansion and a buffer against Russia. Manchuria was dominated by the Russians from 1898 to 1905, by the Japanese from 1905 to 1945, and again by the Russians from 1945 to 1950 when they handed over their concessions and privileges to the Chinese communist government. Korea was dominated by Japan after her victories over China in 1895 and over Russia in 1905. After World War II, Korea was promised independence but was divided at the 38th parallel into a Russian occupation zone and an American zone. After the Korean War (1950–1953, see pp. 995–996) the country remained divided at roughly the same parallel with a communist regime in the north and a Western-sponsored regime in the south.*

War broke out in 1904, undeclared, by Japanese naval attack on Russian installations at Port Arthur. Both sides sent large armies into Manchuria. The battle of Mukden, in the number of men engaged, which was 624,000, was the largest battle which human experience had thus far witnessed. Military observers were present from all countries, anxiously trying to learn what the next war in Europe would be like. The Russians sent their Baltic fleet around three continents to the Far East, but to the world's amazement the Russian fleet was met and destroyed at Tsushima Strait by the new and untested navy of Japan. Russian communications by sea were thereby broken, and since the Trans-Siberian Railway was unfinished, and since the Japanese also won the battle of Mukden, Russia was beaten.

At this point the president of the United States, Theodore Roosevelt, stepped upon the scene. With an outpost in the Philippines and growing interests in China, it was to the American advantage to have neither side win too overwhelming a victory in the Far East. The most imperially minded of all American presidents offered his mediation, and plenipotentiaries of the two powers met at Portsmouth, New Hampshire. By the treaty of Portsmouth, in 1905, Japan recovered from Russia what it had won and lost in 1895, namely, Port Arthur and the Liaotung peninsula, a preferred position in Manchuria, which remained nominally Chinese, and a protectorate in Korea, which remained nominally independent, although a few years later, in 1910, it was annexed by Japan. Japan also received from Russia the southern half of the island of Sakhalin. Much of what Russia lost to Japan in 1905 was regained forty years later at the end of the Second World War.

The Russo-Japanese war was the first war between Great Powers since 1870. It was the first war fought under conditions of developed industrialism. It was the first actual war between westernized powers to be caused by competition in the exploitation of backward countries. Most significant of all (except for the Ethiopian rout of the Italians), it was the first time that a nonwhite people had defeated a white people in modern times. Asians had shown that they could learn and play, in less than half a century, the game of the Europeans.

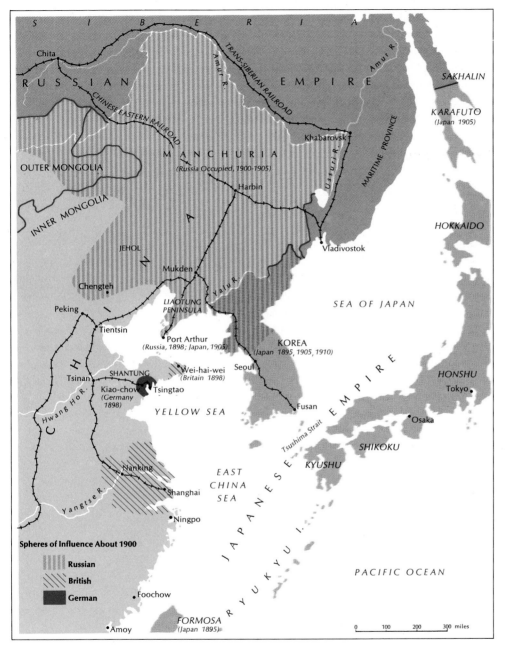

SIBERIA

Chita

TRANS-SIBERIAN RAILROAD

Amur R.

RUSSIAN EMPIRE

Amur R.

SAKHALIN

KARAFUTO
(Japan 1905)

CHINESE EASTERN RAILROAD

Khabarovsk

MANCHURIA
(Russia Occupied, 1900-1905)

OUTER MONGOLIA

Harbin

MARITIME PROVINCE

Ussuri R.

INNER MONGOLIA

HOKKAIDO

JEHOL

Vladivostok

Chengteh

Mukden

SEA OF JAPAN

Peking

LIAOTUNG
PENINSULA

Yalu R.

Tientsin

Port Arthur
(Russia, 1898; Japan, 1905)

KOREA
(Japan 1895, 1905, 1910)

Seoul

HONSHU

Tsinan

SHANTUNG

Wei-hai-wei
(Britain 1898)

Tokyo

Kiao-chow
(Germany 1898)

Tsingtao

Hwang Ho R.

YELLOW SEA

Fusan

JAPANESE EMPIRE

Osaka

Tsushima Strait

SHIKOKU

Nanking

EAST
CHINA
SEA

KYUSHU

Yangtse R.

Shanghai

Ningpo

Spheres of Influence About 1900

	Russian
	British
	German

Foochow

PACIFIC OCEAN

RYUKYU Is.

FORMOSA
(Japan 1895)

Amoy

0   100   200   300 miles

The Japanese victory set off long chains of repercussions in at least three different directions. For one thing, the Russian government, frustrated in its foreign policy in East Asia, shifted its attention back to Europe, where it resumed an active role in the affairs of the Balkans. This contributed to a series of international crises in Europe, of which the result was the First World War. Second, the tsarist government was so weakened by the war, both in prestige and in actual military strength, and opinion in Russia was so disgusted at the clumsiness and incompetency with which

707

the war had been handled, that the various underground movements were able to come to the surface, producing the Revolution of 1905. This in turn was a prelude to the great Russian Revolution twelve years later, of which Soviet communism was the outcome. Third, news of Japan's victory over Russia electrified those who heard of it throughout the non-European world. The fact that Japan was itself an imperialist power was overlooked in the excited realization that the Japanese were not white. Only half a century ago the Japanese, too, had been "backward"—defenseless, bombarded, and bulldozed by the Europeans. The moral was clear. Everywhere leaders of subjected peoples concluded, from the Japanese precedent, that they must bring Western science and industry to their own countries, but that they must do it, as the Japanese had done, by getting rid of control by the whites, supervising the process of modernization themselves, and preserving their own native national character. Nationalist revolutions began in Persia in 1905, in Turkey in 1908, in China in 1911. In India and Indonesia many were stirred by the Japanese achievement. In the face of rising agitation, the British admitted an Indian to the Viceroy's executive Council in 1909, and in 1916 the Dutch created a People's Council, to include Indonesian members, in the Indies. The self-assertion of Asians was to grow in intensity after the First World War.

The Japanese victory and Russian defeat can therefore be seen as steps in three mighty developments, the First World War, the Russian Revolution, and the Revolt of Asia. These three together put an end to Europe's world supremacy and almost to European civilization; or at least they so transmuted them as to make the world of the twentieth century far different from that of the nineteenth.

The British presence in India, reaching over three centuries, spanned the whole period from the early trading empires to the latest phases of European imperialism. In the seventeenth century the Indian subcontinent was held together by a Moslem empire whose ruler was known in Europe as the Great Mogul. His revenues, in 1605, were some twenty times greater than those of the King of England. The Europeans were for a long time only handfuls of foreigners operating out of small coastal stations. After 1700 the Mogul authority fell to pieces, leaving a disorganized situation in which the British emerged as the supreme power throughout the country.

India in the nineteenth century represented, in its fullest form, the European imperialism which by 1900 reached throughout Asia and Africa. Parts of it were ruled by the British directly, parts through the rajahs and maharajahs of native states. British power prevented internal warfare and subordinated the conflicts between Hindus and Moslems. Peace generally prevailed except for the great Mutiny, or rebellion, of 1857, which was quickly suppressed. The British introduced their own ideas of law, government, civil service and education. With food production increased by irrigation, and famine relieved by transport of provisions by railroad, population grew very rapidly.

The British invested a great deal of capital in India, in railroads, coal mines, and tea plantations. There was also much development of Indian capital, especially in the new jute, cotton and steel industries. As the railroad opened the interior to the cheaper products of Lancashire, the old handicraft and village industries were destroyed, to be symbolically revived by Gandhi and his spinning wheel in the 1920s, and in fact replaced by an extensive development of modern manufactures. India moved into the twentieth century as a land of violent contrasts, of endless villages interrupted by teeming cities, with staggering problems of poverty and over-population, yet also an important industrial country with a heavy involvement in world trade.

The British, throughout their rule in India, lived very much to themselves, occasionally mixing with the Indian upper classes but avoiding intimate or even equal relationships. For many Indians, nevertheless, English became a second language, used both for contacts with the Western world and as a common medium among themselves. A modern Indian upper class, largely English-speaking, grew up with the development of business, government and the professions. It ultimately took the lead in the national movement against foreign rule. But historic divisions within the country, between Hindu and Moslem, dating back to the Mogul empire and before, brought it about that upon the British withdrawal, in 1947, what had formerly been known as India became the separate states of India and Pakistan.

THE BRITISH IN INDIA

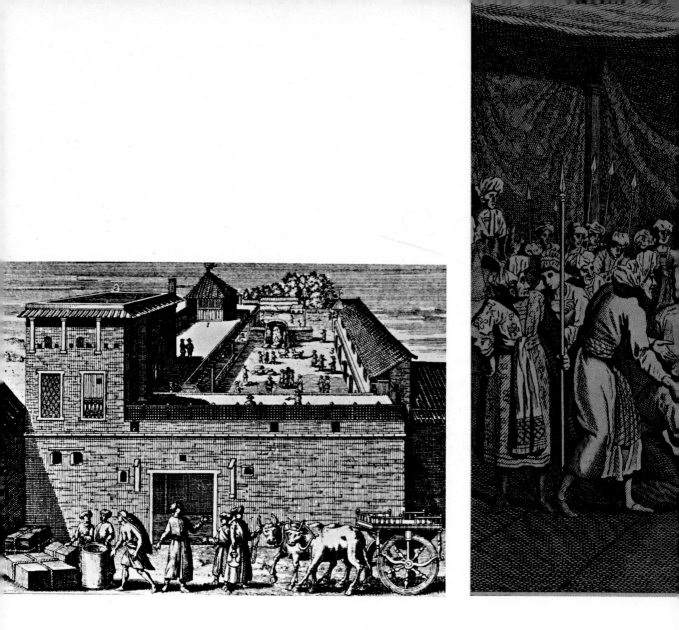

The gorgeous East, as Milton called it, had been fabled in Europe for its riches since ancient times. Above, right, we see the weighing of the Great Mogul on his birthday, upon which he was to receive an equal weight in gold and jewels. The picture is from an English geography of 1782. As the French "Encyclopédie" put it at about this time: "The most solemn day of the year was when the emperor was weighed in golden balances in the presence of the people; on that day he received over 50 millions in presents."

At the left is the English factory at Surat, near Bombay, in the early seventeenth century. A "factory" was only a trading center where the agents, or factors, of the East India Company stored their goods.

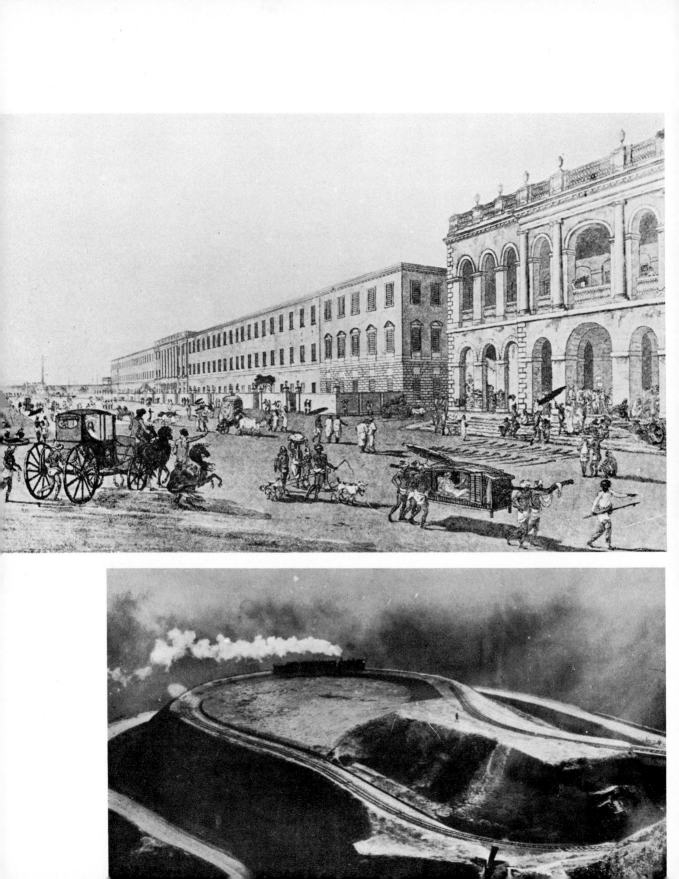

Calcutta, now the largest city in India, is far from being one of the oldest. It was founded by the English East India Company in 1690, and acquired many Western-style buildings in the two following centuries. At the left above is the Old Court House; at the right the early nineteenth-century Government House, with a large British lion astride the neoclassic gate. At the left an English lady is carried in a palanquin, and in both pictures important persons ride by in carriages, surveyed at a distance by some of the plain people of India, one of them with a bullock cart. The two cultures never really merged.

Darjeeling, in the mountains 300 miles north of Calcutta, grew up after 1840 as a cool retreat for Britons in refuge from the Indian heat. At the left is the "big loop" of the Darjeeling Railway, a substantial feat of engineering, by which the imperial rulers were able to make the journey more comfortably. The clouds probably obscure a view of the Himalayas for which Darjeeling is famous.

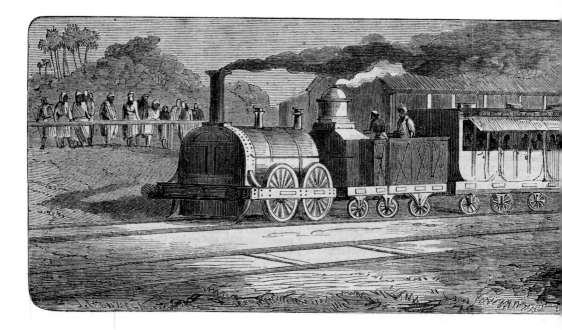

The railroad also had a transforming impact on India as a whole. By carrying goods it brought the interior into the world market, breaking up old native industries while creating new ones, and by transporting persons it drew together the members of diverse religions, castes and linguistic groups. A passenger train of 1863 appears above. In its crowded coaches Indians who in former times would have kept scrupulously apart, for fear of pollution, had to rub elbows together, and on long journeys even eat together and breathe the same tainted air. Such proximity, together with the increasing adoption of English, produced a new basis for Indian unity which in the end was to make the British position untenable.

At the right, before the track is laid, a team of elephants hauls the first locomotive into Indore in Central India.

Above left: Queen Victoria is proclaimed Empress of India at Bombay in 1877. The neo-Gothic canopy, built for the occasion, under which the queen is enthroned, seems incongruous in the circumstances. It reminds us, together with the more permanent church in the background, that the British maintained their own ways with supreme confidence, making few concessions to the alien culture over which they presided.

In the nineteenth century the traveling Englishwoman became legendary for her indomitability. At the right, two of them go on a jungle picnic. The pith helmets of their escorts, and the bearer carrying the refreshments on his head, may be taken as symbols of the heyday of empire.

716

The drawing above represents the administration of justice, with a British magistrate at the left, a native magistrate at the right. They seem much alike, and their purpose may be to show how under British rule the Indian judicial system was brought up to British standards of legal procedure.

Many Indians received a thoroughly English education. At the right is Jawaharlal Nehru at Harrow about 1905. Nehru, born in 1889 of Brahmin parents, his father a wealthy lawyer, was educated at home by English tutors, then sent to Harrow and Cambridge. He joined Gandhi in the independence movement in the 1920s, and served as first prime minister of independent India from 1947 until his death in 1964. British India dug its own grave, or prepared its own successors.

XVI: THE FIRST WORLD WAR

When a traveler has wandered off his course it is easy for him, if he has a good map and if the country is well marked with road signs, to retrace his steps, find the point where he went astray, and resume the route to his destination. It would not be so easy if he had no map, if there were no signs, and if he could never under any circumstances go backward.

Somewhere before 1914 Europe went off its course. Europeans believed themselves to be heading for a kind of high plateau, full of a benign progress and more abundant civilization, in which the benefits of modern science and invention would be more widely diffused, and even competitive struggle worked out somehow for the best. Instead, Europe stumbled in 1914 into disaster. It is not easy to see exactly where Europe went astray, at what point, that is, the First World War became inevitable, or (since the human mind does not know what is truly inevitable) so overwhelmingly probable that only the most Olympian statesmanship could have avoided it. History is not as exact as a map, its road signs are read differently by different people—and the traveler can never go backward.

Chapter Emblem: A German medal to celebrate the sinking of the Lusitania in 1915, showing the Cunard Line as a skeleton selling tickets, under an inscription, "Business First."

AAfter 1870 Europe lived in a repressed fear of itself. The great questions of the mid-century had been settled by force. The German Empire was only the strongest and most obvious of the new structures which armed power had reared. Never had the European states maintained such huge armies in peacetime as at the beginning of the twentieth century. One, two, or even three years of compulsory military service for all young men became the rule. In 1914 each of the Continental Great Powers had not only a huge standing army but millions of trained reserves among the civilian population. Few people wanted war; all but a few sensational writers preferred peace in Europe, but all took it for granted that war would come some day. In the last years before 1914 the idea that war was bound to break out sooner or later probably made some statesmen, in some countries, more willing to unleash it.

Rival Alliances:
Triple Alliance
Versus Triple Entente

Political diagnosticians, from Richelieu to Metternich, had long thought that an effective union of Germany would revolutionize the relationships of Europe's peoples. After 1870 their anticipations were more than confirmed. Once united (or almost united), the Germans entered upon their industrial revolution. Manufacturing, finance, shipping, population grew phenomenally. In steel, for example, of which Germany in 1865 produced less than France, by 1900 Germany produced more than France and Great Britain combined. Germans felt that they needed and deserved a "place in the sun," by which they vaguely meant some kind of acknowledged supremacy like that of the British. Neither the British nor the French, the leaders of modern Europe since the seventeenth century, could share wholeheartedly in such German aspirations. The French had the chronic grievance of Alsace and Lorraine, annexed to Germany in 1871. The British as the years passed saw German salesmen appear in their foreign markets, selling goods often at lower prices and by what seemed ungentlemanly methods; they saw Germans turn up as colonial rivals in Africa, the Near East, and the Far East; and they watched other European states gravitate into the Berlin orbit, looking to the mighty German Empire as a friend and protector to secure or advance their interests.[1]

Bismarck after 1871 feared that in another European war his new German Empire might be torn to pieces. He therefore followed, until his retirement in 1890, a policy of peace. We have seen him as the "honest broker" at the Berlin Congress of 1878, helping to adjudicate the Eastern Question, and again offering the facilities of Berlin in 1885 to regulate African affairs. To isolate France, divert it from Europe, and keep it embroiled with Britain, he looked with satisfaction on French colonial expansion. He took no chances, however; in 1879 he formed a military alliance with Austria-Hungary, to which Italy was admitted in 1882. Thus was formed the Triple

[1]See map, "Anglo-German Industrial Competition," p. 725.

Alliance, which lasted until the First World War. Its terms were, briefly, that if any member became involved in war with two or more powers its allies should come to its aid by force of arms. To be on the safe side, Bismarck signed a "reinsurance" treaty with Russia also; since Russia and Austria were enemies (because of the Balkans), to be allied to both at the same time took considerable diplomatic finesse. After Bismarck's retirement his system proved too intricate, or too lacking in candor, for his successors to manage. The Russo-German agreement lapsed. The French, faced by the Triple Alliance, soon seized the opportunity to form their own alliance with Russia, the Franco-Russian Alliance signed in 1894. In its time this was regarded as politically almost impossible. The French Republic stood for everything radical, the Russian empire for everything reactionary and autocratic. but ideology was thrown to the winds, French capital poured into Russia, and the tsar bared his head to the *Marseillaise.*

The Continent was thus divided by 1894 into two opposed camps, the German-Austrian-Italian against the Franco-Russian. For a time it seemed that this rigid division might soften. Germany, France and Russia cooperated in the Far Eastern crisis of 1895.[2] All were anti-British at the time of Fashoda and the Boer War.[3] The Kaiser, William II, outlined tempting pictures of a Continental league against the global hegemony of England and her empire.

Much depended on what the British would do. They had long prided themselves on a "splendid isolation," going their own way, disdaining the kind of dependency that alliance with others always brings. Fashoda and the Boer War came as a shock. British relations with France and Russia were very bad. Some in England, including Joseph Chamberlain, therefore thought that a better understanding with Germany was to be sought. Arguments of race, in this exceedingly race-conscious age, made Englishmen and Germans feel akin.[4] But politically it was hard to cooperate. The Kaiser's Kruger Telegram of 1896 was a studied insult.[5] Then in 1898 the Germans decided to build a navy.

A new kind of "race" now entered the picture, the naval competition between Germany and Great Britain. British sea power for two centuries had been all too successful. The American Admiral Mahan, teaching at the Naval War College, and taking his examples largely from British history, argued that sea power had been the foundation of Britain's greatness, and that in the long run sea power must always choke off and ruin a power operating on the land. Nowhere were Mahan's books read with more interest than in Germany. The German naval program, mounting rapidly after 1898, in a few years became a source of concern to the British, and by

---

[2] See pp. 703–704.

[3] See pp. 692–694.

[4] The will of Cecil Rhodes, who died in 1902, illustrates this point. Rhodes left most of his fortune (£6,000,000) to establish scholarships at Oxford to be awarded to students in the United States, as an Anglo-Saxon country, the British dominions and colonies, and Germany. The German Rhodes Scholarships were suspended from 1914 to 1930 and again after 1938. The same feeling that Germans were racially akin was common in the United States also; a prominent example of this viewpoint was President Theodore Roosevelt.

[5] See p. 693.

1912 was felt as a positive menace. The Germans insisted that they must have a navy to protect their colonies, secure their foreign trade, and "for the general purposes of their greatness." The British held with equal resolution that England, as a densely populated industrial island, dependent even for food upon imports, must at all costs control the sea in both peace and war. They adhered stubbornly to their traditional policy of maintaining a navy as large as the next two combined. The naval race led both sides to enormous and increasing expenditures. In the British it produced a sense of profound insecurity, driving them as the years passed ever more inescapably into the arms of Russia and France.

Slowly and cautiously the British emerged from their diplomatic isolation. In 1902 they formed a military alliance with Japan against their common enemy, Russia.[6] The decisive break came in 1904, from which may be dated the immediate series of crises issuing in the World War ten years later.

In 1904 the British and French governments agreed to forget Fashoda and the accumulated bad feeling of the preceding twenty-five years. The French recognized the British occupation of Egypt, and the British recognized the French penetration of Morocco. They also cleared up a few lesser colonial differences and agreed to support each other against protests by third parties. There was no specific alliance; neither side said what it would do in the event of war; it was only a close understanding, an *entente cordiale.* The French immediately tried to reconcile their new friend to their ally, Russia. After defeat by Japan the Russians proved amenable. The British, increasingly uncertain of German aims, proved likewise willing. In 1907 Britain and Russia, the inveterate adversaries, settled their differences in an Anglo-Russian Convention. In Persia, the British recognized a Russian sphere of influence in the north, the Russians a British sphere in the south and east. By 1907 England, France, and Russia were acting together. The older Triple Alliance faced a newer Triple Entente, the latter somewhat the looser, since the British refused to make any formal military commitments.

[6] See p. 705.

Anglo-German Industrial Competition 1898 and 1913. *This diagram really shows two things: first, the huge increase in world trade in the last fifteen years before the First World War, shared in by all countries; and second, the fact that German exports grew more rapidly than British. The exports of both countries together, as shown on the diagram, multiplied no less than threefold in these fifteen years. The increase, while due in small part to a slight rise of prices, was mainly due to a real increase in volume of business. If the reader will compare the shaded bands within the large arrows he will see that, for the countries shown, British exports about doubled, but those of Germany multiplied many times. In 1913 total German exports about equalled the British, but German exports to the United States and Russia greatly exceeded the British. Note how the Germans even gained in exports to British India, where the liberalism of British policy freely admitted competitive goods. In merchant marine, though the Germans doubled their tonnage, the British continued to enjoy an overwhelming lead.*

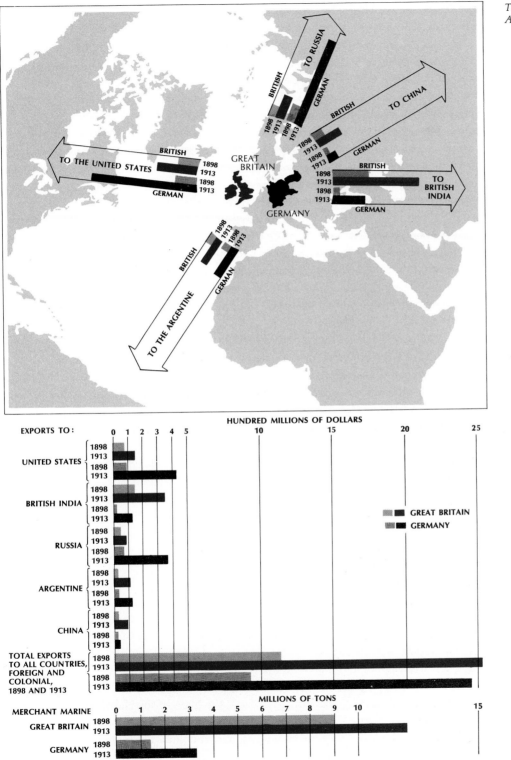

The Germans, who already felt encircled by the alliance of France and Russia, naturally watched with concern the drift of England into the Franco-Russian camp. The Entente Cordiale was barely concluded when the German government decided to test it, to find out how strong it really was, or how far the British would really go in support of France. The French, now enjoying British backing, were taking over more police powers, concessions, and loans in Morocco. In March 1905 William II disembarked from a German warship at Tangier, where he made a startling speech in favor of Moroccan independence. To diplomats everywhere this carefully staged performance was a signal: Germany was attempting not primarily to keep France out of Morocco, nor even to reserve Morocco for itself, but to break up the new understanding between France and England. The Germans demanded and obtained an international conference at Algeciras (at which the United States was represented), but the conference, which met in 1906, supported the French claims in Morocco, only Austria voting with Germany. The German government had thus created an incident and been rebuffed. The British, disturbed by German diplomatic tactics, stood by the French all the more firmly. French and British army and naval officers now began to discuss common plans. Distrust of Germany also inclined the British to bury the hatchet with Russia in the next year. The German attempt to break the Entente simply made it more solid.

In 1911 came a second Morocco crisis. A German gunboat, the *Panther*, arrived at Agadir "to protect German interests." It soon developed that the move was a hold-up: the Germans offered to make no further trouble in Morocco if they could have the French Congo. The crisis passed, the Germans obtaining some trifling accessions in Africa. But a member of the British cabinet, David Lloyd George, made a rather inflammatory speech on the German menace.

Meanwhile a series of crises rocked the Balkans. Here at the opening of the twentieth century the situation was very confused. The Ottoman Empire, in an advanced state of dissolution, still held a band of territory from Constantinople westward to the Adriatic.[7] South of this band lay an independent Greece. North of it, on the Black Sea side, lay an autonomous Bulgaria and an independent Rumania. In the center and west of the peninsula, north of the Turkish belt, was the small, land-locked independent kingdom of Serbia, adjoined by Bosnia-Herzegovina, which belonged legally to Turkey but had been "occupied and administered" by Austria since 1878. Within the Austro-Hungarian Empire, adjoining Bosnia on the north, lay Croatia and Slovenia.

Serbs, Bosnians, Croats, and Slovenes all spoke basically the same language, the main difference being that Serbs and Bosnians wrote with the eastern or Cyrillic alphabet, the Croats and Slovenes with the western or Roman. With the Slavic Revival and general growth of nationalism these peoples came to feel that they were really one people, for which they took the term South Slavs or Yugoslavs. We have seen how, when the Dual Monarchy was formed in 1867, the Slavs of the Habsburg empire were kept subordinate to the German Austrians and to the Magyars. By 1900 the most radical Slav nationalists within the empire had concluded that the Dual Monarchy

[7]See maps, pp. 478, 684, and 728.

would never grant them equal status, that it must be broken up, and that all South Slavs should form an independent state of their own. Concretely, this meant that an element of the Austro-Hungarian population, namely, the Croatian and Slovenian nationalists, wished to get out of the empire and join with Serbia across the border. Serbia became the center of South Slav agitation. The Serbs conceived of their small kingdom as the Sardinia of a South Slav Risorgimento, the nucleus around which a new national state could be formed, at the expense of Austria-Hungary, which, to repeat, contained Croatia-Slovenia within its own frontiers and "occupied" Bosnia.

This brew was brought to a boil in 1908 by two events. First, the Young Turks, whose long agitation against Abdul Hamid has been noted, managed in that year to carry through a revolution.[8] They obliged the sultan to restore the liberal-parliamentary constitution of 1876. They showed, too, that they meant to stop the dissolution of the Ottoman Empire, by taking steps to have delegates from Bulgaria and Bosnia sit in the new Ottoman parliament. Second, Russia, its foreign policy in the Far East ruined by the Japanese war, turned actively to the Balkan and Turkish scene. Russia, as always, wanted control at Constantinople. Austria wanted full annexation of Bosnia, the better to discourage Pan-Yugoslav ideas. But if the Young Turks really modernized and strengthened the Ottoman Empire, Austria would never get Bosnia, nor the Russians Constantinople.

The Russian and Austrian foreign ministers, Isvolsky and Aehrenthal, at a conference at Buchlau in 1908 came to a secret agreement: they would call an international conference, at which Russia would favor Austrian annexation of Bosnia, and Austria would support the opening of the Straits to Russian warships. Austria, without waiting for a conference, proclaimed the annexation of Bosnia without more ado. This infuriated the Serbs, who had marked Bosnia for their own. Meanwhile, that same year, the Bulgarians and the Cretans broke finally with the Ottoman Empire, Bulgaria becoming fully independent, Crete uniting with Greece. Isvolsky was never able to realize his plans for Constantinople. His partners in the Triple Entente, Britain and France, refused to back him; the British in particular were evasive on plans for opening the Straits to the Russian fleet. The projected international conference was never called. In Russia itself public opinion knew nothing of Isvolsky's secret deal. The known fact in Russia was that the Serbs, the little Slav brothers of Russia, had had their toes rudely stepped on by the Austrians by the annexation of Bosnia.

This "first Balkan crisis" presently passed. The Russians, weakened by the Japanese war and by recent revolution,[9] accepted the Austrian *fait accompli*. Russia protested but backed down. Austrian influence in the Balkans seemed to be growing. And South Slav nationalism was frustrated and inflamed.

In 1911 Italy declared war on Turkey, from which it soon conquered Tripoli and the Dodecanese Islands. With the Ottomans thus embarrassed, Bulgaria, Serbia, and Greece joined forces in their own war against Turkey, hoping to annex certain Balkan territories to which they believed they had a right. Turkey was soon defeated, but the

[8] See pp. 681–685.
[9] See pp. 705–706, 775–777.

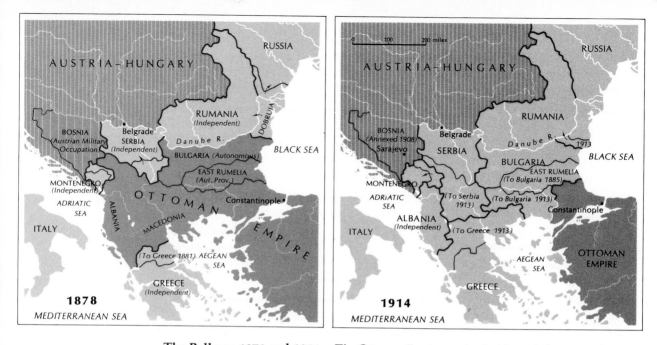

The Balkans 1878 and 1914. *The Ottoman Empire, under the blows of Austria and Russia, had been receding from Europe since 1699 (see map, p. 684). The Congress of Berlin of 1878 undertook to stabilize the situation by recognizing Rumania, Serbia, and Montenegro as independent monarchies, and northern Bulgaria as an autonomous principality within the Ottoman Empire. The ambitions of these new states (and of Greece, independent since 1829), together with the discontents of all non-Turkish peoples remaining under Ottoman rule, led to successive altercations culminating in the Balkan wars of 1912–1913. Albania then became independent, and Serbia, Bulgaria, and Greece contiguous. Austrian and Russian pressures meanwhile continued; in 1908 Austria annexed Bosnia, where the South Slav population was related to the Serbs. In Bosnia, at Sarajevo, six years later, the assassination of an Austrian archduke by a South Slav patriot precipitated the First World War.*

Bulgarians claimed more of Macedonia than the Serbs would yield, so that the first Balkan war of 1912 was followed in 1913 by a second, in which Serbia, Greece, Rumania, and Turkey turned upon and defeated Bulgaria. Albania also, a mountainous region on the Adriatic, mainly Moslem, and known as the wildest place in all Europe, was the subject of angry discord. The Serbs occupied part of it in the two Balkan wars, but the Greeks also claimed a part, and it had also on several occasions been vaguely promised to Italy.[10] Russia supported the Serbian claim. Austria was determined to shut off the Serbs from access to the sea, which they would obtain by annexation of Albanian territory. An agreement of the great powers, to keep the peace, conjured up an independent kingdom of Albania. This confirmed the Austrian policy, kept Serbia from the sea, and aroused vehement outcries in both Serbia and Russia. But Russia again backed down. Serbian expansionism was again frustrated and inflamed.

728   [10]See p. 683.

The third Balkan crisis proved to be the fatal one. It was fatal because two others had gone before it, leaving feelings of exasperation in Austria, desperation in Serbia, and humiliation in Russia.

On June 28, 1914, a young Bosnian revolutionary, a member of the Serbian secret society called "Union or Death," and commonly known as the Black Hand, acting with the knowledge of certain Serbian officials, assassinated the heir to the Habsburg empire, the Archduke Francis Ferdinand, in the streets of Sarajevo, the Bosnian capital, in the Austrian Empire. The world was shocked at this terroristic outrage and at first sympathized with the protests of the Austrian government. Francis Ferdinand, who would soon have become emperor, was known to favor some kind of transformation of Austria-Hungary, in which a more equal place might be given to the Slavs; but the reformer who makes a system work is the most dangerous of all enemies to the implacable revolutionary, and it is perhaps for this reason that the archduke was killed by the Black Hand.

The Austrian government was determined to make an end to the South Slav separatism that was gnawing its empire to pieces. It decided to crush the independence of Serbia, the nucleus of South Slav agitation, though not to annex it, since there were now thought to be too many Slavs within the empire already. The Austrian government consulted the German to see how far it might go with the support of its ally. The Germans, issuing their famous "blank check," encouraged the Austrians to be firm. The Austrians, thus reassured, dispatched a drastic ultimatum to Serbia, demanding among other things that Austrian officials be permitted to collaborate in investigating and punishing the perpetrators of the assassination. The Serbs counted on Russian support, even to the point of war, judging that Russia could not again yield in a Balkan crisis, for the third time in six years, without losing its influence in the Balkans altogether. The Russians in turn counted on France; and France, terrified at the possibility of being some day caught alone in a war with Germany, and determined to keep Russia as an ally at any cost, in effect gave a blank check to Russia. The Serbs rejected the critical item in the Austrian ultimatum as an infringement on Serbian sovereignty, and Austria thereupon declared war upon Serbia. Russia prepared to defend Serbia and hence to fight Austria. Expecting that Austria would be joined by Germany, Russia rashly mobilized its army on the German as well as the Austrian frontier. Since the power which first mobilized had all the advantages of a rapid offensive, the German government demanded an end to the Russian mobilization on its border and, receiving no answer, declared war on Russia on August 1, 1914. Convinced that France would in any case enter the war on the side of Russia, Germany also declared war on France on August 3.

The German decisions were posited on a reckless hope that Great Britain might not enter the war at all. England was bound by no formal military alliance. Even the French did not know for certain, as late as August 3, whether the British would join them in war. The British clung to scraps of their old proud isolation; they hesitated to make a final choice of sides; and as the foreign secretary, Sir Edward Grey, repeatedly explained, in England only Parliament could declare war, so that the foreign office could make no binding promise of war in advance. It has often been said that, had the German government known as a positive fact that England would fight, the war might not have come. Hence the evasiveness of British policy is made a contributing cause of the war. In reality, the probability that England would fight was so great that to underestimate it, as the Germans did, was an act of supreme and even criminal folly. The British were deeply committed to France, especially through naval agreements. As the German High Seas Fleet grew, the British had been obliged to concentrate naval forces in the North Sea. They had therefore had to withdraw forces from the Mediterranean. In 1914, by agreement with France, the French fleet was concentrated in the Mediterranean, watching over British interests, while the British fleet attended to French interests in the north. The French Channel coast was therefore open to German naval attack, unless the British defended it. Sir Edward Grey accepted this moral obligation, but what swept the British public was the invasion of Belgium. The German plan to crush France quickly was such that it could succeed only by crossing Belgium. When the Belgians protested, the Germans invaded anyway, violating the treaty of 1839 which had guaranteed Belgian neutrality. England declared war on Germany on August 4.

The mere narration of successive crises does not explain why the chief nations of Europe became locked in combat over the murder of an imperial personage within a few days. Among more obvious general causes, the alliance system may be singled out. Europe was divided into two camps. Every incident tended to become a test of strength between the two. A given incident, such as German intervention in Morocco, or the assassination of Francis Ferdinand, could not be settled on its own merits, merely by the parties concerned; however it was dealt with, one of the two camps was deemed to have lost or gained and hence to have lost or gained in influence in other incidents, of perhaps greater purport, that would arise in the future. Each power felt that it must stand by its allies whatever the specific issue. This was because all lived in the fear of war, of some nameless future war in which allies would be necessary. The Germans complained of being "encircled" by France and Russia. They dreaded the day when they might have to face a war on two fronts. Willing to accept even a European-wide war to break their threatened "encirclement" by the Entente powers, they were obliged to hold to their one ally, Austria-Hungary, which was in turn able to sell its support at its own price. The French dreaded a coming conflict with Germany, which in forty years had far surpassed France in population and industrial strength; they were obliged to cling to their ally Russia, which therefore could oblige the French to yield to Russian wishes. As for Russia and Austria, they were both tottering empires. Especially after 1900, the tsarist regime suffered from endemic revolutionism, and the Habsburg empire from chronic nationalistic agitation. Authorities in both empires became desperate. Like the Serbs, they had little to lose and were therefore reckless. It was Russia that drew France and hence England into war in 1914, and Austria that drew in Germany. Seen in this light, the tragedy of 1914 is that the most backward or politically bankrupt parts of Europe, through the alliance system, dragged the more advanced parts automatically into ruin.

The German Empire, too, faced an internal crisis. The Social Democrats became the largest party in the Reichstag in 1912. Their sentiments for the most part were antimilitarist and antiwar. But the German imperial government recognized no responsibility to a majority in the chamber. Policy was determined by men of the old unreconstructed upper class, in which army and navy interests, now reinforced by the new business interests, were very strong; and even moderates and liberals shared in the ambition to make Germany a world power, the equal of any. The perplexities the ruling groups faced at home, the feeling that their position was being undermined by the Social Democrats, may have made them less unwilling to view war as a way out. And while it is not true that Germany started the war, as its enemies in 1914 popularly believed, it must be granted that its policies had for some years been rather peremptory, arrogant, devious and obstinate. In a broad sense, the failure of Europe to assimilate the consolidated industrial Germany which arose after 1870, and which therefore made its bid for world-power status relatively late, was a distant and basic cause of the war.

The alliance system was only a symptom of deeper trouble. In a word, the world had an international economy but a national polity. Economically, each European people now required habitual contact with the world as a whole. Each people was to that extent dependent, and insecure. Industrial countries were especially vulnerable, relying as they did on import of raw materials and food, and on export of goods, services, or capital in return. There was, however, no world state to police the world-wide system, assuring participation in the world economy to all nations under all conditions. Each nation had to take care of itself. Hence came much of the drive for imperialism, in which each Great Power tried to stake out part of the world-system for itself. And hence also came the quest for allies and for binding alliances. The alliances, in a world that was in the strict sense anarchic (and seemed likely to remain so), were a means by which each nation attempted to bolster up its security; to assure that it would not be cut off, conquered, or subjected to another's will; to obtain some hope of success in the competitive struggle for use of the world's goods.

The First World War lasted over four years, from 1914 to the end of 1918, the United States entering with effective result in the last year. Germany and its allies were called the Central Powers, while the Entente governments were termed the Allies.

At first a short war, as in 1870, was universally expected. The German General Staff had its plans ready for a two-front struggle against France and Russia. The disadvantage of fighting on two fronts was offset by the possession of good rail lines, which allowed the rapid shuttling of troops from one front to the other. The German war plan, called the Schlieffen Plan, rested upon this fact. Since it was foreseen that

86
**The Marne
and the New Face
of War**

*The Schlieffen Plan
and Battle of
the Marne, 1914*

731

World War I. *Land fighting in the First World War was confined to the areas shown by the darker horizontal shading. The huge battles on the Western Front, which in expenditure of manpower exceeded those of the Second World War in the West, for four years swayed back and forth over the small area indicated, less than a hundred miles wide.*

Russia would be the slower of the two enemies in developing its full power, the plan called for holding the eastern front defensively in the early stages, to permit concentration of maximum forces in the West for a quick sharp victory over France, after which Russia could be disposed of at leisure. In the West the German armies were to swing in a great wheeling movement. The hub of the wheel was near the

Swiss border; the moving wing, the German right, was to march rapidly through Belgium into northern France, catch the French army on its left, and roll the whole French force backward against the Swiss frontier. The Schlieffen Plan required that the German right wing be kept very strong. By this plan the German commander Moltke declared in May 1914 that he could crush France in six weeks.

On August 3, 1914, the Germans launched 78 infantry divisions in the West. They were opposed by 72 French divisions, 5 British and 6 Belgian. The Germans swept irresistibly forward. The Schlieffen Plan seemed to be moving like clockwork. The civilian authorities made plans for the conquest and annexation of large parts of Europe. Then a hitch occurred: the Russians were fulfilling the terms of their alliance; the 10,000,000,000 francs invested by Frenchmen in Russia now paid its most significant dividend. The Russians pushed two armies into Germany, penetrating into East Prussia. Moltke withdrew forces from the German right wing in France, on August 26, for service in the east. The Germans moved on, but their striking arm was weakened, and their lines of communication were already overextended. Joffre, the French commander, regrouping his forces, with strong support from the relatively small British contingent, and at exactly the right moment, ordered a counterattack. The ensuing battle of the Marne, fought from September 5 to 12, changed the whole character of the war. The Germans were obliged to retreat. The hope of felling France at a single blow was ended. Both sides now tried to outflank and destroy each other until the battle lines extended to the sea. The Germans failed also to win control of the Channel ports; French and British communications remained uninterrupted. For these reverses the great victories meanwhile won by the Germans in the east, though of gigantic proportions (the battles of Tannenberg and the Masurian Lakes, at which 225,000 Russians were captured), were in the long run small consolation.

In the West the war of movement now settled into a war of position. The armies on the western front became almost immobile. The units of horse cavalry, the uhlans, hussars, and lancers that had pranced off to war in high spirits, disappeared from the field. Since motor transport was still new (the armies had trucks, but no self-propelled guns, and no tanks until very late in the war), the basic soldier more than ever was the man on foot. Airplanes were used for reconnaissance, artillery observation, and occasional bombing; not till the last months of the war did concentrated bombing of rear areas begin. The Germans raided London many times with Zeppelins, long cigar-shaped airships, but did little damage. Hostilities were confined to the front, and on the whole it was only soldiers who were killed or wounded.

The queen of battles was the machine gun. Against it infantry could advance only after elaborate preparations. Infantry on both sides dug into trenches, long zigzag slits higher than a man's head, which soon formed connected mazes from Switzerland to the North Sea. Dugouts, or caves where men might sleep or eat, communicated with the trenches. And between hostile trenches lay No Man's Land,

and in front of its trenches, to protect them from attackers, each side set up thick entanglements of barbed wire, on which assailants could be impaled, and then easily bayoneted or shot. Before infantry could attack it was necessary to break up the barbed wire, silence the machine guns, and disarrange the enemy's trenches and dugouts. This was a task for heavy artillery, of which altogether unprecedented quantities came to be used. If the wind was right, an attack might also be prepared by the discharge of poison gases, first used by the Germans in the spring of 1915; but the vagaries of wind, the quick adoption of gas masks, and its ineffectiveness against guns and entrenchments made gas an indecisive weapon. An artillery preparation preceded every advance. At the Somme, in 1916, the Allies placed 2,000 heavy cannon behind a ten-mile front, and the preliminary bombardment lasted continuously for seven days and nights. If the destruction by shellfire was sufficient, the infantry might struggle forward five or ten miles, using bayonets and hand grenades in addition to fire, and often wearing gas masks, but it would soon find the enemy again entrenched and be unable to go farther, because the indispensable artillery moved forward far more slowly than the foot soldier. Only when the British introduced the tank in the last months of the war, and employed new infiltration tactics rather than mass attack, was an answer found to the problem posed by the machine gun.

Such conditions gave every advantage to the defensive. Attack was laborious, costly in lives, and at best achieved small results. With opposing forces dug in in continuous lines almost face to face, there was little opportunity for slashing action by small units. Vast armies had to be employed as heavy masses; it was a war of the battering ram rather than the stiletto. Each side nevertheless attempted repeatedly to achieve a breakthrough. But the defending line seldom broke; even when it did, the defenders could pour in reserves faster than the attackers could advance, because, where an advancing force had to find its way slowly through country wrecked by artillery, a retreating force could use western Europe's superb network of roads and railroads, which aviation as yet scarcely disturbed. Battle therefore was unprofitable, but casualties were enormous, and they came wholesale in tremendous holocausts. More men were used and killed on the western front in the First World War than in the Second.

87
**The Deadlock of
1915–1916: Naval,
Diplomatic, Military**

*Naval Blockade
and Naval Warfare*

734

After the battle of the Marne it became evident that the war would be a long one. For a long war no power had made any plans. In a long war Germany and the Central Powers were at a disadvantage, because they were exposed to the slow effects of blockade by sea. Naval blockade was a deadly weapon, if only one could wait, and so long as Russia and France, by remaining unconquered, prevented Germany from exploiting the resources of Europe and Asia. To the Allies, on the other hand, a long war gave an advantage; their control of the sea allowed them to import food, as usual, from Canada, Australia, and the Argentine, and munitions from the United States. A long war also gave time to the Allies to develop their manpower. The French had virtually all their manpower in readiness in 1914; but the British, who in 1914 could send only five divisions to the Continent, required two years to produce a mass army. The British long resisted conscription, which they considered, even in wartime, ill suited to their free institutions. For over a year they relied on volunteers, but by the beginning of 1916 they too turned to compulsory service, and by the spring of that year they had an army of seventy divisions. Moreover, of course, had the war not been a long one, the United States would never have entered it, nor, once entered, would it have had time to raise, train, equip, and transport its forces.

The British and French lost no time in developing the naval blockade. International law at the time placed goods headed for a country at war into two classes. One class was called "contraband"; it included munitions and certain listed raw materials which might be used in the manufacture of military equipment. The other class, including foodstuffs and raw cotton, was defined as noncontraband. A country was supposed, by international law, to be able to import noncontraband goods even in wartime. Contraband goods could be stopped by a blockading power; if on an enemy ship, the whole ship and cargo could be seized, but if on a neutral ship it had to be proved from the ship's papers, before confiscation, that the contraband goods were destined for the enemy. These terms of wartime law had been set forth as recently as 1909 at an international conference held in London. The purpose was to make it impossible for a sea power (that is, the British) to starve out an enemy in wartime, or even to interfere with normal civilian production. The jealousy of Continental Europe for British sea power was an old story.

Such law, if observed, would make the blockade of Germany entirely ineffective, and the Allies did not observe it. To starve out the enemy and ruin his economy was precisely their purpose. Economic warfare took its place alongside armed attack as a military weapon—as in the days of Napoleon.[11] The Allies announced a new international law. The distinction between contraband and noncontraband was gradually abolished. The British navy (aided by the French) proceeded to stop all goods of whatever character destined for Germany or its allies. Neutrals, among whom the Americans, Dutch, and Scandinavians were the ones mainly affected, were not allowed to make for German ports at all. Neutrals could still, of course, import into their own countries. Goods destined for resale to Germany therefore moved into Rotterdam and Copenhagen. It was, in fact, largely to use these cities as ports of entry that the Germans refrained from occupying Denmark and the Netherlands in the First World War. The Allies retorted by placing Denmark and the Netherlands under strict quotas, allowing them only the kind and quantity of imports that they had customarily received before the war. They even attempted to prevent the Netherlands and Scandinavia from selling their own domestic products to Germany. The Germans, for example, feeling the food shortage, took to buying large amounts of Norwegian fish. But the Norwegian fishing fleet depended on British coal and its canning industry on imported tin. The British, by rationing coal and tin for Norway, soon checked the flow of fish into Germany. The whole system was enforced by

[11] See pp. 438–442.

requiring neutral vessels to stop at Gibraltar or other Allied points, have their cargoes and papers examined, and obtain clearance. Thus all sea-borne imports into Germany were prevented, and imports into Germany's neutral neighbors were controlled.

The United States protested vehemently against these regulations. It defended the rights of neutrals. It reasserted the distinction between contraband and noncontraband, claimed the right to trade with other neutrals, and upheld the "freedom of the seas." Much mutual bad feeling resulted between the American and British governments in 1915 and 1916. But when the United States entered the war it adopted the Allied position *in toto,* and its navy joined in enforcing exactly the same regulations. International law was in fact changed. In the Second World War the very words "contraband" and "freedom of the seas" were never heard.

The Germans also attempted to blockade England. A few isolated German cruisers were able for some time to destroy British shipping in the several oceans of the world. But the Germans relied mainly on the submarine, against which the preponderant British naval power at first seemed helpless. The submarine was an unrefined weapon; a submarine commander could not always tell what kind of ship he was attacking, nor could he remove passengers, confiscate cargo, escort the vessel, nor indeed do much except sink it. Citing British abuses of international law in justification, the German government in February 1915 declared the waters surrounding the British Isles to be a war zone, in which Allied vessels would be torpedoed and neutral vessels would be in grave danger. Three months later the liner *Lusitania* was torpedoed off the Irish coast. About 1,200 persons were drowned, of whom 118 were American citizens. The *Lusitania* was a British ship; it carried munitions of war manufactured in the United States for Allied use; and the Germans had published ominous warnings in the New York papers that Americans should not take passage upon it. Americans then believed that they should be able to sail safely, on peaceable errands, on the ship of a belligerent power in wartime. The loss of life shocked the country. President Wilson informed the Germans that another such act would be considered "deliberately unfriendly." The Germans, to avoid trouble, refrained for two years from making full use of their submarines. For two years the Allies enjoyed an only partly impeded use of the sea.

Allied access to the sea was confirmed by the one great naval engagement of the war, the battle of Jutland. The German admirals, especially when deprived of the full use of their submarine arm, became restless to see their newly built navy skulking behind mine fields on the German shores. The High Seas Fleet could not presume to challenge the superior British Grand Fleet, posted watchfully at Scapa Flow. It hoped, however, to decoy smaller formations of British ships in turn, destroy them one by one, and perhaps eventually obtain enough of a naval balance in the North Sea to loosen the British blockade, by which Germany was slowly being strangled. In May 1916 the Germans believed that they had trapped a squadron of British cruisers, under Admiral Beatty, into a surprise engagement with the High Seas Fleet. The British, however, whose intelligence services were excellent, knew the German plan. Beatty was really, at great risk to himself, luring the Germans into a trap. The

Germans found too late that the entire Grand Fleet of 151 ships under Admiral Jellicoe was bearing down upon them. They tried to withdraw, but Jellicoe maintained contact. For several hours the two navies, whose rivalry had been a main cause of the war, enjoyed their one opportunity to inflict destruction upon each other. But Jellicoe, who has been called the one man who could have lost the war in a single day, was too prudent to jeopardize his enormous command, and all it stood for, without good reason. The Germans were able to break off and withdraw into mined waters. They had lost less tonnage and fewer men than the British. They had proved themselves to be dangerously proficient in naval combat. But their fleet never came out again. The British retained command of the sea.

With the war virtually deadlocked, both sides looked about for new allies, to open new fronts, or add even the small increment of strength that might turn the balance. Germany and Austria-Hungary had been joined in October 1914 by the Ottoman Empire, whose enemy was Russia, and in 1915 by Bulgaria, which felt itself outraged by Serbia in the Balkan war of 1913.

The leading new prospect was Italy, which, although formally a member of the Triple Alliance, had long ago drifted away from it and took no part in the crisis of 1914. Both sides solicited the Italian government, which was willing to bargain imperturbably with both. The Italian public was divided. Probably most people wanted to stay at peace, which was recommended both by Catholic and by socialist leaders. Extreme nationalists saw in the war a chance to obtain their *irredenta*, the border regions in which Italians lived, but which had not been incorporated in the time of Cavour.[12] The Italian government opened negotiations with Austria-Hungary, offering to refrain from attacking Austria if the Trentino and south Tyrol were ceded. The negotiations with Austria were used also to frighten the Allies, which in the end Italy joined on terms very advantageous to itself. By the secret treaty of London of 1915, between England, France, Russia, and Italy, it was agreed that if the Allies won the war Italy should receive the Trentino, the south Tyrol, Istria and the city of Trieste, and some of the Dalmatian Islands; that, if Turkey were partitioned, Italy should receive Adalia in Asia Minor; and that if England and France took over Germany's African colonies, Italy should receive territorial increases in Libya and Somaliland. The treaty of London, in short, carried on the most brazen prewar practices of territorial expansionism. It must be remembered that the Allies were desperate. Italy, thus bought, and probably against the will of most Italians, opened up a front against Austria-Hungary in May 1915.

Each side tampered with minorities and discontented groups living within the domains of the other. The Germans promised an independent Poland, to embarrass Russia. They stirred up local nationalism in the Ukraine. They raised up a pro-German Flemish movement in Belgium. They persuaded the Ottoman sultan, as caliph, to proclaim a holy war in North Africa, hoping that irate Moslems would drive

---

[12] See pp. 565–566.

the British from Egypt and the French from Algeria. This had no success. German agents worked in Ireland, and one Irish nationalist, Sir Roger Casement, landed in Ireland from a German submarine, precipitating the Easter Rebellion of 1916, which was suppressed by the British.

To Americans the most amazing of similar activities was the famous Zimmermann telegram. In 1916 an American military force had crossed the Mexican border in pursuit of bandits, against protests by the Mexican government. Relations between the United States and Germany were also deteriorating. In January 1917 the German state secretary for foreign affairs, Arthur Zimmermann, dispatched a telegram to the German minister at Mexico City, telling him what to say to the Mexican president. He was to say that if the United States went to war with Germany, Germany would form an alliance with Mexico and if possible Japan, enabling Mexico to get back its "lost territories." These latter referred to the region conquered by the United States from Mexico in 1848—Texas, New Mexico, and Arizona (California was not mentioned by Zimmermann, who was no doubt somewhat vague on the exact history and location of these Alsace-Lorraines of America). Zimmermann's telegram was intercepted and decoded by the British, and passed on by them to Washington. Printed in the newspapers, it shocked public opinion in the United States.

The Allies were more successful in appealing to nationalist discontent, for the obvious reason that the most active national minorities were within the lands of their enemies. They were able to promise restoration of Alsace-Lorraine to France without difficulty. They promised independence to the Poles, though with some difficulty as long as the tsarist monarchy stood. They gave a haven, though as yet no official recognition or support, to various "committees" of émigrés who, fleeing mainly from Austria-Hungary during the war, set up national councils—a Czech national council in Moscow and a more important one in London, to which Masaryk and Beneš belonged; a Yugoslav national council in London; a Polish national council in Paris, led by the great pianist Paderewski. These councils worked to have independence for their respective nations included in the Allied war aims. They drew much of their support and funds from the United States, to which millions of Poles, Czechs, Slovaks, and South Slavs had emigrated in the preceding thirty years. Czechs in the Austrian army deserted in great numbers to the Russians, and South Slavs fought with great reluctance except against the Italians, so that national discontent from the beginning undermined the military power of the Austrian monarchy.

The Allies made plans for a final partition of the Ottoman Empire. The British aroused Arab hopes for independence. The British Colonel T. E. Lawrence led an insurrection in the Hejaz against the Turks; and the emir Hussein of Hejaz, with British support, in 1916 took the title of king of the Arabs, with a kingdom reaching from the Red Sea to the Persian Gulf. Zionists saw in the impending Ottoman collapse the opportunity to realize their dream for Palestine.[13] Since Palestine was an Arab country (and had been for over 1,000 years) the Zionist program conflicted with British plans to sponsor Arab nationalism. Nevertheless, in the Balfour note of 1917,

[13] See p. 658.

the British government promised to support the idea of a Jewish "homeland" in Palestine.

Nor was the very center of the Ottoman Empire overlooked. In the first months of the war the Russians brought up the eternal question of the Turkish Straits. Russia in 1915 bore the brunt of the German attack; the Western Allies needed the respite thus given them and feared that Russia might, if unsatisfied, make a separate peace. Britain and France themselves, in 1915, were attacking the Straits at the Dardanelles.[14] They therefore had to reassure their Russian ally as to their ultimate intentions. By a secret agreement of March 1915 the British and French accepted the Russian terms. Russia, after the war, was to annex Constantinople, together with the Bosporus, Sea of Marmora and Dardanelles—i.e., the entire Straits. The Western powers thus abandoned a policy to which they had clung stubbornly for generations—many Russians, indeed, doubted whether, if the Allies emerged victorious, they would ever live up to the bargain. As for the rest of Turkey, another agreement of 1916, made at the time when Hussein became king in Arabia, divided it into spheres of influence: Mesopotamia was to go to Britain, Syria and southeastern Asia Minor to France, Armenia and Kurdistan to Russia. Adalia and Smyrna were reserved for Italy.

Meanwhile the British and French easily conquered the German colonies in Africa. Early in the war the British foreign secretary, Sir Edward Grey, revealed to Colonel House, President Wilson's personal emissary, that it was not the intention of the Allies for Germany ever to get its colonies back.

In China, too, the third important area of imperialist competition, the war accelerated the tendencies of preceding years. The Japanese saw their own opportunity in the self-slaughter of the Europeans. Japan had also been allied to Britain since 1902. In August 1914 Japan declared war on Germany. It soon overran the German concessions in China and the German islands in the Pacific, the Marshalls and Carolines. In January 1915 Japan presented its Twenty-One Demands on China, a secret ultimatum most of which the Chinese were obliged to accept. Japan thereby proceeded to turn Manchuria and north China into a kind of exclusive protectorate.

All these developments, whether accomplished facts or secret agreements, affecting Europe, Asia, or Africa, became very troublesome later on at the peace conference. They continued some of the most unsettling tendencies of European politics before the war. It does not appear that the Allies, until driven by Woodrow Wilson, gave any thought to means of controlling anarchic nationalism or of preventing war in the future. As for the Germans, their war aims were even more expansionist. Early in September 1914, when a quick victory seemed within grasp, Bethmann-Hollweg, who remained chancellor until the summer of 1917, drew up a list of German war aims which stayed unaltered until the end of hostilities. The plans called for an enlarged German Empire dominating all central Europe, and annexations or satellites in both western and eastern Europe. In the West, Belgium was to become

---

[14] See pp. 740–741.

a German dependency to provide more direct access to the Atlantic, and French Lorraine with its rich iron ore was to be added to the already German parts of Alsace-Lorraine. In the East, Lithuania and other parts of the Baltic were to become German puppets, large sections of Poland directly annexed, and the remainder joined with Austrian Galicia to form a German-dominated Polish state. Rumania was to become an economic dependency, and the Netherlands and the Scandinavian countries were expected to be drawn into the orbit of the German political and economic bloc. Colonial adjustments, including the acquisition of most of central Africa from coast to coast, were also projected. The political map of Europe and of colonial Africa would thus be transformed.

Wilson, though his personal sympathies lay with England and France, saw politically little to choose between the warring alliances, and in his public utterances spoke as if they were Tweedledum and Tweedledee. Both sides were indignant that he saw no difference between them. In 1916 he attempted to mediate, entering into confidential discussions with both; but both still hoped to win on their own terms, so that negotiation was fruitless. Wilson judged that most Americans wished to remain uninvolved, and in November 1916 was reelected to a second term, on the popular cry that "he kept us out of war." He urged a true neutrality of thought and feeling. As late as January 1917, three months before going to war, he called for a "peace without victory," one in which neither side should be altogether crushed.

Campaigns of 1915–1916 Meanwhile the fighting dragged on. The Germans and Austro-Hungarians, early in 1915, began the operation which they hoped would put Russia out of the war. Some expressed misgivings, remembering the fate of Napoleon. They were reassured by the German General Hoffmann: "If Napoleon had had the railroad, telephone, motor convoy, telegraph, and airplane he would still be in Moscow today." The offensive opened with much promise. On the eastern front the western conditions of immobility did not obtain. The front was too long to be thoroughly entrenched, and the Russians lacked machine guns and heavy artillery. The attackers pressed on into Lithuania and White Russia. The Russian losses were of truly Asiatic proportions—2,000,000 killed, wounded, or captured in 1915 alone. But at the end of the year the Russian army was still fighting. Peace could not be imposed.

On the western front, in 1915, the Allies tried to take advantage of German concentration in the east. They too mounted an offensive, but they could not pierce the German lines. With 250,000 Allied casualties (almost twice as many as those of the German defenders) the campaign was a failure.

In January 1915 Winston Churchill, First Lord of the Admiralty, proposed that Britain use its control of the sea to select its own point of attack. He recommended an onslaught at the Dardanelles. It was at first thought that purely naval action would suffice, so that no forces need be diverted from France. The battleships were to demolish the fortifications with their great guns, then push through the narrow passage (only a mile wide) and seize Constantinople. Thus the deadlock in France would be circumvented, Turkey driven out of the war, aid brought to Serbia, the

Balkan front built up, and communications opened with Russia—all at small cost. There was some opposition to the plan, especially by the French, and by some British naval officers, who objected to such a dispersion of effort from the main theater; but the opposition was overruled. The fleet, after initial successes, reached the narrowest part of the strait. After a naval bombardment of five days it was decided that army units must land to clean out the Turkish forts on the peninsula of Gallipoli. First one division was sent, and ultimately five—as many as the British had been able to send against the Germans in the preceding August. German officers supervised the defense of the Turkish forts. The most terrific pounding by both army and navy was of no use. Repeatedly the British refused to withdraw, fearing loss of prestige throughout the Moslem world. In the end, all told, 450,000 men were poured into the Dardanelles. There were 145,000 Allied killed and wounded. After almost a year the enterprise was given up as a failure. Poor coordination, between British and French and between army and navy, ruined a plan which if more vigorously prosecuted in its early stages might have been successful. Since in the end it consumed a huge outlay of Allied men and material, as well as time, the only person to express satisfaction was Falkenhayn, who in September 1914 had succeeded Moltke as chief of the German High Command.

For 1916 both sides turned again to France as the scene of their main effort. The Allies planned a great offensive along the river Somme while the Germans prepared one in the neighborhood of Verdun. The Germans disconcerted the Allies by moving first. Verdun occupied a salient in the French line, protruding in such a way that it could be shelled and assaulted from several directions. Falkenhayn selected it for attack because he believed that the French would defend it to the last ditch. His aim was not to find a weak spot, break through, restore mobile warfare, and obtain a quick decision—all these he had given up as impossible in the West. His aim was to pick a strong spot, hammer at it incessantly, draw in wave after wave of French reserves, and methodically slaughter them. He expected to inflict five casualties for every two he lost, and so to bleed his adversary slowly to death. It was a strategy of pure attrition. Verdun was a piece of flypaper on which the French army would be caught.

The Germans attacked Verdun in February 1916. The French commander, Joffre, put in General Pétain to defend it but resisted letting his main reserves become committed, holding as many as he could for the coming offensive on the Somme. Pétain and his troops, held to minimum numbers, thus had to take the full weight of the German army. The battle of Verdun lasted six months, it drew the horrified admiration of the world, and it became a legend of determined resistance ("they shall not pass"), until the Germans finally abandoned the attack because they sustained almost as many casualties as the French—330,000 to 350,000—so that their purpose was baffled.

While the inferno raged at Verdun (and a month after the battle of Jutland) the Allies opened their offensive on the Somme on July 1. The outlook seemed good. The Germans were still involved at Verdun. The Russians, according to plan, had attacked in the East, showing surprising strength after the disasters of 1915, so that three German divisions had already been withdrawn from France. During the summer of 1916 the Central Powers were to lose almost 400,000 men in Russia. On the Somme, the Allies brought up unheard of amounts of artillery, and the newly trained British army was present in force. The idea was to break through the German line simply by stupendous pressure; on both sides, Allied and German, the art of generalship had perforce sunk to an all-time low. Despite a week-long artillery bombardment the British lost 60,000 men on the first day of the attack. In a week they had advanced only a mile along a six-mile front. In a month they had advanced only two miles and a half. As at Verdun, the superiority of the defensive was again demonstrated. The battle of the Somme, lasting from July to October, cost the Germans about 500,000 men, the British 400,000, and the French 200,000. Nothing of any value had been gained. It was, indeed, at the Somme that the British first used the tank, an armored vehicle with caterpillar tracks that could crush through barbed wire, lunge over trenches, and smash into machine-gun nests; but the tanks were introduced in such small numbers, and with such skepticism on the part of many commanders, that they had no effect on the battle.

Meanwhile in 1916 the Italians held off repeated Austrian blows. The Germans and Austro-Hungarians overran Serbia, despite ill-coordinated efforts of an Allied expeditionary force to defend it. They also overran Rumania, which somewhat inopportunely entered the war on the side of the Allies in the hope of enlarging its territories. On the eastern front, in 1916, the Russians lost another million men, but 1916 was not a good year for the Germans. In the West, Verdun and the Somme were both signal failures for those who planned them and proved again the superiority of the defensive. At sea, the naval blockade continued. Germany and its allies controlled central Europe from the North Sea to the Turkish Straits. There was no fighting on the soil of Germany or Austria-Hungary. But they were a beleaguered fortress, cut off from the sea, hemmed in by Russians, Italians, French, and British. The deadlock was confirmed for both sides, and the slow murderous futility of the war of attrition became more apparent.

As of the end of 1916, it is hard to see how the First World War would have turned out, had not two new sets of forces been brought in.

88
The Collapse of Russia and the Intervention of the United States

The Withdrawal of Russia: Revolution and the Treaty of Brest-Litovsk

The first victim of the First World War, among governments, was the Russian empire. As the Russo-Japanese War had led to the Revolution of 1905 in Russia, so the more ruinous war in Europe led to the far greater Revolution of 1917. The story of the Russian Revolution is told in the following chapter. It is enough to say here, as part of the history of the war, that war offered a test that the tsarist government could not meet. Bungling, dishonest, and secretive, incapable of supplying the materiel required for modern fighting, driving hordes of peasants into battle in some cases even without rifles, losing men by the millions yet offering no goal to inspire sacrifice, the tsarist regime lost the loyalty of all elements of its people. In March 1917 the troops in St. Petersburg mutinied, while strikes and riots desolated the city. The Duma, or Russian parliament, used the occasion to press its demands for reform. On

March 15 Nicholas II abdicated. A Provisional Government took over, made up of liberal noblemen and middle-class leaders, generally democrats and constitutionalists, with at first only one socialist. The Provisional Government remained in office from March to November 1917. Its members, who shared in the liberalism of western Europe, believed that a liberal and parliamentary regime could not succeed in Russia unless the German Empire were defeated. They took steps, therefore, to prosecute the war with a new vigor. In July 1917 an offensive was opened in Galicia, but the demoralized Russian armies again collapsed.

The mass of the Russian people were wearied of a war in which they were asked to suffer so much for so little. Nor did the Russian peasant or workingman feel any enthusiasm for the westernized intellectuals and professional men who manned the Provisional Government. The ordinary Russian, so far as he had any politics, was drawn to one or another of numerous forms of socialism, Marxist and non-Marxist. The Russian Marxist party, the Social Democrats, was divided between Menshevik and Bolshevik factions, the latter being the more extreme. The Bolshevik leaders had for some time lived as exiles in western Europe. Their principal spokesman, V. I. Lenin, with a few others, had spent the war years in Switzerland. In April 1917 the German government offered safe passage to Lenin through Germany to Russia. A railway car full of Bolsheviks, carefully "sealed" to prevent infection of Germany, was thus hauled by a German train to the frontier, whence it passed on to St. Petersburg, or Petrograd, as the city was renamed during the war. The aim of the Germans in this affair, as in the sending of Roger Casement to Ireland in a submarine, was of course to use a kind of psychological warfare against the enemy's home front. It was to promote rebellion against the Provisional Government and thus at last to eliminate Russia.

The position of the Provisional Government became rapidly more untenable, from many causes, until by November 1917 the situation was so confused that Lenin and the Bolsheviks were able to seize power. The Bolsheviks stood for peace with Germany, partly to win popular favor in Russia, and partly because they regarded the war impartially, as a struggle between capitalist and imperialist powers which should be left to exhaust and destroy each other for the benefit of socialism. On December 3, 1917, a peace conference opened between the Bolsheviks and the Germans at Brest-Litovsk. Meanwhile the peoples within the western border of the old Russia—Poles, Ukrainians, Bessarabians, Estonians, Latvians, Finns—with German backing, proclaimed their national independence. The Bolsheviks, since they would not or could not fight, were obliged to sign with Germany a treaty to which they vehemently objected, the treaty of Brest-Litovsk of March 3, 1918. By this treaty they acknowledged the "independence," or at least the loss to Russia, of Poland, the Ukraine, Finland, and the Baltic provinces. In May the Rumanians also were forced to sign a harsh treaty at Bucharest.

For the Germans the treaty of Brest-Litovsk represented their maximum success during the First World War; it accomplished some of the war aims formulated at the beginning of hostilities. Not only had they neutralized Russia; they also now dominated eastern Europe through puppets placed at the head of the new independent states. They relieved the effects of the naval blockade by drawing considerable quantities of foodstuffs from the Ukraine, though less than they expected. A certain number of German troops remained in the East to preserve the new arrangements. But it was no longer a two-front war. Masses of the German army were shifted from east to west. The High Command, under Hindenburg and Ludendorff since August 1916, prepared to concentrate for a last blow in France to end the war in 1918.

The year 1918 was essentially a race to see whether American aid could reach Europe soon enough, in sufficient amount, to offset the added strength which Germany drew from the collapse of Russia. In March of that year the Germans, beginning with gas attacks and a bombardment by 6,000 artillery pieces, opened a formidable offensive before which the French and British both recoiled. On May 30, 1918, the Germans again stood at the Marne, thirty-seven miles from Paris. At this time there were only two American divisions in action, though the United States had been at war over a year. At this point in the story there are therefore two open questions: how the United States entered the war, and the length of time required for the buildup of its forces overseas.

The United States and the War

We have seen how President Wilson clung persistently to neutrality. The American people were divided. Many had been born in Europe or were the children of immigrants. Those of Irish origin were anti-British; those of German origin were often sympathetic to Germany. On the other hand, since the time of the Spanish-American and Boer Wars, a noticeable current of friendliness to the English had been running, more than ever before in American history. The sale of war materials to the Allies, and the purchase of the bonds of Allied governments, had given certain limited though influential circles a material interest in an Allied victory. The idealism of the country was on the side of England and France, so far as it was not isolationist. An Allied victory would clearly advance the cause of democracy, freedom, and progress far more than a victory of the German Empire. On the other hand, England and France were suspected of somewhat impure motives, and they were allied with the Russian autocracy, the reactionary and brutal tsardom.

The fall of tsarism made a great impression. Democratic and progressive men now came forward even in Russia. No one had ever heard of Lenin or foresaw the Bolshevik Revolution. It seemed in the spring of 1917 that Russia was struggling along the path that England, France, and America had already taken. An ideological barrier had dropped away, and the demand for American intervention to safeguard democracy became more insistent.

The Germans gave up the attempt to keep the United States out. Constricted ever more tightly by the blockade, and failing to get a decision on land, the German government and High Command listened more readily to the submarine experts, who declared that if given a free hand they could force British surrender in six months. It was the chief example in the First World War of the claim that one branch of the service could win the war alone. Civilian and diplomatic members of the government objected, fearing the consequences of war with the United States. They were overruled; it was a good example of the way in which, in Germany, the army and navy had taken the highest policy into their hands. It was decided to reopen unrestricted submarine warfare on February 1, 1917. It was foreseen that the United States would declare war, but it was believed that this would make no immediate difference. The Germans in 1917 estimated (correctly) that between the time when the United States entered a European war and the time when it could take part with its own army a time lag of about a year must intervene. Meanwhile, the planners said, in six months they could force Britain to accept defeat, after which neither the United States nor any other power could fight in Europe. Their error was in exaggerating the role of the submarine.

On January 31, 1917, the Germans notified Wilson of the resumption of unrestricted submarine attacks. They announced that they would sink on sight all merchant vessels found in a zone around the British Isles or in the Mediterranean. Wilson broke off diplomatic relations, and ordered the arming of American freighters. Meanwhile, the publication of the Zimmermann telegram convinced many Americans of German aggressiveness. German secret agents also had been at work in America, fomenting strikes and causing explosions in factories engaged in the manufacture of munitions for the Allies. In February and March several American ships were sunk. Americans regarded all these activities as an interference with their rights as neutrals. Wilson at last concluded that Germany was a menace. He seems to have felt not so much that it menaced the actual military security of the United States, as that it menaced everything that was right, lawful, decent, and progressive in modern civilization. He did not think in material terms. Even to protect commerce, in his view, was not a matter of material self-interest or profit; it was a matter of principle, of protecting the right of neutral nations to go about their affairs, normally, safely, and lawfully, even though other nations happened to be at war. Having made his decision Wilson saw a clear-cut issue between right and wrong. The American people now saw it in the same way, and Wilson obtained a rousing declaration of war from Congress, on April 6, 1917, with a speech notable for its eloquence and solemnity:

It is a fearful thing to lead this great peaceful people into war, into the most terrible and disastrous of all wars, civilization itself seeming to be in the balance. But the right is more precious than peace, and we shall fight for the things which we have always carried nearest our hearts—for democracy, for the right of those who submit to authority to have a voice in their own Government, for the rights and liberties of small nations, for a universal dominion of right by such a concert of free peoples as shall bring peace and safety to all nations and make the world itself at last free.

The United States went to war "to make the world safe for democracy."

At first the German campaign realized and even exceeded the predictions of its sponsors. In February 1917 the Germans sank 540,000 tons of shipping, in March 578,000 tons, in April, as the days grew longer, 874,000 tons. Something akin to terror, with difficulty concealed from the public, seized on the government in

London. Britain was reduced to a mere six-weeks' reserve of food. Gradually countermeasures were developed—mine-barrages, hydrophones, depth-charges, airplane reconnaissance, and most of all the convoy. It was found that a hundred or more freighters together, though all had to steam at the pace of the slowest, could be protected by a sufficient concentration of warships to keep submarines away. The United States navy, which, unlike the army, was of considerable size and ready for combat, supplied enough additional force to the Allies to make convoying and other antisubmarine measures highly effective. By the end of 1917 the submarine was no more than a nuisance. For the Germans the great plan produced the anticipated penalty without the reward—its net result was only to add America to their enemies.

On the western front in 1917, while the Americans desperately got themselves ready for the war they had entered, the French and British continued to hold the line. The French, finding in General Nivelle a commander who still believed in the breakthrough, launched an offensive so unsuccessful and so bloody that mutiny spread through the French army. Pétain then replaced Nivelle; he restored discipline to the exhausted and disillusioned soldiers, but he had no thought of further attack. "I am waiting for the Americans and the tanks," he said. The British then assumed the main burden. For three months late in 1917 they fought the dismal battle of Passchendaele. They advanced five miles, near Ypres, at a cost of 400,000 men. At the very end of 1917 the British surprised the Germans with a raid by 380 tanks, which penetrated deep into the German lines but then had to withdraw, since no reserve of fresh infantry was at hand to exploit their success. Meanwhile the Austro-Hungarians, strongly reinforced by German troops, overwhelmed the Italians at the disastrous battle of Caporetto. The Central Powers streamed into northern Italy, but the Italians, with British and French reinforcements, were able to hold the line. The net effect of the campaigns of 1917, and of the repulse of the submarine at the same time, was to reemphasize the stalemate in Europe, incline the weary Allies to await the Americans, and give the Americans what they most needed—time.

The Americans made good use of the time that was given them. Conscription, democratically entitled selective service, was adopted immediately after the declaration of war. The United States army, whose professionals in 1916 numbered only 130,000, performed the mammoth feat of turning over 3,500,000 civilians into soldiers. With the navy, the United States came to have over 4,000,000 in its armed services (which may be compared with over 12,000,000 in the Second World War). Aid flowed to the Allies. To the loans already made through private bankers were added some $10,000,000,000 lent by the American government itself. The Allies used the money mainly to buy food and munitions in the United States. American farms and factories, which had already prospered by selling to the Allies during the period of neutrality, now broke all records for production. Civilian industry was converted to war uses; radiator factories turned out guns, and piano factories airplane wings. Every possible means was employed to build up ocean shipping, without which neither American supplies nor American armies could reach the theater of war. Available shipping was increased from 1,000,000 to 10,000,000 tons. Civilian consumption was drastically cut. Eight thousand tons of steel were saved in the manufacture of women's corsets and 75,000 tons of tin in the making of children's toy wagons. Every week people observed Meatless Tuesday, and sugar was rationed. Daylight-saving time, invented in Europe during the war, was introduced to save coal. By such means the United States made enormous stocks available for its Allies as well as itself, though for some items, notably airplanes and artillery ammunition, the American armies, when they reached France, drew heavily on British and French manufactures.

The Germans, as we have seen, victorious in the East, opened a great final offensive in the West in the spring of 1918, hoping to force a decision before American participation turned the balance forever. To oppose it, a new unity of command was at last achieved, for the first time, when a French general, Ferdinand Foch, was made commander-in-chief of all Allied forces in France, with the national commanders subordinate to him, including Pershing for the Americans. In June the Germans first made contact with American troops in significant force, meeting the Second Division at Château-Thierry. The German position was so favorable that civilians in the German government thought it opportune to make a last effort at a compromise peace. The military, headed by Hindenburg and Ludendorff, successfully blocked any such attempts; they preferred to gamble on one final throw. The German armies reached their farthest advance on July 15 along the Marne. There were now nine American divisions in the Allied line. Foch used them to spearhead his counterattack on July 18. The badly overstrained Germans began to falter. Over 250,000 American troops were now landing in France every month. The final Allied offensive which opened in September, with American troops in the Argonne occupying an eastern sector, proved more than the Germans could withstand. The German High Command notified its government that it could not win the war. The German foreign office made peace overtures to President Wilson. An armistice was arranged, and on November 11, 1918, firing ceased on the western front.

Since Germany's allies had surrendered during the preceding weeks, the war, or at least the shooting war in western Europe, was now over. The horror it brought to individual lives cannot be told by statistics, which drily report that almost 10,000,000 men had been killed, and 20,000,000 wounded. Each of the European Great Powers (except Italy) lost from 1,000,000 to 2,000,000 in killed alone. The United States, with some 330,000 casualties of all types (of whom 115,000 died) lost in the entire war fewer men than the main combatants had lost in such a single battle as Verdun or Passchendaele.[15] American assistance was decisive in the defeat of Germany. But it came so late, when the others had been struggling for so long, that the mere beginnings of it were enough to turn the scale. On the date of the armistice there

---

[15]Of the 115,000 American deaths only 50,000 represented men killed in battle, the remainder representing mainly deaths by disease. The great influenza epidemic of 1918, which brought death to millions, civilians and military alike, in all parts of the world, probably accounted for 25,000 deaths in the American army.

were 2,000,000 American soldiers in France, and another 1,000,000 were on the way. But the American army had really been in combat only four months. During the whole year 1918, out of every hundred artillery shells that were fired by the three armies, the French fired 51, the British 43 and the Americans only 6.

89
The Collapse of the Austrian and German Empires

The war proved fatal to the German and Austro-Hungarian empires, as to the Russian. The subject Habsburg nationalities, or the "national councils" representing them in the Western capitals, obtained increasing recognition from the Allies, and in October declared their independence. The last Austrian emperor, Charles I, abdicated on November 12, and on the next day Austria was proclaimed a republic, as was Hungary in the following week. Before any peace conference could convene, the new states of Czechoslovakia, Yugoslavia, an enlarged Rumania, a republican Hungary, and a miniature republican Austria were in existence by their own action.

The German Empire stood solid until the closing weeks. Liberals, democrats, and socialists had lately begun to press for peace and democratization. Yet it was the High Command itself that precipitated the débacle. In the last years of the war dictatorial powers had become concentrated in the hands of General Ludendorff, and in September 1918 only he and his closest military associates realized that the German cause was hopeless. On September 29, at supreme headquarters at Spa in Belgium, Ludendorff informed the Kaiser that Germany must ask for peace. He urged that a new government be formed at Berlin, reflecting the majority in the Reichstag, on democratic parliamentary principles.

In calling for immediate peace negotiations, he seems to have had two ideas in mind. First, he might win time to re-form his armies and prepare a new offensive. But if worst came to worst, if collapse became unavoidable, then the civilian or democratic elements in Germany would be the ones to sue for peace.

The liberal Prince Max of Baden was found to head up a cabinet in which even socialists were included. In October various reforms were enacted, the Bismarckian system was ended, Germany became a liberal constitutional monarchy. For Ludendorff the changes were not fast enough. What was happening was essentially simple. The German military caste, at the moment of Germany's crisis, was more eager to save the army than to save the empire. The army must never admit surrender; that was an affair for small men in business suits. Emperor, High Command, officers, and aristocrats were unloading frantically upon civilians.

President Wilson unwittingly played into their hands. Speaking now as the chief of the Allied coalition, the one to whom peace overtures were first made, he insisted that the German government must become more democratic. It may be recalled how Bismarck, after defeating France in 1871, demanded a general election in France before making peace.[16] Wilson, unlike Bismarck, really believed in democracy; but in a practical way his position was the same. He wanted to be sure

[16] See p. 574.

that he was dealing with the German people itself, not with a discredited elite. He wanted it to be the real Germany that applied for and accepted the Allied terms. In Germany, as realization of the military disaster spread, many people began to regard the Kaiser as an obstacle to peace. Or they felt that Germany would obtain better terms if it appeared before the Allies as a republic. Even the officer corps, to halt the fighting before the army disintegrated, began to talk of abdication. Sailors mutinied at Kiel on November 3, and councils of workers and soldiers were formed in various cities. The socialists threatened to withdraw from the newly formed cabinet (i.e., go into opposition and end the representative nature of the new government) unless William II abdicated. A general strike, led by minority socialists and syndicalists, began on November 9. "Abdication," Prince Max told the emperor, "is a dreadful thing, but a government without the socialists would be a worse danger for the country." William II abdicated on November 9, and slipped across the frontier into Holland, where despite cries to try him as a "war criminal" he lived quietly until 1941. Germany was proclaimed a republic on the same day. Two days later the war stopped.

The fall of the empire in Germany, with the consequent adoption of the republic, did not arise from any basic discontent, deep revolutionary action, or change of sentiment in the German people. It was an episode of the war. The republic (soon called the Weimar Republic) arose because the victorious enemy demanded it, because the German people craved peace, because they wished to avoid forcible revolution, and because the old German military class, to save its face and its future strength, wished at least temporarily to be excused. When the war ended, the German army was still in France, its discipline and organization still apparently unimpaired. No hostile shot had been fired on German soil. It was said later, by some, that the army had not been defeated, that it had been "stabbed in the back" by a dissolving civilian home front. This was untrue; it was the panic-stricken Ludendorff who first cried for "democracy." But the circumstances in which the German republic originated made its later history, and hence all later history, very troubled.

European society was forced by the First World War into many basic changes that were to prove more lasting than the war itself. First of all, the war profoundly affected capitalism as previously known. Essential to the older capitalism (or economic liberalism, or free private enterprise) had been the idea that government should leave business alone, or at the most regulate certain general conditions under which businessmen went about their affairs. Before 1914 governments had increasingly come into the economic field. They had put up tariffs, protected national industries, sought for markets or raw materials by imperialist expansion, or passed protective social legislation to benefit the wage-earning classes. During the war all belligerent governments controlled the economic system far more minutely. Indeed, the idea of the "planned economy" was first applied in the First World War. For the first time (with such rare and archaic precedents as the French dictatorship of

1793) [17] the state attempted to direct all the wealth, resources, and moral purpose of society to a single end.

Since no one had expected a long war, no one had made any plans for industrial mobilization. Everything had to be improvised. By 1916 each government had set up a system of boards, bureaus, councils, and commissions to coordinate its war effort. The aim was to see that all manpower was effectively utilized, and that all natural resources within the country, and all that could possibly be imported, were employed where they would do the most good. In the stress of war free competition was found to be wasteful and undirected private enterprise too uncertain and too slow. The profit motive came into disrepute. Those who exploited shortages to make big profits were stigmatized as "profiteers." Production for civilian use, or for mere luxury purposes, was cut to a minimum. Businessmen were not allowed to set up or close down factories as they chose. It was impossible to start a new business without government approval, because the flotation of stocks and bonds was controlled, and raw materials were made available only as the government wished. It was equally impossible to shut down a business engaged in war production; if a factory was inefficient or unprofitable the government kept it going anyway, making up the losses, so that in some cases management came to expect government support. Here too the tests of competition and profitableness were abandoned. The new goal was coordination or "rationalization" of production in the interests of the country as a whole. Labor was discouraged from protesting against hours or wage rates, and the big unions generally agreed to refrain from strikes. For the upper and middle classes it became embarrassing to show their comforts too openly. It was patriotic to eat meagerly and to wear old clothes. War gave a new impetus even to the idea of economic equality, if only to enlist rich and poor alike in a common cause.

Military conscription was the first step in the allocation of manpower. Draft boards told some men to report to the army, granting exemptions to others to work safely in war industries. Given the casualty rates at the front, state determination over individual life could hardly go farther. With the insatiable need for troops, drawing in men originally exempted or at first rejected as physically inadequate, great numbers of women poured into factories and offices, and in Britain even into newly organized women's branches of the armed forces. Women took over many jobs which it had been thought only men could do. Since their invasion proved to be permanent, the labor force of all countries was enlarged, women's place in society was revolutionized, the institution of marriage and the relations of husband and wife were transformed, and the lives, liberty, and outlook of millions of individual women were turned outward from the home. Governments did not directly force men or women to drop one job and take another. There was no systematic labor conscription except in Germany. But by influencing wage scales, granting draft exemptions, forcing some industries to expand and others to contract or stand still, and propagandizing the idea that work in an arms factory was patriotic, the state shifted vast numbers of workers to war production. Impressed or "slave" labor was not used in the First

[17]See pp. 402–404.

World War nor were prisoners of war obliged to give labor service, though there were some abuses of these rules of international law by the Germans, who were possibly the least scrupulous and certainly the most hard-pressed.

Governments controlled all foreign trade. It was intolerable to let private citizens ship off the country's resources at their own whim. It was equally intolerable to let them use up foreign exchange by importing unneeded goods, or to drive up prices of necessities by competing with one another. Foreign trade became a state monopoly, in which private firms operated under strict licenses and quotas. Even neutrals were affected, as when the Netherlands Overseas Trust was set up to monopolize and administer the rigid quota of imports allowed to enter Holland through the Allied blockade. The greatest of the exporting countries was the United States, whose annual exports rose from $2,000,000,000 to $6,000,000,000 between 1914 and 1918. The endless demand for American farm and factory products naturally drove up prices, which, however, were fixed by law in 1917, for the most important items, before reaching the level to which free competition would have naturally driven them.

As for the European Allies, which even before the war had exported less than they imported, and were now exporting as little as possible, they could make purchases in the United States only by enormous loans from the American government. British and French citizens, under pressure from their own governments, sold off their American stocks and bonds, which were bought up by Americans. The former owners received pounds sterling or francs from their own governments, which in return took and spent the dollars paid by the new American owners. In this way the United States ceased to be a debtor country (owing some $4,000,000,000 to Europeans in 1914), and became the world's leading creditor country, to which by 1919 Europeans owed about $10,000,000,000. Europe's "dollar shortage," or inability to find means of payment for all the American goods that it needed, was to become a troublesome problem on future occasions.

The Allies controlled the sea, but they never had enough shipping to meet rising demands, especially with German submarines taking a steady though fluctuating toll. Each government set up a shipping board, to expand shipbuilding at any cost and to assign available shipping space to whatever purposes—troop movements, rubber imports, foodstuffs—the government considered most urgent in view of overall plans. Control and allocation eventually became international, in the Interallied Shipping Council of which the United States was a member after entering the war. In England and France, where all manufactures depended on imports, government control of shipping and hence of imports was itself enough to give control over the whole economy.

Germany, denied access to the sea and also to Russia and western Europe, was obliged to adopt unprecedented measures of self-sufficiency. The oil of Rumania and grain of the Ukraine, which became available late in the war, were poor substitutes for the world trade on which Germany had formerly depended. The Germans were hungrier than other belligerents. Their government controls became more thorough and more efficient, producing what they called "war socialism." In

Walter Rathenau they found a man with the necessary ideas. He was a Jewish industrialist, son of the head of the German electrical trust. One of the first to foresee a long war, he launched a program for the mobilization of raw materials. Early in the war it seemed that Germany might be soon defeated by lack of nitrogen, necessary to make explosives. Rathenau sweepingly requisitioned every conceivable natural source, including the very manure from the farmers' barnyards, until German chemists succeeded in extracting nitrogen from the air. The German chemical industry developed many other substitute products, such as synthetic rubber. German production was organized into War Companies, one for each line of industry. Each company was a kind of trust, representing the various business firms engaged in one industry. Under government supervision, each War Company strove for maximum production, fixed common prices, allotted raw materials to member firms and individual plants, and determined how much each mine or factory should produce. The War Companies represented the negation of competition, the triumph of the trend toward trusts and monopolies that had gone on in Europe and America since 1890.

Rathenau thought his War Companies a good halfway house between private corporations and socialist bureaucracy, and believed that something like them might be instituted permanently after the war. In his book, *In Days to Come,* he sketched a democratic future for industrial society, in which the waste of competition and profit-seeking would be done away with, with management and labor organized together in each industry to plan and divide up the work and assure a fair return for all. His ideas were much discussed inside and outside Germany after the war. In Germany the war destroyed for a long time, for almost everybody, faith in a freely competitive private capitalism.

The other belligerent governments also replaced competition between individual firms and factories with coordination. "Consortiums" of industrialists in France allocated raw materials and government orders within each industry. The War Industries Board, under Bernard Baruch, did the same in the United States. In Britain, similar methods became so efficient that by 1918, for example, the country produced every two weeks as many shells as in the whole first year of the war and turned out seventy times as much heavy artillery.

Inflation,
Industrial Changes,
Control of Ideas

No government, even by heavy taxes, could raise all the funds it needed except by printing paper money, selling huge bond issues, or obliging banks to grant it credit. The result, given heavy demand and acute shortages, was rapid inflation of prices. Prices and wages were regulated but were never again so low as before 1914. The hardest hit by this development were those whose money income could not easily be raised—people living on "safe" investments, those drawing annual salaries, professional people, government employees. These classes had been one of the most stabilizing influences in Europe before the war. Everywhere the war threatened their status, prestige, and standard of living. The huge national debts meant higher taxes for years to come. The debt was most serious when it was owed to a foreign country. During the war the Continental Allies borrowed from Britain, and they and the British both borrowed from the United States. They thereby mortgaged their future. To pay the debt, they were bound for years to export more than they imported—or, roughly, to produce more than they consumed. It may be recalled that in 1914 every advanced European country habitually imported more than it exported.[18] That fact, basic to the European standard of life, was now threatened with reversal.

Moreover, with Europe torn by war for four years, the rest of the world speeded up its own industrialization. The productive capacity of the United States increased immensely. The Japanese began to sell in China, in India, in South America the cotton textiles and other civilian goods which these countries for the time being could not obtain from Europe. The Argentine and Brazil, unable to get locomotive parts or mining machinery from England, began to manufacture them themselves. In India the Tata family, a group of wealthy Parsees controlling $250,000,000 worth of native Indian capital, developed numerous manufacturing enterprises, one of which became the largest iron and steel works in the British Empire. With Germany entirely out of the world market, with Britain and France producing desperately for themselves, and with the world's shipping commandeered for war uses, the position of western Europe as the world's workshop was undermined. After the war Europe found new competitors in its own traditional business. The economic foundations of the nineteenth century had slipped away. The age of European supremacy was in its twilight.

All the belligerent governments during the war attempted to control ideas as they did economic production. Freedom of thought, respected everywhere in Europe for half a century, went into the discard. Propaganda and censorship became more effective than any government, however despotic, had ever been able to devise. No one was allowed to sow doubt by raising any basic questions.

It must be remembered that the facts of the prewar crises, as related above, were then largely unknown. People were trapped in a nightmare whose causes they could not comprehend. Each side wildly charged the other with having started the war from pure malevolence. The long attrition, the fruitless fighting, the unchanging battle lines, the appalling casualties were a severe ordeal to morale. Civilians, deprived of their usual liberties, working harder, eating dull food, seeing no victory, had to be kept emotionally at a high pitch. Placards, posters, diplomatic white papers, schoolbooks, public lectures, solemn editorials, and slanted news reports conveyed the message. The new universal literacy, the mass press, the new moving pictures, proved to be ideal media for the direction of popular thinking. Intellectuals and professors advanced complicated reasons, usually historical, for loathing and crushing the enemy. In Allied countries the Kaiser was portrayed as a demon, with glaring eyes and abnormally bristling mustaches, bent on the mad project of conquest of the world. In Germany people were taught to dread the day when Cossacks and Senegalese should rape German women and to hate England as the inveterate enemy

---

[18] See p. 619.

which inhumanly starved little children with its blockade. Each side convinced itself that all right was on its side and all wrong, wickedness, and barbarity on the other. An inflamed opinion helped to sustain men and women in such a fearsome struggle. But when it came time to make peace the rooted convictions, fixed ideas, profound aversions, hates, and fears became an obstacle to political judgment.

91
The Peace of
Paris, 1919

The late ally, Russia, was in the hands of Bolsheviks, ostracized like a leper colony, and taking no part in international relations. The late German and Austro-Hungarian empires were already defunct, and more-or-less revolutionary regimes struggled to establish themselves in their places. New republics already existed along the Baltic coast, in Poland, and in the Danube basin but without effective governments or acknowledged frontiers. Europe east of France and Italy was in a state approaching chaos, with revolution on the Russian style threatening. Western Europe was wrenched out of all resemblance to its former self. The Allied blockade of Germany continued. In these circumstances the victors assembled in Paris, in the bleak winter of 1919, to reconstruct the world. During 1919 they signed five treaties, all named after Paris suburbs—St.-Germain with Austria, Trianon with Hungary, Neuilly with Bulgaria, Sèvres with Turkey (1920), and most especially, with Germany, the Treaty of Versailles.

The world looked with awe and expectation to one man—the president of the United States. Wilson occupied a lone eminence, enjoyed a universal prestige. Victors, vanquished, and neutrals admitted that American intervention had decided the conflict. Everywhere people who had been long tried, confused, bereaved, were stirred by Wilson's thrilling language in favor of a higher cause, of a great concert of right in which peace would be forever secure and the world itself at last free. Wilson reached Europe in January 1919, visiting several Allied capitals. He was wildly acclaimed, and almost mobbed, greeted as the man who would lead civilization out of its wasteland.

The Fourteen Points
and the Treaty
of Versailles

Wilson's views were well known. He had stated them in January 1918 in his Fourteen Points—principles upon which, after victory, peace was to be established. The Fourteen Points demanded an end to secret treaties and secret diplomacy (or in Wilsonian language, "open covenants openly arrived at"); freedom of the seas "alike in peace and in war"; removal of barriers and inequalities in international trade; reduction of armaments by all powers; colonial readjustments; evacuation of occupied territory; self-determination of nationalities and a redrawing of European boundaries along national lines; and, last but not least, an international political organization to prevent war. On the whole, Wilson stood for the fruition of the democratic, liberal, progressive, and nationalistic movements of the century past, for the ideals of the Enlightenment, the French Revolution, and of 1848. As Wilson saw it, and as many believed, the World War should end in a new type of treaty. There was thought to be something sinister about peace conferences of the past, for example the Congress of Vienna of 1815.[19] The old diplomacy was blamed for leading to war. Lenin in his own way and for his own purposes was saying this in Russia too. It was felt that treaties had too long been wrongly based on a politics of power and the balance of power or on unprincipled deals and bargains made without regard to the people concerned. Democracy having defeated the Central Powers, people hoped that a new settlement, made in a democratic age, might be reached by general agreement in an atmosphere of mutual confidence. There was a real sense of a new era.

Wilson had had some difficulty, however, in persuading the Allied governments to accept his Fourteen Points. The French declared that something about making Germany pay for war damages must be added. The British vetoed the freedom of the seas "in peace and war"; it was naval rivalry that had estranged them from Germany, and they had fought the war, in a basic sense, to preserve British command of the sea. But with these two reservations the Allies expressed their willingness to follow Wilson's lead. The Germans who asked for the armistice believed that peace would be made along the lines of the Fourteen Points with only the two modifications described. The socialists and democrats now trying to rule Germany thought also that, having thrown out the Kaiser and gotten rid of the warlords, they would be treated by the victors with some moderation, and that a new democratic Germany would reemerge into the place in the world which they considered to be due it.

Twenty-seven nations assembled at Paris in January 1919, but the full or plenary sessions were unimportant. Matters were decided by conferences among the Big Four—Wilson himself, Lloyd George for England, Clemenceau for France, Orlando for Italy. The conjunction of personalities was not a happy one. Wilson was sternly and stubbornly righteous; Lloyd George a fiery and changeable Welshman; Clemenceau an aged patriot, the "tiger of France," who had been not exactly young in the War of 1870 (he was born in 1841); Orlando a passing phenomenon of Italian politics. None of them was especially equipped for the task in hand. Clemenceau was a pronounced nationalist, Lloyd George had always been concerned with domestic reforms, Orlando was by training a professor like Wilson, and Wilson, a former college president, lacked concrete knowledge or intimate feeling for peoples other than his own. However, they democratically represented the governments and peoples of their respective countries, and thus spoke with an authority denied to professional diplomats of the old school.

Wilson first fought a hard battle for a League of Nations, a permanent international body in which all nations, without sacrificing their sovereignty, should meet together to discuss and settle disputes, each promising not to resort to war. Few European statesmen had any confidence in such a League. But they yielded to Wilson, and the covenant of the League of Nations was written into the treaty with Germany. In return, Wilson had to make concessions to Lloyd George, Clemenceau, Orlando, and the Japanese. He was thus obliged to compromise the idealism of the Fourteen Points. Probably compromise and bargaining would have been necessary

[19] See pp. 454–460.

anyway, for such general principles as national self-determination and colonial readjustment invariably led to difference of opinion in concrete cases. Wilson allowed himself to believe that, if a League of Nations were established and operating, faults in the treaty could later be corrected at leisure by international discussion.

The great demand of the French at the peace conference was for security against Germany. On this subject the French were almost rabid. The war in the West had been fought almost entirely on their soil. To trim Germany down more nearly to French size, they proposed that the part of Germany west of the Rhine be set up as an independent state under Allied auspices. Wilson and Lloyd George objected, sagely observing that the resulting German resentment would only lead to another war. The French yielded, but only on condition that they obtain their security in another way, namely, by a promise from both Britain and the United States to join them immediately if they were again attacked by the Germans. An Anglo-French-American guarantee treaty, with these provisions, was in fact signed at Paris. France obtained control over the Saar coal mines for fifteen years; during that time, a League commission would administer the Saar territory and in 1935 a plebiscite would be held. Lorraine and Alsace were returned to France. German fortifications and troops were banned from a wide belt in the Rhineland. Allied troops would occupy the Rhineland for fifteen years to assure German compliance with the treaty.

In the east the Allies wished to set up strong buffer states against Bolshevism in Russia. Sympathies with Poland ran very high. Those parts of the former German Empire that were inhabited by Poles, or by mixed populations of Poles and Germans—Posen and West Prussia—were assigned to the new Polish state. This gave Poland a corridor to the sea, but at the same time cut off the bulk of Germany from East Prussia.[20] Danzig, an old German town, became a free city, belonging to no country. Memel also was internationalized; it was soon seized by Lithuania. Upper Silesia, a rich mining country, went to Poland after a disputed plebiscite. In Austria and among the Sudeten Germans of Bohemia, now that there was no longer a Habsburg empire (whose existence had blocked an all-German union in 1848 and in the time of Bismarck),[21] a feeling developed for annexation to the new German republic. But the feeling was unorganized, and in any case the Allies naturally refused to make Germany bigger than it had been in 1914. Austria remained a dwarf republic, and Vienna a former imperial capital cut off from its empire—a head severed from its body, and scarcely more capable of sustaining life. The Bohemian Germans became disgruntled citizens of Czechoslovakia.

Germany lost all its colonies. Wilson and the South African General Smuts, to preserve the principle of internationalism against raw conquest, brought it about that the colonies were actually awarded to the League of Nations, which in turn, under "mandates," assigned them to various powers for administration. In this way France and Great Britain divided the best of the African colonies; the Belgian Congo received a slight enlargement; and the Union of South Africa took over German Southwest

[20]See maps, pp. 760–761 and 259, panel 4.
[21]See pp. 528–532, 567–572.

Africa. In the colonial world, Italy got nothing. Japan received the mandate for German Pacific islands north of the equator, Australia for German New Guinea and the Solomon Islands, New Zealand for German Samoa. The Japanese claimed rights over the German concessions in China. The Chinese at the Paris conference tried to get all special concessions and extraterritorial rights in China abolished.[22] No one listened to such proposals. By a compromise, Japan received about half the former German rights. The Japanese were dissatisfied. The Chinese walked out of the conference.

The Allies took over the German fleet, but the German crews, rather than surrender it, solemnly scuttled it at Scapa Flow. The German army was limited to 100,000. Since the Allies forbade conscription, or the annual training of successive groups of young civilians, the army became exclusively professional, the officer class retained political influence in it, and the means used by the Allies to demilitarize Germany served if anything the contrary purpose. The treaty forbade Germany to have any heavy artillery, aviation, or submarines. Wilson saw his plan for universal disarmament applied to Germany alone.

The French, even before the armistice, had stipulated that Germany must pay for war damages. The other Allies made the same demand. Wilson, at the conference, was stupefied at the size of the bills presented. The Belgians suggested, for their own share, a sum larger than the entire wealth of all Belgium according to officially published Belgian statistics. The French and British proposed to charge Germany with the entire expenses, including war pensions, incurred by them during the war. Wilson observed that "total" reparation, while not strictly unjust, was absolutely impossible, and even Clemenceau noted that "to ask for over a trillion francs would lead to nothing practical." The insistence on enormous reparations was in fact largely emotional. No one knew or considered how Germany would pay, though all dimly realized that such sums could only be made up by German exports, which would then compete with the Allies' own economic interests. The Germans, to avoid worse, even offered to repair physical damages in Belgium and France, but were brusquely refused on the ground that the Belgians and French would thereby lose jobs and business. No total at all was set for reparations in the treaty; it was made clear that the sum would be very large, but it was left for a future commission to determine. The Allies, maddened by the war, and themselves loaded with fantastic debts to the United States, had no desire in the matter of reparations to listen to economic reason and regarded the reparations as simply another means of righting a wrong and of putting off the dangers of a German revival. As a first payment on the reparations account the treaty required Germany to surrender most of its merchant marine, make coal deliveries, and give up all property owned by German private citizens abroad. This last proviso ended Germany's prewar career as an exporter of capital.

It was with the specific purpose of justifying the reparations that the famous "war guilt" clause was written into the treaty. By this clause Germany explicitly "accepted

---

[22] See pp. 702–705.

the responsibility" for all loss and damage resulting from the war "imposed upon them (the Allies) by the aggression of Germany and her allies." The Germans themselves felt no such responsibility as they were now obliged formally to accept. They considered their honor as a people to be impugned. The "war guilt" clause gave a ready opening to agitators in Germany and made even moderate Germans regard the treaty as something to be escaped from as a matter of self-respect.

The Treaty of Versailles was completed in three months. The absence of the Russians, the decision not to give the Germans a hearing, and the willingness of Wilson to make concessions in return for obtaining the League of Nations, made it possible to dispose of intricate matters with considerable facility. The Germans, when presented with the completed document in May 1919, refused to sign. The Allies threatened a renewal of hostilities. A government crisis ensued in Berlin. No German wished to damn himself, his party, or his principles, in German eyes, by putting his name to a document which all Germans regarded as outrageous. A combination drawn from the Social Democratic and Catholic parties finally consented to shoulder the hateful burden. Two abashed and unknown men, with the plain names of Müller and Bell, appeared at the Hall of Mirrors at Versailles, and signed the treaty for Germany in the presence of a large concourse of Allied dignitaries.

The other treaties drafted by the Paris conference, in conjunction with the Versailles treaty, laid out a new map for eastern Europe and registered the recession of the Russian, Austrian, and Turkish empires. Seven new independent states now existed: Finland, Estonia, Latvia, Lithuania, Poland, Czechoslovakia, and Yugoslavia. Rumania was enlarged by adding areas formerly Hungarian and Russian; Greece was enlarged at the expense of Turkey. Austria and Hungary were now small states, and there was no connection between them. The Ottoman Empire presently disappeared: Turkey emerged as a republic confined to Constantinople and Asia Minor, Syria and Lebanon went to France as mandates of the League of Nations, Palestine and Iraq to Great Britain on the same basis.[23] The belt of states from Finland to Rumania was regarded as a *cordon sanitaire* (sanitary zone) to prevent the westward expansion of communism. The creation of Yugoslavia realized the aims of the South Slav or Pan-Serb movement which had set off the fatal crisis of 1914. The fact, however, that Italy received Trieste and some of the Dalmatian Islands (in keeping with the secret treaty of 1915) left the more ambitious Yugoslavs discontented.

Significance of the Paris Peace Settlement

The most general principle of the Paris settlement was to recognize the right of national self-determination, at least in Europe. Each people or nation, as defined by language, was in principle set up with its own sovereign and independent national state. Nationalism triumphed in the belief that it went along naturally with liberalism and democracy. It must be added that the peacemakers at Paris had little choice in this matter, for the new states had already declared their independence. Since in eastern Europe the nationalities were in many places intermixed, and since

[23] The secret treaty of 1915 (p. 739) promising the Straits to Russia lapsed with the Revolution, neither the Bolsheviks nor the Allies recognizing an agreement made with the tsarist government.

the peacemakers did not contemplate the actual movement and exchange of populations to sort them out, each new state found alien minorities living within its borders or could claim that people of its own kind still lived in neighboring states under foreign rule. There were Hungarians in Czechoslovakia, Ruthenians in Poland, Poles in Lithuania, Bulgars in Rumania—to cite only a few examples. Hence minority problems and irredentism troubled eastern Europe, as they had before 1914. Eventually it was the complaint of Germans in Czechoslovakia that they were an oppressed minority, together with the irredentist demand of Germany to join these outlying brothers to the Fatherland, that produced the Munich crisis preceding the Second World War.[24]

The Treaty of Versailles was designed to put an end to the German menace. It was not a successful treaty. The wisdom of it has been discussed without end, but a few comments can safely be made. For practical purposes, with respect to Germany, the treaty was either too severe or too lenient. It was too severe to conciliate and not severe enough to destroy. Possibly the victors should have dealt more moderately with the new German republic, which professed their own ideals, as the monarchical victors over Napoleon, in 1814, had dealt moderately with the France of the restored Bourbons, regarding it as a regime akin to their own. As it was, the Allies imposed upon the German republic about the same terms that they might have imposed upon the German Empire. They innocently played the game of Ludendorff and the German reactionaries; it was the Social Democrats and liberals who bore the "shame" of Versailles. The Germans from the beginning showed no real intention to live up to the treaty. On the other hand, the treaty was not sufficiently disabling to Germany to destroy its economic and political strength. Even the degree of severity that it incorporated soon proved to be more than the Allies were willing to enforce. The treaty-makers at Paris in 1919, working hastily and still in the heat of war, under pressure from press and propaganda in their own countries, drafted a set of terms which the test of time showed that they themselves did not in the long run wish to impose. As the years passed, many people in Allied countries declared various provisions of the Versailles treaty to be unfair or unworkable. The loss of faith by the Allies in their own treaty only made easier the task of those German agitators who demanded its repudiation. The door was opened for Adolf Hitler.

[24]See pp. 885–887.

Europe 1923. *The map shows European boundaries between the two World Wars. They are as established by the Treaty of Versailles of 1919, the other treaties of the Peace of Paris, the settlement of the Irish troubles, the outcome of the Russo-Polish war of 1920, the termination of the Greek-Turkish war, and the end of Allied intervention in Russia and in Turkey. By comparison with the language map on p. 478, it may be seen to what extent these boundaries set up various nationalities as independent states. The boundaries here shown began to collapse in 1938 with the German annexation of Austria and with the Munich conference, by which Germany annexed the Sudeten areas of Czechoslovakia. On the Polish question, which precipitated the Second World War, see also panel 4 of the map on p. 259.*

ARCTIC OCEAN

0   100   200   300 miles

Narvik

Reykjavik• ICELAND
(Denmark)

NORWAY

SWED•

FAEROE I.
(Denmark)

Oslo•

Stockhol•

ORKNEY I.
SCAPA FLOW

•Edinburgh   NORTH SEA   DENMARK   •Copenhagen

ULSTER
IRISH   GREAT BRITAIN
FREE STATE   Dan•
•Dublin   •Liverpool   POLISH-
                                                   CORRIDOR

ATLANTIC OCEAN   •Hamburg
                         NETHERLANDS   •Bremen   GERMANY •Berlin
                    •London Amsterdam• Rhine WEIMAR REPUBLIC
                                        RUHR •Weimar •Dresden
                         Brussels•   Cologne•   •Prague
                         BELGIUM   •Frankfurt CZECHO
                              LUX.•   •Stuttgart
                    Paris• Metz• SAAR
                    •Versailles   •Strasbourg
                                        •Munich   Vienna•
                                                        AUSTRIA Bu•

F R A N C E   SWITZERLAND
                    Geneva• •Locarno
            •Bordeaux   •Trent   •Trieste
                                              •Fiume

                              •Marseilles •Florence ADRIATIC S
        •Bilbao   •Zara
                                                        (Italy)
PORTUGAL   CORSICA   YU
        Madrid•   •Barcelona (France)
•Lisbon S P A I N   Rome• ITALY
                                              •Naples
        •Seville   BALEARIC I.
Cadiz•   (Spain)   SARDINIA
Tangier• •Gibraltar (Britain)
        SPANISH   SICILY
        MOROCCO   •Algiers   MALTA (B•

        MOROCCO   ALGERIA   TUNISIA   MEDITERRANE
        (France)   (France)   (France)

760

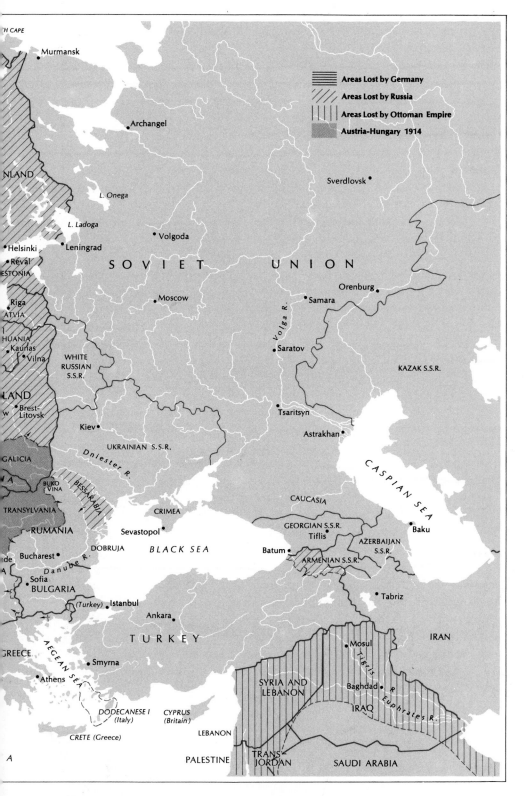

'H CAPE

• Murmansk

• Archangel

Sverdlovsk •

NLAND

L. Onega

L. Ladoga

•Helsinki   • Leningrad   • Volgoda

S O V I E T   U N I O N

•Reval

ESTONIA

Riga   • Moscow   Orenburg •

ATVIA   • Samara

HUANIA   Volga R.

•Kaunas   • Saratov   KAZAK S.S.R.

•Vilna   WHITE
RUSSIAN
S.S.R.

LAND   •Brest–
W   Litovsk   • Tsaritsyn

Kiev •   Astrakhan •

UKRAINIAN S.S.R.

GALICIA   Dniester R.   C A S P I A N   S E A

BUKO
VINA   BESSARABIA

A   CAUCASIA

TRANSYLVANIA   CRIMEA   GEORGIAN S.S.R.   Baku •

RUMANIA   Sevastopol •   Tiflis •

DOBRUJA   B L A C K   S E A   Batum •   AZERBAIJAN
S.S.R.

Bucharest •   ARMENIAN S.S.R.

de   Danube R.

•Sofia   • Tabriz

BULGARIA

(Turkey) • Istanbul   • Ankara   IRAN

T U R K E Y

GREECE   A
E
G
E
A
N   • Smyrna   • Mosul

• Athens   S
E
A   SYRIA AND
LEBANON   Baghdad •   Tigris R.

DODECANESE I   CYPRUS
(Italy)   (Britain)   IRAQ   Euphrates R.

CRETE (Greece)   LEBANON

A   PALESTINE   TRANS
JORDAN   SAUDI ARABIA

Even at the beginning the Allies showed doubts. Lloyd George, in the last weeks before signature, tardily called for certain amendments, though in vain; for in 1919 British opinion shifted somewhat from fear of Germany to the fear of Bolshevism, and already the idea of using Germany as a bulwark against communism was expressed. The Italians disliked the whole settlement from the beginning; they observed that the spoils of Africa and the Near East went only to France and Great Britain. The Chinese were also dissatisfied. The Russians, when they reentered the international arena some years later, found a situation that they did not like and had had no part in making. They objected to being faced with a *cordon sanitaire* from Finland to Rumania and soon remembered that most of this territory had once belonged to the Russian empire.

The United States never ratified the Treaty of Versailles at all. A wave of isolationism and disgust with Europe spread over the country; and this feeling, together with some rational criticism of the terms, and a good deal of party politics, caused the Senate to repudiate Wilson's work. The Senate likewise refused to make any advance promises of military intervention in a future war between Germany and France, and hence also declined to ratify the Anglo-French-American guarantee treaty on which Wilson had persuaded Clemenceau to rely. The French considered themselves duped, deprived both of the Rhineland and of the Anglo-American guarantee. They raised more anguished cries over their insecurity. This led them to try to hold Germany down while it was still weak, in turn raising many further complications.

The League of Nations was established at Geneva. Its mere existence marked a great step beyond the international anarchy before 1914. Wilson's vision did not die. But the United States never joined; Germany was not admitted until 1926, or Russia until 1934. The League could handle and dispatch only such business as the Great Powers were willing to allow. It was associated with a west-European ascendancy that no longer corresponded to the facts of the world situation. Its covenant was part of the Versailles treaty, and many people in many countries, on both sides in the late war, saw in it, not so much a system for international adjudication, as a means for maintaining a new status quo in favor of Britain and France.

The First World War dealt a last blow to the ancient institutions of monarchy and aristocratic feudalism. Thrones toppled in Turkey, in Russia, in Austria-Hungary, in the German Empire and the individual German states; and with the kings went the courtly retainers and all the social preeminence and special advantage of the old landed aristocracies. The war was indeed a victory for democracy, though a bitter one. It carried further a process as old as the French and American revolutions. But for the basic problems of modern civilization, industrialism and nationalism, economic security and international stability, it gave no answer.

XVII: THE RUSSIAN

REVOLUTION

No less powerful than the First World War as a force shaping the twentieth century has been the revolution in Russia, of which the decisive step was the seizure of power by Lenin in November 1917. The Russian Revolution of 1917 can be compared in its magnitude only with the French Revolution of 1789. Both originated from deep-lying and distant causes, and both made their repercussions felt in many countries for many years. The present chapter will set forth the revolutionary process in Russia over half a century. We shall begin with the old regime before 1900, pass through the two revolutions of 1905 and 1917, and survey the Union of Soviet Socialist Republics down to 1939, at which time a new order had been consolidated under Joseph Stalin, a form of "planned economy" successfully realized, and the last of the true revolutionaries, or Old Bolsheviks, either silenced or put to death.

The comparison of the Russian Revolution to the French is enlightening in many ways. Both aimed at liberation, the one from feudalism, the other from capitalism.

Chapter Emblem: One of a series of bronze medals issued by the Leningrad mint in honor of Lenin and the Russian Revolution of 1917.

Neither was a strictly national movement dealing with merely domestic troubles; both addressed their appeal to all men regardless of creed or color. Both attracted followers in all countries. Both became international. Both aroused a strong reaction on the part of those in all countries whose view of life was endangered. Both showed the same pattern of revolutionary politics: a relative unity of opinion so long as the problem was to overthrow the old regime, followed by disunity and conflict over the founding of the new, so that one set of the original revolutionaries eliminated others, until a small, organized, and determined minority (Jacobin democrats in 1793, Bolshevik communists in 1918) suppressed all opposition in order to defend or advance the revolutionary cause; and in short order (within a matter of months in France, years in Russia), many of the dominant revolutionary party were themselves suppressed or liquidated.

The differences are equally deserving of notice. Relatively speaking, or compared in general civilization with other European countries, Russia in 1900 was in the rear, and France in 1780 in most ways in the lead. Nor is the difference merely relative. Illiteracy was probably more widespread in Russia in 1900 than in France in 1780. The last tsar, Nicholas II, was horsewhipped as a young man by his own father, Alexander III; the last tsarina, Alexandra, was a superstitious woman much given to consultation with necromancers. The private life of Louis XVI and Marie Antoinette was less primitive. Moreover, the French Revolution of 1789 broke out in time of peace, whereas both in 1905 and in 1917 revolution came in Russia in conjunction with an unsuccessful war. This may signify that under modern conditions stable governments have little to fear from revolution in peacetime. On the other hand, the French Revolution led to a series of European wars. Russia after its revolution (largely because Europe was exhausted in 1918) fought no major foreign war until 1941, when the German Adolf Hitler invaded the Soviet Union.

In France, to pursue the contrast, the revolution just "happened," in that ordinary people from many walks of life unexpectedly found themselves in a revolutionary situation, and even the Jacobin dictatorship was improvised by men who had spent their lives thinking of other things. In Russia bands of professional revolutionaries worked for the revolution long in advance, and the dictatorship of the Bolsheviks realized the plans and preparations of twenty years. In France the revolution was followed by a reaction in which émigrés returned, dispossessed classes reappeared in politics, and even the Bourbons were restored. The Russian Revolution effectively wiped out its opposition; no once discredited class ever came back, few émigrés returned, no Romanovs regained their throne. The Russian Revolution was in this sense more immediately successful. Yet it may be that the effects of the French Revolution were deeper and more subtle.

It has just been said that professional revolutionists worked for revolution in Russia. They did not, however, "cause" it. Lenin and the Bolsheviks did not bring about the Russian Revolution. They captured it after it had begun. They boarded the ship in midstream. The Russian Revolution, like all great revolutions, originated in a totality of previous history.

W̶e have seen in earlier chapters how the tsarist autocracy arose, how it ruled as a machine superimposed upon its subjects, how the upper class became westernized while the masses sank further into serfdom, and how an intelligentsia developed, divorced both from the work of government and the activities of the people.[1] It has been explained in Chapter XIII how Alexander II freed the serfs in 1861 and created provincial and district councils or zemstvos, elected mainly by landowners, which attended to such matters as roads, schools and hospitals.[2]

In 1881 Alexander II was assassinated by members of the People's Will. His son, Alexander III (1881–1894), tried to stamp out revolutionism and to silence even peaceable criticism of the government. Revolutionaries and terrorists were driven into exile. The People's Will as an organized group became extinct. Jews were subjected to pogroms, by far the worst of any (until then) in modern times. For the first time the empire adopted a program of systematic Russification. Poles, Ukrainians, Lithuanians, Caucasians, the scattered German communities, the various Moslem groups, all faced the prospect of forcible assimilation to the Great Russian culture. The philosopher and chief official of this movement was Pobiedonostsev, procurator of the Holy Synod, or layman head, under the tsar, of the Russian Orthodox Church. Pobiedonostsev saw in the West something alien and doomed. Drawing on such old enemies of the French Revolution as Edmund Burke, he attacked Western rationalism and liberalism in his writings, declared that Slavs had a peculiar national character of their own, and dreamed of turning Holy Russia into a kind of churchly community, in which a disciplined clergy should protect the faithful from the insidious influences of the West.

This is not, however, what happened. In the closing decades of the nineteenth century Russia became more than ever before a part of European civilization. Almost overnight it presented Europe with great works of literature and music that Europeans could understand. The Russian novel became known throughout the Western world. All could read the novels of Tolstoy (1828–1910) without a feeling of strangeness; and if the characters of Turgenev (1818–1883) and of Dostoievski (1821–1881) behaved more queerly, the authors themselves were obviously within the great European cultural family. The melodies of Tchaikovsky (1840–1893) and songs of Rimsky-Korsakov (1844–1908) became familiar throughout Europe and America; if they sometimes seemed hauntingly wild, distant, or sad, they still betrayed no more than the usual amount of national idiosyncrasy. Russians also contributed to the sciences, notably chemistry. They were considered to be especially talented in the more abstruse intellectual exercises, such as higher mathematics, physics, or chess.

[1] See pp. 244–256, 346–352, 581–586.
[2] See pp. 583–586.

Russia also, from the 1880s, began to pass through the industrial revolution and take its place as an integral part of the world economic system. European capital entered the country, financing railways, mines, and factories (as well as government and the army) until by 1914 Europeans had about the same amount invested in Russia as in the United States, some four billion dollars in each case.[3] In 1897, under the reforming ministry of Count Witte, Russia adopted the gold standard, making its currency readily convertible with all others. In the quarter-century between 1888 and 1913 the Russian railway mileage more than doubled, the miles of telegraph wires multiplied fivefold, the number of post offices trebled, and the number of letters carried by the mails multiplied seven times. Although still industrially backward by Western standards, without, for example, any machine tool industry or chemical plants, Russia was industrializing rapidly. Exports rose in value from 400,000,000 rubles in 1880 to 1,600,000,000 in 1913. Imports, though smaller, grew more rapidly, quintupling in the same period. They consisted of such items as tea and coffee and of the machines and industrial goods made in western Europe. For a long time after the Revolution, the Soviet Union conducted less foreign trade than did the Russian empire on the eve of the First World War. The Soviet regime, to keep control over its own economic system, tried to depend as little as possible on outside markets and sources of supply.

Industrialization, in Russia as in all countries, brought an increase both of the business and of the wage-earning classes, or, in socialist terminology, of the bourgeoisie and of the proletariat. Though growing, they were still not numerous by standards of the West. Factory workers, laboring for eleven or more hours a day, for low wages under hard conditions, were in somewhat the same position as in England or France before 1850.[4] Unions were illegal, and strikes prohibited. Nevertheless, great strikes in the 1890s called attention to the misery of the new industrial workers. There was one distinctive feature to the Russian proletariat. Russian industry was heavily concentrated; half of Russia's industrial workers were employed in factories employing over 500 persons. It was easier for workers under such circumstances to be organized economically and at the proper time to be mobilized politically. As for the Russian business and capitalist class, it was relatively the weaker because of several features in the situation. Ownership of much of Russia's new industrial plant was in foreign hands. Much was owned by the tsarist government itself; Russia already had the largest state-operated economic system in the world. Moreover, in Russia (unlike the United States at the time) the government itself was a heavy borrower from Europe; hence it was less dependent financially on its own people and more able to maintain an absolutist regime.

Nevertheless, the rising business and professional classes, reinforced by enterprising landowners, were strong enough to form a liberal segment of public opinion, which emerged in 1903 as the Constitutional Democratic party (the K.D.'s or "Cadets"). Many of those who were active in the provincial zemstvos also became Constitutional Democrats. They were liberals, progressives, or constitutionalists in

[3] See pp. 620–622, 671.
[4] See pp. 469–470, 506–509, 513–516.

the Western sense, thinking less about the troubles of factory workers and peasants than about the need of a nationally elected parliament to control the policies of state.

Russia remained predominantly agricultural. Its huge exports were mainly farm and forest products. The peasants formed four-fifths of the population. Free from their former lords since 1861, they lived in their village communes or *mirs*.[5] In most communes the land was divided and redivided among peasant households by agreement of the village community, nor could anyone leave without communal permission. The peasants still carried a considerable burden. Until 1906 they paid redemption money arising from the Emancipation of 1861, and even after that other forms of onerous payments. They also paid high taxes, for the government defrayed the interest on its foreign loans from taxes raised at home. The constantly rising export of cereals (also used to pay off debts contracted by Russia in the West) tended to keep food from the farmer's table; many a peasant raised the best wheat for sale and ate black bread himself. The farm population, in short (as in other countries in similar stages of their development), bore a considerable share of the costs of industrialization.

Under such pressures, and because of their incredibly crude methods of cultivation, the peasants were forever demanding more land. "Land hunger" was felt both by individual families and by the *mirs*. The Emancipation had turned over roughly half the land to peasant ownership, individual and collective; and in the following half-century the peasants added to their share by buying from nonpeasant owners. The *mirs* were by no means obsolescent. They were in fact flourishing; they acquired far more land by purchase than did individual buyers, and perhaps half or more of the peasants valued communal security above the uncertain pleasures of private property. The exceptions were the minority of more enterprising and wealthier peasants, later called the *kulaks*. Such a one was Leon Trotsky's father, who, a hard-working, rude, and illiterate man, owned or leased the equivalent of a square mile of land, employed scores of field hands at harvest time, and permanently maintained a large domestic staff. That such a "big farmer" could afford so many employees suggests the poverty in which the bulk of the peasants lived. Not all of the well-to-do peasants were as affluent as Trotsky's father, but the big farmers stood out conspicuously from the mass, by whom they were not liked.

The peasants were the ancient source of revolutionary disturbance in Russia. Fables about Pugachev and Stephen Razin circulated in peasant legend.[6] After the Emancipation the peasants continued to believe that they had some kind of rights in *all* the land of former estates on which they had formerly been serfs—not merely in the portion that had been allotted to peasant possession. They demanded (and obtained) credit from the government to buy from the big landowners or former masters. Their land hunger could not be appeased. They remained jealous of the landed aristocrat's very existence. In Russia, as elsewhere in Europe, and unlike the United States, the

[5] See pp. 583–584.
[6] See pp. 248–249, 348–349.

rural population was divided into two sharply distinct classes, on the one hand the peasants of all types, who worked the soil, and on the other the gentry who resided upon it. The two never intermarried. They differed not merely economically, but in speech, dress, and manners, and even in the looks of their faces and hands. But in the last three decades of the nineteenth century the Russian peasants were notably quiet, insurrectionism seemingly having subsided.

The other traditional source of revolutionary disturbance lay among the intelligentsia.[7] In the conditions in which the Russian empire had grown up, many of the best and purest spirits were attracted to violence. Revolutionary intelligentsia (as distinguished from those who were simply liberal or progressive) yearned for a catastrophic overthrow of the tsardom. Since the days of the Decembrists[8] they had formed secret organizations, comprising a few hundreds or thousands of members, engaged in outwitting the tsarist police, by whom they were bafflingly inter-penetrated. For example, at a Bolshevik party congress held in 1913, out of twenty-two delegates present, no less than five, unknown to the others, were government spies.

The revolutionary intelligentsia, since there was normally little that they could do, spent their time in vehement discussion and interminable refinement of doctrine. By 1890 the terrorism and nihilism of the 1870s were somewhat passé. The great question was where these willing officers of a revolutionary movement could find an army. Disputation turned upon such topics as whether the peasants or the new factory workers were the true revolutionary class, whether the peasants were potentially proletarian or incurably petty bourgeois, whether Russia was bound to experience the same historical process as the West, or whether it was different; and, specifically, whether Russia had to go through capitalism or might simply skip the capitalist stage in reaching the socialist society.

Most of the revolutionary intelligentsia were "populists." Some had once belonged to the now broken People's Will. Some continued to approve of terrorism and assassination as morally necessary in an autocratic country. They generally had a mystical faith in the vast inchoate might of the Russian people, and since most Russians were peasants, the populists were agrarians interested in peasant problems and peasant welfare. They believed that a great native revolutionary tradition existed in Russia, of which the peasant rebellion of Pugachev, in 1773, was the chief example.[9] The populists put their faith in the peasant commune or *mir*, which they called "naively socialistic," seeing in it a basic institution that had saved the Russians from self-seeking Western individualism and upon which a more developed socialism might be built. They read and respected Marx and Engels; indeed, a populist first translated the *Communist Manifesto* into Russian; but they regarded Marxism as suited to the conditions of western Europe. They did not believe that an urban proletariat was the only true revolutionary class. They did not believe that capitalism, by creating such a proletariat, had inevitably and logically to precede

[7] See pp. 582–583.
[8] See p. 493.
[9] See pp. 348–349.

socialism. They said that, in Russia, the horrors of capitalism could be skipped.
They addressed themselves to the plight of the farmer and the evils of landlordism,
favored strengthening the *mir* and equalizing the shares of all peasants in it, and, since
they did not have to wait for the prior triumph of capitalism in Russia, they thought
that revolution might come quite soon. This populist sentiment crystallized in the
founding in 1901 of the Social Revolutionary party. Agrarian populism, rather than
Marxism or communism, long remained the chief spontaneous form of radicalism in
eastern Europe.

Two populists, Plekhanov and Axelrod, fleeing to Switzerland in the 1870s, there
became converted to Marxism. In 1883 they founded in exile the organization from
which the Russian Social Democratic or Marxist party was to grow. A few Marxists
began to declare themselves (though not publicly) in Russia itself. When the
youthful Lenin met his future wife Krupskaya in 1894, she already belonged to a circle
of argumentative Marxists. The fact that the peasants in the 1890s were dis-
appointingly quiescent, while machine industry, factory labor, and strikes were
developing rapidly, turned many of the revolutionary intelligentsia, though only a
minority, from populism to Marxism. To Plekhanov and Axelrod were added, as
younger leaders, Lenin (1870–1924), Trotsky (1879–1940), Stalin (1879–1953) and
others.

Of these it was Lenin who, after Marx, was to be claimed by communism as a
father. Lenin was a short almost rotund man, with a small man's bounding quickness
and intense, penetrating gaze. High cheekbones and somewhat slanting eyes showed
an Asiatic strain on the paternal side; Russian friends at first said that he looked "like
a Kalmuck." His hair receded in early youth, leaving a massive forehead, behind
which a restless mind was inexhaustibly at work. Even in his twenties he was called
the Old One. He was of upper middle-class origin, son of an inspector of schools
who rose in the civilian bureaucracy to a rank equivalent to major-general. His
boyhood was comfortable and even happy, until the age of seventeen, when his elder
brother, a student at St. Petersburg, became somewhat incidentally involved in a plot
to assassinate Alexander III, for which he was put to death by order of the tsar
himself. Because of the blot on the family record it became impossible for Lenin to
continue with his law studies. He soon joined the ranks of professional revolutionaries, having no other occupation and living precariously from the party funds,
which came mainly from the donations of well-to-do sympathizers.

Arrested as a revolutionary, he spent three years of exile in Siberia. Here the
tsarist government treated educated political prisoners with an indulgence not later
shown by the Soviet regime. Lenin and most of the others lived in cottages of their
own or boarded with natives. No labor was required of them. They borrowed books
from Europe; met and visited with one another; debated, played chess, went hunting,
meditated, and wrote. They chafed, however, at being cut off from the mainstream of
Russian political life back home. Lenin, his term over, proceeded in 1900 to western
Europe, where except for short secret trips to Russia he remained until 1917. His
intellectual vigor, irresistible drive, and shrewdness as a tactician soon made him a
force in the party. Genius has been called the faculty for everlasting concentration

upon one thing.   Lenin, said his one-time close associate Axelrod, "for twenty-four hours of the day is taken up with the revolution, has no thoughts but thought of revolution, and even in his sleep dreams of nothing but revolution."

In 1898 the Marxists in Russia, spurred on by émigrés, founded the Social Democratic Labor party.   They were not more revolutionary than the larger group of Social Revolutionaries.   They simply had a different conception of the revolution. First of all, as good Marxists, they regarded the revolution as an international movement, part of the dialectical process of world history in which all countries were involved.   Russia for them was no different from other countries except that it was less advanced.   They expected the world revolution to break out first in western Europe.   They particularly admired the German Social Democratic party, the largest and most flourishing of all the parties that acknowledged the fatherhood of Marx.[10]

Where, in Russian terms, the populist Social Revolutionaries were Slavophiles, the Social Democrats were westernizers.   Indeed, most of the leaders lived in Europe.   They held that Russia must develop capitalism, an industrial proletariat, and the modern form of class struggle before there could be any revolution.   Seeing in the urban proletariat the true revolutionary class, they looked upon all peasantry with suspicion, ridiculed the *mir,* and abhorred the Social Revolutionaries. "Marxism," said Lenin, "has forever shaken itself loose from the nonsensical patter of the populists and anarchists to the effect that Russia can escape a capitalist development."   (Russian Marxists were on this point more Marxist than Marx and Engels, both of whom, when urged, refused to pronounce on the merits of the *mir* or on the need of capitalism as a precondition to socialism in Russia.)   Like Marx himself, the Russian Marxists disapproved of sporadic terrorism and assassination. For this reason, and because their doctrine seemed somewhat academic and their revolution rather conditional and far in the future, the Marxists were for a time actually favored by the tsarist police, who regarded them as less dangerous than the Social Revolutionaries.

Split in the Social Democrats: Bolsheviks and Mensheviks

The Russian Marxists held a second party congress in Brussels and London in 1903, attended by both émigrés like Lenin and delegates from the underground in Russia, and by both Social Democrats and members of lesser organizations.   The purpose of the congress was to unify all Russian Marxism, but in fact it split it forever.   The two resulting factions called themselves Bolsheviks, or majority men, and Mensheviks, or minority men.   Lenin was the main author of the split and hence the founder of Bolshevism.   Although he obtained his majority after one participating organization, the Jewish Bund, had seceded in indignation, and by calling for surprise votes on tactical issues, and although after 1903 it was usually the Mensheviks who had the majority, Lenin clung proudly and stubbornly to the term Bolshevism, with its favorable connotation of a majority in his support.   For a number of years after 1903 the Social Democrats remained at least formally a single Marxist party, but they were

[10] See pp. 635–636, 642–645.

irreconcilably divided into two wings. In 1912 the Bolshevik wing organized itself as
a separate party.

Bolshevism, or Leninism, originally differed from Menshevism mainly on matters of organization and tactics. Russian Marxists referred to each other as "hards" and "softs." The "hards" were attracted to Lenin, the "softs" repelled by him. Lenin believed that the party should be a small revolutionary elite, a hard core of reliable and zealous workers. Those who wished a larger and more open party, with membership for mere sympathizers, became Mensheviks. Lenin insisted upon a strongly centralized party, without autonomy for national or other component groups. Lenin demanded strong authority at the top, by which the central committee would determine the doctrine (or "party line") and control personnel at all levels of the organization. The Mensheviks favored a greater degree of influence by the membership as a whole. Lenin thought that the party would strengthen itself by purges, expelling all who developed deviations of opinion. The Mensheviks favored covering up or bridging over all but the most fundamental disagreements. The Mensheviks came to recommend cooperation with liberals, progressives, and bourgeois democrats. Lenin regarded such cooperation as purely tactical and temporary, never concealing that in the end the Bolsheviks must impose their views through a dictatorship of the proletariat. The Mensheviks, in short, came to resemble the Marxists of western Europe, so far as that was possible under Russian conditions.[11] Lenin stood for the rigid reaffirmation of Marxian fundamentals, dialectical materialism, and irreconcilable class struggle.

If we ask what Leninism added to the original Marxism,[12] the answer is not easy to find. Lenin accepted Marx's governing ideas: that capitalism exploited the workers, that it necessarily produced and preceded socialism, that history was logically predetermined, that class struggle was the law of society, that existing forms of religion, government, philosophy, and morals were weapons of the ruling class. He did, however, develop and transform into a first-rank element of Marxism certain theories of "imperialism" and of the "uneven development of capitalism" that had been propounded in only general terms by Marx and Engels. In the Marxist-Leninist view, "imperialism" was exclusively a product of monopoly capitalism, that is, capitalism in its big-business, "highest," and "final" stage, which develops differently and at different times in each country. Monopoly capitalism is bent on exporting surplus capital and investing it in underdeveloped areas for greater profits.[13] The unceasing drive for colonies and markets in a world already almost completely partitioned leads inevitably to international "imperialist" wars for the "redistribution" of colonies, as well as to intensified national colonial struggles for independence; both provide new revolutionary opportunities for the proletariat. In other respects, Lenin roundly denounced all who attempted to "add" anything to the fundamental principles of Marx. Nothing infuriated him so much as revisionist

---

[11] See pp. 643–645.
[12] See pp. 535–542.
[13] See pp. 670–671.

efforts to tone down the class struggle, or hints that Marxism might in the last analysis perhaps find room for some kind of religion.   He wrote in 1908:

Marx's theory is the objective truth.   Following the path of this theory, we will approach the objective truth more and more closely, while if we follow any other path we cannot arrive at anything except confusion and falsehood.   From the philosophy of Marxism, cast of one piece of steel, it is impossible to expunge a single basic premise, a single essential part, without deviating from objective truth, without falling into the arms of bourgeois-reactionary falsehood.[14]

Lenin was a convert.   He discovered Marxism; he did not invent it.   He found in it a theory of revolution which he accepted without reservation as scientific and on which he was more outspokenly dogmatic even than Marx himself.   His powers of mind, which were very great, were spent in demonstrating how the unfolding events of the twentieth century confirmed the analysis of the master.

But it was by his powers of will that Lenin was most distinguished, and if Leninism contributed little to Marxism as a theory it contributed a great deal to it as a movement.   Lenin was an activist.   He was the supreme agitator, a field commander in the class war, who could dash off a polemical pamphlet, dominate a party congress, or address throngs of workingmen with equal ease.   Beside him, Marx and Engels seem almost to be mere recluses or sociologists.   Marx and Engels had preferred to believe that the dictatorship of the proletariat, when it came, would represent the wishes of the great majority in a society in which most people had become proletarians.   Lenin more frankly foresaw the possibility that the proletarian dictatorship might represent the conscious wishes of a small vanguard and might have to impose itself on great masses by an unshrinking use of force.

Above all, Lenin developed Marx's idea of the role of the party.   He drew on the rich experience of pre-Marxist revolutionaries in Russia—the mysterious use of false names, invisible ink, secret ciphers, forged passports, and hidden rendezvous—the whole conspiratorial wonderland which, when it existed to a lesser degree in the West before 1848, drew Marx's scorn and laughter.   Lenin's conception of the party was basically Marx's, reinforced by his own experience as a Russian.   The party was an organization in which intellectuals provided leadership and understanding for workers, who could not see for themselves.   For trade unionism, concerned only with the day-to-day demands of workingmen, Lenin had even less patience than Marx.   "The unconscious growth of the labor movement," he wrote, "takes the form of trade unionism, and trade unionism signifies the mental enslavement of the workers to the bourgeoisie."   The task of intellectuals in the party, the elite, or experts, was to make the trade unions and the working class "conscious" and hence revolutionary.   Armed with "objective" knowledge, known to be correct, the party leadership naturally could not listen to the subjective opinions of others—the passing ideas of laboring men, of

[14]David Shub, *Lenin* (New York, 1948), p. 69.   Many other quotations in the present chapter are taken from Mr. Shub's biography, and many are from B. D. Wolfe, *Three Who Made a Revolution* (New York, 1948).

peasants, of mistaken party subordinates, or of other parties pretending to know more than Marx himself. The idea that intellectuals supply the brains and workers the brawn, that an elite leads while the toilers meekly follow, is understandable enough in view of the Russian background, which had created on the one hand a painfully self-conscious intelligentsia, and on the other a repressed working class and peasantry deprived of all opportunity for political experience of their own. It was one of the most distinctive traits of Leninism and one of the most foreign to the democratic movement of the West.

Leninism accomplished the marriage of Russian revolutionary traditions with the Western doctrine of Marxism. It was an improbable marriage, whose momentous offspring was to be communism. But at the time, when Bolshevism first appeared in 1903, it had little or no effect. A real revolution broke out in Russia in 1905. It took the revolutionary émigrés almost entirely by surprise.

T he almost simultaneous founding at the turn of the century of the Constitutional Democratic, Social Revolutionary, and Social Democratic parties was clearly a sign of mounting discontent. None of these was as yet a party in the Western sense, organized to get men elected to office, for there were no elections in Russia above the provincial zemstvo level. All three parties were propaganda agencies, made up of leaders without followers, intellectuals who followed, respectively, the liberal, agrarian, or Marxian lines of thought. All, even the liberal Constitutional Democrats, were watched by the police and obliged to do most of their work underground. At the same time, after 1900, there were signs of growing popular unrest. Peasants were trespassing on lands of the gentry and even rising in local insurrections against landlords and tax collectors. Factory workers sporadically refused to work. But with these popular movements none of the new parties had formed any solid links.

The government refused to make concessions of any kind. The tsar, Nicholas II, who had mounted the throne in 1894, was a man of narrow outlook. To the Little Father all criticism seemed merely childish. Tutored in his youth by Pobiedonostsev,[15] he regarded all ideas questioning autocracy, Orthodoxy, and Great Russian nationalism as un-Russian. That persons in the government should be controlled by interests outside the government—the mildest liberalism or most orderly democracy—seemed to the tsar, the tsarina, and the leading officials to be a monstrous aberration. Autocracy, for them, was the best and only, as it was the God-given, form of government for Russia.

The chief minister, Plehve, and the circles at court, hoped that a short successful war with Japan would restore sympathy for the government. The war went so badly that its effect was the reverse.[16] Critics of the regime (except for the handful of the most internationalist Marxists) were sufficiently patriotic to be ashamed at the ease

**93
The Revolution
of 1905**

*Background and
Revolutionary Events*

[15] See p. 767.
[16] See pp. 705–706.

with which Russia was defeated by an upstart and Asiatic power. As after the Crimean War, there was a general feeling that the government had exposed its incompetence to all the world. Liberals believed that its secret methods, its immunity to criticism or control, had made it sluggish, torpid, obstinate, and inefficient, unable either to win a war or to lead the economic modernization that was taking place in Russia. But there was little that the liberals could do.

The police had recently allowed a priest, Father Gapon, to go among the St. Petersburg factory workers and organize them, hoping thus to counter the propaganda of revolutionaries. Father Gapon took up their grievances in all seriousness. They believed, as simple peasants only recently transplanted to the city, that if only they could reach the ear of the Little Father, the august being high above all hard capitalists and stony officials, he would hear their complaints with shocked surprise and rectify the evils that afflicted Russia. They drew up a petition, asking for an eight-hour day, a minimum daily wage of one ruble (fifty cents), a repudiation of bungling bureaucrats, and a democratically elected Constituent Assembly to introduce representative government into the empire. Unarmed, peaceable, respectful, singing "God save the Tsar," a crowd of two hundred thousand—men, women, and children—gathered before the tsar's Winter Palace one Sunday in January 1905. But the tsar had fled, and his officials were afraid. Troops marched up and shot down the demonstrators in cold blood, killing several hundred.

"Bloody Sunday" in St. Petersburg snapped the moral bond upon which all stable government rests. The horrified workers saw that the tsar was not their friend. The autocracy stood revealed as the force behind the hated officials, the tax collectors, the landlords, and the owners of the industrial plants. A wave of political strikes broke out. Social Democrats (more Mensheviks than Bolsheviks) appeared from the underground or from exile to give revolutionary direction to these movements. Councils or "soviets" of workers were formed in Moscow and St. Petersburg. The peasants, too, in many parts of the country spontaneously began to erupt, overrunning the lands of the gentry, burning manor houses and doing violence to their owners. Social Revolutionaries naturally tried to take this movement in charge. The liberal Constitutional Democrats, professors, engineers, business people, lawyers, leaders in the provincial zemstvos founded forty years before, tried also to seize leadership or at least use the crisis to force the government's hand. All agreed on one demand—that there should be more democratic representation in the government.

The tsar yielded grudgingly and as little as possible. In March 1905 he promised to call to office men "enjoying the confidence of the nation." In August (after the ruinous battle of Tsushima) he agreed to call a kind of Estates General, for which peasants, landowners, and city people should vote as separate classes. Still the revolution raged unchecked. The St. Petersburg Soviet, or workers' council, led mainly by Mensheviks (Lenin had not yet reached Russia), declared a great general strike in October. Railroads stopped, banks closed, newspapers ceased to appear, and even lawyers refused to go to their offices. The strike spread to other cities and to the peasants. With the government paralyzed, the tsar issued his October

Manifesto. It promised a constitution, civil liberties, and a Duma to be elected by all classes alike, with powers to enact laws and control the administration.

The tsar and his advisers intended to divide the opposition by releasing the October Manifesto, and in this they succeeded. The Constitutional Democrats, with a Duma promised, allowed themselves to hope that social problems could henceforth be dealt with by parliamentary methods. Liberals were now afraid of revolutionaries; industrialists feared the strength shown by labor in the general strike, and landowners demanded a restoration of order among the peasants. Aroused peasants and workingmen were not yet satisfied; the former still wanted more land and less taxation, the latter a shorter working day and a living wage. The several branches of revolutionary intellectuals worked upon the continuing popular agitation, hoping to carry matters forward until the tsarist monarchy was abolished and a socialist republic established with themselves at its head. They believed also (and correctly) that the October Manifesto was in any case a deception, which the tsar would refuse to adhere to as soon as revolutionary pressure was removed. The soviets continued to seethe, local strikes went on, soldiers mutinied at Kronstadt and sailors in the Black Sea fleet.

But the government was able to maintain itself. With the middle-class liberals now inactive or demanding order, the authorities arrested the members of the St. Petersburg Soviet. Peace was hastily made with Japan, and reliable troop units were recalled from the Far East. The revolutionary leaders fled back to Europe, or again went underground, or were caught and sent to prison or to Siberia; executions were carried out in the countryside.

The chief apparent result of the Revolution of 1905 was to make Russia, at least ostensibly, into a parliamentary type of state, like the rest of Europe. The promised Duma was convoked. For ten years, from 1906 to 1916, Russia had at least the superficial attributes of a semiconstitutional monarchy. The year 1905 was Russia's 1789, with its 1793 held for twelve years in abeyance.

But Nicholas II soon showed that he did not intend to yield much. He drew the teeth of the new Duma before the creature could even be born, by announcing in advance, in 1906, that it would have no power over foreign policy, the budget, or government personnel. His attitude toward constitutional monarchy continued until 1917 to be entirely negative; the one thing that tsarism would not allow was any real participation in government by the public. Within this "public" the two extreme fringes were equally impervious to liberal constitutionalism. On the right, stubborn upholders of pure autocracy and the Orthodox church organized the Black Hundreds, terrorizing the peasantry and urging them to boycott the Duma. On the left, in 1906, the Social Revolutionaries and both the Bolshevik and Menshevik wings of the Social Democrats likewise refused to recognize the Duma, urged workers to boycott it, and refused to put up any candidates for election.

The short-lived first Duma was elected in 1906 by a system of indirect and unequal voting, in which peasants and workers voted as separate classes, and with proportionately far less representation than was granted to the landlords. In the absence of socialist candidates, workers and peasants voted for all sorts of people, including the liberal Constitutional Democrats (the "Cadets"), who obtained a sweeping majority. The Cadets, when the Duma met, found themselves still fighting for the bare principle of constitutional government. They demanded true universal suffrage and the responsibility of ministers to a parliamentary majority. The tsar's response was to dismiss the Duma after two months. The Cadets fled to Viborg in autonomous Finland, which the tsarist police generally let alone. It is significant that these constitutional liberals and democrats, in council at Viborg, again appealed for a general strike and nonpayment of taxes—that is, for mass revolution. But real revolutions are not easy to start, and nothing happened.

A second Duma was elected in 1907, with the government trying to control the elections through suppression of party meetings and newspapers, but since Social Revolutionaries and Mensheviks now consented to take part some eighty-three socialists were elected. The Cadets, now afraid of the revolutionary left, and concluding that constitutional progress must be gradual, showed a willingness to cooperate with the government, which, however, denouncing and arresting some fifty socialists as revolutionaries bent only on destruction, again abruptly put an end to the Duma itself. A third Duma, elected after an electoral change that gave an increased preponderance of representation to the landed propertied class and guaranteed a conservative majority for the government, managed to hold several sessions between 1907 and 1912; so, similarly, did a fourth Duma from 1912 to 1916. The deputies, by following the lead of the government, by addressing themselves only to concrete issues, by losing themselves in committee work, and by avoiding the basic question of where supreme power lay, kept precariously alive a modicum of parliamentary institutions in the tsarist empire.

The Stolypin Reforms

Some officials believed that the way to checkmate the revolutionaries, and strengthen the hold of the monarchy, was for the government, while keeping all controls in its own hands, to attract the support of reasonable and moderate people by a program of reforms. One of these was Peter Stolypin, whom the tsar retained as his principal minister from 1906 to 1911. It was Stolypin who dissolved the first two Dumas. But it was not his policy merely to stand still. His aim was to build up the propertied classes as friends of the state. He believed, perhaps rightly, that a state actively supported by widespread private property had little to fear from doctrinaire intellectuals, conspirators, and émigrés. As he said in a speech to the Third Duma in 1908: "The government has placed its wager, not on the needy and the drunken, but on the sturdy and the strong—on the sturdy individual proprietor who is called upon to play a part in the reconstruction of our Tsardom."

Stolypin therefore favored and broadened the powers of the provincial zemstvos, in which the larger landowners took part in administering local affairs. For the peasantry he put through legislation more sweeping than any since the Emancipation.

Seeing in the *mir* the source of communal agrarian restlessness, Stolypin hoped to replace this ancient institution with a regime of private individual property. He abolished what was left of the redemption payments for which the *mirs* had been collectively responsible.[17] He allowed each peasant to sell his share of the communal rights and to leave the commune at will. He authorized peasants to buy land freely from the communes, or from each other, or from the gentry. He thus favored the rise of the class of "big farmers," the later *kulaks*, men who obtained control of large tracts, worked them with hired help, and produced cash crops for the market. These were "the sturdy and the strong" upon whom Stolypin pinned his hopes. At the same time, by allowing peasants to sell out and leave the *mir* (it would generally be the worst farmers or most improvident persons who did so) he hastened the formation of a migratory wage-earning class, which would either seek work from the big farmers or go off to take jobs in the city. The creation of a mobile labor force, and of a food supply raised by big farmers for the market, would thus advance the industrialization of Russia.

The Stolypin policy was successful. Between 1907 and 1916, 6,200,000 families out of 16,000,000 who were eligible applied for legal separation from the *mir*. There was no mistaking the trend toward individual property and independent farming. But the results of the Stolypin program must not be exaggerated. The *mir* was far from broken. A vast majority of peasants were still involved in the old system of common rights and communal restrictions. The land shortage was still acute in the agricultural areas where yields were highest. Land hunger and poverty continued in the countryside. There were *kulaks*, to be sure, to be resented and envied, but the largest landed proprietors were still the gentry. About 30,000 landlords owned nearly 200,000,000 acres of land, and another 200,000,000 acres made up other large landed estates.

Stolypin was not left long to carry on his program. The tsar gave him only an unwilling support. Reactionary circles disliked his tampering ways and his Western orientation. Social Revolutionaries naturally cried out against dissolution of the communes. Even Marxists, who should in theory have applauded the advance of capitalism in Russia, feared that Stolypin's reforms might do away with agrarian discontent. "I do not expect to live to see the revolution," said Lenin in these years. Stolypin was shot dead while attending the theater in Kiev, in the presence of the tsar and tsarina, in 1911. The assassin, a member of the terrorist wing of the Social Revolutionaries, is thought also to have been a secret agent of the reactionary tsarist police. It may be added that Stolypin's predecessor, Plehve, and about a dozen other high officials within the past few years had similarly died at the hands of assassins.

But all in all, violent and half barbaric though it still was, the Russian empire on the eve of the First World War was moving in a Western direction. Its industries were growing, its railways expanding, its exports almost half as great in value as those of the United States. It had a parliament, if not a parliamentary government. Private

[17] See pp. 582–584.

property and individualist capitalism were spreading to new layers of the people. There was a guarded freedom of the press, illustrated, for example, by the legal and open establishment of the Bolshevik party paper, *Pravda*, in St. Petersburg in 1912. It is not possible to say how far this development might have gone, for it was menaced on both the right and the left by obstinate and obscurantist reactionaries upholding the absolute tsardom and by revolutionaries whom nothing but the end of tsardom and wholesale transformation of society could appease. But both extremes were discouraged. The desperation of extreme reactionaries in the government, the feeling that they might in any case soon lose their position, perhaps made them the more willing to precipitate a European war by armed support of Serbian nationalists. As for the revolutionary parties, and especially the Bolsheviks, they were losing in membership on the eve of the war, their leaders lived year after year in exile, dreaming of the great days of 1905 which stubbornly failed to repeat themselves and sometimes pessimistically admitting, as Lenin did, that there might be no revolution in their time.

94
The Revolution
of 1917

End of the Tsardom: The Revolution of March 1917

War again put the tsarist regime to a test that it could not meet. In this war, more "total" than any had ever been, willing cooperation between government and people was indispensable to success. This essential prerequisite the tsarist empire did not have. National minorities, Poles, Jews, Ukrainians, Caucasians, and others, were disaffected. As for the socialists, who in every other European parliament voted for the war credits, the dozen otherwise disunited socialists in the Duma refused to do so and were promptly jailed.[18] The ordinary workingman and peasant marched off with the army, but without the sense of personal conviction felt by common people in Germany and the West. More decisive was the attitude of the middle class. Because they patriotically wished Russia to win, the glaring mismanagement of the government was the more intolerable to them. The disasters with which the war opened in 1914, at Tannenberg and the Masurian Lakes, were followed by the advance of the Central Powers into Russia in 1915, at the cost of 2,000,000 Russian soldiers killed, wounded, or captured.[19]

At the war's outbreak middle-class people, as in all countries, offered their assistance to the government.[20] The provincial zemstvos formed a union of all zemstvos in the empire to facilitate the mobilization of agriculture and industry. Business groups at Petrograd (St. Petersburg lost its Germanic name at this time) formed a Commercial and Industrial Committee to get the factories into maximum production. The government distrusted these signs of public activity arising outside official circles. On the other hand, organized in this way, middle-class people became conscious of their own strength and more critical of the bureaucracy. Some officials in the war ministry itself were known to be at heart pro-German,

[18] See pp. 778, 806.
[19] See pp. 733, 740.
[20] See p. 750.

reactionaries who feared the liberalism of England and France, with which Russia was allied.

Life at court was bizarre even for Russia. The tsarina Alexandra, by origin a German woman, looked upon all Russians outside her own circle with contempt, incited her husband to play the proud and pitiless autocrat, and took advice from a self-appointed holy man, the bearded and weird Rasputin. She was convinced that Rasputin possessed supernatural and prophetic powers, because he had apparently cured her young son, the tsarevitch, of hemophilia. Rasputin, by his influence over her, had a voice in appointments to high office. All who wished an audience with the imperial pair had to go through him. Patriotic and enlightened persons of all classes vainly protested. In these circumstances, and given the military defeats, the union of zemstvos and other such war-born bodies complained not merely of faults of administration but of fundamental conditions in the state. The government responded by holding them at arm's length. The tsarist regime, caught in a total war, was afraid of the help offered by its own people.

During the war, in September 1915, the Duma was suspended. It was known that reactionaries—inspired by the tsarina, Rasputin, and other sinister forces—expected that a victory in the war would make it possible to kill liberalism and constitutionalism in Russia. The war thus revived all the basic political issues that had been latent since the Revolution of 1905. The union of zemstvos demanded the assembly of the Duma. The Duma reassembled in November 1916 and, conservative though it had always been, expressed loud indignation at the way affairs were conducted. Among all elements of the population dissatisfaction with the course of the war and the government's ineptitude mounted. In December Rasputin was assassinated by nobles at the court. The tsar began to consider repression and again adjourned the Duma. Machine guns were issued to the police. Members of the Duma, and of the new extragovernmental bodies, concluded that the situation could be saved only by force. It is when moderate persons, normally concerned with their own business, come to such conclusions that revolution becomes a political possibility. The shift of moderates and liberals, their need of a coup d'état to save themselves from reactionaries, likewise raised the long failing prospects of the minority of professional revolutionaries.

Again it was the workers of Petrograd who precipitated the crisis. Food had become scarce, as in all the belligerent countries. But the tsarist administration was too clumsy and too demoralized by graft to institute the controls that had become usual elsewhere, such as maximum prices and ration cards. It was the poorest who felt the food shortage most keenly. On March 8, 1917, food riots broke out, which soon developed, doubtless with the help of revolutionary intellectuals, into political insurrections. Crowds shouted, "Down with the tsar!" Troops within the city refused to fire on the insurgents; mutiny and insubordination spread from unit to unit. Within a few days, on the model of 1905, a Soviet of Workers' and Soldiers' Deputies had been organized in Petrograd.

Middle-class leaders, with the government now helpless, demanded dismissal of the ministry and formation of a new one commanding the confidence of a majority of the Duma. The tsar retaliated by disbanding the Duma. The Duma set up an executive committee to take charge until the situation clarified. There were now two new authorities in the city: one, the Duma committee, essentially moderate, constitutionalist, and relatively legal; the other, the Petrograd Soviet, representing revolutionary forces arising by spontaneous upsurge from below. The Petrograd Soviet (or workers' "council") was to play in 1917 a role like that of the Paris Commune of 1792, constantly pushing the supposedly higher and more nationwide authority to the left. The Soviet became the public auditorium and administrative center of the working-class upheaval. Since it was generally socialist in its outlook, all the factions of doctrinaire socialists—Social Revolutionaries, Mensheviks, Bolsheviks—tried to win it over and utilize it for their own ends.

The Duma committee, under pressure from the Petrograd Soviet, on March 14 set up a Provisional Government under Prince Lvov. The Duma liberals, as a concession to the Soviet, admitted one socialist to the new government, Alexander Kerensky, a moderate, legal-minded Social Revolutionary, and they furthermore consented to demand the abdication of Nicholas II. The tsar was then at the front. He tried to return to his palace near Petrograd, but the imperial train was stopped and turned back by troops. The army, fatefully, was taking the side of the revolution. The very generals in the field, unable to vouch for the loyalty of their men, advised abdication. Nicholas yielded; his brother the grand duke declined to succeed him; and on March 17, 1917, Russia became a republic.

The Bolshevik Revolution: November 1917

The Provisional Government, following the best precedents of European revolutions, called for elections by manhood suffrage to a Constituent Assembly, which was to meet late in the year and prepare a constitution for the new regime. It tried also to continue the war against Germany. In July an offensive was mounted but the demoralized armies were quickly routed. Pending final decision by the Constituent Assembly, the Provisional Government promised wholesale redistribution of land to the peasants but took no action. Meanwhile, the peasants, driven by the old land hunger, were already overrunning the rural districts, burning and looting. At the front the armies melted away; many high officers refused to serve the republic, and masses of peasant soldiers simply turned their backs and went home, unwilling to be absent while farmlands were being handed out. The Petrograd Soviet, opposing the Provisional Government, called for speedy termination of the war and, fearing reactionary officers, issued on March 14 its Order No. 1, entrusting command within the army to committees elected by both officers and men. Discipline collapsed.

The revolution was thus already well advanced when Lenin and the other Bolsheviks arrived in Petrograd in the middle of April.[21] They immediately took sides with the Petrograd Soviet against the Provisional Government, and with similar soviets that had sprung up in other parts of the country. In July an armed uprising

[21] See pp. 771–775.

of soldiers and sailors, which the Bolshevik central committee disapproved of as premature, was put down. The Bolsheviks were blamed, and Lenin had to flee to Finland. But as a bid for popular support the Provisional Government named the socialist Kerensky as its head in place of Prince Lvov in an uneasy coalition of moderate socialists and liberals. Kerensky's middle position was next threatened from the right. The newly appointed military commander General Kornilov dispatched a force of cavalry to restore order. Not only conservatives but liberals wished him success in the hope that he would suppress the soviets. Kornilov's movement was defeated, but with the aid of the Bolsheviks, who rallied with other socialists, and of revolutionary-minded soldiers in the city who offered armed resistance. Radicals denounced liberals as accomplices in Kornilov's attempt at counterrevolution, and both camps blamed Kerensky for having allowed the plot to be hatched under his government. Both liberals and moderate socialists abandoned Kerensky, and he had to form a government of uncertain political support. Meanwhile the food shortage worsened, with transport disarranged and the farm population in turmoil, so that workers in the city listened more willingly to the most extreme speakers.

The Bolsheviks adapted their program to what the most aroused elements in a revolutionary people seemed to want. Lenin concentrated on four points: first, immediate peace with the Central Powers; second, redistribution of land to the peasants; third, transfer of factories, mines, and other industrial plants from the capitalists to committees of workers in each plant; and, fourth, recognition of the soviets as the supreme power instead of the Provisional Government. Lenin, though a rigid dogmatist on abstract questions, was a flexible and bold tactician; and his program in 1917 was dictated more by the immediate situation in Russia than by considerations of theoretical Marxism. What was needed was to win over soldiers, peasants, and workers by promising them "peace, land, and bread." With this program, and by infiltration and parliamentary stratagems, and by their accuracy as political prophets—predicting the Kornilov counterrevolution and "unmasking" the trend of middle-way liberals to support it—the Bolsheviks won a majority in the Petrograd Soviet and in soviets all over the country.

Lenin thereupon raised the cry, "All power to the Soviets!" to crush Kerensky and forestall the coming Constituent Assembly. Kerensky, to broaden the base on which he stood, and unable to wait for the Constituent Assembly, convoked a kind of preparliament representing all parties, labor unions, and zemstvos. Lenin and the Bolsheviks boycotted this preparliament. Instead they called an all-Russian congress of soviets.

Lenin now judged that the hour had come for the seizure of power. The Bolsheviks themselves were divided, many like Zinoviev and Kamenev opposing the move, but Lenin was backed by Trotsky, Stalin, and a majority of the party central committee. Troops garrisoned in Petrograd voted to support the soviets, which the Bolsheviks now controlled. On the night of November 6–7, 1917, the Bolsheviks took over telephone exchanges, railway stations, and electric lighting plants in the city. A warship turned its guns on the Winter Palace, where Kerensky's government sat. The latter could find almost no one to defend it. The hastily assembled Congress of Soviets pronounced the Provisional Government defunct and named in its place a "council of people's commissars," of which Lenin became the head. Trotsky was named "commissar for foreign affairs," Stalin "commissar for nationalities." Kerensky fled, eventually arriving in the United States, where he lived until 1970.

At the congress of soviets Lenin introduced two resolutions. One called upon the belligerent governments to negotiate a "just democratic peace," without annexations and without indemnities; the second forthwith, and without compensation, abolished "all landlord property." Determined to establish a proletarian dictatorship, the Bolsheviks knew the importance of the Russian peasants. The millions of acres belonging to the large estates which were now expropriated under the first act of the revolutionary government provided a base of support for the new regime without which it could hardly have survived.

Thus was accomplished the Bolshevik or November Revolution.[22] But the long awaited Constituent Assembly remained to be dealt with. It met in January 1918. Thirty-six million persons had voted for it. Of these, 9,000,000 had voted for Bolshevik deputies, showing that the Bolshevik program, launched less than a year before by a small band of émigrés, had a widespread mass appeal. But almost 21,000,000 had voted for Kerensky's party, the agrarian-populist, native Russian, peasant-oriented Social Revolutionaries. However, said Lenin, "to hand over power to the Constituent Assembly would again be compromising with the malignant bourgeoisie." The Assembly was broken up on the second day of its sessions; armed sailors dispatched by the people's commissars simply surrounded it. The dissolution of the Constituent Assembly was a frank repudiation of majority rule in favor of "class rule"—to be exercised for the proletariat by the Bolsheviks. The dictatorship of the proletariat was now established. Two months later, in March 1918, the Bolsheviks renamed themselves the Communist party.

The New Regime: The Civil War, 1918–1922

In these same months the Communists, or Bolsheviks, made the peace of Brest-Litovsk with Germany, surrendering to Germany control over the Baltic provinces, Poland, and the Ukraine. The conquests of two centuries were thus abandoned; not since the days of Peter the Great had the Russian frontier been so far from central Europe. To Lenin it made no difference. He was convinced that the events that he had just mastered in Russia were the prelude to a general upheaval; that the war, still raging in the west, would bring all Europe to the inevitable proletarian or Marxist revolution; that Imperial Germany was therefore doomed; and that Poles, Ukrainians, and others would soon emerge, like the Germans themselves, as free socialist peoples. In any case, it was largely by promising peace that Lenin had won enough backing to overthrow Kerensky, who on this deep popular demand had delayed

---

[22] Also known as the October Revolution, since according to the Julian calendar, used in Russia until 1918, the events described took place in October.

too long, waiting for England and France to release Russia from its treaty obligations as an ally. But real peace did not come, for the country sank immediately into civil war.

Not only old tsarist reactionaries, and not only liberals, bourgeois, zemstvo men, and Constitutional Democrats, but all types of anti-Leninist socialists as well, Mensheviks and Social Revolutionaries, scattered in all directions to organize resistance against the regime of soviets and people's commissars, and they obtained aid from the Western Allies. Both sides competed for the support of the peasants.

As for the new regime, the oldest of its institutions was the party, founded as a wing of the Social Democrats in 1903, the next oldest were the soviets, dating from 1905 and 1917, and then came the council of people's commissars set up on the day of the coup d'état. The first institution founded under the new order was a political police, an Extraordinary All-Russian Commission of Struggle Against Counterrevolution, Speculation, and Sabotage, commonly known from its Russian initials as the Cheka and in later years, without basic change of methods or purpose, under such successive names as the OGPU, the NKVD and the MVD. It was established on December 7, 1917. In January 1918 the Red Army was founded, with Leon Trotsky as war commissar and virtually its creator. In July a constitution was promulgated.

In social policy the Bolsheviks at first adopted no long-range plans, contenting themselves with a mixture of principle and expediency known as "war communism." They nationalized some of the largest industrial enterprises but left the bulk under the control of workers' committees. The pressing problem was to find food, which had ceased to move through any normal channels. The peasants, very much as in the French Revolution under similar conditions—worthless money, insecure property titles, unruly hired men, armed marauding, and a doubtful future—were producing less food than usual, consuming it themselves, or hoarding it on their own farms. The response of the government and city workers was also much as in 1793. The new government levied requisitions, required the peasants to make stated "deliveries," and invited labor unions to send armed detachments into the country to procure food by force. Since it was naturally the big farmers who had the surplus, these came into disrepute as starvers of the people. Class war broke out, rabid, ferocious, and elemental, between farmers who feared that their very subsistence as well as their property would be taken away, and city people, often supported by hungry agricultural laborers, who were driven to desperation by famine. Many peasants, especially the larger farmers, therefore rallied to anti-Bolshevik political leaders.

Centers of resistance developed on every side. In the Don valley a small force assembled under Kornilov and Denikin, with many army officers, gentry landowners, and expropriated business people taking part in it. The Social Revolutionaries gathered followers on the middle Volga. At Omsk a disaffected group proclaimed the independence of Siberia. As a military organization the most significant was a force of some 45,000 Czechs, who had deserted or been captured from the Austro-Hungarian armies and had then been organized as a Czech Legion to fight on the side of Russia and the Allies.   After the November Revolution and the peace of Brest-Litovsk, these Czechs decided to leave Russia by way of the Trans-Siberian railroad, return to Europe by sea, and resume fighting on the western front.   When Bolshevik officials undertook to disarm them they allied with the Social Revolutionaries on the Volga.

The Allied governments believed that Bolshevism was a temporary madness that with a little effort could be stopped.   They wished above all to bring Russia back into the war against Germany.   So long as the war in Europe lasted, they could not reach Russia by the Black or Baltic Sea.   A small Allied force took Murmansk and Archangel in the north.   But for Allied military intervention the best opening was in the Far East, through Vladivostok.   The Japanese, who had declined military aid to their Allies in any other theater, received this proposal with enthusiasm, seeing in the ruin of the Russian empire a rare opportunity to develop their sphere of influence in East Asia.   It was agreed that an interallied military force should land at Vladivostok, cross Siberia, join with the Czechs, break up Bolshevism, and fall upon the Germans in eastern Europe.   For this ambitious scheme Britain and France could supply no soldiers, engaged as they were on the western front; the force turned out to be American and Japanese, or rather almost purely Japanese, since Japan contributed 72,000 men and the United States only 8,000.   They landed at Vladivostok in August 1918.

The civil war lasted until 1920, or even later in some places.   It became a confused melee in which the Bolsheviks struggled against dissident Russians and against foreign intervention.   They fought in the Ukraine first against the Germans, and then against the French, who occupied Odessa as soon as the war ended in Europe. They reconquered the Ukraine, Armenia, Georgia, and Azerbaijan, which had declared their independence; put to flight a hundred thousand "Whites" under Wrangel in the south; and fought off Admiral Kolchak, who, with a White army in Siberia, proclaimed himself ruler of all Russia.   In 1920, the Bolsheviks carried on a war with the new republic of Poland, which was scarcely organized when it set out to recover the huge Ukrainian and White Russian territories that had been Polish before 1772.[23]   British, French, and American troops remained at Archangel until the end of 1919, the Japanese at Vladivostok until the end of 1922.

But the anti-Bolshevik forces could never unite.   The anti-Communist Russians represented every hue of the political spectrum from unregenerate tsarists to left-wing Social Revolutionaries.   Many of the rightist anti-Bolsheviks openly antagonized the peasants by proceeding to restore expropriated landed estates in areas they occupied; many engaged in vindictive reprisals in a kind of "white terror." The Allies themselves could not agree; the French sent troops to the Ukraine and gave aid to the Poles, but the British and Americans wanted to be rid of all military entanglements as soon as the armistice with Germany was signed.   Leon Trotsky, on the other hand, forged in the crucible of the civil wars the hard and solid metal of the Red Army, recruiting it, organizing it, restoring its discipline, equipping it as best he could, assigning political commissars to watch it, and assuring that trustworthy of-

[23] See map, p. 259.

ficers occupied its high command. The Bolsheviks could point to the foreign intervention and appeal to national patriotism; and they could win peasant support
by the distribution of land. By 1922 the Bolsheviks, or Communists, had established
themselves up to the frontiers of the former tsarist empire in every direction except
on the European side. There the band of Baltic states in the *cordon sanitaire* remained
independent; Rumania had acquired Bessarabia, the new Rumanian frontier reaching now almost to Odessa; and Poland, as a result of the war of 1920, retaining a
frontier farther east than the Allies themselves had intended. Russia had lost
thousands of square miles of territory and buffer areas acquired over the centuries by
the tsars. They were to remain lost until the Second World War. But peace was
won and the regime stood.

It was during these civil wars that the Red Terror broke out in Russia. Like the
famous Terror in France in 1793, it was in part a response to civil and foreign war.
Before the Bolshevik Terror, the old Jacobin Terror paled. They differed as the
cruelty and violence endemic in the old Russia differed from the more humane or law-
abiding habits of western Europe. Thousands were shot merely as hostages (a practice unknown to Europe for some centuries); and other thousands without even the
summary formalities of revolutionary tribunals. The Cheka was the most formidable political police that had yet appeared. The Bolshevik Terror was aimed at the
physical extermination of all who opposed the new regime. A bourgeois class background would go far to confirm the guilt of the person charged with conspiring against
the Soviet state. As a chief of the Cheka said: "The first questions you should put to
the accused person are, To what class does he belong, what is his origin, what was
his education, and what is his profession? These should determine the fate of the
accused. This is the essence of the Red Terror." But a working-class background
made little difference. In 1918 a young woman named Fanny Kaplan shot at Lenin
and wounded him. She deposed that she had favored the Constituent Assembly,
that her parents had emigrated to America in 1911, that she had six working-class
brothers and sisters; and she admitted that she had intended to kill Lenin. She was
of course executed, and a massacre followed in Petrograd. When the sailors at
Kronstadt, who were among the first adherents won by the Bolsheviks, rose in 1921,
objecting to domination of the soviets by the party (threatening a kind of leftist
renewal of the revolution, like the Hébertists who had opposed Robespierre), they
were branded as petty-bourgeois and shot down by the thousands. The Terror
decimated the revolutionists themselves quite as much as it did the bourgeoisie; it
was to continue to do so long after the Revolution was secured.

The Terror succeeded in its purpose. Together with the victories of the Red
Army, it established the new regime. Those "bourgeois" who survived took on
the protective coloration of "toilers." No bourgeois as such ever again presumed to
take part in the politics of Russia. Mensheviks and other socialists fleeing to Europe
told appalling stories of the human toll taken by Lenin. Horrified European socialists repudiated communism as an atrocious, Byzantine, Asiatic perversion of Marxism.
But, at whatever cost, Lenin and his followers were now able to start building the
socialist society as they understood it.

95

The Union of
Soviet Socialist
Republics

Government:
The Nationalities
and Federalism

W ith the end of the civil wars and foreign intervention, and with the termination of the war with Poland, it became possible in 1922 to establish the Union of Soviet Socialist Republics. Its first members were four in number: the Russian Soviet Federated Socialist Republic, the Ukrainian Soviet Socialist Republic, the White Russian Soviet Socialist Republic, and the Transcaucasian Soviet Socialist Republic.[24] In the new Union, which geographically replaced the old Russian empire, the name Russia was not officially used. The guiding conception was a blend of the national and the international: to recognize nationality by granting autonomy to national groups, while holding these groups together in a higher union and allowing new groups to enter regardless of historic frontiers. In 1922 the expectation of world revolution was still alive. The constitution, formally adopted in 1924, pronounced the founding of the U.S.S.R. to be "a decisive step by way of uniting the workers of all countries into one World Soviet Socialist Republic." It made the Union, in principle, fluid and expansible, declared that any member republic might secede (none ever has) and that newly formed soviet socialist republics might join. When, in connection with the Second World War, the U.S.S.R. took back territories detached from tsarist Russia after the First World War—Bessarabia from Rumania, Karelia from Finland, parts of White Russia and the Ukraine from Poland, and Estonia, Latvia, and Lithuania after two decades of independence—these territories were sovietized and added to the Union as republics on a footing of legal equality with the old ones.

[24] The original Russian and Transcaucasian federal republics were subsequently reorganized to create additional soviet republics, so that by the constitution of 1936 the S.S.R.'s were eleven in number, to which five more were added in 1940; the Karelo-Finnish S.S.R. lost this status, however, in 1956. There are today fifteen soviet republics in the U.S.S.R., with population figures in 1940 and as estimated for 1970, as follows:

	1940	1970 (est.)
Russian S.F.S.R.	109,000,000	130,000,000
Ukrainian S.S.R.	40,000,000	46,500,000
White Russian (Byelorussian) S.S.R.	10,000,000	9,000,000
Armenian S.S.R.	1,250,000	2,350,000
Georgian S.S.R.	3,500,000	4,800,000
Azerbaijan S.S.R.	3,200,000	5,000,000
Uzbek S.S.R.	6,300,000	11,500,000
Turkmen S.S.R.	1,200,000	2,070,000
Tadjik S.S.R.	1,500,000	2,790,000
Kazakh S.S.R.	6,100,000	12,800,000
Kirghiz S.S.R.	1,500,000	2,890,000
ADDED IN 1940:		
Karelo-Finnish S.S.R.	500,000	————
Moldavian S.S.R.	2,500,000	3,550,000
Lithuanian S.S.R.	2,900,000	3,120,000
Latvian S.S.R.	2,000,000	2,300,000
Estonian S.S.R.	1,100,000	1,330,000
TOTAL U.S.S.R.	195,000,000	240,000,000

The federal principle in the U.S.S.R. was designed to answer the problem of nationalism. The tsardom, in its last decades, had tried to deal with this problem by systematic Russification. The nationalities had resisted, and nationalist discontent had been one of the forces fatally weakening the empire. Nationalism, or the demand that national groups should have their own political sovereignty, had not only broken up the Austro-Hungarian empire but "Balkanized" central and eastern Europe. In 1922 the U.S.S.R., occupying a sixth of the world's land area, was adjoined on the west by a Europe which in one twenty-seventh of the world's land surface contained twenty-seven independent states.

A hundred languages were spoken in the Soviet Union, and fifty distinct nationalities were recognized within its borders. Many of these were extremely small, splinter groups or isolated communities left by the ebb and flow of mankind in inner Asia over thousands of years. Many were very primitive, without political consciousness. All recognized nationalities received a cultural autonomy, or the right to use their own language, have their own schools, wear their own dress, and follow their own folkways without interference. Indeed, the Soviet authorities favored the growth of cultural nationalism. Some fifty languages were reduced to writing for the first time, and the new regime encouraged the singing of national songs, performance of dances, and collection of folklore. Administratively the nationalities were put on various levels, with varying degrees of separate identity according to their size, degree of civilization, or importance. Some constituted only "national districts," others "autonomous regions"; still others "autonomous republics" within a federated soviet republic. The most important were the federated soviet republics themselves. The second constitution, adopted in 1936, created an upper legislative house, the Soviet (or Council) of Nationalities, to which each Union republic sent twenty-five delegates, each "autonomous republic" eleven, each "autonomous region" five, and each "national district" one. In practice, the Russian S.F.S.R., with over half the population and three-quarters of the territory of the Union, predominated over the others. When to the Russian were added the Ukrainian (or Little Russian) and White Russian republics, whose people were not very different from the Great Russians, the overwhelmingly Russian and Slavic character of the Union became marked.

The federal structure undoubtedly gave some dignity, self-respect, and sense of equal cooperation to many of the numerous minorities. Yet political rights were severely limited by the centralization of authority in the hands of the federal government and the Communist party, as well as by the overwhelming Slavic preponderance. There was no substance to the formal claim that each constituent republic was sovereign, had the right to secede, and had the right to conduct its own foreign affairs, on the basis of which the Soviets demanded sixteen (and received three) votes in the United Nations when it was formed in 1945. Moreover, there was evidence in the Second World War that separatism had not wholly died down, remaining especially alive in the Ukraine. Four autonomous republics and one autonomous region were officially dissolved for separatist as well as collaborationist activities. Grievances persisted on the part of many minorities on political and even

Areas Annexed Since 1939

0   100 200 300 400 500 Miles

ATLANTIC OCEAN

SPITZBERGEN (Norway)

NORTH SEA

NORWAY

SWEDEN

FINLAND

FRANZ JOSEF LAND

NORTH CAPE

BARENTS SEA

NOVAYA ZEMLYA

KARA SEA

Murmansk

Berlin

BALTIC SEA

KARELIA

LITHUANIAN S.S.R.

ESTONIAN S.S.R.

Viborg

Leningrad

Archangel

Kara

POLAND

LATVIAN S.S.R.

Dvina R.

Warsaw

Minsk

Salekhard

WHITE RUSSIAN S.S.R.

Moscow

RUMANIA

Kiev

Kirov

MOUNTAINS

MOLDAVIAN S.S.R.

UKRAINIAN S.S.R.

Gorki

Kazan

Perm

Samarovo

Sverdlovsk

Odessa

RUSSIAN

SOVIET FEDERAT

Kuibyshev

URAL

Tobolsk

Sevastopol

Rostov

Volgograd

Magnitogorsk

Omsk

To

Istanbul

BLACK SEA

Novosibirs

Ankara

Astrakhan

Volga R.

CASPIAN SEA

TURKEY

GEORGIAN S.S.R.

Batum

ARAL SEA

KAZAK S.S.R.

Semipalatinsk

MEDITERRANEAN SEA

ARMENIAN S.S.R.

AZERBAIJAN S.S.R.

L. Balkhash

SYRIA

Baku

TURKESTAN

UZBEK S.S.R.

Tashkent

Alma Ata

IRAQ

TURKMEN S.S.R.

Ashkhabad

KIRGIZ S.S.R.

SINKIA

Teheran

TADJIK S.S.R.

SAUDI ARABIA

RED SEA

PERSIAN GULF

IRAN

AFGHANISTAN

on cultural grounds. Yet, on balance, the Soviets had accomplished much to prevent the disintegration of their multinational state by granting the nationalities a measure of political and cultural self-expression while on fundamental matters consolidating central authority and control within the communist framework as a whole.

Government: Parallelism of State and Party

790

Government in the Union, and in each component republic, followed a pattern worked out during the Revolution and written into the constitution of 1924 and the later constitution promulgated in 1936. Its chief feature was a system of parallelism. On the one hand was the state; on the other, paralleling the state but technically not part of it, was the party. There was a close interlocking relationship between the two.

RCTIC OCEAN
ALASKA
BERING STRAIT
WRANGEL I.
Anadyr
BERING SEA
SEVERNAYA ZEMLYA
NOVO SIBIRSK I.
Kolyma R.
Khatanga
Verkhoyansk
Lena R.
KAMCHATKA
Petropavlovsk
PACIFIC OCEAN
B E R I A
Yakutsk
Okhotsk
SEA OF OKHOTSK
OCIALIST REPUBLIC
Nikolaevsk
Vitim
SAKHALIN
KURILE I. (from Japan 1945)
Yeneseisk
Kirensk
Sovetskaya Gavan
Tygda
L. Baikal
Amur R.
Birobijan
Khabarovsk
Chita
Irkutsk
MANCHURIA
Harbin
Ulan Bator
MONGOLIAN REPUBLIC
MOUNTAINS
Vladivostok
SEA OF JAPAN
Mukden
JAPAN
NORTH KOREA
SOUTH KOREA
Peking
Lü-Ta (Dairen Port Arthur)
YELLOW SEA
C H I N A

The Union of Soviet Socialist Republics. *The U.S.S.R. is over 5,000 miles long and covers one-sixth of the land area of the globe, including 42 percent of Europe and 43 percent of Asia, though the conventional distinction between Europe and Asia is not officially recognized in the Soviet Union. It is the only state which immediately adjoins so many important political regions —Europe in the west, the Near and Middle East in the south, China along a long frontier, Japan across a narrow sea, and the United States on the side toward Alaska and the Aleutian islands. The Union has fifteen member republics, of which the Russian is by far the largest, embracing more than three-fourths of the territory and over half the population. Most of it lies farther north than Lake Superior, but around Tashkent, in the latitude of New York and Chicago, cotton and citrus fruits are grown.*

On the side of the state, the distinctive institution was the council or soviet. Here elections took place, and authority proceeded from the bottom upward to the top. Under the constitution of 1924 only "toilers" had the right to vote. Surviving bourgeois, private traders, "persons using the labor of others to make a profit," as well as priests, were excluded from the suffrage. An indirect system of elections prevailed. In each village and town the voters chose a local soviet; the local soviet elected delegates to a provincial soviet, which in turn sent delegates to a soviet of the republic (Russian or other); the soviets of these republics sent delegates to a Union-wide Congress of Soviets, the supreme law-enacting body of the country. Soviets at all levels chose executive officials; the Congress of Soviets chose the Council of People's Commissars, or ministry.

In the constitution of 1936 a more direct democratic procedure was introduced—for the state side of the parallelism. Voters henceforth directly elected members of the higher soviets, a secret ballot was adopted, and no class was any longer denied the vote. A bicameral parliament was created, with an upper chamber, the Soviet of Nationalities mentioned above, and a lower chamber, a Soviet of the Union, in which there was one representative for every 300,000 persons in the whole country. The Supreme Soviet, with its two chambers, chose a smaller body, a Presidium, to function while the chambers were not in session. The chairman of the Presidium served as "president," or nominal head, of the U.S.S.R. The Presidium supervised the Council of People's Commissars or Council of Ministers, as it came to be called after 1946, which the Supreme Soviet continued to elect. The chairman of the Council of Ministers was in Western terms the premier or prime minister. On the state side, as set forth in the constitution, especially the constitution of 1936, the government embodied many seemingly democratic features.

Yet alongside the state, at all levels and in all localities, was the party. Only one party was allowed, the Communist, though nonparty members might be elected to the soviets or to other official positions. In the party, authority began at the top and proceeded downward. At its apex stood the Central Committee, whose membership varied from about seventy in the 1930s to more than double that in later years. The Central Committee worked through an executive secretariat headed by a general secretary and through an Orgburo and a Politburo, subcommittees handling, respectively, matters of party organization and party policy. The Central Committee itself, or an inside group within it, and especially the general secretary, determined the membership of the Committee and of its subcommittees. It likewise assigned, transferred, and gave orders to party members through the successive lower levels of its organization. Although party congresses were held every few years before the Second World War, they generally simply registered decisions already made by the Central Committee. Actually it was the Politburo of about a dozen men that dominated the Central Committee.[25] Power and authority flowed downward and outward, as in an army, or as in a highly centralized government agency or large private

[25] In 1952–1953 the Politburo was replaced by a Presidium of the Central Committee; in 1966 it was restored.

corporation in the West, except that the party was not subject to any outside control. Discipline was likewise enforced in ways not used in liberal countries, the fearsome machinery of the secret police being available for use in extreme cases against party members as well as those outside.

The number of party members, men and women, which could not have been more than 70,000 at the time of the Revolution, rose to about 2,000,000 by 1930, 3,000,000 by 1940, 8,000,000 by 1960, and over 12,000,000 by 1970. The Leninist ideal of a small, compact, and manageable party, made up of faithful and zealous workers who willingly carried out orders, the ideal on which the Bolsheviks had separated from the Mensheviks in 1903, continued to characterize the Communist party in the Soviet Union. Old Bolsheviks, those who had been members in the lean years before 1917, long continued to occupy the seats in the Politburo and other important party positions. The problem, once it was clear that the Revolution had come to stay, was to prevent an inrush of careerists, persons who simply wished to belong to the new governing elite, old Mensheviks, Social Revolutionaries, or even former bourgeois now flying Communist colors. A party of 2,000,000 members, though small in contrast to the population of the U.S.S.R., still represented an enormous growth for the party itself, in which for each old member (who had joined before 1917) there were thousands of new ones. To preserve party unity under the new conditions strict uniformity was enforced. Members made an intensive study of the principles of Marxism-Leninism, embraced dialectical materialism as a philosophy and even a kind of religion, learned how to take orders without question or compunction, and to give authoritative leadership, assistance, or explanations of policy to the mass of nonparty members among whom they worked. The bottom of the party structure consisted in small nuclei or cells. In each factory, in each mine, in each office, in each class at the universities and technical schools, in each labor union, in each at least of the larger villages, one, two, or a dozen of the local people (factory workers, miners, office workers, students, etc., as the case might be) belonged to the party and imparted party views and party momentum to the whole.

The function of the party, in Marxist terms, was to carry out the dictatorship of the proletariat. It was to lead the people as a whole to the realization of socialism and, in day-to-day affairs, to coordinate the ponderous mechanism of government and make it work. Party members were present at all levels. The same men sat, in the party, in the Politburo of the Central Committee, and, in the state, in the Council of People's Commissars. At the next lower level, in the soviets of the Union and of the component republics, party members were numerous. Lower down, party members became more rare. In a small rural soviet there might be no one belonging to the party at all; the village councilmen would receive instructions, exhortations, or "pep talks" from itinerant party members. In any event, throughout the whole structure, the party decided what the state should do.

The role of the party in the U.S.S.R. has been called, at its best, a "vocation of leadership." Those joined it who were willing to work hard, to devote themselves to party matters day and night, to absorb and communicate the party policy (or "line"), to go where they were sent, to attend meetings, speak up, and remain until all others had left for home, to perceive and explain the significance of small passing events for the future of Russia or the world revolution, to master intricate technical details of farming, manufacturing, or the care of machinery, so that others would look to them willingly for advice. The party was a specially trained elite whose members were in constant touch with each other. It was the thin stream of life blood which, circulating through all the diverse tissues of the U.S.S.R.—the multitudinous republics, soviets, bureaus, army, industrial and other enterprises owned under socialism by the state—kept the whole complex body unified, organic, functioning, and alive.

To the country as a whole the party undoubtedly represented the vocation of leadership. The corollary was that more than ninety-five out of a hundred persons were condemned to be followers, and while it is perhaps true (as apologists for the system have said) that under any system true leadership is exercised by a tiny fraction of people, the difference between Communist and non-Communist in the U.S.S.R. became a clear matter of social status. As the years passed, by the 1930s, many Communists in the U.S.S.R. were less of the type of revolutionary firebrand than of the successful and the efficient man or woman in any social system. They represented the satisfied, not the dissatisfied. Frequently they enjoyed material privileges, such as access to the best jobs, better housing, special food coupons, or priorities on trains. They worked faithfully for recognition and promotion in the party. They developed a bourgeois concern for the advantages of their own children. They became a new vested interest. Within the party, members had to be not so much leaders as followers. A homogeneous and monolithic organization was desired, presenting a solid front to the far more numerous but unorganized outsiders. Within the party, from time to time, a great deal of difference of opinion and open discussion was tolerated (indeed, since there was only one party all political questions were intraparty disputes), but in the end the entire membership had to conform. The party favored a certain initiative of action, and a certain fertility of mind in inventing ways to get things done, but it did not favor, and in fact repressed, originality, boldness, or freedom of thought or action.

The New Economic Policy, 1921–1927

By 1920 "war communism," as we have seen, had hopelessly antagonized the peasants, who, it was estimated, were cultivating only 62 percent as much land as in 1914.[26] This fact, together with a severe drought and the breakdown of transportation, produced a great famine. Four or five million people died. The ravages of eight years, of the World War, the Revolution, the civil wars, the Terror, had left the country in ruins, its productive facilities thrown back by decades as compared with the point reached in 1914. The rising of the Kronstadt sailors in 1921 revealed profound disillusionment in the revolutionary ranks themselves. Lenin concluded that socialization had advanced too fast. He openly advocated a compromise with capitalism, a strategic retreat. The New Economic Policy, or Nep,

[26] See p. 785.

adopted in 1921, lasted until 1927. Most of the decade of the 1920s saw a relaxation of tempo for most people in the U.S.S.R.

Under the Nep, while the state controlled the "commanding heights" of the economy, maintaining state ownership of the basic productive industries, it allowed a great deal of private trading for private profit. The basic problem was to restore trade between town and country. The peasant would produce nothing beyond the needs of his own subsistence unless he could exchange his surplus for city-made wares such as clothing or tools. The city people had to be fed from the country if they were to turn out factory products or even continue to live in the city. Under the Nep, peasants were allowed to sell their farm products freely. Middlemen were allowed to buy and sell farm products and manufactured articles at will, to whom they pleased, at market prices, and at a profit to themselves. The Nep therefore favored the big individualist farmer or *kulak*. Indeed, rural changes initiated before 1914 were still at work;[27] peasant families consolidated millions of acres as private property in 1922, 1923, and 1924. Correspondingly, other peasants became "proletarians," wage-earning hired hands. The Nep also favored the sprouting of a new-rich commercial class, neobourgeois who ate expensive dinners in the cafés of Moscow, and whose very existence seemed to explode the dream of a classless society. Under the Nep the worst damages of war and revolution were repaired. But there was no real progress, for in 1928 Russia was producing only about as much grain, raw cotton, cattle, coal, and oil as in 1913, and far less than it presumably would have produced (given the rate of growth before 1913) had there been no revolution.

Lenin died in 1924 prematurely at the age of fifty-four after a series of paralyzing strokes that left him incapacitated in the last two years of his life. His embalmed remains were put permanently on view in the Kremlin; Petrograd was renamed Leningrad; a leader cult was built up around his name and image; the party presented him as a deified equal of Marx himself; and it became necessary for all schools of communist thought to claim unflinching fidelity to the Leninist tradition. Actually, in his own lifetime, the Old Bolsheviks had never regarded Lenin as infallible. They had often differed with him and with each other. As he lay dying, and after his death, his old companions and contemporaries, men in their prime, carrying on the feuding habits of the émigré days, fought with each other for control of the party in Lenin's name. They disputed over Lenin's intentions. Had he secretly thought of the Nep as a permanent policy? If not, how would he have modified it, and, most especially, how soon? Quietly, behind the scenes, as secretary of the party, without much attention to broader problems, a hitherto relatively modest member named Joseph Stalin, of whom Lenin had never had an enthusiastic opinion, was drawing all the strings of party control into his own hands. More openly and vociferously Leon Trotsky, who

[27] See pp. 778–779.

as war commissar in the critical years had been only less conspicuous than Lenin himself, raised the basic issues of the whole nature and future of the movement.

Trotsky, in 1925 and 1926, inveighed against the lassitude that had descended upon socialism.[28] The Nep with its tolerance of bourgeois and *kulaks* excited his contempt. He developed his doctrine of "permanent revolution," an incessant drive for proletarian objectives on all fronts in all parts of the world. He stood forth as the exponent of world revolution, which many in the party were beginning to discard in favor of first building socialism in one country. He denounced the tendency to bureaucratic ossification in the party and urged a new movement of the masses to give it life. He called for more forceful development of industry and for the collectivization of agriculture, which had figured in Communist manifestos ever since 1848.[29] Above all, he demanded immediate adoption of an overall plan, a central control and operation of the whole economic life of the country.

Trotsky failed to carry the party with him. He was charged with leftist deviationism, machinations against the Central Committee, and inciting to public discussion of issues outside the party. Stalin wove his web. At a party Congress in 1927, 854,000 members dutifully voted for Stalin and the Central Committee and only 4,000 for Trotsky. Trotsky was first exiled to Siberia, then banished from the U.S.S.R.; he lived first in Turkey, then France, then Mexico, writing and propagandizing for the "permanent revolution," stigmatizing developments in the U.S.S.R. as "Stalinism," a monstrous betrayal of Marxism-Leninism, organizing an underground against Stalin as he had done in former days against the tsar. He was murdered in Mexico in 1940 under mysterious circumstances, presumably by a Soviet agent or sympathizer.

96

Stalin: The Five-Year Plans and the Purges

Economic Planning

Hardly had the party expelled Trotsky when it appropriated certain fragments of his program. In 1928 it launched the First Five-Year Plan, aimed at rapid industrialization and the collectivization of agriculture. "Planning," or the central planning of a country's whole economic life by government officials, was to become the distinctive feature of Soviet economics and the one which was to have the greatest influence in the rest of the world.

In retrospect, it seems strange that the Communists waited ten years before adopting a plan. The truth seems to be that the Bolsheviks had only confused ideas of what to do after their seizure of power. Marxism for the most part gave only

---

[28]For communists, though not for socialists, the terms "communism" and "socialism" are almost interchangeable, since Russian Communists regard their own system as true socialism and all other socialism as opportunistic, reactionary, or false. Communism is also defined, in the U.S.S.R., as a future state of society toward which socialism, i.e., Soviet socialism, is the intermediate stage.

[29]See p. 536.

general hints.   Marxism was primarily an analysis of existing or bourgeois society. It was also a theory of class war.   But to portray any details of a future society, or specify what should be done after the class war had been won by the proletariat, was according to Marx and Engels sheer utopian fantasy.   The bourgeoisie, to be sure, would be destroyed; there would be "social ownership of the means of production," and no "exploitation of man by man"; everyone would work, and there would be neither leisure class nor unemployment.   This was not much to go on in the operation of a modern industrial system.

One great constructive idea had been mapped out, most clearly by Engels. *Within* each private enterprise, Engels had observed, harmony and order reigned; it was only *between* private enterprises that capitalism was chaotic.   In the individual factory, he noted, the various departments did not compete with each other; the shipping department did not purchase from the production department at prices fluctuating according to daily changes in supply and demand; the output of all departments was planned and coordinated by management.   In a larger way, the great capitalist mergers and trusts, controlling many factories, prevented blind competition between them, assigned specific quotas to each, anticipated, coordinated, and stabilized the work of each plant and each person by an overall policy.   With the growth of large corporate enterprise, observed Engels, the area of economic life under free competition was constantly reduced, and the area brought under rational planning was constantly enlarged.   The obvious next step, according to Engels and other socialists, was to treat *all* the economic life of a country as a single factory with many departments, or a single enormous monopoly with many members, under one unified, vigorous and far-seeing management.

During the First World War the governments of belligerent countries had in fact adopted such centralized controls.[30]   They had done so not because they were socialistic, but because in time of war people were willing to give up their usual liberties and willing to do as they were told by the government, and because all else was subordinated to a single overwhelming and undisputed social purpose—victory. The "planned society" therefore made its first actual (though incomplete) appearance in the First World War.   It was partly from socialist doctrine as exemplified by Engels, partly from experience of the war, and in even larger measure from the irresistible pressure to meet the continuing chronic problems of the country by raising its productive level that Stalin and the party in Russia gradually developed the idea of a plan.   The war experience was especially valuable for the lessons it gave on technical questions of economic planning, such as what kind of bureaus to set up, what kind of forecasts to make, and what kind of statistics to collect.

In the U.S.S.R. it was decided to plan for five years into the future, beginning with 1928.   The aim of the plan was to strengthen and enrich the country, make it militarily and industrially self-sufficient, lay the groundwork for a true workers'

---

[30] See pp. 749–752.

society, and overcome the Russian reputation for backwardness. As Stalin said in a speech in 1929:

> We are advancing full steam ahead along the path of industrialization to Socialism, leaving behind the age-long Russian "backwardness." We are becoming a country of metal, a country of automobiles, a country of tractors. And when we have put the U.S.S.R. in a motor car and the *muzhik* in a tractor . . . we shall see which countries may then be "classified" as backward and which as advanced.

The First Five-Year Plan was declared fulfilled in 1932, and a Second Five-Year Plan was launched, lasting until 1937. The Third, inaugurated in 1938, was interrupted by the war with Germany in 1941. New plans were introduced after 1945.[31]

The First Five-Year Plan (like its successors) listed the economic goals to be achieved. It was administered by an agency called the Gosplan. Within the frame of general policy set by the party, the Gosplan determined how much of every article the country should produce, how much of the national effort should go into the formation of capital, and how much into producing articles for daily consumption, what wages all classes of workers should receive, and at what prices all goods should be exchanged. At the bottom level, in the individual factory, the local management drew up its "requirements," or estimates of what it would need, in raw material, machinery, trained workers, plant facilities and fuel, if it was to deliver the planned quantity of its product at a stated date. These estimates were passed up the planning ladder (or, thousands of such estimates up thousands of ladders) until they reached the Gosplan, which, balancing them against each other and against other needs as seen at the top, determined how much steel, coal, etc., should be produced, and in what qualities and grades; how many workers should be trained in technical schools and in what particular skills; how many machines should be manufactured and how many spare parts; how many new freight cars should be constructed and which lines of railway track needed repair; and how, where, when, and to whom the steel, coal, technicians, machines, and rolling stock should be made available. The plan, in short, undertook to control, by conscious management, the flow of resources and manpower which under free capitalism was regulated by shifts in demand and supply, through changes in prices, wage levels, profits, interest rates, or rent.

The system was exceedingly intricate. It was not easy to have the right number of ball bearings, for example, arrive at the right place at the right time, in exact correspondence to the amounts of other materials or to the number of workers waiting to use them. Sometimes there was overproduction, sometimes underproduction. The plan was often amended as it was applied in action. Countless reports, check-ups, and exchanges of information were necessary. A huge class of white-collar office workers came into existence to handle the paper work. The plan achieved some of its goals, exceeded a few, and failed in some.

[31] See pp. 944–945.

The primary objective of the First Five-Year Plan was to build up the heavy industry, or capital wealth, of the U.S.S.R. The aim was to industrialize without the use of foreign loans.[32] Russia in 1928 was still chiefly an agricultural country. The world offered hardly any case of a country shifting from agriculture to industry without borrowing capital from abroad. Great Britain, the original home of the Industrial Revolution, was the best example, although even there, in the eighteenth century, a great deal of capital invested in England was owned by the Dutch. An agricultural country could industrialize from its own resources only by drawing upon agriculture itself. An agricultural revolution had been prerequisite to an industrial revolution in England.[33] By enclosure of land, the squeezing out of small independent farmers, and the introduction of scientific cultivation, under the auspices of a growing class of wealthy landowners, England had both increased its production of food and released many of the rural population to find employment in industry. The First Five-Year Plan called for a similar agricultural revolution in Russia, without benefit to landlords and under the auspices of the state.

Stalin: The Five-Year Plans and the Purges

The plan, as originally conceived, called for the collectivization of only one-fifth of the farm population, but it was suddenly revised in the winter of 1929 to include the immediate collectivization of the greater part of the peasantry. The plan set up collective farms, averaging a few thousand acres apiece, which were considered to be the property not of the state but of the peasants collectively who resided on them. Individual peasants were to pool their privately owned fields and livestock in these collectives. Those peasants who possessed fields or stock in considerable amount, the prosperous peasants or *kulaks,* resisted surrendering them to the new collectives. The *kulaks* were therefore liquidated as a class. Zealous detachments of Communists from the cities often used more violence than the plan envisaged; poor peasants turned upon rich ones; hundreds of thousands of *kulaks* and their families were killed and many more transported to labor camps in remote parts of the Soviet Union. The trend that had gone on since Stolypin and indeed since the Emancipation, building up a class of property-owning, labor-hiring, and "bourgeois" peasants, was now abruptly reversed. Politically, the obstinate obstruction of individualistic farmers was removed, and the peasantry was converted into a class more nearly resembling the proletariat of Marxian doctrine, a class of people who as individuals owned no capital and employed no labor, and so were better able to feel the advantages of a proletarian state. The year 1929, not 1917, was the great revolutionary year for most people in Russia.

Collectivization was accomplished at the cost of village class war in which the most capable farmers perished, and at the cost also of a wholesale destruction of livestock. The big farmers slaughtered their horses, cattle, pigs, and poultry rather

The Collectivization of Agriculture

[32] The Bolsheviks had repudiated the entire debt of the tsarist empire. Their credit in capitalist countries was therefore not good, so that, in addition to fearing dependence upon foreign lenders, they were in any case unable to borrow large sums.

[33] See pp. 464–466.

than give them up. Even middling and small farmers did the same, caring nothing about animals that were no longer their own, or naively expecting that under collectivism the state would soon furnish a new supply. The ruinous loss of animals was the worst unforeseen calamity of the First Five-Year Plan. Agricultural disorder, together with two summers of bad weather, was followed in 1932 by temporary but deadly famine in southeast Russia that took the lives of an estimated 2,000,000 to 3,000,000 persons; the government meanwhile refused to cut back on export quotas because they were needed to pay for industrial imports under the Five-Year Plan. Agriculture long remained the weakest sector of the Soviet economy despite all efforts to increase production.

By introducing thousand-acre units in place of very small ones, collectivization made it possible to apply capital to the soil. Formerly the average peasant had been far too poor to buy a tractor and his fields too tiny and dispersed for him to use one, so that only a few rare *kulaks* had employed any machinery. In the course of the First Five-Year Plan hundreds of Machine Tractor Stations were organized throughout the country. Each, in its region, maintained a force of tractors, harvesting combines, expert agronomists, etc., which were dispatched from one collective farm to another by local arrangement. The application of capital increased the output per peasant. It was also much easier administratively for higher authorities to get control over the agricultural surplus (products not consumed by the village itself) from a single collective farm than from numerous small and unorganized peasants. Each collective was assigned a quota on which it contracted in advance to make delivery. Members of the collective could sell in a free market any products they raised beyond this quota; but meanwhile the government knew the quantity of agricultural produce it could count on, either to feed the cities and other regions that did not produce their own food, or for export in the world market to pay for imports of machinery from the West. By 1939 all but a negligible fraction of the peasantry were collectivized. Although collectivization failed to increase agricultural output, it accomplished the goal of insuring state control over agricultural production. Simultaneously, it made possible the success of industrialization by augmenting the supply of industrial workers. Since the villages needed less labor, 20,000,000 people moved from country to city between the years 1926 and 1939 and were available for jobs in the new industries.

It was the peasants who bore the burden of collectivization. Not only had they been subjected to violence and expropriation, but the new collectives threw the peasant back into something like the *mir,* condemning him to the rounds of communal living, robbing him of the chance to make any decisions of his own. By obliging peasants to make "deliveries" below market prices, it even revived some features of the type of serfdom and forced labor that had prevailed a century before over most of eastern Europe. On the other hand, although the collectives varied widely in their degree of prosperity, it is probable that by 1939 a great many of the rural people were better housed and better fed than they had been before the Revolution. *Kulaks* who might have remembered better conditions had not survived.

While the agricultural base was being revolutionized, industrialization went rapidly forward. At first there was considerable dependence on the capitalist countries. Engineers and other technicians from western Europe and the United States took service in the Soviet Union. Much machinery was at first imported. But the world-wide depression that set in about 1931, bringing a catastrophic fall of agricultural prices, meant that foreign-made machines became more costly in terms of the cereals that were the chief Soviet export. The international situation also deteriorated. Both Japan and Germany in the 1930s showed an increasing hostility to the U.S.S.R. From the beginning the Five-Year plans had as one of their objectives the industrial and military self-sufficiency of the country. The Second Five-Year Plan, launched in 1933, though in some ways less ambitious than the first, showed an even greater determination to cut down imports and achieve national self-sufficiency, especially in the heavy industry that was basic to war production.

No ten years in the history of any Western country ever showed such a rate of industrial growth as the decade of the first two plans in the Soviet Union. In Great Britain industrialization had been gradual; in Germany and the United States it had been more rapid, and in each country there had been decades in which output of coal or iron doubled; but in the U.S.S.R., from 1928 to 1938, production of iron and steel expanded four times and that of coal three and a half times. In 1938 the U.S.S.R. was the world's largest producer of farm tractors and railway locomotives. Four-fifths of all its industrial output came from plants built in the preceding ten years. Two plants alone, at the new cities of Magnitogorsk in the Urals and Stalinsk 1,000 miles farther east, produced as much iron and steel as the whole Russian empire in 1914. In 1939 the U.S.S.R. was surpassed in gross industrial output only by the United States and Germany.

The plans called for a marked development of industry east of the Urals, and so brought a modernization of life for the first time to inner Asia, in a way comparable only to the movement of machine industry into the once primitive Great Lakes region of the American Middle West. Pittsburghs, Clevelands, and Detroits rose in the old Turkestan and Siberia. Copper mines were opened in the Urals and around Lake Balkhash, lead mines in the Far East and in the Altai Mountains. New grain-producing regions were developed in Siberia and in the Kazakh S.S.R., whence grain was shipped westward to Russia proper, or southward to the Uzbek S.S.R., which was devoted mainly to cotton. Tashkent, the Uzbek capital, formerly a remote town of bazaars and caravans, grew to be a city of over half a million, a center of cotton culture, copper mining, and electrical industries, connected with the north by the newly built Turksib railway. The Kuznetsk basin, 2,000 miles inland from every ocean, was found to possess coal deposits of high grade. Kuznetsk coal and the iron ores of the Urals became complementary, though separated by a thousand miles, somewhat like Pennsylvania coal and Minnesota iron in the United States. The opening of all these new areas, requiring the movement of food to Uzbekistan in exchange for cotton, or of Ural iron to the new Kuznetsk cities, demanded a revolution in transportation. The railroads in 1938 carried five times as much freight as in 1913.

These astounding developments were enough to change the relative economic strength of the world's peoples with respect to one another. It was significant that inner Asia was for the first time turning industrial. It was significant, too, that although the U.S.S.R. had less foreign trade than had the Russian empire, it had more trade than the old Russia with its Asian neighbors, with which it formed new and close connections. The Russia that went to war with Germany in 1941 proved to be a different antagonist from the Russia of 1914. Industrialization in the Urals and in Asia enabled the U.S.S.R. (with a good deal of Allied assistance) to survive the German occupation and destruction of the older industrial areas in the Don valley. The new "socialist fatherland" proved able to absorb the shock and strike back. A great deal of the increased industrial output had gone to equip and modernize the Red Army.

At the same time, the degree of industrialization of the U.S.S.R. should not be exaggerated. It was phenomenal because it started from so little. Qualitatively, by Western criteria, standards of production were low. Many of the hastily constructed, new plants were shoddy and suffered from rapid depreciation. In efficiency, as shown by output per worker employed, the U.S.S.R. continued to lag behind the West. In intensity of modernization, as shown by output of certain items in proportion to the whole population, it also lagged. Per capita of its huge population, in 1937, the U.S.S.R. produced less coal, electricity, cottons, woolens, leather shoes, or soap than did the United States, Britain, Germany, France, or even Japan, and less iron and steel than any of them except Japan. Production of paper is revealing because paper is used in so many "civilized" activities—in books, newspapers, magazines, correspondence, placards, maps, pictures, charts, business and government records, and household articles and amenities. Where the United States about 1937 produced 103 pounds of paper per person, Germany and Great Britain each 92, France 51, and Japan 17, the U.S.S.R. produced only 11.

Social Costs and
Social Effects
of the Plans

Industrialization in Russia, as formerly in other countries, was put through at great sacrifice on the part of the people. It was not merely that *kulaks* lost their lives, or that others, whose numbers have never been known except to Soviet authorities, were found to be enemies of the system and sent off to correctional labor camps. All were required to accept a program of austerity and self-denial, going without the better food, housing, and other consumers' goods that might have been produced, in order that the capital wealth and heavy industry of the country might be built up. As much as a third of the national income was reinvested in industry every year—twice as much as in the England of 1914, though probably not more than in the England of 1840. The plan required hard work, and low wages. People looked to the future, to the time when, the basic industries having been built, better housing, better food, better clothing, and more leisure would follow. Morale was sustained by propaganda. One of the chief functions of party members was to explain why sacrifices were necessary. In the late 1930s life began to ease; food rationing was abolished in 1935, and a few more products of light industry, such as dishes and fountain pens, began to appear in Soviet retail stores. Living standards were at least up to those of 1927 with prospects brighter for raising them. But the need for war preparations, as the world again approached chaos, again drove back the vision of the Promised Land.

Socialism, as realized in the plans, did away with some of the evils of unrestrained free enterprise. There was no unemployment. There was no cycle of boom and depression. There was no misuse of women and children as in the early days of industrialism in the West. There was no absolute want or pauperization, except for political undesirables and except for temporary conditions of famine. There was a minimum below which no one was supposed to fall. On the other hand, there was no economic equality. Marxism, indeed, had never seen equality of income as a virtue. While there was no handful of very rich people, as in the West (where the income of the rich came from property), the differences in wages and salaries were as great as in Europe or the United States. Managers, engineers, and intellectual workers received the highest pay. People with large incomes, by buying government bonds or accumulating personal possessions, could build up little fortunes for themselves and their children. They could not, however, under socialism, own any industrial capital.

Competition persisted. In 1935 a miner named Stakhanov greatly increased his daily output of coal by devising improvements in his methods of work. He also greatly increased his wages, since Soviet workers were paid at piece rates. His example proved contagious; workers all over the country began to break records of all kinds. The government publicized their achievements, called them Stakhanovites and "labor heroes," and pronounced the movement to be "a new and higher stage of socialist competition." In labor circles in the United States such straining to increase output would be called a speed-up, and piecework wages had long been anathema to the organized labor of all countries. Nor was management free from competitive pressure. A factory manager who failed to show a profit upon which the plan counted, or who failed to meet his quota of output, might lose not only his job but his social status or even his life. Poor management was often construed as sabotage. Poor use of the men and resources allocated to a factory was considered a betrayal of Soviet workers and a waste of the property of the nation. The press, not otherwise free, freely denounced whole industries or individual executives for failures to meet the plan.

The sense of competition or emulation, the feeling that everybody was busily toiling and struggling to create a socialist fatherland, was perhaps the most distinctive achievement of the new system. Workers had a real belief that the new industrial wonders were their own. The sense of participation, of belonging, which democracy had given to the average man in the West in political matters, was widely felt in the U.S.S.R. in economic matters also. People rejoiced at every new advance as a personal triumph. It became a national pastime to watch the mounting statistics, the fulfilling of quotas or hitting of "targets." Newspaper readers read no comic strips; they read eagerly of the latest doings (or misdoings) on the economic front. Never had there been such unalloyed delight in material and mechanical progress, not even in America in the Gilded Age. No class difference was felt between labor and management. There was apparently little envy, since differences of income, being socialistic, were regarded as necessary and fair. In creating this solidarity, this widely shared willingness to contribute, this trust in one's economic superiors and pride in collective accomplishment, the U.S.S.R. offered one of its most serious challenges to the private enterprise and private capitalism of the West.

How real this feeling was, how much of it was spontaneous, and how much was inculcated by a watchful and dictatorial government, are questions on which there has been much difference of opinion. There is no doubt that solidarity was purchased at the price of totalitarianism.[34] The government supervised everything. There was no room for skepticism, eccentricity of thought, or any basic criticism that weakened the will to achieve. As in tsarist times, no one could leave the country without special permission, which was given far more rarely than before 1914. There was only one party. There were no free labor unions, no free press, no freedom of association, and at best only an irritable tolerance for religion. Art, literature, and even science became vehicles of political propaganda. Dialectical materialism was the official philosophy. Conformity was the ideal, and the very passion for solidarity made for fear and suspicion of all who might go astray. As for the number of people sacrificed to the Juggernaut, liquidated bourgeois, liquidated *kulaks*, purged party members, disaffected persons sentenced to long terms in labor camps, not even an approximate estimate can be made, but it certainly reached many millions over the years.

The Purge Trials of the 1930s

In 1936 socialism was judged to have proved so successful that a new constitution for the U.S.S.R. was proclaimed. It enumerated, as rights of Soviet citizens, not merely the usual civil liberties of Western democracy but the rights to steady employment, rest, leisure, economic security, and a comfortable old age. All forms of racism were condemned. It reorganized the soviet republics and granted equal and direct universal suffrage, as explained above.[35] The new constitution of 1936 was favorably commented upon in the West, where it was hoped that the Russian Revolution, like former revolutions, had at last turned into more peaceable and quiet channels. It was nonetheless apparent that the Communist party remained the sole governing group in the country, that Stalin was tightening his dictatorship, and that the party was racked by internal troubles.

It was natural that the complex and multifarious operations of the Five-Year plans should produce divergences of opinion among the men who carried them out. The party elders, however, were engaged not merely in discussions of policy but in the older game of the seizure of power. On the right, led by Bukharin, was a group that believed in more gradual methods of collectivizing the peasants. More important was the element described as leftist. Its mastermind and rallying point was the exiled Trotsky. Probably there was some kind of secret Trotskyist machine within the U.S.S.R. and within the party, even if there is no evidence for the charge

[34] See also totalitarianism, Fasicst, Nazi, and Soviet, pp. 872–876.
[35] See p. 792.

that some Trotskyists had intrigued with Germans and other foreigners to overthrow and replace Stalin. As early as 1933 the party underwent a drastic purge, in which a third of its members were expelled. Even faithful associates of Stalin were appalled at his growing ruthlessness. Serge Kirov, an old friend and revolutionary companion of Stalin since 1909, recently elected a key member of the party secretariat, showed signs of leading the disaffected; in 1934 he was assassinated in his office, very probably by a police agent of Stalin's. Stalin used the assassination to strike out at his opponents, imagined or real, by a revival of terror, immediately executing over a hundred persons and launching the extraordinary "purges" of the 1930s.

A series of sensational trials took place. In 1936 sixteen Old Bolsheviks were brought to trial. Some, like Zinoviev and Kamenev, had been expelled from the party in 1927 for supporting Trotsky and subsequently, after the proper recantations, had been readmitted. Now they were charged with the murder of Kirov, with plotting the murder of Stalin, and with having organized, in 1932, under Trotsky's inspiration, a secret group to disorganize and terrorize the Central Committee. To the amazement of the world, all the accused made full confession to the charges in open court. All blamed themselves as unworthy and erring reprobates. All were put to death. In 1937, after similar trials, seventeen other Old Bolsheviks met the same fate or received long prison sentences; and in 1938 Bukharin and the rightists, charged with wanting to restore bourgeois capitalism and conspiring with Trotsky to revolutionize the U.S.S.R., were executed. The same confessions and self-accusations followed in almost every case, with no other verifiable evidence adduced. How these confessions were obtained in open court, from men apparently in full possession of their faculties and bearing no sign of physical harm, long remained one of the great mysteries of modern statecraft. Later revelations of psychological torture and physical mistreatment that broke their will and destroyed their reasoning powers gave some insight into the techniques used. In addition to these public trials there were thousands of arrests, private inquisitions, and executions. In 1937, in a secret court-martial, Marshal Tukhachevski and seven other ranking generals were accused of Trotskyism and of conspiring with the Germans and Japanese and were shot. The purges included not only men who had held the highest rank in party, government, and military circles but reached down into the lesser echelons of all these groups as well. Before the purges were over late in 1938, an unknown number of persons, but probably in the millions, were either executed or sent off into prison labor camps. Years later the innocence was established of many of the victims of Stalin's almost paranoid suspicion, and their reputations were posthumously restored.

By these famous "purge trials" Stalin's dictatorship and party discipline were reinforced. It is likely that a real danger of renewed revolution was averted. Had the tsarist government dealt as summarily with Bolsheviks as Bolsheviks dealt with one another there could have been no November Revolution. Above all, Stalin rid himself by the trials of all possible rivals for his own position. He disposed of the embarrassment of having men about him who could remember the old days, who could quote Lenin as a former friend, or belittle the reality of 1937 by recalling the dreams of 1917. After 1938 there were virtually no Old Bolsheviks left. The aging but still explosive professional revolutionaries were now dead. A younger group, products of the new order, successful men of affairs, practical, constructive, impatient of "agitators," and acquiescing in Stalin's dictatorship, were operating what was now an established system.

97

The International
Impact of
Communism,
1919–1939

*Socialism and the
First World War*

Marxism had always been international in its outlook. To Marx, and the early Marxists, existing states (like other institutions) owed their character to the class struggle. They were committees of the bourgeoisie to govern the proletariat. National states were regarded as frameworks, destined to be dismantled and pass away in the course of inevitable historic processes. After Marx's death, as Marxist parties grew in numbers, and as states of western Europe became more democratic, most people who called themselves Marxists actually accepted the national state, seeing in it a means by which the workingman's lot could be gradually improved. This view was part of the movement of "revisionism," or what more rigorous Marxists called "opportunism."[36] In the First World War national loyalty proved its strength. The socialist parties in the Reichstag, the French Chamber, and other parliamentary bodies voted for war credits without hesitation. Socialist workingmen reported for mobilization like everyone else. In Germany socialists said that the reactionary Russian tsardom must be resisted; in France, that the Germans menaced all Frenchmen alike. In general, all political parties, including the socialists, declared a moratorium on party politics during the war.

Small minorities of socialists in every country, however, refused to accept the war. Marxian socialism had long taught that workingmen of all nations were bound by the supreme loyalty of class, that their real enemies were the capitalists of their own countries, that international wars were capitalist and "imperialist" quarrels, and that class struggle was the only kind of warfare that the proletarian should accept. These socialists denounced the action of the socialist majorities as a sellout to capitalism and imperialism. They met in international conferences with each other and with socialists from the neutral countries. Active among them were Lenin and other Russian Social Democrats then in Switzerland. "The only task for socialists," wrote Lenin in 1914, "is to convert the war of peoples into a civil war." The minority or antiwar socialists met at the small Swiss town of Zimmerwald in 1915, where they drew up a "Zimmerwald program," calling for immediate peace without annexations or indemnities. This had no effect on most socialists in the belligerent countries. The Zimmerwald group itself soon began to split. Most Zimmerwalders regarded peace, or the repudiation of the war, as their aim. But a "Zimmerwald Left" began to develop, inspired mainly by Lenin and the Russian émigrés. This faction made its aim not peace but revolution. It hoped that the war would go on until it caused social revolution in the belligerent countries.

[36] See pp. 542, 643–645.

Then in April 1917, with the German imperial government wishing them *bon voyage,* Lenin and the other Bolsheviks went back to Russia and accomplished the November Revolution. Lenin, until his death in 1924, believed that the Russian Revolution was only a local phase of a world revolution—of *the* revolution of strict Marxian doctrine. Russia, for him, was the theater of currently most active operations in the international class war. Because he expected proletarian upheaval in Germany, Poland, the Danube valley, and the Baltic regions, he accepted without compunction the treaty of Brest-Litovsk. He took no pride in Russia; he was no patriot or "social-chauvinist," to use his own term. In the founding of the U.S.S.R. in 1922 he saw a nucleus around which other and greater soviet republics of any nationality might coalesce. "Soviet republics in countries with a higher degree of civilization," he wrote, "whose proletariat has greater social weight and influence, have every prospect of outstripping Russia as soon as they start upon the road of proletarian dictatorship."

The First World War was in fact followed by revolutions in Germany and eastern Europe. With the German and Austro-Hungarian empires wrecked, socialists and liberals of all descriptions strove to establish new regimes. Among socialists the old differences persisted, between Social Democrats favoring gradual, nonviolent, and parliamentary methods, and a more extreme (and smaller) group which saw in postwar disintegration a chance to realize the international proletarian revolution. The first group looked upon the Bolshevik Revolution with horror. The second looked upon it with admiration. The first group included not only trade union officials and practical socialist politicians, but such prewar giants of Marxian exegesis as Karl Kautsky and Eduard Bernstein. Even Kautsky, who had upheld pure Marxism against the revisionism of Bernstein, could not stomach the methods of Lenin. The mass of European socialists, with their fiercest leaders removed, were to remain characterized by relative moderation. Marxist in principle, they were in fact more than ever wedded to gradual, peaceable, and parliamentary methods.

In the second group, the sifted residue of uncompromising Leninist neo-Marxists, who accepted the Bolshevik Revolution, were Karl Liebknecht and Rosa Luxemburg. Organizing the Spartacist[37] movement in Germany, they attempted, in January 1919, to overthrow the majority-socialist government in Germany, as Lenin had overthrown the Provisional Government in Russia in November 1917. In the second group also was Béla Kun, who had turned Bolshevik during a sojourn in Russia, and who set up and maintained a soviet regime in Hungary for several months in 1919.

Lenin and the Bolsheviks, though absorbed in their own revolution, gave all possible aid to the fringe of left socialists of Europe. They sent large sums of money to Germany, to Sweden, to Italy. When the Bolshevik Radek was arrested in Berlin he was said to have a plan for proletarian revolution in all central Europe in his possession. The party considered sending Russian troops to Hungary to support

[37] See p. 822 and note.

Bela Kun.   But the chief instrument of world revolution, created in March 1919, was the Third or Communist International.

*The Founding of the
Third International*

The Second International, which since its foundation in 1889 had met every two or three years until 1914, held its first postwar meeting at Berne in 1919.[38] It represented socialist parties and labor organizations of all countries.   The Berne meeting was stormy, for a small minority vehemently demanded "revolution as in Russia, socialization of property as in Russia, application of Marxism as in Russia." Overruled at Berne, they repaired to Moscow and there founded a new International in conjunction with the Russian Communist party, and with Lenin and the Russians dominating it completely.   It was Lenin's hope, by founding a new International of his own, to discredit moderate socialism and to claim for the Communists the true line of succession from the First International of Karl Marx.   The First International, he declared, had laid the foundations for proletarian struggle, the Second had broadened it, the Third "took over the work of the Second International, cut off its opportunistic, social-chauvinist, bourgeois and petty-bourgeois rubbish, and began to carry into effect the dictatorship of the proletariat."

The first congress of the Third International in 1919 was somewhat haphazard, but at the second, in 1920, the extreme left parties of thirty-seven countries were represented.   The Russian party was supposedly only one component.   Actually, it supplied most of the personnel and most of the funds; the Bolshevik Zinoviev was its first president, remaining in this office until his disgrace as a Trotskyist in 1927.   The Third or Communist International—the Comintern—was in part a spontaneous rallying of Marxists from all countries who accepted the Bolshevik Revolution as the true fruition of Marxism and so were willing to follow the Russian lead; but, even more, it was the creation and weapon of the Bolsheviks themselves, by which to discredit and isolate the moderate socialists and effectuate world revolution.   Of all enemies the Communists hated the socialists most, reserving for them even choicer epithets than they bestowed upon capitalists and imperialists, because Communists and socialists were competing for the same thing, the leadership of the world's working class.

Parties adhering to the Comintern were obliged to drop the old name "socialist" and call themselves Communist.   They were obliged to accept strong international centralization.   Where the Second International had been a loose federation, and its congresses hardly more than forums, the Third International put strong powers in the hands of its Executive Committee, whose orders the Communist parties of all countries had to obey.   Since there was a kind of interlocking directorate by which members of the Central Committee of the party in Russia sat also as members of the Executive Committee of the Third International, the top Communists in Russia had, in the Comintern, an "apparatus" by which they could produce desired effects in many countries—the use of party members to penetrate labor unions, foment strikes, propagandize ideas, or interfere in elections.

[38] See pp. 643–645.

The second congress of the International, in 1920, endorsed a program of Twenty-One Points, written by Lenin. These included the requirements that each national party must call itself Communist, repudiate "reformist" socialism, propagandize labor unions and get Communists into the important union offices, infiltrate the army, impose an iron discipline upon members, require submission of each party worker to his national committee and to the orders of the international Executive, use both legal channels and secret underground methods, and expel promptly any member not hewing to the party line. Making no pretense of respect for parliamentary democracy, the second congress ruled that "the only question can be that of utilizing bourgeois state institutions for their own destruction." As for the labor movement, Lenin wrote that "the struggle against the Gomperses, the Jouhaux, the Hendersons [39] . . . who represent an *absolutely similar* social and political type as our Mensheviks . . . must be waged without mercy to the end." The Comintern was not an assemblage of humanitarians engaged in welfare work; it was a weapon for revolution, organized by revolutionaries who knew what revolution was.

For several years the U.S.S.R., using the Comintern or more conventional diplomatic channels, promoted world revolution as best it could. Communists from many countries went to Russia for indoctrination. Native-born or Russian agents proceeded to the Dutch Indies, to China, to Europe, to America. Until 1927 the Chinese revolutionists welcomed assistance from Moscow; the Russian Borodin became an adviser in their affairs. In 1924, in England, publication of the "Zinoviev letter," in which, at least allegedly, the Comintern urged British workers to provoke revolution, led to a great electoral victory for the Conservative party. The Bolshevik menace, real and imagined, produced everywhere a strong reaction. It was basic to the rise of fascism described in the following chapters.

In 1927, with the suppression of Trotskyism and world revolutionism in Russia, and with the concentration under Stalin on a program of building socialism in one country, the Comintern entered upon a period of inaction. About 1935, as fascist dictators became more noisily bellicose, the U.S.S.R. turned to a policy of international collective security, and the Comintern instructed all Communist parties, each in its own country, to enter into coalitions with socialists and advanced liberals, in what were called "popular fronts," to combat fascism and reaction. During the Second World War (in 1943), as a gesture of good will to Great Britain and the United States, the U.S.S.R. abolished the Comintern entirely, but it reappeared for a few years from 1947 to 1956 under a new name, the Communist Information Bureau or Cominform.[40]

---

[39] Samuel Gompers (1850–1924), began as a cigar maker, president of the American Federation of Labor, 1886–1924; Léon Jouhaux (1879–1954), began as a factory worker, secretary-general of the French General Confederation of Labor, 1909–1947, resigned in 1947 to found a new labor organization in opposition to communism; Arthur Henderson (1863–1935), began as an ironmolder's apprentice, chairman of the Parliamentary Labour Party, 1908–1910, 1914–1917, Member of Parliament, 1903–1931, Secretary of State for Foreign Affairs, 1929–1931.

[40] For the U.S.S.R. and for international communism after 1945, see pp. 940–953.

It was not through the Comintern that the U.S.S.R. exerted its greatest influence on the world. It exerted its influence by the massive fact of its very existence. By 1939 it was clear that a new type of economic system had been created. However one judged the U.S.S.R., no one could dismiss its socialism as visionary or impracticable. An alternative to free enterprise and capitalism had been brought into being. Marxism was not merely a theory; there was an actual society, embracing a sixth of the globe, which called itself Marxist. In every country those who were most critical of capitalist institutions compared them unfavorably to those of the Soviet Union. Many believed, or hoped, that something like Soviet results might be obtained without the use of Soviet methods, which were dismissed as typically Russian, a deplorable heritage from the Byzantine Empire and the tsars. With the appearance of an extreme Communist left, socialism and socialist ideas seemed in contrast to be middling and respectable. Everywhere in the 1930s the idea of "planning" began to find favor. Everywhere workers obtained more security against the fluctuations of capitalism. The so-called backward peoples, especially in Asia, were particularly impressed by the achievement of the U.S.S.R., which had shown how a backward country could develop a scientific industrial civilization without falling under the influence of foreign capital or foreign guidance.

Those in the 1930s who hoped to profit from the Soviet experience were not generally communist, and had no intention of following the dictates of Moscow. Wholly accepting neither Russian Communism nor historic Western capitalism, they hoped to combine the best attributes of both. Even to say this much is to suggest the tremendous implications of the Russian Revolution. Before 1917 no one in Europe or Asia had thought that anything was to be learned from Russia. Twenty years later even critics of the U.S.S.R. feared that it might represent the wave of the future. Its sheer power was soon demonstrated in the Second World War. While undeniably violent and terroristic, and ruthless in its disregard for individual persons and individual liberties, the U.S.S.R., in its prestige, its ideas, its appeal to many of the earth's peoples, was a force on which all had to reckon.

XVIII: THE APPARENT

VICTORY OF DEMOCRACY

We have followed events in Russia down to about the year 1939 but have left the story of Europe and the rest of the world at the signing of the peace treaties of 1919. We must deal now with the period of just twenty years that elapsed between the formal close of the First World War in 1919 and the outbreak of the Second World War in 1939. In these twenty years the world made a dizzy passage from confidence to disillusionment and from hope to fear. It went through a few years of superficial prosperity, abruptly followed by unparalleled economic disaster. For a time, in the 1920s, democracy seemed to be almost everywhere advancing; then, in the 1930s, the new phenomenon of totalitarianism began to spread. Let us first examine the apparent triumphs of democracy in the 1920s, turn next to the devastating world-wide effects of the great depression that began in 1929, and then, in the following chapter, trace the painful decade of the 1930s.

Chapter Emblem: A medal struck in honor of the Peace of Versailles, 1919.

813

The first years following the war were troubled. Even the victors faced serious difficulties in reconversion from war to peace. Men demobilized from the huge armies found themselves unemployed and psychologically restless. Farms and factories geared to maximum production during the war faced a sudden disappearance of markets. They produced more than could now be sold, so that the war was followed by a sharp postwar depression, which, however, had run its course by 1922. Basically, the economic position even of the victors was seriously damaged, for the war had disjointed the world of 1914, in which industrial western Europe had lived by exchange with eastern Europe and with overseas countries.

The war, President Wilson had said, had been fought to make the world safe for democracy. Political democracy now made advances everywhere. The new states that emerged from the war all adopted written constitutions and universal manhood suffrage. Democracy made advances even in countries that had long been in large measure democratic. The last significant steps toward manhood suffrage were taken in Great Britain in 1918. The most conspicuous innovation was the enfranchisement of women. Women now voted in Britain, the United States, Germany, and in most of the smaller states of Europe. The United States Senate, by constitutional amendment of 1913, was elected directly by the voters instead of by state legislatures, as formerly. Proportional representation—a system of marking and counting ballots in such a way as to make the elected legislature exactly reflect the strength of all parties—was introduced in the new German republic, in some of the smaller states, and, in a way, in France. It was thought more democratic for all minorities, even small ones, to be able to differentiate themselves and be represented freely and accurately in a parliament. The referendum, initiative, and recall were widely discussed and in many countries adopted. The "referendum" permitted referral to the electorate of measures passed by a legislature. The "initiative" was a process by which voters might initiate legislation without waiting for the legislature, the "recall"

Autour d'Elle *by Marc Chagall (Russian, then French, 1887–   )*
Where some painters departed from the Western tradition by cultivating pure abstraction or geometrized patterns (see pp. 652–655, 984–989), others did so by evoking unconscious or dream-like mental phenomena. This picture was painted by Chagall in France in 1945 in memory of his wife. The houses in the center represent the Russian city of Smolensk, where they had been married thirty years before. The surrounding faces and figures are individually quite distinct, but they float disconnectedly like the vivid images in a dream, without location in space or time, or any rational relationship to each other. Past and present, memory and perception, fantastic and real objects flow together in a kind of free play of the unconscious mind. These qualities characterized surrealism, of which Chagall in his younger days had been a forerunner. Courtesy of the Musée d'Art Moderne, Paris (Service Photographique). Permission A.D.A.G.P. 1970 by French Reproduction Rights, Inc.

a process by which voters might depose unfit public servants without awaiting the expiration of an elective term.

In most European countries the successors of the old prewar socialists gained in strength. With the left of the old socialists generally seceding, calling themselves communists, and affiliated with each other and with Moscow in the Communist International, the European socialists or social democrats were preponderantly a party of peaceable or revisionist Marxism, entirely willing to carry on the class conflict by parliamentary and legislative methods. Labor unions, with new self-confidence gained from the role they had played in the war, grew in membership, prestige, and importance.

Social legislation which before the war would have seemed radical was now enacted in many places. An eight-hour legal working day became common, and government-sponsored insurance programs against sickness, accident, and old age were either adopted or extended; an act of 1930, in France, insured almost 10,000,000 workers. An air of progressive democracy pervaded Europe and the European world. The social service, or welfare, state, already under way in the late nineteenth century, was becoming more firmly established.

Only in Italy in the early postwar years, of the states that might have been expected to continue their prewar democratic gains, did democracy receive a sharp setback. Italy had been a parliamentary state since 1861 and had introduced a democratic suffrage in the elections of 1913. In 1919 the Italians held their second elections under universal manhood suffrage. But Italian democracy was abruptly ended. In 1922 an agitator named Benito Mussolini, leading a movement which he called Fascism, killed off the Italian parliament.[1] Lenin had already founded the first single-party state; Mussolini became the first of the personal dictators of postwar Europe outside Russia. Fascist Italy, in the 1920s, was the chief exception in what seemed to be a rising tide of democracy.

[1] See pp. 565–566, 862–867.

The Assembly Line *by Diego Rivera (Mexican, 1886–1957)*
Not all twentieth-century artists have been attracted to pure abstraction or exploration of the unconscious. Among others, social activists and revolutionaries have continued to engage in narrative painting and realistic representation. Diego Rivera was one of the great painters of the Mexican Revolution. Regarded as the greatest living muralist and known also for his Marxist opinions, he was commissioned in 1931 by The Detroit Institute of Arts to decorate the walls of a large new hall. The fragment reproduced here shows part of the assembly line in an automobile plant, with workers of various races working speedily and as a team, while "bourgeois" visitors in the background somewhat stupidly watch and marvel. It was the machine age that Rivera meant to portray, rendering it with a mixture of realism and artistic heightening, and a sense of automatism, movement and power. Courtesy of The Detroit Institute of Arts.

In central and east-central Europe—in Germany, in the territory of the former Austro-Hungarian empire, and in the western fringe of former tsarist Russia—entirely new states and new governments struggled to establish themselves. The new states included, besides republican Germany, the four successor states to the Habsburg empire—Austria, Hungary, Czechoslovakia, and Yugoslavia; and the five states that had broken away from the Russian empire—Poland, Finland, Estonia, Latvia, and Lithuania.[2] The other small states in eastern Europe, Rumania, Bulgaria, Greece, and Albania, had already been independent before 1914; their boundaries underwent some modification and their governments considerable reorganization after the war. The Turkish republic is considered elsewhere.[3]

The new states were to a large extent accidents of the war. Nowhere, except possibly in Poland, did they represent a deeply felt, long-maturing, or widespread revolutionary sentiment. Only an infinitesimal number of Germans in 1914 would have voted for a republic. Even among the nationalities of Austria-Hungary in 1914 few persons would have chosen the complete break-up of the Habsburg empire. The republicans, moderate socialists, agrarians, or nationalists who now found themselves in power had to improvise governments for which there had been little preparation. They had to contend with reactionaries, monarchists, and members of the old aristocracy. They had also to deal with the real revolutionaries, who, inspired by Lenin's success, hoped to bring about the dictatorship of the proletariat. A communist revolt broke out in Germany in 1919 but was quickly suppressed; soviet regimes were actually set up but soon crushed in Hungary and in the German state of Bavaria; and as late as 1923 there was a communist uprising in the German state of Saxony.

The new states all embodied the principle of national self-determination, which held that each nationality should enjoy political sovereignty—one nation, one government. But people in this region were and always had been locally intermixed.[4] Each of the new states therefore included minority nationalities; for, with the exception of an exchange of populations between Greece and Turkey, arranged in 1923, there was no thought of the actual physical removal of "alien" groups. Poland and Czechoslovakia were the most composite of the new states. Each of these two possessed, in particular, among its several minorities, a considerable population of disaffected Germans. The new states also disputed with each other over places of mixed nationality to which two or more laid claim. Poland and Lithuania clashed over the largely Jewish city of Vilna, Poland and Czechoslovakia over the Teschen district, Poland and Russia went to war because the Poles claimed the far-spreading boundaries of 1772;[5] Austria and Hungary quarreled over the border province of Burgenland, Hungary and Rumania over Transylvania, Yugoslavia and Italy over Fiume, Rumania and Czechoslovakia over Bukovina, which was mainly Ukrainian;

[2] See map, pp. 760–761.
[3] See pp. 830–831.
[4] See map, p. 478.
[5] See map, p. 259.

and the Greeks invaded what was left of Turkey. Each of these incidents was "settled," but in each case one party continued to nurse a grievance.

The Advance of Democracy after 1919

Nevertheless, despite economic and nationalist troubles, the new states and governments attempted at the outset to make themselves democratic. Except for the German republic they were all relatively small. All the newly created states were republics except Yugoslavia, which was under the older Serbian dynasty. Hungary started out in 1918 as a republic, but the attempt of Bela Kun to found a Hungarian Soviet Republic in 1919 brought back the counterrevolutionaries who restored the Habsburg monarchy in principle, though they were prevented by foreign pressure from restoring the king in person. Hungary emerged in 1920 as a monarchy with a perennially vacant throne, under a kind of dictatorship exercised by Admiral Horthy. All smaller states of Europe, including Hungary, possessed at least the external apparatus of democracy until the 1930s; that is, they had constitutions, parliaments, elections, and a diversity of political parties. If civil liberty was sometimes violated, the right to civil liberty was not denied; and if the elections were sometimes rigged, they were at least in principle supposed to be free.

Economic Problems of Eastern Europe: Land Reform

Eastern Europe for centuries had been an agrarian region of large landed estates, which supported on the one hand a wealthy landowning aristocracy of almost feudal outlook, and on the other an impoverished mass of agricultural workers with little or no property of their own. The landed aristocracy had been the chief support of the Austro-Hungarian empire and an important pillar of the old order in the tsarist empire and in eastern Prussia. The mass of the rural population, through all this region, had been free from serfdom, or released from subjection to manorial landlords, only since the middle of the preceding century.[6] The middle class of business and professional men was small except in Austria and Bohemia, the western portion of Czechoslovakia. In general, the whole region was conscious of lagging behind western Europe, not only in industry, factories, railroads, and great cities, but also in literacy, schooling, reading habits, health, death rates, length of life, and material standard of living.[7]

The new states set out to modernize themselves, generally on the model of the West. They introduced democratic and constitutional ideas. They put up protective tariffs, behind which they tried to develop factories and industries of their own. But the new national boundaries created difficulties. Where Europe in 1913 had had 6,000 miles of frontiers, after the war it had almost 10,000, and all the increase was in eastern Europe. Goods circulated much less easily. Protected industries in the old agricultural regions produced inefficiently and at high cost. Old and established industries, in Austria, Czechoslovakia, and western Poland, cut off by the new frontiers and new tariffs from their former markets, fell upon hard times. The

[6]See p. 533 and map, p. 217.
[7]See p. 608.

working class of Vienna lived in misery, because Vienna, a city of 2,000,000 persons, formerly the capital of an empire of 50,000,000, was now the capital of a republic of 6,000,000. In Czechoslovakia the German minority, the Sudetens, complained that in hard times the German businessmen and workers, because of government policies, always suffered more than their Czech counterparts. Economically, the carving up of eastern Europe into a dozen independent states was self-defeating.

The greatest of reforms undertaken by the new east-European states was the reform of landownership. Although it far from solved basic economic problems in the area, it did have substantial effect on the pattern of land distribution. The whole traditional agrarian base of society was overturned. The work of the Revolution of 1848, which, in the Habsburg lands, had liberated the peasants but left them landless, was now carried a step further. The example of the Russian Revolution gave a powerful stimulus, for in Russia in 1917 peasants had driven off landlords, and communists and communist sympathizers won a hearing among discontented and propertyless peasants from Finland to the Balkans. Not until 1929, it should be recalled, did the Soviet Union embark on the collectivization of agriculture; until then, communism appeared to favor the small individual farmer. But it may be said with equal truth that the model for agrarian reform lay in the West, especially in France, the historic land of the small peasant proprietor.

Land reform worked out differently in different countries. In the Baltic states the big properties belonged almost entirely to German families, the "Baltic barons," descendants or at least successors to the medieval Teutonic Knights.[8] In Estonia, Latvia, and Lithuania, the nationalist dislike for Germans thus made it easier to liquidate landlords. Small farms here became the rule. In Czechoslovakia over half the arable land was transferred from large to small owners; here again, the fact that many great landowners had been German, in some cases since the days of the Thirty Years' War,[9] made the operation in a sense more palatable, though it inflamed the German minority in Bohemia. In Rumania and Yugoslavia the break-up of large estates, though considerable, was less thorough. In Finland, Bulgaria, and Greece the issue hardly arose, since small landownership was already common.

Land reform had least success in Poland and Hungary. In both countries, indeed, reforms were announced. A Polish law of 1925 promised to redistribute some 5,000,000 acres to some hundreds of thousands of families, and the Hungarian republic of 1919 actually began to divide up the great estates. But in both Poland and Hungary the landed magnates were exceptionally strong and well rooted. They had been the leaders, literally for centuries, of the nationalist movement in their respective countries. In both countries, in the 1920s, nationalistic sentiment appealed to more people than did social reform. The Poles, consumed with a desire to restore the immense Poland that had existed before the partitions of the eighteenth century, became involved at first in an actual war with Soviet Russia, and thereafter supported a dictatorial and reactionary government which made no attempt to carry out the laws

[8] See p. 42.
 [9] See pp. 144, 232.

of 1925. The Hungarians were frightened by Béla Kun into a fear of all lower-class movements, and all Hungarians, rich and poor, felt a sense of national outrage at the treaty of Trianon, which had cut to pieces the former Apostolic Kingdom of St. Stephen. After ten years' talk, in 1930, a third of the cultivated land in Hungary still belonged to a few hundred families.

After the land reforms, political parties of peasants or small landholders became the chief democratic force within the various states on the western border of Russia. Often they inclined to socialism, especially since capitalism was to them a foreign thing. On the other hand, the great landowners, the former aristocrats of the prewar empires, whether already expropriated or merely threatened with expropriation, were confirmed in a reactionary outlook, frightened by the neighboring communism of Russia but equally opposed to democracy, disposed to favor what was soon to be known generically as fascism. The land reforms did not solve basic economic problems. The new small farms were very small, frequently no more than ten acres. The peasant owners lacked capital, agricultural skill, and knowledge of the market. Farm productivity did not rise. In place of old differences between landlord and tenant there developed new differences between the more comfortable peasant and the proletarian hired man—between the *kulak* and the toiler, in communist parlance. The continuance of relative poverty, the obstinacy of reactionary upper classes, the new stresses and strains among the peasants themselves, the economic distortions produced by numerous tariff walls, and the lack of any sustained tradition of self-government all helped to frustrate the democratic experiments launched in the 1920s.

The keystone of Europe was Germany. Germany, too, had its revolution in 1918. But it was a revolution without revolutionaries, a negative revolution caused more by the disappearance of the old than by any vehement arrival of the new. The emperor and the High Command of the army, in the last weeks of the war, had bowed themselves out of the picture, leaving it to others to face defeat and humiliation.[10] For a time, after November 1918, the men in charge of affairs were mainly Social Democrats. The Social Democrats were Marxists, but their Marxism was the tamed, toned down, and revisionist Marxism that had prevailed for twenty years before the advent of Lenin. They were trade union officials and party managers. They could look back, in 1918, on decades spent in developing labor organizations and building up the Social Democratic party, which in 1912 had become the largest single party in the Reichstag.[11] Now, in 1918, they were a cautious and prudent group, essentially conservative, more anxious to preserve what they had already achieved than to launch audacious new social experiments. Before 1917 the Social Democrats considered themselves well to the left. But the Bolshevik Revolution in Russia, and the emergence of a pro-Bolshevik or communist element in Germany, put the Social Democrats

99
The German Republic and the Spirit of Locarno

[10] See pp. 748–749.
[11] See pp. 635–637, 642–644.

in the middle. The middle is an awkward spot, especially in disturbed times; the Communists regarded the Social Democrats as reactionaries, despicable traitors to the working-class movement; whereas the true reactionaries, recruited from old monarchists, army officers, Junker landowners, and big business groups, saw in social democracy, or professed to see in it, a dangerous flirtation with Bolshevism.

The middle group in Germany, the Social Democrats reinforced by the Catholic Center party and others, were more afraid of the left than of the right. They were appalled, in 1918 and 1919, by the stories brought out of Russia, not merely by fugitive bourgeois or tsarist aristocrats, but by refugee Social Democrats, Mensheviks, and anti-Leninist Bolsheviks, men whom all socialists had long known and trusted in the Second International. In January 1919 the Spartacists,[12] led by Karl Liebknecht and Rosa Luxemburg, attempted to bring about a proletarian revolution in Germany, like that in Russia. Lenin and the Russian Bolsheviks lent their aid. For a time, there seemed to be a possibility that Germany might go communist, that the Spartacists might succeed in imposing a dictatorship of the proletariat. But the Social Democratic Provisional Government crushed the Spartacist uprising, turning for that purpose to demobilized army officers and volunteer vigilantes recruited from the disbanding army. The Spartacist leaders Liebknecht and Luxemburg were arrested and shot while in police custody. The events of "Spartacus Week" widened a chasm between Social Democrats and Communists which was not to be bridged even in Hitler's concentration camps.

Shortly after, elections were held for a National Constituent Assembly. No single party received a majority, but the Social Democrats were the leading party. A coalition of Social Democrats, Center party, and liberal democrats dominated the Assembly. After several months of deliberations at the city of Weimar, in July 1919, a constitution was adopted establishing a democratic republic. The Weimar republic (as the regime in Germany from 1919 to the advent of Hitler in 1933 is called) was soon threatened ominously from the right. In 1920 a group of disaffected army officers staged a *Putsch,* or armed revolt, put the republican government to flight, and attempted to place a puppet of their own, one Dr. Kapp, at the head of the state. The Berlin workers, by turning off public utilities, stopped the Kapp *Putsch* and saved the republic. But the Weimar government never took sufficiently firm measures to put down private armed bands led by reactionary or outspokenly antidemocratic agitators. One of these was soon to be Adolf Hitler, who as early as 1923 staged an abortive revolt in Munich.[13] Nor, being democratic and liberal, did it ever deny the rights of election to the Reichstag, and of free speech in the Reichstag and in public, either to communists or to antidemocratic reactionaries.

The Weimar republic was in principle highly democratic. The constitution embodied all the devices then favored by the most advanced democrats, not only universal suffrage including the vote for women, but proportional representation and

---

[12] So named from Spartacus, a Roman slave who led a slave revolt in south Italy in 72 B.C.
[13] See p. 868.

the initiative, referendum, and recall.[14]   But except for the legal eight-hour day and a few other such safeguards to the workers' welfare (and traditional demands of organized labor) the republic of which the Social Democrats were the main architects in its formative years was remote from anything socialistic.   No industries were nationalized.   No property changed hands.   No land laws or agrarian reforms were undertaken, as in the new states of eastern Europe; the East-Elbian Junkers remained untouched in their landed estates.   There was almost no confiscation even of the property of the former kaiser and other ruling dynasties of Bismarck's federal empire.   The very statues of emperors, kings, princes and grand dukes were left standing in the streets and squares.   Officials, civil servants, police agents, professors, schoolteachers of old imperial Germany remained at their respective duties.   The army, though limited by the Versailles treaty to 100,000 men, remained the old army in miniature, with all its essential organs intact, and lacking only in mass.   The soldiers were peasant youths enlisted for long terms and soon formed to German and Prussian military traditions.   In the officer corps the old professional and aristocratic influences remained strong.

Never had there been a revolution so mild, so reasonable, so tolerant.   There was no terror, no fanaticism, no stirring faith, no expropriation, no émigrés.   There had in truth been no revolution at all, in the sense in which France, England, the United States, Russia, and other countries, either recently or in the more distant past, had experienced revolutions.

The supreme question, for Europe and the world, was how Germany would adjust itself to the postwar conditions.   How would the Germans accept the new internal regime of democracy?   How would they accept the new German frontiers and other provisions of the Treaty of Versailles?   These two questions were unfortunately interconnected.   The Weimar republic and the Treaty of Versailles were both products of the defeat of Germany in the war.   There were many in Germany who favored democracy, notably the numerous Social Democrats, and many more possibly could have been won over to it, given time and favorable conditions.   But no one, not even the Social Democrats, accepted the Treaty of Versailles or the new German frontiers as either just or final.   If "democracy" in Germany meant the perpetual acceptance of the treaty without amendment, or if it meant economic distress or hardship which could either reasonably or unreasonably be explained as consequences of the treaty, then "democracy" would lose such appeal as it had for the Germans.

The German republicans, we have seen, protested against the Versailles treaty before signing, and signed only under pressure.[15]   The Allies continued the wartime naval blockade after the armistice; this confirmed, in German eyes, the argument that the Treaty of Versailles was a *Diktat*, a dictated peace, Carthaginian, ruthless, and vengeful.   The "war guilt" clause, while it perhaps on the one hand satisfied a peculiar Anglo-American sense of morality, on the other hand offended a peculiar

[14] See pp. 814–816.
[15] See p. 758.

German sense of honor. Neither the reparations demanded of them, nor the new frontiers, were accepted by the Germans as settled. Reparations they regarded as a perpetual mortgage on their future. They generally expected, some day, to revise their eastern frontier, get back at least the Polish corridor, and incorporate Austria. In Austria, now purely German, no longer joined with Slavs and Hungarians, there was through the 1920s a strong movement for union with Germany. But plans for union, even for a tariff union, were blocked by the Allies.

The French lived in terror of the day when Germany would recover. Their plans for their own security, and for the collective security of Europe against a German revival, had been disappointed. They had been unable to detach the Rhineland from Germany. The United States Senate had refused to ratify the treaty, signed at Paris by Wilson, by which the United States was to guarantee France against German invasion in the future.[16] Both Britain and the United States showed a tendency to isolation, to pull away from the Continent, to get back to "normalcy," to work mainly for a restored trade in which a strong Germany would be a large customer. The League of Nations, of which the United States was not a member, and in which every member nation had a veto, offered little assurance of safety to a people so placed as the French. The French began to form alliances, against a potentially resurgent Germany, with Poland, Czechoslovakia, and other east-European states. They insisted also on German payment of reparations. The amount of reparations, left unstated in the treaty, was fixed by a Reparations Commission in 1921 at 132,000,000,000 gold marks. This sum, the equivalent of $35,000,000,000, was soon pronounced by various Western economists to be more than Germany could possibly contrive to pay.

The Weimar government in these circumstances looked to Russia, which had been no party to the Versailles treaty and claimed no reparations. The Soviet government meanwhile, concluding from the failure of proletarian revolution in Germany and Hungary that the time was not ripe for the sovietizing of Europe, prepared to enter into normal diplomatic relations with established governments. Germany and Russia, despite ideological repugnance, thus signed the treaty of Rapallo in 1922. In the following years the Soviet Union obtained needed manufactures from Germany, and German factories and workingmen were kept busy by orders from Russia. The German army dispatched officers and technicians to give instruction to the Red Army. Obliged by the Treaty of Versailles to restrict its activities, the German army was in fact able, through its work in Russia, and through a number of subterfuges at home, to maintain a high standard of training, planning, technical knowledge, and familiarity with new weapons and equipment. The good understanding between Germany and Russia naturally caused apprehension in the West.

The French, baffled in the attempt to collect reparations, and assisted by the Belgians, in 1923 sent units of the French army to occupy the industrial sites of the Ruhr valley. The Germans responded by general strikes and passive resistance. To sustain the

[16] See pp. 756, 762.

workmen in this patriotic idleness the Weimar government paid them benefits, grinding paper money off the printing presses for this purpose. Germany, like other belligerent countries, had suffered from inflation, i.e., rising prices, during and after the war; neither the imperial government nor the Weimar statesmen had been willing to impose heavier taxes to offset inflation. But what now swept Germany was different from ordinary inflation. It was of catastrophic and utterly ruinous proportions. Paper money became literally worthless. By the end of 1923 it took over four trillion paper marks to equal a dollar.

This inflation brought far more of a social revolution than the fall of the Hohenzollern empire had ever done. Debtors paid off debts in worthless money. Creditors received baskets full of meaningless paper. Salaries even when raised lagged behind the soaring cost of living. Annuities, pensions, proceeds of insurance policies, savings accounts in the banks, income from bonds and mortgages—every form of revenue which had been arranged for at some time in the past, and which often represented the economy, foresight and personal planning of many years—now turned to nothing. The middle class was pauperized and demoralized. Middle-class people were now materially in much the position of day-workers and proletarians. Their whole view of life, however, made it impossible for them to identify themselves with the laboring class or to accept its Marxist or socialist ideologies. They had lost faith in society itself, in the future, in the old burgher codes of self-reliance and rational planning of their own lives in an understandable world. A kind of moral void was created, with nothing for them to believe in, hope for, or respect.

The inflation, however, by wiping out all outstanding indebtedness within the country, made it possible, once the losses were written off and accepted, to start up economic production afresh. The United States was persuaded to play a reluctant role. The United States, in these years, demanded payment of the huge war debts owed to it by the Allies.[17] The Allies—Britain, France, Belgium—insisted that they could not pay debts to the United States unless they collected reparations from Germany. In 1924 the Dawes Plan, named for the American Charles G. Dawes, was instituted in Germany to assure the flow of reparations. By the Dawes Plan the French evacuated the Ruhr, the reparations payments were cut down, and arrangements made for the German republic to borrow abroad. A good deal of American private capital was invested in Germany in the following years, both in German government bonds and in German industrial enterprises. Gradually, so at least it seemed, Germany was put on its feet. For four or five years the Weimar republic even enjoyed a bustling prosperity, and there was a good deal of new construction in roads, housing, factories, and ocean liners. But the prosperity rested in good measure on foreign loans, and the great depression that began in 1929 reopened all the old questions.

These years of economic prosperity were years also of relative international calm. No issue, in truth, was dealt with fundamentally. The universal German hatred

The Spirit of Locarno

[17] See pp. 751, 753, 757.

for the Treaty of Versailles elicited no concessions from the Allies. Conceivably, had the Allies been willing at this time to amend the treaty by international agreement, they might have taken wind from the sails of nationalistic rabble-rousers in Germany and so spared themselves much later grief. It may be, however, that no possible concession would have sufficed. The great problem was to prevent a German overthrow of the treaty structure by violence, especially in eastern Europe where the Germans regarded the new frontiers as basically subject to reconsideration. After the Ruhr incident, and adoption of the Dawes Plan, a group of moderate and peace-loving men shaped the foreign policy of the principal countries—Gustav Stresemann in Germany, Édouard Herriot and Aristide Briand in France, Ramsay MacDonald in England.

The charter of the League of Nations provided for international sanctions against potential aggressors. Like the system of congresses after the Peace of Vienna, the League was supposed to assure peaceable compliance with the peace treaties, or their modification without resort to force.[18] No one expected the League, by any authority of its own, to prevent war between Great Powers, but the League achieved various minor pacifications in the 1920s, and in any case its headquarters at Geneva offered a convenient meeting place in which statesmen could talk. In 1924 Ramsay MacDonald, then prime minister of the Labour government in England, brought forward his Geneva Protocol. This provided for compulsory arbitration of international disputes, called for joint military action by members of the League of Nations against an aggressor, and explicitly defined the aggressor as the power unwilling to accept arbitration. Opinion in England was hesitant to make such a guarantee for Europe as a whole. The British overseas dominions, each of which was free to form its own foreign policy, feared entanglement in Europe. Britain preferred to go along with its own dominions. The Conservative British government that followed MacDonald declined to sign the Geneva Protocol, which was abandoned.

In its place, in 1925, the European powers signed a number of treaties at Locarno. These marked the highest point in international good will reached between the two World Wars. Germany signed a treaty with France and Belgium guaranteeing their respective frontiers unconditionally. It signed arbitration treaties with Poland and Czechoslovakia—not guaranteeing these frontiers as they stood, but undertaking to attempt changes in them only by international discussion, agreement, or arbitration. France signed treaties with Poland and Czechoslovakia promising military aid if they were attacked by Germany. France thus fortified its policy of balancing German power in the East by its own diplomatic alliances and by supporting the Little Entente, as the postwar alliance of Czechoslovakia, Yugoslavia, and Rumania was called. Great Britain "guaranteed"—i.e., promised military aid in the event of violation—the frontiers of Belgium and France against Germany. It did not give an equivalent guarantee with respect to Czechoslovakia or Poland. The British took the view that their own basic security would be threatened by German expansion westward, but not by German expansion to the east. It was on the borders of Czechoslovakia and Poland, fourteen years later, that the

[18] See pp. 487–493.

Second World War began. Had Britain gone along with France in 1925 in guaranteeing these two countries, then stuck to the guarantee, the Second World War might possibly have been prevented. On the other hand, no war ever depends on any single decision; it is the accumulation of many decisions that matters.

In 1925 people talked with relief of the "spirit of Locarno." In 1928 international harmony was again strengthened when the French foreign minister Briand and the United States Secretary of State Frank B. Kellogg arranged for the Pact of Paris. Ultimately signed by sixty-five nations, it condemned recourse to war for the solution of international controversies. Although no measures of enforcement were provided and a number of reservations were added before certain countries signed, the Pact solemnly affirmed the will of the nations to renounce war as an instrument of national policy. Meanwhile, the idea of general disarmament, pledged by Wilson in his Fourteen Points, was kept alive by a number of conferences. Some agreement was reached by the powers on naval construction at the Washington Conference of 1921–1922 and at subsequent, less successful, meetings at Geneva and London. Agreement on land disarmament was more difficult to arrive at; a League of Nations preparatory commission began consultations in 1925, but no general disarmament conference was held until 1932; by then the atmosphere had changed.

In the mid-1920s the outlook was indeed full of hope. At Locarno, Germany had of its own volition (and not by the *Diktat* of Versailles) accepted its borders both east and west, to the extent of abjuring violence and unilateral action even in the east. In 1926 Germany joined the League of Nations. Germany was a going concern as a democratic republic. Democracy seemed to work, as well as could be expected, in most of the new states of eastern Europe—the *cordon sanitaire* against Communist Russia, which itself had halted its postwar revolutionary offensive. The world was again prosperous, or seemed to be so. World production was at or above the prewar level. In 1925 the world's production of raw materials, it was estimated, was 17 percent greater than in 1913. World trade, by 1929, measured in hard money—gold—had almost doubled since 1913. The war and the postwar troubles were remembered as a nightmare escaped from. It seemed that, after all, the world had been made safe for democracy.

But complacency was shattered by the great world depression, by the growth of a malignant nationalism in Germany, due in some part to the depression, and by the assertion of a new militancy in Japan, which also was not unrelated to the depression. But let us turn first to the postwar years in Asia.

The peoples of Asia had never been satisfied with the position in which the great European expansion of the nineteenth century had placed them.[19] Increasingly they condemned everything associated with "imperialism." In this respect there was little difference between countries actually governed by Europeans as parts of European empires, such as British India, the Netherlands Indies, French Indo-

**100
The Revolt
of Asia**

Resentments in Asia

---

[19] See Chapter XV, pp. 665–708.

china (or the American Philippines), and countries which remained nominally independent under their own governments, such as China, Persia, and the Ottoman Empire. In the former, as political consciousness awakened, there was objection to the monopoly of Europeans in the important offices of government. In the latter, there was objection to the special rights and privileges enjoyed by Europeans, the widespread impounding of customs revenues to pay foreign debts, the capitulations in Turkey, the extraterritorial rights in China, the spheres of influence in Persia which divided the country between British and Russians.

By imperialism, in either case, aroused Asians meant a system whereby the affairs of their own country were conducted, its resources exploited, its people employed, for the benefit of foreigners, Europeans or white men. They meant the system of absentee capitalism, by which the plantations, docks, or factories before their eyes, and on which they themselves labored, were the property of owners thousands of miles away whose main interest in them was a regular flow of profits. They meant the constant threat that an alien civilization would disintegrate and eat away their own ancient cultures. They meant the nuisance of having to speak a European language, or the calamity of having to fight in wars originated by Europeans. And they meant the airs of superiority assumed by white men, the race-consciousness exhibited by all whites, though perhaps most of all the British and Americans, the color line that was everywhere drawn, the attitudes varying between contempt and condescension, the relation of native "boy" and European "sahib." Imperialism to them signified the gentlemen's clubs in Calcutta to which no Indian was ever admitted, the hotels in Shanghai from which Chinese were carefully kept out, the park benches in various cities on which no "native" could ever sit. In deeper psychology, as well as in economics and in politics, the revolt of self-conscious Asians was a rebellion against social inferiority and humiliation.

The revolt against the West was generally ambivalent or two-sided. It was a revolt against Western supremacy, but at the same time, in most cases, those who revolted meant to learn from and imitate the West, in order that, by taking over Western science, industry, organization, and other sources of Western power, they might preserve their own identity and emerge as the West's equals.

The crisis in Asia had broken out with the Russo-Japanese War, when an Asian people, in 1905, defeated a great European power for the first time.[20] In 1906 revolution began in Persia, leading to the assembly of the first majlis, or parliament. In 1908 the Young Turks staged a successful revolution in Constantinople and summoned a parliamentary assembly to represent all regions then in the Ottoman Empire. In 1911 the revolutionists in China, led by Sun Yat-sen, overthrew the Manchu dynasty and proclaimed the Chinese republic. In each case the rebels charged their old monarchs—shah, sultan, emperor—with subservience to Western imperialists. In each case they summoned national assemblies on the prevailing democratic model of Europe, and they proposed to revive, modernize and westernize their countries to the degree necessary to avoid domination by the West.

[20] See pp. 705–708.

In the First World War almost all the Asian peoples were somehow involved. The Ottoman Empire, allied with Germany, immediately repudiated all the capitulations, or special legal rights of Europeans. Persia attempted to remain neutral and to get rid of the partition made in 1907 between British and Russian spheres, but it became a battleground of British, Russian, and Turkish forces. China, which joined the Allies, attempted at the peace conference to have the extraterritorial rights in China abolished. We have seen how this request of the Chinese republic was refused, and how the Allies, instead, transferred many of the prewar German concessions to the Japanese.[21] The dependent regions of Asia, the Dutch, French, and British possessions, were stimulated economically by the war.[22] The Netherlands Indies, though remaining neutral, increased its output of foodstuffs, oil, and raw materials. India developed its steel industry and textile manufactures and contributed over a million soldiers, combat and service troops, to the British cause. All the dependent regions were stirred by Woodrow Wilson's call to make the world safe for democracy. By this they understood gaining more democracy, or at least more national independence, for themselves.

The home governments made concessions. They were naturally afraid to go too far; they insisted that their subject peoples were not yet capable of self-government; they had huge investments at stake; and the whole world economy depended on the continuing production of tropical and subtropical countries. But they did compromise. In 1916 the Dutch created a legislative assembly to advise the governor-general of the Indies; half its members were elected from native races. In 1917 the British agreed to a measure of self-government in India; an Indian legislative assembly was set up with 140 members, of whom 100 were elected, and in the provinces of British India the number of elected representatives and of native Indian officials was increased. The French in 1922 provided for a somewhat similar assembly in Indochina. Thus all three imperial powers, at about the same time, began to experiment with consultative bodies whose membership was partly elective, partly appointive, and partly native, partly European. The United States introduced an elected assembly in the Philippine Islands in 1916.

The Russian Revolution added a new stimulus to unrest in Asia. The Bolsheviks denounced not only capitalism but also imperialism. In Marxist-Leninist ideology imperialism was an aspect of capitalism.[23] Colonial peoples also tended to identify the two, not so much for Marxist reasons as because modern capitalism was a foreign or "imperialist" phenomenon in colonial countries, where the ownership and the management of large enterprises were both foreign. Nationalism in Asia, the movement for independence or for more equality with the West, thus easily shaded off into socialism and the denunciation of capitalistic exploitation. The Bolsheviks were quick to see the advantages for themselves in this situation. As it became clear that the world revolution, as expected by Lenin, would not soon come to pass in Europe, the Russian communists turned to Asia as the theater in which

[21] See p. 757.
[22] See p. 753.
[23] See p. 773.

world capitalism might be attacked by a great flanking movement. In September 1920 a "congress of oppressed Eastern peoples" assembled at Baku, on the coast of the Caspian Sea. Zinoviev, head of the Communist International, called for war upon "the wild beasts of British capitalism." Not much was accomplished at the conference. But a few extremists from Asian countries in the following years sojourned in Moscow, and a few communists dispatched from Moscow stirred up the discontents which existed, quite without Russian instigation, all over Asia.

The postwar situation in Asia was thus extremely fluid. Men who were not communists hailed communism as a liberating force. Anti-westerners declared that their countries must westernize. Nationalism overshadowed all other isms. In the Indian National Congress rich Indian capitalists consorted with socialist leaders, with whom they were held together in relative harmony so long as the common enemy was the British.

The Turkish Revolution: Kemal Ataturk

The most immediately successful of the revolutionary movements was the one in Turkey. The Young Turks at first, in 1908, had meant to prevent the further dissolution of the Ottoman Empire.[24] This proved to be impossible. In the Balkan wars of 1912–1913 the Ottoman power was almost totally excluded from the Balkan peninsula. In the World War, in which the Turks were on the losing side, the Arabs with a great deal of British assistance broke away. After the war the Greeks invaded the Anatolian peninsula. They dreamed of a Great Greece embracing both sides of the Aegean. Europeans still regarded Turkey as the sick man of Europe, the Ottoman state as doomed to extinction, and the Turkish people as barbarous and incompetent. The Allies had agreed in 1915 to partition Turkey; and after the war the Western powers favored the Greek invasion, Italian and French forces occupied parts of Anatolia, and Italians, French and British undertook to take Constantinople from Turkish rule, though its disposition remained uncertain. (It had been promised to Russia in 1915, before the Bolshevik Revolution.[25]) In these circumstances a powerful army officer named Mustapha Kemal rallied Turkish national resistance. Gradually, and with aid from Soviet Russia, the Turks drove the Greeks and the Western Allies away. They affirmed their hold on the Anatolian peninsula, and on both shores of the Straits, including Constantinople, which was renamed Istanbul.[26]

The Nationalists, under the energetic drive of Mustapha Kemal, now put through a revolution scarcely paralleled in any country at any time. They abolished the sultanate and the caliphate, since the sultan had somewhat compromised himself with foreigners, and was also, as caliph or commander of the faithful, a religious functionary for all Islam and hence a conservative influence. The Turkish republic was promulgated in 1923.

[24] See pp. 681–685, 727.
[25] See p. 739.
[26] See map, p. 684.

Where the Ottoman Empire had been a composite organization made up of diverse religious communities, among which the Moslems were the ruling group, the Turkish republic was conceived as a national state in which the "people," i.e., the Turkish people, were sovereign. Universal suffrage was introduced, along with a parliament, a ministry, and a president with strong powers. Non-Turks in Asia Minor now became "foreign" in a way they had not been before. Chief among these were the Greeks. About 1,400,000 Greeks either fled or were officially transported from Asia Minor to Greece, and, in exchange, some 400,000 Turks residing in northern Greece were transported to Turkey. The exchange of populations caused great hardship, it uprooted most of the Greek element that had lived in Asia Minor since 1000 B.C., and it overwhelmed the impoverished Greek kingdom by obliging it suddenly to absorb a mass of destitute refugees, who were a quarter as numerous as the population of Greece itself. But it enabled the Turkish republic to acquire a relatively homogeneous population, ending minority disputes between Greece and Turkey until Cyprus posed new problems after the Second World War.

For the first time in any Moslem country the spheres of government and religion were sharply distinguished. The Turkish republic affirmed the total separation of church and state. It declared religion to be a private belief, and it tolerated all religions. Government was reorganized on secular and nonreligious principles stemming from the French Revolution. The law of the Koran was thrust aside. The new law was modeled on the Swiss Code, the most recently codified European legislation, itself derived from the Code Napoleon.

Mustapha Kemal urged women to put aside the veil, to come out of the harem, to vote, and to occupy public office. He made polygamy a crime. Men he required by law to discard the fez. He fought against the fez as Peter the Great had fought against the beard, and for the same reason, seeing in it the symbol of conservative and backward habits. The hat, "headgear of civilization," correspondingly became the symbol of progress. The people shifted to Western dress. The Western alphabet became mandatory; literate Turks had to learn to read again, and illiteracy was reduced. The Western calendar and the metric system were adopted. Turks were required to assume hereditary family surnames, like Westerners; Kemal himself took the name Ataturk, or Great Turk. The capital was moved from Istanbul to Ankara. The republic put up a high tariff. In 1933 it adopted a five-year plan for economic development. The Turks, having shaken off foreign influence, were determined not to become again dependent on Western capital or capitalism. The five-year plan provided for mines, railroads, and factories, mainly under government ownership. At the same time, while willing to accept Russian aid against the Western powers, the republic had no patience with communism, which it suppressed. The Turks wanted a modern Turkey—by and for the Turks.

Persia experienced a similar revolution, somewhat less drastic. The old concessions, capitulations, and spheres were done away with, and the Persian government renegotiated its oil contracts, asserting more control over foreign corporations and receiving a larger return from them in taxes and royalties. In 1935, to emphasize its break with the past, Persia took the name of Iran.

831

India at the close of the World War was on the verge of revolution against British rule.[27]   Discontented Indians looked for leadership to Mohandas K. Gandhi, the Mahatma, or Holy One, who in the following decades, though hardly typical of modern Asia, attained a world-wide eminence as the spokesman of subjected peoples.   Gandhi had been educated in England in the 1890s and had practiced law in South Africa, where he became aware of racial discrimination as a world-wide problem.   In India, after 1919, he led a movement for self-government, for economic and spiritual independence from Great Britain, and for greater tolerance within India itself both between Hindus and Moslems and between upper-caste Hindus and the depressed outcastes and untouchables.   The weapons he favored were those of the spirit only; he preached nonviolence, passive resistance, civil disobedience, and the boycott.   He took to self-imposed fasts and hunger strikes to break the firmness of British jailers, and later of Indians themselves.   He and his most loyal followers, as the troubles mounted, refused to be elected or take part in the partially representative institutions that the British cautiously introduced and also boycotted the British economic position in India, by refusing to buy or use goods imported from England. The latter touched the British in a sensitive spot.   Before the World War half of all exports of British cotton cloth had gone to India.   By 1932 this proportion fell to a quarter.   Gandhi turned against all industrialism, even the mechanized industry that was growing up in India itself.   He put aside Western costume, took to using a spinning wheel and living on goat's milk, urged Indian peasants to revive their old handicrafts, and appeared on solemn occasions clad in no more than a homespun loin-cloth.   By the high level of his principles Gandhi made himself an inspiration to many groups which differed on more mundane matters.   Even in the West he was regarded as one of the great religious teachers of all time.

India was very much divided within, and the British maintained that because of these divisions the ending of British rule would precipitate anarchy.   There were Hindus and Moslems, between whom clashes and terrorist outrages were chronic. (Gandhi was himself murdered in 1948 by an anti-Moslem Hindu fanatic.)   There were the hundreds of oriental potentates of the native states.   There were Indian capitalists, like the Tata family, and growing masses of proletarians produced by Indian industrialization.[28]   There were the higher castes and the outcastes, and there were hundreds of millions of peasants living in a poverty unimaginable in the West. In politics, there were those who demanded full independence, boycotted the British, and spent years in jail, as did Gandhi and his more practical-minded but devoted follower, Jawaharlal Nehru; and there were the moderates who believed that they might best advance the welfare of India by accepting government office, cooperating with the British, and working for dominion status within the British Empire. Marxism exerted a strong appeal, not indeed on the spiritual and pacific Gandhi, but on Nehru and even many of the less radical leaders.   In the 1920s the Soviet Union stood in their eyes for the overthrow of imperialism; in the 1930s it pointed the way by

[27] See pp. 694–698, 708.
[28] See p. 753.

its adoption of five-year plans. For a people wishing to raise itself by its own bootstraps, to move from poverty to industrial strength and higher living standards without loss of time, and without dependence on foreign capital and capitalism, the Soviet Union with its economic planning seemed to offer a more appropriate model and more practical lessons than the rich democracies of the West, with their centuries of gradual progress behind them.

The twenty years between world wars were years of repeated disturbance, of rioting and repression, of sporadic violence despite the exhortations of Gandhi, of conferences and round tables, reforms and promises of reform, with a drift in the 1930s toward more participation of Indians in the affairs of the Indian empire. Independence was not won until after the Second World War; with it took place a partition of the Indian subcontinent into two new nations, a predominantly Hindu India and a predominantly Moslem Pakistan.[29]

In the Netherlands Indies, where the nationalist movement was less developed than in India,[30] the interwar years were more quiet. A serious rebellion, in which communists took part, broke out in 1922 but was suppressed by the Dutch. The peoples of the archipelago were almost as diverse as those of India. Only the Dutch empire had brought them politically together. Opposition to the Dutch gave them a common program. In 1937 the legislative council petitioned for the grant of dominion status within ten years. After a good deal of trouble the Dutch conceded independence, as in the case of the British and India, after the Second World War.[31]

The Chinese Revolution: The Three People's Principles

The Chinese revolution had opened in 1911 with the overthrow of the Manchu dynasty, which itself had belatedly begun to introduce westernizing reforms. The Chinese republic was proclaimed, but the first immediate result was the establishment in Peking of a military dictatorship exercised by General Yuan Shih-kai, who had been a close adviser to the Manchus and who, until his death in 1916, never ceased to cast covetous eyes on the now empty imperial throne itself. In the south the veteran revolutionary Dr. Sun Yat-sen reorganized the Kuomintang (National People's, or Nationalist party), successor to the prerevolutionary network of underground societies of which he had been the chief architect. Sun, elected the first president of the republic by a revolutionary provisional assembly, resigned within a few months in favor of General Yuan, who he mistakenly believed would unite the country under a parliamentary regime. Subsequently, in the confusion that followed the struggle for power in Peking after Yuan's death in 1916, Sun was proclaimed president of a rival government in the south at Canton, which exercised a nominal power over the southern provinces. Not until 1928 could any government have any basis for claiming actual rule over China—and even then, there were important exceptions. For most of these years the country was virtually in the hands of

[29]See pp. 954–955.
[30]See p. 695.
[31]See pp. 955–956.

contending war lords, each of whom pocketed the customary taxes in his own locality, maintained his own army, and recognized no superior authority.

It was Sun Yat-sen who best expressed the ideas of the Chinese revolution. Born in 1867 and educated under American influence in the Hawaiian Islands, he had received a medical degree at Hong Kong, had traveled extensively about the world, studied Western ideas, lectured to Chinese audiences in America, collected money for his conspiracies against the Manchus, and had returned from Europe to take part in the revolution. Shortly before his death in 1925 Sun gathered the lectures which he had been expounding for years into a book, *The Three People's Principles.* The book sheds much light on the revolt of China, and of all Asia, against the supremacy of the West.

The three people's principles, according to Sun Yat-sen, were democracy, nationalism, and livelihood. Livelihood meant social welfare and economic reform—a more equitable distribution of wealth and land, a gradual end to poverty and unjust economic exploitation. By nationalism Dr. Sun meant that the Chinese who had always lived mainly in the clan and family had now to learn the importance of the nation and the state. They were in fact a great nation, he thought, the world's most cultured, and had once prevailed from the mouth of the Amur to the East Indies. But they had never been cohesive; they had enjoyed too much liberty, each doing as he pleased, and for this reason the Westerners had been able to assault and invade them, occupy their cities, impose one-sided treaties, and extort humiliating rights and concessions. True freedom was freedom within an organized whole. The Chinese had been "a sheet of loose sand"; they must now "break down individual liberty and become pressed together into an unyielding body like the firm rock which is formed by the addition of cement to sand."

By democracy Sun Yat-sen meant the sovereignty of the people. Like Rousseau, he gave little attention to voting, elections, or parliamentary processes. Western democracy he thought in many ways old-fashioned. "Let us not, as we pursue democracy, copy the West; let us make a clear distinction between sovereignty and ability." He meant that, while the people were sovereign, the able should govern. He thought that government must be conducted by experts in government and criticized the West for neglecting this maxim.

Dr. Sun felt a warm sympathy for Lenin. All countries except Russia were governed by capitalists, he declared shortly before his death. Yet he was by no means a doctrinaire Marxist; he thought Marxism inapplicable to China and argued that the Chinese must take Marxism as they took all other Western ideas, avoiding slavish imitation, using, adapting, amending, rejecting as they saw fit. He insisted that Marxism was unsuited to China because China had no native capitalism in any Marxist or Western sense. The "capitalists" in China, he said, were owners of land, and especially the owners of land in the cities, such as Shanghai, where the coming of Westerners had raised land values to dizzy heights. Hence if China could get rid of imperialism it would take a long step toward getting rid of capitalism also; it could set about an equalization of landowning and a confiscation by the state of unearned rents. Since China, he observed, had no true capitalists the state itself must undertake capitalist and industrial development. He acknowledged that it would need loans of foreign capital and the services of foreign managers and technicians. This simply added another reason why the Chinese state, to maintain control, must be strong.

With Sun Yat-sen, in short, democracy easily shaded off into a theory of benevolent and constructive dictatorship; Marxism, communism, socialism, "livelihood," the planned society, welfare economics, and antiforeign and anti-imperialist sentiment were all mixed together.

The first aim of Sun Yat-sen and of the revolutionists in China was to shake off the "treaty system" which had bound China to outside interests since 1842.[32] In this respect the Paris peace conference had been disappointing; the Chinese not only failed to obtain the abolition of Western privileges and extraterritorial rights but could not block the retention by Japan of many of the former German concessions which the Japanese had taken over during the war. Like the United States, China never accepted the Treaty of Versailles.[33] After the war the Western powers remained obdurately attached to their treaty rights, especially the British, who had the greatest stake in investments in China. At the Washington Conference of 1921–1922, convened to consider naval disarmament and the general situation in the Pacific, the question of foreign withdrawal from China appeared on the agenda; it was dismissed with a reaffirmation of the "open door" policy,[34] a nine-power guarantee of the territorial integrity of China, and a few promises for the future.

Disappointed in the attempt to liberate China from foreign interests and frustrated in the effort to impose unity and effective government on the country as a whole, Sun and the Kuomintang turned to Russia. They declared the Russian and Chinese revolutions to be two aspects of the same world-wide movement of liberation. Members of the Chinese Communist party, which had been organized in 1921, were now in 1924 allowed to join the Kuomintang. The latter accepted Russian communist advisers, notably the veteran revolutionist Borodin, whom Sun Yat-sen had known years before in the United States.[35] The Soviet Union, following its strategy of outflanking world capitalism by penetrating Asia, sent military equipment, army instructors, and party organizers into China. It also surrendered the Russian concessions and extraterritorial rights acquired in China by the tsars. The Chinese policy of friendliness to Russia began to produce the hoped for effects; the British, to draw China from Russia, gave up a few of their lesser concessions at Hankow and other cities.

The Kuomintang, its armies reorganized and strengthened, now displayed a fresh vitality and after 1924 launched a military and political offensive, planned by the ever active Russian advisers, supported by the Chinese communists, and headed by Chiang Kai-shek who soon succeeded to the leadership of the Kuomintang upon

[32] See pp. 702–705.
[33] See p. 757.
[34] See pp. 704, 827.
[35] See p. 809.

Sun's death in 1925. Chiang's main objectives were to compel the independent war lords and the regime still holding office in Peking to accept the authority of a single Nationalist government. By the end of 1928 Chiang's armies had swept northward, occupied Peking (renaming it Peiping, or "Northern Peace"), and transferred the new government to Nanking. Chiang now exercised at least nominal control over most of China, although effective control was still limited by the recalcitrance of many provincial war lords. The outside powers, acknowledging the accomplishments of the Kuomintang, extended diplomatic recognition to the Nanking government and conceded its right to organize and run the country's tariff and customs affairs; they also partially surrendered their extraterritorial privileges and pledged to abolish them completely in the near future.

But during these events, and while a measure of national unity was being forged in the country, a new division had emerged. The Kuomintang split internally between a right wing, made up mainly of Chinese financiers, merchants, and officeholders who were more nationalist than socially minded, and a left wing made up of pro-Russians, communists, semicommunists, agrarian radicals, and dissatisfied students and intellectuals. The Russians also, after Stalin's victory over Trotsky in 1927, turned from world revolution and began to concentrate upon socialization in Russia; they withdrew from the ideological offensive in China.

In 1927 an open break occurred between the Kuomintang and its left wing. In the course of the northern military campaign, and particularly in the seizure of Nanking, popular disturbances and excesses, including the killing of a number of foreigners, had taken place, allegedly fomented by the Communists. These radical disturbances frightened and alienated the wealthier and more conservative element in the Kuomintang and so jeopardized Chiang's chief source of financial assistance for his government and army. Chiang himself, also, had never apparently considered the alliance with either the Communists or the Russians as anything more than one of convenience. Now Chiang took decisive action. Communists, and Russian advisers, were forthwith purged from the Kuomintang; many were executed; Borodin and others fled to Moscow; and a Communist-led uprising in Canton was forcefully suppressed. A number of armed Communist groups fled to the safety of the mountain regions in the south and joined other guerrilla contingents; in that way the Chinese Red Army was formed; among its leaders were Mao Tse-tung, a former librarian, teacher, newspaper editor, and union organizer, and Chu Teh who had held high rank in the Kuomintang armies and who had traveled and studied in Germany and elsewhere in Europe.

Chiang, with the renewed financial and moral support of the Kuomintang bankers, thereupon resumed the northern offensive whose success by 1928 has been described. But the original revolutionary impulse of the Kuomintang was now very much dissipated. Made up of men who feared social upheaval and who often regarded their own maintenance in power as their chief problem, it exercised a kind of one-party dictatorship over most of China under Chiang's leadership. Chiang, it must be said, himself recognized mounting popular dissatisfaction with the reluctance or inability of the Kuomintang to initiate deep-seated reforms. But

Chiang was still busy consolidating the regime; after 1931 he had to contend with Japanese aggression; and he had conceived a deadly hatred for Communists and those who actively agitated for revolutionary reform.

The Communists, operating now in southeast China, fed on popular discontent and drew support from the poor peasantry by a systematic policy of expropriation and distribution of large landed estates as well as by intensive propaganda. They succeeded in fighting off Chiang's armies and even in winning over part of his troops. They organized a network of local soviets and in 1931 proclaimed a Chinese Soviet Republic in the southeast. When after many years the Nationalist armies succeeded in dislodging them, they undertook in 1935 an amazing 5,000-mile fighting retreat over near-insuperable terrain to north-central China around Yenan, closer, it was said, to Soviet supply lines and in a position to outflank the Japanese invaders. Here they entrenched themselves again, fought off the Nationalist armies, and built up a strong popular following among the rural masses. With the Japanese invasion of north China well under way they abandoned their revolutionary offensive and pressed Chiang to end the civil war and to create a united front against the Japanese aggressor. Chiang, torn between his desire to destroy the Communists and to stave off the Japanese conquest of the country, had his decision made for him by the failure of his military campaigns against the Communists and by the pressure brought to bear upon him by his subordinates (he was even temporarily kidnapped in 1936). By 1937 an alliance was formed between the Kuomintang and the Communists; the Chinese Red Army was placed under Nationalist control and disposition; a united China would face the Japanese. But the uneasy alliance between Kuomintang and Communists was not to last even until the defeat of the common Japanese foe in the Second World War, and the Chinese revolution was about to enter a new, dynamic, and vastly different phase.[36]

The Nationalist movement in China caused apprehension in Japan, whose rise as a modern power has already been traced.[37] The Japanese, at least since the Sino-Japanese war of 1895, had looked upon the huge disintegrating area of China as a field for expansion of their own interests, in this scarcely differing from Europeans, except that they were closer to the scene. During the World War they had presented their Twenty-One Demands on China, taken over the German concessions in Shantung, and sent troops into eastern Siberia.[38] During the war the industrialization of Japan proceeded apace; Japan captured many markets while the Europeans were locked in the struggle; and after the war the Japanese remained one of the chief suppliers of textiles for the rest of Asia. The Japanese could produce at lower prices than the Europeans, prices at which the penniless masses of Asia were more able to buy. Densely packed in their mountainous islands, they sustained their standard of living by importing raw materials and selling manufactures. But the Chinese

[36] See pp. 947–953.
[37] See pp. 594–600.
[38] See pp. 739, 757, 786.

Nationalists hoped to erect a protective tariff; it was for this reason, among others, that they denounced the treaty system, which for almost a century had bound China to international free trade. The Chinese, like the Turks, hoped to industrialize and westernize their own country behind a high tariff wall, which would shut out Japanese manufactures as well as others.

During the 1920s the civilian, liberal, Western-oriented element in Japan remained in control of the government. In 1925 universal manhood suffrage was adopted. It was still the fashion in Europe and America to view the Japanese with sympathetic approval, as the most progressive of all non-Europeans, the one Asian people who had ably learned to play its part in the advancing world-wide civilization. But there was another facet to Japan. The constitution of 1889 and parliamentary operations were but a façade that concealed political realities. Only in Japan of all modern countries did a constitutional law prescribe that the war and navy ministers must be active generals or admirals, making it possible for the military to control the formation of all cabinets. The diet itself had sharply restricted powers. Ministers governed in the name of the supreme and sacred authority of the emperor, to whom they were alone responsible. Economically, the government's sponsorship of industrial growth had resulted in a tremendous concentration of economic power in the hands of four family trusts known collectively as the Zaibatsu. The business interests and the civilian political leaders all looked to an expanding empire and growing markets, but the most restless element in Japan drew its strength from the nationalist revival which, even before the "opening" of Japan in 1854, had cultivated Shinto, emperor-worship, and the way of the warrior as a new and modern way of life.[39] This element was recruited in large part from the old clansmen and samurai, whom the "abolition of feudalism" had uprooted from their accustomed ways, and who in many cases found no satisfying field of effort in the new regime. Many of these men now served as officers in the army. Often they regarded the West as decadent. They dreamed of the day when Japan would dominate all East Asia.

About 1927 this group began to hold ministries in the Japanese government and to turn Japanese policy into increasingly aggressive and militaristic attitudes toward China. In 1931 Japanese army units stationed in Southern Manchuria (where the Japanese had been since defeat of the Russians in 1905), alleging the mysterious murder of a Japanese officer at Mukden, began to seize Chinese arsenals and spread northward over all Manchuria. In 1932, charging the Chinese with economic warfare against Japan (Chinese boycotts were in fact damaging the Japanese export trade materially), the Japanese landed 70,000 troops at Shanghai. They soon withdrew, preferring to concentrate at this stage on the occupation of the northern part of China. They declared Manchuria to be an independent state under an emperor picked by themselves, renaming it Manchukuo.

After the Manchurian invasion the Chinese appealed to the League of Nations. The League sent a commission of inquiry. The commission, under Lord Lytton, found Japan at fault for disturbing the peace. The small powers in the League

[39] See pp. 597, 599.

generally cried for military sanctions, but the Great Powers, knowing that they would be the ones to bear the burden of military intervention against Japan, and in any case inclined to see no threat to their own immediate security, forced the League to adopt a compromise proposed by the Lytton Commission, so that, in effect, the Japanese remained in occupation of Manchuria and northeast China. The League also adopted a resolution, formulated originally by the American Secretary of State Henry L. Stimson, that no conquests achieved by force of arms in violation of existing agreements should receive diplomatic recognition; it was equally ineffectual. But the world at this time was also stunned by economic depression. Each government was preoccupied with its own internal social problems. The League, in the first clear test to be raised by a Great Power, failed to assure security to a member-state, in this case China, or to prevent open and undisguised aggression, in this case by Japan. The latter defiantly announced its withdrawal from the League. The Chinese remained in a state of war with Japan (not yet declared, and termed by the Japanese an "incident") from 1931 until 1945, a renewed large-scale invasion of China taking place in 1937. In a sense the Second World War began as early as 1931 with the Japanese seizure of Manchuria. One tributary of the torrent had begun to flow.

The capitalist economic system was a delicate and interlocking mechanism, in which any disturbance was rapidly transmitted with accelerating impact through all the parts.[40] For many basic commodities prices were determined by the free play of supply and demand in a world-wide market. There was much regional division of labor; large areas lived by producing a few specialized articles for sale to the world as a whole. A great deal of production, both local and international, especially in the 1920s, was financed by credit, which is to say by promises of repayment in the future. The system rested upon mutual confidence and mutual exchange—on the belief of the lender, creditor, or investor that he would get his money back, on the belief of the borrower that he could pay his debts, on the ability of farms and factories to market their products at prices high enough to bring a net return, so that farmers and factory people might purchase the output of other factories and farms, and so on round and round in countless circles of mutual interdependence, and throughout the world as a whole.

101
The Great Depression: Collapse of the World Economy

The five years after 1924 were a period of prosperity, in that there was a good deal of international trade, building, and development of new industries. The automobile, for example, still an oddity in 1914, became an article of mass production after the war; and its widespread use increased the demand for oil, steel, rubber, and electrical equipment, caused the building or rebuilding of tens of thousands of miles of roads and created whole new secondary occupations for thousands of men as

The Prosperity
of the 1920s
and Its Weaknesses

[40] See pp. 618–625, 659–660, 749–753.

truckdrivers, garage mechanics, or filling-station attendants. Similarly the mass popularity of radios and moving pictures had repercussions in all directions. The ensuing expansion was most phenomenal in the United States, but almost all countries enjoyed it in greater or lesser degree. "Prosperity" became a mystic term, and some thought that it would last indefinitely, that the secret of human plenty and of progress had been found, and that science and invention were at last realizing the hopes of ages.

But there were weaknesses in this prosperity, various imperfections in this or that gear or valve of the mechanism, flaws which, under stress, were to bring the whole intricate structure to a halt. The expansion was largely financed by credit, or borrowing. Laboring people received less than a balanced share; wages lagged behind profits and dividends, so that mass purchasing power, even when inflated by installment buying (another form of credit) could not absorb the vast output that it was technically possible to produce. And throughout the world the whole decade of the 1920s was a time of chronic agricultural depression, so that farmers could neither pay their debts nor purchase manufactures to the degree required for the smooth functioning of the system.

During the war wheat fields under cultivation in Europe were reduced by a fifth. The world price of wheat went up, and farmers in the United States, Canada, and elsewhere increased their acreage. Often, to acquire land at high prices, they gave mortgages which in later years they were unable to repay. After the war Europe restored its own wheat production, and eastern Europe reentered the world market. Agriculture was increasingly mechanized. Where, in the nineteenth century, one man could cut ten times as much grain with a single horse-drawn reaper as with a scythe, and where, before 1914, he could cut fifty times as much with a combined reaper and binder, he could again increase his output fivefold after the war, by using a tractor-drawn harvester-thresher combine. At the same time dry farming opened up new land, and agronomic science increased the yield per acre. The result of all these numerous developments was a superabundant output of wheat. But the demand for wheat was what economists call "inelastic." By and large, within the area of the Western world, people already ate as much bread as they wanted and would buy no more; and the undernourished masses of Asia, who in pure theory could have consumed the excess, could not pay even low costs of production or transportation. The world price of wheat fell incredibly. In 1930 a bushel of wheat, in terms of gold, sold for the lowest price in four hundred years.

Wheat-growers in all continents were faced with ruin. Growers of many other crops faced the same dismal prospect. Cotton and corn, coffee and cocoa all collapsed. Brazilian and African planters were caught by overproduction and falling prices. In Java, where not only had the acreage in sugar been extended, but the unit yield of sugar from the cane had multiplied ten times under scientific cultivation over the past century, the bottom dropped out of prices in the world market. There were indeed other and more profitable forms of agricultural production—for example, in oranges and eggs, of which world consumption was steadily growing. But the coffee planter could not shift to eggs, nor the Iowa farmer to oranges. Not to mention the requirements of climate, the ordinary farmer or peasant lacked the capital, the special knowledge, or the access to refrigerated transportation that these newer branches of agriculture demanded. For the one thing that the average farmer or peasant knew how to do—grow wheat and other cereals—the new wonderful world of science and machinery had too little place.

The acute phase of the great depression, which began in 1929, was made worse by this chronic background of agricultural distress, since there was no reserve of purchasing power on the farms. Contrariwise the farmer's plight became even worse when the city people, struck by depression in industry, cut down their expenditures for food. Agricultural depression, rather than industrial depression, was at the bottom of widespread troubles in the interwar years throughout eastern Europe and the colonial world.

The depression, in the strict sense, began as a stock-market and financial crisis. Prices of stocks had been pushed upward by years of continuing expansion and high dividends. At the beginning of 1929 prices on the European stock exchanges began to weaken. But the real crisis, or turning point, came with the crash on the New York Stock Exchange in October 1929. Here values had been driven to fantastic heights by excessive speculation. Not only professional speculators, but quite ordinary people, in the United States, as an easy way to make a good deal of money, bought stock with borrowed funds. Sometimes, trading on "margin," they "owned" five or ten times as much stock as the amount of their own money put into it; the rest they borrowed from brokers, and the brokers borrowed from banks, the purchased stock in each case serving as collateral. With money so easy to obtain, people pushed up stock prices by bidding against each other and enjoyed huge fortunes on paper; but if prices fell, even a little, the hapless owners would be obliged to sell their stock to pay off the money they had borrowed. Hence the weakening of values on the New York Stock Exchange set off uncontrollable tidal waves of selling, which drove stock prices down irresistibly and disastrously. In a month stock values dropped by 40 percent, and in three years, from 1929 to 1932, the average value of fifty industrial stocks traded on the New York Stock Exchange dropped from 252 to 61. In these same three years 5,000 American banks closed their doors.

The crisis passed from finance to industry, and from the United States to the rest of the world. The export of American capital came to an end. Americans not only ceased to invest in Europe but sold the foreign securities that they had. This pulled the foundations from under the postwar revival of Germany and hence indirectly of much of Europe. Americans, their incomes falling, ceased to buy foreign goods; from Belgium to Borneo people saw their American markets slip away, and prices tumbled. In 1931 the failure of a leading Vienna bank, the *Creditanstalt*, sent a wave of shivers, bankruptcies, and business calamities over Europe. Everywhere business firms and private people could not collect what was owed them, or even draw on money that they thought they had in the bank. They could not buy, and so the factories could not sell. Factories slowed down or closed entirely. Between 1929 and 1932, the latter year representing the depth of the depression, world production is estimated to have declined by 38 percent, and the world's international trade fell by two-thirds. In the United States the national income fell from $85,000,000,000 to $37,000,000,000.

Unemployment, a chronic disease ever since the war, now assumed the proportion of pestilence. In 1932 there were 30,000,000 unemployed persons statistically reported in the world; and this figure did not include the further millions who could find work only for a few hours in the week, or the masses in Asia or Africa for whom no statistics were to be had. The worker's wages were gone, the farmer's income now touched bottom; and the decline of mass purchasing power forced more idleness of machinery and more unemployment. Men in the prime of life spent years out of work. Young men could not find jobs or establish themselves in an occupation. Skills and talents of older people grew rusty, young people found no opportunity to learn. Millions were reduced to living, and supporting their families, on the pittances of charity, doles, or relief. Great modern cities saw an outburst of sidewalk-art, in which, at busy street corners, jobless able-bodied men drew pictures on the pavement with colored chalk, in the hope of attracting a few sixpences or dimes. People were crushed in spirit by a feeling of uselessness; months and years of fruitless job-hunting left them demoralized, bored, discouraged, embittered, frustrated, and resentful. Never had there been such waste, not merely of machinery which now stood still, but of the trained and disciplined labor force on which all modern societies were built. And people chronically out of work naturally turned to new and disturbing political ideas.

Reactions to
the Crisis

Optimists at the time, of whom President Herbert Hoover in the United States was one, declared that this depression, though a severe one, was basically only another periodic low point in the business cycle, or alternation of expansion and contraction, which had ebbed and flowed in the Western world for over a century. Prosperity, they plaintively said, was "just around the corner." Others felt that the crisis represented the breakdown of the whole system of capitalism and free private enterprise. These people, in many cases, looked for signs of the future in the planned economy then being introduced in the U.S.S.R. There was something in both views. After 1932, in part for purely cyclical reasons—because the depression cut down indebtedness and reduced the costs of doing business—it again became possible to produce and sell. World steel production, for example, which had stood at 121,000,000 tons in 1929, and then collapsed to 50,000,000 in 1932, by 1936 again reached 122,000,000. (To what degree revival was due to armament building is debated.) On the other hand, the great depression did put an end to the old economic system in the old sense. Even if such a stricken economy had internal powers of full recuperation after a few years, still people would not stand for such terrifying insecurity in their personal lives. The horrors of mass unemployment were long remembered.

All governments took steps to provide work and incomes for their people. All, in one way or another, strove to free themselves from dependency on the uncertainties of the world market. The interlocking world economy collapsed both from the depression itself and from the measures adopted to cure it. The most marked economic consequence of the depression was a strong movement toward economic nationalism—toward greater self-sufficiency within the sphere which each government could hope to control.

The internationalism of money, the gold standard, and the free convertibility of currencies one into the other were gradually abandoned. Countries specializing in agricultural exports were among the first to be pinched. Agricultural prices were so low that even a large quantity of exports failed to produce enough foreign currency to pay for needed imports; hence the exporting country's currency fell in value. The currencies of Argentina, Uruguay, Chile, Australia, and New Zealand all depreciated in 1929 and 1930. Then came the turn of the industrial countries. England, as the depression went on, could not sell enough exports to pay for imports. It had to pay for imports in part by sending gold out of the country; thus the gold reserve supporting the pound sterling declined, and people who had pounds sterling began to convert their pounds into dollars or other currencies for which they thought the gold basis was more secure. This was known, in the poetic language of economics, as the "flight from the pound." In 1931 Great Britain went off the gold standard, which is to say that it devalued the pound. The Briton or foreigner holding pounds sterling now could not get gold at all; he could use his sterling to buy British goods, or he could convert it to dollars or francs at depreciated rates. A pound was now worth a smaller number of dollars, or, contrariwise, fewer dollars (francs, marks, pesos, etc.) sufficed to buy a pound sterling. Hence other peoples were better able to buy British goods; one purpose of devaluation was in fact to restore Britain's export trade. But after Britain devalued, some twenty-odd other countries, to protect their own exports and their own industries, did the same. Hence somewhat the same relative position reappeared. Even the United States, which possessed most of the world's gold supply, abjured the gold standard and devalued the dollar in 1934. The purpose was mainly to help American farmers, for with dollars cheaper in terms of foreign currencies, foreigners could afford to buy more American agricultural products. But it became harder for foreigners to sell to the United States.

Hence the depression, adding its effects to those of the World War and postwar inflation, led to chaos in the international monetary exchanges. Governments manipulated their currencies to uphold their sagging exports. Or they imposed definite exchange controls: they required that foreigners from whom their own people purchased, and to whom they thus gave their own currency, should use this currency to buy from them in return. Trade, which had been multilateral, became increasingly "bilateral." That is, where a Brazilian importer of steel, for example, had formerly bought steel wherever he wished, at such price or of such quality as he preferred, he now had to obtain steel, often regardless of price or precise quality, from a country to which Brazil had sold enough of its own products to make payment possible. Sometimes, notably in the relations between Germany and east-European countries in the 1930s, bilateralism degenerated into actual barter. The Germans would exchange a certain number of cameras with Yugoslavia in return for a certain number of pigs. In such cases the very conception of a market disappeared.

Currency control was one means of keeping one's own factories from idleness, by holding or capturing export markets in time of depression. Another way of keeping one's own factories going (or farms, or mines, or quarries) was to shut out competitive imports by the old device of protective tariffs. The United States, hit by depression in 1929, enacted the unprecedentedly high Hawley-Smoot tariff in 1930. Other countries, equally or more distressed, now could sell less to America and hence buy less American goods. Other countries likewise raised their own tariffs, in the desperate hope of reserving national markets for their own people. Even Great Britain, citadel of free trade in the nineteenth century, turned to protectionism. It likewise revived and adopted Joseph Chamberlain's old idea of an imperial tariff union, when in 1932, by the Ottawa agreements, Britain and the British dominions adopted a policy of having lower tariffs against one another than against the world outside.[41] Thus the British manufacturers strove to hold a privileged market in the empire, and the harassed wheat-growers of Canada, or wool-growers of Australia, tried to assure themselves of a reliable outlet in Great Britain.

Even tariffs were not always enough. Quotas or quantitative restrictions were adopted in many states. By this system a government said in effect not merely that goods brought into the country must pay a high tariff duty, but that above a certain amount no goods could be brought in at all. Increasingly both importers and exporters worked under government licenses, in order that a country's entire foreign trade could be centrally planned and managed. Such methods approached those of the Soviet Union, which asserted a government monopoly of all foreign trade, exported only in order to finance imports and determined, without the bother of tariffs, the exact quantity of imported commodities that it would take.

Thus the world economy disintegrated into fiercely competing national economic systems. In the oceanic wreckage of the great depression, each state tried to create an island of economic security for its own people. Even before the great depression the new states of eastern Europe, and such other new states as the Turkish republic, had surrounded themselves with tariffs in order to make themselves more modern, industrial, Western, or up-to-date. This process, by depriving the older industrial countries of former markets, had in fact been one cause of depression. Now, with the depression, old and established industrial countries also retreated within their own borders. There were, indeed, attempts to break down the rising barriers, to unfreeze a world economy that was congealing into separate national blocks. An International Monetary and Economic Conference met at London in 1933. It attempted to open the clogged channels of world trade; but it ended in failure because each national delegation was afraid to entrust its people to the ups and downs of a world market. Plans to stabilize the exchange rates of various currencies

844   [41] See p. 672.

were especially blocked by the attitude of the United States. One sequel to the failure of the London Conference was an aggravation of the old war debts-reparations issue.[42] After the conference there was a general default on war debt payments to the United States by the wartime Allies; German reparations payments to these countries had already been all but totally abolished the year before. The United States in the retaliatory Johnson Act of 1934 now denied to the defaulting wartime Allies the right to float bonds in the American security market. Since the vast lending and purchasing power of the United States made it the world's economic center of gravity, the actions taken by the United States at this time reinforced the trend to economic nationalism everywhere else.

The era that had opened with Woodrow Wilson's dream of international economic cooperation was ending with an unprecedented intensification of economic rivalry and national self-centeredness; it was only one of the many promises of the twentieth century to be blasted by the Great Depression.

[42] See pp. 751, 757–758, 823–825.

POSTA AEREA

DUE POPOLI
UNA GUERRA

1 LIRA AFRICA ORIENTALE ITALIANA

XIX: DEMOCRACY AND

DICTATORSHIP

In the 1920s, people in a general way had believed that the twentieth century was realizing all those goals summed up in the idea of progress; in the 1930s, they began to fear that "progress" was a phantom, to speak the word self-consciously with mental quotation marks, and to be content if only they could prevent a relapse into positive barbarization and a new world war.

The Great Depression ushered in the nightmare of the 1930s. Everywhere the demand was for security. Each nation tried to live economically, so far as possible, within itself. Each, increasingly regulating, controlling, guiding, planning or rescuing its own economic system, tried to be as little influenced as possible by the unpredictable behavior of other countries, or by the free rise and fall of prices in an uncontrolled world market. On the one hand, where democratic institutions were strong, well established, and flexible, this trend advanced the principles of the welfare state and social democracy; it protected the individual against the worst evils of unemployment and destitution and committed itself to protecting him from future catastrophes. But on the other hand the same economic trend became one aspect of the totalitarianism which spread alarmingly in the 1930s. For democracy was said to

Chapter Emblem: A postage stamp featuring Hitler and Mussolini, and reading "Two Peoples, One War," for use in Italian East Africa about 1940.

be suited only to wealthy countries. Unemployed people, especially where democracy was not established or taken for granted, cared far more for economic help, or for promises of economic help, than for any theory of how persons wielding public power should be selected. The cry was for a leader, someone who would act, make decisions, assume responsibilities, get results. Even in the United States this feeling contributed to the popularity of Franklin D. Roosevelt, who became president in 1933; in other countries it opened the way for true dictators, unscrupulous and ambitious political adventurers whose purposes, to put it mildly, were less benign than the American Roosevelt's and whose final solution to all problems, economic and political, it turned out, was war.

102
The United States:
Depression and
New Deal

Profound changes took place in the United States, where the stock market crash of 1929 had precipitated the great economic collapse. In 1932 national income had dropped to less than half of what it had been in 1929; 12,000,000 to 14,000,000 were unemployed; there was despair in all quarters. The Republican President Herbert Hoover, elected in 1928 at the floodtide of prosperity, was identified in the public mind with the hard times. Hoover viewed with disfavor any large-scale government intervention, convinced that the business cycle that had brought the depression would in turn bring prosperity, and that once business confidence was restored recovery would begin. Eventually his administration did act, proposing for the world economy a one-year suspension of payments on all intergovernmental debts and at home giving financial assistance to banks and railroads, expanding credit facilities, and helping to save the mortgages of some farmers and small home owners. But further Hoover would not go; he opposed anything like immediate direct federal relief to the jobless; some 12,000 to 14,000 veterans seeking payment of their wartime bonuses to tide them over the bad times were ejected from Washington; unemployment, business failures, and farm foreclosures continued. In the election of 1932 the millions of unemployed workers, disheartened urban lower middle classes, and distressed farmers swept the Republican administration from office and elected the first Democratic president since Woodrow Wilson. The new president was Franklin Delano Roosevelt. The combination of recovery, relief, and reform legislation that he inaugurated is known as the New Deal.

The new president embarked on a program of improvisation and experimentation, but with such dispatch and vigor as to generate at once an electric enthusiasm. Within a short time an impressive array of legislation was put through the Congress. The program of assistance to farmers, small home owners, and industry initiated under the Hoover administration was expanded so that it was no longer recognizable.

The government provided financial assistance for the relief of the unemployed and sponsored a broad public works program to absorb the jobless; at first it gave loans to the states for such construction projects as housing, roads, bridges, and schools; later it organized a direct federal program of works projects. To meet the financial crisis, the banks were temporarily closed and then reopened under stricter supervision. The dollar was taken off the gold standard and devaluated in order to generate a moderate and controlled inflation, designed especially to help the farmers compete in foreign markets. The economic program of the New Deal was, at least at first, intensely nationalistic; we have noted how at the London Economic Conference in 1933 Roosevelt refused to tie the American currency to any international stabilization proposals. In agriculture the government gave subsidies to farmers who would curtail farm production, even going so far as to subsidize the destruction of crops and livestock, so that ruinous surpluses which had been one cause of the agricultural distress might be eliminated. It was a paradox, to be sure, for the government to reduce acreage and destroy agricultural products while city populations were in want. But the administration was endeavoring not only to cope with the immediate situation but also to meet the deep-seated agricultural crisis which antedated the depression. Subsequently, farmers received subsidies for devoting part of their land to soil-conserving crops. A Civilian Conservation Corps also promoted conservation and reforestation, and relieved unemployment by giving jobs to almost 3,000,000 young people. For industry a National Recovery Administration (the NRA) encouraged business firms to set up voluntary "codes of fair competition" and to decide on prices and production; in return they accepted certain regulations and made concessions to labor.

The purpose of these relief and rehabilitation measures was to set the ailing capitalist system on its feet again, to create purchasing power and to stimulate industry. The major technique was government spending or "deficit financing." Although never following any consistent economic philosophy, the New Deal policies indirectly reflected the theoretical formulations of the British economist, J. M. Keynes, who insisted that if private investment funds were idle, government funds must be employed to encourage industrial activity and to increase purchasing power until such time as private funds were flowing again. In order to get money into circulation and to "prime the pump" of industrial production the government undertook its huge borrowing and spending program. Unorthodox as "deficit financing" was, it seemed then, and even later, the only direct or active method of meeting, or preventing, economic collapse in a capitalist system. In all these recovery and reform measures the federal government assumed a role that it had hitherto played only in wartime. Alphabetical agencies proliferated; the federal payroll grew; the government debt mounted—between 1932 and 1940 it more than doubled.

From the beginning, longer-range reform measures were initiated in addition to the recovery measures. A Securities and Exchange Commission was created to regulate the issuance of stock and to supervise the operations of the stock exchange; the aim was to prevent overspeculation and the recurrence of a crash such as that of 1929. Bank deposits were guaranteed by federal insurance so that depositors would never again lose their lifetime savings. A Tennessee Valley Authority served as a pilot program in flood control, regional economic development, and cheap public power production—a yardstick, it was said, for the private utility companies.

Increasingly, after 1935, the government seemed to shift toward an emphasis on regulation and reform. Sound economic recovery had not been achieved; there were still at least 5,000,000 persons who could not find jobs in private industry. The NRA had not worked to the satisfaction of either labor or industry; it seemed only to have accentuated the concentration of economic power in the hands of bigger business firms. At first it had aroused enthusiasm, but no one was greatly concerned when the Supreme Court in 1935 declared it unconstitutional on technical grounds. Businessmen who at first had been responsive to the government's leadership were now increasingly resisting the government's regulation of finance and industry. Ambitious demagogues, not unlike those in Europe who at this very moment were building totalitarian dictatorships out of the chaos of the depression, were active—the Louisiana Senator Huey Long, the Catholic radio-priest Father Charles E. Coughlin, the rabble-rousing Gerald L. K. Smith, and others. Many liberals and intellectuals, always skeptical of the permanence of prosperity and disrespectful toward the worship of material success in the 1920s, viewed with admiration the Soviet "experiment," then in the midst of the industrial expansion of its second Five-Year Plan.

The tempo of New Deal reform after 1935 quickened and moved in the direction of aiding labor and the little man. A broad national Social Security Act in 1935 provided for unemployment, old-age, and disability insurance. The United States followed in the footsteps of imperial Germany, Britain, and other European countries which had had such legislation since before the First World War. Pioneer in democracy, America had hitherto not shown much tendency to advance in social legislation; nor had there ever been much demand for it even from labor ranks. Now, except for some details, the new program came to command almost universal respect. A Fair Labor Standards Act established forty hours as a maximum normal work week and set a minimum hourly wage; child labor was abolished. With the passage of a third measure, the National Labor Relations (or Wagner) Act, the American industrial scene was virtually transformed. For the first time the unions found the federal government and the law solidly aligned on their side in the campaign to organize labor. In the United States, far more effectively than in other industrial countries, employers had succeeded, in the 1920s and earlier, in preventing unionization by a variety of methods ranging from welfare paternalism to brute violence. Moreover, organized labor itself had not been enterprising. The American Federation of Labor, set up in 1886, had generally confined itself to the organization of skilled workers into craft-wide unions.

Under the new act, which guaranteed the right of workers to set up and bargain through unions of their own choice, company unions were outlawed and employers were forbidden to interfere with union organization or to discriminate against union members. Under its aegis the older AFL was revitalized and a new vigorous organization came into being, the Congress of Industrial Organizations (CIO), organizing workers on an industry-wide basis and reaching down to unskilled workers in such industries as automobile, steel, textile, maritime, and rubber. Millions never before organized, including women and black workers, became part of powerful labor unions with expanding treasuries. Total union membership rose from about 4,000,000 in 1929 to 9,000,000 by 1940; in the 1970s it was over 17,000,000.

Militant and conscious of its new strength but hardly touched by revolutionary ideology, American labor chose not to create a third party but to operate within the traditional two-party system.

Other reforms were introduced too. A program of slum clearance and low-cost housing made a start toward providing adequate housing. Aid was given to the tenant farmer and the sharecropper. All this was undertaken to help those whom the president described in 1937 as "one-third of a nation ill-nourished, ill-clad, ill-housed." If the New Deal did not feed, clothe, and house them, or strike at the deeper roots of American poverty, urban decay, and racial discrimination, it at least demonstrated that the national community cared.

In keeping with the same reform orientation after 1935, a tax revision bill, called by its opponents a "soak the rich" scheme, arranged for steeply graduated income taxes, levies on corporate profits, and the plugging of various corporate tax-evasion loopholes. The New Deal later tried also to reverse the trend toward the concentration of economic power, which it had itself stimulated under the NRA, by an investigation into monopoly and monopoly practices, and a trust-busting campaign.

Government spending and renewed confidence in the soundness of the country's institutions did create a slow, gradual, and partial recovery. In mid-1937, however, a recession occurred, i.e., business activity slid backward, when government spending slowed down; the recession did not end until 1938 when government spending was resumed. National income reached $71,000,000,000 by 1939, double what it had been at the depth of the depression but still short of 1929. Despite substantial recovery, business activity did not once reach the high-water mark of June 1929. Resistance from the business community itself may have played a part. The rising public debt, antibusiness pronouncements by the government, heavier corporate and income taxes, and the many concessions to labor undoubtedly frightened off business investments and led to what was called a "sit-down strike" of capital. Some claimed even that wage rates had gone up too sharply, adding to production costs and therefore discouraging business expansion. The New Deal did much to help the patient get back on his feet. But he was not yet the same man. The New Deal did not end the depression. Complete recovery, the elimination of unemployment, the full use (and expansion) of the nation's productive capacity had to wait upon the huge war expenditures, by which depression spending was to be dwarfed. By 1938 or so the New Deal was over; the administration turned its attention from domestic reform to the gathering storm in Europe and the Far East.

The changes had been great under what some called the Roosevelt Revolution. Carrying forward a process that went back at least to the Theodore Roosevelt era, but enlarging the role of the federal government as no previous administration had done, the New Deal transformed the noninterventionist state into a social service or welfare state. The government had imposed controls on business, entered business itself, used its powers to redistribute wealth, and established a broad social security system. Labor's power and political influence had grown. The basic premise that seemed to emerge from the New Deal, the responsibility of public authority for the social and economic welfare of the people, was clearly established. Here perhaps was the real essence of the New Deal. After it no party would wish to question or could question certain innovations—the regulation of the stock exchange, social security, wages and hours legislation, the existence of the unions, protection to the farmer, the need for government watchfulness over the economy to prevent any new collapse, including even the willingness to spend government funds to prevent such a collapse. The Republican party, when it returned to power after the war, retained and even extended these various reforms. It was a tacit admission, despite fulminations at the time, that the New Deal had not aimed at destroying the system of capitalism but at rehabilitating and strengthening it by regulation and reform.

The New Deal, however, had engendered violent feelings, which lingered on. Roosevelt, himself of patrician and well-to-do background, denounced the "economic royalists"; in turn he was called a "traitor to his class," and even worse. Despite vociferous opposition, in the election of 1936 Roosevelt won all but two states in the most decisive victory in modern American history; and he was subsequently reelected in 1940 and 1944 (during the wartime emergency, to be sure, and with increasingly smaller majorities) for a totally unprecedented four terms. Such an occurrence was later barred for the future by a constitutional amendment of 1951. Roosevelt battled with the Supreme Court as David Lloyd George had with the British House of Lords. When the Supreme Court declared certain measures unconstitutional, for various technical reasons but generally on the grounds that they exceeded the constitutional powers of the executive and of the federal government, the New Dealers denounced the Court as acting not as a judicial body but as a policy-making agency, and one insensitive to the emergency facing the country. Roosevelt made plans to reorganize and "pack" it, i.e., enlarge the bench and fill the new vacancies; gradually, however, the Court itself softened in its hostility, and death and retirement made it possible for Roosevelt to appoint new justices sympathetic to the New Deal. His conflict with the Court was the closest Roosevelt came to tampering with any of the fundamental constitutional structure of the country; even then he was only carrying forward a long tradition of conflict between the executive and the judicial branches of the government, and he had attempted to secure his goal through proper legislative channels.

No one could be neutral about Roosevelt. By some it was argued that he had created an enormous, regulatory, governmental bureaucracy, expensive and cumbersome, a positive threat to the freedom and self-reliance of the individual citizen; that taxation had become unfair and oppressive and served to choke initiative and enterprise; that labor had come to overshadow the American economy. To some, like Hoover, the New Deal was a "vast casualty to liberty." But not even his bitterest foes could deny that he had gained and retained power through untrammeled free elections and an unaltered two-party system. Nor could anyone deny his great popularity with the masses of the American people; nor deny that he restored their confidence in the American democracy and the American system of private enterprise at a time when both were in a state of collapse. Despite its waste and inconsistencies, its costliness and unorthodox financial policies, its enlargement of the executive power and expansion of the governmental bureaucracy, the New Deal represented a bold and humanitarian way of meeting the greatest crisis the American republic had ever faced short of the challenge of arms; it preserved and reaffirmed American faith in its democratic system—and that at a time when democracy was succumbing elsewhere.

B ritain, like the United States, even in the troubles of the depression, remained firmly attached to representative institutions and democratic principles. The Great Depression aggravated and intensified Britain's older economic difficulties. More dependent on overseas markets than any other people, the British until 1914 had managed to hold their lead, exporting industrial products and capital, selling insurance and other services, and importing foodstuffs. But in the years before 1914 the British were increasingly losing their markets because of a combination of circumstances, among which must be included the emergence of other economically aggressive industrial powers, the growth of tariff barriers, the development of native textile and other industries in India and elsewhere in the East, the substitution of new textile products for British cottons and woolens, and the substitution of new sources of fuel for British coal. The losses were accelerated by the economic disruption of the First World War, the disappearance of many investments, and the postwar disorganization and impoverishment of markets, though British trade for about a year enjoyed a short-lived boom caused by pent-up demands that could not be satisfied during the war. Exports were hurt too by the general rise in tariffs after the war and the customs barriers raised in the new small states of Europe. Increasingly, after 1918, Britain lived in a world no longer dependent on, or eager for, her manufactures. Britain's very historical primacy as the pioneer industrial country was also a handicap. The British had antiquated machinery and techniques that were easily improved upon by the younger industrial countries starting afresh.

The net result of all this was that in the interwar years, even in times of relative prosperity for the rest of the world, Britain was in depression and suffered severely from unemployment. The unemployment insurance adopted in 1911 was called heavily into play. By 1921 over 2,000,000 unemployed were receiving benefit payments, contemptuously called the "dole" by those who disliked it. Unemployment insurance, an expanded old-age pension system, medical aid, government subsidized housing, and other social welfare measures helped to relieve economic distress and to prevent any drastic decline in the living standards of British workingmen. The welfare state was well under way in Britain before the Labour party took office after the Second World War.

The labor unions made a strenuous effort to retain wage gains and other concessions won in wartime. Industry, hard-pressed itself, resisted. This situation reached a climax in 1926 in the coal mining industry, which was in a particularly bad plight; government subsidies had not helped and even conservative investigators

British Politics: The 1920s and the Depression

had recommended some form of amalgamation and public management. A strike by the coal miners led to a "general strike" supported by the other British unions; about half of the 6,000,000 organized workingmen in Britain left their jobs as a token of their sympathy and solidarity. But the government declared a state of emergency and made use of army and navy personnel and middle-class volunteers to man essential services. The strike ended in failure, and even in a setback for the trade unions, which were put under stricter control by the Trades Disputes Act of 1927, a measure that declared all general or sympathy strikes illegal and even forbade the unions from raising money for political purposes. The act remained in effect until repealed after the Second World War.

After the election of 1922, the Labour party[1] replaced the Liberal party as the second of the two great parties of the country and faced the Conservatives as the official opposition. It was not easy to explain the decline in fortunes of the Liberals. In the election of December 1918 internal dissension over allowing Lloyd George and the party to continue the wartime coalition had led to secession by one group of Liberals; other Liberals were alienated when Lloyd George's postwar coalition government partially abandoned free trade in 1921. But there was perhaps a deeper explanation. The transformation of the Liberals before the war into a party sponsoring labor reform and active government intervention in economic matters has been described.[2] Now, after the war, they were outdistanced by a Labour party which could more consistently and more actively champion both labor legislation and bolder measures to offset Britain's troubled economic state. The Labour party, moreover, which had been no more than a loose federation of trade union and socialist organizations before the war, tightened its organizational structure and, bridging the gap between the trade unionists and the socialists, committed itself in 1918 to a program of socialism. But it was a program of gradualist, democratic socialism operating through customary British parliamentary and political procedures and hence able to gain and retain the good will of large sections of the middle classes.

Twice, in 1924 and in 1929, Labour governed the country with Ramsay MacDonald as prime minister, in each case as a coalition government with Labour dependent on the support of the Liberals for its majority. In 1924 the Labourites proved their moderation; their administration went no further than an extension of unemployment relief and the inauguration of housing and public works projects; indeed the Labour government acted rather firmly in the face of a series of strikes which broke out. Its overthrow was precipitated by its diplomatic recognition of the Soviet Union and the pledge of a loan to the Soviets for the purchase of British goods. Defeat was ensured by the preelection publication of the so-called Red (or Zinoviev) letter purporting to be secret instructions to British labor groups from the head of the Communist International urging preparations for a Communist uprising in Britain.[3] The document's authenticity has never been established, but the Conservatives successfully exploited it and easily won the election of 1924.

[1] See pp. 641, 643.
[2] See pp. 632–633, 662.
[3] See p. 809.

In the election of May 1929, however, Labour's representation almost doubled, and the Conservative representation dropped proportionately. MacDonald again became prime minister of a Labour-dominated coalition government. Thus the Wall Street crash and the world-wide depression broke while the Labour party government was in office. The effects of the depression were quickly felt. Unemployment, which had hovered about the 1,000,000 mark in 1929, soon was approaching the 3,000,000 figure. The government expended large sums to supplement the unemployment insurance payments. Gold was flowing out of the country; tax receipts were declining; the public debt was growing. Alarmed at the mounting deficit, MacDonald took the advice of a committee of financial experts and made plans to introduce a severe economy policy, even to the extent of reducing the "dole" payments. The Labour party was outraged; some of the Labour ministers in his cabinet refused to support him. He and those ministers who went along with him were read out of the party. MacDonald thereupon formed an all-party coalition cabinet known as the National government. In an election in 1931 the new coalition won an overwhelming victory, the Conservative members of the coalition alone winning a majority of the seats in Parliament. MacDonald continued to head the National government. A Conservative-dominated coalition cabinet remained in office thereafter until it was broadened during the Second World War to include the official Labour party too. Thus, as in the United States, the depression led to the ousting by the voters of those in office. The new government, though Conservative in essence, represented an effort to maintain national unity in the face of economic emergency, within the framework of the British parliamentary democracy. Not a single seat in Parliament in this depression election of 1931 went to either the Communists or to a British Fascist party organized by Sir Oswald Mosley; in 1935 the Communists won one seat.

The National government coped with the depression chiefly along retrenchment lines, under Ramsay MacDonald from 1931 to 1935, Stanley Baldwin to 1937, and Neville Chamberlain after 1937. When the economy measures were adopted, protest demonstrations were held in the larger cities and a group of sailors even "mutinied" in protest against their pay cuts; but these were passing events. In addition to its retrenchment policy and budget-balancing, the government made some efforts to encourage industry to reorganize and rationalize production by providing low interest loans. Mainly, the government concentrated on the kind of economic nationalist measures that have already been described—the abandonment of the gold standard and devaluation of the pound in 1931, the curtailment of free trade and the adoption of protectionism in 1932; along with the latter went the system of "imperial preferences" adopted at Ottawa, providing advantageous treatment for British manufactures in the dominions and for dominion agricultural products in Britain.[4] As in the United States, despite some recovery from the depths of the depression, none of the measures taken brought full recovery or full employment. Unemployment persisted until military conscription and an expanded armament program ab-

[4]See p. 843–844.

sorbed the jobless.   The Labour party, partially recovering its strength in the election of 1935, denounced the timid expedients of the Conservatives, whom it held responsible for the apathy and gloom gripping the country.

To the older British Empire, India, the crown colonies, protectorates, and spheres of influence, the postwar settlement added a number of League of Nations mandates. British rule in its various forms extended to almost a half-billion people, a fourth of the earth's population and land surface.   It was principally in Ireland, Egypt, India, and Palestine that the British faced complex imperial problems after the First World War.   In Palestine, where the British exercised a League of Nations mandate, Arabs and Jews fought with each other and with Britain.   In Egypt, in 1922, Britain, although retaining the right to station some troops there, formally ended the protectorate it had established forty years earlier; but many questions, especially the status of the Sudan, remained unresolved.   In India the agitation for national independence, as we have seen, grew more intense.   In these areas nothing resembling a solution was arrived at until after the Second World War.   In Ireland the independence movement largely accomplished its ends.

The Irish question had disoriented English politics for forty years.[5]   Irish home rule, authorized by Parliament in 1914, had been deferred for the duration of the war.   Irish Nationalists, during the war, had accepted German support and had risen in rebellion in 1916.   After the war, in 1919 and 1920, the Irish Nationalist or Sinn Fein party fought a small but savage war of independence against the British forces known as "Black and Tans."   The British blocked independence, but in 1922 recognized the Irish Free State, granting it dominion status.   The Protestant majority in Ulster, the northern counties where Presbyterians of Scottish origin had lived for three centuries, preferred to remain outside the Free State and continued to be joined in the United Kingdom of Great Britain and Northern Ireland, to the vehement dissatisfaction of the Irish republicans.   In 1937 a new constitution for the Irish Free State affirmed the full sovereignty of Ireland (or Eire, as it was now called), the country remaining, however, in the British Commonwealth of Nations.   Politics remained unsettled, for the Irish agitated for the annexation of Ulster, conducted tariff wars with a Britain from which they were now cut off, strove to revive Celtic in place of the English language, and fell into disputes in which Irish moderates were pitted against Irish extremists, the latter perpetrating an occasional assassination, or other outrage, to further their cause.   The last formal ties with the British Commonwealth were severed in 1949, when the Republic of Ireland was proclaimed.   The Irish continued to claim jurisdiction over Ulster and to protest discrimination against the Irish Catholic minority there.

As for the dominions, the political status of these areas of white settlement overseas was now more clearly defined than ever before.   The dominions—Canada, Australia, New Zealand, and the Union of South Africa—had long pursued their own policies, even levying tariffs against British goods.   They had all joined loyally

[5]See pp. 633–634, 662, 738.

with Great Britain in the First World War, but all were stirred by a nationalism of their own and desired their virtual independence to be regularized and promulgated to the world. An imperial conference of 1926 defined "dominion status," which was corroborated by the Statute of Westminster of 1931. The dominions became legally equal with each other and with Great Britain. All alike were "autonomous communities within the British empire, equal in status, in no way subordinate one to another in any aspect of their domestic or external affairs, though united by a common allegiance to the crown, and freely associated as members of the British Commonwealth of Nations." This meant that each of the countries concerned conducted its own affairs in its own way through a parliament and ministry of its own choosing, with the king or his governor-general playing a merely nominal role, as had long been the practice in Great Britain. No act passed by the British Parliament could apply to a dominion save by the dominion's own consent. It was the decision of the Commonwealth ministers as much as that of the British cabinet itself that forced the abdication of Edward VIII in 1936 when he insisted on marriage to a twice divorced woman of American birth, an alliance which it was held would tarnish the prestige of the crown. Despite independent policies in economic matters and even in foreign affairs, the bonds between the dominions and Britain were firm; the support of the dominions in the Second World War was to be vital in Britain's survival. After the war the Commonwealth was to become a larger and even more flexible institution than hitherto.

When the depression came to France, agitation of fascist type made more headway there than in Britain or the United States. Earlier, in the 1920s, France was preoccupied with recovery from the physical destruction of the war, the instability of public finances, and the fear of a resurgent Germany. Immediately after 1919, and for most of the 1920s, the government was run by coalitions of parties of the conservative right, i.e., parties supported by business and financial interests, well disposed toward the army and church, and interested, above all else, in economy and stability in domestic affairs. For about two years, from 1924 to 1926, the Radical Socialists were in control; this party of the moderate left, whose leader was Edouard Herriot, served as spokesman for the lower middle classes, the small businessmen and farmers; it advocated progressive social legislation so long as that did not involve increased taxes. Despite its name, a carry-over from an earlier era, it was firmly committed to private enterprise and private property; it was staunch in its defense of individual liberties and was fervently anticlerical; sometimes, it seemed, its anticlericalism was a substitute for any more positive program. Although the Radical Socialists could cooperate in elections with the Socialists, the other major party of the left, the two parties differed too profoundly on economic policies to preserve stable coalitions. In the 1920s, the Socialists, led by Léon Blum, were still recovering from the postwar secession of the more orthodox Marxists who had formed a French Communist party. Both left and right in France shaded off into antidemocratic groups that were hostile to the parliamentary republic as such. These included the Communists on the left, who sat in parliament and took part in all elections; and on the extreme right, royalists of the

Action Française and other antirepublican organizations, which operated principally outside the Chamber as militant and noisy pressure groups.

The outstanding figure of the moderate conservative right was Raymond Poincaré; it was he who sent troops into the Ruhr in 1923, when the Germans failed to pay reparations; and it was he who now "saved" the franc. The reparations question was extremely important for French finances. The country had undertaken a large-scale reconstruction program to repair the wartime devastation of northern and eastern France and had counted upon the defeated enemy to pay. When German reparations were not paid as anticipated, the public debt mounted, a balanced budget became an impossibility, and the franc declined precipitously. Other factors, too, contributed to French financial difficulties, among them, the huge war expenditures, heavy wartime investment losses notably in Russia, and an outmoded taxation program which invited widespread evasion. Finally, after 1926, when the financial crisis reached a climax, a "national union" ministry under Poincaré took firm action; it inaugurated many new taxes, tightened tax collection somewhat, cut down drastically on government expenditures in order to balance the budget, and eventually stabilized the franc at about one-fifth of its prewar value. The internal debt was thus in effect largely repudiated, to the despair of many bondholders, but the threat of a runaway inflation, like that of the Weimar republic, and national bankruptcy were avoided. From 1926 to 1929 the country prospered. Industry grew; it was still, to be sure, predominantly small-scale and concerned mainly with luxury items, but the war had stimulated heavy industry and mass production; and Alsace and Lorraine were again French. New factories, replacing those destroyed in the war, were modern and up-to-date. The index of industrial production rose; tourists flocked in. As in many other countries, workingmen did not share proportionately in the prosperity of the 1920s. The unions received a sharp setback when, immediately following the war, a series of strikes of major proportions ended in failure; the unions were also divided between a Communist and non-Communist national confederation; collective bargaining in the country was virtually unknown. The workers were not mollified by a social insurance program adopted by a reluctant parliament, which went into effect in 1930.

The Great Depression came later to France than to other industrial countries, partly because the French economy was more evenly balanced between industry and agriculture. After 1930 the effects of the depression were felt, not to the same extent, to be sure, as in the United States or Germany, but still in a telling way. Trade declined. Unemployment and part-time employment increased; at the worst period, in 1935, close to 1,000,000 workers were unemployed; perhaps half of those employed worked part-time. Industrial production, which in 1930 was 40 percent above the prewar level, sank by 1932 back to the 1913 figure. The government displayed the usual pattern of unstable, shifting, short-lived ministries; in 1933 no fewer than five ministries rapidly succeeded one another (there were some forty all told in the twenty interwar years). In 1932, as in 1924, the Radical Socialists again emerged from the elections as the leading party but were unable to maintain a stable left coalition with the Socialists. The cabinets formed after 1932 followed a policy of retrenchment and economy and clung to the gold standard. Meanwhile, in Germany Adolf Hitler had become chancellor in 1933; all France's domestic difficulties were intensified by mounting international tension.

In the uneasy years of the depression, the latent hostility to the republic always present in the country came to the surface. Fascist-type "leagues" appeared in open imitation of Italian and German fascist organizations, many obtaining funds from wealthy industrialists; the older *Action Française* and right-wing veterans' associations like Colonel de la Rocque's *Croix de Feu* were also active. The same elements that had been antirepublican, antidemocratic, or monarchist since the Great Revolution, and which had rallied behind Boulanger and denounced Dreyfus,[6] now grew more strident in their attacks on the parliamentary republic, denouncing its instability and its impotence.

In 1934 it seemed for a moment that the opportunity awaited by the anti-republican elements had come. A political and financial scandal, of the kind familiar in prewar French public life, broke over the country. A financial manipulator and adventurer with excellent political connections, Stavisky by name, induced the municipal authorities at Bayonne to launch a flotation of worthless bonds. Faced with exposure, he fled and then apparently committed suicide; the sensationalist press encouraged the rumor that he had been shot by the police to prevent the implication of high-ranking politicians. A clamor went up accusing the government of involvement in the financial scandal. Where elsewhere such an affair would have called merely for turning the rascally incumbents out of office, in France it supplied ammunition for those who demanded the guillotining of the constitutional regime itself; the republic was equated with corruption and venality.

The agitation reached a climax in the riots of February 1934. A mob of fascist tendency assembled in the Place de la Concorde, threatened the Chamber, and battled with the police; several were killed and hundreds injured. French liberals and democrats, organized labor, and the Socialist party were outraged by the threat to the republic. The Communists were hostile to the fascist groups but were unfriendly to the government too; soon, along with the Comintern, they sensed the danger to themselves and to the Soviet Union in the event of a French fascist triumph and joined with the antifascists. As elsewhere, in the 1930s they emerged from their sectarian revolutionary isolation, became intensely patriotic, and grew considerably in prestige, influence, and appeal. An impressive labor-sponsored general strike was held a week after the riots. Shortly thereafter, the Radical Socialists, Socialists, and Communists drew together in a political coalition that came to be known as the Popular Front, of the kind that was being organized, or advocated, in many countries in the 1930s. It campaigned on a pledge to defend the republic against fascism, to take measures against the depression, and to introduce labor reforms. In the spring of 1936 it won a decisive victory at the polls. The French Socialists for the first time in

---

[6] See pp. 628–631.

their history became the leading party in the Chamber; their chief, Léon Blum, long an eloquent spokesman for democratic and reformist socialism, became premier of a coalition cabinet of Socialists and Radical Socialists; the Communists, who had increased their representation in the Chamber from 10 to 72 seats, did not join the cabinet but pledged their support.

The Popular Front and After

Blum's Popular Front ministry, although it lasted little more than a year, put through a program of legislation unprecedented in French parliamentary annals. In part, this was due to the Popular Front election program; in part it was due to unforeseen events, for the tremendous enthusiasm generated by the victory led to a spontaneous nationwide wave of "sit-down strikes," which did not subside until Blum pledged a number of immediate reforms.

Through Blum's mediation, industry at once awarded a blanket wage increase to all workers and promised to cooperate with social legislation passed by parliament. Parliament in short order passed laws providing for a forty-hour week, vacations with pay, and a collective bargaining law. As in the case of the Wagner Act in the United States, the encouragement now given to collective bargaining led to the nationwide signing of collective contracts for the first time in the country's history; similarly, the government protection and encouragement given to union organizing led to an enormous growth in trade union membership, which grew from about 1,000,000 to 5,000,000 in about a year. Labor's strength was increased also by a reunification of the Communist and non-Communist labor confederations. Other legislation was important too. Steps were taken to nationalize the armaments and aviation industry; the fascist armed leagues were, at least in theory, dissolved; the Bank of France was reorganized and placed under government control to break the power of the "two hundred families." Machinery was established for the arbitration of labor disputes. Aid was given to farmers through price fixing and government purchases of wheat. As in the United States all these measures aimed at both recovery and reform; Blum spoke openly of his program as a "French New Deal." Like the American program, it was intended to create mass purchasing power, absorb the unemployed, and stimulate industry. No large-scale public works program was launched, however, nor was "deficit financing" resorted to; and the Blum government was too dependent on its middle-class Radical Socialist allies to introduce any fundamental, or "structural," reforms. Still, French workers and the little man took heart: the "social republic" again seemed a possibility. But French conservatives, and the quasi-fascists to their right, cried revolution; they uttered dark predictions that a French Lenin would follow Blum. They did not conceal their sullen resentment at what had come to pass: the fate of Catholic France was in the hands of a leftist, a Socialist, and a Jew. Even salvation by a warrior from outside the country, one who had demonstrated his anti-Bolshevism, would be preferable. They envied the protection given to established interests by Mussolini; and there were those who even muttered "better Hitler than Léon Blum."

In all truth the Popular Front reform program, long overdue as it was, came to France at a time when the sands were rapidly running out. While France had a forty-hour week, German arms plants were operating at full capacity. In the shadow of Nazi remilitarization a rearmament program had to be undertaken at the very same time as reform; even moderates argued that the country could not afford both. Opposition from many quarters hindered success. French employers balked at cooperating in the new reforms and tried to pass on rising production costs to the consumer. Labor was disgruntled at the rise in prices that canceled out their wage gains. Both employers and labor applied the forty-hour week in such a manner that plants were shut down for two days a week instead of operating in shifts, as the law had intended. Nothing could check the flight of gold from the country. Industrial production hardly rose; even in 1938, when it had shown substantial recovery in other countries, it was only 5 percent higher in France than at the depth of the depression. The Communists attacked the Blum government for refusing aid to the hard-pressed Spanish Popular Front government across the Pyrenees; Blum, following the lead of Britain and fearing involvement, resisted. In 1937, after a year in office, the Blum government was overthrown by the Senate, which refused to grant it emergency financial powers. The Popular Front coalition rapidly disintegrated. By mid-1938 the Radical Socialists had abandoned their allies on the left, and under Édouard Daladier formed a conservative ministry, whose attention was increasingly occupied by the international crisis. Little remained of the Popular Front, or indeed of the strength of labor, which declined rapidly and exhausted itself further by a general strike in 1938 in protest against nullification of the forty-hour week; the strike was broken by the government and was followed by retaliatory legal measures. For the French workingman, 1936 had gone the way of other "great years"; the comfortable classes had been thrown into panic by the social turmoil; internal division and class hatreds had grown sharper. Yet the French democracy, the Third Republic itself, had been successfully preserved and its domestic enemies repulsed, at least for a time.

Trials and Adjustments of Democracy in Britain and France

Britain and France, and indeed all western Europe, Europe's "inner zone," never fully recovered from the Great Depression before the Second World War came. When economic expansion later resumed after the war, the interwar years seemed like a deep trough in Europe's economic history. Western Europe barely maintained its old inherited equipment in the depression and was unable to utilize even its existing machinery to capacity. Moreover, as the events of 1929 had clearly shown, Europe's economic dependence on the United States was pronounced, and the U.S.S.R. was becoming an industrial giant. The economic destiny of Europeans in the 1930s was very much in doubt.

Western Europe and the Depression

There were other signs of decline. The birth rate in western Europe in the 1930s declined to its lowest recorded levels as young people postponed marriage and married people limited the size of their families because of economic and psychological stresses. Birth rates did not run significantly higher than death rates, the population stagnating and growing older.   Politically neither British nor French democratic political leaders were able to cope successfully with the economic dilemmas of the depression era.   Nor could the Socialists, who found neither Marxian economics nor class struggle ideas helpful but who failed to renew or reinvigorate their doctrines in any significant way.   The economic ideas of Keynes, whose *General Theory of Employment, Interest, and Money* appeared in 1936, were hardly known outside academic circles and had little impact.   Yet parliamentary and democratic institutions survived the challenge they faced in western Europe (and in the Scandinavian countries), although the increased power of the executive and the frequent resort to full or emergency powers were alarmingly symptomatic of a general parliamentary decline.   Elsewhere, in eastern, central, and southern Europe the political outcome was very different; here the democratic machinery introduced after 1919 was being replaced by dictatorship and in some cases by the new phenomenon of fascism or totalitarianism.

Though they shade into each other imperceptibly, it is well to distinguish dictatorship from totalitarianism.   Dictatorship, an old phenomenon in history, has commonly been regarded as a mere expedient, designed for emergencies and believed to be temporary; at most, it is a theory of government.   Totalitarianism, as it arose after the World War, was not merely a theory of government but a theory of life and of human nature.   It claimed to be no expedient but a permanent form of society and civilization, and so far as it appealed to emergency for justification, it regarded life itself as an everlasting emergency.   Let us first review the pertinent events in Italy and Germany, return next to the general ideas of totalitarianism, and then, in the final section of the chapter, trace the story of totalitarian foreign aggression and crises which in 1939 again led to a world war.

The belief widely held in the 1920s, that democracy was generally advancing, was not deeply disturbed by the failure of Russia or Turkey or China to develop effective parliaments or liberal institutions.   These were backward countries, in the throes of revolution; some day, when conditions quieted down, it could be supposed, they would move forward to democracy as known in the West.   The first jarring exception to the apparent victory of democracy was furnished by Italy, a country that was part and parcel of civilized Europe, one which since 1861 had accepted parliamentary liberalism, but where, as early as 1922, Benito Mussolini seized control of the government and proclaimed *Fascismo.*

Mussolini, born in 1883, the son of a blacksmith, was a fiery and pugnacious character, who before the war had followed the career of professional revolutionary, left-wing socialist, and radical journalist.   He had read and digested such works as Sorel's *Reflections on Violence* and Nietzsche's writings.[7]   During the war he turned intensely nationalist, clamored for intervention on the side of the Allies, and

[7]See pp. 651, 661–662.

demanded the conquest from Austria of *Italia irredenta,* the "unredeemed" Italian lands to the north and across the Adriatic. In the war he rose to the rank of corporal. In March 1919 he organized, mainly from demobilized and restless ex-soldiers, his first fighting band or *Fascio di Combattimento. Fascio* meant a bunch or bundle, as of sticks; it called to mind the Latin *fasces,* or bundles of rods, carried by the lictors in ancient Rome as a symbol of state power—for Mussolini loved to conjure up ancient glories.

In 1919 Italian glories were dim. Italy had entered the war on the side of the Allies quite frankly for territorial and colonial spoils; the secret treaty of London in 1915 promised the Italians certain Austrian lands and a share in German and Turkish possessions. During the war Italian arms did not especially shine; Italian troops were routed at Caporetto in 1917. Yet Italy lost over 600,000 lives in the war, and the Italian delegates came to the peace conference confident that their sacrifices would be recognized and their territorial aspirations satisfied. They were rapidly disappointed. Wilson refused to honor the provisions of the London secret treaty and other demands of the Italians. Britain and France displayed no eagerness to side with Italy. The Italians received some of the Austrian territories promised to them, but they were given no part of the former German or Turkish possessions as mandates.

After the war Italy, like other countries, suffered from the burden of wartime debt and from acute postwar depression and unemployment. Social unrest spread. In the countryside land seizures took place, not in any significant proportions but enough to spread concern among landowners; tenant farmers refused to pay rents; peasants burned crops and destroyed livestock. In the cities great strikes broke out in heavy industry and in such vital services as transportation. Some of the strikes turned into sit-down strikes, the workers refusing to leave the plants; demands were raised even for worker control of the factories. Moderate socialist and labor leaders disavowed all such extremism, but left-wing socialists who, as elsewhere, had turned communist and joined the Third International, fanned the existing discontents. Meanwhile, armed bands of young men, most prominent of whom were the Blackshirts or Fascists, brawled with communists and ordinary workingmen in the streets. By the late summer of 1920 the strikes and the agrarian unrest had subsided, although violence in the streets persisted.

During the months of turmoil the government itself refrained from any bold action. The Italian parliamentary system in the prewar years had never functioned impressively nor commanded widespread esteem; now respect for parliament and the weak, shifting, postwar coalition ministries sank even lower. In 1919 the first postwar election had been held, under a law that added proportional representation to the manhood suffrage introduced in 1913. The Socialists and a new Catholic Popular, or Christian Socialist, party made an impressive showing. In 1921, in the wake of the postwar disturbances, new elections were held. Liberals and democrats, moderate socialists, and the Catholic Popular party were all returned in large numbers. Mussolini's Fascist movement won 35 of the 500-odd seats. Despite this less than impressive showing (the best ever made by the Fascists in a totally free election), the Fascist ranks had been swelling, in the backwash, as it were, of the postwar unrest.

Although the social agitation had died down, burning itself out on its own, and there had in actuality never been any real threat of a Soviet-style revolution, the propertied classes had gone through a great fright; they found comfort in the Fascist movement and were willing to lend it financial support.

Mussolini and the Fascists had at first gone along with the radical tide; they had not disapproved the factory seizures; they had inveighed against plutocracy and war profiteers and called for a high levy on capital and profits. But Mussolini, never one to sacrifice opportunity to save principles or doctrine, had soon come forward with his Fascists as the upholders of national law and order, and hence property; he pledged battle "against the forces dissolving victory and nation." The propertied interests gave financial aid to the self-styled bulwark against Bolshevism; patriots and nationalists of all classes rallied to it; and the lower middle class, pinched by economic inflation and, as elsewhere, unable to find protection or solace in labor unions or socialist movements, joined too. The black-shirted upholders of national order meanwhile proceeded methodically to administer beatings (and doses of castor oil) to Communists and alleged Communists, to Socialists and Christian Socialists, and to ordinary persons who did not support them; nor did they refrain from arson and murder. Vigilante squadrons, the *squadristi*, broke up strikes, demolished labor union headquarters, and drove from office duly elected Socialist and Communist mayors and town officials. Mussolini reinforced his claim as paladin of law, authority, and order by declaring his loyalty to king and church; a few years earlier he had been a rabid republican and anticlerical.

In October 1922 took place the "March on Rome." The Blackshirts mobilized for a threatened coup and began to converge from various directions on the capital; Mussolini remained at a safe distance in Milan. The liberal-democratic coalition cabinet had viewed the events of the past two years with disapproval but at the same time with the undeniable satisfaction that the Blackshirts were serving something of a useful national purpose by suppressing trouble-makers on the left. Now they made belated but ineffectual gestures to save the situation by an effort to have martial law declared; the king refused to approve. The cabinet resigned and Mussolini was named premier. It was all quite legal, or almost so. Indeed Italy was still in form a constitutional and parliamentary government. Mussolini headed only a coalition ministry and received from parliament no more than a year's grant of full emergency powers to restore order and introduce reforms.

But soon it was clear in whose hands power rested. Before the expiration of his emergency powers Mussolini forced through parliament a law providing that any party securing the largest number of votes in an election should automatically receive two-thirds of the seats in the legislature. This was Mussolini's solution to the instability of coalitions and blocs in parliamentary governments like those of Italy and France, and indeed most other Continental democracies, where a single party hardly ever enjoyed a majority. The two-thirds law was not even necessary. In the 1924 elections, aided by government control of the electoral machinery and use of the *squadristi*, but still in relatively uncontrolled elections in which seven opposition slates appeared, the Fascists received well over three-fifths of the total vote.

Within a few years after 1924 Mussolini reduced the Italian parliament to a non-entity, curtailed universal male suffrage, put the press under censorship, destroyed the labor unions and deprived labor of the right to strike, and abolished all other political parties. A secret police was established and special tribunals set up to try opponents of the regime; a new official Fascist militia replaced the *squadristi*—it continued to employ many of the old methods.

Fascism in the 1920s was an innovation which the rest of the world was slow to understand. In 1924 (when dissenters were still allowed in the parliament) the socialist deputy Matteotti publicly exposed hundreds of cases of armed Fascist violence, and of fraud and chicanery in elections. He was soon murdered by Fascists. For a government in civilized Europe to dispose of its critics by assassination was something of a novelty. Mussolini strutted, stuck out his jaw, and glared ferociously; he jumped through flaming hoops to show his virility and had his chief subordinates do likewise; to the outside world this seemed an odd way of demonstrating fitness for public office. He denounced democracy as historically outmoded and declared that it accentuated class struggle, split people into countless minority parties, and led to selfishness, futility, evasion, and empty talk. In place of democracy he preached the need of vigorous action, under a strong leader; he himself took the title of Leader or *Duce.* He denounced liberalism, free trade, laissez faire, and capitalism, along with Marxism, materialism, socialism, and class-consciousness, which he said were the evil offspring of liberal and capitalistic society. In their place he preached national solidarity and state management of economic affairs, under the same Leader's far-seeing and audacious vision. And in fact Mussolini seemed to bring a kind of efficiency to easy-going Italy; as the saying went, at least he made the trains run on time.

Mussolini introduced, at least in theory, the syndical, or corporative state. This had been discussed in both left- and right-wing circles for many years. Left-wing syndicalism, especially before the First World War, looked to revolutionary labor unions to expropriate the owners of industry and then to assume the direction of political and economic life. A more conservative syndicalism was endorsed and encouraged by the Catholic church, with which, as has been noted in a previous chapter, Mussolini made his peace with the signing of the Lateran accord in 1929.[8] The conservative type looked nostalgically toward a revival of the medieval gilds, or "corporations," in which master and journeymen, employer and employees, had labored side by side in a golden age of collaboration and social peace. The Fascist corporative system really resembled neither, because in it the hand of the state was writ large, something which none of the older corporative doctrines had anticipated. It went through a number of complicated stages, but as it finally emerged by the 1930s it provided for the division of all economic life into twenty-two major areas, for each of which a "corporation" was established. In each corporation representatives of the Fascist-organized labor groups, the employers, and the government determined working conditions, wages, prices, and industrial policies; and in a national council

[8] See p. 656.

these representatives were supposed jointly to devise plans for Italy's economic self-sufficiency. In each case the role of government was decisive and the whole structure was under the jurisdiction of Mussolini's Minister of Corporations. As a final step, these corporative economic chambers were integrated into the government proper so that in 1938 the old Chamber of Deputies was superseded by a Chamber of Fasces and Corporations representing the corporations and the Fascist party, its members selected by the government and not subject to popular ratification.

None of this was democratic, but this was an improvement over democracy, the Fascists asserted. A legislature in an advanced economic society, they said, should be an economic parliament; it should represent not political parties and geographical constituencies but economic occupations. Organization along such lines would do away with the anarchy and class conflict engendered by free capitalism, which only sap the strength of the national state. Real authority in any event rested with the government—the Head of the Government, who settled most matters by decree. In point of fact, social unrest and class conflict were "ended," not by the corporative system as such, but by the prohibition of strikes and lockouts and the abolition of independent labor unions. The corporative system represented the most extreme form of state control over economic life within a framework of private enterprise and a relatively capitalistic economy, that is, one in which ownership rested in private hands. It was the Fascist answer to Western-style democracy and to Soviet proletarian dictatorship. Fascism, said Mussolini, is the "dictatorship of the state over many classes cooperating."

When the depression struck, none of Italy's economic controls availed very much. Mussolini was eager to lay upon the world depression the blame for Italy's continuing economic ills. He turned to a vigorous program of public works and to increasing economic self-sufficiency. A "battle of wheat" was launched as a campaign to increase food production; progress was made in reclaiming swamp areas in central Italy and in developing hydroelectric power as a substitute for the coal which Italy lacked. Throughout the Fascist era no fundamental reform took place in the position of the peasants. The existing structure of society, which in Italy meant social extremes of wealth and poverty, remained unaltered. Fascism failed to provide either the economic security or the material well-being for which it had demanded the sacrifice of individual freedom. But it undeniably substituted a widespread psychological exhilaration, a feeling that Italy was undergoing a heroic national revival; and after 1935 to support that feeling Mussolini turned increasingly to military and imperialist adventures.

Fascism came to be regarded in other countries as a possible alternative to democratic or parliamentary government, as an actual corrective to troubles whose reality no one could deny. All communists hated it, and so did all socialists, labor leaders, moderate leftists, and idealistic liberals; wealthier or established people, because of fear of Bolshevism, made more allowances in its favor. In east-European countries, often highly nationalistic, or influenced by disgruntled landowners, or simply unused to settling questions by majority vote, Fascism made a considerable appeal. In the Latin countries, in Spain, Portugal, and France, Mussolini's corporative state found champions and admirers. Sometimes, in Europe and elsewhere, intellectuals spun refined, respectable theories about the new order of discipline and authority, forgetting how Mussolini himself with unusual candor had written, "Fascism was not the nursling of a doctrine worked out beforehand with detailed elaboration; it was born of the need for action."

I t was in Germany that Mussolini found his aptest pupil. Born in Austria in 1889, Adolf Hitler was too young to have done much before the war. He was not an intellectual, like the prewar journalist Mussolini. He was never a socialist, but he fell into a restless and somewhat ignorant type of radicalism. Son of a small government employee, orphaned at an early age, he came at nineteen to the great metropolis of Vienna, without friends, money, or means of making a living, often going hungry, or sleeping in what Americans would call flop houses, a good example of uprooted humanity which the preceding half-century had thrown pell-mell into huge industrial cities. The young Hitler did not like what he saw in Vienna: neither the trappings of the Habsburg court, nor the noblemen of eastern Europe who rode by in their carriages, nor the mixed nationalities of the Danubian empire, nor the Vienna workingman's attachment to international Marxism, nor above all the Jews, who thanks to a century of liberal influences had become assimilated to the German culture and now occupied many distinguished positions in business, law, medicine, and journalism in the city. He became exceedingly race-conscious, like many others in many countries at the time,[9] but to the youthful Hitler it gave a special satisfaction to think of himself as a pure German of the good old German stock. He became violently anti-Semitic, and he also disliked aristocracy, capitalism, socialism, cosmopolitanism, internationalism, and "hybridization."

His aversion for Austria led him to move to the south German state of Bavaria in 1913. Here he followed no particular trade but managed to sell a few watercolors. In the war he served in the German army. Like Mussolini, he rose no further than corporal. It is quite possible that in a more democratic society both Hitler and Mussolini, who were both of lower middle-class families, would have received commissions and enjoyed promotion. For Hitler, as for Mussolini, and for countless others, the war was a thrilling, noble, and liberating experience. The average man, in modern society, led a pretty dull existence. Peace, for many, was a drab routine from which war was an exciting emancipation. Human atoms, floating in an impersonal and unfriendly world, they were stirred by the nationalism which the war aroused into a sense of belonging to, believing in, fighting for something greater than themselves, but which was yet their own. When peace returned, they felt a moral letdown.

After the war the demobilized Hitler, with no future, and no place in society to which to return, drifted back to Bavaria. Bavaria in 1919 was a main focus of the Communist offensive in central Europe; a Bavarian Soviet Republic even existed for

---

[9]See pp. 648, 657–658, 673, 723, 828.

105
**Totalitarianism:
Germany's
Third Reich**

*The Rise of
Adolf Hitler*

about three weeks until crushed by the predominantly Social Democratic German federal government. But the Communist threat made Bavaria a busy center of all kinds of counterrevolutionary agitation—anticommunist, antisocialist, antirepublican, and antidemocratic. A transposition in fact occurred after the World War, by which south Germany, always in the past more liberal than the north, became the seat of a disgruntled illiberalism, while Prussia became the main pillar of German democracy because of the large working-class population in Berlin and the Ruhr. Bavaria in particular swarmed with secret societies led by discontented army officers or others who fitted with difficulty into the new regime. One tiny group pretentiously called itself the German Workers' party, and of this "party," in 1919, Adolf Hitler became one of the early members. In 1920 it renamed itself the National Socialist German Workers' party, though Hitler at this time, it is said, would have preferred the term Social Revolutionary. Thus were born the Nazis, so called from the German way of pronouncing the first two syllables of *National*.

In earlier pages we have noted the beginnings of the Weimar republic and the burdens it was compelled to bear from the start—the Versailles peace, reparations, the catastrophic inflation of 1923.[10] Something has been said also of the failure of the republicans to inaugurate the kind of deep social changes that might have democratized the political and social structure of German society and thereby strengthened republican forces. For five years after the war, violence remained sporadic in Germany. Communist agitation continued; but more dangerous, because they attracted more sympathy among the Germans, were the maneuvers of monarchist and antirepublican organizations, which maintained armed bands and threatened uprisings like the Kapp *Putsch* of 1920.[11] (One such private "army" was the Brownshirts or Storm Troopers maintained by the Nazis.) Such bands even resorted to assassination. Thus Walter Rathenau was murdered in 1922; he had organized German production during the war, and in 1922 he was foreign minister, but he had democratic and internationalist inclinations—and was a Jew. Another victim was Matthias Erzberger, a leading moderate politician of the Catholic Center party—he had helped "betray" the army by signing the armistice.

In 1923, when reparations payments were not forthcoming, the French army occupied the Ruhr. A clamor of national indignation swept over Germany. Hitler and the National Socialists, who since 1919 had obtained a considerable following, denounced the Weimar government for shameful submission to the French. They judged the moment opportune for seizing power, and at the end of 1923, in imitation of Mussolini's march on Rome the year before, the Brownshirts staged the "beer-hall *Putsch*" in Munich. Hitler jumped on the platform, fired a revolver at the ceiling, and shouted that the "national revolution has broken out." But the police suppressed the disturbance, and Hitler was sentenced to five years in prison. He was released in less than a year; the Weimar democracy dealt mildly with its enemies. In prison he wrote his book, *Mein Kampf* (*My Struggle*), a turbid stream of personal recollection, racialism, nationalism, collectivism, theories of history, Jew-baiting, and political comment.

[10] See pp. 824–825.
[11] See p. 822.

The former corporal was not alone in his ideas; no less a person than General Luden-dorff, who had distinguished himself in the war,[12] and after the war became one of the most grotesquely unbalanced of the old officer class, gave his warm support to Hitler and even took part in the beer-hall *Putsch*.

Beginning in 1924, with the French out of the Ruhr, reparations adjusted, a new and stable currency adopted, and loans from foreign countries, mainly America, Germany began to enjoy an amazing economic revival. National Socialism lost its appeal, the party lost members, Hitler was regarded as a charlatan and his followers as a lunatic fringe. All seemed quiet. Then came the great depression in 1929. Adolf Hitler, who without the depression might have faded out of history, was made by the circumstances attending the depression in Germany into a figure of Napoleonic proportions.

No country suffered more than Germany from the world-wide economic collapse. Foreign loans abruptly ceased or were recalled. Factories ground to a halt. There were 6,000,000 unemployed. The middle class had not really recovered from the great inflation of 1923;[13] when struck again, after so brief a respite, they lost all faith in the economic system and in its future. The communist vote steadily mounted; the great middling masses, who saw in communism their own death warrant, and who are extremely numerous in any highly developed society, looked about desperately for someone to save them from Bolshevism. The depression also stirred up the universal German loathing for the Treaty of Versailles. Many Germans explained the ruin of Germany by the postwar treatment it had received from the Allies—the constriction of its frontiers, the loss of its colonies, markets, shipping, and foreign investments, the colossal demand for reparations, the oc-cupation of the Ruhr, the inflation, and much else.

Any people in such a trap would have been bewildered and resentful. But the way out chosen by the Germans was perhaps distinctively German, arising from deeper attitudes formed by German experience in the past centuries. Democ-racy—the agreement to obtain and accept majority verdicts, to discuss and compromise, to adjust conflicting interests without wholly satisfying or wholly crushing either side—was hard enough to maintain in any country in a true crisis. In Germany democracy was itself an innovation, which had yet to prove its value, which could easily be called un-German, an artificial and imported doctrine, or even a foreign system foisted upon Germany by the victors in the late war.

Hitler inflamed all such feelings by his propaganda. He denounced the Treaty of Versailles as a national humiliation. He denounced the Weimar democracy for producing class struggle, division, weakness, and wordy futility. He called for "true" democracy in a vast and vital stirring of the people, or *Volk*, behind a Leader who was a man of action. He declared that Germans, pure Germans, must rely only on themselves. He inveighed against Marxists, Bolsheviks, communists, and socialists, throwing them all together in a deliberate beclouding of the issues; but he claimed to favor the right kind of socialism for the little man, i.e., the doctrine of the National

---

[12] See pp. 747, 748.
[13] See pp. 824–825.

Socialist German Workers' party. He ranted against unearned incomes, war profits, the power of the great trusts and chain stores, land speculators, interest slavery, and unfair taxes. Above all, he denounced the Jews. Jews, like others, were found in all political camps. To the left, Jewish capitalists were anathema. To the right, Jewish revolutionaries were a horror. In anti-Semitism Hitler found a lowest common denominator upon which to appeal to all parties and classes. The thoughtless and the ignorant, who comprehended nothing of economics or social forces, found it easy enough to identify a Jew; and on being told that the Jews caused the country's troubles, they experienced a new sense of political understanding. At the same time the Jews were a small minority (only 600,000 in all Germany), so that in an age of mass politics it was safe enough to attack them.

In the election of 1930 the Nazis won 107 seats in the Reichstag; in 1928 they had won only 12; their popular vote went up from 800,000 to 6,500,000. The Communist representation rose from 54 to 77. The depression went on, hopelessness and desperation became deeper. Frequent elections had to be held because no workable majority was possible; the Center-Right combination under Bruening governed weakly. In July 1932 the Nazis more than doubled their popular vote, won 230 seats, and were now by far the largest single party though because of the multiplicity of parties they fell well short of a majority. In another election, in November 1932, the Nazis, though still well out in front, showed some loss of strength, losing two million votes, and dropping to 196 seats. The Communist vote had risen progressively to a peak of 100 in November 1932.

After the relative setback of November 1932 Hitler feared that his moment was passing. But certain conservative, nationalist, and antirepublican elements—old aristocrats, Junker landowners, army officers, Rhineland steel magnates, and other industrialists—had conceived the idea that Hitler could be useful to them. From such sources came a portion of Nazi funds. This group of big men, mainly of the small Nationalist party, imagined that they would be able to control Hitler and hence control the wave of mass discontent of which in such large measure he had made himself the leader; they were little disturbed by his anticapitalist program.

After Bruening's resignation in June 1932, Franz von Papen headed a Nationalist cabinet with the backing of the influential army leader, General Kurt von Schleicher, but in December 1932 Schleicher forced Papen's downfall and succeeded him. When he, too, was compelled to resign a month later, both men, intriguing separately, prevailed upon President Hindenburg to name Hitler chancellor of a coalition cabinet. On January 30, 1933, by entirely legal means, Adolf Hitler became chancellor of the German Republic; other positions in the new cabinet were occupied by the Nationalists, with whom the Nazis were to share power. But to share power was not their aim. Hitler called for another election. A week before election day the Reichstag building caught fire. The Nazis, without any real evidence, blamed it on the communists. They raised up a terrific Red scare, suspended freedom of speech and press, and set loose the Brownshirts to bully the voters. Even so, in the election, the Nazis won only 44 percent of the vote; with their Nationalist allies, they had 52 percent. Hitler, trumpeting a national emergency, was voted dictatorial powers by a pliant Reichstag from which the Communist deputies had been excluded. The Nazi Revolution now began.

Hitler called his new order the Third Reich. He declared that, following on the First Reich or Holy Roman Empire, and the Second Reich or empire founded by Bismarck, the Third Reich carried on the process of true-German history, of which, he said, it was the organic outgrowth and natural culmination. The Third Reich, he prophesied, would last a thousand years.

Like Mussolini, Hitler took the title of Leader, or, in German, the *Führer*. He claimed to represent the absolute sovereignty of the German People. Jews were considered un-German. Democracy, parliamentarianism, and liberalism were stigmatized as "Western" and together with communism labeled as "Jewish." The new "racial science," whose high priest was Alfred Rosenberg, classified Jews as non-Aryan [14] and included as Jewish anyone who had had one Jewish grandparent. The Nuremberg laws of 1935 deprived Jews of all citizenship rights and forbade intermarriage between Jews and non-Jews. Jews were beaten up, hounded, driven from public office, ruined in private business, fined as a community, put to death, or allowed to flee the country after being stripped of all their possessions. The anti-Semitism of some fanatics descended to positive bestiality; it foreshadowed the wartime physical extermination of millions of German and east-European Jewry.

The new order was thought of as absolutely solid, or monolithic, like one huge single slab of rock in which no particle had any separate structure. Germany ceased to be federal; the old states such as Prussia and Bavaria were abolished, so that the historic process of German unification was carried forward. All political parties except the National Socialists were destroyed. The Nazi party was itself violently purged on the night of June 30, 1934, when many of the old Brownshirt leaders, those who represented the more social-revolutionary wing of the movement, were accused of plotting against Hitler and were summarily shot. A secret political police, the Gestapo (*Geheime Staatspolizei*), together with People's Courts, and a system of permanent concentration camps in which thousands were detained without trial or sentence, suppressed all ideas at variance with the Leader's. Law itself was defined as the will of the German people operating in the interests of the Nazi state. Churches both Protestant and Catholic were "coordinated" with the new regime; their clergy were forbidden to criticize its activities, international religious ties were discountenanced, and efforts were made to keep children out of religious schools. The government encouraged anti-Christian pagan movements, in worship of the old Teutonic gods, but nothing was sponsored so much as worship of Nazism and its Führer. A Nazi Youth Movement, and schools and universities, indoctrinated the rising generation in the new concepts. Meanwhile, the severe repression thwarted the efforts of a few dedicated men to develop a broad resistance movement.

[14]See note p. 6.

Labor unions also were "coordinated": they were replaced by a National Labor Front. Strikes were forbidden. Under the "leadership principle" employers were set up as small-scale Führers in their factories and industries and given extensive control subject to the closest government supervision. An extensive public works program was launched, reforestation and swamp-drainage projects were organized, housing and super-highways were built. A vast rearmament program absorbed the unemployed and within a short time unemployment had significantly declined. Even under Nazi statistics labor's share in the national income was reduced, but workingmen had jobs; and an organization called Strength Through Joy attended to the needs of people with small incomes, providing entertainment, vacations, and travel for many who could never otherwise afford them.

The government assumed increasing controls over industry, while leaving ownership in private hands. In 1936 it adopted a Four-Year Plan of economic development under the supervision of Hermann Göring. All countries after the great depression tended to economic nationalism, but Nazi Germany set up the goal of autarchy and self-sufficiency—absolute independence from foreign trade. German chemists developed artificial rubber, plastics, synthetic textiles, and many other substitute products to enable the country to do without raw materials imported from overseas. Germany took advantage of its position as the chief market on which east Europeans were dependent. Mixing political threats with ordinary business, the Nazis bartered for Polish wheat, Hungarian lumber, or Rumanian oil, often giving in return such articles as it was convenient for Germany to dispose of, rather than those that the east Europeans wanted. For Europe as a whole one of the basic economic problems, especially after the World War, was that while the Continent was economically a unit dependent on exchange between diverse regions, politically it was cut to pieces by tariff restrictions, currency differences and hot-house industries artificially nurtured by nationalist ambition. The Nazis claimed to have a solution for this problem in a network of bilateral trade agreements assuring all neighboring peoples an outlet for their products. But it was a solution in which Germans were to be the most industrial, most advanced, most powerful and most wealthy, and other Europeans relegated to permanently inferior status. And what could not be accomplished under trade agreements and economic penetration could be accomplished by conquest and war. Within a few years after 1933 the Nazi Revolution had turned Germany into a huge disciplined war machine, its internal foes liquidated or silenced, its munitions plants going full blast, its mesmerized masses roaring their approval in giant demonstrations, ready to follow the Führer in storming new Valkyrian heights. "Today Germany," went an ominous Nazi phrase, "tomorrow the whole world."

Totalitarianism:
Some Origins
and Consequences

Totalitarianism was a many-sided thing. It had appeared first with the Bolshevik Revolution, for in the denial of individual liberty the Soviet regime did not differ from the most extreme anti-Soviet or fascist totalitarianism as manifested in Germany. There were at first important differences in principle. Theoretically, the proletarian dictatorship was temporary; it did not glorify the individual Leader-Hero; and it was not nationalistic, for it rested on a principle of world-wide class struggle in all nations alike. It adopted a democratic-sounding constitution and paid at least lip service to the idea of a bill of rights. Its constitution officially condemned racism, and it did not deliberately and consciously cultivate an ethics of war and violence. But as time passed, Soviet totalitarianism became harder to distinguish from others. The Soviet dictatorship and one-party state seemed as permanent as any political system; the hollowness of the constitution and bill of rights became more apparent; a leader cult developed around the person of Stalin; and the emphasis became more nationalistic, falling less on the workers of the world and more on the glories of the Soviet Fatherland.

Totalitarianism, as distinct from mere dictatorship, though it appeared rather suddenly after the First World War, was no historic freak. It was an outgrowth of a good deal of development in the past. The state was an institution that had continuously acquired new powers ever since the Middle Ages; step by step, since feudal times, it had assumed jurisdiction over law courts and men at arms, imposed taxes, regulated churches, guided economic policy, operated school systems, and devised schemes of public welfare. The First World War had continued and advanced the process.[15] The twentieth-century totalitarian state, mammoth and monolithic, claiming an absolute domination over every department of life, now carried this old development of state sovereignty to a new extreme. For centuries, for example, the state had clashed with the church; from Philip the Fair of France in 1303, down through Henry VIII, the enlightened despots, the French Revolutionaries, Napoleon, Mazzini, Bismarck—the list was a long one of those who had come into conflict with the Christian churches. The twentieth-century dictators did the same. In addition, however, they were in most cases not merely anticlerical but explicitly anti-Christian, offering, or rather imposing, a "total" philosophy of life.

This new philosophy drew heavily upon a historic nationalism which it greatly exaggerated. It derived in part from the organic theory of society, which held that society (or the nation or state) was a kind of living organism within which the individual person was but a single cell. The individual, in this theory, had no independent existence; he received life itself, and all his ideas, from the society, people, nation, or culture into which he was born and by which he was nurtured. In Marxism, the absolute subordination of the individual to his class came to much the same thing. The individual was a microscopic cell, meaningless outside the social body. He was a little particle within a monolithic slab. He was but clay to be molded by the imprint of his group. It made little sense, given such theories, to speak of the individual's "reason" or "freedom," or to allow individuals to have their own opinions (which were formed for them by environment), or to count up individual opinions to obtain a merely numerical majority. Valid ideas were those of the group as a whole, of the people or nation (or, in Marxism, the class) as a solid block. Even science was a product of specific societies: there was a "Nazi science" which was bound to differ in

[15] See pp. 749–754.

its conclusions from democratic, bourgeois, Western, or "Jewish" science; and for the Soviets there was a Soviet science, consistent with dialectical materialism, and better equipped to see the truth than the decadent bourgeois, capitalistic, or "fascist" science of the non-Soviet world. All art, too—music, painting, poetry, fiction, architecture, sculpture—was good art insofar as it expressed the society or nationality in which it grew.

The avowed philosophy of totalitarian regimes (like much modern thought) was basically subjective. Whether an idea was held to be true depended on whose idea it was. Ideas of truth, or beauty, or right were not supposed to correspond to any outer or objective reality; they had only to correspond to the inner nature, interests, or point of view of the people, nation, society, or class that entertained such ideas. The older concepts of reason, natural law, natural right, and the ultimate alikeness of all mankind, or of a common path of all mankind in one course of progress, disappeared.[16]

The totalitarian regimes did not simply declare, as a dry finding of social science, that peoples' ideas were shaped by environment. They set about shaping them actively. Propaganda became a principal branch of government. Propaganda was hardly new; but in the past, and still in the democratic countries, it had been a piecemeal affair, urging the public to accept this or that political party, or to buy this or that brand of coffee. Now, like all else, it became "total." Propaganda was monopolized by the state, and it demanded faith in a whole view of life and in every detail of this coordinated whole. Formerly the control of books and newspapers had been mainly negative; under Napoleon or Metternich, for example, censors had forbidden statements on particular subjects, events, or persons. Now, in totalitarian countries, control of the press became frighteningly positive. The government manufactured thought. It manipulated opinion. It rewrote history. Writers were required to present whole ideologies, and books, newspapers, magazines, and the radio diffused an endless and overwhelming cloud of words. Loudspeakers blared in the streets, gigantic blown-up photographs of the Leader looked down in public places. The propaganda experts were sometimes fanatics; but often they were cynics like Dr. Goebbels in Germany, too intelligent to be duped by the rubbish with which they duped their country.

The very idea of truth evaporated. No norm of human utterance remained except political expediency—the wishes and self-interest of the men in power. No one could learn anything except what the government wanted him to know. No one could escape the omnipresent official doctrine, the insidious penetration of the very recesses of his mind by ideas planted by outsiders for their own purposes. People came to accept, and even to believe, the most extravagant statements when they were endlessly repeated, year after year. Barred from all independent sources of information, having no means by which any official allegation could be tested, the peoples of totalitarian countries became increasingly in fact, and not merely in sociological theory, incapable of the use of reason.

[16] See pp. 317–318, 322, 326–327, 334–336, 603–606, 658–659.

Racism, more characteristic of Nazi Germany than of totalitarianism in general, was a further exaggeration, or degradation, of older ideas of nationalism and national solidarity. It defined the nation in a tribal sense, as a biological entity, a group of persons possessing the same physical ancestry and the same or similar physical characteristics. Anti-Semitism was the most venomous form of racism in Europe. While a latent hostility to Jews had always been present in the Christian world, modern anti-Semitism had little to do with Christianity. It arose in part from the fact that, in the nineteenth century, with the general removal of religious disabilities, the Jews entered into general society and many of them achieved positions of prominence, and nowhere more so than in Germany, so that from the point of view of any individual non-Jew they could be represented as dangerous competitors in business or the professions. But most of all, anti-Semitism was inflamed by propagandists who wished people to feel their supposed racial purity more keenly or to forget the deeper problems of society, including poverty, unemployment, and economic inequities.

For totalitarianism was an escape from the realities of class conflict. It was a way of pretending that differences between rich and poor were of minor importance. Typically, a totalitarian regime came into power by stirring up class fears, then remained in power, and represented itself as indispensable, by declaring that it had settled the class problem. Thus Mussolini, Hitler, and certain lesser dictators, before seizing office, pointed alarmingly to the dark menace of Bolshevism; and, once in power, declared that all classes stood shoulder to shoulder in slab-like solidarity behind the Leader. Nor were events in Russia altogether different. The Bolsheviks in 1917, armed with the ideas of Karl Marx, aroused the workers against capitalists, landlords, middle-class people, and rich peasants; then, once in power, and after extensive liquidations, they declared that the classless society had arrived, that no true social classes any longer existed, and that all Soviet citizens stood solidly behind a regime from which, they said, all good citizens benefited equally. Only the democracies admitted that they suffered from internal class problems, from maladjustments between rich and poor or between favored and unfavored groups in society.

The dictatorships blamed their troubles on forces outside the country. They accused dissatisfied persons of conspiring with foreigners or refugees—with being the tools of Trotskyism, imperialism, or international Jewry. Or they talked of the struggle between rich nations and poor nations, the "have" and the "have-not" countries, and thus transformed the problem of poverty into an international struggle. In the distinction between "have" and "have-not" countries there was, of course, more than a grain of truth; in more old-fashioned language some countries (in fact the European democracies, as well as the United States and the British dominions of the 1930s) had "progressed" farther than others. It is probable that any propaganda is more effective if partly true. But when the totalitarians blamed their troubles on other countries and transformed the conflict between "have" and "have-not" into a struggle between nations, they gave the impression that war might be a solution for social ills.

Violence, the acceptance and even glorification of violence, was indeed the characteristic most clearly distinguishing the totalitarian from the democratic systems. We have seen how a cult of violence, or belief that struggle was beneficial, had arisen before the First World War.[17] The war itself habituated people to violence and direct action. Lenin and his followers showed how a small group could seize the helm of state under revolutionary or chaotic conditions. Mussolini in 1922 taught the same lesson, with further refinements; for the Italy in which he seized power was not at war, and it was merely the threat or possibility of revolution, not revolution itself, that provided him with his opportunity. In the 1920s, for the first time since the seventeenth century, some of the most civilized parts of Europe, in time of peace, saw private armies marching about the country, bands of uniformed and organized ruffians, Blackshirts or Brownshirts, who manhandled, abused and even killed law-abiding citizens with impunity. Nor would anyone in the 1920s have believed that, by the 1930s, Europe would see the reintroduction of torture.

The very ethics of totalitarianism was violent and neopagan. It borrowed from Nietzsche and other prewar theoreticians, who, safe and civilized, had declared that men should live dangerously, avoid the flabby weakness of too much thought, throw themselves with red-blooded vigor into a life of action. The new regimes all instituted youth movements. They appealed to a kind of juvenile idealism, in which young people believed that by joining some kind of squad, donning some kind of uniform, and getting into the fresh air they contributed to a great moral resurgence of their country. Young men were taught to value their bodies but not their minds, to be tough and hard, to regard mass gymnastics as patriotic demonstrations, and camping trips as a preparation for the world of the future. Young women were taught to breed large families without complaint, to be content in the kitchen, and to look with awe upon their virile mates. The body-cult flourished while the mind decayed. Especially in National Socialism the ideal was to turn the German people into a race of splendid animals, pink-cheeked, Nordic, and upstanding. Contrariwise, euthanasia was adopted for the insane and was proposed for the aged. Later, in the Second World War, when the Nazis overran eastern Europe, they committed Jews to the gas chambers, destroying some 6,000,000 human beings by the most scientific methods. Animals were animals; one bred the kind one wanted and killed the kind one did not.

The trend to dictatorship or totalitarianism spread over Europe in the 1930s. By 1939 only ten out of twenty-seven European countries remained democratic, in the sense that different political parties honestly competed for office, and that citizens within generous limits thought and acted as they pleased. They were Great Britain and France; Holland, Belgium, and Switzerland; Czechoslovakia and Finland; and the three Scandinavian countries. The Soviet Union still exemplified the dictatorship of the proletariat, and all other European countries possessed more or less dictatorial regimes somewhat vaguely called, with more or less accuracy, "fascist."

[17]See pp. 661–662.

The promise of the early 1920s that constitutional and democratic government would flourish was thwarted. The weakness or absence of a parliamentary or democratic tradition, low education and literacy standards, the hostility of reactionary elements, the fear of Bolshevism, and the dissatisfaction of existing national minorities, all of which were coupled with economic strains, many resulting from the Great Depression, contributed to the collapse of the new representative institutions. Apart from the avowedly totalitarian or fascist regimes of Germany and Italy, the new dictatorships and authoritarian systems rested generally on a combination of personal and military power. To name but a few, this was true of Poland under Marshal Pilsudski and his successor, General Smigly-Rydz; Hungary under General Julius Gömbös, successor to Count Bethlen; Greece under General Metaxas; Spain (after a bloody civil war to be described), under General Franco; and Yugoslavia, Bulgaria, and Rumania under their respective kings. In Portugal, Salazar began a clerical-corporative dictatorship in 1932 which continued for over three decades. In Austria, Dollfuss fused various right-wing political and military elements into a clerical-fascist "Christian" dictatorship which violently suppressed the Socialists and sought in vain with this dictatorship to counter the German threat; assassinated in July 1934, he was succeeded by Kurt von Schuschnigg, who headed a similar regime until the German annexation of Austria in 1938. In many respects the dictatorships of Latin America under a diversity of *caudillos* and military juntas, in both origin and character, resembled the European dictatorships.

The authoritarian regimes were all alike in the repression of individual liberties, in the banning of opposition parties, and in the abolition or nullification of parliamentary institutions. Many borrowed features of the corporative state, outlawing independent labor organizations and forbidding strikes; many like Hungary, Rumania, and Poland instituted anti-Semitic legislation. None went so far in the total coordination of all political, economic, intellectual, and biological activities in a revolutionary mass-based dictatorship as did Hitler's Third Reich.

The acceptance and glorification of violence, it has been noted, was the feature most clearly distinguishing the totalitarian from the democratic systems. War in the Nazi and Fascist ethics was a noble thing, and the love of peace a sign of decadence. (The Soviet regime, while by its own theory it regarded war with non-Soviet powers as inevitable some day, did not preach it as a positive moral good.) The exaltation of war and struggle, the need for maintaining national solidarity, the habit of blaming foreign countries for social troubles, together with the considerable armaments program in which totalitarian states engaged, plus the personal ambition and egotistical mania of individual dictators, made the decade of the 1930s a time not only of domestic reaction and economic stagnation but of recurrent international crises, of which the last one led to war.

XX: THE SECOND

WORLD WAR

Peace in the abstract, the peace which is the mere absence of war, does not exist in international relations. Peace is never found apart from certain conditions; it means peaceable acceptance of given conditions, or peaceable and orderly transformation of conditions by negotiation and agreement. The conditions, in the 1930s, were basically those laid down by the Paris peace conference of 1919—the states recognized, the frontiers drawn, the terms agreed to, at the close of the First World War. In the 1930s neither Germany, Italy, Japan, nor the U.S.S.R. was content with these conditions; they were "revisionist" or dissatisfied powers; and the first three were willing to undertake war itself to make a change. Great Britain, France, and the United States were satisfied powers, expecting no benefit from change in the conditions; but on the other hand they had lost faith in the conditions and were unwilling to risk war for the sake of upholding them. They had made a treaty in 1919 which a dozen years later they were unwilling to enforce. They stood idly by, as long as they could, while the dissatisfied powers tore to pieces the states recognized, the frontiers drawn, and the terms agreed to at the Peace of Paris. From the Japanese invasion of Manchuria in 1931 to the outbreak of European war in 1939, force was used by those who wished to upset international order, but never by those who wished to maintain it.

106
The Weakness of
the Democracies:
Again to War

*The Pacifism
and Disunity
of the West*

While dictators stormed, the Western democracies were swayed by a profound pacifism, which may be defined as a somewhat doctrinaire insistence on peace regardless of consequences. Many people now believed, especially in England and the United States, that the First World War had been a mistake, that little or nothing had been gained by it, that they had been deluded by wartime propaganda, that wars were really started by armaments manufacturers, that Germany had not really caused the war of 1914, that the Treaty of Versailles was too hard on the Germans, that vigorous peoples like the Germans or Italians needed room for expansion, that democracy was after all not suited to all nations, that it took two to make a quarrel, and that there need be no war if one side resolutely refused to be provoked—a whole system of pacific and tolerant ideas in which there was perhaps the usual mixture of truth and misunderstanding. Taunted by enemies, the Western democracies behaved like Ferdinand the Bull, who "would not fight and be fierce no matter what they did," and who, in the story, because he would not fight, was allowed to go home and "just smell the flowers" and be "very happy." Unfortunately the Western democracies found pacifism less rewarding.

The pacifism of the West had other roots, most evident in France. One million, four hundred thousand Frenchmen had died in World War I; half of all French males between the ages of 20 and 32 in 1914 had been killed. To the French it was inconceivable that such a holocaust should be repeated. French strategy was therefore defensive and sparing of manpower. If war came, the French expected to fight it mainly in the elaborate fortifications, called the Maginot Line, which they built on their eastern frontier facing Germany, from the Swiss to the Belgian border; to its north the Ardennes forest was to be a barrier to any invader. Moreover, as we have seen, during the depression France was torn by internal class conflict and by fascist and quasi-fascist agitation.[1] Many Frenchmen of the right, historically unsympathetic to the republic and seeing, or claiming to see, in such movements as the Popular Front the threat of social revolution, did not conceal their admiration for Mussolini or even for Hitler. Abandoning their traditional role as ardent nationalists, they would do nothing to oppose the dictators. On the other hand, many on the left looked with sympathy upon the Soviet Union. France was ideologically too divided in the 1930s to possess any firm foreign policy, and all elements took false comfort from the supposed impregnability of the French Chinese Wall.

A similar situation, in less degree, prevailed in Great Britain and the United States. The loss and bloodshed of the First World War were remembered. It was well known that another world war would be even more horrible; there was an

[1]See pp. 859–861.

unspeakable dread of the bombing of cities. Typical of the time was a resolution adopted by students at Oxford in 1933 that they would never take up arms for their country under any conditions; peace movements appeared among American college students too. The pull between left and right was felt in England and America. In the 1930s, when any international action seemed to favor either the U.S.S.R. on the one hand, or Hitler and Mussolini on the other, it was hard to establish any foreign policy on a firm basis of national unity. In Britain some members of the upper classes were overtly sympathetic to the fascist dictators, or at least saw in them a bulwark against communism. The government itself tried to be noncommittal; it believed that some means of satisfying or appeasing the more "legitimate" demands of the dictators might be found. Neville Chamberlain, prime minister after 1937, became the principal architect of the appeasement policy.

The Weakness of the Democracies: Again to War

The United States government, despite President Roosevelt's repeated denunciation of the aggressors, followed in practice a policy of rigid isolation. Neutrality legislation, enacted by a strong isolationist bloc in Congress in the years 1935 to 1937, forbade loans, export of munitions, and use of American shipping facilities to any belligerent once the president had recognized a state of war in a given area. It was then believed, by many, that the United States had been drawn into the First World War by such economic involvement. From this American neutrality legislation the aggressors of the 1930s were to derive great benefit, but not the victims of their aggression.

As for the men who ruled the U.S.S.R., they were revisionist and dissatisfied in that they did not accept the new frontiers of eastern Europe nor the territorial losses incurred by Russia in the First World War. They resented the *cordon sanitaire* created in 1919 against the spread of Bolshevism, the ring of small states on their borders from Finland to Rumania, which were almost without exception vehemently anti-Soviet. They had no fondness for the international status quo nor had they abandoned their long-range revolutionary objectives. But, as communists and as Russians, they were obsessed by fear of attack and invasion. Their Marxist doctrine taught the inherent hostility of the entire capitalist world; the intervention of the Western Allies in the Revolution and civil wars confirmed their Marxist theory. And long before the Bolshevik Revolution, in the days of Napoleon and earlier, the fertile Russian plains had tempted ambitious conquerors. Resentful and suspicious of the outside world, in the 1930s the men in the Kremlin were alarmed primarily by the signs of aggressive intentions in Germany. Hitler, in *Mein Kampf* and elsewhere, had declared that he meant to obliterate Bolshevism and subordinate large stretches of eastern Europe to Germany.

The Soviets became interested in collective security, in international action against aggression. In 1934 they joined the League of Nations. They instructed communist parties to work with socialists and liberals in popular fronts.[2] They offered assistance in checking fascist aggressors, signing mutual assistance pacts with France and Czechoslovakia in 1935. But many people fled from the Soviet embrace

[2] See p. 809.

with a shudder. They distrusted Soviet motives; or they were convinced that the purges and trials of the 1930s had left the Soviets weak and undependable as allies; or they felt that the fascist dictators might be diverted eastward against the Soviets and so spare the Western democracies. Here again, though the Russians were ostensibly willing, no effective coalition against aggression could be formed.

The March of Nazi and Fascist Aggression

Adolf Hitler perceived these weaknesses with uncanny genius. Determined to wreck the whole treaty system, he employed tactics of gradual encroachment which played on the hopes and fears of the democratic peoples. He inspired in them alternating tremors of apprehension and sighs of relief. He would rage and rant, arouse the fear of war, take just a little, declare that it was all he wanted, let the former Allies naively hope that he was now satisfied and that peace was secure; then rage again, take a little more, and proceed through the same cycle.

Each year he precipitated some kind of emergency, and each time the French and British saw no alternative except to let him have his way. In 1933, soon after seizing power, he took Germany out of the League and out of the Disarmament Conference then taking place. He successfully wooed Poland, long France's ally, and in 1934 the two countries signed a nonaggression treaty. That same year the Nazis of Austria attempted a *Putsch*, assassinated the Austrian chancellor, Dollfuss, and demanded the union of Austria with Germany. The Western powers did nothing. It was Mussolini who acted. He had no desire to see Germany installed at the Brenner Pass and mobilized large Italian forces on the frontier; he thus discouraged Hitler from intervening openly in Austria and so preserved the independence of Austria for four more years. In January 1935 a plebiscite was conducted in the Saar by the League of Nations as stipulated under the Versailles treaty. Amidst intense Nazi agitation, the Saar voted for reunion with the Reich. Two months later, in March 1935, Hitler dramatically repudiated those clauses in the Versailles treaty intended to keep Germany disarmed; he now openly built up the German armed forces. France, England and Italy protested at such arbitrary and one-sided denunciation of an international treaty, but did nothing specifically about it. Indeed, Great Britain entered into a naval agreement with Germany, to the consternation of the French.

On March 7, 1936, using as his justification the new Franco-Soviet pact, Hitler repudiated the Locarno agreements[3] and reoccupied the Rhineland; i.e., he sent German troops into the German territory west of the Rhine, which by the Treaty of Versailles was supposed to be a demilitarized zone. There was talk in the French government of action, and at this time Hitler might have been fairly easily checked, for German military strength was still weak and the German army was prepared to withdraw, or at least consult, at signs of resistance. But the French government was divided and unwilling to act without Britain; and the British would not risk war to keep German troops from occupying German soil. The next year, 1937, was a quiet one, but Nazi agitation flared up in Danzig, which the Treaty of Versailles had set up

[3] See pp. 826–827.

as a free city. In March 1938 German forces moved into Austria, and the union of Austria and Germany, the *Anschluss,* was at last consummated. In September 1938 came the turn of Czechoslovakia and the Munich crisis. To understand it we must first pick up other threads in the story.

Mussolini, too, had his ambitions and required sensational foreign triumphs to magnetize the Italian people. Since 1919 the Italians had been dissatisfied with the peace arrangements. They had received nothing of the former Turkish territories and former German colonies which had been liberally parceled out, as mandates, to Great Britain, France, Belgium and Japan, and even to South Africa, Australia and New Zealand.[4] They had never forgotten the humiliating defeat of Italian forces by Abyssinia at Adowa in 1896.[5] Ethiopia, as Abyssinia was now called, remained the only part of Black Africa (with the exception of Liberia) that was still independent.

In 1935 Italy went to war with Ethiopia. The League of Nations pronounced the Italian action an unwarranted aggression and imposed sanctions on Italy, by which members of the League were to refrain from selling Italy either arms or raw materials—oil was excepted. The British even gathered large naval forces in the Mediterranean in a show of strength. In France, however, there was considerable sympathy for Mussolini in important quarters, and in England there was the fear that if sanctions became too effective, by refusal of oil or by closure of the Suez Canal, Italy might be irritated into a general war. Mussolini was thus able to defeat Ethiopia in 1936 and to combine it with Italian Somaliland and Eritrea in an Italian East African empire. The Ethiopian Emperor Haile Selassie made futile pleas for further action at Geneva. The League of Nations again failed, as in the case of the occupation of Manchuria by Japan, to provide machinery for disciplinary action against a wayward Great Power.[6]

Hardly had the Ethiopian crisis been disposed of, to the entire satisfaction of the aggressor, when an even more serious crisis broke out in Spain. In 1931, after a decade of political disturbance, a rather mild revolution had driven out Alfonso XIII, the last Bourbon, and brought about the establishment of a democratic Spanish republic. Old hostilities within the country came to a head. The new republican government undertook a program of social and economic reform. To combat the ancient entrenched power of the church, anticlerical legislation was enacted: church and state were separated, the Jesuit order was dissolved and its property confiscated, and the schools were removed from clerical control. The old movement for Catalonian independence was somewhat mollified by the grant of considerable local autonomy. To placate the peasantry the government began to break up some of the larger landed estates and to redistribute the land. The government's program was never pushed vigorously enough to satisfy extremist elements who manifested their

---

[4] See pp. 756–757, 762, 863.
[5] See p. 691.
[6] See pp. 838–839.

dissatisfaction in strikes and uprisings, particularly in industrial Barcelona and the mining areas of the Asturias; but it was radical enough to antagonize the great property-owners and the churchmen. After 1933 the government fell into the hands of rightist and conservative parties, who ruled through ineffective and unpopular ministries. An insurrection of the miners in the Asturias was put down with much brutality. Agitation for complete Catalonian independence was repressed.

In February 1936 new general elections were held. All elements of the left—republicans, socialists, syndicalists, anarchists, communists—joined in a Popular Front against monarchists, clericals, army officers, other adherents of the old regime, and Falangists, or Spanish fascists. The left won a victory at the polls. Thereupon, in July 1936, a group of military men led an insurrection against the republican government; General Francisco Franco emerged as leader. The parties of the left united in resistance and the whole country fell into civil war. It was a considerable war, in which over 600,000 human beings lost their lives, and was attended by extreme cruelties on both sides. For nearly three years the republican or loyalist forces held their own before finally succumbing to the insurgents led by Franco, who in March 1939 established an authoritarian, fascist-type rule over the exhausted country.

Spain provided a rehearsal for the greater struggle soon to come. The republican government could legitimately have looked forward to the purchase of arms abroad to suppress the rebellion, but Britain and France were resolved not to let the war expand into a general conflict. They forbade the shipment of war materials to the republican government; even the French Popular Front government put obstacles in the way of aid to the hard-pressed Spanish Popular Front. The United States extended its neutrality legislation to cover civil wars and placed an embargo on the export of arms to Spain despite much pressure in the country for support to the loyalists. At British and French instigation twenty-seven nations, including all the major European powers, agreed not to intervene or take sides. But the non-intervention policy proved a fiasco. Germany, Italy, and the Soviet Union intervened anyway. The former two supported Franco and denounced the republicans as the tools of Bolshevism, while the U.S.S.R. supported the republic and stigmatized the rebels under Franco as the agents of international fascism. Germans, Italians, and Russians sent military equipment to Spain, testing their tanks and planes in actual battle. The fascist bombings of Madrid and Barcelona horrified the democratic world. The Germans and Italians sent troops (the Italians over 50,000); the Soviets if only for geographical reasons could not do likewise but sent technicians and political advisers. Thousands of volunteers of leftist or liberal sympathy, from the United States and Europe, went to Spain as individuals to serve with the loyalist republican forces. Spain became the battlefield of contending ideologies. The Spanish civil war split the world into fascist and antifascist camps.

Like Ethiopia, the war in Spain helped bring Germany and Italy together. Mussolini had at first, like others, feared the revival of a militant Germany. He had been the one who outfaced Hitler when the latter threatened to absorb Austria in 1934. The Ethiopian war, Italian ambitions in Africa, and a clamorous Italian demand for ascendancy in the Mediterranean, the *mare nostrum* of the ancient Romans, estranged

Italy from France and Britain. In 1936, soon after the outbreak of the Spanish war, Mussolini and Hitler came to an understanding, which they called the Rome-Berlin Axis, the diplomatic axle around which they hoped the world might turn. That year Japan signed with Germany an Anti-Comintern Pact, soon ratified by Italy too; ostensibly an agreement to oppose communism, it was actually the foundation for a diplomatic alliance. Each, thus furnished with allies, was able to push its demands with more success. In 1938 Mussolini accepted the German absorption of the very Austria which in 1934 he had denied to Hitler.

And in 1937 Japan, using as a pretext the firing upon Japanese troops at the Marco Polo Bridge near Peiping, launched a new full-scale invasion of China. Within a short time despite valiant and united resistance from the Chinese forces, both Kuomintang and communist, the invader controlled most of China. The Chinese fought on from the hinterland, obtaining equipment and supplies by difficult and devious routes. The League again ineffectually condemned the Japanese action. The United States refrained from applying its neutrality legislation, since no war was officially declared. This made possible the extension of loans to the Chinese government, but it also made possible the purchase by the Japanese of vitally needed scrap iron, steel, oil, and machinery from American industrial firms. The Japanese profited from the tension in the Western world; and in 1938 the tension in Europe was rapidly mounting.

By annexing Austria in March 1938 Hitler added about 6,000,000 Germans to the Reich. Another 3,000,000 Germans lived in Czechoslovakia.[7] All those who were adults in 1938 had been born under the Habsburg empire. They had never, since 1918, been contented with their new position as a minority in a Slavic state, and they had long complained against various forms of subtle discrimination. There were Polish, Ruthenian and Hungarian minorities also, and since even the Slovaks felt a basic separatism from the Czechs, there was in truth no preponderant national majority of any kind. The fact that Czechoslovakia had one of the most enlightened minorities policies in Europe, enjoyed the highest living standard east of Germany, and was the only country in central Europe in 1938 that was still democratic, only demonstrated the difficulty of maintaining a multinational state under the most favorable of conditions.

Czechoslovakia was strategically the keystone of Europe. It had a firm alliance with France, which had repeatedly guaranteed to defend it against German attack, and an alliance with the Soviet Union; Soviet aid was made dependent on the functioning of the French alliance. With Rumania and Yugoslavia it formed the Little Entente, upon which France relied to maintain the existing boundaries in that part of Europe. It had a well-trained army, important munitions industries, and strong fortifications against Germany, which, however, were located in precisely the Sudeten border area where the population was almost all German. When Hitler annexed Austria—since

[7]See pp. 756, 758–759, 818–820, and map, pp. 760–761.

Vienna is further east than Prague—he enclosed Czechoslovakia in a vise. From the German point of view it could now be said that Bohemia-Moravia, which was almost one-third German anyway, formed a bulge protruding into the German Reich.

The Sudeten Germans of Czechoslovakia, whether Nazis or not, fell under the influence of agitators whose aim was less to relieve their grievances than to promote National Socialism. Hitler fomented their demands for union with Germany. In May 1938 rumors of an imminent German invasion caused the Czechs to mobilize; Russia, France, and England issued warnings. Hitler, not actually intending to invade at that time, was forced to issue assurances but was furious and was determined to smash the Czechs in the autumn. France and England, instead of rejoicing in having prevented aggression, were appalled by their narrow escape from war. The French were nervous and acquiesced in the leadership of Britain, which in the following months strove to avoid any firm stand that might precipitate war. The Czechs, under pressure from Britain and France, accepted British mediation on the Sudeten issue and in the summer of 1938 offered wide concessions to the Sudeten Germans amounting to regional autonomy; but these were never enough to satisfy Hitler, who loudly proclaimed that the plight of the Germans in Czechoslovakia was intolerable and must be corrected. The Soviets urged a firm stand, but the Western powers had little confidence in Soviet military strength and, given the Soviet geographical situation, their ability to render assistance; moreover, they feared a firmness that might mean war. They could not be sure whether Hitler was bluffing. He might, if opposed, back down; but it seemed equally likely, or indeed more so, that he was entirely willing to fight. The Western powers discounted intelligence reports, which happened to be true, of a military-civilian plot to unseat Hitler if, in the event of Western firmness, a war broke out over Czechoslovakia.

As the tension mounted in September 1938, the British prime minister, Neville Chamberlain, who had never flown in his life before, flew to Germany twice to sound out Hitler on his terms; the second time Hitler raised his demands so that even the British and French could not accept them. Mobilization began; war seemed imminent. Suddenly, in the midst of the unbearable tension, Hitler invited Chamberlain and Édouard Daladier, the French premier, to a four-power conference at Munich, to be attended also by his ally, Mussolini. The Soviet Union, and Czechoslovakia itself, were excluded. At Munich Chamberlain and Daladier accepted Hitler's terms and then put enormous pressure on the Czech government to yield, to sign its own death warrant in cold blood. France, urged on by England in a pacific course that it was only too willing to follow, repudiated its treaty obligation to protect Czechoslovakia, ignored the Russians who had reaffirmed their willingness to aid the Czechs if the French acted, and abandoned its whole system of a Little Entente in the East. It was agreed at Munich that Germany should annex the adjoining fringe of Bohemia in which the majority of the people were Germans. This fringe contained the mountainous approaches and the fortifications, so that its loss left Czechoslovakia militarily defenseless. After promise of guarantees, by all concerned, of the integrity of what remained of Czechoslovakia, the conference disbanded. Chamberlain and Daladier were received with cheers at home. Chamberlain happily reported that he had brought "peace in our time." Again the democracies sighed with relief, hoped that Hitler had made his last demand, and told themselves that, with wise concessions, there need be no war.

The Munich crisis, with its death sentence to Czechoslovakia, revealed the helpless weakness into which the Western democracies had fallen by 1938. There was, in fact, little that the French and British could do, at Munich, to save Czechoslovakia. Their countries lagged behind Germany in military preparedness. They were impressed by the might of the German army and air force. Bolder men than Daladier and Chamberlain, knowing the state of their own armed forces, would have declined to risk a quarrel. They loved peace and would buy it at a high price, not daring to believe that they were dealing with a blackmailer whose price would be always raised. They suffered, too, from another moral uncertainty: by the very principle of national self-determination, accepted by the victors after the First World War, Germany had a right to all that it had hitherto demanded. Hitler, in sending German troops into the German Rhineland, in annexing Austria, stirring up Danzig, incorporating the Bohemian Germans, had only asserted the right of the German people to have a sovereign German state. Moreover, if Hitler could be diverted eastward, enmeshed in a war with Russia, then communism and fascism might destroy each other—so one might hope. Possibly it was one of Hitler's motives, in the Munich crisis, to isolate Russia from the West and the West from Russia. If so, he succeeded well enough.

In the weeks following Munich the international commission set up to arrange the new boundaries worked further injustices on Czechoslovakia, dispensing even with the plebiscites which had been agreed to for disputed areas. Meanwhile the Poles and Hungarians brought forth their demands on the hapless Czechs. The Poles seized the Teschen district; and Hungary, under a German and Italian award, took 7,500 square miles of Slovakia. France and Britain were not consulted and did not seriously protest.

The final disillusionment came in March 1939. Hitler marched into Bohemia-Moravia, the really Czech part of Czechoslovakia, which he transformed into a German protectorate. Exploiting Slovak nationalism, he declared Slovakia "independent." Czechoslovakia, merely trimmed down at Munich, now disappeared from the map. Having promised to take only a bite, Hitler swallowed the whole. He then seized Memel from Lithuania and raised demands for Danzig and the Polish Corridor. A horrible realization now spread in France and Britain. It was clear that Hitler's most solemn guarantees were worthless, that his designs were not limited to Germans, but reached out to all eastern Europe and beyond, that he was essentially insatiable, that he could never be appeased. In April 1939 his partner in aggression Mussolini took over Albania.

The Western powers now began to make military preparations. Britain, changing its east-European policy at the eleventh hour, now gave a guarantee to Poland, and followed that with guarantees to Rumania and Greece. The guarantee to Poland was made under the worst possible circumstances, the military bastion of Czechoslovakia having been already surrendered and the Soviet Union alienated from the West by its exclusion at Munich.

In the spring and summer of 1939, the British and the French tried to form an anti-German alliance with Russia. Poland and the Baltic states were unwilling to allow Soviet armies within their borders, even for the purpose of defending them against the Germans. The Anglo-French negotiators, clinging to a few shreds of international propriety, refused to throw Poland and the Baltic states to Stalin in the way in which they had just thrown Czechoslovakia to Hitler. Since the Poles, in 1920, had conquered more territory than the Allies had meant them to have,[8] pushing their eastern border well into White Russia, almost to Minsk, the Anglo-French scruples seemed to the Soviets unnecessarily delicate. The Russians did not wish the Germans to launch an attack on them from a point as far east as Minsk. They thought, too, with good reason, that what the French and British really wanted was for Russia to take the brunt of the Nazi attack. They considered it an affront that the British sent lesser officials as negotiators to Moscow when the prime minister himself had three times flown personally to treat with Hitler. Having quietly undertaken negotiations earlier that spring, the Soviets now, on August 23, 1939, openly signed a treaty of nonaggression and friendship with Hitlerite Germany. In a protocol kept secret at the time, it was agreed that in any future territorial rearrangement Russia and Germany would divide Poland between them, that Russia would enjoy a preponderant influence in the Baltic states and have its claim to Bessarabia, lost to Rumania in 1918, recognized. In return the Soviets were pledging to stay out of any war between Germany and Poland, or between Germany and the Western democracies.

The Nazi-Soviet Pact of August 23, 1939 stupefied the world. Communism and Nazism, supposed to be ideological opposites, had come together. A generation more versed in ideology than in power politics was dumbfounded. The pact was recognized as the signal for war; all last minute negotiations failed. The Germans invaded Poland on September 1. On September 3 Great Britain and France declared war on Germany. The second European war in a generation, soon to be a world war, had begun.

[8] See pp. 786, 787, and map, p. 259.

The Survivor *by George Grosz (German, then American, 1893–1959)*
George Grosz, born in Germany, came to the United States in 1932 to avoid the Nazis. He painted this powerful picture in 1945 at the close of the Second World War. It suggests what is meant by the collapse of civilization. The hideous figure crawling out of the wreckage, according to the artist's own explanation, is insane with fear. He is starving, filthy, abandoned, and alone. In his teeth he desperately clasps a knife, which he will use to fight another terrified survivor, should he meet one, or to hunt for and cut up food. Note the symbolism of a broken swastika in the arrangement of the man's body and the debris. The picture is of course meant to be repulsive, to show the depths to which humanity can be degraded, and so shock people into constructive action. The tormenting question is whether this picture will prove a true prophecy of the twentieth century. Courtesy of Mrs. Marc J. Sandler.

107
The Years of
Axis Triumph

*Nazi Europe,
1939–1940: Poland and
the Fall of France*

The Second World War opened with the assault on Poland. German forces totaling over 1,000,000 men, spearheaded by armored divisions and supported by the massed air power of the *Luftwaffe*, rapidly overran western Poland and subdued the ill-equipped Polish armies. The outcome of the campaign, a spectacular, perfectly executed example of *Blitzkrieg*, or lightning warfare, was clear within the first few days; organized resistance ended within a month. The Germans undertook at once the integration of their Polish conquest into the Reich.

Simultaneously, in the East, the Russians, acting under the secret clauses of the German-Soviet pact, moved into the eastern half of Poland two weeks after the German invasion; the territory occupied was roughly equivalent to that lost to Poland in 1920. The Russians proceeded also to establish fortified bases in the Baltic states—Estonia, Latvia, and Lithuania. Finland alone resisted Soviet demands. The Finns refused to cede border territories sought by the Russians or to yield military rights within their country. The Soviets insisted; Leningrad, the second major city of the U.S.S.R., lay only twenty miles from the Finnish frontier. When negotiations foundered in November 1939 the Soviets attacked. Finnish resistance was valiant and at first effective, but the small country was no match for the U.S.S.R., even though the latter used only limited forces in the war. Western democratic sympathies were with the Finns; the British and French sent equipment and supplies and even planned an expeditionary force. Russia was expelled from the League of Nations for the act of aggression—the only power ever to be so expelled. By March 1940 the fighting was over. The Finns had to yield somewhat more territory to the U.S.S.R. than originally demanded.

Meanwhile all was deceptively quiet in the West. The pattern of 1914, when the Germans reached the Marne in the first month of hostilities, failed to repeat itself. Unlike 1914, the opening phase of the war was one of position at the outset. The French sat behind their Maginot Line; the British had few troops; the Germans did not stir from behind their Siegfried Line, or West Wall, in the Rhineland. Hardly any air action took place. It was called the "phony war." The two great Western

Classic Landscape *by Charles Sheeler (American, 1883–1965)*
This landscape is "classic" in its balance, its repose, its clear delineation, its array of familiar mathematical forms, and the universality of its message. It depicts the River Rouge plant of the Ford Motor Company; but all local color has been removed, so that what results is a picture of pure industrialism. It is a stark symbol of the technological civilization which has been emerging in all parts of the world in the twentieth century. The plant seems rational and precise, but the absence of human beings is to be noted: it is as if the machine had a life of its own and could do without human hands, or with very few of them—the ultimate triumph of automation. The sharp shadows suggest bright sunshine, despite the smoke pouring from the tall chimney. When the picture was painted no one was alarmed about atmospheric pollution. Courtesy of Mrs. Edsel B. Ford.

democracies rejected Hitler's peace overtures after the conquest of Poland but still clung to their peacetime outlook. The mad hope still lingered that somehow a real clash might even yet be averted. During this same strange winter, a cold and bitter one, the Germans put their forces through special training, whose purpose became apparent in the spring.

On April 9, 1940, the Germans suddenly attacked and overran Norway, ostensibly because the British were laying mines in Norwegian waters in an endeavor to cut off German sources of Swedish iron ore. Denmark, too, was overrun, and an Allied expeditionary force with inadequate air strength had to withdraw. Then on May 10, the Germans delivered their main blow, striking at the Netherlands, Belgium, Luxembourg, and France itself. Nothing could stand against the German armored divisions and dive bombers. The Nazi use of massed armor, though already demonstrated in Poland, took the French and British by surprise. Strategically, the Allies expected the main advance to be in central Belgium, as in 1914, and indeed as in the original German plan, which had been altered only a few months earlier. Hence the French and British sent into Belgium the best equipped troops they had. But the Germans delivered their main armored thrust, seven panzer divisions, through Luxembourg and through the Ardennes forest, long considered by the French General Staff impassable to armor. In France, skirting the northwestern end of the Maginot Line, which had never been extended to the sea, the German panzer divisions crossed the Meuse, drove deep into northern France against confused and ineffective resistance and, racing westward toward the Channel ports, cut off the Allied armies in Belgium. The Dutch, fearful of further air attack on their crowded cities, capitulated; the Belgian king sued for an armistice; and a large part of the French armies surrendered. The British fell back upon Dunkirk and could hope only to salvage their broken forces before the trap closed completely. They were able to accomplish their rescue operation only because Hitler, for some inexplicable combination of reasons, political and military, had some days earlier halted the advance of his armored divisions. In the week ending June 4 an epic evacuation of over 330,000 British and French troops was successfully executed from the beaches of Dunkirk, under air cover, with the help of all kinds of British vessels, manned in part by civilian volunteers, but the precious equipment of the shattered army was all but totally abandoned.

In June the German forces drove relentlessly southward. Paris itself was occupied on June 13, Verdun two days later; by June 22 France had sued for peace and an armistice had been signed. Hitler danced with glee.

France, obsessed by a defensive military psychology at the outset of the war, its armies unprepared for mechanized warfare, lacking armored divisions and an adequate air force, its government divided, its people split into hostile and suspicious factions, had fallen into the hands of a group of men who were openly defeatist. The fall of France left the world aghast. Everyone knew that France was no longer its former self, but it had still been considered a great power, and its collapse in one month seemed inconceivable. Some Frenchmen, fleeing to England, established a Free French movement under General Charles de Gaulle; others formed a Resistance movement in France. The British made the bitter decision to destroy a part of the French fleet anchored in the Algerian harbor of Oran to prevent its falling into enemy hands.

France itself under the terms of the armistice was occupied in its northern half by the Germans. The Third Republic, its capital now at Vichy in the unoccupied southern half, was transformed by vote of a confused and stunned parliament into an authoritarian regime headed by the eighty-four-year-old Marshal Pétain and the cynical and unscrupulous politician Pierre Laval. The republic was dead; the very slogan *Liberty, Equality, and Fraternity* was banned from official use. Pétain, Laval and others proceeded to collaborate with the Nazis and to integrate Vichy France into the Nazi new order in Europe.

Mussolini attacked France in June 1940, as soon as it was clear that Hitler had defeated it. Shortly thereafter, he invaded Greece and moved against the British in Africa. The Duce tied his own destinies, for good or ill, to those of the Führer. Since the Germans were emphatically the senior partner in this combination, since they were on good terms with Franco in Spain, and since Russia was benevolently neutral, they now dominated the entire European continent. History seemed to repeat itself, in the distant and unreal way which is the only way in which it ever repeats. The Germans controlled almost exactly the same geographical area as Napoleon. Organizing a new "continental system," which they called the "new order," they made plans to govern, exploit, and coordinate the resources, industry, and labor of Europe. Not having made plans for a long war, and only belatedly mobilizing their own resources, they had to intensify the exploitation of their conquered subjects. They garrisoned virtually the whole of Europe with their soldiers, creating what they called *Festung Europa,* the Fortress of Europe. In every country they had their sympathizers, collaborators, or "quislings"—Vidkun Quisling, who had organized a Norwegian fascist party in 1933, and was premier of Norway from 1942 to 1945, was typical of the group.

But Hitler never commanded the following of Napoleon. It is significant that he never remotely approached Napoleon in raising an international army to fight his battles. Instead, by what the West called slave labor, he impressed millions of Frenchmen, Poles, Czechs, and others, prisoners of war or civilians, to work under close control in his war industries. It became one of the largest forcible displacements of population in all history. No liberating reforms, political, social, legal, like those of Napoleon and the French Revolution, followed in the wake of Hitler's armies. A generation reared to mistrust the fabricated atrocity tales of the First World War painfully became aware of the very real German horrors of the Second—hostages rounded up and shot in reprisal for resistance; a whole village like Lidice in Czechoslovakia razed to the ground and its inhabitants killed or deported; concentration camps converted into mass extermination centers, with gas chambers and crematory ovens, at Maidanek, Treblinka, Dachau, Buchenwald, Auschwitz, and elsewhere, where "inferior" peoples could be systematically liquidated. Before the six-year war was over, in the areas of Nazi domination, over 6,000,000 human beings were so destroyed; by far the largest proportion were some 5,700,000 European

Jews, but Poles, Russians, and other peoples were killed as well. All this was done in the effort to "Germanize" Europe, to make it work and sacrifice for the greater glory of the *Herrenvolk*, the master race. Genocide, the attempted destruction of whole ethnic groups or peoples, was the greatest of the Nazi sins against mankind.

The Battle of Britain
and American Aid

In 1940, as in 1807, only Great Britain remained at war with the conqueror of Europe. After Dunkirk the British awaited the worst, momentarily expecting invasion. Winston Churchill, who had replaced Chamberlain as prime minister in May 1940 during the military débacle, rose to the summit of heroic leadership in adversity. To Parliament and the British people he promised nothing but "blood, toil, tears, and sweat." He pledged implacable war against "a monstrous tyranny, never surpassed in the dark, lamentable catalogue of human crime." To the American democracy across the Atlantic he appealed "Give us the tools, and we will finish the job." The United States began to respond.

Since 1939, and even before, the American government had been anything but neutral. Opinion was excitedly divided. One group, called isolationist, opposed any involvement in the European war, believing either that Europe was hopeless, or that the United States could not save it, or that the Germans would win anyway before America could act, or that Hitler, even if victorious in Europe, constituted no danger to the United States. Another group, the interventionists, urged immediate aid to the Allies, believing that Hitler was an actual menace, that fascism must be destroyed, or that the Nazis, if they subjected all Europe, would soon begin to tamper with the American republics. President Roosevelt was an interventionist, convinced that American security was endangered; he tried to rally national opinion by declaring that the United States might openly assist the Allies without itself fighting, by using "measures short of war." His Republican opponent in 1940, Wendell Willkie, took an identical stand.

The neutrality legislation of the mid-1930s was amended in November 1939, when the ban on the sale of arms was repealed. Britain and the British Empire the President described as "the spearhead of resistance to world conquest"; the United States was to be "the great arsenal of democracy." Both were fighting for a world, he said, in which the Four Freedoms were to be secure—freedom of speech, freedom of worship, freedom from want, and freedom from fear. In June 1940, immediately after Dunkirk, the United States sent a small initial shipment of arms to Britain. A few months later the United States gave the British fifty over-age destroyers in return for the right to maintain American bases in Newfoundland, the Bermudas, and the British Caribbean islands. In 1941 it adopted Lend-Lease, a policy of providing arms, raw material, and food to powers at war with the Axis. At the same time, in 1940 and 1941, the United States introduced conscription, built up its army and air force, and projected a two-ocean navy. Plans for joint hemisphere defense were developed with the Latin American republics. To protect its shipping it secured bases in Greenland and Iceland and convoyed Allied shipping as far as Iceland. In October 1941 German submarines sank an American destroyer. It is likely that the Germans, as in 1917, would have eventually provoked war with the United States to stop the flow of aid to their enemies even had war not come from another quarter.

Meanwhile, after the fall of France, the Germans stood poised for the invasion of Britain. But they had not calculated on such rapid and easy successes in Europe, they had no immediately practical plan for an invasion, and they needed to win control of the air before a sea invasion could take place. Moreover, there was always the hope that the British might sue for peace, or even become an ally of Germany—so Hitler's mind ran. The assault on Britain, which began that summer and reached its climax in the autumn of 1940, took the form of an air offensive. Never until then had any bombing been so severe. But the Germans were unable to win control over the air in the battle of Britain. Gradually the British Royal Air Force fought off the bombers with more success; new radar devices helped detect the approach of enemy planes. Although Coventry was wiped out, and the life and industry of other cities badly disrupted, and thousands of people killed (20,000 in London alone), still the productive activity of the country carried on. Nor, contrary to the predictions of most theorists of air power, did the bombings break the morale of the civilian population.

In the winter of 1940–1941 the Germans began to shift their weight to the east. Hitler postponed indefinitely the planned invasion of Britain for which he seems never to have had much enthusiasm anyway. He had already decided, like Napoleon before him, that before committing his resources to an invasion of England he must dispose of Russia, a project much closer to his heart.

The Nazi-Soviet Pact of 1939 which had precipitated the war, like the alliance between Napoleon and Alexander I, was never a warm or harmonious understanding. Both parties, foreseeing war with each other, probably entered it mainly to gain time. The Soviets gained space as well, pushing their borders westward. The two soon began to dispute over eastern Europe. The Soviets, with their Nazi ally preoccupied by the war, hoped to win more influence in the Baltic, as promised them, and in the Balkans. They had already occupied eastern Poland and the three Baltic states and won territory from Finland. In June 1940, to the chagrin of the Germans, they had quietly sovietized and converted the three Baltic states into member republics of the U.S.S.R. The old German landowning class, the famous "Baltic barons," who had lived there for centuries, were uprooted and were returned to German soil. At the same time the Soviets seized from Rumania the Bessarabian province which they had lost in the First World War and incorporated it as a Soviet republic. The Russians were expanding toward the Balkans, another area of historic Russian interest, and seemed bent on winning control over eastern Europe.

This the Germans viewed with dismay. They wished to reserve eastern Europe for themselves as a counterpart to industrial Germany. Hitler moved to bring the Balkans under German control. By early 1941 he had blackmailed or, by territorial concessions, cajoled Rumania, Bulgaria, and Hungary into joining the Axis; they became Axis lesser partners and were occupied by German troops; Yugoslavia also was occupied despite resistance by the army and population. Greece too was subjugated, the Germans coming to the rescue of Mussolini's hard-pressed troops. Hitler thus barred Russian expansion in the Balkans and made them part of the Nazi new order. The Balkan campaigns delayed his plans, but now, to end the threat from the East, and to gain the wheat harvests of the Ukraine and the oil wells of the Caucasus, the core of the Eurasian "Heartland," Hitler struck. After mutual deception that had continued since the pact of 1939, on June 22, 1941, he invaded Russia.

The war, which for two years had been only sporadic combat, now began in earnest. In the latter half of 1941 the queer war in Europe turned into the Second World War.

The German army, supplemented by Finnish, Rumanian, Hungarian, and Italian contingents, threw 3,000,000 men into Russia along a vast 2,000-mile front. One swift moving battle melted into another. The Russians resisted but gave way. By the autumn of 1941 the Germans had overrun White Russia and most of the Ukraine. In the north, Leningrad was in a state of siege; in the south, the Germans had entered the Crimean peninsula and were besieging Sebastopol. And toward the center of the vast front, the Germans stood, exhausted, but apparently victorious, within twenty-five miles of Moscow. But the overconfident German forces had not calculated on the stubbornness of Russian resistance, nor were they prepared to fight in the bitter Russian winter, which suddenly came upon them. A counteroffensive, launched by the Russians in the winter of 1941, saved Moscow. Hitler, disgusted and impatient with his subordinates, took over direct command of military operations; he shifted the main attack to the south and began a great offensive in the summer of 1942 directed toward the oil fields of the Caucasus. Sebastopol soon fell; the siege of Stalingrad began.

1942, The Year of Dismay: Russia, North Africa, the Pacific

A year after the invasion, in the fateful summer of 1942, the German line reached from beleaguered Leningrad in the north, past the western outskirts of Moscow, past Stalingrad on the Volga southward to the Caucasus mountains; the Germans were within a hundred miles of the Caspian Sea. But the Russians had traded space for time. Though the industrial Don basin and the food-producing Ukraine were overrun, and deliveries of Caucasus oil rendered hazardous and uncertain, still the Russians continued to fight; industries were shifted to the new Ural and Siberian cities; and neither the Soviet economy nor the Soviet government was yet struck in a vital spot. A "scorched earth" policy, in which the retreating Russians destroyed crops and livestock and guerrilla units wrecked industrial and transportation facilities, guaranteed that Russian resources would not fall into the hands of the advancing conqueror.

Simultaneously, late in 1942 the Axis also was moving forward in North Africa. Here the desert campaigns had started in September 1940 with an Italian eastward offensive mounted from Libya, which succeeded in crossing over into Egypt. The stakes here too were high—control over Suez and the Mediterranean. At the height of the battle of Britain, Churchill had made the decision to send vitally needed supplies and men to North Africa. To the satisfaction of the British, a counteroffensive against vastly superior numbers swept the Italians out of Egypt and by early 1941 the British moved deep into Libya. Shortly thereafter the British overran Ethiopia and ended entirely Mussolini's short-lived East African empire; the Italian navy suffered reverses as well. But in North Africa fortunes were fickle. A German elite force, the Afrika-Korps under General Rommel, reorganized the Axis armies and in the spring of 1941 attacked in Libya. The British, their forces depleted by transfers that had been made to the Greek front, were driven back to the Egyptian frontier. Then, a few months later, in a second successful offensive, the British once more advanced into Libya. Again fortunes shifted. By mid-1942 Rommel had repulsed the British and penetrated Egypt. The British took up a stand at El Alamein, seventy miles from Alexandria, their backs to the Suez Canal. Here they held the Germans.

But it seemed in 1942 that the Axis armies, breaking through the Soviet Caucasus and across the isthmus of Suez in North Africa, might enclose the whole Mediterranean and Middle East in a gigantic vise, and then, moving farther east, join forces with their allies the Japanese, who were at this time penetrating into the Indian Ocean.

For the Pacific situation in the latter half of 1941 had also exploded. It was Japan that finally drew the United States into war.

The Japanese, in 1941, had conducted a war against China for ten years. In the second war in Europe, as in the first, Japanese expansionists saw a propitious moment to assert themselves throughout the Far East. In 1940 they had cemented their alliance with Germany and Italy in a new three-power pact; the following year they had concluded a neutrality treaty with Russia. From the Vichy French government the Japanese obtained a number of military bases and other concessions in Indochina and began the occupation of that area. The United States placed an embargo on the export of such materials as scrap iron and steel to Japan. Hesitating to precipitate any all-out drive of the Japanese toward the Dutch East Indies and elsewhere, the United States government still sought some definition of Japanese ambitions in southeast Asia. The new Japanese prime minister General Hideki Tojo, a staunch champion of the Axis, publicly proclaimed that the influence of Britain and the United States was to be totally eliminated from the Orient, but he agreed to send representatives to Washington for negotiations. At the very time that the Japanese representatives in Washington were carrying on conversations with the American Secretary of State Cordell Hull, on December 7, 1941, without warning, the Japanese launched a heavy air raid on the American naval base at Pearl Harbor in Hawaii and began to invade the Philippines. Simultaneously, they launched attacks on Guam,

Europe 1942. *The map shows Europe at the height of Axis military successes during World War II, just before the Soviet victory at Stalingrad and the Western invasion of North Africa. Austria, the Sudetenland, Bohemia-Moravia, Poland, and Alsace-Lorraine were all joined to Hitler's Reich. The Atlantic coast from southern France to northern Norway was under German military occupation, as was much of Russia almost to the Caspian Sea. Southern Europe from Vichy France to Rumania was also occupied or allied.*

ARCTIC OCEAN

ICELAND
Reykjavik

Hitler's "Empire"

Allied With Germany

Occupied by the Axis

At War Against the Axis

Relations between the Axis and Vichy France
were governed by the Armistice of June 1940,
but Germany occupied the whole of France
in November 1942.

0   100   200   300 miles

FAEROE I.
(Denmark)

NORWAY

Narvik

SWEDEN

SHETLAND I.
(Britain)

Bergen

Oslo

ORKNEY I.

Stockholm

NORTH
SEA

DENMARK

Copenhagen

BALT

NORTHERN
IRELAND

UNITED
KINGDOM

EIRE

ATLANTIC OCEAN

Hamburg

Elbe R.

Dan

NETHERLANDS

Rotterdam

Coventry

London

Berlin

ENGLISH CHANNEL   Dunkirk

BELGIUM

Essen

GERMANY

Breslau

Cologne

Brest

LUX.

Nuremburg

SUDETEN-
LAND

BOHEMIA

Sedan

Paris

MORAV

Rhine R.

Munich

Vienna

FRANCE

Vichy

SWITZERLAND

AUSTRIA

Bu

Bordeaux

CROA

Bilbao

ADRIATIC SEA

Toulon

PORTUGAL

Madrid

ITALY

Lisbon

SPAIN

Barcelona

CORSICA
(Vichy France)

Rome

Anzio

Cassino

Salerno

Taranto

Cadiz

BALEARIC I.
(Spain)

SARDINIA
(Italy)

Tangier

Gibraltar (Britain)

Palermo

SPANISH
MOROCCO

Oran

Algiers

Bizerte

SICILY

Casablanca

MALTA (Br

MEDITERRANEAN

MOROCCO
(Vichy France)

ALGERIA
(Vichy France)

TUNISIA
(Vichy France)

Farthest Axis Penetration
—— December 1941
· · · · November 1942

RTH CAPE

•Murmansk

WHITE SEA

•Archangel

FINLAND

L. Onega

L. Ladoga

Leningrad•
•Helsinki

ESTONIA

•Riga

TVIA

THUANIA
nel

BYELO-RUSSIA

SUWALKI

•Smolensk

S O V I E T   *U N I O N*

•Moscow

Tula•

•Kuibyshev

Volga R.

Donetz R.

•Stalingrad

rsaw

POLAND

•Kiev

•Kharkov

UKRAINE

•Rostov

Don R.

•Astrakhan

Dniester R.

BESSARABIA

ARY

•Maikop

•Grozny

C A S P I A N   S E A

•Baku

RUMANIA

grade

•Bucharest

BIA

Danube R.

•Sofia

BULGARIA

•Sevastopol   •Yalta

B L A C K   S E A

•Batum

TRANSCAUCASIA

•Istanbul

Ankara•

T   U   R   K   E   Y

•Tabriz

IRAN

A E G E A N   S E A

Athens•
GREECE

CRETE

CYPRUS
(Britain)

SYRIA

•Baghdad

IRAQ

LEBANON

PALESTINE

TRANS-
JORDAN

SAUDI ARABIA

EA

899

Midway, Hong Kong, and Malaya. The Americans were caught off guard at Pearl Harbor; close to 2,500 were killed; the fleet was crippled; and the temporary disablement of the American naval forces allowed the Japanese to roam at will in the western Pacific. The United States, and Great Britain, declared war on Japan on December 8. Three days later Germany and Italy declared war on the United States, as did the Axis puppet states.

The Japanese, working overland through Malaya, two months later captured Singapore, a British naval base long fabulous for its supposed impregnability, the veritable Gibraltar of the East. The sinking by air of the mighty British battleship *Prince of Wales*, a feat often pronounced by naval experts to be impossible, added to the general consternation. In 1942 the Japanese conquered the Philippines, Malaya, and the Netherlands Indies. They invaded New Guinea and threatened Australia; they moved into the Aleutians. They streamed into the Indian Ocean, occupied Burma, and seemed about to invade India. Everywhere they found ready collaborators among enemies of European imperialism. They held up the idea of a Greater East Asia Co-Prosperity Sphere under Japanese leadership, in which the one clear element was that the European whites should be ejected. Meanwhile, as noted, the Germans stood at the Caucasus and almost at the Nile. And in the Atlantic, even to the shores of the United States and the American republics, German submarines were sinking Allied ships at an unprecedented and disastrous rate. The Mediterranean was unusable. For the Soviet-Western alliance, 1942 was the year of dismay. Despite Allied naval victories, the late summer and autumn of 1942 was the worst period of the war. Few realized, wrote the United States Chief of Staff General George C. Marshall some years later, how "close to complete domination of the world" were Germany and Japan and "how thin the thread of Allied survival had been stretched."

108
The Western-Soviet Victory

Plans and Preparations, 1942–1943

But by January 1942 twenty-six nations, including the three Great Powers—Britain, the United States, and the U.S.S.R.—and representing Europe, Asia, and both Americas, were aligned against the Axis, a combination to which President Roosevelt gave the name the United Nations. Each pledged to use all its resources to defeat the Axis and never to make a separate peace. The Grand Alliance against the Axis aggressors, which could not be created in the 1930s, had at last been consummated.

The two Atlantic democracies, the United States and Great Britain, pooled their resources under an organization called the Combined Chiefs of Staff. Never had any two sovereign states formed so intimate a coalition. In contrast with the First World War an overall strategy was in effect from an early date. It was decided that Germany was the main enemy, against which it was necessary to concentrate first. For the time being the Pacific war was relegated to the background. Australia became the chief base for operations against the Japanese. The American General Douglas MacArthur, who had been ordered to abandon the doomed American garrison in the Philippines, assumed command in the southwest Pacific; Admiral Chester Nimitz was in command of the Pacific naval forces. A separate organization was established for the China-Burma-India theater. The American navy and air force soon brought Japanese southward expansion to a halt and frustrated Japanese efforts to cut off supply lines to Australia; impressive naval and air victories were won in the spring of 1942 in the battle of the Coral Sea and at Midway, the only relief to the overall gloom of that period. In the summer American forces landed at Guadalcanal in the Solomon Islands. A long ordeal of "island-hopping" with inadequate forces began.

In Europe it was decided to concentrate first on the air bombardment of Germany. The Russians, dissatisfied, called for a true "second front," an immediate invasion by ground forces that would relieve the pressure of the many German divisions that were devastating their country. Suspicious of the West as ever, doubly suspicious since the Munich conference of 1938, in which they saw a Western attempt to deflect the Germans into an attack on Russia, they regarded the failure to establish a second front as new evidence of anti-Soviet feeling. Throughout the war, they took what aid they could get but never learned to like or trust their Allies.

But the United States, in 1942, was not ready to undertake land action by a direct assault on *Festung Europa.* Although in the Second World War, as in the First, more than two years elapsed between the outbreak of war in Europe and the intervention of the United States, and although in the second war American military preparations began much sooner, the United States in 1942 was still involved in the cumbersome processes of mobilization, converting industry to the production of war materials for itself and its Allies, imposing controls on its economy to prevent a runaway inflation, and giving military training to its profoundly civilian-minded people, of whom over 12,000,000 eventually served in the armed forces—over three times as many as in the First World War. In any case, for a year after the United States entered the war, German submarines enjoyed enough control of the Atlantic to make large shipments of troops too risky. In effect, they blockaded the American army in the United States. The American and British navies gradually won the battle of the Atlantic; the submarine menace was reduced to tolerable proportions by the first part of 1943. It was decided to begin the assault upon Germany, from Great Britain as a base, with a massive and prolonged air bombardment of its factories and cities. Since not everything could be shipped across the Atlantic at the same time, and since the United States and Britain were engaged in war with Japan as well, this meant the deferment of land invasion until 1944. The embattled Russians were dissatisfied; their suspicions were aroused again; they professed to doubt whether the Western Allies meant ever really to face the German army at all.

Meanwhile, at the end of 1942 the tide began to turn. In November an Anglo-American force effected a surprise invasion of Algeria and Morocco in an amphibious operation of hitherto unparalleled proportions. The Allies, failing to win the cooperation of the French in North Africa as they had hoped to do, turned to the Vichy French political leader Admiral Darlan in a calculated act of expediency that brought a loud outcry of protest in many quarters. Darlan assisted the Allies in assuming control but was assassinated in late December. In the competition that developed in the succeeding months for leadership of the French liberation committee, newly established in Algiers, General de Gaulle, though mistrusted and virtually ignored by President Roosevelt, easily bested his rival General Giraud.

On the Continent, after the North African landings, the Germans took over control of unoccupied France as well; they were frustrated, however, in the effort to obtain possession of the remainder of the French fleet by the action of French crews which scuttled the ships at Toulon. In North Africa the invading forces under the command of General Dwight D. Eisenhower fought their way eastward into Tunisia. Meanwhile the British forces under General Montgomery, having held the Germans at El Alamein in June 1942, had already launched their third (and final) counteroffensive in October, even before the invasion; they now pushed the Germans westward from Egypt until a large German force was crushed between the two Allied armies and destroyed in Tunisia. By May 1943 Africa was cleared of Axis forces. Mussolini's dream of an African empire had been thwarted; the Mediterranean was open; the threat to Egypt and the Suez Canal was ended.

At the same time it became clear, in the winter of 1942–1943, that the Germans had suffered a catastrophic reversal in Russia in the titanic battle of Stalingrad. In August 1942 massive German forces began an all-out assault on Stalingrad, the vital key to all transport on the lower Volga; by September they had penetrated the city itself. Stalin, who from the start of the war personally commanded military operations in Russia, ordered his namesake city held at all costs; Russian soldiery and the civilian population took a desperate stand. Hitler was as obstinate in ordering the city taken. After weeks of fighting the Germans had occupied most of the city when suddenly the Russians began a great counterattack, led by General Zhukov; twenty-two German divisions were forced to capitulate; over 330,000 Germans were lost. The Russians followed up their victory with a new counteroffensive, a great westward drive that netted them wholesale advances and regained for them what they had initially lost in the first year of the war. After Stalingrad, despite some setbacks, the Russians were on the offensive for the remainder of the war. Stalingrad (or Volgograd as it was later renamed) was a turning point not only in the history of the war but in the history of central and eastern Europe as well.

American equipment meanwhile all through 1943 was arriving in Russia in prodigious quantities. The terms of Lend-Lease were liberally extended to the Soviets; a stream of American planes, guns, vehicles, clothing, and food made its way laboriously to Russia through the Arctic Ocean and through the Persian Gulf. Machinery and equipment were sent for the Soviet arms plants, which were themselves tremendously increasing their output. Anglo-American bombing was crippling the German aviation industry at home. The Allied contribution to the Soviet war effort was indispensable but Russian human losses were tremendous. It was not forgotten in later years by the Russians that they lost more men in the battle of Stalingrad than the United States lost in combat during the entire war in all theaters combined.

With contemporary American successes in the Solomon Islands at the end of 1942 and the slow throttling of German submarines in the Atlantic, the beginning of the year 1943 brought new hope for the Allies in all quarters. In a spectacular campaign of July–August 1943, the British, Canadians, and Americans conquered the island of Sicily. Mussolini immediately fell; the twenty-one-year-old Fascist regime came to an end. Mussolini set up an "Italian Social Republic" in the north, but it was no more than a German puppet government. Some months later, in April 1945, the Duce, as he attempted to flee the country, was seized, shot, and strung up like a slaughtered pig by anti-Fascist Italians. The new Italian government under Marshal Badoglio, in August 1943, tried to make peace. The German army then occupied Italy. The Allies, having crossed to the Italian mainland, attacked from the south. In October the Badoglio government declared war on Germany, and Italy was recognized by the Allies as a "cobelligerent." But the Germans stubbornly blocked the advance of the Allies to Rome despite new Allied landings and beachheads. The Italian campaign turned into a long and disheartening stalemate because the Western Allies, concentrating troops in Great Britain for the approaching cross-Channel invasion, could never spare enough for the Italian front.

Festung Europa, especially along its western approaches, the coasts of Holland, Belgium, and France, bristled with every kind of fortification that German scientific and military ingenuity could devise. A seaborne attack upon Europe was an operation of wholly unprecedented kind. It differed from the earlier amphibious attacks on Algeria, Sicily, or the Pacific islands in that the defender in Europe, in the very part of Europe where the road and railway network was thickest, could immediately rush overwhelming reserves to the spot attacked—except insofar as feinting tactics kept him uncertain, air power destroyed his transport, or the Russians held the bulk of his forces in the East. Precise and elaborate plans had been worked out. Ten thousand aircraft were to provide aerial protection, scores of warships were to bombard the coast, 4,000 ships were to carry the invading troops and their supplies across the Channel, artificial harbors were to be created where none existed.

The invasion of Europe began before dawn on June 6, 1944. The spot selected was the coast of Normandy directly across the Channel from England. An unparalleled combination of forces, British, Canadian, and American, land, sea, and air, backed up by huge accumulations of supplies and reserves of men assembled in Great Britain, and the whole under the unified command of the American General Eisenhower, assaulted the French coast, established a beachhead and maintained a front. The Allies poured in their strength, over 130,000 men the first day, 1,000,000 within a month. The Germans were at first thrown back more easily than had been expected. By August Paris was liberated, by September the Allies crossed the frontier of Germany itself. In France, Italy, and Belgium the Resistance movements, which had grown up in secret during the later years of German occupation, now came into the open and drove out Germans and pro-German collaborators. In Germany

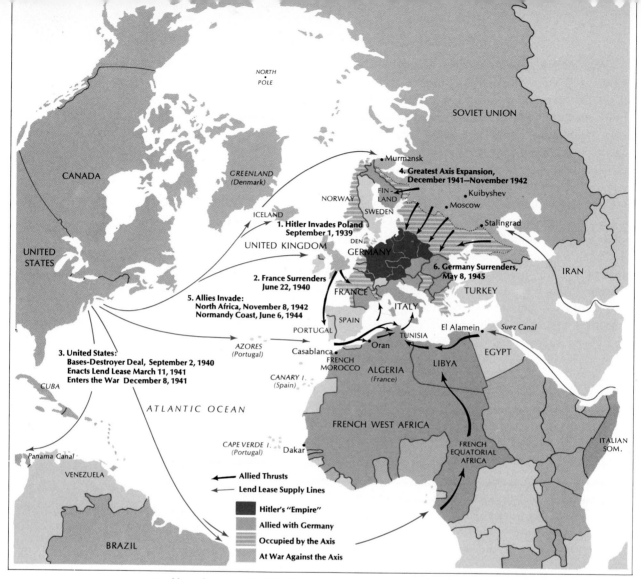

NORTH POLE

SOVIET UNION

CANADA

GREENLAND
(Denmark)

• Murmansk

**4. Greatest Axis Expansion,
December 1941–November 1942**

NORWAY

FIN-
LAND

• Kuibyshev

• Moscow

ICELAND

SWEDEN

• Stalingrad

**1. Hitler Invades Poland
September 1, 1939**

UNITED KINGDOM

DEN.

GERMANY

**6. Germany Surrenders,
May 8, 1945**

UNITED
STATES

IRAN

**2. France Surrenders
June 22, 1940**

FRANCE

TURKEY

**5. Allies Invade:
North Africa, November 8, 1942
Normandy Coast, June 6, 1944**

ITALY

SPAIN

El Alamein

Suez Canal

PORTUGAL

TUNISIA

**3. United States:
Bases-Destroyer Deal, September 2, 1940
Enacts Lend Lease March 11, 1941
Enters the War December 8, 1941**

AZORES
(Portugal)

Casablanca

Oran

EGYPT

FRENCH
MOROCCO

ALGERIA
(France)

LIBYA

CUBA

CANARY I.
(Spain)

ATLANTIC OCEAN

FRENCH WEST AFRICA

ITALIAN
SOM.

Panama Canal

CAPE VERDE I.
(Portugal)

Dakar

FRENCH
EQUATORIAL
AFRICA

VENEZUELA

Allied Thrusts

Lend Lease Supply Lines

BRAZIL

Hitler's "Empire"

Allied with Germany

Occupied by the Axis

At War Against the Axis

itself no deep-rooted Resistance movement ever developed, but a small group of men, military and civilian, formed an underground group. On July 20, 1944, it attempted to assassinate Hitler by exploding a bomb at his military headquarters in East Prussia; Hitler was only injured and took a fearsome revenge.

In August, in another amphibious operation, the Allies landed on the French Mediterranean coast and swept up from southern France to join the Allied forces advancing against stiffening resistance. At one point, momentarily, the Allied offensive even suffered a serious reversal. A sudden German drive, launched under Hitler's direct personal orders in December 1944 against thinly held American lines on the Belgian sector in the Ardennes, created a "bulge" in the advancing armies and caused heavy losses and confusion. But the Allies rallied. Neither Hitler's Ardennes counteroffensive nor the use of new destructive weapons rained on Britain, jet-propelled flying bombs and rockets, availed the Germans. The Western Allies pushed on and smashed through the heavily fortified Siegfried Line. The last natural

904

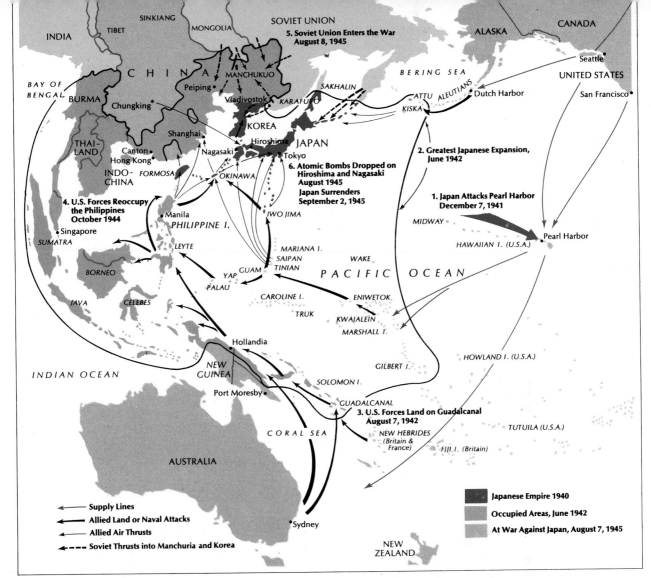

World War II. *These two maps show the global character of the war and the central position of the United States with respect to the European and Pacific theaters. The numbered legends summarize the successive stages of the war in both the Eastern and Western hemispheres. In 1942, with the Germans reaching as far east as Egypt and Stalingrad, and the Japanese as far west as Burma, the great danger to the Soviet-Western alliance was that these two might join forces, dominate southern Asia, control the oil resources of the Persian Gulf, and stop the flow of Western supplies to the Soviet Union from this direction. The almost simultaneous Soviet-Western successes, late in 1942, at Stalingrad and El Alamein, and in the invasion of Morocco-Algeria and of Guadalcanal, proved to be the turning point of the war. In 1943 the German submarine campaign in the Atlantic was defeated, so that American troops and supplies could move more freely to Europe. The invasion of Normandy in June 1944, with continuing Soviet pressure from the east, brought about German surrender in May 1945. Meanwhile, in the Pacific, American occupation of the islands and reoccupation of the Philippines prepared the way for the surrender of Japan, consummated by two atomic bombs in August 1945.*

905

obstacle, the Rhine, was crossed when in March 1945 American forces by a stroke of luck discovered an undestroyed bridge at Remagen; they poured troops over it and established a bridgehead—the first troops to cross the Rhine in combat since the armies of Napoleon. The main crossing, under the British, subsequently took place farther to the north. Soon the Allies were accepting wholesale surrenders in the Ruhr valley.

Meanwhile in 1944 the Russian armies swept the Germans from the Ukraine, White Russia, the Baltic states, and eastern Poland. By August they reached the suburbs of Warsaw. The Polish underground rose against the Germans but the Russians, determined that Poland must not be liberated by noncommunist Polish leadership, refused to permit aid to the rising, and it was crushed. The Russians, their lines overextended, and checked for several months by German strength in Poland, pushed southward into Rumania and Bulgaria; both countries changed sides and declared war against Germany. Early in 1945 the Russians, reopening their offensive, forced their way into East Prussia and Silesia and by February they reached the Oder, forty miles from Berlin, where Zhukov paused to regroup his forces. In March and April Russian forces occupied Budapest and Vienna.

The final drive on Germany began. Hitler moved troops from the collapsing western front to reinforce the stand on the Oder and to protect his capital. The German population did little to impede Western advances, hopeful that the Western allies might reach Berlin and indeed occupy as much of their country as possible, before the Russians. In April the Americans drew up on the Elbe, about sixty miles from Berlin, with hardly any obstacles before them; but here they halted, by decision of General Eisenhower who was without any firm political guidance from home. The Americans wanted a clear line of demarcation from the Russians, their supply lines were overextended, and they believed it necessary to divert some forces southward against a possible German last stand in an Alpine redoubt that never materialized, but mainly the decision was a gesture of good will toward the Russians who were to be permitted to take Berlin as compensation for their heavy sacrifices in the common cause. Similarly, the American troops that moved southward were held back from taking Prague and the Russians were permitted to take the Czech capital too. By some it was later said that the fate of central Europe was determined by the war in the Far East; the Americans sought Russian aid against Japan, which it turned out, could readily have been dispensed with. In any event, the Russians were in control of all the major capitals of central and eastern Europe; in the case of Berlin and Prague it need not have been that way.

The Western Allies and the Soviets offered no terms to Hitler, nor to any Germans. They demanded unconditional surrender, and the Germans fought on in the very streets of Berlin. On the last day of April Hitler perished by his own hand in the ruins of his capital after denouncing some of his closest party subordinates, including Göring, as traitors. Admiral Doenitz, designated by Hitler as his successor, went through the formalities of surrender on May 8, 1945. Since fighting had already ceased on the Italian front a few days earlier, the war in Europe was now over.

In the Pacific, against Japan, operations had dragged on for three years, hampered by the strategic decision to concentrate against Germany first. Slowly, from points in the Solomon Islands, the easternmost fringe of the Indonesian archipelago, American forces, at first very small, worked their way in a northwesterly direction toward faraway Japan. They had to fight in turn for Guadalcanal, for New Guinea, for the reconquest of the Philippines. They had to fight for the Japanese islands and atolls in the mid-Pacific (taken by Japan from the Germans after the First World War and converted into powerful naval bases), the Gilbert Islands, the Marshalls, the Carolines, the Marianas. In October 1944 they won a great naval victory at the battle of Leyte Gulf. Finally, in one of the war's greatest and final battles, they won the island of Okinawa, only 300 miles from Japan itself. Okinawa was captured just as the Germans collapsed in Europe. From the new Allied bases that had been won, from Saipan, from Iwo Jima, and from Okinawa, and from aircraft carriers a heavy bomber offensive was launched against Japan, such as had devastated Germany in the preceding two years, shattering Japanese industry, destroying the remnants of the Japanese navy, and compelling the Japanese government to give serious thought to suing for peace. The Allied leaders refused to believe that Japanese defenses were ready to crumble or that the Japanese were ready to negotiate. The American army prepared to shift combat troops from the European theater to the Far East. The stage was being set for a full-scale invasion of Japan itself.

Then, on August 6, 1945, an atomic bomb, prepared in utmost secrecy by American and European scientists, hit the city of Hiroshima, with a population of 200,000 people, which it destroyed by a single explosion with the loss of over 70,000 lives. Two days later, the Soviet Union, which had pledged itself to enter the conflict in the East within three months after the surrender of Germany, declared war on Japan and invaded Manchuria. On August 9 an even more powerful atomic bomb struck Nagasaki. The Japanese made peace at once. On September 2, 1945, the formal surrender was signed. The emperor was permitted to remain as head of the state, but the Japanese islands were placed under the rule of a United States army of occupation.

The Second World War of the twentieth century was over. The same cold impersonal statistics that had recorded 10,000,000 killed in the First World War now reported some 15,000,000 military deaths and at least that many civilian fatalities. Russian military deaths were estimated at over 7,000,000, German at 3,500,000, Chinese at 2,200,000, Japanese at 1,300,000; British and Commonwealth losses were about 350,000, American about 300,000, French about 200,000. The death figures would have been greater except that one of every two soldiers seriously wounded was saved by new sulfa and penicillin drugs and by blood plasma transfusions. None of these military statistics could be more than approximate and no one could begin to estimate the complete toll of human lives lost in the war, directly or indirectly, from the bombings, the mass-extermination and deportation policies of the Germans, the postwar famines and epidemics. Perhaps the losses came to 35,000,000 or 40,000,000, but at such figures the human mind retreats and human sensitivities are dulled. It is enough to say that peace had come.

The foundations of the peace had been laid, it was thought, during a number of major wartime Allied conferences. In August 1941 Roosevelt and Churchill had met at sea off the coast of Newfoundland and had drawn up the Atlantic Charter. There were meetings in 1943 at Casablanca, at Cairo, and at Teheran (in the latter Stalin participated for the first time); and in the final phase of the war, in February 1945, at Yalta, and in July 1945, at Potsdam, in the environs of shattered Berlin.

The Atlantic Charter, issued jointly by Roosevelt and Churchill at their first meeting, resembled in spirit the Fourteen Points of Woodrow Wilson. It pledged that sovereign rights and self-government would be restored to all who had been forcibly deprived of them, that all nations would have equal access to world trade and world resources, that all peoples would work together to achieve improved living standards and economic security. The postwar peace, it promised, would assure for men in all lands freedom from fear and want and would guarantee an end to force and aggression in international affairs. Here, and in the Four Freedoms enunciated earlier by President Roosevelt, the ideological basis of the peace was proclaimed. At the 1943 conferences, and through other consultations, the Allies endeavored to concert their military plans. At Casablanca, in January 1943, it was resolved to accept nothing less than the "unconditional surrender" of the Axis powers. The vague formula, adopted somewhat cavalierly at American initiative, and without much thought to possible political implications, was intended mainly to prevent a recurrence of anything like the ambiguity surrounding the armistice of 1918.[9] Though much criticized in later years (and not fully applied in the case of Japan), it is doubtful whether the decision had any true bearing on the outcome of events. German resistance was stubbornly prolonged because of Hitler's mad will, and his support by the military, not because responsible leaders would have been willing or able to sue for peace if the Allies had offered them appropriate terms. At Teheran, in December 1943, the occupation and demilitarization of Germany was discussed and plans laid for the establishment of a postwar international organization.

Meanwhile, as the Russian armies advanced against the Germans in 1944, the fate of central and eastern Europe became a very important question. Throughout the war Roosevelt and the Americans, unwilling to disturb the unity of the Western-Soviet coalition in the global struggle, followed a policy of postponing controversial territorial and political decisions until victory was assured. Churchill was more apprehensive. Steeped in traditional balance-of-power politics, he sensed that, without bargaining and prior political arrangements, the victory over the Nazis would leave Russia dominant over all eastern Europe. Acting on his own, he visited Stalin in October 1944 and sketched out a demarcation of spheres of influence for the Western powers and the Soviets in the Balkan states (a Russian preponderance in Rumania and Bulgaria, a Western preponderance in Greece, and an even division of influence in Hungary and Yugoslavia). Russian control over the Baltic states had

°See p. 755.

virtually been conceded by the British earlier. But Roosevelt and the State Department would not ratify any such agreement; it was considered old-fashioned and a dangerous revival of the worst features of pre-1914 diplomacy. Soon, however, political decisions had to be made. The two conferences that arrived at the most important political decisions were the meetings at Yalta and at Potsdam in 1945.

The Yalta meeting in February 1945 took place when the Allies were close to final victory—closer, events disclosed, than anyone at the time realized. The three Allied statesmen met at an old tsarist Crimean summer resort on the Black Sea, toasted their common triumphs, and took the measure of each other. Roosevelt thought of himself in the role of a mediator between Churchill and Stalin where European issues were involved. He took pains to avoid giving Stalin the impression that he and Churchill were in any sense united against him; in point of fact, Roosevelt was even suspicious of Churchill's devotion to empire and colonial ties, which he considered anachronistic for the postwar world. Despite differences, agreements were reached between the Big Three, at least formally, on Poland and eastern Europe, Germany, the war in the Far East, and the projected postwar international organization, the United Nations.

The discussion of Poland and eastern Europe raised the most serious difficulties. Stalin's armies, having driven the Nazi forces to within forty miles of Berlin, were in control of Poland and almost all eastern and central Europe. The Russians remembered these areas as anti-Soviet, and Poland particularly as the perpetrator of aggression against Soviet territory in 1920 and as the ancient corridor of attack upon Russia. Stalin had already taken steps to establish a "friendly" government in Poland, i.e., a government subservient to the Soviets. Neither Roosevelt nor Churchill had fought the war against the Nazis to leave Russia the undisputed master of all eastern Europe and in a position to impose a totalitarian political system on all this vast area. At Yalta, Roosevelt and Churchill extracted from Stalin a number of promises for the areas he controlled. In accordance with the Atlantic Charter, the liberated states were to be permitted provisional governments "broadly representative of all democratic elements in the population," i.e., not consisting merely, as in the case of the provisional government of Poland already established, of authorities subservient to the Soviets. They pressed Stalin to pledge also the "earliest possible establishment through free elections of governments responsive to the will of the people." The pledge was a verbal concession that cost the Russian leader little; he rejected the suggestion of international supervision over the elections. The Declaration on Liberated Europe, promising sovereign rights of self-determination, provided a false sense of agreement.

A number of territorial changes were also accepted, pending final settlement at the postwar peace conference. It was agreed that the Russian-Polish, or eastern, boundary of Poland should be set roughly at the so-called Curzon line, the frontier contemplated by the Allies in 1919 before the Poles conquered territory to its east. The Poles were to be compensated, in the north and west, at the expense of Germany.[10] On this and on other matters relating to Germany there was a large area of accord; the three were united in their hatred of German Nazism and militarism.

[10] See maps, p. 259 and front end papers; and see p. 787.

Germany was to be disarmed and divided into four occupation zones, to be administered by the Big Three powers and by France—the latter at the insistence of Churchill. There was vague talk, at Yalta and earlier, of dismembering Germany, of undoing the work of Bismarck, but the difficulties of such an undertaking were understood and the proposal was postponed, later to be discarded completely. Also discarded, as impracticable, was the Morgenthau plan, seriously considered as late as 1944, which was designed to transform industrial Germany back into an eighteenth-century pastoral and agricultural economy. The demand for reparations raised by the Soviets, in the total amount of $20,000,000,000, to be paid in kind, half to go to the Soviets, was rejected as excessive, but it was agreed that reparations would go to those countries that had borne the main burden of the war and suffered the heaviest losses; the Soviet Union would receive half the total sum; details were to be worked out later.

To the satisfaction of everyone, the participants agreed on plans for a postwar international organization, to be called the United Nations. Roosevelt believed it essential to win the Soviets over to the idea of an international organization. He was convinced that the big powers, cooperating within the framework of the United Nations, and acting as international policemen, could alone preserve the future peace and security of the world. No less than Stalin or Churchill, he emphasized the importance of the big powers in the new organization although he accepted a dignified role for the smaller nations as well. It was agreed that each of the big powers, the permanent members of the new organization's Security Council, would have a veto power on all important decisions. The Soviets pressed for more than one vote in the General Assembly of the new organization, arguing that their constitution gave sovereign rights to each of their constituent republics and that the British dominions would each have a seat. It was agreed not to contest their claim for three seats. To Roosevelt this was a small concession; the American president rejoiced that an international organization was to come into being and that the Soviets were to participate.[11]

Critical agreements were reached on the Far East. Here political and military decisions were inextricably linked. In April 1941 the Soviets had concluded a nonaggression treaty with Japan and had remained neutral in the Pacific war despite their historic interests in the Far East. Given the magnitude of the war effort on the European front, no one pressed the Soviets to enter the Pacific war. It was agreed to wait at least until the Germans were on the verge of defeat. Now, at Yalta, it was hoped by the most important American military advisers that Russia could be persuaded to join the war against the Japanese. Though Japan was badly battered and its morale sinking, it was still estimated that Japanese resistance would last some eighteen months after Germany's fall; and a bloody invasion of the Japanese homeland was projected. The atomic bomb was in an advanced state of preparation but had not yet been tested. Russian participation, it was felt, would pin down the Japanese armies on the Chinese mainland and save Allied lives.

[11]See pp. 932–933.

Stalin agreed to enter the war against Japan, but he sought compensation; Russian "public opinion," the Soviet dictator averred, would demand it. It was stipulated that the U.S.S.R. would enter the war against Japan "two to three months" after Germany had surrendered. In return, the Soviets were to have restored to them territories and rights which tsarist Russia had lost to Japan forty years before in the Russo-Japanese war of 1904–1905—the southern half of Sakhalin Island, and in Manchuria special concessions at the warm-water port of Dairen and at the naval base of Port Arthur, as well as joint control with China over the Manchurian railroads leading to these ports; in addition, the Soviets were to receive the Kurile Islands, which had not been Russian before.[12] The Russian position in Outer Mongolia was also to remain unaltered. Meanwhile Stalin confirmed Chinese political sovereignty over Manchuria despite the privileges granted to the Soviets, and pledged Soviet support for the Nationalist government of China, then on uneasy terms with the Chinese Communists.[13]

But China was not a party to any of these concessions, which for a time were kept secret. Roosevelt took it upon himself to secure the consent of Chiang Kai-shek, which he subsequently did. By the territorial concessions to the Soviets in the Far East, the Western powers seemed to be sanctioning the replacement of Japanese imperialism by Russian imperialism in the long contested area of northeast China, and without China having any voice in the matter at all. The concessions were the price to be paid for Soviet assistance against the Japanese, assistance then considered indispensable for the final defeat of Japan. What really exasperated so many in later years was that Russia's entry into the war, as pledged, was not of the slightest military consequence; it came two days after the atomic bomb had been dropped, and at a time when the Japanese were in a desperate state, near to collapse and surrender, even without the dropping of the atomic bomb. The concessions in the Far East need not have been made. Even without the Yalta agreement, nothing perhaps except outright force could have deterred Stalin from moving into Manchuria after the Japanese collapse, or indeed from controlling eastern Europe as he wished. The Yalta agreement lent, however, an aura of respectability to Soviet expansion.

Roosevelt made concessions at Yalta not only because he esteemed the Soviet war effort against the Germans but because he believed that he needed their support in the last phase of the war against the Japanese; he wished to preserve the Western-Soviet coalition until the final victory was guaranteed. Above all else, he believed that wartime harmony would produce postwar cordiality, especially if all the participating personalities remained alive to assure it. Churchill was somewhat less certain of the future and of "diplomacy by friendship" and would have preferred a franker recognition and definition of spheres of influence. Such ideas were ruled out as the thinking of a bygone era. Yet the spirit of the Atlantic Charter, so closely identified with the American president, the pledge of sovereign self-determination for all peoples, was contravened at Yalta in many ways. Like the Versailles treaty of

[12] See pp. 705–706 and map, p. 707.
[13] See pp. 836–837, 946–948.

1919, the decisions at Yalta would not have been so disappointing had the ideals not been set so high.

At Potsdam, in July 1945, after the German collapse, the Big Three met again. A new American president, Harry S Truman, represented the United States; President Roosevelt had died in April, on the eve of final victory. Churchill, in the midst of the conference, was replaced by the new British prime minister Clement Attlee after the Labour party's victory at the polls. Stalin still represented Russia. By now, disagreements between the Western Allies and the Soviets had deepened, not only over Soviet control in Poland, eastern Europe, and the Balkans, but over German reparations and other matters. Yet the Western leaders were still prepared to make concessions in the hope of establishing harmonious relations. Agreements were announced on the postwar treatment of Germany, on German disarmament, demilitarization, "denazification," and the punishment of war criminals. It was agreed that each power might take reparations in kind from its occupation zone and that the Russians would get substantial additional deliveries from the Western zones so that the original $10,000,000,000 Soviet demand was virtually met. Pending the final peace treaty, German territory east of the Oder-Neisse rivers was committed to Polish administration. The details of this decision had earlier been postponed; now the Polish-German boundary was set at the western Neisse, even further west than originally envisaged. Poland thus extended its territorial boundaries about a hundred miles westward as compensation for Russian westward expansion at Polish expense. German East Prussia was similarly divided between Russia in the north and Poland in the south. Königsberg, founded by the Teutonic Knights, for centuries the ducal seat of Prussian dukes and the coronation city of Prussian kings, became the Russian city of Kaliningrad. The ancient German cities of Stettin and Breslau became the Polish cities of Szczecin and Wroclaw. The *de facto* administration of these areas hardened into permanent rule. The transfer of the German population in these eastern areas was supposed to be effected in an orderly and humane fashion; but millions of Germans were soon driven from their homes or fled within a few months. For them (and for the Germans who were expelled from the Sudetenland) it was the final consummation of the war that Hitler had unleashed.

It was agreed at Potsdam that peace treaties would be signed as soon as possible with the former German satellite states; the task of preparing them was entrusted to a Council of Foreign Ministers representing the United States, Britain, France, the Soviet Union, and China. In the months that followed, the widening chasm between the Soviets and the West manifested itself in stormy meetings of the Foreign Ministers' Council in London, Paris, and New York, as well as in the Peace Conference held in Paris in 1946 at which were represented the twenty-one states that had contributed substantial military forces to the defeat of the Axis powers. Eighteen months after Potsdam, in February 1947, treaties were finally signed with Italy, Rumania, Hungary, Bulgaria, and Finland. All these states paid reparations and agreed to certain territorial adjustments. In 1951 a peace treaty was signed with Japan, but not by the Soviets, who made their own peace in 1956. The years went by but no final peace treaty was signed with Germany, a Germany divided into two. For the wartime Western-Soviet coalition had fallen apart, shattering the dreams and aspirations of those who had fought the Second World War to a resounding triumph over one kind of aggression and totalitarianism, and now found themselves confronted with a new age of crisis.

"Modernization" is an experience that peoples throughout the world are undergoing in the later twentieth century. It takes many forms, but among its most obvious signs are airplanes and supermarkets, computer technology and urban congestion. That these can now be found in all continents is suggested in the following pages.

One consequence is a new global uniformity in certain aspects of civilization. It is no longer a matter of Westernization, as used to be said of what happened in Japan and Russia, nor of the Americanization of the world that has sometimes been pointed to with alarm. It is a process in which Americans and Europeans have been instrumental, but which arises from the effects of modern science, engineering, medicine, transportation, and electronic communications wherever they are introduced. It seems that human beings of all cultures and races may develop an aptitude to pursue these activities, and that they have wants which such activities can supply.

But as modern civilization becomes more widespread, paradoxical countercurrents are set up. Cultures interpenetrate one another. While Asia and Africa adopt new techniques from the West, Europeans and Americans seek out Eastern religions or find a new meaning in West African tribal art. Older cultures are eroded in Asia and Africa, and in the West itself, where practices that have characterized Europe at least since the Renaissance—in painting, sculpture, architecture, literature, religion, personal values, child-rearing and family life—have been increasingly called into question. Some peoples, on the other hand, feel a new attachment to their own background as a means of heightening their own identity. Accepting the interdependence of a world civilization, they strive not only for political but for cultural or spiritual independence.

To operate an airline, or any other appurtenance of modern civilization, requires a high degree of accuracy, division of labor, and the synchronization of the efforts of many persons who must perform certain actions at a given time. These in turn presuppose the objectivity of knowledge and rationality of behavior, and an acceptance of discipline, foresight, organization and management. But these very qualities generate their opposites. It is a further paradox that new philosophies of subjectivity and irrationalism, revolts against form and demands for free self-expression, have been thought of as signs of modernity in the twentieth century. Organization restricts liberty, yet is necessary to modern life. It is not easy for man to adapt to the social environment that he has himself created to improve his condition. The paradox is as old as Rousseau, yet is felt increasingly every day.

PARADOXES OF MODERNITY

The office of International Business Machines seems in strange company alongside the mosque in Istanbul, Turkey, but it would seem no more so alongside a Gothic church in Europe. Here there is the additional juxtaposition of East and West.

At the right, two youths work on a computer problem at Ibadan University in Nigeria. Their costume reflects their own time and place, but the young man at the right shows a concentration and perplexity that are universal. Ibadan University is a new institution, dating from 1962, but the multiplication of universities, with their attendant problems, is a sign of modernization in all countries.

Above, the king of Akure, who is actually a British-trained lawyer, is seated in his robes conducting a seminar in law for Nigerian civil servants. The students are in Western garments, even to the wristwatch and necktie. The books are in English; familiarity with the English or French language is the most useful legacy that Black Africa has received from the colonial period.

At the right, three Yoruba women shop in a supermarket at Lagos, Nigeria. Urbanization has proceeded so rapidly in Africa that Lagos now has about a million people in its metropolitan area. Most of them were born in rural villages under very different conditions.

The assumptions underlying Western art since the Renaissance have perhaps been abandoned most fully in sculpture. The statue which celebrated a great man or an allegorical figure from the fifteenth century through the nineteenth has become even more rare than the realistic portrait painting; it might even be thought ludicrous today.

Henry Moore, at the left, born in England in 1898, is one of the leading sculptors of the twentieth century. He is shown in a room where he keeps his collection of plaster maquettes, the working models for the finished products over his long career. As early as 1920, breaking with European traditions of sculpture, he became interested in the art of pre-Columbian America, Black Africa and archaic or preclassical Greece. The models on these shelves reveal influences of this kind. In the quest for a new accent, for boldness of line or emphatic abstraction, the modern and the primitive come together.

Above: An exhibit of contemporary American painting and sculpture at Moscow in 1959. The Russian woman is puzzled by what she sees, as many Americans would also be. The Soviet regime has frowned upon modern art, seeing in it a sign of decadence, and has favored a socialist realism which is believed to be more attuned to the plain working people. The hostility between communism and avant-garde movements in the arts is another paradox of modernity, since both arose in revolt against the bourgeois society of nineteenth-century Europe.

At the right, workmen decorate the base of a new building in Lagos. The building itself, the 25-story Independence House, is a monument to modernization, but the façade shown here, with its bas-relief by the Nigerian sculptor Relix Idubor, represents three figures from traditional folklore or history.

At the left: Rush hour in Tokyo. Except for the three Japanese characters, and the Japanese faces, this could be a picture from many other cities in the world, where thousands of men and women must start for home over considerable distances at exactly the same time.

Above: Paper work, with overflowing in-baskets and out-baskets, reinforced by the telephone, is another sure indication of modern times. This busy executive is at work in Nigeria.

Above: Five disciples consult a guru or religious teacher in an obscure retreat in the foothills of the Himalayas. The two in front are from Latin America, and have come to India in the belief that the philosophies of Hinduism and the ancient Mayas may have much in common. They are in any case seeking for something that they do not find in modern civilization.

Left: A Japanese super-express passes Mt. Fuji between Tokyo and Osaka. If not a paradox, it is at least worthy of comment, that some forms of modernization have gone further in Japan than in Europe or North America.

XXI: THE CONTEM

ORARY AGE

A cataclysm, according to Webster's dictionary, is "any violent change involving sudden and extensive alterations of the earth's surface; hence, any upheaval, especially a social or political one." A cataclysm in nature, as we may imagine it, is a time when volcanoes erupt, earthquakes rumble, old mountain systems are broken down, new peaks and ranges thrust themselves upward, the very coastlines assume new shapes, living creatures flee from destruction, old forms of life become extinct, and new forms of life, at first unnoticed, enter upon careers in which they are later to flourish. The human world has been in the grip of such a cataclysm since 1914. The First World War, the postwar troubles, the Russian Revolution, the Great Depression, the parade of the dictators, the Second World War, the expansion of communism in eastern Europe, the rise of communist China, the birth of new nations in Asia and Africa, and the emergence of the Soviet and American superpowers are all part of the same process of readjustment, which has altered the very coastlines of human society beyond recognition, and for which "cataclysm" is not too strong a word.

With the awareness that no mere chapter can do justice to the complexities of the world since 1945, nor keep abreast of the onrushing events of our own day, the

Chapter Emblem: The earth as seen from a satellite 22,300 miles away, transmitting a photograph to a station in North Carolina.

present chapter attempts to sketch the most memorable developments of what we have called the contemporary age.

Broadly speaking, the world in the second half of the twentieth century faced no wholly new problems, yet certain basic problems that had troubled mankind for over a century had become both more complex and more urgent. Three can be singled out—the problem of science, the problem of industrialism, and the problem of national sovereignty.

The problem of science was dramatized by the atomic bomb. The world shuddered at the instantaneous destruction of Hiroshima. With the war ending on this note, and with postwar improvements of atomic and hydrogen bombs, it was realized that a third world war would be unimaginably more awful. The use of intercontinental guided missiles, radio controls, proximity fuses, and probably biological warfare could be foreseen. Man, it was said, now possessed the means to annihilate not only his civilization but the very existence of human life on the planet. This thought was appalling to a world which had set its highest values on social progress. And in truth, the reflective person wondered more than ever before how he or his family might meet their deaths, or what sufferings they might be called upon to endure.

The problem of science was not new. Science, with its partner, invention, had for a long time transformed the methods used in both industry and war. It had conquered many of the dread plagues and diseases of mankind. Observant people had long known that science could be applied either constructively or destructively, that knowledge was power, that the intelligence was the instrument of the will. It was the magnitude of destructive possibilities that made people formerly indifferent now see and worry over the problem. Scientists themselves rushed forward, after the first atomic explosion, to affirm the need of a moral regeneration. They insisted that science was neutral, that it was free from blame for the horror of Hiroshima, that scientific investigation must remain free, that the trouble lay only in the uses to which scientific knowledge was put. Not since the days of Galileo had scientists been so embarrassed or so aroused over moral and social issues. Somehow science, or the exaggerated reliance on science, had misfired. The dream of those prophets of a scientific civilization, Bacon and Descartes, the idea that accumulation of scientific knowledge would automatically bring more human welfare, had taken on the ghastly distortions of a nightmare.

One answer was that there must be more social science. With better understanding of society and of human behavior, it seemed, men need not use physical science to kill each other. It was certainly true that the more fully society was understood, the better for all concerned. But here too lay a danger. From the scientific understanding of human behavior it could be a short step to the scientific control of human behavior. We have seen how, in totalitarian states, governments not merely accepted the fact that people were shaped by environment but undertook to monopolize the environment and do the shaping themselves. A society in which science was pursued as one of many interests was one thing. A purely "scientific" society was another. In the latter, people might simply be manipulated by experts. Prophets of a scientific civilization had formerly drawn alluring pictures of a New Atlantis. Now, prognosticators were more likely to portray a drab and mechanized world of the future, in which a ruling elite governed the masses by scientific "techniques," using plenty of carbon paper, long-distance telephones, and computers, poring over statistical reports, card indexes, photographs and fingerprints, advised by social psychologists, public opinion pollsters, and propaganda technicians, and exercising a new technocratic despotism with the help of the police. George Orwell's *1984* and Aldous Huxley's *Brave New World* were the best known of the "antiutopias" that appeared.

The problem of science passed over into the political problem. It was not science, but the practical uses of science, and the question of who should determine its practical uses, that created the difficulty. Scientific understanding of nuclear fission produced the atomic bomb not because of anything in the nature of science or of nuclear fission, but because of something in the nature of human society and the clash of human wills.

The problem of industrialism and of security in an industrial society also persisted. Industrialism produced a high degree of division of labor. Specialization reigned among persons within the same small community and among the great regions of the earth. Each was dependent on continuing interchange with others. Each person, moreover, could perform his task only with the use of a great deal of capital. Railroad workers had to have a railroad; the farmer had to have access to a tractor; even the musician, after composing a symphony, could not hear it played unless someone paid a hundred performers' wages. There were in theory two opposite social poles. At one, best represented by the U.S.S.R., all capital was owned by the state and supplied to workers as needed, and all interchange was planned out in detail by public authorities in advance. At the other pole, best represented by the United States, capital was owned by private persons, who chose the channels of investment and hence determined the availability of jobs, and interchange took place through the mechanism of the market. Neither system was in practice logically pure, and in fact mixed economies became the rule in many countries, but the difference remained pronounced. The drawback in the Soviet system was its lack of freedom, in the American system its lack of stability or of economic security. Americans spent a good deal more time trying to correct the lack of security than the Soviets did in trying to correct the lack of freedom.

The devastation of western Europe in 1945, the problem of a ruined industrialism in one of the world's chief industrial areas, of a society unable to produce with efficiency yet obliged to produce enough to satisfy a civilized population, led, like the problem of science, straight into the thick of political questions. Nor was Europe the only center of trouble. In Asia and Africa the impact of Western ideas and Western technologies had helped create societies that sought Western technological proficiency but also at the same time sought independence from the West. In Asia especially the conditions of a world-wide industrialism, and advances in medicine, sanitation, and public health, had helped to build up dense populations which after the war were multiplying at unprecedented rates. The new governments, in India and Pakistan, or in Indonesia and Malaysia, or in the People's Republic of China, had to feed and satisfy these great multitudes of people. They believed that only by industrializing could they raise their living standards. They needed machinery, loans, advisers; they looked in part to the Soviet Union and in part to the United States and to an economically recovered Europe. Colonialism in Asia and Africa was dead, but the need of Asians and Africans for assistance was very much alive, and in the furnishing of assistance there was bound to be competition.

Another question hinged on the unity and diversity of the modern world. Was the modern world really "one world," or was it not? It was one world in the sense that it required a good deal of mutual exchange, and in the sense that political repercussions traveled over it rapidly. But it was far from homogeneous. Half a dozen great cultures and hundreds of little ones clung to their identities. All admired the steam turbine, and stood in awe of atomic fission, but beyond the material level their schemes of values widely diverged. None wished to be subordinated to another, or to lose its own way of life in the gray vagueness of a uniform world civilization. Here lay the root of the problem of national independence and of its corollary, world organization.

After the Second World War, as after the First, a concerted effort was made to set up an international organization to prevent war in the future.[1] A conference of all anti-Axis powers, held at San Francisco in 1945, established the United Nations on the basis of wartime cooperation. The United Nations, like the League of Nations which it superseded, had numerous organs of which two were central: a General Assembly in which all recognized sovereign states, however small, were considered equal; and a Security Council made up of the five states regarded as great powers—the United States, Great Britain, France, the Soviet Union, and China—plus six elected members chosen by the Assembly for two-year terms. Each great power enjoyed a veto. The Security Council could act on important matters only if the great powers were unanimous.

Since only a great power could bring about a great war, and since any great power bent on war would obviously veto any measures aimed against it, it was clear that the United Nations could not prevent a large-scale war if one were actually imminent. Hence many people criticized the provision in the United Nations charter for a great-power veto. They declared that it recognized the very national sovereignty which led to international war, and they urged some kind of world state in its place, which should have the authority to put down violence anywhere in the world as the national state puts down violence within its own borders. It was certain, however, that the veto was necessary. The U.S.S.R. demanded it most frankly and used it most freely, but no other great power, including the United States, would have consented to enter or remain in the United Nations without this safeguard to its own freedom of

[1]See pp. 755–756, 762, 910.

action. In practice, without the veto, one or more great powers would withdraw, and the United Nations would become a mere alliance against nonmembers. The chief weakness of the old League, it was remembered, was the fact that all the great powers had not belonged to it, and that the United States never joined. In the following years even small countries on occasion refused to abide by judgments of the United Nations. It seemed likely that no people, large or small, possessing a state of its own was yet willing, in a matter considered vital, to forego its independence. Yet in the grave international tension that marked the postwar years, the United Nations stood as a testimonial to the human hope for international cooperation and peace.

Although the United Nations Security Council provided permanent seats for five powers, the war, in effect, left only two great powers still standing in any strength, the United States and the Soviet Union. Since the seventeenth century the world has normally had some half a dozen great powers. That there were only two in 1945 made a great difference. Moreover, the two were superpowers, continental land giants, possessing enormous resources and military strength, overshadowing all other states, including the great powers of Europe that had long dominated events in the modern centuries. The characteristic of a two-state system, not found in a multiple-state system, is that each superpower knows in advance who its only dangerous enemy can be. In such a situation diplomatic delicacy breaks down. All measures that either power takes for its own security seem to be provocations to the other. After the war the United States and the U.S.S.R. fell into this unpleasant dualistic relationship. From 1945 on, there set in a diplomatic and ideological clash of interests and ideas which came to be known as the Cold War, which, with many alterations and vicissitudes, persisted on into the second half of the twentieth century.

We have already noted the state of affairs at the close of hostilities.[2] Russian armies occupied eastern Europe as far west as the river Elbe; American, British, and French armies held the remainder of Germany, most of Austria, and all of Italy. The movement of ground armies during the fighting generally determined the spheres of influence after the peace, except that the four powers effected the necessary transfer of troops in order to occupy the zones of Germany agreed upon at Potsdam. The Soviets at the last moment, in August 1945, had declared war on Japan and moved into Manchuria and Korea. Soon, in the months that followed, from 1945 to 1947, they lent aid to separatists in northern Iran; pressed the Turks for joint control of the Turkish Straits; favored the communists in a civil war in Greece; forced a communist government upon the countries of eastern Europe; communized their occupation zone in East Germany; refused to cooperate in economic policies toward occupied Germany; rejected atomic disarmament proposals; and called for an active offensive of the communist parties of war-torn western Europe. All this time they actively supported the revolutionary offensive in Asia, aiding the Chinese communists,

[2] See pp. 906–907.

supporting the communist-led rebels in Indochina and elsewhere, and establishing a puppet communist regime in North Korea.

It was not possible for anyone (even in Russia) to know what Stalin and the men in the Kremlin really believed or intended in 1945. Probably, as confirmed Marxist-Leninists, they considered a clash between the U.S.S.R. and the Western powers to be inevitable at some indefinite future date. Probably they were disturbed by American monopoly of the atomic bomb. Probably they felt that the fluid postwar situation gave them a chance to establish an outer buffer zone favorable to Russia, a program on which they had already embarked in their alliance with Germany in 1939, which had allowed them to absorb eastern Poland and the Baltic states—or to reabsorb them, since these regions had been Russian for over a century before 1918. Probably they also saw in the aftermath of the Second World War, as they had seen in the aftermath of the First, an opportunity to advance the international Marxist revolution in Europe and in Asia.

The U.S.S.R. rejected a plan put forward by the United States, and accepted by other powers, to put the manufacture of atomic weapons under international supervision and control. Disarmament in the past had always failed because some disarmed and some did not. The United States proposal therefore carried a condition: that the international control body, to prevent the manufacture of atomic bombs by national governments, should have the right to send inspectors at will into all countries, and to enforce sanctions, regardless of the veto, against any country found guilty of unauthorized uses of atomic power. To the Soviets the idea of having foreigners freely examine their society had always been repugnant. They declared that inspection would violate national sovereignty. They questioned the good faith of the American proposal. Preferring to rely on themselves, they proceeded with their own atomic research, as did the United States. By 1949 the U.S.S.R. was equipped to conduct atomic warfare. The atomic armaments race, universally dreaded, began.

The Soviet Union, to protect its interests in an international body where the overwhelming majority was consistently against it, made increasingly frequent use of its veto in the United Nations. Although action by the United Nations resulted in Soviet withdrawal from Iran, the United States found the United Nations alone inadequate to check communist expansion. It began to develop a positive national policy of its own to "contain" communism. In 1947, by the "Truman Doctrine," it supplied military equipment and professional military advisers to Greece and Turkey and announced a policy of assisting all peoples to prevent forcible capture of their governments by minority parties. At the same time, under a plan announced in 1947 by the American Secretary of State George Marshall, a program of broad economic aid to all European countries was projected, including the Soviet satellites if they would accept it; the hope was that the economic reconstruction of Europe would check communist gains from hunger and distress.

The Soviets for their part denounced the American "warmongers." With the United States arming Greece and Turkey, with American carriers able to sail the

length of the Mediterranean or lie off the coast of Murmansk, with American air bases established or easy to establish in the Middle East, with the Americans in occupation of southern Korea and Japan, and virtually annexing Okinawa, and with the bulk of the United States lying across the North Pole from the vital centers of the Soviet Union, and the American capacity for long-range bombardment already sufficiently demonstrated, the Soviets not unnaturally felt encircled. Soviet suspicions, dating from Munich, and even from the civil war of 1918–1919, from the second-front controversy in the Second World War and the friction immediately after the war, became inflamed.

The great object of rivalry in the early postwar years was Europe. Europe, the main protagonist of this long history, was in ruins in 1945. The Second World War left it in a worse state of shock and disorder than the First. Physical destruction was incomparably greater. In the First World War trench warfare had thoroughly destroyed limited regions. In the Second the ground fighting made a ruin of western Russia, and the air bombing reduced whole cities, especially in Germany, to piles of debris. The so-called strategic bombing had blighted the productive industry and the transport facilities of the Continent. Goods, even if produced, could not be moved; millions of refugees from bombed-out cities or from hostile political regimes sought miserably for an asylum. More people died of starvation or cold, in civilized Europe in 1945 and 1946, than at any time in generations or even in centuries.

The war had ruined one of the world's chief industrial areas and brought its industrial system to collapse. The dense European population could support itself only by an industry and exchange that had broken down. The war damage, chiefly bomb damage, destroyed the capital accumulation of generations—housing, paved streets, utilities plants, foundries, factories. And the ruin of freight yards, rolling stock, and bridges brought the interchange of commodities to a standstill. Town was cut off from country. City people dispersed to live with their country cousins or reverted to primitive methods of hunting for food and fuel. In a year or two the worst local devastation was repaired, but for a time the basic problem remained. Industrial Europe was unable to exchange with agricultural eastern Europe or with the world. The Continent was in the position in which the First World War had left Vienna. Europe was a world metropolis, a kind of huge continental city, cut off from the trading area with which it had exchanged. It was a former world capital in danger of becoming a slum. It lived by large and uninterrupted imports for which it could no longer afford to pay. It could not pay because in the second war, as in the first, Europeans lost most of their overseas investments, and overseas countries built up their own industries and had less need of those of Europe. Europe's capacity to manufacture for export was also injured by the war. At the same time, as an advanced industrial region, Europe had a politically awakened population. Europeans would not starve or suffer in mute resignation. The European economy, at the very time when its own productivity was badly impaired, had to carry a rising burden of social services and maintain the welfare state.

But Europe was not to be written off; its combined population exceeded that of either of the superpowers, and even in ruins it possessed one of the world's leading industrial plants. One of the chief postwar questions was therefore the rescue of

Europe, or, in practical politics, who Europe's "rescuer" was to be. There were only two candidates, the U.S.S.R. and the United States. Europeans did not relish the prospect of being rescued by either. Most Europeans regarded communism as slavery. In France and Italy, to be sure, a quarter of the people voted the communist ticket, and communists held important positions in labor unions, but the number of those actually desirous of a communist society was not large. Social cleavages existed between the classes, but short of catastrophe, Europe would not go communist. Nor was the number large of those who wished to be remodeled according to the economy or culture of the United States. Dependency even on the benefactions of the United States they feared as a wild gamble; remembering the depression of 1929, and how all Europe had then gone down after the cessation of American loans, they had no desire to be dependent upon American capitalism. Europe, like the world's other great aggregates, wanted to preserve its identity and its spiritual independence. But between the programs of the two superpowers there was this difference: the Soviets had more to gain by chaos in Europe, and the United States had more to gain by its rebuilding. The United States immediately after the war sent billions of dollars' worth of goods to relieve the distress of Europe and then embarked on an even more extensive recovery program, the Marshall Plan. Its motives were much discussed and even impugned. In effect, the Americans satisfied their humanitarian impulse, found markets for their own industries (at the American taxpayers' expense), reduced the drift of working-class Europeans into the communist camp, and soon made possible an amazing and rapid revival of industrial Europe.

The key to the rebuilding of Europe was Germany. The Ruhr was still Europe's industrial heartland. The former Allies had at first agreed to occupy Germany jointly. They agreed that Germany should pay reparations, especially to Russia, which had suffered most heavily from German attack. Gradually the American government, to make Europe self-supporting and less dependent on American aid, came to favor the economic reconstruction of Germany. The Russians became apprehensive. They wished to use Germany to rebuild the Soviet Union. The Americans wished to use it to rebuild Europe; they did not wish to pour aid into Germany to have it drained off as reparations to the U.S.S.R. By 1946 joint administration of Germany broke down. The Russians reaffirmed their hold on eastern Germany; the Americans, British, and French went their own way in the western zones. Each side competed for the good will of the late enemy. Each accused the other of partitioning the country in violation of their agreements. In the division between the victors, the Germans found the chance to reassert their own national identity although their homeland remained divided.

After 1947 relations between the two superpowers went from bad to worse. Early in 1948 communists seized power in Prague, ending a democratic coalition government and turning Czechoslovakia completely into a satellite state. The Soviets forbade their satellites to participate in the American-sponsored economic reconstruction program; they encouraged quasi-insurrectionary strikes in France and Italy in 1947 and 1948. In the summer of 1948, retaliating for the American, British, and French unification of western Germany and the introduction of currency reform there, the Soviets blockaded Berlin, cutting off all rail and road routes through East Germany to the western sectors of Berlin. The Western powers, notably the United States, responded with a mass "air lift," daily flying in thousands of tons of supplies to prevent starvation among the Berlin populace; eventually, after almost a year, the blockade was lifted; but it was only the first of several crises over Berlin. Meanwhile, the United States and the western European powers proceeded with their plans for the economic reconstruction and defense of Europe, and the U.S.S.R. drew its satellites closer together.

Under the Marshall Plan, which went into effect in 1948, the huge grants to western Germany and to Europe continued, but the grants no longer were regarded as stop-gap relief. American aid was henceforth to be so apportioned among the various countries, and so coordinated with each country's policies and with joint policies of the European countries acting together, as to enable Europe to stand on its own feet and play its own part in international trade. American officials urged Europeans to reduce their tariff barriers and currency controls against each other. They stressed that only by creating a free and Europe-wide internal market could Europeans obtain the advantage of mass production and lower costs such as prevailed in the United States.

The results of the Marshall Plan, the industrial revival of western Europe and the movement toward European economic cooperation, exceeded the boldest anticipations of its sponsors. The trend after the First World War toward high tariffs and economic rigidity, with the United States taking the lead, had culminated in the Great Depression and with it had come a further intensification of economic nationalism. With the Marshall Plan the trend was reversed. There was now a freer movement of world trade and an almost complete liberalization of trade between the participating western European countries. A European "payments union" provided a channel for the conversion of currencies. Industrial production rose dramatically; by 1950, within two years of the inauguration of the plan, industrial production in West Germany reached and exceeded prewar levels and continued upward; by the early 1950s the boom spread to France and Italy and, though to a lesser extent, to Britain. Western Europeans began to enjoy a remarkable prosperity; their economies were growing at unprecedented rates, and living standards and consumption levels rose strikingly, even if not rapidly enough to satisfy all the expectations aroused.

The Marshall Plan was in a sense revolutionary; it had proposed nothing less than that a wealthy country like the United States should use its economic resources to revive its competitors; it was an act of creative generosity and shrewd statesmanship, a recognition of the mutual interdependence of all members of the world-wide economy. For Asia, Africa, and Latin America, the underdeveloped areas, where the problem was not to revive a sick industrial economy but to create industry, other American programs of long-range capital investment, and the British Commonwealth Colombo Plan, were counterparts to the Marshall Plan for Europe. Communism would be combated, under this theory, by removing its breeding grounds of poverty and want; it was a long-range program; the verdict would rest with generations still unborn.

The countries of western Europe, receiving their initial impulse from the Marshall Plan but then acting boldly and imaginatively on their own, took further steps toward economic integration. In 1952, under a plan developed by Robert Schuman and Jean Monnet, six industrial countries, France, Italy, West Germany, Belgium, the Netherlands, and Luxembourg, established a European Coal and Steel Community to make it possible to pool their coal and steel resources. Not only were the production results significant but the supranational agencies established to supervise the Coal and Steel Community became the groundwork for later economic and political integration. In 1957, under treaties signed at Rome, an even more far-reaching step was taken when the same six countries established the European Economic Community or Common Market, which aimed at the elimination of all internal tariff barriers, the establishment of a common tariff system with respect to the outside world, and a free movement of labor and capital; moreover, it pronounced European economic integration the avenue to political unity.

The Common Market, in operation in 1958, became one of the thriving economic aggregates of the world. Britain, at first undecided whether its Commonwealth ties and dependence on low-priced agricultural imports made it possible to join with western Europe, held back for a time from seeking membership. In 1963 the British bid for membership was blocked by France, the French seeing the prospects of Continental unity weakened by British membership and regarding Britain as a bridgehead for excessive United States influence on the Continent. In 1960 Britain and six other small nations on the European continent (Austria, Switzerland, Portugal, and the Scandinavian countries) formed a seven-member European Free Trade Association but it lacked the dynamism of the Common Market. The Common Market countries formed also a European Atomic Community to pool west-European atomic resources and research. The same countries meanwhile moved toward political integration. The executive and legislative machinery established first for the Coal and Steel Community was joined with that of the Common Market and "Euratom" to create a "European Parliament." Each country chose its representatives but they then sat in the parliament at Brussels on the basis of political affiliation, not nationality; it was planned that one day they would be elected by a European-wide electorate. For a time western Europe seemed to be moving from customs union to political unity as individual nations once had done. The supranational economic and political machinery of the Common Market, the day-to-day labors of a European bureaucracy in Brussels and in Luxembourg, the close consultation on common interests, were unifying western Europe. The purely political Council of Europe, established earlier at Strasbourg in 1949, continued to champion the federation of Europe by political action. The likelihood of any real European unity, however, was still far from established. The European governments showed no haste to surrender their national sovereignty and independence. France, which had been a pioneer in building European internationalism, later showed signs of a stubborn and persistent older nationalism.

Meanwhile the nations of western Europe cooperated closely in the military area, with each other and with the United States. There were, at first, preliminary arrangements to insure against any military revival of Germany but soon these were directed at Soviet expansion. Under the Brussels treaty of 1948, Britain, France, Belgium, the Netherlands and Luxembourg agreed to consult with each other on mutual defense matters. In 1949 the United States took the lead in creating the North Atlantic Treaty Organization. Under the treaty, signed by twelve nations originally, with West Germany, Greece, and Turkey soon joining, the United States agreed to supply equipment for European rearmament and guaranteed western Europe against invasion, the unspecified but only enemy being the U.S.S.R. In 1950 the Korean War broke out. The United States pressed to rearm West Germany. The French, seeking to allay persistent anxieties over German rearmament, sponsored a plan for a European Defense Community with a common "European army" in which the German military would serve as "European" soldiers. The powers principally involved ratified it, but it failed to pass the French National Assembly itself in 1954; the French had second thoughts over rearming Germany and were apprehensive because the British were not firmly enough committed to the projected military structure. The Western European Union came into existence instead. Using the Brussels treaty as a nucleus, it joined together the five Brussels powers, and the United States, Canada, Italy, and West Germany, and authorized the West German government, the German Federal Republic, to create a national army under the overall command of NATO. Britain, the United States, and Canada were now firmly committed to the defense of the Continent. British, like American, isolationism was ending. With British and American commitments on the Continent, and with European anxiety directed exclusively at Soviet expansion, alarm at the possibility of a resurgent German militarism was laid to rest; there remained only a common agreement that Germany would be prohibited from manufacturing atomic weapons and missiles.

In less than a decade after the most devastating war in its history western Europe had recovered and regained its identity and seemed to be moving toward economic and political unity. The U.S.S.R. could not be expected to view with equanimity the creation of a new superpower on its own western border—for it was as a superpower that a restored and unified Europe was taking shape in the 1950s. Any power, not merely the Soviet Union, might object to such consolidation among its neighbors. The American encouragement to the unification of Europe thus seemed to Russia another hostile act. The Russians countered by drawing their own satellites closer together. Emulating the European Economic Community, they moved toward the economic integration of the east-European satellites by creating a Council for Economic Mutual Aid in 1949 and a network of military alliances consummated in the Warsaw Pact of 1955. But these were only a small part of the vast changes taking place in the new communist world that had come into being after 1945.

111
The Communist
World in Eastern
Europe

*Eastern Europe,
1945–1953*

The Second World War, like the First, was followed by a wave of revolutionary change and communist expansion. If there was nothing so epochal as the Russian Revolution of 1917, the triumph of communism in eastern Europe in the years after 1945 and in China by 1949 was, if anything, even more momentous. Where communism in 1918 was chaos, in 1945 it was the way of life of an organized Great Power. The communist scares in eastern and central Europe in 1919 had flickered out, but in 1945 communism materialized in these areas, not through spontaneous revolution but through Soviet military strength and the backing the Soviets gave to local communist leaders.

The Soviets came to control eastern Europe in the sweep of military operations against the Germans in the last months of the Second World War. The states which fell into the orbit of Soviet influence included Poland, Hungary, Rumania, Bulgaria, and Czechoslovakia; Eastern Germany was also shaped into a Soviet satellite. In all these states, with varying timetables between 1945 and 1948, communist-dominated "people's republics" were established, closely bound to the Soviet Union. Yugoslavia and Albania, liberated by their own partisan leaders and not by the Red Army, became communist-style people's republics too, but not tied to the Soviet Union. Since the three Baltic states had been incorporated into the Soviet Union earlier, in 1940, an additional 100,000,000 Europeans and eleven European states were under communist-style governments after the Second World War. The areas considered in 1919 a protective buffer against Bolshevism were now under Russian domination. An "iron curtain" was said to have descended, roughly along the old Elbe-Trieste line, sharpening and deepening the centuries-old divergencies in the development of western and eastern Europe.[3] Finland, Austria, and Greece escaped communist domination, Greece only after a fierce civil war that dragged on to 1949, in which anticommunist forces, aided by a British occupation army, defeated the communists and restored the Greek monarchy. Elsewhere after 1945, as after the First World War, monarchies fell—in Italy, and in the people's republics of Yugoslavia, Bulgaria, Rumania, and Albania, where the new revolutionary regimes could not be expected to retain their royalty.

In the consolidation of communist control in eastern Europe, a similar pattern tended to repeat itself. It was understood during the war that the power or powers emancipating an area from the enemy would temporarily exercise political control until the peace treaties were signed. In that way the Western powers controlled political events in Italy without consultation with the Soviets. In Poland, Bulgaria, Rumania, and Hungary, Soviet military occupation made it possible for local communist leaders, many trained in Moscow and returning from exile, to help form united front coalition governments. In the case of Poland and Yugoslavia, pressure at Yalta and Potsdam forced the Soviets to give representation to the Western-spon-

[3] See pp. 215–261, 608–609, and map, p. 217.

sored governments-in-exile then in London; the leader of the agrarian party, Stanislaw Mikolajczyk, returned to Poland as deputy premier. At first the communists were only a minority in these coalition governments, but they held the key ministries of interior and justice and controlled the police, propaganda, and the courts. All elements alleged to be "fascist" or to have collaborated with the Nazis were barred from public life and even from voting. Although many of the nationalist and rightist political elements so excluded were probably guilty of fascist sympathies and even of collaboration, the loose definition of "fascist" and even of "reactionary" made it possible to bar many who were merely anticommunist. In the first elections held, the purges and disfranchisement of political "undesirables" made a mockery of Stalin's pledge at Yalta to hold free and unfettered elections in these areas. This the United States and Great Britain pointed out in strong but ineffectual protests.

In the second stage the communist leaders succeeded in ousting or reducing to impotence their political rivals in the provisional governments, pushing aside the agrarian, socialist, and other leaders, ending the coalitions, and taking full control. From these maneuvers the "people's republics" or "people's democracies" formally emerged, with constitutions modeled more or less on the Soviet pattern. In Czechoslovakia, where liberal leaders like Eduard Beneš and Jan Masaryk hoped for a time that their country would serve as a bridge between the Soviets and the West, the coalition government lasted longer than elsewhere but ended with a communist coup in February 1948, and with the young Masaryk a suicide or victim of political murder.

With the communists in control, the leaders of the opposition political parties, especially the agrarian leaders who opposed the threat of land collectivization, were forced into flight or in other ways silenced. The agrarian leader, Petkov, was hanged in Bulgaria in 1947; Mikolajczyk fled Poland the same year; scores of people in these countries and in other satellites were imprisoned. The new regimes, like earlier revolutionary orders, clashed also with the churches; high-ranking prelates of the Catholic church, Cardinal Mindszenty in Hungary, Archbishop Stepinac in Yugoslavia, and others elsewhere, were denounced, brought to public trial and imprisoned, and church property confiscated. From 1949 to 1953, reflecting the tightening repression within the Soviet Union in Stalin's last years, there occurred the familiar Soviet pattern of purges, arrests, trials, confessions, and executions in the highest ranks of the communist leaders themselves once they fell from Stalin's grace. They were accused of nationalist deviations, of which they were undoubtedly guilty, and of conspiring with Tito, the independent-minded communist leader of Yugoslavia. Among the victims of these purges were the Rumanian woman revolutionary Ana Pauker, the Bulgarian Kostov, the Hungarian Rajk, and the Czechoslovak leaders Clementis and Slansky. Later, after Stalin's death, many of these victims received the somewhat dubious vindication of posthumous rehabilitation. The Polish leader, Wladislaw Gomulka, purged from the party in 1949, imprisoned in 1951, released in 1954, lived on to return to power in 1956.

Meanwhile profound economic and social changes took place as the new regimes launched industrialization projects similar to the Soviet Five-Year plans and made visible progress in moving from agrarian to industrial societies. With the emphasis on heavy industry rather than on consumer goods, industrialization, however, brought little immediate improvement in living standards. Important landholding changes were introduced too. Whatever landed estates still existed were liquidated; the day of the landed aristocracy in East Prussia (now divided between the U.S.S.R. and Poland), Hungary, and Poland was ended. The new regimes hesitated to collectivize the land, knowing the deep-rooted opposition to collectivization in eastern Europe. They contented themselves at first with establishing cooperatives, but after 1955, with varying speed and intensity, they embarked on collectivization programs. Poland remained an exception; here the initial collectivization program was halted and almost all agriculture remained in private hands.

For a time the policies of the new regimes were coordinated through a new international organization created in 1947 and given the innocuous name of the Cominform or Communist Information Bureau. Although more loosely organized than the Comintern, which had been dissolved by Stalin in 1943 as a gesture of ideological wartime harmony with the West, it became the chief center of the propaganda war against the West until its dissolution in 1956.[4] The relationship of the people's republics to the Soviets was formalized also, as we have seen, by a network of military alliances under the Warsaw Pact and by trade agreements and economic cooperation projects under the Council for Economic Mutual Aid which, to the chagrin of the satellite states, principally benefited the Soviet Union.

In the early postwar years, Yugoslavia, freed from the Nazis largely by its own partisan armies, made a remarkable and successful show of resistance to the Soviets. Tito, as the Yugoslav communist leader Joseph Broz was called, demonstrated the centrifugal power of nationalism even in the communist international order and openly defied Moscow. The Soviet leadership first excommunicated and anathematized the heretic in 1948 and then after Stalin's death sought unsuccessfully to woo him back to the fold.

The Soviet Union:
The Post-Stalin Era

In March 1953 Russia's twentieth-century Peter the Great died. Stalin's accomplishments had been massive—the industrialization of Russia, the rallying of the country in the Fatherland War, the promotion of Russian national interests and of world communism in the years after 1939.[5] At the same time it was Stalin's mistrust of the West and his inflexibility that contributed to the poisoning of the postwar international atmosphere. Inside his own country his dictatorial ruthlessness and paranoid suspicions, growing sharper with the passage of years, filled even his closest associates with dismay. With Andrei Zhdanov, who died in 1948, and Lavrenti Beria as his principal lieutenants, controls over all phases of intellectual life multiplied and grew more repressive. The orientation was vehemently nationalistic and xenophobic; deviations in economics, music, genetics, linguistics were condemned on grounds of "cosmopolitanism," i.e., internationalism. An officially inspired anti-

[4]See pp. 808–809.
[5]See pp. 796–806, 895–912, 933–934.

Semitism made an appearance, thinly disguised as anti-Zionism. Plots were fabricated to create an atmosphere of terror, as in the revelation of an alleged "doctors' plot" in 1952, most of the doctors being Jewish, to poison Stalin and other Kremlin leaders. The Soviets claimed also a leadership in technological inventiveness, denying even that the Russia of Peter the Great ever had to be "Europeanized" by borrowings from the West.[6] Three years after Stalin's death, Nikita S. Khrushchev, his successor as party secretary, in a speech to the party on the "crimes of the Stalin era," made startling disclosures of his dictatorial rule which confirmed the worst speculations of Western critics over the years. Stalin had been personally responsible for the purges and executions of the 1930s, had built up a cult of personality around himself, and had created an atmosphere of terror so that his most intimate colleagues lived in fear for their very lives.

After Stalin's death in 1953, a struggle for power within the party and regime culminated by 1958 in the triumph of Nikita S. Khrushchev—rotund, jovial, and ebullient but in actuality a shrewd, tough, pragmatic realist who had helped carry out Stalin's purges in the Ukraine in the 1930s, even if he later seemed genuinely appalled at the terrorist atmosphere he had helped to create. At first Georgi Malenkov served as premier, but others exercised collective control behind the scenes and vied for supreme power. Almost at once Molotov, Bulganin, and Khrushchev, along with Malenkov, combined against Beria, head of the dreaded secret police, and arrested and executed him. Malenkov was ousted in February 1955. In trying to satisfy the great popular demand for consumer goods, he had reduced expenditures for heavy industry and for the military and had raised up an opposition against himself.

For three years, from 1955 to 1958, Bulganin, spokesman for the army, served as premier, but he was only a figurehead. Khrushchev, like Stalin before him, steadily consolidated power as secretary of the party, systematically building up support in the Central Committee. His strength was apparent when he made his speech in February 1956 on the crimes of the Stalin era. By 1958, all his competitors had been ousted from office, discredited, and relegated to obscure posts. On the other hand, Stalin's methods were not favored; rivals, after the Beria episode, were no longer executed. By March 1958 Khrushchev seemed to be the unchallenged leader, serving both as premier and first secretary of the party, his ascent as much a personal victory as a triumph of the party over other competing institutions in Soviet society—the army, the bureaucracy, and the secret police. Then, in 1964, he too fell swiftly from command, the victim of rebellion in the party leadership at his accumulation of power and of discontent over many of his domestic and foreign policies. In replacing him, the party apparatus made sure to separate the top governmental and top party posts. Leonid I. Brezhnev became party secretary and Aleksei N. Kosygin premier; within a few years Brezhnev was the dominant figure.

After Stalin, the Soviet leaders softened many aspects of the older tyrant's reign of almost thirty years, curbing the power of the secret police, closing slave labor

[6] See pp. 244–256, 581–583.

camps, releasing political prisoners, and rehabilitating the reputations of many of Stalin's victims. They permitted something of "a thaw," a greater freedom in literary and intellectual activity and even in political criticism, but vigilantly supervised it lest it get out of hand. Controls alternated between relaxation and repression; in 1958 Boris Pasternak was forbidden to accept the Nobel Prize in literature because his writings, notably *Dr. Zhivago*, condemned Soviet society at least implicitly by ignoring it and stressing individual freedom; other writers were similarly repressed and some imprisoned. Although the arbitrary controls and extreme repression of the Stalin era diminished, the essential features of Soviet totalitarianism persisted, the control of the party in all aspects of life remained pervasive, and many ugly features of intolerance and even anti-Semitism were still virulent. But a new generation, faithful to a Soviet society now over a half-century old, could, like the poet Eugene Yevtushenko or the novelist Alexander Solzhenitsyn, at least attack the perversions of the Revolution under Stalin and guard against such perversions under his successors. Scornful of the capitalist world, they sought rising living standards and greater intellectual freedom within their own communist society.

As under the earlier Five-Year plans,[7] the Soviet economy continued to expand after the war at a rapid rate of growth even if the rate slackened in the 1960s. A fourth and a fifth Five-Year Plan (1946–1950, 1951–1955) successfully repaired the tremendous devastation wrought by the war and enlarged the country's industrial potential. New plans followed, designed to strike a balance between consumer goods and heavy industry, with housing receiving special attention. One feature was an experiment with decentralization, i.e., delegating more authority for decision-making to regional planning agencies in the various republics and other territorial subdivisions, and even to factory managers. The Soviet average annual rate of growth was estimated at 6 or 7 percent in the 1950s, but it fell off in the 1960s. Although Soviet leaders boasted that the Soviet Union would overtake the United States in per capita output by 1970, the fact remained that the gross national product of the country in the early 1970s was still less than half that of the United States. Moreover, consumer goods and services were still slighted in favor of heavy industry, and it remained a fact that while the Soviet standard of living was significantly rising, the Soviet citizen at the beginning of the 1970s could purchase only about 50 percent as much goods and services as the average American. The economic center of gravity continued to move eastward. For cities like Kazakhstan, Samarkand, and Tashkent the pace of modernization proceeded rapidly. Asiatic Russia was furnishing over one-half the country's iron and steel, cement, and electrical energy, and almost all of its magnesium and aluminum.

Soviet industrial advances were crowned by remarkable achievements in nuclear power and space technology. In 1949 the Soviets exploded their first atomic bomb, and their subsequent progress in atomic energy was demonstrated in record-breaking experimental blasts. In 1957 they successfully launched the *sputnik*, the world's first

[7]See pp. 796–804.

artificial earth satellite, alerting even the most skeptical to the advanced state of Soviet technology and science. In the early 1960s they launched manned space flights of an extent and endurance that for a time overshadowed American accomplishments.

Agriculture persisted as the weakest part of the economy; the failure of production to rise at the rate demanded by industrial and urban growth and population increase remained the most serious single problem. The Stalinist system of collective farms, although administered after 1953 so as to provide greater benefits to the collectivized peasantry, still did not seem to provide proper incentives for increasing production. Its original political purpose, to control the peasantry and guarantee food deliveries to the cities, seemed to justify its economic inefficiency even in the eyes of Stalin's successors.

The changes in the Soviet Union after Stalin's death in 1953 directly affected the Soviet satellites. Stalin's successors, agreeing that the brutal exploitation of eastern Europe could not continue, and reinforced in that attitude by riots in East Berlin in June 1953, began to encourage a relaxation of controls and economic concessions. But the program was by no means consistent or clear; moreover, the measures of relaxation led to growing pressure for more freedom. Discontent mounted over forced industrialization and land collectivization and over continued repression by Stalinist-type leaders who continued to rule even after Stalin's death. The ferment rose to the surface after Khrushchev himself in 1956 denounced the brutal character of the Stalin dictatorship and, in addition, made the official concession, directed then toward Yugoslavia, that "different roads to socialism" were possible. The "de-Stalinization" program opened a Pandora's box; destroying Stalin's infallibility destroyed Soviet infallibility as well. In October open revolt broke out in Poland and Hungary against Stalinist leaders and their ties to the Soviets.

In Poland the demand for greater independence emerged within the Polish party itself. Gomulka, once discredited and imprisoned for his nationalist deviationism, returned to power and pressed for Polish independence. Khrushchev blustered and threatened military action but backed down, convinced that at least in foreign affairs Poland could be counted an ally. Gomulka soon received wide backing in Poland, even from the church, most of the population viewing him as a desirable alternative to the return of Moscow control. He in turn proceeded to end collectivization of the farms, check police terror, and create a freer political and intellectual atmosphere. Poland's "October Revolution" was relatively successful.

In Hungary events took a different course. Only a few days after the news of the Polish success, rioting broke out in the streets of Budapest and other cities. The moderate-minded communist leader Imre Nagy, who had tried to liberalize the Hungarian regime from 1953 to 1955 but had been dismissed, returned to power. He undertook a policy of liberal concessions, even freeing political prisoners like Cardinal Mindszenty, but the very concessions increased the revolutionary pressures from workers and students who once again rioted in the streets of Budapest and threatened to drive out the communist regime, restore parliamentary government, and cut the ties with Moscow. Khrushchev, thereupon, dispatched an army of tanks and artillery and forcefully reestablished communist rule. The revolt was suppressed; the tougher Janos Kádár, subservient to Moscow, took over; two years later Nagy himself was executed. The Hungarian Revolution of 1956 was crushed by Russian troops like the revolution of 1848–1849 a century before.[8] The open show of force by Moscow in Budapest destroyed illusions about the benevolence and liberality of Stalin's successors and shook the communist faithful in western Europe and elsewhere.

Despite the Hungarian episode and the limits to which the Soviets would permit independence in the satellites, liberalizing changes took place for about a dozen years after 1956. The Soviets allowed economic policies to be adapted to the needs of each country; the pace of industrialization and of collectivization slowed down. The east-European states traded with countries outside the Soviet sphere, including the United States, and invited foreign tourists. A freer atmosphere, even in Hungary, came to prevail. Rumania showed signs of independence in foreign affairs and resisted Soviet pressures for supranational economic planning. Czechoslovakia democratized its regime, permitting freedom of the press and noncommunist political organizations.

The Soviet leaders grew nervous as they saw their grip on eastern Europe threatened. Czechoslovakia became the Hungary of the 1960s. The Soviet leaders saw the liberalization of the regime under Alexander Dubcek as a threat to socialism and even more, as a subversion of the Warsaw Pact military network, threatening the dissolution of the Soviet hegemony in eastern Europe. In August 1968 the Soviets sent 250,000 troops, including token Polish, Hungarian, Bulgarian, and East German contingents, into the hapless country to crush the incipient revolution. The Czechs were stunned and infuriated but were forced to accept the Soviet political dictates; they had to restore censorship and make governmental changes designed to thwart any new rebellion. The "Brezhnev doctrine" served notice that the Soviets reserved the right to intervene in the affairs of any member of the socialist commonwealth if socialism seemed threatened, and that the satellites were to enjoy only a qualified sovereignty. It served notice also of the strictly circumscribed limits within which freedom and independence would be tolerated in eastern Europe. Yet it was obvious that the Soviet Union could turn back the tides of internal liberal change and of national self-assertiveness in eastern Europe only by its continued military presence. Even more than the events in Hungary the intervention in Czechoslovakia shattered the unity of the world communist movement. The large Western communist parties in France and Italy protested the intervention. The once monolithic communist world was becoming fragmented. And the greatest challenge came from the new communist power that had risen in the East.

[8]See p. 525.

The emergence of communist China by the end of 1949 was among the most momentous of postwar events. The communist triumph was the final episode in the long civil war that had been going on between the Kuomintang, or Nationalists, and the communists since 1927.[9] An uneasy alliance, formed between the two groups in 1937 to fight the Japanese, barely held together through the war years, to the consternation of American advisers who sought a unified military effort against the common enemy. The communists had placed their armies under the nominal command of Chiang Kai-shek and the Kuomintang, but retaining actual control and waging successful guerrilla warfare against the Japanese, they moved into vast rural areas deep in the Japanese zones, organized villages and local governments along communist lines, and mobilized wide support among the peasants through popular land reforms. Toward the end of the war a Nationalist China, a communist China, and a Japanese-occupied China confronted each other. The Nationalists began to deteriorate in morale and efficiency, and to lose popular support. Expelled by the Japanese from their industrial and financial bases in eastern China, they suffered from chaotic economic conditions, inflation, heavy taxation, and outright corruption. To the growing strength of the communists, the Nationalist government responded with repression that transformed it into an increasingly authoritarian regime.

In the last stage of the Pacific war, Chiang Kai-shek offered the communists representation in his government if they agreed to scale down the Chinese Red Army and incorporate it fully into his Kuomintang forces. The communists refused, demanding instead a constitutional convention to decide on the form of the postwar government and insisting on an equitable allotment of military supplies to their own army, which, in many areas, had been fighting more effectively against the Japanese than the Nationalists. The victory over Japan set the stage for renewed civil war. Nationalist troops, with United States aid, took over the big cities in eastern and northern China but the communist forces, moving out from their guerrilla bases, poured into the hinterland of the northern Chinese provinces and moved also into Manchuria, where they made contact with the Russians. The Soviets at this juncture, however, were maintaining scrupulously correct relations with the Kuomintang and refused direct encouragement to the communists. Mao Tse-tung, the communist leader, declined to surrender the northern provinces, disband his army, and accept Kuomintang political control over the country as a whole, and in the autumn of 1945 fighting between the two groups broke out. A truce mediated by the American General George Marshall temporarily halted hostilities, but with the withdrawal of the U.S.S.R. from Manchuria in the spring of 1946, many months after it had pledged to do so and after it had removed Manchurian industrial assets as reparations, Kuomintang and communists again clashed over control of the important border

[9] See pp. 836–837.

province. As Marshall noted, the communists were quite willing to plunge the country into civil war to achieve their ends; but, as he also noted, political power in the Kuomintang, despite the promulgation of a constitution in 1946, remained concentrated in the hands of an inner group bent on repressing all opposition, even noncommunist. One of the tragedies of the postwar era was that the anticommunist forces in China, and in many other parts of Asia, were themselves far from democratic.

In the fighting which lasted from the spring of 1946 to September 1949, the Nationalists lost ground steadily. The United States gave almost $2,000,000,000 to bolster the Kuomintang but to no avail; the Nationalists seemed to lack the ability and will to resist. On the other hand, the Red Army, equipped with captured Japanese arms, now receiving aid from the Soviets, and indirectly obtaining American supplies through mass surrenders and sales by corrupt Kuomintang functionaries, moderated their propaganda so as to attract wide sections of the population and pressed forward victoriously, routing the Kuomintang armies in the north and then, moving south, occupying the Nationalist capital at Nanking. By the end of 1949 Nationalist resistance had ended on the Chinese mainland. Chiang withdrew his shattered forces to the island of Taiwan, or Formosa, to use the European name that Portuguese explorers had given it in 1590. Here, and on a few small offshore islands, Chiang in subsequent years regrouped and revitalized his armies with American aid, and governed in considerably more enlightened fashion; the Nationalists awaited their day of retribution.

The New Regime The Chinese communist leader, Mao Tse-tung, and his lieutenants proceeded to consolidate control in the new Chinese People's Republic which they proclaimed in September 1949. Mao Tse-tung guided the destinies of the new state with a tight grip on party and government. For a time Liu Shao-sh'i, party theoretician and government leader, was his closest lieutenant and heir apparent; Chou En-lai was for many years premier and foreign minister; Chu Teh, the hero of the Chinese Red Army's exploits in the 1930s, successively held key military and civilian posts. The new regime reestablished the national capital in the ancient northern city of Peking, restoring the old name which the Nationalists in the 1930s had changed to Peiping.

For the first time since the Chinese Revolution of 1911, and indeed for generations, a unified central government controlled all China, able to direct and mobilize one-fourth of the world's population for its purposes. The Chinese communists might be a small hardened group of successful Marxist-Leninist revolutionaries exercising supreme power over the submissive Chinese masses, but they were not so alien to the Chinese cultural tradition as most Westerners believed. They continued a long familiar pattern of bureaucratic despotism in government that stretched back for centuries; they were articulate spokesmen for a universal hostility to Western imperialism [10] that had all but carved their country to pieces in the

[10] See pp. 699–704, 828, and maps, pp. 700–701 and 707.

nineteenth century; they were the legatees of an ancient tradition of Chinese political and cultural preeminence in the east Asian world. With traditional social and religious patterns already disrupted in the twentieth century by revolutions, civil war, and the war against the Japanese, the communists accelerated the disintegration of older Confucian values but provided an apparent stability unknown to the country in the first half of the twentieth century.

The Chinese communists leaned on Russian experience but added innovations of their own. They promulgated a Soviet-type constitution with a parallel structure for party and government, and with party officials naturally controlling each level of governmental organization.[11] The apparatus of totalitarianism appeared; the party manipulated all organs of information for purposes of indoctrination, reaching wide sections of the population in its political education program. Political education was accompanied by a secret police, mass arrests and executions, forced labor, the liquidation of anticommunist opponents, and internal party purges which were styled "rectification" drives. In 1957 Mao, then echoing the "de-Stalinization" program in the U.S.S.R., conceded that in the first five years of the revolution excesses had been committed and that some 800,000 opponents had been executed. Whatever leniency he then introduced was succeeded by renewed oppression, though not as severe as in the earlier years.

As the Soviet Union had earlier, the leaders of the new communist regime mobilized the nation in a vast program of economic development designed to transform China from an agricultural country into an industrial power. As a first step, from 1949 to 1952, they restored and rehabilitated the war-devastated economy which they had inherited. At the same time they inaugurated a vast land redistribution program, establishing cooperatives as a preliminary to collectivization and eliminating the old landlord class. The country's initial Five-Year Plan, scheduled to begin when reconstruction was complete, was postponed because of the outbreak of the Korean War in 1950 but was launched in 1953. Concentrating on heavy industry, the plan, with some Soviet economic and technical assistance, had a considerable success; substantial advances were recorded in the output of coal, electric power, iron ore, and steel. Not all targets were reached, especially not in agriculture, where the same floods and droughts that had troubled China for centuries refused to obey government decrees. Yet the first Five-Year Plan, running from 1953 to 1957, inaugurated a period of industrial expansion and economic growth.

In 1958 a second plan, more ambitious and heralded as the "great leap forward," was launched. Faced with a serious lack of balance between the growth of industry and the lag in agriculture, the planners were determined to continue industrial expansion and simultaneously to revolutionize agricultural production by a mass mobilization of the countryside, which in some ways was to exceed even the earlier collectivization drives of the Soviet Union. On the premise that Soviet-style agricultural cooperatives and collectives were inadequate for Chinese purposes, the government began to amalgamate the existing cooperatives into far larger and more

[11]See pp. 790–794.

comprehensive units, "people's communes," which would be responsible not only for agricultural mechanization and improvement but for local industrialization and many other social and economic functions as well. Intended to be a self-sufficient rural city, tightly organized in military fashion with a hierarchy of production brigades and battalions, the commune was to use the reservoir of local labor and resources to raise agricultural and industrial production. Women were important too in the endeavor. Communal kitchens, nurseries, and boarding schools were projected to free them from household chores and child care for the supposedly more edifying labors of factories and fields. The disruption of family living and the loosening of traditional family ties were held to be a necessary concomitant to progress; at the same time they clearly involved political advantage to the regime.

All kinds of obstacles thwarted the continuation of the revolutionary communal experiment. In 1959 and 1960 the government, acknowledging the stubborn resistance it was encountering from a recalcitrant peasantry which had learned over the centuries to reject external compulsion, backed down. By 1961 the "great leap forward" was in full retreat. With successive years of crop failures and deficiencies, some of which were caused by natural disasters, the government abandoned the communal program. Agriculture continued to be organized along collective lines, but peasants were permitted to sell or barter surplus products as an added incentive to production; the nonagricultural functions of the communes were allowed to atrophy. The government now stressed the fundamental importance of agriculture as the necessary prerequisite for future economic development; it suspended but did not abandon its ambitious plans for industrial growth. By the 1960s, however, the Chinese economy had already made significant progress toward industrialization. In the years before the communist regime, annual steel production had never reached 1,000,000 tons; by 1960 the official figures set it at over 18,000,000 tons. Although per capita output was understandably low, given its huge population, China by 1960 ranked among the top ten industrial powers in the world in total industrial output. With various forms of economic dislocation appearing, and with Soviet aid suspended after 1960, progress became uneven and production sharply declined in the 1960s. But an industrial base for further expansion had been built even if only a modest 3 to 4 percent annual growth rate could be expected. Nor was the country's scientific prowess to be minimized; it successfully tested an atomic bomb in 1964 and a hydrogen bomb in 1967. The most serious long-term production problem remained, as elsewhere, the ability of the economy to keep pace with the expanding population—an estimated 750,000,000 people in 1970 and growing at a rate of 2 to 3 percent each year.

Meanwhile the regime was transforming life in many ways apart from industrialization. Road, rail, and air transport were physically unifying the country. Impressive strides were made in public sanitation and public health; the housefly was said to have disappeared, presumably by government edict. The government made deliberate efforts to combat illiteracy by reforming and simplifying the written Chinese language and by moving toward a single spoken tongue. As with the Soviets, women were given full equality with men and played a larger role in political and professional life than in most parts of the Western world, sharing equally in the sacrifices imposed and the progress achieved in the new regime. Old abuses like child marriage and concubinage were outlawed. Perhaps more profoundly than the Russian, the Chinese Revolution was refashioning the habits and ethos of an entire population, reaching remote villages and hamlets untouched for centuries.

In the two and a half years from 1966 to the end of 1968, when the country went through a period of turbulence known as the Great Proletarian Cultural Revolution, the stability of the regime received its severest test. The aging Mao, fearful that he would lose his grip after the failure of the country's economic experiments, or that the revolution would not survive him, called for a purge of the highest ranks of government and party directed against all who lacked the zeal to push on with the revolution or who had succumbed to bureaucratic routine and inertia. A principal target of abuse was Liu Shao-sh'i, president of the republic since 1959, and once Mao's heir apparent. The purge, as begun by party leaders, was judged too moderate. Thereupon Mao and his closest followers, including his wife Chiang Ching, mobilized hundreds of thousands of young people and galvanized them into action as Red Guards or shocktroops to take up the Maoist revolutionary cause. Converging on Peking in the spring of 1966, they denounced and attacked the old ways and denounced the vestiges of Western imperialist culture. They turned on newspaper editors, writers, professors, university presidents, and government officials, harassing and humiliating their opponents. Rival factions emerged among the revolutionists and bloody clashes took place in the south around Canton. When the uncontrolled mobs threatened to tear the country apart, committees were set up consisting of party and army leaders and government officials who gradually restored order in the capital and in the provinces. The high school and college students were urged to return to their homes in 1967, and even to school. By the time the great purge was over by the end of 1968, numerous lives were lost, the economy disrupted, and more than two-thirds of the party's central committee had been replaced. Mao's control seemed assured and his revolutionary legacy reinforced. But his heir apparent was now Lin Piao, defense minister and head of the armed forces, and the army emerged stronger than before. Liu survived but with diminished influence. All continued to pay lip service to Chairman Mao, the continuing revolution, and his "living thoughts," but strenuous efforts were needed to restore stability and calm, and undo the economic damage.

Although proclaiming peace, the new regime from the beginning followed an ac- tive, aggressive foreign policy. In 1951, pressing old claims of Chinese suzerainty, the communist republic occupied Tibet, the proletarian revolution thus passing to the land of the Dalai and Panchen Lamas. When Tibetan restlessness broke into open revolt in 1959, the Chinese forcibly suppressed it, forcing the Dalai Lama to seek asylum in India. Relations with India became strained even though India looked with favor on the efforts of the Chinese to modernize and considered itself in fraternal and friendly competition to demonstrate what Asian nations could accomplish, the one under a parliamentary democracy, the other under communism. But border disputes along India's northeastern frontier led to an open clash and undeclared war in the autumn of 1962. The Chinese invaded the border areas, easily overran Indian defenses, and then suddenly called off the fighting. The episode shook the Indian leaders out of the illusion that Chinese military power had been built only for defense against Western encroachments in Asia. The intervention of the Chinese communists in the Korean War at the end of 1950 will be recounted shortly.

The existence of a second major communist power, with the world's largest population and the world's largest communist party (18,000,000 members by the 1970s), with a militant program and ambitions for world revolutionary leadership, and self-appointed as champion of the nonwhite peoples of the world, undermined the ideological leadership of the Soviet Union in the communist world. The Soviets had not wholeheartedly encouraged the Chinese communists in their civil war with the Kuomintang at the end of the Second World War. Once the communist victory was an established fact, the U.S.S.R. accepted it and surrendered by a treaty of 1950 the rights and concessions in Manchuria which it had won under the Yalta agreement in 1945 and confirmed by a treaty with the Nationalists that year. Relations between Mao and Stalin remained cool but correct. The Korean War made the Chinese dependent on the Soviets for military aid, the Five-Year Plan for capital loans and technical assistance. Increased hostility to the United States also caused the Chinese communists to draw closer to the Soviets. The Chinese communists resented the persistent refusal of the United States to grant their regime diplomatic recognition, the efforts to block them from securing representation in the United Nations, and the continued aid to the Nationalists on Formosa and the offshore islands which they considered their *irredenta*.

In the first critical years of the new regime Mao relied on Soviet assistance and grudgingly submitted to Stalin's guidance, but he never considered himself subordinate to Stalin and certainly not to his successors. Indeed Mao projected himself as a new prophet of Marxism-Leninism, adapting the "revolution" to Asian conditions where the peasant masses and not the proletariat were to be the engine for social change. Just as they had ended Western intrusion in their affairs, the Chinese communists began openly to assert their independence of Soviet control under Stalin's successors. Mao echoed Khrushchev's pronouncement in 1956 that there were "different roads to socialism" with "Let a hundred flowers bloom, let a hundred schools of thought contend." But neither believed in toleration of differences nor in mere ideological debate.

Mao became the spokesman for a more orthodox hard-shell Marxism-Leninism.[12] He and the Chinese communists vehemently denounced Stalin's successors as arch-revisionists who were abandoning the class struggle, capitulating to capitalism and Western imperialism, tolerating such deviations from true Marxism as Titoism, and advancing appeasement-like theories of coexistence with the Western military powers out of a cowardly and un-Marxist fear of nuclear war. The Chinese com-

[12] See pp. 772–775.

munists also openly pressed their claim to leadership of the nonwhite peoples in Asia, Africa, and elsewhere in their struggle for equality. Not yet a giant industrial or military power, although on the way to becoming one, they were using the racial issue to further their ends. The Soviets, viewed as "half-Asian" by many in the West, were repudiated as Westerners by the Chinese communists. The friction between the two major communist states not only reflected ideological and political rivalry, and competition for the allegiance of the communist world, but also territorial conflict over the lands of inner Asia into which Russia had expanded in the age of the tsars. In 1960 the Chinese communists and the Soviets were hurling polemics at each other; in 1968 they clashed in armed conflict over disputed border territory on the Ussuri River dividing Manchuria and Russia's maritime provinces, each side inflaming the episode to denounce the other as a mortal enemy.

In Europe the only Chinese communist outpost was tiny Albania which thus protected itself from falling into either the Soviet or Yugoslav orbit. For a time the Chinese communists made headway in winning support in Algeria, Cuba, central Africa, Indonesia, and southeast Asia; by the mid-1960s their influence in these areas showed signs of waning. But the Chinese communists were patient and were geared to their own timetable. Just as the Bolsheviks had forged a world-wide revolutionary movement out of the Russian revolutionary experience, so the Chinese communists were applying the hard lessons of the Long March and the relentless struggle against the Kuomintang to the new world challenge. The struggle for ideological leadership, once carried on within the old Russian party, was now mounted on a world scale. With the emergence of China as a vast new center of communist power, with Yugoslavia maintaining its own independent form of communism, with the satellite states of eastern Europe openly reasserting their national identity, with the west-European communist parties pronouncing their freedom of decision, and with all these elements profiting from the growing Soviet-Chinese tension, Moscow no longer exerted the ideological monopoly it had once enjoyed. A new "polycentrism" had emerged, unheard of in Stalin's day.

The colonial revolt in Asia and Africa, having built up pressure in the years after the First World War, reached a veritable flood tide in the years after the Second.[13] The British, French, Dutch, and Belgian empires in Asia and Africa all but disappeared in an amazingly short span of about fifteen years, from 1947 to 1962. In some instances the liquidation of these empires occurred peacefully, with the imperial power resigned to the end of colonial rule, as in the case of the British withdrawal from the Indian subcontinent; in other instances the Western powers withdrew only after long and protracted bloody wars, as in the case of the Dutch in Indonesia and of the French in Indochina and Algeria. Everywhere the end of empire came as a result of rising nationalist agitation inspired by principles of self-determination, anti-

Empires into Nations: Asia and Africa

113 Empires into Nations: Asia and Africa

[13] See pp. 827–837.

imperialism, and the wartime Atlantic Charter. Western political ideas of sovereignty, independence, and freedom were compounded with racial hatred of European whites and denunciation of imperialism and capitalism. After the war Europeans could rule in their Asian and African empires only at prohibitive military cost, if at all, and in blatant contradiction to their own professed ideas of self-government.

Asia: End of the British and Dutch Empires

The peaceable end in 1947 of British rule in India, the largest and most populous of all colonial areas directly ruled by Europeans, was epoch-making. The drive for self-government and independence gathered momentum in the 1930s and resulted in the grant of a constitution, a legislature, and numerous other concessions to self-government. The British had trained an Indian civil service prepared to carry on the functions of a modern state. In the Second World War, even more than in the First, India rendered substantial aid to the British. To rally the Indian war effort and to counteract Japanese propaganda demanding the expulsion of all Europeans from Asia, the British promised dominion status to take effect at the war's end, a pledge which did not satisfy the Indian nationalist leaders who sought independence immediately. Meanwhile the Moslem League, which claimed to speak for 100,000,000 Moslems unwilling to live in an independent India dominated by the Hindus and the Congress party, insisted on a state of their own. After the war the British decided on partition. In 1947 the Indian empire was dissolved, the British sovereign giving up the title of emperor; in the process Indian unity was lost.

A dominion of India, predominantly Hindu, emerged with some 350,000,000 inhabitants, and a dominion of Pakistan, mainly Moslem, with some 75,000,000 inhabitants. India became a republic in 1950, Pakistan in 1956. Because of the Moslem distribution in the old Indian empire, Pakistan (the made-up name means Land of the Pure in Urdu) had to be established in two disconnected parts separated by 1,000 miles of Indian territory; even so, some 40,000,000 Moslems were left in India, which helped keep India a multireligious and secular state. Independence resulted, as the British had warned, in bloody riots between the religious communities, forcible mass expulsions and migrations, and the deaths of almost 1,000,000 persons. The uglier features of the communal rivalry soon subsided, however, although religious tension remained high and flared up on several occasions in the decades after independence. Relations between the two nations were strained because of a quarrel that dragged on for years over the status of the disputed border state, Kashmir.

Politically, the Republic of India under Jawaharlal Nehru and the Congress party offered to Asia an example of parliamentary democracy, humanitarian leadership, and slow evolutionary progress in meeting enormous problems of poverty, overpopulation, and linguistic and cultural diversity. After Nehru's death in 1964 his successors continued his policies, but there was growing restlessness at the near-monopoly of political power exercised by the Congress party. The pace of economic development remained slow despite various five-year plans, while the population grew to an estimated 530,000,000 by 1970. Pakistan after an initial decade of turmoil was governed under the paternalistic dictatorship of General Mohammed Ayub Khan from 1958 to 1969. His government provided stability and some economic improvement, but the reforms did not benefit the country as a whole and resentment at his high-handed rule led to widespread riots and strikes that forced his resignation. Here too population growth outpaced economic growth; the population grew to an estimated 125,000,000 by 1970.

Both India and the Islamic Republic of Pakistan retained a connection with the British Commonwealth of Nations. Of the remaining parts of the British Empire in Asia, Ceylon became independent in 1948 and retained its ties with the Commonwealth; Burma chose independence outside the Commonwealth. Malaya, after a decade of internal strife and warfare, became independent in 1957 and six years later joined with other former British dependencies in southeast Asia to create a larger Federation of Malaysia linked to the Commonwealth. With the adherence of the newly independent Asian and African states, the Commonwealth of Nations, as the British Commonwealth was now more accurately styled, became even more flexible an institution than it had been under the earlier definitions of 1926 and 1931.[14] In the two decades after 1947 it grew into an association of some twenty-eight independent communities, most of them republics, which accepted the British sovereign as symbolic head of the Commonwealth but as nothing more and agreed to consult, though not necessarily to act in concert, on matters of common concern. The new Asian and African members of the Commonwealth lacked the tie of sentiment that bound white Australians, New Zealanders, and Canadians of European descent to Great Britain, and many of these states possessed only the machinery of parliamentary democratic self-government. The Commonwealth remained one of the world's informal political groupings, a transmission belt for the communication of Western technology, political institutions, and economic aid, and for the interaction of Western and non-Western ideas and values in parts of the world as far flung as the British Empire once had been. In 1961 the Commonwealth lost a second of its original members (having lost Ireland in 1949): the political leaders of South Africa, the Afrikaner descendants of the old Boer settlers, withdrew, finding the Commonwealth incompatible with the white supremacy policy of *apartheid,* or racial segregation, which they alone with small stubborn governing groups in Rhodesia and other parts of the world, were endeavoring to uphold.

Another great empire in the East, the Netherlands Indies, which the Dutch had been consolidating since the early modern centuries, also came to an end.[15] In 1942 the Dutch had to abandon the Indonesian archipelago to the Japanese under humiliating circumstances. When the Japanese evacuated it at the war's end they proclaimed its independence; the Indonesian nationalist leader, Sukarno, who had been agitating for independence since the 1920s, took control. The Dutch tried to return and reconquer the country, and open warfare continued for four years. In 1949 the Dutch recognized Indonesia with its 75,000,000 peoples (110,000,000 two

[14] See pp. 594, 856–857.
[15] See pp. 170, 694–695, 833.

decades later) as an independent republic, joined in a tenuous union with the Dutch crown; in 1954 even these ties were dissolved. The Dutch insisted on retaining Netherlands New Guinea or West Irian but finally ceded it too in 1963. Often these last outposts were only token reminders of past grandeur. Portugal, for example, clung stubbornly to a few enclaves in India until forcibly expelled in 1961.

In Indonesia, as elsewhere in the former colonial world, independence was won but constitutional democracy and economic welfare were not assured. Sukarno, elected president in 1949, governed dictatorially under a policy variously called "guided democracy" and "Indonesian socialism," setting aside the constitution, suspending the elected parliament, and exercising unrestricted powers as "president for life." Here and elsewhere, the leadership which the former colonial countries relied on in the struggle for national independence turned into personal dictatorship and authoritarianism after independence was won. Sukarno was overthrown in 1966 after an abortive communist coup the year before, which he for his own purposes had backed; it was crushed in a giant bloodbath resulting in the execution of a staggering number of rebels. His military successors promised a return to fiscal responsibility, the restoration of parliamentary government, and the resumption of unfulfilled economic programs.

End of the French Empire in Indochina

European domination ended in 1954 in the former French colonial union of French Indochina but not until after seven and a half years of full-scale fighting between French armies and communist-led nationalist forces. The leader of the nationalist forces in Vietnam was the Paris-educated, Moscow-trained communist, Ho Chi Minh who, after waging guerrilla warfare against the Japanese during the war, proclaimed an independent republic at the war's end. The Japanese, as they withdrew, also proclaimed Indochinese independence under an emperor. The French in Paris were willing to concede a large measure of self-rule to the peoples of Indochina, but negotiations broke down and fighting began at the end of 1946. Because the leadership of the independence movement soon fell into the hands of Ho Chi Minh and the communists, the French could claim that they were bent not on preserving nineteenth-century colonial privileges but on stemming the tide of world communism. Yet the advance of communism in Asia, as distinct from its advance in eastern Europe, was closely linked to nationalism and to genuine native discontent.

The United States, anticolonialist but ready to champion anticommunist movements, gave considerable financial aid to the French but after its own involvement in the Korean War shrank from open intervention. The war severely drained the morale and resources of the French Republic. In the end the French forces suffered a disastrous defeat at the battle of Dien Bien Phu in 1954 and shortly thereafter negotiated a truce. At an international conference at Geneva an armistice was arranged and the independence of Vietnam, Laos, and Cambodia recognized. Vietnam, the state most seriously contested, was partitioned at the 17th parallel into a communist North Vietnam and a noncommunist South Vietnam. The partition was considered temporary, to last only until a referendum could be held. The armistice of 1954 proved to be an uneasy one. Vietnam remained in turmoil and hostilities soon reopened, as will shortly be related.

In the Moslem states communism made little headway, but nationalism grew in intensity as did the self-consciousness of the Islamic world as a political entity. The Moslem world included Arabs and non-Arabs and stretched from Morocco on the Atlantic Ocean to Pakistan and Indonesia in Asia; it embraced the Arab states of the Middle East and stretched north to Afghanistan and Iran on the borders of the Soviet Union. Within the Moslem world the Arab states made efforts to form a united bloc. Syria, Lebanon, and Jordan, which had emerged from the old Turkish empire in 1919 as European-mandated areas, emerged from the Second World War as independent countries; Iraq had been independent since 1937. Egypt, where the British for a time retained treaty rights, was in other respects independent.[16] In 1945, the chief Arab states, Egypt, Iraq, Syria, Jordan, Saudi Arabia, and Yemen formed an Arab League to act jointly in international affairs and to advance Arab interests. In the following decade the new Arab states of North Africa, Morocco, Tunisia, and Algeria, whose independence movements the Arab League had openly encouraged, joined it.

The Arab countries were aroused most by the emergence of a Jewish state in Israel. After the war the homeless survivors of the Nazi barbarism in Europe sought out Palestine as a place of refuge which they considered pledged to them as a Jewish homeland in the First World War.[17] The Arabs objected to making territorial sacrifices because of Europe's persecution of the Jews. Britain, which held a mandate over Palestine, unsuccessfully sought to placate the Arabs by limiting Jewish immigration. In 1948, the British, after much discussion and negotiation, announced the end of their mandate and the partition of Palestine. The Zionist leaders thereupon proclaimed the republic of Israel and took up arms against sizable invading Arab armies, which they succeeded in defeating quickly. In setting up the Israeli state almost 1,000,000 Arabs were dispossessed and remained disgruntled; Israeli offers to relocate the refugees were spurned. To the Arabs, Zionism seemed like a new form of Western invasion of the Middle East. The Israelis maintained that their new state would serve as a bridgehead for Western scientific, technological, and democratic advances in an economically underdeveloped, semifeudal area. With imagination and boldness they succeeded in developing modern industry and in reclaiming vast stretches of the Negev desert, where they grew citrus fruits and other crops. They succeeded also in creating a democratic society out of widely disparate elements and in developing powerful modern military forces. The Arab countries refused even to recognize the state. Egypt took the lead in the holy war against Israel.

Egypt, after a military revolution in 1952 which drove out the Egyptian monarch and inaugurated a military-dominated republic, emerged as the chief Arab state.

[16] See pp. 685–687, 758, 856.
[17] See pp. 657–658, 738–739, 893–894.

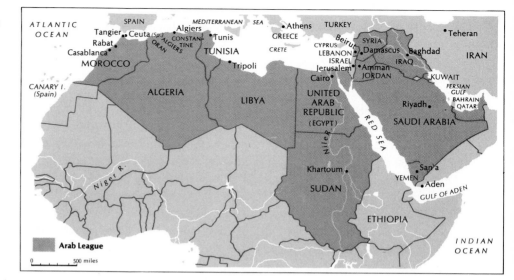

The Arab World 1970. *The Arabic language zone is one of the most extensive in the world, reaching from the Atlantic Ocean to the Persian Gulf. In 1945 the Arab states formed a League whose members are shown on the map as of 1970. The League has proved to be rather loose, with much disagreement among its members, but concerns itself with common cultural and economic matters and with opposition to the establishment of an Israeli state in the midst of an otherwise predominantly Arab world.*

The army colonel Gamal Abdel Nasser concentrated power in his own hands after the revolution and created a personal, military dictatorship. To build his country's economic and military strength, Nasser, though vehemently anticommunist, sought and obtained arms and economic aid from the Soviet Union as well as from the United States; he was incensed when the United States, in retaliation for his friendship with the Soviets, cut off some of the funds he needed to construct the Aswan Dam.

In 1956 matters came to a head. The British, as they had promised earlier, evacuated the Suez Canal zone and surrendered the remaining military rights they still held in Egypt. To a startled world Nasser then announced that the Suez Canal would be nationalized and placed under Egyptian control. The outraged British prime minister, Anthony Eden, haunted by the memories of British appeasement of European dictators in the 1930s, resolved to punish Nasser by military intervention. He acted in concert with the French, who were irritated at the flow of Egyptian aid to Algerian nationalists, and with Israel, which saw its security imperiled by permanent Egyptian control over the Canal. The United States, however, refused to support the British, French, and Israeli action when it occurred, and the Soviet Union backed Nasser, as did many of the states of Asia and Africa which saw Nasser resisting an old-fashioned imperialist invasion. Britain, France, and Israel were compelled to withdraw their forces; Nasser was left in control of the Canal. Although he agreed to operate it on an impartial basis, he continued to bar Israeli shipping.

In 1967 the Egyptians moved to close the Gulf of Aqaba. This action, combined with the continued barring of the Suez Canal to Israeli shipping, threatened

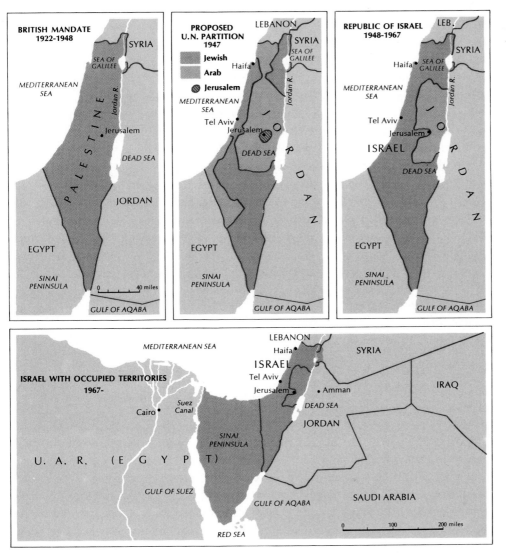

Israel and the Middle East. *"Palestine" is the term by which Europeans long designated a small region of mixed population, but predominantly Arab, which belonged to the Ottoman Empire until the First World War. European Jews, with the Zionist movement, began to migrate to it in the nineteenth century. In 1922 the League of Nations "mandated" it to the British, who tried to restrict Jewish immigration in an attempt to satisfy the Arabs. After the death of millions of Jews during the Second World War the Zionist idea of an independent Jewish state won increasing numbers of adherents. In 1947 the United Nations proposed a partition between Jewish and Arab states, with Jerusalem as a separate zone. The Arabs rejected the plan, and in the Arab–Israeli war of 1948 the Israelis won recognition of more liberal boundaries than those first proposed. The Arab states still refused recognition of Israel. In the Six Day War of 1967 the Israelis occupied additional territory. Among the Arabs a guerrilla movement developed against Israel, threatening even some of the Arab governments themselves. The rival interests of the United States and the Soviet Union in the Middle East made the situation dangerously explosive.*

to strangle the Israeli economy. In a quick six-day offensive the Israelis destroyed the Egyptian air forces, shattered the Egyptian, Syrian, and Jordanian armies, captured vast amounts of equipment, mostly of Soviet origin, and occupied extensive territories belonging to the three Arab states, including the Jordanian sector of hitherto partitioned Jerusalem. The Arab states, smarting under the humiliating defeat, refused to sign a peace treaty or recognize Israel and received new arms, equipment, and advisers from the Soviet Union. Arab guerrilla border raids, Israeli reprisals, and the involvement of the Great Powers unsettled the entire Middle East.

Although firmly entrenched in his own country, Nasser's Pan-Arab ambitions did not prosper. In 1958, to dramatize his plans for an Arab union, he officially renamed Egypt the United Arab Republic; for three years Syria joined the republic under provisions for joint Arab citizenship but seceded in 1961. Other Arab states remained cool to Nasser whom they suspected of using Pan-Arab aspirations for personal ambitions.

In all of the Moslem world, Arab and non-Arab, in Asia and in Africa, the older age of imperialism had ended. In the Middle East, although the powers no longer sought territorial control, they competed for access to the incredibly rich oil resources of the area. The Islamic world, proud of its cultural heritage and rejecting outside political domination, sought to modernize and to share in Western material advances on its own terms. With many religious and cultural barriers to overcome, including traditional barriers to the full absorption of women into society, the pace of modernization remained slow but social changes were irresistibly under way.

The French in North Africa: The Algerian War

The postwar history of Morocco, Tunisia, and Algeria (the Maghreb, as these Arab states of North Africa along with Libya sometimes call themselves) belongs at once to the history of the Moslem world, the history of emergent Africa, and the history of France. Morocco and Tunisia were never outright colonial dependencies but were French protectorates under their traditional native rulers, the Moroccan sultan and the Tunisian bey. The North African nationalists who had been educated in France and discussed ideas of freedom and independence in Paris cafés after the First World War were now intent on achieving these goals.[18] The decision by the wartime Allies to grant independence to the former Italian colony of Libya in 1951, and rising agitation for the British to end the vestiges of their control in Egypt, galvanized all North Africa. In order to mollify the rising nationalist agitation, the French tried various political maneuvers but they soon yielded, and by 1956 granted complete independence to Morocco and Tunisia.

The course of events was different in Algeria. The French considered Algeria not a colony but an integral part of France, providing it representation in the French national assembly like any other constituency in metropolitan France save that the vote was heavily weighted in favor of the European settlers in Algeria and to the disadvantage of the Arab majority. Of the 9,000,000 inhabitants, at least 1,000,000 were

[18] See pp. 686, 827–830.

European settlers, or *colons,* mostly French; like the family of the great French writer Albert Camus, they had planted roots and lived there for generations. Since the settlers controlled the economy and owned most of the land and industry, they feared for their political and economic privileges if Algeria were cut loose from France and governed by an Arab Moslem majority smarting from years of unequal treatment. They were adamant, therefore, on keeping Algeria French. At a moment when France and the French army had barely recovered from the disastrous rout in Indochina, large-scale revolt broke out in Algeria in the autumn of 1954.

The French-Algerian war lasted seven and a half years, involving 400,000 French troops and costing some 25,000 lives. The Algerian Liberation Front received aid and support from Egypt and other sympathetic Arab states. Torture and cruelty were common on both sides; the violence spread to Paris itself as extremist Algerians attacked moderates. The French were confronted with a choice between losing Algeria, which after Indochina would be an intolerable blow to their already declining prestige in world affairs, and the military, financial, and moral strain of continuing a miserable colonial war. The army, the settlers in Algeria, and rightists in France wished to press on with the war and subdue the rebels. By the spring of 1958 it became impossible for any French cabinet of the Fourth Republic even to suggest concessions to the Algerian nationalists. At that point, in the midst of a cabinet crisis, an insurrection led by die-hard settlers and army leaders in Algiers on May 13, 1958, brought General de Gaulle to power with a grant of emergency powers, which he soon used to establish the Fifth Republic.

Although no one knew how de Gaulle would meet the Algerian crisis, and many saw him and his entourage as ardent nationalists who would not abandon Algeria, he slowly and pragmatically moved to solve the crisis at his own tempo and in his own style. At first continuing the war, he made allusions to autonomy and self-determination for the Algerians after the rebellion was ended, offering a long-range program of economic aid and other reforms to attract them to France. He then began to pronounce the words self-determination more clearly and promised a referendum once a truce had been arranged. In 1961 he won the backing of the French electorate for his proposal of independence. Army leaders openly rebelled against him, and some of his closest political associates helped form a secret army of terrorists which bombed and killed and plotted his assassination. Undaunted, he moved ahead. In July 1962 the Algerian population voted for independence; French rule of a century and a quarter ended. The new Algerian regime was beset with political instability and a civil war was narrowly averted with the establishment of a military-type dictatorship. After independence there was a mass exodus of Europeans from Algeria but most Frenchmen and Algerians were grateful that de Gaulle had ended the Algerian ordeal.

In Asia and in North Africa the nationalist agitation for independence and the end of colonial empires might have been expected. But in Africa south of the Sahara the movement for liberation and its success was nothing short of breath-taking. In 1945, and even in 1950, the political complexion of Africa was scarcely different from what it had been in 1914 in the sense that with the exception of Ethiopia, Liberia, and Egypt, it was all European-governed or controlled. By 1960 the exact opposite was true: all of Africa except for a few scattered areas was independent or close to achieving independence. By 1970 there were over thirty-five independent sovereign states in Africa, and the number was still slowly growing.[19]

The granting of independence to the former Italian colony of Libya in 1951 by international agreement, the announced end of British treaty rights in Egypt in 1954, the establishment of an independent Sudan in 1956, and the events in French North Africa all spurred nationalist movements in sub-Saharan Africa where the black population lived in empires carved out by Europeans either in the early modern centuries or, even more significantly, in the decade and a half of imperialist scramble for Africa after the Berlin congress of 1885.[20] The British led the way in the liberation of the continent. Having freed their Indian empire, and cutting their other imperial commitments for economic reasons, they took steps to prepare the way for African self-rule through a gradual transfer of authority to local officials and through economic development programs. Still, agitation for independence mounted.

The Gold Coast, in West Africa, was the first British African colony to achieve its independence. Here the independence movement was uncomplicated by the presence of any sizable white settler minority as was the case elsewhere; moreover the inhabitants enjoyed a relative degree of economic stability. By 1948 it had a legislative council with an African majority. That year riots and demonstrations broke out in the capital city of Accra. The nationalists found a dedicated and eloquent leader in the American-educated Kwame Nkrumah who stirred up agitation for immediate independent status as a dominion. The British first jailed Nkrumah but then released him and in 1951 made him prime minister, arranging for a transitional period of a few years before independence. In 1957 the country became an independent dominion, the first of the new African members of the Commonwealth. It immediately shed a name identified with imperialist exploitation and took for itself the name of Ghana, recalling an African kingdom which had flourished on the Niger River from the fourth to the eleventh century A.D. In 1960 Ghana became a republic, retaining its association with the Commonwealth. After independence Nkrumah gathered extensive powers into his own hands. He became president for life, banned opposition parties, and governed as a dictator. Here, too, a colorful and dominant personality came to lead and even personify the independence movement and then after independence ruled as a dictator. After a decade of Nkrumah's dictatorial rule, his unbridled extravagances and pro-Chinese communist foreign policy led to his overthrow in 1966 by military leaders.

In the early 1960s Nigeria also moved from colonial status to independence, first as a dominion and then as a republic linked to the Commonwealth. Nigeria, with the largest area and population of the new African states, for a time offered the most successful example of political stability and democratic self-government, but in the mid-1960s tribal and regional antagonisms flared up. The Ibos, mainly Christian and

[19] See pp. 687–694.
[20] See pp. 689–690.

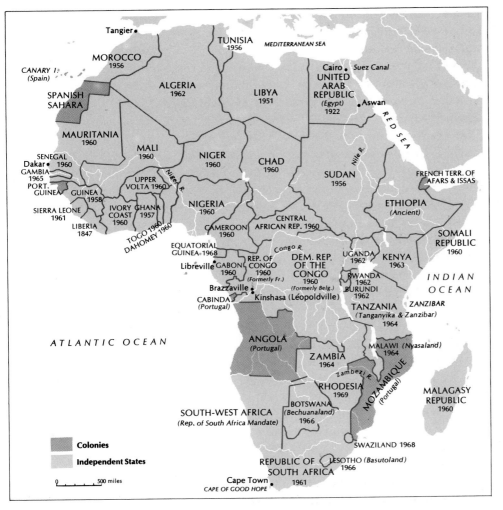

Africa 1970. *This map should be compared with those for Pre-Colonial Africa (p. 688) and for Africa in 1914 at the height of European colonialism (p. 693). The first of the new states was Ghana, the former British Gold Coast, which became independent in 1957 and took its name from a medieval African kingdom that had been located further north. The 1960s saw the independence of Algeria, an Arabic country (French for over a century), and of numerous republics in Black Africa in place of the French, British, and Belgian colonial empires. In the south the long-settled white population broke its British connection, proclaimed the Republic of South Africa, and enforced a regime of white supremacy over the far more numerous blacks. Whites in the former Southern Rhodesia set up a de facto independent republic and followed the same doubtful course.*

one of the most economically advanced peoples in the country, believed themselves the victims of intolerable persecution. After an unsuccessful attempt at a coup that led to bloody reprisals, they fled to the eastern region, their homeland, which in 1967 seceded and declared its independence as the new republic of Biafra, with a population of some 10,000,000. In the fighting that followed until the crushing of

963

the rebellion in 1969, thousands of civilians, mainly children, cut off from food supplies in the isolated bushland, died a slow death from starvation or malnutrition. In the age of African independence Africans, tragically, were destroying Africans.

In East Africa the independence movement itself encountered obstacles. In Kenya, as in South Africa and in Southern Rhodesia, an influential and economically privileged minority of white settlers set themselves against a government of nonwhite Africans. The nationalist movement retorted with violence and terrorism which reached a climax in the early 1950s with the activities of the secret Mau Mau society. The British imprisoned nationalist leaders and forcibly suppressed the extremists, resettling the entire Kikuyu tribe. After a decade of unrest, in 1963 they granted independence to Kenya, which under the leadership of Jomo Kenyatta, once imprisoned and exiled by the British, launched its experiment in self-government. In the process of Africanization, which was directed against Asians as well as against Europeans, Indians who had come in the days of British rule and served as the country's merchants, shopkeepers, and bankers were gradually forced out and much of their property expropriated. Of the other leading states of East Africa Uganda became independent in the early 1960s, as did Tanganyika and Zanzibar which, merging in 1964, took the name Tanzania and for a time served as a bridgehead for Chinese communist influence on the continent.

The French, like the British, also dissolved their colonial empire in western and Equatorial Africa, reacting very differently here than in Algeria. In the 1950s these French colonies were quiet. For years the French had hoped that a French-educated African elite would maintain strong political and cultural ties to France. Under the French Union of the Fourth Republic the overseas territories had representation in the French assemblies even though effective control remained centralized in Paris. The French republican leaders announced plans to extend the suffrage and to provide self-governing institutions in Africa, but by the mid-1950s the African colonies, inspired by the example of events elsewhere on the Continent, sought full independence.

In 1958 de Gaulle, at the time he established the Fifth Republic, though still fighting the war in Algeria, offered the African colonies the right of self-determination and voluntary association with France, which they all accepted. Guinea alone insisted on secession. The French African states moved in two or three years from autonomy to complete independence and sovereignty, some choosing to remain associated with France and with each other in a loosely organized association known as the French Community; even those who withdrew retained economic and cultural ties with France. It was a tribute to the older empires, French and British, that many of the new states voluntarily retained ties with the former imperial powers. Indeed, French and English remained the only common tongues for the continent of Africa, and English for the Indian subcontinent. But some Asians and Africans, alarmed by the continuing cultural and economic relationships with the West, saw themselves threatened with a revival of imperialism, or "neocolonialism."

By the early 1960s there sat in the General Assembly of the United Nations delegates of over a dozen new sovereign and independent states which had once been under French suzerainty—Dahomey, Guinea, the Ivory Coast, Niger, Upper Volta, Mauritania, and Mali; Cameroon and Togo (the former German colonies held since 1919 as mandates or trusteeships); Senegal, the Malagasy Republic (Madagascar), Chad, Gabon, the Central African Republic, and the Congo Republic (Brazzaville). The poet-president of Senegal, Leopold Senghor, spoke of *négritude,* a powerful and far-reaching black self-consciousness and self-assertiveness, a pride in ancient cultural roots and modern independence, which struck responsive chords in Americans of African descent whose ancestors had been brought in chains from some of the very lands now emerging as nations.

European withdrawal was accompanied by tragedy in the Belgian Congo. The Belgian Congo had once been a byword for imperialist abuse and exploitation.[21] The most abusive features were removed before the First World War and progressive reforms instituted, but political control remained concentrated in Brussels and no provision was made for self-administration or for training a native civil service. When nationalist agitation for independence burst forth in 1959, the Belgian government in panic decided against gradualism and, without the slightest preparation, precipitously announced withdrawal in six months' time. The native nationalist leadership was itself divided. Some favored a unitary state, others a federal state; some immediately arranged for the secession of Katanga, the wealthiest province. There were tribal and regional antagonisms, and hardly anyone was prepared to take over the functions of government. The Belgian withdrawal and the proclamation of the Congo Republic in June 1960 led to anarchy, riots, looting, and atrocities. Katanga province seceded; Europeans fled; Belgian troops were flown back to restore order; and the Soviet Union threatened to intervene to defend the Congo against the Western imperialists. In the midst of the crisis the executive secretary-general of the United Nations organized an international police force, composed chiefly of Africans, and averted what might have been a civil war of potentially grave danger because of Soviet-Western complications. The worst of the initial crisis over, the secession of Katanga province ending after two and a half years, and with a United Nations emergency force remaining for a time to assist in maintaining order, the Congo Republic still faced an uncertain future. The African continent remained one of the battlegrounds of the Cold War.

The British, French, and Belgian empires in Africa were ended. Portugal alone, forcibly expelled in 1961 from its old imperial enclaves in India, clung to Angola and Mozambique, the one on the western, the other on the eastern coast of Africa, two large colonies which had once flourished on the slave trade and were tokens of Portuguese grandeur in the first age of European expansion. Portugal, itself authoritarian, set itself against the tide of colonial liberation and repressed the rising agitation for independence.

By the early 1960s the old style empires were gone. The German and Turkish empires had disappeared with military defeat in the First World War, the Italian in the Second. In a decade and a half after 1947, the British, French, Dutch, and Belgian

---

[21] See pp. 687–690.

empires in Asia and Africa had been liquidated. The United States had withdrawn from the Philippines, granted Puerto Rico its freedom as a commonwealth, taken in Alaska and Hawaii as equal members of the federal union. The age of imperialism, dating back to the fifteenth century when the Europeans first set sail on their voyages of discovery, and reaching a new climax from 1885 to 1900 when Europeans penetrated the interior of Africa and expanded their holdings or spheres of influence in Asia, and Americans took over the Philippines and asserted themselves in the Caribbean and in Latin America, was ended. A new chapter in world history opened, and all contemporary history was now world history.

114
The Democracies
since 1945

In the domestic affairs of the Western countries there were again, as after the First World War, decisive democratic advances. It was an indubitable triumph for democracy to rid the world of Nazism in Germany and Fascism in Italy. Constitutional and parliamentary government was restored where it had been suspended or destroyed, civil liberties strengthened, woman suffrage introduced in France and Italy. The prewar trend toward the welfare state was accelerated. The memories of the Great Depression, the sacrifices demanded in the war, the ambitions and hopes raised in the Resistance movements, and the desire to protect the citizens of democracies against economic insecurity of all kinds laid new burdens and responsibilities on democratic governments everywhere.

The United States

For the United States, and indeed for much of the world, the most important single fact in the early postwar years was the productivity of the American economic system. The American economy, after recovering partially from the Great Depression during the New Deal years and expanding enormously to meet military needs during the Second World War, continued to grow after 1945 in defiance of gloomy predictions that conversion to peacetime production would bring disaster. War damage in such industrial countries as the U.S.S.R., Germany, Britain, and Japan made United States economic leadership for a time greater than ever. Income per capita in the United States in 1938 had been only a little higher than in Great Britain, Sweden, or Switzerland, the next wealthiest countries. In 1948 it was about twice as high. A few years later western Europe, the U.S.S.R., and Japan had recovered from the war and experienced rapid industrial expansion in the 1950s and 1960s. Even so, the United States had a substantial lead in per capita output, wealth, and consumption levels. Per capita output in the United States at the start of the 1970s was still twice as high as that of western Europe, its closest competitor. To take one example of consumer levels, there were still 335 automobiles owned per 1,000 inhabitants in the United States and less than 100 per 1,000 in the countries of western Europe. With 6 percent of the world's population, the United States at the beginning of the 1970s owned and produced one-half the world's wealth.

The great wealth and vast resources of the United States often provoked in other countries a suspicious and hostile view of American policies and culture, but it was

American wealth that made possible a program of financial aid to the European countries under the Marshall Plan, amounting to many billions of dollars, without which the Europeans could not have overcome the ravages of the war and then proceeded to modernize their economies and expand their productive output in so sensational a way. The United States program after the war was aimed at strengthening democratic governments abroad while keeping its own industries busy and employment high. At the same time the economic ascendancy of the United States produced problems. Exporting profusely yet unwilling or not needing to import in the same proportion, the United States by its very productivity tended to unbalance world exchanges. Until 1957 there was a chronic "dollar shortage"; that is, other countries could not earn the dollars to buy American goods and found themselves frustrated when they asked for "trade, not aid" in their relations with the United States. The United States at that time, as it had for two decades, held almost half of the noncommunist world's gold and foreign exchange, an amount disproportionate to its share of world production and trade; western Europe held about one-fourth. With the recovery and remarkable expansion of western Europe and with other shifts in the world economy, by the end of 1962 United States holdings of gold and foreign exchange declined sharply, and the country was compelled to devise measures to check the decline and to meet its unfavorable balance of payments. On the whole, however, Americans recognized the interdependence of the world economy and few voices were raised in favor of restoring tariffs or repeating the economic nationalism of the 1920s or of the depression years.

The rapid rate of industrial growth in continental western Europe as well as in the Soviet Union made Americans anxious lest their economy fail to keep pace with other industrial countries. In the decades after 1950 production in the United States rose at a rate of less than 3 percent annually, more slowly than in the Soviet Union or in western Europe. Economic growth had to keep step also with the nation's expanding population, which grew from 132,000,000 in 1940 to exceed 200,000,000 in 1968. The population increase showed signs of slowdown about 1957 but with an approximate increase of over 1 percent the country was still growing by over 2,000,000 each year. There was concern, too, that private affluence and expenditures on consumer goods would obscure the need for public commitment to expenditures on education, housing, urban redevelopment, and the elevation of living standards in depressed areas; large military expenditures also diverted funds from domestic needs. The very efficiency of American technology, and the beginnings of automation, threatened to displace workers and create additional social problems.

President Truman, coming into office on Roosevelt's death in 1945, and reelected in 1948, attempted in his Fair Deal to continue the New Deal of his predecessor.[22] The labor unions remained a powerful force in American life although measures were taken under Republican auspices to curtail what were alleged to be unfair industrial practices of the unions. When the Republican party took over the presidency for eight years after 1952 under the wartime hero Dwight D. Eisenhower, the orientation

[22] See pp. 848–853.

was closer to that of the business community but no fundamental steps were taken to nullify the changes inaugurated by the New Deal; social security coverage was extended, legal minimum wages raised, and public housing built. In the election of 1960 a Democratic administration was returned to office with the election of John F. Kennedy, the first Catholic president and the youngest president ever to be elected. Tragically assassinated toward the end of his third year in office, he was succeeded by his vice-president, Lyndon B. Johnson, who in the presidential election of 1964 won a landslide victory. Both Kennedy and Johnson favored strong executive leadership and government action to combat lagging economic growth, persistent pockets of poverty, and racial discrimination. Under Johnson federal aid to education was increased and medical and health services, especially for the aged, expanded. His intense commitment to the war in Vietnam cost him his large popular following, and he did not run for reelection. In 1968 Richard M. Nixon defeated the Democratic candidate by a narrow margin of the popular vote.

The United States remained the vigorous champion of free private enterprise, but the American people had come to accept the responsibility of the federal government for the state of the economy as a whole and the need for government vigilance to prevent the recurrence of anything like the crash of 1929 and the depression. It was said with some accuracy that the giant industrial combinations of the United States, the giant labor unions, and the large apparatus of government, together with other economic groupings, exerted countervailing pressures that helped distribute economic power in the country and prevented any single group or groups from an excessive voice in economic decisions.

Domestic developments in the United States were overshadowed in the postwar years by the country's new world-wide international commitments, by its anxiety over the intentions and deeds of the U.S.S.R. and international communism, and for a time in the 1950s by an obsessive concern with internal subversion and disloyalty. After the First World War, raids had taken place on left-wing organizations and the government had deported some radical aliens. After the Second World War the government embarked on a more extensive program of curbing leftist organizations and activities; the Attorney General's office drew up lists of subversive organizations, loyalty hearings were undertaken, government officials were dismissed, and espionage trials were held. The "red scare," fanned by the Wisconsin Senator Joseph McCarthy, flared amidst the country's chagrin and humiliation at communist triumphs in the Far East and American setbacks in the Korean War. By many it was argued that the toleration of dissent, long the hallmark of American freedom, was threatened by repression aimed only ostensibly at communist activities; by others it was argued that the foundations of American security were menaced by internal sedition and world conspiracy. The most abusive features of the McCarthy era faded after 1953.

The United States continued to grapple with its special "American dilemma," the very crucial question whether the American democracy could effectively absorb its black citizens into American society. For the black population, over 22,000,000 at the end of the 1960s, the myth of the American melting pot did not quite apply.

Chafing at continuing forms of discrimination, they became increasingly militant in the 1960s; civil rights demonstrations and pressures grew. In May 1954 a Supreme Court decision prescribed equal access of the races to the nation's public schools. President Eisenhower and President Kennedy used federal troops to enforce the ruling. Despite progress, segregation in the schools persisted in the South and in the large urban concentrations in other parts of the country. In 1964 Congress adopted legislation to prevent discrimination in employment, housing, and public accommodations.

The new American role in world affairs made equality especially urgent. The United States had to appear in a favorable light to the majority of the world's population which was not white; events in Little Rock and Birmingham were followed closely by men and women in Bandung and Nairobi. The emergence of independent states in Africa led to a strong sense of identity in young Afro-Americans who took pride in the new states and their ancient culture. Moreover, the American conscience was sorely troubled. Expanded economic and educational opportunities, the Supreme Court rulings, federal action, and the determination of the great majority of the American people to work toward a peaceful remedy to the most glaring defect in the American democracy held promise for the future. But in the late 1960s there were grim warnings that the United States was moving toward "two societies, black and white, increasingly separate and scarcely less unequal." Extremists were at work in all camps; demonstrations, some peaceful but many violent, and taking the form of urban riots, were becoming a feature of the American landscape. There was danger that the revolutionary class struggle which America in some ways had escaped might be fought out in racial terms, or that the Afro-American agitation would take on the aspects of a colonial independence movement. It already had its militant leadership and its martyrs like Martin Luther King whose assassination in 1968 shocked the country. Racial inequity, assassinations and violence, and the fighting in Asia perturbed young white people in America as well and aroused them to unprecedented militancy.

Great Britain

In Great Britain, even before the war had ended in the Far East, an election in July 1945, the first in ten years, unseated Winston Churchill and voted in a Labour government under Clement Attlee. Once the center of high capitalism, Britain for a time became the world's chief exemplar of parliamentary socialism. The Labour party, governing from 1945 to 1951 for the first time in history with a majority of its own, put through a broad social program which left permanent changes in British society.[23] Insisting that in an ailing economy the country's basic industries, the "commanding heights" of the economy, could not be left to the unplanned anarchy of capitalism and free competition, the Labour government brought under public ownership an important segment of the British economy, including the Bank of England, the coal mines, such public utilities as electricity and gas, communications and transportation, and iron and steel production. Since it nationalized only a

[23] See pp. 641, 643, 854–856.

relatively small proportion of British industry, what emerged was not socialism but a mixed economy. Even in the private branches of the economy steps were taken to influence the direction and amount of private investment; the national interest was to supplement the self-interest of private enterprise and the profit motive. At the same time the Labour government greatly expanded and revamped the program of social insurance inherited from the Liberal reforms of 1906–1914.[24] Both the Labour and the Conservative parties had committed themselves during the war to an extension of these welfare services as the just due of a population that had accepted wartime rigors and sacrifices. The Beveridge report on social insurance in 1942 had sketched a program designed to guarantee full employment in a free society and to provide social security for all from cradle to grave. The Labour government now extended insurance coverage for unemployment, old age, and other contingencies and also inaugurated a comprehensive free medical and health service for the entire population.

All of this program, the public ownership of the basic industries of the economy, government controls over the economy as a whole, the extensive social security system, and the use of taxation to redistribute wealth furthered the idea of the welfare state, described by some as an oppressive, regimented, bureaucratic apparatus, and the road to a "new serfdom," and by others as a demonstration that political democracies could protect the social and economic welfare of their citizens and thereby insure an even greater devotion to democratic processes. The only constitutional change under the Labour government was an act of 1949 to reduce the power of the House of Lords to delay legislation from three years to one. Restrictions on labor activities dating from the general strike of 1926 were repealed.[25]

The electorate, growing restive at the continuation of wartime austerity controls, gave Labour a renewed but smaller majority in 1950 and then in 1951 returned the Conservatives with a small majority, but that majority grew substantially in two succeeding elections, in 1955 and 1959. The Conservatives in office halted the nationalization program and denationalized the iron, steel, and trucking industries, but they continued without perceptible change the structure of the social security and health insurance program. The Conservative prime ministers, Churchill, Eden, Macmillan, and Douglas-Home, although dropping many governmental controls, remained committed to welfare democracy.

Both parties in Britain had to cope with the country's deteriorating international trade position. Britain was in an even worse state after the Second World War than after the First because most of its foreign holdings, amounting to some $40,000,000,000 before the war, had to be liquidated in the course of the fighting; in addition a large part of the British merchant marine had been lost. For Britain, dependent on imports for its food and raw materials, this loss of interest on its investments and of income from its shipping services cut into the country's invisible exports and increased its adverse balance of payments.[26] The disappearance of a

[24] See pp. 632–633.
[25] See p. 854.
[26] See pp. 618–624, 843–845, 853.

universally convertible currency, such as the gold standard had provided, created further obstacles to multilateral trade. Adopting a stern austerity program at home and foregoing its own products, Britain girded to expand its exports and to compete with aggressive competitors in the world market. With American financial aid and an intensified export drive, and with the postwar European economic cooperation program, the threat of economic collapse was averted and the British economy and trade position improved in the 1950s. Great Britain experienced a prosperity which despite some dark spots exceeded anything the country had known since before the First World War.

Still very much dependent on imports of food and raw materials, the country could pay for its imports and sustain its prosperity only with a modernized expanding economy. The Labour party argued that the Conservatives, lacking in economic dynamism, were responsible for a lag in British industrial growth compared to that of other west-European countries. In the general elections of 1964, after three successive defeats, Labour was returned to office, but with a precarious majority. Although this majority was increased in 1966, the Labour government of Harold Wilson faced continued economic pressures. There were renewed balance of payments difficulties, despite mounting exports, and in 1967 the government devalued the pound and extended its austerity measures. In 1970, in an upset victory even more surprising because of Labour's overwhelming self-confidence, the Conservatives were returned to office with Edward Heath as prime minister. Throughout the postwar years Britain showed continued intellectual and cultural vitality; it had its share of restless intellectuals and angry young men who took satisfaction in assaulting the vested interests and the status quo, socialist or conservative, all of which were vaguely identified as the Establishment.

France's Fourth Republic, which lasted from the liberation of France in 1944 to May 1958, inherited most of the weaknesses of the Third. Whereas the Third Republic lasted seventy years, the Fourth survived barely fourteen before it fell victim to its constitutional defects and the burden of colonial wars.[27] For two and a half years, from 1944 to 1946, a provisional government was in office while constitution-making proceeded. In January 1946 General de Gaulle resigned as head of the provisional government to protest the parliamentary regime and the contest of political parties which he saw as reappearing. Later that year the constitution, which he opposed, was adopted unenthusiastically in a popular referendum by a narrow margin, and only after an earlier, Communist-backed draft providing for a single assembly had been rejected. The constitution of 1946, which formally inaugurated the Fourth Republic, differed only in a few details from the parliamentary machinery of the Third Republic. One innovation adopted without debate was the extension of the suffrage to women. The president of the republic was again a ceremonial figure and the premier and his cabinet were responsible to the whims of the legislature with only a few technical but ineffective safeguards against cabinet instability. A second

[27] For the Third Republic, see pp. 627–631, 857–861, 892–893.

house, the Council of the Republic, had somewhat less power than the former Senate. The new republican regime came to be dominated, as the Third Republic had been, by an all-powerful National Assembly, jealous of its prerogatives and deeply suspicious of a strong executive.

As head of the provisional government, General de Gaulle governed in cooperation with three major parties of the left, the Communist party, the Socialist party, and the Popular Republican Movement (or MRP), the latter a new phenomenon in republican history, a Catholic progressive party devoted to the republic. All three had emerged from the Resistance movement enhanced in strength and prestige, but the Communists emerged as the leading party, largely on their well advertised but undeniably heroic record in the wartime Resistance movement after the German invasion of the Soviet Union in 1941. Almost a fourth of the electorate voted for candidates of the Communist party in France, as in Italy, but this seemed to represent the maximum which communism in western Europe seemed able to attain. De Gaulle and his successors refused the Communists the key ministries in the cabinet which they had sought but gave them several posts vital to the rehabilitation of the national economy. After de Gaulle resigned, the three parties continued to cooperate in governing; but in May 1947 the Communists, reflecting the heightening tension between the Soviet and Western camps, fomented a series of strikes directed against the government and were expelled from the cabinet.

After 1947 parliamentary and ministerial instability grew worse; the Socialists and MRP formed unstable coalitions with the once moribund but now reviving Radicals, and with other center parties. After an election in June 1951 the National Assembly was hopelessly split into six parties virtually equal in representation. Periodically de Gaulle returned to the political scene, heading a movement called the Rally of the French People which he described as "above parties." Inveighing with good cause against the instability of the regime, he nonetheless alarmed the democratic parties of the noncommunist left who saw the republic threatened by communism on the left and a threatened dictatorship on the right. By 1953 the Rally of the French People had faded and de Gaulle had returned to retirement. The immediate threat to the constitutional regime seemed to have subsided. The country had traveled full cycle from a leftist orientation at the moment of liberation to one in which the conservative parties dominated the political scene. In the next few years parliamentary instability and ineffectiveness filled the public with cynicism, hostility, and indifference; the spirit of enthusiasm and regeneration carried forward from the Resistance movement died out, save for a brief revival under the eight-months ministry of the reforming Radical, Pierre Mendès-France, in 1954–1955.

Yet despite its uninspiring political record, the economic and social accomplishments of the Fourth Republic were substantial. The provisional governments under de Gaulle and the tripartite combination of left parties laid the foundation for a modern welfare democracy. The government nationalized a number of key industries, including the coal mines, gas and electricity, and the major banking, credit, and insurance facilities. As in Britain, a mixed economy emerged. The government expanded the existing body of social security legislation and added the innovation of family allowances as a supplement to the wages of heads of family. In 1946 it launched a farsighted economic plan drawn up by Jean Monnet, which channeled investments into six key sectors of the economy, enlarging and modernizing the economic base and creating the potential for industrial expansion. The Monnet plan, along with American financial aid under the Marshall Plan, helped to modernize the French economy and to make possible a spectacular economic growth that no one a generation earlier would have thought possible. By 1952 production levels were one and a half times those of 1938, and industrial output began to grow at an average annual rate of 5 percent. Frenchmen like Monnet and Robert Schuman took the lead also in many of the imaginative proposals for European economic integration launched in the 1950s such as the European Coal and Steel Community. The country also showed a remarkable demographic vitality that confounded earlier pessimists.[28] The population decline in the years before the war gave way to regular annual increases so that the prewar French nation of 40,000,000 exceeded the 50,000,000 mark by the late 1960s. There were many weak spots in the economy; public finances and tax evasion remained serious problems; and labor unrest persisted, in part provoked by the Communists, in part motivated by genuine grievances, including inflation. But the economic record and the rise in living standards were impressive.

What rendered the Fourth Republic's political problems insoluble was the strain of trying to preserve the old French empire. The regime was unable to cope with the exhausting colonial wars that it waged first in Indochina from 1946 to 1954 and then in Algeria from 1954 to 1962.[29] France alone, of all the major powers, was almost continuously at war for almost fifteen years in the postwar era. France could envy the lot of the losers in the Second World War, Germany and Italy, which had no restless colonies to subdue.

As promised during the war, the constitution of 1946 democratized the government of the French Union but, as we have seen, the limited reforms did not satisfy national revolutionaries pressing for independence in Tunisia, Morocco, Madagascar, Indochina, or Algeria. From December 1946 to June 1954, the French army fought the nationalists in Indochina until finally after the disastrous defeat at Dien Bien Phu, almost as severe a blow to French military pride as the fall of France in June 1940, the French had to withdraw. Then, only a few months after the rout in Indochina, the Algerian war broke out, the main outlines of which have been described. As the fighting dragged on, savagery and brutality mounted on both sides. With over 400,000 troops in Algeria, three-fourths of whom were young conscripts, with the Algerian nationalists waging elusive guerrilla operations in the hills, with the war spilling over into the very streets of Paris, the police raiding the homes of Algerian sympathizers, and Algerian extremists striking at moderates, the war drained the financial resources, morale, and self-esteem of the French. The French participated in the ill-fated Suez expedition in 1956 to stop the flow of aid from Egypt to the

[28] See p. 611.
[29] See pp. 946–947, 956.

Algerian nationalists, but nothing availed. The settlers in Algeria, and the army leaders smarting under their previous defeats, adamantly opposed French withdrawal and, taking matters into their own hands, in May 1958 staged an insurrectionary demonstration in Algiers. A new cabinet, hastily invested in Paris, proved impotent against the junta in control in Algeria, feared a paratroop invasion of the capital and civil war, and welcomed the one man who could save the situation, General de Gaulle. The vast majority of the French people hailed his return. The army leaders, the settlers in Algeria, and the parties of the right were convinced that with his solicitude for the army and for French national greatness he would keep Algeria French. He also mollified the left, except for the Communists and a tiny group of stubborn, inflexible republicans, by recalling the democratic way in which he had governed after liberation and by insisting that he would return to power only in a legal way. In June 1958 the National Assembly invested de Gaulle as premier with emergency powers for six months and with the authority to prepare a new constitution.

In that way the Fifth Republic was born. In quick succession in the autumn of 1958 the new constitution was prepared and accepted overwhelmingly by a popular referendum, elections held, a new Gaullist party (the Union for the New Republic) emerging as the leading party, and de Gaulle elected president. The presidency was the key office and focus of power in the Fifth Republic. The president appointed the premier, although the latter remained technically responsible to the legislature. The president was empowered to dissolve the Assembly and call for new elections, submit important questions to popular referendums, and assume emergency powers, all of which de Gaulle did in his years in office. Political instability disappeared; in the first ten years of the Fifth Republic there were only three premiers; in the fourteen years from 1944 to 1958 under the Fourth Republic there had been twenty-five.

We have already noted how de Gaulle settled the Algerian crisis and how an independent Algeria came into existence in July 1962. Even earlier, de Gaulle granted self-determination and independence to the former French colonies in sub-Saharan Africa. With French self-confidence restored because of the stability of the new regime, with economic prosperity continuing, and with France playing an active and independent role in world affairs, Frenchmen reconciled themselves to the loss of empire and took pride in their heightened importance on the world scene. In 1960 France became the fourth nation to develop a nuclear capacity, following in the steps of the United States, the U.S.S.R., and Britain. Rejecting the rigid patterns of the Cold War and viewing postwar international affairs as a traditional struggle between Great Powers rather than a clash of ideologies, de Gaulle declined to follow the American or British lead in Europe or Asia and aspired to a large diplomatic role for France on the European continent, in Asia, and elsewhere.

With the settlement of the Algerian crisis de Gaulle made himself an even stronger master of the French domestic scene. He continued to build a kind of plebiscitary democracy by frequent direct appeals to the people and by ignoring parliament. Bypassing parliament, he secured a constitutional amendment providing for the direct popular election of future presidents. In the elections of 1962 his party won an absolute majority in the Assembly, the first time any party had done so in republican history. Although civil liberties were preserved, and free speech and free elections guaranteed, the old democratic ferment seemed to be disappearing; the political parties, including the Communist, seemed paralyzed or impotent. A sterility and torpor settled over French political life, skilled technicians ran the affairs of state, and de Gaulle, an uncrowned republican monarch, presided for eleven years as arbiter over the nation's destinies.

But the nation was growing restless. In 1965 de Gaulle was reelected president, but a runoff was necessary when he failed to secure a majority on the first ballot. The labor unions chafed at inflation and inadequate attention to housing; students objected to government expenditures on nuclear arms instead of on educational facilities; opposition political leaders criticized the government's control over the mass information media. The country as a whole grew impatient with the General's extravagant posturing in world affairs as when he called for Quebec to free itself from Canada, or allied himself with the Arab cause against Israel, or upheld doctrinaire anti-British and anti-American attitudes. Suddenly in May 1968 unrest in the universities sparked a revolt that led to demonstrations by hundreds of thousands of students and then brought 10,000,000 workers out on strike, paralyzing the economy. De Gaulle survived the revolt but only after assuring himself of army support and promising wage increases and broad educational and labor reforms.

New elections in June 1968 in which de Gaulle held out the threat of communism and chaos resulted in an overwhelming majority for his party. For a time the country seemed to forget the outburst. Educational reforms were inaugurated, and de Gaulle weathered an assault on the franc despite the economic disruption of the spring. But in April 1969 he chose to make a referendum on a complicated series of constitutional reforms a vote of confidence in himself. When it was defeated at the polls by a small margin he resigned in pique and retired to his country estate, an august, heroic, and austere figure whose exploits in war and peace had even during his own lifetime assured him a place in history. The Gaullist Republic continued without de Gaulle.

In 1945 Germany was in ruins, its cities gutted, three-fourths of the homes in its great cities destroyed, its industrial plants burned and bombed, its land divided into four zones and occupied by United States, British, French, and Soviet troops. Economic chaos, a worthless currency, food and housing scarcities, an active black market, shattered morals and morale combined to create a grim picture. Moreover, under the arrangements at Potsdam, Germany surrendered control to Poland and the U.S.S.R. of an area along its eastern borders roughly equivalent to one-fourth the German territory as defined at Versailles.[30] Some 12,000,000 refugees, expelled or in flight from these eastern areas, as well as from former German population centers such as the Sudetenland, had to find homes in the bombed-out German cities.

The four powers cooperated in 1946 in holding an international trial at Nuremberg of twenty-two major Nazi leaders charged with crimes against humanity

[30]See pp. 909, 912, maps, pp. 760–761, and front end papers.

and world peace and executed all but a few of the defendants. The evidence of evil deeds, massive and incontrovertible, was set down for posterity in many volumes of testimony but misgivings arose in many quarters about the precedent of punishing the leaders of a defeated enemy and even over the propriety of one totalitarian power sitting in judgment over another. A "denazification" program, carried out by the occupation authorities, each in its own way, and by German courts under Allied supervision, had mixed results; sometimes lesser offenders were punished because their cases were less complicated while more serious offenders benefited from postponements and delays. Since so many technically trained and professional Germans had in some way been identified with Nazi organizations, it became impossible to exclude them all from public life. In general, the Allied countries rejected the notion of collective or mass guilt for Nazi misdeeds; the sins of the Nazis were not to be visited on the German people as a whole. Individuals guilty of the more heinous crimes associated with the Third Reich were still being apprehended and tried over two decades after the war's end—in German courts and, in the spectacular case of Adolf Eichmann, who played a leading role in the Jewish liquidation program, in Israel. In 1947, the Allied authorities formally dissolved the historic state of Prussia; the spirit of Prussian militarism and authoritarianism was thus to be exorcised from the German body politic; on this Western and Soviet authorities were in agreement.[31]

Late in 1946 the Americans and British fused their occupation zones; the French followed in 1948. The Soviets went their separate way in their zone in East Germany. They encouraged the East German Communists to swallow up the Social Democrats and in 1949 oversaw the establishment of a German Democratic Republic. Under the stern rule of Moscow-controlled Communists, East Germany followed the general pattern of the iron curtain satellites, industrializing, collectivizing the land, creating a one-party state. Even under Stalin's successors there was less liberalization here than in any of the other satellites. The riots in East Berlin in June 1953 and the continued mass flight to West Germany were symptoms of unrest and dissatisfaction with the regime.

In West Germany, after state governments were first established, a constitutional convention representing the state diets met in 1948–1949 with the encouragement of the Western occupying powers and established the Federal Republic of Germany, its capital in the Rhineland city of Bonn. The liberals, democrats, and socialists of Bonn were resolved to create an enduring German democracy which their predecessors at Frankfurt in 1848–1849 and at Weimar in 1919 had failed to do.[32] The political fortunes of the new republic from the beginning rested largely in the hands of the Christian Democrats, heir to the old Catholic Center party. The dominating personage in postwar Germany was Konrad Adenauer, a patriarchal, strong-willed figure and powerful personality recalling Bismarck, who took office as chancellor at the age of seventy-three and governed with skill and shrewdness for fourteen years

---

[31] See pp. 235–245, 447–448, 568–578.
[32] See pp. 528–532, 821–823.

from 1949 to 1963, reluctantly resigning at the age of eighty-seven. Elections held every four years after 1949 confirmed the Christian Democrats in office although a reinvigorated and modernized Social Democratic party supported by one-third of the voters provided a strong and energetic opposition; West Germany seemed headed toward a two-party system. Adenauer realistically relegated to an indefinite future the question of German unification and the lost eastern territories. He strengthened ties of friendship with France, cooperated in the movement of European political and economic integration, won the support and confidence of the Western powers, and provided the domestic stability and continuity that made possible a phenomenal German economic recovery.

The most spectacular achievement of West Germany was its industrial recovery and subsequent expansion, which was justifiably styled the "German miracle." After the chaos of the first two postwar years, from 1945 to 1947, conditions began to improve. The damage to German industry, whose capacity had been greatly expanded during the war, proved less extensive than appeared on the surface; many of the German plants were usable after repairs to which Germans set themselves with diligence and ingenuity. The influx of deportees and refugees from the East turned into an asset, adding to the labor force. Reparations, over which the Western powers and the Soviets wrangled, were soon halted in the Western zone. In 1948 the Western powers effected a much needed currency reform in their zone. Then, with over $3,000,000,000 provided by the United States under the Marshall Plan, carefully allocating resources and planning capital investments, and cooperating closely with other European countries in lowering trade barriers, West Germany embarked on an unprecedented industrial expansion. Essentially the economic system remained capitalist although the government shaped economic policies, guiding and channeling investments into the vital sectors of the economy. Ludwig Erhard served as Adenauer's economics minister and for five years as his successor. In 1968 Kurt Georg Kiesinger became chancellor, continuing the Christian Democratic ascendancy. But in 1969 the Social Democratic party won its first victory at the polls and Willy Brandt, long a popular figure as mayor of West Berlin, assumed the chancellorship.

With the population accepting a relatively modest scale of living and thereby making imports less necessary, the industrial scene undisturbed by labor strife, the country free from the burden of military expenditures and profiting from the increased demand created by the Korean War in 1950–1953, a substantial proportion of the national product was reinvested year after year and made possible the continuous industrial growth and full employment. By 1950 industrial production had surpassed prewar German levels; by 1958 Germany had all but doubled its output of 1938 and was the leading industrial country of western Europe. By the 1960s it was producing well over twice as much as before the war, even though its industrial rate of growth showed signs of slowing down, largely because of a labor shortage. At the same time the West German population grew in the two decades after 1945 from 48,000,000 to 58,000,000 while the population of East Germany, despite important economic progress there too, declined from 19,000,000 to 17,000,000. Only a few years after a disastrous military defeat, the German Federal Republic was an impressive industrial and political power, a coveted ally of the Western camp, an equal member, after 1955, of such Western military structures as the North Atlantic Treaty Organization. A new generation appeared that felt little responsibility for the crimes of the Nazis. Once burning political issues faded, material progress seemed triumphant over ideology, at least so far as older and middle-aged people were concerned. A small National Democratic party tried to agitate the burned-out ashes of Nazism but with limited success. The real sources of discontent appeared among students and young people who, like their counterparts elsewhere, rebelled and embraced a vaguely defined anarchism.

Just as Germany remained divided, so did Berlin, which lay one hundred miles deep within East Germany, partitioned into a Western and a Soviet sector, the scene of continuing international friction. In 1961 the Soviet and East German authorities erected a physical wall to check the exodus of East Berliners, thousands of them having already fled in pursuit of the more democratic atmosphere and material plenty of the West. At heart, liberals, democrats, and socialists in West Germany and in West Berlin, and communists in East Germany, were at one in their determination some day to reunite their divided nation. The West Germans insisted that it be by free elections throughout German territory; the East Germans and their Soviet overseers insisted that it be by negotiations between the two governments. Although consultations were undertaken, reunification remained remote; the issue was less in German hands than in the larger framework of postwar power rivalries.

The Japanese Revival

In Japan, as in Germany, the Americans used military occupation after 1945 to inculcate democracy. A new constitution promulgated in 1946 ended the divine right rule of the emperor and transformed him into a constitutional sovereign. Under the firm hand of General Douglas MacArthur the political machinery of democratic government was established; women voted; local self-government was encouraged. Labor unions grew in size and militancy. The large industrial and banking combinations known collectively as the Zaibatsu were ordered dissolved although new forms of economic concentration took their place. A sweeping program of land redistribution was inaugurated; unfortunately, many peasants lacked the means to purchase the holdings offered them, and there was resistance to the program from the larger landowners. Although the moderate socialists, the Social Democrats, emerged as an important party, political control remained largely in the hands of conservative groups drawn from the upper social classes who had long ruled Japan. Japan, like Germany, profited from the tension between the Soviets and the Western world. In the peace treaty signed in 1951, to which the Soviets were not a party, no reparations were exacted nor were any drastic limitations on armaments imposed. Japanese sovereignty was reestablished, although the United States, by treaty, retained some military rights in Japan and occupied Okinawa and the Ryukyus. A militant peace movement, stirring up memories of Hiroshima, tried to steer Japan on a neutralist course and opposed mutual defense arrangements with the United States;

anti-American demonstrations and riots, led by dissatisfied university students, occurred frequently.

In 1968 Japan celebrated the centennial of the Meiji restoration which had launched the country into the mainstream of world history. Only a quarter of a century after its disastrous defeat in the Second World War, with a population surpassing 100,000,000 but having successfully stabilized its rate of population growth, Japan was the third leading industrial power of the world, surpassed only by the United States and the U.S.S.R. Prospering and intent on making its democratic machinery work, it seemed, despite social ferment, a bastion of stability in the troubled Orient of the postwar years.

In Italy, after more than two decades of fascism, democratic processes were resumed.[33] The country adopted a new constitution, voted the Savoy monarchy out of existence in favor of an Italian republic, and extended the suffrage to women. In the first postwar elections, held in June 1945, three left parties, the Christian Democratic, the Communist, and the Socialist, came forward as the strongest. Communism was a powerful force in Italian political life, emerging, as in France, with great prestige from the partisan movement of the Resistance and successfully exploiting existing economic and social grievances, of which there were many in Italy; until 1947 the Communists held seats in the cabinet. In the divided Socialist party a majority led by Pietro Nenni insisted on close ties with the Communists while a minority insisted on an independent democratic socialism. The Christian Democrats, as in the case of West Germany, dominated the political scene. A revival of the Catholic Popular party of the prefascist 1920s, the party was sparked initially by a high sense of Christian idealism and social justice yet was moderate enough in its social and economic outlook to attract conservatives who saw their own parties disappear in the wake of the democratic reaction to fascism.

The dominating figure in postfascist Italy was the Christian Democratic leader, Alcide de Gasperi, who survived the Mussolini years as a librarian in the Vatican. He provided strength and stability in the first chaotic period after the war, and for seven formative years in the life of the republic, from 1946 to 1953, presided over a strong government which advanced political freedom and introduced moderate reforms. In 1947, in the context of the Cold War, de Gasperi dismissed the Communists from his cabinet. The general elections of 1948 followed shortly thereafter. In Italy, as in France, the Communists wished to force their way back into the seats of government. Adopting a revolutionary militancy, and winning the support of the Nenni Socialists, they made a concerted bid for power. De Gasperi triumphed, backed by the conservative parties, the Vatican, and the United States, which for the first time in its history openly intervened to influence the outcome of a European election; the Communists and their Left Socialist allies received only one-third the vote.

[33] See pp. 862–867, 903.

The Christian Democrats continued to govern in coalition with minor democratic parties. From the beginning the Christian Democrats moved slowly and cautiously in their reform program, taking care not to alienate propertied interests. Although they attempted to break up the larger landed estates, especially in the south, to redistribute the land, and to elevate living standards in the backward south, the tempo of change was slow. The Christian Democrats continued to win the elections held every five years after 1948, but after de Gasperi resigned in 1953, no firm hand was at the helm. The Christian Democratic party was itself divided by factionalism and depended on support from the reviving conservative parties and propertied interests. The result was cabinet instability, governmental sluggishness, and an inability to move ahead on needed reforms. When the Nenni Socialists, repelled by the Soviet repression in Hungary in 1956, abandoned the Communists, it became possible in the early 1960s for the Christian Democrats to govern in coalition with the Socialists to their left and to embark on a new program of reform. But the Socialists, compromised by their association in the cabinet with conservatives, found themselves losing working-class support. The Communists, manifesting increasing independence from Moscow after 1956, remained a powerful latent force, gaining substantial strength in the elections after 1958. Supported by over one-fourth the electorate, they profited from popular restlessness with the unstable, routine Christian Democratic coalitions. The fact that in 1963 Pope John XXIII spoke openly for a rapprochement with the Soviet world in the interests of preserving peace also made it easier for many Italians to vote Communist.

In the two decades after the war, for reasons that baffled economists, Italy, like Germany, enjoyed an unprecedented economic expansion. By 1949, with Marshall Plan aid, industrial production reached prewar levels. From 1953 on, Italian industrial growth, in some years as high as a 10 percent annual increase, rivaled that of West Germany and France. Benefiting from the west-European free trade Common Market established in 1958 and with foreign capital confidently streaming in, the Italian economy was flourishing; by the 1960s economic output was well over double the level of the prewar years. The rate of growth slackened, but the economy continued to boom. Italian automobiles and motor scooters, shoes and other leather goods, typewriters, calculating machines, sewing machines, and Italian film stars enjoyed popular esteem in the United States and elsewhere. Although the economic development of the south made some progress, disparity still existed. A steady migration of southern workers to the more advanced northern industrial areas created problems; an industrial city like Milan had to absorb a stream of untrained, often illiterate, immigrants who seemed to be coming from a foreign country.

Postfascist Italy had been transformed into a political democracy with a thriving capitalist economy, a quiet revolution elevating living standards for all classes of the population. Most Italians hoped that the continuing growth of a prosperous middle class, the progress in industrialization of the south, and close political and economic ties with the rest of democratic western Europe would allay social and labor unrest, extinguish the flickering ambitions of any revived neofascism, and frustrate the growth of a still powerful Communist party.

A long with the sweeping political and economic changes that engulfed nations and continents in the contemporary age, there emerged some strikingly new cultural manifestations. Much of contemporary twentieth-century culture had its origins in the years 1871–1914.[34] But since those years science, philosophy, the arts, and religion have forged new frontiers, or taken new directions, and require our attention.

In science the preponderant theme of the years since 1914 has been the acceleration of scientific discovery and its technological application, a virtual snowballing of scientific discovery and invention. Although modern science and technology expanded rapidly in the half-century before the First World War, more scientific progress can be said to have taken place in the years since 1919, and at a more rapid rate, than in all previous human history, and the progress is a continuing one. More scientists are at work, too, in the contemporary era than ever before. About 15,000 trained scientists, it is estimated, were exploring scientific problems at the opening of the twentieth century; fifty years or so later, over 500,000 scientists were engaged in research, more than the accumulated total of all previous centuries.

The average person experienced the triumphs of science most dramatically in medicine and public health. Sulfa drugs, penicillin, cortisone, and antibiotics were used to combat infections and ailments that were formerly crippling or deadly; vitamins, hormones, adrenalin, and insulin were available to promote health or relieve suffering. Vaccines were invented to combat a number of dread diseases, including, after 1955, infantile paralysis. The advances in medicine were accompanied by advances in surgery. Surgical techniques were developed to save or prolong human life; and vital organs, including the heart, could be transplanted. Apart from the advances in medical science, the citizen in an industrial society benefited from modern technology in ways too familiar to need recounting. For entertainment he had radio and the motion picture, and, after the Second World War, television; it was hinted that the revolution in electronics would spell an end to the age of Gutenberg. Since 1947 airplanes could fly faster than the speed of sound. Tourist travel to distant parts of the earth became commonplace. A new world of computers, rocketry, and space technology also opened up; and it was possible, too, that the world was on the threshold of a new industrial age based on atomic power.

We have already noted the profound transformation in physics in the opening years of the twentieth century, comparable to the scientific revolution of the early modern centuries and the impact of Darwinian evolution in the nineteenth.[35] After 1919 a new series of discoveries led to a deeper understanding of the structure of the atom and its nucleus. The cyclotron, developed in 1932, made it possible to penetrate

---

[34] See pp. 645–663.
[35] See pp. 649–650; and pp. 295–308 and 646–647.

or "bombard" the nucleus of the atom with high-speed particles and explore it further. The atom, it appeared, was not simply a nucleus of protons surrounded by electrons. In 1932 the British physicist Sir James Chadwick discovered that the atomic nucleus, or nucleon, consisted not only of protons but of neutrons as well. At the turn of the century scientists had discovered the natural radioactivity of certain elements and Einstein had propounded his formula for the equivalence of energy and mass.

Now it was discovered that the atomic nucleus of elements like uranium, when bombarded by neutrons, could release unprecedented energy. Scientists explained that when a certain form, or isotope, of the uranium atom absorbs a neutron it becomes violently unstable and splits into two parts, not only releasing energy but also releasing neutrons of its own which then trigger the splitting of other atoms in a giant chain reaction, all resulting in the emission of energy in prodigious amounts. In 1938 German scientists for the first time succeeded in accomplishing the fission or splitting of the uranium atom in the laboratory. By then the advance of atomic science, though still the achievement of men of many different nationalities, was geared to war. Learning of the German developments, some scientists, including Albert Einstein who had himself fled the Nazis in 1934, prevailed upon the United States government to explore the use of atomic energy for military purposes before the Germans succeeded in doing so. In 1942 American and British scientists, aided by numerous European refugee scientists including the Italian Enrico Fermi, accomplished the first sustained nuclear chain reaction; this in turn led to the secret preparation of the atomic bomb and, as has been related, its use in August 1945.[36]

The destructive power of the atomic bomb dropped at Hiroshima heralded the atomic age. The first use of atomic energy was for military purposes, but it could be used for constructive peacetime purposes as well, and the enormous energy controlled and converted into industrial power to serve mankind; a tiny gram of uranium could produce power equal to almost three tons of coal. Even more staggering technical developments followed in the 1950s, involving nuclear fusion or the joining together of lighter atoms to form heavier ones at great heat with accompanying thermonuclear chain reactions. This was the basis of the hydrogen bomb developed in the 1950s in which atomic fission bombs were used as detonators. Such thermonuclear fusion was believed to be the source of the energy of the sun itself. Twentieth-century nuclear physics had uncovered the cosmic secret that the production of all energy in the universe depended on nuclear transformation.

The Implications of Science

As in the case of nuclear physics, science in the contemporary age was more closely allied with technology than ever before. There was a conscious organized effort to exploit new scientific findings. It became necessary for government or industry to subsidize most scientific research in an age of expensive laboratory equipment and complex investigation requiring large-scale collaborative efforts; the solitary scien-

[36]See p. 907.

tific investigator or even inventor was disappearing. As scientific research came to be subsidized for national purposes, scientists for the first time were compelled to keep some of their conclusions secret and were subject to questioning about their own personal loyalties. Even so, because scientists worked with common funds of knowledge it was difficult to keep scientific findings secret; espionage agents merely hastened the flow of information by a few months or years. With science tied to national considerations as never before, anxiety grew that scientific discoveries would serve political and not human goals.

Science had always affected man's thinking about himself and his universe. The Copernican revolution had removed the earth from its position of centrality in the scheme of things; Darwinian evolution had demonstrated that man was biologically no more than a species that had survived. The philosophical implications of twentieth-century physics were only vaguely understood, yet they reinforced theories of relativism in all spheres. Ironically, at the very time that the average man was awed by the capabilities of science, scientists themselves recognized that they had no magic key to the nature of things. Generally they claimed no more than to determine, or guess at, relationships. Some of these within the world of the atom were mysterious and uncertain indeed.

Among some observers, there was a growing tendency to question the value of scientific and technological advance as such, and to ask whether modern technology, like some Frankenstein monster, had not grown beyond human control. Ecologists pointed to the wastage and spoliation of natural resources and to the pollution of the atmosphere by smoke, soot, and smog. They spoke of the threat to the human environment and the menace even to continued biological existence on the planet. The very life-preserving features of modern medicine and public health threatened to result in overpopulation and in unmanageable pressure upon the limited resources of the globe for sustaining life. Some critics condemned modern technology and extolled the virtues of a prescientific and preindustrial age; others more reasonably called for sharper awareness of the dangers involved and for increased controls by society.

Meanwhile, in the quest to understand nature the old divisions between the sciences were breaking down and new sciences were appearing; biochemistry, biophysics, astrophysics, geophysics, and other subdisciplines appeared, and all made intensive use of mathematics. The study of genetics made great advances. While physicists explored the atom, biochemists isolated the organic substance found in the genes and chromosomes of all living cells, the chemical carriers of all hereditary characteristics. When they discovered a genetic "code" for each cell, and when they synthesized the basic substance of heredity, the implications of genetic engineering for the future evolution of mankind were staggering. Here, too, science was more than ever linked to the destiny of man.

The other life sciences and sciences of man that made their appearance in the late nineteenth century also grew in importance. The new psychology and its exploration of human behavior, especially of human irrationality, as well as the applied medical sciences of psychiatry and psychoanalysis, expanded rapidly. Freud, who had first

Spatial Picture *by Antoine Pevsner (Russian, then French, 1886–1962)*

Antoine Pevsner, like Kandinsky and Chagall (see pp. 653 and 815), left his native Russia after the Soviet regime began to disapprove of "modern" art. Pevsner is known more as a sculptor than as a painter, but the present painting resembles his sculptural pieces, which are designed to represent space, or multi-dimensionality, in an abstract way. As reproduced here this "Spatial Picture" looks like a diagram in pure mathematics or engineering. Actually it is a painting in oil, with the lower part-circle bright red and the fan-like arrangement of conical lines a soft blue. Art is used to set forth the world as known to science, not the world of appearances. Space here is not the familiar medium in which human beings live and move, but space as it may "really" be apart from man's peculiarities of size and physical senses. In a way such a painting is more realistic and objective than the scenic beauties of the Western pictorial tradition. Courtesy of the Musée d'Art Moderne, Paris (Service Photographique).

developed his theories of psychoanalysis before 1914, became a household byword from the 1920s on; his emphasis on the human sex drive, and particularly infantile sexuality, was much modified by disciples like Adler, Jung, and others, but the original creative concepts persisted. The new psychology continued to search out the unconscious, nonrational sources of man's ideas, tastes, ambitions, and even his ethics. The techniques developed by Freud and his disciples became especially common in the United States.

As in the late nineteenth century, sociology and anthropology increasingly stressed the relativism of all culture. They denied notions of cultural superiority or hierarchies of cultural values, or even that there were objective criteria of historical progress. If Western society, they argued, made notable progress in science and technology, other cultures accomplished more in self-discipline, individual integrity, or human happiness. The very adjective "primitive," as opposed to "advanced," tended to disappear, and a new cultural humanism emerged that recognized and emphasized values distinct from the Western tradition.

The Creative Arts

The revolution against the older tradition in the creative arts continued. At least since the Renaissance artists had followed certain traditional norms of representation and space perspective. But modern, or contemporary, art prided itself on being nonobjective; it rejected the idea of imitating or reconstructing nature, or mirroring it with realism or photographic fidelity. The fundamental innovations of the artistic revolution began in the decade before 1914. They grew out of the French postimpressionist painters like Gauguin and Van Gogh who at the turn of the century made color the prime element in their art, and were forwarded by the cubists like Braque who rejected representational art even more thoroughly and placed their primary emphasis on abstract form. After 1919 the revolution in painting picked up in intensity; it seemed to mirror the political turbulence of the times and the disillusionment with rationalism and optimism. It even reflected psychoanalysis and the emphasis on the unconscious and irrational elements in man, and the relativism of the new physics which taught that there was no one nature or one universe valid for all time for all men. The surrealists like Dali openly derided rationality and reality, focusing on the artist's subconscious in an orgy of uncontrolled subjectivism.

Matisse, Braque, Picasso, and others continued the pre-1914 experimentation in color and in form. Picasso systematically distorted and deformed his objects as in the famous painting memorializing the German bombing of Guernica in 1937 during the Spanish Civil War, striving for effects of anguish and intensity by these very distortions. Chagall, too, deliberately painted the exaggerations of a dream world. At the same time the possibilities inspired earlier by the cubists led to a stricter sense of geometry and a focus on form alone. The results were sometimes pleasing, as in the case of Mondrian, but often strange; but here too, science taught that solid everyday objects have a different kind of reality in space and in movement. After the Second World War, in Europe and especially in the United States, artists like Jackson Pollock developed a new school of abstract art; it included techniques of artistic improvisation in which the artist's subconscious was said to dictate his work. Other even broader experimentation followed.

For the first time, beginning with the decade of the 1950s, the United States took the leadership from France in the new artistic developments. The results were bold and original expressions of form and color, but all of this conscious subjectivism widened still further the gap between artist and public. The artist, painter, and sculptor (and the poet, musician, and novelist who were also rejecting the older conventions) were conveying their own vision of the world, not an objective reality shared by others. Perhaps the greatest innovation was that the public, baffled as it was by much of contemporary art, came to recognize an avant-garde as normal. Or at least this was so in freer societies; in totalitarian societies like Nazi Germany in the 1930s or in the Soviet Union such experimentation and innovation were frowned upon and banned as degenerate or socially dangerous.

The focus on subjectivism and on the unconscious and the stress on the transformation and turbulence of Western society were reflected in literature too. The artistic reconstruction of lost time and the unfolding of the individual's innermost experience through a stream of consciousness and a flood of memories appeared first, as everyone knows, in the work of Proust and Joyce. Perhaps T. S. Eliot reflected best the spiritual malaise of the contemporary age in the tone of his famous long poem, *The Waste Land*, written in 1922 but just as relevant fifty years later. After the Second World War advanced writers, particularly in France, experimented with the "antinovel," a novel without heroes or plots in a conventional sense, efforts to reconstruct little closed worlds shut off from the realities of the present. Here too the writers' subjectivism deliberately reflected a world of crumbling certainties. All of this was in sharp contrast to the literature and entertainment provided through the mass communications media and hardly touched the average citizen.

Philosophy in the twentieth century seemed to contribute less to an understanding of contemporary problems than at almost any time in the past. Whereas it had formerly focused on metaphysics and ethics, and shared common concerns with theology, it now sought, at least for a time, to adopt the precision of mathematics and the methodology of science. The effort to understand the fundamentals of philosophy in terms of empirical science, mathematics, and symbolic logic was known as logical positivism (or logical empiricism). It received its first full expression in the self-consciously monumental work, the *Principia Mathematica*, completed the year before the First World War by Bertrand Russell and Alfred North Whitehead. About the same time the Viennese philosopher Ludwig Wittgenstein, who before the war had studied at Cambridge, completed and then communicated to Russell the manuscript of his own work. In 1922 it appeared in English as the *Tractatus Logico-Philosophicus,* and Wittgenstein shortly thereafter moved to Cambridge permanently. In the 1920s a group of Viennese philosophers headed by Rudolf Carnap further developed logical positivism. Opposed to all that was metaphysical, it insisted that the traditional questions of philosophy and theology were invalid,

Autumn Rhythm *by Jackson Pollock (American, 1912–1956)*

Work of this kind is called Abstract Expressionism or Action Painting. This piece illustrates an extreme development of abstraction; it shows no objects, real or imaginary, or even any clearly defined images; it conveys neither feeling, nor thought, nor geometric conception, nor depth, nor volume. What it represents is the painter's "action." Pollock produced it by fastening a huge canvas (9 × 17 feet) to the floor, and then dripping, squirting or flinging paints in many colors over the surface, to achieve a kind of random effect in which no plan or rational arrangement would be apparent. The painting is supposed to emerge from an automatic or instinctive activity, but actually the uniformity of the field, the selection of colors and a certain delicacy in the blobs and curves, suggest that the artist, whatever his doctrine, was actually working for a premeditated effect. If, in a minimal definition, art is the calculated use of means for ends, then no art can be wholly unconscious. Courtesy of the Metropolitan Museum of Art, George A. Hearn Fund, 1957.

fruitless, and senseless, that one could not speak of "God, death, what is higher," in Wittgenstein's phrase, and that the search for philosophical truth depended on the logic of language itself. The Cambridge philosopher A. J. Ayer summed up the argument for the general reader in his *Language, Truth, and Logic* published in 1936.

There was a second major development that received its widest currency after the Second World War. Wittgenstein, in the course of lectures at Cambridge, which were faithfully copied down by disciples and posthumously published as the *Philosophical Investigations* (1953), further developed linguistic philosophy, or linguistic analysis. Rejecting the mathematical formulations of logical positivism, including much of his own early work, he now argued that philosophical questions and statements could not be similar to those of science and mathematics. The main focus had to be on language and the ambiguities of language. Following his lead and rejecting both traditional metaphysics and logical positivism, contemporary philosophy, especially in Great Britain and the United States, placed emphasis on language and semantics. It abandoned speculation for analysis. It no longer debated metaphysical problems but explored the meaning of the words used in the ancient debates. All of this was somewhat remote for the layman. When he asked for the light the philosophers could throw on the meaning of human freedom, they replied that the question was unfruitful and misleading and that the inquirer might more profitably inquire how many ways and in what ways men used the word "free." Although there were some exceptions, contemporary philosophy was no reassuring guide in the uncertainties of the modern age.

Religion: Protestantism, Catholicism, Judaism

Christianity was in great flux. With the continued advance of secularism, the end of the European colonial empires in Asia and Africa, and the triumphs of communism in eastern Europe and other parts of the world, Christianity suffered a number of setbacks. Intellectually the Christian churches continued to grapple with the pressures of adjustment to modern civilization.[37] From the nineteenth century they inherited the problem of reconciling religious insights or traditional teachings with the conclusions of natural science, biblical scholarship, and comparative religion. A challenge now arose from the followers of Freud, Jung, and others who saw in religion a kind of universal neurosis and suggested that it was part of the collective subconscious of mankind.

In Protestantism in the years before the First World War liberal, or modernist, thought tended to dominate. The churches absorbed the new scientific findings, minimized the supernatural and dogmatic aspects of their faith, and tried to adapt the religious teachings of the gospel to the social needs of the contemporary world. But the First World War and the disillusionment that followed dealt a blow to the ideal of the social gospel and its inherent optimism. Sometime in the 1920s, as a reaction, there set in a revived emphasis on revealed religion, the supernatural, and the mystical. The Swiss theologian Karl Barth, whose writings from 1919 to the 1960s exerted great influence, sought to lead Protestantism back to the root principles of the

[37] See pp. 652–658.

Reformation. After the Second World War, as a result of the work of Barth, Paul Tillich, and others, a powerful movement in Protestantism reasserted its dependence on revealed truth and denied that human reason with its fallibility and corruption could ever properly judge divine revelation. Some theologians turned also to the nineteenth-century Danish theologian Søren Kierkegaard who, like Luther, had resolved his own deep anguish by a complete personal commitment to religious experience. Despite these developments the liberal, or modernist, trend remained strong. A world council of churches was established in 1948 to further the ecumenical movement, an effort to unite all branches of Protestantism and even to work out a rapprochement with the Roman Catholic Church, and eventually embrace all Christianity.

The Roman Catholic Church seemed to be in one of its great historic phases. Like Protestantism, it suffered from the advances of secularism in the twentieth century. It lost followers, and church attendance and recruitment for the clergy declined. With the vast increase in global population, mainly in the non-Western areas, the world proportion of Catholics was reduced, to the disadvantage of a religion that laid a claim to universality.

The papacy became the center of ferment. After the Second World War many criticized Pius XII (1939–1958) for having failed to protest, as "God's deputy," against the Nazi destruction of European Jewry; his defenders insisted on the need to preserve the church from temporal quarrels in order to preserve its eternal mission. The church took firm measures against the advance of communism, prohibiting Catholics in 1949 from even reading the Communist press and suppressing in the 1950s the "worker-priest" movement in which a number of priests, especially in France, had taken their social missions seriously enough to live and work among ordinary workingmen and even study Marxism. Although the church no longer sought to stamp out modernism, i.e., the reconciliation of religion with science and scholarship, there was still a heavy emphasis on dogmatic training in the seminaries. In 1950 the newly pronounced dogma of the Assumption, i.e., the bodily assumption of Mary to heaven, was a blow to liberal Catholics and to ecumenical-minded Protestants. But both Catholics and Protestants absorbed without great shock the Dead Sea Scrolls, the first manuscripts of which were discovered in 1947, and which cast significant new light on the origins of Christianity.

When Pius XII died in 1958, he was succeeded by John XXIII. Although elected at the age of seventy-seven, and reigning for only four and a half years, John was one of the most remarkable popes of modern times. He enlarged the College of Cardinals and increased its non-Italian majority. He took important steps to renew the Catholic church in its organization and doctrine by convening in 1962 a Second Vatican Council, the first since 1870. John, along with a reforming majority in the council, consciously sought to modernize, to bring the church into harmony with the political and social changes of contemporary times. He issued a series of powerful encyclicals, one reaffirming the social reform doctrine of the church, *Mater et Magistra* (1961) and another appealing for international peace and the protection of human rights through world organization, *Pacem in Terris* (1963). He sought to forward the ecumenical movement by encouraging a dialogue with non-Catholics and to establish fraternal ties with all faiths. Non-Catholics, Protestants, and Orthodox Christians, were present as observer-delegates at the council.

In 1963 a change took place when John was succeeded by Paul VI. The Second Vatican Council continued its labors until 1965. It revised some practices; the Mass, for example, could henceforth be said in the vernacular. Above all, it affirmed the principle of collegiality, i.e., that the pope must share authority with the bishops of the church. Paul, more conservative than his predecessor, was unhappy about these developments. Although he reaffirmed the Catholic commitment to social progressivism and applied it to the world's underprivileged peoples in the encyclical *Progressio Populorum* (1967), he opposed the attempts to impugn or repudiate either orthodox theology or papal supremacy. A synod of bishops convened in 1967 found its agenda severely restricted. On the critical question of birth control, a vital matter in Latin America and in all Catholic countries, Paul rejected the recommendations of a commission he had himself appointed and in a much discussed encyclical, *Humanae Vitae* (1968), condemned the use of artificial, i.e., scientific, birth control methods. A modernist catechism, prepared by Dutch bishops, was also condemned. The result was a great deal of restlessness in the church and impatience with the failure to pursue the modernization of ancient rules and practices. Many Catholics advocated abandoning the injunction of celibacy for the clergy; some monks, nuns, priests, and even two bishops set aside their vows and married. Theologians continued to reaffirm the principle of shared authority. Paul's insistence on papal obedience went unheeded, and his strictures against artificial birth control were openly criticized. It was widely said that the church had not faced so severe a crisis since the days of the Reformation.

Judaism, the third important faith of the Western world, was haunted in the years after 1945 by the great traumatic experience of the 1930s and 1940s, the Nazi attempt at genocide, the holocaust, as it was called. Although the older trend of assimilation to a secular society persisted, there was a revived adherence to religion, both orthodox and reform. There was also unprecedented support by Jews in Europe and the United States for the new state of Israel, and not only among Jews who were Zionists. Support for Israel was reinforced by new Jewish harassment and persecutions in the Soviet Union and eastern Europe and in the Arab countries; in turn these countries used Jewish allegiance to Israel as grounds for their attacks.

Like the Western religions, Islam, Hinduism, and the other great non-Western faiths, of which little can be said in these pages, all faced serious challenges to their doctrinal orthodoxy and were making efforts to adjust millennial old doctrines to the secularism of the contemporary age.

Existentialism

Outside organized religion, and generally outside professional philosophy too, a loosely organized body of ideas called existentialism made an effort to grapple with the human predicament. The existentialists formed no one school of thought and held no coherent body of principles; there were Christian existentialists, agnostic and atheist existentialists. Yet all held some beliefs and attitudes in common. All reflected a troubled civilization, a world disturbed by war, totalitarianism, and oppression, a world of material progress and moral uncertainty in which the individual could be crushed by the very triumphs of science and technology. The existentialists questioned the idea of progress or dismissed it as an illusion, and they rejected traditional metaphysical or religious formulations about the meaning of human existence. Going beyond relativism, they emphasized the fact of "existence" in the present and doubted whether a living generation could learn from the past or contribute to the future. Accepting what they liked to call the "absurdity" of man's situation, they sought to reconcile the discrepancy between human ideals and a universe which they considered devoid of purpose.

Existentialist thought owed a debt to thinkers like Pascal in the seventeenth century and Nietzsche in the nineteenth, and to many others who throughout Western history had underscored the tragic element in human existence and the limitations on the power of human reason. More directly it owed a debt to Kierkegaard, the Danish religious philosopher whose writings became better known when translated into German in 1909. Kierkegaard rebelled at abstract metaphysics and at the formalism and complacency of the Danish Lutheran church. He insisted on the anguished ethical and religious choices confronting every individual, choices that could never be made for him, and that had to be made not merely intellectually but with a total commitment of the human will. Only by such commitment, he maintained, could the individual escape being overwhelmed by dread and despair.

Existentialism was further explored in Germany after the First World War by Martin Heidegger, Karl Jaspers, and other philosophers. But it was French writers, after the emergence of their country from defeat, occupation, and resistance in the Second World War, who developed it in literature and philosophy in a form that gave it wide intellectual following. The novelist, dramatist, and essayist Jean-Paul Sartre was an outstanding exemplar, as was Albert Camus. These writers drew especially upon the Resistance experience. In a hostile world, they contended, man had to reassert his freedom. Man was "condemned to be free," said Sartre, totally free and entirely responsible for the choices he made. The authentic existentialist, moreover, was not merely contemplative but *engagé*, committed to action even though his deeds, he knew, could not change the world. Camus drew upon the myth of Sisyphus to communicate his message, Sisyphus condemned to roll his stone uphill, his very humanity growing out of courage and perseverance at a hopeless and absurd task. The existentialists rejected the perfectibility of man and society and rejected the utopian (and Marxian) idea that perfect social systems could somehow be established to suit future unborn generations.

Some of these beliefs were shared by Christian existentialists who adopted Nietzsche's nineteenth-century assertion that "God is dead." The universe, they asserted, was no longer ruled by a deity who decreed and revealed the rules men must live by; man had to make his own choices and commitments. They spoke even of a post-Christian era. But mainly the existentialist ideas were part of an atheistic humanism, like that of Sartre. In their emphasis on the anguish of human existence, the frailty of human reason and human institutions, and the reassertion of human freedom the existentialists carried forward an old theme but gave it new meaning. It is not surprising that the Western world in the twentieth century should evoke doctrines emphasizing both the tragic element of man's destiny and his irrepressible individualism.

The New Activism

Sometime in the 1960s a new activism, somewhat related to existentialism, emerged, especially among young people. A generation was coming to maturity in the Western world that knew nothing first-hand of the depression or of the war against the dictators, which their elders had lived through. Young people grew up in an age of rapid political and social change, amidst revolutionary advances in science and technology, and in a globe that was shrinking dramatically; and they were made aware of all these developments by the new mass communications media. The younger generation tended to take for granted the scientific, technological, and other accomplishments of their society and pointed instead to its deficiencies—the flagrant contradictions of wealth and poverty within nations and between nations, racial inequities, the impersonal quality of mechanized society and large institutions, the violence that destroyed men in continuing wars, and the threat of universal nuclear destruction.

The rebelliousness of the young developed into more than the traditional manifestation of a generation gap. It burst forth in the late 1960s in widely separate parts of the world. Students demonstrated and rioted in Paris, Berlin, San Francisco, New York, Mexico City, Tokyo, and many other places. They made heroes of the sworn foes of the established order: Fidel Castro and his martyred lieutenant Ernesto Che Guevara, Ho Chi Minh, Mao Tse-tung, American black leaders like the assassinated Malcolm X, the heralds of the colonial revolution like Franz Fanon, and others. They read the neo-Marxian philosopher Herbert Marcuse who warned that the very tolerance of bourgeois society was a trap to prevent true protest against injustice. They dismissed the older revolutionists in the Soviet Union as timid bureaucrats who were unaware that the revolution had entered a post-Marxian phase and that the genuine ferment was to be found in the underdeveloped third world. They attacked material comfort, affluence, and conformity. Sometimes they turned to violence themselves; more often, they sang its praise. Championing a new anarchism and nihilism, and a commitment to the present, they called on each other to destroy in order to purify and to restore creative freedom by releasing men from the "burdens" of the past. No one could say how much the youth rebellion was a passing phenomenon or indeed whether it was typical of most young people. Older people shuddered at the assault on established institutions and rational processes but found it less easy to be complacent about social inequities of all kinds. The youth rebellion seemed to be part of a transitional stage through which all modern civilization seemed to be passing in the second half of the twentieth century, and whose meaning could only be vaguely grasped.

994

H aving surveyed the domestic developments in the years since 1945, we must go back to the major international rivalries that troubled the postwar years and continued to disturb the contemporary era.

We have already noted the origins and course of the Cold War in Europe.[38] In 1950 the Cold War turned to actual fighting in Asia. In June 1950, to the consternation of the Western world, the Soviet-sponsored regime of North Korea crossed the thirty-eighth border parallel and launched an attack on the republic in the south established under the aegis of the United Nations. During the Second World War it had been agreed that Korea, once a source of imperialist rivalry between Japan and Russia, and since 1910 under Japanese rule, would again become free and independent; for temporary occupation purposes Soviet troops were to occupy the northern part of Korea down to the thirty-eighth parallel and the United States troops the area south of that parallel. In the months after the end of the Pacific war the U.S.S.R. created a puppet government on the order of the European "people's republics," proceeded to sovietize its occupation zone, and trained a large North Korean army. The Soviets put obstacles in the way of an American proposal to hold elections for all Korea under United Nations international supervision; elections were held only in South Korea. By early 1949, however, both the U.S.S.R. and the United States had withdrawn their occupation troops from their respective zones.

In June 1950 came the attack; it was hard to believe that the move was not incited or encouraged by the larger communist powers, the U.S.S.R. and the newly established Chinese People's Republic.[39] Undoubtedly the attackers calculated on a quick victory because of their superior forces and gambled that the outside world would do no more than lodge a moral protest, as in the Japanese invasion of Manchuria in 1931. But the United States under President Truman initiated the firmest action ever taken under international auspices against overt aggression in the twentieth century. Taking advantage of a temporary Soviet boycott of the Security Council to secure the adoption of its resolution without a Soviet veto, it prevailed upon the United Nations to take prompt military measures against the aggressor and committed American combat units to the fighting.

For many weeks, in the summer of 1950, the United Nations forces under the command of General MacArthur were compelled to retreat and faced the danger of expulsion from the peninsula. A successful amphibious landing at Inchon changed the picture. The United Nations forces hurled the communist armies northward and then, in a momentous decision, crossed the thirty-eighth parallel in hot pursuit, driving rapidly toward the Yalu River, the boundary line between Korea and the

[38] See pp. 933–939.
[39] See pp. 951–953.

Manchurian province of communist China. At that juncture, in November 1950, the Chinese People's Republic entered the fighting; hundreds of thousands of Chinese communist troops supported by Russian-made jet planes drove the United Nations forces southward in what looked like a repetition of the early phase of the war. But the United Nations forces held; they fought their way back to the thirty-eighth parallel, and even slightly to its north.

President Truman and his advisers, along with Britain and the majority of the nations in the United Nations, were determined to resist the North Korean act of aggression, but they were resolved also not to permit the conflict to develop into a third world war, which they feared might happen if Manchuria or other parts of China were bombed. When General MacArthur pressed that course of action, President Truman relieved him of his command. The American people were stunned, hurt, and infuriated by the worst military reverses in their history; many wanted to punish communist China but most saw the wisdom, or feasibility, of restricting the fighting. In July 1951 a cease-fire agreement ended large-scale fighting. But the negotiations dragged on for two full years, principally over the exchange and repatriation of prisoners of war, while sporadic fighting continued. In July 1953 an armistice was signed. It had been an extensive war; fifteen nations had participated along with the United States in the United Nations combat forces; counting both sides, a total of over 2,000,000 men were estimated dead, wounded, or missing; the United States suffered some 33,000 battle deaths, about three-fifths as many as in the First World War.

Politically, conditions reverted to what they had been before 1950. Korea was again divided roughly at the same parallel. The North Korean government, the Chinese People's Republic, and the U.S.S.R. persisted in rejecting international supervision of free elections for the entire country. The armistice remained an uneasy one, numerous border, and other, incidents occurring. In Western eyes a flagrant act of aggression had been checked; to the communist world, and to many noncommunists in Asia, the great capitalist power, the United States, had been prevented from reasserting Western imperialist supremacy in the East. The truth was that the United States, in the Korean War, and in its efforts to create regional security pacts in the East, found little enthusiasm among the larger noncommunist Asian powers—India, Indonesia, Burma. Most of them disliked communism but refused to be involved in war; most distrusted the West; and in the years of Asian revolution the United States, although the least involved of all the Great Powers in nineteenth-century Asian imperialism, was held in many Asian quarters, by virtue of its new leadership in the Western world, to be the symbol of Western oppression and exploitation, a picture assiduously cultivated by the Soviets and even more belligerently, as time went on, by the Chinese communists.

From Korea to Vietnam

In the early 1950s something of a change took place in Soviet-American relations and in the Cold War. The political leaders of the U.S.S.R. who took over after Stalin's death in 1953 seemed at times more conciliatory or at least were willing to pursue their ends in less ruthless ways.[40]   Although they kept the Western powers and the world oscillating between tension, relaxation, and renewed tension, the alternative of a peaceful coexistence of competing world systems seemed to open up.   There were signs, too, that in the United States not all compromise and conference were to be shunned as appeasement.   At Geneva, in 1955, President Eisenhower, along with British and French leaders, met face to face with the heads of the Russian state in a friendlier atmosphere than any since the Second World War.   But the Geneva spirit did not last.   The Soviets reopened crises over Western access to Berlin.   In 1960 a new summit conference at Paris broke up when Khrushchev brought forth evidence of American reconnaissance flights over Russian territory which the Americans did not deny.   The tension shifted to the Western hemisphere.   In Cuba Fidel Castro had ousted a rightist dictatorship in 1959 and established a procommunist regime to which both Soviet and Chinese communists lent support.   In 1961 Cuban anticommunist exiles, encouraged by the United States, invaded the island but met with disaster. The following year President Kennedy, charging that Soviet missile bases installed in Cuba represented a menace to American security, placed a naval quarantine on the further shipment of military equipment to Cuba and issued stern warnings to the Soviets to withdraw.   The world held its breath but Khrushchev backed down and agreed to dismantle the bases (for which he was berated as a capitulationist by the more belligerent Chinese communists).   Berlin, where a huge concrete and barbed wire "wall" was thrown up in 1961 to prevent East Germans from traveling to West Berlin, remained a recurrent source of friction.   In Korea border incidents and the seizure in 1968 of an American ship, avowedly on an intelligence-gathering mission, disturbed the armistice.   The Middle East, as we have seen, broke out in open warfare in 1956 and again in 1967, the Soviets wooing and arming the Arab states.   Above all, Southeast Asia, after the withdrawal of the French in 1954, remained a troubled area.

In Southeast Asia an undeclared war developed in the 1960s in which the United States but not the Soviet Union was directly involved.   The agreement at Geneva in 1954 partitioned Vietnam at the seventeenth parallel into a communist North Vietnam with its capital at Hanoi and presided over by Ho Chi Minh and a noncommunist South Vietnam established at Saigon.   The partition was to last only until a referendum was held, but the referendum did not take place.   Communist guerrilla activities, supported by North Vietnam, and with the backing of the Chinese People's Republic, harassed the republic in South Vietnam.   A communist-sponsored National Liberation Front, the Vietcong, operating in the south, grew in strength, terrorizing and coercing the South Vietnamese peasantry but more often than not winning their support.

The United States, under Republican and Democratic administrations, from President Eisenhower on, took the position that it was necessary to check communist aggression in South Vietnam in order to prevent the other states in Asia from being toppled one by one—like a set of dominoes, the theory went.   Accordingly, the United

[40] See pp. 943–944.

States bolstered the South Vietnam regime in Saigon with military advisers, financial backing, and arms and at the same time sought to democratize the regime whose undemocratic practices and widespread corruption it found embarrassing.

American involvement became deeper. In 1960 a few hundred military advisers were present; in 1962, 4,000 soldiers were in combat and the first battle deaths reported. In 1964, on the ground that North Vietnamese torpedo boats had attacked United States ships in the Gulf of Tonkin, President Johnson authorized heavy bombing raids on supply bases in the north in retaliation. The bombing raids mounted in intensity. In searching for the elusive Vietcong in the south, napalm was used to burn and destroy entire villages; the result was the defoliation of hundreds of thousands of acres of land; the survivors became homeless refugees. The commitment of American ground troops and the number of casualties rose steadily. By the end of the 1960s the United States had over 500,000 troops committed; by 1970 American battle deaths, exceeding those in Korea and surpassed only by casualties in the two world wars, rose above 40,000. More tons of explosives had been dropped than had been used against all the Axis powers in the Second World War. The Vietnamese death toll, counting both sides, was estimated at 750,000.

The other Western powers were unenthusiastic and gave little support. Domestic dissatisfaction in the United States swelled; the war in Vietnam became a root cause of riots and disorders in American universities and cities. The question was widely debated whether the United States had the responsibility or capability, despite its enormous strength, to police the world against communist aggression, whether the American presence in Vietnam was an unwanted foreign presence reminiscent of Western intrusion in the age of imperialism, whether bombing raids that reached to within ten miles of the Chinese border might not provoke Chinese direct intervention and provoke a third world war, whether the South Vietnam regime could be stabilized and democratized to make the sacrifices worthwhile, and whether the continued hostilities might not end in the utter destruction of the entire hapless country. Critics with a knowledge of Asian history argued, too, that the Vietnamese had a long record of self-protection from their Chinese neighbors and that even a Vietnam united under communist preponderance would not necessarily mean complete subjugation by the Chinese. Although many continued to believe in the

Vietnam and its Neighbors. *French Indochina, for about sixty years before World War II, comprised the old Asian territories of Cambodia, Laos, and Vietnam, though the French called northern Vietnam Tonkin and southern Vietnam Annam. Shaken by Japanese invasion in World War II, the French proved unable after a long struggle to resist the Vietnamese movement for independence which drew strength also from communist affiliations. When the French withdrew in 1954 an international agreement (the Geneva Accords) provided for partition of Vietnam until unity could be restored. Since the north was now communist, the United States undertook to strengthen South Vietnam by favoring reforms and by measures of economic and military assistance which grew in the 1960s into a large-scale though undeclared war. North Vietnam was supported by the communist powers and by revolutionary sympathizers in the south.*

necessity of the American intervention in order to halt communist aggression, by the
end of the 1960s the United States took steps to cease its bombing operations, to begin
a scheduled withdrawal of troops, and to encourage peace negotiations.   The Hanoi
government and the Vietcong which now called itself a provisional government were
willing to undertake negotiations with South Vietnam and the United States, but on
their own terms.   Although preliminary peace talks opened in Paris in the spring of
1968, the fighting continued mercilessly.

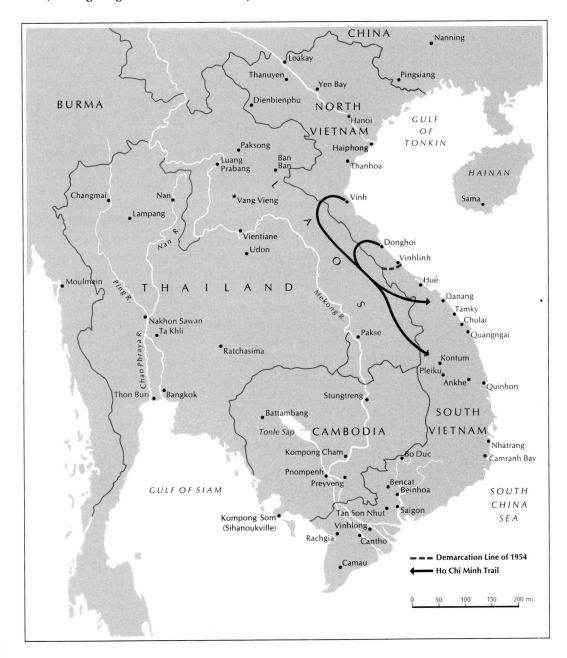

Over every crisis, large or small, hung the threat that armed conflict might "escalate," as one now said, into nuclear catastrophe. The early atomic disarmament negotiations had been broken off in 1948. In 1949, as we have seen, the Soviets exploded their first atomic bomb. In 1952 the United States successfully tested the first hydrogen bomb, which by its chain reaction and thermonuclear effect had an incalculably greater destructive capacity than the atomic bomb; a year later the Soviets tested a hydrogen bomb of their own. The threat existed that testing alone would poison the atmosphere and damage the genetic endowment of unborn generations; at stake was the biological as well as the political and cultural heritage of mankind. In 1958 the powers agreed to a truce on the testing of nuclear weapons, but in 1961 the Soviets tested a 50-megaton bomb, i.e., one with the explosive power of 50,000,000 tons of T.N.T., dwarfing the mere 20,000 tons of T.N.T. of the Hiroshima bomb. No one doubted that the United States could do the same. Thermonuclear strategists calculated the potential casualties of an atomic clash in millions of deaths, or "megadeaths," and evaluated the effects of deterrents and counterdeterrents, of "first strikes" and "second strikes," on a nation's ability to wage atomic war and survive. The balance of power was spoken of as a balance of terror; military experts referred to doctrines of "mutual superiority." In 1963 as a hopeful prospect the United States, the Soviet Union and Britain signed a treaty to ban nuclear testing in the atmosphere, to which eventually a hundred additional states subscribed. But the French, who in 1959 had become an atomic power, insisted on continuing their testing; in 1968 they developed a hydrogen bomb. In 1964 China, exploding its first atomic bomb, and three years later developing a hydrogen bomb, became a fifth atomic power. It was only a matter of time before other nations would have atomic weapons too. The United States and the Soviet Union possessed not only the ultimate weapons but the delivery systems that could make annihilation possible. So thinly suspended over mankind was the nuclear sword of Damocles that in 1963 a direct communication link or "hot line" was installed between the Kremlin and the White House to prevent the outbreak of an accidental nuclear war that might result from some human error or mechanical failure; direct communication between the tribal chieftains was necessary now that the safety of the planet was at stake.

Less dangerous to mankind was the competition in space technology that developed between the Russians and the Americans in putting artificial satellites and manned space ships into the earth's orbit and outer space preparatory to the exploration of lunar frontiers and beyond. In the late 1960s man had made the quarter-million mile journey to the moon and in 1969 two Americans set foot on the moon itself. The Americans had outdistanced the Soviets in the race to reach the moon although the Soviets had pioneered in orbital flight; the Soviets proceeded with the deployment of manned space stations and other feats.

At the end of the 1960s the world was no longer as neatly polarized into two camps, each led by one of the superpowers, as at the beginning of the Cold War. In the communist world, we have noted, the ideological and diplomatic rift that opened up after 1963 between the Soviet Union and the Chinese People's Republic set the two countries on increasingly hostile courses. Moreover, the Soviet Union faced growing restlessness among its east-European satellites and, as the invasion of Czechoslovakia in 1968 made clear, could control its empire only by military force. The major communist parties outside the Soviet Union were demonstrating their independence from Moscow. In the Western camp the United States had to take into account the independence and pride of the "new Europe." The political and economic revival of western Europe led to a rebirth of confidence and self-reliance. The Europeans insisted on more of an equal partnership with the United States if the Atlantic Alliance were to survive.

De Gaulle, president of France from 1958 to 1969, made himself the spokesman for European self-assertiveness and called for Europe to act as a counterpoise to the "dual hegemony" of the superpowers. He vetoed British entry into the Common Market because it would mean transatlantic, i.e., American, influences at work on the Continent. He ended French participation in the North Atlantic Treaty Organization military command and caused the removal of its headquarters from Paris to Belgium, viewing the Atlantic Alliance as a mere instrument for American dominance of the Continent. He adopted an independent, generally anti-American, stance in Asian affairs, in Africa, and in the Middle East. He sought to bridge the gap between western Europe and eastern Europe, to end the Cold War at French initiative, and to reunite Europe "from the Atlantic to the Urals." At the same time he set obstacles in the path of west-European integration which had so hopefully been inaugurated in the 1950s. The economic cooperation of the Common Market remained on a solid base, but he made sure that no steps toward political integration or supranational control took place. The result of his policies in the 1960s was to revive an older European nationalism.

Although de Gaulle's pronounced anti-American and anti-British views failed to persuade France's Continental partners, and even alarmed them by what at times seemed a bid for French hegemony, his assertion of independence from the United States struck a sympathetic chord among many Europeans. Many new factors disturbed them. The Americans, it was acknowledged, were committed to the defense of western Europe but since 1960 or so the Soviet Union had achieved the capability of launching direct nuclear attacks on the United States and, in the event that the United States defended western Europe, could threaten to incinerate American cities and their inhabitants. In such an emergency the Americans would undoubtedly have to consult their interests. Nor did the Europeans have a voice, they complained, in American nuclear strategies and policies; so far as they could, the French and the British developed nuclear deterrents of their own. Moreover, the United States had acted unilaterally in the Cuban missile crisis, and it fought in Asia with what was considered a reckless disregard at times for the risks involved. Supported by their booming economy and enormous military strength, with an exaggerated notion of their omnicompetence and with their excessive anticommunist zeal, they might continue to act without consulting their European partners. Then too, American interests might shift to the Pacific, to the detriment of Europe. Europeans, long accustomed to a central role in world affairs, had to adjust to a world balance of power in which the Americans and the Russians were preponderant, and

1001

they had to reckon on the possibility that under the new conditions of warfare the superpowers might agree to localize or avoid conflicts to prevent their own mutual destruction.

The independence demonstrated by the countries of western Europe was in part traceable to their continued economic successes. They had absorbed with a minimum of shock the loss of their colonial empires. The European Economic Community or Common Market (and to a lesser extent the European Free Trade Association under British leadership) was thriving, providing a mobility of men, machinery, and capital that made possible trade and productivity for a large market and benefits for businessmen and consumers. The Europeans, as they had in the past, played a central international role in the world's global economy. With 10 percent of the world's population, western Europe in 1970 accounted for one-fourth the world's productive output, surpassed in per capita output only by the North Americans. Once again, the countries of western Europe were at the center of the network of world trade, accounting for a fourth of all world exports and a third of all imports; at the end of the 1960s they held half the world's gold and had the power to influence the world's money market in many ways.

These very economic successes masked the failure of the European economy to maintain its pace in other areas. For the world itself had entered a new phase of the industrial revolution. Progress was no longer measured in coal and steel or in ships and textiles but in atomic energy, electronics, computer sciences, and space technology. Here the Europeans found themselves sharply outdistanced by the two superpowers, and especially by the United States. In addition, the economic penetration of Europe by American giant industrial firms, the glaring fact that the computer market was almost entirely in American hands, concerned them. Most Europeans hoped to meet the "American challenge" by emulating American techniques and by maintaining increased and not fewer contacts with America, but they were not optimistic about catching up.

Europe, the homeland of modern and Western civilization, and the protagonist of this long history, still faced many dilemmas in its new world setting. Its main hope lay through continued economic cooperation. Although the Common Market provided an experience in sharing sovereignty and responsibility, the move toward political integration, even after the passing of de Gaulle, remained remote. Europe would continue to be a Europe of nation-states. Yet only unity of the twenty-five European states, eastern and western, could make it possible to meet the Russian challenge, or the American challenge, absorb a reunified Germany that might come into being one day, and end old nationalist jealousies that had brought grief in the past.

The Emergent Nations

Another development, not to be overlooked, also ending the bi-polarity of the early postwar years, was the refusal of the Asian, African, and Latin American nations to align themselves with either of the superpowers. Here too a new self-assertiveness and pride affected world affairs. The Asians, Africans, and Latin Americans made their voice clearly heard in the United Nations, where they constituted a majority in the General Assembly and exercised an independent influence of their own. They were especially vocal in combating the remnants of colonialism, racism, and discrimination where these still persisted.

But all the new regimes in Asia and Africa faced desperate problems of expanding population and mass poverty at home despite their newly won political freedom. Having made promises and aroused hopes, they had to find better answers than the older authorities had offered. With less experience in government they had to deliver more. The new states learned that freedom from colonial rule did not automatically produce stability, welfare, and sound government. Some of the political leaders had come to power on a program of anticolonialism and little else, and now needed positive answers for pressing problems. The new succession states of Africa suffered from political fragmentation; many were small, with populations no larger than a good-sized American or European city. Their national boundaries were often artificially drawn and followed the lines of European conquest. They were handicapped by linguistic, religious, and regional disunity, sometimes by persistent tribalism. The more farsighted of the African leaders looked to some form of federation to create larger and more viable nations, and even one day to build a federated "Africa," but questions of leadership were delicate. Most states had the forms of constitutional government but many fell quickly into civil strife and then into dictatorships or quasi-dictatorships; power became highly concentrated and centralized; single-party governments were common, or government fell into the hands of the military. Everywhere, in Africa and in Asia, communists, Russian and Chinese, stood in the wings ready to expropriate the colonial revolution.

By the early 1960s, as we have seen, the old style empires had disappeared. The age of imperialism had its share of exploitation, brutality, and degradation that left a permanent scar, yet it was also the instrument whereby the scientific, material, intellectual, and humanitarian advances of western Europe had been spread to the rest of the world. The West no longer dominated these areas politically but Western civilization, technology, and institutions were still important everywhere. In that sense it was truer to speak of the rise of the West than of its decline. Modernization, generally speaking, meant Westernization, the spread of the industrial revolution and of democratic self-government. Industry, science, secularization, social mobility, individual freedoms had long been characteristic as actual accomplishments, or as goals, of the West; now they were reaching remote parts of the world. The impact of the new upon older values and institutions brought dislocations and tensions but the processes of change seemed inevitable and were transforming the landscape of the non-Western world. At the same time the Western world came to prize and appreciate non-Western thought, literature, music, and art forms. The merging of Western and non-Western culture in the contemporary age meant cultural interaction, not the domination of the one by the other.

With improved health and sanitation measures, and improvements in food production and distribution, all of which involved Western techniques, a decline in death rates led to vast population increases in the underdeveloped areas of the

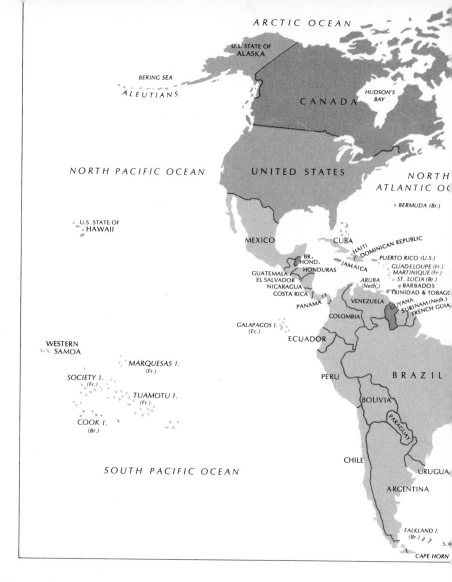

The World 1970. *On a small political map of the world in 1970 the most readily visible changes, as compared to a map of the world before the Second World War, are the breakup of the European colonial empires in Asia and Africa, the emergence of several new states in Asia and of over thirty-five independent republics in Africa, the enlargement of the Commonwealth of Nations to include such new Asian and African members as India, Pakistan, and Nigeria, the peripheral expansion of the Soviet Union to include the Baltic states, and the rise of a communist China.*

world. The populations of China, India, Indonesia, Egypt, and the Latin American countries were growing at an annual population increase of over 2 percent; China and India, which already had a huge population base to begin with, had some 10,000,000 new mouths to feed each year. The population explosion had global dimensions. At the beginning of the 1970s the world's population was 3,400,000,000; increasing at unprecedented rates, it was expected to double every thirty-three years. The mere

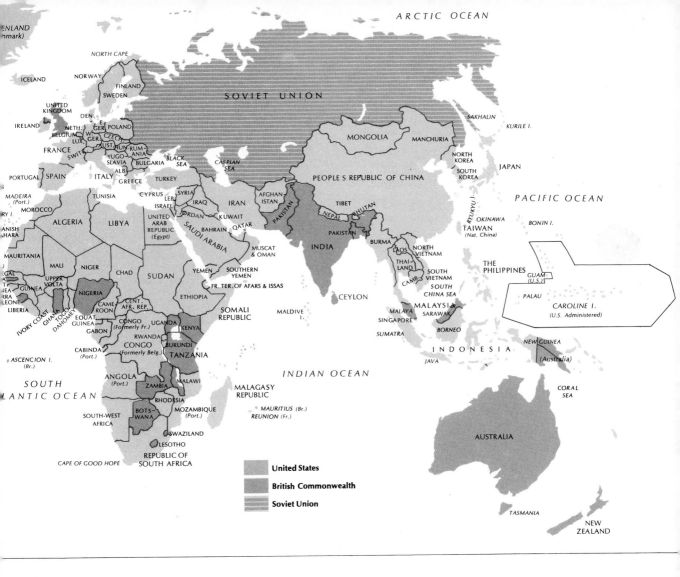

	United States
	British Commonwealth
	Soviet Union

gain in population since the opening of the twentieth century was greater than the total world population had been in 1900. By the end of the century, barring some unforeseeable developments, total world population was expected to reach 7,500,000,000, over three-fourths of whom would be non-Western peoples.

Economic development programs designed to increase industrial and agricultural output, feed burgeoning populations, and raise living standards were under way everywhere, but the question remained whether economic advances could keep pace with population growth. The dissemination and popularization of birth control techniques was a partial answer, but it required reaching into remote villages, overcoming popular resistance, and, for Latin America at least, an adjustment of attitude on the part of one of the world's major religions. Even so, it could not be expected to check the explosion but only to help in a gradual leveling off. There was the hope that one day, with growing standards of comfort and security at stake, the size of families would be deliberately controlled as had happened in western Europe, the United States, Japan, and increasingly in the Soviet Union, but that day was distant. It was distant because growing standards of comfort and security were not in sight for two-thirds of the world's peoples. Hundreds of millions still lived on inadequate and unrelieved rations of grain or rice. With more people inhabiting the globe, it was accurate to say that in the mid-twentieth century, despite all scientific achievements, more people in the world were suffering from hunger and want than ever before, and no easy solution was on the horizon. Even where economic progress was a fact, what made matters worse was that the gap which existed at the end of the Second World War between the economies of the advanced countries and those of the less developed countries was widening rather than narrowing. Even when these underdeveloped economies were growing, as they were, they were not advancing as fast as the highly productive countries, certainly not as fast as continental western Europe after 1953, the Soviet Union, or the United States.

Under the aegis of the United Nations, economic planners projected development programs for former colonial countries. The aim was to help the underdeveloped areas achieve an annual growth rate of 5 percent by the end of the 1960s and 6 percent by the end of the 1970s. Of the eighty-six states designated by the United Nations as developing countries only a third were reaching the 5 percent goal; the average was 4 percent. Given the continuing population growth and the low economic levels at which they were starting, these were modest goals. Even if, as the planners hoped, they could double per capita income in the next twenty-five or thirty years, only a limited improvement in living standards could be expected because for three-fifths of the world in 1970, annual per capita income was barely $300 (as compared with $3,680 in the United States). But here were goals to strive for and to raise hopes in parts of the world where such hopes had never before been raised. To accomplish even these objectives the advanced nations would have to give economic and technical aid of many kinds and the governments of the new countries would have to establish strict priorities between consumption and capital investment. Many old habits of life, ingrained attitudes, and traditional values would have to be modified, if not overturned. Sacrifice, patience, and forbearance would be necessary. If most of the world's population still lived on a bare subsistence level as they had for millennia, the difference was that they now looked forward to a better day and that they could count on the assistance of the more favored nations to help them. Given the revolution of rising expectations in the emergent nations, it was a vital question whether they would accept long-range solutions and resist the blandishments of authoritarian panaceas.

Despite the changed relations between the United States and the U.S.S.R., there persisted the solemn threat that war might break out at any of the numerous points of friction over the globe. Such conflicts might involve the leading powers or take some other form. With sharp divisions in the communist world, with communist China growing in power and importance, with Europe insisting on equal partnership in the Atlantic Alliance, with the Latin American republics and the new Asian and African nations becoming independent aggregates as a third world of their own, new international combinations and a new balance of power might be possible. The world might be saved from warfare or it might contend in deadlier hostilities than ever before.

The United Nations remained, despite its shortcomings, a first step toward rational world organization and peace. In the years after its founding important changes took place in its composition. As the former Axis countries, their satellites, and the wartime neutral countries entered, and as the new nations of Asia and Africa gained independence, over seventy-five states were added to the original fifty-one. The equality of all states within the General Assembly remained the rule: the tiny Arab kingdom of Kuwait, admitted in 1963 as the one hundred and eleventh member with full dignities and privileges, had a population of 350,000; Swaziland, in southern Africa, the one hundred and twenty-fifth state, admitted in 1968, had a population of 385,000. On the other hand, the communist government of China, governing since 1949 the world's most populous country, was not represented at all; the Nationalist government continued to occupy China's seat, largely at the insistence of the United States. The General Assembly grew not only in membership but in function. In 1950, because decisions of the Security Council were being repeatedly thwarted by the Soviet use of its veto power, the United States took the lead in strengthening the powers of the General Assembly so that if the Security Council were stymied by a Great-Power veto, the General Assembly could take emergency action on its own without a Great-Power veto being possible. The executive arm of the United Nations, the General Secretariat, gained in importance also through the accomplishments, initiative, and resourcefulness of its first general secretaries, the Norwegian Trygve Lie, the Swede Dag Hammarskjöld, and the Burmese U Thant, who organized United Nations emergency police forces and in other ways helped to confine or liquidate disputes and even armed conflicts in Korea, Indonesia, Kashmir, the Suez Canal, the Congo, Cyprus, the Sinai peninsula, and elsewhere.

Against all the frightening eventualities of the contemporary age one hope lay in international organization, in the actual or in an improved United Nations. Organization was important, but in the end it was only a mechanism. Just as parliaments did not work in countries where people wished each other's ruin, so international organizations did not work where nations feared each other's designs upon their very existence. The world needed smoothly functioning mechanisms, but above all it needed confidence. Confidence is a matter of mind and spirit. Of all things, once lost, it is the hardest to create.

All the problems of the contemporary age, the awesome implications of science, the challenges of industrial development, the explosive rivalries of the nations, remained aspects of the one and only superproblem, the question of man's fate. How could the human person, man, woman, or child, regardless of color or creed—the being said by some to be made in the image of God, by others to have a natural right to liberty and happiness, by still others to have the freedom to create meaning in a meaningless universe—live out his life and fulfill his humanity in a world where science, technology, and national sovereignty pressed upon him from every side?

◉ So the cataclysm carried on. But even a cataclysm, as already intimated, is not a time of downfall only. Mountains crumble, but others are thrust up. Lands vanish, but others rise from the sea. So it is with the social cataclysm of our times. Old landmarks are worn down. The British Empire and the gold standard pass away. The ascendancy of Europe, of the West, of the white races nears its close; all these must learn to negotiate with others, not to rule them. Upper- and middle-class people lose their former ease of life; but times are better for coal miners and industrial workers. Young people rebel at conformity and complacency. Everywhere there is a new crudeness, a disregard for amenities, from the conduct of diplomacy to the writing of plays and novels; but both diplomacy and literature grapple boldly with real problems. Never has war been so scientifically destructive, and it is certain that another world war would blight some centers of civilization; but it would be parochial to suppose that no civilization anywhere would survive. Individual lives are fragile. But man as such is a tough animal, and a very widespread one. To close this book on a note of placidity would indeed be foolish, but so would it be to close it on a note of universal doom. It is highly probable that if everybody in the world could vote on the question, provided only that literally everybody were included, as many or more would say that the land is rising as that it sinks.

APPENDIX I: CHRONOLOGICAL

EUROPE AS A WHOLE: POLITICAL AND SOCIAL	EUROPE AS A WHOLE: THOUGHT AND LETTERS	BRITISH ISLES
	500–300 B.C. Classical Greek civilization	
146 B.C. Greeks conquered by Rome	427–347 B.C. Plato	
31 B.C. Roman Empire	384–322 B.C. Aristotle	
306–337 Emperor Constantine	106–43 B.C. Cicero	
5th century: Germanic migrations	2nd century: Ptolemy and Galen	43–410 Roman Empire in Britain
476 Roman Empire in West ends	354–430 Saint Augustine	
7th century: spread of Islam		596 Conversion of Anglo-Saxons
800 Coronation of Charlemagne		
9th century: Norse and Magyar invasions		871–899 Alfred the Great
1054 Schism of West and East		
	1033–1109 Anselm	
1073–1085 Pope Gregory VII (Hildebrand)		1066 Norman conquest
1095 First Crusade	1079–1142 Abelard	
12th century: rise of towns	12th century: coming of Arabic and Greek science	12th century: development of the monarchy in England
1189 Third Crusade		

TABLES

TABLE ONE: TO 1517

WESTERN EUROPE	CENTRAL EUROPE	EASTERN EUROPE
		6th–4th century B.C. Greek city states
		4th–1st century B.C. Hellenistic Age
31 B.C.–476 Roman Empire	31 B.C.–476 Roman Empire in western and southern Germany	31 B.C.–1453 Roman Empire in East
		330 Constantinople founded
496 Conversion of Franks	568 Founding of Venice	
711 Moslems in Spain		
732 Moslem defeat at Tours		
768–814 Charlemagne	768–814 Charlemagne	10th century: conversion of Swedes, Poles, Hungarians to Rome; Russians to Constantinople
987–1792 Capetian monarchy in France	*962–1806 Holy Roman Empire*	
	1056–1106 Emperor Henry IV	*1001–1918 Kingdom of Hungary*
		1054 Schism of East and West
	1075–1122 Investiture struggle	
12th century: development of the monarchy in France		12th century: Teutonic Knights in Prussia

EUROPE AS A WHOLE: POLITICAL AND SOCIAL	EUROPE AS A WHOLE: THOUGHT AND LETTERS	BRITISH ISLES
1198–1216 Pope Innocent III	12th–13th century: universities, scholasticism	
13th century: rise of parliaments	1215 Fourth Lateran Council	1215 Magna Carta
1294–1303 Pope Boniface VIII	1225–1274 Thomas Aquinas	
		1295 Model Parliament
1348 Black Death		1337–1453 Hundred Years' War
1378–1417 Schism of the West	1384 John Wycliffe died	
1414–1415 Council of Constance		1381 Wat Tyler's rebellion
	1438 Printing	
1453 Roman Empire in East ends	15th century: the Renaissance at its height	1455–1485 Wars of the Roses
	1452–1519 Leonardo	
1492 Discovery of America	1466–1536 Erasmus	1485–1603 *The Tudors*
1498 Portuguese reach India	1469–1527 Machiavelli	1485–1509 Henry VII
1517 Beginnings of Reformation	1517 Luther's 95 Theses	1509–1547 Henry VIII

EUROPE AS A WHOLE: POLITICAL AND SOCIAL	EUROPE AS A WHOLE: THOUGHT AND LETTERS	BRITISH ISLES
1517 Beginnings of Reformation	1517 Luther's 95 Theses	1509–1547 Henry VIII
1519–1556 Charles V		
1519–1648 Habsburg supremacy		1521 Henry VIII's *Defense of Seven Sacraments*
1519–1522 Magellan circumnavigates globe		
1529 Turks besiege Vienna	1530 Loyola's *Spiritual Exercises*	
1531 First stock exchange at Antwerp	1534 Luther's German Bible	1534 Act of Supremacy
	1536 Calvin's *Institutes of the Christian Religion*	1536–1539 Dissolution of Monasteries
		1539 Six Articles
1540 Founding of Jesuits	1543 Copernicus' *Revolutions of Heavenly Orbs* and Vesalius' *Structure of the Human Body*	1547–1553 Edward VI
1541–1564 Calvin at Geneva		
1545–1563 Council of Trent		1553–1558 Mary
1555 Peace of Augsburg		1558–1603 Elizabeth I
1556–1598 Philip II of Spain		1559 Knox and the Reformation in Scotland
	1561–1626 Francis Bacon	1563 The 39 Articles
	1564–1642 Galileo	
	1564–1616 Shakespeare	1569 Norfolk's rebellion
1571 Defeat of Turks at Lepanto	1576 Bodin's *Republic*	
		1577 Alliance with Netherlands

WESTERN EUROPE	CENTRAL EUROPE	EASTERN EUROPE
1208 Albigensian Crusade	13th century: failure of the Empire to organize Germany and Italy	13th century: conversion of East Baltic peoples to Rome
1303–1417 Papacy at Avignon		1236 Tartars in Russia
1337–1453 Hundred Years' War	1356 Golden Bull	1389 Turks in Balkan Peninsula
1412–1431 Joan of Arc	1420–1431 Hussite Wars	
	1438–1918 Habsburg Emperors	
		1453 Turks take Constantinople; end of Byzantine Empire
1461–1489 Louis XI of France		
1479–1516 Ferdinand and Isabella of Spain		1480 Ivan the Great ends Tartar control over Russia
1494 French invasion of Italy		
1515–1547 Francis I of France	1519–1556 Charles V	

TABLE TWO: 1517-1618

WESTERN EUROPE	CENTRAL EUROPE	EASTERN EUROPE
1515–1547 Francis I of France	1519–1556 Charles V Emperor	
1516 Concordat of Bologna		1520–1566 Suleiman the Magnificent
	1521 Luther banned	
	1526 Charles V at war with Turks	1526 Turks occupy Hungary
	1529 Turks besiege Vienna	
		1533–1584 Ivan the Terrible, first Tsar of Russia
1536 Franco-Turkish alliance against Charles V		1535 First French capitulations in Turkey
1547–1559 Henry II of France	1546–1547 Schmalkaldic War	1553 English in White Sea
1556–1598 Philip II of Spain	1555 Peace of Augsburg	
	1556–1564 Ferdinand I	
1559–1589 Weakness of monarchy in France		
1562–1598 Wars of Religion in France		
1566 Netherlands revolt begins	1564–1576 Maximilian II	
1572 Massacre of St. Bartholomew		1571 Defeat of Turks at Lepanto
1574–1589 Henry III	1576–1612 Rudolf II	1574 Turks take Tunis

EUROPE AS A WHOLE: POLITICAL AND SOCIAL	EUROPE AS A WHOLE: THOUGHT AND LETTERS	BRITISH ISLES
	1580 Montaigne's *Essays* 1582 Gregorian Calendar	
1588 Spanish Armada		1588 Spanish Armada
	1596–1650 Descartes	
		1603–1714 The Stuarts 1603–1625 James I
1607 English found Virginia 1608 French found Quebec 1609 Spanish found Santa Fé 1612 Dutch found New York	1611 King James' Bible	

EUROPE AS A WHOLE: POLITICAL AND SOCIAL	EUROPE AS A WHOLE: THOUGHT AND LETTERS	BRITISH ISLES
	1561–1626 Francis Bacon 1564–1642 Galileo 1596–1650 Descartes	*1603–1714 The Stuarts* 1603–1625 James I
1618–1648 Thirty Years' War		
17th century: English, French, Dutch in America; Dutch in South Africa and Indonesia	1623–1662 Pascal 17th century: flowering of English, French, and Dutch literature 1625 Grotius' *Law of War and Peace*	1625–1649 Charles I
	1642–1727 Isaac Newton	1637 Ship money case 1640–1660 Long Parliament 1642–1648 Puritan rebellion and Civil War 1649 Execution of Charles I 1649–1658 Rule of Cromwell 1649–1653 Commonwealth 1653–1660 Protectorate
1648 Peace of Westphalia		
1650 World population estimate: 500 million	1660s Beginnings of scientific societies	1660 Restoration 1660–1685 Charles II
1661–1715 Age of Louis XIV		
		1670s Rise of Whigs and Tories 1673 Test Act
1683 Turks threaten Vienna	1687 Newton's *Principia*	1685–1688 James II
		1688 "Glorious Revolution"
1689–1697 War of League of Augsburg		1688–1702 William and Mary
	1690 Locke's *Treatises on Government; Human Understanding* 1697 Bayle's *Dictionary*	

TABLE THREE: 1618-1714

EUROPE AS A WHOLE: POLITICAL AND SOCIAL	EUROPE AS A WHOLE: THOUGHT AND LETTERS	BRITISH ISLES
1701–1714 War of Spanish Succession		1702–1714 Anne
		1707 Union of England and Scotland
1713–1714 Treaties of Utrecht and Rastadt		

EUROPE AS A WHOLE: POLITICAL AND SOCIAL	EUROPE AS A WHOLE: THOUGHT AND LETTERS	BRITISH ISLES
1713–1714 Treaties of Utrecht and Rastadt	18th century: Age of Enlightenment	*1714–1837 Hanoverians* 1714–1727 George I 1720 South Sea Bubble 1721 Walpole's ministry
1740–1763 British-French colonial wars	1740–1789 Enlightenment at its peak	1727–1760 George II 1739 War of Jenkins' Ear
1740–1748 War of Austrian Succession	1740–1760 Voltaire at his height	
1740–1789 Enlightened Despotism in Europe	1748 Montesquieu's *Spirit of Laws*	
		1745 Jacobite Rebellion
1750 World population estimate: 700 million	1751–1768 French *Encyclopedia*	
1754–1763 French and Indian War in America		
1756 Diplomatic Revolution		
1756–1763 Seven Years' War	1761 Rousseau's *Social Contract*	1760–1820 George III
1763 Treaties of Paris and Hubertusburg: British supremacy in Canada and India		1769 Watt's steam engine 1769 Arkwright's waterframe
1776 American Declaration of Independence	1776 Adam Smith's *Wealth of Nations*	1776 American Revolution
1778–1783 War of American Independence		
		1782–1806 Ministries of the Younger Pitt
1789 French Revolution begins	1784 Herder's *Philosophy of History of Mankind*	

WESTERN EUROPE	CENTRAL EUROPE	EASTERN EUROPE
		1699 Austro-Turkish Peace of Karlowitz
1700–1931 Bourbons in Spain 1700–1746 Philip V of Spain		
	1701–1918 Hohenzollern kings in Prussia 1701–1713 Frederick I of Prussia	

TABLE FOUR: 1714-1815

WESTERN EUROPE	CENTRAL EUROPE	EASTERN EUROPE
1715–1774 Louis XV of France 1715–1723 Regency in France 1720 Mississippi Bubble	1711–1740 Charles VI of Austria 1713–1740 Frederick William I of Prussia 1713–1740 Pragmatic Sanction	1682–1725 Peter the Great 1709 Battle of Poltava
		1721 Russo-Swedish Treaty of Nystadt 1733–1738 War of Polish Succession 1739 Austro-Turkish Peace of Belgrade
18th century: "Old Regime" in France	1740–1786 Frederick II of Prussia 1740–1780 Maria Theresa of Austria 1740–1745 Silesian Wars	
	1756 Habsburg-Bourbon Alliance 1756–1763 Seven Years' War	1762–1796 Catherine II of Russia 1768–1774 Russo-Turkish War
1774–1793 Louis XVI of France		1772 First Partition of Poland 1773–1774 Pugachev rebellion 1774 Russo-Turkish Treaty of Kuchuk Kainarji
	1780–1790 Joseph II of Austria 1780s Cultural revival of Germany	1787–1792 Russo-Turkish War
1789 French Revolution begins		

EUROPE AS A WHOLE: POLITICAL AND SOCIAL	EUROPE AS A WHOLE: THOUGHT AND LETTERS	BRITISH ISLES
	1790 Burke's *Reflections on the French Revolution* 1790s Spread of French revolutionary ideas Beginnings of romanticism	
1792–1815 Revolutionary and Napoleonic Wars 1792–1797 War of First Coalition		1793–1814 War with France
1798–1801 War of Second Coalition		1798 Rebellion of Ireland 1801 Union of Great Britain and Ireland 1802–1803 Peace of Amiens
1803–1805 War of Third Coalition		
1804–1814 "Grand Empire" 1806–1812 Continental System	1804–1811 Napoleonic codes	
1809–1811 Napoleon at height 1812 Invasion of Russia 1812 U.S.-British War 1813 Battle of Leipzig 1814–1815 Congress of Vienna 1815 Waterloo		1808–1813 Peninsular War in Spain 1814 Alliance of Chaumont

WORLD AS A WHOLE	EUROPE AS A WHOLE	BRITISH ISLES
		1760–1820 George III 1760–1830 Beginnings of modern industry
1806–1825 Latin American independence	1814–1815 Congress of Vienna	1815 Higher Corn Laws
	1818 Congress of Aix-la-Chapelle	1819 Peterloo
	1820 Congress of Troppau 1822 Congress of Verona	
1823 Monroe Doctrine	1830 Revolutions	
	1833 Lyell's *Principles of Geology*	1832 First Reform Bill
1841 Anglo-Chinese (Opium) War		1837–1901 Victoria 1838–1848 Chartism 1842 Mines Act 1846 Repeal of Corn Laws 1847 Ten Hours Act
1842–1858 "Treaty System" established in China	1848 Revolutions; Marx and Engels' *Communist Manifesto*	

WESTERN EUROPE	CENTRAL EUROPE	EASTERN EUROPE
1792 First French Republic established		1793 Second Partition of Poland
1793–1794 The Terror	1797 Treaty of Campo Formio	1795 Third Partition of Poland
1795–1799 Directory		1796–1801 Paul I of Russia
1799 Bonaparte's coup	1798–1814 French predominance	
1799–1804 Consulate		1801–1825 Alexander I of Russia
1804–1814 Napoleon I: The Empire		
1807 Peace of Tilsit	1806 End of Holy Roman Empire	1806–1812 Russo-Turkish War
	1806 Confederation of the Rhine	1807 Franco-Russian Alliance
		1812 Napoleon's invasion of Russia
1814 Restoration of Bourbons	1813–1814 German War of Liberation: Leipzig	
1815 Hundred Days; Waterloo		

TABLE FIVE: 1815-1871

WESTERN EUROPE	CENTRAL EUROPE	EASTERN EUROPE
		1801–1825 Alexander I of Russia
1814–1830 Restored Bourbons in France	1814–1848 Influence of Metternich	
1814–1824 Louis XVIII of France		
	1819 Carlsbad Decrees	
1824–1830 Charles X of France		1825 Decembrists in Russia
		1825–1855 Nicholas I of Russia
1830 Revolution in France and Belgium	1830 Revolutionary flurries	1828–1829 Russo-Turkish War
		1829 Independence of Greece
1830–1848 July Monarchy in France: Louis Philippe		1830 Revolution in Poland
1848 Revolution: Second French Republic	1848 Revolution: Frankfurt Assembly	
	1848–1916 Francis Joseph of Austria	

WORLD AS A WHOLE	EUROPE AS A WHOLE	BRITISH ISLES
1850 World population estimate: 1.2 billion		1850–1873 Golden age of British capitalism
1850–1864 Tai-Ping Rebellion in China		
1854–1868 Westernizing of Japan	1854–1856 Crimean War	
1857 Indian Rebellion	1859 Austro-Italian War	
	1859 Darwin's *Origin of Species*	
1860 Russians found Vladivostok		
1861–1865 American Civil War		
1863–1867 French in Mexico		
	1864–1876 First International	
	1866 Austro-Prussian War	
1867 Dominion of Canada	1867 Marx's *Capital*	1867 Extension of suffrage
1870 Vatican Council I	1870 Franco-Prussian War	1870–1874 Gladstone's first ministry
	1871–1918 German Empire	

WORLD AS A WHOLE	EUROPE AS A WHOLE	BRITISH ISLES
	1871 Darwin's *Descent of Man*	
	1878 Congress of Berlin, Austro-German Alliance	1874–1880 Disraeli's ministry
1880–1914 Height of imperialism	1880s Socialist parties founded: revisionism	
	1882 Triple Alliance	
1883–1893 French in Indochina		1884 Extension of suffrage
1885 Berlin Conference on Africa		
1885–1898 Partition of Africa		
	1889 Second International	
1895–1898 Far Eastern crisis	1894 Franco-Russian Alliance	
1898 Fashoda crisis; Spanish-American War		
1899–1902 Boer War		1899–1902 Boer War
1900 World population estimate: 1.6 billion	1900 Freud's *Interpretation of Dreams*	
1902 Anglo-Japanese Alliance		
1904 Russo-Japanese War	1904 Anglo-French Entente	
	1905 Einstein's relativity theory	
	1905 Morocco crisis	
		1906–1911 Social insurance and parliamentary reform
1907 Anglo-Russian division of Persia	1907 Triple Entente	
	1908 Bosnian crisis	
1911 Chinese Revolution	1911 Agadir crisis	
	1912–1913 Balkan crisis	
1914–1918 First World War	1914–1918 First World War	1914 Ulster Crisis

WESTERN EUROPE	CENTRAL EUROPE	EASTERN EUROPE
1852 Napoleon III: Second French Empire	1852–1890 Bismarck active	1853 Russo-Turkish War 1854–1856 Crimean War 1855–1881 Alexander II of Russia 1858 Formation of Rumania
	1859–1870 Unification of Italy	
1860 Free trade with England 1860–1870 Liberal Empire		1861 Emancipation of Russian serfs
1870–1940 Third Republic in France	1866–1871 Unification of Germany 1867 Dual Monarchy in Austria-Hungary	1870s Populism and Nihilism in Russia

TABLE SIX: 1871-1919

WESTERN EUROPE	CENTRAL EUROPE	EASTERN EUROPE
1870–1940 Third Republic in France 1871 Paris Commune	1871–1918 German Empire 1871–1883 *Kulturkampf* 1878–1890 Bismarck's Anti-Socialist laws 1883–1889 Bismarck's social insurance laws 1888–1918 William II of Germany	1877 Russo-Turkish War 1878 Autonomy of Bulgaria; independence of Serbia 1881 Assassination of Alexander II
1889 Boulanger in France 1894–1906 Dreyfus affair in France		
	1898–1914 German naval race with England	
1901–1905 Laic laws separate church and state in France 1900ff. Growth of democracy: universal suffrage in Netherlands 1896, etc.	1900ff. Growth of democracy: universal suffrage in Austria 1907, etc.	1903 Bolshevik-Menshevik split 1904 Russo-Japanese War 1905 Revolution in Russia
		1908 Bosnian crisis 1908 Young Turk Revolution
1914 Battle of Marne	1914 Assassination of Francis Ferdinand	1912–1913 Balkan Wars 1914 Battle of Tannenberg

WORLD AS A WHOLE	EUROPE AS A WHOLE	BRITISH ISLES
1917 United States enters War 1917 Russian Revolution 1919 Peace of Paris	1919 Peace of Paris	1916 Battle of Jutland 1916–1922 Irish troubles 1918 Universal suffrage

WORLD AS A WHOLE	EUROPE AS A WHOLE	BRITISH ISLES
1919 Peace of Paris	1919 Peace of Paris 1919 Spread of democracy	1918 Universal suffrage
1922–1929 "Prosperity Decade" 1923 Turkish Republic	1922–1943 Fascism in Italy 1923 Ruhr crisis 1925 Locarno Pacts	1922 Irish Free State 1924 First Labour coalition government 1926 General Strike 1926 Definition of Dominion status 1929–1931 Second Labour Government
1929 Great Depression begins 1930 World population estimate: 2 billion 1931–1932 Manchurian crisis 1931–1945 Japanese in China	1930s Depression 1930s Decline of democracy; rise of dictators	1931–1940 National Government 1931 Britain leaves gold standard 1932 Britain adopts Empire tariff protection
1933–1945 F. D. Roosevelt's presidency 1933 Failure of World Economic Conference 1935–1936 Ethiopian crisis 1936–1939 Spanish Civil War	1933–1945 Hitler in Germany 1933 Germany leaves League of Nations and rearms 1936–1939 Popular fronts 1937 Rome-Berlin-Tokyo Axis	1936 Edward VIII abdicates; George VI
1938 Munich crisis 1939–1945 Second World War 1940–1945 Japan aims at "Greater East Asia" 1941 U.S.S.R., U.S.A. enter war	1939 Nazi-Soviet Pact 1940–1944 German domination of Europe	1939–1945 Britain at war 1940 Churchill replaces Chamberlain 1940 Battle of Britain
1944 Allies invade Europe 1945 Yalta and Potsdam conferences 1945 First atomic bomb 1945 United Nations	1945 Death of Hitler and Mussolini	1945 Labour election victory

WESTERN EUROPE	CENTRAL EUROPE	EASTERN EUROPE
1916 Verdun and the Somme		1917 Fall of Tsardom; Bolshevik Revolution
1918 Armistice	1918 Fall of German and Austro-Hungarian Empires	

TABLE SEVEN: 1919-1945

WESTERN EUROPE	CENTRAL EUROPE	EASTERN EUROPE
1919 Paris Peace Conference	1919 Treaty of Versailles, etc.	1918–1920 Russian Civil War
		1919–1923 Greek-Turkish War
	1919–1933 Weimar Republic	
		1920–1943 Third International
		1920–1921 Russo-Polish War
		1921–1928 Nep in Russia
	1922–1943 Mussolini in power in Italy	1922 Founding of U.S.S.R.
	1923 French occupy Ruhr	1922 Russo-German treaty of Rapallo
	1923 Inflation in Germany	
	1924 Dawes Plan	1924 Death of Lenin; emergence of Stalin
		1927 Expulsion of Trotsky
		1928–1933 First Five-Year Plan
1930s Depression	1930s Depression	
1931 Spanish revolution		
1934 Stavisky riots in Paris	1933–1945 Hitler in power	
1936–1939 Spanish Civil War	1934 First Austrian crisis	
1936–1937 Popular Front in France	1936 Germany re-militarizes Rhineland	
	1938 Germany annexes Austria	1934 U.S.S.R. joins League of Nations
	1938–1939 Germany annexes Czechoslovakia	1936–1937 New Soviet constitution; purge trials
		1939–1941 Nazi-Soviet Pact
1940 Fall of France		1939–1940 Russo-Finnish War; Soviets expand in Baltic
1940–1944 German occupation of Western Europe	1941–1944 Allies bomb Germany	1941 Germans invade Russia
		1942 Battle of Stalingrad
	1943 Allies invade Italy; fall of Mussolini	1943–1945 Russian offensives
1944–1945 Allies liberate Western Europe	1944–1945 Allied and Russian offensives	

WORLD AS A WHOLE	ASIA	AFRICA
1945 United Nations established: 51 members	1945 Arab League formed: 7 states	1945 Colonial empires continue; only four independent African states
1945–1947 Peacemaking breaks down: Cold War begins		
1945–1953 U.S.: Truman presidency; Marshall Plan, Truman Doctrine		
1947 British leave India	1946–1954 French war in Indochina	
	1947 India and Pakistan independent	
	1948 Assassination of Gandhi	
	1948 Burma an independent republic	
	1948 Israel established	
	1948–1949 Arab-Israeli war	
1949 Communist triumph in China	1949 Chinese People's Republic established	
1949 North Atlantic Treaty Organization	1949 Dutch leave Indonesia	
1950 World population estimate: 2.5 billion	1950 India a republic	
1950–1953 Korean War	1950–1953 Korean War	
	1950s Japan: regains sovereignty; economic expansion	
1951 Japanese peace treaty		1951 Libya independent
		1952 Egypt a republic; monarchy ousted
1953–1961 U.S.: Eisenhower presidency		
1954 U.S. hydrogen bomb tested	1954 French leave Indochina; Vietnam partitioned	1954–1962 French war in Algeria
		1954 British surrender Suez Canal treaty rights
	1955 Bandung Afro-Asian conference	
1956 Suez Canal crisis	1956 Islamic Republic of Pakistan	1956 Suez crisis: Britain, France, Israel vs. Egypt
		1956 Morocco, Tunisia independent
1957 U.S.S.R. launches space satellites		1957 Ghana: first British African colony to gain independence
		1957–1962 About 25 states gain independence: Ghana, Nigeria, Congo, Algeria, etc.
1958–1963 Pope John XXIII: reforms in Catholic Church	1958–1961 Syria part of United Arab Republic	1958 French colonies vote independence; French Community formed
		1958 Egypt becomes United Arab Republic
1959 Cuban revolution: Castro in power		

TABLE EIGHT: 1945-1959

WESTERN EUROPE	CENTRAL EUROPE	EASTERN EUROPE
1945–1946 De facto split of Europe: east and west	1945 Allied occupation of Germany	1945–1948 Communist satellites established
1945–1951 Britain: Labour government		
1946–1958 Fourth French Republic	1946 Italian Republic	
	1946 Nuremberg trials	
	1946–1953 Italy: De Gasperi premier	
1947 Marshall Plan	1947 Peace treaties with Italy, Hungary, etc.	1947–1956 Cominform
	1948–1949 Berlin blockade and airlift	1948 Communist takeover in Czechoslovakia
	1948 Italian elections: Communist setback	1948–1955 Yugoslavia splits with U.S.S.R.
1949 Council of Europe	1949 German Federal Republic (West Germany); German Democratic Republic (East Germany)	1949 Council of Mutual Economic Assistance
1949 North Atlantic Treaty Organization	1949–1963 West Germany: Adenauer chancellor; economic expansion	1949 Russian atomic explosion
1951 European Coal and Steel Community		1951–1955 Fifth Five Year Plan
1951–1964 British Conservatives in office		
1952 Britain: Elizabeth II succeeds George VI	1952 Allied occupation of West Germany ends	
1953 West European economic recovery begins	1953 East Berlin uprising	1953 Death of Stalin
		1953 Russian hydrogen bomb
1954 Western European Union; West German rearmament		1953–1955 Malenkov premier; emergence of Khrushchev
1954 French defeat in Indochina; war in Algeria begins	1955 Austrian peace treaty	1955 Warsaw Pact
	1955 West Germany sovereign	
		1956 20th party congress: Khrushchev denounces Stalin regime
		1956 Polish, Hungarian risings crushed
		1956 U.S.S.R.–Japan peace treaty
1957 Rome treaties: Common Market; European Atomic Energy Community		1957 U.S.S.R. launches Sputnik I and II
1957 Britain tests hydrogen bomb		
1957–1962 End of British, Belgian, French colonial empires in Africa		
1958 Fifth French Republic; De Gaulle president		1958–1964 Khrushchev in power
1959 British back European Free Trade Association		

WORLD AS A WHOLE	ASIA	AFRICA
1960 World population estimate: 3 billion		1960–1962 Congo civil war
1960–1962 Congo civil war	1960s North-South Vietnam war continues	
1961 U.S.S.R. and U.S. space flights begin; Soviets launch first man in space		1961 South Africa a republic: white minority government
1962 U.S.-Russian crisis over Cuba	1962 Arab League: Algeria becomes 13th member	1962 Algeria independent
1962 Chinese-Soviet rift	1962 Chinese-Soviet rift	
1962–U.S.: civil rights and race crises	1962 China-India border war	
1962–1965 Vatican Council II: reforms in Catholic Church		
1963–Pope Paul VI		1963 Organization of African Unity: 31 states
1963 Partial nuclear test ban agreement		
1963 President John F. Kennedy assassinated		
1963–1969 Lyndon B. Johnson presidency		
1964 Cyprus crisis	1964 Death of Nehru	
1964–Vietnam war: U.S. involvement deepens	1964 Vietnam war: U.S. commits large scale air and ground forces	
	1964 China tests atomic bomb	
1965 United Nations: 110 members	1965–1966 Indonesia crushes communists; Sukarno ousted	1965 Rhodesia: white minority government proclaims independence
		1966 Nkrumah overthrown in Ghana
1967–1968 China and France join U.S., U.S.S.R., and Britain as thermonuclear powers	1967 Israel defeats Arab states in six-day war	1967–1969 Nigeria suppresses Biafra secession
	1967 China explodes hydrogen bomb	
	1968 Arab-Israeli clashes continue	
1968–Student riots: U.S., France, Japan, etc.		
1968 Vietnam peace talks in Paris; war continues	1968 Chinese "cultural revolution": disorders and unrest	
1968 Treaty to prevent spread of nuclear weapons: 61 nations sign		
1969 U.S.: Richard M. Nixon presidency	1969 Death of Ho Chi Minh	
1969 Man lands on moon: 3 Americans in lunar flight	1969 20th anniversary of Chinese People's Republic	
	1969 Chinese-Soviet border clashes in Manchuria	
1970 United Nations: 126 members		1970 43 independent African states
1970 World population estimate: 3.5 billion		
1970 Vietnam war continues		

WESTERN EUROPE	CENTRAL EUROPE	EASTERN EUROPE
1960 Belgium withdraws from Congo 1960 France a nuclear power		1960s Liberalization in Soviet satellites 1961 U.S.S.R. launches first man in space
	1961 Berlin Wall	
1962 French leave Algeria		1962–1963 Chinese Communists split with U.S.S.R.
1963 Common Market: French veto British entry	1963 Erhard succeeds Adenauer	
1964–1970 Britain: Labour in office		1964 Khrushchev ousted; replaced by Brezhnev, Kosygin
1965 De Gaulle reelected president		
		1967 Military dictatorship in Greece 1967 50th anniversary of Russian Revolution
1968 France: massive student and labor demonstrations 1968 France tests hydrogen bomb		1968 Soviets invade Czechoslovakia; end liberal Czech regime
1969 De Gaulle resigns; succeeded by Pompidou 1969–Northern Ireland: Catholic-Protestant clashes	1969 Willy Brandt heads Socialist coalition government	1969 World communist parties meet in Moscow
1970 Britain: Conservatives win election		

APPENDIX II: RULERS & REGIMES

HOLY ROMAN EMPIRE

Habsburg Line

MAXIMILIAN I	1493–1519
CHARLES V	1519–1556
FERDINAND I	1556–1564
MAXIMILIAN II	1564–1576
RUDOLPH II	1576–1612
MATTHIAS	1612–1619
FERDINAND II	1619–1637
FERDINAND III	1637–1657
LEOPOLD I	1658–1705
JOSEPH I	1705–1711
CHARLES VI	1711–1740

Charles VI was succeeded by a daughter, Maria Theresa, who as a woman could not be elected Holy Roman Emperor. French influence in 1742 secured the election of

Bavarian Line

CHARLES VII	1742–1745

On Charles VII's death the Habsburg control of the Emperorship was resumed.

Lorraine Line

FRANCIS I	1745–1765

(husband of Maria Theresa)

Habsburg-Lorraine Line

JOSEPH II	1765–1790

(son of Francis I and Maria Theresa)

LEOPOLD II	1790–1792
FRANCIS II	1792–1806

The Holy Roman Empire became extinct in 1806.

AUSTRIAN DOMINIONS

The rulers of Austria from 1438 to 1740, and at least titular kings of Hungary from 1526 to 1740, were the same as the Holy Roman Emperors.
After 1740:

Habsburg Line (through female heir)

MARIA THERESA	1740–1780
JOSEPH II	1780–1790

In Principal European Countries since 1500

Leopold II   1790–1792
Francis II   1792–1835

In 1804 Francis II took the title of Emperor, as Francis I of the Austrian Empire. Austria was declared an "empire" because Napoleon proclaimed France an empire in that year, and because the demise of the Holy Roman Empire could be foreseen.

Ferdinand I   1835–1848
Francis Joseph   1848–1916
Charles I   1916–1918

The Austrian Empire became extinct in 1918.

✠ ✠ ✠

BRITISH ISLES

Tudor Line

Kings of England and Ireland

Henry VII   1485–1509

Henry VIII   1509–1547
Edward VI   1547–1553
Mary I   1553–1558
Elizabeth I   1558–1603

In 1603 James VI of Scotland, a great-great-grandson of Henry VII, succeeded to the English throne.

Stuart Line

Kings of England and Ireland, and of Scotland

James I   1603–1625
Charles I   1625–1649

Republican Interregnum

The Commonwealth   1649–1653

The Protectorate
Oliver Cromwell   1653–1658
Lord Protector
Richard Cromwell   1658–1660

Restored Stuart Line

Charles II   1660–1685
James II   1685–1688

In 1688 James II was forced out of the country, but Parliament kept the crown in a female branch of the Stuart family, calling in Mary, the daughter of James II, and her husband William III of the Netherlands.

WILLIAM III 1689–1702,
AND MARY II 1689–1694
ANNE 1702–1714

In 1707, through the Union of England and Scotland, the royal title became King (or Queen) of Great Britain and Ireland. The Stuart family having no direct Protestant heirs, the throne passed in 1714 to the German George I, Elector of Hanover, a great-grandson of James I.

Hanoverian Line

Kings of Great Britain and Ireland

GEORGE I 1714–1727
GEORGE II 1727–1760
GEORGE III 1760–1820
GEORGE IV 1820–1830
WILLIAM IV 1830–1837

William IV having no heirs, the British throne passed in 1837 to Victoria, a granddaughter of George III. In Hanover no woman could rule, and an uncle of Victoria inherited. Though the British family has continued in direct descent from George I, it has dropped the title of Hanoverian and is now known as the House of Windsor. From 1877 to 1947 the British rulers bore the additional title of Emperor of India.

VICTORIA 1837–1901
EDWARD VII 1901–1910
GEORGE V 1910–1936
EDWARD VIII 1936
GEORGE VI 1936–1952
ELIZABETH II 1952–

✠ ✠ ✠

FRANCE

Valois Line

LOUIS XI 1461–1483
CHARLES VIII 1483–1498
LOUIS XII 1498–1515
FRANCIS I 1515–1547
HENRY II 1547–1559
FRANCIS II 1559–1560
CHARLES IX 1560–1574
HENRY III 1574–1589

In 1589 the Valois line became extinct, and the throne passed to Henry of Bourbon, a remote descendant of French kings of the fourteenth century.

Bourbon Line

HENRY IV 1589–1610
LOUIS XIII 1610–1643
LOUIS XIV 1643–1715
LOUIS XV 1715–1774
LOUIS XVI 1774–1792

The Republic

Convention 1792–1795
Directory 1795–1799
Consulate 1799–1804

The Empire

NAPOLEON I 1804–1814
Emperor of the French
and King of Italy

Restored Bourbon Line

LOUIS XVIII 1814–1824

(Royalists count a Louis XVII, 1793–1795, and date the reign of Louis XVIII from 1795.)

CHARLES X 1824–1830

The Revolution of 1830 gave the throne to the Duke of Orleans, descendant of Louis XIII.

Orleans Line

LOUIS-PHILIPPE 1830–1848

The Second Republic

1848–1852

The Second Empire

NAPOLEON III 1852–1870
Emperor of the French

The Third Republic

1870–1940

Vichy Regime

1940–1944

Provisional Government

1944–1946

The Fourth Republic

1946–1958

The Fifth Republic

1958–

✠ ✠ ✠

PRUSSIA (AND GERMAN EMPIRE)

A continuous Hohenzollern line ruled until 1918.

Electors of Brandenburg and Dukes of Prussia

GEORGE WILLIAM   1619–1640
FREDERICK WILLIAM   1640–1688
the "Great Elector"
FREDERICK III   1688–1713

In 1701 Frederick III was permitted by the Holy Roman Emperor to entitle himself King in Prussia, as Frederick I.

Kings of Prussia

FREDERICK I   1701–1713
FREDERICK WILLIAM I   1713–1740
FREDERICK II, the "Great"   1740–1786
FREDERICK WILLIAM II   1786–1797
FREDERICK WILLIAM III   1797–1840
FREDERICK WILLIAM IV   1840–1861
WILLIAM I   1861–1888

In 1871 William I took the title of German Emperor.

German Emperors

WILLIAM I   1871–1888
FREDERICK III   1888
WILLIAM II   1888–1918

The German Empire became extinct in 1918. It was succeeded by the

Weimar Republic

1919–1933

(an unofficial title for what was still called the Deutsches Reich, a phrase not easy to translate accurately)

The Third Reich

1933–1945

(an unofficial title for the Deutsches Reich under Adolf Hitler)
Allied Military Government in 1945 eventuated in

German Federal Republic (West Germany)

1949–

German Democratic Republic (East Germany)

1949–

SARDINIA (AND KINGDOM OF ITALY)

In 1720 Victor Amadeus II, Duke of Savoy, took the title of King of Sardinia, having acquired the island of that name.

Kings of Sardinia

VICTOR AMADEUS II   1720–1730
CHARLES EMMANUEL III   1730–1773
VICTOR AMADEUS III   1773–1796
CHARLES EMMANUEL IV   1796–1802
VICTOR EMMANUEL I   1802–1821
CHARLES FELIX   1821–1831
CHARLES ALBERT   1831–1849
VICTOR EMMANUEL II   1849–1878

In 1861 Victor Emmanuel II took the title of King of Italy.

Kings of Italy

VICTOR EMMANUEL II   1861–1878
HUMBERT I   1878–1900
VICTOR EMMANUEL III   1900–1946
HUMBERT II   1946

In 1936 Victor Emmanuel III took the title of Emperor of Ethiopia, which became meaningless with British occupation of Ethiopia in 1941. In 1946 the Kingdom of Italy became extinct and was succeeded by the

Italian Republic

1946–

SPAIN

Isabella died in 1504, but Ferdinand lived until 1516, whereupon the Spanish thrones were inherited by their grandson Charles, who became Charles V of the Holy Roman Empire, but was known in Spain as Charles I.

Habsburg Line

With Charles II the Spanish Habsburg line became extinct, and the throne passed to the French Bourbon grandson of Louis XIV of France and great-grandson of Philip IV of Spain.

Bourbon Line

Bonaparte Line

(brother of Napoleon)

Restored Bourbon Line

In 1868 Isabella abdicated; after a regency, and a brief reign by Amadeus I (Savoy), 1871–1873, there was a short-lived Republic, 1873–1874, succeeded by

In 1931 a republican revolution unseated Alfonso XIII.

Spanish Republic

1931–1936

Spanish Civil War

1936–1939

Regime of Francisco Franco

1939–

RUSSIAN EMPIRE

Grand Dukes of Moscow

In 1547 Ivan IV took the title of Tsar of Russia.

Tsars of Russia

Time of Troubles

1604–1613

Romanov Line

In 1917 the tsardom became extinct.

Provisional Government

1917

Communist Revolution

1917

Union of Soviet Socialist Republics

1922–

BIBLIOGRAPHY

The following reading lists are intended for the convenience of general readers, students, and classroom teachers. Professional students of history may find them useful too, but no attempt has been made to provide comprehensive coverage of any areas or topics. The aim throughout has been to call attention to the leading and most reliable works, to which the reader may also turn for additional specialized bibliographies and for information on source materials. Classification follows the plan of chapters in the present book. Few titles are intentionally repeated; to find books on some topics it will often be necessary to look in several places. For reasons of space works in foreign languages have been excluded. Excluded also (with a few exceptions) are general textbooks, articles in periodicals, and primary source materials. Many biographies and memoirs are listed, but no effort has been made to provide inclusive lists.

Many of the titles listed below are available or are becoming available in paperback; up-to-date lists of such paperbacks may be found in the *Paperback book guide for colleges* published and distributed by the R. R. Bowker Company. An asterisk indicates availability in a paperback edition.

1034

There are literally hundreds of thousands of books on historical subjects, and it is difficult to find the titles and authors of those one wants on a particular topic. An important bibliographical tool is the American Historical Association's *Guide to historical literature* (1961), the successor to a similar volume published thirty years earlier. It makes no effort at exhaustive coverage and is already out of date, but it contains some 20,000 items, mostly annotated, in all fields and periods of history. It also lists the most useful reference sources for the study of history, specialized bibliographies [some of which are cited in the appropriate chapters below], and professional periodicals. More limited in scope is J. Roach (ed.), *A bibliography of modern history* (1968). Of professional periodicals, the *American Historical Review* and the *Journal of Modern History* are valuable sources for lists and reviews of current historical literature; the annual *International Bibliography of Historical Sciences* also provides comprehensive lists. Some of the most discerning appraisals of new history books are to be found in the unsigned reviews in the *Times Literary Supplement* (London).

In a special category of bibliographical assistance for teachers and students are the series of pamphlets that have been appearing under the auspices of the American Historical Association's Service Center for Teachers of History (1957 ff.). These are bibliographical essays presenting a summary of recent research and interpretations prepared by authorities on a variety of subjects; over seventy have appeared to date, and many have appeared in revised editions. A number of these essays are cited in the appropriate sections below.

W. L. Langer, *An encyclopedia of world history: ancient, medieval, and modern, chronologically arranged*

(4th ed., 1968), is a vast table of dates and important events. A similar service is performed by S. H. Steinberg, *Historical tables, 58 B.C.–A.D. 1965* (1966). Two convenient one-volume reference tools are *Webster's biographical dictionary* (1948, 1962) and the *Columbia encyclopedia* (3rd ed., 1963).

For historical atlases the following are recommended: W. R. Shepherd, *Historical atlas* (rev., 1956); *Muir's historical atlas—medieval and modern* (rev., 1952); E. W. Fox, *Atlas of European history* (1957); and R. R. Palmer and others, *Atlas of world history* (1957). Convenient and economical atlases for student use are J. B. Breasted and others, *European history atlas** (10th ed., 1954); *Hammond's historical atlas** (1953); and R. R. Palmer and others, *Abridged historical atlas** (1958). Geographical information may readily be located through *Webster's geographical dictionary* (1955) and the *Columbia Lippincott gazetteer of the world* (1955).

Among the most useful are the *Encyclopaedia Britannica* [for many historical purposes the eleventh edition (1910–1911) is still to be recommended], the *Encyclopedia Americana, Collier's Encyclopedia,* and the *New International Encyclopedia.* Each publishes an annual Yearbook as well. The *Encyclopedia of the social sciences* (1930–1935) has been completely revised (with biographical coverage sharply reduced) and is now available as D. L. Sills (ed.), *International encyclopedia of the social sciences* (17 vols., 1968). The *Dictionary of national biography* (1885–1949) is informative on notable Britons; a shorter version is the *Concise dictionary of national biography* (2 vols., 1961).

The number of anthologies for classroom use has been multiplying rapidly. New titles are amply publicized through publishers' releases and advertisements, and the following titles are intended to give only a sampling of those available [all except the first are available in paperback]: Columbia University, *Introduction to contemporary civilization in the West* (2 vols., rev., 1960), a collection of fairly lengthy source selections; J. H. Hexter and others, *The traditions of the Western world* (1967); R. P. Stearns, *Pageant of Europe: sources and selections from the Renaissance to the present day* (rev., 1961); F. L. Baumer, *Main currents of Western thought: readings in Western European intellectual history from the Middle Ages to the present* (rev., 1964); E. Weber, *The Western tradition from the ancient world to the atomic age* (1959); L. S. Stavrianos, *The epic of modern man: a collection of readings* (1966), globally oriented; and G. L. Mosse and others, *Europe in review* (rev., 1964).

Multivolumed anthologies or series include T. H. Greer (gen. ed.), Classics of Western Thought (3 vols., 1968); N. F. Cantor (gen. ed.), Ideas and Institutions in Western Civilization (5 vols., rev., 1968); H. H. Rowen (gen. ed.), Sources in Western Civilization (10 vols., 1964); W. H. McNeill and J. W. Sedlar (eds.), Readings in World History (1968 ff.); and E. C. Black and L. W. Levy, Documentary History of Western Civilization (50 projected vols., 1965 ff.). H. V. White is general editor of Major Traditions of World Civilization (1965 ff.), and J. H. Hexter of The Traditions of the Western World (1966 ff.).

Among anthologies or series that focus on source problems or on conflicting interpretations of historical issues there are S. B. Clough, P. Gay, C. K. Warner, and J. M. Cammett, *The European past: reappraisals in history* (2 vols., rev., 1970); B. D. Gooch (ed.), *Interpreting European history* (2 vols., 1967); T. C. Mendenhall and others, *Select problems in historical interpretation* (2 vols., 1948, and in briefer form, under different titles, 1952); O. Ranum, *Searching for modern times* (2 vols., 1969); L. F. Schaefer and others, *Problems in Western civilization: the challenge of history* (2 vols., 1968); K. M. Setton, H. R. Winkler, and others, *Great problems in European civilization* (1954); L. W. Spitz and R. W. Lyman (gen. eds.), *Major crises in Western civilization* (2 vols., 1965); R. E. Sullivan (gen. ed.), *Critical issues in history* (2 vols., 1967); and B. Tierney, D. Kagan, and L. P. Williams (eds.), *Random House Great issues in Western civilization* (2 vols., 1967), available also in twenty-four separate pamphlets (1968). The Great

Lives Observed series (1968 ff.) consists of sources, contemporary judgments, and latter-day interpretations relating to leading historical personalities. N. F. Cantor and M. S. Werthman are general editors of a series in six volumes, The Structure of European History: Studies and Interpretations (1967), and J. F. Naylor and R. Bienvenu of Problems in European History: A Documentary Collection (1968 ff.). The Wiley Major Issues in History series is projected in fifteen volumes.

A series maintaining a high level of quality is the Heath Problems in European Civilization (1958 ff.), edited by R. W. Greenlaw and D. E. Lee; over forty titles have appeared to date; the volumes often contain useful biographical essays and sometimes offer materials not otherwise available in English. A similar series is being published as European Problem Studies, edited by H. B. Hill (Holt, Rinehart and Winston, 1963 ff.).

Anthologies of more specialized coverage include N. F. Cantor and M. S. Werthman (eds.), *The history of popular culture* (2 vols., 1968); and by the same editors, *The English tradition: modern studies in English history* (2 vols., 1967); H. Ausubel and R. L. Schuyler, *The making of English history* (1952); J. Friguglietti and E. Kennedy, *The shaping of modern France: writings on French history since 1715* (1969); and M. Kranzberg and C. W. Pursell, Jr. (eds.), *Technology in Western civilization* (2 vols., 1967).

Brief volumes on selected topics, especially suitable for undergraduate reading, are to be found in the following series: the Berkshire Studies in European History (Holt, Rinehart and Winston, 1927 ff., revisions in progress); the Cornell University Narrative Essays in the History of Our Tradition (1950 ff.); Teach Yourself History (Macmillan, 1948 ff.), a British series, edited by A. L. Rowse, successfully using a biographical approach to lure the general reader to historical topics; the Rand McNally European History series (1968 ff.); and Europe Since 1500: a paperbound series (Crowell, 1967 ff.). The Anvil series (Van Nostrand, 1955 ff.), edited by L. L. Snyder, consists of introductory essays on given topics by a professional authority and selected readings; over ninety-five booklets covering a wide variety of subjects have appeared to date. Three highly recommended series, written and edited by British authorities but published also in this country, with each volume covering a segment of European history, are: G. Barraclough (gen. ed.), History of European Civilization Library (Harcourt, Brace and World, 1965 ff.); D. Hay (gen. ed.), A General History of Europe (Holt, Rinehart and Winston, 1966 ff.); and J. H. Plumb (gen. ed.), History of Europe (Harper and Row, 1967 ff.). They are referred to below as the "Barraclough series," "Hay series," and "Plumb series," respectively. F. Gilbert is general editor of the Norton History of Modern Europe (6 paperbound vols., W. W. Norton, 1969–1970). B. Mazlish (gen. ed.), Main Themes in European History (Macmillan, 1964 ff.), brings together reprints of articles by leading authorities on selected important "themes" of European history since 1500; booklets have appeared so far on religion, technology, labor, the modern state, science, agriculture, population, and imperialism. The New Dimensions in History series (Wiley, 1966 ff.) focuses on selected cities in various historical eras.

Among manuals on methods of research and on the writing of history, a spirited introduction is J. Barzun and H. F. Graff, *The modern researcher** (1957, rev., 1970). Other introductions include A. Nevins, *The gateway to history** (rev., 1962); S. Kent, *Writing history** (1941, rev., 1967); L. Gottschalk, *Understanding history** (1950, rev., 1969); and the older but still useful C. V. Langlois and C. Seignobos, *Introduction to the study of history* (1904). There is practical information in W. Gray and others, *Historian's handbook** (1959); N. F. Cantor and R. I. Schneider, *How to study history** (1967); and in K. L. Turabian, *A manual for writers of term papers, theses, and dissertations** (1955 ed.), an adaptation of a standard guide, The University of Chicago,

Bibliography   *A manual of style* (12th ed., 1969). Examples of books affording insight into the study and writing of history are C. Gustavson, *A preface to history** (1955); M. Bloch, *The historian's craft** (1953); A. L. Rowse, *The use of history** (Teach Yourself History series, 1946); G. R. Elton, *The practice of history* (1967); and H. S. Hughes, *History as art and science: twin vistas on the past** (1967). A fascinating anthology on historians at work is R. W. Winks (ed.), *The historian as detective* (1969).

The great historians of the past and the evolution of history are discussed in the encyclopedic M. A. Fitzsimons, A. G. Pundt, and C. E. Nowell (eds.), *The development of historiography* (1954), and in H. Butterfield, *Man on his past: the study of the history of historical scholarship* (1955). Three older basic studies are H. E. Barnes, *A history of historical writing* (1938); J. T. Shotwell, *The history of history* (1939); and J. W. Thompson and B. J. Holm, *A history of historical writing* (2 vols., 1942). A good introductory anthology is F. Stern (ed.), *The varieties of history: from Voltaire to the present** (1956). Special studies of the historical craft and its practitioners include G. P. Gooch, *History and historians in the nineteenth century* (1913); E. E. Neff, *The poetry of history* (1947); B. E. Schmitt (ed.), *Some historians of modern Europe* (1942); S. W. Halperin (ed.), *Some twentieth-century historians: essays on eminent historians* (1961); J. R. Hale (ed.), *The evolution of British historiography: from Bacon to Namier* (1967); and an intriguing journalistic account of some contemporary British historians, V. Mehta, *The fly and the fly bottle* (1962).

Theories of History   The historical manuals listed above all provide some introduction to the philosophy and theory of history, and generally have useful bibliographies. A convenient introduction is the anthology edited by H. Meyerhoff, *The philosophy of history in our time** (1959); also useful is P. Gardiner (ed.), *Theories of History* (1959). There are valuable contributions and extensive bibliographies on the role and nature of historical studies in the Social Science Research Council's Bulletin 54, *Theory and practice in historical study* (1946), and Bulletin 64, *Social sciences in historical study* (1954), and in L. Gottschalk (ed.), *Generalization in the writing of history: a report of the committee on historical analysis of the Social Science Research Council* (1963). Of the many other volumes on the subject, mostly for the advanced student, there may be mentioned: M. Mandelbaum, *The problem of historical knowledge* (1938); R. Aron, *Introduction to the philosophy of history* (1948, trans. 1961); R. G. Collingwood, *The idea of history** (1946); E. H. Carr, *What is history?** (1962); F. E. Manuel, *Shapes of philosophical history* (1964); B. Mazlish, *The riddle of history: the great speculators from Vico to Freud* (1966); N. O. Brown, *Life against death: the psychoanalytical meaning of history** (1959); J. Lukacs, *Historical consciousness: or the remembered past* (1968); and J. T. Marcus, *Heaven, hell, and history: a survey of man's faith in history from antiquity to the present* (1967).

Among thoughtful reflections by practicing historians the following sampling of titles may be suggested: H. S. Commager, *The search for a usable past and other essays in historiography* (1967); Page Smith, *The historian and history** (1964); G. Kitson Clark, *The critical historian* (1967); C. V. Wedgwood, *The sense of the past: thirteen studies in the theory and practice of history* (1960); G. Jackson, *Historian's quest* (1969); M. Duberman, *The uncompleted past* (1970); and J. H. Plumb, *The death of the past* (1970).

The current state of historical studies and newer approaches may be explored in J. Higham and others, *History* (1965), a volume in a series examining humanistic scholarship in America; B. C. Shafer and others, *Historical study in the West: France, Western Germany, Great Britain, and the United States* (1968); and W. Laqueur and G. L. Mosse (eds.), *The new history: trends in historical research and writing since World War II** (1968), originally a volume of the *Journal of Contemporary History*. Examples of the new approaches are to be found in D. K. Rowney and J. Q. Graham, Jr. (eds.), *Quantitative history: selected readings in the quantitative analysis of historical data** (1969); B. Mazlish (ed.), *Psychoanalysis and history* (1963); and R. F. Berkhofer, Jr., *A behavioral approach to historical analysis* (1969). The contributions of two important social sciences may be approached through M. Harris, *The rise of anthropological theory* (1968), and R. A. Nisbet, *The sociological tradition* (1967).

Histories recounting and analyzing the human story in order to show that it follows a certain pattern or system, or obeys certain laws, are generally regarded with distrust by historians, who are not convinced by the evidence offered. In the present generation the most important such grand-scale interpretive account has been A. J. Toynbee's monumental *A study of history** (12 vols., 1934–1961, of which vol. 12 consists of *Reconsiderations*) [abridgment edited by D. C. Somervell, 2 vols., 1947–1957]. Some objections to Toynbee are discussed in M. F. Ashley-Montagu (ed.), *Toynbee and history: critical essays and reviews* (1956); in E. T. Gargan and others, *The intent of Toynbee's history* (1961); and in P. Geyl, *Debates with historians* (1956), and *Encounters in history* (1961). Pattern histories are to be distinguished from efforts to recount the scope of man's history in a more purely narrative way. Here two works stand out: H. A. L. Fisher, *A history of Europe* (3 vols., 1935–1936; 2 vols., 1949), a notable effort by a single author to tell the whole Western story from the Greeks to the twentieth century, and W. H. McNeill, *The rise of the West: a history of the human community* (1963), a brilliant presentation of Western history in its world setting stressing the interrelationships of human civilization at all stages. A multivolumed collaborative UNESCO History of Mankind is currently under way; it suffers from a commitment to political consensus on all of its conclusions. Not always abreast of modern scholarship but colorful and eminently readable are the volumes of W. Durant, *The story of civilization* (10 vols., 1935–1967), covering from early times to the late eighteenth century. J. Bowle (ed.), *The concise encyclopedia of world history* (1958), despite its title, is an overall view of history since early times with contributions by various authorities; it may be compared with the *Larousse encyclopedia of modern history from 1500 to the present day* (1965). S. Barr, *The pilgrimage of Western man* (1949), and P. L. Ralph, *The story of our civilization* (1954), are two brief, well-written surveys. Some analytical studies include S. B. Clough, *The rise and fall of civilization: an inquiry into the relationship between economic development and civilization* (1951); H. J. Muller, *The uses of the past: profiles of former societies** (1952); the same author's *Freedom in the Western world: from the Dark Ages to the rise of democracy** (1963) and *Freedom in the modern world** (1966); and C. Quigley, *The evolution of civilizations: an introduction to historical analysis* (1961).

Interpretive and Large-Scale Histories

The Cambridge Modern History (14 vols., 1902–1912), of which Lord Acton was general editor, has long been a standard work, authoritative but usually dry, with numerous contributors writing for each volume, each on his specialty. The New Cambridge Modern History has been launched (1957 ff.) under the general editorship of Sir George Clark, and many of the fourteen projected volumes have appeared; they are described in the appropriate sections below. The volumes contain valuable chapters by renowned specialists from all over the world but often fail to provide a suitable synthesis for the period covered. In that respect the venture is less successful than the French series *Peuples et civilisations: histoire générale* (20 vols., 1926 ff.), in which one, two, or three scholars have prepared each volume and synthesized the period under consideration; some of the volumes in this French series are unsurpassed for coverage and insight. An Oxford History of Modern Europe is also appearing. A valuable series by American scholars on Europe since 1250 [still incomplete for the years between the Reformation and 1610 and for the years since 1900] is The Rise of Modern Europe (1936 ff.), also known as the "Langer series" for its editor, W. L. Langer; each volume contains a rich bibliography for the years covered; the individual volumes are described below in the appropriate chapters. The University of Michigan History of the Modern World (15 vols. projected, 1958 ff.), edited by A. Nevins and H. M. Ehrmann, is a series of histories of individual nations of which several have appeared to date. A similar series, The Modern Nations in Historical Perspective, gen. ed. R. W. Winks (1964 ff.), aims at encompassing all parts of the globe. British scholars have launched the first volumes of a History of Civilization to consist of thirty-five volumes, edited by R. Syme (1963 ff.). Two useful collaborative works are E. Barker, G. N. Clark, and P. Vaucher (eds.), *The European inheritance* (3 vols., 1954), and E. Eyre (ed.), *European civilization, its origin and development* (7 vols.,

Multivolumed Collaborative Works and Series on Modern European History

1934–1939), a work under Catholic auspices by many contributors, some of them non-Catholic. Remarkable as the work of a single author, in forty volumes in the English translation, is L. von Pastor's *History of the popes . . .* (1891–1953). J. H. Plumb is editor of the History of Human Society series. There are numerous informative volumes for the general reader, with illustrations, in the Time-Life Great Ages of Man series, complete in twenty-one volumes. Somewhat similar is the British Hamlyn History of the World in Colour (1969 ff.), derived from the French illustrated series *Connaissance de l'histoire.*

General Histories in Special Areas [A number of books are relevant to many or all of the chapters of the present work and provide additional specialized bibliographies as well.] For European economic history the following are most useful: H. Heaton, *Economic history of Europe* (1936, 1948); S. B. Clough and C. W. Cole, *Economic history of Europe* (1941, 1952); S. B. Clough, *The economic development of Western civilization* (1959, rev., 1968); and A. Birnie, *An economic history of Europe, 1760–1939* (rev. ed., 1951). On economic thought: E. Roll, *A history of economic thought* (rev., 1946); C. Gide and C. Rist, *A history of economic doctrines* (2nd ed., 1948); and R. L. Heilbroner, *The worldly philosophers** (1953). On rural and agrarian history: N. S. B. Gras, *A history of agriculture in Europe and America* (2nd ed., 1940), and B. H. S. van Bath, *The agrarian history of western Europe, 500–1850 A.D.* (trans. from the Dutch, 1963).

On political thought: G. H. Sabine, *A history of political theory* (1937); F. Watkins, *The political tradition of the West: a study in the development of modern liberalism* (1948); and J. H. Hallowell, *Main currents in modern political thought* (1950).

On general intellectual and cultural history and related subjects: B. Russell, *A history of Western philosophy* (1945); J. H. Randall, *Making of the modern mind* (1926, 1940); the same author's *The career of philosophy* (2 vols., 1962–1965), from the Middle Ages to the age of Darwin; and C. Brinton, *Ideas and men: the story of Western thought* (1950, 1963), which for the postmedieval period has been published as *The shaping of the modern mind** (1953). Recommended also: J. Bronowski and B. Mazlish, *The Western intellectual tradition: from Leonardo to Hegel* (1960); E. N. Johnson, *An introduction to the history of the Western tradition* (2 vols., 1961); G. L. Mosse, *The culture of western Europe: the nineteenth and twentieth centuries* (1961); E. Friedell, *A cultural history of the modern age* (3 vols., trans. 1947); B. Dunham, *Heroes and heretics: a political history of Western thought* (1964); R. W. Stromberg, *An intellectual history of modern Europe* (1966); W. H. Coates, H. V. White, and J. S. Schapiro, *The emergence of liberal humanism* (1966); and the sequel volume by Coates and White, *The ordeal of liberal humanism* (1969).

On military history and related themes: T. Ropp, *War in the modern world** (1959, 1962); A. Vagts, *A history of militarism; romance and realities of a profession** (1937); L. Montross, *War through the ages* (rev., 1946); J. U. Nef, *War and human progress* (1950); R. A. Preston and others, *Men in arms* (1956); and Q. Wright, *A study of war* (2 vols., 1942; 1 vol. abr., 1965). More specifically on strategy there are *Makers of modern strategy: military thought from Machiavelli to Hitler** (1944), edited by E. M. Earle; B. H. Liddell Hart, *Strategy: the indirect approach* (3rd ed., 1954); J. F. C. Fuller, *Decisive battles: their influence upon history and civilization* (2 vols., 1940), and *A military history of the Western world* (1954 ff.). D. Eggenberger, *A dictionary of battles* (1969), is a useful reference book, and F. L. Israel has edited *Major peace treaties of modern history, 1648–1967* (4 vols., 1967).

Miscellaneous On certain unclassifiable but important subjects, readers may turn to Mary R. Beard, *Woman as a force in history: a study in traditions and realities* (1946); Miriam Beard, *A history of the business man* (1938, rev., 1964); E. P. Prentice, *Hunger and history: the influence of hunger on human history* (1939); R. N. Salaman, *The history and social influence of the potato* (1949); C. Brinton, *A history of Western morals* (1959); K. E. Olson, *The history makers: the press of Europe from its beginnings through*

1965 (1966); W. H. Armytage, *A social history of engineering* (1966); P. P. Aries, *Centuries of childhood* (1962); and M. Foucault, *Madness and civilization* (1961, trans. 1965).

For prehistory and related subjects an authoritative treatment is J. Hawkes and L. Wooley, *Prehistory and the beginnings of civilization** (1963), the first volume in the UNESCO *History of mankind;* the two parts of the volume are also available separately. Other recommended works are G. G. Simpson, *The meaning of evolution* (1949); H. Bastin, *And then came man* (trans. 1963); R. J. Braidwood, *Prehistoric men* (1967); L. S. B. Leakey, *Adam's ancestors: the evolution of man and his cultures** (1953); A. Montagu, *Man: his first million years* (1958); C. Bibby, *Four thousand years ago* (1961); V. C. Childe, *What happened in history** (1954), *The dawn of European civilization** (1925, 1958), and other writings; W. W. Howells, *Back of history** (1954); G. Daniel, *The idea of prehistory* (1963); S. Pigott, *Ancient Europe** (1965); and G. Clark, *World prehistory** (1961, rev., 1969).

One of the best introductions to anthropology is still A. L. Kroeber, *Anthropology* (1923, 1948); E. Hooton, *Up from the ape* (rev., 1954), stresses physical anthropology. G. Daniel provides a survey of archaeological advances in *A hundred years of archaeology* (1950), and some examples of archaeologists at work are provided in: C. Ceram, *Gods, graves, and scholars* (1951, rev., 1967); J. Alsop, *From the silent earth: a report on the Greek Bronze Age* (1964); J. Chadwick, *The decipherment of linear B** (1958, rev., 1967); and P. MacKendrick's two books, *The Greek stones speak* (1962) and *The mute stones speak: the story of archaeology in Italy* (1960). Geographical influences on history are discussed in D. S. Whittlesey, *Environmental foundations of European history* (1949), and in C. T. Smith, *An historical geography of western Europe before 1800* (1967).

A convenient general introduction is T. B. Jones, *From the Tigris to the Tiber: an introduction to ancient history** (1969). Recommended books on the ancient Near East are J. A. Wilson, *The burden of Egypt** (1951); H. Frankfort's two volumes, *The birth of civilization in the Near East** (1956) and *Before philosophy** (1949); A. Gardiner, *Egypt of the pharaohs* (1961); and H. M. Orlinsky, *Ancient Israel** (1954). E. A. Speiser, *The United States and the Near East* (rev., 1950), is an effort to relate the ancient Near Eastern past to the present. For authoritative treatment of various subjects one may turn to appropriate portions of the Cambridge Ancient History (12 vols., 1923–1939, revision in process); the revision of vol. I, part I, has appeared as *Prolegemona and prehistory* (1969).

Excellent introductions to Greek civilization are M. I. Finley, *The ancient Greeks: their life and thought** (1963), and *The world of Odysseus** (1954); H. D. F. Kitto, *The Greeks* (1951); C. M. Bowra, *The Greek experience* (1957); A. Andrewes, *The Greeks* (1967); and F. Hooper, *Greek realities* (1967). Among the best surveys of Greek history are those by N. G. L. Hammond (1959, rev., 1967), A. R. Burn* (1965), J. B. Bury (rev., 1951), and M. L. W. Laistner (rev., 1957). On politics one may turn to A. Andrewes, *The Greek tyrants* (1956); A. H. M. Jones, *Athenian democracy* (1957); and W. B. Forrest, *The emergence of Greek democracy, 800–400 B.C.* (1966). An interesting popular account is S. Barr, *The will of Zeus* (1961). On the world created by Alexander there are W. W. Tarn and C. T. Griffith, *Hellenistic civilization* (3rd ed., 1952); M. Cary, *The legacy of Alexander* (2nd ed., 1951); and M. Hadas, *Hellenistic culture: fusion and diffusion* (1959). A remarkable biography is W. W. Tarn, *Alexander the Great* (1948), which may be compared with P. Bamm, *Alexander the Great: power as destiny* (trans. from the German, 1968).

Among the most useful histories of Rome and Roman civilization are those by M. Cary (1935), A. E. R. Boak (4th ed., 1955), H. H. Scullard* (1935, 1969), and D. R. Dudley (1960). A superb volume on the end of the republic is R. Syme, *Roman revolution** (1939), which may be supplemented by A. H. MacDonald, *Republican Rome* (1966). Two valuable introductions to the history of the empire are M. P. Charlesworth, *The Roman Empire** (1951), and M. Grant, *The world of Rome* (1960). A provocative popular account is S. Barr, *The mask of Jove: a history of Graeco-Roman civilization from the death of Alexander to the death of Constantine* (1966). Highly recommended is the authoritative A. H. M. Jones, *The decline of the ancient world** (1966), in the Hay series, a summary of his exhaustive longer work, *The later Roman empire 284–602* (2 vols., 1964). The second volume of the UNESCO *History of mankind* by L. Pareti and others, *The ancient world: 1200 B.C. to A.D. 500* (1965), has some informative chapters. On the late Greek and Roman worlds there are also, among others, the magisterial social and economic histories of M. I. Rostovtzeff, *A history of the ancient world* (2 vols., 1926–1928).

On the coming of Christianity, N. H. Baynes, *Constantine the Great and the Christian church* (1931), is of fundamental importance, but there is a good brief account in A. H. M. Jones, *Constantine and the conversion of Europe** (Teach Yourself History series, 1948). On St. Augustine and his times there is a sensitive account by P. Brown, *Augustine of Hippo: a biography** (1967), and a useful study, F. Van der Meer, *Augustine the bishop: church and society at the dawn of the Middle Ages* (1961). The *Oxford classical dictionary* (1949) is a valuable one-volume collaborative encyclopedia. For further titles and discussion see M. Chambers' bibliographical essay in the AHA Service Center series, *Greek and Roman history* (1958).

Among the most useful surveys are those by N. F. Cantor (1963), R. H. C. Davis (1957), S. Painter (1953), C. Stephenson and B. Lyon (rev., 1962), J. R. Strayer* (1955), and Strayer and D. C. Munro (1942, rev., 1959). J. W. Thompson, *Economic and social history of Europe in the Late Middle Ages, 1300–1530* (rev., 1965), is a detailed account. Volumes focusing on the various factors that produced medieval (and early modern) Europe are C. Dawson, *The making of Europe: an introduction to the history of European unity* (1937); W. C. Bark, *Origins of the medieval world** (1958); H. R. Trevor-Roper, *The rise of Christian Europe** (1965), in the Barraclough series; D. Hay, *Europe: the emergence of an idea** (1957, rev., 1968); H. Moss, *The birth of the Middle Ages, 395–814** (1935); C. Brooke, *Europe in the Central Middle Ages, 962–1154* (1968), in the Hay series; J. M. Wallace-Hadrill, *The barbarian West, 400–1000** (1952); A. R. Lewis, *Emerging medieval Europe, A.D. 400–1000** (1967); and C. Duby, *The making of the Christian West, 980–1140* (trans. 1968). An important work by an economic historian is R. S. Lopez, *The birth of Europe* (1967). Two outstanding older interpretations are F. Lot, *The end of the ancient world and the beginnings of the Middle Ages** (1931), and A. Dopsch, *The economic and social foundations of European civilization* (1924). A useful brief introduction is S. Katz, *The decline of Rome and the rise of medieval Europe** (Cornell University series, 1955). C. W. Previté-Orton in the *Shorter Cambridge medieval history* (2 vols., 1952) has condensed for the general reader the eight volumes of the Cambridge medieval history (1911–1936). Colorful portraits of medieval life are found in G. G. Coulton's *Medieval panorama* (1938) and his other writings, and in E. E. Power, *Medieval people** (1924, 1935). B. Lyon has prepared a bibliographical essay, *The Middle Ages in recent historical thought** (AHA Service Center series, 1959, rev., 1965).

Intellectual developments are discussed with insight in R. W. Southern, *The making of the Middle Ages** (1953); D. Knowles, *The evolution of medieval thought** (1962); F. B. Artz, *The mind of the Middle Ages, 200–1500* (rev., 1958); P. Wolff, *The awakening** (1970), vol. I of the Pelican History of European Thought; and in the older work by H. O. Taylor, *The medieval mind* (2 vols., 1911, 1925). Other valuable studies include E. K. Rand, *Founders of the Middle Ages* (1928, re-issued 1957); M. L. Laistner, *Thought and letters in western Europe, A.D. 500 to 900* (rev., 1957); the same author's *The intellectual heritage of the Early Middle Ages* (1957); and G. Leff, *Medieval thought* (1958). The best survey of medieval political philosophy is still C. H. McIlwain, *The growth of political thought in the West: from the Greeks to the end of the Middle Ages* (1932), and a good brief introduction is J. B. Morrall, *Political thought in medieval times* (1958). One may also consult F. C. Copleston, *Medieval philosophy* (1952), and *Aquinas* (1955); and R. S. Hoyt (ed.), *Life and thought in the Early Middle Ages* (1967).

There are innumerable books dealing with various regions and institutions during the Middle Ages, or covering specific centuries, of which the titles given here are only a sampling. G. Barraclough, *Origins of modern Germany** (1947), is the most valuable introduction to medieval Germany, but F. Heer, *The Holy Roman Empire* (trans. 1968), also merits reading. C. Petit-Dutaillis, *The feudal monarchy in France and England, from the tenth to the thirteenth century* (1933, trans. 1936), is a comparative study of the two monarchies, and S. Painter, *Rise of the feudal monarchies** (1951), is an excellent brief introduction. F. M. Powicke, *The thirteenth century, 1216–1307* (1953), and various other volumes in the Oxford History of England provide detailed coverage for advanced students. Two interesting accounts are E. Duckett, *Death and life in the tenth century* (1968), and R. E. Lerner, *The age of adversity: the fourteenth century** (Cornell University series, 1968). On English developments there are B. Lyon, *A constitutional and legal history of medieval England* (1960); G. O. Sayles, *Medieval foundations of England* (1948); G. L. Haskins, *The growth of English representative government* (1948); C. H. McIlwain, *The High Court of Parliament and its supremacy* (1910); F. Thompson, *A short history of Parliament, 1295–1642* (1953); H. Cam, *England before Elizabeth** (1950); and the many detailed volumes on constitutional history by B. C. Wilkinson. For social developments see D. W. Robertson, Jr., *Chaucer's London** (1968). On the Carolingian era and on France see H. Fichtenau, *The Carolingian empire: the age of Charlemagne** (1949, trans. 1957); A. D. Bullough, *The age of Charlemagne* (1965); and R. Fawtier, *The Capetian kings of France* (1960).

Economic developments are discussed in the provocative books of H. Pirenne, *Economic and social history of medieval Europe** (1936), and *Medieval cities: their origins and the revival of trade* (1925, 1939). They may be compared with the more modern treatment by Lopez cited earlier; with R. Latouche, *The birth of the Western economy** (1961), the most useful survey of social and economic developments available; and with F. Rörig, *The medieval town** (1967). An important special subject is examined in L. White, Jr., *Medieval technology and social change** (1962). The guilds and other organizations are discussed in P. Boissonnade, *Life and work in medieval Europe from the fifth to the fifteenth century* (trans. 1927), and in S. L. Thrupp, *The merchant class of medieval London, 1300–1500* (1948). The first three volumes of the collaborative Cambridge Economic History of Europe provide authoritative specialized accounts: *The agrarian life of the Middle Ages* (1941, rev., 1966); *Trade and industry in the Middle Ages* (1952); and *Economic organization and policies in the Middle Ages* (1952). On the complex subjects of feudalism, vassalage, and manorialism one may also turn to F. L. Ganshof, *Feudalism** (1952); C. Stephenson, *Medieval feudalism* (1942); S. Painter, *Medieval society** (1953); the same author's *French chivalry** (1940); and for a comparative study emphasizing the diversity of feudalism in various ages and places, R. Coulborn (ed.), *Feudalism in history* (1956). M. Bloch's great contributions are available in translation as *Feudal society** (1939–1940, trans. 1961), *French rural history: an essay on its basic characteristics* (trans. 1966), and *Land and work in medieval Europe: selected papers** (trans. 1967).

For the Byzantine world one may turn to G. Ostrogorsky, *History of the Byzantine state* (1950), translated in 1956 by J. M. Hussey, who herself has written a good introduction in briefer compass, *The Byzantine world** (1957), and has edited *The Byzantine empire*, vol. IV (rev., 1966–1967) in the Cambridge Medieval History. A. Vasiliev has written a comprehensive *History of the Byzantine empire, 324–1453* (2 vols., 1928–1929). Among other narrative and topical accounts there are C. Diehl's books: *History of the Byzantine empire* (trans. 1925), *Byzantium: greatness and decline* (1919, trans. 1957), and *Byzantine portraits* (1927); N. H. Baynes, *The Byzantine empire* (1925, 1946), and *Byzantine studies and other essays* (1955); the essays edited by N. H. Baynes and H. Moss, *Byzantine: introduction to East Roman civilization* (1945); P. Lemerle, *A history of Byzantium* (1964); S. Vryonis, Jr., *Byzantium and Europe** (1967), in the Barraclough series; D. J. Geanakoplos, *Byzantine East and Latin West: two worlds of Christendom in Middle Ages and Renaissance** (1966); and R. Jenkins, *Byzantium: the imperial centuries*, A.D. *619–1071* (1966).

A good starting point for the study of Islam is H. A. R. Gibb's succinct *Mohammedanism:*

an historical survey (1949, 1953) and his *Islamic society and the West* (1951). Another good introduction is H. Lammens, *Islam: beliefs and institutions* (trans. 1926). The best interpretive account of the founder of Islam is Tor Andrae, *Mohammed: the man and his faith* (trans. 1936, reprinted 1957), which may be compared with the detailed biographical accounts of W. M. Watt, *Muhammad at Mecca* (1953), and *Muhammad at Medina* (1956). An excellent short survey of Arab history, mostly on the period to the eleventh century, is B. Lewis, *The Arabs in history* (1950, rev., 1958); more detailed is P. K. Hitti, *History of the Arabs* (6th ed., 1956), available in briefer form as *The Arabs: a short history* (1943, rev., 1968). G. E. von Grunebaum compares Islamic with Byzantine and Christian civilization in his masterful *Medieval Islam: a study in cultural orientation* (1946); and D. L. E. O'Leary examines the influence of Islamic philosophy and science on Europe in *Arabic thought and its place in history* (2nd ed., 1939). H. Pirenne in his *Mohammed and Charlemagne* (1937, trans. 1939), and in his two economic histories cited earlier, propounded the thesis that Islamic expansion brought on the final collapse of western Roman civilization, an argument challenged in many quarters.

Some biographical accounts that may be recommended are R. Winston, *Charlemagne: from the hammer to the cross** (1954); E. S. Duckett, *Alcuin, friend of Charlemagne* (1951); F. Barlow, *William I and the Norman Conquest* (Teach Yourself History series, 1965); A. R. Kelly, *Eleanor of Aquitaine and the four kings** (1950); and E. F. Jacob, *Henry V and the invasion of France** (Teach Yourself History series, 1950).

The classic expression of the spiritual unity and harmony of medieval Europe is Henry Adams, *Mont-Saint-Michel and Chartres** (1912, many reprintings). C. Dawson, in *The making of Europe*, already cited, *Medieval religion* (1934), and *Medieval essays* (1954), also examines the close communion between medieval European culture and the Christian religion, as does P. Hughes in the relevant chapters of *A history of the church* (3 vols., 1935–1949). Among several valuable introductions to the church as an institution are M. W. Baldwin, *The medieval church** (Cornell University series, 1953), and G. Barraclough, *The medieval papacy** (1968), in the series edited by the author. R. H. Bainton, *The Penguin history of Christianity** (1960 ff.), and H. Chadwick, *The Pelican history of the church** (1967 ff.), both multivolume works now appearing, are highly recommended. The most comprehensive study of the development of the papacy from the fourth to the twelfth century is W. Ullmann, *The growth of papal government in the Middle Ages: a study in the ideological relation of clerical to lay power* (1955; 2nd ed., 1962).

Specialized subjects are treated in W. E. Lunt, *Papal revenues in the Middle Ages* (2 vols., 1934); A. S. Turberville, *Medieval heresy and the Inquisition* (1920, 1932); and S. Runciman, *The medieval Manichee* (1961). Both the latter books are more balanced treatments of their subject than H. C. Lea's pioneer work *A history of the Inquisition of the Middle Ages* (3 vols., 1888; abr. ed., 1969*).

Three notable contributions to the study of medieval secular culture are by C. H. Haskins: *Normans in European civilization** (1915), *The Renaissance of the twelfth century* (1927), and *The rise of universities** (1923). The last may be supplemented by H. Rashdall, *Universities of Europe in the Middle Ages* (1895, rev., 1936), and by G. Leff, *Paris and Oxford universities in the thirteenth and fourteenth centuries* (1968).

The Crusades may be approached through the brief Berkshire study, R. A. Newhall, *The Crusades** (1927, rev., 1963), and the detailed, colorful S. Runciman, *A history of the Crusades** (3 vols., 1951–1954). Runciman has also written *The fall of Constantinople, 1453* (1965). The first two volumes of a collaborative, scholarly *History of the Crusades* (K. M. Setton, gen. ed.) have appeared (1955, 1962). For all aspects of the expansion of Christianity the works of K. S. Latourette are indispensable, especially his *History of Christianity* (1953) and his longer *History of the expansion of Christianity* (7 vols., 1937–1945), of which vol. II, *The thousand years of*

uncertainty, A.D. 500–A.D. 1500, covers the Middle Ages.   S. W. Baron's monumental history *A*
social and religious history of the Jews covers the years 1200 to 1650 in vols. IX–XIV (rev.,
1967–1969); see also, on the same general subject, L. Finkelstein (ed.), *The Jews* (2 vols., 1960).

Several pamphlets in the various problems series are relevant to this chapter: D. Kagan (ed.),
Decline and fall of the Roman Empire (1962); A. F. Havighurst (ed.), *The Pirenne thesis: analysis,*
criticism, and revision (rev., 1969); J. F. Benton (ed.), *Town origins: the evidence from medieval England*
(1968); R. E. Sullivan (ed.), *The coronation of Charlemagne* (1959); R. S. Lopez (ed.), *The tenth*
century: how dark the Dark Ages? (1959); C. W. Hollister (ed.), *The twelfth-century Renaissance*
(1969); C. R. Young (ed.), *The Renaissance of the twelfth century* (1970); S. Williams (ed.), *The*
Gregorian epoch (1966); J. A. Brundage (ed.), *The Crusades* (1964); J. M. Powell (ed.), *Innocent III*
(1963); R. E. Herzstein (ed.); *The Holy Roman Empire in the Middle Ages* (1965); and G. P. Bodet
(ed.), *Early English parliaments: high courts, royal councils, or representative assemblies?* (1968).   In the
Anvil series there are available: R. H. Bainton, *Early Christianity* (1960); S. C. Easton and
H. Wieruszowski, *The era of Charlemagne* (1961); J. A. Corbett, *The papacy: a brief history* (1956);
R. H. Bainton, *The medieval church* (1962); H. L. Adelson, *Medieval commerce* (1962); P. K. Hitti,
Islam and the West (1962); and J. H. Mundy and P. Riesenberg, *The medieval town* (1958).

Two valuable syntheses on the Renaissance period are W. K. Ferguson, *Europe in transition,* **II: The Revolution**
1300–1520* (1963), and M. P. Gilmore, *The world of humanism, 1453–1517** (1952), the latter in **in the Christian**
the Langer series.   Other recommended syntheses covering the beginnings of the early **Church, 1300–1560**
modern period are D. Hay, *Europe in the fourteenth and fifteenth centuries** (1966), in the series
edited by Professor Hay; M. Aston, *The fifteenth century: the prospect of Europe** (1968), in the
Barraclough series; H. G. Koenigsberger and G. L. Mosse, *Europe in the sixteenth century** (1968),
in the Hay series; and E. P. Rice, Jr., *The foundations of early modern Europe, 1460–1559** (1970), in
the Norton History of Modern Europe.   E. P. Cheyney, *Dawn of a new era, 1250–1453** (1936), is
an older, somewhat dated volume in the Langer series.   G. R. Potter (ed.), *The Renaissance,*
1493–1520 (1957), and G. R. Elton (ed.), *The Reformation, 1520–1559* (1958), vols. I and II of the
New Cambridge Modern History, have many informative chapters, but as indicated earlier,
they do not present as integrated a picture of the periods covered as might be desired.   On a
special subject G. Mattingly, *Renaissance diplomacy** (1955), is highly recommended.   Two
useful bibliographical essays in the AHA Service Center series are W. J. Bouwsma, *The*
interpretation of Renaissance humanism* (1959), and H. J. Grimm, *The Reformation in recent historical*
thought* (1963).

The growing restlessness within the church is described in P. Hughes, *The revolt against the* *The Decline*
church: Aquinas to Luther (1947), the third volume of *A history of the church* (1934 ff.), an *of the Church*
outstanding Catholic account; E. F. Jacob, *Essays in the conciliar epoch* (1943, 1953); G. J. Jordan,
The inner history of the Great Schism in the West (1930); and J. N. Figgis, *Studies of political thought*
from Gerson to Grotius (1923), a classic study of the difficulties of "peaceful reform" within the
church.   Two national heresies of the fourteenth century may be studied in J. Herben, *Hus and*
his followers (1926), a popular account; F. G. Heymann, *George of Bohemia: king of heretics* (1965);
H. Kaminsky, *A history of the Hussite revolution* (1967); B. Workman, *John Wyclif: a study of the*
English medieval church (2 vols., 1926); and the lively K. B. McFarlane, *John Wycliffe and the*
beginnings of English nonconformity* (Teach Yourself History series, 1952).

In addition to the accounts cited at the beginning of this chapter one may turn to F. B. Artz, *Renaissance humanism, 1300–1550* (1966); G. C. Sellery, *The Renaissance: its nature and origins** (1950); D. Hay, *The Italian Renaissance in its historical background** (1961); and J. A. Mazzeo, *Renaissance and revolution: the remaking of European thought* (1969). The origins and development of the concept "Renaissance" are masterfully explored in W. K. Ferguson, *The Renaissance in historical thought: five centuries of interpretation* (1948), in which he examines, among other things, the classical account of the Italian Renaissance by J. A. Symonds (7 vols., 1875–1886) and J. Burckhardt (1860; new ed., 1944), both of which stressed the originality and uniqueness of Italy. There is also a valuable symposium on the historiography of the Renaissance: T. Helton (ed.), *The Renaissance: a reconsideration of the theories and reinterpretations of the age** (1961). The fusion of politics and humanism in Renaissance Italy is brilliantly traced in H. Baron, *The crisis of the early Italian Renaissance: civic humanism and republican liberty in an age of classicism and tyranny** (2 vols., 1955; rev. 1 vol. ed., 1966). On this subject one may also read E. Garin, *Italian humanism: philosophy and civic life in the Renaissance* (1941, trans. 1965). The specialist cannot neglect P. O. Kristeller, *Renaissance thought: the classic, scholastic, and humanist strains* (1961), and *Eight philosophers of the Italian Renaissance* (1964). On Machiavelli there are studies by F. Chabod, *Machiavelli and the Renaissance* (trans. 1958); J. R. Hale, *Machiavelli and Renaissance Italy** (Teach Yourself History series, 1960); and F. Gilbert, *Machiavelli and Guicciardini: politics and history in sixteenth-century Florence* (1965). Three recent valuable studies focusing on Florence are G. Holmes, *The Florentine enlightenment, 1400–1450* (1969); V. Cronin, *The Florentine Renaissance* (1967); and G. A. Brucker, *Renaissance Florence* (1969). Two lavishly illustrated books with chapters contributed by experts are D. Hay (ed.), *The Renaissance* (1967), and G. Martinelli (ed.), *The world of Renaissance Florence* (1964, trans. 1967). Older studies include A. C. Krey, *A city that art built* (1936); F. Schevill, *History of Florence** (2 vols., 1936), and *The Medici** (1949); and G. F. Young, *The Medici* (1910). Two specialized subjects are explored in R. DeRoover, *The rise and decline of the Medici Bank, 1307–1494** (1963); and F. C. Lane, *Venetian ships and shipping of the Renaissance* (1934).

A number of monographs based on archival sources have recently appeared illuminating the "world of humanism." Two examples are G. A. Brucker, *Florentine politics and society, 1343–1378* (1962), and M. Becker, *Florence in transition* (2 vols., 1967–1969); other contributions may be sampled in the collaborative N. Rubinstein (ed.), *Florentine studies: politics and society in Renaissance Florence* (1969).

J. Huizinga, *The waning of the Middle Ages . . . life, thought, and art in France and the Netherlands in the fourteenth and fifteenth centuries** (1924), an outstanding work, and P. S. Allen, *The age of Erasmus* (1914), remain excellent introductions to the Northern Renaissance. On Erasmus there are available P. Smith, *Erasmus** (1923), a sympathetic biography; the discerning J. Huizinga, *Erasmus** (1924); the brief, spirited M. M. Phillips, *Erasmus and the Northern Renaissance** (Teach Yourself History series, 1950); and R. M. Bainton, *Erasmus of Christendom* (1969). On Christian humanism one may also turn to E. H. Harbison, *The Christian scholar in the age of the Reformation** (1956); L. Spitz, *The religious Renaissance of the German humanists* (1963); and A. Hyma, *The Christian Renaissance: a history of the "Devotio Moderna"* (1924).

The relations between banking and culture in Germany and elsewhere are shown in R. Ehrenberg, *Capital and finance in the age of the Renaissance: a study of the Fuggers and their connections* (1928), and in J. Strieder, *Jacob Fugger the Rich* (1931). G. M. Trevelyan's *Illustrated English social history* (4 vols., 1949 ff.) and *English social history: a survey of six centuries** (rev., 1946) discuss Chaucer's England and the influence of the Continental Renaissance. A thoughtful monograph illuminating aspects of the English Renaissance is A. B. Ferguson, *The articulate citizen and the English Renaissance* (1965). For France, L. Batiffol, *The century of the Renaissance* (1916), remains useful. M. L. Bush, *Renaissance, Reformation, and the outer world, 1450–1660**

(1967), stresses political developments; other books on England, France, and Spain in this period are listed in the next chapter.

Besides the accounts listed at the beginning of this chapter, among the best syntheses focusing on the Reformation proper are G. R. Elton, *Reformation Europe, 1517–1559** (1963), in the Plumb series; A. G. Dickens, *Reformation and society in sixteenth century Europe** (1960), in the Barraclough series; O. Chadwick, *The Reformation** (1963), in the Pelican History of the Church; and K. Holl, *The cultural significance of the Reformation* (1959). Other recommended accounts include H. J. Grimm, *The Reformation era* (rev., 1965); R. H. Bainton, *The Reformation of the sixteenth century* (1952); N. Sykes, *The crisis of the Reformation** (1946); G. L. Mosse, *The Reformation** (rev., 1963), a Berkshire study; E. H. Harbison, *The age of Reformation** (1955), in the Cornell University series; and H. J. Hillerbrand, *Men and ideas in the sixteenth century** (1969). P. Hughes, *A popular history of the Reformation** (1957), and J. Lortz, *How the Reformation came* (1964), are accounts by eminent Catholic scholars. P. Smith, *The age of the Reformation** (1920), is still useful. For the political background see H. Holborn, *A history of modern Germany: the Reformation* (1959), the first volume of a three-volume history of Germany; F. L. Carsten, *Princes and parliaments in Germany* (1959); W. L. McElwee, *The reign of Charles V, 1516–1558* (1936); and the masterly biography by K. Brandi, *The Emperor Charles V** (1939). An outstanding biographical account of Luther is E. G. Schwiebert, *Luther and his times* (1950); there are also biographies by H. Boehmer (1925, trans. 1946); H. Grisar (1926, trans. 1930), an unsympathetic Catholic account; and L. Febvre (1929). E. H. Erikson, *Young man Luther: a study in psychoanalysis and history** (1958, 1962), is a pioneering psychoanalytical study. Other lively, scholarly accounts are R. Bainton, *Here I stand: a life of Martin Luther** (1950); A. G. Dickens, *Martin Luther and the Reformation** (Teach Yourself History series, 1967); E. G. Rupp, *The progress of Luther to the Diet of Worms, 1521* (1951); R. H. Fife, *The revolt of Martin Luther* (1957); and J. Atkinson, *Martin Luther and the birth of Protestantism** (1968).

Among the best accounts of Calvin and his influence are J. T. McNeill, *The history and character of Calvinism* (1954); F. Wendel, *Calvin: the origins and development of his religious thought* (trans. 1963); and Q. Breen, *John Calvin: a study in French humanism* (1931). There are biographical studies by G. Harkness (1931), R. N. Carew Hunt (1933), and J. MacKinnon (1936). An interesting study of Servetus is R. H. Bainton, *Hunted heretic: the life and death of Michael Servetus** (1960). Two valuable studies of the cities in which the major events of the Reformation occurred are G. Strauss, *Nuremberg in the sixteenth century** (1966), and W. Monter, *Calvin's Geneva** (1967).

The course of the Reformation in England may be approached through three brief and able accounts: T. M. Parker, *The English Reformation to 1558** (1950), in the Home University Library; A. G. Dickens, *Thomas Cromwell and the English Reformation* (1959); and F. E. Hutchinson, *Cranmer and the English Reformation** (Teach Yourself History series, 1951). Fuller treatment is provided in A. G. Dickens, *The English Reformation** (1964), the best synthesis now available; H. M. Smith, *Henry VIII and the Reformation* (1948); F. M. Powicke, *The Reformation in England* (1941); and P. Hughes, *The Reformation in England* (3 vols., 1950–1954), a judicious Catholic account. Two surveys covering all phases of English religious history are N. Sykes, *The English religious tradition* (1953), and E. O. James, *A history of Christianity in England* (1949). A. F. Pollard's older biography of Cardinal Wolsey (1929) may be compared with the more popular C. W. Ferguson, *Naked to my enemies** (1958). R. W. Chambers, *Thomas More* (1948), is a sympathetic, moving biography. D. Knowles, *The religious orders in England: the Tudor age* (1959), is informative on an important subject, as is G. W. O. Woodward, *The dissolution of the monasteries* (1967). A distinguished biography focusing on the king as well as on the events of

Bibliography his reign is J. J. Scarisbrick, *Henry VIII* (1968), which in many ways supersedes the older biography by A. F. Pollard (1902); and a detailed account of the famous divorce is provided in G. deC. Parmiter, *The king's great matter: a study of Anglo-papal relations, 1527–1534* (1967).

The various forms of Protestantism are placed in historical perspective in E. Troeltsch's masterpiece *The social teachings of the Christian churches* (2 vols., reissued 1949); J. S. Whale, *The Protestant tradition* (1959); and E. G. Léonard, *A history of Protestantism* (1965). The radical movements of the era may be studied in G. H. Williams, *The radical Reformation* (1962), and N. Cohn, *The pursuit of the millennium* (1957, rev., 1964); and an important subject is explored in H. Kamen, *The rise of toleration* (1967).

On the much debated question concerning the relation between economic change and religious doctrine, see M. Weber, *The Protestant ethic and the spirit of capitalism** (1904, reissued 1948), which opened the controversy; R. H. Tawney, *Religion and the rise of capitalism** (1926, 1947), a brilliant work; J. Brodrick, *The economic morals of the Jesuits* (1934); and K. Samuelsson, *Religion and economic action** (trans. 1961), a balanced treatment of the subject. B. N. Nelson examines a special phase of religion and economic change in *The idea of usury* (1949, rev., 1969).

Two provocative books dealing with the social implications of the Reformation for England, and many other subjects, are H. R. Trevor-Roper, *Religion, the Reformation and social change* (1967), and C. Hill, *Reformation to industrial revolution: the making of modern English society* (1967).

Catholicism Reformed and Reorganized On the Counter Reformation one may turn to A. G. Dickens, *The Counter Reformation* (1969), in the Barraclough series; O. Evennett, *The spirit of the Counter Reformation* (1968); B. J. Kidd, *The Counter Reformation, 1550–1600* (1933); and a Catholic account, P. Janelle, *The Catholic Reformation* (1949). H. Jedin, *The Council of Trent* (2 vols., 1957–1961), is an excellent objective account, narrating much more than the council itself. Of the large literature on the Jesuits the following may be mentioned: C. Hollis, *The Jesuits* (1968); T. J. Campbell, *The Jesuits, 1534–1921* (2 vols., 1921); H. Boehmer, *The Jesuits* (1914, 1928); R. Fülöp-Miller, *The power and the secret of the Jesuits* (1930); and A. H. Rowbotham, *Missionary and mandarin: the Jesuits at the court of China* (1943), as one example of the overseas activities of the order. There are biographies of Loyola by C. Hollis (1931), P. Dudon (1933), and J. Brodrick (1956).

Problems and Readings* Among pamphlets in various problems series sampling divergent interpretations of subjects covered in this chapter are K. H. Dannenfeldt (ed.), *The Renaissance: medieval or modern?* (1959); D. Hay (ed.), *The Renaissance debate* (1963); D. L. Jensen (ed.), *Machiavelli: cynic, patriot, or political scientist?* (1960); L. W. Spitz (ed.), *The Reformation: material or spiritual?* (1962); K. C. Sessions (ed.), *Reformation and authority: the meaning of the Peasants' Revolt* (1968); A. J. Slavin (ed.), *The new monarchies* (1964), and *Henry VIII and the English Reformation* (1968); and R. W. Green, *Protestantism and capitalism: the Weber thesis and its critics* (1959). In the Anvil series there are R. H. Bainton, *The age of the Reformation* (1956), and E. M. Burns, *The Counter Reformation* (1964). Source material and commentary are provided in H. J. Hillerbrand (ed.), *The Protestant Reformation: a narrative history related by contemporary observers and participants* (1964); L. W. Spitz (ed.), *The Protestant Reformation* (1966); and G. R. Elton (ed.), *Renaissance and Reformation, 1300–1648* (1963).

III: The Wars of Religion, 1560–1648 C. J. Friedrich, *The age of the baroque, 1610–1660** (1952), in the Langer series, covers institutional and international developments as well as the arts and is useful for many subjects covered in this chapter and the next. The following also treat many of the topics discussed in this chapter: H. G. Koenigsberger and G. L. Mosse, *Europe in the sixteenth century** (1968), in the Hay series, cited earlier; R. B. Wernham (ed.), *The Counter Reformation and price revolution, 1559–1610* (1968), vol. III of the New Cambridge Modern History; J. H. Elliott, *Europe divided, 1559–1598** (1969), in the Plumb series; R. S. Dunn, *The age of religious wars, 1559–1689** (1970), in the Norton History of Modern Europe; T. Aston (ed.), *Crisis in Europe, 1560–1660** (1965); and H. R. Trevor-Roper (ed.), *The age of expansion: Europe and the world, 1559–1660* (1968), a richly illustrated collaborative work with chapters on the non-Western world as well. Three accounts stressing European power politics are C. Petrie, *Earlier diplomatic history, 1492–1713* (1949); L. Dehio, *The precarious balance: the politics of power in Europe, 1494–1945* (1948, trans. 1962); and R. B. Mowat, *A history of European diplomacy, 1451–1789* (1928). The changing art of war may be studied in C. Oman, *A history of the art of war in the sixteenth century* (1937), and J. R. Partington, *A history of Greek fire and gunpowder* (1960).

The best introductory account is J. H. Parry, *The age of reconnaissance** (1963); and the same author has written *Europe and a wider world, 1415–1715** (1949). A brief account is C. E. Nowell, *The great discoveries and the first colonial empires** (1954), in the Cornell University series. The older classic study, W. C. Abbott, *The expansion of Europe* (2 vols., 1918), should be supplemented by D. F. Lach, *Asia in the making of Europe* (vol. I, 1965). C. M. Cipolla stresses the importance of technology for the explorations in *Guns, sails, and empires: technological innovation and the early phases of European expansion, 1400–1700** (1965). Challenging on the broader implications of European expansion is the essay by W. P. Webb, a student of the American frontier, *The great frontier* (1952). Other useful works include P. Sykes, *History of exploration* (3rd ed., 1950), beginning with ancient times; J. N. L. Baker, *A history of geographical discovery and exploration* (1931, 1948); B. Penrose, *Travel and discovery in the Renaissance, 1420–1620** (1952, 1955); A. P. Newton (ed.), *The great age of discovery* (1932); J. A. Williamson, *Maritime enterprise, 1485–1558* (1913), and his more compact *Europe overseas* (1925); J. B. Brebner, *The explorers of North America, 1492–1806* (1933); and H. H. Hart, *Sea route to the Indies* (1950).

Portuguese maritime and colonial enterprises are recounted in C. R. Boxer, *Four centuries of Portuguese expansion, 1415–1825** (1961); E. Prestage, *The Portuguese pioneers* (1933); C. R. Beazley, *Prince Henry the Navigator* (1895); H. M. Stephens, *Albuquerque* (1892, 1897); and two fascinating books by E. Sanceau, *The land of Prester John* (1944), about Portuguese interest in Abyssinia, and *Knight of the Renaissance: a biography of D. João de Castre, soldier, sailor, scientist and viceroy of India, 1500–1548* (1949). G. Freyre, *Brazil: an interpretation* (1945), is the best short account in English of Brazil. An important special point is discussed in A. Marchant, *From barter to slavery: the economic relations of Portuguese and Indians in the settlement of Brazil, 1500–1580* (1942). On Portugal itself there are sound histories by H. V. Livermore (1947, rev., 1966) and by C. E. Nowell (1952).

Two solid books reflecting modern scholarship on Spain in the early centuries are J. H. Elliott, *Imperial Spain, 1469–1716* (1964); and J. Lynch, *Spain under the Habsburgs*, vol. I, *Empire and absolutism, 1516–1598* (1964), and vol. II, *Spain and America, 1598–1700* (1969). Elliott has also written *The revolt of the Catalans: a study in the decline of Spain, 1598–1640* (1963). An earlier work still not superseded, R. B. Merriman, *Rise of the Spanish empire in the old world and the new* (4 vols., 1918–1934), traces the evolution of Spanish policy to the death of Philip II; two other older works still useful are J. H. Mariéjol, *The Spain of Ferdinand and Isabella* (1904, ed. and rev. by B. Keen, 1961), and R. T. Davies, *The golden century of Spain, 1501–1621** (1937, rev., 1965). Also useful are J. B. Trend, *The civilization of Spain* (1944, rev., 1967); and two books by J. Vicens Vives, *An economic history of Spain from earliest times to the end of the nineteenth century* (1955, trans. 1969), and *Approaches to the history of Spain** (1962, trans. 1967). C. Petrie, *Philip II of Spain*

(1963), is an account of Spanish affairs in the sixteenth century rather than a biography; and G. Mattingly, *The Armada** (1959), is a superb treatment placing the dramatic episode in its European setting.

S. E. Morison, *Admiral of the Ocean Sea* (1942), reconstructs the life and voyages of Columbus. S. Zweig, *Conqueror of the seas* (1938), is a readable biography of Magellan, as is C. M. Parr, *So noble a captain* (1953). For the Spanish empire in the new world excellent accounts are available in C. H. Haring, *The Spanish empire in America* (1947); C. Gibson, *Spain in America** (1966); and J. H. Parry, *The Spanish seaborne empire* (1966), in the Plumb History of Human Society series; interesting but less reliable is S. de Madariaga, *Rise of the Spanish American empire* (1947). A picturesque account is F. A. Kirkpatrick, *The Spanish conquistadores* (1934, 1949). The argument that absolutism in the empire destroyed constitutionalism in Spain is presented in J. H. Parry, *The Spanish theory of empire in the sixteenth century* (1940). L. Hanke, *The Spanish struggle for justice in the conquest of America** (1949), questions some of the older views on the role of the Inquisition, and a defense of Spanish colonial administration based upon the literature of the time is offered in I. A. Leonard, *Books of the brave* (1949). Spanish treatment of subject peoples in Latin America is discussed in L. B. Simpson, *The encomienda in New Spain: forced native labor in the Spanish colonies, 1492–1550* (1929), and in F. Tannenbaum, *Slave and citizen: the Negro in the Americas** (1947), where it is argued that in Latin America (unlike North America) there was recognition of the "moral personality" of the slave. See also, on the North American attitudes, W. D. Jordan, *White over black: American attitudes toward the Negro, 1550–1812** (1968). An important study is B. D. Davis, *The problem of slavery in Western culture* (1966). The grim story of the slave trade is told in J. Pope-Hennessy, *Sins of the fathers: a study of the Atlantic slave traders, 1441–1807** (1968), and in D. P. Mannix and M. Cowley, *Black cargoes* (1962). An important analysis of the impact of the discoveries upon economic changes in Europe is E. J. Hamilton, *American treasure and the price revolution in Spain, 1501–1650* (1934).

[The general economic histories cited at the beginning of this bibliography and the works cited at the opening of this chapter should also be consulted.] There are valuable contributions in E. E. Rich and C. H. Wilson (eds.), *The economy of expanding Europe in the sixteenth and seventeenth centuries* (rev. ed., 1967), vol. IV of the Cambridge Economic History of Europe, the first of two projected volumes on the subject. On the emergence of capitalism see H. E. Sée, *Modern capitalism: its origin and evolution* (1928); F. L. Nussbaum, *History of the economic institutions of modern Europe* (1933), which is based largely on the work of the German historian W. Sombart; and M. Dobb, *Studies in the development of capitalism** (rev., 1963). R. L. Heilbroner, *The quest for wealth* (1956), is interesting and informative. On mercantilism E. Hecksher has written the most authoritative work, *Mercantilism* (2 vols., 1935); other studies are J. W. Horrocks, *A short history of mercantilism* (1925); C. Wilson, *Profit and power* (1957); and P. Buck, *The politics of mercantilism* (1942), the latter drawing some comparisons to twentieth-century totalitarianism. E. S. Furniss, *The position of the laborer in a system of nationalism: a study in the labor theories of the later English mercantilists* (1920), is a provocative study. J. E. Nef, *Industry and government in France and England, 1540–1640** (1957), presents the case for an early "industrial revolution."

The characteristic economic institutions of the period are described in G. Renard and G. Weulersse, *Life and work in modern Europe: the fifteenth to the eighteenth centuries* (1926); D. Hannay, *The great chartered companies* (1926); G. Unwin, *Industrial organization in the sixteenth and seventeenth centuries* (1904), and *Gilds and companies of London* (1909, 1925); and S. Kramer, *The English craft gilds: studies in their progress and decline* (1927).

P. Geyl, *The revolt of the Netherlands, 1555–1609* (1932, 1958), seeks to show that the split between Belgium and Holland originated not in language or religion but in the fortunes of war;

the sequel, *The Netherlands in the seventeenth century 1609–1715* (2 vols., trans. 1961–1964), describes the extreme particularism that grew up in the separated provinces. C. V. Wedgwood, *William the Silent** (1944), is an excellent, laudatory biography, and R. B. Merriman, *Six contemporaneous revolutions* (1938), relates events in the Netherlands to similar stirrings elsewhere in seventeenth-century Europe. The classic study by J. L. Motley covering the years 1555 to 1609 (7 vols., 1856–1867) may still be read with profit.

Among many good books the best introductions are C. Read, *The Tudors: personalities and practical politics in sixteenth century England** (1936); S. T. Bindoff, *Tudor England** (1952); J. D. Mackie, *The earlier Tudors, 1485–1558* (1952); G. R. Elton, *England under the Tudors* (1955); J. B. Black, *The reign of Queen Elizabeth, 1558–1603* (1936); and J. A. Williamson, *The Tudor age* (1953). The relevant chapters of M. Ashley, *Great Britain to 1688* (1961); K. Feiling, *England under the Tudors and Stuarts* (1935); and R. Lockyer, *Tudor and Stuart Britain* (1964), are also to be recommended. An excellent brief introduction to the Elizabethan age is J. Hurstfield, *Elizabeth I and the unity of England** (1966), and a fresh examination of the early years of Elizabeth's reign is provided in W. MacCaffrey, *The shaping of the Elizabethan regime* (1968). R. B. Wernham, *Before the armada: the emergence of the English nation, 1485–1588,* is strong on foreign affairs, and L. B. Smith, *The Elizabethan world* (1967), is a colorful account. The outstanding biography of Elizabeth remains J. E. Neale's distinguished study, *Queen Elizabeth I** (1934, 1966), but two recent scholarly and readable books deserve mention: E. Jenkins, *Elizabeth the Great** (1959), and N. Williams, *Elizabeth the first, queen of England* (1968); there are other brief biographies by M. Waldman (1952) and D. B. Chidsey (1955). A. L. Rowse crowds many subjects into *The Elizabethan age* (2 vols., 1950–1955) and has also written a highly controversial *William Shakespeare: a biography** (1963). There is a well-written biography of Mary Tudor by H. F. M. Prescott (rev., 1953) and of Mary Stuart by A. Fraser, *Mary Queen of Scots* (1969). C. Read's books focusing on Elizabeth's ministers, *Mr. Secretary Walsingham* (3 vols., 1925), *Mr. Secretary Cecil* (1955), and *Lord Burghley and Queen Elizabeth* (1960), are masterful accounts of the determination and execution of English policy; the latter volume may be compared with the less detailed B. W. Beckingsale, *Burghley: Tudor statesman, 1520–1598* (1967).

On the naval and imperial side three works by J. A. Williamson may be recommended: *The age of Drake* (1938, 1946), *The ocean in English history* (1941), and *Sir Francis Drake* (1951). D. Quinn has written *Raleigh and the British empire** (1947), in the Teach Yourself History series. Some religious connections of English expansionism are pointed out in L. B. Wright, *Religion and empire: the alliance between piety and commerce in English expansion, 1558–1625* (1943). T. W. Rabb, *Enterprise and empire: merchant and gentry investment in the expansion of England, 1575–1630* (1967), is an important economic work and a pioneering effort to apply computer techniques to the study of early modern history.

Social and economic features of the age are treated in L. Stone, *The crisis of the aristocracy, 1558–1641* (1965; abr. ed., 1967), stressing the decline of the nobility; H. R. Trevor-Roper, *The gentry, 1540–1640* (1953); and J. H. Hexter, *Reappraisals in history: new views on history and society in early modern Europe** (1961). Older studies include R. H. Tawney, *Agrarian problem in the sixteenth century** (1912); L. B. Wright, *Middle class culture in Elizabethan England* (1935); and the numerous volumes of Trevelyan. On religious subjects one may turn to P. Collinson, *The Elizabethan Puritan movement* (1967), and P. McGrath, *Papists and Puritans under Elizabeth I* (1968).

The religious and dynastic turmoil in sixteenth-century France is discussed in the volume by Batiffol cited earlier and in the following works: F. C. Palm, *Calvinism and the religious wars* (1932), a Berkshire study, and his fuller study, *Politics and religion in sixteenth century France* (1927); R. M. Kingdon, *Geneva and the coming of the wars of religion in France* (1956); J. W.

Bibliography   Thompson, *Wars of religion in France, 1559–1576* (1909, 1914); A. J. Grant's able little study *The Huguenots* (1934); P. Van Dyke, *Catherine de Medicis* (2 vols., 1922); J. E. Neale, *The age of Catherine de Medici** (1943); R. Roeder, *Catherine de Medici and the lost revolution** (1937); and J. Héritier, *Catherine de Medici* (1941, trans. 1963). S. L. England describes an important episode in *The massacre of Saint Bartholomew* (1938); and there are biographies of Henry of Navarre by Q. Hurst (1938) and H. Pearson (1964). Governmental and constitutional developments are explored in W. F. Church, *Constitutional thought in sixteenth century France* (1941), and in J. R. Major, *Representative institutions in Renaissance France, 1421–1559* (1960). D. Bitton, *The French nobility in crisis, 1560–1640* (1969), describes arguments for and against nobility two centuries before the French Revolution.

The revival of France is described in L. Batiffol, *Marie de Médicis and the French court in the seventeenth century* (1908); in R. Kierstead, *Pomponne de Bellièvre: a study of the king's men in the age of Henry IV* (1968); and in D. Buissert, *Sully and the growth of centralized government in France, 1598–1610* (1968). On Richelieu one may turn to A. Bailly, *The cardinal-dictator: a portrait of Richelieu* (1936), a superpatriotic account which rejoices in Richelieu as a successful Machiavellian; C. V. Wedgwood's better-balanced *Richelieu and the French Monarchy** (Teach Yourself History series, 1949); and an older, still valuable account, C. J. Burckhardt, *Richelieu: his rise to power** (1936, trans. 1940, reissued 1964). Two important specialized studies are O. Ranum, *Richelieu and the councillors of Louis XIII* (1963), and, by a Russian scholar, A. D. Lublinskaya, *French absolutism: the crucial phase, 1620–1629* (trans. 1968).

The Thirty Years' War   Two vivid and authoritative accounts are C. V. Wedgwood, *The Thirty Years' War** (1938), and S. H. Steinberg, *The Thirty Years' War** (1966), although the older study of S. R. Gardiner (1897) may still be profitably read. See also F. Watson, *Wallenstein; soldier under Saturn* (1938); N. Ahnlund, *Gustav Adolf the Great* (1932, 1940); and A. T. Anderson, *Sweden in the Baltic* (1947). Detailed treatment of all aspects of Swedish history is to be found in the books of M. Roberts, *The early Vasas* (1968), *Gustavus Adolphus* (2 vols., 1953–1958), and *Essays in Swedish history* (1967); he has also edited the relevant documentary material in *Sweden as a great power, 1611–1697* (1968). The story of the conversion to Catholicism of Gustavus Adolphus's daughter and her abdication is well told in G. Masson, *Queen Christina* (1968), and in S. Svolpe, *Christina of Sweden*, edited by A. Randall (1966), a condensation of the untranslated larger work by the Swedish historian.

Problems and Readings*   The following will be found useful: D. L. Jensen (ed.), *The expansion of Europe: motives, methods, and meanings* (1967); J. H. Parry (ed.), *The European reconnaissance: selections and documents* (1968); W. E. Minchitan (ed.), *Mercantilism: system or expediency?* (1969); J. M. Levine (ed.), *Elizabeth I* (Great Lives Observed, 1969); J. C. Rule and J. J. TePaske (eds.), *The character of Philip II: the problem of moral judgments in history* (1963); J. J. TePaske (ed.), *Three American empires* (1967); J. F. Bannon (ed.), *Indian labor in the Spanish Indies* (1966); J. H. Salmon (ed.), *The French wars of religion* (1967); and T. K. Rabb (ed.), *The Thirty Years' War: problems of motive, extent and effect* (1964). Literary and historical subjects are treated in the Folger Booklets on Tudor and Stuart Civilization, published by the Folger Shakespeare Library, Washington, D.C. A bibliographical essay relevant to this and succeeding chapters is C. F. Mullett, *Men and movements in Europe since 1500* (AHA Service Center series, 1964).

Among informative syntheses of these years there are D. Ogg, *Europe in the seventeenth century**
(1925, 1961); G. N. Clark, *The seventeenth century** (1929, 1961); M. Beloff, *The age of absolutism,
1660–1815** (1954), in the Home University Library; R. N. Hatton, *Europe in the age of Louis XIV**
(1969); and M. Ashley, *The golden century: Europe, 1598–1715* (1969). Other useful introductions
are J. Stoye, *Europe unfolding, 1648–1689** (1969), in the Plumb series; C. J. Friedrich and C.
Blitzer, *The age of power, 1610–1713** (1957); and J. B. Wolf, *Toward a European balance of power,
1620–1715** (1970). Three volumes in the Langer series provide excellent coverage for the
period: C. J. Friedrich, *The age of the baroque, 1610–1660,** already cited; F. L. Nussbaum, *The
triumph of science and reason, 1660–85** (1953); and J. B. Wolf, *The emergence of the great powers,
1685–1715** (1951). W. F. Reddaway's *History of Europe, 1610–1715* (1948) is also recommended.

F. L. Carsten (ed.), *The ascendancy of France, 1648–1688* (1961), and J. S. Bromley (ed.), *The
rise of Great Britain and Russia, 1688–1725* (1970), vols. V and VI of the New Cambridge Modern
History, provide authoritative treatment of many topics. Two other works of general
character which bear on this period are A. T. Mahan, *The influence of sea power on history,
1660–1783* (1890, 1906), and E. Barker, *The development of public services in western Europe,
1660–1930* (1944).

The second part of P. Geyl, *The Netherlands in the seventeenth century, 1609–1715*, already cited,
covers the years from 1648 to 1715; for seventeenth-century Netherlands' history one may
turn also to the relevant portions of G. J. Renier, *The Dutch nation* (1944), and to C. Wilson,
*The Dutch Republic and the civilization of the seventeenth century** (1968), an attractive, brief introduction. Dutch economic influence is ably explored in V. Barbour, *Capitalism in Amsterdam
in the seventeenth century** (1950). On William of Orange the best study is by S. B. Baxter,
William III and the defense of European liberty, 1650–1702 (1966). N. A. Robb, *William of Orange:
a personal portrait* (2 vols., 1963–1966), is stronger on biographical than on political details; and
D. Ogg, *William III** (1956), is a brief sketch.

On Dutch overseas exploration and colonization the most illuminating introduction is C.
R. Boxer, *The Dutch seaborne empire, 1600–1800* (1965), in the Plumb History of Human Society
series. See also A. Hyma, *The Dutch in the Far East: a history of the Dutch commercial and colonial
empire* (1942); B. H. Velkke, *Nusantara: a history of the East Indian archipelago* (1943); and J. J. van
Klaveren, *The Dutch colonial system* (1953). The imperial rivalry of England and Holland in
Malaya and India is outlined in S. A. Khan, *The East India trade in the seventeenth century* (1923);
and phases of Dutch-French relations are examined in G. N. Clark, *The Dutch alliance and the
war against French trade, 1689–1697* (1923), and in H. H. Rowen, *The ambassador prepares for
war: the Dutch embassy of Arnauld de Pomponne, 1669–1671* (1957).

[See also the books on England cited in Chapter III.] An excellent introduction is J. P. Kenyon,
*The Stuarts** (1958), and one of the most interesting general books on this period is still G. M.
Trevelyan, *England under the Stuarts** (1904, 1947). Other general histories of high quality are
G. Davies, *The early Stuarts, 1603–60* (1937), G. N. Clark, *The later Stuarts, 1660–1714* (1934),
both being volumes in the Oxford History of England; C. Hill, *The century of revolution,
1603–1714** (1962); and M. P. Ashley, *England in the seventeenth century** (Pelican History of
England, 1950, 1961). Ashley also has prepared a survey of seventeenth-century social history
with many contemporary illustrations in *Life in Stuart England* (1964). For economic
developments one may turn to C. Wilson, *England's apprenticeship, 1603–1763* (1965), while the

Bibliography   European setting is presented in J. R. Jones, *Britain and Europe in the seventeenth century** (1966). Constitutional questions are explored in detail in J. R. Tanner, *English constitutional conflicts of the seventeenth century, 1603–1689* (1928, 1948); and religious questions are treated in R. G. Usher, *The reconstruction of the English church* (2 vols., 1910), and in W. K. Jordan, *The development of religious toleration in England* (4 vols., 1932–1940). Three monographs, F. C. Dietz, *English public finance, 1558–1641* (1932), showing the financial dilemma faced by the crown; G. N. Clark, *The wealth of England from 1496 to 1760* (1947); and L. A. Harper, *The English Navigation Laws: a 17th century experiment in social engineering* (1939), should also be examined. The books by L. Stone and by H. R. Trevor-Roper have already been cited. The English background to settlement in America is ably sketched in W. Notestein, *The English people on the eve of colonization, 1603–1630** (1954), and in C. W. Bridenbaugh, *Vexed and troubled Englishmen, 1590–1642* (1968).

On the Great Rebellion and subsequent developments L. von Ranke and S. R. Gardiner's older histories of seventeenth-century England are justly regarded as classics, and from them the reader can still profit. But some of the most vivid and perceptive writing on these events has come in recent years from C. V. Wedgwood, a strong advocate of the theory that analysis (the "why") ought to flow from detailed, accurate, and lively narrative (the "how"); among her works are *The King's peace, 1637–1641** (1955), *The King's war, 1641–1647* (1959), *A coffin for King Charles: the trial and execution of Charles I* (1964), *Strafford, 1593–1641* (1935, 1949), *Velvet studies* (1946), and *Oliver Cromwell** (1939, 1947).

C. Firth, *Oliver Cromwell and the rule of the Puritans in England** (1900, 1925), is still the best biographical account, but there are other valuable studies by S. R. Gardiner, J. Morley, J. Buchan, and M. Ashley.* C. D. Bowen has sketched a vivid portrait in *The lion and the throne: the life and times of Sir Edward Coke, 1552–1634* (1957). Two important studies are H. R. Trevor-Roper's unsympathetic *Archbishop Laud, 1573–1645* (1940) and J. H. Hexter, *The reign of King Pym* (1941). D. Willson has written a biography of the first Stuart, *King James VI and I** (1956), E. C. Wingfield-Stratford, a biography of his successor, *Charles I* (3 vols., 1949–1950), as has C. Hibbert (1969). B. H. Wormald provides an important study in *Clarendon: politics, history, and religion, 1640–1660* (1951). B. Willey, *The seventeenth century background; studies in the thought of the age in relation to poetry and religion* (1934, 1949); D. M. Wolfe, *Milton in the Puritan revolution* (1941); and F. E. Hutchinson, *Milton and the English mind** (Teach Yourself History series, 1946), show something of the effect of the political turmoil upon the English imagination.

Much of the interest in Stuart and Commonwealth England is directed to the emergence during that period of some recognizably modern political and social problems. The provocative books by C. Hill are especially worth examining: *Puritanism and revolution** (1958), *The century of revolution, 1603–1714** (1962), cited earlier, *Society and Puritanism in pre-revolutionary England** (1964), and *Intellectual origins of the English Revolution* (1966). They may be compared with the views in the symposium edited by E. W. Ives, *The English Revolution, 1600–1660* (1968). Other interesting books include M. Walzer, *The revolution of the saints: a study in the origins of radical politics** (1965), seeking a model in Puritanism for latter-day radicalism; P. G. Rogers, *The Fifth Monarchy men* (1966); G. P. Gooch, *English democratic ideas in the seventeenth century** (1898; ed. H. J. Laski, 1927); M. James, *Social policy and problems during the Puritan revolution* (1930); W. Schenk, *The concern for social justice in the Puritan revolution* (1948), stressing religious rather than economic compulsions as basic in Puritan thought; W. Haller, *The rise of Puritanism** (1938); E. Bernstein, *Cromwell and communism: socialism and democracy in the Great English Revolution* (trans. 1930); T. C. Pease, *The Leveller movement* (1916); M. Ashley, *John Wildman, plotter and postmaster: a study of the English republican movement in the seventeenth century* (1947); and C. Firth, *Cromwell's army* (1905). A. S. P. Woodhouse (ed.), *Puritanism and liberty* (1938), includes important material on the seventeenth-century army debates on democracy.

1054   For additional titles a valuable bibliographical essay is E. C. Furber, *Changing views on British history* (1966). On the Irish question a useful introduction is provided in J. C. Beckett, *The making of modern Ireland* (1966).

The background to the Restoration is ably traced in G. Davies, *The restoration of Charles II, 1658–1660* (1955). The best treatment of the Restoration period itself is D. Ogg, *England in the reign of Charles II* (2 vols., 1934), and *England in the reigns of James II and William III* (1955). Written from a Tory viewpoint, A. Bryant, *King Charles II* (1932, 1949), makes the best possible case for Charles' relations with Louis XIV. F. C. Turner, *James II* (1948), is fair and factual. Various special topics are covered in A. A. Seaton, *The theory of toleration under the later Stuarts* (1911); J. Pollock, *The Popish plot* (1903, 1945); D. Mathew, *The social structure in Caroline England* (1948); H. G. Plum, *Restoration Puritanism* (1943); A. Bryant, *Samuel Pepys* (3 vols., 1933–1939); and J. H. Wilson, *Court wits of the Restoration* (1948).

G. M. Trevelyan's brilliant little book *The English Revolution 1688–1689** (1939, 1946) argues that the immediate result of the revolution was to strengthen conservatism for the eighteenth century but that the long-run consequences made the revolution a turning point in history; it may be compared with L. Pinkham, *William III and the respectable revolution* (1954), and M. Ashley, *The Glorious Revolution of 1688* (1967). S. B. Baxter's valuable study of William III has been cited earlier. Trevelyan's *England under Queen Anne* (3 vols., 1930–1934) vividly portrays the succeeding age. For foreign and military affairs, it can be supplemented by W. S. Churchill, *Marlborough, his life and times* (4 vols., 1933–1938). J. Clapham, *The Bank of England* (2 vols., 1944), covers the period 1694–1944.

Many of the general accounts cited at the beginning of this chapter focus on the French predominance in this age. In addition, the following books explore various aspects of Louis XIV and his reign: J. B. Wolf, *Louis XIV** (1968), the most comprehensive biography; D. Ogg, *Louis XIV* (1933), somewhat hostile; V. Buranelli, *Louis XIV** (Europe Since 1500 series, 1966), a brief, sympathetic account; and M. Ashley, *Louis XIV and the greatness of France** (Teach Yourself History series, 1948). P. Goubert, *Louis XIV and twenty million Frenchmen** (1970), is not a biography but a study of French society and the ordinary people. Some special studies are P. R. Doolin, *The Fronde* (1935); J. E. King, *Science and rationalism in the government of Louis XIV, 1661–1683* (1949); E. E. Reynolds, *Bossuet* (1963); G. H. Dodge, *The political theory of the Huguenot dispersion* (1947); and L. Rothkrug, *Opposition to Louis XIV: the political and social origins of the Enlightenment* (1965). The older studies of J. B. Perkins (1886, 1897) and H. M. Baird (1895) have now been superseded. Other important interpretive volumes are A. Guérard, *The life and death of an ideal: France in the classical age** (1928); W. H. Lewis, *The splendid century** (1953); G. Treasure, *Seventeenth-century France** (1966); V. L. Tapié, *The age of grandeur* (rev., 1966); and O. Ranum, *Paris in the age of absolutism** (1969).

On the development of the French economy and empire, see C. W. Cole, *Colbert and a century of French mercantilism* (2 vols., 1939), also his earlier volume and a sequel which carries the story to 1700; E. C. Lodge, *Sully, Colbert, and Turgot: a chapter in French economic history* (1931); P. Bamford, *Forests and French sea-power, 1660–1789* (1956); and W. Scoville, *The persecution of the Huguenots and French economic development, 1680–1720* (1960). On the empire see H. I. Priestley, *France overseas through the old regime: a study of European expansion* (1939); S. L. Mims, *Colbert's West Indian policy* (1912); and W. J. Eccles, *Canada under Louis XIV, 1663–1701* (1964).

For the debate over events in England see P. A. M. Taylor (ed.), *The origins of the English Civil War: conspiracy, crusade, or class conflict?* (1960); L. Stone (ed.), *Social change and revolution in England, 1540–1640* (1965); R. E. Boyer (ed.), *Oliver Cromwell and the Puritan revolution: failure of a*

Bibliography man or a faith? (1966); M. Ashley, *Cromwell* (Great Lives Observed series, 1969); and G. M. Straka (ed), *The Revolution of 1688: Whig triumph or palace revolution?* (1963). In the Anvil series there is R. L. Schuyler and C. C. Weston, *Cardinal documents in British history* (1961). For France one may turn to W. F. Church (ed.), *The impact of absolutism in France: national experience under Richelieu, Mazarin, and Louis XIV* (1969); W. F. Church (ed.), *The greatness of Louis XIV: myth or reality?* (1959); and H. G. Judge (ed.), *Louis XIV* (1965).

V: The Transformation of Eastern Europe, 1648–1740

The following are helpful general introductions to the complexities of eastern and east central Europe: F. Dvornik, *The making of central and eastern Europe* (1949), and *Slavs in European history and civilization* (1962); R. Portal, *The Slavs: a cultural and historical survey of the Slavonic people* (1965, trans. 1970); O. Halecki, *Borderlands of Western civilization: a history of east central Europe* (1952); S. H. Cross, *Slavic civilization through the ages* (1948); and W. H. McNeill, *Europe's steppe frontier, 1500–1800* (1964). L. S. Stavrianos, *The Balkans since 1453* (1958), is invaluable and may be supplemented by the background portions of R. L. Wolff, *The Balkans in our time** (1956), and T. Stoianovich, *A study in Balkan civilization** (1967). J. S. Bromley (ed.), *The rise of Great Britain and Russia, 1688–1725* (1969), vol. VI of the New Cambridge Modern History, has already been cited. Two bibliographical essays in the AHA Service Center series are useful: R. V. Burks, *Some elements of East European history* (1961), and J. Blum, *The European peasantry from the fifteenth to the nineteenth centuries* (1960).

The Ottoman Empire

There is no comprehensive volume on the Ottoman Empire. The best concise coverage of the empire in the years between 1453 and 1918 may be found in Stavrianos, *The Balkans since 1453*, cited above. A careful account of the Turkish role in European affairs is available in D. M. Vaughan, *Europe and the Turk: a pattern of alliances, 1350–1700* (1954), and in P. Coles, *The Ottoman impact on Europe, 1350–1699** (1968), in the Barraclough series. An interesting special study is R. Schwoebel, *The shadow of the crescent: the Renaissance image of the Turk, 1453–1517* (1967). The older volumes by A. Sorel (1898) and J. A. R. Marriott (1917) on the Eastern question are now outdated. A popular but sound account of the empire is F. W. Fernau, *Moslems on the march* (trans. 1954). On the earlier period, R. O. Merriman, *Suleiman the Magnificent, 1520–1566* (1944), is the best general introduction, although it should be supplemented by A. H. Lybyer, *Government of the Ottoman Empire in the time of Suleiman the Magnificent* (1913), and by N. Sousa [Susa], *The capitulatory regime of Turkey* (1955), which explains the special status of various Christian and other minorities in the Turkish empire. B. H. Sumner, *Peter the Great and the Ottoman Empire* (1949), describes some of the early relations of Turkey with Russia. C. E. Bosworth, *The Islamic dynasties: a chronological and genealogical handbook* (1967), is a useful reference tool.

Austria and the Habsburgs to 1740

The most helpful study now available is A. Wandruszka, *The house of Habsburg* (1956, trans. 1964). There are older general narrative histories of Austria-Hungary by H. W. Steed (1914) and L. P. Léger (1889), and of Hungary by H. Marczali (1910) and C. A. Macartney (1934). P. Frischauer, *The imperial crown: the rise and fall of the Holy Roman and the Austrian empires* (1939), is an interesting work, primarily biographical in nature, on the house of Habsburg to the death of Leopold II in 1792. For Eugene of Savoy one may turn to Frischauer's lively but not entirely adequate biography *Prince Eugene, 1663–1736* (1934) or, preferably, to N. Henderson, *Eugene of Savoy* (1964); the detailed multivolumed study in German by M. Braubach in progress is not available in translation (5 vols., 1963–1965). Two scholarly well-written studies of' the Turkish siege of 1683, informative on the Habsburgs and on the Ottoman Empire, are J. Stoye,

The siege of Vienna (1964), and T. M. Barker, *Double eagle and crescent: Vienna's second Turkish siege and its historical setting* (1967).

The most convenient introductions are F. L. Carsten, *The origins of Prussia* (1954); S. B. Fay and K. Epstein, *The rise of Brandenburg-Prussia to 1786** (1937, rev., 1964), a Berkshire study; and J. A. R. Marriott and C. G. Robertson, *The evolution of Prussia* (1915, 1946). C. T. Atkinson, *Germany 1715–1815* (1908), is an older account of military and political history. H. Holborn in his *History of modern Germany,* vol. II, *1648–1840* (1964), covers the fluid situation in the Holy Roman Empire after the Thirty Years' War, as do the relevant portions of V. Valentin, *The German people: their history and civilization from the Holy Roman Empire to the Third Reich* (1946), and R. Flenley, *Modern German history* (rev., 1964).

The economic aspects of the Prussian state-building process are analyzed in G. F. von Schmoller, *The mercantile system and its historical significance* (1884, 1896), which may be supplemented by A. Small, *The cameralists* (1909). On the earlier Hohenzollerns see C. E. Maurice, *The life of Frederick William: the Great Elector of Brandenburg* (1926); F. Schevill, *The great elector* (1947); R. Ergang, *The Potsdam Führer: Frederick William I, father of Prussian militarism* (1941); and R. A. Derwart, *The administrative reforms of Frederick William I of Prussia* (1953). An invaluable study going well beyond the scope of this chapter is G. A. Craig, *The politics of the Prussian army, 1640–1945** (1956, 1964); it may be supplemented by K. Demeter, *The German officer corps in society and state, 1650–1945* (1930, rev., 1962, trans. 1965). Important also, especially for the sociological dimension it adds, is H. Rosenberg, *Bureaucracy, aristocracy, and autocracy: the Prussian experience, 1660–1815* (1960).

There are many excellent narrative accounts of Russian history, most of which give good coverage of the early years; among those written or revised in recent years are volumes by B. H. Sumner, B. Pares, M. T. Florinsky, J. D. Clarkson, S. Harcave, A. G. Mazour, N. V. Riasanovsky, G. Vernadsky, W. B. Walsh, and M. C. Wren. A fascinating, though impressionistic, cultural history is J. H. Billington, *The icon and the axe: an interpretive history of Russian culture* (1966). M. T. Florinsky, *Russia: a history and an interpretation* (2 vols., 1953), is perhaps the best general account for the period to 1917. G. Vernadsky, *A history of Russia* (5 vols. to date, 1943–1969), covers early Russian history in great detail to 1682, while in *The origins of Russia* (1959) he analyzes the background of the Russian people and the formation of the Russian state. F. Nowak, *Medieval Slavdom and the rise of Russia** (1930), is a useful introduction in the Berkshire series. G. P. Fedotov, *The Russian religious mind* (1946), sketches the early interplay of pre-Christian paganism, Byzantinism, and Russian political forms. There are vivid popular narratives by H. Lamb, *The march of Muscovy: Ivan the Terrible and the growth of the Russian empire, 1400–1648* (1948), and *The city and the Tsar: Peter the Great and the move to the West, 1648–1762* (1948). On the early rulers there are available J. Fennell, *Ivan the Great of Moscow* (1961); H. von Eckhardt, *Ivan the Terrible* (1949); and I. Grey, *Ivan III and the unification of Russia* (1965), and the same author's *Ivan the Terrible* (1964). On Peter and his age one may read a masterful brief account by B. H. Sumner, *Peter the Great and the emergence of Russia** (1950), in the Teach Yourself History series; a readable longer biography, I. Grey, *Peter the Great* (1962); V. Kliuchevsky, *Peter the Great** (trans. 1958); and L. J. Oliva, *Russia in the era of Peter the Great** (1969). Russian expansion is discussed in R. J. Kerner, *The urge to the sea: the course of Russian history* (1942), which emphasizes the significance of trade routes, and in F. A. Golder, *Russian expansion on the Pacific, 1641–1850* (1914). An important subject is well covered in J. Blum, *Land and peasant in Russia from the ninth to the nineteenth century** (1961), and in R. E. F. Smith, *The origins of farming in Russia* (1960).

On Russian relations with Sweden R. N. Bain's older studies are inadequate, but there are

Bibliography   few other books to recommend except general histories of the two countries. Voltaire's *History of Charles XII* (1731) still merits reading, but an outstanding modern biography of the Swedish monarch is R. M. Hatton, *Charles XII of Sweden* (1969).

Poland   The best balanced treatment of Poland in these years is in the appropriate chapters of W. F. Reddaway (ed.), *The Cambridge history of Poland* (2 vols., 1941–1950); they may be supplemented by R. Dyboski, *Poland in world civilization* (1950), and O. Halecki, *A history of Poland* (rev., 1961). The background chapters of F. Heymann, *Poland and Czechoslovakia** (1966), are useful. On the eighteenth-century partitions one may consult D. B. Horn, *British public opinion and the first partition of Poland* (1945); and H. H. Kaplan, *The first partition of Poland* (1962); and R. H. Lord, *The second partition of Poland* (1915). Three biographies are also instructive: O. Laskowski, *Jan III Sobieski, King of Poland, 1629–1696* (1941); R. N. Bain, *The last king of Poland and his contemporaries* (1909), on Stanislaus II; and M. M. Gardner, *Kosciuszko* (1920). On an important aspect of Polish history, S. Konovalov, *Russian-Polish relations: an historical survey* (1945), is a brief, well-organized account.

Problems and Readings*   Various volumes of readings in Russian history and Russian civilization from earliest times to the present are available, among them those edited by W. B. Walsh (3 vols., 4th ed., 1963) and T. Riha (3 vols., rev., 1969). In the Heath Problems series there is a pamphlet edited by M. Raeff, *Peter the Great: reformer or revolutionary?* (1964), and L. J. Oliva has edited a useful anthology of articles, *Russia and the West from Peter to Khrushchev* (1965).

VI: The Struggle for Wealth and Empire

For the years covered in this chapter, 1713–1763, there are available in the Langer series: P. Roberts, *The quest for security, 1715–1740** (1947), not entirely satisfactory in its coverage and interpretation, and a masterful volume by W. L. Dorn, *Competition for empire, 1740–1763** (1940), particularly good on the relation of the European state system to the overseas expansion and rivalry of the time. Other helpful syntheses include M. S. Anderson, *Europe in the eighteenth century, 1713–1783** (1961), in the Hay series; R. J. Whyte, *Europe in the eighteenth century** (1965); and D. Ogg, *Europe of the ancien régime, 1715–1783** (1965), in the Plumb series. J. O. Lindsay (ed.), *The old regime, 1713–1763* (1957), vol. VII in the New Cambridge Modern History, has informative chapters on many domestic and international developments; and J. S. Bromley and A. Goodwin have prepared a bibliography for these years, *A select list of works on Europe and Europe overseas, 1715–1815* (1956).

The Colonial Empires   [Several of the books on European overseas expansion listed for Chapter IV also discuss the eighteenth century.] To these must be added G. Williams, *The expansion of Europe in the eighteenth century: overseas rivalry, discovery, and exploitation* (1960); the relevant chapters of D. K. Fieldhouse, *The colonial empires: a comparative survey from the eighteenth century* (1966); the comprehensive C. E. Carrington, *The British overseas: exploits of a nation of shopkeepers* (1950, rev., 1968); and K. M. Pannikar, *Asia and Western dominance** (1959). The eighteenth-century impact on India is explored in H. Furber, *John Company at work: a study of European expansion in India in the late eighteenth century* (1948). In addition, the following works on India are recommended for the general reader, though not confined to the eighteenth century: S. Wolpert, *India** (1965), one of the best brief introductions; M. Naidis, *India: a short introductory history* (1960); W. N. Brown, *The United States and India and Pakistan* (rev., 1963), with some perceptive pages on the historical background. In addition there are E. Thompson and G. T.

Garratt, *Rise and fulfillment of British rule in India* (1934); P. Woodruff [Mason], *The men who ruled*
*India** (2 vols., 1954–1957); and M. Andrewes, *British India* (1964). Among biographical
studies there are A. M. Davies, *Warren Hastings* (1935), and *Clive of Plassey* (1939); P. Moon,
*Warren Hastings and British India** (1947), in the Teach Yourself History series; K. Feiling,
Warren Hastings (1945); P. J. Marshall, *The impeachment of Warren Hastings* (1965); and H. H.
Dodwell, *Dupleix and Clive, the beginning of empire* (1920). More specialized and advanced
studies are suggested in H. H. Dodwell (ed.), *The Cambridge shorter history of India* (1943), and in
V. A. Smith, *The Oxford history of India* (rev. by P. Spear and others, 1958). An account of these
years by Indian scholars is to be found in R. C. Majumdar (ed.), *The struggle for empire* (1957), the
fifth volume in a longer work on Indian history. J. Nehru, *The discovery of India** (1946), by the
Indian statesman, is recommended as one of the most stimulating introductions to all Indian
history. For other books on early and later Indian history one may consult R. I. Crane's
bibliographical essay, *The history of India: its study and interpretation** (AHA Service Center
pamphlets, 1958).

The numerous volumes by Francis Parkman on the French regime in Canada are classics
of nineteenth-century historiography; the standard twentieth-century account is G. M.
Wrong, *The rise and fall of New France* (2 vols., 1928), and his various other writings. The works
of Priestley and Cole, cited for Chapter IV, should also be consulted on French policy before
and after Colbert. Also recommended are M. Bishop, *Champlain: life of fortitude* (1949); W. J.
Eccles, *Frontenac: the courtier governor** (1959, 1965); two studies by N. M. Crouse, *French pioneers
in the West Indies, 1624–1664* (1940), and *The French struggle for the West Indies 1665–1713* (1944); R.
Pares, *War and trade in the West Indies* (1936), on the war of 1739; J. O. McLachlan, *Trade and
peace with old Spain, 1667–1750: a study of the influence of commerce on eighteenth century diplomacy*
(1940); and C. L. Lokke, *France and the colonial question, 1763–1801* (1932).

A good geographically focused introduction is H. J. Mackinder, *Britain and the British seas* (1902,
1914). W. B. Willcox, *Star of empire: a study of Britain as a world power, 1485–1945* (1950), fills in
the narrative and also analyzes the main forces involved. Older studies by G. L. Beer, C. M.
Andrews, and H. L. Osgood of the old colonial system and of mercantilism in operation are
still valuable. For the mid-eighteenth century, from 1748 to 1776, there is L. H. Gipson's
monumental work now completed in thirteen volumes, *The British Empire before the American
Revolution* (1936–1967); vol. XIII contains in part II a summary of the entire work, and a
fourteenth volume (1969) serves as a bibliographical guide to the literature and sources.
Another important large-scale treatment is The Cambridge History of the British Empire (9
vols., 1929–1959). A wealth of economic data is to be found in L. C. A. Knowles and C. M.
Knowles, *The economic development of the British overseas empire* (3 vols., 1924–1936); and J. R.
Seeley, *The expansion of England* (1883, 1895), is a classic essay on its theme. C. G. Robertson,
*Chatham and the British Empire** (1948), and J. A. Williamson, *Cook and the opening of the Pacific**
(1948), are two lively studies in the Teach Yourself History series. J. R. Muir, *The life and
achievements of Captain James Cook* (1939), may also be recommended. M. G. Lawson, *Fur: a
study in English mercantilism, 1700–1775* (1943); R. G. Albion, *Forests and sea power: the timber
problem of the Royal Navy, 1652–1862* (1926); C. Wilson, *Anglo-Dutch commerce and finance in the
eighteenth century* (1941, 1966); and J. S. Corbett, *England in the Seven Years' War* (2 vols., 1907), illustrate other aspects, as does E. Williams, *Capitalism and slavery** (1944).

[Books on eighteenth-century France are listed below in Chapter VIII.] Good introductions to
British politics and the origins of political parties after 1688 include G. Holmes, *British politics
in the age of Anne* (1967); C. H. Robertson, *England under the Hanoverians* (rev., 1948); J. H. Plumb,
*England in the eighteenth century** (Pelican History of England, 1953); the same author's *The*

first four Georges* (1956); B. Williams, *The Whig supremacy, 1714–1760* (Oxford History of England, 1939); the early chapters of K. B. Smellie, *Great Britain since 1688* (University of Michigan series, 1962), and similarly of R. K. Webb, *Modern England: from the eighteenth century to the present** (1968). Other recommended books on personalities and events are J. H. Plumb, *Sir Robert Walpole* (2 vols., 1956, 1961), with a third volume projected; J. Morley, *Walpole* (1889); B. Williams, *The life of William Pitt, Earl of Chatham* (2 vols., 1913); O. A. Sherrard, *Lord Chatham* (3 vols., 1952–1955); the briefer J. H. Plumb, *Chatham* (1953); and E. Eyck, *Pitt versus Fox: father and son, 1735–1806* (trans. 1950). Two other works of interest are F. S. Oliver, *The endless adventure* (3 vols., 1930–1935), and L. Kronenberger, *Kings and desperate men: life in eighteenth century England** (1942).

For a more institutional approach one may turn to L. B. Namier's seminal work *The structure of politics at the accession of George III* (2 vols., 1920); E. Porritt, *The unreformed House of Commons* (2 vols., 1903); A. S. Turberville, *The House of Lords in the eighteenth century* (1927); W. T. Laprade, *Public opinion and politics in eighteenth century England* (1936); A. S. Foord, *His majesty's opposition, 1714–1830* (1964); and a provocative book by J. H. Plumb, *The growth of political stability in England, 1675–1725* (1967). The first volumes have appeared from an enormous collective effort to reconstruct in minute biographical detail the composition of the modern English parliaments, a project inspired and inaugurated by L. B. Namier during his lifetime: L. B. Namier and J. Brooke, *The history of Parliament: The House of Commons, 1754–1790* (3 vols., 1964, others to follow). A compact statistical overview is G. Judd, *Members of Parliament, 1734–1832* (1955).

On social and economic conditions the following monographs are instructive: E. B. Chancellor, *The eighteenth century in London: an account of its social life and arts* (1920), with excellent contemporary illustrations; D. George's books: *London life in the eighteenth century* (1925), *Eighteenth-century England* (1962), and *Dr. Johnson's London* (1967); E. W. Gilboy, *Wages in the eighteenth century* (1934); D. Marshall, *The English poor in the eighteenth century* (1926), on the administrative difficulties of dealing with poverty; and B. Rodgers, *Cloak of charity: studies in eighteenth century philanthropy* (1949). Other relevant books are listed in Chapter XI in connection with the industrial revolution. On economic and financial subjects a far-reaching book is P. G. M. Dickson, *The financial revolution in England: a study in the development of public credit, 1688–1756* (1967); and the celebrated speculative venture of the age is graphically described in J. Carswell, *The South Sea bubble* (1960).

Religious matters are covered in N. Sykes, *Church and state in England in the eighteenth century* (1934); M. L. Edwards, *John Wesley and the eighteenth century* (1933), primarily concerned with Wesley's social and political influence; and H. Townsend, *The claims of the free churches* (1949), a detailed account of how the "left-wing Puritanism" of earlier centuries affected religious thought and action.

In addition to various titles listed at the beginning of this chapter and of Chapter V, and in Chapter VIII for enlightened despotism, the following books deal with mid-eighteenth-century European international relations: A. Sorel, *Europe under the old regime** (trans. 1947), the introduction to his study of Europe and the French Revolution (8 vols., 1895 ff.), excellent on the European balance of power; C. Petrie, *Diplomatic history, 1713–1933* (1946), opinionated but generally reliable; R. Lodge, *Great Britain and Prussia in the eighteenth century* (1923), and *Studies in eighteenth century diplomacy, 1740–1748* (1930); J. F. Chance, *The alliance of Hanover, a study of British foreign policy in the last years of George I* (1923); and H. W. V. Temperley, *Frederick the Great and Kaiser Joseph: an episode of war and diplomacy in the eighteenth century* (1915).

The relations of Britain and France are examined in the Berkshire study A. H. Buffinton, *The second hundred years' war, 1689–1815* (1929), and in the following specialized accounts: A. M. Wilson, *French foreign policy during the administration of Cardinal Fleury, 1726–43* (1936); H.

Richmond, *The navy in the war of 1739–1748* (3 vols., 1920); and S. Conn, *Gibraltar in British diplomacy in the eighteenth century* (1942). On the negotiations ending the war Z. E. Rashed has written *The Peace of Paris, 1763* (1952), and on a special subject M. Savelle has written *The origins of American diplomacy: the international history of Angloamerica, 1492–1763* (1967).

A number of the works cited in the introductory section of this bibliography are concerned with various aspects of the history of thought; a few of them are repeated here. The most stimulating general guides to intellectual history from medieval Christendom to the eighteenth century are J. H. Randall, *The making of the modern mind* (1926, 1940), and the same author's *The career of philosophy* (2 vols., 1962–1965). A useful account focusing on the leading personalities and intellectual climate of each age is J. Bronowski and B. Mazlish, *The Western intellectual tradition from Leonardo to Hegel* (1960). The introductory comments and selections in F. L. Baumer's anthology *Main currents of Western thought* (rev., 1964) and C. Brinton's *Ideas and men* (1950, 1963) are also of considerable value. To the works previously cited may be added W. E. H. Lecky, *History of the rise and influence of the spirit of rationalism in Europe* (2 vols., 1865, rev., 1872), on the declining sense of the miraculous and the secularization of politics; P. Smith, *A history of modern culture** (2 vols., 1930–1934), a useful but rather heavy review of the years 1543–1776; J. M. Robertson, *Short history of free thought, ancient and modern* (2 vols., 1906, rev., 1936), especially for the period before the eighteenth century; and F. L. Baumer, *Religion and the rise of skepticism* (1960), which traces the skeptical tradition from the seventeenth century to the present.

The fundamental reorientation of thinking about nature in early modern times has probably had far more influence on the later world than any of the specific inventions or technical advances of the period. The best introductions are A. R. Hall, *The scientific revolution, 1500–1800: the formation of the modern scientific attitude** (1954, rev., 1962); H. Butterfield, *The origins of modern science, 1300–1800** (1949); M. Boas, *The scientific Renaissance, 1450–1630* (1962); and W. P. D. Wightman, *Science and the Renaissance* (1963). The most important study of the nature and implications of the contributions in astronomy is T. S. Kuhn, *The Copernican revolution: planetary astronomy in the development of Western thought* (1956); also interesting is M. Davidson, *The stars and the mind: a study of the impact of astronomical developments on human thought* (1948).

E. A. Burtt, *The metaphysical foundations of modern philosophical science** (1925, 1948), is a searching examination of the ideas of scientists from Copernicus to Newton. Other books exploring the theoretical foundations of science include E. W. Strong, *Procedures and metaphysics* (1936); J. B. Conant, *On understanding science: an historical approach* (1947), and *Science and common sense* (1951); F. S. Marvin (ed.), *Science and civilization* (1923); S. E. Toulmin, *The philosophy of science* (1953); R. G. Collingwood, *The idea of nature* (1945); A. N. Whitehead, *Science and the modern world* (1925); C. C. Gillispie, *The edge of objectivity: an essay in the history of scientific ideas* (1960); and T. S. Kuhn, *The structure of scientific revolutions* (1962).

One may profitably consult the bibliographical essay by M. Boas, *History of Science* (AHA Service Center series, 1958). The most useful introduction is A. R. and M. B. Hall, *Brief history of science* (1961), with a more detailed account of the scientific revolution available in A. R. Hall, *From Galileo to Newton, 1630–1730* (1963). A valuable general history of science is W. C. D. Dampier, *A history of science and its relations with philosophy and religion* (1929, 1949). Other studies include C. J. Singer, *A short history of scientific ideas to 1900* (rev., 1949); A. C. Crombie,

Bibliography   *Medieval and early modern science* (2 vols., 1959); H. T. Pledge, *Science since 1500: a short history of mathematics, physics, chemistry, and biology* (1939, 1947), a good but mechanical account; and F. S. Taylor, *A short history of science and scientific thought* (1949). Two monumental studies on this field deserve special mention: G. Sarton, *Introduction to the history of science* (3 vols., 1927–1948), from classical times to the fourteenth century [with some of the author's more general ideas presented in *The life of science: essays in the history of civilization* (1948), and in *Six wings: men of science in the Renaissance* (1957)]; and L. Thorndike, *A history of magic and experimental science* (8 vols., 1923–1958), carrying the account to the seventeenth century. Two interesting compilations are F. R. Moulton and J. Schifferes (eds.), *The autobiography of science* (1945), from the sixteenth to the twentieth century, and F. S. Taylor, *The march of mind* (1939). A collaborative four-volume French history, encyclopedic in nature, is being made available in English translation: G. Taton (ed.), *A general history of the sciences;* vol. II is entitled *The beginnings of modern science from 1450 to 1899* (1966).

On the science so profoundly affected in the early modern centuries, in addition to the studies cited above, see E. Whittaker, *From Euclid to Eddington: a study of conceptions of the physical world* (1949); A. Koyré, *From the closed world to the infinite universe* (1957); P. Doig, *A concise history of astronomy* (1950); and G. Abetti, *A history of astronomy* (trans. 1952). The classic study by R. Grant, *History of physical astronomy: from the earliest ages to the middle of the nineteenth century* (1852), is still read by specialists.

A sampling of histories of other specific sciences are H. Leicester, *The historical background of chemistry* (1956), the best comprehensive study; J. R. Partington, *A short history of chemistry* (2nd ed., 1945); J. M. Stilman, *The story of early chemistry* (1924), to the middle of the eighteenth century; C. J. Singer, *A history of biology* (rev., 1950), and *The evolution of anatomy* (1925); F. D. Adams, *Birth and development of the geological sciences* (1938, 1954); C. T. Chase, *The evolution of modern physics* (1947); A. Einstein and L. Infeld, *The evolution of physics* (1938); and I. B. Cohen, *The birth of the new physics* (1960). On the history of medicine A. Castiglioni, *A history of medicine* (1927, 1949); R. H. Shryock, *The development of modern medicine* (1947); and H. E. Sigerist, *A history of medicine* (1951), are recommended. H. W. Haggard has written the interesting, popular account *Devils, drugs, and doctors* (1929), and H. Zinsser, *Rats, lice, and history* (1935).

Scientific   On the organization of scientific activity and the spread of new ideas, see the following: M. Organizations in the   Ornstein, *The role of scientific societies in the seventeenth century* (1928); H. Brown, *Scientific Seventeenth Century   organizations in seventeenth-century France, 1620–1680* (1934); H. Lyons, *The Royal Society, 1660–1940* (1944); D. Stimson, *Scientists and amateurs: a history of the Royal Society* (1948); A. E. Shipley, *The revival of science in the seventeenth century* (1906); S. Bethell, *The cultural revolution of the seventeenth century* (1951); and R. F. Jones, *Ancients and moderns: the rise of the scientific movement in seventeenth-century England** (1936, rev., 1961).

The following bear on the technological implications of the new science: A. Wolf, *A history of science, technology, and philosophy in the sixteenth and seventeenth centuries* (1935), and . . . *in the eighteenth century* (1939); G. N. Clark, *Science and social welfare in the age of Newton* (1937); and the stimulating but not always accurate L. Mumford, *Technics and civilization* (1934).

An interesting one-volume introduction to applied science and technology is R. J. Forbes, *Man the maker* (1950). On technology one may consult C. Singer and others, *A history of technology* (5 vols., 1954–1958), and the briefer T. K. Derry and T. I. Williams, *A short history of technology from the earliest times to* A.D. *1900* (1961).

Biographical Accounts   The contribution of the pioneer astronomers are described in A. Armitage, *Copernicus: the founder of modern astronomy* (1938), and *The world of Copernicus* (1947, 1951); J. A. Gade, *The life and times of Tycho Brahe* (1947); M. Caspar, *Kepler* (1948, trans. 1959); and the briefer C. Baumgardt,

Johannes Kepler: life and letters (1951). F. S. Taylor, *Galileo and the freedom of thought* (1938), is a dispassionate, carefully documented work; and the opposition that Galileo aroused is well described in G. de Santillana, *The crime of Galileo* (1955, 1959). A brief biographical study is L. Fermi and G. Bernardini, *Galileo and the scientific revolution** (1961).

Both F. H. Anderson, *The philosophy of Francis Bacon* (1948), and B. Farrington, *Francis Bacon: philosopher of industrial science* (1949), are more concerned with Bacon's ideas and impact than with the story of his life, whereas C. D. Bowen in her usual fashion has written a sound vivid biography, *Francis Bacon: the temper of man* (1963). E. S. Haldane, *Descartes, his life and times* (1905), is primarily biographical; and S. H. Mellone, *The dawn of modern thought: Descartes, Spinoza, Leibniz* (1930), explains the Cartesian system and its influence. For Pascal see M. Bishop, *Pascal: the life of genius* (1936); and for Pierre Bayle, H. Robinson, *Bayle the skeptic* (1931). The other leading seventeenth-century scientists are ably placed in their intellectual setting in L. T. More, *The life and works of the Honourable Robert Boyle* (1944); M. Boas, *Robert Boyle and seventeenth century chemistry* (1958); and A. E. Bell, *Christian Huygens and the development of science in the seventeenth century* (1947). For Newton the biography by L. T. More (1934) is most complete, but there are good brief ones by S. Brodetsky (1927), J. Sullivan (1938), and E. N. da C. Andrade* (1954); and a somewhat startling psychoanalytical interpretation by F. E. Manuel, *A portrait of Isaac Newton* (1968).

The appropriate chapters in G. Sabine, *A history of political theory*, cited earlier, and E. A. Burtt, *The English philosophers from Bacon to Mill* (1939), are the best introductions. W. Seagle, *The quest for law* (1941), treats historically the formulation of law and jurisprudence. G. P. Gooch's two works, *The history of English democratic ideas in the seventeenth century* (1898, edited by H. J. Laski, 1927) and *Political thought from Bacon to Halifax* (1914, 1923), are still basic.

Some aspects of early modern political theory are analyzed in O. von Gierke, *Natural law and the theory of society, 1500–1800* (2 vols., 1934); J. W. Gough, *The social contract: a critical study of its development* (1936); E. Barker's introduction, as editor, to the volume *Social contract: essays by Locke, Hume, and Rousseau* (1947); D. G. Ritchie, *Natural rights: a criticism of some political and ethical conceptions* (1894, 1916); and C. G. Haines, *The revival of natural law concepts* (1930), concerned especially with American ideas of natural law.

W. A. Dunning, *A history of political theories from Luther to Montesquieu* (1905), and F. J. C. Hearnshaw (ed.), *The social and political ideas of some great thinkers of the sixteenth and seventeenth centuries* (1926), and similar volumes for other periods edited by Hearnshaw, contain helpful short summaries and criticisms. On Locke one may read M. Cranston, *John Locke: a biography* (1957); M. Seliger, *The liberal politics of John Locke* (1969); J. Dunn, *The political thought of John Locke* (1969); as well as many specialized monographs. W. S. M. Knight has written *The life and works of Hugo Grotius* (1925).

One pamphlet is relevant: G. Basalla, *The rise of modern science: external or internal factors?* (1968). A useful anthology is M. B. Hall (ed.), *Nature and nature's laws: documents of the scientific revolution* (1969).

For background the eighteenth-century accounts listed at the beginning of Chapter VI should be consulted, and to them should be added A. Goodwin (ed.), *The American and French Revolutions, 1763–1793* (1965), vol. VIII of the New Cambridge Modern History; L. Gershoy, *From despotism to revolution, 1763–1789** (1944), in the Langer series, one of the most informative accounts of European civilization in the generation before 1789; and the brief L. Krieger, *Kings* *and philosophers, 1689–1789** (1970), in the Norton History of Modern Europe. Some additional general accounts are listed in this chapter and at the beginning of the next.

The Thought of
the Enlightenment

Among general studies of the European Enlightenment, the works of two French scholars remain indispensable: D. Mornet, *French thought in the eighteenth century* (1929); and P. Hazard's two books, *The European mind: the critical years 1680–1715* (1935, trans. 1953), a study of the "crisis of the European conscience," and *European thought in the eighteenth century: from Montesquieu to Lessing* (1946, trans. 1954). The most ambitious effort in recent years to interpret the thought of the era on a European-wide scale is P. Gay, *The Enlightenment: an interpretation* (2 vols., 1966–1969), vol. I, *The rise of paganism,* on the use of the classical past to support the struggle for freedom, and vol. II, *The science of freedom,* on the application of science to all areas of human activity, especially the problems of society. Gay's earlier books also merit attention: *Voltaire's politics** (1959) and *The party of humanity: essays on the French Enlightenment* (1964). In many ways these books refute the famous interpretation by Carl Becker, *The heavenly city of the eighteenth-century philosophers** (1932), who argued that Enlightenment thought, essentially utopian, represented merely a secularized version of medieval Christian views; additional criticisms of Becker are summarized in R. O. Rockwood (ed.), *Carl Becker's heavenly city revisited* (1958). Other stimulating interpretations of the Enlightenment are to be found in A. Cobban, *In search of humanity: the role of the Enlightenment in modern history* (1960); L. G. Crocker, *An age of crisis: man and world in eighteenth century thought* (1959), a valuable work by an American literary scholar; and N. Hampson, *A cultural history of the Enlightenment** (1969). Three introductory surveys are R. B. Mowat, *The age of reason* (1934); F. E. Manuel, *The age of reason** (Cornell University series, 1951); and F. B. Artz, *The Enlightenment in France* (1968). The political thought of the Enlightenment is discussed in K. Martin, *French liberal thought in the eighteenth century** (1929; rev. ed., 1954), and in H. J. Laski, *Political thought in England from Locke to Bentham* (1920). On the important Enlightenment theme of progress see J. B. Bury, *The idea of progress: an inquiry into its origin and growth* (1920, 1932); C. Frankel, *The faith of reason: the idea of progress in the French Enlightenment* (1938); and R. V. Sampson, *Progress in the age of reason: the seventeenth century to the present day* (1956). J. B. Black, *The art of history: a study of four great historians of the eighteenth century* (1926), studies Voltaire, Hume, Robertson, and Gibbon and should be supplemented by J. H. Brumfitt, *Voltaire historian* (1958). On economic thought H. Higgs has written *The physiocrats* (1897, 1952), and M. Beer, *An inquiry into physiocracy* (1939). The volume by L. Rothkrug, *Opposition to Louis XIV: the political and social origins of the Enlightenment* (1965), cited in Chapter IV, also examines economic ideas.

On a special subject A. Hertzberg, *The French Enlightenment and the Jews* (1968), argues unconvincingly but with much learning that by stressing universal values the philosophes contributed to modern anti-Semitism. On European Jewry in this age and since, see H. M. Sachar, *The course of modern Jewish history* (1958).

The Philosophes

There are numerous good books on the leading thinkers of the Enlightenment. On Voltaire, P. Gay, *Voltaire's politics: the poet as realist* (1959), has already been mentioned; in lively fashion it reveals Voltaire's pragmatic, nondoctrinaire reactions to the events of his day. Other studies of Voltaire include accounts by G. Lanson* (1906, trans. 1966), H. N. Brailsford (1935), A. Noyes (1936), N. L. Torrey (1938), I. O. Wade (1970), and a comprehensive biography by T. Bestermann (1969), a leading Swiss authority and editor of Voltaire's correspondence. An outstanding account by R. Shackleton, *Montesquieu: a critical biography* (1961), supersedes A. Sorel's older *Montesquieu* (1888). On Diderot two fine studies are available: L. G. Crocker, *The embattled philosopher: a biography of Denis Diderot* (1954); and the first part of a two-volume study, A. M. Wilson, *Diderot: the testing years, 1713–1759* (1957). On Rousseau and the "Rousseau problem" a good introduction is F. C. Green, *Jean-Jacques Rousseau: a critical study of his life and writings* (1955); in addition to older studies by C. E. Vaughan (1915, 1925), E. Cassirer (1954), C. W. Hendel (1934), and A. Cobban (1934), there are also available J. Guéhenno, *Jean-Jacques Rousseau* (2 vols., 1948, 1962, trans. 1966); W. H. Blanchard, *Rousseau and the spirit of revolt* (1968); R. Grimsley, *Jean-Jacques Rousseau: a study in self-awareness* (1961); the same author's *Rousseau and the religious quest* (1968); and numerous other specialized studies. For a sampling of books on other thinkers there are A. L. Lindsay, *Kant* (1934, 1946); D. M. Low, *Edward Gibbon* (1937); H. P. Adams, *The life and writings of Giambattista Vico* (1935), on the leading Italian philosopher of the Enlightenment; N. K. Smith, *The philosophy of David Hume* (1949); and C. Van Doren, *Benjamin Franklin* (1938). F. E. Manuel links the eighteenth century to the age that follows in *The prophets of Paris: Turgot, Condorcet, Saint-Simon, Fourier, Comte** (1962).

B. Willey continues his study of English intellectual history in *The eighteenth century background* (1940); and G. R. Cragg has written an excellent study of the Enlightenment in its English setting, *Reason and authority in the eighteenth century* (1964).

In addition to the books on British church problems suggested for Chapter VI, the following concern various aspects of eighteenth-century religion: G. R. Cragg, *The church and the age of reason** (1961), a volume in the Pelican History of the Church; J. M. Creed and J. S. Boys Smith, *Religious thought in the eighteenth century* (1934), primarily on English writers; C. E. Elwell, *The influence of the Enlightenment on the Catholic theory of education in France, 1750–1850* (1944); R. R. Palmer, *Catholics and unbelievers in eighteenth century France** (1939); and S. Todsvig, *Emanuel Swedenborg: scientist and mystic* (1948). F. E. Manuel discusses the attitudes of the age toward mythology and religion in *The eighteenth century confronts the gods** (1959), and D. D. Bien provides a case study on an important episode in *The Calas affair: persecution, toleration, and heresy in eighteenth century Toulouse* (1960).

The volume by Gershoy cited at the beginning of the chapter and vols. VII and VIII of the New Cambridge Modern History should be consulted. An important fresh look at the old regime is provided by C. B. A. Behrens, *The ancien régime** (1967), in the Barraclough series, where she studies the era for its own sake and not merely as prologue to the revolutionary age. J. Lough, *An introduction to eighteenth-century France* (1960), is also useful. Several good books on modern France begin with developments in the eighteenth century, among them A. Cobban, *A history of modern France** (3 vols., 1957–1965), of which vol. I is *The old regime and revolution 1715–1799**; and G. Wright, *France in modern times: 1760 to the present* (1960), with outstanding bibliographical chapters throughout the book. For France under the old regime a good starting place in many ways is Alexis de Tocqueville's study (1856), a translation of which has appeared as *The old regime and the French Revolution** (1947). H. Sée, *Economic and social conditions in France during the eighteenth century* (1927), gives a detached analysis of the various institutions of the period. A number of special studies may also be recommended: D. Dakin, *Turgot and the ancien régime in France* (1939); J. M. S. Allison, *Lamoignon de Malesherbes, defender of the French monarchy* (1938); S. T. McCloy, *Government assistance in eighteenth century France* (1946), and *The humanitarian movement in eighteenth century France* (1957); A. Bachman, *Censorship in France from 1715 to 1750: Voltaire's opposition* (1934); P. H. Beik, *A judgment of the old regime* (1944); G. T. Matthews, *The royal general farms in eighteenth century France* (1958); G. P. Gooch, *Louis XV, the monarchy in decline* (1956); and J. H. Shennan, *The parlement of Paris* (1968). On the social classes there are F. L. Ford, *Robe and sword: the regrouping of the French aristocracy after Louis XIV** (1953); E. G. Barber, *The bourgeoisie in eighteenth century France** (1955); and R. Forster, *The nobility of Toulouse in the eighteenth century* (1960).

An informative brief introductory synthesis is J. G. Gagliardo, *Enlightened despotism** (Europe Since 1500 series, 1967); a useful Berkshire study is G. Bruun, *Enlightened despots* (1929, 1967).

A. Goodwin (ed.), *The European nobility in the eighteenth century* (1953), is an important collection of essays. Frederick the Great has attracted many biographers: W. F. Reddaway, *Frederick the Great and the rise of Prussia* (1904), still useful; F. J. P. Veale, *Frederick the Great: his life and place in history* (1935), sympathetic; P. Gaxotte, *Frederick the Great* (1941); G. P. Gooch, *Frederick the Great: the ruler, the writer, the man* (1947), a rather favorable view, drawn in considerable part from Frederick's own words; G. Ritter, *Frederick the Great: a historical profile* (1954, trans. 1968), by the German scholar; and D. B. Horn, *Frederick the Great and the rise of Prussia* (1969). C. V. Easum has written *Prince Henry of Prussia, brother of Frederick the Great* (1942). The best general account of German political fragmentation and cultural stirrings is W. H. Bruford, *Germany in the eighteenth century: the social background of the literary revival** (1935); an important study also is F. Hertz, *The development of the German public mind, a social history of German political sentiments, aspirations and ideas: the age of Enlightenment* (1962), part of a larger work. The nature of the Enlightenment and enlightened despotism in the Spanish framework is well portrayed in R. Herr, *The eighteenth century revolution in Spain* (1958).

Habsburg affairs between 1740 and 1792 are recounted in the following books: J. F. Bright, *Maria Theresa* (1897), and *Joseph II* (1897), companion volumes stressing political and diplomatic affairs; E. Cruikshank, *Maria Theresa* (1969); C. L. Morris, *Maria Theresa, the last conservative* (1937), anecdotal and popular; P. P. Bernard, *Joseph II** (1968), a brief, balanced account; S. K. Padover, *The revolutionary emperor: Joseph the Second, 1741–90* (1934, rev., 1967), arguing that Joseph was the typical enlightened despot; M. C. Goodwin, *The papal conflict with Josephinism* (1938); W. C. Langsam, *Francis the Good: the education of an emperor, 1768–1792* (1949); E. M. Link, *The emancipation of the Austrian peasant, 1740–1798* (1949); and R. J. Kerner, *Bohemia in the eighteenth century* (1932).

Enlightened despotism in Russia is examined in A. Kornilov, *Modern Russian history from the age of Catherine the Great to the end of the nineteenth century* (1917, 1943); G. S. Thomson, *Catherine the Great and the expansion of Russia** (Teach Yourself History series, 1947); and G. P. Gooch, *Catherine the Great and other studies* (1954). There are biographies of Catherine by K. Anthony (1925), G. Kaus (1935), I. Grey (1962), and Z. Oldenbourg (1965). Other studies of eighteenth-century Russia include G. Soloveytchik, *Potemkin: a picture of Catherine's Russia* (1938); M. Raeff, *Origins of the Russian intelligentsia: the eighteenth century nobility** (1966); H. Rogger, *National consciousness in eighteenth century Russia* (1960); and P. Dukes, *Catherine the Great and the Russian nobility* (1966).

The attempt to explore the American and French revolutions in a broader eighteenth-century revolutionary setting is described in more detail at the beginning of the next chapter. Efforts to examine the origins and nature of North American civilization in the eighteenth century include R. B. Perry, *Puritanism and democracy* (1944), on the convergence of Puritanism and the Enlightenment; L. B. Wright, *The Atlantic frontier: colonial American civilization, 1607–1763* (1947); M. Savelle, *Seeds of liberty: the genesis of the American mind* (1948); C. Rossiter, *Seedtime of the Republic: the origin of the American tradition of political liberty* (1953); M. Kraus, *The Atlantic civilization: eighteenth century origins* (1949); J. R. Alden, *Pioneer America* (1960), in the Plumb History of Human Society series; and two books by B. Bailyn, *The ideological origins of the American Revolution* (1967), and *The origins of American politics* (1968). R. L. Schuyler, *The fall of the old colonial system: a study in British free trade, 1770–1870* (1945), should be read in conjunction with books listed on mercantilism and empire in Chapters III and VI. M. Beloff (ed.), *The debate on the American Revolution 1761–83* (1949), a collection of source materials, discusses the Revolution within the context of the British Empire. C. L. Becker, *The Declaration of Independence: a study in the history of political ideas* (1922, 1942), is an engaging essay. There are numerous narrative and analytical accounts of the American Revolution; for discussion by a leading scholar of current interpretations see R. B. Morris, *The American Revolution reconsidered**

(1967), and for additional titles and analysis, J. P. Greene, *The reappraisal of the American Revolution in recent historical literature** (1967), a bibliographical essay in the AHA Service Center series.

Important books that relate the events in America to British internal politics include L. B. Namier, *England in the age of the American Revolution* (1930); G. H. Guttridge, *English Whiggism and the American Revolution* (1942); H. Butterfield, *George III, Lord North, and the people 1779–80* (1949), and *George III and the historians* (1957); C. R. Ritcheson, *British politics and the American Revolution* (1954); A. B. Donoughue, *British politics and the American Revolution: the path to war, 1773–1775* (1964); R. Pares, *King George III and the politicians* (1953); J. S. Watson, *The reign of George III, 1760–1815* (1960); and R. J. Whyte, *The age of George III* (1968). In addition one may turn to J. R. Pole, *Political representation in England and the origins of the American Revolution* (1967), and to E. C. Black, *The Association: British extra-parliamentary political organization 1769–93* (1963). On parliamentary reform see also G. Rudé, *Wilkes and political liberty* (1962), and I. A. Christie, *Wilkes, Wyvill, and reform* (1963), and items listed in Chapter IX for the impact of the French Revolution in England. On diplomacy and international affairs one may consult W. C. Stinchcombe, *The American Revolution and the French alliance* (1969); S. F. Bemis, *The diplomacy of the American Revolution* (1935); I. de Madariaga, *Britain, Russia, and the armed neutrality of 1780* (1962); and on the peace negotiations, R. B. Morris, *The peacemakers; the great powers and American independence* (1965).

Relations between France and America are also discussed in B. Fäy, *The revolutionary spirit in France and America* (1927); W. Stark, *America, ideal and reality: the United States of 1776 in contemporary European philosophy* (1947); and the various books (1935 ff.) by L. Gottschalk on Lafayette during the revolutionary era. Professor Gottschalk has also given a short expression of his views in *The place of the American Revolution in the causal pattern of the French Revolution* (1948). Three special studies may also be noted: C. D. Hazen, *Contemporary American opinion of the French Revolution* (1897); A. O. Aldridge, *Franklin and his French contemporaries* (1957); and D. Echevarria, *Mirage in the West: a history of the French image of American society to 1815** (1957).

Pamphlets relevant to this chapter and to the next include R. Wines (ed.), *Enlightened despotism: reform or reaction?* (1967); E. A. Reitan (ed.), *George III: tyrant or constitutional monarch?* (1964); and W. F. Church (ed.), *The influence of the Enlightenment on the French Revolution* (1964). In the Anvil series there are L. L. Snyder, *The age of reason* (1955); P. Gay, *Deism: an anthology* (1968); and M. Kraus, *The North Atlantic civilization* (1957). A useful anthology is I. Schneider (ed.), *The Enlightenment* (1965).

A. Goodwin (ed.), *The American and French Revolutions, 1763–1793*, vol. VIII of the New Cambridge Modern History, has already been cited; its sequel volume is also relevant: C. W. Crawley (ed.), *War and peace in an age of upheaval, 1793–1830* (1965). Some stimulating surveys for the years beginning with the American and French revolutions are G. Rudé, *Revolutionary Europe, 1783–1815* (1964), in the Plumb series; E. J. Hobsbawm, *The age of revolution: Europe, 1789–1848** (1962); N. Hampson, *The first European revolution, 1776–1815** (1969); and C. Breunig, *The age of revolution and reaction, 1789–1850** (1970), in the Norton History of Modern Europe. On the revolutionary developments in France a valuable synthesis, from a point of view critical of the Revolution, is C. Brinton, *A decade of revolution, 1789–1799** (1934), in the Langer series. An important balanced account by a great French scholar is G. Lefebvre, *The French Revolution* (1951, 2 vols. in trans., 1962–1964), and a sequel volume combining *The Thermidorians** (1937, trans. 1964) and *The Directory** (1946, trans. 1964). Among other important accounts are L. Gershoy, *The French Revolution and Napoleon* (1932, rev., 1964); J. M.

Bibliography   Thompson, *The French Revolution** (1943); N. Hampson, *A social history of the French Revolution** (1963), a judicious history covering more than its title implies; M. J. Sydenham, *The French Revolution** (1965); and A. Goodwin, *The French Revolution** (1953, rev., 1956). There are numerous older volumes now more relevant to the historiography of the Revolution than to its history, by such writers of vastly differing viewpoints as Jules Michelet, Jean Juarès, Hippolyte Taine, L. Madelin, P. Gaxotte, A. Aulard, and A. Mathiez. Two bibliographical essays in the AHA Service Center series are useful: S. J. Idzerda, *The background of the French Revolution** (1959), and J. H. Stewart, *The French Revolution: some trends in historical writing, 1945–1965** (1967); the latter has also gathered together many of the key documents in *A documentary survey of the French Revolution* (1951).

      Considerable attention has been given in recent years to the Revolution as part of a European-wide and transatlantic movement. The most extensive treatment of the subject is R. R. Palmer, *The age of the democratic revolution: a political history of Europe and America, 1760–1800** (2 vols., 1959–1964); the first volume, *The challenge,* carries the account to 1792, the second, *The struggle,* to 1800; and see also by the same author, *The world of the French Revolution** (1970). Some of the conclusions of a French scholar, Jacques Godechot [*La grande nation* (2 vols., 1956), and other works], are available in summary form as *France and the Atlantic revolution, 1770–1799* (1965). Four analytical books exploring the significance of the Revolution at the time and since are H. Arendt, *On revolution** (1963); A. Cobban, *The myth of the French Revolution* (1953), and *The social interpretation of the French Revolution** (1964); and J. L. Talmon, *The origins of totalitarian democracy* (1952), the latter a somewhat unfair attempt to read back into the eighteenth century the roots of modern dictatorship. C. Brinton, *The anatomy of revolution** (1938), is a comparative study of four revolutions, the English, American, French, and Russian.

Developments   A good introduction to France in 1789 is G. Lefebvre, *The coming of the French Revolution** (1939, Within France   trans. 1947). See also, in addition to many of the books listed above and numerous other monographs: B. F. Hyslop, *French nationalism in 1789, according to the general cahiers* (1934), and *A guide to the general cahiers of 1789, with texts of unedited cahiers* (1936); C. Brinton, *The Jacobins: an essay in the new history* (1930), which sees the Revolution as a kind of religion; M. J. Sydenham, *The Girondins* (1961); R. M. Brace, *Bordeaux and the Gironde, 1789–1794* (1947), for concrete details on middle-class participation and misgivings. D. Thomson, *The Babeuf plot: the making of a republican legend* (1947), is on the extremist group crushed by the Directory, and I. Woloch, *Jacobin legacy: the democratic movement under the Directory* (1970), analyzes the more numerous constitutional democrats. F. L. Nussbaum, *Commercial policy in the French Revolution: a study of the career of G. J. A. Ducher* (1923), explains how, under the Committee of Public Safety, the Revolution turned from economic liberalism to revived mercantilism; and S. E. Harris, *The assignats* (1930), shows that the paper money was a fairly effective instrument of war finance. On religion and the Revolution one may turn to A. Dansette, *Religious history of modern France* (2 vols., 1948–1951, trans. 1961), of which the first volume covers the years from the Revolution to 1870; to F. V. A. Aulard, *Christianity and the French Revolution* (1927); and to C. S. Phillips, *The church in France, 1789–1848* (1929). E. E. Y. Hales, *Revolution and papacy 1769–1846* (1960), deals with the Catholic world as a whole. An aspect of the religious question is explored in B. C. Poland, *French Protestantism and the French Revolution . . . 1685–1815* (1957); and on a special subject P. Beik has written *The French Revolution seen from the right . . . 1789–1799* (1956).

      The war and various diplomatic aspects are discussed in S. T. Ross, *European diplomatic history 1789–1815: France against Europe** (1969). H. Mitchell, *The underground war against revolutionary France 1794–1800* (1965), traces British diplomacy, espionage, and the war against the French Revolution. On the emergence of Bonaparte one may turn to G. Ferrero, *The gamble: Bonaparte in Italy, 1796–1797* (1939); P. G. Elgood, *Bonaparte's adventure in Egypt* (1931); and J. C. Herold's vivid *Bonaparte in Egypt* (1962). Additional books on Napoleon are listed in the following chapter.

Most of the general works listed above give close consideration to the motives, course, and effects of the Terror, and in addition the following books illustrate important phases of it: A. Mathiez, *The fall of Robespierre and other essays* (1927), and *After Robespierre: the Thermidorian reaction* (1929, trans. 1965); R. R. Palmer, *Twelve who ruled: the Committee of Public Safety during the Terror** (1941, 1958); A. Soboul, *The Parisian sans-culottes and the French Revolution, 1793–1794* (trans. 1964); G. Rudé, *The crowd in the French Revolution** (1959); and R. B. Rose, *The enragés: socialists of the French Revolution?* (1965). More specialized studies include W. B. Kerr, *The Reign of Terror, 1793–1794; the experiment of the democratic republic, and the rise of the bourgeoisie* (1927); D. M. Greer, *The incidence of the Terror during the French Revolution; a statistical interpretation* (1935), a revealing study of who was actually executed and by what procedures; its sequel, *The incidence of the emigration during the French Revolution* (1951); and J. B. Sirich, *Revolutionary committees in the departments of France, 1793–1794* (1943), on the relations between Paris and the country during the Terror. S. Loomis, *Paris in the Terror* (1964), is a sensationalized popular account, C. Tilly, *The Vendée** (1964), an important sociological analysis of the counterrevolution of 1793. Two books focusing on popular unrest in both France and England are G. A. Williams, *Artisans and sans-culottes* (1968), and G. Rudé, *The crowd in history: a study of popular disturbances in France and England, 1730–1848* (1964).

The Reign of Terror and After

On Sieyès, the constitution maker, see J. Claphan, *The Abbé Sieyès: an essay in the politics of the French Revolution* (1912), and G. C. Van Deusen, *Sieyès: his life and his nationalism* (1932). J. M. Thompson, *Leaders of the French Revolution* (1932), gives sketches of the outstanding personalities which may be filled out with the following biographies: the somewhat sensational A. Vallentin, *Mirabeau* (1948), which does not entirely supersede L. Barthou, *Mirabeau* (1913); H. Wendel, *Danton* (1935); E. S. Scudder, *Prince of the blood: a life of Philippe Egalité* (1937); J. C. Dawson, *Lakanal the regicide* (1948), on an earnest reformer and his program; D. L. Dowd, *Pageant-master of the republic: Jacques-Louis David and the French Revolution* (1948), a good picture of art and propaganda during a period of rapid changes; E. Ellery, *Brissot de Warville* (1915); J. S. Schapiro, *Condorcet and the rise of liberalism* (1934), on the ideas of the leading Girondin philosopher and his unsinkable optimism; L. Gottschalk, *Jean-Paul Marat: a study in radicalism* (1927); E. N. Curtis, *Saint-Just, colleague of Robespierre* (1935); and H. Dupré, *Lazare Carnot, republican patriot* (1940), on the "organizer of victory." In the multivolumed biography of Lafayette, mentioned in the previous chapter in connection with the American Revolution, there is now L. Gottschalk and M. Maddox, *Lafayette in the French Revolution: through the October Days* (1969), on the climactic year 1789. There are biographies of Mme. Roland by C. Young, *A lady who loved herself* (1930); by M. Jacquemaire, *The life of Mme. Roland* (1930); and a more recent study, G. May, *Madame Roland and the age of revolution* (1970). The best-rounded biography of the most prominent figure on the Committee of Public Safety is J. M. Thompson, *Robespierre* (2 vols., 1935), on which the same author has an excellent brief study in the Teach Yourself History series, *Robespierre and the French Revolution** (1953); there are other biographies of Robespierre by R. S. Ward (1934), R. Korngold (1937), and J. M. Eagan (1938). G. Rudé has edited *Robespierre** in the Great Lives Observed series (1967). On one of Robespierre's associates L. Gershoy has written a sensitive biography, *Bertrand Barère: a reluctant terrorist* (1962).

Biographies

In addition to Palmer, *The age of the democratic revolution*, cited above, there are a number of specialized studies. For Germany there is the excellent recent work of K. Epstein, *The genesis of German conservatism* (1966). The older book of G. P. Gooch, *Germany and the French Revolution* (1920), and his subsequent work, *Studies in German history* (1948), are valuable. Various studies on Goethe and other intellectual leaders of the time should be consulted, as should the books on the revival of Germany cited in the following chapter. H. W. Van Loon, *The fall of the Dutch*

Effects of the Revolution Outside France

Bibliography   *Republic* (1913, 1924), and *The rise of the Dutch kingdom, 1795–1813* (1915), give a running account of events in the Netherlands through the eighteenth century. The general histories of the United States on this period cover such topics as the diplomatic complications, the positions of Jefferson, Paine, Gouverneur Morris, and so forth. For effects in Haiti and the black world, see C. L. R. James, *The black Jacobins: Toussaint l'Ouverture and the San Domingo Revolution* (1938).

Of the sizable literature on British relations with revolutionary France and on the impact of the French Revolution on Britain, the following titles are suggested: *The Cambridge history of British foreign policy, 1783–1919* (3 vols., 1922–1923), edited by A. W. Ward and G. P. Gooch; J. Ehrman, *The British government and commercial negotiations with Europe, 1783–1793* (1962); W. T. Laprade, *England and the French Revolution, 1789–1797* (1909); P. A. Brown, *The French Revolution in English history* (1918); L. S. Marshall, *The development of public opinion in Manchester, 1780–1820* (1946); A. Cobban, *Edmund Burke and the revolt against the eighteenth century: a study of the political and social thinking of Burke, Wordsworth, Coleridge, and Southey* (1929); H. N. Brailsford, *Shelley, Godwin and their circle* (1913); R. J. S. Hoffman and P. Levack (eds.), *Burke's politics: selected writings and speeches* (1949); C. Cone, *The English Jacobins: reformers in late 18th century England* (1968), and *Burke and the nature of politics* (2 vols., 1957–1964). A. Cobban has edited a useful anthology, *The debate on the French Revolution, 1789–1799* (1949).

Problems and Readings*   Several studies in various problems series are relevant to this chapter: R. W. Greenlaw (ed.), *The economic origins of the French Revolution—poverty or prosperity?* (1958); P. Amann (ed.), *The eighteenth century revolution: French or Western?* (1963); and R. Bienvenu (ed.), *The ninth of Thermidor: the fall of Robespierre* (1968). For a comprehensive survey examining divergent appraisals of all aspects of the Revolution, see F. A. Kafker and J. M. Laux (eds.), *The French Revolution: conflicting interpretations** (1968); and for sociologically oriented analyses of various problems, see J. Kaplow (ed.), *New perspectives on the French Revolution: readings in historical sociology** (1965), and R. Cobb (ed.), *French Revolution documents* (1966). In the Anvil series, L. Gershoy has an essay and documents on *The era of the French Revolution, 1789–1799: ten years that shook the world* (1957). Useful for this and the following chapter is D. H. Pinkney (ed.), *Napoleon: historical enigma* (1969).

X: Napoleonic Europe

The most convenient general survey of Europe in the age of Napoleon is G. Bruun, *Europe and the French imperium, 1799–1814** (1938), in the Langer series, but see also the books on the revolutionary and Napoleonic age cited in the previous chapter. A remarkable historical tour de force has been achieved by the Dutch historian Pieter Geyl in his *Napoleon: for and against** (1949), a brilliant interpretation of what French historians since 1815 have said about Napoleon. *Napoleon self-revealed in 300 selected letters* (1934), edited by J. M. Thompson, gives the man's own words, as does J. C. Herold (ed.), *The mind of Napoleon* (1955); the same author has written a colorful account of the period in *The age of Napoleon* (1963).

Napoleon and Napoleonic France   Of the innumerable biographies of Napoleon, the following are recommended: J. M. Thompson, *Napoleon Bonaparte: his rise and fall* (1952); F. M. Markham, *Napoleon** (1964); the same author's *Napoleon and the awakening of Europe** (1954), in the Teach Yourself History series; and G. Lefebvre, *Napoleon* (2 vols., 1935, trans. 1969), a major work by a distinguished French historian. R. Holtman, *The Napoleonic revolution** (1967), is a brief, judicious assessment. E. V. Tarlé, *Bonaparte* (1937), is a Soviet view of unusual interest, emphasizing economic influences. F. Pratt's two volumes, *The road to empire* (1939) and *The empire and the glory: Napoleon Bonaparte 1800–1806* (1949), are popular narratives; and L. Madelin, *The consulate and* *the empire* (2 vols., 1934–1936), is eulogistic of Napoleon. Napoleon as a military leader may be studied in D. G. Chandler, *The campaigns of Napoleon* (1966).

Other studies of the Napoleonic age include E. Heckscher, *The continental system* (1922); H. C. Deutsch, *The genesis of Napoleonic imperialism* (1938); and H. H. Walsh, *The Concordat of 1801* (1933). O. Connelly has written *The gentle Bonaparte: a biography of Joseph, Napoleon's elder brother* (1968), and S. Zweig, *Joseph Fouché: the portrait of a politician* (1930). Biographical studies of Talleyrand have been written by A. Duff Cooper* (1932), C. Brinton* (1936), E. Dard (1937), and L. Madelin (1948).

On the last phase of Napoleon's career, E. Saunders has written a lively account, *The hundred days* (1964), and A. Brett-James has edited an anthology of eyewitness accounts under the same title (1964). C. Hibbert has written *Waterloo: Napoleon's last campaign* (1967). Three biographies of notable ladies of the era deserve mention: E. J. Knapton, *Empress Josephine* (1963); the same author's *The lady of the Holy Alliance: the life of Julie de Krüdener* (1939); and J. C. Herold's *Mistress to an age** (1955), on the influential Mme. de Staël.

The concluding chapters of C. G. Robertson, *England under the Hanoverians* (1911), are still useful as a general introduction. On a much larger scale there are the patriotic British volumes of A. Bryant, *The years of endurance, 1793–1802* (1942), *The years of victory, 1802–1812* (1944), and *The age of elegance, 1812–1822* (1950). J. H. Rose's many studies of the period, notably *William Pitt and the national revival* (1911), *William Pitt and the great war* (1911), and *The indecisiveness of modern war* (1927), illuminate many general and special problems of the period. Among other useful studies are G. S. Graham, *Sea power and British North America, 1783–1820* (1941); A. Hope-Jones, *Income tax in the Napoleonic wars* (1939); W. F. Galpin, *The grain supply of England during the Napoleonic period* (1925); and C. Oman [Lenanton], *Napoleon at the Channel* (1942), which has also appeared as *Britain against Napoleon* (1944). Miss Oman has also written a biography of Nelson (1946), as have A. T. Mahan (1897), C. S. Forester (1929), W. James (1948), R. Grenfell (1949), and others. P. Guedalla and R. Aldington have each written good popular biographies of Wellington (1931, 1943, respectively).

An outstanding student of nationalism, H. Kohn, has written *Prelude to nation-states: the French and German experience, 1789–1815* (1967), especially useful for German nationalism in this era. The following works also deal with German and Prussian nationalism: R. Aris, *History of political thought in Germany from 1789–1815* (1936); E. N. Anderson, *Nationalism and the cultural crisis in Prussia, 1806–1815* (1939); E. F. Henderson, *Blücher and the uprising of Prussia against Napoleon, 1806–1815* (1911); R. R. Ergang, *Herder and the foundations of German nationalism* (1931); F. McEachran, *The life and philosophy of Johann Gottfried Herder* (1939); A. G. Pundt, *Arndt and the nationalist awakening in Germany* (1935); H. C. Engelbrecht, *Johann Gottlieb Fichte* (1933); and W. C. Langsam, *The Napoleonic wars and German nationalism in Austria* (1930). [See the books suggested for Chapter XI for other studies on nationalism.]

For the political, diplomatic, and military developments of the age see J. Seeley, *Life and times of Stein, or Germany and Prussia in the Napoleonic age* (3 vols., 1878), an old but valuable general history of the period; G. S. Ford, *Stein and the era of reform in Prussia, 1807–1815* (1922); C. de Grunwald, *Napoleon's nemesis: the life of Baron Stein* (1936); H. A. L. Fisher, *Studies in Napoleonic statesmanship: Germany* (1903); H. Rosinski, *The German army* (1939, 1944—the two editions contain different material), a history from Frederick the Great to Hitler; W. O. Shanahan, *Prussian military reforms, 1786–1813* (1945); and the acute assessment of W. M. Simon, *The failure of the Prussian reform movement, 1807–1819* (1955). The able and cynical Gentz has been the subject of biographies by P. F. Reiff (1912), P. R. Sweet (1941), and G. Mann (1946).

B. Perkins has written a three-volume study of Anglo-American relations in the three decades from 1795 to 1823: *The first rapprochement: England and the United States, 1795–1805* (1955), *Prologue to war . . . 1805–1812* (1961), and *Castlereagh and Adams . . . 1812–1823* (1964). The general diplomatic study of H. C. Allen, *Great Britain and the United States . . . Anglo-American relations, 1783–1952* (1955), is valuable. The American domestic scene is presented in M. Smelser, *The democratic republic 1801–1815* (1968); and a recent account of the United States–British military conflict is R. Horsman, *The War of 1812* (1969). Other ramifications in the Western hemisphere during the revolutionary era are examined in W. Spence Robertson, *The life of Miranda* (2 vols., 1929), and *France and Latin American independence* (1939); and in the general histories of Latin America by J. E. Fagg (rev., 1969), H. Herring (rev., 1968), and others. On Napoleonic influences in other countries, the following may also be mentioned: A. Lobanov-Rostovsky, *Russia and Europe, 1789–1825* (1947); E. Tarlé, *Napoleon's invasion of Russia, 1812* (1942), an account by a leading Soviet historian; G. B. McClellan, *Venice and Bonaparte* (1931); O. Connelly, *Napoleon's satellite kingdoms* (1965); and R. J. Rath, *The fall of the Napoleonic kingdom of Italy* (1941). The best account of Spain in the Napoleonic era is G. H. Lovett, *Napoleon and the birth of modern Spain* (2 vols., 1965), but the opening chapters of R. Carr, *Spain, 1808–1939* (1966), are a good introduction.

Excellent guides are C. K. Webster, *The foreign policy of Castlereagh, 1812–1815: Britain and the reconstruction of Europe* (1931); C. S. B. Buckland, *Metternich and the British government from 1809 to 1813* (1932); his shorter parallel study on Gentz (1933); and L. I. Strakhovsky, *Alexander I of Russia: the man who defeated Napoleon* (1947). E. F. Kraehe, *Metternich's German policy*, vol. I, *The contest with Napoleon, 1799–1814* (1963), is an important account, of which a second volume is projected for the contest with Alexander.

C. K. Webster, *The Congress of Vienna, 1814–1815* (1919), is a technical diplomatic study, whereas G. Ferrero, *The reconstruction of Europe: Talleyrand and the Congress of Vienna, 1814–1815* (1941), and H. Nicolson, *Congress of Vienna: a study in allied unity, 1812–1822** (1946), are works for the general reader. H. Kissinger, *A world restored: Metternich, Castlereagh and the problems of peace, 1812–1822* (1957), is valuable for this and for the period that follows. Informative on an important subject is H. A. Straus, *The attitude of the Congress of Vienna toward nationalism in Germany, Italy, and Poland* (1949).

XI: Reaction versus Progress, 1815–1848

The resettling of European institutions after the great French outburst in many ways marked the opening of a new historical era. There are numerous general, national, and topical histories, accordingly, that take their starting point in 1815. For bibliographical guidance see A. Bullock and A. J. P. Taylor, *A select list of books on European history, 1815–1914** (rev., 1957); L. J. Ragatz, *A bibliography for the study of European history, 1815–1939* (1942 and later supplements); E. N. Anderson, *Nineteenth century Europe: crises and contributions** (AHA Service Center series, 1959); and W. N. Medlicott, *Modern European history: a short bibliography* (1961).

Among general accounts there may be mentioned D. Thomson, *Europe since Napoleon* (1957, 1962), a valuable synthesis; J. McManners, *European history, 1789–1914: men, machines and freedom** (1967); and J. J. Saunders, *The age of revolution: a survey of European history since 1815* (1967). Accounts focusing on selected aspects include P. N. Stearns, *European society in upheaval: social history since 1800** (1967); E. N. and P. R. Anderson, *Political institutions and social change in continental Europe in the nineteenth century* (1967); G. L. Mosse, *The culture of western Europe: the nineteenth and twentieth centuries* (1961); and R. Stromberg, *European intellectual history since 1789** (1968). Three anthologies, useful for the nineteenth and twentieth centuries, are E. C.

Black, *The posture of Europe, 1815–1940: readings in European intellectual history** (1964); E. C. Weber (ed.), *Paths to the present: . . . European thought from romanticism to existentialism** (1960); and P. N. Stearns (ed.), *A century for debate: problems in the interpretation of European history, 1789–1914** (1969).

The most useful general guides to the immediate era of reconstruction and reorientation after 1815 are F. B. Artz, *Reaction and revolution, 1814–1832** (1934), in the Langer series; E. L. Woodward, *Three studies in European conservatism: Metternich, Guizot, the Catholic church in the nineteenth century* (1930); and G. de Bertier de Sauvigny, *Metternich and his times* (1959, trans. 1967). Useful brief treatments in various historical series include J. Droz, *Europe between revolutions, 1815–1848** (1967), in the Plumb series; J. L. Talmon, *Romanticism and revolution in Europe, 1815–1848** (1967), in the Barraclough series; A. J. May, *The age of Metternich, 1815–1848** (rev., 1963), a Berkshire study; H. Hearder, *Europe in the nineteenth century, 1830–1880** (1966), in the Hay series; and B. D. Gooch, *Europe in the nineteenth century* (1970). E. J. Hobsbawm has written a provocative Marxist survey cited earlier, *The age of revolution: Europe, 1789–1848** (1962). For this and the following two chapters there are valuable sections in vol. X of the New Cambridge Modern History: J. P. T. Bury (ed.), *The zenith of European power, 1830–70* (1960), with useful survey chapters by the editor. An important theme is developed in C. Morazé, *The triumph of the middle classes** (trans. 1966).

For Britain the following one-volume accounts focus on the nineteenth century: G. M. Trevelyan, *British history in the nineteenth century and after* [1782–1919], (1922, 1937); A. Wood, *Nineteenth century Britain, 1815–1914* (1960); D. Thomson, *England in the nineteenth century** (Pelican series, 1950, 1964); and R. W. Seton-Watson, *Britain in Europe, 1789–1914: a survey of foreign policy* (1937). E. Halévy's classic, *History of the English people in the nineteenth century* (6 vols., 1912 ff.), is a work of breadth and imagination by a French scholar. Books on economic and social history are listed below. R. K. Webb, *English history, 1815–1914** (AHA Service Center series, 1967), is an informative bibliographical essay.

The following general histories, some of which have been cited earlier, will be found to be useful: A. Cobban, *A history of modern France** (3 vols., 1957–1965); P. A. Gagnon, *France since 1789* (1964); A Guérard, *France: a modern history* (1959, rev., 1969); D. Harvey, *France since the Revolution** (1968); and G. Wright, *France in modern times: 1760 to the present* (1960). In addition the following take the post-Napoleonic years as their starting point: J. P. T. Bury, *France, 1814–1940: a history* (1940); J. B. Wolf, *France, 1815 to the present* (1940); P. Maillaud, *France* (1942); and D. W. Brogan, *The French nation, 1814–1940: from Napoleon to Pétain** (1957), brilliant but often too allusive for the general reader. Interpretive studies include G. L. Dickinson, *Revolution and reaction in modern France* (1892, 1927); E. L. Woodward, *French revolutions* (1934); G. Elton, *The revolutionary idea in France, 1789–1871* (1923); J. Plamenatz, *The revolutionary movement in France, 1815–1871* (1952); and R. H. Soltau, *French political thought in the nineteenth century* (1931). On economic development and policies see A. L. Dunham, *The industrial revolution in France, 1815–48* (1955); S. B. Clough, *France, a history of national economics, 1789–1939* (1939); J. Clapham, *The economic development of France and Germany, 1815–1914* (1921, 1936); and R. E. Cameron, *France and the economic development of Europe, 1800–1914* (1961, rev., 1968). J. T. Joughin has prepared a bibliographical essay of writings in English on French developments: *France in the nineteenth century, 1815–1914** (AHA Service Center series, 1968).

For France in the years immediately after Napoleon the best introductions are F. B. Artz, *France under the Bourbon Restoration, 1814–1830* (1931), and G. de Bertier de Sauvigny, *The Bourbon Restoration* (1955, trans. 1966). The somewhat anecdotal J. Lucas-Dubreton, *The Restoration and the July Monarchy* (1929), may be compared with M. R. D. Leys, *Between two*

Empires (1955), on the same subject. An informative monograph is D. P. Resnick, *The white terror and the political reaction after Waterloo* (1966). Of J. M. S. Allison's various studies of nineteenth-century France, the widest in scope is his *Monsieur Thiers* (1932). Centering around Guizot, another historian-statesman, there is an admirable study, D. Johnson, *Guizot: aspects of French history, 1787–1874* (1963); and on Guizot and others, S. Mellon, *The political uses of history: a study of historians in the French Restoration* (1958). For a biography of Louis Philippe one may turn to T. Howarth, *Citizen-King* (1961). Studies of conservative ideas and activities are C. T. Muret, *French royalist doctrines since the Revolution* (1933); N. E. Hudson, *Ultra-royalism and the French Restoration* (1936); P. Spencer, *Politics of belief in nineteenth century France* (1954); P. N. Stearns, *Priest and revolutionary: Lamennais and the dilemma of French Catholicism* (1967); and R. Rémond, *The right wing in France: from 1815 to de Gaulle* (1954, trans. 1966). A special subject is examined in I. Collins, *The government and the newspaper press in France, 1814–1881* (1959).

Germany In addition to the histories by R. Flenley, *Modern German history* (rev., 1964); H. Holborn, *History of modern Germany* (3 vols., 1959–1968); and V. Valentin, *The German people* (1946), the following general accounts may be recommended for this and the chapters that follow: E. J. Passant and others, *A short history of Germany, 1815–1945** (1959); K. S. Pinson, *Modern Germany: its history and civilization* (1954, rev., 1966); A. J. P. Taylor, *The course of German history . . . since 1815** (1946), shrewd but sometimes antagonistic: M. Dill, Jr., *Germany: a modern history* (1961), in the University of Michigan series; A. Ramm, *Germany, 1789–1914: a political history* (1967), with considerable attention to political thought; W. Carr, *A history of Germany, 1815–1945* (1969); and the impressionistic G. Mann, *History of Germany since 1789* (1959, trans. 1968). E. Vermeil, *Germany's three Reichs: their history and culture* (1945), is a French interpretation. G. A. Craig, *The politics of the Prussian army, 1640–1945** (1955), deals in good part with the nineteenth and twentieth centuries. Political and economic issues are examined in T. Hamerow, *Restoration, revolution, and reaction: economics and politics in Germany, 1815–1871** (1958), and in R. H. Thomas, *Liberalism, nationalism and the German intellectuals, 1822–1847* (1952). A useful bibliographical essay is N. Rich, *Germany, 1815–1914** (AHA Service Center series, 1968).

Austria, Poland, Greece, Spain, and Italy On the Habsburg monarchy after 1815, the best study in any language is C. A. Macartney, *The Habsburg empire, 1790–1918* (1969), a masterful survey. Recommended also are A. Wandruszka, *The house of Habsburg* (1956, trans. 1964), cited earlier; A. J. P. Taylor, *The Habsburg monarchy, 1809–1918** (1943, 1948 revision changes some conclusions), less paradoxical than his history of Germany; and R. Kann, *The multinational empire: nationalism and national reform in the Habsburg monarchy, 1840–1918* (2 vols., 1950–1964). An informative brief introduction is B. Jelavich, *The Habsburg empire in European affairs, 1814–1918** (1969). Other titles are cited in Chapter XIV.

Other European countries in the years 1815 to 1848 are treated in numerous books. For Poland see in addition to the books cited earlier [O. Halecki, *A history of Poland* (rev., 1956); R. Dyboski, *Poland in world civilization* (1950); and the collaborative *Cambridge history of Poland* (2 vols., 1941–1950]: W. J. Rose, *The rise of Polish democracy* (1944), and R. F. Leslie, *Polish politics and the revolution of November 1830* (1956). For Greece the best introductions are C. M. Woodhouse, *A short history of modern Greece* (1968); J. Campbell and P. Sherrard, *Modern Greece* (1968); E. S. Forster, *A short history of modern Greece, 1821–1945* (1941, 1946); and the portions on Greece in L. Stavrianos, *The Balkans since 1453* (1958), and in R. L. Wolff, *The Balkans in our time** (1956). The volume by Stavrianos is available also in briefer form as *The Balkans since 1815** (Berkshire

series, 1965). Valuable also for the Balkans and the Near East is M. S. Anderson, *The Eastern*
question, 1774–1923 (1966).

For Spain see R. Carr, *Spain, 1808–1939* (1966), a volume in the Oxford History of Modern Europe; S. G. Payne, *Politics and the military in modern Spain* (1967); and the general histories of Spain by H. L. Livermore (1948), R. Altamira (trans. 1949), S. de Madariaga (1943, 1958), and W. C. Atkinson, *A history of Spain and Portugal* (1960). For Italy one may turn to A. J. B. Whyte, *The evolution of modern Italy, 1715–1920** (1944, 1950); H. Hearder and P. Waley (eds.), *A short history of Italy** (1963); R. Albrecht-Carrié, *Italy from Napoleon to Mussolini* (1950); S. B. Clough, *The economic history of modern Italy* (1964); and S. B. Clough and S. Saladino, *A history of modern Italy: documents, readings, and commentary* (1968). [Many other books on nineteenth-century developments in these countries are cited also in the next three chapters.]

Authoritative treatment is to be found in the collaborative Cambridge Economic History of
Europe, vol. VI, *The industrial revolutions and after* (2 parts, 1965), to which D. S. Landes' contribution has been published separately, in expanded form, as *The unbound Prometheus: technological change and industrial development in western Europe from 1750 to the present** (1969). The complexities of the industrial revolution may also be approached through four brief, informative books: T. S. Ashton, *The industrial revolution, 1760–1830** (1948, rev., 1962); W. O. Henderson, *The industrialization of Europe, 1780–1914** (1969), in the Barraclough series; P. Deane, *The first industrial revolution** (1965); and G. N. Clark, *The idea of the industrial revolution* (1953). Advanced technical studies, investigating rates of industrial growth in Britain, include: W. G. Hoffmann, *British industry, 1700–1950* (trans. 1955); W. W. Rostow, *British economy of the nineteenth century* (1948); and P. Deane and W. A. Cole, *British economic growth, 1688–1959: trends and structure* (1962). Miss Deane and B. R. Mitchell have also edited *Abstract of British historical statistics* (1962). Rostow has utilized the British experience as a model for other areas in *The process of economic growth* (1952) and *The stages of economic growth: a non-communist manifesto** (1960). There are older studies of the rise of industrialism by L. C. A. Knowles, *The industrial and commercial revolution in Great Britain* (4th ed., 1926); J. L. and B. Hammond, *The rise of British industry* (1926, 1937); P. Mantoux, *The industrial revolution in the eighteenth century** (1906, 1937); and A. P. Usher, *A history of mechanical inventions* (1929, 1954). British economic history in these years is also studied in great detail in T. S. Ashton, *The economic history of England: the eighteenth century* (1955); W. H. B. Court, *A concise economic history of Britain** (1954); and J. H. Clapham, *An economic history of modern Britain* (3 vols., 1926–1938), which is also available as *A concise economic history of Britain** (1949). For these years one may also turn to J. D. Chambers, *The workshop of the world: British economic history from 1820 to 1880* (rev., 1969); S. G. Checkland, *The rise of industrial society in England, 1815–1885* (1964); P. Gregg, *A social and economic history of Britain, 1760–1950** (1950); and W. O. Henderson, *Britain and industrial Europe, 1750–1870* (1954). S. Pollard and C. Holmes have edited a volume of documents, *The process of industrialization, 1750–1870* (1968); and E. Lampard has prepared a useful bibliographical essay, *Industrial revolution: interpretations and perspectives** (AHA Service Center series, 1957).

Changes in British agriculture are analyzed in R. E. Prothero [Lord Ernle], *English farming, past and present* (5th ed., 1936), an older survey which may now be supplemented by M. E. Seebohm. *The evolution of the English farm* (2nd ed., 1952); R. Trow-Smith, *English husbandry, from the earliest times to the present day* (1951); and C. S. Orwin and E. H. Whetham, *History of English agriculture, 1846–1914* (1949, rev., 1964). On the changes in the countryside see also E. C. Wingfield-Stratford, *The squire and his relations* (1956); G. E. and K. R. Fussell, *The English countryman: his life and work*, A.D. *1500–1900* (1955); and F. M. L. Thompson, *The English landed gentry in the nineteenth century* (1963).

There is a large and controversial literature on the effects of industrial change upon the well-being of the British working classes. J. L. and B. Hammond in several vehement books written in the years before 1919 [such as *The town labourer, 1760–1832: the new civilization** (1919)] demonstrated indignantly that the common people were exploited. E. P. Thompson, *The making of the English working class** (1964), marshals much evidence to reinforce the picture of exploitation and of working-class militancy, as does E. J. Hobsbawm in *Industry and empire: 1750 to the present day* (1968), vol. II of *The making of modern English society*, written with C. Hill. Hobsbawm has also written *Labouring men: studies in the history of labour** (1964). The books by Ashton, Clark, Deane, and others cited above provide a less bleak view, as do M. C. Buer, *Health, wealth, and population in the early days of the industrial revolution* (1926), and J. T. Ward, *The factory system, 1830–1855* (1962); but the debate continues. An extremist viewpoint minimizing the evil effects of early industrialism is set forth in a collection of essays edited by F. A. von Hayek, *Capitalism and the historians** (1954).

For the social and political implications behind the growth of an industrial civilization one may read with profit J. McManners, *European history: men, machines and freedom** (1967), cited earlier. For the impact on Britain the reader may turn to G. D. H. Cole and R. Postgate, *The British people, 1746–1946** (1957), and to Cole, *British working class politics, 1832–1914* (1941), both written from a Labour point of view. A. Briggs, *The age of improvement* (1959), is recommended, as are E. L. Woodward, *The age of reform, 1815–1870* (1938), a solid volume of the Oxford History of England; N. Gash, *Politics in the age of Peel, 1830–1850* (1953); and G. S. R. Kitson Clark, *An expanding society: Britain, 1830–1900* (1968). On the Chartists see M. Hovell, *The Chartist movement* (1918, 1925), and J. L. and B. Hammond, *The age of the Chartists, 1832–1854* (1930), of which their *The bleak age** (1934, 1947), is a shorter version. R. J. Cruikshank, *Charles Dickens and early Victorian England* (1949), is a colorful, well-illustrated study of the novelist and the people he wrote about. Some protest movements of the era are well conveyed in R. J. White, *Waterloo to Peterloo* (1957); D. Rend, *Peterloo: the massacre and its background* (1958); and E. J. Hobsbawm and G. Rudé, *Captain Swing* (1969), a study of the rural poor and agrarian unrest in the years 1815 to 1830.

The widening functions of government are analyzed in E. W. Cohen, *The growth of the British civil service, 1780–1939* (1941); M. P. Hall, *The social services of modern England* (3rd ed., 1955); K. B. Smellie, *History of local government* (1946); surveys by H. Finer (4th ed., 1950) and W. A. Robson (3rd ed., 1954); the monumental S. and B. Webb, *English local government* (9 vols., 1906–1929), and D. Owen, *English philanthropy, 1660–1960* (1964). Reform legislation is discussed in the old but still valuable A. Harrison and E. L. Hutchins, *A history of factory legislation* (1903); M. W. Thomas, *The early factory legislation* (1948), and J. T. Ward, *The factory system, 1830–1855*, cited above. Other reform movements are examined in D. G. Barnes, *A history of the English Corn Laws, from 1660 to 1846* (1930); N. McCord, *The Anti-Corn-Law League, 1838–1846* (1958); R. Radzinowicz, *A history of English criminal law: the movement for reform, 1750–1833* (1948); M. M. Law, *British slavery and its abolition, 1823–38* (1926); and F. J. Klingberg, *The anti-slavery movement in England* (1926). Books on socialism and trade unionism are cited elsewhere in this chapter and in Chapter XIV.

For thinkers and reformers of the age there are available E. Halévy, *The growth of philosophic radicalism* (3 vols., 1901–1904; in 1 vol., 1949); L. Stephen, *The English utilitarians* (3 vols., 1900); S. Maccoby, *English radicalism* (5 vols., 1935–1955); J. Bowle, *Politics and opinion in the nineteenth century** (1954); D. C. Somervell, *English thought in the nineteenth century** (1929, 1962); and C. Brinton, *English political thought in the nineteenth century** (1933, 1950). An interesting study is S. R. Letwin, *The pursuit of certainty: David Hume, Jeremy Bentham, John Stuart Mill, Beatrice Webb* (1965). Among biographies there are M. Packe on John Stuart Mill (1954); M. Mack on Jeremy Bentham (1963); G. D. H. Cole on William Cobbett (1924) and Robert Owen (1930); studies of Owen by F. Podmore (1924) and M. Cole (1953); G. M. Trevelyan, *Lord Grey of the Reform Bill* (1920, 1929); C. R. Fay, *Huskisson and his age* (1951); G. Wallas, *The life of Francis Place,*

1771–1854 (1898, 1925); C. Driver, *Tory radical: the life of Richard Oastler* (1946); J. L. and B. Hammond, *Lord Shaftesbury* (4th ed., 1936); and B. Blackburn, *Noble lord: the seventh Earl of Shaftesbury* (1949).

   Among important studies of the Victorian age, some going beyond the scope of this chapter, are G. M. Young, *Victorian England: portrait of an age** (2 vols., 1934); A. Briggs, *Victorian cities* (1965), and *Victorian people** (1955); O. Chadwick, *The Victorian church, 1829–1860* (1966); and W. E. Houghton, *The Victorian frame of mind, 1830–1870* (1957).

Among a number of works stressing nineteenth-century social thought are C. Brinton, *Political ideas of the English romanticists* (1926); J. Barzun, *Romanticism and the modern ego* (1943); the same author's *Berlioz and the romantic century* (2 vols., 1950); D. O. Evans, *Social romanticism in France 1830–1848* (1951); and B. Croce, *European literature in the nineteenth century* (1924). G. Brandes, *Main currents in nineteenth century thought* (6 vols., 1872–1890, trans. from Danish, 1901–1906), is still useful. Political and other meanings of romanticism are analyzed in R. F. Gleckner and G. E. Ensco (eds.), *Romanticism* (1962). Other notable studies of the interplay of ideas and politics include H. Marcuse, *Reason and revolution: Hegel and the rise of social theory* (1941); F. Wiedemann, *Hegel* (1968); G. O. Griffith, *Interpreters of man: a review of secular and religious thought from Hegel to Barth* (1943); T. Whittaker, *Reason: a philosophical essay with historical illustrations: Comte, Mill, Schopenhauer, Vico, Spinoza* (1943); P. Roubiczek, *The misrepresentation of man: studies in European thought in the nineteenth century* (1947); M. Peckham, *Beyond the tragic vision: the quest for identity in the nineteenth century** (1962); and J. L. Talmon, *Political messianism: the romantic phase* (1960). On conservative and nationalist implications of "scientific" history, see T. H. Von Laue, *Leopold Ranke: the formative years* (1950), and G. G. Iggers, *The German conception of history . . . from Herder to the present* (1968). D. Thomson, *Equality* (1949), and A. Rosenberg, *Democracy and socialism: a contribution to the political history of the past 150 years* (1939), both explore some of the problems posed by the French Revolution for the nineteenth and twentieth centuries. F. E. Manuel, *The prophets of Paris** (1962), cited earlier, stresses the link between Enlightenment ideas and nineteenth-century social thought. P. Viereck, *Metapolitics: the roots of the Nazi mind** (1941, rev., 1961), and R. D. O. Butler, *The roots of national socialism* (1942), are two attempts to explain Nazism in historical terms—a procedure which can, of course, be quite unfair to the nineteenth century. E. Golob, *The "isms": a history and evaluation* (1954), is useful but less comprehensive than the title would imply. On political alignments D. Caute, *The left in Europe since 1789** (1966), may be supplemented by H. Rogger and E. Weber (eds.), *The European right: a historical profile** (1965).

The vast literature on this subject may be approached through the following: C. J. H. Hayes, *Essays on nationalism* (1926), *The historical evolution of modern nationalism* (1931, 1948), and *Nationalism: a religion* (1960); H. Kohn, *The idea of nationalism: a study in its origin and background* (1944), from Hebraic and Hellenic times; his *Prelude to nation-states: the French and German experience, 1789–1815* (1967), already cited; and his briefer *Prophets and peoples: studies in nineteenth century nationalism** (1946); L. L. Snyder, *The meaning of nationalism* (1954); and B. C. Shafer, *Nationalism: myth and reality* (1955). Other studies include E. Barker, *National character and the factors in its formation* (1927); S. W. Baron, *Modern nationalism and religion* (1947); H. M. Chadwick, *Nationalities of Europe: the growth of national ideologies* (1945, rev., 1966); E. H. Carr, *Nationalism and after* (1944); F. Hertz, *Nationality in history and politics* (1944); A. Cobban, *National self-determination* (1948); K. W. Deutsch, *Nationalism and social communication** (1953); K. Deutsch and W. J. Folz (eds.), *Nation-building** (1963); and K. R. Minogue, *Nationalism* (1967). F. M. Barnard, *Herder's social and political thought: from Enlightenment to nationalism* (1965), focuses on cultural nationalism, and R. Schlesinger, *Federalism in central and eastern Europe* (1945), examines

Bibliography | the interrelationship of various nationalities living close together.   On language the following are suggested: J. Vendryes, *Language: a linguistic introduction to history* (1925, 1949); K. Vossler, *The spirit of language in civilization* (1932); and F. Bodmer, *The loom of language* (1944).   C. Lévi-Strauss, *Structural anthropology** (trans. 1963), and other writings are also of prime importance.

The following works are suggestive of developments outside the major Western countries of Europe: R. W. Seton-Watson, *The rise of nationality in the Balkans* (1917), and a short essay, *The historian as a political force in central Europe* (1922); S. B. Clough, *A history of the Flemish movement in Belgium: a study in nationalism* (1930); O. J. Falnes, *National romanticism in Norway* (1933); and H. Kohn, *Pan-Slavism: its history and ideology** (1953).   B. C. Shafer has prepared a useful bibliographical essay in the AHA Service Center series, *Nationalism: interpreters and interpretations** (1959).

Liberalism | A fundamental work on this subject is G. de Ruggiero, *The history of European liberalism* (1927), a comparative analysis of English, French, German, and Italian liberalism.   L. T. Hobhouse, *Liberalism* (1911), is a valuable little companion to the sections on England, and J. H. Hallowell, *The decline of liberalism as an ideology* (1943), argues on the basis of German experience that liberalism is lost if separated from ideas of absolute truth and value.   B. Croce, *History of Europe in the nineteenth century* (1933), is a philosophical and historical treatment of the idea of liberty; it may be compared with H. J. Muller, *Freedom in the modern world** (1966), the final volume of a three-volume study.   On German political ideas one may profitably compare L. Krieger, *The German idea of freedom* (1957); H. Kohn, *The mind of Germany: the education of a nation* (1960); and K. Epstein, *The genesis of German conservatism* (1966).   There are studies of de Tocqueville by J. P. Mayer (1939) and by R. Herr (1960).   J. S. Schapiro, *Liberalism and the challenge of fascism: social forces in England and France, 1815–1870* (1949), deals with the concurrent growth of liberal and antiliberal ideas; and B. Russell, *Freedom vs. organization, 1814–1914** (1934, 1947), shows the dilemma of liberalism in a period of rapid economic change.   The most provocative book of all on liberalism remains H. J. Laski, *The rise of European liberalism** (1936, 1947), which presents the story as one of the gradual taming of a revolutionary doctrine.   A useful anthology is A. Bullock and M. Shock (eds.), *The liberal tradition* (1957).

Socialism | Among general surveys are H. W. Laidler, *History of socialism* (rev., 1968); P. Taft, *Movements for economic reform* (1950); and N. I. Mackenzie, *Socialism: a short history* (1949).   A. Gray, *The socialist tradition: Moses to Lenin** (1946), is a witty, penetrating, but unsympathetic account.   G. Lichtheim, *A short history of socialism** (1970), and other writings by the same author are recommended highly.

A large-scale comprehensive study, stressing the interaction of men, movements, and ideas, is G. D. H. Cole, *A history of socialist thought* (4 vols., 1953–1956), covering the years 1789–1939; C. Landauer, *European socialism: a history of ideas and movements from the industrial revolution to Hitler's seizure of power* (2 vols., 1959), is also useful.   A valuable bibliography as well as thoughtful essays are available in D. D. Egbert, S. Persons, and T. Bassett (eds.), *Socialism and American life* (2 vols., 1952), a good part of which is concerned with the European setting; vol. II is entirely devoted to a descriptive and critical bibliography of socialism. Egbert has also written *Social radicalism and the arts* (1970), on cultural changes affected by political developments since 1789.   E. H. Carr, *Studies in revolution* (1950), is a series of incisive essays on earlier and later socialists.   Some useful studies of pre-Marxian anticapitalism are E. M. Butler, *The Saint-Simonian religion in Germany: a study of the Young Germany movement* (1926); G. G. Iggers, *The cult of authority: the political cult of the Saint-Simonians* (1958); F. E. Manuel, *The new world of Henri Saint-Simon* (1956); D. W. Brogan, *Proudhon* (1934); and H. de Lubac, *The un-*

Marxian socialist: a study of Proudhon (1948). British reform activities, including those of
Robert Owen, are referred to at the beginning of this chapter, and additional literature on
Marxism appears in Chapters XII and XIV. A. Fried and R. Sanders, *Socialist thought: a
documentary history** (1964), is a useful anthology.

For the development of economic ideas one may turn to C. Gide and C. Rist, *History of economic
doctrines* (rev., 1948), and E. Roll, *A history of economic thought* (rev., 1946), mentioned in the
introductory section; E. Whittaker, *Schools and streams of economic thought* (1960), contains an
illuminating section on Adam Smith's moral and economic ideas, which may be read along
with J. Rae's older biography (1895). R. Heilbroner, *The worldly philosophers** (1953), cited
earlier, is also useful on the economic liberals. Smith's influence can be seen in *Free trade
and other fundamental doctrines of the Manchester School* (1903), ed. by F. W. Hirst, a collection of
speeches and writings. M. E. Hirst, *The life of Friedrich List and selections from his writings* (1909),
studies the German advocate of economic nationalism.

In addition to the books cited at the end of Chapter X and the beginning of this chapter the
reader may turn to W. A. Phillips, *The confederation of Europe: a study of the European alliance
1813–1823* (1914, 1920); E. L. Woodward, *War and peace in Europe, 1815–1870, and other essays*
(1931); and H. G. Schenk, *The aftermath of the Napoleonic wars: the Concert of Europe—an experiment*
(1947). H. Kissinger, *A world restored: Metternich, Castlereagh and the problems of peace, 1812–1822*
(1957), already cited, is especially stimulating. P. Viereck, *Conservatism revisited: the revolt
against revolt, 1815–1949** (1949, rev., 1965), attempts to rehabilitate the reputations of the
post-1815 conservatives, especially Metternich. On the latter there are sympathetic
biographies by A. Herman (1932) and H. du Coudray (1935), and a valuable study, P. W.
Schroeder, *Metternich's diplomacy at its zenith, 1820–1823* (1962).

British foreign affairs may be followed through these books and through C. K. Webster,
The foreign policy of Castlereagh, 1815–1822 (1925); C. J. Bartlett, *Castlereagh* (1967); H. Temperley,
The foreign policy of Canning, 1822–1827 (1925); H. C. F. Bell, *Lord Palmerston* (2 vols., 1936); P.
Guedalla, *Palmerston, 1784–1865* (1927, 1942); and D. Southgate, *'The most English minister'* . . . :
the policies and politics of Palmerston (1966).

The situation arising from the interest of European powers in Latin America is presented
in D. Perkins, *A history of the Monroe Doctrine* (1941, rev., 1963); C. K. Webster, *Britain and the
independence of Latin America, 1812–1830* (1944); W. P. Cresson, *The Holy Alliance: the European
background of the Monroe Doctrine* (1922); A. P. Whitaker, *The United States and the independence of
Latin America, 1800–1830* (1941); and the detailed study of Anglo-American relations in the
years 1775–1823 by B. Perkins, cited earlier (3 vols., 1955–1964). Two biographical
introductions to the subject are J. B. Trend, *Bolivar and the independence of Spanish America**
(Teach Yourself History series, 1948), and J. Kinsbrunner, *Bernardo O'Higgins** (1968).

Other important stirrings in the same period are described in C. W. Crawley, *The question
of Greek independence* (1930); C. M. Woodhouse, *The Greek war of independence* (1952); J. H. Brady,
Rome and the Neapolitan revolution of 1820–21 (1937); G. T. Romani, *The Neapolitan revolution of
1820–1821* (1950); A. G. Mazour, *The first Russian revolution, 1825: the Decembrist movement**
(1937); M. Zetlin, *The Decembrists* (1958); and M. Raeff, *The Decembrist movement* (1966), a
narrative with documents.

Two stimulating books on international affairs transcending this chapter are L. C. B.
Seaman, *From Vienna to Versailles** (1956), and W. N. Medlicott (ed.), *From Metternich to Hitler:
aspects of British and foreign history, 1814–1939** (1963). A useful reference tool is G. A. Kertesz
(ed.), *Documents in the political history of the European continent, 1815–1939* (1969).

Relevant pamphlets include P. A. M. Taylor (ed.), *The industrial revolution in Britain: triumph or disaster?* (1958); G. A. Cahill (ed.), *The great Reform Bill of 1832: liberal or conservative?* (1969); J. B. Halsted (ed.), *Romanticism: definition, explanation, and evaluation* (1965); H. F. Schwarz (ed.), *Metternich: the "coachman of Europe": statesman or evil genius?* (1962); and M. Walker (ed.), *Metternich's Europe, 1815–1848* (1968). Many pamphlets of essays and readings in the Anvil series are useful: H. Kohn, *Nationalism: its meaning and history* (1955); P. Viereck, *Conservatism: from John Adams to Churchill* (1956); J. S. Schapiro, *Liberalism: its meaning and history* (1958); the same author's *Movements of social dissent in modern Europe* (1962); J. H. Stewart, *The Restoration era in France, 1814–1830* (1968); and P. Beik, *Louis Philippe and the July Monarchy* (1965). On Latin American subjects two titles are useful: R. A. Humphreys and J. Lynch, *The origins of the Latin American revolutions, 1808–1826* (1967), and J. J. Johnson, *Simon Bolivar and Spanish-American independence, 1783–1830* (1968).

Problems and Readings*

XII: 1848: A Revolution That Misfired

The best introductions to the events of 1848 and their aftermath are W. L. Langer, *Political and social upheaval, 1832–1852** (1969), in the Langer series; G. Duveau, *The making of a revolution** (trans. 1968); P. S. Robertson, *Revolutions of 1848: a social history** (1952); and the brief G. Fasel, *Europe in upheaval: the revolutions of 1848** (1970). Other studies include F. Fejtö, *The opening of an era: 1848, an historical symposium* (1948); A. Whitridge, *Men in crisis: the revolutions of 1848* (1949), studies of leading personalities in various countries; and J. Eastwood and P. Tabori, *'48, the year of revolutions* (1948), a journalistic survey garnished with *Punch* cartoons. Two studies opening with this period are G. Woodcock, *A hundred years of revolution: 1848 and after* (1948), and R. J. Cruikshank, *Roaring century, 1846–1946* (1946), colorful sketches from the files of the London *Daily Mail*. A special subject is well treated in C. B. Woodham-Smith, *The great hunger: Ireland, 1845–1849* (1962).

Revolutions in Various Countries

In addition to the general accounts described above and in the previous chapter, the following will be found useful on the ferment of 1815–1850 in the various European countries:

FRANCE. R. Arnaud, *The Second Republic and Napoleon III* (1930), a narrative account; F. A. De Luna, *The French republic under Cavaignac* (1969); A. Lamartine, *History of the French Revolution of 1848* (trans. 1891), by one of the participants; J. Marriott, *The French Revolution of 1848 in its economic aspect* (2 vols., 1913), emphasizing the ideas of Louis Blanc and Émile Thomas; D. C. McKay, *The national workshops: a study in the French Revolution of 1848* (1933); and L. Loubère, *Louis Blanc: his life and his contribution to the rise of French Jacobin socialism* (1961).

ITALY. G. F. H. and J. Berkeley, *Italy in the making* (3 vols., 1932–1940); B. King, *A history of Italian unity* (2 vols., 1912); G. M. Trevelyan, *Garibaldi's defense of the Roman republic, 1848–1849* (1907, 1949); and the same author's *Manin and the Venetian revolution of 1848* (1923). Also recommended: M. C. Wicks, *The Italian exiles in London, 1816–1848* (1937); R. J. Rath, *The provisional Austrian regime in Lombardy-Venetia, 1814–1815* (1968); K. R. Greenfield, *Economics and liberalism in the Risorgimento: a study in nationalism in Lombardy, 1814–1848* (1934); R. Grew, *A sterner plan for Italian unity: the Italian National Society and the Risorgimento* (1963); A. J. P. Taylor, *The Italian problem in European diplomacy, 1847–1849* (1934); and three books by E. E. Y. Hales: *Pio Nono* [Pius IX], *a study in European politics and religion in the nineteenth century* (1954), *Revolution and papacy, 1769–1846* (1960), and *Mazzini and the secret societies* (1956).

HABSBURG LANDS. J. Redlich, *Emperor Francis Joseph of Austria* (1929), an absorbing biography; J. Blum, *Noble landowners and agriculture in Austria, 1815–1848: a study in the origins of the peasant* emancipation of 1848 (1948); A. Schwarzenberg, *Prince Felix zu Schwarzenberg, prime minister of Austria, 1848–1852* (1947); C. Sproxton, *Palmerston and the Hungarian revolution* (1919); and R. J. Rath, *The Viennese revolution of 1848* (1957). Metternich's career and fall are recounted in books listed earlier.

GERMANY AND THE FRANKFURT ASSEMBLY. V. Valentin, *1848: chapters of German history* (1940), an abridgement of the author's larger study in German; L. B. Namier, *1848: the revolution of the intellectuals** (1946), sharply critical of the Frankfurt Assembly; and F. Eyck, *The Frankfurt Parliament, 1848–1849* (1968), a detailed account of the assembly itself. The impact of the failure of 1848 upon German society is explored in E. Kohn-Bramstedt, *Aristocracy and the middle-classes in Germany: social types in German literature, 1830–1900* (1937). Many works relevant to the revolution of 1848 in various countries are also listed in the following chapter in connection with the successful unification movements.

The best brief biography of Marx is I. Berlin, *Karl Marx: his life and environment** (1948). There are numerous others, including studies by M. Beer (1921, 1935), E. H. Carr (1938), F. Mehring (1918, 1948), R. Payne (1968), O. Rühle (1929, 1943), L. Schwarzschild (1947), and C. J. Sprigge* (1949). J. H. Jackson, *Marx, Proudhon, and European socialism** (Teach Yourself History series, 1958), helps to provide the European setting. G. Mayer, *Friedrich Engels: a biography* (1920, 1936), shows that Engels played a far greater role than previously realized; and D. Footman, *Ferdinand Lassalle: romantic revolutionary* (1946), is a colorful picture of the early Social Democrat that by no means supersedes earlier biographies by E. Bernstein (1893), W. H. Dawson (1899), and G. Brandes (1925). The story of Marx's daughter is skillfully told in C. Tsuzuki, *The life of Eleanor Marx, 1885–1898* (1967).

On the theoretical foundations and concrete manifestations of socialism, there is, of course, an enormous and highly controversial literature, to which the books cited under socialism for Chapter XI and those cited for Chapter XIV offer a certain amount of guidance; much current discussion stresses the relationship between Marx's mature thought and his early writings. Informative interpretive accounts include A. G. Meyer, *Marxism: unity of theory and practice** (1957); G. Lichtheim, *Marxism: an historical and critical study** (1961), and *A history of socialism** (1970), already cited; S. Avineri, *The social and political thought of Karl Marx* (1969); B. D. Wolfe, *Marxism: one hundred years in the life of a doctrine* (1965); G. D. H. Cole, *The meaning of Marxism** (1948); and two books by S. Hook: *Towards the understanding of Karl Marx* (1933), and *From Hegel to Marx** (1936). H. J. Laski wrote widely and incisively on socialism, and some of his keenest observations appear in his centennial edition of the Manifesto, *The Communist Manifesto: socialist landmark* (1948), which also contains the original text and prefaces by Marx and Engels. E. Wilson, *To the Finland station: a study in the writing and acting of history** (1940), is an imaginative discussion of the way in which early and later socialists, and nonsocialists, interpreted the past to influence the present. M. M. Bober, *Karl Marx's interpretation of history** (1927, 1948), is a technical study, as is H. Lefebvre, *The sociology of Marx* (1966, trans. 1968). A. G. Meyer has a valuable bibliographical essay in the AHA Service Center series, *Marxism since the Communist Manifesto** (rev., 1969).

Readable and informative works are J. M. Thompson, *Louis Napoleon and the Second Empire** (1954); R. Williams, *The world of Napoleon III** (1957, rev., 1965); T. A. B. Corley, *Democratic despot: a life of Napoleon III* (1961); and B. D. Gooch, *The Second Empire: the reign of Napoleon III** (1969). There are older accounts, still useful, by R. Arnaud (1940), O. Aubry (1940), F. A. Simpson (2 vols., 1909, 1923), and P. Guedalla (1922, 1937). Other recommended studies include T. Zeldin, *The political system of Napoleon III* (1958); G. P. Gooch, *The Second Empire* (1960),

Bibliography

a series of judicious essays; and H. C. Payne, *The police state of Louis Napoleon Bonaparte, 1851–1860* (1966), although the title is misleading. Interesting interpretations appear in H. A. L. Fisher, *Bonapartism* (1908, 1914); A. Guérard's two books, *Reflections on the Napoleonic legend* (1924), and *Napoleon III: an interpretation* (1943); and J. S. Schapiro's *Liberalism and the challenge of fascism*, already cited. Economic aspects are studied in A. L. Dunham, *The Anglo-French treaty of commerce of 1860* (1930), and the same author's *The industrial revolution in France*, already cited. On the rebuilding of Paris one may turn to D. Pinkney, *Napoleon III and the reconstruction of Paris* (1958), and J. M. and B. Chapman, *The life and times of Baron Haussmann* (1957). A scholarly effort to rehabilitate the empress is H. Kurtz, *The Empress Eugénie, 1826–1920* (1964), which may be supplemented by N. N. Barker, *Distaff diplomacy: the Empress Eugénie and the foreign policy of the Second Empire* (1967).

*Problems and Readings**

Three booklets are relevant: M. Kranzberg (ed.), *1848: a turning point?* (1959); S. M. Osgood (ed.), *Napoleon III: buffoon, modern dictator, or sphinx?* (1963); and B. D. Gooch (ed.), *Napoleon III, man of destiny: enlightened statesman or proto-fascist?* (1963). In the Anvil series there are G. Bruun, *Revolution and reaction, 1848–1852: a midcentury watershed* (1958), and S. Hook, *Marx and the Marxists: the ambiguous legacy* (1955).

XIII: The Consolidation of Large Nation-States, 1859–1871

R. C. Binkley, *Realism and nationalism, 1852–1871** (1935), in the Langer series, is a valiant effort to clarify the segment of European history that followed the revolutions of 1848; a brief synthesis of the era is provided in N. Rich, *The age of nationalism and reform, 1850–1890* (1970), in the Norton History of Modern Europe. J. P. T. Bury (ed.), *The zenith of European power, 1830–1871*, already cited, in the New Cambridge Modern History, has many relevant chapters. An outstanding attempt to view the period 1848–1918 as a whole, from the point of view of international affairs, is A. J. P. Taylor, *The struggle for mastery in Europe, 1848–1918* (1954). [Books on nationalism and on the earlier phases of national unification have been cited in Chapters XI and XII.]

The Crimean War

Some salient features of the Eastern question and of the Crimean War are treated in detail in H. Temperley, *England and the Near East: the Crimea* (1936); V. J. Puryear, *England, Russia, and the Straits question, 1844–1856* (1931); C. K. Webster, *The foreign policy of Palmerston, 1830–1841* (2 vols., 1951); the volume by D. Southgate on Palmerston (1966), cited in Chapter XI; and G. B. Henderson, *Crimean War diplomacy, and other historical essays* (1947). A dramatic episode of the war is skillfully recounted in C. B. Woodham-Smith, *The reason why** (1953), and the same author has written a biography of Florence Nightingale (1957). The impact on England is discussed in O. Anderson, *A liberal state at war: English politics and economics during the Crimean War* (1967). Other treatments of the Crimean War period will be found in the general accounts cited in the previous paragraph. On the changing nature of warfare opening up in this era see C. B. Falls, *A hundred years of war* (1954).

Unification of Italy

In addition to the works cited on Italy for the two foregoing chapters, the following are suggested: W. R. Thayer, *The life and times of Cavour* (2 vols., 1911); A. J. Whyte, *The political life and letters of Cavour, 1848–1861* (1930); two lively studies by G. M. Trevelyan; *Garibaldi and the Thousand, May 1860* (1909, 1920) and *Garibaldi and the making of Italy, June–November 1860* (1911, 1920); and C. Hibbert, *Garibaldi and his enemies: the clash of arms and personalities in the making of Italy* (1966), a sound, popular account. Highly recommended also are D. Mack

Smith, *Cavour and Garibaldi in 1860: a study in political conflict* (1954), and his succinct biography, *Garibaldi: a great life in brief* (1956). G. O. Griffith, *Mazzini: prophet of modern Europe* (1932), is the best biography of Mazzini, but S. Barr, *Mazzini: portrait of an exile* (1935), is stimulating, and G. Salvemini, *Mazzini** (1910, 1957), still useful. An informative special study is L. M. Case, *Franco-Italian relations, 1860–1865* (1932).

The outstanding study of the economic basis for unification is W. O. Henderson, *The Zollverein* (1939), but see also A. H. Price, *The evolution of the Zollverein* (1949). H. Friedjung, *The struggle for supremacy in Germany, 1859–1866* (1897, trans. 1935), is a detailed diplomatic and military account by an Austrian historian; and on the key campaign of 1866 G. A. Craig has written *The battle of Königgrätz* (1964). On the events of 1870 recommended studies include L. D. Steefel, *Bismarck, the Hohenzollern candidacy, and the origins of the Franco-German War of 1870* (1962); R. H. Lord, *The origins of the war of 1870* (1924); H. Oncken, *Napoleon III and the Rhine: the origin of the war of 1870–71* (1928); W. E. Mosse, *The European powers and the German question* (1958); and R. Millman, *British foreign policy and the coming of the Franco-Prussian War* (1965). The relevant documents on the origins of the war of 1870 are available in G. Bonnin (ed.), *Bismarck and the Hohenzollern candidature for the Spanish throne* (1957).

E. Eyck's extensive biography of Bismarck (3 vols., 1941–1944) is not translated, but a summary of Eyck's conclusions, *Bismarck and the German empire** (1950), is available. W. N. Medlicott, *Bismarck and modern Germany** (Teach Yourself History series, 1965), is an excellent brief introduction. Other studies of Bismarck include C. G. Robertson, *Bismarck* (1919); A. J. P. Taylor, *Bismarck: the man and the statesman** (1955); F. Darmstaedter, *Bismarck and the creation of the Second Reich* (1949); L. L. Snyder, *The blood and iron chancellor: a documentary biography of Otto von Bismarck* (1967); and W. Richter, *Bismarck* (trans. 1965). The Prussian phase is studied in E. N. Anderson, *The social and political conflict in Prussia, 1858–1864* (1954). Two important works on the entire period are O. Pflanze, *Bismarck and the development of Germany: the period of unification, 1815–71* (vol. I, 1963), with a second volume projected on the period of consolidation, 1871–1890; and T. S. Hamerow, *The social foundations of German unification, 1858–1871* (1969). An admirable study of military and other phases of the Franco-Prussian War is M. Howard, *The Franco-Prussian War: the German invasion of France, 1870–1871** (1961).

For Austria-Hungary the volumes by C. A. Macartney and by A. J. P. Taylor, cited in Chapter XI, should be consulted, as well as O. Jászi, *The dissolution of the Habsburg monarchy* (1929), and A. J. May, *The Habsburg monarchy 1867–1914** (1951).

An authoritative treatment of nineteenth-century Russia is provided in H. Seton-Watson, *The Russian empire, 1801–1917* (1967), in the Oxford History of Modern Europe, and in his *Decline of imperial Russia, 1855–1914** (1952). M. Karpovich, *Imperial Russia, 1801–1917** (1932), is a handy sketch in the Berkshire series. On the reign of the five emperors from Alexander I to Nicholas II, S. Harcave has written *Years of the golden cockerel: the last Romanov tsars, 1814–1917* (1968). On the reforms of Alexander II one may turn to W. E. Mosse, *Alexander II and the modernization of Russia** (1958); and S. Graham, *Tsar of freedom: the life and reign of Alexander II* (1935), is a sympathetic biography. The place of the peasant emancipation in Russian history may be studied in J. Blum, *Lord and peasant in Russia from the ninth to the nineteenth century,** already cited, which carries the story to emancipation; G. Pavlovsky, *Agricultural Russia on the eve of the Revolution* (1930); G. T. Robinson, *Rural Russia under the old regime** (1930, 1949); T. Emmons, *The Russian landed gentry and the peasant emancipation of 1861* (1968); and W. S. Vucinich (ed.), *The peasant in nineteenth century Russia** (1968). Useful also for these years are F. H. Skrine, *The expansion of Russia, 1815–1900* (1903); M. B. Petrovich, *The emergence of Russian Pan-Slavism, 1856–1870* (1956); W. L. Blackwell, *The beginnings of Russian industrialization,*

Bibliography   1800–1860 (1968); and J. S. Curtiss, *The Russian army under Nicholas I, 1825–1855* (1965). A special subject is explored in R. F. Leslie, *Reform and insurrection in Russian Poland, 1856–1865* (1963). The intellectual world is studied in D. Hecht, *Russian radicals look to America, 1825–1894* (1947); E. H. Carr's books, *The romantic exiles: a nineteenth century portrait gallery** (1933, 1949) and *Michael Bakunin* (1937); and N. V. Riasanovsky, *Russia and the West in the teaching of the Slavophiles* (1952). Other books on prerevolutionary Russia are described in Chapter XVII.

The United States   The reconstruction period may be approached through K. M. Stampp, *The era of reconstruction, and Canada   1865–1877* (1965), and invaluable on an important special subject is J. H. Franklin, *From slavery to freedom: a history of Negro Americans* (1947, 1967). Standard works on the European implications of the American struggle include E. D. Adams, *Great Britain and the American Civil War* (2 vols., 1925), and D. Jordan and E. J. Pratt, *Europe and the American Civil War* (1931).

    The growth of Canadian self-government within an imperial framework is discussed in D. G. Creighton, *Dominion of the North, a history of Canada* (1944); C. W. New, *Lord Durham* (1929); and C. P. Stacey, *Canada and the British army, 1846–1871: a study in the practice of responsible government* (1936). External affairs are discussed in J. B. Brebner, *North Atlantic triangle: the interplay of Canada, the United States and Great Britain* (1945), and in G. Glazebrook, *Canadian external relations: an historical study to 1914* (1942). A useful introduction to all subjects relating to Canada is G. M. Craig, *The United States and Canada* (1968), in the American Foreign Policy Library series. R. W. Winks has a bibliographical essay in the AHA Service Center series, *Recent trends and new literature in Canadian history** (1959).

Japan and the West   G. B. Sansom's two books, *Japan: a short cultural history* (1931, 1944) and *The Western world and Japan* (1950), describe Japanese civilization before and during the nineteenth century, respectively. His detailed multivolumed history carries the narrative to 1867 (3 vols., 1958–1964). Two excellent accounts by E. O. Reischauer, *Japan: past and present* (1946, 1953) and *The United States and Japan** (rev., 1957), are highly recommended. Also recommended are H. Borton, *Japan's modern century* (1955); R. Storry, *A history of modern Japan** (1960); W. G. Beasley, *The modern history of Japan** (1963); E. H. Norman, *Japan's emergence as a modern state* (1940); W. L. Neumann, *America encounters Japan: from Perry to MacArthur** (1963); and I. Nish, *The story of Japan* (1968). Two specialized treatments are R. E. Ward (ed.), *Political development in modern Japan* (1968), and B. S. Silberman, *Ministers of modernization: elite mobility in the Meiji restoration, 1868–1873* (1964). J. W. Hall has a valuable bibliographical essay in the AHA Service Center series, *Japanese history: new dimensions of approach and understanding** (1961).

Problems and   A number of booklets will be useful for subjects touched on in this chapter. On the Crimean Readings*   War: B. D. Gooch (ed.), *The origins of the Crimean War* (1969). On Italy: C. F. Delzell (ed.), *The unification of Italy, 1859–1861* (1965); M. Walker (ed.), *Plombières: secret diplomacy and the rebirth of Italy* (1968); D. M. Smith (ed.), *The making of Italy, 1796–1870* (1968); the same author's *Garibaldi* (Great Lives Observed series, 1969); and M. Salvadori, *Cavour and the unification of Italy* (Anvil series, 1961). On Germany: T. S. Hamerow (ed.), *Otto von Bismarck: a historical assessment* (1962); O. Pflanze (ed.), *The unification of Germany, 1848–1871* (1968); and F. B. M. Hollyday, *Bismarck* (Great Lives Observed series, 1970). On Japan: A Tiedemann, *Modern Japan: a brief history* (Anvil series, rev., 1962).

An indictment of the late nineteenth century (and by implication of the age that followed) is C. J. H. Hayes, *A generation of materialism, 1871–1900** (1941), in the Langer series, arguing that liberalism, tainted by materialism and nationalism, opened the way to destructive totalitarianism. The final two volumes in the New Cambridge Modern History cover those years, the titles indicating their emphases: F. H. Hinsley (ed.), *Material progress and world-wide problems, 1870–1898* (1962), and R. L. Mowat (ed.), *The shifting balance of world forces, 1898–1945* [1968, a revision of the original vol. XIII edited by D. Thomson under the title *The era of violence, 1898–1945* (1960)]. B. W. Tuchman, *The proud tower: a portrait of the world before the war, 1890–1914** (1966), provides picturesque selected vignettes; and F. Gilbert, *The end of the European era, 1890 to the present** (1970), in the Norton History of Modern Europe, is a thoughtful, brief synthesis. J. M. Roberts, *Europe, 1880–1945** (1967), the final volume in the Hay series, is a somewhat encyclopedic survey, but useful on economic and demographic subjects. G. Barraclough, *An introduction to contemporary history** (1964), is a provocative essay, calling for a global approach to contemporary history. C. F. Ware, K. M. Pannikar, and J. Romein, *The twentieth century* (1966), vol. VI of the UNESCO History of Mankind, is useful on cultural subjects but lacks coherent treatment.

An introduction to historical demography is provided in C. M. Cipolla, *The economic history of world populations* (1962), and the sources for demographic studies are described in T. H. Hollingsworth, *Historical demography* (1969). H. Moller (ed.), *Population movements in modern European history** (1964), is a useful anthology of articles. Up-to-date discussion of the subject may be found in D. V. Glass and D. E. C. Everseley (eds.), *Population in history* (1965), an important collection of essays, and in E. A. Wrigley, *Industrial growth and population change* (1961). A. M. Carr-Saunders, *World population: past growth and present trends* (1936), is dated but still valuable. Other studies include H. P. Fairchild, *People: the quantity and quality of population* (1939); R. E. Dickinson, *The west European city: a study in urban geography* (1951, 1961); W. E. Moore, *Economic demography of eastern and southern Europe* (1945); and D. Kirk, *Europe's population in the inter-war years* (1946).

Population movements are interpreted in the massive volumes by W. F. Wilcox and others, *International migrations* (2 vols., 1929, 1931); J. Isaac, *Economics of migration* (1947); D. R. Taft and R. Robbins, *International migrations: the immigrant in the modern world* (1955); M. L. Hansen, *The Atlantic migration, 1607–1860: a history of the continuing settlement of the United States** (1940); and W. D. Forsyth, *The myth of open spaces: Australian, British, and world trends of population and migration* (1942).

Population statistics can be brought up-to-date by consulting the United Nations, *Statistical Yearbook* (1948 ff.), and *Demographic Yearbook* (1948 ff.).

In addition to general economic histories the following are recommended: W. Ashworth, *A short history of the international economy since 1850* (rev., 1963); the same author's *An economic history of England, 1870–1939* (1960); J. B. Condliffe, *The commerce of nations* (1950); and on European agriculture since the 1800s, M. Tracy, *Agriculture in western Europe* (1963). Two important institutional studies are C. Wright and C. E. Fayle, *A history of Lloyd's* (1928), on the great English marine insurance center, and J. Clapham, *The Bank of England, a history* (2 vols., 1945), already cited.

Economic studies stressing the role of European capital include L. H. Jenks, *The migration of British capital to 1875* (1927, 1938); H. Feis, *Europe, the world's banker, 1870–1914** (1930); D. C. M. Platt, *Finance, trade, and politics in British foreign policy, 1815–1914* (1968); and R. E. Cameron, *France and the industrial development of Europe, 1800–1914* (1961, rev., 1968). Economic growth in the major European countries is studied in C. P. Kindleberger, *Economic growth in France and Britain, 1851–1950* (1963), which may be compared with W. W. Rostow, *The stages of economic growth* (1960), cited earlier; A. L. Levine, *Industrial retardation in Britain, 1880–1914* (1967); and G. Stolper and others, *The German economy, 1870 to the present* (1940, trans. 1967). American developments in these years may be studied in T. C. Cochran and W. Miller, *The age of enterprise** (1949); R. H. Wiebe, *The search for order, 1877–1920* (1967); and J. A. Garraty, *The new commonwealth* (1968). Two studies of combinations and cartels are H. Levy, *The new industrial system: a study of the origins, forms, finance, and prospects of concentration in industry* (1936), and E. Hexner, *International cartels* (1945).

The general histories of modern France described in Chapter XI should be consulted and the bibliographical chapters in G. Wright, *France in modern times* (1960). On the years since 1870 one may turn to D. W. Brogan, *France under the republic, 1870–1939** (1940), and to his *The French nation, 1814–1940,** cited earlier, although both are difficult for the general reader. A. Sedgwick, *The Third French Republic, 1870–1914** (1968), is a useful brief introduction. D. Thomson's *Democracy in France since 1870** (1946, rev., 1969), is a penetrating analytical study, and G. Chapman, *The Third Republic of France: the first phase, 1871–1894* (1962), a detailed narrative.

French political thought may be examined in J. P. Mayer, *Political thought in France from the Revolution to the Fourth Republic* (1943, 1949), and in A. Scott, *Republican ideas and the liberal tradition in France, 1870–1914* (1951). Other recommended studies on France not strictly confined to the years before 1914 are G. Wright, *Rural revolution in France: the peasantry in the twentieth century** (1964); R. Challener, *The French theory of the nation in arms, 1866–1939* (1952); P. M. de la Gorce, *The French army: a military-political history* (1963); D. G. Ralston, *The army of the republic: the place of the military in the political evolution of France, 1871–1914* (1967); and R. Shattuck, *The banquet years: the arts in France, 1885–1918* (1958). Religious questions since 1870 are treated comprehensively in A. Dansette's *Religious history of modern France,* vol. II, *Under the Third Republic* (trans. 1961); and special aspects are explored in E. Acomb, *The French laic laws, 1879–1889* (1941), and in A. Sedgwick, *The Ralliement in French politics, 1890–1898* (1965).

The tumultuous beginnings of the Third Republic are discussed from various points of view in A. Horne, *The fall of Paris: the siege and the Commune, 1870–1871** (1968); R. L. Williams, *The French Revolution of 1870–1871* (1969); M. Kranzberg, *The siege of Paris, 1870–1871* (1950); E. S. Mason, *The Paris Commune* (1930); F. Jellinek, *The Paris Commune of 1871** (1937); F. H. Brabant, *The beginnings of the Third Republic in France* (1940); J. P. T. Bury, *Gambetta and the national defence: a republican dictatorship in France* (1936); and J. T. Joughin, *The Paris Commune in French politics, 1871–1880* (2 vols., 1955).

On the Dreyfus affair there are detailed and detached accounts by D. Johnson, *France and the Dreyfus Affair* (1967), the best now available, and by G. Chapman, *The Dreyfus case: a reassessment* (1955); and more impassioned accounts by N. Halasz, *Captain Dreyfus: the story of a mass hysteria** (1955), and M. Josephson, *Zola and his time* (1928). R. F. Byrnes presents part of the background in *Antisemitism in modern France: prologue to the Dreyfus affair* (1950).

On political men and movements of the right there are valuable studies, many reaching beyond 1914, among them: M. Curtis, *Three against the Third Republic: Sorel, Barrès and Maurras* (1959); W. C. Buthman, *The rise of integral nationalism in France,* focusing on Charles Maurras (1939); E. Weber, *Action Française: royalism and reaction in twentieth century France** (1963), a remarkably full account; the same author's *The nationalist revival in France, 1905–1914* (1959); and E. R. Tannenbaum, *The Action Française* (1962). R. Rémond, *The right wing in France: 1815 to de Gaulle* (1954, trans. 1966), has already been cited; and it may be supplemented by D. Shapiro (ed.), *The right in France, 1890–1914* (St. Antony's Papers, 1962). Biographical studies include R. Binion, *Defeated leaders: the political fate of Caillaux, Jouvenel and Tardieu* (1960); two biographies of Clemenceau: J. H. Jackson, *Clemenceau and the Third Republic** (Teach Yourself History series, 1948), and G. Bruun, *Clemenceau* (1943); M. L. Brown, Jr., *The comte de Chambord: the Third Republic's uncompromising king* (1967); and H. A. Schmitt, *Charles Péguy: the decline of an idealist* (1967). [Additional studies of men and movements of the left are described below under Socialist Movement and Socialist Parties.]

Bibliography

The best narrative account of Italy since unification is D. Mack Smith, *Italy: a modern history* (1959, rev., 1969), in the University of Michigan series; economic developments are ably presented in S. B. Clough, *The economic history of modern Italy* (1964), cited in Chapter XI. For the years after unification C. J. Sprigge, *The development of modern Italy* (1944), is useful, but the best-balanced account is C. Seton-Watson, *Italy from liberalism to fascism, 1870–1925* (1967), which may be supplemented by J. A. Thayer, *Italy and the Great War: politics and culture, 1870–1915* (1964), and a brief, readable introduction, S. Saladino, *Italy from unification to 1919: growth and decay of a liberal regime** (Europe since 1500 series, 1970). Two specialized studies for this era are A. W. Salomone, *Italian democracy in the making: the political scene in the Giolittian era, 1900–1914* (1945); and A. C. Jemolo, *Church and state in Italy, 1850–1950* (1960).

Italy

The general histories of Germany cited in Chapter XI and the studies on Bismarck in the preceding chapter are also to be consulted, as is G. Stolper, *The German economy, 1870 to the present*, cited earlier in this chapter. W. H. Dawson, *The German empire, 1867–1914, and the unity movement* (2 vols., 1919), is still valuable. Another substantial study is W. F. Bruck, *Social and economic history of Germany, 1888–1938* (1938). Special insights are provided in R. H. Lowie, *The German people: a social portrait to 1914* (1945); H. Kohn, *The mind of Germany: the education of a nation** (1960), cited earlier; and W. M. Simon (ed.), *Germany in the age of Bismarck* (1968). Other studies include J. A. Nichols, *Germany after Bismarck** (1959), on the Caprivi era; J. C. G. Röhl, *Germany without Bismarck: the crisis of government in the Second Reich, 1890–1900* (1968); N. Rich, *Friedrich von Holstein: politics and diplomacy in the era of Bismarck and Wilhelm II* (2 vols., 1965); L. Cecil, *Albert Ballin: business and politics in imperial Germany, 1888–1918* (1967); F. B. M. Hollyday, *Bismarck's rival: General and Admiral Albrecht von Stosch* (1960); H. Levy, *Industrial Germany: a study of its monopoly organizations and their control by the state* (1935); A. Gerschenkron, *Bread and democracy in Germany* (1943); L. W. Muncy, *The Junker in the Prussian administration under William II, 1888–1914* (1944); M. Kitchen, *The German officer corps, 1890–1914* (1968); and F. Lilge, *The abuse of learning: the failure of the German university* (1948). Two biographies of William II are V. Cowles, *The Kaiser* (1963), and M. Balfour, *The Kaiser and his times* (1963). H. C. Meyer examines American historical writings on Germany in *Five images of Germany: half a century of American views on German history** (1960), in the AHA Service Center series.

To the books on Austria cited in Chapter XIII may be added three books by W. A. Jenks: *The Austrian electoral reform of 1907* (1950), *Austria under the iron ring, 1879–1893* (1965), and *Vienna and the young Hitler* (1960).

Germany, 1870–1914

R. C. K. Ensor, *England, 1870–1914* (1936, 1949), provides the best general account of the period, although it is stronger on domestic than on foreign affairs. Important too is the epilogue to E. Halévy's *History of the English people*, cited earlier, covering the years 1895 to 1914. G. Dangerfield, *The strange death of liberal England** (1935), is a searching study of tensions in English society between 1910 and 1914; it may be supplemented by S. Hynes, *The Edwardian turn of mind* (1968). A. P. Thornton, *The habit of authority: paternalism in British history* (1966), is a provocative essay. Two syntheses moving on into the twentieth century are D. C. Somervell, *British politics since 1900* (1950), and K. Hutcheson, *Decline and fall of British capitalism*

Great Britain, 1870–1914

(1950). Recommended also are the following, of which some have been cited in Chapter XI: R. J. Evans, *The Victorian age, 1815–1914* (1950); G. M. Young, *Victorian England: portrait of an age* (2 vols., 1934); G. Kitson Clark, *The making of Victorian England* (1962); W. E. Houghton, *The Victorian frame of mind* (1957); and W. L. Burn, *The age of equipoise** (1964). H. M. Lynd, *England in the eighteen eighties: toward a social basis for freedom* (1945), is an attempt to apply the "Middletown" technique of sociological investigation to history.

Almost every major figure in British life in this period has been the subject of at least one biography. Among biographical accounts are L. Strachey, *Queen Victoria** (1921), and *Eminent Victorians** (1918, 1933); A. Cecil, *Queen Victoria and her prime ministers* (1952); biographies of Victoria by E. F. Benson (1935), R. Fulford (1951), and E. Longford* (1965); A. Ponsonby, *Henry Ponsonby: Queen Victoria's private secretary* (1942); and P. Magnus, *King Edward the Seventh* (1964). On Gladstone: the older work of J. Morley (3 vols., 1903); W. P. Hall, *Mr. Gladstone* (1931); J. L. Hammond and M. R. D. Foot, *Gladstone and liberalism** (1953), in the Teach Yourself History series; and P. Magnus, *Gladstone: a biography** (1955). On Disraeli: the older work by W. F. Monypenny and G. E. Buckle (6 vols., 1913–1920), now superseded by R. Blake, *Disraeli** (1967), a distinguished biography. The same author has also written *The unknown prime minister: the life and times of Andrew Bonar Law* (1955). Joseph Chamberlain is the subject of an exhaustive multivolumed biography, *The life of Joseph Chamberlain*, the first four volumes by J. L. Garvin (1932–1951) and the latter two by J. Amery (1968–1969). An introduction to the lives of Austin and Neville Chamberlain is provided in the somewhat adulatory D. H. Elletson, *The Chamberlains* (1966). D. C. Somervell has written *Disraeli and Gladstone, a duo-biographical sketch* (1927), and R. Jenkins, *Asquith** (1964). Recommended also are W. Irvine, *The universe of G. B. S.* (1949), on George Bernard Shaw; M. Cole (ed.), *The Webbs and their work* (1949); K. Muggeridge and R. Adam, *Beatrice Webb: a life, 1858–1943* (1968); H. Ausubel, *In hard times: reformers among the late Victorians* (1960); and the same author's *John Bright: Victorian reformer** (1966). R. Kelley, *The transatlantic persuasion: the liberal-democratic mind in the age of Gladstone* (1969), is of special interest.

Political and party issues are examined in depth in M. Cowling, *1867: Disraeli, Gladstone and revolution: the passing of the Second Reform Bill* (1967); F. B. Smith, *The making of the Second Reform Bill* (1966); and P. Smith, *Disraelian conservatism and social reform* (1967). The vicissitudes of the Liberals in the era after Gladstone and their accomplishments are studied in P. Stansky, *Ambitions and strategies: the struggle for the leadership of the Liberal party in the 1890's* (1964); M. Richter, *The politics of conscience* (1964); C. Cross, *The Liberals in power, 1905–1914* (1963); B. D. Gilbert, *The evolution of national insurance in Great Britain* (1966); and M. Bruce, *The coming of the welfare state* (1961, rev., 1966). A pioneer work in electoral sociology is H. Pelling, *Social geography of British elections, 1885–1910* (1967).

On the women's rights movement in this era see two earlier books: R. Strachey, *The cause* (1928), and I. Clephane, *Towards sex freedom* (1935); and three more recent works: J. Kamm, *Rapiers and battleaxes: the women's movement and its aftermath* (1966); C. Rover, *Women's suffrage and party politics in Britain, 1866–1914* (1967); and D. Mitchell's somewhat popular account, *The fighting Pankhursts: a study in tenacity* (1967).

The Irish question is discussed in detail in J. O'Connor, *History of Ireland, 1798–1924* (2 vols., 1926); J. E. Pomfret, *The struggle for land in Ireland, 1800–1923* (1930); J. C. Beckett, *The making of modern Ireland* (1966), cited earlier; and L. J. McCaffrey, *The Irish question, 1800–1922** (1968).

[General histories of socialism are listed for Chapter XI, and works on Marx and Marxism for Chapter XII.] On the modern translation of Marxist ideas into institutional form, the books by G. D. H. Cole, *A history of socialist thought,* and by C. Landauer, *European socialism,* both already cited, are indispensable. In addition there are many specific studies of socialist parties and leaders in each country.   For France: A. Noland, *The founding of the French socialist party, 1893–1905* (1956); S. Bernstein, *The beginnings of Marxian socialism in France* (1933), on the period roughly 1860–1880; H. R. Weinstein, *Jean Jaurès: a study of patriotism in the French socialist movement* (1936); J. H. Jackson, *Jean Jaurès: his life and work* (1943); and an outstanding biography by H. Goldberg, *A life of Jean Jaurès* (1962).   For Germany: C. E. Schorske, *German social democracy, 1905–1917** (1955), a masterful study; A. J. Berlau, *The German Social Democratic party, 1914–1921* (1949); P. Gay, *The dilemma of democratic socialism: Eduard Bernstein's challenge to Marx** (1952), a perceptive study of Bernstein's revisionism; G. Roth, *The Social Democrats in imperial Germany* (1963); and V. L. Lidtke, *The outlawed party: social democracy in Germany, 1878–1890* (1966).   An important biographical work is J. P. Nettl, *Rosa Luxemburg* (2 vols., 1966; abr. 1 vol., 1969).   On Britain: M. Beer, *History of British socialism* (1912, 1948); H. Pelling, *The origins of the Labour party, 1880–1900* (1954, 1965); other studies of early labor history by J. H. S. Reid (1955) and P. Poirier (1958); E. R. Pease, *The history of the Fabian society* (2nd ed., 1925); G. D. H. Cole, *Fabian socialism* (1943); and A. H. McBriar, *Fabian socialism and English politics, 1884–1918** (1962), the most objective account.   Christian socialism is explored in P. d'A. Jones, *The Christian Socialist revival, 1877–1914: religion, class, and social conscience in late-Victorian England* (1968); and for Marx's somewhat negligible impact on the British labor scene see H. Collins and C. Abramsky, *Karl Marx and the British Labour movement* (1965).   On the Internationals there are L. L. Lorwin, *Labor and internationalism* (1929); J. Joll, *The Second International, 1889–1914* (1955); and J. Braunthal, *History of the International* (1961; trans. 2 vols., 1966).   The most comprehensive introduction to anarchism is G. Woodcock, *Anarchism: A history of libertarian ideas and movements* (1962), but also useful is J. Joll, *The anarchists** (1964).

An indispensable classic treatment is S. Perlman, *Theory of the labor movement* (1928, 1949). Useful surveys are W. Galenson (ed.), *Comparative labor movements* (1952), and W. A. McConagha, *The development of the labor movement in Great Britain, France, and Germany* (1942). H. Pelling, *A history of British trade unionism* (1963), supersedes G. D. H. Cole's earlier study (1927), as well as F. Williams, *Magnificent journey: rise of the trade unions* (1955).   The pioneer work of S. and B. Webb, *History of trade unionism* (1894, 1920), remains important.   H. A. Clegg, A. Fox, and A. F. Thompson, *A history of British trade unions since 1889*, vol. I, *1889–1910* (1964), is the first volume of a detailed history.   On the British cooperatives there are G. D. H. Cole, *A century of co-operation* (1944), and F. Hall and W. P. Watkins, *Co-operation* (1934).   For French trade union development the background chapters of V. R. Lorwin, *The French labor movement* (1954), are recommended as are two earlier studies: L. L. Lorwin, *Syndicalism in France* (1912, 1914), and P. T. Moon, *The labor problem and the Social Catholic movement in France* (1921).   For Germany one may turn to W. H. Dawson's old but still valuable treatments of labor and labor problems, *Bismarck and state socialism* (1890) and *Social insurance in Germany, 1883–1911* (1912); W. R. Sanders, *Trade unionism in Germany* (1916); and E. Anderson, *Hammer or anvil: the story of the German working-class movement* (1945), mostly on the period after 1914.   On Italy an important study, despite its extravagant title, is M. F. Neufeld, *Italy, school for awakening countries: the Italian labor movement in its political, social, and economic setting from 1860 to 1960* (1961).   Finally, J. Kuczynski, *A short history of labour conditions under industrial capitalism* (4 vols., 1942–1946), is a comprehensive treatment, written from a Marxian viewpoint, and arguing with statistical detail that labor conditions deteriorated markedly under capitalism.

The best general history of science in the nineteenth century is W. P. D. Wightman, *The growth of scientific ideas* (1951).   On biology, evolution, and Darwinism one may turn to P. Fothergill, *Historical aspects of organic evolution* (1952); J. C. Greene, *The death of Adam: evolution and its impact on Western thought* (1959); P. B. Sears, *Charles Darwin: the naturalist as a cultural force* (1950); G.

Labor Movement and Labor Unions

The New Movement in Science

Bibliography   Himmelfarb, _Darwin and the Darwinian revolution*_ (1959); L. Eiseley, _Darwin's century_ (1961); and G. R. deBeers, _Charles Darwin_ (1958). C. C. Gillispie, _The edge of objectivity_ (1960), is important for Darwinism and other subjects. On the impact of the scientific developments on religion, the classic account is A. D. White, _A history of the warfare of science and theology*_ (1896, many eds.); more recent studies include J. A. O'Brien, _Evolution and religion_ (1932); C. C. Gillispie, _Genesis and geology_ (1951); W. Irvine, _Apes, angels, and Victorians_ (1955); and J. W. Burrow, _Evolution and society: a study in Victorian social theory_ (1966).

On the rise of twentieth-century physics there are E. Zimmer, _The revolution in physics_ (1936); C. T. Chase, _The evolution of modern physics_ (1947); and A. Einstein and L. Infeld, _The evolution of physics_ (1938). Einstein may best be approached through L. Infeld, _Albert Einstein: his work and its influence on our world*_ (1950); L. Barnett, _The universe and Dr. Einstein_ (1952); and the brief H. Cuny, _Albert Einstein*_ (1962). F. Wittels, _Freud and his time_ (1931, 1948), and P. Rieff, _Freud: the mind of the moralist_ (1959), are two of the best studies of Sigmund Freud; they may be compared with the masterful biography by E. Jones (3 vols., 1953–1957; 1 vol. abr., 1961). B. P. Babkin has written _Pavlov: a biography_ (1949); a study of Pavlovian techniques in their practical and political aspects is W. Sargent, _Battle for the mind_ (1957).

Social Thought   The relations between science and social thought, and other subjects, are elucidated in considerable detail in J. T. Merz, _A history of European thought in the nineteenth century_ (4 vols., 1897–1914), and in H. Höffding, _A history of modern philosophy_ (1900, 1924); but two outstanding modern contributions on the latter part of the century are H. S. Hughes, _Consciousness and society: the reorientation of European social thought, 1890–1930*_ (1958), and G. Masur, _Prophets of yesterday: studies in European culture, 1890–1914*_ (1961). Other works on the period include E. Barker, _Political thought in England_ (1915, 1947); J. Bowle, _Politics and opinion in the nineteenth century*_ (1954), already cited; E. Wilson, _Axel's castle: a study in the imaginative literature of 1870–1930_ (1931); W. M. Simon, _European positivism in the nineteenth century_ (1963); D. G. Charlton, _Positivist thought in France during the Second Empire_ (1959); and J. Higham and others, _The origins of modern consciousness_ (1965). More specialized studies are W. Irvine, _Walter Bagehot_ (1939); H. Alpert, _Emile Durkheim and his sociology_ (1939), on a leading French systematizer; J. P. Mayer, _Max Weber and German politics: a study in political sociology_ (1944); J. Freund, _The sociology of Max Weber_ (1966, trans. 1968); R. Humphrey, _Georges Sorel: prophet without honor_ (1951). The best study of Nietzsche is by W. A. Kaufmann, _Nietzsche: philosopher, phychologist, antichrist*_ (1950); and on one of Nietzsche's intimates, Lou Andreas Salomé, R. Binion has attempted a psychoanalytical biography, _Frau Lou: Nietzsche's wayward disciple_ (1968). R. A. Nisbet, _The sociological tradition*_ (1966), cited earlier, is useful for these years.

Racism, Integral Nationalism, and the Cult of Violence   The later development of totalitarianism is dealt with in connection with Chapter XIX. Books examining the revolt against rationalism in politics beginning with the late nineteenth century are H. Kohn, _The twentieth century_ (1957); H. Arendt, _The origins of totalitarianism*_ (1951, 1958), a somewhat abstruse work which finds the roots of totalitarianism in late-nineteenth-century imperialism, nationalism, and anti-Semitism; J. Barzun, _Darwin, Marx, Wagner: critique of a heritage*_ (1941), which points out resemblances in the assumptions and conclusions of the three men; E. Heller, _The disinherited mind_ (1957); and K. Löwith, _From Hegel to Nietzsche: the revolution in nineteenth century thought_ (1941, trans. 1964). Specific studies along similar lines are H. W. C. Davis, _Political thought of Heinrich von Treitschke_ (1915); A. Dorpalen, _Heinrich von Treitschke_ (1957); P. W. Massing, _Rehearsal for destruction: a study of political anti-Semitism in imperial Germany_ (1949); P. G. J. Pulzer, _The rise of political anti-Semitism in Germany and Austria_ (1964); and K. von Klemperer, _Germany's new conservatism: its history and dilemma in the twentieth century*_ (1968). On racism one may consult J. Barzun, _Race: a study in modern ethnic theories_

(1937); L. L. Snyder, *Race: a history of modern ethnic theories* (1939); R. Benedict, *Race, science, and politics* (1941); and the UNESCO publication, *The race question in modern science* (1956).

Two scholarly surveys with considerable attention to contemporary Protestantism are J. H. Nichols, *History of Christianity, 1650–1950* (1956), and E. E. Cairns, *Christianity through the centuries* (1954).

More specifically on the Catholic church, in addition to the study by E. L. Woodward cited at the beginning of Chapter XI, are C. C. Eckhardt, *The papacy and world affairs, as reflected in the secularization of politics* (1937); E. E. Y. Hales' sympathetic study of Pius IX, *Pio Nono* (1954), cited earlier; L. P. Wallace, *The papacy and European diplomacy 1869–1878* (1948); C. Butler, *The Vatican Council: the story told from inside in Bishop Ullathorne's letters* (2 vols., 1930); and R. Fülöp-Miller, *Leo XIII and our times* (1937).

Several books on aspects of Jewish affairs, including Zionism, by J. W. Parkes, are valuable: *The emergence of the Jewish problem, 1878–1939* (1946), *The Jewish problem in the modern world* (rev., 1946), *Anti-Semitism** (1963), and *A history of the Jewish people* (1952). The syntheses of Jewish history by H. M. Sachar, *The course of modern Jewish history** (1958), and L. Finkelstein (ed.), *The Jews: their history, culture and religion* (2 vols., 1949), have already been cited.

Pamphlets relevant to this chapter are R. L. Williams (ed.), *The Commune of Paris, 1871* (1969); L. Derfler (ed.), *The Dreyfus affair: tragedy of errors?* (1964); H. R. Kedward (ed.), *The Dreyfus affair: catalyst for tensions in French society* (1965); and E. C. Helmreich (ed.), *A free church in a free state: the Catholic church, Italy, Germany, France, 1864–1914* (1964). In the Anvil series there are H. Ausubel, *The late Victorians: a short history* (1955); R. L. Schuyler and C. Weston, *British constitutional history since 1832* (1957); L. L. Snyder, *The idea of racialism: its meaning and history* (1962); and J. S. Schapiro, *Anticlericalism: conflict between church and state in France, Italy, and Spain* (1967). On intellectual developments a useful anthology is R. Stromberg (ed.), *Realism, naturalism, and symbolism: modes of thought and expression in Europe, 1848–1914* (1968).

W. L. Langer, *The diplomacy of imperialism, 1890–1902* (2 vols., 1935), contains a full, balanced discussion of imperialism in all aspects. Other valuable studies are D. K. Fieldhouse, *The colonial empires* (1966), already cited; H. Gollwitzer, *Europe in the age of imperialism, 1880–1914** (1969), in the Barraclough series; R. F. Betts, *Europe overseas: phases of imperialism** (1968); and two older accounts: M. E. Townsend, *European colonial expansion since 1871* (1941), and P. T. Moon, *Imperialism and world politics* (1926). Motives and justifications for imperialist activities are analyzed in E. M. Winslow, *The pattern of imperialism: a study in the theories of power* (1948); R. Koebner and H. D. Schmidt, *Imperialism: the story and significance of a political word, 1840–1960* (1964); A. P. Thornton, *Doctrines of imperialism* (1965); T. Kemp, *Theories of imperialism* (1968); J. A. Schumpeter, *Imperialism and social classes* (trans. 1951); W. Woodruff, *Impact of Western man* (1967); and T. Geiger, *The conflicted relationship: the West and the transformation of Asia, Africa, and Latin America* (1967). Other important discussions and studies include G. Clark's two books, *A place in the sun* (1936) and *The balance sheets of imperialism* (1936); L. C. Robbins, *The economic causes of war* (1939); E. Staley, *War and the private investor* (1935); R. Maunier, *The sociology of colonies: an introduction to the study of race contact* (2 vols., 1949); and D. Mannoni, *Prospero and Caliban** (1956), stressing the psychological impact of colonial rule on both rulers and governed. Two key books that later stimulated much inquiry into the nature of imperialism are J. A. Hobson's *Imperialism: a study** (1902), an incisive critique by an English self-styled "economic heretic," and V. I. Lenin's *Imperialism, the highest stage of capitalism** (1916). British

Bibliography

imperialism is analyzed in R. Faber, *The vision and the need: late Victorian imperialist aims* (1966); R. Robinson and J. Gallagher, *Africa and the Victorians: the official mind of imperialism** (1961); B. Semmel, *Imperialism and social reform: English social imperial thought, 1895–1914** (1960); A. P. Thornton, *The imperial idea and its enemies: a study in British power** (1959); and M. Beloff, *Imperial sunset: vol. I, Britain's liberal empire, 1897–1921* (1970). There are valuable chapters in vol. III of The Cambridge History of the British Empire (1959), and in P. Knaplund, *The British Empire, 1815–1939* (1941), an older survey. Biographical accounts include J. L. Garvin's multivolumed *The life of Joseph Chamberlain,* cited in the previous chapter; W. L. Strauss, *Joseph Chamberlain and the theory of imperialism* (1942); and V. Halperin, *Lord Milner and the empire: the evolution of British imperialism* (1952). Special subjects are explored in G. S. Graham, *Great Britain in the Indian Ocean: a study of maritime enterprises, 1810–1850* (1968); J. B. Kelly, *Britain and the Persian Gulf, 1795–1880* (1968); B. C. Busch, *Britain and the Persian Gulf, 1895–1914* (1968); and F. Kazemzadeh, *Russia and Britain in Persia, 1864–1914* (1968).

The imperial activities of the other leading European powers [except Russia—discussed at the end of this chapter and under Chapter XVII] are described in M. E. Townsend, *The rise and fall of Germany's colonial empire, 1884–1918* (1930); W. O. Henderson, *Studies in German colonial history* (1963); H. Brunschwig, *French colonialism, 1871–1914: myths and realities* (1960, trans. 1966); T. F. Power, Jr., *Jules Ferry and the renaissance of French imperialism* (1944); H. I. Priestley, *France overseas: a study of modern imperialism* (1938); S. H. Roberts, *History of French colonial policy, 1870–1925* (2 vols., 1929); and C. Hollis, *Italy in Africa* (1941). Two helpful bibliographical essays are L. J. Ragatz, *The literature of European imperialism, 1815–1939* (rev., 1947), and D. Healy, *Modern imperialism: changing styles in historical interpretation** (AHA Service Center series, 1967).

The Americas

On the expansion of the United States, A. K. Weinberg, *Manifest destiny** (1935), is a standard general work. E. R. May, *Imperial democracy* (1961), and *American imperialism: a speculative essay* (1968), are indispensable on American motivations. Other phases of American foreign policy are treated in United States diplomatic histories and in M. W. Williams, *Anglo-American Isthmian diplomacy, 1815–1915* (1916); J. W. Pratt, *Expansionists of 1898** (1936), and *America's colonial experiment* (1950); W. Millis, *The martial spirit** (1931), an ironic discussion of the Spanish-American War; M. Tate, *The United States and the Hawaiian kingdom* (1965); and H. and M. Sprout, *The rise of American naval power, 1776–1918* (1939). D. Dawson, *The Mexican adventure* (1935), is a careful account of Napoleon III's fiasco during the 1860s; and F. Tannenbaum's *Mexico: the struggle for peace and bread* (1950) provides a running narrative of Mexican history, with a detailed examination of twentieth-century events. J. F. Rippy, *Latin America and the industrial age* (1944), may be added to the works on South and Central America previously cited.

The Ottoman Empire and the Balkans

Two general accounts are G. E. Kirk, *A short history of the Middle East* (rev., 1957), and H. Kohn, *A history of nationalism in the East* (1929). B. Lewis, *The emergence of modern Turkey* (1961, rev., 1969), an outstanding work, treats nineteenth-century developments as background. Other valuable studies are J. Haslip, *The Sultan: the life of Abdul Hamid II* (1958), a vivid scholarly account with much insight into the empire; S. Mardin, *The genesis of Young Ottoman thought* (1963), on the decade 1867–1878; W. W. White, *The process of change in the Ottoman Empire* (1937); R. H. Davison, *Reform in the Ottoman Empire, 1856–1876* (1963); H. Dodwell, *The founder of modern Egypt: a study of Muhammad Ali* [Mehemet Ali] (1931); L. Ostrorog, *The Angora reform* (1928); D. C. Blaisdell; *European financial control in the Ottoman Empire* (1929); D. S. Landes, *Bankers and pashas: international finance and economic imperialism in Egypt** (1958); and R. L. Tignor,

Modernization and British colonial rule in Egypt, 1882–1914 (1966). The diplomacy surrounding the construction of the Suez Canal may be studied in J. Marlowe, *World ditch: the making of the Suez Canal* (1964); J. Pudney, *Suez: de Lesseps' canal* (1969); and P. Balfour [Lord Kinross], *Between two seas* (1969).

The best introduction to the diplomatic status of Turkey in modern times is M. S. Anderson, *The Eastern question, 1774–1923* (1966), cited in Chapter V; other studies include F. E. Bailey, *British policy and Turkish reform: a study in Anglo-Turkish relations, 1826–1853* (1942); R. W. Seton-Watson, *Disraeli, Gladstone, and the Eastern question* (1935); W. N. Medlicott, *The Congress of Berlin and after: a diplomatic history of the Near Eastern settlement, 1878–1880* (1938, rev., 1963); E. M. Earle, *Turkey, the Great Powers, and the Bagdad railway* (1923); and M. K. Chapman, *Great Britain and the Bagdad railway* (1948).

On the Balkans L. Stavrianos, *The Balkans since 1453*, and R. J. Wolff, *The Balkans in our times,** have already been cited; in addition one may turn to B. H. Sumner, *Russia and the Balkans, 1870–1880* (1937); C. Sforza, *Fifty years of war and diplomacy in the Balkans* (1941); J. A. Levandis, *The Greek foreign debt and the Great Powers, 1821–1898* (1944); T. W. Riker, *The making of Roumania: a study of an international problem, 1856–1866* (1931); W. C. Vucinich, *Serbia between East and West: the events of 1903–1908* (1954); C. Jelavich, *Tsarist Russia and Balkan nationalism* (1958); and C. E. Black, *The establishment of constitutional government in Bulgaria* (1943).

A valuable introductory survey for Africa as a whole is G. P. Murdock, *Africa: its peoples and their culture history* (1959). R. Hallett, *The penetration of Africa: European exploration in North and West Africa to 1815* (1965), is an effort to examine the inner workings of African societies as well as European exploration in the earlier years; and the use of "oral tradition" in the reconstruction of early African history is brilliantly demonstrated in J. Vansina, *Kingdoms of the savanna** (1966). On European exploration and expansion useful introductions include H. H. Johnston, *The opening up of Africa* (1911); H. L. Hoskins, *European imperialism in Africa* (1930), in the Berkshire series; and H. A. Wieschoff, *Colonial policies in Africa* (1944). P. Curtin, *The image of Africa: British ideas and action, 1780–1850* (1964), is an important study in political and cultural interaction. W. E. B. Du Bois, *The world and Africa* (1947), presents ideas and historical materials not readily accessible elsewhere; it may be read in connection with R. L. Buell, *The native problem in Africa* (2 vols., 1928), and J. A. Noon, *Labor problems of Africa* (1944). P. Duignan and L. H. Gann's *Burden of empire: an appraisal of Western colonialism south of the Sahara* (1967) attempts to demonstrate that the benefits of European expansion outweighed the debits. The same writers are coeditors of a projected four-volume collaborative history of modern Africa, *Colonialism in Africa, 1870–1960*, of which vol. I, *The history and politics of colonialism, 1870–1914* (1969), has appeared.

A monumental history of missionary activity in Africa since 1840 is C. P. Groves, *The planting of Christianity in Africa* (4 vols., 1948–1959). Biographical studies include J. Simmons, *Livingstone and Africa* (1955); G. Seaver, *David Livingstone, his life and letters* (1957); F. Debenham, *The way to Ilala: David Livingstone's pilgrimage* (1955); R. Oliver, *Sir Harry Johnston and the scramble for Africa* (1957); G. Elton, *Gordon of Khartoum* (1954); J. Marlowe, *Mission to Khartum* (1969); and M. F. Perham, *Lugard: the years of adventure, 1858–1898* (1936). There are biographies of Cecil Rhodes by B. Williams (1921), A. Maurois (1953), and S. G. Millin (1933). B. Williams has written *Botha, Smuts, and South Africa* (1948), in the Teach Yourself History series. The best study of the Congo to 1908 is R. Slade, *King Leopold's Congo* (1962). R. Anstey has written *Britain and the Congo in the nineteenth century* (1962). Other important monographs are R. Coupland, *East Africa and its invaders* (1938), to 1856, and *The exploitation of East Africa, 1856–1890: the slave trade and the scramble* (1939); M. M. Knight, *Morocco as a French economic venture: a study of open door imperialism* (1937); H. Rudin, *Germans in the Cameroons, 1884–1914; a*

Bibliography   *case study in modern imperialism* (1938); and S. E. Crowe, *The Berlin West-African conference, 1884–1885* (1942).

Asia   [Japan is discussed mainly in Chapter XIII, and Asian problems in general after 1918 are treated in Chapters XVIII and XXI.]   Among the most informative general discussions of the European impact on the Far East are J. Pratt, *The expansion of Europe in the Far East* (1947); and *China and Britain* (1944); P. H. Clyde and B. F. Beers, *The Far East: a history of the impact of the West on eastern Asia* (1948, 1966); and F. H. Michael and G. E. Taylor, *The Far East in the modern world* (1956).   An excellent introduction to Chinese history is J. K. Fairbank, *The United States and China** (1948, 1958), in the American Foreign Policy Library series.   Other useful short surveys include those by K. S. Latourette, *The Chinese: their history and culture* (3rd ed., 1940); the same author's *A history of modern China* (1954); L. C. Goodrich, *A short history of the Chinese people* (1943, 1951); and C. P. Fitzgerald, *China: a short cultural history* (1938, 1954).

European relations with China are taken up in G. F. Hudson, *Europe and China* (1930); E. R. Hughes, *The invasion of China by the Western world* (1938); J. K. Fairbank, *Trade and diplomacy on the China coast: the opening of the treaty ports, 1842–1854** (2 vols., 1953); Ssu-yu Teng and J. K. Fairbank, *China's response to the West: a documentary survey, 1839–1923** (1954, 1963); Li Chien-nung, *The political history of China, 1840–1928* (trans. 1956); M. Collis, *Foreign mud: being an account of the opium imbroglio in Canton in the 1830's and the Anglo-Chinese war that followed* (1947); N. A. Pelcovits, *Old China hands and the Foreign Office* (1948); and V. Purcell, *The Boxer uprising* (1963).

For nineteenth-century developments in India see, in addition to books already described in Chapters IV and VI: P. J. Griffiths, *The British impact on India* (1952); P. Moon, *Strangers in India* (1942); S. Sen, *Eighteen fifty-seven* (1957); T. R. Metcalf, *The aftermath of revolt: India, 1857–1870* (1964); and T. W. Wallbank, *India: a survey of the heritage and growth of Indian nationalism* (1948), a Berkshire study.   M. Edwardes, *British India, 1772–1947* (1968), is especially useful.   On Indochina C. Robequain, *The economic development of French Indo-China* (1944), and J. F. Cady, *The roots of French imperialism in eastern Asia* (1954, rev., 1967), may be consulted.

In addition to the works on Russian foreign policy cited in the chapters that follow, there may be mentioned here: A. Lobanov-Rostovsky, *Russia and Asia* (1933), and B. H. Sumner, *Tsardom and imperialism in the Far East and the Middle East, 1880–1914* (1942).   For the story of the Russian fleet that eventually was defeated at Tsushima by the Japanese, one may read A. Nobikov-Priboy, *Tsushima* (trans. 1944); F. Thiess, *The voyage of forgotten men* (1947); and R. Hough, *The fleet that had to die* (1958).   The diplomatic history of the war is recounted in J. A. White, *The diplomacy of the Russo-Japanese War* (1964).

There are bibliographical essays in the AHA Service Center series by R. H. Davison on the Near and Middle East (1959), by R. I. Crane on India (1958), by C. O. Hucker (1958) and by J. K. Fairbank (1968) on China, and by P. D. Curtin on Africa (1963).

Problems and   Relevant booklets include H. M. Wright (ed.), *The "new imperialism": analysis of late nineteenth
Readings*   century expansion* (1961); R. W. Winks (ed.), *British imperialism: gold, God, glory* (1963); R. F. Betts (ed.), *The scramble for Africa: causes and dimensions of empire* (1966); T. C. Caldwell (ed.), *The Anglo-Boer War* (1965); and R. A. Austen (ed.), *Modern imperialism: Western overseas expansion in the age of industrialism* (1969).   On India there are M. D. Lewis (ed.), *The British in India* (1962); P. J. Marshall (ed.), *Problems of empire: Britain and India, 1757–1813* (1968); and A. T. Embree (ed.), *1857 in India: mutiny or war of independence?* (1963).   In the Anvil series D. N. Rowe has
1094   written *Modern China: a brief history* (1959).

For the diplomatic history of the years 1870–1914, A. J. P. Taylor, *The struggle for mastery in Europe, 1848–1918* (1954), cited earlier, is the best general account; also useful is the older R. J. Sontag, *European diplomatic history, 1871–1932* (1933). On diplomacy in the two decades after 1870 there is the masterful study by W. L. Langer, *European alliances and alignments, 1871–1890** (1931, 1950); the same author's *The Franco-Russian alliance, 1880–1894* (1929) and *The diplomacy of imperialism, 1890–1902* (2 vols., 1935), already cited. Two books by Medlicott, *The Congress of Berlin and after*, already cited, and *Bismarck, Gladstone, and the concert of Europe* (1956), are more critical of Bismarck than is Langer. G. A. Craig, *From Bismarck to Adenauer* (1958), is informative on Bismarck's direction of foreign policy.

Two thoughtful analyses for the student and general reader incorporating the latest scholarship on the background to the First World War are L. Lafore, *The long fuse: an interpretation of the origins of World War I** (1965), and J. Remak, *The origins of World War I, 1871–1914** (Berkshire series, 1967). Among the leading comprehensive treatments are S. B. Fay, *The origins of the World War** (1928, 1930); B. E. Schmitt, *The coming of the war, 1914* (2 vols., 1930); P. Renouvin, *The immediate origins of the war* (1928); N. Mansergh, *The coming of the First World War: a study in the European balance, 1878–1914* (1949); and L. Albertini, *The origins of the War of 1914* (3 vols., 1942–1943, trans. 1952–1957). G. P. Gooch, *Before the war* (2 vols., 1936–1938), *Recent revelations of European diplomacy* (4th ed., 1940), and his other writings provide much bibliographical information and insight.

The war-guilt controversy has been reopened by the German scholar Fritz Fischer, who on the basis of new archival materials has reaffirmed German culpability in *Germany's aims in the First World War** (1961, trans. 1967), the title somewhat modified in translation from the original German *Griff nach der Weltmacht*. The question of German insecurity or German ambition is also debated among other topics in W. Laqueur and G. L. Mosse (eds.), *1914: The coming of the First World War** (1969), published originally as a volume of the *Journal of Contemporary History*.

Among many specialized accounts the following are concerned primarily with the Allied powers: A. F. Pribram, *England and the international policy of the European Great Powers, 1871–1914* (1929, 1941); G. Michon, *The Franco-Russian alliance, 1891–1917* (1929); E. M. Carroll, *French public opinion and foreign affairs, 1870–1914* (1931); J. E. Tyler, *The British army and the Continent, 1904–1914* (1938); G. Monger, *The end of isolation: British foreign policy, 1900–1907* (1963); J. A. S. Grenville, *Lord Salisbury and foreign policy* (1964); T. Iiams, *Gabriel Hanotaux at the quai d'Orsay, 1894–1898* (1962); C. Andrew, *Théophile Delcassé and the making of the entente cordiale: a reappraisal of French foreign policy, 1898–1905* (1968); and S. R. Williamson, *The politics of grand strategy: Britain and France prepare for war, 1904–1914* (1969). The position of the Central Powers is discussed in E. Brandenburg, *From Bismarck to the World War: a history of German foreign policy, 1870–1914* (1927); E. M. Carroll, *Germany and the Great Powers 1866–1914* (1938); A. F. Pribram, *Austrian foreign policy, 1908–1918* (1923); A. von Wegerer, *A refutation of the Versailles war guilt thesis* (1930); and Count von Montgelas, *The case for the Central Powers* (1925). R. W. Seton-Watson, *Sarajevo* (1926); E. C. Helmreich, *The diplomacy of the Balkan wars, 1912–1913* (1938); and V. Dedijer, *The road to Sarajevo* (1966), examine the Balkan antecedents of the war.

Anglo-German relations are discussed in H. Kantorowicz, *The spirit of British policy and the myth of the encirclement of Germany* (1931); R. J. Sontag, *Germany and England: background of conflict, 1848–1894** (1938); P. R. Anderson, *The background of anti-English feeling in Germany, 1890–1902* (1939); and R. J. S. Hoffman, *Great Britain and the German trade rivalry, 1875–1914* (1933). The naval race is discussed in the memoirs of Tirpitz, Grey, Fisher, Haldane, and other participants; in J. Steinberg, *Yesterday's deterrent: Tirpitz and the birth of the German battleship* (1965); in A. J. Marder, *The anatomy of British sea power . . . 1880–1905* (1940), on the pre-dreadnought era, and *From the dreadnought to Scapa Flow: the Royal Navy in the Fisher era, 1904–1919* (4 vols. to date, 1961–1969), now complete through 1917; and in E. L. Woodward, *Great Britain and the German navy* (1935).

Two books seeking to capture the mood of the era are J. Remak, *Sarajevo: the story of a political murder* (1959), and J. Cameron, *1914* (1959). W. S. Churchill, *The world crisis* (5 vols., 1923–1929), remains of interest even though it must be read with caution when it deals with events in which the author participated. N. Angell, *The great illusion* (1911), was a widely read book whose antiwar message went unheeded.

On the involvement of the United States in the war one may consult the various general diplomatic histories of the United States, for example, those by S. F. Bemis, T. A. Bailey, R. Ferrell, A. DeConde, and R. Leopold, and the numerous works they cite. Of interest also is B. Perkins, *The great rapprochement: England and the United States, 1895–1914* (1968). An outstanding study is E. F. May, *The World War and American isolation, 1914–1917** (1959), which may be supplemented by A. Link, *Woodrow Wilson and the progressive era, 1910–1917* (1954); and on a special subject there is B. W. Tuchman, *The Zimmerman telegram** (1958).

Here again the available material is staggering. The biographical notes in T. Ropp, *War in the modern world*, should be consulted. There are general narratives by B. H. Liddell Hart (1934), C. R. M. Cruttwell (1934), H. Baldwin* (1962), C. B. Falls* (1959), and A. J. P. Taylor* (1964). Recommended also is the *American Heritage history of World War I* (1964), superbly illustrated, with the narrative by S. L. A. Marshall. Decisions on strategy are studied in F. Maurice, *Lessons of Allied co-operation: naval, military and air, 1914–1918* (1942), and the same author's *The Supreme Command 1914–1918* (2 vols., 1961). The most complete history in English is the official *British History of the Great War based on official documents by the historical section of the Committee of Imperial Defence* (32 vols., 1920 ff.).

On the opening phase of the war B. W. Tuchman, *The guns of August* (1962), has been justly praised for its colorful writing and mastery of materials. G. Ritter, *The Schlieffen plan* (trans. 1958), is a valuable analysis. A sampling of literature on episodes of the war would include A. M. Moorehead, *Gallipoli* (1958); J. E. T. Harper, *The truth about Jutland* (1927); A. Horne, *The price of glory: Verdun, 1916** (1963); and R. M. Watt, *Dare call it treason* (1963), on the French army mutinies of 1917.

[The Russian Revolution is discussed in Chapter XVII, and additional books on the German revolution and on the long-range effects of the war are described in Chapter XIX.] On the economic and social aspects of the war, one may turn to the multivolumed Carnegie Endowment series, Economic and Social History of the World War (1921 ff.), under the general editorship of J. T. Shotwell. Representative titles include J. A. Salter, *Allied shipping control: an experiment in international administration* (1921); W. Beveridge, *British food control* (1928); F. W. Hirst, *Consequences of the war to Great Britain* (1934); A. Fontaine *French industry during the war* (1926); A. Mendelssohn-Bartholdy, *The war and German society: the testament of a liberal* (1938); J. Redlich, *Austrian war government* (1929); and D. Mitrany, *The effect of the war in southeastern Europe* (1936). The best one-volume account of developments on the home front in the various countries is F. P. Chambers, *The war behind the war, 1914–1918* (1939). Internal developments are also treated in E. L. Woodward, *Great Britain and the War of 1914–1918* (1967); P. Guinn, *British strategy and politics, 1914–1918* (1965); J. C. King, *Generals and politicians: conflict between France's high command, parliament and government, 1914–1918* (1951); G. D. Feldman, *Army, industry, and labor in Germany, 1914–1918* (1966); R. B. Armeson, *Total warfare and compulsory labor* (1964), also on Germany; A. J. May, *The passing of the Hapsburg monarchy, 1914–1918* (2 vols., 1966); and Z. A. B. Zeman, *The breakup of the Habsburg empire, 1914–1918* (1961). An illuminating study is J. M. Read, *Atrocity propaganda* (1941); and on the human costs of the war see T. J. Mitchell and G. M. Smith, *Medical services: casualties and medical statistics of the Great War* (1931).

Among books dealing with wartime diplomatic maneuvers there are H. W. Gatzke, *Germany's drive to the West: a study of Germany's Western war aims during the First World War** (1950); J. W. Wheeler-Bennett, *The forgotten peace: Brest-Litovsk, March 1918* (1939); H. C. Meyer, *Mitteleuropa in German thought and action* (1955); and U. Trumpener, *Germany and the Ottoman Empire, 1914–1918* (1968). Two provocative studies focusing on the diplomatic duel between the United States and Russia are V. S. Mamatey, *The United States and east central Europe, 1914–1918* (1957), and A. J. Mayer, *Political origins of the new diplomacy, 1917–1918* (1959). T. E. Lawrence, *Seven pillars of wisdom: a triumph** (1926, 1935), on the revolt of the Arabs against the Turks, is a fascinating account that must be used with caution. Other studies focusing on the Middle East and on developing Arab-Zionist rivalries are E. Kedourie, *England and the Middle East* (1956), on the years 1914–1921; H. M. Sachar,*The struggle for the Middle East, 1914–1924* (1969); and L. Stein, *The Balfour declaration* (1961).

For the armistice one may turn to H. R. Rudin, *Armistice, 1918* (1944), and F. Maurice, *The Armistice of 1918* (1943).

On the conference the best brief account is P. Birdsall, *Versailles twenty years after* (1941), sympathetic to Wilson. H. Nicolson, *Peacemaking, 1919* (1933, 1939), and G. B. Noble, *Policies and opinions at Paris, 1919* (1935), describe the intellectual climate in which the momentous decisions were reached. H. W. V. Temperley, *A history of the peace conference of Paris* (6 vols., 1920–1924), is a massive technical study, comparable to the official papers published by various governments from time to time on the conference and related topics, whereas F. S. Marston, *The peace conference of 1919* (1944), is a brief, readable guide dealing mainly with organizational aspects.

A brilliant though not entirely convincing study arguing with massive detail that the unconscious preoccupation underlying decisions at Versailles was the threat of Bolshevism and domestic radicalism is A. J. Mayer, *Politics and diplomacy of peacemaking: containment and counterrevolution at Versailles, 1918–1919* (1967); it may be compared with J. M. Thompson, *Russia, Bolshevism, and the Versailles peace* (1966), which views the revolutionary threat as important but not dominating. Other studies examining aspects of the peace conference include S. P. Tillman, *Anglo-American relations at the Paris peace conference of 1919* (1961); A. Luckau, *The German delegation at the Paris peace conference* (1941); S. Bonsal, *Suitors and suppliants: the little nations at Versailles* (1946); R. Albrecht-Carrié, *Italy at the Paris peace conference* (1938); I. Morrow, *The peace settlement in the German-Polish borderlands* (1936); and A. Cobban, *National self-determination* (1944). There are monographs on many of the smaller countries at the conference: F. Deak on Hungary (1942), D. Perman on Czechoslovakia (1962), D. Spector on Rumania (1962), T. Komarnicki on Poland (1957), and I. J. Lederer on Yugoslavia (1963). J. C. King explores a special subject in *Foch versus Clemenceau: France and German dismemberment, 1918–1919* (1960).

One of the most hotly disputed issues was reparations, and on this J. M. Keynes's *The economic consequences of the peace* (1920) has been the most influential single book. Etienne Mantoux, *The Carthaginian peace—or the economic consequences of Mr. Keynes* (1946), is a vigorous reply to Keynes. C. Bergmann, *The history of reparations* (1927), is a scholarly presentation of a German point of view; and in *The end of reparations* (1931), H. Schacht attempts to vindicate his own policy. A wider point of view is found in A. L. Bowley, *Some economic consequences of the Great War* (1930). On the colonial question see W. R. Louis, *Great Britain and German's lost colonies, 1914–1919* (1967); and an important special subject is explored in H. R. Winkler, *The League of Nations movement in Great Britain, 1914–1919* (1952).

There are innumerable biographies, which vary widely in quality, of the civil and military figures of the period. Some of the better biographical studies are G. Wright, *Poincaré and the French presidency* (1943); L. B. Namier, *In the margin of history* (1939); K. Tschuppik, *Ludendorff: the*

Bibliography   *tragedy of a military mind* (1932); W. K. Hancock, *Smuts* (2 vols., 1962–1968); R. S. Baker, *Woodrow Wilson: life and letters* (8 vols., 1927–1939); and A. Link's multivolumed biography of Wilson (1947 ff., 5 vols. to date) and his other books on Wilson. The attempt to apply techniques of psychoanalysis in S[igmund] Freud and W. Bullitt, *Thomas Woodrow Wilson* (1967), has led to strange and unconvincing results; a more successful psychological approach is achieved in A. L. and J. L. George, *President Wilson and Colonel House: a personality study** (1956). On David Lloyd George the best biographical account is T. Jones, *Lloyd George* (1951), superior to those by M. Thomson (1948) and F. Owen (1954). M. Gilbert has edited *Lloyd George* (1968), in the Great Lives Observed series.

Problems and   D. E. Lee (ed.), *The outbreak of the First World War: who was responsible?* (1963); I. J. Lederer (ed.),
Readings*   *The Versailles settlement: was it foredoomed to failure?* (1960); and T. P. Greene (ed.), *Wilson at Versailles* (1957), are useful, as is J. J. Roth (ed.), *World War I: a turning point in modern history* (1967), a brief anthology of essays. In the Anvil series L. L. Snyder has edited *Historic documents of World War I* (1958).

XVII: The Russian Revolution

Russia Before 1917

[Many books on tsarist Russia, Russian imperialism, and World War I are listed for Chapters XIII, XV, and XVI.] R. V. Daniels, *Russia** (1964), is an excellent brief introduction to twentieth-century events, and J. H. Billington, *The icon and the axe: an interpretive history of Russian culture* (1966), cited earlier, is rewarding and stimulating for cultural developments. New books on Russia are listed in the quarterly *Russian Review* and other professional publications, and G. B. Carson has prepared a bibliographical essay, *Russia since 1917** (AHA Service Center series, 1962).

The political situation in late tsarist Russia is best approached through H. Seton-Watson, *The Russian empire, 1801–1917* (1967), and *The decline of imperial Russia, 1855–1914** (1952), both cited earlier; B. H. Sumner, *Russia and the Balkans, 1870–1880* (1947), an analysis offering much more than the title suggests; A. Levin, *The Second Duma* (1940); and M. T. Florinsky, *The end of the Russian empire* (1931), one of several Russian studies in the Carnegie series described in Chapter XVI. R. F. Byrnes, *Pobedonostsev: his life and thought* (1968), describes in detail an outstanding exemplar of tsarist obscurantism.

In addition to books on late-nineteenth-century Russia listed for Chapter XIII, economic and institutional topics are discussed in P. I. Liashchenko, *History of the Russian national economy to the 1917 revolution* (1949); L. A. Owen, *The Russian peasant movement, 1906–1917* (1937); J. S. Curtiss, *Church and state in Russia: the last years of the empire, 1900–1917* (1940); and T. H. von Laue, *Sergei Witte and the industrialization of Russia** (1963). The intellectual ferment may be studied in T. G. Masaryk, *The spirit of Russia* (2 vols., 1919; 3rd posthumous vol., 1968), a profound and difficult work of extraordinary value; E. H. Carr, *Dostoevsky, 1821–1881, a new biography* (1931); E. J. Simmons, *Leo Tolstoy* (1946); and W. H. Bruford, *Chekhov and his Russia: a sociological study* (1948). Valuable also is R. Hare, *Pioneers of Russian social thought** (1951). H. Kohn has edited selections from the most important Russian writers in the years 1815 to 1917 in *The mind of modern Russia** (1954). On the political side valuable studies include G. Fischer, *Russian liberalism: from gentry to intelligentsia* (1958); S. H. Baron, *Plekhanov: the father of Russian Marxism** (1963); D. W. Treadgold, *Lenin and his rivals: the struggle for Russia's future, 1898–1906* (1950); L. Haimson, *The Russian Marxists and the origins of Bolshevism* (1955); F. Venturi, *Roots of revolution* (1960); A. P. Mendel, *Dilemmas of progress in tsarist Russia* (1961); J. Walkin, *The rise of democracy in pre-revolutionary Russia* (1962); and P. Avrich, *The Russian anarchists* (1967). The best short study of the events of 1905 is S. Harcave, *First blood: the Russian revolution of 1905* (1964).

Biographical introductions for the general reader are B. D. Wolfe, *Three who made a revolution: a biographical history* [Lenin, Trotsky, Stalin]* (1948, rev., 1964); C. Hill, *Lenin and the Russian Revolution** (Teach Yourself History series, 1947); and the lives of Lenin by D. Shub* (1948) and L. F. Fischer* (1964), the latter the most authoritative available. The biography by R. Payne* (1964) is an unbalanced, unsympathetic account. An outstanding study focusing on Lenin is A. B. Ulam, *The Bolsheviks: the intellectual and political history of the triumph of communism in Russia** (1965). I. Deutscher has written two outstanding biographies: *Stalin: a political biography** (1949, rev., 1967), and a remarkably vivid, though perhaps overly sympathetic, three-volume life of Trotsky (1954–1963). E. E. Smith has put together the fragmentary evidence on Stalin's early life in *The young Stalin* (1967); and T. H. Rigby has edited *Stalin** (1966), in the Great Lives Observed series. A fascinating effort to apply Freudian techniques to an important subject is E. V. Wolfenstein, *The revolutionary personality: Lenin, Trotsky, Gandhi* (1967).

On the Revolution W. H. Chamberlin, *The Russian Revolution, 1917–1921** (2 vols., 1935), is still valuable; other important studies are G. Vernadsky, *The Russian Revolution, 1917–1921* (1932); B. Pares, *The fall of the Russian monarchy* (1939); G. Katkov, *Russia 1917: the February Revolution* (1967); and R. V. Daniels, *Red October* (1967). Emphasizing personal relations at the court is the scholarly and well-written R. K. Massie, *Nicholas and Alexandra* (1967). A. Moorehead, *The Russian Revolution* (1958), is a popularly written account, not completely dependable. The most comprehensive account in any language, written from the sources, is E. H. Carr's as yet unfinished *A history of Soviet Russia** (1950 ff.), of which seven volumes have appeared to date, carrying the history from 1917 to 1929.

On the early years three monographs are helpful: O. H. Radkey, *The elections to the Russian constituent assembly of 1917* (1950); L. Schapiro, *The origins of the communist autocracy: political opposition in the Soviet state, 1917–1922* (1955); and R. E. Pipes, *The formation of the Soviet Union: communism and nationalism, 1917–1923** (1954).

Foreign relations in the crucial early years are discussed in the following works: J. W. Wheeler-Bennett, *The forgotten peace: Brest-Litovsk*, already cited; L. I. Strakhovsky, *Intervention at Archangel* (1944); J. A. White, *The Siberian intervention* (1950); G. Stewart, *The White armies of Russia: a chronicle of counter-revolution and Allied intervention* (1933); G. A. Brinkley, *The volunteer army and Allied intervention in south Russia, 1917–1921* (1966); P. S. Wandycz, *Soviet-Polish relations, 1917–1921* (1969); and R. H. Ullman, *Anglo-Soviet relations, 1917–1921* (2 vols. to date, 1961–1968), a remarkably detailed account. The ties with Germany are described in G. Freund, *Unholy alliance* (1957); K. Rosenbaum, *Community of fate: German-Soviet diplomatic relations, 1922–1928* (1965); and H. L. Dyck, *Weimar Germany and Soviet Russia, 1926–1933* (1966). Important documents and other source materials are printed in *Intervention, civil war, and communism in Russia, April–December 1918* (1936), edited by J. Bunyan. The most comprehensive study focusing on American relations to these events are G. F. Kennan's volumes: *Russia leaves the war** (1956) and *The decision to intervene** (1958).

For general guidance see the *Foreign Affairs Bibliographies*, described at the beginning of the next chapter; in addition, T. T. Hammond has prepared a specialized guide: *A bibliography of Soviet foreign relations and world communism* (1964). Three important and provocative books extending to the end of World War II are E. H. Carr, *The Soviet impact on the Western world** (1947); G. F. Kennan, *Russia and the West under Lenin and Stalin* (1961); and F. L. Schuman's lengthy narrative and analysis, *Soviet politics at home and abroad* (1946), which manages to put about as good a construction on Russian policy as possible. The best surveys are M. Beloff, *The foreign policy of Soviet Russia, 1929–1941* (2 vols., 1947–1949), a solid and dispassionate narrative; the same author's *Soviet policy in the Far East, 1944–1951* (1953); two books by L. F. Fischer: *The Soviets in world affairs . . . 1917–29* (2 vols., 1930; 1 vol., 1960) and *Russia's road from peace to war: Soviet*

Bibliography

foreign relations, 1917–1941 (1969); and R. D. Warth, *Soviet Russia in world politics* (1963). An important volume focusing on the historical background to post-1945 events is A. B. Ulam, *Expansion and coexistence: the history of Soviet foreign policy, 1917–1967** (1968). [Other books, emphasizing the years since 1939, are cited in the chapters that follow.]

U.S.S.R.—Political and Economic Developments

A valuable introduction is P. Sorlin, *The Soviet people and their society: from 1917 to the present* (1969). On the structure and functioning of the Soviet government at various stages the most useful books are S. N. Harper and R. Thompson, *The government of the Soviet Union* (1938, 1949); J. Towster, *Political power in the U.S.S.R., 1917–1947* (1948); M. Fainsod, *How Russia is ruled* (1953, rev., 1963); M. T. Florinsky, *Towards an understanding of the U.S.S.R.* (1952); B. Moore, Jr., *Soviet politics: the dilemma of power** (1950), and *Terror and progress in the U.S.S.R.** (1954); J. N. Hazard, *The Soviet system of government* (1957, rev., 1960); and Z. B. Brzezinski, *The permanent purge: politics in Soviet totalitarianism* (1956). An important monograph is M. Fainsod, *Smolensk under Soviet rule** (1958). On the party itself there are J. S. Reshetar, *A concise history of the Communist party of the Soviet Union* (1960); L. Schapiro, *The Communist party of the Soviet Union** (1960); J. A. Armstrong, *The politics of totalitarianism: the Communist party of the Soviet Union* (1961); and R. V. Daniels, *The conscience of the Revolution** (1960), on the opposition within the party from 1917 to 1929. A stimulating essay is T. H. Von Laue, *Why Lenin? Why Stalin?: a reappraisal of the Russian Revolution, 1900–1930** (1964); and a comprehensive analysis of the purges, stressing the enormity of the blood bath, is R. Conquest, *The great terror: Stalin's purges of the thirties* (1968). The life of an Old Bolshevik is recounted in W. Lerner, *Karl Radek: the last internationalist* (1970). For insight into the party and regime one may also profitably sample, and compare, the 1938 and later versions of the official *History of the Communist party of the Soviet Union*.

Two thoughtful books assessing the accomplishments of the regime are J. P. Nettl, *The Soviet achievement* (1967), in the Barraclough series, and I. Grey, *The first fifty years: Soviet Russia 1917–1967* (1967). The most successful effort to assess economic progress (and the methods used to achieve it) is A. Nove, *An economic history of the U.S.S.R.* (1969), an intensive study which supersedes M. Dobb, *Soviet economic development since 1917** (1948). Other technical studies include A. Baykov, *The development of the Soviet economic system* (1946); N. Jasny, *The socialized agriculture of the U.S.S.R.* (1949); the same author's monumental *Soviet industrialization, 1928–1952* (1961); and A. Bergson, *The real national income of Soviet Russia since 1928* (1961).

Various important matters are taken up in D. F. White, *Growth of the Red Army* (1944); J. Erickson, *The Soviet high command* (1962); R. Kolkowicz, *The Soviet military and the Communist party* (1967); P. B. Anderson, *People, church and state in modern Russia* (1944); J. S. Curtiss, *The Russian church and the Soviet state, 1917–1950* (1953); S. W. Baron, *The Russian Jew under tsars and soviets* (1964); R. Schlesinger, *Soviet legal theory: its social background and development* (1946); J. N. Hazard, *Law and social change in the U.S.S.R.* (1953); I. Deutscher, *Soviet trade unions: their place in Soviet labor policy* (1950); and S. Wolin and R. M. Slusser (eds.), *The Soviet secret police* (1957). The following works are also suggested: R. Schlesinger, *The spirit of post-war Russia: Soviet ideology, 1917–1946* (1947); J. Somerville, *Soviet philosophy: a study of theory and practice* (1946); and A. Inkeles and R. A. Bauer, *The Soviet citizen: daily life in a totalitarian society** (1960). There are, in addition, many journalistic accounts and numerous polemical works of uneven quality.

World Communism

On the transformation of earlier socialism and Marxism into communism, a number of studies have been described at the beginning of this chapter and in Chapters XI, XII, and XIV. In addition, there are A. Rosenberg, *A history of Bolshevism from Marx to the first Five Year Plan* (1934); R. N. C. Hunt, *Theory and practice of communism** (1950), and *Marxism: past and present* (1954); J. Plamenatz, *German Marxism and Russian communism** (1954); R. Schlesinger, *Marx: his* time and ours (1950), written from a Marxian viewpoint; A. B. Ulam, *The unfinished revolution: an essay on the sources of influence of Marxism and communism** (1960); and A. G. Meyer, *Leninism* (1957), and *Communism** (1960). R. T. deGeorge, *Patterns of Soviet thought: the origins and development of dialectical and historical materialism* (1966), is a technical but valuable study. E. H. Carr's *Studies in revolution* (1950), cited earlier, presents thoughtful essays ranging from Saint-Simon to Stalin. M. Salvadori, *The rise of modern communism** (1952, rev., 1963), is a brief study in the Berkshire series. Personal testimonies of the impact of communism may be found in A. Balabanoff, *My life as a rebel* (1938), and in R. H. Crossman (ed.), *The God that failed** (1950). On the Comintern one may turn to H. Seton-Watson, *From Lenin to Khruschev: the history of world communism** (1953, 1960). F. Borkenau, *The Communist International* (1938), and *World communism** (1953); and L. L. Lorwin, *The international labor movement* (1953). Special studies include J. W. Hulse, *The forming of the Communist International* (1964); R. Fischer, *Stalin and German communism* (1948); and K. E. McKenzie, *Comintern and world revolution, 1928–1943* (1964).

Pamphlets in various problems series include R. H. McNeal (ed.), *Russia in transition, 1905–1914: evolution or revolution?* (1969); A. E. Adams (ed.), *Imperial Russia after 1861: peaceful modernization or revolution?* (1965); the same author's *The Russian Revolution and Bolshevik victory* (1960); B. M. Unterberger (ed.), *American intervention in the Russian civil war* (1969); S. W. Page (ed.), *Lenin: dedicated Marxist or pragmatic revolutionary?* (1969); and R. V. Daniels (ed.), *The Stalin revolution: fulfillment or betrayal of communism?* (1965). Two booklets in the Anvil series are J. S. Curtiss (ed.), *The Russian Revolutions of 1917* (1957); and A. G. Mazour (ed.), *Soviet economic development: operation outstrip, 1921–1965* (1967).

[Books on internal developments in the major countries outside Asia and on international relations between the two wars are listed in Chapters XIX and XX respectively.] As a tool for serious study of the forces and events of the twentieth century one must turn to *Foreign affairs bibliography: a selected and annotated list of books on international relations, 1919–1932* (1933), and subsequent volumes published in 1945, 1955, and 1964; these volumes are careful compilations of books on international affairs and domestic affairs, for which space is utterly lacking in the present bibliography. New publications are listed as they appear in the current issues of the quarterly *Foreign Affairs* and provide the basis for future cumulative volumes.

Among several general surveys of twentieth-century history focusing on Europe there may be mentioned C. E. Black and E. C. Helmreich, *Twentieth-century Europe* (1950, 1959); F. P. Chambers, *This age of conflict* (3rd ed., 1962), good on diplomatic and military events; and H. S. Hughes, *Contemporary Europe: a history* (1961, rev., 1966), with attention to cultural and intellectual developments. An interesting overview is provided in A. J. P. Taylor, *From Sarajevo to Potsdam** (1966), in the Barraclough series, and C. Horne is editing a series of brief volumes by British writers, The Making of the Twentieth Century* (Macmillan, 1967 ff.). Q. Howe has completed two of the projected three volumes of *A world history of our times* (1949, 1953). A subjective and occasionally stimulating book is C. Quigley, *Tragedy and hope: a history of the world in our time** (1966). G. Barraclough, *Introduction to contemporary history** (1961), cited earlier, focuses on the twentieth century and the need to place European events in world perspective. Volume XII (rev. ed., 1968) of the New Cambridge Modern History, *The shifting balance of world forces, 1898–1945*, has already been cited.

Of various anthologies of readings and source problems on twentieth-century history, there are useful ones by G. Wright and A. Mejia* (1963), A. Baltzly and W. Salamone (1950), A. L. Funk* (1953, rev., 1968), W. C. Langsam (1951), and E. N. Anderson* (1958).

For a study of the human resources of Europe in the interwar years one must turn to D. Kirk, *Europe's population in the inter-war years* (1946), cited in Chapter XIV. The general economic problems facing the world after 1919 are discussed in J. E. Barker, *Economic statesmanship* (1920); W. S. Culbertson, *International economic policies: a survey of the economics of diplomacy* (1925); the League of Nations, *Commercial policy in the inter-war period: international proposals and national policies* (1942); and I. Svennilson, *Growth and stagnation in the European economy* (1954).

On the League of Nations there are innumerable studies published by the League itself, and the following general accounts may also be mentioned: F. P. Walters, *A history of the League of Nations* (2 vols., 1952); J. T. Shotwell and M. Salvin, *Lessons on security and disarmament from the history of the League of Nations* (1949); W. E. Rappard, *The quest for peace since the World War* (1940); and B. Dexter, *The years of opportunity: the League of Nations, 1920–1926* (1967). Books on disarmament include J. M. Wheeler-Bennett, *Disarmament and security since Locarno, 1925–1931* (1932), and *The pipe dream of peace: the collapse of disarmament* (1935); and R. H. Ferrell, *Peace in their time: the origins of the Kellogg-Briand pact** (1952). S. R. Smith, *The Manchurian crisis, 1931–1932: a tragedy in international relations* (1948), is a discriminating study of the League's most disastrous defeat, and W. W. Willoughby, *The Sino-Japanese controversy and the League of Nations* (1935), is a comprehensive treatment.

[See also the discussion of various peoples of the world in the age of imperialism in Chapter XV.] An introduction to the ferment in Asia is provided in J. Romein and J. E. Romein, *The Asian century: a history of modern nationalism in Asia* (1956, trans. 1962); and the American Universities Field Staff has prepared a useful list of books, *A select bibliography: Asia, Africa, eastern Europe, Latin America* (1960).

A good historical survey of the Middle East with attention to modern developments is S. N. Fisher, *The Middle East: a history* (1959, rev., 1969). On the modernization of Turkey two valuable books are B. Lewis, *The emergence of modern Turkey* (1961, rev., 1969), cited earlier, and L. Thomas and R. N. Frye, *The United States and Turkey and Iran* (1951). Other studies include H. N. Howard, *The partition of Turkey, 1913–1923* (1931); A. J. Toynbee, *The Western question in Greece and Turkey: a study in the contact of civilizations* (1922); D. E. Webster, *The Turkey of Atatürk: social process in the Turkish reformation* (1939); H. E. Allen, *The Turkish transformation: a study in social and religious development* (1935); and P. Balfour (Lord Kinross), *Atatürk: a biography of Mustafa Kemal* (1965).

Stirrings in the Middle East are also discussed in G. Antonius, *The Arab awakening** (1965); Z. B. Zeine, *Struggle for Arab independence* (1960); H. A. R. Gibb, *Modern trends in Islam* (1947); A. H. Hourani, *Syria and Lebanon* (1946); S. Longrigg, *Syria and Lebanon under French mandate* (1958); A. Williams, *Britain and France in the Middle East and North Africa, 1914–1967* (1969); R. O. Collins and R. L. Tignor, *Egypt and the Sudan** (1967); and T. Little, *Modern Egypt** (1964).

For the Indian subcontinent a number of books have been listed in Chapter XV. The best introduction to twentieth-century developments is W. N. Brown, *The United States and India and Pakistan* (1953, rev., 1963), already cited, and T. G. Spear, *India, Pakistan, and the West** (1952, rev., 1967). Other useful books are D. R. Gadgil, *The industrial evolution of India in recent times* (1924, 1944); T. W. Wallbank, *India** (1948), in the Berkshire series; the same author's *India in the new era: a study of the origin and development of the Indian Union and Pakistan* (1951); H. Tinker, *India and Pakistan: a political analysis** (1962, rev., 1968); C. F. Andrews and G. Mookerji, *The rise and growth of the Congress in India* (1938); A. Seal, *The emergence of Indian nationalism* (1968); and F. Hutchins, *The illusion of permanence: British imperialism in India* (1967). Nehru's autobiography, *Toward freedom** (1941); his *Glimpses of world history* (1942); and other writings make absorbing reading, as does Gandhi's *Autobiography: the story of my experiments with truth* (1948). To the standard biography of Gandhi by L. Fischer* (1951) one may add G. Ashe, *Gandhi: a study in revolution** (1968); E. H. Erikson, *Gandhi's truth: on the origins of militant nonviolence** (1969); and E. V. Wolfenstein, *The revolutionary personality*, already cited; the latter two utilize psychoanalytical approaches. Two recommended biographies of Nehru are by F. Moraes (1957) and M. Brecher* (1959).

The ferment in East and Southeast Asia in general is discussed in E. H. Jacoby, *Agrarian unrest in Southeast Asia* (1949), and in B. Lasker, *Asia on the move: population pressure, migration, and resettlement in eastern Asia under the influence of want and war* (1945), and *Peoples of Southeast Asia* (1944). The historical background is sketched in B. Harrison, *Southeast Asia: a short history* (1954).

On China from 1911 to the 1930s the best introduction is J. K. Fairbank, *The United States and China** (2nd ed., 1958), already cited. O. E. Chubb, *Twentieth century China** (1964), is a good survey of the years from 1911 to the present. On the 1920s one may read H. F. McNair, *China in revolution: an analysis of politics and militarism under the republic* (1931); H. R. Isaacs, *The tragedy of the Chinese revolution** (3rd ed., 1961); and Leng Shao-chuan and N. D. Palmer, *Sun Yat-sen and communism* (1961). Biographical studies include L. Sharman, *Sun Yat-sen: his life and its meaning: a critical biography** (1934); H. Z. Schiffrin, *Sun Yat-sen and the origins of the 1911 revolution* (1969); and E. Hahn, *Chiang Kai-shek: an unauthorized biography* (1955). The first volume of a projected four-volume encyclopedia has appeared: H. L. Boorman (ed.), *Biographical dictionary of republican China* (1967). [Books on the communist triumph in China are listed in Chapter XXI.]

On the rise of militarism in Japan in the 1930s, R. Benedict, *The chrysanthemum and the sword** (1946); D. M. Brown, *Nationalism in Japan* (1955); and R. Storry, *The double patriots* (1957), may be cited. [Other books on Japan have been listed in Chapter XIII.]

A useful background study for twentieth-century economic developments is A. Harrison, *The framework of economic activity** (1967). On the coming of the depression J. K. Galbraith has written a vivid history in *The great crash: 1929** (1955); and C. Bird, *The invisible scar** (1966), is a moving social history of the depression's impact on the United States. The two most useful economic surveys covering the world economy are H. V. Hodson, *Slump and recovery, 1929–1937* (1938), and W. A. Lewis, *Economic survey, 1919–1939* (1948); there are valuable contributions in W. Laqueur and G. L. Mosse (eds.), *The great depression** (1970), originally a volume of the *Journal of Contemporary History.* Other studies include M. J. Bonn, *The crumbling of empire: the disintegration of world economy* (1938); H. W. Arndt, *The economic lessons of the nineteen thirties* (1944); G. Haberler, *Prosperity and depression* (3rd ed., 1941); L. C. Robbins, *The great depression* (1934); W. Röpke, *International economic disintegration* (1942); and E. Bennett, *The diplomacy of the financial crisis, 1931* (1962). [For the impact of the depression on politics and society in various countries see the following chapter.]

In the Anvil series L. L. Snyder has edited *The world in the twentieth century* (rev., 1964) and *Fifty major documents of the twentieth century* (1955); and on economic developments S. B. Clough, T. Moodie, and C. Moodie have edited *Economic history of Europe: twentieth century* (1968). In the Heath Problems series there are M. D. Lewis (ed.), *Gandhi: maker of modern India?* (1965), and on the depression, R. F. Himmelberg (ed.), *The great depression and American capitalism* (1968).

Books on international relations in the interwar years are listed in the following chapter, and books on the general economic problems of the 1920s and 1930s are listed in Chapter XVIII. The national histories of Britain, France, Germany, and Italy described in Chapters XI and XIV should also be consulted.

On the general concept of the welfare state, these books may be recommended: J. M. Keynes, *The end of laissez-faire* (1927); J. A. Schumpeter, *Capitalism, socialism, and democracy** (1942); G. Soule, *A planned society* (1934); B. Wooton, *Freedom under planning* (1945); and M. Bruce, *The coming of the welfare state* (1961, rev., 1966). F. A. von Hayek, in *The road to serfdom** (1944) and other writings, subjects the welfare state to an unsympathetic appraisal. A. Sturmthal, *The tragedy of European labor, 1918–1939* (1943, 1951), is a penetrating study criticizing labor in the interwar period as too narrow in vision to be politically effective; it may be supplemented for other leaders of the left by the essays in W. Laqueur and G. L. Mosse (eds.), *The left-wing intellectuals between the wars, 1919–1939** (1966), originally a volume of the *Journal of Contemporary History*.

The American New Deal   The background and nature of the New Deal can best be approached through two volumes by W. E. Leuchtenburg: *The perils of prosperity** (1958) and *Franklin D. Roosevelt and the New Deal** (1964); other useful introductions are D. W. Brogan, *The era of Franklin D. Roosevelt* (1950), by an acute British writer; B. Rauch, *History of the New Deal, 1933–1938** (1944); B. Mitchell, *Depression decade: from New Era through New Deal, 1929–1941** (1947); D. Wecter, *The age of the great depression, 1929–1941* (1948); and the multivolumed study by A. M. Schlesinger, Jr., *The age of Roosevelt** (1957 ff.), of which three lively volumes have appeared to date. Many biographical accounts and memoirs have appeared as well. Two outstanding studies of Roosevelt are J. M. Burns, *Roosevelt: the lion and the fox** (1956), and F. Freidel's multivolumed *Franklin D. Roosevelt* (3 vols. to date, 1952 ff.).

Britain Between the Wars   Three thorough and balanced accounts are available: W. N. Medlicott, *Contemporary England, 1914–1964* (1967); C. L. Mowat, *Britain between the wars, 1918–1940* (1955); and A. J. P. Taylor, *English history, 1914–1945* (1965). Briefer surveys are D. Thomson, *England in the twentieth century, 1914–1963** (1964), and B. B. Gilbert, *Britain since 1918* (1967). These books may be supplemented by the impressionistic R. Graves and A. Hodge, *The long week-end: a social history of Great Britain, 1918–1939** (1940); R. Blythe, *The age of illusion* (1963); J. Symons, *The thirties: a dream revolved* (1960); M. Muggeridge, *The thirties: 1930–40 in Great Britain* (1940, rev., 1967); and W. McElwee, *Britain's locust years, 1918–1940* (1962). Something of the impact of the 1914–1918 war upon British culture and economy is revealed in A. Siegfried, *Post-war Britain, a French analysis* (1924); A. C. Pigou, *Aspects of British economic history, 1918–1925* (1947); F. W. Hirst, *Consequences of the war to Great Britain* (1934), in the Carnegie series, described in Chapter XVI; P. B. Johnson, *Land fit for heroes: the planning of British reconstruction, 1916–1919* (1968); and A. Marwick's two books: *The deluge: British society and the First World War* (1965) and *Britain in the century of total war: war, peace, and social change, 1900–1967* (1968).

On some specific interwar developments and episodes consult T. Wilson, *The downfall of the Liberal party, 1914–1935* (1966); C. F. Brand, *The British Labour party: a short history* (1964); S. Graubard, *British Labour and the Russian Revolution, 1919–1924* (1941); R. Lyman, *The first Labour government* (1924); L. Chester, S. Fay, and H. Young, *The Zinoviev letter* (1967); J. Symons, *The general strike* (1957); E. Windrich, *British Labour's foreign policy* (1941); and M. Bowley, *Housing and the state, 1919–1944* (1945). British politics in the depression years are ably explored in R. S. Bassett, *1931: political crisis* (1958), and R. Skidelsky, *Politicians and the slump: the Labour government of 1929–1931* (1967). There are biographies of Ramsay MacDonald by G. E. Elton (1939); of Stanley Baldwin by G. M. Young (1952), D. C. Somervell (1953), A. W. Baldwin (1956), and K. Middlemas and J. Barnes (1969); of Neville Chamberlain by K. Feiling (1946), I. Macleod (1961), and W. R. Rock (1969); of Winston Churchill by his son R. S. Churchill [to 1914] (2 vols., 1966), and L. Broad (1956); of Anthony Eden (1955) by L. Broad; and of Halifax by Lord Birkenhead (1965). H. Nicolson has written a biography of George V (1953), and J. W.

Wheeler-Bennett one of George VI* (1958). A. Bullock has published the first volume of a
two-volume study, *The life and times of Ernest Bevin: trade union leader, 1881–1940* (1960). The
best introduction to Keynes is R. F. Harrod, *The life of John Maynard Keynes** (1951); R.
Lekachman, *The age of Keynes** (1966), is mostly on post-1945 Keynesian influence in the
United States. T. Jones, *Diary with letters, 1931–1950* (1954), is valuable on many subjects; and
there are other memoirs by Hugh Dalton (1953), Clement Attlee (1954), Anthony Eden (3 vols.,
1960–1965), A. Duff-Cooper (1953), L. S. Amery (3 vols., 1952–1955), Samuel Hoare (1954),
Harold Macmillan (2 vols., 1966–1967), and others. On personalities in the Labour
movement, F. Williams, *Fifty years' march: the rise of the Labour party* (1949), is colorful.

Among useful studies of the Commonwealth of Nations there are A. B. Keith, *The
dominions as sovereign states* (1938); E. A. Walker, *The British Empire: its structure and spirit* (1943);
G. E. Elton, *Imperial Commonwealth* (1946); K. C. Wheare, *The statute of Westminster and dominion
status* (1938), and *The constitutional structure of the Commonwealth* (1960); and two valuable
accounts covering the interwar years, W. K. Hancock, *Survey of British Commonwealth affairs* (2
vols., 1937–1942), and N. Mansergh, *Survey of British Commonwealth affairs: problems of external
policy, 1931–39* (1952). A brief informative essay is F. H. Underhill, *The British Commonwealth:
an experiment in cooperation among nations* (1956).

There are two useful bibliographical essays in the AHA Service Center series: H. R.
Winkler, *Great Britain in the twentieth century** (1960), and C. F. Mullett, *The British Empire-Commonwealth** (1961).

Histories of the Third Republic as a whole appear under Chapter XIV, and to these may be
added two brief syntheses for the interwar years: N. Greene, *From Versailles to Vichy: the Third
Republic, 1919–1940** (1970), and E. J. Knapton, *France since Versailles** (1952). S. Hoffman and
others, *In search of France: the economy, society and political system in the twentieth century** (1963), has
several incisive essays. In addition to studies by M. R. Clark (1930) and D. J. Saposs (1931),
the best introduction to French labor in the twentieth century is through V. R. Lorwin, *The
French labor movement* (1954), already cited, and H. W. Ehrmann, *French labor: from Popular
Front to liberation* (1947); see also R. Wohl, *French communism in the making, 1919–1924* (1966).

Invaluable for the stormy events of the 1930s, the Popular Front years, and the
background to the fall of France is A. Werth, *The twilight of France, 1933–1940* (1942), a
condensation of his earlier volumes, all of which may be read with profit. There are some
interesting essays in J. Joll (ed.), *The decline of the Third Republic* (St. Antony's papers, 1959).
On some specific subjects there are C. A. Micaud, *The French right and Nazi Germany, 1933–1939*
(1943); P. J. Larmour, *The French Radical party in the 1930's* (1964); J. T. Marcus, *French socialism in
the crisis years, 1933–36* (1958); N. Greene, *Crisis and decline: the French Socialist party in the Popular
Front era* (1969); D. R. Brower, *The new Jacobins: the French Communist party and the Popular Front*
(1968); J. Colton, *Compulsory labor arbitration in France, 1936–39* (1951); and M. Wolfe, *The French
franc between the wars, 1919–39* (1951). Léon Blum, *For all mankind* (trans. 1946), is a moving
testimony and analysis of France's weaknesses in the 1930s as the Socialist leader saw them.
On Blum himself, in addition to various journalistic books, there is a study by L. Dalby (1963),
an illuminating chapter in J. Joll, *Intellectuals in politics: three biographical essays* [Blum,
Rathenau, Marinetti] (1960), and a full-length political biography, J. Colton, *Léon Blum:
humanist in politics* (1966).

Three well-balanced narrative accounts of the Weimar Republic and its fall are S. W.
Halperin, *Germany tried democracy: a political history of the Reich from 1918 to 1933** (1946); R.
Grunberger, *Germany, 1918–1945** (1964); and A. J. Nicholls, *Weimar and the rise of Hitler**
(1968). A valuable bibliography has been published by the Wiener Library (London), *From*

Weimar to Hitler: Germany 1918–1932 (rev., 1964). E. Eyck, *A history of the Weimar Republic** (2 vols., trans. 1963), is a detailed narrative account by a distinguished liberal German historian. A. Rosenberg, *Imperial Germany: the birth of the German republic, 1871–1918* (1931), provides the background for the same author's *A history of the German republic* (1936). Works on the uneasy early years include R. Watts, *The kings depart* (1968); A. J. Ryder, *The German revolution of 1918: a study of German socialism in war and revolt* (1967); W. T. Angress, *Stillborn revolution: the communist bid for power in Germany, 1921–1923** (1963); A. Mitchell, *Revolution in Bavaria* (1965); and R. G. L. Waite, *Vanguard of Nazism: the Free Corps movement in postwar Germany, 1918–1923** (1952). G. Freund, *Unholy alliance* (1957), already mentioned, covers German-Soviet relations in the early years of the republic. Cultural developments are sympathetically treated in P. Gay, *Weimar culture: the outsider as insider* (1968); and many valuable insights are provided in R. Dahrendorf, *Society and democracy in Germany* (1967).

The personalities of the Weimar Republic are discussed in a number of books, among which are J. W. Wheeler-Bennett, *Wooden Titan: Hindenburg in twenty years of German history, 1914–1934* (1936); A. Dorpalen, *Hindenburg and the Weimar Republic* (1964); H. Kessler, *Walter Rathenau* (1929); K. Epstein, *Matthias Erzberger and the dilemma of German democracy* (1959); A. Vallentin, *Stresemann* (1931); H. W. Gatzke, *Stresemann and the rearmament of Germany** (1954); and H. A. Turner, *Stresemann and the politics of the Weimar Republic** (1963). The much-debated question of army loyalties is studied in G. A. Craig, *The politics of the Prussian army, 1640–1945** (1955), already cited; J. W. Wheeler-Bennett, *The nemesis of power: the German army in politics, 1918–1945** (1954, rev., 1964); H. J. Gordon, *The Reichswehr and the German republic, 1919–1926* (1957); R. J. O'Neill, *The German army and the Nazi party, 1933–1939* (1968); and F. L. Carsten, *The Reichswehr and politics, 1918 to 1933* (1966).

On the coming to power of the Nazis one may also profit from D. Orlow, *The history of the Nazi party, 1919–1933* (1969); T. Eschenburg and others, *The path to dictatorship, 1919–1933* (1966); and an intriguing special study, W. S. Allen, *The Nazi seizure of power: the experience of a single German town, 1930–1935** (1965). On the Nazi era [aspects of Nazism are also discussed below under totalitarianism] there are many studies. There is a good survey in the general histories of Germany, cited earlier, by E. J. Passant (1959 ed.) and by R. Flenley (1964 ed.); in H. Mau and H. Krausnick, *German history, 1933–1945* (trans. 1958); in H. Vogt, *The burden of guilt: a short history of Germany, 1914–1945** (trans. 1964); and in the widely read popular account by the journalist W. L. Shirer, *The rise and fall of the Third Reich** (1960), a vivid narrative which uses the available sources but makes no pretense of objectivity. A similar vigorous but oversimplified account is R. Goldston, *The life and death of Nazi Germany** (1969). Among older analytical and interpretive accounts are F. L. Neumann, *Behemoth: the structure and practice of national socialism** (1942), and K. Heiden, *A history of national socialism* (1935). Some indispensable newer treatments are D. Schoenbaum, *Hitler's social revolution: class and status in Nazi Germany, 1933–1939** (1966); M. Broszat, *National socialism* (1960, trans. 1967); H. Krausnick and others, *Anatomy of the SS state* (trans. 1965); and E. N. Peterson, *The limits of Hitler's power* (1969). A valuable symposium by international scholars is M. Baumont and others, *The Third Reich* (1955). In F. Meinecke, *The German catastrophe: reflections and recollections* (1950), a great German historian analyzes the modern history of his country; his book may be compared with the chapters in H. Kohn (ed.), *German history: some new German views* (1954).

A. Bullock has written a brilliant biography of the Fuehrer, in some ways the best introduction to the history of the era, *Hitler: a study in tyranny** (1952, rev., 1964). K. Heiden, *Der Fuehrer: Hitler's rise to power* (1944), is still valuable, and some psychological insights are provided in J. H. McRandle, *The track of the wolf: essays on national socialism and its leader, Adolf Hitler* (1965). Hitler's early years are reconstructed in F. Jetzinger, *Hitler's youth* (1956, trans. 1958), and in B. F. Smith, *Adolf Hitler: his family, childhood, and youth** (1967); and the end of the leader and his regime is vividly recounted in H. R. Trevor-Roper, *The last days of Hitler** (1947, rev., 1966). Also recommended is H. Heiber, *Adolf Hitler* (1960, trans. 1961). The proceedings of the Nuremberg war crimes trials have been published as International Military Tribunal, *Trial of the major war criminals before the International Military Tribunal, 1945–1946* (42 vols., 1947–1949), and as *Nazi conspiracy and aggression* (8 vols., 2 supplements, 1946–1948). Discussions of the trial are found in P. de Mendelssohn, *Design for aggression* (1946); W. R. Harris, *Tyranny on trial: the evidence of Nuremberg* (1954); J. L. Stipp (ed.), *Devil's diary: the record of Nazi conspiracy and aggression* (1955); P. Calvacoressi, *Nuremberg: the facts, the law, and the consequences* (1948); and E. Davidson, *The trial of the Germans: Nuremberg, 1945–1946* (1966).

Special phases of the Nazi era are discussed in numerous books, among them: E. Crankshaw, *Gestapo: instrument of tyranny** (1956); T. Taylor, *Sword and swastika: generals and Nazis in the Third Reich** (1952); P. Seabury, *The Wilhelmstrasse: a study of German diplomats under the Nazi regime* (1955); J. S. Conway, *The Nazi persecution of the churches, 1933–1945* (1968); G. Lewy, *The Catholic church and Nazi Germany* (1964); S. Friedlaender, *Pius XII and the Third Reich: a documentation* (1966); G. A. Ziemer, *Education for death: the making of the Nazi* (1942); O. J. Hale, *The captive press in the Third Reich* (1964); Z. A. B. Zeman, *Nazi propaganda* (1964); A. Schweitzer, *Big business in the Third Reich* (1964); G. Reitlinger, *SS: alibi of a nation, 1922–1945** (1956); and on the concentration camps, E. Kogon, *The theory and practice of hell** (1950). A popular overdrawn history of a special subject is W. Manchester, *The arms of Krupp, 1587–1968* (1968). G. L. Mosse (ed.) illustrates facets of the Nazi era in *Nazi culture* (1966), and M. Mayer, *They thought they were free* (1955), provides some insight into the attitudes of men and women living under the Nazi dictatorship. [Other books on wartime Germany and German-dominated Europe are listed in the next chapter.] On the still incomplete story of the opposition to Hitler, the best introductions are H. Rothfels, *The German opposition to Hitler* (1949); C. FitzGibbon, *20 July* [published in England under the title *The shirt of Nessus*] (1956); G. Ritter, *The German resistance: Carl Goerdeler's struggle against tyranny* (1954, trans. 1959); T. Prittie, *Germans against Hitler* (1964); R. Manvell and H. Fraenkel, *The July plot* (1964); the same authors' *The Canaris conspiracy* (1969); E. Zeller, *The flame of freedom* (trans. 1968); H. C. Deutsch, *The German conspiracy against Hitler in the twilight war* [1939–1940] (1968); and R. Manvell and H. A. Jacobsen (eds.), *July 20, 1944: Germans against Hitler* (1969).

[Communism is discussed mainly in Chapter XVII, and Italian fascism is discussed separately below.]

Some attempts to explore the ideological roots of the German experience (in addition to several books listed for earlier chapters) are W. M. McGovern, *From Luther to Hitler* (1941); P. Viereck, *Metapolitics: the roots of the Nazi mind** (1941, rev., 1961), cited earlier; R. D. O'Butler, *The roots of national socialism 1783–1933* (1941), also cited earlier; and L. L. Snyder, *German nationalism: the tragedy of a people* (1952); some of these books are less than fair to the earlier Germans. Other important efforts to explore the origins of Nazism include F. Stern, *The politics of cultural despair: a study in the use of the Germanic ideology** (1961); R. H. Bowen, *German theories of the corporative state* (1947); G. L. Mosse, *The crisis of German ideology: intellectual origins of the Third Reich** (1964); and W. Laqueur, *Russia and Germany: a century of conflict** (1965), which, despite its title, deals with Russian influences on Nazi ideology.

Among important recent efforts to examine totalitarian attitudes and institutions on a comparative basis and to establish definitions are F. L. Carsten, *The rise of fascism** (1967); H. R. Kedward, *Fascism in western Europe, 1900–1945* (1969); E. Nolte, *Three faces of fascism: Action Française, Italian fascism, national socialism** (1963, trans. 1966), a difficult book for most readers; J. Weiss, *The fascist tradition: radical right-wing extremism in modern Europe** (1967); H. Rogger and E. Weber (eds.), *The European right: a historical profile** (1965), cited earlier; W. Laqueur and G. L. Mosse (eds.), *International fascism, 1920–1945** (1966), originally a volume of the *Journal of Contemporary History*; and S. J. Woolf and others, *European fascism* (1968), and *The nature of fascism* (1968). To these may be added A. Cobban, *Dictatorship: its history and theory* (1939); C. J.

Bibliography Friedrich and Z. K. Brzezinski, *Totalitarian dictatorship and autocracy** (1956); K. R. Popper, *The open society and its enemies* (2 vols., rev., 1963); E. Fromm, *Escape from freedom** (1941), a psychological inquiry into the reasons for submission to tyranny; H. Arendt, *The origins of totalitarianism,** already cited; G. W. F. Hallgarten, *Why dictators?* (1954); J. L. Talmon, *The origins of totalitarian democracy** (1952), cited earlier; S. Neumann, *Permanent revolution* (1942); E. Halévy, *The era of tyrannies** (1938, trans. 1965); and H. Buchheim, *Totalitarian rule: its nature and characteristics* (trans. 1968).

Italy, 1919–1945 The relevant chapters in D. Mack Smith, *Italy: a modern history* (rev., 1969), are valuable; three other useful introductions to the Italian experience are A. Cassels, *Fascist Italy** (1968), in the Europe Since 1500 series; E. Wiskemann, *Fascism in Italy: its development and influence* (1969); and F. Chabod, *A history of Italian fascism* (1963). On the rise of fascism and the nature of the fascist state the following are also recommended: A. Rossi [pseud. A. Tasca], *The rise of Italian fascism, 1918–1922* (1938), a detailed account by a well-informed Italian ex-Communist; G. A. Borgese, *Goliath: the march of fascism* (1937); G. Salvemini, *The fascist dictatorship in Italy* (1927), and *Under the axe of fascism* (1936). The following books also discuss both the theory and practice of Italian fascism: H. W. Schneider, *Making the fascist state* (1928); H. Finer, *Mussolini's Italy* (1935); C. T. Schmidt, *The plough and the sword* (1938), and *The corporate state in action: Italy under fascism* (1939); J. Meenan, *The Italian corporative system* (1945); H. L. Matthews, *The fruits of fascism* (1943); and D. Germino, *The Italian fascist party in power* (1959).

On *Il Duce* himself there is a detailed biography by I. Kirkpatrick, *Mussolini: study of a demagogue** (1964). The older G. Megaro, *Mussolini in the making* (1938), remains valuable. There are also accounts by L. Fermi* (1961); C. Hibbert (1962), mostly on the latter phases of the dictator's career; and R. MacGregor-Hastie, *The day of the lion: the life and death of fascist Italy, 1922–1945* (1963), the latter not entirely reliable. The multivolumed biography of Mussolini in progress (2 vols. to date, 1965 ff.) by the Italian historian R. de Felice is not available in translation. An outstanding account of the underground struggle from 1924 to 1943 is C. F. Delzell, *Mussolini's enemies: the Italian anti-fascist resistance* (1961). F. Deakin, *The brutal friendship: Mussolini, Hitler, and the fall of Italian fascism** (1962, rev., 1966), is a detailed account of the last phase of Mussolini's career from his overthrow to his death.

Other European [Spain and the Spanish Civil War are discussed in the following chapter.] Useful books on
Developments eastern Europe after 1918 are H. Seton-Watson, *Eastern Europe between the wars, 1918–1941** (1946); C. A. Macartney and A. W. Palmer, *Independent eastern Europe* (1962); R. L. Wolff, *The Balkans in our time,** already cited; and C. and B. Jelavich, *The Balkans** (1965). Other general accounts include J. S. Roucek, *Balkan politics: international relations in no man's land* (1948), and two valuable surveys by the Royal Institute of International Affairs, *The Balkan states* (1936) and *Southeastern Europe: a political and economic survey* (1939). The best treatment of the economic disruption following the end of the Austro-Hungarian empire is L. Pasvolsky, *Economic nationalism of the Danubian states* (1928). More specialized accounts of various countries and selected topics include C. A. Gulick, *Austria from Habsburg to Hitler* (2 vols., 1948), a fully documented and detailed account sympathetic to the Austrian socialists; M. MacDonald, *The Republic of Austria, 1918–1934: a study in the failure of democratic government* (1946), a constitutional analysis; J. Braunthal, *The tragedy of Austria* (1948); C. A. Macartney, *Hungary and her successors: the treaty of Trianon and its consequences, 1919–1937* (1937), and *Problems of the Danube basin* (1942); A. Basch, *The Danube basin and the German economic sphere* (1944); S. H. Thomson, *Czechoslovakia in European history* (1943, 1953); R. W. Seton-Watson, *A history of the Czechs and Slovaks* (1943, 1965); E. Wiskemann, *Czechs and Germans* (1938, 1967);

H. L. Roberts, *Rumania: political problems of an agrarian state* (1951); and R. West, *Black lamb and grey falcon: a journey through Yugoslavia* (2 vols., 1941), a sensitive and discriminating description. On the Scandinavian countries good studies are F. D. Scott, *The United States and Scandinavia* (1950); M. W. Childs, *Sweden: the middle way* (rev., 1947); and J. H. Wuorinen, *Scandinavia** (1965).

On the American New Deal a selection of conflicting interpretations is conveniently presented in E. C. Rozwenc (ed.), *The New Deal: revolution or evolution?* (rev., 1959), and in M. Keller (ed.), *The New Deal* (1963). For Britain see J. A. Thompson, *The collapse of the British Liberal party: fate or self-destruction?* (1969). For Italy: S. W. Halperin, *Mussolini and Italian fascism* (1964), in the Anvil series. For Weimar Germany: R. N. Hunt (ed.), *The creation of the Weimar Republic: stillborn democracy?* (1969), and F. K. Ringer (ed.), *The German inflation of 1923* (1969). For the Nazi era: J. L. Snell (ed.), *The Nazi revolution: Germany's guilt or Germany's fate?* (1959); and R. G. L. Waite (ed.), *Hitler and Nazi Germany* (rev., 1969). G. H. Stein has edited *Hitler* in the Great Lives Observed series, and J. Remak, *The Nazi years* (1969). On totalitarianism there are available: P. T. Mason, *Totalitarianism: temporary madness or permanent danger?* (1967); E. Weber, *Varieties of fascism: doctrines of revolution in the twentieth century* (Anvil, 1964); N. Greene (ed.), *Fascism: an anthology** (1968); and C. F. Delzell (ed.), *Mediterranean fascism** (1970).

There is no one comprehensive treatment taking into account the sources now available for the diplomacy of the interwar years and the background to the Second World War. Useful introductions for the general reader are E. Wiskemann, *Europe of the dictators, 1919–1945** (1966), in the Plumb series; K. Eubank, *The origins of World War II** (1969), in the Europe Since 1500 series; and L. Lafore, *The end of glory: an interpretation of the origins of World War II** (1970). Older surveys are G. M. Gathorne-Hardy, *A short history of international affairs, 1920–1939* (1942); E. H. Carr, *International relations between the two world wars** (1940, rev., 1948); and R. M. Rayner, *A twenty-years' truce, 1919–1939* (1945). Many other titles are listed below. The war is placed in historical perspective in L. Dehio, *The precarious balance: four centuries of the European power struggle** (1948, trans. 1952), and in H. Holborn, *The political collapse of Europe* (1951), a provocative essay. For the war itself, in all aspects, G. Wright, *The ordeal of total war, 1939–1945** (1968), in the Langer series, is indispensable. Of special value are the annual volumes for the interwar years edited for the Royal Institute of International Affairs by A. Toynbee and others, *Survey of international affairs* (1920 ff.), and the accompanying *Documents on international affairs;* a survey has been issued to cover the years 1939–1946 (1954), and the annual volumes have been resumed for the years since 1946.

An outstanding work is G. Jackson, *The Spanish republic and the Civil War, 1931–1939** (1965), which may be compared with the equally informative H. Thomas, *The Spanish Civil War** (1961). Stressing the communist role is B. Bolloten, *The grand camouflage: the Spanish Civil War and revolution, 1936–1939* (1961, rev., 1968). The turbulent background is ably conveyed in G. Brenan, *The Spanish labyrinth** (1943); in the relevant chapters of R. Carr, *Spain, 1808–1939* (1966), already cited; and in S. G. Payne, *Politics and the military in modern Spain* (1967), also cited earlier. Payne has, in addition, written an informative monograph, *Falange: a history of Spanish fascism** (1961), and a brief account of the Civil War in *The Spanish revolution** (1969). On the international aspects of the war there are P. van der Esch, *Prelude to war: the international repercussions of the Spanish Civil War, 1936–1939* (1951); H. Feis, *The Spanish story: Franco and the nations at war** (1948); N. J. Padelford, *International law and diplomacy in the Spanish civil strife* (1939); D. A. Puzzo, *Spain and the Great Powers, 1936–1941* (1962); D. T. Cattell's two volumes,

Communism and the Spanish Civil War (1955) and *Soviet diplomacy and the Spanish Civil War* (1957). Three studies of the American response to the war are F. J. Taylor, *The United States and the Spanish Civil War* (1956); A. Guttmann, *The wound in the heart: America and the Spanish Civil War* (1962); and R. P. Traina, *American diplomacy and the Spanish Civil War* (1968). Other memorable aspects are touched upon in P. Stansky and W. Abrahams, *Journey to the frontier: Julian Bell and John Cornford: their lives and the 1930's** (1966); G. Orwell, *Homage to Catalonia** (1938), by one who fought and became disillusioned; V. Brome, *The international brigades* (1966); and S. Weintraub, *The last great cause: the intellectuals and the Spanish Civil War* (1968). On events since the Nationalist victory see S. G. Payne, *Franco's Spain** (1967).

In addition to the general accounts listed above dealing with the two decades as a whole, the following, which focus on one or two countries, are recommended: A. Wolfers, *Britain and France between two wars: conflicting strategies of peace since Versailles** (1940); R. W. Seton-Watson, *Britain and the dictators: a survey of post-war British policy* (1938), and *From Munich to Danzig* (1939); W. M. Jordan, *Great Britain, France, and the German problem, 1918–1939* (1943); E. H. Carr, *Britain: a study of foreign policy from Versailles to the outbreak of the war* (1939), and *The twenty years' crisis, 1919–1939* (2nd ed., 1946); W. N. Medlicott, *British foreign policy since Versailles* (1940); P. A. Reynolds, *British foreign policy in the inter-war years* (1954); and F. S. Northedge, *The troubled giant: Britain among the great powers, 1916–1939* (1966). Focusing on France are R. Albrecht-Carrié, *France, Europe, and the two world wars* (1961); E. R. Cameron, *Prologue to appeasement: a study in French foreign policy* (1942); W. E. Scott, *Alliance against Hitler: the origins of the Franco-Soviet Pact* (1962); and A. H. Furnia, *The diplomacy of appeasement* (1966). Two valuable books of essays by L. B. Namier review the documents and memoirs as they began to appear in the postwar period: *Diplomatic prelude, 1938–1939* (1948) and *Europe in decay: a study in disintegration, 1936–1940* (1950). Four provocative books, highly critical of the appeasement policy, are F. L. Schuman, *Europe on the eve: the crises of diplomacy, 1933–1939* (1939); A. L. Rowse, *Appeasement: a study in political decline, 1933–1939** (1961); M. Gilbert and R. Gott, *The appeasers* (1963); and M. George, *The warped vision: British foreign policy, 1933–1939* (1965). W. R. Rock, *Appeasement on trial: British foreign policy and its critics, 1938–1939* (1966), analyzes the opposition to the policy at the time, of which the most effective account is W. S. Churchill, *The gathering storm** (1948), the first volume of his *The Second World War** (6 vols., 1948–1953), covering the years when he was in the opposition.

On specific episodes and subjects one may turn to E. Wiskemann, *The Rome-Berlin Axis: a history of the relations between Hitler and Mussolini* (1949), and the same author's *Undeclared war* (1939). The Ethiopian conquest is studied in G. Salvemini, *Prelude to World War II* (1954); P. Cremona, *Italy's foreign and colonial policy, 1914–1937* (1938); and G. W. Baer, *The coming of the Italo-Ethiopian war* (1967). On the annexation of Austria one may read G. Brook-Shepherd, *Anschluss: the rape of Austria* (1963); the same author's *Austrian odyssey* (1957) and *Dollfuss* (1961); and J. Gehl, *Austria, Germany and the Anschluss, 1931–1938* (1963). J. W. Wheeler-Bennett, *Munich: prologue to tragedy** (1948, reissued 1963), is one of the best books on the entire era, but also useful are K. Eubank, *Munich* (1963); H. Noguères, *Munich: "peace for our time"* (trans. 1963); and K. Robbins, *Munich 1938* (1968). W. Strang, *Home and abroad* (1956), and *The Foreign Office* (1955), are autobiographical and historical accounts by a British diplomat; F. Gilbert and G. A. Craig (eds.), *The diplomats, 1919–1939** (1953), includes many valuable chapters on the men who made foreign policy in the era.

Books dealing with eastern Europe, in addition to those listed for Soviet foreign policy in Chapter XVII, include J. A. Lukacs, *The great powers and eastern Europe* (1952); P. Wandycz, *France and her Eastern allies, 1919–1925* (1962); L. Kochan, *The struggle for Germany, 1914–1945* (1963), on the rivalry between the West and Russia; G. Hilger and A. G. Meyer, *The incompatible allies: a memoir history of German-Soviet relations, 1918–1941* (1953); J. Korbel, *Poland between East and West:*

Soviet and German diplomacy towards Poland, 1919–1933 (1963); and A. Cienciala, *Poland and the Western powers, 1938–1939* (1968). The first volume of an important longer study focusing on eastern Europe is J. E. McSherry, *Stalin, Hitler, and Europe: the origins of World War II, 1933–1939* (vol. I, 1968). The German-Soviet pact (and its subsequent history) may be studied in A. Rossi [pseud. A. Tasca], *The Russo-German alliance, August 1939–June 1941* (1950), and in G. L. Weinberg, *Germany and the Soviet Union, 1939–1941* (1954). On the events immediately preceding the outbreak of the war a Swiss historian, W. Hofer, has written *War premeditated, 1939* (1955); and C. Horne, the brief, informative *The approach of war, 1938–9** (1967).

The opening guns in a campaign to "revise" the general picture of Nazi war responsibility have been launched with A. J. P. Taylor's dazzling but unconvincing performance in *The origins of the Second World War** (1961, 1963), in which he depicts Hitler as one who did not desire war but merely took advantage of the uncertainty of his opponents. A second book in the same category is D. L. Hoggan, *When peaceful revision failed: the origins of World War II* (1964), an English version of a book by an American scholar that appeared first in German translation (1961), and which goes even further in blaming the British.

The role of the United States in these years is traced in two comprehensive volumes by W. L. Langer and S. E. Gleason, *The challenge to isolation, 1937–1940* (1952) and *The undeclared war, 1940–1941* (1953); in R. Ferrell, *American diplomacy in the great depression* (1957); and in S. Friedlaender, *Prelude to downfall: Hitler and the United States, 1939–1941* (trans. 1967). The events in the Far East may be studied through David J. Lu, *From the Marco Polo Bridge to Pearl Harbor: Japan's entry into World War II* (1961); R. Butow, *Tojo and the coming of the war* (1961); and J. B. Crowley, *Japan's quest for autonomy: national security and foreign policy, 1930–1938* (1966). On American involvement one may turn to H. Feis, *The road to Pearl Harbor* (1950); P. W. Schroeder, *The Axis alliance and Japanese-American relations, 1941* (1963); and R. Wohlstetter, *Pearl Harbor: warning and decision** (1962).

An invaluable source for diplomatic history of the interwar years are the German Foreign Office archives captured during the Second World War and edited by an international group of distinguished historians; many volumes on the years since 1933 have already appeared in English translation under the auspices of the U.S. Department of State as *Documents on German foreign policy, 1918–1945* (1949 ff.); other portions will remain available on microfilm for scholars. Guides have been edited by G. L. Weinberg (1952) and by G. O. Kent (3 vols., 1962–1965).

G. Wright, *The ordeal of total war,** has already been cited. W. S. Churchill, *The Second World War** (6 vols., 1948–1953; authorized 1-vol. condensation, 1959), is a full-dress treatment by a historian with unrivaled opportunities; in some ways, however, the work is as much autobiographical as historical and should be used with caution. For a thoughtful evaluation of Churchill as wartime leader one may read with profit the essays in A. J. P. Taylor and others, *Churchill revised: a critical assessment* (1969).

Three attempts to cover the events of the war in brief compass are L. L. Snyder, *A concise history: the war, 1939–1945** (1960); P. Young, *World War, 1939–1945* (1966); and B. Collier, *A short history of the Second World War* (1967). H. Baldwin discusses with verve eleven major battles in *Battles lost and won: great campaigns of World War II* (1966). There are also narrative histories by J. F. C. Fuller (1948), W. P. Hall (1946), R. W. Shugg and H. A. DeWeerd (1946), H. C. O'Neill (1950), and C. B. Falls (rev., 1950). Many volumes of the detailed official histories of the United Kingdom, Canada, and the United States have appeared. Of special note is the official U.S. Navy history in fifteen volumes prepared by S. E. Morison (1947 ff.) and published in a one-volume abridgment as *The two-ocean war: a short history of the United States navy in the Second World War* (1963). On naval warfare there are also S. W. Roskill, *The war at sea, 1939–1945* (1954), and J. Creswell, *Sea warfare, 1939–1945* (1967).

On overall strategy a valuable discussion of high-level decisions, Allied and Axis, by the Office of the U.S. Chief of Military History is K. R. Greenfield (ed.), *Command decisions* (1959). Also useful on strategy are the following: J. R. M. Butler's volume in the U.K. official history, *Grand strategy* (1957); the succeeding volume on strategy in the same series by J. M. A. Gwyer and J. R. M. Butler (1964), covering the 1941–1942 period; S. E. Morison, *American contributions to the strategy of World War II* (1958); F. H. Hinsley, *Hitler's strategy* (1951); E. Robertson, *Hitler's pre-war policy and military plans* (1963); and B. H. Liddell Hart, *The other side of the hill** (1951, rev. ed. of *The German generals talk,* 1948).

For studies of the wartime domestic scene there are some excellent volumes in the U.K. official history: W. C. Hancock and M. M. Gowing, *British war economy* (1949); R. M. Titmuss, *Problems of social policy* (1950); and M. M. Postan, *British war production* (1950). Various phases of the American domestic scene are treated in many books, of which one attempt at a synthesis is A. R. Buchanan, *The United States and World War II** (2 vols., 1964). B. H. Klein, *Germany's economic preparations for war* (1959), stresses inefficiency and the belatedness of full-scale mobilization, as do A. S. Milward, *The German economy at war* (1965), and B. E. Carroll, *Design for total war: arms and economics in the Third Reich* (1968). The German front is also discussed in C. K. Webster and N. N. Frankland, *Strategic air offensive against Germany, 1939–1945* (1961), and H. R. Trevor-Roper (ed.), *From Blitzkrieg to defeat* (1965). The German military may be examined in H. Rosinski, *The German army* (1940, 1966), and one special aspect in G. H. Stein, *The Waffen SS: Hitler's élite guard at war, 1939–1945* (1966). For the Russian front one may read A. Werth, *The year of Stalingrad* (1947), and *Russia at war, 1941–1945** (1964); A. Clark, *Barbarossa: the Russian-German conflict, 1941–1945* (1965); and T. Higgins, *Hitler and Russia: the Third Reich in a two-front war, 1937–1943* (1966). The war in the Pacific is ably sketched in C. Bateson, *The war with Japan* (1968). A useful bibliographical essay is L. Morton, *Writings on the Second World War** (AHA Service Center series, 1967).

[The books dealing with France in the 1930s listed in Chapter XIX and earlier in this chapter should also be consulted.] The political and military background to the fall of France may now be approached through J. Williams, *The Ides of May: the defeat of France, May–June 1940* (1968); A. Horne, *To lose a battle: France, 1940* (1969); G. Chapman, *Why France fell: the defeat of the French army in 1940* (1969); and the massive, popularly written W. L. Shirer, *The collapse of the Third Republic: an inquiry into the fall of France in 1940* (1969). They may be supplemented by A. Goutard, *The fall of France* (trans. 1940); A. Beaufre, *1940: the fall of France* (trans. 1968); and L. Thompson, *1940* (1966). A moving memoir is M. Bloch, *Strange defeat** (1940), by the eminent medievalist who was executed as a member of the Resistance. An outstanding study relating to these years is P. C. F. Bankwitz, *Maxime Weygand and civil-military relations in modern France* (1967). A volume by a French journalist is informative but must be read with caution, A. Géraud [Pertinax], *The gravediggers of France* (2 vols., trans. 1944), and A. Rossi [A. Tasca] analyzes the role of the Communists in the opening phase of the war in *A Communist party in action* (1949). Paul Reynaud has written many volumes of self-vindicating memoirs of which one has been translated as *In the thick of the fight, 1940–45* (trans. 1955). On the Vichy regime recommended books are R. Aron, *The Vichy regime, 1940–44* (1958); P. Farmer, *Vichy: political dilemma* (1955); D. Pickles, *France between the republics, 1940–1945* (1946); A. D. Hytier, *Two years of French foreign policy: Vichy, 1940–1942* (1959); and R. O. Paxton, *Parades and politics at Vichy* (1966). Defensive on the controversial question of American relations with Vichy is W. L. Langer, *Our Vichy gamble** (1947). There is a biography of Laval by H. Cole (1963), and a detailed biographical study focusing on diplomatic events, G. Warner, *Pierre Laval and the eclipse of France, 1931–1945* (1968). Although there is no general treatment of the Resistance movement in English, A. Werth provides a useful introduction in *France, 1940–1955* (1957); and a special aspect is explored in P. Novick, *The Resistance versus Vichy: the purge of* collaborators in liberated France (1969). For the years from the 1930s to liberation, the volumes of Charles de Gaulle, *War memoirs** (3 vols., 1954-1956, trans. 1958-1960), are incomparable; specifically on de Gaulle's unsatisfactory wartime relations with London and Washington, there are two able studies: A. L. Funk, *Charles de Gaulle: the crucial years, 1943-1944* (1959), and M. Viorst, *Hostile allies: FDR and Charles de Gaulle* (1965).

Bibliography

[See also the many books on the Third Reich listed in Chapter XIX.] The volume of the *Survey of international affairs* covering the years 1939-1946, *Hitler's Europe* (1954), is valuable on all aspects of the German domination. A special subject is well treated in A. Dallin, *German rule in Russia, 1941-1945: a study of occupation policies* (1957), demonstrating the ineptitude of the Germans in exploiting discontent; it may be supplemented by J. A. Armstrong, *Ukrainian nationalism, 1939-1945* (1955). On the Jewish question two books serve as a good introduction to a grim subject: G. Reitlinger, *The final solution: the attempt to exterminate the Jews of Europe, 1939-1945* (1953, rev., 1968), and R. Hilberg, *The destruction of the European Jews** (1961). On other ethnic policies there are R. L. Koehl, *RKFDV: German resettlement and population policy, 1939-1945* (1957); J. B. Schechtman, *European population transfers, 1939-1945* (1946); E. M. Kulischer, *Europeans on the move: war and population changes, 1917-1947* (1948); and M. J. Proudfoot, *European refugees, 1939-1952* (1957).

Hitler's New Order

Wartime diplomacy and the successes and failures of the Soviet-Western coalition are discussed in the latter volumes of Churchill's history; in J. L. Snell, *Illusion and necessity: the diplomacy of global war, 1939-1945** (1963); the same author's *Wartime origins of the East-West dilemma over Germany* (1959); W. H. McNeill, *America, Britain, and Russia: their cooperation and conflict, 1941-1946* (1953); C. Wilmot, *The struggle for Europe** (1952); G. Smith, *American diplomacy during the Second World War** (1965); B. Gardner, *The wasted hour: the tragedy of 1945* (1963); and M. F. Herz, *Beginnings of the Cold War* (1966). Invaluable are the superb volumes of H. Feis: *Churchill, Roosevelt, Stalin: the war they waged and the peace they sought** (1957), covering the years from 1941 to the collapse of Germany and including Yalta; *Between war and peace: the Potsdam Conference** (1960); and on the last phase, *The atomic bomb and the end of the war in the Pacific** (1961, rev., 1966). On the last phase in the Pacific see also R. Butow, *Japan's decision to surrender** (1954), and W. Craig, *The fall of Japan* (1968). Hitler's relations with his two major allies are discussed in F. W. Deakin's detailed *The brutal friendship** (1962, rev., 1966), already cited, and in J. Menzel, *Hitler and Japan: the hollow alliance* (1966). E. L. Woodward, *British foreign policy in the Second World War* (1962), is based on the Foreign Office archives to which the author was given early access. On Yalta there are good chapters in J. L. Snell (ed.), *The meaning of Yalta: Big Three diplomacy and the new balance of power** (1956). On the early postwar efforts at settlement there are R. Opie and others, *The search for peace settlements* (1951), a Brookings Institution study, and F. W. Pick, *Peacemaking in perspective: from Potsdam to Paris* (1950). [For other volumes on the origins and nature of the Cold War see the titles listed for the following chapter.]

Wartime Diplomacy and Origins of the Cold War

In the various problems series there are available: L. F. Schaefer (ed.), *The Ethiopian crisis: touchstone of appeasement?* (1961); G. Jackson (ed.), *The Spanish Civil War: domestic crisis or international conspiracy?* (1967); A. Guttman (ed.), *American neutrality and the Spanish Civil War* (1963); F. L. Loewenheim (ed.), *Peace or appeasement: Hitler, Chamberlain, and the Munich crisis* (1965), an especially full selection of source materials; D. E. Lee (ed.), *Munich: blunder, plot, or tragic necessity?* (1969); J. L. Snell (ed.), *The outbreak of the Second World War: design or blunder?* (1962); S. M. Osgood (ed.), *The fall of France, 1940* (1965); I. Morris (ed.), *Japan, 1931-1945:*

*Problems and Readings**

Bibliography   *militarism, fascism, Japanism?* (1963); and G. O. Totten (ed.), *Democracy and prewar Japan: groundwork or façade?* (1965). W. C. Langsam has edited *Historic documents of World War II* (Anvil, 1958), and M. Gilbert, *Churchill* (1967), in the Great Lives Observed series.

XXI: The Contemporary Age

It is difficult to assess the durable value of the literature dealing with the events and developments of the recent era. The listings in this chapter therefore have been kept brief. Useful in keeping up with current developments, in addition to obvious periodical and newspaper sources, are the annual volumes published by the Royal Institute of International Affairs, the *Survey of international affairs*; the Yearbooks published by the leading encyclopedias; the *Annual register;* and *Keesing's contemporary archives: weekly diary of important world events* (1931 ff.). A stimulating symposium is the Scott, Foresman publication, *Contemporary civilization** (1959 ff.), which every few years attempts an overview of world affairs by leading authorities.

The Communist Worlds in Europe and Asia

[The books listed for the U.S.S.R. in Chapter XVII and for eastern Europe in Chapter XIX should be consulted.] Informative on post-1945 developments are R. C. Wolff, *The Balkans in our time,** and C. and B. Jelavich, *The Balkans** (1965), both cited earlier; and F. G. Heymann, *Poland and Czechoslovakia** (1966). To these may be added H. Seton-Watson, *The East-European revolution* (1950, 1956); Z. K. Brzezinski, *The Soviet bloc: unity and conflict* (1960, rev., 1967); R. V. Burks, *The dynamics of communism in eastern Europe* (1961); and H. L. Roberts, *Eastern Europe: politics, revolution, and diplomacy* (1970).

    On the emergence of communism in China and on the regime since 1949 some books have already been cited in Chapter XVIII. Good introductions are J. K. Fairbank, *The United States and China** (rev., 1958), already cited; R. C. North, *Moscow and Chinese Communists** (1953); C. Tuan-sheng, *The government and politics of China, 1912–1949** (1961); and G. Moseley, *China: Empire to People's Republic* (1968). In addition there are A. D. Barnett, *Communist China and Asia* (1960); C. Brandt, B. Schwartz, and J. Fairbank, *A documentary history of Chinese communism* (1952); C. P. Fitzgerald, *The birth of communist China** (1952, rev., 1966); B. Schwartz, *Chinese communism and the rise of Mao** (1951); C. Brandt, *Stalin's failure in China** (1958); and C. B. McLane, *Soviet policy and the Chinese Communists 1931–1946* (1958). The most reliable biography of Mao is S. Schram, *Mao Tse-tung** (rev., 1967). The best book on the role of the United States is H. Feis, *The China tangle: the American effort in China from Pearl Harbor to the Marshall mission** (1953). On other aspects of international affairs there are M. Lindsay, *China and the Cold War: a study in international politics* (1955); R. G. Boyd, *Communist China's foreign policy* (1962); K. Mehnert, *Peking and Moscow* (1964); and D. S. Zagoria, *The Sino-Soviet conflict** (1962). There are bibliographical essays in the AHA Service Center series by A. B. Cole, *Forty years of Chinese communism** (1962), and by J. K. Fairbank, *New views of China's tradition and modernization** (1968).

The Emergent Nations: Asia and Africa

The literature here is enormous and one should also consult the books cited in Chapter XV and in Chapter XVIII. Some works of a general nature that serve as a useful introduction are R. Emerson, *From empire to nation: the rise to self-assertion of Asian and African peoples** (1960); S. C. Easton, *The twilight of European colonialism: a political analysis* (1960); J. Strachey, *The end of empire* (1960); H. Tinker, *Ballot box and bayonet: people and government in emergent Asian nations* (1964); L. L. Snyder, *The new nationalism* (1968); M. Perham, *Colonial sequence, 1930–1949* (1967); and V. M. Dean and H. D. Harootunian (eds.), *West and non-West: new perspectives* (1963), contributions by some forty experts. An impressive, and discouraging, study is G. Myrdal, *Asian drama: an inquiry into the poverty of nations** (3 vols., 1968).

The impact of modernization is examined historically and comparatively in C. E. Black, *The dynamics of modernization: a study in comparative history** (1966); I. R. Sinai, *The challenge of modernization** (1964), and *In search of the modern world* (1968); B. Moore, *Social origins of dictatorship and democracy: lord and peasant in the making of the modern world* (1966); D. A. Rustinow, *A world of nations: problems of political modernization** (1967); and W. W. Rostow, *The stages of economic growth: a non-communist manifesto** (1960), cited earlier. There are informative volumes on many of the developing nations in the Modern Nations in Historical Perspective* series. For the Middle East and its international implications see J. C. Hurewitz, *Middle East dilemmas* (1953), and *Middle East politics: the military dimension** (1969); W. R. Polk, *The United States and the Arab world* (1965); F. J. Khouri, *The Arab-Israeli dilemma* (1968); and A. Williams, *Britain and France in the Middle East and North Africa, 1914–1967* (1969).

For Africa one may turn for guidance to D. L. Wredner, *A history of Africa south of the Sahara** (1962); R. Oliver and S. D. Fage, *A short history of Africa** (1962); G. Carter, *Independence for Africa* (1960); J. Hatch, *A history of postwar Africa** (1965); and B. Davidson, *Africa in history* (1969). There is a growing literature on specific areas and subjects, among which may be mentioned: M. Crowder, *West Africa under colonial rule* (1968); R. W. July, *The origins of modern African thought: its development in West Africa during the nineteenth and twentieth centuries* (1967); J. D. Hargreaves, *West Africa: the former French states* (1967); E. Mortimer, *France and the Africans, 1944–1960* (1969); R. I. Rotberg, *The rise of nationalism in central Africa: the making of Malawi and Zambia, 1873–1964* (1965); and T. O. Ranger (ed.), *Aspects of central African history* (1968). The best study of events in the Congo is J. Gérard-Libois, *Katanga secession* (1966); and R. Emerson examines the significance for the United States of the rapidly changing continent in *Africa and United States policy* (1967).

BRITAIN. [Many of the books cited for Chapter XIX should also be consulted.] W. Beveridge, *Full employment in a free society* (1944), is an expanded version of the wartime report on which subsequent welfare state developments were based. For these and other developments since 1945 one may turn to K. Hutcheson, *The decline and fall of British capitalism* (1951), cited earlier; S. H. Beer, *British politics in the collectivist age* (1965); A. Sampson, *Anatomy of Britain** (1962); W. M. Stern, *Britain yesterday and today* (1962); and P. Gregg, *The welfare state: an economic and social history of Great Britain from 1945 to the present day* (1969). The changing Commonwealth may be studied in N. Mansergh, *The multi-racial Commonwealth* (1955), and *Commonwealth perspectives* (1958); J. B. D. Miller, *The Commonwealth in the world* (1959); and W. B. Hamilton (ed.), *A decade of the Commonwealth, 1955–1964* (1966). R. W. Winks has edited *The historiography of the British Empire-Commonwealth: trends, interpretations and resources* (1966).

FRANCE. The establishment and subsequent history of the Fourth Republic are best approached through the following: G. Wright, *The reshaping of French democracy* (1948); E. M. Earle (ed.), *Modern France: problems of the Third and Fourth Republics* (1951); P. M. Williams, *Crisis and compromise: politics in the Fourth Republic** (1964); A. Werth, *France, 1940–1955* (1956), cited earlier; F. deTarr, *The French Radical party from Herriot to Mendès-France* (1961); A. J. Rieber, *Stalin and the French Communist party, 1941–1947* (1962); E. S. Furniss, *France: troubled ally* (1960); and D. MacRae, Jr., *Parliament, politics, and society in France, 1946–1958* (1967).

For the Fifth Republic one may turn to A. Werth, *The de Gaulle revolution* (1960); P. M. Williams and M. Harrison, *De Gaulle's republic* (1960); P. M. Williams, *The French Parliament: politics in the Fifth Republic, 1958–1967* (1968); H. W. Ehrmann, *Politics in France** (1968); and D. Pickles, *The Fifth French Republic* (1960), and *Algeria and France* (1963). For the social and economic changes in postwar France, many antedating the Fifth Republic, see E. R. Tannenbaum, *The new France* (1961); S. Hoffman and others, *In search of France** (1963), cited earlier; P. Bauchet, *Economic planning: the French experience* (trans. 1964); J. Ardagh, *The new French revolution: a social and economic study of France, 1945–1968** (1969); J. J. Servan-Schreiber, *The*

American challenge (trans. 1968); R. Gilpin, *France in the age of the democratic state* (1968); and C. Brinton, *The Americans and the French* (1968). Recent developments are placed in historical perspective in J. C. Cairns, *France** (1965), and D. Johnson, *France* (1969). Two studies emphasizing foreign affairs are A. Grosser, *French foreign policy under de Gaulle** (1967), and W. W. Kulski, *De Gaulle and the world: the foreign policy of the Fifth French Republic* (1968). There are biographical accounts of de Gaulle by D. Schoenbrun * (1966), A. Werth * (1966), and J. Lacouture (trans. 1966). Aspects of French thought are explored in H. S. Hughes, *The obstructed path: French social thought, 1930–1960** (1968), and in G. Lichtheim, *Marxism in modern France* (1966).

GERMANY, WEST AND EAST. Two useful introductions are M. Balfour, *West Germany* (1968), and L. J. Edinger, *Politics in Germany** (1968). On the occupation years and first postwar decade there are E. Davidson, *The death and life of Germany: an account of the American occupation* (1959); H. Zink, *The United States in Germany, 1945–1955* (1957); G. A. Almond (ed.), *The struggle for democracy in Germany* (1949); and J. F. Golay, *The founding of the Federal Republic of Germany* (1958). Two informative studies on German economic recovery are H. C. Wallich, *Mainsprings of the German revival* (1955), and A. Grosser, *The colossus again: Western Germany from defeat to rearmament* (1953). For the Adenauer years see E. Alexander, *Adenauer and the new Germany* (1957), and R. Hiscocks, *The Adenauer era** (1966). L. J. Edinger applies newer psychological techniques in a biography of the Social Democratic leader, *Kurt Schumacher: a study in personality and political behavior* (1965); and K. P. Tauber studies an important subject in detail in *Beyond eagle and swastika: German nationalism since 1945* (2 vols., 1967). G. A. Craig, *From Bismarck to Adenauer: aspects of German statecraft* (1959), cited earlier, places recent German diplomacy in historical perspective. On the Eastern zone the best introduction is J. P. Nettl, *The Eastern zone and Soviet policy in Germany, 1945–1950* (1951).

ITALY. On the Italian republic see M. Grindrod, *The new Italy: transition from war to peace* (1947), and *The rebuilding of Italy: politics and economics, 1945–1955* (1955); H. S. Hughes, *The United States and Italy** (1953, rev., 1965), in the American Foreign Policy Library series; N. Kogan, *A political history of postwar Italy* (1966); and M. Salvadori, *Italy** (1965).

JAPAN. E. O. Reischauer, *The United States and Japan,** already cited, is invaluable. The best study of the occupation is K. Kawai, *Japan's American interlude* (1960). Two important studies of economic developments are J. B. Cohen, *Japan's post-war economy* (1958), and G. C. Allen, *Japan's economic recovery* (1958).

THE UNITED STATES. Although no listing on the contemporary United States is possible here, an introduction to the depression, war, and postwar years is provided in G. E. Mowry, *The urban nation, 1920–1960** (1965), and in C. N. Degler, *Affluence and anxiety: the United States since 1945** (1968). The black experience in America is told in J. H. Franklin, *From freedom to slavery* (1947, 1967), cited earlier, and in A. Meier and E. M. Rudwick, *From plantation to ghetto** (1966).

On European recovery and postwar movements toward economic and political unification good introductions are M. M. Postan, *An economic history of western Europe, 1945–1964** (1967), a valuable survey; G. Lichtheim, *The new Europe** (1963); A. J. Zurcher, *The struggle to unite Europe, 1940–1955* (1958); J. Freymond, *Western Europe since the war* (1964); D. W. Urwin, *Western Europe since 1945* (1968); M. Curtis, *Western European integration** (1965); S. R. Graubard (ed.), *A new Europe?** (1964); and A. Buchan (ed.), *Europe's futures, Europe's choices* (1969). The historical background to unification may be explored in R. Albrecht-Carrié, *One Europe: the historical background of European unity* (1965), and in J. Lukacs, *Decline and rise of Europe* (1965). Special studies include W. Diebold, Jr., *The Schuman plan* (1959); H. A. Schmitt, *The path to European union: from the Marshall Plan to the Common Market;* W. O. Henderson, *The genesis of the Common Market* (1963); F. R. Willis, *France, Germany and the new Europe, 1945–1967** (1968); and U. W. Kitzinger, *The politics and economics of European integration* (1963).

Several books on the wartime origins of the Soviet-Western rift have been described at the end of the previous chapter. Other attempts to reconstruct historically the major aspects of the Cold War with varying success include P. Calvacoressi, *International politics since 1945** (1968); L. Halle, *The Cold War as history* (1967); W. Knapp, *A history of war and peace, 1939–1965* (1967); W. LaFeber, *America, Russia, and the Cold War, 1945–1966* (1967); J. Lukacs, *A new history of the Cold War** (1961, rev., 1966); D. Rees, *The age of containment: the Cold War** (1967); D. Donnelly, *Struggle for the world: the Cold War, 1917–1965* (1965); A. Fontaine, *History of the Cold War*, vol. I, *1917–1950* (trans. 1968; vol. II, *1950–1967*, translation in progress); J. L. Clayton, *The economic impact of the Cold War* (1970); and P. Seabury, *The rise and decline of the Cold War* (1967). Two books by G. Kennan are invaluable: *Russia and the West under Lenin and Stalin** (1961) and *American diplomacy, 1900–1950** (1951); two other stimulating books are E. H. Carr, *The Soviet impact on the Western world** (1947), and L. F. Fischer, *Russia, America, and the world* (1961). Studies vehemently critical of United States policy include K. Ingram, *History of the Cold War* (1955); D. F. Fleming, *The Cold War and its origins, 1917–1960* (2 vols., 1961); W. A. Williams, *The tragedy of American diplomacy* (1959), and *American-Russian relations, 1781–1947* (1952); and G. Kolko, *The politics of war* (1969). Two useful surveys of American foreign policy are J. W. Spanier, *American foreign policy since World War II** (1960, rev., 1968), and P. Y. Hammond, *The Cold War years: American foreign policy since 1945* (1969).

A comprehensive study of the founding of the United Nations is R. B. Russell, *A history of the United Nations Charter: the role of the United States, 1940–1945* (1958); and the organization's subsequent history may be traced in C. M. Eichelberger, *The UN: the first twenty years* (1965). On nuclear weapons and international relations the following interesting, and disturbing, books are recommended: P. M. S. Blackett, *Atomic weapons and East-West relations* (1956); H. A. Kissinger, *Nuclear weapons and foreign policy* (1957); G. F. Kennan, *Russia, the atom, and the West* (1958); H. Kahn, *On thermonuclear war** (1960); D. E. Lilienthal, *Change, hope and the bomb** (1963); and M. Lerner, *The age of overkill* (1964). H. D. Smyth, *Atomic energy for military purposes* (1945), is a history of the wartime development of the bomb.

The best general account of the Korean War is D. Rees, *Korea: the limited war* (1964), which may be supplemented by G. Henderson, *Korea: the politics of the vortex* (1968). On Vietnam the background is provided in V. Purcell, *The revolution in Southeast Asia* (1963); E. J. Hammer, *The struggle for Indochina** (1966); and two books by B. B. Fall, *The two Vietnams: a political and military analysis* (1963, rev., 1967) and *Hell in a very small place: the siege of Dien Bien Phu* (1967). An informative but impassioned account is J. Buttinger, *Vietnam: a dragon embattled* (2 vols., 1967); a more balanced treatment is W. R. Fishel, *Anatomy of a conflict* (1968).

[The books described in Chapter XIV should be consulted as well as the histories of science listed in Chapter VII.] On the scientific background to the new physics, in addition to titles cited earlier, see B. Schonland, *The atomists, 1805–1933* (1968), and B. Cline, *The questioners: physicists and the quantum theory** (1965). R. Clowes, *The structure of life* (1967), is informative on the biological revolution, and J. Watson, *The double helix* (1968), describes himself and other biologists at work. Various scientific developments and their implications are discussed in A. E. E. McKenzie, *The major achievements of science* (2 vols., 1960); B. Barber, *Science and the social order* (1952); C. D. Darlington, *The evolution of man and society* (1969); and K. Coutts-Smith, *The dream of Icarus* (1969). Useful introductions to the activities of the professional philosophers

Bibliography   are provided in J. Passmore, *A hundred years of philosophy* (1968); in A. J. Ayer and others, *The revolution in philosophy* (1956); and in M. White (ed.), *The age of analysis** (1955), a convenient anthology. Aspects of modern religious thought are explored in S. P. Schilling, *Contemporary continental theologians* (1966), and an introduction to the complexities of contemporary art is provided in A. Neumeyer, *The search for meaning in modern art* (trans. 1964), and in H. Rosenberg, *The anxious object: art today and its audience* (1964). Many of the volumes listed in the following paragraph are also relevant to science, religion, thought, and society.

Past, Present,   Although no attempt can be made to list the many assessments of contemporary problems, *and Future*   there may be some point in asking the reader to consider the titles and intents of these books: T. H. Von Laue, *The global city: freedom, power and necessity in the age of world revolutions* (1969); R. A. Nisbet, *Social change and history* (1969); B. Moore, Jr., *Social origins of democracy and dictatorship** (1966), already mentioned, and broader than its title implies; B. Ward, *The West at bay** (1948), *Faith and freedom** (1954), *The rich nations and the poor nations** (1962), and *Five ideas that changed the world** (1959) [which she identifies as nationalism, industrialism, colonialism, communism, and internationalism]; E. Fischer, *The passing of the European age: a study of the transfer of Western civilization and its renewal in other continents* (1943, 1948); V. Bush, *Modern arms and free men: a discussion of the role of science in preserving democracy** (1949); C. P. Snow, *The two cultures and the scientific revolution* (1959, rev., 1963); J. Barzun, *Science: the glorious entertainment* (1964); P. R. and A. H. Ehrlich, *Population, resources, environment: issues in human ecology* (1970); P. M. Hauser, *The population dilemma* (1963); C. B. Hoover, *The economy, liberty, and the state* (1959); A. Shonfield, *Modern capitalism: the changing balance of public and private power** (1965); F. S. C. Northrop, *The meeting of East and West* (1946), and *The taming of the nations* (1952); R. Aron, *The century of total war* (1954); H. S. Hughes, *An essay for our times* (1950); A. J. Toynbee, *Civilization on trial* (1948), and *The world and the West* (1953); H. Arendt, *The human condition** (1958); K. E. Boulding, *The meaning of the twentieth century* (1964); K. W. Deutsch, *Nationalism and its alternatives* (1969); M. Katz, *The things that are Caesar's* (1966) [on government and the governed]; and J. K. Galbraith, *The new industrial state* (1967); and L. S. Feuer, *The conflict of generations* (1969).

Problems and   In the Anvil series a number of titles are relevant to this chapter: L. L. Snyder, *The world in the Readings**   *twentieth century* (rev., 1964); T. W. Wallbank, *Contemporary Africa: continent in transition* (rev., 1964), and *Documents on modern Africa* (1964); C. A. Buss, *Southeast Asia and the world today* (1958), and *The People's Republic of China* (1962); O. I. Janowsky, *The foundations of Israel: emergence of a welfare state* (1959); G. F. Kennan, *Soviet foreign policy, 1917–1941* (1960); N. A. Graebner, *Cold War diplomacy: American foreign policy, 1945–1960* (1962); and V. S. Mamatey, *Soviet Russian imperialism* (1964). Problem studies include N. A. Graebner (ed.), *The Cold War: ideological conflict or power struggle?* (1964); T. W. Wallbank (ed.), *The partition of India: causes and responsibilities* (1966); and P. P. Y. Loh, *The Kuomintang debacle of 1949: conquest or collapse?* (1965). Materials on science and intellectual developments are presented in L. P. Williams (ed.), *Relativity theory: its origins and impact on modern thought* (1968); and in W. W. Wagar (ed.), *Science, faith, and man: European thought since 1914* (1968).

ILLUSTRATION SOURCES

INDEX

ABOUT THE AUTHORS

ROBERT ROSWELL PALMER, Professor of History at Yale University, was born in Chicago in 1909. After graduating from the University of Chicago, he received his doctorate from Cornell University in 1934. From 1936 to 1963 he taught at Princeton University, and was Dean of the Faculty of Arts and Sciences at Washington University in St. Louis from 1963 to 1966. He was President of the American Historical Association in 1970. Professor Palmer worked with the Historical Section of the Army Ground Forces from 1943 to 1945. He is the author of *Catholics and Unbelievers in Eighteenth Century France* (1939), *Twelve Who Ruled: The Year of the Terror in the French Revolution* (1941, 1958), and the two-volume *Age of the Democratic Revolution* (1959 and 1964), both volumes of which were History Book Club selections and the first of which won the Bancroft Prize in 1960. He has likewise written *The World of the French Revolution* (1970), which was also published in French in 1968. He edited the *Rand McNally Atlas of World History* (1957) and translated Georges Lefebvre's *Coming of the French Revolution* (1947). He has contributed to a variety of journals and collaborative volumes in this country and Europe.

JOEL COLTON was born in New York City in 1918. He received his A.B. from the City College of New York in 1937, his A.M. from Columbia University in 1940, and his Ph.D. from Columbia in 1950. In 1947 he joined the Department of History at Duke University and since 1967 has been chairman of the department. He is also on the Board of Editors of the *Journal of Modern History* and has served as Consultant to the Advanced Placement Program of the College Entrance Examination Board. He was awarded a Guggenheim Fellowship, 1957–1958, a Rockefeller Foundation Fellowship, 1961–1962, and a National Humanities Endowment Senior Fellowship, 1970–1971. His articles and reviews have appeared in numerous professional publications such as the *American Historical Review* and the *Journal of Modern History*. He is the author of *Compulsory Labor Arbitration in France, 1936–1939* (1951), *Léon Blum: Humanist in Politics* (1966), and *Twentieth Century* (1968), a volume in the Great Ages of Man series. In 1969 his biography of Léon Blum appeared in a French translation.

A NOTE ON THE MAKING OF THIS BOOK

The text of this book was set by means of modern photocomposition. The text type selected is ELEGANTE, *the film counterpart of* PALATINO. *The display type is* MICHELANGELO *and was set by hand in foundry type. Both are contemporary creations of the German type designer* HERMANN ZAPF. *Elegante is distinguished by broad letters and vigorous, inclined serifs typical of the work of a sixteenth century Italian master of writing. Michelangelo expresses the simplicity and clarity of the classic form. Both Elegante and Michelangelo reflect the early Venetian scripts influencing Zapf's creations.*

This book was composed by Graphic Techniques, Inc., Linden, N.J. and printed and bound by Kingsport Press, Inc., Kingsport, Tenn. on Northwest Charter Enamel paper supplied by Alan & Gray, New York, N.Y. The camera work for the illustrations and maps was performed by Westcott & Thomson, Philadelphia, Pa.

Manuscript editing was handled by Suzanne Thibodeau and photo research by Shareen Brysac.

The design concept was directed by Hermann Strohbach with the cooperation of the following designers and artists:

The maps were executed by Jean Paul Tremblay

Typography by Karl Leabo

Cover design by R. Scudellari